Taxati

102 096 801 X

D1766555

Sixteenth edition

This book is due for return on or before the last date shown below.

Taxation of Employments

Sixteenth edition

Robert W Maas FCA, FTII, FIIT, TEP
CBW Tax

Bloomsbury Professional

Bloomsbury Professional Ltd, Maxwelton House, 41–43 Boltro Road, Haywards Heath, West Sussex, RH16 1BJ

© Dawn Publishing Ltd and Bloomsbury Professional Ltd 2015

Previously published by Tottel Publishing Ltd

Bloomsbury Professional is an imprint of Bloomsbury Publishing plc

British Library Cataloguing-in-Publication Data

A CIP Catalogue record for this book is available from the British Library.

ISBN   978 1 78043 681 4

Typeset by Phoenix Photosetting, Chatham, Kent
Printed and bound in Great Britain by CPI Group (UK) Ltd, Croydon, CR0 4YY

Preface

This book aims to explain the UK tax issues that relate specifically to employers and their staff. It deals not only with those working in the UK but also the special rules that apply to those who work overseas while remaining resident in the UK.

It is two years since the previous edition and there have been significant changes in that period. Amongst other changes, both the *Finance Acts 2013* and *2014* made significant changes to the legislation on employee share schemes and on pensions. The *Finance Act 2013* introduced a new tax-advantaged employer-shareholder shares scheme. The *Finance Act 2014* significantly extended the scope of the rules on agency workers and removed the need for prior approval of the various tax-advantaged share schemes, replacing it with extensive powers for HMRC to investigate compliance with the rules subsequent to the implementation of the scheme. It also brought many junior members of LLPs into the scope of PAYE.

There have also been some important court decisions, in particular the Upper Tribunal decisions in *Reed Employment LLP* and in the *Glasgow Rangers FC* EBT and the decision of the Court of Appeal in *ITV Services Ltd*.

A preface is an author's opportunity to acknowledge the help of others involved in the production of a book. In particular, I would like to thank Jill Holland for the updating of this edition. I also acknowledge the help of my partners and colleagues at CBW Tax, in particular Tom Adcock for his help on points of interpretation. I would like to thank Nathan Steinberg who continues to challenge me with obtuse technical points which have influenced my thoughts.

The law referred to in this book in general reflects the position at 30 July 2014.

Robert W Maas

London EC1
October 2014

Contents

Contents

Table of Statutes

Table of Statutory Instruments

[All references are to paragraph number]

Table of Cases

[All references are to paragraph number]

C

H

S

Abbreviations and References

ABBREVIATIONS

CA	=	Contributions Agency
CAA 2001	=	Capital Allowances Act
CGT	=	Capital Gains Tax
CGTA	=	Capital Gains Tax Act 1979
CIR	=	Commissioners of Inland Revenue
CSOP	=	Company Share Option Plan
DSS	=	Department of Social Security
EFTA	=	European Free Trade Area
ECJ	=	European Court of Justice
EMI	=	Executive Management Incentive
ESC	=	Extra Statutory Concession
ESI	=	Employment Status Indicator
ESOT	=	Employee Share Option Trust
EU	=	European Union
FA	=	Finance Act
FURBS	=	Funded Unapproved Retirement Benefits Scheme
HMRC	=	Her Majesty's Revenue & Customs
ICAEW	=	Institute of Chartered Accountants in England and Wales
ICTA 1988	=	Income and Corporation Taxes Act 1988
IRPR	=	Inland Revenue Press Release
ITA 2007	=	Income Tax Act 2007
ITTOIA 2005	=	Income Tax (Trading and other Income) Act 2005
MEP	=	Member of the European Parliament
MSC	=	Managed Service Company
NIC	=	National Insurance Contributions
NICO	=	National Insurance Contributions Office
Para	=	Paragraph
PAYE	=	Pay As You Earn
PEP	=	Personal Equity Plan
PRP	=	Profit-related pay
PSA	=	PAYE Settlement Agreement
PSO	=	Pension Schemes Office
Reg	=	Regulation
s	=	Section
SAYE	=	Save As you Earn
SCD	=	Simon's Special Commissioners' Decisions
SSCBA 1992	=	Social Security and Contributions Act 1992
Sch	=	Schedule
SI	=	Statutory Instrument
SIP	=	Share Incentive Plan
SMP	=	Statutory Maternity Pay

SP	=	Statement of Practice
SpC	=	Special Commissioners' decision
SSP	=	Statutory Sick Pay
TCGA 1992	=	Taxation of Chargeable Gains Act 1992
TMA 1970	=	Taxes Management Act 1970
UITF	=	Urgent Issues Task Force Abstract
VAT	=	Value Added Tax
VATA 1994	=	VAT Act
VTD	=	VAT Tribunal Decision

REFERENCES

AC	=	Law Reports, Appeal Cases (Incorporated Council of Law Reporting for England and Wales, 3 Stone Buildings, Lincoln's Inn, London WC2A 3XN)
All ER	=	All England Law Reports (Butterworth & Co (Publishers) Ltd, Halsbury House, 35 Chancery Lane, London WC2A 1EL
BTC	=	British Tax Cases, (CCH Editions Ltd, Telford Road, Bicester, Oxon OX6 0XD)
Ch	=	Law Reports, Chancery Division
Ch	=	Law Reports, Chancery Division
DLR	=	Dominion Law Reports (Canada)
EWHC	=	England and Wales High Court
ICR	=	Law Reports, Industrial Cases Reports
IR	=	Irish Reports (Law Reporting Council, Law Library, Four Courts, Dublin)
ITC	=	Irish Tax Cases (Government Publications, 1 & 3 GPO Arcade, Dublin 1)
KB	=	Law Reports, King's Bench Division
QB	=	Law Reports, Queen's Bench Division
STC(SCD)	=	Simon's Special Commissioners' Decisions (Butterworth & Co (Publishers) Ltd, as above)
STC	=	Simon's Tax Cases (Butterworth & Co (Publishers) Ltd, as above)
TC	=	Official Reports of Tax Cases (HMSO, PO Box 276, London SW8 5DT)
TLR	=	Times Law Reports
UKHL	=	UK House of Lords
WLR	=	Weekly Law Reports (Incorporated Council Law Reporting, as above)

Chapter 1

Introduction

Introduction of income tax

1.1   Income tax was first introduced in the UK in 1799. It was a temporary tax to help finance the Napoleonic wars and was abolished in 1802 when the Treaty of Amiens was signed. It was, however, reimposed a year later when England again declared war on France and continued until the final defeat of Napoleon in 1815, when the tax was again abolished. It was reintroduced as a temporary measure in 1842, but unfortunately over 150 years later the needs that prompted its reintroduction are still with us and Parliament has thought fit to reimpose the tax every year since then.

Schedular system

1.2   From its inception in its modern form in 1842 until the enactment of the *Income Tax (Earnings and Pensions) Act 2003 (ITEPA 2003)* the tax was assessed on a Schedular system. In other words, tax was charged 'in respect of all property, profits or gains respectively described or comprised in the Schedules marked A, B, C, D and E, contained in the First Schedule to this Act and in accordance with the Rules respectively applicable to those Schedules'. The words up to the last comma in the above quotation are those in *section 1(1)* of the *Income and Corporation Taxes Act 1988 (ICTA 1988)* with the exception that Schedule B was abolished by the *Finance Act 1988 (FA 1988)* and Schedule C by the *Finance Act 1996 (FA 1996)* and Schedule F has been added. The quotation is in fact from *section 1* of the *Income Tax Act 1918 (ITA 1918)*, but the five Schedules actually derive from the *Income Tax Act 1842 (ITA 1842)*.

1.3   Under a Schedular system it is necessary to determine into which Schedule a particular source of income falls before the tax on it can be calculated, as the rules of each Schedule can differ quite radically. If the source of an item of income cannot be brought within the scope of the rules of any of the Schedules it will be outside the scope of the tax. Although the Schedular system has disappeared under the Tax Law Rewrite Project, a basic condition of that project was that it should not change the law (except in minor ways) so this principle remains. *ITEPA 2003*, the rewrite Act in relation to Schedule E income, has dropped the expression, 'Schedule E', albeit that it has largely retained the computational rules. One important exception is that, unlike with most sources of income, the UK taxes employment income even after the source of such income has ceased, if the income was within the scope of UK tax at the time that the right to it arose.

The charge to tax on employment income

1.4   This Act now charges income tax on employment income, pension income and social security income. [*ITEPA 2003, s 1(1)*]. In 1842 Schedule (E) charged tax 'upon every public Office or Employment of Profit, and upon every Annuity, Pension or Stipend payable by Her Majesty out of the Public Revenue of the United Kingdom, except Annuities before charged to the Duties in Schedule (C)'. [*ITA 1842, s 1*]. In other words it was limited to public offices and employments. This did not mean that the salary from a non-public employment escaped tax; Schedule (D) imposed tax 'upon the annual Profits or gains arising or accruing to any Person residing in Great Britain from any Profession, Trade, Employment or Vocation'. *Section 146* of the *ITA 1842* contained ten rules for calculating the taxable income under Schedule E.

Pay As You Earn

1.5   Over the years the shape of the taxation of employment income has obviously changed significantly but most of the basic principles laid down in 1842 remain relatively unscathed. The first major change was introduced by *section 18* of the *Finance Act 1922 (FA 1922)* which provided that 'such profits or gains arising or accruing to any person from an office, employment or pension as are, under the *ITA 1918* chargeable to tax under Schedule D ... shall cease to be chargeable under that Schedule and shall be chargeable to tax under Schedule E'. The next significant change was the enactment of the *Income Tax (Employments) Act 1943* which introduced for 1944/45 onwards the deduction of tax at source under the PAYE rules. Deduction of tax from earnings had actually been introduced a few years earlier, by *section 11* of the *Finance (No 2) Act 1940 (F(No.2)A 1940)*, but the PAYE system represented a great simplification.

Expenses and benefits

1.6   The next major change was the introduction in *ss 38–46* of the *Finance Act 1948 (FA 1948)* of rules for the taxation of expenses and benefits in kind in respect of directors and employees earning £2,000 or more. These special rules were in general designed to ensure that tax was charged on the cost of providing benefits to such people not merely on the realisable value, if any, of such benefits. The rules were substantially recast in the mid-1970s, starting with the *Finance (No 2) Act 1975 (F(No.2)A 1975)*, and continuing in the *Finance Act 1976 (FA 1976)* (which recast much of the previous year's legislation) and the 1977 and 1978 *Acts* (which supplemented the 1976 rules).

Other Changes

1.7   The introduction of voluntary self-assessment in 2004 significantly changed the operation of the tax system. *ITEPA 2003* has rewritten the legislation in a way that is thought to be easier to understand, although that is of course a change in nomenclature not in substance. 2004 saw pension reform. The change to the remittance basis rules for non-UK domiciled taxpayers in 2008 and the introduction of a statutory residence test in 2013 have significant implications for those working overseas or coming to this country from overseas.

1.8   The major changes have been supplemented along the way with other less drastic ones, such as the granting of relief for expenses (by *Finance Act 1853, s 51*), for pension contributions [*Finance Act 1921, s 32*], and retirement annuities [*Finance Act 1956, s 22*], and the introduction of special rules on share options in 1966, employee shareholdings in 1972, approved profit sharing schemes in 1968, approved share options in 1971 and again in 1984, the short-lived profit-related pay in 1987, employee share ownership trusts in 1989 and employee share ownership plans (since renamed share incentive plans) and enterprise management incentives in 2000, and employee shareholder shares in 2013.

1.9   There has also been a great deal of anti-avoidance legislation in recent years. There is a widespread perception that the self-employed are taxed less heavily than employees. Whilst this is not wholly true, it has spawned many attempts by taxpayers to seek to shed employed status. There have also been numerous attempts to alleviate the tax charge on employees by means of indirect payments of remuneration. The response of successive governments has been to seek to tax some categories of self employed workers as if they were employees and to bring indirect payments into eth employment income net. This started in 1999 with legislation aimed at the provision of services through intermediaries (generally known as IR35), followed by legislation on managed service companies in 2007 income provided through third parties (disguised remuneration) in 2011 and a major reform of the agency rules (disguised remuneration) in 2014.

1.10   The overall result is a complex set of rules which interrelate with one another and reflect changes in government policy from time to time rather than a coherent attempt to formulate a sensible system of taxing income from employment. In particular, many of the changes in recent years seem to have been prompted more by a desire to minimise the workload of Her Majesty's Revenue and Customs (HMRC) than to produce a fair and comprehensible system of taxation. *ITEPA 2003* is akin to a consolidation act. It has not changed the scope of the legislation but has reproduced it in more modern and readily understandable language. Furthermore, the legislation cannot be looked at in isolation. It is supplemented by a large number of court decisions, which interpret areas of difficulty in the legislation (*Tolley's Tax Cases 2011* covers no fewer than 289 cases on employment and pension income and a further 65 on PAYE), and by HMRC concessions and statements of practice, which alleviate some of the areas where the legislation can cause unfairness or anomalies.

1.11   Income tax and National Insurance (a social security charge imposed on earnings) are administered by HMRC, which is itself an amalgamation of the Inland Revenue which formerly dealt with the direct taxes, such as income tax, and the stamp duties, and HM Customs & Excise which administered the remaining indirect taxes. This amalgamation took place in 2005. In this book, HMRC is used to refer to the tax authorities both before and after that date, except in references to case law where the actual name of the parties to the case is retained. One side effect of this reorganisation is that HMRC are moving away from calling their senior staff Inspectors of Taxes and increasingly using the generic word Officer to cover all of their employees, with the use of certain powers being restricted to senior Officers. The terms Inspector and Officer have been used indiscriminately in this book; there is no significance in which term is used in a particular place.

1.12   Most taxpayers' major source of income is from an employment. Accordingly, the tax law in relation to employments has an impact on the vast majority of taxpayers. Because of the system of deduction of tax at source most salary and wage-earners give little thought to whether anything might be done to minimise their tax burden – or indeed whether the calculation for those within the scope of self-assessment submitting returns before the 30 September deadline (and in practice also for those submitting returns later) that has been done by HMRC is correct.

Wages or salaries

1.13   It may be appropriate to mention here, that at least as far as HMRC are concerned there is no distinction between wages and salaries – if indeed there is any real difference between the two terms. This was well expressed over 70 years ago by Lord Sumner in one of the landmark cases on Schedule E, *Great Western Rly Co v Bater 8 TC 231.* 'It is, however, a purely arbitrary distinction and so indefinite as to be really accidental. For economic purposes it is convenient to treat wage-earners as a class, and for political purposes the receipt of a salary is often supposed to involve a different point of view from that which attaches to the earning of wages, but the first term really refers more to the nature and condition of manual work done than to the remuneration paid for it, and the second denotes social aspirations rather than any HMRC category. Fashions change fast in this matter and many a man or woman, who took wages without objection thirty years ago, receives a salary now of no greater amount than the service would command under the old name.' This is, of course, as true today as it was in 1922.

1.14   This book is not intended to enable the average salary or wage-earner to check his tax bill as such. Nor does it cover in depth the operation of the PAYE system. It would be hard to rival the HMRC's own booklets in this area, CWG2 (2014) (*Employer's Further Guide to PAYE and NICs*) and 480 (2014) (*Expenses and Benefits: A Tax Guide*), which are issued free to employers.

1.15   The intention is to explain the legislation in depth, to point to tax planning opportunities, and to illuminate anomalies and danger areas in the legislation.

Self-assessment

1.16   Self-assessment, ie calculating the tax payable, applies to employees like anyone else. There is an obligation to notify chargeability of untaxed income and capital gains within six months after the end of the tax year and an obligation to complete a tax return if HMRC request an employee to do so. There is no obligation to complete a tax return if HMRC decide not to issue one. Their practice is to issue tax returns to all company directors and to employees in receipt of significant amounts of untaxed income but not to issue returns generally where a person's income can be wholly dealt with through PAYE – including where small amounts of untaxed income can be taxed by an adjustment in the employee's PAYE coding notice. HMRC also occasionally issue returns to other employees to check that there are no sources of untaxed income which have not been notified to them.

1.17   Prior to the introduction of self-assessment, benefits in kind and any taxable element of expenses were generally calculated by HMRC based on information provided by employers via the form P11D. For 1996/97 onwards the form P11D has been redesigned and employers are required to calculate the taxable benefits for their employees in relation to some types of benefit. The employee is entitled to a copy of his form P11D so that he can put the appropriate figures on his tax return if he is required to complete one, although as the form is now a cross between an information return and a statement of taxable earnings it is probably confusing to most employees. Those who are employed at 5 April in a tax year are entitled to the copy P11D information automatically by 6 July following or within 30 days whichever is later (*Income Tax (Paye as You Earn) Regulations 2003 (SI 2003 No 2682), Reg 94*); those who left during the year must be given it on request within 30 days of the request if that is later than 6 July. The employer is entitled to calculate the benefits on the basis of the information he has, which may well be incomplete. The employee is nevertheless required to put the correct benefit figure on his return – which means he will need to recalculate it if he disagrees with his employer's figure as can happen in respect of interest free loans where the employer may not know that the money was spent for a qualifying purpose. In such circumstances he should obviously put a note on his return to explain why he has not adopted the P11D figure. He is still not entitled to a detailed breakdown of the figures on his P11D, so unless the employer volunteers this he will, in practice, be forced to rely on many of the employer's figures. Although the employer has to calculate the taxable benefits, the expenses figures that go on the form are still total expenses. It is then up to the employee to formulate a claim for relief for bona fide business expenses. There is clearly a risk of over taxation where the P11D is not intended to give the tax return figure, such as in relation to expenses which may or may not have a personal element and, where they do, that element might be an incidental (non-taxable) one or may breach the wholly exclusively and necessarily test and give rise to a tax liability. This probably sounds daft to most readers, but generations of MPs (including one assumes your own MP, as otherwise you might expect him to seek to change it) have thought it eminently reasonable.

1.18   Self-assessment is voluntary. However, as a taxpayer is required to calculate and return each item of his income and capital gains, the only thing that those who choose not to self-assess escape is the need to add up the figures on their returns and calculate the tax thereon. As the price for avoiding these chores is a need to submit the tax return four months earlier – by 30 September following the end of the tax year – many people choose to self-assess.

1.19   Self-assessment did not merely shift the burden of assessing from HMRC to the taxpayer. It was a radical reform of the entire system of personal taxAn individual has had to file his tax return by 31 January after the end of the tax year if he files it online, the return for the year to 5 April 2015 being due on 31 January 2016. A person who manually files his return needs to do so by 31 October, the return for the year to 5 April 2015 needing to be filed by 31 October 2015. The return must be complete. Previously it was common to show against the space for earnings, 'per PAYE' (or sometimes for directors, 'per accounts') and against expenses and benefits, 'per P11D'. HMRC now regard such returns as incomplete and ask the taxpayer to complete the form with the possibility of missing the 31 January deadline, thereby incurring interest and penalties.

1.20   At the same time as he submits his 2014/15 return a taxpayer must also send a cheque for the balance of the tax payable for that year. In the case of employees this will be primarily the tax on benefits in kind. He may also need to send a cheque for his first instalment of tax for 2015/16. This is because income tax (but not capital gains tax) is payable in three instalments, the first interim payment on 31 January in the year of assessment, ie 31 January 2015 for 2014/15; the second interim payment on the following 31 July, ie 31 July 2015 for 2014/15; and the third and final payment with the tax return on the following 31 January, ie 31 January 2016 for 2014/15. The first two instalments are based on the tax payable (not the taxable income) for the previous year, ie on the 2013/14 tax liability for 2014/15. These payment dates apply even where the 31 October filing date has to be used. There is a right to reduce the tax if the taxpayer thinks his liability for the current year is less, but penalties will be imposed for making such a reduction without good reason. The interim payments do not have to be made if at least 80 per cent of the income of the previous year was received under deduction of tax. Accordingly, most full time employees do not need to make interim payments as the PAYE deduction should satisfy this test unless benefits in kind are very high, or the employee has other sources of untaxed income.

1.21   Under self-assessment, although HMRC review all returns, they do not look at them in detail unless a return contains something that raises questions. This does not mean there is no check. HMRC have been given extensive powers to obtain information including a right to randomly enquire into returns.

From 5 December 2005 it has been possible for two people of the same sex to enter into a civil partnership. A civil partnership carries with it the tax benefits and disadvantages of marriage. Accordingly references in this book to a spouse should be read as also including a civil partner where appropriate.

Format of this book

1.22   The format adopted has been to consider first the basic rules of assessment to give the reader an understanding of the scope of the taxation of income from employments and pensions. As mentioned above, tax is chargeable on the emoluments from an office or employment. Accordingly, **Chapters 3** and **4** expand on the basic principles by considering the meaning of emoluments and of employment, and attempting to distinguish employment from self-employment. A new concept of deemed employment income has also been introduced from 2011 and the rules for identifying such deemed income are also considered in **Chapter 3**. The special rules on expenses and benefits are then dealt with in **Chapters 5** to **9**.

1.23   The basic rules having been covered, the book then looks at ancillary matters; **Chapter 10** dealing with pensions and **Chapter 11** with termination payments, signing-on fees and similar lump sum payments. Rather than scatter throughout the book the variants to the basic rules that relate to people who are resident or not domiciled in the UK, those are collected together in **Chapter 12**. The following chapter deals with the special rules applying to UK residents working overseas.

1.24   Chapters **14–16** deal with the special provisions in relation to employee shareholdings and similar incentives for employees. Income tax and National Insurance are deducted at source by the employer from most payments of earnings. The tax deduction system, PAYE, is considered in **Chapter 17**. **Chapter 18** covers the special anti-avoidance rules that are designed to prevent employments being disguised as self-employment by the interposition of a company or other intermediary. A brief mention is made of National Insurance. Although not nominally part of the tax system, an appreciation of the taxation of income from employment is incomplete without at least a brief survey of this impost. Finally, a chapter is included on the VAT implications of certain benefit payments.

1.25   Parliament has in the past rarely changed tax law retrospectively. However the then Minister in a Parliamentary Statement on 2 December 2004 said that she was 'giving notice of our intention to deal with any arrangements that emerge in future designed to frustrate our intention that employers and employees should pay the proper amount of tax and NIC on the rewards of employment. Where we become aware of arrangements which attempt to frustrate the intention we will introduce legislation to close them down where necessary from today'. Subsequent anti-avoidance changes to the share scheme rules in particular have sometimes been made with effect from 2 December 2004 although not in the last few years.

Chapter 2

The Basic Rules

Meaning of 'employee'

2.1   *Income Tax (Earnings and Pensions) Act 2003 (ITEPA 2003)* imposes tax on employment income, pension income and those social security benefits which are taxable. For simplicity reference will normally be made below to 'employees' as meaning persons taxable on employment income. It must be borne in mind however that, unless the context indicates otherwise, this expression also includes an office holder, such as the director of a company.

2.2   The basic rules that then existed were recast in the *Finance Act 1989 (FA 1989)*, when the then Chancellor indicated that his changes would 'greatly simplify' the tax affairs of those taxpayers who regularly receive pay some time after the year for which it is earned.

Basis of assessment

2.3   Prior to the change it was necessary to ascertain the period to which remuneration related, determine its taxability by reference to the taxpayer's position at that time, and tax it as income of the period to which it related. Now it is necessary 'simply' to ascertain the period to which remuneration relates, determine its taxability by reference to the taxpayer's position at that time, and tax it as income of the year of assessment in which it is paid, unless it is a pension, in which case it is taxed as income of the year of assessment for which it was earned, ie a one-stage process has been 'simplified' into a two-stage one. Under the new system statutory rules are obviously needed to determine when remuneration is paid, which was relatively unimportant under the pre-1989 rules, as in family companies in particular, remuneration may well not be physically paid over as such.

2.4   It is important to realise that there is a two-stage process. Whether remuneration is assessable must be determined by reference to the time it is earned. When it is assessable depends on the date it is paid (a concept that has a technical meaning – see **2.47**).

The charging provisions

2.5   For most people the *ITEPA 2003* charges tax on 'general earnings' plus 'specific employment income' for the tax year. [*ITEPA 2003, ss 6, 9(2),*

(4)]. General earnings is defined as earnings within *Chapter 1, Part 3* of that Act. [*ITEPA 2003, s 7(3)*]. This in turn defined as any salary, wages or fees, any gratuity or other profit or incidental benefit of any kind obtained by the employee if it is money or money's worth, or anything else that constitutes an emolument of the employment. [*ITEPA 2003, s 62(2)*]. General earnings are normally charged to tax under *ITEPA 2003, s 15* (see **2.47**). Specific employment income is defined as any amount which counts as employment income by virtue of Part 6 of that Act (income which is not earnings or share related – mainly receipts from pension schemes and payments on termination of employment) or Part 7 (share related income) or any other enactment. [*ITEPA 2003, s 7(4), (6)*]. The amount taxed is the net taxable earnings from the employment in the tax year, which is the total amount of any taxable earnings from the employment in that year less the total amount of any deductions allowed from the earnings under the provisions listed in *ITEPA 2003, s 327(3)–(5)*] [*ITEPA 2003, s 11(1)*]. If that amount is negative, the net taxable earnings are nil and the loss is relievable under *ITEPA 2003, s 128* (see **2.55A**) [*ITEPA 2003, s 11(2)(3)*]. This calculation has to be done separately for each employment [*ITEPA 2003, s 11(4)*]. *ITEPA 2003, s 327* allows deductions from general earnings under the following chapters of *ITEPA 2003*, Part 5

(a)   *Chapter 2 (ss 333–360A)* (expenses),

(b)   *Chapter 3 (ss 361–365)* (deductions from benefits code earnings),

(c)   *Chapter 4 (ss 336–368)* (fixed allowances for employee expenses),

(d)   *Chapter 5 (ss 369–371)* (deductions for earnings representing benefits or reimbursed expenses),

(e)   *Chapter 1 (ss 378–385)* (deductions from seafarers' earnings),

(f)   *s 232* (giving effect to mileage allowance relief),

and also under

(g)   *ITEPA 2003, Part 12 (ss 71–715)* (payroll giving),

(h)   *Capital Allowances Act 2001 (CAA 2001), s 262* (capital allowances), and

(i)   *Finance Act 2004 (FA 2004), ss 188–194* (contributions to registered pension schemes).

The amount taxed in relation to specific employment income is the net taxable specific income from the employment for the year (ie the deemed income under the relevant provision) less any allowable deductions from that income (excluding deductions from earnings generally) [*ITEPA 2003, ss 9(4), (5),12*]. A major anti-avoidance provision to tax what the government describe as employment income provided through third parties, or 'disguised remuneration', was introduced in the *Finance Act 2011 (FA 2011)*. This is something of a misnomer; it aims to tax loans and other items that would not normally be considered to be earnings at all. This legislation applies from 6 April 2011 although it imposes a charge on that date in relation to some transactions undertaken after 8 December 2010 unless they have been unwound by 5 April 2012. The legislation is considered at **3.26** onwards.

2.6   Special rules apply to employees who are resident, ordinarily resident or domiciled outside the UK. [*ITEPA 2003, s 20*]. 'Overseas earnings' of a person who is resident and ordinarily resident in the UK but not domiciled here are taxed only when and to the extent that they are brought into the UK, although some long-term residents cannot use the remittance basis after 5 April 2008 (see **12.17** onwards). [*ITEPA 2003, s 23*]. Earnings are overseas earnings if the employment is with a foreign employer and the duties of the employment are performed wholly outside the UK. [*ITEPA 2003, s 23(2)*]. 'Wholly' is interpreted very restrictively for this purpose.

2.7   Where an employee is resident but not ordinarily resident in the UK general earnings other than in respect of duties performed in the UK (and earnings from overseas Crown employment subject of UK tax) are also normally taxable only when, and to the extent that, they are remitted to the UK. [*ITEPA 2003, s 26(2)*].

2.8   If an employee is not resident in the UK for a tax year he is taxable here only in relation to earnings for duties performed in the UK (and earnings from an overseas Crown appointment), and only to the extent that such earnings are remitted to the UK. [*ITEPA 2003, s 27*].

2.9   A person who is taxable on overseas earnings whether they are remitted or not, eg someone who is resident, ordinarily resident and domiciled in the UK or someone who is non-resident and works partly in the UK but is paid wholly overseas or some long-term residents after 5 April 2008, can be taxable on money that he is unable to bring into the UK to pay the tax because of foreign currency controls. Such a person will nevertheless have to raise the money to pay the tax from other sources. There is no relief for delayed remittances corresponding to that which applies to the remittance basis (see **12.48**).

2.10   If a person who is not UK resident, or is resident but not ordinarily resident in the UK, has an employment where some of the duties are performed in the UK (the UK including Eire for this purpose) and some are performed elsewhere, the remuneration has to be apportioned to ascertain the amount applicable to the UK duties. The part attributable to non-UK duties will be taxable if the employee is UK resident, but outside the scope of UK tax if he is not. It is in fact most unusual for a person to be ordinarily resident in the UK but not resident there. The converse is far more common. If the duties of the employment of such a person are carried on wholly outside the UK, they are not taxable (unless and until they are remitted to the UK) as the charging provisions only tax remuneration for UK work. Where the remuneration from an employment is taxable partly on an earnings basis and partly on a remittance basis the apportionment between the two is essentially a question of fact. However, HMRC will accept time apportionment based on the number of working days in and outside the UK. Strictly speaking, the apportionment should probably be based on the total number of days in the UK (including non-working days) as, unless the contract provides otherwise, the law treats salary as accruing on a daily basis. It is worth considering if such an apportionment may be more beneficial to the employee. Where the remuneration is wholly paid abroad HMRC are prepared to treat remittances to the UK as representing the emoluments taxed on an earnings basis rather than those taxed only on a remittance basis. Where part is paid in the UK, and part abroad HMRC regard overseas earnings as having been remitted only if the aggregate of the emoluments paid in the UK, benefits enjoyed in the UK, and remittances to the UK, exceed the taxable UK earnings for the year of assessment (*SP 1/09*).

Meaning of 'residence' and 'domicile'

2.11   In order to determine whether and how income is taxable in the UK it is obviously necessary to know what is meant by residence and domicile. The UK introduced a statutory residence test (or more correctly a series of tests) from 6 April 2013. Although these rules are complex, they do at least provide certainty. A person is UK resident in a tax year if he meets one of six tests of residence. The first four cover specific situations. They are called the automatic tests because if a person meets one of these tests he is automatically UK resident for the year concerned. The last two are the sweep up test that will apply in other circumstances. There are two tests because there are different rules for a person who emigrates from the UK and one who moves to the UK. The tests are:

(*a*)   The individual is present in the UK for more than 183 days in the tax year *Finance Act 2013 (FA 2013, Sch 45, para 7)*.

(*b*)   The individual has a home in the UK during the tax year, he spends some time there (however short) on at least ten days in the tax year, and for a period of at least 91 days (30 of which fall in the tax year) either he has no home outside the UK or, if he does, he spends time there on fewer than 30 days in the tax year (*FA 2013, Sch 45, para 8*).

(*c*)   He works 'sufficient hours in the UK' over a 365-day period (all or part of which falls into the tax year), during that period there are no significant breaks from UK work, and more than 75% of the total number of days in the 365-day period on which he does more than three hours' work are days of work in the UK (*FA 2013, Sch 45, para 9*). Whether a person works sufficient hours in the UK is calculated by reference to a formula. Start from 365, deduct disregarded days, ie days on which the person works at least three hours overseas (even if he does three hours here as well). Deduct annual leave, parenting leave, sickness, and non-working days embedded in a block of such days. Divide the resulting figure by seven and round down to the nearest whole number (or round up to 1). Ascertain the total hours that the person works in the UK (other than on disregarded days) during the 365-day period and divide that by the number previously calculated. If this gives 35 or more, the person worked sufficient hours in the UK for both of the tax years 2013/14 and 2014/15.

(*d*)   The individual dies during the tax year, was UK resident for each of the previous three years under one of the above tests, had a home in the UK during the tax year and, if he were not resident in the tax year, the previous year would not have been a split year (*FA 2013, Sch 45, para 10*).

(*e*) The individual was resident here in any one of the previous three tax years, spends at least 15 days in the UK in the tax year and satisfies one or more of five connecting factors (see below). The number of factors that count vary with the time spent in the UK, namely:

Days spent in UK	Impact of connection factors on residence status
Fewer than 16 days	Always non-resident
16–45 days	Resident if individual has 4 factors or more (otherwise not resident)
46–90 days	Resident if individual has 3 factors or more (otherwise not resident)
91–120 days	Resident if individual has 2 factors or more (otherwise not resident)
121–182 days	Resident if individual has 1 factor or more (otherwise not resident)
183 days or more	Always resident

The five connecting factors are:

● Family – the individual's spouse or civil partner (or common law equivalent) or minor children are resident in the UK.

● Accommodation – the individual has accessible accommodation in the UK and makes use of it during the tax year (subject to an exclusion for a short stay with a relative).

● Substantive work in the UK – The individual does substantive work in the UK (but does not work here full time).

● UK presence in the previous year – The individual spent more than 90 days in the UK in either of the previous two tax years.

● More time in the UK than in other countries – The individual spent more days in the UK in the tax year than in any other single country.

(*FA 2013, Sch 45, para 17*).

(*f*) If the individual was not resident in the UK in any of the previous three tax years, he is present here for more than 45 days in the tax year and meets one or more of the first four of the above five factors. Again the number of factors that count vary with the time spent in the UK but the table differs from that at (4). The rules are:

Days spent in UK	Impact of connection factors on residence status
Fewer than 46 days	Always non-resident
46–90 days	Resident if individual has 4 factors or more (otherwise not resident)
91–120 days	Resident if individual has 3 factors or more (otherwise not resident)

Days spent in UK	Impact of connection factors on residence status
121–182 days	Resident if individual has 2 factors or more (otherwise not resident)
183 days or more	Always resident

The connecting factors appear to apply throughout the year if they apply on a single day in the year, although split-year treatment (see **2.11B**) will often apply in the year that a person comes to, or leaves, the UK. Split-year treatment will not apply where a person ceases to be, or becomes, UK resident because of a change in the connecting factors taken into account.

2.11A Even if he would be UK resident under one of the above tests a person is not UK resident for a tax year if either:

(*a*) He was UK resident in at least one of the previous three tax years, spends less than 16 days here in the tax year concerned and does not die in that year (*FA 2013, Sch 45, para 12*).

(*b*) He was not UK resident in any of the three previous tax years and spends less than 46 days here in the tax year concerned (*FA 2013, Sch 45, para 13*).

(*c*) He works sufficient hours overseas in the tax year, there are no significant breaks from overseas work in that year, he does more than three hours' work in the UK on no more than 30 days and he spends no more than 90 days here in the tax year (ignoring days on which he is deemed to be in the UK) (*FA 2013, Sch 45, para 14*). Sufficient hours overseas is calculated in the same way as sufficient hours in the UK (see above) but by reference to the tax year, not by reference to any 365-day period.

(*d*) He dies during the tax year, he was not UK resident for either of the two previous years (or was not UK resident for the previous year and the year before that was a split year) and he spent less than 46 days in the UK in the tax year (*FA 2013, Sch 45, para 15*).

(*e*) He dies during the tax year, was not UK resident in either of the two previous years by virtue of head 3 above (or was not UK resident in the previous year by virtue of that head and the year before that was a split year) and he would have been non-UK resident under head (*c*) if it applied only by reference to the part of the tax year up to the date of his death (*FA 2013, Sch 45, para 16*).

2.11B Although residence status normally applies for the entire tax year there are a number of circumstances in which the year can be split into two, the individual being then treated as resident during the part that he lives in the UK and as non-resident during the part for which he was resident elsewhere. There are eight circumstances in which this can apply. The two that are employment related are:

(*a*) The taxpayer was resident in the previous tax year, is non-resident during the following year by virtue of **9.3**(3), and in the current year there is a period that begins within the tax year on a day on which the taxpayer does more than three hours' work overseas, ends at the end of the tax year, and during which the taxpayer works sufficient hours overseas, has no significant breaks from overseas work, works in the UK for no more than the permitted limit and does not spend more than the permitted number of days in the UK (*FA 2013, Sch 45, para 44*). Sufficient hours overseas is calculated in a similar way to that at **9.2**(3). The permitted limit is 30 days reduced proportionately for the number of whole months in the tax year prior to the start of the non-resident period. The permitted number of days in the UK is 90 reduced for the number of whole months in the tax year prior to the start of the non-resident period.

(*b*)   The taxpayer was UK resident for the previous tax year, is not UK resident in the following year, has a spouse or partner who meets the above condition, moves overseas during the current tax year so that they can continue to live together, and for the remainder of the year has no home in the UK (or if he does, spends more time in an overseas home than in the UK one) and spends no more than the permitted number of days in the UK (calculated as above).

2.11C   The above is a brief summary of the main features of the test. There are a great many nuances and caveats that space does not permit to be dealt with here. Residence is a complex area on which it is advisable to seek advice in the light of the individual's specific circumstances.

2.12   For years prior to 2013/14 there were no statutory tests. It was necessary to rely on the application of court decisions. The cases that have come before the courts, whilst helpful, have not sought to formulate definitions but have been determined very much on their own facts. Based on these cases HMRC evolved a set of rules for deciding whether or not a person is resident in the UK. Although these are generally accepted they are amenable to challenge in the courts. These rules are broadly as follows:

(*a*)   A person is resident in the UK if he is present in the UK for 183 days or more during a year of assessment. HMRC say that there are no exceptions to this rule. Strictly speaking the 183-day period should probably be arrived at by aggregating hours and minutes where a person is in the UK for parts of days (*Wilkie v IRC 32 TC 495*). In practice HMRC ignore parts of days and count a day as a day of presence in the UK only if the person is present there throughout that entire day. It does not matter why the 183-day limit is breached. If a person intends to leave after 182 days but is prevented from doing so by illness or by a transport strike he will be resident in the UK for the year of assessment even though he had no intention of remaining in the UK for over 182 days.

(*b*)   A person is also resident in the UK for a year of assessment if he is present here on average for more than 90 days a year. This is normally looked at over a four-year period including the relevant year. It could well be that a person who regularly visits the UK for 88 or 89 days would be held to be UK resident, so this test should be approached with caution. For this purpose (but not for (*a*) above), any days which are spent in the UK because of exceptional circumstances beyond an individual's control, such as illness, will be excluded from the calculation (*SP 2/91*). Although *SP 2/91* states that such days 'will' be excluded, it goes on to say that 'each case where this relaxation of the normal rules may be appropriate will be considered in the light of its own facts'. This suggests that this practice is very much at the discretion of HMRC and cannot be relied upon. As the 90-day figure is not statutory in any event, *SP 2/91* does not seem much of a concession. In recent years HMRC seem to have become a lot more aggressive and seem reluctant to follow these rules where they feel they impinge unfairly on them.

(c)   Although the above reflects HMRC's long-standing position, they contend that mobile workers, such as long-distance lorry drivers and salesmen who make frequent trips abroad, and who are present in the UK for less than 90 days a year on average but whose home is in the UK are resident in the UK. This accords with the decisions in some very old cases, such as the 1875 decision in In *Re Young 1 TC 57* and the 1879 case of *Lloyd v Sulley 2 TC 37* (*Tax Bulletin 52*, April 2001). These cases related to master mariners who might be away for an entire year on a voyage but who were none the less held to be UK resident as their homes and families were in the UK.

In recent years HMRC have taken the stance that whilst these rules apply to someone coming to the UK they do not necessarily apply to a person who emigrates from the UK. Such a person needs to demonstrate that he has made a major change in his pattern of life before HMRC will accept that he has left the UK. Until he has done so they will regard him as remaining UK resident even if his average days in the UK are below 90 per year. If a person goes abroad to work full time under a contract of employment that spans a complete tax year he will, however, be regarded as having ceased to be both UK resident and ordinarily resident from the time he leaves provided that his visits back do not average more than 90 days a year (if they were to do so it is hard to envisage the employment being a full-time one). It is proposed to replace this test with a new statutory residence test from 6 April 2013.

Ordinary residence

2.13   Up to 2012/13 there was a secondary test of ordinary residence. Some of the special rules that apply to non-UK domiciled individuals also applied if a person was resident but not ordinarily resident in the UK. Ordinary residence implied a slightly greater degree of permanence than residence. HMRC regarded someone as being ordinarily resident in the UK once he had been here for three consecutive fiscal years (and often earlier where it appeared probable that he would stay for over three years). It is probably possible for a person to have been ordinarily resident in the UK without being physically present there at all during a year of assessment but as it would be impossible for him to have performed UK duties in such circumstances, this is not relevant in the context of taxing employment income. The availability of accommodation in the UK, which was abolished as a test for residence purposes in 2003, may still be relevant for the purpose of ordinary residence. HMRC's initial Press Release of 16 March 1993 suggested that its abolition affected only temporary visitors to the UK – which does not seem apt to cover emigrants – but the 1996 and subsequent editions of their booklet *IR20, Residents and non-residents*, indicated that the rule has been completely abolished. IR20 was replaced by new guidance, HMRC6, from April 2009. HMRC6 stated that the availability of accommodation is a factor to be taken into account. It describes a person as being ordinarily resident here if his presence in the UK forms part of the regular and habitual mode of his life for the time being. The concept of ordinary residence is no longer used for tax purposes although it can be relevant for national insurance.

Domicile

2.14   Domicile is also a non-statutory concept. It is a very difficult concept. As a very rough rule of thumb, a person who was born in the UK (or rather in either England and Wales, Scotland or Northern Ireland as each has their own legal system and domicile ties a person to an appropriate legal system) is likely to be domiciled here and a person who was born overseas will normally not be domiciled here, unless he has come to the UK with the intention of staying here either for the rest of his life or indefinitely. A person is domiciled in the country that he regards as his home. A person starts life with a domicile of origin, which is the father's domicile at the time of the child's birth. That domicile can be replaced by a domicile of choice by going to another country with the intention of living there permanently or indefinitely. If a domicile of choice is lost, the original domicile of origin automatically revives. A person born overseas to a non-UK domiciled father who comes to England to work and intends to return to his home country when his working life is over is most unlikely to acquire a new English domicile of choice.

2.15   A full consideration of the meaning of these expressions is outside the scope of this book. It is hoped that the above will suffice to enable one to determine which particular rules apply to a person's employment income.

Year of payment

2.16   To decide whether or not emoluments fall within the charging provisions it is necessary to determine the year to which they relate. This is normally relatively simple as remuneration is generally paid for a specific week, month or year. However, it is possible for remuneration or other emoluments not to be specifically related to any period. For example, a company may decide to pay a loyalty bonus to all employees who have been with it for at least five years. In such circumstances the bonus will be regarded as being in respect of the year in which it is paid. This can give rise to problems if the employment does not exist in the year of payment. In *Bray v Best [1989] STC 159* the assets of an employee trust were distributed to ex-employees in 1979/80, the employment having ceased in 1978/79 following a takeover and the transfer of the staff to another group company. It was held that, although the funds distributed were emoluments of the employment, as they were not referable to a specific period they could only be emoluments of 1979/80, and thus escaped tax as the employees did not hold the employments at any time in 1979/80 (and thus the emoluments did not fall within the employment income charging provisions).

2.17 To prevent this state of affairs recurring, it is now provided that where emoluments would otherwise be for a year of assessment in which the recipient does not hold the employment:

(*a*)   they must be treated as emoluments for the first year of assessment in which the employment is held, if they are paid in respect of a prospective employment; and

(*b*)   they must be treated as emoluments for the year of assessment in which the employment ceased if they relate to a past employment.

[*ITEPA 2003, ss 17, 30*].

2.18 In *Griffin v Standish [1995] STC 825* a taxpayer was awarded a bonus for 1987 payable on 14 April 1988. The taxpayer contended that following *Bray v Best* it was assessable for 1988/89. It was held that although the bonus was not paid for a specific tax year it was clearly in respect of the calendar year 1987 and so should be apportioned between 1986/87 and 1987/88.

2.19 The residence status of the taxpayer at the time he receives the emoluments appears irrelevant. It is only necessary to ascertain whether or not the receipt constitutes emoluments from the employment, not whether they would have been assessable on him had the employment existed at the time of receipt.

Place of performance of duties

2.20 If a person ordinarily performs all or part of the duties of his employment in the UK, the emoluments for any period of absence from the office or employment must be treated as being for duties performed in the UK (unless it can be shown that, but for that absence, they would have been for duties performed outside the UK). [*ITEPA 2003, s 38(2)*]. For example, suppose that an employee of a UK company is given by his employer a sabbatical (spanning a complete tax year) which he spends wholly overseas. He cannot claim that the salary for that year relates to non-UK work and is therefore not taxable. The position might be different if the employer asked the employee to work for a period in, say, the firm's Japanese branch and gave him a sabbatical prior to his actually taking up the position in Japan. In *Leonard v Blanchard [1993] STC 259* Nourse LJ indicated that the provision has a fairly narrow application. To come within it the taxpayer would need to show that if he had turned up for duty he would have performed the duties outside the UK.

2.21 If the duties of an employment in a chargeable period are mainly performed outside the UK, any duties performed in the UK which are merely incidental to the performance of those overseas duties are also taken to be performed outside the UK. [*ITEPA 2003, s 39(2)*]. This presumption does not deem the employee to be present in the UK for the purpose of determining whether there is a 365-day qualifying period when he is actually abroad carrying out such duties, nor does it prevent the employment from being one the duties of which are performed partly outside the UK for the purpose of *section 193(1)* (see **13.15** below). [*ITEPA 2003, s 39(3)*].

2.22   It was held in *Robson v Dixon 48 TC 527* that duties are not merely incidental to other duties if, although they may be small in terms of time, they are an essential ingredient of the duties. In that case it was held that a few flights to UK airports by an airline pilot based in Amsterdam and normally flying internationally were not merely incidental to his employment in Holland.

2.23   The following duties must be treated as performed in the UK irrespective of where they are actually performed:

(*a*)   the duties of an office or employment under the Crown which is of a public nature and the emoluments of which are payable out of the public revenue of the UK or of Northern Ireland [*ITEPA 2003, ss 25(1), 27(1), 28*]; and

(*b*)   any duties which a person performs on a ship or other vessel engaged on a voyage between two ports both of which are in the UK, or which a UK resident performs on a vessel or aircraft engaged on a journey beginning or ending in the UK (or on a part beginning or ending in the UK of a longer voyage or journey). [*ITEPA 2003, s 40*].

Head (*a*) above does not apply to employees engaged locally (ie not based in the UK) if they are not UK resident and the maximum pay for their grade is less than that of an executive officer employed in the same department of the UK Civil Service working in Inner London [*ITEPA 2003, s 28(5)–(7)* and Board's Order of 6 April 2003].

2.23A   Where the remittance basis applies to earnings and a single overseas bank account contains both earnings which are taxable as arising in the UK and earnings which are taxable only if remitted, a special rule applies for 2013/14 onwards to determine what moneys are remitted to the UK. For this rule to apply, the earnings must be paid into a qualifying account [*Income Tax Act 2007, s 109RA(1)* inserted by *FA 2013, Sch 6, para 1*]. In practice the taxpayer needs to open a separate bank account into which his earnings are paid. The is because the taxpayer has to nominate an account as his qualifying account and can nominate only one account; an account cannot be a qualifying one if at the time earnings is first paid into it there is a credit balance of more than £10, and the only payments that can be made into the account are earnings, interest on the account and proceeds of sale of employment-related securities (or options) [*ITA 2007, ss 109RB(1)(10), 10RC(6)*].

2.23B   The remittances from a qualifying account during a tax year are aggregated. So are payments out of the account which are not remitted [*ITA 2007, s 109RA(2)*]. The normal rules to identify payments out of a mixed fund (*ITA 2007, s 109Q(3)(4)*) are then applied to the two amounts as if they were a single transfer made at the end of the tax year. This identifies what types of income or gains are deemed to have been remitted. Each transfer out of the account during the year which is remitted to the UK is treated as a proportion of the total remittances and each other payment out of the account is treated as a proportion of the total unremitted amount [*ITA 2007, s 109RA(2)*].

2.23C *ITA 2007, s 109Q(3)(4)* treat UK employment income as remitted first and overseas employment income as remitted next. Accordingly the effect of *ITA 2007, s 109RA* is to identify remittances as far as possible with income that is taxable in the UK on an arising basis and to treat overseas earnings as remitted only after all of the UK earnings have been either remitted or identified with unremitted withdrawals from the account. There are detailed rules governing the operation of qualifying accounts. In particular if non-earnings are accidentally paid into the account, they must be transferred out as soon as the error is discovered and if there are more than three such errors during a tax year, the account will cease to be a qualifying account. It is very important that these rules are complied with. However as they are of limited application, they are not considered further here. They can be found in *FA 2013, ss 809RA–809RD*.

2.23D General earnings in respect of duties performed in the UK sector of the continental shelf (as designated under the *Continental Shelf Act 1964 (CSA 1964), s 1(7)*) in connection with exploration or exploitation activities must be treated as in respect of duties performed in the UK. Exploration and exploitation activities means activities carried on in connection with the exploration or exploitation of so much of the seabed and subsoil and their natural resources as is situated in the UK or the UK sector of the continental shelf [*ITEPA 2003, s 41*].

Directors' fees

2.24 Where fees are received in respect of directorships held by members of a professional partnership HMRC are prepared to treat the fees as partnership trading income provided that the directorship is a normal incidence of the profession (and the practice), the fees are small in relation to the practice's profits, and the fees are pooled for division among the partners (*ESC A37*). Also, the director will not be assessed on the reimbursed travelling expenses provided that either the partnership recognises them as income and claims a deduction or it does not claim a deduction as a trading expense and the expenses are reasonable in amount (*ESC A4*). Similarly, where a company appoints a director to the board of another company and requires the director to pay over the fees, the nominating company can opt to treat the fees as its own trading income (*ESC A37*).

Members of the European Parliament

2.25 The Statute for Members of the European Parliament (2005/884/EC) sets out common pay and conditions for MEPs with effect from the 2009 European Parliamentary elections. This provides that the pay of MEPs is taxable by the European Community. However if an MEP is UK resident it is also taxable in the UK. To prevent double taxation, double tax relief applies to payments to MEPs under Articles 9.1 and 10 (salaries), 13 (transitional allowances) and 14, 15 and 17 (pensions) of the Statute [*Finance Act 2009 (FA 2009), s 56*].

Pensions

2.26   Tax in respect of an annuity (other than one taxable as an annual payment), pension or stipend payable by the Crown or out of the public revenue of the UK or Northern Ireland is taxable under *ITEPA 2003, s 566*. This includes the social security retirement pension, widow's pension, and industrial death benefit pensions [*ITEPA 2003, s 577*] but not war widow's pension or, to the extent that it relates to death due to service in the armed forces of the Crown, wartime service in the merchant navy or war injuries, any other pension or allowance payable by or on behalf of the Ministry of Defence under the *Defence (Local Defence Volunteers) Regulations 1940*, the War Pensions (Coastguards) Scheme 1944, the War Pensions (Naval Auxiliary Personnel) Scheme 1964, the Pensions (Polish Forces) Scheme 1964, the War Pensions (Mercantile Marine) Scheme 1946, the *Home Guard Orders 1964*, the *Ulster Defence Regiment Order 1964*, the Personal Injuries (Civilians) Scheme 1983 or the *Naval Military and Air Forces etc (Disablement and Death) Service Pensions Order 1983*. The Treasury have power to amend this list by statutory instrument. Such pensions are exempt from tax [*ITEPA 2003, s 639*]. Any other pension paid by a person in the UK unless it is paid on behalf of a non-UK resident. [*ITEPA 2003, s 569*]. In some cases so is a lump sum paid under an unapproved pension scheme. [*ITEPA 2003, s 394*]. The detailed rules are considered at **10.123–10.135**.

2.27   Similarly no tax liability arises in respect of a wounds pension granted to a member of the British Armed Forces (ie the armed forces of the Crown); retired pay of a disabled officer granted on account of medical unfitness attributed to (or aggravated by) service in the British Armed Forces; a disablement or disability pension granted to a member of the British Armed Forces; a disablement pension granted to a person who has been employed in the nursing services of any of the British Armed Services on account of medical unfitness attributable to (or aggravated by) service in those Services; an injury or disablement pension under the *Injuries in War (Compensation) Acts 1914*; an injury or disablement pension under a War Risks Compensation Scheme for the Mercantile Marine; a pension granted on account of disability under a scheme under the *Pensions (Navy, Army, Air Force and Mercantile Marine) Act 1939*; or for 2005/06 onwards a benefit by reason of illness or injury payable by way of a lump sum or following the termination of the person's service in the armed forces or reserve forces under a scheme established by an order under the *Armed Forces (Pensions and Compensation Act 2004)*. If the Minister certifies that the pension or retired pay is only partly attributable to disablement or disability the exemption applies only to that part [*ITEPA 2003, s 641* as amended by *Finance Act 2005 (FA 2005), s 19(6)*]. For 2005/06 onwards a lump sum provided under a scheme established by the *Armed Forces Early Departure Payments Scheme Order 2005* is also exempted from tax [*ITEPA 2003, s 640A* inserted by *FA 2005, s 19(5)*]. *ITEPA 2003, s 566* also taxes any other pension paid by (or on behalf of) a person in the UK [*ITEPA 2003, s 569*]. In some cases it also includes a lump sum paid under an unapproved pension scheme [*ITEPA 2003, s 394*]. The detailed rules are considered at **10.80–10.89**.

2.28   The *Pensions Act 2004* (*PA 2004*) introduced a bonus for those who defer their state pension for at least 12 months. This can be paid either as an increase in pension or as a lump sum. Such a lump sum can be either a state pension lump sum, a shared additional pension lump sum or a graduated retirement benefit lump sum, depending on what pension rights the individual elects to defer [*Finance (No 2) Act 2005* (*F No.2) A 2005*), *s 9(1)*]. If the individual opts for the lump sum this is still treated as income for tax purposes but is ignored in calculating his total income (so will not affect either the rate of tax on that lump sum itself or any top slicing relief on other income). The amount is taxable for the 'applicable year of assessment' and is taxable on the pensioner irrespective of whether he is resident, ordinarily resident or domiciled in the UK [*F (No 2) A 2005, s 7(1)–(4)*]. The rate of tax is dependent on the pensioner's total income (ignoring the lump sum). If this is nil the tax on the lump sum is nil. If it does not exceed the starting rate for the year the lump sum is taxed at the starting rate. If it does so but does not exceed the basic rate limit the lump sum is taxed at the basic rate and if it exceeds that limit the lump sum is taxed at the higher rate [*F (No 2) A 2005, s 7(5)*].

2.29   The applicable year of assessment is that in which the first benefit payment day falls (ie the day on which the deferred pension starts to be paid) [*F (No 2) A 2005, s 8(1)–(3)*]. If the individual dies before the beginning of the tax year in which the pension starts to be paid (eg it is paid to his widow) the applicable year of assessment is the year in which he dies [*F (No 2) A 2005, s 7(2)(b)*]. If the election to defer the pension was made by a deceased spouse and on the death of that spouse the surviving spouse was in receipt of a state pension in her own right, the first benefit payment day is the date of death of the deceased spouse, because the surviving spouse can bring the deferment to an end [*F (No 2) A 2005, s 8(4)*]. If the surviving spouse is not yet entitled to a state pension she cannot claim the lump sum until she first becomes entitled to a pension, so the normal rule which will fix the date her own pension starts to be paid on the first benefit payment day will apply. If the Secretary of State for Work and Pensions makes regulations to enable a pensioner to elect to defer taking his lump sum until the tax year after that in which the deferred pension starts to be paid (as he has done by *Regulation 8* of the *Social Security (Deferral of Retirement Pensions, Shared Additional Pension and Graduated Retirement Benefit) (Miscellaneous Provisions) Regulations 2005 (SI 2005 No 2677)*), the applicable year of assessment will be that later year. If the pensioner dies during that later year and at the date of his death has not made the election but the regulations enable his personal representatives to do so the applicable year will be that later year. (The above regulations do not contain such a provision.) If the individual dies before the beginning of that later tax year the applicable year will be the tax year in which he dies [*F (No 2) A 2005, s 8(5)–(7)*].

Sickness benefits

2.30   Sickness or disability benefits paid to an employee on a weekly or monthly basis (as opposed to a lump sum, which would not normally constitute income) and which are financed by the employer, eg through insurance premiums, are regarded as emoluments from the employment.

2.31   Where an ex-employee receives a pension awarded on retirement through disability caused by injury on duty, by a work-related illness (eg pneumoconiosis) or by war wounds, and this exceeds the pension he would have received had he retired on the grounds of ordinary ill health, the excess is not treated as income. [*ITEPA 2003, s 644* enacting *ESC A62*].

Voluntary pensions

2.32   A pension arising from a past employment of the pensioner (or of the spouse, parent or a relative or dependant of the pensioner) and which is paid by the ex-employer or his successor, is under the employment income rules even if it is voluntary and even though it is capable of being discontinued. [*ITEPA 2003, s 633*]. If the pension is paid by or on behalf of a non-UK resident it may still be taxable in the UK, but the taxable amount is limited to the amount on which tax would have been chargeable if the pension were income from a foreign possession. [*ITEPA 2003, s 635*]. This not only applies the remittance basis to such a pension but also may take it outside the scope of UK tax completely, as if the pension is truly voluntary it is probably not a foreign 'possession'.

Foreign pensions

2.33   Any other government pension receivable by a UK resident is also taxable under the employment income rules if it is payable in the UK by (or through) any public department, officer or agent of:

(*a*)   a country forming part of Her Majesty's dominions;

(*b*)   any other country for the time being mentioned in *Schedule 3* to the *British Nationality Act 1981 (BNA 1981)*; and

(*c*)   any other territory under Her Majesty's protection,

and is payable either to:

(i)   a person who has been employed in the service of the Crown (or service under the government of one of the above territories) outside the UK; or

(ii)   a widow, child, relative or dependant of any such person, and is in respect of that service.

[*ITEPA 2003, s 615*].

2.34   Only 90 per cent of such a pension is taxable however – or, to be precise, one-tenth of it may be deducted in charging the pension to tax. [*ITEPA 2003, s 617*]. This does not apply if the pension is payable by the UK Government as such pensions are regarded as UK, not foreign pensions.

2.35 The residence and domicile status of the recipient is irrelevant in relation to pensions, except, of course, to the extent that his tax treatment may be affected by one of the UK's double taxation agreements with other countries. The OECD model double tax agreement, which the UK normally follows, provides that pensions are taxable only in the country in which the recipient is resident, with the exception of government (or local authority, etc.) pensions. These are taxable only by the paying country unless the recipient is both a national and a resident of the other country, in which case they are instead taxed in that country. For example a pension paid by a UK company to a US resident will be exempt from UK tax (and taxed in the USA). One paid by the UK government or a local authority is taxable in the UK (and exempted in the USA) unless the recipient is a US national in which case it is taxed in the US instead. The State social security retirement pension is not regarded as a government pension for this purpose.

2.36 A pension not falling within any of the above categories, such as one paid by a non-UK and non-government employer in respect of services performed overseas, is not taxable as employment income but as income from a foreign possession.

2.37 Certain pensions payable by the German and Austrian governments to victims of Nazi persecution are exempt from tax. [*ITEPA 2003, s 642*]. The main ones are those payable under the following:

(*a*)   the Law for Compensation to Members of the Public Service (BWGoD);

(*b*)   the Equalisation of Burdens Law (LAG);

(*c*)   the Law to Compensate Austrian Public Servants;

(*d*)   the Law Concerning Compensation for National Socialist Injustice in Social Insurance (WGSVG);

(*e*)   pensions paid to victims of National Socialist Persecution whose social security contributions were paid in the German Reich outside the Federal Republic or in Danzig and to certain others whose entitlement derives from contributions in the territories annexed by Germany in 1938 and 1939 (under *s 99, Employers Insurance Law* (AVG), *s 1320, Reich Insurance Code* (RVO) or *s 9, Refugees and Foreign Pensions Law* (FAG), *s 108, Miners Pension Law* (RGK) or *ss 18* and *19* of the law to regulate compensation for National Socialist injustice in social insurance (WGSVG).

(Inspector's Manual, para 1584).

Other assessable items

Sick pay

2.38 In certain trades, such as the building industry, where it is common for a person to work for short periods in a succession of employments, employers contribute to a central industry-wide fund during the period they employ a person, so that if he is off sick the cost of sick pay is effectively spread amongst all the employers and is not a burden on the one for whom the individual happens to be working at a particular point in time. Without such an arrangement few employers would be prepared to pay sick pay, or holiday pay, where they engage a worker for only a few weeks. With such centralised schemes the sick pay is not paid by the employer but by the central fund. Furthermore, it would not be attributable to any one of the employments, and in the absence of special provisions might escape tax as there would be no source from which it derives.

2.39   It is accordingly provided that if a person holding an employment is absent from work by reason of sickness or disability, any sick pay or similar payment to the employee (or to his order, or for his benefit or that of a member of his family or household, ie his spouse, his children and their spouses, his parents and his dependants) is taxable as earnings of the employment if it arises as a result of any arrangements entered into by his employer. [*ITEPA 2003, s 221*]. If the fund for making such payments is contributed to partly by the employee and partly by employers, only a proportion of the payment is taxable, namely the part that it is just and reasonable to attribute to the employer's contributions. [*ITEPA 2003, s 221(4)*].

2.40   This ensures that where sick pay is paid not by the employer but, for example, by a trade association, the amount constitutes taxable income.

Other taxable payments

2.41   It is specifically provided that the following statutory payments under social security and other legislation are taxable income. [*ITEPA 2003, s 660*].

(*a*)   Statutory sick pay under *section 1* of the *Social Security and Housing Benefits Act 1982* (or the corresponding Northern Ireland legislation).

(*b*)   Statutory maternity pay under the *Social Security Act 1986* (*SSA 1986*) (or the corresponding Northern Ireland enactment).

(*c*)   Statutory paternity pay and statutory adoption pay under *ts 12ZA* or *s 12ZB* of the *Social Security Contributions and Benefits Act 1992* (*SSCBA 1992*).

(*d*)   Income support under the *SSA 1986* which is paid in respect of a period during which the claimant:

   (i)   is one of a married or unmarried couple (as defined in the *SSA* 1986) and although he is engaged in a trade dispute the other person is not. [*ITEPA 2003, s 665*].

   If the income support paid for a week (or part of a week) exceeds the 'taxable maximum' for that period the excess is not taxable. [*ITEPA 2003, s 667*]. The taxable maximum is 50 per cent of the 'applicable amount' under the *SSA 1986* [*ITEPA 2003, s 668*]. Where a single person or both of a couple are on strike no income support is due except in respect of any addition for dependants, so there is nothing to tax.

(*e*) Jobseeker's allowance under the *Jobseekers Act 1995* (*JSA 1995*). If it exceeds the taxable maximum the excess is not taxable. Where an income-based jobseeker's allowance is paid to one of a married or unmarried couple the taxable maximum is the portion of the applicable amount (as defined in the Regulations under that Act) included therein. Where such an allowance is paid to anyone else it is the age-related amount that would be applicable if a contribution-based allowance had been paid. Where a contribution-based jobseeker's allowance is paid to one of a couple it is the portion of the applicable amount that would have applied had an income-based jobseeker's allowance been paid. For other contribution-based jobseeker's allowance recipients it is the age related amount applicable to him. If an income-based jobseeker's allowance is paid to one of a couple the other of which is barred from allowance because of a trade dispute the taxable maximum is half of the applicable amount. [*ITEPA 2003, ss 670–676*].

(*f*) Unemployment benefit (up to 6 October 1996) and supplementary benefit under the *Social Security Act 1975* (*SSA 1975*), the *Social Security Pensions Act 1975* (*SSPA 1975*) (both now consolidated into the *Social Security Contributions and Benefits Act 1992*) and the corresponding Northern Ireland legislation. Also invalid care allowance and widowed mother's allowance, in each case apart from any dependent child addition. [*Hansard 7 June 1993, col 49*].

(*g*) Incapacity benefit under the *Social Security (Incapacity for Work) Act 1994* other than benefit for a period for which short-term incapacity benefit is payable otherwise than at the higher rate (ie other than under *SSCBA 1992, ss 30B(5), 40(8)* or *41(7)*) and any increase in benefit in respect of a child, and the continuing benefit where the period of incapacity began before 13 April 1995. [*ITEPA 2003, ss 663, 664*].

(*h*) Contributory Employment and Support Allowance (ESA) under the *Welfare Reform Act 2007* (*WRA 2007*) [*ITEPA 2003, s 658* as amended by the *WRA 2007, s 28(1)*]. From 27 October 2008 ESA replaced Incapacity Benefit and Income Support on the basis of incapacity for new claimants. It consists of two parts, one of which is taxable and the other of which is not.

2.42   The following social security benefits are not taxable: attendance allowance, back to work bonus, bereavement payment, child benefit, child's special allowance, child tax credit, council tax benefit, disability living allowance, guardian's allowance, housing benefit, industrial injuries benefit (other than death benefit), pensioner's Christmas bonus, payments out of the Social Fund, severe disablement allowance, state maternity allowance, state pension credit, universal credit, working tax credit, payments to reduce underoccupation by housing benefit claimants, in-work credit, in-work emergency discretion fund payments, in-work emergency fund payments and return to work credits. [*ITEPA 2003, s 677* as amended by *FA 2013, s 13*]. Short-term incapacity benefit, disability living allowance, invalidity benefit, compensation payments where child support is reduced due to a change in legislation, child maintenance bonus and increases in other benefits attributable to a child, all of which are no longer payable, were also not taxed. [*ITEPA 2003, s 677*]. Employment Retention and Advancement Scheme payments and Return to Work Credit Scheme payments under those government pilot schemes are also exempt from tax [*Taxation of Benefits under Government Pilot Schemes (Return to Work Credit and Employment Retention and Advancement Schemes) Order 2003 (SI 2003 No 2339)*]. Better off in Work Credit, which was introduced as a pilot scheme from 27 October 2008, is also exempt from income tax (*Taxation of Benefits under Government Pilot Schemes (Better off in Work Credit) Order 2008 (SI 2008 No 2603)*). Return to Work Credit ceased in 1 October 2013. Better off in Work credit appears not to have been proceeded with.

2.43　There is a special appeals procedure for taxable unemployment benefit, jobseeker's allowance or income support. Under this a Department for Work and Pensions Benefits Officer notifies the recipient of the amount on which he is taxable. Such notice must state the date of issue and contain a statement that the recipient is entitled to object to the notice within 60 days. [*Section 152(1)*]. The benefits officer has power to extend this 60-day period if he is satisfied that there was a reasonable excuse for an objection not having been made in time. [*Section 152(5)*]. If no objection is made (or one is made but subsequently withdrawn) the taxable amount cannot subsequently be challenged on an appeal against the assessment. [*Section 152(2)*]. If an objection is made and an amended figure is subsequently agreed (and confirmed in writing by the benefits officer) there is again no further right of appeal, although the recipient can repudiate or resile from the agreement within 60 days of its having been made. [*Section 152(3), (4)*]. If, having issued a notice, the benefits officer changes his mind as to the amount, he can issue a notice of alteration which will supersede the original notice – but that notice will not give a fresh right of appeal. [*Section 152(6)*]. Presumably if the original figure was acceptable but the new one is not, the issue of the amended notice would be a reasonable ground for not having appealed within the 60-day limit. Where the amount is not agreed it can of course be challenged before the appeal Commissioners in the normal way.

2.44　Curiously, there appears to be no procedure for the General or Special Commissioners to hear an appeal against such a notice. The objection simply preserves the taxpayer's right to challenge the amount on an appeal against the assessment when it is eventually raised. There is a right of appeal against a benefits officer's refusal to accept a late objection [*Section 152(5)*], but again it appears that the Commissioners can merely determine whether or not there is a reasonable excuse for it not having been submitted on time, and cannot consider what the true amount should be unless at the same time they hear an appeal against the assessment.

2.45　Payments made by foreign governments which correspond to UK social security benefits which are exempt from tax, or to child benefit, are also not taxed. [*ITEPA 2003, s 681*].

2.46　It should also be mentioned at this stage that some other statutory provisions deem certain receipts to be income taxable as earnings. [*ITEPA 2003,* *s 7(5)*]. Such a provision can operate independently. It may not be necessary to bring the circumstances within the employment income charging provisions to trigger the tax charge. (*Nichols v Gibson [1996] STC 1008* – see **11.31**).

The receipts basis of assessment

2.47 Having ascertained that emoluments fall within the charging provisions, it is next necessary to discover the year in which they are to be assessed. Tax on employment income is normally charged on the amount of the earnings from the employment received in a year of assessment (subject to a possible 100 per cent reduction for overseas employments of seafarers extending for over 12 months – see **Chapter 12** below). [*ITEPA 2003, s 15*]. If the employee is resident and ordinarily resident but not domiciled in the UK tax on overseas earnings (see **2.6**) is chargeable on the amount received in (or remitted to) the UK in the year of assessment. [*ITEPA 2003, s 23*]. If he is resident but not ordinarily resident in the UK his chargeable earnings are again the amount received in the UK in the tax year, except to the extent that they derive from duties performed in the UK where the taxable amount is the amount received (whether in the UK or elsewhere) in the tax year. [*ITEPA 2003, s 26*]. A non-resident individual is taxable only on earnings which both relate to duties performed in the UK and are received in the UK during the tax year. [*ITEPA 2003, s 27*].

2.48 It does not matter whether the emoluments relate to the year of assessment in which they are received or to some other year nor, indeed, whether the employment is held in the year of receipt (or the year of remittance). They will be assessable in the year of receipt even if this is before the employment starts or after it has ceased provided that the remuneration relates to a year of assessment for which the charging provisions impose a tax charge, or is deemed to relate to such a year under *sections 17* or *30* [*ITEPA 2003, ss 15(3), 21(3), 26(3), 27(3)*]. It does not even matter that the money may be received after the employee's death (or, as the case may be, may be remitted to the UK by his executors or administrators). In such circumstances the tax charge is made on the estate of the deceased employee. [*ITEPA 2003, s 13(4), (4A)*]. The receipt basis does not apply to pension income, social security income or employment income arising before 1989/90. Where such income is received more than six years after the year to which it relates it can nevertheless be assessed to tax at any time during the six tax years following that in which it was received. [*TMA 1970, s 35*].

Determining date of receipt

2.49 For the purpose of establishing the appropriate tax year for remuneration taxable the following rules apply to determine when an amount is received. If more than one of them applies, the earliest date fixed by any of them must be adopted. [*ITEPA 2003, ss 18, 31*].

(*a*)   The time when payment is made of, or on account of, the emoluments. Although on this wording a payment on account appears to trigger tax on the entire emoluments the intention is obviously that it should trigger tax only on the payment on account itself, and that is how HMRC interpret it.

(b) The time when a person becomes entitled to payment of or on account of the earnings. For example, if a person is entitled under his contract of employment to receive his March 2010 salary on 31 March 2010 but because of a shortage of funds his employer does not actually pay it until after 6 April 2010 it will nevertheless be assessable for 2009/10. The employer must deduct tax under PAYE and account for it to HMRC as if the remuneration had been paid on 31 March 2010. It is possible to structure a contract of employment so that a person becomes entitled to a bonus on the termination of the employment or such earlier time as he may request. In such circumstances he would not become entitled to payment of the emoluments until he makes such a request. If a person is entitled to commission on sales that he makes during March 2010 but his contract provides that this will be paid with his April salary he will not become entitled *to payment of* the commission until April, even though legally he may well be entitled to the commission immediately on making the sales.

(c) The time when sums on account of the earnings are credited in the company's accounts or records. This only applies if the recipient is a company director and the earnings are from an office or employment with the company. The most obvious example is where an amount is credited to a director's current account. However, this head is wider than that. It would also apply, for example, if the amount is simply included as a general creditor in the company's accounts – provided, of course, that the amount is identifiable as being in respect of emoluments for a particular individual.

For this purpose any restriction on the right to withdraw the money must be disregarded. [*ITEPA 2003, s 18(2)*]. Suppose, for example, remuneration is credited to a director's current account but he has agreed with the company's bankers that he will not withdraw the money until the company's overdraft falls below a specified sum. The remuneration is nevertheless to be treated as paid when it is credited. Remuneration being credited subject to a restriction must be distinguished from sums conditionally credited, which will not trigger a tax charge. Thus, if the remuneration was voted conditional on the overdraft falling below the specified level, and provisionally credited to the account it would not be regarded as paid at the time of crediting as it is not 'earnings' until such time as the condition is satisfied.

(d) If the amount of the earnings is determined during the course of a company's accounting year (or other period in respect of which the emoluments are paid) it is deemed to be paid at the end of that year or period. Again this only applies if the recipient is a company director and the earnings are from an office or employment with the company.

(e) If the amount of the emoluments for a period is not known until it is determined after the end of that period, then the emoluments are deemed to be paid at the time the amount is determined. This test also applies only where the recipient is a company director and the earnings are from an office or employment with the company. The obvious example is the common situation under *Table A* of the *Companies Act 1948* where a director is not entitled to any remuneration until it is determined by the company in general meeting, which is usually done at the time the accounts are approved.

2.50 Heads (*c*), (*d*) and (*e*) in **2.49** above, apply irrespective of whether the remuneration relates to the office of director. [*ITEPA 2003, s 18(1)*]. For example, if a person is a director of a company, for which he is paid director's fees, and in addition is employed by the company as a sales executive these heads will apply to his salary as sales executive by reason of the fact that he is a director of the company. Furthermore, these three heads apply if the person is a director of the company at any time in the year of assessment in which the remuneration falls. [*ITEPA 2003, s 18(2)*]. For example, suppose a person is an employee until 31 March 2006 and is appointed a director on 1 April 2006. Suppose also that a bonus for the year to 31 March 2006 is credited for him to an account in the company's books during March 2006, and that this sum is paid over to him in May 2006. Because he became a director during 2006/07 the remuneration will be deemed to be paid in March 2006 even though at that time he was not a director. The converse also seems to apply. If a person was a director at 31 March 2006 but then resigns and a bonus for him is credited to the company's books in December 2006 and paid over to him in May 2007 it will be remuneration of 2006/07 (under head (*a*) of **2.49** above) as he was not a director at any time during 2006/07 when the remuneration was credited and determined, so heads (*c*) and (*e*) would not apply to it. The reason that these rules are repeated in both *sections 18* and *31* is that *section 18* is dealing with employees who are resident, ordinarily resident and domiciled in the UK and *section 31* with employees who are resident, ordinarily resident or domiciled elsewhere (see **2.6–2.8**).

Meaning of 'director'

2.51 For the purpose of heads (*c*), (*d*) and (*e*) of **2.49** above, a 'director' means:

(*a*) in relation to a company whose affairs are managed by a board of directors or similar body, a member of that board or body;

(*b*) in relation to a company whose affairs are managed by a single director or similar person, that person; and

(*c*) in relation to a company whose affairs are managed by the members themselves, a member of the company.

[*ITEPA 2003, s 18(3)*].

2.52 The word 'director' also includes any person in accordance with whose directions or instructions the company's directors are accustomed to act.

However, a person cannot be deemed to be a director under this test by reason only that the directors act on advice given by him in a professional capacity. [*ITEPA 2003, s 18(3), (4)*]. This is the same definition as that of a 'shadow director' under the *Companies Act 1985 (CA 1985)*. This provision does not exclude all outside advisers, however. The person concerned must be carrying on a profession. In *Currie v* and *Durant v IRC* (both *12 TC 245*) it was held that an income tax repayment agent was not carrying on a profession and neither was an insurance broker. There are also a number of VAT tribunal decisions on what is a profession, but these are not concerned with the types of people that might be expected to act as outside advisers to a company.

Special provisions

2.53   Some legislative provisions deem certain types of emoluments to be paid at specific dates. Such provisions obviously override the five basic rules set out above.

2.54   The sections of *ITEPA 2003* concerned are:

s 87(1) non-cash vouchers (see **6.20** below)

s 94 credit tokens (see **6.30** below)

s 81 cash vouchers (see **6.16** below)

s 327 living accommodation (see **8.4** below)

s 401 compensation for loss of office, etc (see **11.15** below)

s 72 benefits in kind (see **6.43** below)

s 114 cars available for private use (see **7.2** below)

s 150 car fuel (see **7.46** below)

s 154 vans available for private use (see **7.98** below)

s 175 beneficial loans (see **9.1** below)

s 188 release of beneficial loans (see **9.25** below)

s 446u disposal of shares acquired at an undervalue (see **14.86** below)

s 223 director's tax paid by employer (see **9.28** below)

s 222 payment by employer where tax deduction not possible (see **17.65** below).

[*ITEPA 2003, ss 19(2)*].

2.55   If emoluments take the form of a benefit not consisting of money (and not within one of the above statutory provisions) the five rules set out in **2.49** above do not apply. Instead, the emoluments are treated as received at the time the benefit is provided. [*ITEPA 2003, s 19(1)*].

Employment Loss Relief

2.55A   If a person is in employment or holds an office in a tax year and makes a loss in the employment or office in that year, he can make a claim to set the loss against general income [*ITA 2007, s 128(1)*]. The loss can be set against income of the tax year in which it is realised, the previous tax year or both. The claim must specify the year for which the loss is to be relieved and, if that is both, which year's income is to be offset first [*ITA 2007, s 128(2)-(4)*]. A claim for both years will eliminate the whole of the taxable income for the 'first' year before anything is set against income for the second. This is because the claim for each year is for the entire loss; it cannot be for part only of the loss so as to keep income in charge to cover the personal allowance and basic rate tax band [*ITA 2007, s 129(2)*]. The claim must be made by the first anniversary of the normal self-assessment filing date (31 January) [*ITA 2007, s 128(5)*]. Making a claim in relation to one year only does not debar a second claim in relation to the other year [*ITA 2007, s 128(6)*]. No claim can be made if (and to the extent that) the loss is made as a result of something done in pursuance of arrangements one of the main purposes of which is the avoidance of tax [*ITA 2007, s 128(5A)*]. If a claim is made for employment loss relief to be set against income of a tax year and a subsequent claim is made to carry back a loss in the next year against that income, the first claim takes priority [*ITA 2007, s 129(2)–(4)*].

2.55B   If the loss cannot be fully relieved against income, the balance can be set against capital gains for the relevant year in the same way as a trading loss [*ITA 2007, s 130, Taxation of Chargeable Gains Act 1992 (TCGA 1992), s 261B*].

2.55C   It is difficult to see how a loss can arise in an employment as deductions are normally limited to the income and it would in any event be unusual for expenses to exceed the income from the employment, particularly in the light of the very restrictive rules on allowability of expenses in relation to an employment (see **5.2**). One instance where the provision was held to apply was in *Martin v HMRC* (TC 2460) (see **11.73A**) where Mr Martin had to repay part of a signing on fee.

Pensions

2.56   Pensions are not affected by the adoption of the receipts basis of taxation. They are taxed as income of the year in which they accrue, irrespective of whether or not they are paid in that year. This applies to pensions chargeable under *ITEPA 2003, s 566* (see **2.26** above); voluntary pensions taxable under *ITEPA 2003, s 633* (see **2.32** above); income support under the *Social Security Act 1986* assessable under *ITEPA 2003, s 665* (see **2.41** above); pensions paid under retirement benefit schemes which are taxable under *ITEPA 2003, s 580* and the National Insurance state pension which is taxable under *ITEPA 2003, s 577* (see **2.26** above). Pensions payable under personal pension and retirement annuity schemes take the form of annuities and as such are not regarded as employment income but are nevertheless earned income [*Income* *and Corporation Taxes Act 1988 (ICTA 1988), ss 643(3), 619(1), (b)]*. They are still, subject to PAYE (see **17.68**). In the case of retirement annuities if the whole of the premiums did not qualify for relief only the proportion attributable to the part that did is earnings. The personal pension rules require any premium not qualifying for relief to be repaid, so that situation cannot arise. If income withdrawals are taken from a personal pension scheme they are taxable as employment income and subject to PAYE (*ITEPA 2003, s 598*). Income withdrawals cannot be taken from retirement annuities. The UK's double tax agreements normally provide that pensions can betaxed only in the country of residence. Accordingly where a UK resident retires abroad his pension (including the State pension) is usually outside the scope of UK tax. Conversely a UK resident who spent his working life overseas will be taxable here on his overseas pension even though it derives from overseas work.

2.57 In *Minto v HMRC [2008] STC (SCD) 121* the appellant was unable to work from September 2000 because of work-related stress. His employer had taken out permanent health insurance (PHI) which met the bulk of his salary. On 1 March 2002 he was made redundant. His employer arranged (under a term of the PHI policy) for the PHI policy in respect of Mr Minto to be transferred to him. Mr Minto claimed that either the transfer of the policy was in settlement of his claim against the employer for work-related stress and the payments under it were instalments of a capital payment due to him, or that the PHI payments constituted a structured settlement of damages which was exempt from tax. The Special Commissioner disagreed. He felt that the payments were more aptly described as pension payments taxable as employment income having regard to their origin as benefits of Mr Minto's employment.

PAYE

2.58 Income tax on salaries and other remuneration taxable as employment income is normally collected by deduction at source under the Pay As You Earn (PAYE) system. This requires the employer to withhold income tax by reference to tax tables published by HMRC and account for it to HMRC. Interest is chargeable from 14 days after the end of the tax year on the amount unpaid at that time [*Regulation 82*]. There is still no interest on late payment of the monthly amounts due during the tax year though. The PAYE system is dealt with in **Chapter 17**.

Chapter 3

The Meaning of 'Earnings'

Money and money's worth

3.1   Prior to 2003/04 there was no exhaustive statutory definition of emoluments, although the word was expressed to include all salaries, fees, wages, perquisites and profits whatsoever. [*Income and Corporation Taxes Act 1988 (ICTA 1988), s 13(1)*]. For 2003/04 onwards there is a definition of earnings from an employment. This means any salary, wages or fee, any gratuity or other profit or incidental benefit of any kind obtained by the employee if it is money or money's worth, and anything else that constitutes an emolument of the employment. [*Income Tax (Earnings and Pensions Act 2003 (ITEPA 2003), s 62(2)*]. Unfortunately, this reverts to the use of the word 'emolument' as a sweep-up term and, like its predecessor, does not attempt to define it. Indeed, it does not use the word anywhere else in the Act, having chosen to replace it by general earnings – a term which it then defines by reference to *s 62(2)*! It is, however, clear that not every benefit received by an employee falls within the scope of earnings. In *Tennant v Smith 3 TC 158* Lord Halsbury states 'Your Lordships are to ascertain not whether Mr Tennant has got advantages which enable him to spend more of his income than if he did not possess them, but whether he has got that which any words in the Statute point out as the subject on which it imposes taxation.' He went on to say 'I came to the conclusion that the Act refers to money payments made to the person who receives them, though, of course, I do not deny that if substantial things of money value were capable of being turned into money they might for that purpose represent money's worth and be therefore taxable.'

3.2   Lord Halsbury was influenced to some extent by the fact that the wording of the legislation in 1890 when this case was heard provided that tax should be charged under Schedule E on all 'salaries, fees, wages, perquisites or profits' and perquisites was defined as 'fees or other emoluments' payable either by the Crown or the subject. The word 'payable' does not appear in the current legislation. Nevertheless, the concept that what is taxable is money or money's worth, and not anything else, is so well established that it is unlikely to be challenged. This is in any event a relatively unimportant limitation as most benefits in kind are now specifically brought within the tax net and the taxpayer is normally indifferent as to whether he is taxed on them because they are emoluments or because they are benefits.

Employer discharging liability

3.3   In *Hartland v Diggines 10 TC 247* Mr Hartland was paid a bonus, and in addition his employer paid to HMRC the tax thereon. Mr Hartland contended – it is not wholly clear why – that only the net sum was income of his; the tax was a voluntary payment by his employer which was nothing to do with him. Lord Pollock analysed the position as follows. 'Mr Hartland is responsible to [HMRC] to pay the tax in respect of his emoluments and salary and perquisites which he receives; and in effect ... he has received a certain amount of money into his hands, and he has received an indemnity against any liability to pay any part of it to [HMRC]. In effect, therefore, what he has received is the money paid into his hands, plus that immunity; and ... one has to look at the substance of the matter ... The substance of the matter is that the salary paid to Mr Hartland is not all he has received. He has received money's worth to the extent of the sum which has been paid in respect of that salary to [HMRC].'

3.4   Although this was a case heard in 1924, long before the introduction of PAYE, the concept that relieving a person of a liability is an emolument was reaffirmed in *Richardson v Worrall 58 TC 642*. That case was concerned with purchases through credit cards. Mr Worrall paid for petrol with a credit card in his employer's name. He contended that this was an expense incurred by his employer and as such was covered by the round sum car use benefit (see **7.2** below – the fuel benefit (see **7.45** below) did not exist at the time). It was held that at the moment he put petrol into his car he had incurred a liability to pay for the petrol. As he had not specifically told the garage attendant that he was filling up the car on behalf of his employer before taking the petrol, this liability was a personal liability (even if he was acting as agent for an undisclosed principal he incurred a joint personal liability). Accordingly, when he paid for the petrol with the company credit card the company was discharging a pre-existing liability of Mr Worrall and the payment was taxable on him as emoluments – so that the benefits in kind provisions, which Mr Worrall was challenging, were not relevant to the taxability.

3.5   In *Perrons v Spackman 55 TC 403* it was held that a mileage allowance paid to an employee when he used his own car on his employer's business was part of his emoluments. The taxpayer claimed that it was a reimbursement of travelling expenses, not an emolument. Not surprisingly this contention was dismissed as it was a cash payment clearly arising from the employment. The real issue was whether an equivalent sum was deductible under what is now *section 336* (see **5.2** below) as an expense. The taxpayer had based his claim on the House of Lords judgment in *Pook v Owen 45 TC 571* (see **5.38**) but Vinelott J felt that that case had proceeded on the basis that the car allowance in *Pook v Owen* was a reimbursement of actual expenses. In Mr Perrons' case there was no evidence that the mileage allowance was a mere reimbursement of expenses actually incurred by Mr Perrons in making journeys in the course of his duties. It included a significant contribution to the overhead costs of putting his car on the road and maintaining it for his own private use as well as for business use. Accordingly the allowance had to be treated as emoluments with Mr Perrons then making a claim for a deduction against it under *section 336*.

Unfortunately, the claim failed because the whole expense of maintaining the car could not be said to be an expense that he was necessarily obliged to incur as part of the expense of travelling in the performance of his duties.

3.6   The breadth of the word 'emoluments' is well illustrated by *Weight v Salmon 19 TC 174*. The managing director of a listed company was entitled to a fixed salary but in addition each year the board of directors by resolution gave him the privilege of applying at par for a specified number of shares in the company. The shares acquired were worth substantially more than par and HMRC assessed him on the difference between the two figures. The House of Lords had no difficulty in holding that the advantage of being able to acquire the shares at an undervalue came within 'or profits whatsoever'. Subject to the special rules on employee shareholdings considered in **Chapter 14**, the acquisition of shares at an undervalue will accordingly trigger a tax charge on the undervalue. The special rules described at **14.121** apply to ascertain the market value at the time of acquisition of shares (or an interest in shares) in a research institution spin-out company for the purpose of calculating any such undervalue. [*ITEPA 2003, s 452(2)(a)*].

3.7   Money does not have to come from the employer for it to be taxable. In *Hunter v Dewhurst 16 TC 605*, which was concerned with compensation for loss of office, Lord Atkin stated that the question was whether the payment was received 'from' the office. He thought that the wording 'appears to me to indicate emoluments either received from the employer or from some third party (such as tips, permitted commission and the like) as a reward for services rendered in the course of the employment'. In the light of this it is not surprising that in *Calvert v Wainwright 27 TC 475* it was held that tips received by an employed taxi driver formed part of his emoluments. Indeed, as early as 1878 it was held that a pecuniary gift received at Christmas by a clergyman from his congregation as a token of their regard for him, although voluntarily paid, accrued to him by reason of his holding his office under the Church of Scotland and in respect of the discharge of his duties of that office. It was accordingly an emolument (*In Re Strong, 1 TC 207*). In *Herbert v McQuade 4 TC 489* and *Cooper v Blakiston 5 TC 347* payments to clergymen by third parties were again held to be part of their emoluments.

3.8   There is no reason why a non-cash reward from a third party should be excluded provided of course that it is capable of conversion into money (so that it is money's worth) and is paid as a result of the individual holding the employment. The amount of the emoluments in such a case is of course the price that could be obtained from a disposal of the item or right in accordance with *Wilkins v Rogerson 39 TC 344* (see **6.70**). There is however an exemption for gifts from a third party if that gift consists of goods (or a voucher or token only capable of being used to obtain goods), the donor is not connected with the employer, the gift is not made in recognition of the performance of particular services in the course of the employment (or in anticipation of such services), it has not been directly or indirectly procured by the employer, and the total cost of all gifts made by the donor to the employee in the tax year does not exceed £250. [*ITEPA 2003, s 324* and *Income Tax (Exemption of Minor Benefits) (Increase in Sums of Money) Order (SI 2003 No 1361)*]. There is also a statutory exclusion from the benefit in kind rules for the higher paid (see **6.37**) for the provision of entertaining (including hospitality of any kind) provided for staff of others provided it is not in recognition of particular services and not procured directly or indirectly by their employer. [*ITEPA 2003, s 265*]. This is intended to cover such things as invitations to social events, football matches, etc.

3.9   More recently the meaning of emoluments fell to be considered by the Special Commissioners in *Sports Club plc v Inspector of Taxes [2000] STC (SCD) 443*. Evelyn and Jocelyn, two international footballers, each entered into service agreements with Sports Club plc. They also entered into promotional agreements with companies unconnected with Sports Club plc. Sports Club plc then made substantial advance payments to the promotional companies for the right to exploit the 'image rights', (ie the right to exploit and use the player's name, image, signature and voice) of Evelyn and Jocelyn respectively. Sports Club plc also entered into a further agreement with Evelyn's company (owned by his manager) under which that company would provide consultancy advice to Sports Club plc. HMRC contended that the payments for the image rights and the consultancy advice were in reality additional remuneration of Evelyn and Jocelyn. The Special Commissioners asked themselves four questions: Did the promotional agreements have independent value? Did the consultancy agreement have an independent value? Were the promotional agreements a smokescreen for additional remuneration? And were the payments under the agreement emoluments 'from' the employment? They answered the first two in the affirmative based on the evidence. They also held that on the facts the promotional and consultancy agreements were not a smokescreen but gave the Club valuable rights that they intended to exploit (albeit that for various reasons they had not in fact derived significant income from them). It was a short step from that to find that the payments under those agreements were made in return for promotional rights and consultancy services respectively, and not in reference to the playing of football which was the service rendered by the players under their service agreement. Accordingly, the payments were not emoluments from the employments of Evelyn or Jocelyn.

3.10   When this decision was first published some people felt that it created a significant tax avoidance opportunity. This is probably not the case. Many sportspeople and entertainers have the ability to generate 'merchandising' income in addition to their performance income. Image rights are simply a form of merchandising. Many sportsmen have substantial promotional contracts with commercial companies such as Nike or Adidas to exploit specific image rights. Indeed, Jocelyn already had contracts with Mizuna (a clothing manufacture) and McDonald's for exploitation of his image when the image rights contract with Sports Club plc was entered into. HMRC have never sought to treat such contracts as derived from the player's performance. It is hard to see why HMRC thought that it should make any difference that in the case of Evelyn and Jocelyn the promotional contracts were with the Club rather than with a third party. Furthermore, it is hard to see on what basis they hoped to recharacterise payments to a third party as emoluments of the players.

3.11   HMRC put forward an alternative contention that the payments were benefits in kind. The Commissioners accepted that the words 'by reason of the employment' in *ITEPA 2003, s 70* (see **6.43**) are wider than the definition of employment income in *ITEPA 2003, s 7* (formerly 'emoluments from the employment' in *ICTA 1988, s 19*). However, they had already held that the payments under the agreements were not made 'by reason of the employment' of Evelyn or Jocelyn; they were paid by reason of the separate commercial contracts to provide promotional and consultancy services. They also felt that the expression 'benefit' in *ITEPA 2003, s 201* 'must exclude anything provided in return for good consideration under a separate commercial contract'. Finally, they did not see how they could lift the corporate veil and consider the ultimate destination of the payments to the companies – and even if they could do so the ultimate destination of the consultancy payments was not Evelyn but his manager.

Payment or present?

3.12   The deciding principle is whether the payment is a voluntary payment for services or a mere present. In *Calvert v Wainwright*, Atkinson J gave the illustration of a person who takes the same taxi every day and, in addition to the ordinary tip he gives, says to the driver at Christmas 'you have been very attentive to me, here is a £10 note'. That £10 would be a present and not assessable 'because it had been given to the man because of his qualities, his faithfulness, and the way he has stuck to the passenger', whereas a tip given in the ordinary way is given as remuneration for services rendered.

3.13   This distinction between a reward for services and a personal testimonial was developed in the Court of Appeal in *Bridges v Bearsley 37 TC 289*. Mr Bearsley was the managing director of Meccano Ltd, a company that he had greatly helped to build. The founder of the company, Frank Hornby, owned the major part of the company. Mr Bearsley and two other directors had from time to time pressed him to allow them to have fairly substantial holdings of shares in the company. From time to time Frank Hornby had transferred to them small numbers of shares. Mr Hornby had promised to 'look after' Mr Bearsley but did not make any significant transfer of shares to him. Mr Bearsley had gained the impression that Mr Hornby would leave him a reasonable number of shares in his will. Unfortunately he did not do so. Mr Bearsley and his fellow directors decided to approach Mr Hornby's sons to express their unhappiness. Mr Donald Hornby thought that his father had been remiss in not leaving them shares in his will. He agreed with the three directors that they ought to have a further 20,000 shares between them. These shares could, however, only come out of his father's estate after the death of his mother, the life tenant. In these circumstances the three directors felt they ought to have a written agreement to this effect. In the mistaken belief that a deed needed consideration the solicitor expressed the gift of shares to be 'in consideration of the Covenantee continuing his present engagement with Meccano Limited until the expiry of four years from the date hereof'. In spite of this the Court of Appeal held that the value of the shares transferred was a personal testimonial, not an emolument of Mr Bearsley's office as a director. Schedule E charged tax 'in respect of any office or employment on emoluments therefrom'. 'The word "therefrom" must be construed in its context … The reference is to what is received by the holder of an office or employment in that capacity: to the holder of the office or employment as such' (Morris LJ). Mr Bearsley would not have received the shares but for what he had done in the past, ie all the years before 1945 when the deed was entered into and the four years after 1945. 'In one sense he received the shares by reason of his office. Had he not held the office he would not have had them. But that merely shows that he would not have had the shares, either as remuneration or as a gift, if he had not given many years' service to the company ... the Hornby brothers made it a condition of their promise that Mr Bearsley would go on serving the company for four years. They did not exact from him a promise that he would continue to serve the company ... the Hornby brothers in effect said "Because of your good work in the past we will at some uncertain future date transfer to you some shares that will come to us provided that you go on serving the company for four years". It does not seem to me that the promise they made has the attributes of remuneration or that it lacks the features of a personal gift.'

3.14   The vital distinction as to whether a payment is made by virtue of the employment, and is thus an emolument of it, or by virtue of something extraneous to the employment, and thus is not an emolument, was considered by the House of Lords in *Hochstrasser v Mayes 38 TC 673*. Mr Mayes was an employee of Imperial Chemical Industries Ltd (ICI). ICI operated a housing agreement under which if an employee was transferred to another part of the country, ICI would either buy his existing house at cost or make good to the employee any loss on sale. Mr Mayes sold his house at a loss of £350 which ICI paid to him. The amount payable to an employee under the housing agreement was completely independent of his salary. The agreement was to facilitate ICI transferring staff between its different sites. Lord Cohen cited with approval the remarks of Morris LJ in *Bridges v Bearsley* with the proviso that 'I am prepared to accept that statement of the law, but it is, I think, clear from the final conclusion of Morris LJ ... that it is not enough for the Crown to establish that the employee would not have received the sum on which tax is claimed had he not been an employee. The court must be satisfied that the service agreement was the *causa causans* and not merely the *causa sine qua non* of the receipt of the profit'. Viscount Simmonds made the same point but added a word of warning: 'If in such cases as these the issue turns, as I think it does, upon whether the fact of employment is the *causa causans* or only the *sine qua non* of the benefit, which perhaps is only to give the natural meaning to the word "therefrom" in the statute, it must often be difficult to draw the line and say on which side of it a particular case falls ... It is for the Crown, seeking to tax the subject, to prove that the tax is exigible, not for the subject to prove that his case falls within exceptions which are not expressed in the Statute but arbitrarily inferred from it'. The distinction between the expressions *causa causans*, the reason for the payment, and *causa sine qua non*, the event without which the payment would not have come about, was brought out clearly by Jenkins LJ in the High Court: 'I think it may well be said here that, while the employee's employment with ICI was a *causa sine qua non* of his entering into the housing agreement ... the *causa causans* was the distinct contractual relationship subsisting between ICI and the employee under the housing agreement'. In other words, the employment merely enabled Mr Mayes to enter into the housing agreement. The payment of £350 arose because he had entered into that agreement. Lord Denning 'tried by the touchstone of common sense – which is perhaps rather a rash test to take in a revenue matter', unlike his colleagues, regarded the case as plain: 'No one coming fresh to it, untrammelled by cases, could regard this £350 as a profit from the employment … It was not a remuneration or reward or return for his services in any sense of the word'.

3.15   In *Rogers v HMRC 2011 SFTD 788* a gift of shares to an employee was held not to constitute emoluments. The case is interesting because the facts are similar to those in *Bridges v Bearsley* but the intervening cases since 1957 might have been felt to have somewhat sidelined that decision. Indeed the Tribunal felt that the case may well have been decided differently today following *Shilton v Wilnshurst* [64 TC 78]. Mr Rogers was one of a small team of individuals who were recruited to a fairly new company and were instrumental in developing it. The owner of the company made vague promises to give them shares at some stage. He owned 51% of the company and clearly was reluctant to lose control. However, he was not very involved in running the business. There was talk of giving Mr Rogers a 9% shareholding. The owner was killed in a plane crash and his father gave Mr Rogers and the other team members the shareholdings that he knew the son had intended. By that stage, Mr Rogers had developed a drink problem and had been sidelined. He had been made chairman of the UK entity, which carried minor duties. It was most unlikely that at the time of the gift his continuing contribution to the business would justify a 9% shareholding worth several million pounds. The Tribunal took as a summary of the current law that set out by the Special Commissioners in *McBride v Blackburn [2003] STC (SCD) 139*:

> 'From these authorities, therefore, we derive the following principles. A voluntary payment is taxable if it is received in respect of the discharge of the duties of an office; or if it accrues by virtue of the office; or if it is in return for acting in the office. However, a gift is not taxable if it retains its characteristic as a gift (which we would describe as an exercise of bounty intended to benefit the donee for reasons personal to him or her), even though it is given in recognition of services rendered, or if it is "peculiarly due" to personal qualities, or if it is to mark participation in an exceptional event. Relevant factors are: whether the payment is made by the employer; whether the office is at an end; whether other remuneration is paid; whether the payment is exceptional; whether there is an element of recurrence; and whether the recipient is entitled to the payment.'

It decided that the payment could not relate to future work as Mr Rogers had been sidelined. It did not relate to past work as Mr Rogers had been fully remunerated for that work. He had no contractual entitlement to the shares. They concluded that the real reason for the transfer was that the deceased shareholder felt a huge sense of gratitude to Mr Rogers since in 1988 when the company had a single customer and no track record he was the guy who went out and won it new customers, something that neither the major shareholder nor the team leader could have done, and the shareholder never forgot that. Accordingly the transfer was a gift, not something caused by the employment.

3.16   The distinction drawn in *Hochstrasser v Mayes* has been blurred somewhat by the Court of Appeal decision in *Hamblett v Godfrey 59 TC 694*. Miss Hamblett was a civil servant employed at GCHQ, Cheltenham. The Government decided that for security reasons, it was necessary to restrict the staff's right to have recourse to industrial tribunals or to be a member of a trade union. They paid Miss Hamblett an ex gratia sum of £1,000 in recognition of her agreeing to give up such rights. She, not unnaturally, contended that whilst her employment was the *causa sine qua non* of her entering into the agreement with the Government the *causa causans* of the payment of £1,000 was her giving up her statutory rights under that agreement. In a unanimous decision the Court of Appeal dismissed this approach. 'The rights, the loss of which was being recognised were rights under the employment protection legislation and the right to join a union … Both those rights … are directly connected with the facts of the taxpayer's employment. If the employment did not exist, there would be no need for the rights in the particular context in which the taxpayer found herself.' (Purchas LJ). Accordingly, as the rights were not severable from the employment it followed in the judge's view that the £1,000 arose from the employment and was thus part of the emoluments of the employment. Quoting both Lord Radcliffe, 'it is assessable if it has been paid to him in return for acting as or being an employee', and Viscount Simmonds, 'the test of taxability is whether from the standpoint of the person who receives it the profit accrues to him by virtue of his office', in *Hochstrasser v Mayes*, Neill LJ thought the cases 'demonstrate to my mind that emoluments from employment are not restricted to payments made in return for the performance of services'. The facts in the *Hamblett* case pointed to the conclusion that 'the source of the payment was the employment. It was paid because of the employment and because of the conditions of employment and for no other reason'.

3.17   Accordingly, the current state of the law is that whilst the principle formulated in *Hochstrasser v Mayes* still holds good if the payment can be shown to be not directly related to the employment, if it arises directly from the employment it will be emoluments. Mr Mayes' £350 arose from the decision of ICI to move him to a different job. It is difficult to know in what circumstances the *Hochstrasser* principle still applies. *Hochstrasser* was a House of Lords decision whereas *Hamblett* stopped at the Court of Appeal, so the *Hamblett* case cannot have overruled the *Hochstrasser* principle entirely.

3.18   Indeed, *Wilcock v Eve [1995] STC 18*, emphasises that the *Hochstrasser v Mayes* principle still lives. Mr Eve was a director of a company, LBUA, which was a wholly-owned subsidiary of Hill Samuel Group plc. In May 1986 there was a management buyout of LBUA. As a result Mr Eve was unable to exercise his rights under the Hill Samuel approved share option scheme. In April 1987 Hill Samuel became concerned about its reputation for fairness and decided to make ex-gratia payments to people in Mr Eve's position to compensate them for the loss of the option rights. The first Mr Eve knew of this was when Hill Samuel sent him a cheque for £10,000 in September 1987. It was held that although Mr Eve remained an employee of LBUA, the payment by Hill Samuel did not derive from that employment and was not an emolument from it. It was also held not to be a benefit within *ICTA 1988, s 154* (now *ITEPA 2003, s 201*). The payment was not 'by reason' of Mr Eve's employment with LBUA.

3.19   Mr McBride was not so lucky. He was a Lloyd's name and following the substantial losses suffered in the early 1990s became involved in the committees of two action groups. Following the settlement these action groups decided to make ex gratia payments to various members of their committees, including Mr McBride, to recognise the substantial amount of work they had done on behalf of the action group. The constitution of both groups provided that members of the committee were not entitled to any remuneration. The Special Commissioners held that the payments were emoluments of an office (*McBride v Blackburn [2003] STC (SCD) 139*).

3.20   The taxpayer also lost in *Kuehne & Nagel Drinks Logistics Ltd v HMRC [2011] STC 576*. Kuehne & Nagel took over the drinks distribution business of Scottish & Newcastle UK Ltd as part of a joint venture. The employees were concerned that the pension scheme of Kuehne & Nagel was inferior to that of Scottish & Newcastle. In addition Scottish & Newcastle had paid each employee a beer allowance that Kuehne & Nagel did not intend to continue. To head off a threat of industrial action, Scottish & Newcastle offered to make a payment to the employees of £5,000 each (on which £200 related to the beer allowance and was agreed to be taxable). The payments were actually made by Kuehne & Nagel, but as Scottish & Newcastle's agent and at its cost. The FTT held that the whole amount was taxable as income as it was paid and received as an incentive to work willingly and without industrial action. This was upheld on appeal. The judge pointed out that to be taxable, a receipt had to be 'from' an employment but that did not mean that it had to be made in return for services. He also accepted that if there is more than one reason for a payment it will be income if one of them makes it from an employment. The Court of Appeal agreed (*[2012] EWCA Civ 34*). Patten LJ rejected an HMRC contention that a contributing cause for a payment which is more than marginal but is employment-based, can bring the payment into charge. The employment must be a substantial cause of the payment. He also said that if the employment causation is a substantial and equal cause of the payment, it becomes open to the judge to say that the statutory test is satisfied. This suggests that the employment needs to be either the main cause of the payment or at least of equal standing to other causes.

3.21   Another interesting case on whether income is received by virtue of the employment is *O'Leary v McKinlay [1991] STC 42*. David O'Leary was resident in England and domiciled in Ireland. His employer, Arsenal FC Ltd, entered into an arrangement designed to pay him an additional £28,985 per annum. To achieve this a third party set up a Jersey trust with a nominal £10. Arsenal lent the trustees £266,000 interest-free and repayable on demand. The trustees invested this to produce £28,985. This money was paid to O'Leary but not remitted by him to the UK. He contended that this income was income from a foreign possession taxable under Case V of Schedule D on a remittance basis. It was held, however, that it was an emolument of his employment and thus assessable under Schedule E on an arising basis. The test posed by Vinelott J was 'how would an ordinary member of the public have perceived the money?'. He would have said without hesitation that it was an emolument of the taxpayer's employment by Arsenal. The judge was very much influenced by the fact that there was an overall scheme. If an employer lent money to an employee interest-free and the employee was free to exploit the money in any manner he chose, his employment could not be said to be the source of the income it generated. However, in O'Leary's case he never had the free use of the £266,000. The purpose of the arrangement was to provide him with the income of £28,985. The trustees could not have invested it in any other manner without O'Leary's consent (and undoubtedly Arsenal's too).

3.22   Although the actual decision has in most cases been superseded by legislation *Abbott v Philbin 39 TC 82* sheds an interesting light on what is meant by money's worth, following on from *Tennant v Smith 3 TC 158*, in which it was held that a non-cash benefit can be emoluments only if it is capable of being turned into money. In 1954 Mr Abbott was granted an option to acquire shares at the market price on the date the option was offered. The option was non-assignable. It was exercised in 1956. HMRC claimed that the option was not money's worth, but on its exercise in 1956 the acquisition of the shares would be. The taxpayer contended that the option was money's worth but that having paid tax on the value in 1954 the difference between the price paid for the shares in 1956 and their value at that time was not taxable. It was common ground that if the tax charge arose on the grant of the option a further charge could not arise at a later date. It was held that the option was money's worth and its value assessable in 1954. The fact that it was non-assignable affected the value but did not mean that it could not be turned to pecuniary account. Indeed, Viscount Simmonds thought that 'if it had no ascertainable value then it was a perquisite of no value'. Lord Denning, whilst agreeing that the charge arose on the grant of the option, added that if no payment had been made for the option, he would have arrived at a different conclusion. The option would then have been unenforceable at law and the taxpayer would only have an expectation, which he could not turn into account, rather than a right, which he could. This demonstrates the importance of getting the documentation right!

3.23   HMRC also considers that if an employer acquires an asset from an employee at a price exceeding its market value that excess constitutes emoluments (*IR Press Release 27 April 1994*).

3.24   HMRC's Statement of Practice on commissions, etc. (*SP 4/97*) states that it is a question of fact whether something is received in the capacity of employee/office-holder or in some other capacity such as the purchaser of an insurance policy, goods or services. It goes on to express the view that if an employee is entitled to commission in respect of goods or services sold to third parties he is assessable on the full amount of that commission even if it is passed to the customer or, indeed, paid direct to the customer. In such circumstances he may be able to claim a deduction for the payment to the customer if he can show that he is 'obliged' to make the payment wholly, exclusively and necessarily in performing the duties of his employment, eg it is a contractual term of the sale to the customer. If the purchaser pays a discounted price there is no income tax liability on the employee unless the purchaser is a member of his family or household of the employee or a member of his household receives something (money or benefits) in consequence of the discounted payment. If the purchaser is a member of the employee's family there is unlikely to be an income tax charge if the price paid covers the cost to the employer of providing the goods or services. Where a commission or discount is available to an employee on the same basis as it is available to the general public, it will not arise from the employment. Subject to that a commission on the employee's own purchase constitutes taxable emoluments. Even if his contractual right is not to a commission but to make a reduced payment HMRC consider that the reduction is an emolument of the employment if it derives from the employer, although not necessarily if it derives from a third party.

Statutory payments

3.25   An interesting area is statutory payments. In *Mairs v Haughey [1993] STC 569* (see **11.56**) the House of Lords held that in law a redundancy payment is not an emolument. The redundancy legislation reflects an appreciation that an employee has a stake in their employment which justifies them receiving compensation if they lose that stake. It is not a payment from being or becoming an employee. In *Hamblett v Godfrey 59 TC 694* (see **3.15**) in contrast, a payment to restrict an employee's right to have recourse to industrial tribunals or to be a member of a trade union, was held by the Court of Appeal to be taxable as the source of the payment was the employment. *Mintec Ltd v CIR [2001] STC (SCD) 101* was concerned with compensation in respect of the employer's failure to comply with its statutory duty to consult with employee representatives regarding proposed redundancies. By agreement with the trade unions it agreed to pay all affected employees 'a payment of £2,500 in recognition of any entitlement under the consultation process including pay in lieu of notice, etc'. In a very brief decision the Special Commissioner (Stephen Oliver QC) held that the payments were not taxable under *s 19*. The *Trade Union and Labour Relations (Consolidation) Act 1992 (TULRCA 1992)* provides for protective awards to employees. Had such awards been made they would not have been emoluments as the source of the awards would have been the 1992 Act. Following *Mairs v Haughey* as a payment in lieu of such an award, the £2,500 should not be treated in any different way from the protective award itself. A word of warning. It is difficult to square this decision with the dicta in *Drummond v Austin Brown 58 TC 67*, a capital gains tax case, which differentiated the receipt of compensation from a payment to head off the litigation which would give rise to that compensation. *Turullois v HMRC (TC 3795)* dealt with an interim order under the Employment Rights Act 1996 (ERA 1996). Ms Turullois was a 'whistle-blower'. She made a protected disclosure and was sacked unlawfully. The interim payment required the employment to be treated as continuing for the purpose of pay only. The payments continued for about a year (until the date of the Employment Tribunal substantive hearing) and were paid under deduction of PAYE and NIC. Ms Turullois was held to have been unfairly dismissed. She contended that the interim payments were compensation for unfair dismissal taxable under *ITEPA 2003, s 401* (see **11.15**) and claimed a refund of the tax on the first £30,000. HMRC accepted that the payments were not earnings but contended that they were emoluments. The FTT held that they could not be emoluments 'from' the employment as the employment had ceased at the date of dismissal. Accordingly they must have been payments on accounts of compensation taxable under *s 401*.

The impact of the schedular system

3.26   The UK tax system is a Schedular system. That is a person is not taxed on income as such; he is taxed on income that falls within a specific schedule or category. Each category has its own rules for ascertaining the amount of taxable income – and in some cases the year in which such income is to be taxed. Although the Tax Law Rewrite has abolished the schedules as terminology, it has retained the distinct rules. This means that it is possible for some income to fall into the gaps between the taxable categories and escape tax. It is also possible for some income to fall into more than one category in which case only the most appropriate one can apply.

3.27   This is what happened in *P A Holdings Ltd v HMRC (2009 UK FTT 95 (TC), 2009 SFTD 209)*. P A Holdings established an employee benefit trust (EBT) in Jersey and paid a substantial contribution to it. The EBT transferred the bulk of its funds to a new Jersey company, Ellastone. It then subscribed for 24 million 1p redeemable preference shares in Ellastone. The shares entitled the owner to only one dividend (if the company chose to make one) and were redeemable at par. The EBT appointed the preference shares to employees in proportion to the bonuses that would otherwise have been paid to them. Ellastone then declared a dividend of 99p a share and redeemed the shares at 1p a share. It was accepted that the 1p was earnings. However the First-tier Tribunal held that the 99p dividend was earnings but agreed with the company that it could not be taxed as earnings because there was a separate tax category (formerly Schedule F) for taxing dividends. The dividends could be taxed only under that category (which attracted a lower rate of tax). However the same answer did not apply for National Insurance (see **Chapter 20**) as National Insurance is not based on a schedular system; it taxes only earnings. As the dividends constituted both 'earnings' and dividends there is nothing to prevent National Insurance being imposed on the basis that they were earnings. The Court of Appeal disagreed with the tax analysis. 'The conventional approach of the courts is to look at all the circumstances of the case in order to answer the one statutory question, namely whether the income receipts of the employee are emoluments or profits from employment (see Russell LJ in *Brumby v Milner* 1976 51 TC 583 at 607G).. . This requires the court not to be restricted to the legal form of the source of the payment but to focus on the character of the receipt in the hands of the recipient. In *Dale v IRC* [1954] AC 11 payments to trustees, which a testator had directed should be paid from a charitable trust for their work as trustees, were held to be earned income... It seems to me that that approach, followed, for example in *White v Franklin* (*q.v.supra* 514), provides the answer to the essential question as to the character of the receipts in the hands of PA's employees. The court should not be seduced by the form in which the payments (that is as dividends declared in respect of the shares in Ellastone) reached the employees. It should focus on the character of the receipt in the hands of the recipients'. Accordingly the dividend was taxable as remuneration. Sadly the company decided not to appeal this worrying decision.

Employment income provided through third parties ('disguised remuneration')

3.28   This legislation was introduced by the *Finance Act 2011 (FA 2011)*. It is intended 'to tackle arrangements using trusts and other vehicles to reward employees which seek to avoid, defer or reduce tax liabilities' (Finance Bill 2011 Explanatory Notes). It was primarily aimed at the use of employee benefit trusts (EBTs) and employer-funded retirement benefit schemes (EFURBSs). These were often based offshore so that the income within the trust or scheme would accumulate free of tax. The employer would make a cash contribution to the trust or scheme and the trust would typically lend the funds to the employee. HMRC have said that they do not believe that such arrangements succeed in avoiding PAYE and that they intend to litigate all open cases. They have been coy as to why they believe they do not work. Accordingly this legislation may not even be needed to achieve its objective as HMRC seem to believe that it is met by existing legislation. Unfortunately, not only has it been enacted but its effect, particularly as regards loans from third parties, can be horrific. It is hard to believe that parliament intended to tax many of the transactions that are caught by the legislation. It applies from 6 April 2011 although it imposes a charge on that date in relation to some transactions undertaken after 8 December 2010 unless they have been unwound by 5 April 2012.

3.29   It applies where:

(*a*)   a person is an employee (or former or prospective employee) of another person;

(*b*)   there is an 'arrangement' (the relevant arrangement) to which the employee (or a person linked with the employee – see **3.33**) is a party (or which wholly or partly covers or relate to the employee);

(*c*)   it is reasonable to suppose that, in essence, the relevant arrangement (so far as it covers or relates to the employee – or to a person linked with the employee – see **3.33**) is (wholly or partly) a means of providing rewards or recognition or loans in connection with the employee's employment (or former or prospective employment), or is otherwise concerned with the provision of such items;

(*d*)   a 'relevant step' is taken by a 'relevant third person' (see **3.34**(*c*)); and

(*e*)   it is reasonable to suppose that, in essence, either:

(i)   the relevant step is taken (wholly or partly) in pursuance of the relevant arrangement; or

(ii)   there is some other connection (direct or indirect) between the relevant step and the relevant arrangement.

[*ITEPA 2003, s 554A(1), (5) inserted by FA 2011, Sch 2, para 1*].

3.30   It treats the 'value of the relevant step' (see **3.37**) as employment income of the employee from the employment for the tax year in which the relevant step is taken [*ITEPA 2003, s 554Z2(1)*]. If the relevant step is taken before the employment starts, it is treated as income for the tax year in which the employment starts.

3.31 The charge under *section 554Z2* takes precedent over the benefits code and over *Income Tax (Trading and Other Income) Act 2005 (ITTOIA 2005), Part 4, Chapter 3* (Dividends from UK Resident Companies) [*ITEPA 2003, s 554Z2(2)*]. In particular where the relevant step is the making of an employment-related loan, the loan is taxed as income under this provision; it is not to be treated as a taxable cheap loan under the benefit rules [*ITEPA 2003, s 554Z2(3)*].

3.32 The following are relevant steps.

(1) A sum of money or asset held by (or on behalf of) the third party is earmarked (however informally) by him with a view to a later relevant step being taken by him, or by any other person (on, or following, the meeting of any condition or otherwise) in relation to that sum or asset (or to any sum of money or asset which might arise or derive, directly or indirectly, from it) [*ITEPA 2003, s 554B(1)(a)*].

(2) A sum of money or asset starts being held by (or on behalf of) the third party in some other manner, specifically with a view (so far as the third party is concerned) to a later relevant step being taken by the third party or by any other person (on, or following, the meeting of, any condition, or otherwise in relation to that sum of money or asset (or to any sum of money or asset which might arise or derive, directly or indirectly, from it)) [*ITEPA 2003, s 554B(1)(b)*].

(3) The third party either:

 (*a*) pays a sum of money to a 'relevant person' (ie the employee, a person chosen by the employee, a person within a class of persons chosen by the employee or a person 'linked with' the employee);

 (*b*) transfers an asset to a relevant person;

 (*c*) takes a step by virtue of which a relevant person acquires securities, an interest in securities or a securities option (as defined in *ITEPA, s 420*, see **14.21**);

 (*d*) makes available a sum of money or asset for use:

  (i) as security for a loan made (or to be made) to a relevant person; or

  (ii) otherwise as security for the meeting of any liability (or the performance of any undertaking) which a relevant person has (or will have) (or makes the money or asset available under an arrangement which permits its use); or

 (*e*) grants to a relevant person a lease of any premises the effective duration of which is likely to exceed 21 years [*ITEPA 2003, s 554C(1), (2), (3), (4)*].

(4) Without transferring the asset to the relevant person, the third party either:

(*a*)   makes an asset available (at any time) for a relevant person to benefit from in a way which is 'substantially similar to' the way in which the relevant person would have been able to benefit from it if the asset had been transferred to him at that time; or

(*b*)   on or after the second anniversary of the cessation of the employment, makes an asset available for a relevant person to benefit from.

[*ITEPA 2003, s 554D(1)*].

3.33   The definition of a relevant person at **3.32**(3)(*a*) above applies for all of these provisions. A person is linked with the employee if:

(*a*)   he is (or has been) connected with the employee or a person within (*a*) to (*d*);

(*b*)   it is a close company in which the employee (or a connected person or a person within (*a*) to (*d*)) is (or has been) a participator;

(*c*)   it is an overseas company in which A (or a connected person or a person within (*a*) to (*d*)) is (or has been) a participator and which would be a close company if it were UK resident; or

(*d*)   it is a 51% subsidiary of a company within (*b*) or (*c*).

[*ITEPA 2003, s 554Z1(1)*].

The *Income Tax Act 2007 (ITA 2007), s 993* definition of a connected person (see Appendix 1) applies but with the modification that a man and woman living together as if they were spouses of each other are treated as spouses, and two people of the same sex living together as if they were civil partners are treated as civil partners [*ITEPA 2003, s 554Z1(2)*]. The definition of 'participator' in *Corporation Tax Act 2010 (CTA 2010), ss 454, 455* applies for this purpose (and in the case of an overseas company as if the company were a close company [*ITEPA 2003, s 554Z1(3)*]. If the third party takes a step on behalf of the employee, or at the direction or request of the employee, any person for whose benefit the step is taken is also regarded as a relevant person if he is not otherwise one [*ITEPA 2003, s 554C(2)*].

3.34   There are a number of additional conditions and modifications attaching to the scope of the above paragraphs.

(*a*)   The provision does not apply if the relevant step is within **3.32**(1) or (2) and is taken on or after the employee's death [*ITEPA 2003, s 554A(4)*].

(*b*)   For the purpose of **3.29**(*c*) it does not matter if the relevant arrangement does not include details of the steps which will be taken (or may be taken) in connection with providing, in essence, the rewards or recognition or loans (eg it does not include details of any sums of money or assets which will (or may) be involved or details of how, or when, or by whom, or in whose favour, any step will or may be taken) [*ITEPA 2003, s 554A(6)*].

(c)   For the purpose of **3.29**(*d*), a relevant third person is any person other than the employee or employer, the employee acting as a trustee, or his employer acting as a trustee, [*ITEPA 2003, s 554A(7)*]. If the employer is a member of a group of companies at the time that the relevant step is taken, any other company which is a member of the group at that time is also treated as the employer. If the employer is an LLP (limited liability partnership), any company which is a wholly owned subsidiary of the LLP is similarly also treated as the employer. Whether a company is a member of a group must be determined in accordance with *Taxation and Chargeable Gains Act 1992, s 170(2)–(11)* (but as if the reference therein to a 75% subsidiary were to a 51% subsidiary [*ITEPA 2003, s 554Z(5), (6)*]. The *Companies Act 2006 (CA 2006), s 1159(2)* definition of a wholly owned subsidiary (a company which has no members except the LLP and the LLP's wholly owned subsidiaries or persons acting on behalf of the LLP or its wholly owned subsidiaries) applies [*ITEPA 2003, s 554A(8), (9)*]. This is a convoluted way of saying that anyone other than the employee, the employer, another member of the employer's group of companies or, if the employer is an LLP, a company (or another LLP) which is wholly owned by the LLP is caught. This extension is important because it takes out of these provisions benefits and loans from other group companies or wholly owned subsidiaries of the LLP. It should however be noted that the exclusion applies only to 51% subsidiaries (over 50% ownership) within a group and 100% subsidiaries of an LLP. The exclusion for group companies and LLP subsidiaries does not apply if there is a connection (direct or indirect) between the relevant step and a tax avoidance arrangement [*ITEPA 2003, s 554A(10)*].

A tax avoidance arrangement is an arrangement (as defined at (*d*) below) which has a tax avoidance purpose, ie if the main purpose (or one of the main purposes) of any party to the arrangement in entering into the arrangement is the avoidance of tax or National Insurance contributions [*ITEPA 2003, s 554Z(13)–(15)*]. A step is connected with a tax avoidance arrangement if, for example, it is taken (wholly or partly) in pursuance of that arrangement or of an arrangement at one end of a series of arrangements with the tax avoidance arrangements being at the other end. It does not matter if the person taking the step is unaware of the tax avoidance arrangement [*ITEPA 2003, s 554Z(16)*].

(d)   For the purpose of **3.29**(*e*) a relevant step is connected with the relevant arrangements (ie the arrangement within **3.29**(*b*)) if, for example, the relevant step is taken (wholly or partly) in pursuance of an arrangement at one end of a series of arrangements with the relevant arrangement being at the other end. It does not matter if the person taking the relevant step is unaware of the relevant arrangements [*ITEPA 2003, s 554A(11)*]. Arrangement includes any agreement, scheme, settlement, transaction, trust or understanding (whether or not legally enforceable) [*ITEPA 2003, s 554Z(3)*].

(e)   For the purposes of **3.29**(*c*) and (*e*) in particular, all relevant circumstances must be taken into account in order to get to the essence of the matter [*ITEPA 2003, s 554A(12)*].

(*f*)   References to the payment of a sum of money include, in particular, payment of a sum of money by way of a loan [*ITEPA 2003, s 554Z(7)*].

3.35   The provisos in relation to **3.32** are:

(*a*)   For the purposes of **3.32**(1) and (2) ('earmarking') it does not matter if:

    (i)   details of the later relevant step have not been worked out (for example, details of the sum of money or asset which will (or may be) the subject of the step, or details of how, or when, or by whom, or in whose favour, the step will (or may) be taken);

    (ii)   any condition which would have to be met before the later relevant step is taken might never be met; or

    (iii)   the employee (or a person linked with the employee) has no legal right to have a relevant step taken in relation to the sum of money or asset.

[*ITEPA 2003, s 554B(2)*].

(*b*)   For the purposes of **3.32**(2) it does not matter whether or not the sum of money or asset in question has previously been held by or on behalf of the third party on a basis which is different to that referred to in paragraph **3.32**(2) [*ITEPA 2003, s 554B(3)*].

(*c*)   For the purpose of **3.32**(3)(*d*):

    (i)   references to making a sum of money or asset available mean making it available in any way, however informal;

    (ii)   it does not matter if the relevant person has no legal right to have the sum or asset used as security; and

    (iii)   it does not matter if the sum of money or asset is never actually used as security.

[*ITEPA 2003, s 554C(5)*].

(*d*)   For the purpose of **3.32**(3)(*e*) if there are circumstances which make it likely that the original lease will be extended for any period, the effective duration of the original lease must be determined on the basis that it will be so extended. If the employee (or the linked person or, if different, the person to whom the original lease was granted) is, or is likely to become, entitled to a later lease (or to the grant of a later lease) of the same premises, or it is otherwise likely that he will be granted a later lease of the same premises, the original lease must be regarded as continuing until the end of the later lease [*ITEPA 2003, s 554C(6)–(10)*]. Lease and premises have the same meaning as in *ITTOIA 2005, ss 276–307* [*ITEPA 2003, s 554C(10)*]. Unfortunately those provisions do not contain a definition of either of those terms.

(*e*)   Where a person is treated as taking a step by virtue of **3.32**(4), that step is deemed to occur on the second anniversary of the cessation of the employment [*ITEPA 2003, s 554D(2)*].

3.36   There are exemptions for:

(*a*)   A relevant step taken under:

    (i)   an approved SIP;

    (ii)   an approved SAYE option scheme;

    (iii)   an approved CSOP scheme;

    (iv)   an arrangement the sole purpose of which is the granting of qualifying share options;

    (v)   an excluded share arrangement (one in relation to a SIP, SAYE or CSOP scheme);

    (vi)   an arrangement the sole purpose of which is the provision of benefits within *ITEPA 2003, s 393B(3)* (benefits in respect of death, disablement or ill-health of an employee during service);

    (vii)   an arrangement the sole purpose of which is the paying of benefits which are excluded in calculating earnings from the employment for the purpose of earnings-related NIC contributions;

    (viii)   a pension scheme set up by a government outside the UK for the benefit of its employees;

    (ix)   a registered pension scheme;

    (x)   an arrangement the sole purpose of which is the making of payments to which *Finance Act 2004 (FA 2004), s 161(4)* applies (a registered pension scheme which has been wound up).

    (See **3.60**.)

(*b*)   A loan on ordinary commercial terms with *ITEPA 2003, s 176* (this will only apply where the loan is made in the ordinary course of a business carried on by the lender which includes the lending of money) (see **3.63**).

(*c*)   A relevant step taken by P for the sole purpose of a transaction which P has with A and which P entered into in the ordinary course of P's business.

    BUT:

    (i)   if the step is a loan this applies only if a substantial proportion of P's business involves making similar loans to members of the public and the loan to A is part of a package of benefits which is available to a substantial proportion of B's employees, and

    (ii)   in any other case the transaction with A is part of a package of benefits which is so available.

    (See **3.67**.)

(*d*)   The earmarking of funds where B has awarded deferred remuneration to A conditional on specific conditions being met within the next five years and there is a reasonable chance that those conditions will not be met (see **3.69**).

(*e*) Earmarking in relation to employee share schemes (in specific circumstances) (see **3.73**).

(*f*) A loan under a car ownership scheme where under the arrangement a loan is made to A by a licenced lender, provided that the loan has to be repaid within four years (see **3.85**).

(*g*) A relevant step to which one of the employment income exemptions in *ITEPA 2003, ss 227–326* (employment income exemptions) applies (see **3.87**).

(*h*) The receipt by P of income from earmarked funds (see **3.88**).

(*i*) The acquisition of assets by P out of earmarked funds (see **3.89**).

(*j*) The provision of pension income (see **3.91**).

(*k*) A contribution to a registered pension scheme of A (eg a personal pension scheme) (see **3.93**).

(*l*) A pre 6 April 2006 contribution to an EFURBS in respect of which A is taxed (see **3.96**).

(*m*) The purchase of annuities out of pension scheme rights (see **3.97**).

(*n*) Payments under registered pension schemes (see **3.99**).

(*o*) Transfers between certain foreign pension schemes (see **3.100**).

(*p*) Any other steps that HMRC may by Regulation specify (see **3.102**).

These are considered in detail at **3.60** onwards. Most are very restrictive.

3.37 If a relevant step involves a sum of money (see **3.32**) its value is the sum of money [*ITEPA 2003, s 554Z3(1)*]. This is subject to *ITEPA 2003, ss 437* and *452* (see **14.59** and **14.121**) [*ITEPA 2003, s 554Z3(3)*]. These two provisions lay down special rules for determining the market value of certain employment-related securities, so 'subject to' presumably means that the figure calculated under these provisions must be used instead of the actual cash payment. If the relevant step does not include a sum of money, its value is the higher of the market value of the asset concerned when the relevant step is taken or the cost of the relevant step [*ITEPA 2003, s 554Z3(2)*]. The cost of the relevant step for this purpose is the expense incurred in connection with the relevant step (including a proper proportion of any expense relating partly to the relevant step and partly to other matters) by the person or persons at whose cost the relevant step is taken [*ITEPA 2003, s 554Z3(6)*]. The value is simply the market value (even if the cost of the relevant step is higher), if the relevant step is one by virtue of which a relevant person acquires employment-related securities, interest in securities or a securities option to which the rules in *ITEPA 2003, ss 422–460* apply, or if *ITEPA 2003, s 554Z7* (see **3.42**) applies [*ITEPA 2003, s 554Z3(4), (5)*].

3.38 This provision is subject to *sections 554Z4* (residence issues), *554Z5* (overlap with earlier relevant step), *554Z6* (overlap with certain earnings), *554Z7* (exercise price of share options) and *554Z8* (cases where consideration given for a relevant step). So far as applicable these provisions must be applied in that order [*ITEPA 2003, s 554Z3(7)*]. Accordingly it is sensible to consider them in that order.

3.39   After determining the value of the relevant step the next step is to determine the year it is for. This is done by applying the normal income tax rules for earnings as if the amount were general earnings [*ITEPA 2003, s 554Z4(1), (2)*]. If this treats it (or part of it) as earnings for a year in which the employee is non-UK resident only so much of the amount as relates, on a just and reasonable basis, to duties performed in the UK is taxable [*ITEPA 2003, s 554Z4(3)–(5)*]. However this attribution does not apply for the purpose of *section 554Z2(1)* (see **3.30**) [*ITEPA 2003, s 554Z4(6)*].

3.40   If there is an overlap between the money or asset that is the subject of the relevant step (sum P) and the sum of money or asset (sum Q) which was the subject of an earlier relevant step (such as earmarking it) relating to the same employment, the value of the relevant step (after applying *section 554Z4* if relevant) is reduced by sum Q. If the overlap covers only part of sum Q, it is obviously reduced only by the corresponding part of sum Q as determined on a just and reasonable basis [*ITEPA 2003, s 554Z5(1), (2)*]. For this purpose there is an overlap between sums P and Q so far as either they are the same sum of money or asset, or sum P essentially replaces sum Q [*ITEPA 2003, s 554Z5(4)*]. If any reduction was previously made under *section 554Z5* to the value of sum Q, sum P is treated as overlapping with any other sum of money or asset so far as that other sum was treated as overlapping with sum Q [*ITEPA 2003, s 554Z5(5)*]. *Section 554Z5* applies after making any reductions under *sections 554Z4* (see **3.37**) or *554Z7* (see **3.42**), but before any reductions under *sections 554Z6* (see **3.39**) or *554Z8* (see **3.45**) [*ITEPA 2003, s 554Z5(3)*].

3.41   If the relevant step gives rise to 'relevant earnings' which are 'for' a tax year in which the employee is UK resident (or 'for' a year in which he is non-resident but the relevant earnings are in respect of duties performed in the UK) the value of the relevant step (after any deductions under *sections 554Z4 or 554Z5*) is reduced by the amount of the relevant earnings [*ITEPA 2003, s 554Z6(1), (2)*]. Relevant earnings for this purpose are earnings within *ITEPA 2003, s 62* (the basic definition of earnings, see **2.5**), deemed earnings under *ITEPA 2003, s 50* (workers employed by intermediaries – see **18.12**), and amounts treated as earnings under *ITEPA 2003, ss 221–226* (payments where employee absent because of sickness or disability; payments by employer on account of tax where deduction not possible; payments on account of director's tax other than by the director and payments for restrictive covenants) [*ITEPA 2003, s 554Z6(3)*]. However no such reduction can be made for anything which is exempt income (as defined in *ITEPA 2003, s 8* – income on which no liability to income tax arises) or which falls within *ITEPA 2003, ss 237–249* (exemptions: other transport, travel and subsistence) [*ITEPA 2003, s 554Z6(4)*]. In other words, if the relevant step has already given rise to taxable income of the employee under the normal employment income rules, it is only any excess of the value of the relevant step over that sum that is taxed under the anti-avoidance rule.

3.42   If:

(*a*)   the relevant step is one within *ITEPA 2003, s 554B* (earmarking) and is not treated as being taken out by *ITEPA 2003, ss 554L(3), (7) or (9)* (see **3.73**) or *554M(4), (6) or (8)* (see **3.71** onwards);

(*b*)   the employer is a company;

(*c*)   there is an arrangement (the employee share scheme) under which, in respect of the employment, a right (a relevant share option) may be granted to the employee to acquire relevant shares or to receive a sum of money the amount of which will be determined by the market value of any relevant shares at the time the sum is to be paid;

(*d*)   in order to exercise the relevant share option the employee would (under its terms) have to pay a sum of money the amount of which can be determined at the time the option is granted;

(*e*)   the subject of the relevant step is relevant shares (earmarked shares) which are earmarked or otherwise start being held (with a view to providing shares are paying a sum of money) pursuant to:

   (i)   a relevant share option granted to the employee under the employee share scheme under (*c*) in relation to which the requirements of (*d*) are met, or

   (ii)   such a relevant share option which is expected to be granted to the employee under the employee share scheme;

(*f*)   the number of relevant shares of any type which are earmarked shares does not exceed the maximum number of relevant shares of that type which might reasonably be expected to be needed for providing shares (or paying a sum of money) pursuant to the relevant share option; and

(*g*)   there is no connection (direct or indirect) between the relevant step and a tax avoidance arrangement;

the value of the relevant step (after any deduction under *ITEPA 2003, ss 554Z4–554Z6*) is reduced by the sum of money payable by the employee under (*d*) above (or the proportion of that sum equal to the proportion of the value of the relevant step left after any reduction under *ITEPA 2003, s 554Z4* (see **3.39**)) [*ITEPA 2003, s 554Z7(1), (3), (4)*]. Relevant shares for this purpose has the same meaning as in *ITEPA 2003, s 554I(4)* (see **3.74**) [*ITEPA 2003, s 554Z7(8)*].

3.43   Similarly if the relevant step is a step treated as being taken by *ITEPA 2003, s 554L(5)(7)-(9)* or (*554M(4),(6)* or (*8*)(see **3.75**) and in order to exercise the relevant share option to which the step relates, the employee would have to pay a sum of money the amount of which can be determined at the time the option is granted, the value of the relevant step is again reduced by that sum of money (or the relevant proportion of it where *ITEPA 2003, s 554Z4* applies) [*ITEPA 2003, s 554Z7(2), (3), (4)*].

3.44   If either:

(*a*)   the relevant step is taken in relation to an expected grant of a relevant share option (see **3.42**(*f*)(ii)), the grant is not made before the end of the final grant date, and at the end of the final grant date any of the earmarked shares continue to be held by or on behalf of the third party solely on the basis mentioned in **3.42**(*e*); or

(*b*)   at any time after the taking of the relevant step any of the earmarked shares cease to be held by or on behalf of the third party solely on the basis mentioned in **3.42**(*e*) but continue to be held by or on behalf of him on the basis mentioned in *ITEPA 2003, s 554B(1)* (see **3.32**);

the anti-avoidance rule applies as if a relevant step within *section 554B* were taken at the end of the final grant date (or when the shares cease to be held on the basis of *section 554B(1)*) and the subject of that step is the earmarked shares referred to in (*a*) or (*b*) above [*ITEPA 2003, s 554Z7(5)–(7)*]. For this purpose the final grant date is the end of the date falling immediately after the period of three months from the date on which the relevant step is taken [*ITEPA 2003, s 554Z7(5)(a)*].

3.45   If:

(*a*)   the relevant step is one within *ITEPA 2003, s 554C(1)(a)–(c)* (see **3.32**(3));

(*b*)   it is for consideration given by the employee (or a person linked with the employee) in the form of the transfer of an asset to the third party by the employee;

(*c*)   the transfer of the asset by the employee (or linked person) is made before (or at or about) the time the relevant step is taken and is not by way of loan; and

(*d*)   there is no connection (direct or indirect) between the transfer of the asset by the employee (or linked person) and a tax avoidance arrangement;

the value of the relevant step (after any reductions under *sections 554Z4–554Z6*) is reduced by the market value of the asset transferred by the employee (or linked person) at the time of its transfer (or the relevant proportion of that market value if the value of the relevant step was reduced under *ITEPA 2003, s 554Z4* (see **3.37**) [*ITEPA 2003, s 554Z8(1), (2)*].

3.46   For the purpose of (*d*) above it must, in particular, be assumed that the transfer by the employee (or linked person) is connected with a tax avoidance arrangement if either before the transfer the asset was transferred to the employee by another person by way of loan, or the asset is (or carries with it) any rights or interests under the relevant arrangement (as defined in *ITEPA 2003, s 554A(1) (b)* – see **3.29**) or any arrangement which is connected (directly or indirectly) with the relevant arrangement [*ITEPA 2003, s 554Z8(3), (4), (8)*].

3.47   If the relevant step is one within *ITEPA 2003, s 554C(1)(b), (c) or (e)* (see **3.32**(3)) or s 554D (see **3.32**(4)), and does not also involve a sum of money, it is for consideration given by the employee (or linked person) in the form of the payment of a sum of money to the third party, and the payment is made before (or at or about) the time the relevant step is taken, the value of the relevant step (after any reductions under *sections 554Z4–554Z6*) is reduced by the amount of the consideration given (or the relevant proportion of the consideration if the value of the relevant step was reduced under *ITEPA 2003, s 554Z4* (see **3.39**) [*ITEPA 2003, s 554Z8(5)–(7), (8)*].

Remittance basis taxpayers

3.48   If:

(*a*)   the value of the relevant step (or a part of it) is 'for' a tax year as determined under *ITEPA 2003, s 554Z4* (see **3.39**) (the relevant tax year);

(*b*)   *ITA 2007, ss 809B, 809D or 809E* (remittance basis) applies to the employee for the relevant tax year;

(*c*)   the employee is ordinarily UK resident in the relevant tax year;

(*d*)   the employee's employment with the employer in the relevant tax year is employment with a foreign employer; and

(*e*)   the duties of the employment in the relevant tax year are performed wholly outside the UK;

the employee's income by virtue of *ITEPA 2003, s 554Z2(1)* (see **3.30**) (or the relevant part of it) is taxable specific income (as defined in *ITEPA 2003, s 10(3)*, see **17.21**) in a tax year so far as it is remitted to the UK in that year [*ITEPA 2003, ss 554Z9(1), (2)*]. *ITEPA 2003, ss 38–41* apply to determine the location of employment duties with the amendments necessary to (*b*) reflect the value of the relevant step [*ITEPA 2003, s 554Z15*].

3.49   Any income remitted before the employment starts is treated for this purpose of being remitted in the year it starts [*ITEPA 2003, s 554Z9(3)*]. If in the relevant year the employee has associated employments (with the employer or employers associated with the employer) the duties of which are not performed wholly outside the UK, the amount of the employment income to which **3.48** applies is limited to such amount as is just and reasonable having regard to the employee's employment income from all of the employments, the proportion of the overall amount which is general earnings to which *ITEPA 2003, s 22* applies (remittance basis) or employment income to which *ITEPA 2003, s 41A* applies (remittance basis employment-related securities), the nature of, and time devoted to, the duties performed outside the UK and those performed in the UK in the relevant tax year and all other relevant circumstances [*ITEPA 2003, s 554Z9(4)–(6)*].

3.50   If:

(*a*)   the value of the relevant step, or a part of it, is 'for' a tax year (the relevant tax year) as determined under *ITEPA 2003, s 554Z4* (see **3.39**) and is not in respect of duties performed in the UK;

(*b*)   *ITA 2007, ss 809B, 809D* or *809E* (remittance basis) applies to the employee for the relevant tax year; and

(*c*)   the employee is not ordinarily resident in the UK in the relevant tax year;

the employee's employment income by virtue of *ITEPA 2003, s 554Z2(1)* (or the relevant part of it) is taxable specific income (as defined in *ITEPA 2003, s 10(3)* – see **17.21**) in a tax year so far as it is remitted to the UK in that year [*ITEPA 2003, s 554Z10(1), (2)*]. Any income which is remitted before the employment starts is treated as remitted in the tax year in which it starts [*ITEPA 2003, s 554Z10(3)*]. The extent to which the value of the relevant step (or any part of it) is not in respect of duties performed in the UK must be determined on a just and reasonable basis [*ITEPA 2003, s 554Z10(4)*].

3.51   If **3.46** or **3.48** applies to a part of the value of a relevant step (the relevant part) any reduction in the value of the relevant step under any of *ITEPA 2003, ss 554Z5–554Z7* must be made so that a percentage of the reduction reduces the relevant part. This percentage is the proportion of the value of the relevant step represented by the relevant part before any reductions under any of *sections 554Z5 to 554Z8* [*ITEPA 2003, s 554Z11(1)–(3)*].

3.52   If the relevant step involves a sum of money, that sum is treated for the purpose of the remittance basis as deriving from the employee's employment income (or the relevant part of it) to which *section 554Z9(2)* (see **3.46**) or *554Z10(2)* (see **3.50**) applies [*ITEPA 2003, s 554Z11(5)*]. In any other case the asset which is the subject of the relevant step is so treated [*ITEPA 2003, s 554Z11(6)*].

3.53   If after the relevant step is taken:

(*a*)   there is another relevant step (the later relevant step) by reason of which these provisions apply in respect of the employee's same employment; and

(*b*)   there is overlap (as defined in *ITEPA 2003, s 554Z5* – see **3.40**) between the sum of money or asset which is the subject of the relevant step (sum R) and the sum of money or asset which is the subject of the later relevant step (sum S);

then for the purpose of the remittance basis, sum S is treated, to the extent of the overlap, as deriving from sum R (except in so far as, in any event, sum S and sum R are the same sum of money or asset or sum S derives from sum R [*ITEPA 2003, s 554Z11(7), (8)*].

3.54   If the relevant tax year (within the meaning of *section 554Z9* (see **3.46**) or *554Z10* (see **3.48**) is the tax year 2007/08 or earlier and the employee was UK resident in that year but was not UK domiciled or not ordinarily resident in the UK in that year:

(*a*)   *section 554Z9* or *554Z10* (as the case may be) applies as if *ITA 2007, s 809B* (claim for remittance basis to apply) applied to the employee for the relevant tax year; and

56

(*b*)   in *section 554Z9(1)(d)* (see **3.48**) the reference to a foreign employer does not include one resident in the Republic of Ireland.

[*ITEPA 2003, s 554Z11(9)–(11)*].

Relevant step taken after the employee's death

3.55   If the relevant step is one within *ITEPA 2003, s 554C* (see **3.32**(3)) or *554D* (see **3.32**(4)) and it is taken on or after the employee's death, or if relevant, any of the employment income arising by virtue of *section 554Z2(1)* (see **3.30**) is remitted to the UK on or after the employee's death, then, unless the employment never started before the employee's death:

(*a*)   if the relevant person is the employee, his personal representatives are liable for the tax;

(*b*)   if the relevant person is another individual, the amount which is treated as employment income of the employee under *section 554Z2(1)*, or is remitted, is treated as employment income of that other individual for the tax year in which the relevant step is taken or the income is remitted; and

(*c*)   if the relevant person is not an individual, the 'relevant taxable person' is chargeable to income tax on the amount which is treated as the employee's income or is remitted.

[*ITEPA 2003, s 554Z12(1), (3)–(5)*].

3.56   References above to the relevant person mean the relevant person (within the meaning of *section 554C(1)* (see **3.32**(3)) or *554D(1)* or *(2)* (see **3.32**(4)) in relation to the relevant step [*ITEPA 2003, s 554Z12(2)*]. For the purpose of (*c*) the 'relevant taxable person' is:

(*a*)   the person (or each of the persons) who took the relevant step (ie the third party) and who are UK resident, or, if there is no such person;

(*b*)   the employer (if still alive or in existence when the relevant step is taken, or, if the employer is dead or has ceased to exist;

(*c*)   the non-UK resident person (or each of the non-UK resident persons) who took the relevant steps.

[*ITEPA 2003, s 554Z12(6)*].

Where (*c*) in **3.55** applies, the rate of tax is that applying under *ITEPA 2003, s 394(2)* (the highest rate of income tax – currently 50%) at the time of the relevant step or remittance, and the tax is charged for the tax year in which the relevant step is taken or the income remitted [*ITEPA 2003, s 554Z12(7)*]. If there is more than one relevant person in relation to a relevant step, the taxable amount is apportioned between them on a just and reasonable basis with (*a*) to (*c*) above then being applied to each apportioned amount [*ITEPA 2003, s 554Z12(8)*].

Subsequent income tax liability

3.57 If after the relevant step is taken, another event (the later event) occurs, the later event would give rise to a liability for income tax on the employee or any other person on an amount (other than by virtue of these provisions, *ITEPA 2003, Part 7, Chapters 2–5* (employment related securities – see **Chapter 14**) or *Part 9* (pension income – see **2.56**), and it is just and reasonable to do so in order to avoid a double charge to income tax in respect of the sum of money or asset, then no liability to income tax arises on the later amount by virtue of the later event so far as is just and reasonable to avoid a double charge [*ITEPA 2003, s 554Z13*].

Relief where earmarking not followed by further relevant step

3.58 An application for relief can be made by the employee (or his personal representatives if he has died) to HMRC if:

(*a*)   these provisions have applied by reasons of a relevant step (the original relevant step) within *ITEPA 2003, s 554B* (see **3.32**(1), (2)) taken by a third party;

(*b*)   there occurs an event which is not a relevant step in relation to a relevant sum or asset;

(*c*)   by reason of the event at (*b*) no further relevant step is, or will be, taken by the third party or any other person in relation to the sum of money or asset which was the subject of the original relevant step (or to a sum of money or asset which, directly or indirectly, has arisen or derived (or may arise or derive) from the sum of money or asset which was the subject of the original relevant step); and

(*d*)   there is no connection (direct or indirect) between the relevant event and a tax avoidance arrangement (which includes in particular the avoidance of tax by way of obtaining relief under the section itself.

[*ITEPA 2003, s 554Z14(1)–(3)*].

3.59 If HMRC are satisfied that (*a*)–(*d*) above are met, they must give such relief as the HMRC Officer concerned considers just and reasonable (if any) in respect of income tax paid on any 'previously charged amount' [*ITEPA 2003, s 554Z14(5)*]. The application for relief must be made within four years of the occurrence of the event at (*b*) [*ITEPA 2003, s 554Z14(4)*]. A previously charged amount is the amount taxed by reference to the original step and any grossing up addition made in respect of it [*ITEPA 2003, s 554Z14(6)*].If the tax liability fo the employee or anyone else was reduced by reference to the original step, such as under *ITEPA 2003, s 554Z5* (see **3.40**) or *s 554Z13* (see **3.57**), HMRC must have regard to that reduction in determining what is just and reasonable [*ITEPA 2003, s 554Z14(7), (8)*].

Exceptions

Steps under certain schemes etc.

3.60   No tax charge arises by reason of a relevant step if that step is taken under either:

(a)   an approved SIP (Share Incentive Plan within *ITEPA 2003, Part 7. Ch 6* – see **Chapter 15**);

(b)   an approved SAYE Option Scheme (within *ITEPA 2003, Part 7, Ch 6* – see **Chapter 16**);

(c)   an approved CSOP scheme (share option scheme within *ITEPA 2003, Part 7, Ch 8* – see **Chapter 16**);

(d)   an arrangement the sole purpose of which is the provision of excluded benefits (ie benefits in respect of ill-health or disablement of an employee during service; in respect of accidental death of an employee during service; under a group life policy (or a life policy on an individual that meets the other conditions of *ITEPA 2003, s 481*) or benefits under regulations prescribed under *ITEPA 2003, s 393B(3)*);

(e)   an arrangement the sole purpose of which is the making of disregarded payments within *Sch 3, Part 10, para 12* of the *Social Security (Contributions) Regulations 2011 (SI 2001 No 1004)*;

(f)   a pension scheme set up by a government outside the UK for the benefit of its employees (or primarily for their benefit);

(g)   a registered pension scheme (see **Chapter 10**);

(h)   an arrangement the sole purpose of which is the making of payments under a registered pension scheme from assets held for the purpose of the scheme within *FA 2004, s 161(4)* [*ITEPA 2003, s 554E(1)*].

Other relevant steps under approved share scheme

3.61   No tax charge arises by reason of a relevant step if that step is taken solely for the purpose of acquiring or holding shares to be awarded under an approved SIP, or to be provided pursuant to options granted under an approved SAYE option scheme or approved CSOP option scheme (or of providing shares pursuant to an award under an approved SIP or an option granted under an approved SAYE option scheme or CSOP scheme), that step is not taken under an arrangement within (a) to (c) in **3.60** and there is no connection (direct or indirect) between the relevant step and a tax avoidance arrangement [*ITEPA 2003, s 554E(2), (3)*]. This exclusion does not apply if (immediately before or after the step is taken) the total number of shares of any type held (in relation to the approved scheme) by the third party and any other persons for purposes within the exemption exceeds the maximum number of shares of that type which might reasonably be expected to be required for those purposes over the 10-year period starting from the day on which the relevant step is taken [*ITEPA 2003, s 554E(4)*]. It appears that this disallowance affects all of the shares, not merely the excess number.

3.62   If a person takes a relevant step within *ITEPA 2003, s 554B* (earmarking) to which this exception (or that in *s 554B(6)* – see **3.63**) applies and the sum of money or asset (or any part of it) subsequently ceases to be held by that person wholly for purposes within *subsection (3) or (6)* but continues to be held by him for purposes within *ITEPA 2003, s 554B* (ie continues to be earmarked with a view to a later relevant step being taken) these provisions apply as if the earmarking has taken place at that time [*ITEPA 2003, s 554E(10), (11)*].

Relevant steps for the purpose of an EMI (Employee Management Incentive) scheme

3.63   No tax charge arises by reason of a relevant step if that step is taken for the sole purpose of either:

(*a*)   granting qualifying EMI options (see **Chapter 16**);

(*b*)   acquiring or holding shares to be granted as EMI options; or

(*c*)   providing shares pursuant to EMI options;

and there is no connection (direct or indirect) between the relevant step and a tax avoidance arrangement [*ITEPA 2003, s 554E(6)*]. This exclusion does not apply to the relevant step if (immediately before or after the step is taken) the total number of shares of any type held in relation to the EMI scheme by the third party and any other persons for the above purposes exceeds the maximum number of shares of that type which might reasonably be expected to be required under the EMI scheme within the following 10 years [*ITEPA 2003, s 554E(7)*]. If the shares cease to be held for the purpose of the EMI scheme but remain earmarked, the rule in **3.62** applies.

MPs

3.64   No tax charge arises to MPs (obviously), ie the charge does not apply be reason of a relevant step being taken by the Independent Parliamentary Standards Authority in relation to a member of the House of Commons [*ITEPA 2003, s 554E(12)*].

Commercial transactions

3.65   No tax charge arises by reason of the payment of a sum of money by way of loan if the loan is one on ordinary commercial terms within *ITEPA 2003, s 176* and there is no connection (direct or indirect) between the making of the loan and a tax avoidance arrangement [*ITEPA 2003, s 554F(1)*]. A loan is within *section 176* only if it is made by a person in the ordinary course of a business carried on by that person which includes the lending of money or the supplying of goods or services on credit and was made on terms generally available to members of the public.

3.66   These provisions also do not apply to a relevant step which is not the payment of a sum of money by way of loan if:

(*a*)   the step is taken for the sole purpose of a transaction which the third party and the employee (or a person linked with the employee) entered into in the ordinary course of the third party's business;

(*b*)   a substantial proportion of the person's business involves similar transactions (ie transactions of the same or a similar type to that with the employee) with members of the public (ie the public at large) with whom the person deals at arm's length;

(*c*)   the terms on which the third party entered into the transaction with the employee are substantially the same as those on which he normally enters into similar transactions with members of the public; and

(*d*)   there is no connection (direct or indirect) between the relevant step and a tax avoidance arrangement.

[*ITEPA 2003, s 554F(2)–(5)*].

Employee benefit packages

3.67   No tax charge arises if:

(*a*)   the relevant step is not taken under a pension scheme;

(*b*)   it is taken for the sole purpose of a transaction between the employee (or a linked person) and the third party which the third party has entered into in the ordinary course of its business;

(*c*)   if the relevant step is a loan, a substantial proportion of the lender's business involves making similar loans to members of the public, the transaction with the employee is part of a package of benefits which is available to a substantial proportion of his employer's employees, and no feature of the package of benefits has (or is likely to have) the effect that benefits under the package will be wholly or mainly conferred on directors, senior employees or employees who receive (or as of a result of the package of benefits are likely to receive) the higher or highest levels of remuneration;

(*d*)   if the relevant step is not a loan, the transaction with the employee (or linked person) is part of a package of benefits which is available to a substantial proportion of the employees of the relevant employees' employer (or to a substantial proportion of those employees whose status as employees is comparable with that of the employee concerned (taking into account, for example, levels of seniority, types of duties and levels of remuneration);

(*e*)   the terms on which similar transactions are offered by the third party under the package of benefits are generous enough to enable substantially all of the employees of the relevant employees' employer to whom the package is offered to take advantage of it;

(*f*)   the terms on which the third party entered into the transaction with the relevant employee are substantially the same as those on which he normally enters into similar transactions with employees of the employer;

(*g*)   if the employer is a company, a majority of its employees to whom the package of benefits is available do not have a material interest (broadly over 5%) in the company; and

(*h*)   there is no connection, direct or indirect, between the relevant step and a tax avoidance arrangement.

[*ITEPA 2003, s 554G(1), (3), (4), (7)*].

3.68   It will be seen that this is a very limited exclusion. It is aimed at excluding only third party benefits which are generally available to most employees of the employer. For the purpose of paragraph (*c*), a loan is similar only if it is made for the same or similar purposes as the loan which is the subject of the relevant step [*ITEPA 2003, s 554G(2)(a)*]. On the face of it this is an odd restriction. Suppose, for example, the package enables loans to be taken for any purpose and the employee borrows to build a greenhouse in his garden. It appears that it needs to be shown that a substantial part of the lender's business is making loans to build greenhouses! The reference in paragraph (*c*) to members of the public means members of the public at large with whom the third party deals at arm's length [*ITEPA 2003, s 554G(2)(b)*]. If the employer is a company and is a member of a group of companies, the package of benefits must not be wholly or mainly conferred on senior or highest earning employees of the group either [*ITEPA 2003, s 554G(4)(d)*]. For the purpose of paragraphs (*e*) and (*f*), a transaction is similar if it is of the same or a similar type to the transaction with the employee in question [*ITEPA 2003, s 554G(5)*]. The full definition of material interest for the purpose of paragraph (*f*) is that in *ITEPA 2003, s 68* – see **8.25** [*ITEPA 2003, s 554G(1)(g)*]. Except in the case of a loan, references in **3.67** and **3.68** to employees of the relevant employee's employer is limited to those employees whose duties are performed in the UK (but for this purpose non-UK duties are treated as UK ones if they are merely incidental to the performance of UK duties) [*ITEPA 2003, s 554G(6)*].

Earmarking of deferred remuneration

3.69   No tax charge arises by reference to the step at (*g*) below if:

(*a*)   on a date (the award date) the employee is awarded deferred remuneration;

(*b*)   the main purpose of the award is not the provision of relevant benefits under an EFURBS (employee financed relevant benefits scheme, ie within *ITEPA 2003, ss 393–400*, but other than benefits taxed as pension income);

(*c*)   the deferred remuneration is awarded on terms the main purpose of which is to defer its provision to the employee to a specified future date while providing that the award will be revoked if specified conditions are not met by the vesting date;

(*d*)   the vesting date is not more than five years after the award date;

(*e*)   at the award date there is a reasonable chance that all of the conditions will not be met and the remuneration will be revoked;

(*f*)   if the remuneration had been paid to the employer at the award date, it would have been subject to PAYE;

(*g*)   on or before the vesting date, someone takes a relevant step within *ITEPA 2003, s 554B* (see **3.32**) which triggers the application of the provision;

(*h*)   on that relevant step the sum of money or asset concerned represents all or part of the deferred remuneration (and nothing else); and

(*i*)   there is no connection, direct or indirect, between the relevant step and a tax avoidance arrangement.

[*ITEPA 2003, s 554H(1), (3)*].

3.70   The conditions at (*c*) above must be included in the award. If desired the terms can also provide for the award to be partly revoked if other specified conditions are not met [*ITEPA 2003, s 554H(2)*].

3.71   If at any time any sum of money or asset held by or on behalf of a third party within *ITEPA 2003, s 554B(1)* which represents any of the 'earmarked deferred remuneration' ceases to do so (because the remuneration is to be provided in a different way or the award has been revoked for any reason) but the sum of money continues to be held by the third party under *s 554B(1)*, a relevant step is deemed to take place at that time. The subject of this is the aggregate of the sum of money or asset and a just and reasonable apportionment of any 'relevant income' [*ITEPA 2003, s 554H(5), (6)*]. For this purpose the earmarked deferred remuneration is the sum or asset that is the subject of the relevant step at (*h*) above [*ITEPA 2003, s 554H(4)*]. The relevant income is any income which before the time mentioned above arises directly or indirectly from the sum or asset representing any of the earmarked deferred remuneration and is the subject of a relevant step (within *ITEPA 2003, s 554B*) by reason of which the provisions would apply (apart from *ITEPA 2003, s 554Q* – see **3.85**) and which at that time continues to be held by the third party on the basis mentioned in *ITEPA 2003, s 554B(1)* [*ITEPA 2003, s 554H(12)*].

3.72   If on or before the vesting day any part of the earmarked deferred remuneration is not either paid to the employer in a form that attracts PAYE (and the award has not been revoked), a relevant step within *ITEPA 2003, s 554B* is deemed to take place on the vesting day, the subject of which is the sum of the notional PAYE amount and a just and reasonable proportion of any relevant income (as defined in *ITEPA 2003, s 554H(12)* – see **3.71**) – but with the substitution of the vesting day for the time mentioned in that paragraph) [*ITEPA 2003, s 554H(8), (10), (11)*]. The notional PAYE amount is the PAYE that would have been due if the earmarked deferred remuneration (or the unpaid and unrevoked part of it) had been paid to the employee on the vesting day [*ITEPA 2003, s 554H(9)*].

Employee share schemes

3.73   There are a number of exclusions in relation to employee share schemes. They apply only if the employer is a company [*ITEPA 2003,* *s 554I(3)*]. No tax charge arises by reason of a relevant step within *ITEPA 2003, s 554B* (see **3.32**(1), (2)) if the subject of the relevant step is relevant shares which are earmarked (or otherwise start being held) solely with a view to meeting an award (or an expected future award) under one of the following types of arrangement in relation to which the appropriate requirements are met, provided that the number of relevant shares of any type which are so earmarked does not exceed the maximum number which might reasonably be expected to be needed to meet the award and there is no connection (direct or indirect) between the relevant step and a tax avoidance arrangement [*ITEPA 2003, ss 554J(3), 554K(3), 554L(3), 554M(2)*]. The arrangements covered by this exclusion are:

(1) Where:

    (*a*) there is an arrangement under which an award can be made to the employee of 'relevant shares' (or of a sum of money the amount of which will be determined by reference to the market value of relevant shares at the time that it becomes payable);

    (*b*) the main purpose of the award is not the provision of relevant benefits (as defined at **3.67**(*b*)) ;

    (*c*) the award will be on terms the main purpose of which is to defer the receipt of the shares by the employee (or the payment of the money to him) to a later specified date (the vesting date) while providing that the award will be revoked if specified conditions are not met by the vesting date;

    (*d*) the vesting date will be within 10 years of the date of the award; and

    (*e*) at the date of the award there will be a reasonable chance that the award will be revoked because not all of the specified conditions are met [*ITEPA 2003, s 554J(1)*].

(2) Where:

    (*a*) there is an arrangement under which an award may be made to the employee of relevant shares (or a sum of money the amount of which will be determined by reference to the market value of relevant shares at the time it becomes payable) ;

    (*b*) the main purpose of the award is not the provision of relevant benefits;

    (*c*) the relevant shares will be of shares or stock in (or instruments within *ITEPA 2003, s 554I(4)* – see **3.74** – issued by) a trading company or a company that controls a trading company;

    (*d*) the award will be on terms the main purpose of which is to ensure that the relevant shares (or sum of money) are received only if a specified 'exit event', or an exit event within a specified description, occurs; and

    (*e*) at the time the award is made there is a reasonable chance that the specified exit event will occur [*ITEPA 2003, s 554K(1)*].

(3) Where:

(*a*) there is an arrangement under which a right (a relevant share option) can be granted to the employee to acquire relevant shares (or a sum of money the amount of which will be determined by reference to the market value of relevant shares at the time that it becomes payable) ;

(*b*) the main purpose of the grant of the relevant share option is not the provision or relevant benefits;

(*c*) the grant will be made on terms the main purpose of which is to ensure that the option is not exercisable by the employee before a later specified date (the vesting date) while providing that it cannot be exercised at all if specified conditions are not met by the vesting date;

(*d*) the vesting date is within 10 years of the date of the grant;and

(*e*) at the date of the grant there is a reasonable chance that the relevant share options will not be exercisable at all because not al: of the specified conditions will be met by the vesting date.

[*ITEPA 2003, s 554L(1)*].

(4) Where:

(*a*) there is an arrangement under which a right (a relevant share option) can be granted to the employee to acquire relevan: shares (or a sum of money the amount of which will be determined by reference to the market value of relevant shares at the time it becomes payable);

(*b*) the main purpose of the grant of the relevant share option is not the provision of relevant benefits;

(*c*) the relevant shares will be shares or stock in (or instruments within *ITEPA 2003, s 554I(4)* issued by) a trading company or a company that controls a trading company;

(*d*) the grant will be made on terms the main purpose of which is to ensure that the relevant share option is exercisable only if a specified exit event (or an exit event within a specified description) occurs; and

(*e*) at the time the grant is made there is a reasonable chance that the exit event will occur.

[*ITEPA 2003, s 554M(1)*].

3.74 For the above purposes 'relevant shares' are shares or stock in the employer company, instruments issued by the employer which are securities within *ITEPA 2003, s 420(1)(b)* (debentures, debenture stock, loan stock, bonds, certificates of deposit and other instruments creating or acknowledging indebtedness (other than contracts of insurance)) and units in a collective investment scheme (within *ITEPA 2003, s 420(2)*) managed by the employer [*ITEPA 2003, s 554I(4)*]. An 'exit event' is:

(*a*)   shares in the relevant company (ie one whose shares are held or which issued the security) being admitted to trading on a stock exchange;

(*b*)   all the shares in the relevant company (or a substantial proportion of them) being disposed of to persons none of whom is connected with any of the persons making the disposal;

(*c*)   if the relevant company is a trading company, the company's trade (or a substantial proportion of it) being transferred to a person who is not a relevant connected person (ie a person who is connected with the relevant company or is a shareholder (or connected with a shareholder) of that company);

(*d*)   the relevant company's assets (or a substantial proportion of them) being disposed of to a person who is not a relevant connected person;

(*e*)   the winding up of the relevant company starting (the date of commencement of a winding up is as defined in *Corporation Tax Act 2009 (CTA 2009), s 12(7)*); or

(*f*)   a person who controls the relevant company ceasing to control it (other than if a person connected with him starts to do so – it is not clear whether this means starts at the same time or if not how big a gap applies).

[*ITEPA 2003, s 554I(6), (7)*].

For the purpose of (*c*) above the trade is transferred to another person if the relevant company ceases to carry on the trade and, on that occurring, the other person starts to carry it on [*ITEPA 2003, s 554I(7)(c)*].

3.75   For the purpose of **3.73**(1), (2) and (3) in addition to the required provision relating to revocation, the award terms can also provide that the award will be partly revoked (or the option can be exercised in part only, as the case may be) if specified conditions are not met by the vesting date [*ITEPA 2003, ss 554J(2), 554K(2), 554L(2)*].

3.76   If the relevant step within **3.73** is taken in relation to an expected award or grant of an option, the award or grant is not made within three months of the date of the relevant step and at the end of the three-year period any of the earmarked shares continue to be held by the third party solely on the basis of the relevant paragraph of **3.73**, a relevant step within *ITEPA 2003, s 554B* is deemed to occur on the three-year anniversary. The subject of that relevant step is the shares which continue to be held plus any relevant income in relation to them. Relevant income in relation to such shares is any income which arises directly or indirectly from the shares, is the subject of a relevant step within *ITEPA 2003, s 554B* and at the time of the deemed relevant step continues to be held by or on behalf of the third party on the basis mentioned in *ITEPA 2003,* *s 554B(1)(a)* or *(b)*) [*ITEPA 2003, ss 554J(4), (5), (13), 554K(3), (4), (12), 554L(4), (5), (15), 554M(3), (4), (14)*].

3.77   If at any time any of the earmarked shares ceases to be held solely on the basis set out in the relevant paragraph of **3.72** but continue to be held on the basis mentioned in *ITEPA 2003, s 554B(1)(a)* or *(b)*, a relevant step is deemed to take place at that time, the subject of that step again being the shares and any relevant income (as defined above) [*ITEPA 2003, ss 554J(6), (7), (13), 554K(5), (12), 554L(6), (7), (15), 554M(5), (6), (14)*]. If the relevant step in *section 554J(3)* (see **3.73**) is taken in relation to an award of relevant shares or money which is made before the final grant date, a relevant step is deemed to have been taken on the vesting date. [*ITEPA 2003, s 554J(8), (9)*]. Similarly, if the relevant step mentioned in *section 554K(2)* is taken in relation to an award of relevant shares or money, a relevant step is deemed to have been taken at the end of the exit period, and if the relevant step in *section 554L(3)* is taken in relation to a grant of a relevant share option and the grant is made by the final grant date, a relevant step is deemed to have been taken on the final exercise date, and if the relevant step in *section 554M(2)* is taken in relation to the grant of a relevant share option and the grant is not make by the final grant date and a specified exit event occurs, a relevant step is deemed to have been taken at the end of the exit period. [*ITEPA 2003, ss 554K(7), (8), 554L(8), (9), 554M(7), (8)*]. In each case the subject matter of that deemed relevant step is any of the earmarked shares not falling within *sections 554J(10)–(12), 554K(9)* or *(10), 554L(10)–(13)* or *554M(9)–(13)* as the case may be (see **3.78**), plus any relevant income in relation to the shares to which the relevant share option relates. [*ITEFA 2003, s 554L(8), (9)*]. This is subject to *section 554A(4)* (relevant step taken after employee's death – see **3.33**(*a*)).

3.78   If the relevant step in one of paragraphs (1) to (4) in **3.71** is taken in relation to an award which has been made (or an option which has been granted, as the case may be), or an expected award or grant which is in fact made within the three-year period referred to or **3.76**, a relevant step is deemed to take place on the vesting date (or the final exercise date). The subject of that deemed step is any of the earmarked shares (and any relevant income (as defined in **3.74**) from them) in relation to which neither:

(*a*)   the shares have been transferred to the employee before that date in such a way as to give rise to employment income of the employee which is chargeable to income tax or is exempt income;

(*b*)   a sum has been paid to the employee which has given rise to employment income and that payment either represents the proceeds of disposal of the shares or the payment has been made from another source and, correspondingly, the shares are no longer held by any person in relation to the award; or

(*c*)   the award has been revoked in accordance with its terms and the shares are no longer held by any person in relation to the award.

[*ITEPA 2003, s 554J(10)–(12)*].

3.79   The exceptions in relation to 3.30(2) are:

(*a*)   an employee receives the shares before the end of the exit period (ie the period of six months following the occurrence of the exit event) and the receipt gives rise to employment income of the employee;

(*b*)   the sum has been paid to the employee before the end of the exit period, the payment gives rise to employment income and either the payment represents the proceeds of the disposal of the shares, or the payment is made from another source and the shares are no longer held by any person in relation to the award.

[*ITEPA 2003, s 554K(9)–(11)*].

3.80   The exceptions in relation to **3.32**(3) are:

(*a*)   the relevant share option became exercisable by the vesting date, the employee exercised it (in whole or in part) by the final exercise date (ie 10 years after the date of the grant) and the receipt of the shares gave rise to employment income which is chargeable to income tax (or would be chargeable apart from *ITEPA 2003, s 474* (exceptions to the employee share scheme rules)) or which is exempt income,

(*b*)   the relevant share option became exercisable by the vesting date, the employee exercised it (in whole or in part) by the final exercise date and as a result a sum of money was paid to him, that sum gives rise to employment income which is chargeable to income tax (or would be chargeable apart from *ITEPA 2003, ss 41F – 41L from 2015/16* or *FA 2004, Sch 7, para 15* in earlier years) or which is exempt income, and the payment either represents the disposal of the shares or the payment is made from another source and the shares are no longer held (by any person) in relation to the relevant share options,

(*c*)   in accordance with its terms the option ceased to be exercisable by the vesting date and the shares are no longer held by any person in relation to the relevant share option, or

(*d*)   the option became exercisable by the employee, in whole or in part, by the vesting date but the employee did not exercise it and it lapsed (in whole or in part) by the final exercise date, and the shares are no longer held by any person in relation to the relevant share option

[*ITEPA 2003, s 554L(10)–(12)* as amended by *Finance Act 2014 (FA 2014), Sch 9, para 18*].

3.81   The exceptions in relation to **3.32**(4) are:

(*a*)   the employee exercised the share option (in whole or in part) before the end of the exit period (ie the period of six months following the date of the exit event – or of five years where the exit event is the admission of the shares to trading on a stock exchange – or, if earlier, the period during which the option is exercisable by the employee in accordance with the terms of its grant) and as a result receives the shares, and the receipt of the shares gives rise to employment income which is chargeable to income tax (or would be but for *ITEPA 2003, ss 41F – 41L* from 2015/16 or *FA 2004, Sch 7, para 15* in earlier years) or which is exempt income; or

(b)   the employee exercised the share option (in whole or in part) before the end of the exit period and as a result a sum of money became payable to him, that payment gave rise to employment income which is chargeable to income tax (or would be but for *ITEPA 2003, s 474*) or which is exempt income, and the payment either represents the proceeds of the disposal of the shares or it is made from another source and the shares are no longer held by any person in relation to the relevant share option; or

(c)   the share option became exercisable before the end of the exit period but it lapsed (in whole or in part) before the end of that period.

[*ITEPA 2003, s 554M(9)–(13)* as amended by *FA 2014, Sch 9, para 19*].

Other cases involving employment-related securities, etc.

3.82   No tax arises:

(a)   by reason of a relevant step, the subject of which is employment-related securities, if by virtue of the step the securities are acquired by a person and *ITEPA 2003, s 425(2)* (exception on acquisition of restricted securities) applies to the acquisition or up to 2015/16 only would apply but for *ITEPA 2003, s 421E(1)* (exclusion where the employee is not UK resident) [*ITEPA 2003, s 554N(1)* as amended by *FA 2014, Sch 9, para 20*];

(b)   by reason of a relevant step the subject of which is an employment-related securities option, if by virtue of that step the option is acquired by a person and *ITEPA 2003, s 475(1)* (no charge in respect of the acquisition of an option) applies or up to 2015/16 only would apply but for *ITEPA 2003, s 474(1)* (employee not UK resident) [*ITEPA 2003, s 554N(2)* as amended by *FA 2014, Sch 9, para 20*];

(c)   by reason of an event which is either:

(i)   a chargeable event within *ITEPA 2003, ss 426, 438* or *476* (employment-related securities);

(ii)   an event which gives rise to the discharge of a notional loan for the purpose of *ITEPA 2003, s 446U*; or

(iii)   a disposal to which *ITEPA 2003, ss 446X–446Z* applies (securities disposed of for more than market value);

if, by virtue of the event, an amount counts as employment income of the employee [*ITEPA 2003, s 554N(4), (5)*].

(d)   by reason of an event which would have been exempted under (c) but for *ITEPA 2003, ss 421B(6)* (death of the employee), *421E(1)* (non-residents

– up to 2015/16 only), *429* (cases outside the charge under *section 426*), *430A(5)* (exchange of restricted securities), *443* (cases outside the charge under *section 438*), *474(1)* (non-residents – up to 2015/16 only), or *477(2)* (death of the employee), or but for an election under *ITEPA 2003, ss 430 or 431* (elections for restrictions to be ignored) [*ITEPA 2003, s 554N(6)* as amended by *FA 2014, Sch 9, para 20*];

(*e*) by reason of a relevant step which is taken after the acquisition (as defined in *ITEPA 2003, s 421B(2)(a)*) of an asset within *ITEPA 2003, s 554C(4)(a) or (b)* (securities or an interest in securities) and either:

 (i) 'relevant consideration' is given by the employee for the asset of an amount equal to or exceeding the market value of the asset at the time of its acquisition; or

 (ii) ignoring any relevant consideration given for the relevant asset, the acquisition gives rise to earnings of the employee the amount of which is equal to or exceeds the market value of the assets and which are not exempt income, if the subject of the relevant step is that asset and there is no connection (direct or indirect) between the relevant step and a tax avoidance arrangement [*ITEPA 2003, s 554N(11), (12)*];

(*f*) by reason of a relevant step taken after the acquisition (as defined in *ITEPA 2003, s 421B(2)(a)*) of an asset within *ITEPA 2003, s 554C(4)(a) or (b)* if:

 (i) the acquisition is pursuant to an employment-related securities option (within *ITEPA 2003, ss 471-484* – securities options) (or would have been had the employee been UK resident) acquired by reason of the employee's employment, or former or prospective employment,

 (ii) the acquisition is a chargeable event for the purposes of *ITEPA* 2003, s 476 (or up to 2015/16 would have been but for *ITEPA 2003, s 474(1)*);

 (iii) the subject of the relevant step is that asset; and

 (iv) there is no connection, direct or indirect, between the relevant step and a tax avoidance arrangement;

[*ITEPA 2003, s 554N(11)–(13)*]

(*g*) by reason of a relevant step within *ITEPA 2003, s 554C(1)(a)* (see **3.32(3)**) taken by a person if:

 (i) the payment of the sum of money is by way of loan;

 (ii) that loan is made and used solely for the purpose of enabling the employee to exercise an employment-related securities option (within *ITEPA 2003, ss 471–484* – securities options);

 (iii) the exercise of the option gives rise to employment income of the employee which is chargeable to income tax (or would be chargeable but for *ITEPA 2003, s 474*) or which is exempt income; and

(iv)   there is no connection, direct or indirect, between the relevant step and a tax avoidance arrangement;

[*ITEPA 2003, s 554N(13)*].

3.83   For the purpose of (*e*) above, relevant consideration is consideration in money or money's worth which is given, before, or at or about, the time of the acquisition, but does not include a promise to do something or the performance of any duties of (or in connection with) an employment [*ITEPA 2003, s 554N(8)*]. If *ITEPA 2003, ss 437(1)* or *452(1)* (which contain special valuation rules) applies to the acquisition (or would do so if *ITEPA 2003, ss 435–444* (convertible securities) or *451–460* (research institution spin-out companies) applied to the acquisition) the market value must be determined on the basis set out *in s 437(1)* or *452(1)* as may be appropriate [*ITEPA 2003, s 554N(9)*].

3.84   If apart from (*d*) in **3.79** these provisions would have applied and the loan is not repaid in full within 40 days of the relevant step occurring, a relevant step is deemed to occur at the end of that 40-day period. The subject matter of that deemed step is an amount equal to the unpaid balance of the loan and the person to whom the loan is deemed to have been made is the employee or other person within *ITEPA 2003, s 554C(2)* ('relevant person', see **3.32**(3) (*a*)) [*ITEPA 2003, s 554N(14)–(16)*].

Employee car ownership schemes

3.85   Where under there is an arrangement which:

(*a*)   provides for an employee to purchase a new car from a third party using a loan to be made to the employee by a licenced lender (ie a person who holds a licence under the *Consumer Credit Act 1974 (CCA 1974)*, is acting within the terms of the licence and is not acting as a trustee);

(*b*)   specifies the date by which the car loan must be fully repaid, being a date within four years of the time of the loan; and

(*c*)   permits the employee, in order to obtain funds to repay the car loan, to sell the car back to the vendor on a specified date at a specified price based on an estimate (made at the time the arrangement is entered into) of the likely outstanding amount of the loan on the specified date;

and the employee purchases the car using the car loan, no tax charge arises by reason of a relevant step taken for the sole purpose of the purchase of the car, or its sale-back under the arrangement, or the making of the car loan (provided that the arrangement is not a tax avoidance arrangement and there is no other connection, direct or indirect, between the relevant step and a tax avoidance arrangement) [*ITEPA 2003, s 554O(1), (2), (5)*].

3.86   If the car loan has not been fully repaid by the specified repayment date, a relevant step is deemed to occur at that date, the subject of which is the outstanding amount of the loan and in relation to which the relevant person is the employee [*ITEPA 2003, s 554O(3), (4)*]. The definition of a car in *ITEPA 2003, s 235(2)* (a mechanically propelled road vehicle which is not a goods vehicle, a motorcycle or a vehicle of a type not commonly used as a private vehicle and unsuitable to be so used) applies [*ITEPA 2003, s 554O(5)*].

Employment income exemptions

3.87 No tax charge arises by reason of a relevant step if an exemption from the employment income charge under *ITEPA 2003, ss 227–326A* applies to the subject of that step [*ITEPA 2003, s 554P(1)*]. If the exemption applies to the relevant step in part only, it must be treated as being two separate relevant steps, one in relation to the exempt part, and the other in relation to the balance and the exclusion of these provisions applies only to the exempt part [*ITEPA 2003, s 554P(2)*]. The apportionment between the two parts must be done on a just and reasonable basis [*ITEPA 2003, s 554P(3)*].

Income arising from earmarked sum or asset

3.88 If a sum of money or asset is held by or on behalf of a person, income arises from that sum or asset, and when it arises it is received by or on behalf of that person and is the subject of a relevant step within *ITEPA 2003, s 554B* taken by that person, no tax charge arises by reason of the relevant step if:

(*a*) before the income arises the sum or asset was the subject of a relevant step taken by that person;

(*b*) these provisions applied by virtue of the relevant step taken at (*a*) (or would have applied but for *ITEPA 2003, ss 554Q, 554R* (see **3.86**), *554H-554M* (see **3.73** onwards) or *554T* (see **3.92**);

(*c*) immediately before the income arose, the sum or asset was still earmarked or otherwise held on the basis mentioned in *ITEPA 2003, s 554B(1)(a)* or *(b)* (see **3.32**(1), (2)); and

(*d*) it is not reasonable to suppose that, taking into account the type of investments from which the income derives, in essence the income represents a return from the sum or asset which might be expected on the assumption that all relevant connected persons (ie persons with a connection, direct or indirect) to the arrangements under which the income arises) are acting at arm's length of each other [*ITEPA 2003, s 554Q*].

Acquisitions out of sums or assets

3.89 If:

(*a*) a sum of money or asset (S) is held by (or on behalf of) a person;

(*b*) a different sum of money or asset (T) is acquired by (or on behalf of) that person wholly out of sum or asset S;

(c)   sum or asset T is not acquired (directly or indirectly) from the employee or any person linked to the employee (see **3.33**),

(d)   it is not reasonable to suppose that, in essence, at the time of the acquisition of sum or asset T its value was greater or less than that of the part of sum or asset S which was used to acquire T and the difference (or any part of the difference) in the values would not have been expected to arise if all relevant connected persons (ie persons having a connection (direct or indirect) to the arrangement under which sum or asset T was acquired) were acting at arm's length to each other; and

(e)   on its acquisition, sum or asset T is the subject of a relevant step within *ITEPA 2003, s 554B* taken by that person,

no tax charge arises by reason of that relevant step if:

(i)   before the acquisition sum or asset S was the subject of a relevant step within *ITEPA 2003, s 554B* taken by that same person;

(ii)   these provisions applied to the employee by reason of his employment by reason of the relevant step at (i) (or would have done so apart from *ITEPA 2003, ss 554R* or *554Q* (see **3.83**) or *554T* (see **3.90**); and

(iii)   immediately before the acquisition of sum or asset T, sum or asset S is still earmarked or otherwise held on the basis mentioned in *ITEPA 2003, s 554B(1)(a)* or *(b)*.

[*ITEPA 2003, s 554R(1)–(6)*].

3.90   If on its acquisition, sum or asset T either:

(a)   was the subject of a relevant step taken by the same person by reason of which these provisions apply (or would do so apart from *subsection (6)* or any of *sections 554H–554M* (see **3.69** onwards), *554Q* (see **3.85**) or *554T* (see **3.93**); or

(b)   where there was no such relevant step, it is held by (or on behalf of) that person on the same basis as that on which sum or asset S was held by him (or on his behalf) immediately before the acquisition of sum or asset T;

and, for the sole purpose of the acquisition, either sum or asset S or sum or asset T is the subject of a relevant step within *ITEPA 2003, s 554C(1)(a)–(c)* (payment of sum or transfer of asset – see **3.32**(3)), no tax charge arises by reason of that relevant step [*ITEPA 2003, s 554R(7), (8)*].

Pension income

3.91   No tax charge arises by reason of a relevant step within *ITEPA 2003, ss 554C* (payment of sum or transfer of assets – see **3.32**(3)) or *554D* (making assets available) (see **3.32**(4) if the step is the provision of pension income which is chargeable to tax under *ITEPA 2003, ss 605–636C* or is exempt income within *ss 637–654*.

Pension scheme transactions

3.92   There are a number of exclusions in relation to pension schemes. These are contained in *ITEPA 2003, ss 554T, 554U, 554V, 554W* and *554X*. Where more than one of these provisions applies, they must be applied in the above order [*ITEPA 2003, s 554S(2)*].

Employee pension contributions

3.93   No tax charge arises by reason of a relevant step within *ITEPA 2003, s 554B* (see **3.30**(1), (2)) if the sum of money or asset which is the subject of the step derives (wholly or partly or directly or indirectly) from an excluded pension contribution (see **3.95**) paid after 5 April 2011 [*ITEPA 2003, s 554T(1)*]. However if it derives only partly from such a contribution, it is treated as two relevant steps (by apportioning on a just and reasonable basis) with the exclusion limited to the part that does so derive [*ITEPA 2003, s 554T(2), (5)*].

3.94   The provisions do not apply by reason of a relevant step within *ITEPA 2003, s 554C* (see **3.32**(3)) *or 554D* (see **3.32**(4)) if the sum of money or asset which is the subject of the relevant step represents 'relevant benefits' (as defined in *ITEPA 2003, ss 393–400* – benefits from non-approved pension schemes) and arises or derives (wholly or partly or directly or indirectly) from an 'excluded pension contribution' (see **3.95**) paid by the employee [*ITEPA 2003, s 554T(3), (7)*]. If it derives only partly from such a contribution it is again treated as two relevant steps (by apportioning on a just and reasonable basis) with the exclusion being limited to the part that does so derive [*ITEPA 2003, s 554T(4), (5)*].

3.95   An excluded pension contribution is a contribution:

(*a*)   which is made to an arrangement by the employee (ie a personal pension scheme) by way of a payment of a sum of money;

(*b*)   by virtue of which the employee acquires rights to receive relevant benefits under the arrangement (and nothing else);

(*c*)   which is neither a relievable pension contribution (one in respect of which an individual is entitled to relief under *FA 2004, s 188* – see **10.27**) nor a tax-relieved contribution (within *FA 2004, Sch 34, para 3(3)* – certain overseas pension schemes); and

(*d*)   which is not a repayment of any loan (and has nothing to do with any loan) and has nothing to do with a sum of money or asset which has been the subject of a relevant step within *ITEPA 2003, s 554C(1)(d)*

[*ITEPA 2003, s 554T(6–(7)*].

Pre-6 April 2006 contributions to EFURBS

3.96   No tax charge arises by reason of a relevant step if the subject of that step is a sum of money or asset which has (wholly or partly) arisen or derived (directly or indirectly) from a sum of money (the taxed sum) which was paid by the employer in accordance with an employer-financed retirement benefit scheme (within *ITEPA 2003, ss 393–400*) with a view to the provision of benefits under the scheme and in respect of which the employee was taxed [*ITEPA 2003, s 554U(1), (3)*]. *ITEPA 2003, Sch 36, para 53(3)* applies for the purpose of determining whether the employee has been taxed in respect of the sum [*ITEPA 2003, s 554U(2)*]. This requires him to have been assessed to tax under *ICTA 1988, s 595(1)* or the sum having counted as employment income under *ITEPA 2003, s 386(1)*. If the sum of money or asset derives only partly from such a sum, it is treated as two relevant steps (by apportioning on a just and reasonable basis) with the exclusion being limited to the part that does so derive [*ITEPA 2003, s 554U(4)–(6)*]. If the employer is a company which is a member of a group at any time, the reference above to the payment of a sum of money by the employer includes a reference to it being paid by any other company that was a member of the group at the time of the payment [*ITEPA 2003, s 554U(7)*].

Purchases of annuities out of pension scheme rights

3.97   If an annuity contract is purchased from an insurance company wholly out of rights which the employee has under a pension scheme and those rights are, wholly or partly, pre-6 April 2011 annuity rights (ie rights which accrued before 6 April 2011 specifically to receive an annuity), no tax charge arises either by reason of the purchaser taking a relevant step for the sole purpose of purchasing the annuity contract (or transferring the beneficiary's rights under the annuity contract to the employee or a person linked with the employee), or otherwise taking a relevant step within *ITEPA 2003, s 554B* on the purchase of the annuity contract, the subject of which is the beneficiary's rights under that contract [*ITEPA 2003, s 554V(1), (2), (6)*]. Similarly if an 'insurance company' takes a relevant step for the sole purpose of selling the annuity contract, or otherwise takes a relevant step within *ITEPA 2003, s 554B* the subject of which is a sum of money or asset representing the purchase price received for the annuity contract, these provisions do not apply by virtue of that step [*ITEPA 2003, s 554V(3)*]. This is intended to exclude the capital value of annuities bought out of pre-6 April 2011 annuity rights. Whether it does so is questionable as it is very rare for the rights to be 'specifically to receive an annuity'; the employee normally has a right to convert part of his annuity rights into a lump sum.

3.98   If the employee's rights are only partly pre-6 April 2011 annuity rights, the relevant step is treated as two relevant steps (by apportioning on a just and reasonable basis) and the exclusion applies only to the part which represents such rights [*ITEPA 2003, s 554U(4), (5)*]. For the purpose of **3.97** an annuity contract means a contract for the provision of an annuity granted for consideration in money or money's worth in the ordinary course of a business of granting annuities on human life, and payable for a term ending at a time ascertainable only by reference to the end of a human life (although it does not matter that the annuity may in some circumstances end before or after the life). An insurance company means a person or EEA (European Economic

Area) firm within *FA 2004, s 275(1)(a)* or *(b)*, or a person resident in a territory outside the EEA whose normal business includes the provision of annuities and who is regulated in the conduct of that business by the government of that territory or by a body established under the law of that territory for the purpose of regulating such business [*ITEPA 2003, s 554V(6)*].

Certain retirement benefits

3.99   If:

(*a*)   a relevant benefit (as defined in *ITEPA 2003, s 393B*) is provided under an employer-financed retirement benefit scheme within *ITEPA 2003, s 393A* (EFRBS) (or a superannuation fund within *ICTA 1988, s 615(3)* – schemes in relation to non-UK trades) by way of the payment of a lump sum wholly out of rights which the employee has under the scheme;

(*b*)   the employee's rights out of which the lump sum is paid are wholly or partly pre-6 April 2011 lump sum rights (rights which accrued before 6 April 2011 specifically to receive relevant benefits by way of lump sum payments); and

(*c*)   the payment of the lump sum is a relevant step within *ITEPA 2003, s 554C*;

no tax charge arises by reason of that relevant step [*ITEPA 2003, s 554W(1), (2), (5)*]. If the employee's rights are only partly pre-6 April 2011 lump sum rights, the payment is treated as two relevant steps (by apportioning on a just and reasonable basis) and the exclusion applies only to the pre-6 April 2011 rights [*ITEPA 2003, s 554W(3), (4)*].

Transfers between foreign pension schemes

3.100   If either:

(*a*)   rights which an employee has under a '*section 390* scheme' are transferred to another *section 390* scheme or to an overseas pension scheme; or

(*b*)   rights which an employee has under an overseas pension scheme are transferred to another overseas pension scheme and some or all of the rights transferred are *section 390* scheme rights;

no tax charge arises by reason of either a relevant step within *ITEPA 2003, s 554C* (see **3.32**(3)) taken for the sole purpose of transferring the rights, or a relevant step within *ITEPA 2003, s 554B* (see **3.32**(1), (2)) taken by the transferee in relation to the transferred rights on their transfer [*ITEPA 2003, s 554X(1)–(3)*]. If not all the transferred rights under (*b*) above are *section 390* scheme rights, the relevant step is treated as two relevant steps (by apportioning on a just and reasonable basis) and the exclusion applies only to the part which relates to the *section 390* scheme rights [*ITEPA 2003, s 554X(4)–(6)*]. If any of the transferred rights derive (directly or indirectly) from contributions to any scheme which are paid by the employer after 5 April 2006 and are neither 'tax relieved contributions' nor 'tax exempt provision' the relevant step is again treated as two relevant steps (by apportioning on a just and reasonable basis) and the exclusion does not apply to the part apportioned to such rights [*ITEPA 2003, s 554X(7)–(9)*]. Where sub-paragraphs (4)–(6) also apply, it is only the exempt *section 390* scheme portion that is apportioned again under this provision [*ITEPA 2003, s 554X(10)*]. If the employer is a company and is a member of a group of companies, the reference to the employer include any other company that was a member of the group at the time that the contribution was paid [*ITEPA 2003, s 554X(11)*].

3.101   A '*section 390* scheme' is a scheme in relation to which a claim was accepted under *ITEPA 2003, s 390* (corresponding overseas pension scheme). *Section 390* was repealed by *FA 2004* with effect from 6 April 2006 and most are likely to have become recognised overseas pension schemes from that date, so the provision aims to exclude a tax charge where rights which accrued in an overseas pension scheme before 6 April 2006 are transferred to another scheme that was approved by HMRC under the pre-*FA 2004* legislation. *Section 390* scheme rights are rights which the employee has under an overseas pension scheme and which have either been transferred to the scheme (directly or indirectly) from a *section 390* scheme, or have arisen or derived (directly or indirectly) from rights that have been so transferred. An overseas pension scheme means one within the meaning of *FA 2004, s 150(7)*. Tax exempt provision and tax relieved contributions are defined in *FA 2004, Sch 34, para 3(3), (4)* [*ITEPA 2003, s 554X(12)*].

Power to exclude other relevant steps

3.102   HMRC have power by regulation to exclude from the charge to tax (wholly or in part) other situations specified in the regulations. They can do so with retrospective effect.

Chapter 4

Employed or Self-employed

4.1   Tax is charged on employment income in relation to offices and employments. Neither of these terms is defined for tax purposes, although an office is expressed to include in particular any position which has an existence independent of the person who holds it and may be filled by successive holders. [*Income Tax (Earnings and Pensions Act 2003 (ITEPA 2003), s 5*]. A good dictionary definition of an office is 'the task or service attaching to a particular post or station'. An office generally continues its existence independent of the persons who from time to time occupy it.

Meaning of 'office'

4.2   The best legal definition is attributed to Rowlatt J in 1920 in *Great Western Rly Co v Bater 8 TC 231*: 'what those who use the language of the *Act* of 1842 meant ... was an office or employment which was a subsisting, permanent, substantive position, which had an existence independent from the person who filled it, which went on and was filled in succession by successive holders' (*8 TC* at p. 235). In fact this definition was put forward by Counsel and although Rowlatt approved it he felt constrained by earlier authorities not to decide that that was the meaning of the word. This definition was however endorsed by Lord Atkinson when the case reached the House of Lords. It has also been endorsed in subsequent cases, in particular by Lord Atkin in *McMillan v Guest 24 TC 190* where it was held that a director of a company holds an office.

Public office

4.3   The *Great Western Rly* case was actually concerned with the interpretation of the phrase 'public offices and employments of profit' and, whilst Rowlatt J treated this as a single phrase, Lord Atkinson thought that it embraced two distinct things, public offices and public employments. At the time only income from public offices and employments was assessed under Schedule E (the old rule for taxing employment income). Income from other employments was assessed under Schedule D. Furthermore, the assessment was on an annual basis, the person assessed having a right of recovery against his predecessor in the office. In the case of a railway company the assessment was on the company, leaving it to recover the tax from the office-holder from time to time. Accordingly the concept of permanence was perhaps implicit in the legislation of the time rather than in the natural meaning of the word 'office'.

Obscurity of legislation

4.4   The problem of definition was compounded by the obscurity of the legislation – a complaint that may, unfortunately, still frequently be made against modern legislation. Thus the Master of the Rolls complained, 'in fact it comes back to be a question of fact. It is an unsatisfactory conclusion at which to arrive, because I should wish, if I could, to be able to lay down some rule which would be a guide in the division of this staff into taxable and non-taxable people under Schedule E, but I do not see my way to do it; I do not think it possible.' (*8 TC* at p. 239). Lord Wrenbury was far more scathing: 'if any useful purpose could be served by censuring the Legislatures of 1842 or 1853, no censure could be too strong, I think, for having expressed an Act, and that a taxing Act, in language so involved, so slovenly and so unintelligible as is the language of the Acts of 1842 and 1853. But there it is. A court cannot say it means nothing and cannot be construed at all ... If parliament had the time, which it has not, the law of Income Tax, which now so vitally affects the subjects of the Realm, ought as speedily as possible to be expressed in a new Statute which should bear and express an intelligible meaning.' (*8 TC* at p. 255).

4.5   As an aside, another dictum from that case, which is unfortunately still true some 70 years later, is that of Lord Sumner in relation to tax litigation: 'Where a decision which limits the right of the Crown has long been unquestioned, far more practical weight attaches to this consideration of lapse of time than would have been the case had the decision been the other way. In these contests the subject is always at a great disadvantage. Decisions in favour of the Crown may often go unchallenged not because their correctness is generally recognised, but because no private person can face the cost of disputing them. Decisions to the contrary effect stand in a different position. The Crown is always very ably advised, in Revenue as in other matters, and for an appeal against the doubtful ruling affecting Income Tax the funds can always be found.' (*8 TC* at p. 253).

Edwards v Clinch

4.6   The meaning of an office fell to be considered again more recently by the House of Lords in the 1981 case of *Edwards v Clinch 56 TC 367*. Mr Clinch, a distinguished civil engineer, was engaged from time to time by the Government to hold public local enquiries. He held the enquiry entirely as he thought fit. He received no salary but rendered a fee account after completion of each enquiry. Each enquiry was of indeterminate duration. It could last several days, or weeks, or months. HMRC accepted that Mr Clinch was not employed by the Secretary of State or by anyone else. They contended, however, that his appointment to hold an enquiry was an office and that accordingly his fees could not be included as part of his profits as a self-employed civil engineer but had to be assessed separately as employment income. The courts accordingly had to consider whether or not continuity was an essential attribute of an office. If it was not, Mr Clinch would be taxable on it as employment income. It was held by a three-to-two majority that Mr Clinch did not hold a series of offices and his fees were properly taxable as part of his self-employment income.

4.7   Ackner LJ thought each enquiry:

> 'was a temporary, *ad hoc*, appointment confined to the taxpayer. He was not appointed to a position which had an existence of its own. It had no quality of permanency about it ... It was ... a transient, indeterminate, once-only, execution of a task for which the taxpayer was peculiarly qualified.' Lord Salmon quoted these words approvingly and added: 'I cannot agree that the dictionary meaning of the word "office" can or was intended to be of any real help in construing the word "office" in Schedule E.' (*56 TC* at p. 415). Lord Lowry thought that 'the mere appointment to perform a function (in this case the statutory function of holding a public local enquiry) does not by itself mean that the person appointed holds an office within the meaning of Schedule E. To say that the alleged office has no name, since the word "inspector" is merely a convenient description, may put the matter too simply, but it is the base from which I set out ... I consider that the ordinary meaning of "office" in this context involves the notion of a specific post to which a person can be appointed, which he can hold and which he can vacate. I concede that this is not the only sense in which the word can be understood, but I feel satisfied that it is the primary sense ... There is a subtler but perhaps more cogent argument in the [taxpayer's] favour than the mere absence of a name. The "office" comes into being with the act of appointment and automatically ceases to exist when the person appointed concludes his task. I think that to regard this as the holding of an office by the appointed person confuses his function with his so-called office. The [taxpayer] here was in one sense "in an official position", but not, in my opinion, in an official post (or office). A genuine office does not lapse because the holder dies, retires or completes his assignment. To be in a position of authority is not necessarily to hold an office, and when you appoint somebody to *do* something you do not thereby appoint him to *be* something (in other words to hold an office) unless the Act or other relevant instrument says so.' (*56 TC* at pp. 418–19).

4.8   Lord Lowry felt that his decision was a logical development from the test formulated by Rowlatt J:

> 'If I may indulge in a metaphor from the occupation of gold mining, I would say (without any disrespect, I hope) that the *Bater* test is the crude ore which has now by a series of processes ... been refined into something of superior quality ... *Bater* was followed by a series of cases which satisfied the *Bater* test, and therefore further refinement was unlikely in the meantime, but, like my noble and learned friend, Lord Bridge, I do not forget the words of Harman LJ in *Mitchell and Edon v Ross 40 TC 11*: "An office is a position or post which goes on without regard to the identity of the holder of it from time to time" ... Thus, when the present case came to be decided, some refining had already been done. The emphasis on

permanence and continuity had lessened and the possibility of a once-only appointment had been recognised. But the concept of an office which exists independently of its holder still held sway ... I think I can fairly summarise the Court of Appeal's attitude by saying that all the Judges recognised the changes since *Bater* and accepted the principle in *Farrell v Alexander [1976] 2 All ER 721* but still considered that a degree of permanence and continuity was essential and were unwilling to disregard a clear thread of supporting opinion which ran through a long line of cases. The characteristic of permanence need only amount to the independent existence of an office, as opposed to its incidental creation and automatic demise with the beginning and end respectively of the appointment of an individual to perform a task. And the continuity required need have no magic beyond the existence of the post (subject always to its abolition *ab extra*) after the holder has left it, with the *possibility* of successors being appointed ... The contrast now, however, is not between public and private occupations but between trade, profession or vocation on the one hand, and office or employment on the other. We might therefore look for logical links between office and employment and should not be too ready to equate an independent contractor with an office holder, since the latter has a deemed employer and his holding of an office has much in common with employment ... a person does *not* hold a so-called office if it comes into being only as the inevitable accompaniment of the fact of the alleged holder's appointment to perform a task ... I respectfully agree that it would be unsound to deny the existence of an office or employment in every case where a post did not exhibit all the *indicia* postulated by Rowlatt J ... Following the example of Lord Wrenbury in *Bater's* case and respectfully sharing his view of the difficulties of the tax legislation, I consider that my only safe course is to decide the individual case before us without showing too much concern for supposed analogies and contradictions, but remembering that the case, if decided in favour of the Crown, would provide the first example of innominate office under Schedule E.' (*56 TC* at pp. 421, 423–24, 426–27).

4.9 Lord Bridge of Harwich, in contrast, in a dissenting judgment felt that *Bater* was no longer good law:

'At first blush, it seems to me that the appointed person holding a public local enquiry ... occupies an "office" ... Under the *Act* of 1842 tax was charged under Schedule D on "the annual profits or gains arising or accruing ... from any profession, trade, *employment* or vocation"; it was charged under Schedule E on "every *public* office or employment of profit" ... These charging words and the distinction they drew between the two Schedules survived unaltered in the consolidating *Income Tax Act 1918*. The *Finance Act 1922* made the important change of transferring from Schedule D to Schedule E ... the charge to tax on the profits of "any office or employment". Hence the public element in Schedule E ceased to be of importance ... all the relevant authorities hark back to *Bater's* case ... I hope I can say without any disrespect that the endorsement of the opinion of Rowlatt J and Lord Atkinson in all the cases following *Bater's* case, has been quite uncritical, since there has been, so far as I can discover ...

no occasion before the instant case when any Court ... has been invited ... to re-examine the foundation on which it rests to see if it is still valid as applied to the phrase "office or employment" in Schedule E in the form it assumed in 1956, which reappears in the consolidating *Act* of 1970. It is precisely such a re-examination that your Lordships now have to undertake. It leads, in my opinion, inevitably to the conclusion that the opinion is no longer good law. The rule on which Rowlatt J and Lord Atkinson based their interpretation has gone. Moreover, now that Schedule E embraces all employments, it would surely be absurd to suggest that "employment" under the Schedule can be limited to "a subsisting, permanent, substantive position which has an existence independent of the person who fills it". If that construction no longer applies to "employment" in Schedule E, I can see no logic whatever in continuing to apply it to "office". So far as authority is concerned, therefore, your Lordships are, in my opinion, wholly unconstrained and free to give to the word "office" its ordinary dictionary meaning.' (*56 TC* at pp. 429–30, 433).

4.10   It is nonetheless likely that there is still some distinction between an office and an employment for tax purposes. A company directorship is an office. So are the positions of company secretary, auditor and, probably, registrar. So are most public appointments such as a judge, or an MP.

4.11   Indeed the question came before the courts again in June 1991 in *McMenamin v Diggles [1991] STC 419*. Mr Diggles was the senior clerk in a set of barristers' chambers and had served under a contract of employment until 7 October 1985. From that date new contractual arrangements were entered into under which, in return for a specified percentage of the gross income of each member of chambers, Mr Diggles agreed to provide at his own cost and expense a full clerking service for each member. Under the agreement he could either act as head clerk himself or provide some other suitably qualified person to act. In practice he filled the role himself. HMRC contended that Mr Diggles held an office on the basis that the code of conduct of the Bar Council required every practising barrister 'to have the services of the clerk of chambers'. It was accepted by both parties that it was possible to have an office without an instrument creating it, to have an office which had no public element, and to which there was no formality of appointment. It was held that the Commissioners had, on weighing up all the facts, correctly concluded that Mr Diggles did not hold an office within the meaning of the statute and their decision was not vulnerable to attack under the principle in *Edwards v Bairstow 36 TC 207*. An interesting feature of this case is that the work Mr Diggles actually did after 7 October 1985 does not appear to have been any different to what he previously did as an employee. This reinforces the importance attaching to the agreement where the nature of the work does not clearly point to either employment or self-employment (see also *Massey v Crown Life Assurance Co* at **4.27–4.29** below).

Meaning of 'employment'

4.12   An employment is easier to define but less easy to recognise. Again it is not exhaustively defined in the legislation but is expressed to include in particular any employment under a contract of service, any employment under a contract of apprenticeship and any employment in the service of the Crown, and 'employed' 'employee' and 'employer' are to have corresponding meanings. [*ITEPA 2003, s 4*]. The problem normally is to distinguish it from a trade, profession or vocation. An employment is the relationship that exists between master and servant, but in the modern world the distinction between a servant and an independent contractor is often blurred. The dictionary defines a servant as 'a person employed by another person or body of persons to work under direction for wages'. In the past the emphasis has been on 'under direction'; if a person is subject to control by another he is his servant. However, in recent years the courts have made it clear that control is just one of a number of tests that need to be looked at. This is sensible. Every relationship under which someone performs a task for another involves an element of control. If someone wants his house painted he will control the colour the painter uses, will exert a degree of control over the time he does the work, etc. However, this will not make the painter an employee of the customer.

Distinguished from self-employment

4.13 The distinction between an employee and a person who is self-employed is one of the most difficult to draw, yet for tax purposes it is vital to do so as the two are taxed under very different rules. The question to be asked is whether the person is engaged under a contract 'of service' or a contract 'for services'. In other words, is the person undertaking to enter the service of another, in which case he is an employee, or is he undertaking to provide a service of some sort to that other person, in which case he will not be? To put it another way, is the person undertaking merely to provide his labour or is he undertaking to provide some service which another person requires, albeit that his labour is a major component of that service? In *Market Investigations Ltd v Minister of Social Security [1968] 3 All ER 732* Cooke J formulated the test as to whether the person is 'in business on his own account'. This was a National Insurance case, as are the majority of the cases on this question. The test is the same for both income tax and National Insurance. In recent years the Government have made clear that once a person's status has been established with one of these authorities the other will accept their decision. HMRC do not however consider themselves bound by decisions of the Secretary of State under the National Insurance rules. They say these are not lawful precedents; they relate to the named contributor only and depend on their individual facts, so cannot be applied even to workers in similar circumstances (*Tax Bulletin 48, August 2000*).

4.14 The HMRC booklet, IR56 concluded 'If you are not sure whether you are employed or self-employed, please get in touch with your local Tax Enquiry Centre, Tax Office or Contributions Agency Office of the DSS for advice. If you can't agree with their decision you can appeal against it'. The author would be interested to hear from any reader who has followed this advice and been told that HMRC think he is self-employed. The author has on a number of occasions approached them on behalf of clients seeking confirmation that they agree with his view that an individual is self-employed, and can think of only one instance where he has had a positive response – the request has normally initiated an argument. Hopefully things will be different following the introduction of the ESI tool (see **4.62**). IR 56 has now been withdrawn and replaced by Help sheets ES/FS1 (for workers) and ES/FS2 (for engagers).

Case law

4.15   Before considering the HMRC guidance it may be helpful to look at some of the cases from which their tests are drawn. The distinction between employment and self-employment has been before the courts on a number of occasions and the approaches taken by the judges are far more helpful in determining the tests to be applied than the brief distillation that HMRC have developed from them.

4.16   The best starting point is probably three National Insurance cases decided in the late 1960s; *Ready Mixed Concrete (South East) Ltd v Minister of Pensions & National Insurance [1968] 1 All ER 433*, *Argent v Minister of Social Security [1968] 3 All ER 208*, and *Market Investigations Ltd v Ministry of Social Security [1968] 3 All ER 732*.

Test for contract of service

4.17   The issue in the *Ready Mixed Concrete* case was whether a person who owned his own lorry and was engaged by the company to deliver concrete to its customers was an employee. MacKenna J formulated the test as to whether or not a contract of service existed, and then sought to identify what such a contract involves. 'A contract of service exists if the following three conditions are fulfilled:

(*a*)   The servant agrees that in consideration of a wage or other remuneration he will provide his own work and skill in the performance of some service for his master;

(*b*)   He agrees, expressly or impliedly, that in the performance of that service he will be subject to the other's control in a sufficient degree to make that other master; and

(*c*)   The other provisions of the contract are consistent with its being a contract of service.'

4.18   He felt that (*a*) did not call for comment other than to make clear that an employment required remuneration, but helpfully expanded upon the other two tests. 'As to (*b*). Control includes the power of deciding the thing to be done, the way in which it shall be done, the means to be employed in doing it, the time when, and the place where it shall be done. All these aspects of control must be considered in deciding whether the right exists in a sufficient degree to make one party the master and the other his servant. The right need not be unrestricted ... If the contract does not expressly provide which party shall have the right, the question must be answered in the ordinary way by implication.'

4.19   He went on to say: 'The third and negative condition is for my purpose the important one, and I shall try with the help of five examples to explain what I mean by provisions inconsistent with the nature of a contract of service.

(*a*)   A contract obliges one party to build for the other, providing at his own expense the necessary plant and materials. This is not a contract of service, even though the builder may be obliged to use his own labour only and to accept a high degree of control: it is a building contract. It is not a contract to serve another for a wage, but a contract to produce a thing (or a result) for a price.

(*b*)   A contract obliges one party to carry another's goods, providing at his own expense everything needed for performance. This is not a contract of service ... it is a contract of carriage.

(*c*)   A contract obliges a labourer to work for a builder, providing some simple tools, and to accept the builder's control. Notwithstanding the obligation to provide the tools, the contract is one of service. That obligation is not inconsistent with the nature of a contract of service. It is not a sufficiently important matter to affect the substance of the contract.

(*d*)   A contract obliges one party to work for the other, accepting his control, and to provide his own transport. This is still a contract of service ... Transport in this example is incidental to the main purpose of the contract ...

(*e*)   The same instrument provides that one party shall work for the other subject to the other's control, and also that he shall sell him his land. The first part of the instrument is no less a contract of service because the second part imposes obligations of a different kind.'

4.20   In other words 'an obligation to do work subject to the other party's control is a necessary, though not always a sufficient, condition of a contract of service. If the provisions of the contract as a whole are inconsistent with its being a contract of service, it will be some other kind of contract ...'. MacKenna J also adopted the tests applied in two earlier cases. The first, on the meaning of control, from *Zuijus v Wirth Bros Pty Ltd (1955) 93 CLR 561*. 'What matters is lawful authority to command, so far as there is scope for it. And there must always be some room for it, if only in incidental or collateral matters.' The second from Denning LJ in *Bank voor Handel en Scheepvaart NV v Slatford [1952] 2 All ER 956*: 'I would observe the test of being a servant does not rest nowadays on submission to orders. It depends on whether the person is part and parcel of the organisation' (*[1968] 1 All ER* at pp. 440–441).

4.21   The importance of the *Ready Mixed Concrete* test was affirmed more recently in the Court of Appeal in *Montgomery v Johnson Underwood Limited [2001] EWCA Civ 318* by Buckley J: 'Clearly as society and the nature and manner of carrying out employment continues to develop, so will the court's view of the nature and extent of "mutual obligations" concerning the work in question and "control" of the individual carrying it out ... However since the concept of the contract of employment remains central to so much legislation which set out to adjust the rights of employers and workers, including employees, it must be desirable that a clear framework or principle is identified and kept in mind ... For my part, I regard the quoted passage from *Ready Mixed Concrete* as still the best guide and as containing the irreducible minimum by way of legal requirement for a contract of employment to exist. It permits Tribunals appropriate latitude in considering the nature and extent of "mutual obligations" in respect of the work in question and the "control" an employer has over the individual. It does not permit those concepts to be dispensed with altogether ... It directs Tribunals to consider the whole picture to see whether a contract of employment emerges. It is though important that "mutual obligation" and "control" to a sufficient extent are first identified before looking at the whole.' MacKenna J's three tests were affirmed by the Court of Appeal in *Nethermere (St Neots) Ltd v Gardiner* (1984 ICR 612) which is often quoted in the courts in place of *Ready Mixed Concrete*. However the basic tests set out in the two cases are identical.

Part-time employment

4.22   The question in the *Argent* case was whether a part-time teacher at a drama school was an employee. Unlike most cases in this area, Mr Argent claimed to be an employee whereas both the school and the Ministry contended that he was not. Roskill J's approach was to look at the reality of the engagement: 'One has a picture of an actor of some experience sometimes going off and doing whole-time or near whole-time acting ... but at other times teaching ... being paid hourly rates or by fixed fees for the work he was doing. It is also relevant to point out that ... the appellant had no administrative or disciplinary duties at the school except to mark a register ... In those circumstances is he a man who can properly be said to have been employed ... under a contract of service, or is the true position ... that he was really working under a services contract doing part-time work ...?' (*[1968] 3 All ER* at p. 215). He concluded that Mr Argent was self-employed.

Test for self-employment

4.23   The *Market Investigations* case was concerned with part-time interviewers for a market research organisation. Cooke J considered a number of previous authorities including that of Denning LJ in the *Bank voor Handel* case mentioned above, Lord Wright in a Canadian case, *Montreal Locomotive Works Ltd v Montreal [1947] 1 DLR 161*, and various US cases from which he concluded: 'The observations of Lord Wright, of Denning LJ and of the judges of the Supreme Court in the USA suggest that the fundamental test to be applied is this: "Is the person who has engaged himself to perform these services performing them as a person in business on his own account?". If the answer to that question is "Yes", then the contract is a contract for services. If the answer is "No" then the contract is a contract of service. No exhaustive list has been compiled and perhaps no exhaustive list can be compiled of considerations which are relevant in determining that question, nor can strict rules be laid down as to the relative weight which the various considerations should carry in particular cases. The most that can be said is that control will no doubt have to be considered, although it can no longer be regarded as the sole determining factor; and that factors, which may be of importance, are such matters as whether the man performing the services provides his own equipment, whether he hires his own helpers, what degree of financial risk he takes, what degree of responsibility for investment and management he has, and whether and how far he has an opportunity of profiting from sound management in the performance of his task.' ([*1968*] *3 All ER* at pp. 737–738).

4.24   This is how the test is nowadays usually phrased. It is, of course, the same test, although in an expanded form, as that adopted in *Argent*. It should also be emphasised that the test of whether a person is in business on his own account seems to be an application of MacKenna J's third condition in *Ready Mixed Concrete* (see **4.17(c)**). As was emphasised in the *Johnson Underwood* case (see **4.21**), the other two of McKenna J's tests need to be satisfied before applying this test. In *Hall v Lorimer* (see **4.84**) Nolan J cast doubt on whether this in business on one's own account test was necessarily the right approach so it needs to be treated with a degree of caution. Where the person already has a business organisation the test is relatively easy to apply. If he does not, particularly if the services to be supplied do not require anything other than the person's labour, it is more difficult. However, Cooke J made it clear that the absence of such an organisation is not fatal: 'A person who engages himself to perform services for another may well be an independent contractor even though he has not entered into the contract in the course of an existing business carried on by him.'

4.25   On the facts, however, he found that the interviewer was an employee: 'It is apparent that the control which the company had the right to exercise in this case was very extensive indeed. It was in my view so extensive as to be entirely consistent with Mrs Irving being employed under a contract of service. The fact that Mrs Irving had a limited discretion when she should do the work was not in my view inconsistent with the existence of a contract of service ... Nor is there anything inconsistent ... in the fact that Mrs Irving was free to work for others during the relevant period.' ([*1968*] *3 All ER* at p 739). It will be apparent from this that the 'overall reality' test is merely a different approach to MacKenna J's three principles set out at **4.17** above.

Other case law

4.26   The decision in the *Argent* case reflects the reality that Mr Argent was a full-time actor who taught drama during such periods as his acting engagements permitted. In a later income tax case, *Sidey v Phillips 59 TC 458*, a part-time lecturer was held to be an employee, as was the taxpayer in a 1956 case, *Fuge v McClelland 36 TC 571*. The status of a teacher was also at issue in *Walls v Sinnett 60 TC 150*. Mr Walls, a professional singer, was appointed to the post of lecturer of music at a technical college. He was required to attend the college four days a week during term time but was permitted – indeed, encouraged – to undertake outside work. Vinelott J felt that, 'What is striking about this case is that the engagement, to use a neutral word, is full-time ... Mr Walls says that, although full-time, he was able to carry on a great deal of other work, but that is neither one way nor the other; it was an engagement ... of employment as a very senior teacher or lecturer, and such teachers frequently have a relatively light teaching load and are encouraged to engage in other activities which can add to their experience ... The other point that is very much stressed by the taxpayer is the degree of control ... In some contexts the degree of control exercised over a man may be very important in deciding whether he is an employee or servant or not, but in the case of a senior lecturer at a college of further education, more particularly one who like Mr Walls came into teaching from active work as a singer, it is not surprising to find he was given a very wide degree of latitude in the organisation of his work and time.' (*60 TC* at p. 165). This emphasises the importance of looking at the overall picture. The fact that an employer does not seek to dictate to an expert how he should utilise his expertise is not inconsistent with a contract being one of service. Nor is the fact that if the duties of an employment do not utilise a person full time he is free to undertake other work which is consistent with his being available to fulfil his obligations under his employment contract.

4.27   Lord Denning, in his normal robust way, thought that the decision is largely a matter of common sense. In *Massey v Crown Life Assurance Co [1978] 2 All ER 576* he simply stated: 'I will not today attempt to formulate the distinction except to repeat what I said in *Stevenson Jordan & Harrison Ltd v McDonald and Evans [1952] 1 TLR 101*. "It is often easy to recognise a contract of service when you see it but difficult to say where the difference lies. A ship's master, a chauffeur and a reporter on the staff of a newspaper are all employed under a contract of service; but a ship's pilot, a taxi-man and a newspaper contributor are employed under a contract for services."'

4.28   It is well established that the label that the parties to a relationship choose to put on it is not conclusive as to what that relationship is. The *Massey* case concerned a branch manager of an insurance company. He originally had a contract of employment. On the advice of his accountant he persuaded his employer to engage him instead as a self-employed contractor. The employer signed a new form of contract engaging him to provide services to the company. Mr Massey was subsequently dismissed and sought to claim unfair dismissal as an employee. Lord Denning would have none of it. 'The law as I see it, is this: If the true relationship of the parties is that of master and servant under a contract of service, the parties cannot alter the truth of that relationship by putting a different label on it. If they should put a different label on it, and use it as a dishonest device to deceive [HMRC], I should have thought it was illegal and could not be enforced by either party and they could not get any advantage out of it, or at any rate not in any case where they had to rely on it as the basis of a claim ... On the other hand if their relationship is ambiguous and is capable of being one or the other, then the parties can remove that ambiguity by the very agreement itself which they make with one another. The agreement itself then becomes the best material from which to gather the true legal relationship between them.'

4.29   Reference should also be made to some of the IR 35 cases considered at **18.4** onwards. The IR35 rules do not apply where a worker would have been self-employed had he worked direct for the end user instead of through an intermediary. Accordingly many of these cases hinge on the distinction between employment and self-employment.

Agreement between parties

4.30   The importance of the wording of the agreement between the parties was emphasised in the Privy Council case of *Narich Pty Ltd v Comr Pay-Roll Tax [1984] ICR 286* where Lord Brandon stated: 'The first principle is that, subject to one exception, where there is a written contract between the parties whose relationship is in issue, a court is confined, in determining the nature of that relationship, to a consideration of the terms, express or implied, of that contract in the light of the circumstances surrounding the making of it; and it is not entitled to consider also the manner in which the parties subsequently acted in pursuance of such contract. The one exception to that rule is that, where the subsequent conduct of the parties can be shown to have amounted to an agreed addition to, or modification of, the original written contract, such conduct may be considered and taken into account by the court.' In other words, if all the terms are contained in a written agreement the courts will look only at that agreement, not what happened in practice, to determine whether or not the relationship was an employment, unless the facts suggest that what happened in practice indicates that the contract was orally varied in some way. Obviously the agreement will also be ignored if HMRC can demonstrate that it is a sham. However the courts tend to take a less stringent approach in relation to employment contracts where the employee does not normally have equal bargaining power with the employer. There are some useful pointers to interpreting employment agreements by the Court of Appeal in the *Reed Employment* case (see **5.38A**)

4.31   It should be borne in mind that the inclusion of some things in an agreement may have the opposite effect to that intended. For example if there is doubt whether a person is really self-employed there is a temptation to include a clause stating that the contractor is responsible for his own tax and National Insurance. However, this would be a very strange clause to find in a genuine arm's length contract with an independent contractor who is providing a service in the course of his business. A businessman would never think that there was the remotest possibility that he could be liable for the tax of his solicitor, accountant, valuer, or other adviser and would not dream of seeking to provide for such an eventuality when engaging the adviser. Accordingly, the inclusion of such a clause in an agreement with his self-employed bookkeeper, salesman, etc. is likely to be taken as an indication – at the least – that in the eyes of the parties the status of the relationship is open to doubt. PAYE Audit division are likely to regard the inclusion of such a provision as an indication that the relationship needs to be scrutinised carefully as it could well be one of master and servant.

4.32   Whether a person is an employee or an independent contractor is a question of law. However, the answer will depend very much on the facts. In *O'Kelly v Trusthouse Forte plc [1983] 3 All ER 456* Sir John Donaldson MR expressed the distinction thus: 'The test to be applied in identifying whether a contract is one of employment or for services is a pure question of law and so is its application to the facts. But it is for the tribunal of fact not only to find those facts but to assess them qualitatively and within limits, which are indefinable in the abstract, those findings and that assessment will dictate the correct legal answer. In the familiar phrase, it is all a question of fact and degree. It is only if the weight given to a particular factor shows a self-misdirection in law that an appellate court with a limited jurisdiction can interfere. It is difficult to demonstrate such a misdirection and, to the extent that it is not done, the issue is one of fact.' (*[1983] 3 All ER* at p. 478). In that case casual employees taken on by a hotel for functions as and when required (regular casuals) were held by a tribunal to be self-employed. The Court of Appeal upheld this decision on the *Edwards v Bairstow 36 TC 207* principle, i.e. that it was not a decision that a reasonable tribunal properly instructed in the law could not have reached and that therefore the courts were not entitled to overturn it.

4.33   Although decisions of the Special Commissioners were not reported prior to 1995, the case of *Specialeyes (Optical Services) Ltd* (see *Taxation 4 July 1991*) is interesting. The company, which traded as optical retailers through a nationwide chain of shops, engaged a large number of self-employed opticians to carry out eye examinations. Most of these had only one client, the appellant, which is in the business of providing sight tests to the public. An optician received a fixed fee for each eye test performed, out of which he paid the company a facility fee to cover the use of its premises and equipment. The opticians were at liberty to stipulate the hours during which they were prepared to attend the branch. They were responsible for their own professional indemnity insurance. The Commissioners upheld the company's contention that the opticians were not employees. The rationale seems largely to have been based on the fact that the company's degree of control is limited to deciding at which branch and on which day the optician will be given the opportunity to carry out sight tests – and even that was obtained only by agreement and sometimes after considerable negotiation. The Commissioners were also influenced by the fact that the opticians were not 'part and parcel' of the company's organisation and by the terms of the contract between the parties. HMRC opted not to take this decision to appeal. They cited only three cases, *Market Investigations* (see **4.23** above), *Global Plant Ltd v Secretary of State for Health and Social Security [1971] 3 All ER 385* and a Privy Council appeal in a Hong Kong case, *Lee Ting Sang v Chung Chi-Keung [1990] 2 AC 374*. The Commissioners felt that the facts in the latter two cases were far removed from the case under consideration. It is intriguing that HMRC seem increasingly to rely on Hong Kong decisions: this suggests that they are unable to draw much comfort from the large number of UK cases considered above.

4.34   The *Lee Ting Sang* case was an industrial injuries case. Mr Sang was a stonemason working for a subcontractor. His tools were provided by the subcontractor. He had worked on the site for 20 days prior to the accident; he was normally paid in accordance with the amount of concrete chiselled as measured by the subcontractor (or sometimes a wage of HK$220 a day); if he finished his work before 5pm he would assist the subcontractor to sharpen chisels – for which he would be paid on an hourly basis; he would give the subcontractor priority if others wanted him; and he gave evidence that he believed he would be sacked if he disappeared from the site. His work was not supervised but was inspected periodically by the main contractor's foreman.

4.35   HMRC probably like the case because the decision reversed that of the Court of Appeal of Hong Kong, as 'the facts ... point out so clearly to the existence of a contract of service that the finding that the applicant was working as an independent contractor was ... a view of the facts which could not reasonably be entertained and is to be regarded as an error of law'.

4.36 The case is important because it is based on English law. Lord Griffiths, giving the judgment of the Privy Council, said, 'The question is to be answered by applying English common law standards to determine whether the workman was working as an employee or as an independent contractor. What then is the standard to apply? This has proved to be a most elusive question and despite a plethora of authorities the courts have not been able to devise a single test that will conclusively point to the distinction in all cases. Their Lordships agree with the Court of Appeal [of Hong Kong] when they said that the matter had never been put better than by Cooke J in *Market Investigations Ltd v Minister of Social Security*.' He then quoted the passage set out at **4.23** above.

4.37 Lord Griffiths placed no weight on the fact that Mr Sang worked from 8am to 5pm each day:

'This accords with the common sense of the matter for if the applicant was free to come and go at will it is difficult to see how the first respondent could carry out timeous performance of his subcontract'; or on the lack of supervision: 'It is true that he was not supervised in his work, but this is not surprising, he was a skilled man and he had been told the beams upon which he was to work and the depth to which they were to be cut and his work was measured to see that he achieved that result. There was no question of him being called upon to exercise any skill or judgement as to which beams required chipping or as to the depth that they were to be cut. He was simply told what to do and left to get on with it.'

4.38 His overall impression of the facts was that:

'The picture emerges of a skilled artisan, earning his living by working for more than one employer as an employee and not as a small businessman venturing into business on his own as an independent contractor with all its attendant risks. The applicant ran no risk whatever save that of being unable to find employment which is, of course, a risk faced by casual employees who move from one job to another. ... It must now be taken to be firmly established that the question of whether or not the work was performed in the capacity of an employee or as an independent contractor is to be regarded by the appellate court as a question of fact to be determined by the trial court. At first sight it seems rather strange that this should be so, for whether or not a certain set of facts should be classified under one legal head rather than another would appear to be a question of law. However ... it was held in a series of decisions in the Court of Appeal and in the House of Lords under the English *Workmen's Compensation Acts 1906* and *1925* that a finding by a county court judge that a workman was, or was not, employed under a contract of service was a question of fact.'

4.39 He played down the weight to be given to *Stevenson Jordan & Harrison Ltd v McDonald & Evans* (see **4.27**) and *Bank voor Handel en Scheepvaart NV v Slatford* (see **4.20**), although it appears solely on the basis of the wording of the Hong Kong legislation, not because what Lord Denning said in those cases was wrong in principle. 'In arriving at his conclusion the district judge relied upon two dicta of Denning J which, whilst no doubt of value in the determination of the cases in which they were spoken, would appear to have little relevance to the facts of the present case and if misapplied may have led to an erroneous conclusion ... To apply the test of whether a person is "part and parcel of the organisation" is likely to be misleading in the context of a statute which expressly contemplates that casual workers and workers working for two or more employers concurrently may be employed under a contract of service.'

Mutuality of obligations

4.40   Another important factor not brought out in the above cases is mutuality of obligations, i.e. that whilst an employee has duties to their employer the employer also has duties to the employee in particular to offer them work to do. This is in fact the first of McKenna J's tests in *Ready Mixed Concrete* (see **4.17(a)**) albeit phrased differently. The absence of such mutuality is a strong pointer to self-employment. Indeed many people feel that it is of itself conclusive that there is not an employment. In *R (on the application of Professional Contractors Group Ltd) v IRC [2001] EWHC Admin 236 [2001] STC 629* the judge was fairly scathing of the HMRC guidance, particularly that on this area. The case itself was a challenge to the validity of the 'IR 35' legislation (see **19.35**) but in the course of his judgment Burton J said, 'It is essential to any consideration of the common law test as to whether an individual is trading as an employee or as an independent contractor, that consideration should be given as to whether he is in business on his own account.' He later says, 'It cannot be right for [HMRC] simply to conclude, as it does in another such guidance document, *ESM 0514*, that "mutuality of obligation" is not a relevant issue: "Do not consider this factor when reviewing a work status unless the engager or worker raises it". It has now recently been emphasised by the House of Lords in *Carmichael v National Power plc [1999] 1 WLR 2042*, that the test adopted in *Nethermere (St Neots) Ltd v Gardner [1984] ICR 612, CA* by Stephenson LJ of an "irreducible minimum of mutual obligation" is another central piece of guidance in the analysis of whether there is employment or self-employment.'

4.41   *Carmichael v National Power plc* involved two part-time guides at Blyth Power Station. They claimed to have a continuing employment with National Power, not a series of individual employments covering only the times when they were actually working as guides. The industrial tribunal held that their case foundered on the rock of absence of mutuality and the House of Lords held that was a correct analysis. The reference in the *Professional Contractors Group* case to *ESM 0514* is to the HMRC *Employment Status Manual*. That paragraph in fact starts, 'This aspect is rarely of practical use from a tax or NIC's point of view and can confuse the issue.' In *Reed Employment* (see **5.38**) the Court of Appeal distinguished two different types of mutuality; that the employee agrees to work in return for payment, and that if the employee is willing to work the employee will provide work. The second can be crucial in relation to over-riding contracts of employment where there is an agreement that one party will provide work for the other from time to time. Unless care is taken the courts could find that although the overriding contract is a contract, it is not a contract of employment, but instead it governs what happens in relation to a series of separate employments that arise each time the provider actually provides work. That is what happened in *Reed*.

4.42   In an employment appeals case, *Montgomery v Johnson Underwood Ltd [2001] EWCA Civ 318*, Buckley J in the Court of Appeal seems to have played down the importance of both mutual obligations and control whilst stressing that they are still fundamental: 'Clearly as society and the nature and manner of carrying out employment continues to develop, so will the court's view of the nature and extent of "mutual obligations" concerning the work in question and "control" of the individual carrying it out ... However since the concept of the contract of employment remains central to so much legislation which sets out to adjust the rights of employers and workers, including employees, it must be desirable that a clear framework or principle is identified and kept in mind ... For my part, I regard the quoted passage from *Ready Mixed Concrete* as still the best guide and as containing the irreducible minimum by way of legal requirement for a contract of employment to exist. It permits Tribunals appropriate latitude in considering the nature and extent of "mutual obligations" in respect of the work in question and the "control" an employer has over the individual. It does not permit those concepts to be dispensed with altogether ... It directs Tribunals to consider the whole picture to see whether a contract of employment emerges. It is thoughimportant that "mutual obligation" and "control" to a sufficient extent are first identified before looking at the whole.'

4.43   As with the *Dacas* and *Muscat* cases (see **4.72–4.79**) this was an agency case. Mrs Montgomery was a part-time receptionist/telephonist. The agency, Johnson Underwood Ltd (JU) found her work with Orenstein & Kopple Ltd (O&K). After two and half years O&K became unhappy with Mrs Montgomery making personal calls and asked JU to terminate the assignment. Mrs Montgomery sought compensation for unfair dismissal. Both companies claimed not to be her employer. The Employment Appeals Tribunal felt that she was not an employee of O&K but was an employee of JU. The Court of Appeal decided she was not an employee of JU either. Longmore LJ stated, 'In a case where (as here) the tribunal has found as a fact that there was "little or no control, direction or supervision" on the part of JU, a conclusion that Mrs Montgomery was the employee of JU cannot stand. Whatever other developments this branch of the law may have seen over the years, mutuality of obligation and the requirement of control on the part of the potential employer are the irreducible minimum for the existence of a contract of employment.'

4.44   In *Parade Park Hotel v HMRC [2007] STC (SCD) 430* the Special Commissioner concluded from the above comment of Buckley J that, 'The question of mutuality of obligation and control must be considered first before looking at the question whether the person engaged to perform the services is doing so as a person in business on his own account (Cooke J in *Market Investigations Ltd v Minister of Social Security* (see **4.23**)), and before standing back and considering the overall effect of all factors relating to the engagement (*Hall v Lorimer* (see **4.24**)).' The facts in the *Parade Park* case were unusual. Mr May worked primarily for Parade Park doing general maintenance jobs. However, he would refuse to do some jobs, would turn up when he pleased and when he turned up would look at the maintenance book which listed what work needed to be done and pick from the list what work he felt like doing. Mr May was paid a daily rate but accepted that he would not be paid if he did not turn up on a day. His attendance was unreliable; sometimes he would not turn up for weeks and other times he would come but not necessarily when he had said he would. The Special Commissioner held that a number of the terms of the relationship were inconsistent with it amounting to a contract of service. In *Sherburn Aero Club Ltd v HMRC [2009] STC (SCD) 450* flying instructors were held to be in business on their own account. Such control as there was, was to meet safety requirements and the instructors were free to decide whether or not to take a particular lesson.

4.45 An interesting recent case decided in favour of the taxpayer is *Castle Construction (Chesterfield) Ltd v HMRC [2009] STC (SCD) 97*. HMRC have decided not to appeal the decision of the Special Commissioner (Mr Nowlen). Castle Construction generally acted as sub-contractors on construction projects. It initially only sub-contracted bricklaying services but had moved into scaffolding services and carpentry and joinery. Its only employees were head office staff, quantity surveyors and trainee bricklayers. All other workers were self-employed. They could be hired and terminated with absolute flexibility. Evidence was given that this suited both the company and the workers, who relished the flexibility to come and go much as they pleased and to work for different contractors when that seemed more attractive. The evidence was that the time worked by individual workers varied considerably. The workers provided their own tools. They had to buy their visibility jackets and hard hats (if needed) from Castle if they wanted to work for Castle. The Commissioner started from the Ready Mixed Concrete tests (see **4.17**). He felt that a substitution clause in the contract 'was a fiction' but that the flexibility was consistent with a contract of employment. He did not feel the control test 'terribly helpful as the main control clearly had to be with the main contractor', not Castle. He also addressed the Market Investigations test of whether the worker is in business on his own account (see **4.13**). He placed emphasis on the fact that the bricklayers provided their own tools but seems to have been swayed by the fact that they 'have all undergone a considerable training and a period of apprenticeship. Many are experienced and many are very good at their trade. They often have great pride in their work'. Accordingly 'the bricklayers do in a real sense have a trade and a business that is broader than their individual engagements'. He was also impressed by the fact that the company trained apprentices but regarded such people as employees. The last quote above is particularly interesting as it puts an unusual slant on being in business on one's own account. The taxpayer was also successful in a subsequent case, *Littlewood and another (t/a Window and Door Services) v HMRC [2009] STC (SCD) 243*. The Commissioner (John Clark) felt that there was not a sufficient degree of control over the workers to make the partnership master. He also found that the workers were in business on their own account, 'albeit in a modest way'. Mr Clark did however comment that following the Court of Appeal decision in

Dacas (see **4.72**) he thought that 'there is some doubt how appropriate it now is to apply the test [of a business on one's own account]'.

4.46   Mention should probably also be made of the 2012 Employment Appeal Tribunal case of *Quashie v Stringfellows Restaurants Ltd* (UKEAT/0289/11/RN). Although not a tax case, the decision is likely to appeal to HMRC. Miss Quashie was a lap dancer. The Employment Tribunal held that she was self-employed but this was reversed on appeal. The Tribunal, Judge McMullen QC, asked himself three questions. Was she an employee on the nights she danced at the club; if so was she also an employee during the gaps between those employments so that she had an umbrella contract; and if she had an umbrella contract, was it tainted by illegality as she had claimed to be self-employed on her tax returns. He answered the first Yes and the second Yes. He thought the third arguable and as the case would have to go back to an Employment Tribunal to determine the issue of unfair dismissal, felt that the Tribunal should consider the question of illegality too. Why was Miss Quashie an employee? The judge said that 'once there is a contract to be paid for work done, the only issue is whether there is sufficient control by the paymaster to connote a contract of employment'. The contract test embraces mutuality of obligations; that is not a separate test (although he did stress that the mutuality of obligations must be 'to do with' the work). The interesting point though is that Miss Quashie was paid nothing by Stringfellows. She received money only from customers to whom she provided a private dance. So where was the mutuality? The judges' view was that Miss Quashie 'gave up her night to be available for something provided by the Respondent'. What was that something? 'She could make the bargain to dance to the Respondent's tune if the Respondent agreed to let her be seen at the club to enhance her reputation, or to keep her hand in, or even just to maintain networking in a congenial workplace'. To work at the club, Angels, Miss Quashie was required to abide by the club rules, to work one Saturday and one Monday twice a month, work one night a week at Angels, turn up for a Thursday meeting (and be fined for not doing so), comply with the Angels image and dress code, perform a number of free dances on the stage/podium/pole (and be fined for not doing so), be told what to do on stage, be required to give compulsory free dances at midnight (and be fined for not doing so), agree to tell the Club manager if a customer agreed to pay over £300 for a dance (with the manager being entitled to reduce the figure if he felt it appropriate to retain the Club's reputation), and seek permission if she wanted to leave the Club before the end of her shift. She could not accept money in cash from customers; she could only accept 'Heavenly Money', ie vouchers which customers buy from the Club. The judge concluded: 'On each night she attended the claimant was obliged to work as directed by the management. If she did not provide the free dances or other duties she could be fined. I infer from the findings that if the Claimant were directed to a customer, she could not refuse. It seems to me that mere attendance on the night is pursuant to a requirement that she work; that is, that she turn up and stay throughout the night shift on pain of fine or deduction … All of these conclusions point ineluctably towards a finding that on the night the Claimant was an employee. The findings on control are critical and they put mutuality of obligation in a secondary position, rather than at the forefront, of the legal analysis in this case'.

The HMRC approach

4.47   HMRC tell employers that 'in general terms [persons] are employed if they work for you and do not have the risk of running a business, or self-employed if they are in business on their own account and are responsible for the success or failure of that business'. They also say that 'an individual worker is likely to be employed if the answer is "yes" to most of the following questions':

(*a*)   Do the workers have to do the work themselves?

(*b*)   Can you tell the worker where to work, when to work, how to work or what to do?

(*c*)   Can you move the worker from task to task?

(*d*)   Does the worker have to work a set number of hours?

(*e*)   Is the worker paid a regular wage or salary?

(*f*)   Can the worker get overtime or bonus payments?

(*g*)   Is the worker responsible for managing anyone else engaged by?

They say that a worker is likely to be self-employed if either:

(*a*)   'The answer is "yes" to one or more of the following questions –

    (i)   Can the worker hire someone to do the work, or take on helpers at their own expense?

    (ii)   Can the worker decide where to provide the services of the job, when to work, how to work and what to do?

    (iii)   Can the worker make a loss as well as a profit?

    (iv)   Does the worker agree to do a job for a fixed price regardless of how long the job may take?' or

(*b*)   'The answer is "yes" to most of the following questions –

    (i)   Does the worker risk his own money?

    (ii)   Does the worker provide the main items of equipment (not the tools that many employees provide for themselves) needed to do the job?

    (iii)   Does the worker have to correct unsatisfactory work in their own time and at their own expense?'

(ES/FS2).

ES/FS2 replaced booklet IR 56 from 17 October 2008. IR 56 gave much more detailed guidance. It said that the distinction between employment and self-employment 'is something to be decided in a commonsense way'. Unfortunately this is not always how they seem to approach the question in practice. They frequently seem to start with the concept that anyone who works on his own in an occupation where his own labour is a major component of the service that he provides is an employee unless there is strong evidence to suggest otherwise. They will normally start from the old, discredited test of control – seizing on the slightest degree of control to reinforce their initial presumption.

Nevertheless, although they do not in practice seem to place much weight on some of the tests, HMRC have formulated some helpful guidelines.

HMRC guidelines

4.48 Factors that 'usually' indicate that a person may be self-employed are as follows.

(*a*) Whether he has the final say in how the business is run. The difficulty with this test is that when dealing with the provision of personal services there is often not a great deal of running to do. There is also the problem of identifying the business. A person who has a skill that he sells to A on Monday, to B on Tuesday and C on Wednesday and to D on Friday, having decided to take Thursday off to play golf, clearly has the final say on how his business is run as he is the only one involved in the entire business. However, HMRC may well take the view that the business is not the aggregation of what the person does during the week but that he works during the course of the week for four businesses, A's, B's, C's and D's, and in looking at how the 'business' is run one needs to look separately at his activities in each of such businesses.

(*b*) Whether he risks his own money in the business. Unfortunately, a business which consists of selling a particular skill of the proprietor often needs no money to be risked. The proprietor risks his time and may be in severe financial difficulties should he not be paid for it, but HMRC are not normally prepared to regard this as a recognisable risk.

(*c*) Whether he is responsible for meeting losses as well as enjoying profits. Again, a business that requires little finance is unlikely to incur losses and losses of time tend to be ignored.

(*d*) Whether he provides the major items of equipment that he needs. HMRC consider that the provision of 'small tools' is not indicative of self-employment. The author has known them to regard equipment costing hundreds of pounds as small for this purpose.

(*e*) Whether the person is free to hire other people on terms of his choice to do the work he has undertaken to perform, and, if so, whether he pays that person out of his own pocket. In practice, of course, a customer will frequently contract with a business because they want a particular expertise which they believe that business to have, and would regard it as a breach of contract if the business were to sub-contract the task to someone else. Accordingly, it seems doubtful whether in modern conditions the absence of a right to delegate is indicative that a person is not self-employed.

(*f*) Whether the person has to correct unsatisfactory work in his own time and at his own expense. This is a rather odd test. Many employees would regard themselves as morally obliged to correct unsatisfactory work in their own time.

4.49   If a positive answer can be given to all of the above questions a person has a strong claim to self-employed status. If such an answer cannot be given, albeit because most of these questions are not relevant to his circumstances, he can expect HMRC to regard him as an employee. Two further factors that HMRC consider relevant are set out at **4.89**.

4.50   Factors that indicate to HMRC that a person is 'probably' an employee are as follows.

(*a*)   Whether the person has to do the work personally rather than hire someone else to do it for him. It seems doubtful whether it is actually indicative of anything in modern conditions. A person is frequently engaged to perform a task because he possesses a particular skill. There is an implied condition in such circumstances that the person will do the work personally, but this could not of itself make him an employee.

(*b*)   Whether someone can tell the person at any time what to do or when and how to do it. Most jobs give the worker a large degree of discretion as to what he does at any time, and if he has a particular skill it would be foolish for anyone to seek to dictate how he performs his task. Of course an employer can tell an employee to do a particular task at a particular time – but a contractor can likewise instruct his subcontractor – as in today's complex society it is necessary for all of the people engaged on a project to work together, albeit that they are all independent contractors, to enable the project to be completed promptly and efficiently.

(*c*)   Whether the person is paid by the hour, the week or the month, and if he gets overtime pay. The author, like most professional advisers, is paid by his clients by the hour, so this is not really indicative of anything. The contrast HMRC are seeking to make is, of course, that they would expect an independent contractor to perform a task for a fixed fee irrespective of how long it took. While some businesses work in this manner, many do not. Lest anyone assumes that if he is not paid an hourly rate or weekly or monthly wage he is unlikely to be an employee, HMRC add, 'even if you are paid by commission or on a piecework basis you may still be an employee'.

(*d*)   Whether the person works set hours or a given number of hours per week or month. Again this is probably a neutral factor. A doctor who agrees to attend at a company's premises every Thursday afternoon to be available for consultation by staff is unlikely to be an employee of the company even though he provides his services at set hours and the number of hours for which he will work has been agreed in advance.

(*e*)   Whether the person works at the premises of the person he is working for, or at a place or places that they decide. This is not always a helpful test. The nature of the services to be provided will often determine where they are performed. If one wants a painter to decorate one's house the painter has to carry out the work at that house. The requirement does not, of course, make him an employee. Nor would the fact that he agrees with the householder when he will do the job or how many coats of paint he will apply or even all of these things.

4.51 Whilst it is easy to denigrate the tests that HMRC have formulated, they do cover the main factors to be taken into consideration and in some cases their application will point clearly to the right answer. The HMRC *Employment Status Manual* is also helpful in defining the principles involved although the strictures of Burton J in *R v CIR ex parte Professional Contractors Group Ltd and others [2001] STC 629* (see **4.40**) emphasise that it does not necessarily present an unbiased view. It must also be appreciated that the nature of the relationship between the parties can only be discerned by weighing up *all* the relevant factors. In an attempt to demonstrate that a subcontractor is not an employee people sometimes include as standard a clause in consultancy contracts which states that a person is entitled to use a substitute. If the contractor is relying on the specific expertise of a subcontractor such a clause is clearly artificial and is likely to do more harm than good as it raises the question as to why it should have been inserted, unless the parties had a genuine doubt as to whether the subcontractor was self-employed. A provision that the subcontractor will be responsible for his own tax and National Insurance is another provision that would not normally be found in a contract for services and thus highlights a doubt as to the status of the arrangement.

4.52 In May 2012, HMRC published a guidance booklet, 'Intermediaries Legislation (IR35)'. These pose a number of tests to determine whether a person is within the IR35 legislation. The answer to that question is whether he would be an employee if he worked directly for the end user without the interposition of a company or other intermediary. As such these tests ought to be equally applicable to the basic question of whether or not someone is an employee. These tests are set out at **10.60**. Unfortunately it is hard to see any real legal basis for the HMRC approach, so it seems concessionary. Nevertheless HMRC indicate that if a person scores more than 20 out of 48 points on their scale and he can evidence his answer, they will accept that IR35 does not apply. HMRC's 'Your Charter' states that a taxpayer can expect HMRC to treat him even-handedly. This must mean that they will treat someone who works direct for a client no more harshly than someone else doing similar work but who seeks to reduce his tax bill by working through an intermediary. Accordingly a self-employed individual who has completed the questionnaire and established a low-risk status must be entitled to tell HMRC of this and expect them to go away.

4.53 The freedom to refuse to undertake a particular task is normally likely to be inconsistent with a contract of employment. In the *O'Kelly* case (see **4.32** above) Ackner LJ pointed out that the casuals there were free to choose whether or not to work for a particular function and that 'however irritating it might have been to the company if faced with refusal, it would have been quite unreal to conclude that either party would have thought it was a breach of contract'.

4.54 In *Horner v Hasted [1995] STC 766* an employee of a firm of chartered accountants had the status within the firm equivalent to that of a partner. He was not a chartered accountant and was prevented by the then rules of the ICAEW from being a partner. He contended that he was not, in fact, an employee. It was held that he plainly was. The duties he undertook were very unusual incidents of a contract of employment, but it was a very unusual contract arising in very unusual circumstances. The circumstances were not incompatible with a contract of employment. Such a contract is well able to subsist in a one-off situation. The lack of 'control' or the relationship of boss and underling, or master and servant was not of the significance today it once might have been. It is not a universal litmus test and the importance and relevance depended on the role to be played by the 'employee' in the employer's business. A contrary decision was reached by the General Commissioners in the case of a journalist, Margaret Leslie who was held to be self-employed in relation to her shifts on a national newspaper, largely because she had no guarantee for future work beyond the immediate eight-hour shift and was not subject to grievance or disciplinary procedures (*Taxline, January 1995, item 19*). This decision appears questionable in the light of the above case.

4.55   Lord Sumner in *Great Western Rly Co v Bater*, while holding that Mr Hall was not within Schedule E ('nor does he hold any office at all; he merely sits in one') added 'I regret this decision, for it will, I fear, lead to persons escaping tax which they ought to pay, because they cannot be traced by the Revenue officials, or can be got at only at a disproportionate expense'. In recent years HMRC appear to have launched a campaign to bring within the employment income net everyone who offers his services for hire and whose business consists primarily in the exploitation of his own talents. It is probable that this is prompted by the same consideration, i.e. that HMRC do not trust the self-employed to account for tax on their earnings: a conclusion undoubtedly based on experience. If, however, a person is an employee, HMRC can collect the tax from his employer, with a right of recourse to the employee in many cases, if the employer does not pay.

4.56   In *Andrews v King [1991] STC 481*, Mr Andrews was engaged by a potato merchant company on various days over a two-year period. The company would contact Mr Andrews and tell him how many men were required on a particular day (it would be six, including Mr Andrews, for potato picking or four for grading). Mr Andrews would put together a team of the appropriate size. He drove them to the site in his own van, all six (or four) sharing the cost of the petrol. The company provided all necessary machinery and equipment. The price for the work was agreed by the company from time to time jointly with Mr Andrews and the rest of the team. Mr Andrews was treated no more favourably than the other members of the team. At the end of a day the company would pay Mr Andrews the agreed consideration in cash, he would deduct from this each member's petrol contribution and divide the balance equally between the other workers and himself. He did not keep any records of what payments he made to the other workers.

4.57   HMRC contended that Mr Andrews was a self-employed gangmaster and that the other workers were employees of his. This seems a very harsh claim in the circumstances. Fortunately, Sir Nicholas Browne-Wilkinson had no hesitation in dismissing their claim. He held that Mr Andrews was not a self-employed gangmaster. He exerted no control over the other workers, who were subject to the supervision of the company. The only equipment that he provided was his van, but this was not used in the work, only in getting to and from it and the cost of doing so was shared by all the workers. Although Mr Andrews selected the workers it could not be said that he hired them. He did not pay them himself and present their services to the company in return for a fee. All of the workers together negotiated their fee with the company. Mr Andrews took no financial risk and had no opportunity to benefit by sound management. In these circumstances the court could not identify any business carried on by the taxpayer on his own account. The Commissioners, in holding that he did, had reached a conclusion that was not possible as a matter of law. An interesting facet of this case is that the court looked at the status of the supposed 'employer' not that of the employee. This emphasises that in a status dispute it is worth considering the position of both parties to determine the nature of the contract.

4.58   HMRC contended as an alternative that, even if Mr Andrews was not in fact the employer of the other workers, he could be deemed to be the employer under the *PAYE Regulations*. *Regulation 2* of the *1993 Regulations* defined an 'employer' as 'any person paying emoluments' (*Reg 12* of the *2003 Regulations* has the same effect). However, *regulation 4* (which has since been repealed and replaced by *ITEPA 2003, ss 687–702*) provided that 'where an employee works under the general control and management of a person who is not his immediate employer, that person ... shall be deemed to be the employer'. The judge held that *Reg 4* overrode *Reg 2* and that, as Mr Andrews worked alongside the other workers, there was nothing to indicate that he had any control over them. He could not therefore be their employer as they worked under the general control and management of the company.

4.59   The Special Commissioners decision in *Lewis t/a MAL Scaffolding v HMRC* Sp C 527; *[2006] STC (SCD) 253* is interesting. Mr Lewis provided the services of scaffolders and labourers to site contractors. The individuals were engaged on an informal basis without documentation or written contracts. The Special Commissioner commented 'I find nothing suspicious from the standpoint of tax or social security in the absence of documents ... But that absence tends to confirm the oral evidence that I was given that ... neither Mr Lewis nor any of the workers (save for the Bligh brothers) wanted formal agreements. And that tends to suggest that the relationships were arm's length relationships between independent contractors and not those of employer and employee'. He concluded on the facts that all of the workers were self-employed. On the other hand, in *HMRC v Wright [2007] STC 1684* Lewison J felt that whether the contracts were oral or written was 'an irrelevant consideration'. He felt that the General Commissioners had not answered the key question, namely whether Mr Wright had sufficient control over his workers to make them his employees. On the basis of the facts found by the Commissioners he felt that the answer to that question did not lead to the inevitable conclusion that he did, and remitted the case to the Commissioners to answer that question.

4.60   Special care needs to be taken where a person who was previously an employee becomes an independent contractor working for his former employer.

In *Demibourne Ltd v CIR* Sp C 486; *[2005] STC (SCD) 667* the Special Commissioner, whilst accepting that it is possible for this to happen, felt that to achieve this there needs to be a clear distinction between the employer/ employee relationship and the new one amounting to a contract between client and independent contractor. In that case the terms of the engagement were very similar to that of this previous employment.There was a change in the terms of payment, but that was a consequence of the way the parties viewed the arrangement rather than a factor deferring its nature. Secondly the worker was no longer entitled to paid holidays. Apart from that the two engagements were virtually identical. The changes were not sufficient to replace the relationship of employer and employee with one between client and independent contractor.

Casual employees

4.61 A particular problem arises with casual employees. Many people assume that an employment implies a degree of continuity. This is not the case. A person who is engaged to work for someone for a few hours only can nevertheless be an employee if the relationship meets MacKenna J's three conditions (see **4.17** above). The HMRC booklet CWG2 (2006), the *Employer's Further Guide to PAYE and NICs,* sets out a procedure for dealing with casuals.

(*a*)   If the person will work for the employer for a week or less and the remuneration is less than the PAYE and National Insurance thresholds, the employer need only keep a record of the person's name and address and the amount paid.

(*b*)   If the pay exceeds the PAYE limit, tax must be deducted on an emergency code basis (unless the employer knows that the worker has other employment, when it must be deducted at basic rate).

(*c*)   If the person will work for more than a week (or he actually works for more than a week – or there is an agreement with him that he will work for the employer again) or the employee produces a form P45, the normal PAYE procedures will apply. This involves deduction of tax under the emergency code if the employee declares on a form P46 that he has no other employment, or at basic rate if he does not.

4.62 HMRC's approach is that anyone who does not follow this procedure cannot complain if HMRC subsequently seek to recover from him tax and National Insurance in relation to casual employees. In practice, of course, at that stage the employer is not in a position to recover the tax from the worker as he is normally no longer in contact with him.

4.62A *Yetis v HMRC and Style Superior Windows & Conservatories Ltd* (TC 2410) is an interesting case if only because it was Mr Yetis who claimed to be an employee and HMRC who claimed that he was self-employed. Mr Yetis succeeded despite having the onus of having to displace the HMRC assessments. He was engaged to man the Style stand at Homebase in Cambridge. He was paid a basic weekly wage plus commission. Mr Yetis had signed a statement saying that he was self-employed but he claimed that did not reflect the true position. Mr Yetis was not a salesman, but was engaged to generate leads. Later Style told Mr Yetis they could no longer afford his weekly wage and he became commission only. He accepted that he was self-employed from that time. Mr Yetis was not free to engage a helper. The FTT held that, on balance, Mr Yetis was an employee. They seem to have mainly asked themselves whether he was in business on his own account. It should be noted that HMRC specifically claimed that receiving a weekly wage was not inconsistent with self-employment.

Employment Status Indicator Tool

4.63 HMRC have produced an employment status indicator (ESI) tool, which can be accessed on their website. This is designed to help determine whether someone is employed or self employed. They claim that 'ESI users will be able to reach the right practical answer without needing to understand how the rules work' and that 'the ESI interactive guidance tool effectively shields the user ... from the complexity of the rules, while still providing an accurate and consistent answer on employment status in all but the most complex case' (Operational Impact Assessment 14.3.2006).

4.64 The Operational Impact Assessment states that the tool is available for customers to obtain a provisional view of employment status but that later in 2006/07 HMRC hope to display an enhanced version of the tool 'which will give external customers binding status decisions (provided that the information supplied is accurate and complete) without any need to contact the department'. To enable HMRC to give a binding opinion HMRC require the taxpayer's personal details and it is this element the current web version cannot capture. The HMRC concern is that currently the user is anonymous so they have no way of knowing what information was given (but as the tool allocates a reference number for each user they can probably check this from their computer if the taxpayer can quote that reference). The author understands that the HMRC position is actually that they regard an answer given by the current version of the ESI tool as binding on them if the taxpayer can show what answers were given. In practice this is not difficult if a note is kept of the answers given to the tool's questions as in the case of dispute that information can be given to HMRC and they can put it through the ESI tool themselves and see what answer it produces.

4.65 Many people have been wary of the ESI tool because the tool itself states 'It will not give a definitive or legally-binding opinion', but it is understood that HMRC do not mean by this that they will not stand by its result but merely that they are not claiming that such result is a definitive legal opinion. In such circumstances it seems sensible to use the tool as the first step in determining whether a person is employed or self employed. It is mandatory for HMRC staff themselves to do this so an initial ruling by HMRC on a person's status will have been produced by the tool – unless the case falls into the most complex category that the tool cannot cope with (complex in this context means out of the ordinary; the tool cannot cope with some simple cases). If you are happy with the answer given by the tool you can either keep a note of the information inputted – and ideally a print-out of the status determined by the tool and of the reasons for its decision, or can ask HMRC for a formal ruling, confident as to what that ruling will be. If you disagree with the status determined by the tool you are not bound by it and are free to argue that the tool is wrong. The tool very helpfully explains the factors that prompted its decision, which is useful information if you want to mount an argument with HMRC. HMRC have confirmed that provided that the information inputted is accurate, a taxpayer 'can rely on the ESI outcome as HMRC's view of the status for that particular engagement' (factsheet ES/FS2). They say that the employer should retain the printed version of the ESI result; the printout of the Enquiry Details Screen showing the engagement details and the replies to the questions asked; the engagement contract where applicable; and any other documentation or information that was relied on when completing the ESI (ES/FS2). They also say that the ESI tool should not be used for determining the status of office holders (such as company directors), or of individuals who provide their services through a limited company to which IR 35 applies (see **18.1**), or to contracts with agencies to provide services to another person (ES/FS2). It is unclear why they think it should not be used in IR 35 cases. The result ought to be valid provided that the facts that are inputted relate to the notional arrangement that IR 35 envisages between the end user and the worker, not to the contract between the worker and his immediate engager.

4.66   HMRC's claims for the tool are exaggerated. Not all of the questions are well phrased and there are a number of important factors that it does not address. However, contrary to the expectation of many cynics it does not invariably produce the answer that the individual is an employee. Indeed the author's experience in trying the Beta version was that it ruled as self employed all of his real cases where HMRC were strenuously arguing that the individual was an employee! Perhaps more important the cases clearly show that status cannot always be determined from the answers to a list of questions. One needs to step back and look at the picture as a whole. Nevertheless if one is satisfied with the close up there is no need to step back. Accordingly in this author's view whilst it would be dangerous to regard the ESI tool as shielding the user from the complexity of the rules, it is a very useful tool for those who start with an understanding of the rules and want guidance as to how HMRC are likely to apply them.

4.67   Whether a person is an employee of another is largely a question of fact. Many potential customers who are reluctant to engage a self-employed person to provide his skills for them for several weeks or months on a virtually full-time basis for fear that he will be regarded by HMRC as an employee, are happy to engage a company that is wholly owned by that person and has no activities other than to exploit his skills, to perform the same task. It is questionable whether, legally, this makes any difference. From a practical point of view, however, HMRC generally seem to be content that the person is taxable under PAYE, albeit only on his salary from his one-man company (or personal services company, or loan-out company, or service company as such companies are alternatively called) and do not normally seek to show that he is really an employee of the person who engages the company to provide the service. Indeed, it can be inferred from the fact that the government felt it necessary to introduce anti-avoidance rules on the provision of services through intermediaries (see **19.33**) that HMRC believed that they could not tackle the perceived problem by attacking the existence of the personal services company or other intermediary.

4.68 There were indications a few years ago that HMRC intended to mount an attack on the film industry, and require the film production company to deduct tax under PAYE from the payments it was contracted to make to the one-man company as if the fee were remuneration due to the worker himself. They appear to have backed away from a confrontation. They have not conceded this point though. Their Schedule E manual used to state, 'To avoid PAYE many film and video workers in Schedule E grades have set up limited companies. Normally the worker is the major shareholder and a director. It is alleged that the service company supplies the services of the individual to a film or video production company. An examination of many such cases has shown that such arrangements often fail. The worker remains an employee of the production company' (para 7324). Paragraph 7329 contained an identical comment in relation to television and radio workers. Whilst experience suggests that 'often' may be an exaggeration, this obviously emphasises the importance of getting the documentation right. The position is likely to depend on the real agreement between the parties and on the nature of the task to be performed. If the nature of the task is that the worker will function as a servant of the ultimate customer, the real terms of the agreement may be that the worker undertakes to be a servant of the customer in consideration of the customer making payments to the one-man company. Such an agreement would be an employment agreement.

4.69 On the other hand, if the one-man company has substance, e.g. a proper board of directors that regularly meets and makes decisions, it should be perfectly feasible to draw up a contract under which the one-man company agrees to provide the customer with the skills of the worker for a fee, with the worker remaining under the control of the one-man company but the one-man company acting in accordance with the directions of the customer. Such an agreement is unlikely to constitute an employment of the worker by the customer. It needs to be remembered that there are two contracts involved in such a case; one between the worker and his company and the other between the company and the person who wants to use its services. Each needs to be approached with great care from a tax point of view even though the first may seem unimportant from a commercial one.

4.70 One interesting case where the interposition of a one-man company proved successful was *Cooke v Blacklaws (1984) 58 TC 255*. The taxpayer in that case, a New Zealander, was not concerned to avoid the ultimate customer, the National Health Service, treating him as an employee, as his activities were clearly a self-employment. His purpose was to pursue the tax advantages that could be obtained by an employee of an overseas company but were not available to a self-employed person. Mr Blacklaws entered into an oral contract with a Panamanian company at a fixed salary and the company orally agreed to make his services available to a UK dental practice for a fee based on a proportion of the NHS fees that Mr Blacklaws generated. HMRC sought to set aside the company and assess Mr Blacklaws on his income as a self-employed individual. In spite of the lack of documentation, the Special Commissioners found that he had carried out dental work for the practice as an employee of the Panamanian company. This decision was upheld in the High Court on the *Edwards v Bairstow* principle (see **4.32** above). This case should not be taken as an indication that a written contract does not matter. The contract provides an opportunity to set out the factual arrangement between the parties. As stated at **4.30**, where there is a written contract the courts will normally limit themselves to construing that contract. If there is no written agreement the court will need to ascertain the facts, or at least those facts that can be proved, and then try to discern the contractual arrangement from such facts.

4.71   On which side of HMRC's line a particular arrangement falls will depend very much on the facts. Some other questions that might be relevant are: can the customer dismiss the worker or must it cancel the contract and require the one-man company to remove its employee from the customer's premises? Does the customer have to pay the one-man company when the worker is sick or on holiday? If so what is the commercial justification? Can the customer tell the worker what to do or does it request him (as director of his one-man company) to arrange for himself (as the company's employee) to do the particular task?

Triangular relationships

4.72   Where an employment is found to exist it might sometimes (but probably very infrequently) be necessary to identify the real employer. It might be thought that ought to be obvious. However, there are two Court of Appeal decisions which give a somewhat surprising answer, namely *Brook Street Bureau (UK) Ltd v Dacas [2004] EWCA Civ 217* and *Cable & Wireless plc v Muscat [2006] EWCA Civ 220.*

4.73   Mrs Dacas was an office cleaner. She entered into what was called a Temporary Worker Agreement with Brook Street. Under this Brook Street contracted to obtain suitable assignments for Mrs Dacas as a temp and contracted to pay her remuneration for each hour worked during an assignment. They duly paid her and deducted PAYE from her remuneration. They found her an assignment with the London Borough of Wandsworth. The assignment was a continuous one. It lasted for over four years. The Council then alleged that she had been rude to a visitor and told Brook Street that she was no longer acceptable to them. Brook Street then told Mrs Dacas that no further work would be found for her. Mrs Dacas claimed unfair dismissal against both the Council and Brook Street. The Employment Tribunal held that Mrs Dacas was not an employee of Brook Street and not an employee of the Council either. Accordingly she was not an employee at all so could not maintain proceedings for unfair dismissal against anyone. Mrs Dacas appealed against the finding that she was not an employee of Brook Street but neither she nor Brook Street joined the Council in the appeal. That was unfortunate for Mrs Dacas as the Court of Appeal agreed that she was not an employee of Brook Street but considered that she was an employee of the Council.

4.74   Mr Muscat was employed by Exodus Internet Ltd. In late 2001 Exodus decided to reduce its number of employees but offered to retain Mr Muscat's services as a contractor although it required him to provide his services through a limited company. Mr Muscat formed a company, E-Nuff Communications Ltd, of which he became an employee. In February 2002 Exodus was taken over by Cable and Wireless. Mr Muscat continued to work as before, indeed as he had initially done as an employee of Exodus. E-Nuff submitted invoices to Cable and Wireless. These went unpaid. After some months Cable and Wireless told Mr Muscat that they did not deal with contractors direct and he would have to deal with them through an agency, Abraxas plc. E-Nuff accordingly entered into an agreement with Abraxas to provide to Abraxas the services of Mr Muscat and Abraxas onward provided those services to Cable and Wireless to whom it had contracted to provide contract personnel. In late 2002 Cable and Wireless told Mr Muscat that they no longer required his services. Mr Muscat claimed unfair dismissal. The Employment Tribunal held that Mr Muscat had an implied contract of service with Cable and Wireless. Cable and Wireless appealed, first to the Employment Appeals Tribunal and then to the Court of Appeal. Both upheld the Employment Tribunal decision.

4.75   At first sight these are extraordinary decisions. Brook Street gave the appearance of employing Mrs Dacas. E-Nuff gave the appearance of employing Mr Muscat. The courts did not contend that those ostensible employments were shams, yet in both cases they found that a third party was the real employer.

4.76   The answer may well lie in the *Employment Rights Act 1996 (ERA 1996)* with which the court was concerned in both cases. This defines a contract of employment as 'a contract of service or apprenticeship, whether express or implied and (if it is express) whether oral or in writing'. It also treats some other contracts as if they were employments. *ITEPA 2003* does not define an employment but states that 'employment includes in particular any employment under a contract of service, any employment under a contract of apprenticeship and any employment in the service of the Crown' [*ITEPA 2003, s 4*]. In construing the *Employment Rights Act* the court felt that as the definition referred specifically to an 'implied contract' the Employment Tribunal was obliged to consider not only the contractual relationships but also whether there might be an implied employment relationship. It also gave the Act a purposive approach. The purpose was to protect the employee against unfair dismissal. It defined commonsense to suggest that Mrs Dacas, whose work was managed and controlled by the Council in the mutual expectation that she would be paid for what she was told to do and had in fact done, was not employed by anyone. The Court of Appeal in *Reed Employment* (see **5.38**) made clear that Employment Tribunal cases need to be approached with caution in interpreting tax law and can be useful only if they relate to the employment leg of the statute.

4.77   Mummery LJ defined the real problem as:

> 'the application of the basic legal requirements to the case where an employment agency is interposed between the applicant and the end-user and where the functions normally found in a single employing entity

are re-distributed between two entities, each of which denies it is the employer … This means that in ascertaining the overall legal effect of the triangular arrangements on the status of Mrs Dacas the Employment Tribunal should not focus so intently on the express terms of the written contracts … that it is deflected from considering finding facts relevant to a possible implied contract of service between Mrs Dacas and the Council in respect of the work actually done by her exclusively for the Council at its premises and under its control, until it took the initiative in terminating the arrangements. The formal written contract … may not tell the whole story about the legal implication of a contract of service between Mrs Dacas and the Council. There may be evidence of a pattern of regular mutual contact of a transactional character between Mrs Dacas and the Council from which a contract of service may be implied by the tribunal. I see no insuperable objection in law to a combination of transactions in the triangular arrangements, embracing an express contract for services between Mrs Dacas and Brook Street, an express contract between Brook Street and the Council and an implied contract of services between Mrs Dacas and the Council, with Brook Street acting in certain agreed respects as an agent for Mrs Dacas and as an agent for the Council under the terms of the express written agreement'.

4.78   The Employment Tribunal in *Muscat* felt itself bound by the *Dacas* decision. Cable and Wireless sought to distinguish the two cases but without success. The Court of Appeal felt that in Dacas its predecessor's concern was that 'by failing to consider the possibility of an implied contract of employment between worker and end-user, Employment Tribunals were not applying the law correctly so as to provide the employment protection which Parliament intended'. This suggests that the 'implied employment' approach may well be limited to employment protection legislation, which specifically envisages an implied contract, and may have no application to tax where the objective of Parliament, which is probably to impose on someone the obligation to deduct and account for tax and NIC, can be met without a need to identify whether an implied employment might exist alongside the contractual employment.

4.79   Furthermore there is not necessarily an implied employment relationship in every triangular situation. The Court in Muscat concluded:

'No doubt if Employment Tribunals apply their minds to the possibility of an implied contract … there will be some cases in which they find that relationship … There will no doubt also be many cases in the future in which Employment Tribunals will conclude that a worker in the triangular relationship is not an employee of the end user. That may be because they find that he or she is an independent contractor. It may be that the Employment Tribunal will conclude … that the worker was employed by the agency. Another possibility is that the worker may be found to have had a series of short employment contracts with different end-users but no continuing contract of employment such as will support employment rights. All will depend on the facts of the individual case. We find it hard to imagine a case in which a worker will be found to have no recognised status at all, either as an employee of someone or as a self-employed independent contractor'.

4.80   *Westek Ltd v HMRC [2008] STC (SCD) 169* concerned a preliminary point on the validity of the assessment. The substantive issue is yet to be heard by the Special Commissioners but it is probably worth highlighting it. Westek paid substantial management fees to companies (in one case a partnership) that HMRC believe to be controlled by directors of the company. HMRC are contending that the companies and partnership were mere conduits and that the payments are in reality remuneration of the directors subject to PAYE and Class 1 NIC.

Employment income taxed as receipts of trades, etc

4.81   A difficult area, in which there would appear to be little consistency of treatment, is what happens where, in the course of a trade or profession, a person enters into engagements that looked at on their own contractually constitute the acceptance of an employment or office.

Davies v Braithwaite

4.82   In *Davies v Braithwaite 18 TC 198* an actress entered into a contract to perform in the USA. At the time earnings of a UK resident from an employment carried on wholly overseas were assessable on a remittance basis. Miss Braithwaite contended that her contract with the US theatre was an employment contract and that as she had not remitted the earnings they were not taxable. HMRC contended that the agreement, albeit in the form of an employment agreement, was merely an incidence of her profession as an actress and that the earnings fell to be treated as part of her self-employment income.

4.83   Upholding HMRC's claim, Rowlatt J sai:

'it seems to me that where one finds a method of earning a livelihood which does not contemplate the obtaining of a post and staying in it, but essentially contemplates a series of engagements and moving from one to the other – and in the case of an actor's or actress's life it certainly involves going from one to the other and not going on playing one part for the rest of his or her life, but in obtaining first one engagement and then another, and a whole series of them – then each of the engagements could not be considered an employment, but is a mere engagement in the course of exercising a profession ...' (*18 TC* at p. 204).

Fall v Hitchen

4.84   In a later case, *Fall v Hitchen 49 TC 433* a ballet dancer was engaged under a standard British Actor's Equity Association form of contract to perform at a theatre in England and following *Davies v Braithwaite*, sought to treat the earnings as part of his Schedule D activities. It was held that the case was distinguishable from the Braithwaite case and that the earnings should be assessed as employment income. It is not clear on what basis the judge saw a distinction. The most likely is that the contract in Braithwaite was of a few weeks duration only whereas that in Hitchen lasted for approximately six months.

4.85   Although *Fall v Hitchen* was decided in 1972 HMRC was content for a long time to leave all such earnings within a performer's Schedule D accounts. However, in 1990, 18 years later, they adopted the stance that not only should they apply the decision in *Fall v Hitchen* rigidly but also, despite the fact that the judge specifically accepted that *Davies v Braithwaite* was still good law, they should regard the decision as applicable to all engagements under Equity contracts, however short in duration. In effect they seemed to be contending that the *Hitchen* case in reality overrode *Braithwaite* and that the latter was wrongly decided. They however exercised their 'care and management' powers (that HMRC have discretion to do what they think necessary for the efficient care and management of the tax system) so as to allow established artists to treat their earnings from Equity contracts as part of their self-employed activities. The cynical might feel that if HMRC choose to ignore those court decisions which they find inconvenient it is a clever ploy to exclude from the effect of such a decision those who can afford to challenge such a stance through the courts! HMRC's change of approach generated some protest in Parliament and, as a slight concession, the Government permitted entertainers to claim tax relief for agent's fees, although the relief in *FA 1990, s 77*, although extended slightly by *Finance Act 1991 (FA 1991), s 69*, is tightly circumscribed.

4.86   In 1993 Equity backed two 'test cases' before the Special Commissioners. These related to Alec McCowan, a long-established actor, and Sam West, a relative newcomer to the profession. The Commissioner held that the *Braithwaite* and *Fall v Hitchen* cases were not contradictory but dealt with different situations, and that both Mr McCowan and Mr West were self-employed.

4.87   Although HMRC did not appeal the *McCowan* and *West* decisions, Ian Lorimer, a film technician (a vision mixer) took his own case to the Court of Appeal where it was held, albeit on *Edward v Bairstow* principles, that he was self-employed (*Hall v Lorimer [1994] STC 23*). HMRC decided not to take the case to the House of Lords.

4.88   A single judgment was given by Nolan LJ. 'The case has been argued before us ... on the agreed basis that the critical issue is whether or not the contracts from which the taxpayer derived his earnings were contracts of service ... The detailed facts of the matter, which are so important in a case of this sort are set out with admirable thoroughness and clarity in the case stated ...'.

4.89   The Crown submitted that 'an employment properly so called is not the less an employment because it is casual rather than regular' and that 'the nature and degree of skill involved in the work cannot alone be decisive'. Nolan LJ accepted both of these propositions. He was hesitant about the Crown's suggestion that he should follow the approach taken in *Market Investigations* (see **4.23**) and affirmed in *Lee Ting Sang* (see **4.34**), as:

'In cases of this sort there is no single path to a correct decision. An approach which suits the facts and arguments of one case may be unhelpful in another.' He endorsed the view of Mummery J in the High Court that 'In order to decide whether a person carries on business on his own account it is necessary to consider many different aspects of that person's work activity. This is not a mechanical exercise of running through items on a check list to see whether they are present in, or absent from, a given situation. The object of the exercise is to paint a picture from the accumulation of detail. The overall effect can only be appreciated by standing back from the detailed picture which has been painted, by viewing it from a distance and by making an informed, considered, qualitative appreciation of the whole ... Not all details are of equal weight or importance in any given situation. The details may also vary in importance from one situation to another ... It is ... impossible in a field where a very large number of factors have to be weighed to gain any real assistance by looking at the facts of another case and comparing them one by one to see what facts are common, what are different and what particular weight is given by another tribunal to the common facts. The facts as a whole must be looked at, and a factor which may be compelling in one case in the light of the facts of that case may not be compelling in the context of another case.'

4.90 He found the distinction between an employee selling his labour and a contractor selling the product of his labour:

'very hard to apply in the case of a professional man. Surely the self-employed barrister advising in his chambers or the doctor advising in his surgery is selling his skill and labour and not its product. If the scene shifts to the court or to the operating theatre can the client or patient really be said to be buying the product which may be disastrous in spite of the best efforts of the advocate or the surgeon ... Again the question, whether the individual is in business on his own account, though often helpful, may be of little assistance in the case of one carrying on a profession or vocation. A self-employed author working from home or an actor or singer may earn his living without any of the normal trappings of a business. For my part I would suggest there is much to be said in these cases for bearing in mind the traditional contrast between a servant and an independent contractor ... it is, I think, in any event plain that Cooke J was not intending to lay down an all-purpose definition of employment. For example, his test does not mention the duration of the particular engagement or the number of people by whom the individual is engaged'.

4.91 Nolan J specifically upheld the continuing relevance of the *Davies v Braithwaite* decision and felt it:

'not surprising that the Special Commissioners attached importance to the case because it concerned an actress ... whose income-earning activities had much in common with those of the taxpayer'. It is worth noting that HMRC were contending that Mr Lorimer had 580 different 'employments' during a four-year period! *Hall v Lorimer* arises from another extra-statutory approach by HMRC to taxation based ostensibly on their interpretation of the decision in *Fall v Hitchen* – or, many think, based on a desire to extend PAYE to as many of the self-employed as they could get away with! In the early 1980s they adopted the view that it was impossible for casual and freelance film technicians and other behind-the-scene workers to be self-employed and insisted that film companies should apply PAYE to all payments to such people – their latest guidance requiring this even where the worker is an employee of someone else such as his own personal services company (although 'by concession' they do not actually require tax to be deducted for assignments lasting less than a week). They gradually relented, looking at the work done by different categories of workers, and accepted that certain types of work did not constitute an employment. As a result they published a list of 'Grades where PAYE need not be applied'.

Most of these were agreed in the early 1980s. They have been extremely reluctant to add to the list since then. Mr Lorimer's grade was not included on the list – and since his victory has not been added to it!

4.92   Following consideration of the *Hall v Lorimer* decision HMRC said the decision adds two further factors to be considered in determining whether someone is an employee. The engagements may need to be looked at in the context of the worker's business activities as a whole including such matters as his exposure to bad debts and the amount of time spent on organising, obtaining or carrying out the work; and it may be appropriate to take into account the length of the individual engagement and the number of other persons for whom similar work is performed. They also conclude that the *Market Investigation* test may not be very relevant to professional people who conduct their occupations without the usual trappings of business such as stock, premises, and equipment. Independence may be a useful pointer in such cases. HMRC will also look at whether the person's services require the exercise of rare skill and judgement, the worker is engaged for a specific task, the worker incurs substantial unreimbursed expenditure in obtaining, organising and carrying out engagements requiring visits to various sites, there is a risk of delayed payment and bad debts, and the extent to which the worker is able to influence pay.

4.93   HMRC have also agreed that in the light of the *McCowan* and *West* decision actors, ballet dancers, opera singers and other performers and artistes who appear in live theatre, etc. or film, TV and video productions under Equity or Musician's Union Contracts may well be engaged under contracts for services, i.e. self-employed. The terms of the contract may not be decisive in themselves. They have indicated that the same principal applies to stage managers. HMRC's current position is that a performer or artiste is normally assessable as a self-employed individual except where he is engaged for a regular salary to perform in a series of different productions over a period of time in such roles as may be stipulated from time to time by the engager, eg permanent members of an orchestra or a ballet, opera or theatre company. This applies also to stage managers but not normally to other non-performing theatrical staff. They also accept that musicians engaged to appear at theatrical performances, those engaged under 'first call' or 'guarantee' contracts, musicians who are shareholder performers in the London Philharmonic, London Symphony, New Philharmonia and Royal Philharmonic Orchestras and other orchestral players who are engaged for individual performances are self-employed *(Employment Status Manual, paras ESM 4.122–4.140)*. In the film and television industries front of camera performers are generally accepted as self-employed. So are certain categories of behind camera workers. HMRC publish a grading list setting out which classes they accept as Schedule D.

4.94   In their booklet IR 175 issued in connection with the IR 35 or personal service company rules (see **19.33**), HMRC appear to accept that *Hall v Lorimer* is not confined to the entertainment industry but is part of the mainstream law on what is an employment. This booklet has since been withdrawn but there is no reason to doubt that this still represents their view.

Offices held by professionals

4.95   The next category of cases in which the same problem arises is in relation to offices held by professionals. The leading case here is *IRC v Brander and Cruickshank 46 TC 574*. A Scottish firm of advocates derived a substantial part of its income from acting as company secretaries and registrars. Following the takeover of one company they were paid compensation for losing their role as registrar. They successfully claimed that as a registrarship was an office the income should strictly not have been included in their trading profits and, although they did not wish to disturb this treatment, the compensation was not part of their trading activities but assessable under the employment income rules – and being less than £30,000 (see **11.19**(a) below) not taxable. The House of Lords upheld this contention. In *Walker v Carnaby Harrower, Barham and Pykett 46 TC 561* a similar claim was upheld in relation to compensation received by a firm of accountants who were asked to resign as auditors of a group of companies.

4.96   In spite of these decisions HMRC have never sought to contend that accountants must exclude audit fees from their accounts or that other similar receipts by professional firms should be taxed as employment income. Indeed on the contrary they have introduced concessions to prevent some such receipts being taxed as employment income where an Inspector of Taxes might have sought to persuade the payer to apply PAYE.

Doctors

4.97   The third category in which the same problem arises concerns doctors. A doctor in general practice works for the National Health Service under a contract for services and is assessable on his earnings as self-employment income. If he has a private practice the receipts from it are obviously also part of his self-employment income. If, however, a doctor also has a part-time hospital appointment with a local Health Authority this is an office or employment taxable as employment income and the hospital pays the earnings under deduction of PAYE. The case that established that the hospital earnings should not be included in the trading profits was a House of Lords decision,

Mitchell and Edon v Ross 40 TC 11. HMRC insist that a doctor's hospital earnings should be distinguished in this way.

4.98   The bulk of the tax litigation involving doctors has not been concerned with the principle of whether hospital earnings are taxable as employment income, but rather with the resultant problem in relation to expenses. The difficulty is that expenses in relation to the hospital appointment are not an allowable deduction in calculating Schedule D profits as they are obviously not wholly and exclusively incurred in earning such profits. Indeed, they are nothing to do with earning such profits, except to the extent that it might be contended that the hospital appointment enhances the reputation of the doctor, and possibly his ability to refer patients to hospital colleagues, and that the holding of the employment (even if it were unpaid) would be a necessary part of practice public relations. Unfortunately, in most cases the expenses are not deductible in calculation net employment income either, as the duties of the employment will not normally start until the doctor arrives at the hospital. In the *Mitchell and Edon* case the expenses were disallowed completely, and this has generally been the outcome of subsequent cases also, the one success being another House of Lords decision, *Pook v Owen 45 TC 571* (see **5.33**). This problem is considered in more detail in **Chapter 5**.

Chapter 5

Expenses

Introduction

5.1   Normally an employer can be expected to provide an employee with whatever facilities he needs to perform his tasks effectively. Accordingly, he will either incur all necessary business expenses or will reimburse the employee for the cost of such expenditure. However, this is not always the case. In many businesses, such as the building or engineering trades, an employee will be expected to bring with him to the job his own basic tools and sometimes even quite expensive equipment. In others, the employee may invent his own equipment to do a job effectively and his employer may be happy for him to use such individual equipment on the job, and may be prepared to reflect the value of such equipment in the wage he pays. Sometimes, while accepting that a job could be done far more effectively if certain expenditure were to be incurred, the employer may feel that he cannot justify that expenditure in the context of his other commitments and the employee may decide to incur it himself. In some instances an employer will agree to pay a general expense allowance (which is effectively treated as part of the employee's salary for tax purposes) but out of which he expects the employee to pay for the expenses he incurs for the purpose of his work.

The statutory provisions

5.2   Specific provisions would therefore be expected to allow an employee to deduct from his salary expenses that he incurs in the course of his employment. These are to be found in *Income Tax (Earnings and Pensions) Act 2003 (ITEPA 2003), ss 327–377*. Unfortunately, *s 336*, the general rule, is very narrowly drawn and over the years the courts have interpreted it extremely restrictively. Because of this a paraphrase of *s 336* would be dangerous and it is accordingly set out in full below:

'The general rule is that a deduction from earnings is allowed for an amount if:

(*a*)   the employee is obliged to incur and pay it as holder of the employment; and

(*b*)   the amount is incurred wholly, exclusively and necessarily in the performance of the duties of the employment'.

5.3   There are then in *ss 337* (travel in performance of duties) and *338* (travel for necessary attendance) two separate general rules for travel expenses.

5.4 *Expenses*

'A deduction from earnings is allowed for travel expenses if:

(*a*)   the employee is obliged to incur and pay them as holder of the employment; and

(*b*)   the expenses are necessarily incurred on travelling in the performance of the duties of the employment'; and

'A deduction from earnings is allowed for travel expenses if:

(*a*)   the employee is obliged to incur and pay them as holder of the employment; and

(*b*)   the expenses are attributable to the employee's necessary attendance at any place in the performance of the duties of the employment'.

5.4   Prior to 2003/04 the wording read 'If the holder of an office or employment is *obliged* to incur and defray out of the emoluments of that office or employment:

(*a*)   qualifying travelling expenses; or

(*b*)   any amount (other than qualifying travelling expenses) expended wholly, exclusively and necessarily in the performance of the duties of the office or employment;

there may be deducted from the emoluments to be assessed the amount so incurred and defrayed.' [*Income and Corporation Taxes Act 1988 (ICTA 1988), s 198(1)*].

5.5   '"Qualifying travelling expenses" meant:

(*a*)   amounts necessarily expended on travelling in the performance of the duties of the office or employment; or

(*b*)   other expenses of travelling which:

    (i)   are attributable to the necessary attendance at any place of the holder of the office or employment in the performance of the duties of the office or employment; and

    (ii)   are not expenses of ordinary commuting (see **5.18**) or private travel.' [*ICTA 1988, s 198(1A)*].

A deduction against employment income cannot be claimed for qualifying travelling expenses in respect of the use of a car if mileage allowance payments (see **7.49**) are made to the taxpayer in respect of use of the vehicle or mileage allowance relief (see **7.51**) is available (*ICTA 1988, s 198(5)*).

5.6   Up to 1997/98 the text read:

'If the holder of an office or employment is *necessarily obliged*:

(*a*)   to incur and defray out of the emoluments of that office or employment the expenses:

116

> (i) of travelling *in the performance* of the duties of the office or employment; or
>
> (ii) of keeping and maintaining a horse to enable him to perform those duties; or
>
> (b) otherwise to expend money *wholly, exclusively and necessarily in the performance of those duties*;
>
> there may be deducted from the emoluments to be assessed the expenses so necessarily incurred and defrayed.'

It will be seen that the changes from 1998/99 related wholly to travelling expenses apart from the consignment to history of the relief for keeping and maintaining a horse.

5.7   If the wording seems a little old-fashioned it is because the provision is virtually unchanged since the time of its original embodiment as the *Income Tax Act 1853, s 51*. The wording of most of the provisions tends to alter on consolidation of the tax statutes (which occurred in 1918, 1952, 1970 and 1988). It is no accident that the draftsman has not sought to make alterations here beyond what is necessary to deal with the new relief for employment-related travelling expenses which do not meet the condition of being in the performance of the duties. It is because there is a great deal of judicial guidance on its interpretation which the draftsman wished to preserve and which any alteration might invalidate.

The three requirements

5.8   There are three main hurdles that need to be overcome to obtain a deduction for an expense.

(a)   The employee must be 'obliged' to incur it.

(b)   It must be incurred 'in the performance of' the duties of the employment (other than travelling expenses within *ss 337 and 338)*).

(c)   Except for travelling expenses, it must be 'wholly, exclusively and necessarily' incurred.

5.9   It is very difficult to meet all three of these tests. 'Obliged' has been held to connote an expense that is not personal to the employee but that each and every holder of the office or employment would have to incur. The leading case is *Ricketts v Colquhoun 10 TC 118*. A barrister who lived and worked in London was appointed to the office of Recorder of Portsmouth. He claimed to deduct his travelling expenses to Portsmouth. It was held that he could not do so as he would not have incurred the expense had he lived in Portsmouth. 'In the performance of the duties' is an equally hard test to satisfy. The very strict interpretation of head (a) is emphasised by the case of *Ling v HMRC [2011] UKFTT 793(TC)* where Miss Ling's salary was increased to recognise that she needed to incur expenses but the Tribunal nevertheless disallowed the expenses as not being required by the duties of her employment.

Travelling expenses

5.10   It will be seen that there are two distinct categories of deductible travelling expenses. Travel in performance of duties and travel attributable to necessary attendance at a place in performance of the duties. The test of travelling in the performance of the duties of the employment can be hard to satisfy. Travelling expenses to one's place of employment are not incurred 'in the performance of' the duties of the employment; they are incurred in order to put the employee in a position to carry out his employment. Sometimes a person has more than one place of employment. In such circumstances it is necessary to determine which, if any, is the base of the employment in order to apply this test. Travel from the base is travel in the performance of the duties of the employment, as once a person has reached his employment base he has commenced his duties. Many employees claim that their home is their base, so that all travel is in the course of the employment. Where a person, such as a travelling salesman, has no fixed place of employment, and rarely visits his company's premises, it may well be possible to show this. In most cases, however, it will not be possible.

5.11   This is well illustrated by *Miners v Atkinson [1997] STC 58* (see **5.35**). HMRC contended that Mr Miners' place of work was the office of a client of his employer company, so the travelling expenses from Mr Miners' home (the company's registered office) was not allowable. The Special Commissioner said that this ignored the fact that the taxpayer was employed by his company not the third party. However, he went on to hold that there was no evidence that the taxpayer's house had been specially designed or adopted as the company's office. Accordingly, it was not necessary for the work of the taxpayer to be carried out from that precise address. The taxpayer and his wife could have moved the registered office closer to the third party's premises. In these circumstances, costs of travel from the registered office/home were not 'necessarily' incurred for the purpose of the employment. Arden J endorsed this view. He suggested that the starting point is that the company's premises was the taxpayer's home. This required one to ask whether the taxpayer is working at home out of choice. He answered that question by quoting the Special Commissioners' view that it was not necessary for the work to be done at that precise address. This actually does not answer whether the taxpayer is working at home out of choice; it answers whether the particular location of the company's office was at the choice of its directors. Once the question is posed in that form it is difficult to see how travelling expenses of a director can ever be allowable, as the location of the business premises will always be at the choice of the board of directors. It is hard to see that it can make any difference whether the choice of location of the offices coincides with the choice of location of the home. It seems an extraordinary concept that a business could move its office closer to its customer, so travel to the customer is not allowable!

5.12   HMRC accepts that, where travel is in the course of the employee's duties allowable expenses 'can include the cost of a reasonable level of refreshments (both alcoholic and non-alcoholic) with the meal and refreshments such as tea, coffee or soft drinks taken between meals'. (*IR Press Release 16*

May 1995). They also accept that travel includes 'the cost of any attributable subsistence, for example an evening meal and hotel room where the employee has to stay away overnight' (*Tax Bulletin 32, December 1997*). It also includes, for example, toll fees, the cost of hiring a car and parking charges. It will not include private expenses such as newspapers and laundry (but see **5.37** for the special relief for personal overnight expenses).

5.13 One interesting case on this theme is *Taylor v Provan 49 TC 579*. A Canadian resident was appointed a director of a UK brewery group. His only responsibility was to bring about a major merger. Most of his work was done from his home in Canada. He received no remuneration but was reimbursed for travel between Canada and the UK. Evidence was given that he was unique and no-one else could have done the job, which was specially created for him. It was held that the job required two places of work, his home in Canada and the company's offices in England, so that the air fares were for travel between the two and thus incurred in the course of the employment.

5.14 In *Wilkinson v HMRC 2010 SFTD 1063*, Mr Wilkinson was appointed to a six-year training programme which consisted of rotational placements with four different NHS trusts, in Portsmouth, Winchester, Southampton and Bournemouth respectively. His base hospital throughout the six years was Winchester. He claimed for excess travel costs when working at the other hospitals, i.e. the difference between the cost of travel to Winchester and that to the other hospitals. This was denied on the basis that each of the hospitals was a permanent workplace, so the travel to each was ordinary commuting.

5.15 Home to work travel is not regarded as private use of a company car – and presumably is regarded as a business expense where public transport is used:

(*a*) where the employee has a travelling appointment;

(*b*) where the employee travels from home to a temporary place of work and the distance travelled is less than that between the normal place of work and the temporary place of work;

(*c*) where, exceptionally, the home qualifies as a place of work and the employee travels from home to another place or work in the performance of his duties, and, by concession;

(*d*) where a disabled person is provided with a car for home to work travel and there is no other private use;

(*e*) where public transport is disrupted; and

(*f*) for late-night journeys within the terms of *ITEPA 2003, s 248* (formerly *ESC A66*) (see **9.116**(t)) (*Hansard 12 May 1993, col 472*).

5.16 The second category is travel which is attributable to the necessary attendance of the employee at a place in the performance of the duties, provided that the expense is not excluded as ordinary commuting or private travel. That word 'necessary' should be noted; but it is not the travelling expense that needs to be necessary in this case, it is the attendance of the employee at a particular place. It remains to be seen how this will be interpreted by the courts. It is not 'necessary' for a director of an English engineering company to do design work from his villa in the South of France; he does it there out of personal choice, so the expense, quite properly, will not be deductible. But what about the worker who is asked to go once a month to deliver stock to the branch office in his home town? It is necessary for someone to undertake that job, but it is not necessary for that particular employee to do it. And what about the employee who delivers an urgent and important document to the office in his home town? It is necessary for the document to be delivered, but in many cases this could have been achieved by consigning the document to a courier company. It is to be hoped that once a business need for something to be done in a particular place is identified HMRC will accept that the 'necessary attendance' test is met and will not seek to become involved in the commercial management decision as to whose attendance it should be.

5.17   The main relaxation for this category of travel is that the travel does not have to be in the performance of the duties; all that has to be shown is that the employee needs to be at the particular place in order to perform duties of the employment there. The main exclusions are for ordinary commuting and private travel. Ordinary commuting is travel between the employee's home (or some other place that is not a workplace in relation to the employment) and a place which is a permanent workplace. [*ITEPA 2003, s 338(3)*]. Private travel is:

(*a*)   travel between the employee's home and a place that is not a workplace in relation to the employment (ie a place at which the employee's attendance is necessary in the performance of the duties of the employment); or

(*b*)   travel between two places neither of which is a workplace in relation to the employment.

[*ITEPA 2003, s 338(5)*].

Travel that is 'for practical purposes' substantially ordinary commuting or private travel is treated as such commuting or travel. [*ITEPA 2003, s 338(4)*]. This appears designed to exclude from relief travel where there is a minimal business need and the substantial reason for the travel is a non-business one. It will exclude relief for the employee who is sent to Australia to deliver a letter that could have easily been sent by post but was hand-delivered solely to provide the employee with a 'perk'.

5.18   Ordinary commuting is commuting to or from a 'permanent workplace'. This is defined as a place which the employee regularly attends in the performance of his duties and which is not a temporary workplace. [*ITEPA 2003, s 339(2)*] A temporary workplace is a place which the employee attends in the performance of the duties of the employment for the purpose of performing a task of limited duration or for some other temporary purpose. [*ITEPA 2003, s 339(3)*].

5.19   The distinction between a permanent and a temporary workplace is an important one. Travel from home to a permanent workplace is always disallowable as ordinary commuting. Travel from home to a temporary workplace is neither ordinary commuting nor private travel and is accordingly deductible provided that the necessary attendance in the performance of the duties test is satisfied.

5.20 A place cannot be a temporary workplace if the employee's attendance there is in the course of 'a period of continuous work' at the place which either lasts more than 24 months or comprises all (or almost all) of the total period for which the employee is likely to hold the employment or the attendance there is 'at a time when it is reasonable to assume' that it will be in the course of such a period. [*ITEPA 2003, s 339(5)*]. A 'period of continuous work' at a place means a period over which, looking at the whole period and considering all the duties of the employment, the duties of the employment fall to be performed to a significant extent at that place. [*ITEPA 2003, s 339(6)*]. HMRC regard duties as performed to a significant extent at a place if the employee spends 40 per cent or more of his working time at that place. The converse does not hold true. A place can be a permanent workplace even though the employee spends less than 40 per cent of his time there, with the result that travel to that place falls to be disallowed as ordinary commuting (*Tax Bulletin 33, February 1998*).

5.21 Note especially the phrase 'at a time when it is reasonable to assume'. This applies the test prospectively as well as historically. If when the travelling expenses are incurred there is an intention, or even a likelihood, that the work at a particular place will extend over more than 24 months, that place cannot be a temporary workplace, even though the period of employment there actually turns out to be less than 24 months. HMRC have said that the converse holds true also. Although the legislation prevents a place being a temporary workplace if the employee in fact spends a period there in excess of 24 months, HMRC have indicated that they propose to ignore this. If when the employee first attends that site he expects to be working there for 24 months or less, they do not regard it as a permanent workplace until either there is a change of intention or the employee has in fact worked there for over 24 months.

5.22 An actual or contemplated modification of the place at which the duties of the employment fall to be performed is disregarded in applying the 24-month rule if it does not have, or would not have, any substantial effect on the employee's journey or on the expenses of travelling to and from the place where the duties are to be performed. [*ITEPA 2003, s 339(7)*]. For example, suppose an employee is sent from London to Edinburgh to open an office, commuting back to London at weekends. He takes premises on a 12-month lease, intending to move to larger premises in Edinburgh after that time. He intends to spend a further 18 months at the new office. It is not permissible to say that the period in the first office will last less than 24 months and so will that at the second. As the journey from London to the new office will be roughly the same as at the old, the two must be looked at as one. As the employee anticipates spending 30 months in Edinburgh the Edinburgh office will not be a temporary workplace, with the result that the whole of the travel will be disallowed as ordinary commuting.

5.23   Mr Phillips was a construction worker. During 2000/01 he had three separate assignments, each with a separate contract, obtained through an agency. The Special Commissioners held that commuting to and from work at a temporary job was ordinary commuting because the place where the work was performed was a permanent workplace. Mr Phillips accordingly had three separate employments. His attendance at each was in the course of a period of continuous work at that place which comprised all of the period for which he held the employment. Accordingly the travel was ordinary commuting (*Phillips v Hamilton [2003] STC (SCD) 286*). Mr Macken was also a construction worker. During 1998/99 he worked for a construction company at a site in Bristol through an agency. The company offered him a permanent job at the same site. It was held that although he had had two jobs he had nevertheless worked continuously at the same site for more than 24 months for the purpose of the 24-month rule (*Macken v Hamilton [2003] STC (SCD) 286*).

5.24   A place which the employee regularly attends in the performance of his duties and which forms the base from which those duties are performed, or which is the place at which the tasks to be carried out in the performance of the duties are allocated, cannot be a temporary workplace. [*ITEPA 2003, s 339(4)*]. For example, suppose a repairman has to go into his employer's office every Monday morning where he obtains his instructions for the week. That will be a permanent workplace, so his travelling expenses to and from the office will be ordinary commuting and disallowed, albeit that the remainder of his travelling expenses are likely to be deductible. If he is passed his instructions by telephone at his home instead of attending the office there would, in contrast, be no disallowance.

5.25   In certain circumstances a person is treated as having a permanent workplace consisting of an area, in which case travel to the edge of that area would be ordinary commuting but travel within it would be deductible. This applies where:

(*a*)   the duties are defined by reference to that area (whether or not they also require attendance at a place outside that area);

(*b*)   in the performance of the duties the employee attends different places within that area; and

(*c*)   none of the places that he so attends within that area is a permanent workplace [*ITEPA 2003, s 339(8)*].

There is no restriction on the size of the defined area. In theory it could be 'the UK' or even 'the world'. However, if it is defined more broadly than the area in which the employee normally works HMRC are likely to contend that the defined area is a sham.

5.26   Travel between two workplaces in the course of a single employment is normally travel in the course of that employment. The position is different where there are separate employers at the two workplaces – and probably even if there are two separate employments with the same employer. There is an exception for expenses of travel between two places at which a person performs duties of different offices or employments under companies in the same group (ie where one is a 51 per cent subsidiary (= 50+ per cent) of the other or both are 51 per cent subsidiaries of a third company). Such expenses are treated as necessarily expended in the performance of the duties which that person is to perform at his destination. [*ITEPA 2003, s 340*]. It should be noted that this only applies within a group. If two companies are associated but do not form a group, travel between the two needs to meet the ordinary tests. Similarly if a person has employments with two partnerships or with a partnership and an associated company, the normal tests need to be met.

5.27   There is still potentially a problem where an employee works from home, particularly where he is the controlling director of a one-man company. HMRC say that 'where employees work at home they usually do so because it is convenient rather than because the nature of the job actually requires them to carry out the duties of their employment there. However, where it is an objective requirement of the employee's duties to carry out substantive duties at the home address then his or her home is a workplace for tax purposes – with the result that travel between there and another permanent workplace in respect of the same employment is in the performance of the duties of the employment (*Tax Bulletin 32, December 1997*). The problem is that this 'objective requirement' test (which is not in the legislation) does not reflect modern practices. It is becoming increasingly common for employees to spend part of their working time at home by agreement with their employer. Indeed it is becoming fairly common for certain 'hot-desking' in large organisations (even including HMRC). This is where the employer has agreed that office employees can work from home so that he does not provide accommodation for all of them at his own premises on the basis that there is likely always to be a 'spare' desk available. The nature of the job does not require such staff to work from home. It is for the convenience of both the employee and the employer. Currently most employees are probably content in such circumstances to accept that travel to the employer's premises is ordinary commuting because that is normally a regular requirement. However, as home-working increases people are likely to increasingly question whether HMRC's view is correct.

5.28   *Warner v Prior [2003] STC (SCD) 109* exemplifies the problem. Ms Warner was employed by Kent County Council as a supply teacher. She was required to do two types of duty, 'directed time' (actual teaching) and 'additional time' (marking work, writing reports and preparing lessons). Because there was rarely a place to do additional time work in a school (as a supply teacher had fewer facilities than permanent teachers) she carried out the bulk of her additional time in an office she maintained at home. The Special Commissioner held that her home office was a place of work and that it was objectively necessary having regard to her duties for her to have such a place of work somewhere other than the schools. However, he held that that fact of itself did not mean that she was entitled to deduct travelling expenses between her two places of work. Where she lived, at least within Kent, had no bearing on her appointment or her ability to perform it. Her secondary place of work at home was dictated by where she lived and not by the requirements of the job itself. The travelling expenses were accordingly not 'necessarily incurred' and were not deductible.

5.29 The position of the director of the one-man company is likely to depend on the facts. The new rules do not negate the *Miners v Atkinson* case (see **5.11** and **5.36**). However, Mr Miners worked largely for one client, so there was a site that the court could discern as his base. If a one-man company has a number of clients none of which can be categorised as the main one, it is probable that if the director's home is not his base and he will be a site-based employee – in which case all his travel will be from home to a temporary workplace and therefore fully deductible. Support for this view can be found in the parliamentary debates on the IR 35 legislation (see **19.35**) and the guidance in that legislation given in *Tax Bulletin 47 (June 2000)*.

5.30 *Lewis v HMRC [2008] STC (SCD) 895* concerned an employee, in fact an employee of HMRC. Mrs Lewis was an international specialist. She had an office at her home in Kenilworth where she worked two to three days a week and an office in HMRC premises in London. The reason for this arrangement was that she had previously worked for HMRC in the Midlands and was not prepared to move to London. HMRC installed IT equipment and a high speed ISDN line and business phone line at Mrs Lewis's home. She claimed that travelling from her home office to HMRC's London office was in the performance of her duties. It was held that each and every international HMRC tax specialist did not need a London office. Accordingly travelling to and from London was ordinary commuting. Sadly where a person has two bases in different parts of the country, working at one some days and the other the remainder of his time there is no relief for the cost of keeping two homes, and if the employee has only one home there is no relief for travel to the distant place of work as it will be ordinary commuting. Curiously parliament recognises a need for Members of Parliament to have a home near Westminster and a home in the constituency and is willing to reimburse expenses for both, albeit that the MP's need for two homes is no different from those of the factory manager in Manchester who has to go to his London head office one day a week

5.31 It will be seen that the tests look at the status of the journey, not the nature of the expense. Once the application of the test gives rise to a deduction, the cost of the travel is allowable irrespective of the mode of transport. There is also no territorial limitation. If a temporary workplace is in Australia, the travel costs will be deductible as much as if it is in Manchester. HMRC say that they will not normally deny relief simply because the employee could have used an alternative cheaper route or could have travelled standard class but went first class. However, if the travel arrangements are 'unusually lavish' they will want to consider whether, on the facts, the expenditure is really attributable to business travel or is, for example, some sort of reward – or perhaps motivated by a private whim of a director (*Tax Bulletin 32, December 1997*).

5.32 HMRC have entered into various Working Rule Agreements with Trade Associations relating to travel and subsistence payments in the construction and allied industries which contain limited concessionary elements. The benefit of such agreements are available to all employees in the industry that meet the relevant conditions, irrespective of whether or not the employer is a member of the relevant trade association (*Taxline, January 1995, item 17*). There are specific exemptions for travel where public transport is disrupted (see **9.116(t)**), travel by disabled persons (see **9.116**(u)) and occasional late night travel and breakdown in car sharing arrangements (see **9.116**(t)). There is also an exemption for offshore oil and gas workers. Where such a person has a permanent workplace at an offshore installation no tax is charged on the provision of transport by sea or air between the UK mainland and the offshore installation provided that the place of arrival and departure on the mainland is one for which such transport is provided for employees generally. The exemption also covers overnight accommodation in the vicinity of the place of arrival and departure on the mainland where that is necessary because of the time that the transfer transport from the installation takes place, local transport to and from the place of accommodation, and the reimbursement of reasonable expenses incurred by the employee on such transport, accommodation or subsistence. [*ITEPA 2003, s 305*]. This replaces an earlier concession (*ESC A65*).

Case law

5.33   The allowability of travelling expenses has spawned a great deal of litigation. In *Nolder v Walters 15 TC 380* an airline pilot was liable to be called for duty at any time. He unsuccessfully sought a deduction for travel between his home and the airport on the basis that once he was called he was on duty and that accordingly his home was his base. It was held that his duties did not start until after he had reached the airport. In *Pook v Owen 45 TC 571*, by contrast, a doctor was allowed a deduction for travel between his home and a hospital. He demonstrated that he had two employment bases, his home and the hospital, so that travel between the two was in the course of his duties. He could show this because he took responsibility for a patient from the moment he received a call at home. He instructed the hospital staff on the telephone as to what treatment to give, jumped in his car, and continued the treatment when he reached the hospital. Call out expenses were similarly held to be allowable in *Wilkinson v HMRC 2010 SFTD 1063*. On the other hand, in *Bhadra v Ellam 60 TC 466* the duties of a relief doctor were held not to start until he reached the hospital. A similar disallowance was made in *Hamerton v Overy 35 TC 73* where the duties of a consultant anaesthetist were held not to start until he reached the hospital. A general practitioner who acted as a clinical officer at three separate hospitals was also denied relief for travelling expenses both to and between the hospitals (*Parikh v Sleeman [1990] STC 233*).

5.34   A non-executive director of an NHS trust with several hospitals received and read trust papers at home. He claimed that reading papers was part and parcel of his duties as a director. The Special Commissioners held that such reading was merely preparatory to carrying out his duties. Furthermore the need to read them at home did not arise from the nature of the duties, it arose from personal choice. The taxpayer was therefore not necessarily obliged to defray travelling expenses from his home to the trust sites in the performance of his duties (*Knapp v Morton [1999] STC (SCD) 13*).

5.35   The fact that it is impossible to live near one's place of work will not help. In *Andrews v Astley 8 TC 589* an employee was compelled by a housing shortage to live outside the town where he worked but was refused a deduction for the cost of maintaining a motorbike to get to work. A deduction was also refused in *Phillips v Keane 1 ITC 69*, an Irish case where the identical tests of deductibility apply. Even if the employee cannot choose his place of work, as in the wartime case where the Government directed a married woman to work for a particular company, travel from home will still not be allowable (*Phillips v Emery 27 TC 90*).

5.36   A worrying decision that adds weight to what appears to be a concerted attack by HMRC on travelling expenses of shareholder/directors of one-man companies based at their homes is that in *Miners v Atkinson [1997] STC 58*. Mr Miners was a computer consultant employed by a one-man company, WCLA, based at his home. During the period in dispute it appears that the only client of WCLA was another company, Lombard, some 80 miles away. It was not disputed that Mr Miners was not an employee of Lombard. He did some of the Lombard work at WCLA's office (at his home) but much of it at Lombard's premises. The Special Commissioner accepted that Mr Miners' base was at WCLA's office but nevertheless held that the travelling expenses to Lombard's offices were not necessarily incurred in the performance of his duties with WCLA. 'Mr and Mrs Miners were the only directors and the shareholders of WCLA. Had they wished they could have moved to Croydon or anywhere else and re-established the registered office of WCLA wherever they wished'. This was upheld by Arden J very succintly:

> 'The starting point is that 4 Sandringham Road was the taxpayer's home. On the authorities, it seems to me that one must ask whether the taxpayer was working at home out of choice. The Special Commissioners answered that question against the taxpayer. "It was not necessary for the work which Mr and Mrs Miners carried out at 4 Sandringham Road to be done at that precise address. It could have been done anywhere". In the light of Lord Reid's speech particularly in *Taylor v Provan* (see **5.12**). ... in my judgment the Special Commissioner was correct in concluding that the taxpayer's travelling expenses were not deductible.'

The passage from Lord Reid's speech in *Taylor v Provan* to which the Judge refers is, 'If the holder of an office or employment has to do part of his work at home the place where he resides is generally still his personal choice. If he could do his home work equally well wherever he lives then I do not see how the mere fact that his home is also a place of work could justify a departure from the Ricketts ratio', i.e. that the expenses with which *section 198* is concerned are only those which each and every occupant of the particular office is necessarily obliged to incur in the performance of his duties. There is, however, a big difference between Mr Taylor and Mr Ricketts and the case of Mr Miners. Their employer had an office elsewhere; they did not have to work at home. In Mr Miners' case the only place of business of WCLA was at Sandringham Road. Thus, while it was true that he was based at home, he was actually based at the sole place of business of his employer. If the suggestion that a two person company can move its place of business near to its major customer if it wishes is carried to its logical conclusion, that similarly applies to any company under the control of one person even where it has established an office away from the home of the controlling shareholder. Where does the dividing line fall? Would Mr Miners have succeeded if he had converted his garage into an office? Or if he had bought the house next door and turned it into an office? Or if he had rented a purpose-built office a few streets away? On the test adopted by the Commissioner and the judge it is hard to see that any of these would have made a difference. Some people think that a separate office a few streets away would have been acceptable, but it is illogical that the trader who can afford to rent an office should be treated more favourably than one who does not have the money to do so.

5.37 An equally worrying case is *Kirkwood v Evans [2002] EWHC 30(Ch), [2002] STC 231* which seems to undermine the growing trend towards homeworking. Mr Evans was a civil servant employed by the DSS in King's Lynn until June 1991. He was then employed on detached duty in Southampton. In June 1991 the DSS decided to transfer the work to Leeds. For five years Mr Evans commuted between King's Lynn and Leeds, for which he received an allowance from the DSS towards his travel costs. The DSS introduced a voluntary homeworking scheme in 1996 at which time they appear to have told Mr Evans that he should either work from home or seek alternative employment. Mr Evans opted for homeworking, which made his home his main work place. He agreed with the DSS that he would attend their office in Leeds once a week to deliver the work he had done and collect new work for the forthcoming week. It was held that:

(*a*)   Mr Evans had two work places, one in King's Lynn and the other in Leeds and travelling between the two was dictated by the place where he chose to live not by the nature of the work;

(*b*)   the office in Leeds was a permanent workplace as the terms of the homeworking scheme required him to attend there on one day a week; and

(*c*)   the travel was ordinary commuting (see **5.18**) because it was between the employee's home and a place which is a permanent workplace and could not therefore fall within *s 198(1A)* (see **5.5**); it was irrelevant that Mr Evans's home was also a workplace.

For good measure the judge also disallowed the costs of heating and lighting the workspace in Mr Evans home on the grounds that these were not wholly exclusively and necessarily incurred in the performance of his duties. That seems particularly harsh. He needed the light to work by. He would not have switched it on were he not working. Accordingly, it is hard to see why the cost of the units of electricity consumed whilst he worked there did not meet that test. It is generally accepted that items like telephone calls and electricity where the cost depends on usage do not have a dual purpose where individual units are consumed for a specific business purpose. The judge also said that as homeworking was optional under the scheme it was not necessary for Mr Evans to incur the expense, as he had chosen to work from home. He could have continued to commute to Leeds albeit that it appears that his employer was no longer prepared to subsidise such commuting.

5.38   The case of *Reed Employment plc v HMRC [2014 UKUT 160(TCC)* raises a number of interesting issues. It relates to 'temps' supplied by Reed to customers. These are employees of Reed under an overarching continuous contract which provides for the temp to be paid only when she is working on an assignment at a client of Reed's. Reed created a salary sacrifice scheme under which a temp was given the option to sacrifice part of her salary in exchange for a 'tax-free' travel allowance. She could opt for the travel allowance only if she actually incurred travel expenses. Reed obtained a dispensation from HMRC in relation to travel expenses. There were, however, some odd features of the scheme. The temp obtained very little benefit from the salary sacrifice; most of the benefit accrued to Reed. The amount sacrificed bore no relationship to the amount of the dispensation. It was virtually impossible for the temp to know what salary she was sacrificing, even if she had realised that she was making a salary sacrifice. A number of issues arose. Was there a salary sacrifice at all? No, said the Tribunal; the temp had sacrificed nothing and did not even know what she was purported to have sacrificed. No, agreed the UT, the FTT had been entitled to conclude that whilst the temps had agreed as a term of their contracts of employment to be paid in accordance with the current scheme, they had not agreed to be paid anything other than a salary derived from multiplying the agreed hourly rate by the number of hours worked. This conclusion reflects the principle in *Heaton v Bell* (see **7.77**). If there was a sacrifice, was it in exchange for an expense payment or simply for a different form of emolument? It was for a different form of earnings said the FTT. The UT agreed. Were the workplaces temporary ones? No, said the Tribunal; the overarching contract is not a contract of employment as Reed has no control over what the worker does in periods between assignments, the temp had no entitlement to consideration and there were no other provisions of the contract consistent with it being a contract of employment; accordingly each assignment was a separate employment, so each workplace was a permanent workplace in relation to that employment. Accordingly the travel expenses were costs of ordinary commuting. That was a conclusion they were entitled to reach agreed the UT. Did the dispensation cover the travel allowances? No, the allowances were not paid in respect of deductible expenses so could not be sums paid in respect of expenses within *ITEPA 2003, s 70* for which HMRC could grant a dispensation. Accordingly Reed should have accounted for PAYE and NIC, either because the travel allowances were emoluments or because, if they were expense allowances, they related to non-deductible expenditure. The UT agreed. The UT has a judicial review jurisdiction. It accordingly went on to consider whether Reed could have had a legitimate expectation that HMRC would abide by the dispensation. To create such an expectation, HMRC's promise that the tax would not be payable must be clear, unambiguous and devoid of relevant qualification (per *R v CIR ex parte, MFK Underwriting Agencies, 62 TC 607*). Could HMRC have lawfully given the dispensation? Yes, that is the whole point of a dispensation; it is an agreement that HMRC will not collect tax that is due. But to establish legitimate expectation, the taxpayer must put all of his cards face upwards on the table. He must make a full disclosure of what he proposed to do. Reed had not done that. They had told HMRC that they proposed to implement dispensations by way of a salary sacrifice and then constructed an arrangement which was ineffective to secure their aim. Accordingly PAYE and NIC remained payable on the allowances.

5.38A   The very fully-reasoned decision in *Reed* is well worth a read, albeit that it extends to over 100 pages. It emphasises a number of important legal principles. The key to determining whether there is a salary sacrifice is to ascertain the true construction of the contractual arrangements between the employer and employee as regards the payment of their remuneration. In Reed's case the temp's contractual terms did not include a provision by which she agreed to accept a reduction in her contractually agreed hourly rate; this was not varied by the agreement put in place under the scheme which created a separate payment to reimburse expenses. The UT commented that the scheme 'failed for the simple reason that Reed did not … make it clear to the Employed Temps that as a result of the scheme, their hourly rate had been reduced from £X to £Y with the reduction being paid as tax-free expenses'. It surmised that had the temps been told this, they would have realised that the scheme was intended primarily to benefit Reed and might well not have agreed to use it.

There was an interesting discussion on the effects of a staff handbook and similar documents that sit outside the contract of employment and are not specifically referenced within it. In *Briscoe v Lubrizol Ltd (2002 EWCA Civ 508)* the Court of Appeal said that, depending on the circumstances, incorporation in the contract of employment will not usually be required by the Court and in an employment context the language of a handbook will frequently be construed as giving rise to binding legal obligations as between employer and employee. The Court of Appeal in *Keeley v Fosroc International Ltd (2006 EWCA Civ 1277)* added that the provisions sought to be incorporated in the contract should not be in conflict with other contractual provisions. In *Carmichael v National Power Plc (1999 AC 1226)* the House of Lords held that in relation to employment contracts, it is not always appropriate to determine the contractual position solely from the written terms agreed at the outset of the relationship. In that case Lord Hoffman said that the normal rule about the construction of documents 'does not apply when the intention of the parties, objectively ascertained, has to be gathered partly from documents but also from oral exchanges and conduct. In the latter case, the terms of the contract are a question of fact. And of course the question of whether the parties intended a document to be the exclusive record of the terms of their agreement is also a question of fact'. In *Royal National Lifeboat Institution v Bushaway (2005 IRLR 674)* the Employment Appeal Tribunal said that even the existence of an entire contract clause is not conclusive.

The charge on emoluments under Chapter 1 of *ITEPA 2003* is separate from that on benefits under Chapter 3. The fact that an expense is incurred 'by reason of the employment' does not take an amount out of Chapter 1. It is only an expense incurred 'in the performance of the duties' that does so. The effect of Chapter 3 'is to impose a basis to charge income tax on payments made to employees which do not constitute Chapter 1 earnings and was not intended at the time it was enacted or since to make any change to what constitutes an "emolument" under Chapter 1'.

Reed's over-arching contract with the temps was held not to be a contract of employment because during the times when the temp was not working 'there was no mutual obligation that the employee will personally work for the employer in return for payment or retainer (the "wage/work") obligation' and that is an irreducible minimum for a contract of employment. This is different to the need for there to be mutuality of obligation between the parties for there to be a contract at all. The UT agreed with HMRC and the FTT 'that it would be wrong to read statutory concepts, such as that of continuity of employment, into the definition in *s 4, ITEPA 2003*, which is concerned with contractual rights. While there may be no employment contract in being in a gap period between assignments, the time may nevertheless count for employment law purposes towards the employee's period of employment for statutory purposes'. In Reed's case there was no obligation on Reed to provide work. This contrasted with the position in the EAT case of *ABC News Intercontinental Inc v Gizbert* (unreported) where there was a commitment for the employer to offer 100 days of work per annum and a commitment on the employee to consider assignments in good faith, which the EAT held gave sufficient mutuality to found a contract of employment.

Lorry drivers

5.39   There are also special concessions for lorry drivers. No tax charge will arise if an employer reimburses to the driver the extra cost of travelling and subsistence which the employee incurs because he is away on duty. Where a driver travels full-time in the course of his duty the additional cost of meals at restaurants and cafes over what he would have spent if he were able to get home for meals can similarly be reimbursed – unless the driver travels only in a limited area. The driver is expected to produce bills or vouchers (*SP 16/80*).

5.40   Even where travel is in the course of the employment it is not sufficient for it to be convenient to use a particular mode of transport. Thus, where a civil servant claimed to deduct the excess of the cost of using his car when travelling on official business over the mileage allowance he received, it was held that he was not 'necessarily obliged' to incur this expense as it was not a condition of his employment that he had to use the car and there was no evidence that he could not have travelled by public transport (*Marsden v IRC 42 TC 326*).

Temporary absence

5.41   As explained at **5.20** an employee who is temporarily sent to work away from his normal place of work can claim a deduction of expenses necessarily incurred in travelling to the temporary place and also for accommodation and subsistence at that place. Two conditions must be met: the absence must not be expected to exceed 24 months (and must not do so in fact) and the employee must return to his normal place of work at the end of the temporary assignment. This rule is not limited to a temporary workplace in the UK and will, accordingly, cover hotel and subsistence expenses if an employee is sent by his employer to work overseas for, say, three or four months.

Personal incidental overnight expenses

5.42   There is a specific exemption from tax for incidental overnight expenses of up to £5 a night in the UK and £10 a night elsewhere. It covers sums paid to, or on behalf of, a director or employee wholly and exclusively for the purpose of defraying any expenses which are incidental to the employee being away from his usual place of abode during a qualifying absence from home and which would not otherwise be deductible as an expense. A qualifying absence from home means a continuous period throughout which the employee is obliged to stay away from his usual place of abode and during which he has at least one overnight stay and all of such stays are at places to which the travelling expenses are deductible in calculating taxable employment income (other than under the special provisions in *sections 371* (see **13.32**), *374* (see **12.57**) and *376* (see **13.25**)) or, if there are no travelling expenses (e.g. because he travels with someone else at no extra cost), such expenses would have been deductible had they been incurred (*ITEPA 2003, ss 240, 241*). The exemption also applies where the stay is at a place to which the employee has gone for training, education, etc. within *ITEPA 2003, ss 250* (see **9.66**) or, *s 255* (see **9.69**). [*ITEPA 2003, s 240(6)*].

5.43   The relief does not apply to expenses borne by the employee; they must be either reimbursed to him or incurred by the employer. The £5 and £10 limits are *de minimis* figures. If the expense is £5.01 the whole amount is taxable. The limit applies to the total payment, aggregating cash payments, payments by non-cash vouchers, credit tokens and payments of expenses (*ITEPA 2003, s 241(2)*). Where the stay covers a number of consecutive nights the aggregate expenses are compared with £5 or £10 multiplied by the total number of nights; each night cannot be considered on its own (*ITEPA 2003, s 241(3)*). A night and an overnight stay are not defined. However, the £5 figure applies if the whole of the night is spent in the UK and the £10 figure if any part of the night is spent outside the UK. As the legislation refers to at least one overnight 'stay' the position on nights' travelling is unclear.

Example

Jack and Jill, two employees of Aquarian Enterprises Ltd, went on a business trip to New York. Jack caught a flight on Monday afternoon which got him into New York at 5.00pm (New York time) as he had a preliminary meeting at 9.00am Tuesday morning. Jill caught a flight on Tuesday morning which got her to New York at 2.30pm local time for their afternoon meeting. They both caught the 9.00pm flight to London on Tuesday night which arrives at Heathrow at 9.00am Wednesday morning.

Jack had an overnight stay in New York on Monday. He had a continuous period from Monday afternoon to Wednesday morning throughout which he was obliged to stay away from his UK place of abode. This absence included two nights, Monday and Tuesday, spent at least partly outside the UK (as most of Tuesday night was spent either in New York or over the Atlantic). His allowance is accordingly £20.

Jill's position is unclear. Depending on how one defines night – as when night starts in the UK it is mid-afternoon in New York – she could be said to have spent part of the night in New York as it would have been about 2.00am London time when her flight home left. She certainly spent part of the night on the aircraft. But is that sufficient? Did she have an overnight stay anywhere? Probably, as she stayed away from her UK home overnight even if she did not stay in any one place during that time.

5.44 This exemption covers personal expenses such as newspapers, hotel videos, telephone calls home, etc. that are not incurred for business purposes. The idea is to relieve employers of the obligation to scrutinise hotel bills and isolate such personal expenses on the form P11D. The limit is so small that it is doubtful whether it achieves that objective. It is likely that in most cases the detailed scrutiny will still be needed to check if the *de minimis* limit is breached. If the employer has a policy requiring repayment of any excess personal expense over the £5 or £10 limit no tax liability will arise provided the excess is actually repaid. HMRC say that in such circumstances there may be reporting consequences, i.e. the amount needs to be shown on the P11D, if the refund is not made within a reasonable time of the payment (*IR Press Release 16 May 1995*). Where an item is covered by the exemption it does not need to be shown on the P11D.

Directors

5.45 By concession, a director of two or more companies in a group or a collection of associated companies (or a person who is a director of one company and an employee of another) is regarded as having one place at which he normally acts as a director of all the companies concerned. This enables travel between the offices or places of business of all the companies to be allowable as being necessarily incurred in the course of his duties. This concession applies only to UK travel (*ESC A4*). It is not expressed to apply to mere employees.

5.46 A director who gives his services free to a company 'not managed with a view to dividends' (which probably means with a view to profit – HMRC instance a company that owns a hall or sports ground or runs a club) is not taxed on any travelling expenses reimbursed to him, even if they are from home to the company's premises (*ESC A4*).

5.47 By concession, if a director or higher-paid employee on an overseas business trip takes his wife with him because his health is so precarious that he cannot undertake foreign travel unaccompanied, and the employer pays the wife's expenses, these are not assessed on the husband (*ESC A4*).

5.48 The expenses of a county surveyor in attending a world road conference in Tokyo were held not to be allowable even though he wanted to discuss with other experts there a problem arising from his work. He went at his own expense and in his own time. His employer did not require him to attend and thus the expense was not necessarily incurred (*Owen v Burden 47 TC 476*).

Benchmark scale rates for day subsistence

5.49   HMRC has introduced an advisory system of benchmark scale rate which employers can use to make subsistence payments to employees who incur subsistence expenses while travelling on a business journey. Payment at or below the scale rate will not attract tax or National Insurance. These rates cannot be used for employees who have to stay overnight. The rates are:

breakfast rate	£5.00
one meal rate	£5.00
two meal rate	£10.00
late evening meal rate	£15.00

The breakfast rate applies only to irregular early starters and only where the worker leaves home earlier than usual and before 6.00am. The meal rate only applies if the worker has been away from his home or normal place of work for at least five hours for the one meal rate or ten hours for the two meal rate. The late evening rate applies to irregular late finishes only and only if the employee has to work later than usual and finishes work after 8.00pm. It can be paid in addition to the meal rate in appropriate cases. In all cases the employee must actually incur cost on a meal (food and drink) after starting his journey and the employee must be absent from his normal place of work or home for a continuous period of at least five hours. These rates can be used only if the employer first applies to HMRC for a dispensation and satisfies them that he has adequate management processes in place to ensure that payments are only made where all of the qualifying conditions are met (HMRC Brief 24/2009). These rates have never been rerated.

Expense allowances

5.50   HMRC frequently contend that if an employer does not pay for an expense, that is *prima facie* evidence that the employee was not necessarily obliged to incur it. Whilst there would appear to be no legal basis for this, it is probably a reasonable starting point in most cases. If an employee is likely to incur expenses that, for one reason or another, he does not wish to ask his employer to reimburse, he should ask his employer to designate part of his salary as an expense allowance. Such an allowance would at least rebut HMRC's *prima facie* inference, as the very payment of the allowance suggests that the employee is expected to incur expenses that will not be specifically reimbursed.

In the performance of duties

5.51   The second hurdle is whether an expense is incurred in the performance of the duties of the employment. This is where most litigants fail. The problems with travel expenses have already been considered but similar problems arise with other expenses. The question that the courts normally pose is whether the person was performing his duties at the time he was reaping the fruits of the expenditure. In *Humbles v Brooks 40 TC 500*, where a history teacher attended weekend lectures to update his knowledge of history, it was held that while he was sitting in the lecture room he was not teaching and thus while the expenditure was of benefit to his duties it was not in the performance of them. Even where a student laboratory assistant was required at his employer's expense to attend classes in preparation for a university degree he was denied relief for travelling expenses and text books as it was held that his attendance at the classes, although a condition of his employment, was not in the performance of it (*Blackwell v Mills 26 TC 468*). In *Lupton v Potts 45 TC 643* examination fees paid by a solicitor's articled clerk were disallowed. He did not need to pass the examination to carry out his duties and the expenditure was not incurred in the course of them. Employment agency fees to obtain a job are to place a person in a position to perform the duties of that job, not incurred in the performance of it (*Shortt v McIlgorm 26 TC 262*). In *Ansell v Brown [2001] STC 1166* dietary supplements taken by a professional Rugby Union player were held, reversing the decision of the General Commissioners, not to have been incurred in the performance of his duties. The employment contract required Mr Brown 'to maintain at all times a high standard of physical fitness'. The judge thought it plain that 'the expenditure on supplements was incurred for the purpose of achieving and maintaining the required level of fitness and the required size and physique for a back-row forward', but held that was expenditure to enable him to perform the duties and not in the performance itself. He also added that in any event the need for the expenditure arose from Mr Brown's own personal circumstances, namely his need to increase his weight, which would have meant that the 'necessary' test was not met either. The taxpayer was similarly unsuccessful in *Emms v HMRC SpC 668*. This concerned another professional rugby player. His contract of employment identified any failure to maintain a high standard of physical fitness as gross misconduct justifying dismissal. He claimed a deduction for protein drinks, multi-vitamins and medicines to repair and protect his joints. The Special Commissioners held that the supplements, etc. were incurred to enable him to perform his duties, not in their performance. They also found duality of purpose as the expenditure was governed by the requirements of a balanced diet and healthy living which secured enduring health benefits for him. The duality point seems questionable. It appears to confuse result with purpose. In *Ben Nevis v IRC [2001] STC (SCD) 144), SpC 281* an employee could work for his employer only if he were registered with the Securities Association. The Association declined to register him because he was under investigation by his previous employer. The new employer agreed to allow his employment to continue but on condition that he kept it informed of developments in the investigation. The taxpayer was ultimately exonerated by the investigation. The legal fees incurred by the employee were held not to be in the performance of the duties of the new employment; the taxpayer was merely putting himself in a position to perform those duties. Course fees incurred by a trainee accountant were disallowed in *Perrin v HMRC SpC 671* even though the employee had to pay for the courses under the terms of his contract and a failure to attend the courses was an event that would justify summary dismissal. It was held that the cost was not incurred in the performance of his duties. The nature of his job did not require the expenditure on the courses even though his attendance at them was required by his contract. This emphasises that the test is whether the nature of the job requires the doing of the act which gives rise to the expenditure: 'The expenses of doing an act is not deductible just because it is made a condition of the contract of employment that the act has to be done' (Lord Browne-Wilkinson in *Fitzpatrick v CIR 66 TC 407* – see **5.71**).

5.52   A particularly harsh case is *Snowdon v Charnock [2001] STC (SCD) 152, SpC 282*. Dr Snowdon was a doctor and a psychiatrist. This qualification enabled him to act as a psychotherapist. He was employed as a Higher Specialist Registrar in Psychotherapy. This is a training post including supervised clinical work. The taxpayer incurred psychotherapy fees for personal analysis, half of the cost of which was reimbursed by his employer. HMRC accepted that that half was not taxable on Dr Snowdon by virtue of *s 251* (see **9.63**), ie work-related training. Dr Snowdon claimed a deduction for the other 50 per cent. His employment contract required him to undergo personal therapy and described this both as a duty of the post and a condition of the employment. The personal therapy was required to enable Dr Snowdon to put himself in the shoes of a patient so as to be able to realise the likely effect of his clinical advice. Although the judge felt the case to be a borderline one, he held that the taxpayer was not required to spend the money in the performance of his duties. 'While he was undergoing personal therapy he was not performing the duties under the contract of employment'. It is hard to see why not if it was a specific duty, but the judge was clearly swayed by the fact that the job was a training post and that the psychotherapy was a training requirement of the Royal College of Psychiatrists and thus enabled the taxpayer to become better qualified to perform his duties.

5.53   The taxpayer was successful in *HMRC v Banerjee (No 1) [2010] STC 2318*. Dr Banerjee was a specialist registrar. She was employed by an NHS Trust and worked at a hospital. Her terms of employment required her to continue to hold a national training number throughout her training period (five years). To do so she was required to attend meetings, courses and conferences as prescribed by the supervisor for dermatology specialist registrars. The hospital did not provide or pay for such courses. The General Commissioners decided in her favour. On appeal Henderson J upheld their decision on the basis that, 'their decision turns on the fact that they identified Dr Banerjee's duties under her contract of employment as including attendance at the relevant courses. That may be a relatively unusual state of affairs, but it is not conceptually impossible or obviously absurd; and where that is the true state of affairs as found by the sole tribunal of fact, I can see no error of law in the conclusion that expenditure incurred on attending the courses is deductible'. He felt that the 'principle that expenditure is deductible only if it is incurred in the performance of the duties … is not in any way undermined by the decision of the General Commissioners in this case'. The Court of Appeal agreed (albeit that there was a split decision on the wholly and exclusively issue). Rimmer J thought it 'tolerably obvious … that the reason why Dr Banerjee attended the courses and incurred the expense she did in doing so was because she was required to attend them as part of the duties of her employment and because if she did not do so, her employment would have been terminated. Had her employment so terminated, she would not have completed her training course and her prospect of qualifying as a consultant would presumably have been either destroyed or diminished. The reality is that it was not the attendance at the individual courses that provided the key to her future professional advancement, it was the completion of the training course as a whole that did so; and the relevant expenditure was incurred so as to enable her to complete it. It therefore appears to me to be artificial to fix upon particular aspects of the training contract and identify the expenditure relating to it as in part incurred for the purpose of obtaining some collateral benefit over and above the purpose of satisfying the obligations of the employment contracts [ie as attributing to the fact that an element of the course would contribute to attaining cnsultant status at some stage as an additional purpose of doing the course, rather than as a collateral benefit arisng from it. Nor, more importantly, do I consider that that is what the General Commissioners in fact found.'

Domestic help

5.54   Domestic help to enable a person to take up or continue in employment is not an allowable expense as the employee is neither necessarily obliged to incur the expense, nor incurs it in the performance of the duties. A married couple employed jointly at a single salary as master and mistress of a school could not deduct the cost of a housekeeper engaged to carry out the household duties while the wife was working (*Bowers v Harding 3 TC 22*). A widower could not deduct a payment to a housekeeper to look after his children while he was at work (*Halstead v Condon 46 TC 289*). The costs of a child minder or of putting a child in a crèche so that the mother can work will similarly not be deductible although, in fairly limited circumstances, there is now an exemption from tax in relation to the provision of crèche facilities by the employer (see **6.39(m)** below).

Duality of purpose

5.55   The third hurdle is that to qualify for a deduction an expense must be wholly and exclusively incurred in the performance of the duties (the word 'necessarily' does not seem to add much in this context as once a person is necessarily obliged to incur an expense, that expense is likely automatically to be necessarily incurred).

Mallalieu v Drummond

5.56   The most important case in this area is the self-employment case of *Mallalieu v Drummond 57 TC 330*. Under the self-employment income rules, expenditure has to meet the 'wholly and exclusively' test (but not the 'necessarily obliged' one). This case is particularly important because it is a House of Lords decision. Miss Mallalieu was a barrister. The Bar Council requires that in court a lady barrister should wear black dresses, suits, tights and shoes and white shirts or blouses. Miss Mallalieu did not wear black and white on social occasions. She had an extensive, colourful wardrobe. She gave evidence that when buying clothes for court work her only motive was to comply with the bar's rules of professional conduct. It was held that the expenditure was not wholly and exclusively incurred in the performance of the duties as she had a dual motive for incurring it. The secondary motive was to meet the normal human requirements of warmth and decency. Although she may have consciously only had in her mind the rules of professional conduct she must have subconsciously realised that she could not have appeared in court naked. In the House of Lords, Lord Brightman sought to draw a distinction between the *Mallalieu* circumstances and cases where a person is required to wear a uniform or a costume, but as he thought the difference was self-evident did not bother to explain it. This is unfortunate. It is by no means self-evident, at least to the author, that a waitress required to wear a uniform or an entertainer wearing a costume do not thereby satisfy their needs of warmth and decency.

5.57   The real answer probably lies in the *Edwards v Bairstow 36 TC 207* principle that the courts can disturb a finding of fact by the Commissioners only if no reasonable body of Commissioners properly instructed in the law could have arrived at it. The General Commissioners having found that Miss Mallalieu had a (subconscious) motive of the preservation of warmth and decency, even though there was no specific evidence presented to this effect, were entitled to reach that conclusion – indeed Lord Brightman was of the opinion that he would have found it impossible to reach any other conclusion. The clothes were 'ordinary' clothes and Miss Mallalieu not only wore them in court but also in her chambers and on the way to and from court. She therefore in practice satisfied to a significant degree her need for warmth and decency. A uniform or a costume is not normally suitable for wear outside the work environment so it is unlikely that a body of Commissioners would find a dual motive in such expenditure. However, some uniforms are suitable for wear outside work – shop assistants employed by Marks & Spencer, for example, frequently wear their uniforms to and from the shop – but these do not seem to have been attacked by HMRC.

Clothing

5.58   The other practical explanation, of course, is that uniform or costume cases are unlikely, in general, to come before the courts. HMRC have long adopted the stance that if clothing is suitable for everyday use it cannot be wholly and exclusively incurred for business purposes. If it is not suitable for everyday use any non-business benefit is incidental to the business purpose. It is improbable, even in the light of *Mallalieu v Drummond*, that suitability or unsuitability for everyday use can be the statutory test as to whether expenditure is incurred wholly and exclusively for business purposes. If, for example, an actor buys a lounge suit to wear in a play and only ever wears it on stage, the fact that he could have worn it on other occasions is unlikely to detract from the fact that his professional use of it is likely to have been the motive for its acquisition. Equally, the fact that clothing is specially reinforced to meet the rigours of a stage performance is likely to support a motive that the expenditure was wholly and exclusively for business purposes even though in outward appearance it may be indistinguishable from a suit for everyday wear. Nevertheless, the *Mallalieu v Drummond* decision has in practice resulted in

HMRC challenging expenditure on clothing – and indeed on other expenditure that satisfies a personal need – far more rigorously than before. On the other hand, they seem to have adopted a test that if a logo or the name of the employer is permanently affixed to the clothes that will satisfy the test of deductibility, even if it is so small that it is not readily readable. It is difficult to discern a statutory justification for this distinction. The *Mallalieu v Drummond* principle is not confined to clothing. HMRC are increasingly putting it forward as an argument over a wide range of cases.

Entertainers

5.59   The problem is, in practice, particularly acute in the entertainment professions as the modern trend is for musicians to wear everyday casual clothing, for many plays to be performed in everyday wear, rather than in period costume, and for other entertainers to adopt an everyday, casual look. Fortunately, many Inspectors of Taxes seem to adopt a commonsense approach to stage clothing, although not all do. Few seem to be sympathetic, however, to the problem that to support a public image a person often has to adopt a far more expensive mode of dress than he or she would ordinarily have chosen on occasions when they are in the public eye, such as at press receptions, film premieres, industry get-togethers, etc.

Earlier court cases

5.60   *Mallalieu v Drummond* was not, of course, the first case where a deduction for clothing was in dispute. A computer engineer who wore a suit and tie only at work because his employer required him to be presentably dressed when working at customers' premises, was refused a deduction for the cost of such clothing seven years before the *Mallalieu* case was heard on the same grounds, namely that he wore the clothing for the private purpose of warmth and decency as well as for a working purpose (*Hillyer v Leeke 51 TC 90*). An engineer who claimed the cost of suits and other clothing for everyday wear on the basis that his expenditure was heavier than normal because of damage by oil from the machinery he was servicing was denied this, although he was allowed a deduction for the cost of overalls (*Woodcock v IRC 51 TC 698*). Similarly a surveyor was refused a deduction for everyday clothing he wore on-site visits (*Ward v Dunn 52 TC 517*) and a plainclothes policeman was taxed on a clothing allowance paid to him, while being refused a deduction for the expenditure (*Fergusson v Noble 7 TC 176*).

5.61   In *Sanderson v Durbidge 36 TC 238*, a local government officer was refused a deduction for the excess of the cost of evening meals eaten out when he attended council meetings over what he would normally have spent on meals. A claim to deduct only part of an expense, as in this case, is invariably fatal as it amounts to an admission of duality of purpose. A civil servant living at an overseas naval base was refused a deduction for the extra costs of living abroad as compared with living in the UK (and was taxed on the allowance the Government paid him towards such costs) (*Robinson v Corry 18 TC 411*).

5.62   The extra cost to a water board employee who was required to live near his work in central London over what he would have paid had he lived in the suburbs was disallowed in *Bolam v Barlow 31 TC 136*, as was the cost of a London flat (provided by the company) for a company director who was required by his employer to move to London (*McKie v Warner 40 TC 65*). Mess expenses of Army officers were held not to be deductible in *Lomax v Newton 34 TC 558* and *Griffiths v Mockler 35 TC 135* and lodging expenses of an army officer allotted a civilian billet in lieu of accommodation at barracks was held not deductible – and the lodging allowance paid to him was held to constitute taxable income – in *Nagley v Spilsbury 37 TC 178*.

5.63   Perhaps one of the unluckiest cases in the duality of purpose area is the trading income case of *Prince v Mapp 46 TC 169*. The taxpayer, a professional guitarist, was also an architect. He cut his finger sharpening a pencil and the guitar strings kept catching in the cut. He claimed the cost of plastic surgery to remedy the problem to enable him to play the guitar properly. This was refused because in cross-examination he admitted that he sometimes played the guitar when with friends – which enabled the Commissioners to find duality of purpose: although the operation was wholly and exclusively to enable him to play the guitar it was not wholly and exclusively to enable him to play it professionally.

Telephone costs

5.64   Another area to fall foul of the duality of purpose test – and one where HMRC are now usually challenging claims for a deduction – is the telephone rental charge. Even where a telephone is installed specifically at an employee's home so that he can be contacted by his employer outside normal working hours, the cost of rental is incurred so that the telephone is available to make and receive both business and private calls and thus has a dual purpose (*Lucas v Cattell 48 TC 353*). A disallowance similarly arose in *Nolder v Walters 15 TC 380* where telephone rental was claimed and in *Hamerton v Overy 35 TC 73* where a proportion of the rental was claimed. Even if an employer were to install a telephone in an employee's home and forbid him to use it for personal calls it is likely that HMRC would still refuse a deduction on the basis that the telephone is available for incoming personal calls. The fear of abuse by allowing a deduction for the, normally, very minor cost of private telephone calls is exemplified by the rules for mobile telephones (see **9.33**). If a mobile telephone is provided by the employer the government are willing to accept that private use is likely to be *de minimis* and have exempted such calls. However if the employee provides his own mobile telephone and the employer picks up the bill any rental or similar cost will be taxable on the employee in the same way as with a fixed phone and the cost of personal calls will constitute a benefit in kind.

5.65   Telephone costs illustrate two important principles in relation to duality of purpose. The first is that the *Act* will not allow a deduction for part of an expense; it is all or nothing. Accordingly, rental costs are, strictly speaking, disallowable in full even if the telephone is used predominantly for business purposes. In practice, HMRC's approach to the 'all or nothing' principle varies considerably from Inspector to Inspector and from one expense to another but they generally adopt a commonsense approach. If an expense is predominantly for business a proportion will normally be allowed; if it is mainly for personal reasons HMRC will generally resist a deduction for any part of the expenses.

The 'motive' test

5.66 It should be borne in mind that the test is a motive test, 'Why was the expenditure incurred?' If the motive was solely a business motive it does not matter that the taxpayer may obtain a personal benefit as a side effect of the expenditure. For example, if an employee is sent to Manchester to visit his company's branch and takes the opportunity to have lunch with a friend who lives there, there is little doubt that the fare was wholly and exclusively incurred for the business purpose and that meeting the friend was not a secondary motive of going to Manchester, but merely an opportunity resulting from the wholly business expenditure. Even the *Mallalieu* decision does not breach this principle; it merely stresses that the professed motive for incurring an expense may not be the sole motive. The test is a subjective one. What matters is why the expenditure was actually incurred rather than why the taxpayer thought that he was incurring it. As indicated earlier, a claim to deduct part of an expense is effectively an admission of duality of purpose. In many cases such a claim might be put forward as a compromise. The possibility of deriving some personal advantage from an expense frequently calls into question whether there may have been a dual motive in incurring it or whether the private benefit merely resulted from the business needs. Neither HMRC nor taxpayers generally want to take disputes over small amounts of expenditure to appeal and the allowance of part of the expenditure is normally a compromise that satisfies both sides. Nevertheless, an initial claim for part will not necessarily be perceived by an Inspector as an offer of a compromise; it is more likely to be seen as an admission of a dual purpose.

Apportionment of expenditure

5.67 The second principle illustrated by telephone expenses is that some expenses are in reality a totality of a series of separate expenditures, each of which might be wholly and exclusively for a specific purpose. In such circumstances it is permissible to break the expense down into its constituent parts. Thus, telephone calls are charged by the call. If a person makes 50 telephone calls in a quarter, of which 30 are for business, a claim to deduct 60 per cent of the cost of calls is not a statement that there was a dual purpose in making any individual call. It merely seeks to segregate the cost of business calls from the extraneous cost of personal calls which, for convenience, the telephone company has included on the same bill. As indicated at **5.46**, the decision in *Kirkwood v Evans ([2002] EWHC 30(Ch)), (2002 STC 231)* may have cast doubt on this principle.

5.68 There are a great many other expenses which vary with usage, such as electricity, gas, petrol, etc. Such items may not be purchased by the unit but nevertheless, where it is possible to attribute part of the cost of an item to wholly business use, it is permissible to do so because they are used by the unit. Where apportionment is not strictly possible, although it frequently occurs in practice, is with items (such as a television licence) where the expenditure permits an item to be used for a fixed period and part of the usage during that period is for non-business purposes. In such a case HMRC consider that the expenditure is incurred to make the item available for the mixed business and private use.

5.69   A chink in the duality of purpose wall was disclosed in *Westcott v Bryan 45 TC 476*. Mr Bryan, the managing director of a major public company, was required by the company to live in a house that reflected his position, as they regarded it as of paramount importance that overseas visitors should be entertained by him at his home. The company purchased a very large house, far larger than Mr Bryan would have chosen, for his occupation and paid all the expenses of it. HMRC sought to tax him on the expenses. The Commissioners found that there was a genuine business use of the house and that Mr Bryan's personal use was restricted in that he was not free to discriminate as to his guests. They allowed 25 per cent of the expenses as being for business purposes and held that Mr Bryan was taxable on the other 75 per cent. HMRC appealed (as far as the Court of Appeal) on the basis that expenses can only be apportioned if the benefit to the company is severable from that to the director, for example, where there is a specific room set aside for business purposes. It was held that this was too strict a test. 'Some part of the expense is for the company's benefit, and not for the director's benefit. It may not be a severable part, but it is undoubtedly some part and there should be an apportionment' (Lord Denning MR, *45 TC* at p. 490). This case illustrates that where there is more than one motive for expenditure this may not be fatal if the reason is that the motive of the employer differs from that of the employee.

Claims disallowed by the courts

5.70   Other claims for deductions for expenses that have been disallowed include the cost of subscription by a bank manager to a club, even though membership was required by the employer, as the employee was not performing the duties of his employment while he was at the club (*Brown v Bullock 40 TC 1*); costs of lighting and heating a separate room in which an insurance agent's sons could do their homework while he interviewed clients at his home (*Roskams v Bennett 32 TC 129*); the expenses of the directors of a family farming company of taking part in an overseas tour organised for British farmers, partly to visit farms and partly for sightseeing, as there was a dual purpose for the expense (*Thomson v White 43 TC 256*); and the costs borne by the employer of defending a company director against a dangerous driving charge which could have led to him going to prison, thus depriving the company of his services (*Rendell v Went 41 TC 641*) and the costs of a qualified registrar in general surgery employed as a specialist registrar in attending training courses and obtaining his Certificate of Specialist Training which enabled him to seek a position as a consultant, even though he was required to do so under the terms of his employment contract (*HMRC v Decadt [2007] All ER(D) 139*). If the taxpayer in *Roskams v Bennett* had set aside a room to interview clients, rather than setting aside one for his children, he would undoubtedly have obtained his deduction. The decision in *Brown v Bullock* can be contrasted with that in favour of the taxpayer in *Ellwood v Utitz 42 TC 482* where the purpose of joining the club was to obtain accomodation when in London more cheaply than at a hotel.

5.71 In *Smith v Abbott* and *Fitzpatrick v IRC 66 TC 407*, two cases on similar facts which were heard together by the House of Lords, it was held that the expenses incurred by journalists in buying newspapers were not incurred in the performance of their duties, in spite of a finding of fact that a newspaper proprietor expected or required his journalists to read widely.

5.72 Some of the reasoning is difficult to follow. Particularly worrying is Lord Templeman's comment that 'If deductions of this kind were allowed in one case every journalist or other similar employee would claim to be entitled to deduct the payment made by him for every newspaper and periodical which he chose to purchase and there would be no end to it. A sports reporter is employed to report sport, not to read newspapers ... A journalist who reads newspapers does so in order to be able to perform his duties to the highest possible standard but he does not read in performance of his duties ... there was some dispute as to whether a journalist was required as a condition of his employment to read newspapers ... But it appears from *Blackwell v Mills* that this dispute is not relevant ... It seems to me impossible to say that when the sports reporter was reading newspapers in the quiet of his home he was performing the duties of a sports reporter either at the offices of the newspaper or on location ... It does not matter therefore whether ... the journalists were contractually bound by their employers to expend money in the purchase of other newspapers and magazines ... Whether or not a journalist thinks it is necessary to read one or more newspaper and periodical his duty is the production of his employer's newspaper and he is not carrying out that duty when he is reading other newspapers.'

5.73 This goes far beyond anything that HMRC have ever sought to claim. It is difficult to see any reason why the duties of a job should have to be performed either at the office or on location. There is no logical reason why an employer should not require a person to carry out a number of duties leaving him free to determine where they are carried out. Nor is it clear why a sports reporter should have only a single duty, to report sport, so that other things that he is required to do which are peripheral or supplementary to that function cease to be duties of the employment. The distinction drawn by Lord Templeman, between the performance of the duties and preparatory work seems suspect as he does not appear to even consider the full scope of the duty. In a dissenting judgment Lord Browne-Wilkinson poses the test that 'whether or not a particular operation is a duty of the employment has to be determined objectively, i.e. by answering the question "Does the nature of the job require the doing of the act which gives rise to the expenditure?"', which seems a far more satisfactory approach and does at least give weight to the finding of fact of the extent of the duties.

5.74   *Hinsley v HMRC* and *Milsom v HMRC [2007] STC (SCD) 63* are interesting. Mr Hinsley and Mr Milsom are airline pilots. It is normal in the airline industry to require a pilot to reimburse training costs if he leaves within a specified period. Both pilots made such a reimbursement and claimed to deduct the payment as an expense. The Special Commissioners held that it was not. It was not paid as a necessary consequence of continuing to perform the duties after notice to terminate was given. Even if the expenses had been incurred ab initio by the employee it was also not a necessary one, albeit that virtually all new pilot entrants to the industry require such training, as that fact looks at the circumstances of the individual not at the requirements of the job. The Commissioners noted that had the remuneration during the notice period been reduced by the reimbursed amount, or had the new employer agreed to reimburse the old and reduced the pilot's earnings to reflect that payment, the pilot would have been taxable only on the amount he actually received, but commented that the fact that two transactions have the same economic result does not mean that they should have the same tax result. Another issue in this case was the year in which relief was due. It was obviously not necessary to answer that question in the circumstances, but the Commissioners nevertheless did so, holding that it is due in the tax year in which the unconditional obligation to incur and defray the expense arose, not in that in which it was paid.

5.75   An example of the strictness of the tests is *Guarantor v HMRC [2008] STC (SCD) 1154*. The taxpayer was a director of a company and owned 5 per cent of its shares. The company got into financial difficulties and the directors had to give personal guarantees. The guarantee was to subsist for four months after a person ceased to be a director. The director's guarantee was called after he had left the company and he was forced to make payments under it of £12,972. He claimed it as a deduction under *ITEPA 2003, s 336(1)* on the basis that as a director he was obliged to enter into the guarantee. HMRC claimed that a person can perform the duties of a director without entering into a guarantee. They accepted that had the directors not done so the company would have ceased to exist but that would have been a consequence of the company's poor financial position. Guaranteeing the debt may have enabled the company to survive and this enabled him to continue to perform his duties, but it was not something he did in the course of those duties. HMRC also pointed out that the payment was made some two years after Guarantor had ceased to be a director. At the time he left office he had no more than a contingent liability, and when it crystallised he was no longer in employment so that the expenses could not be incurred in the course of carrying out his duties. Finally HMRC said that, whatever Guarantor's primary purpose and motive in entering into the guarantee, he also had the purpose of protecting his investment in the company and his own position as a director and employee. The Special Commissioner agreed with HMRC. He pointed out in particular both that the expense was incurred only after the employment came to an end so was not in the course of the employment. He also commented that, 'the taxpayer gained some benefit, albeit in the event very short-lived from the company's ability to continue to trade'. This last comment is worrying. 'Incurred wholly and exclusively', looks at the motive or purpose for making a payment. It does not look at benefit. If the motive is wholly employment-related, any incidental benefit, however significant, ought to be irrelevant. To treat the receipt of a benefit as evidence of a dual purpose seems to greatly extend the 'unconscious motive' test in *Mallalieu v Drummond* (see **5.56**).

Trading income cases

5.76   Trading income cases where a claim to deduct expenses was disallowed and which have relevance for employees include the cost of a visit to North America partly to attend a professional conference and partly for a holiday (*Bowden v Russell and Russell 42 TC 301*); the cost of medical expenses where the ill health arose from the taxpayer's working conditions (*Norman v Golder 26 TC 293*); medical expenses of an architect and guitarist (*Prince v Mapp 46 TC 169* – see **5.63**) and the cost of a private room in a nursing home so that the taxpayer could carry on his business whilst recovering from medical treatment (*Murgatroyd v Evans-Jackson 43 TC 581*). The problem in each case was duality of purpose.

5.77   One item that the taxpayer succeeded in deducting was the cost to a solicitor of business lunches with clients (the food and drink of the partner was a side benefit derived from the solely business purpose of entertaining the client) (*Bentleys, Stokes and Lowless v Beeson 33 TC 491*). Unfortunately, such expenditure is now non-deductible by statute.

Expenses where remittance basis applies

5.78   If the income is assessable on a remittance the expense must either have been paid out of the earnings (ie out of the amount remitted) or must have been paid in the UK either in the year of remittance or an earlier year in which the employer was a UK resident and must be such that it would have qualified as a deductible expense if the earnings of the year in which the expense was incurred had been taxable when received. [*ITEPA 2003, s 353*]. Obviously the same expense cannot be deducted twice if part of the emoluments from an employment are taxable on a remittance basis and part on a receipts basis. [*ITEPA 2003, s 354*].

Members of Parliament

5.79   A Member of Parliament cannot claim a deduction for expenditure on (or in connection with) the provision or use of residential or overnight accommodation to enable him to perform his duties as an MP, whether that accommodation is in his constituency or near the Houses of Parliament. [*ITEPA 2003, s 360*]. This is because he is paid an allowance to cover the additional expenses necessarily incurred in staying overnight away from his main residence for the purpose of performing his parliamentary duties and that allowance is exempt from tax. [*ITEPA 2003, s 292* as originally enacted]. From 7 May 2010, the tax exemption (and the *section 360* restriction) applies to a payment under the *Parliamentary Standards Act 2009, s 5(1)*, which is either expressed to be made in respect of accommodation expenses (expenses necessarily incurred on overnight accommodation that is required for the performance of the member's parliamentary duties in or about the Palace of Westminster or the member's constituency) or related to, or in consequence of, a payment expressed to be so made [*ITEPA 2003, s 292(1), (2)* as substituted by *Finance (No 2) Act 2010 (F (No 2) Act 2010), Sch 4, para 2*]. The cost of an overnight stay in a hotel that was required only because the House was sitting late does not count as accommodation expenses unless it was sitting beyond 1.00am [*ITEPA 2003, s 292(3)*]. The tax exemption does not apply to a loan for a deposit payable at the commencement of a tenancy [*ITEPA 2003, s 292(4)*]. Presumably as such a loan will be made by the Independent Parliamentary Standards Authority but the MP is an employee of the House of Commons, such a loan will accordingly attract tax under the disguised remuneration provisions (see **3.28** onwards). From 1 November 2010, the exemption is extended to a payment made to a third party at the direction of a member (as permitted by the *Parliamentary Standards Act 2009, s 5(1)*) [*ITEPA 2003, s 292(5)* inserted by *Finance Act 2011 (FA 2011), s 37*].

5.80   There is a similar exemption for payments expressed to be in respect of relevant UK travel expenses (expenses necessarily incurred on journeys within the UK made by the member that are necessary for the performance of the member's parliamentary duties, and, if he shares caring responsibilities with his spouse or partner, journeys made by the spouse between the member's London Area residence and his Constituency residence) or relevant subsistence expenses (expenses necessarily incurred on an evening meal eaten on the Parliamentary Estate where the member is required to be at the House because it is sitting beyond 7.30pm (but excluding alcoholic drinks)) [*ITEPA 2003, s 293A* inserted by *F(No 2) A 2010, Sch 4, para 2*].

5.81   There is a further exemption for expenses paid to an MP (or member of the Scottish Parliament, Welsh Assembly or Northern Ireland Assembly), which is expressed to be made in respect of European travel expenses, namely the cost of travel between the UK and either a European Union institution or agency or the national parliament of another EU country, a candidate or applicant country or any other country which is a member of the Council of Europe [*ITEPA 2003, s 294* as amended by *F(No 2)A 2010, Sch 4, para 3*]. This is because the government regard such travel as in the course of the MP's parliamentary business so that it should be exempt from tax in the same way as expenses of travel on parliamentary duties within the UK. Up to 6 May 2010 the reference to countries of the Council of Europe was limited to EFTA (European Free Trade Association) countries.

5.82   There is a special exemption from some of the benefits in kind rules for government Ministers and holders of other salaried office under the *Ministerial and other Salaries Act 1975 (MOSA 1975)*, i.e. the Speaker and Opposition office-holders. The exemption covers:

(*a*)   transport or subsistence provided by the Crown to the office-holder or to any member of his family or household; and

(*b*)   the payment (or reimbursement) by the Crown of any expenses incurred in connection with the provision of transport or subsistence to the office-holder or members of his family.

The exemption applies even if the Minister is not actually paid a salary, as long as he is entitled to one. Head (*b*) includes the provision of a car (with or without a driver), the provision of car fuel and of any other benefit in connection with the car. It also includes food, drink and temporary living accommodation. [*ITEPA 2003, s 295*]. This provision was introduced 'to clarify the treatment of such items to avoid any uncertainty'.

5.83 All of these exemptions also apply to Ministers of the Scottish Parliament, the National Assembly for Wales and the Northern Ireland Assembly (*ITEPA 2003, ss 293, 294, 295*, formerly *Finance Act 1999 (FA 1999), s 52* and *Sch 5*).

Detached national experts, etc.

5.84 The daily subsistence allowances paid by the European Commission to persons whose services are made available by the Commission by their employers under the 'detached national experts scheme' established by the Commission on 26 July 1988 (or any replacement scheme) is exempt from tax. [*ITEPA 2003, s 304*]. Such allowances were previously not taxed by virtue of *ESC A84*.

5.85 From 1 January 2011, the tax exemption is extended to subsistence allowances paid by a 'relevant UK body' to persons who because of their expertise in matters relating to the subject matter of the functions of the relevant EU body, have been seconded to the body by their employees. The relevant EU bodies are the European Medicines Agency, the European Police College and the European Banking Authority. The Treasury have power by statutory instrument to add other designated EU bodies [*ITEPA 2003, s 304A* inserted by *FA 2011, s 38*]. There does not appear to be a tax exemption for salary payments (if any) by the body, but they are likely to be exempt under the *International Organisations Acts 1968* and *2005* (see **19.32**). The relief has been introduced because such secondments normally exceed two years, so the relief for a temporary workplace may not apply. The three EU bodies concerned are located in the UK. The exemption creates a level playing field with employees seconded to non-UK bodies (*Finance Bill 2011* Explanatory Notes).

Resettlement grants

5.86 There is also an exemption from tax for any grant or payment made or authorised by parliament:

(*a*)   to a person ceasing to be a member of the House of Commons on a dissolution of parliament;

(*b*)   to a person ceasing to hold certain ministerial and other offices;

(*c*)   as a resettlement grant for persons ceasing to be an MEP; or

(*d*)   to a person ceasing to be a member of the Scottish, Welsh or Northern Irish parliaments on a dissolution or ceasing to hold certain ministerial or other offices.

[*ITEPA 2003, s 241*].

Flat rate deductions

5.87   The Treasury are given power to fix a sum which in their opinion is a fair average annual expenditure by persons in a class that they specify, being people in receipt of earnings payable out of the public revenue, who are obliged to lay out and expend money wholly, exclusively and necessarily in the performance of their duties. That sum can then automatically be deducted as allowable expenses irrespective of the amount actually spent. If the employee can show that his actual expenditure exceeds the fixed sum he can deduct the actual expenditure instead. [*ITEPA 2003, s 368*]. This provision will apply to civil servants, to members of the armed forces and to people such as judges or MPs holding public offices. The idea is obviously to avoid a profusion of claims.

5.88   In practice HMRC are also prepared informally to agree Flat Rate Expense Allowances (FREA) with individual employers or with groups of employers. The employee can then either deduct the FREA without having to demonstrate what expenses he had incurred or alternatively can if he wishes establish the actual allowable expenses deductible under *s 336* (see **5.2**). HMRC entered into such an agreement with the airline My Travel in June 2004 covering pilots and cabin staff. On 30 November 2004 they resiled from that agreement. It had been reviewed by a Head Office specialist (apparently at the instigation of a different local office which was concerned at the receipt of a large number of claims for tax refunds resulting from the agreement) who thought it too generous and that some of the items covered related to capital expenditure not expenses. He also objected that it was retrospective. An employee of My Travel, Mr Bamber (who was the BALPA representative at My Travel) sought judicial review of the decision to withdraw the agreement, both for himself and on behalf of My Travel pilots in general. Whilst describing the HMRC action as at least 'a bit rich', the judge held that HMRC's legitimate aim of recovering in the public interest tax that, strictly speaking, ought by statute to be recovered outweighs any contrary argument that the June agreement should in a general way be kept in force. However, Mr Bamber had alleged that he had relied to his detriment on the agreement (he had pre-spent his tax refund on a new kitchen). He had not produced evidence to prove this and the court deferred his personal application for a month to give him an opportunity to do so.

5.89   The My Travel FREA was retrospective to 1997/98, it did not merely apply to 2004/05 onwards. Whilst the judge pointed out that the HMRC manuals did not say that FREAs could not be retrospective, he accepted that 'it has been [HMRC's] practice, nor a wholly invariable but an almost universal practice, to allow FREAs to apply only for what are in each case the current and future years'. The Employment Income Manual has been amended to specifically state that 'a locally agreed flat rate expenses deduction should apply for the current and future years. It should not be applied retrospectively' (EIM para 32725).

5.90   The Treasury also have power to fix a round sum deduction which in their opinion represents the average annual expenses incurred by a class of employees in respect of the repair and maintenance of work equipment, i.e. tools and special clothing. The Treasury must be satisfied that the employees are generally responsible for incurring the expense and that they could have claimed a deduction for the actual expense. No deduction can be claimed if the employer pays or reimburses the expense to which the lump sum relates, or would do so if requested. [*ITEPA 2003, s 367*]. This enacts a previous concession, *ESC A1*. HMRC agree such fixed expense allowances with trade unions and similar bodies. An employee can either claim this agreed figure irrespective of his actual expenditure or can make a *s 336* claim for his actual expenditure. However, if he opts to make a *s 336* claim, rather than accept the flat rate deduction, HMRC may be reluctant to allow a claim to the flat rate deduction in later years. The amounts agreed under such arrangements are normally relatively small and the figures are not regularly revised.

Professional subscriptions

5.91   Subscriptions to professional and similar bodies will not normally meet the requirements of *s 336* as the expense will not normally be incurred in the performance of the duties of the employment. Accordingly, it is specifically provided that certain fees or subscriptions can be deducted from the emoluments of an employment if they are defrayed out of those emoluments. [*ITEPA 2003, ss 343–345*].

The fees are those payable for registration, licensing or other matters payable as a condition of being able to practice the profession and can be deducted only if the duties of the employment involve the practice of the relevant profession. The professions concerned are:

Health professionals

> Chartered Psychologists (including the practising certificate fee)
>
> Chiropractors
>
> Dental auxiliaries
>
> Dentists Dispensing Opticians
>
> Members of the Health Professions Council
>
> Members of the Hearing Aid Council
>
> Medical Practitioners
>
> Members of the Nursing and Midwifery Council
>
> Ophthalmic Opticians
>
> Osteopaths
>
> Pharmaceutical Chemists
>
> Social Care Workers

Animal health professionals

Farmers

Veterinary Surgeons

Entrants on the supplementary veterinary register

Applicants for the Animal Medicines Training Regulatory Authority Register

Legal professionals

Licensed Conveyancers

Solicitors (fee for practising certificate)

Architects Teachers (General Teaching Council and (from 6 April 2005) General Teaching Council for Northern Ireland Registers)

Patent and Trade Mark agents

Patent agents (registration and practising fees)

Trade Mark agents (registration and practising fees)

Transport sector

Driving instructors

Aircraft maintenance engineers (1) (2)

Air traffic controllers (and student air traffic controllers) (1) (2)

Aircraft flight crew (1) (2)

Flight information service officers (1) (2)

Drivers of large goods vehicles or passenger carrying vehicles (1)

The fee payable by a person employed (or to be employed) at a UK airport for a criminal records check required for the issue of a security pass

Seamen (certificate of competence or licence)

Seafarers (cost of medical fitness certificate)

Security

Fees payable in applying for a licence from the Security Industry Authority under the *Private Security Industry Act 2001 (PSIA 2001)*.

For the professionals marked (1) the cost of the related medical examination is also allowable. So is the cost of the technical examination for those marked (2). HMRC have power to add items to the above list. [*ITEPA 2003, s 343*]. They added airport criminal record checks by the *Income Tax (Professional Fees) Order 2003 (SI 2003 No 1652)*, fees for those in the private security industry by the *Income Tax (Professional Fees) Order 2004 (SI 2004 No 1360)* and social care workers and applicants for AMTRA registration by the *Income Tax (Professional Fees) Order 2008 (SI 2008 No 836)*.

5.92   The deduction for annual subscriptions is for subscriptions paid to a body of persons approved by HMRC. They can approve a body, only if it applies for approval, its activities are not of a mainly local character, they are carried on otherwise than for profit, and they are mainly directed to all or any of:

(*a*)   the advancement or spreading of knowledge – either generally or among persons belonging to the same or similar professions (or occupying the same or similar positions);

(*b*)   the maintenance or improvement of standards of conduct and competence among the members of a profession; and

(*c*)   the indemnification or protection of members of any profession against claims in respect of liabilities incurred by them in the exercise of their profession.

[*ITEPA 2003, s 344(1)–(3)*].

5.93   If the activities of a body are directed mainly to such a purpose but are also to a significant extent directed to some other purpose, HMRC can approve the deduction of such part of the annual subscription as they think fit (having regard to all relevant circumstances and in particular the amount of the body's expenditure or its different activities). [*ITEPA 2003, s 344(5) (6)*]. Approval can be given with effect from the beginning of the tax year in which the body applies for approval. HMRC have power to withdraw or vary approval. [*ITEPA 2003, s 345(1)*]. The body has a right of appeal against a refusal of approval. [*ITEPA 2003, s 345(2)*].

5.94   As well as the body qualifying for approval, the employee has to show that membership of it is relevant to the employment. A fee within **5.91** above is deductible if it is a condition, or one of the alternative conditions, of the performance of the duties of the employment that the employee's name is maintained on the register or that he holds the practising certificate. [*ITEPA 2003, ss 343(1), 344(1)*]. A subscription is deductible only if the activities of the professional or other body are relevant to the employment, i.e. the performance of the duties of the employment is directly affected by the knowledge concerned or involves the exercise of the profession concerned. [*ITEPA 2003, s 344(1) (b)*]. In *Singh v Williams [2000] STC (SCD) 404* a retired medical practitioner sought to set a professional subscription against his civil service pension but the Commissioner felt that although on first sight the word 'profits' in *ITEPA 2003, s 62(2)* (see **3.1**) might encompass pension payments it is plain that the scheme of the legislation in respect of expenses excludes pensions from being emoluments for that purpose.

5.95   HMRC periodically publish a list of bodies approved under *s 344*, the latest of which was issued in December 2002 and can be found on the HMRC website. If a body is not on this list Inspectors of Taxes are likely to refuse a deduction. However, *s 344* does not override *s 336*; it supplements it. If a subscription to a professional or other body can be brought within *s 336* the taxpayer is entitled to deduct it as an expense irrespective of whether that body has applied for approval under *s 344*.

Overseas professional bodies

5.96   A particular difficulty arises with subscriptions to overseas professional bodies as they do not, in general, seek approval under *s 344*. Most, but not all, Inspectors of Taxes generally use their commonsense and allow a deduction if the activities are similar to those of a UK approved body. However, it needs to be realised that this is a concessional treatment. If a body is not on the HMRC list, irrespective of the reason, it is for the taxpayer either to persuade the body to seek approval or to bring his expenditure within the tight rules of *s 336*.

5.97   It should also be noted that *s 344* applies only to an annual subscription to an approved body; it does not grant relief for an initial admission fee or for other payments such as examination fees for post-qualification examinations where these are not specifically allowed by *s 343*.

Armed forces' exemptions

5.98   Travel facilities provided for army, navy or air force personnel going on leave or returning from it are specifically exempted from tax. [*ITEPA 2003, s 296*]. This applies not only to travel vouchers and warrants for specific journeys but also to allowances irrespective of leave travel. The exemption applies regardless of whether the tax charge would otherwise have arisen under *section 62(2)* (see **3.1** above), *section 84* (see **6.20** below) or *section 201* (see **6.43** below). Travel for leave is, of course, equivalent to home to office travel for a civilian.

5.99   There is also an exemption from tax for armed forces' food, drink and mess allowances payable out of the public revenue to (or in respect of) any description of members of the armed forces of the Crown which the Treasury certifies are payable either instead of food or drink normally supplied to members of the armed forces or as a contribution to the expenses of a mess. [*ITEPA 2003, s 297*]. This exemption also applies to any Operational Allowance (designated as such under a Royal Warrant), whether paid before or after the introduction of this provision [*ITEPA 2003, s 297A as amended by Finance Act 2012 (FA 2012), s 16(2)*].

5.100   There is also an exemption from tax for training expenses, allowances and bounties payable in consideration of undertaking certain training and attaining a particular standard of efficiency which are payable out of the public revenue to members of the reserve and auxiliary forces of the Crown. [*ITEPA 2003, s 218*]. Payments to members of the armed forces of the Crown of Council Tax Relief after 31 March 2008 are also exempt [*ITEPA 2003, s 297B inserted by Finance Act 2008 (FA 2008), s 48*]. From 2011/12, there is a further exemption for payments of the Continuity Education Allowance (as designated under Royal Warrant) paid to members of the armed forces or paid in respect of such a person after his death [*ITEPA 2003, s 297A* inserted by *FA 2012, s 16(4)*].

Crown employee foreign service allowance

5.101 Any allowance paid to a person in employment under the Crown is tax free if it is certified (by the Treasury or certain specified ministers) to represent compensation for the extra cost of being obliged to live outside the UK in order to perform the duties of the employment. [*ITEPA 2003, s 299*].

Agent's commission paid by entertainers

5.102 Where a person is employed as an actor, singer, musician, dancer or theatrical artist, a deduction can be claimed for agent's commission – up to a maximum of 17.5 per cent – and VAT thereon. The commission must be paid by the employee under an agency contract to a properly licensed agent (under the *Employment Agencies Act 1973 (EAA 1973)*) and must be calculated as a percentage of the emoluments (or part thereof). The emoluments must obviously themselves be taxable. It should be noted that if an agent agrees to accept a round sum fee instead of a percentage that fee will not be deductible. Such commission paid to a *bona fide* non-profit co-operative society which acts as the agent will also qualify. [*ITEPA 2003, s 352*].

Capital allowances

5.103 An employee can claim capital allowances for his expenditure on plant and machinery which is 'necessarily provided' for use in the performance of his duties (unless the earnings are taxable on a remittance basis). [*Capital Allowances Act 2001 (CAA 2001), s 36*]. The 'necessarily provided' test does not apply to cars, vans or other mechanically propelled road vehicles if the expenditure is incurred partly for the purpose of the employment and partly for other purposes. [*CAA 2001, s 36(3), s 80*]. From 6 April 2002 expenditure on the provision of a mechanically propelled road vehicle or a cycle cannot attract capital allowances even if it meets the necessarily provided test. [*CAA 2001, s 36(1)(a)*]. Where capital allowances were being claimed on such items there was a deemed disposal of the asset at market value at 6 April 2002. [*CAA 2001, s 59(4)*]. This deemed disposal of course triggered a balancing charge or allowance. HMRC have indicated that if it created a charge they will in practice not seek to collect the tax until the vehicle is sold, albeit that they are statutorily entitled to collect it in 2002/03. It is understood that HMRC regard equipment as necessarily provided only if:

(*a*)   the taxpayer is paid entirely or largely by results (for example, by commission);

(*b*)   the method by which the employee is to achieve the results is not stereotyped; and (*c*)   the employee is required to bear the cost of such equipment performing functions or activities intended to achieve his objective in his job and the employer does not provide or pay for such equipment. (*Taxation, 10 March 1994, p. 507*).

There is no statutory basis for these three tests and they seem of doubtful validity.

Employee liability and indemnity insurance

5.104   A specific deduction is allowed for expenditure in relation to certain employee liabilities which are defrayed out of the emoluments, i.e., the deduction cannot exceed the emoluments. It covers:

(*a*)   a payment of (or towards) damages or compensation or in settlement of a claim for damages or compensation;

(*b*)   costs or expenses in relation to such a claim and proceedings arising from it;

(*c*)   indemnity insurance premiums, but only to the extent that the premium relates to indemnifying the employee against the above matters.

[*ITEPA 2003, s 346(1)*].

However, no deduction can be made for liabilities or costs which the employer could not lawfully insure against, e.g., costs arising from a criminal conviction (*ITEPA 2003, s 346(2)*). Nor can any deduction be made for a payment after 11 January 2009 (irrespective of when arrangements were made) if the payment is made in pursuance of arrangements one of the main purposes of which is the avoidance of tax [*ITEPA 2003, s 346(2A)* inserted by *Finance Act 2009 (FA 2009), s 67*]. This blocks a tax avoidance scheme that was designed to create a deduction by an employee deliberately defaulting on a liability and making a payment to his employer out of funds borrowed from another scheme entity (HMRC Technical Note 12.1.2009). HMRC do not think that the device works but the amendment avoids any doubt.

5.105   The liability must be imposed in respect of some act or omission (or of proceedings arising out of a claim) in the director's or employee's capacity as employee, or in some other capacity in which he acts in the performance of the duties of his employment, eg as an employee of a subsidiary company to which his services are seconded. In the case of indemnity insurance premiums the policy must not be for a period exceeding two years, must not entitle the employee to receive any benefit in addition to the risks insured against and the right to renew the policy (other than a benefit to which no significant part of the premium can be attributed), must not be connected with any other contract, and must relate exclusively to one or more of:

(*a*)   indemnifying a person (which will include both the employer and employee) against a liability in one of the above capacities;

(b)   indemnifying a person against any vicarious liability in such a capacity in relation to acts or omissions of someone else;

(c)   the payment of costs or expenses (including those incurred by a third party) in relation to a claim under the policy;

(d)   indemnifying an employer against any loss from the payment by him to an employee of his in relation to a liability within (a) or (b).

[*ITEPA 2003, s 346, 348, 349*].

5.106   An insurance contract is connected with another if one is entered into by reference to the other or with a view to enabling (or facilitating) the other to be entered into on particular terms, and the terms of either would otherwise have been significantly different. If the two contracts are both indemnity insurance contracts (satisfying **5.99**) and the difference in terms simply reflects a reasonable reduction of premium either because they are entered into together and cover different proportions of the same risks or the second is entered into under a renewal right in the first, they are not regarded as connected (*ITEPA 2003, s 350*).

5.107   Relief is also given – in this case against total income – for such expenditure by an ex-director or employee. The payment must be made within six years following the end of the year of assessment in which the employment ceased and the amount must have been deductible under *s 346* had the employment continued and the payment been defrayed out of emoluments for the year in which the payment was in fact made. [*ITEPA 2003, ss 555–564*, formerly *Finance Act 1995 (FA 1995), s 92(1)–(3)*]. This appears to limit the deduction to what the emolument would have been had the employment continued, although it is unclear how such a limitation is to be calculated. Obviously, relief cannot be claimed if the expenditure is covered by insurance or is reimbursed by the ex-employer, a successor to his business, or a connected person of the ex-employer or a successor. [*ITEPA 2003, s 557*]. If such a reimbursement itself constitutes an unapproved retirement benefit under *s 596A* (see **10.86**) or is taxable as an emolument of the former employment, the expenditure can be deducted from the taxable amount [*ITEPA 2003, s 555(1) (b)*]. If the expenditure exceeds the amount from which it is deductible – as indicated above, it is not clear if this means the ex-employee's total income for the year of payment or the salary he would have earned for that year had the employment continued – the ex-employee can claim to set the excess against any capital gains of the same tax year (before off-setting any brought forward CGT losses) [*Taxation of Chargeable Gains Act 1992 (TCGA 1992), s 261E* inserted by *Income Tax Act 2007 (ITA 2007), Sch 1, para 329*].

Chapter 6

Benefits in Kind

Quantum of the benefit

6.1   As indicated in **Chapter 3**, a payment to an employee of 'money's worth' constitutes emoluments. However, the quantum of such emoluments is the amount of money into which the benefit or payment in kind can be converted. This is generally far below the cost of providing the benefit, either because the market price of second-hand goods, even if unused, is generally well below the original retail price of those goods, or because the benefit is not easily saleable because a vendor cannot pass the legal title, there is no evidence of title, or the benefit is of a restrictive nature. Accordingly, in the absence of special provisions there would be a great incentive to ask to be paid in kind, either in whole or in part, by the employer purchasing goods or services and assigning these to the employee.

6.2   It is therefore not surprising to find specific rules covering the taxation of benefits in kind. Where a benefit falls within these special rules its money's worth value will of course cease to constitute emoluments.

Three categories of benefit

6.3   Benefits in kind effectively fall into three categories.

(*a*)   Those that apply to all employees.

(*b*)   Those that apply only to 'higher-paid' employees and company directors.

(*c*)   Those for which there are no special provisions, and are thus taxable only to the extent that they constitute emoluments, and which can be taxed on their money's worth value.

Who are 'higher-paid employees'?

6.4   Before considering how a benefit is to be taxed it is obviously necessary to determine whether the employee is a director or is 'higher-paid' and thus within the special rules applicable to such people. The expression 'higher-paid' is used below for convenience. It was a statutory term from 1976 to 1989 but was replaced in the *Finance Act 1989 (FA 1989)* by the more accurate, but very much more unwieldy, expression 'employees earning £8,500 per annum or more' and 'employment to which Chapter II of Part V of the principal Act applies'. [*FA 1989, s 53*]. This change of nomenclature was made because the Government felt that 'the expression "higher paid employment" has become inappropriate, and can be misleading, since £8,500 is well below the national average for full-time earnings and the benefit rules now apply to the great majority of employees'. The *Rewrite Act* has taken the reverse approach. It provides that benefits are taxable on everyone unless they are in excluded employment. [*Income Tax (Earnings and Pensions) Act 2003 (ITEPA 2003), s 63*]. It then calls those in excluded employment 'lower-paid'. [*ITEPA 2003, s 216(1)*].

6.5 In considering whether a person who is not a director (or who is a full-time working director) earns over £8,500 per annum, or rather, to be precise, is in an employment with emoluments at the rate of £8,500 a year or more (ie averages over £23.29 for each day worked), emoluments must be calculated as if they include all benefits (and other amounts) taxable under the higher-paid employee rules, and also all those benefits that are taxable on all employees. Furthermore, no deduction can be made for mileage allowances, most allowable expenses, professional subscriptions or under the special rules for ministers of religion in *s 290*. [*ITEPA 2003, s 218*]. Where a car is made available for private use (as mentioned in *s 114* – see **7.2**) and an alternative to the benefit is offered the amount to be included in respect of the benefit is the higher of the scale charge or the value of the alternative, plus any non-cash vouchers, credit tokens or expenses payments given in respect of the car (even though such sums are excluded from tax by *ITEPA 2003, s 269(1)*) [*ITEPA 2003, s 219*]. This could lead to unfairness as is illustrated by *Allcock v King [2004] STC (SCD) 122, SpC 396*). Mrs Allcock had a salary for 1998/99 of £3,440. She was also provided with a car. This was available for private use. Petrol was provided by the company and some at least was paid for using a company credit card. HMRC contended that the car use and car fuel benefit (£4,680 in aggregate) brought the earnings up to £8,120. To this had to be added the credit card payments of £491 giving a total of £8,611. As this was over £8,500 Mrs Allcock fell within the benefit legislation. The Commissioner, Graham Aaronson QC, thought this 'an anomaly – and a very unfair one – in the benefits-in-kind provisions'. Nevertheless with the greatest reluctance he concluded that HMRC were correct in law and that 'there is in law no escape from the trap that the statutory language has set'. Someone in HMRC obviously listened to him as ESC A104, which applies from 5 July 2004, excludes the credit card payment if it would be excluded from charge to tax by virtue of *s 239* (see **7.35**) or *269* (see **6.22**) and that ESC was given statutory effect by *Finance Act 2007 (FA 2007), s 62* which repealed the offending provision, [*ITEPA 2003, s 219(5), (6)*]. If a person has two or more employments with the same employer they must all be treated as higher-paid if either the higher-paid rules apply to one of them by virtue of holding a directorship or the aggregate emoluments exceed £8,500 per annum. [*ITEPA 2003, s 220*]. If an individual, partnership, company or other body has control of another partnership, company or other body, all employees of the controlling body are to be treated (for the purpose of *section 218* only) as if they were employees of the individual or the controlling body – so that if they have employments with both the controlling and controlled entity such employments need to be looked at together. [*ITEPA 2003, s 220(3)*].

6.6   These special rules were introduced in 1979 and the figure of £8,500 has never been changed, despite a 364 per cent increase in inflation in 1979 and 2006. They replaced a previous system of taxing benefits of higher-paid employees that started in 1948 when higher-paid meant earning £2,000 per annum or more. The limit was increased to £5,000 in 1975 and to £7,500 in 1978. It appears that the intention is that, in time, these special provisions will apply to all employees. Presumably it is politically inexpedient to be seen to impose additional tax burdens on the lower-paid, so this ultimate intention will be achieved by allowing inflation continually to whittle away the number of employees who are not covered by these rules. At £25,006, national average earnings are getting on for three times the threshold. A person on the national minimum wage of £5.80 who works a 35-hour week for 48 weeks in the year will earn £9,744, so the only people who can benefit from the rules for lower-paid employees are likely to be part-time workers and spouses of directors of family businesses who are paid a nominal wage to entitle them to National Insurance benefits!

Directors

6.7   It should be noted that employment as a director is automatically within the special rules irrespective of the level of earnings – and even if the director has no earnings – unless the director does not have a 'material interest' in the company and either:

(*a*)   his employment is as a full-time working director; or

(*b*)   the company is non-profit making (ie does not carry on a trade and its functions do not consist wholly or mainly in the holding of investments or other property) or it is established for charitable purposes only.

[*ITEPA 2003, s 216(1)–(3)*].

6.8   References below to higher-paid employees should be read as including directors brought within the higher-paid employee rules under these provisions.

Meaning of 'director'

6.9   Some of the expressions used above are specially defined for the purpose of these rules. A 'director' means:

(*a*)   in relation to a company whose affairs are managed by a board of directors or similar body, a member of that board;

(*b*)   in relation to a company whose affairs are managed by a single director or similar person, that person; and

(*c*)   in relation to a company whose affairs are managed by the members themselves, a member of the company.

[*ITEPA 2003, s 67*].

6.10   Any person in accordance with whose directions or instructions the directors (as defined above) are accustomed to act is also a director of the company, unless the directors merely act on advice given by him in a professional capacity. [*ITEPA 2003, s 67(1), (2)*]. The application of this provision was challenged unsuccessfully in the House of Lords in *R v Allen [2001] STC 1537, [2001] UKHL 45*. It was admitted in that case that Mr Allen was a 'shadow director' of a non-UK company that owned a house that he occupied. However, he contended that the benefit provisions (and the special rules on accommodation described in **Chapter 8** which adopt the same definition) did not apply, as although *s 67* states that a director includes a shadow director it does not deem such a person to hold an office, so unless the individual holds an employment the benefit rules could not apply. Alternatively if he did hold an office it is not one the emoluments of which fall to be taxed as employment income as it would be a non-UK one with no UK duties and to construe a benefit from it as taxable would breach the territorial limitation of the UK's taxing jurisdiction. Both of these arguments were dismissed fairly briefly on the basis that the legislative intent was clearly that accommodation and benefits received by a shadow director should be taxed in the same way as those received by a director.

Meaning of 'full-time'

6.11   A director is a full-time working director if he is required to devote substantially the whole of his time to the service of the company in a managerial or technical capacity. [*ITEPA 2003, s 67(3)*]. The *Act* does not say what is meant by 'substantially the whole of his time'. It presumably does not mean 20-odd hours a day seven days a week. HMRC's *Employment Income Manual* states that 'substantially the whole' has its normal meaning. It will allow for the director working slightly less than the full normal working hours of the company. They also refer their staff to *IRC v D Devine & Sons Ltd 41 TC 210)* where the Court of Appeal held that a taxpayer who worked three full days a week was not a full-time director (although that case dealt with different legislation). They also say that a director of several companies can be regarded as a full-time working director of the company which occupies the largest proportion of his time provided that he works for that company for more than 50 per cent of its full normal working hours and works in aggregate for all the companies for at least 75 per cent of those normal working hours (*Employment Income Manual, para 20202*). If an employee-type director does not have a managerial or technical role – as can happen with a small company where, say, the company's only salesman is appointed a director – he cannot qualify as a full-time working director. It is unclear why Parliament should have wanted to discriminate in favour of people with management responsibilities and against those without. One might have expected that if a class of person was to be excluded from the special rules the latter had a stronger claim than the former rather than the other way around.

6.12   In early 1993 HMRC expressed the view that 'full-time' in the context of full-time employment abroad under *ESC A11* means something like a 35–40 hour week (*Tax Bulletin, Issue 6, page 57*). However, they specifically stated that this view 'is not concerned with other instances where the term "full-time" appears in statute, for example "full-time working director" in the benefit in kind rules'. Their Employee Shares and Securities Unit seem to define a full-time employee or a full-time director by reference to a working week in excess of 25 hours, but as their concern is that a company should not be able to exclude too many people from all-employee share schemes it is probably unwise to rely on this test in different circumstances. The long repealed capital gains tax retirement relief and taper relief contained a definition of full-time, namely that the person 'must be required to devote substantially the whole of his time to the service of the company' (*Taxation of Chargeable Gains Act 1992 (TCGA 1992),Sch A1, para 22(1), Sch 6, para 1(2)*). In *Palmer v Maloney [1999] STC 890* the Court of Appeal found it hard to put a meaning on this, one judge interpreting the words literally and the other two stating that whatever it meant Mr Palmer, who worked 42 hours a week for one company, was required to devote substantially the whole of his time to it but disagreeing on any general principle. Aldous LJ thought it a jury question to be decided on the facts of each case as, while HMRC's test of 75 per cent of the full hours worked by other employees (*Capital Gains Manual para 63621*) may be appropriate as a matter of pragmatism, he doubted that it always gives the right answer. Clarke LJ thought 'there seems to be much to be said for a rule of thumb such as that adopted by [HMRC]'.

Meaning of 'material interest'

6.13 A person has a material interest in a company if, either on his own or with one or more of his associates:

(*a*)   he is the beneficial owner of (or able directly or indirectly to control) more than five per cent of the ordinary share capital of the company; or

(*b*)   the company is a close company and he possesses (or is entitled to acquire) such rights as would in the event of a winding up of the company or in any other circumstances, give an entitlement to receive more than five per cent of the assets which would then be available for distribution among the participators,

or if any associate of his (with or without other associates) fulfils either of the above conditions. [*ITEPA 2003, s 68(2), (3)*].

Meaning of 'participator'

6.14 For this purpose the definition of participator in *Corporation Tax Act 2010 (CTA 2010), s 454* and that of associate in *s 448* apply with the modification that (as well as such relatives of the employee himself) the parents or remoter forebear, child or remoter issue or brother or sister of the director's spouse, and the spouses of such relatives of either the director or his spouse, are also associates (such persons are not associates under *section 448*). The definition of control in *Income Tax Act 2007 (ITA 2007), s 995* applies, and it also applies (with the necessary modifications) in relation to an unincorporated association. [*ITEPA 2003, s 69*].

The provisions applicable to all employees

6.15   The special provisions that apply to all employees, lower-paid as well as higher-paid, cover cash vouchers, non-cash vouchers, credit tokens and living accommodation. The first three of these are considered below. Living accommodation is dealt with in **Chapter 8**.

Cash vouchers

6.16   A cash voucher is any voucher, stamp or similar document capable of being exchanged (either on its own or together with other vouchers, stamps or documents) for a sum of money equal to (or greater than, or not substantially less than) the expense incurred in providing the voucher. It includes a voucher exchangeable only after a time and also a voucher that is capable of being exchanged either for cash or for goods or services. [*ITEPA 2003, s 75*]. As a cash voucher can be exchanged for cash it is, not surprisingly, treated as cash and the employee taxed at the time he receives it as if he had received a cash sum equal to the amount for which the voucher can be exchanged. [*ITEPA 2003, s 81*]. The cash itself is, of course, not then taxable as a benefit or under the basic definition of emoluments. [*ITEPA 2003, s 95*]. If a person incurs an expense in or in connection with cash vouchers for two or more employees as members of a group, it must be apportioned amongst them on a just and reasonable basis. [*ITEPA 2003, s 77*].

6.17   A document intended to enable a person to obtain payment of a sum mentioned in it is not a cash voucher if that sum would not have been constituted employment income had the cash been paid direct without the interposition of the voucher. [*ITEPA 2003, s 80(a)*]. This ensures that, for example, an expenses claim or a petty cash slip cannot be regarded as a cash voucher and create an unanticipated tax charge. Similarly, a savings certificate, the accumulated interest on which is exempt from tax (or would be exempt if certain conditions were satisfied) is not a cash voucher. [*ITEPA 2003, s 80(b)*]. It is obviously not the Government's intention that a person given a national savings certificate by his employer should immediately be taxed on its face value, which includes a large element of tax-free growth that is obtainable only by holding the certificate for five years. For 2003/04 onwards there is also an exclusion for a cash voucher which is of a kind made available to the public generally and which is provided to the employee or a member of the employee's family on no more favourable terms than to the public generally. [*ITEPA 2003, s 78*].

6.18   If a voucher is capable of being exchanged for cash but for an amount substantially less than its cost and the difference represents (in whole or part) the cost of providing sickness, personal injury or death benefits (a sickness benefits-related voucher), the cost of providing such benefits is ignored for the purpose of determining whether the voucher is a cash voucher. [*ITEPA 2003, s 76*]. Once it is established that the voucher is a cash voucher PAYE is still applied only to the sum for which the voucher can be exchanged. [*ITEPA 2003, s 81(2)*]. This provision will ensure that industry-wide holiday stamp schemes where the stamp also provides insurance cover against sickness, etc. are brought within the cash voucher rules so that PAYE is applied to the holiday pay element. HMRC are given power to exempt such schemes from the cash voucher provisions entirely if they are satisfied that PAYE can be (and, presumably, will be) applied when the voucher is actually exchanged for cash. [*ITEPA 2003, s 79*]. It appears that if a scheme is so exempted the employee is doubly taxable to a degree as he is then not entitled to the benefit of *ITEPA 2003, s 95(2)*, which prevents the market value of the voucher being an emolument. Undoubtedly, HMRC would not collect such tax by concession.

6.19   If a cash voucher is appropriated to an employee without being given to him, for example, a stamp is attached to a card held for him, the tax charge will arise at the time of such appropriation. [*ITEPA 2003, s 73(3)*]. If a cash voucher is given not to an employee but to his spouse, parent, child, the spouse of one of his children, or a dependant of the employee it must of course be treated as having been given to the employee. [*ITEPA 2003, s 74*].

Non-cash vouchers

6.20   A 'non-cash voucher' is any voucher, stamp or similar document or token capable of being exchanged for money, goods or services (or any combination of the three) and which is not a cash voucher. It includes a transport voucher, which is a ticket, pass or other document or token intended to enable a person to obtain passenger transport services, even though the voucher does not have to be given up. The most common type of transport voucher is, of course, a Rail or London Transport season ticket or travelcard. It also includes a cheque voucher, which is a cheque provided for an employee and intended for use by him wholly or mainly for payment for particular goods or services or for goods or services of one or more particular classes. The most common type of cheque voucher will be a cheque given to an employee to pay for goods or services ordered on behalf of the employer for the benefit of the employer. A voucher does not cease to be a non-cash voucher if it can only be exchanged together with other vouchers, etc. or if it can be exchanged only after some time has elapsed. [*ITEPA 2003, s 84*].

6.21   If an employee is given a non-cash voucher he must be treated as having received emoluments from his employment equal to the cost of the voucher (or of the money, goods or services for which it can be exchanged) to the employer (or the person who provided it, or, from 1994/95, the person at whose cost it was provided). [*ITEPA 2003, s 87(1)–(3)*]. If the employee makes any payment for the voucher, the assessable amount is reduced by that payment. [*ITEPA 2003, s 87(2)(b)*]. The chargeable amount is deemed to be emoluments for the year of assessment in which the voucher is given to the employee or, if later, in which the employer incurs the expense – unless it is a cheque voucher in which case it is the year in which the cheque is handed over to the shop, or is posted to it. [*ITEPA 2003, s 88*]. A curious result of this provision is that only the employee and not the employer will know the year in which a cheque voucher is assessable, and only the employer – not the employee – will know when any other non-cash voucher is assessable. A non-cash voucher does not of itself trigger a PAYE liability.

Exemptions from charge

6.22   Because of these special rules to tax the cost of a cash voucher the goods or services obtained with the voucher are of course excluded from being earnings to avoid double taxation. [*ITEPA 2003, s 95(2)*]. Where specific benefits are exempted from tax the legislation normally also exempts the use of a voucher to provide that benefit. Such provisions are:

s 269	–	use of a voucher to obtain goods or services in connection with a car, van or heavy goods vehicle (see **7.2**);
s 296	–	travel facilities for the armed forces (see **5.96**);
s 242	–	works bus services (see **9.88**);
s 243	–	employer subsidised public transport services (see **9.90**);
s 244	–	cycles and safety equipment (see **9.92**);
s 319		mobile telephones (from 2006/07) (see **9.33**);
s 261	–	sporting and recreational facilities (see **9.32**);
s 210	–	minor exempt benefits (see **6.44**);
s 237(1)	–	parking provision (see **7.79**);
s 246	–	transport for disabled employees (see **9.116**);
s 247	–	cars for disabled employees (see **9.116**);
s 248	–	transport home in certain cases see **9.116**);
s 265	–	third party entertainment (see **6.38**);
s 345	–	travel during transport strikes (see **9.116**);
s 264	–	annual parties (see **9.116**);
s 317	–	subsidised meals (see **9.67**); and
s 320A	–	eye tests and glasses, etc (from 2006/07) (see **9.113**)

[*ITEPA 2003, s 266*].

6.23   The Treasury have been given power by Regulation to exempt from tax any liability that would otherwise arise on earnings or under the benefits code in respect of non-cash vouchers which are (or can be) used to obtain exempt benefits (ie benefits the direct provision of which would have been exempt from tax) specified in the regulations, or which evidence an employee's entitlement to specified exempt benefits [*ITEPA 2003, s 96A* inserted by *Finance Act 2006 (FA 2006), s 63*].

6.24   If a non-cash voucher is used to pay business expenses the employee can claim a deduction of the lessor of the amount treated as earnings under the non cash voucher rules or the amount that would have been deductible under

ITEPA 2003, ss 336, 337 or *370–376* if he had paid the expenditure himself. [*ITEPA 2003, s 362*]. If a non-cash voucher is appropriated to a person without being given to him, eg it is attached to a card for his benefit or is retained by the employer for safekeeping, it is treated as being received by the employee at the time of such appropriation. [*ITEPA 2003, s 82(3)*].

6.25 A non-cash voucher is also exempted from tax to the extent that it is used to obtain entertainment (including hospitality of any kind) for the employee or a member of his family or household (prior to 2003/04 a relation of his) if it is provided at the cost of someone other than his employer (or a connected person of the employer); the employer (or a connected person) has not directly or indirectly procured the provision of the voucher; and the entertainment is not provided in recognition of particular services which have been performed by him in the course of his employment (or in anticipation of particular services to be so performed). [*ITEPA 2003, ss 265, 266(1)*]. This will cover such things as the provision to an employee by a customer of his employer of an admission ticket to a football match or other sporting event in the course of entertainment by the customer. A member of a person's family (or a relation), for this purpose, means the spouse, parent, child or dependant of the employee or the spouse of an employee's child. [*ITEPA 2003, s 721(4)*]. *Section 839* applies to determine whether a person is connected with the employer.

6.26 There is also an exemption in relation to transport vouchers provided for an employee of a passenger-transport undertaking (such as British Airways and the privatised railway companies although as they did not exist in 1982 they cannot satisfy the second test – but see **6.54**) under arrangements in operation on 25 March 1982 and intended to enable that employee or a relation of his (as defined above) to obtain passenger transport services provided by his employer, its subsidiary or parent company, or another passenger transport undertaking. [*ITEPA 2003, s 86*]. This was intended to ensure that where an airline pilot gets cheap flights for his family or a train driver cheap travel on continental railways, the document by which he achieves it would continue to escape tax. This concession was based on the premise that there is probably no cost to the transport undertaking in any event as the marginal cost of transporting an extra passenger is probably nil.

6.27 There is also an exemption for non-cash vouchers used for incidental overnight expenses while the employee is working away from home. The goods or services in question must be incidental to the employee being away from his usual place of abode for a period including at least one overnight stay, must not otherwise be deductible as an employment income expense and must not exceed an average £5 a night in the UK or £10 a night elsewhere. [*ITEPA 2003, s 268*]. The detailed rules are the same as apply to expenses and are considered at **5.4**.

6.28 Where a person incurs expense in relation to the provision of non-cash vouchers for a group of employees the amount must be apportioned in such manner as is just and reasonable. [*ITEPA 2003, s 77*]. A non-cash voucher is automatically deemed to be provided by reason of a person's employment

– which is, of course, essential for it to be taxable as employment income – if it is provided by his employer. [*ITEPA 2003, s 82(2)*]. There is an exception where the employer is an individual and the provision is made in the normal course of the employer's domestic, family or personal relationships. [*ITEPA 2003, s 83(2)*]. This exception does not apply where the employer is a family owned company though. A non-cash voucher provided for a member of the employee's family (within **6.19** above) must be treated as having been provided for the employee. [*ITEPA 2003, s 83*]. A non-cash voucher is also not taxable if it is of a kind made available to the public generally and is not provided to the employee or relative on more favourable terms than to the public generally. [*ITEPA 2003, s 85*]. There is also a reduction in the taxable amount for a meal voucher where it is provided for an employee for use on a working day if meal vouchers are made available to all employees who are employed by the same employer and in lower-paid employment. The cash equivalent of the benefit is to be reduced by 15p for each working day for which the voucher is provided. A meal voucher is a non-cash voucher which can only be used to obtain meals, is not transferable and is not of the kind in respect of which no liability to income tax arises under *s 317* (subsidised meals) (see **9.59**). The relief does not extend to a meal voucher provided for a relative of the employee. [*ITEPA 2003, s 89*]. This provision applies only until 5 April 2013; it has been repealed from that date by *Finance Act 2012 (FA 2012), Sch 38, para 50*.

6.29 *Section 87* has virtually blocked the provision of benefits to lower-paid employees in a tax advantageous form. It requires a great deal of ingenuity (and a lot of administrative trouble) for most employers to provide benefits to employees without bringing some sort of voucher into existence to evidence to the supplier that the employee is entitled to the goods or services and that the employer will pay for them.

Credit tokens

6.30 A 'credit token' is a credit card, debit card or other card, token, document or other thing given to a person by another person who undertakes either that on the production of it he will supply money, goods or services on credit, or that, if on the production of it to a third party that third party supplies money, goods or services, he will pay that third party for them. [*ITEPA 2003, s 92(1)*]. A cash voucher or non-cash voucher is not a credit token. The use of an object to operate a machine is treated as the production of that object, eg if an employer provides his staff with tokens to operate the firm's coffee machine they will be credit tokens. [*ITEPA 2003, s 92(3)*]. A document will still be a credit token even if some other action is required in addition to its production to obtain the money, goods or services and even if the employer gets a commission from the third party who accepts the voucher. [*ITEPA 2003, s 92(2)*].

6.31 On each occasion that an employee (or a relation of the employee within **6.14** above) uses a credit token to obtain money, goods or services the employee is treated as having received employment income equal to the expense incurred by the employer (or other person providing the credit token or the person at whose cost it was provided) in connection with the provision of the money, goods or services obtained. [*ITEPA 2003, s 94*]. It is irrelevant when the credit token is given to the employee. In theory, if an employee does not drink coffee very often he needs to count up the coffee machine tokens sitting in his drawer at 5 April and notify HMRC of their total value as the employer will doubtless declare to HMRC the issue of them to the employee not their usage. It seems improbable that this happens in practice. The most obvious example of a credit token is a company credit card. Where goods are obtained using a credit card it should be noted that the assessable date is the time the card is used, not the later date when the employer settles the bill.

6.32   Where the use of a credit token is taxable under *section 94* no charge on the goods or services obtained by that use will arise under any other provision. [*ITEPA 2003, s 95*]. If a credit token is used to pay business expenses the employee can submit a *s 336* claim (see **5.2** above) or one under *ITEPA 2003, ss 343–346* or *351* (see **5.91** and **5.104** above and **19.17** below) and in the same way as if he had incurred the expense himself. [*ITEPA 2003, s 363*]. If the employee reimburses any part of the cost, such as where he has to pay for personal expenditure on his company credit card, the assessable amount is reduced by the payment he makes. [*ITEPA 2003, s 94(2)*]. PAYE does not apply on the use of credit tokens.

6.33   No assessment will arise to the extent that a credit token is used by the employee to obtain the use of a car parking space at or near his place of work; travel or subsistence during a transport strike; for commuting by a disabled employee, to obtain a car for a disabled employee; to obtain transport home after late night working or the failure of a car sharing arrangement; to obtain the use of a mobile phone (for 2006/07 onwards); for eye tests and glasses etc (from 2006/07); or to obtain entertainment (including hospitality) provided at the cost of a third party without any prompting by the employer, ie which qualifies for the same exemption under the non-cash voucher rules (see **6.22** above). [*ITEPA 2003, s 267* as amended by *FA 2006, ss 60(2)* and *62(4)*].

6.34   There is also an exemption for credit tokens used for incidental overnight expenses while the employee is working away from home. The goods or services in question must be incidental to the employee being away from his usual place of abode for a period including at least one overnight stay, must not otherwise be deductible as a Schedule E expense and must not exceed an average £5 a night in the UK or £10 a night elsewhere. [*ITEPA 2003, s 268*]. The detailed rules are the same as apply to expenses and are considered at **5.40**.

6.35   The Treasury have power by Regulation to exempt from tax any liability that would otherwise arise on earnings or under the benefit code in respect of credit-tokens which are used to obtain exempt benefits (ie benefits the direct provision of which would have been exempt from tax) specified in the regulations [*ITEPA 2003, s 96A* inserted by *FA 2006, s 63*].

6.36   Where a person incurs expense in relation to the provision of credit tokens for more than one employee the amount must be apportioned in such manner as is just and reasonable. [*ITEPA 2003, s 94(4)*]. A credit token is automatically deemed to be provided by reason of a person's employment if it is provided by his employer. [*ITEPA 2003, s 90(2)*]. No benefit arises where the employer is an individual and the provision is made in the normal course of the employer's domestic family or personal relationships. [*ITEPA 2003, s 90(2)*]. A credit token provided for a relation of the employee (as defined at **6.19** above) must be treated as having been provided for the employee. [*ITEPA 2003, s 91*]. No benefit arises if the credit token is of a kind made available to the public generally and it is not provided to the employee on more favourable terms than to the public generally. [*ITEPA 2003, s 93*].

Dispensations

6.37   An employer (or any other person) can apply, in effect, for a dispensation from the non-cash voucher and credit token provisions. To do this he must send to the Inspector of Taxes a statement of the cases and circumstances in which such vouchers or tokens are provided for employees. If the Inspector is satisfied that no tax would be payable on them, eg because they can only be used to meet bona fide business expenses or because the employee will reimburse the full cost of personal expenses, he can exempt them from these provisions. The Inspector may revoke such a dispensation at any time if in his opinion it is reasonable to do so. He can revoke it with retrospective effect to the day it was originally given if he thinks fit, or with effect from any later date that he feels appropriate. [*ITEPA 2003, s 96*]. Dispensations are considered in more detail at **6.79** onwards.

Benefits applicable only to higher-paid employees

The basic rules

6.38   If by reason of his employment any payments are made to a higher-paid employee (see **6.4** above) in respect of expenses and those amounts are not otherwise taxable on him as income, they must be treated as earnings from his employment and taxed on him accordingly. [*ITEPA 2003, ss 70(1)*]. For this purpose any sum put at an employee's disposal and paid away by him is treated as paid to him in respect of expenses. [*ITEPA 2003, s 70(2)*]. This is, on the face of it, a somewhat startling proposition. It is tempered to some extent by the fact that the employee is entitled to make any appropriate claim to deduct expenses under *ITEPA 2003, s 336* (see **5.2** above) (or under *ITEPA 2003, s 351* if he is a clergyman) or for relief for subscriptions under *ITEPA 2003, s 343*, (see **5.87**) or for employee liability payments (see **5.100**) under *ITEPA 2003, s 346* as if he had expended the money himself. [*ITEPA 2003, s 72(2)*]. Mileage allowance payments (see **7.48**) and passenger payments (see **7.56**) in respect of an employee's own car were specifically excluded from *Income and Corporation Taxes Act 1988 (ICTA 1988), s 153* but the format of *ITEPA 2003* no longer makes such a provision necessary.

6.39   In *Wicks v Firth [1983] STC 25* Lord Denning expressed the view that the words 'by reason of' are far wider than the word 'therefrom' used in *ICTA*

1988, s 19(1) and are deliberately designed to close the gap in taxability left by the House of Lords in *Hochstrasser v Mayes*. Oliver LJ agreed but suggested that the words require one to ask the question 'What is it that enables the person concerned to enjoy the benefit?'. This question was adopted in *Mairs v Haughey* (see **11.55**) and also in *Wilcock v Eve* (see **3.17**), in both of which the disputed item was held not to be taxable as a benefit in kind.

Treatment of expenses

6.40 In other words, all expenses paid to higher-paid employees are treated with suspicion, and are assumed not to be business expenses. It is then up to the employee to displace that presumption by showing that the expenses meet the strict rules to attract a deduction.

6.41 Strictly speaking, as payments to the employee are assessable income, such expense payments should be subject to PAYE but HMRC have not been known to take the point.

Payments to third parties

6.42 It should be noted that *section 70* applies only to payments made to the employee (or into an account under his control). It does not apply to payments to third parties. If payments to third parties in respect of expenses satisfy an existing liability of the employee it should not be overlooked that such payments already constitute emoluments under general principles as they constitute amounts of money's worth provided for the employee by reason of his employment. This is emphasised by the decision in *Sports Club plc v Inspector of Taxes [2000] STC (SCD) 443* which is considered at **3.9–3.11**.

The assessable amount

6.43 Where a person is in higher-paid employment and by reason of his employment any benefit is provided for him or for members of his family or household an amount equal to the cash equivalent of the benefit must be treated as income from his employment. [*ITEPA 2003, s 201*]. If the same benefit would give rise to an amount taxable as earnings under the basic rules and an amount being treated as earnings under the benefits code the earnings rule takes precedence and the amount taxed under the benefit code is limited to the excess of the benefit code figure over the amount already taxed as earnings. [*ITEPA 2003, s 64*].

Exceptions

6.44 There are a number of exceptions.

(*a*) The right to receive (or the prospect of receiving) a sum which is itself taxable under *section 221* (sick pay under industry-wide arrangements) see **2.40** above). [*ITEPA 2003, s 202(1)(c)*].

(*b*)   A benefit to which the round sum car use (see **7.2** below), van use (see **7.76** below) or petrol (see **7.45** below) benefits apply. [*ITEPA 2003, s 202(1)(a)*].

(*c*)   A benefit which is taxable under the special rules applying to beneficial loans (see **9.1** below) and employee shareholdings (see **Chapter 14**). [*ITEPA 2003, s 202(1)(a)*].

(*d*)   If a person is taxable on the car use benefit (see **7.2** below), or van use benefit (see **7.76** below) *ITEPA 2003, s 201* does not apply to any benefit in connection with that car, other than a benefit in connection with a driver for the car, ie the car use benefit does not cover the wages, uniform, subsistence, etc. of a chauffeur. [*ITEPA 2003, s 239(4) (5)*]. It also does not cover a car telephone, if it is portable (but does so if it is fixed: see **7.79** and **9.33** below).

(*e*)   The provision of a car parking space at or near the employee's place of work. [*ITEPA 2003, s 237*]. From 2005/06 this exemption also precludes any charge under the general employment income charging rules [*ITEPA 2003, s 237(1)*].

(*f*)   If living accommodation is provided for a person by reason of his employment *ITEPA 2003, s 201* does not apply to:

   (i)   alterations and additions to the premises which are of a structural nature – as these are really expenses of the company as 'landlord' rather than of the employee as occupier; and

   (ii)   repairs to the premises such that if the premises were let under a lease to which *section 11, Landlord and Tenant Act 1985* applies they would be obligations of the landlord, not the occupier. *Section 11* imposes on the landlord the obligation, at his own cost, to keep in repair the structure and exterior of the dwelling including the drains, gutters and external pipes; and to keep in repair and proper working order the installations in the dwelling for the supply of water, gas, electricity, sanitation, space heating and hot water. [*ITEPA 2003, s 313*].

(*g*)   The provision by the employer for either the employee himself or his spouse, children or dependants, of any pension, annuity, lump sum, gratuity or similar benefit to be given on the employee's death or retirement. This will cover not only an actual payment on retirement but also, for example, the payment of an insurance premium on a policy to provide for such a payment. [*ITEPA 2003, s 307*].

(*h*)   The provision by the employer of meals in a canteen in which meals are provided for the staff generally. [*ITEPA 2003, s 317(1)(a)*]. The exemption also applies if the meals are provided for the employees at a particular location. [*ITEPA 2003, s 317(1)(a)*]. It also covers other meals provided on the employee's business premises if:

   (i)   the meals are on a reasonable scale;

   (ii)   all of the employees (or all of them at a particular location) can obtain either a free or subsidised meal or a meal voucher or token enabling them to obtain a meal;

(iii) if the meals are provided in the restaurant or dining room of a hotel or catering business at a time when meals are being served to the public, the employees eat only in a part of the room designated for staff only; and

(iv) for 2011/12 onwards the provision is not pursuant to either relevant salary sacrifice arrangements or relevant flexible remuneration arrangements. Relevant salary sacrifice arrangements are arrangements (whenever made) under which the employee gives up a right to receive an amount of general earnings or specific employment income in return for the provision of free or subsidised meals, and relevant flexible remuneration arrangements are arrangements (whenever made) under which the employer and employee agree that the employee is to be provided with free or subsidised meals rather than receive some other description of employment income [*ITEPA 2003, s 317(5A) inserted by Finance Act 2010 (FA 2010), s 60(4)*].

[*ITEPA 2003, s 317(1)(b), (2)–(5)* as amended by *FA 2010, s 60*].

(*i*) The provision for the employee of medical treatment outside the UK (or of insurance cover against the cost of such treatment) where the need for the treatment arises while the employee is outside the UK for the purpose of performing the duties of the employment. Medical treatment for this purpose includes all forms of treatment for, and all procedures for diagnosing, any physical or mental ailment, infirmity or defect. and the cost of such treatment includes the costs of providing for the employee to be an in-patient in a hospital. [*ITEPA 2003, s 325*]. If the employee is so ill that his doctors feel that he should be flown back to the UK for treatment, this exception would not cover the cost of treatment in the UK or the cost of flying him back. It would, however, cover the cost of treatment in a different overseas country to that in which he was initially taken ill.

(*j*) The provision of entertainment (including hospitality of any kind) for the employee, or for members of his family or household, if:

(i) the person providing the benefit is not his employer, nor a connected person of the employer within *section 839*;

(ii) neither the employer (nor a connected person of his) has directly or indirectly procured its provision; and

(iii) it is not provided either in recognition of particular services which have been performed by the employee in the course of his employment or in anticipation of his performing such services. [*ITEPA 2003, s 265*].

This exempts, for example, the cost incurred by a customer or supplier of the employer who entertains the employee for his own, rather than the employer's, purposes.

(*k*) If an asset or service which improves personal security is provided for an employee by his employer by reason of his employment the cost is not taxed on the employee (or, to be precise, it is taxed on him but offset by an equivalent deduction). Similarly, no charge arises if the employer reimburses such expenditure by the employee. [*ITEPA 2003, s 377(2)*]. This exemption applies only if the asset or service is provided to meet a special threat to the employee's personal security which arises wholly or mainly from the employment concerned. [*ITEPA 2003, s 377(1)*]. The meeting of the threat must be the sole object of the employer in bearing the cost. The asset must be intended for use solely to improve personal physical security (eg not partly to improve security to property of the employee) and the benefit resulting from a security service must consist wholly or mainly of an improvement to the employee's personal physical security. [*ITEPA 2003, s 377(3)*]. A proportion of the cost is exempted from tax if the asset is partly provided to meet a threat to the employee's personal security. [*ITEPA 2003, s 377(4)*]. The fact that the expenditure also improves the physical security of the employee's family or household as well as himself will not restrict the relief. [*ITEPA 2003, s 377(7)*]. Relief is not given for the cost of a car, ship, aircraft or a dwelling-house and its grounds. [*ITEPA 2003, s 377(8)*]. It will be given for additions to such assets, eg bulletproof windows for a car, a perimeter wall round the house, etc. This relief is intended to be very restrictive. It is intended to meet threats from terrorists and other extremist groups. It will not apply, therefore, to such things such as rape alarms provided to female staff who work late or similar items for protection against the criminal activities that the average citizen may have to face. For 2011/12 onwards, most security features on cars installed to meet a threat to the employees' physical security are ignored when calculating the benefit in respect of the car [*ITEPA 2003, s 125A* inserted by *FA 2012, s 14*]. The detailed rules are considered at 7.21.

These provisions were considered by the Special Commissioners in *Lord Hanson v Mansworth [2004 STC] (SCD) 288*. Hanson plc expanded into Northern Ireland in 1978. Lord Hanson was perceived to be close to the Conservative Party although he did not make any contributions to it. The company was concerned about his safety and provided him with a 24-hour security service at his country home (eight dog handlers and dogs and three guards) from 1989/90 to 1997/98. He was put on the police 'reserve' list in 1990. The Commissioners held that Lord Hanson met the profile of the type of person who could well be an IRA target. There was therefore a threat. They thought that 'special' means 'out of the ordinary' and a terrorist threat is out of the ordinary. The threat arose wholly or mainly by reason of Lord Hanson's employment as his high profile arose only by virtue of his name and role in Hanson plc. They thought that the test of whether meeting the threat was the sole object of the provider is a subjective one, ie what was the employer's belief. They further held that the security service was clearly not provided to protect the house from a generalised criminal threat (it already had a burglar alarm system) and that the benefit to Lord Hanson was certainly mainly an improvement in his personal physical security. The Commissioners also held that although the relief is automatic and does not have to be claimed Lord Hanson was negligent in not having shown the benefit of the security services on his tax return and an offsetting deduction. This is, at least a little, startling as there is no box for such a deduction on the tax return.

(*l*)   There are also specific exemptions for the first £8,000 of certain removal expenses (see **9.50**), sports and recreation facilities (see **9.82**) redundancy counselling (see **9.82**), and the payment by an employer on behalf of an employee of amounts in respect of employee liabilities or officers' indemnity insurance (see **5.100**). [*ITEPA 2003, s 334*].

(*m*)   Incidental overnight expenses where a person is working away from home for a period which includes at least one overnight stay. The expenditure must not exceed an average of £5 a night in the UK or £10 a night elsewhere. [*ITEPA 2003, s 240, 241*]. The detailed rules that must be met are the same as for such reimbursed expenses and are considered at **5.40**.

(*n*)   The provision in premises occupied by the employer (or others providing it) of accommodation, supplies or services used by the employee solely in performing the duties of the employment. [*ITEPA 2003, s 316(1)*].

(*o*)   Making available the use of a mobile telephone to the employee or to a member of his family or household (see **9.33**).

(*p*)   Making available computer equipment provided that specified conditions are met (see **9.89**).

(*q*)   The use of a works bus provided that certain conditions are met (see **9.89**).

(*r*)   There are some exemptions for cycles (see **9.93**).

(*s*)   The provision of accommodation, supplies or services used by the employee in performing the duties of his employment. If the benefit is provided on premises occupied by the employer (or by the provider of the benefit if different) any use of it for private purposes by the employee or members of his family or household must not be significant. Use is for private purposes if it is not in performing the duties of the employment and simultaneous use for performing the duties of the employment and for some other purpose is treated as private. [*ITEPA 2003, s 316(2), (3)*]. No guidance has been given as to the meaning of not significant. If the benefit is not provided on the employer's premises it needs to be shown that the sole purpose of providing the benefit is to enable the employee to perform the duties of his employment, that any use for private purposes is not significant and that the benefit is not an excluded benefit [*ITEPA 2003, s 316(4)*]. A motor vehicle, boat, aircraft, or any benefit that involves the extension, conversion or alteration of any living accommodation (or the construction, extension, conversion or alteration of a building or other structure on land adjacent to and enjoyed with such accommodation) are excluded benefits. [*ITEPA 2003, s 316(5)*]. The Treasury has power to amend this list of excluded benefits. [*ITEPA 2003, s 316(6)*]. This provision exempts incidental private use of business assets.

(*t*)   Where an employer makes a payment to an employee in respect of reasonable additional household expenses which the employee incurs in carrying out duties of the employment at home under homeworking arrangements the payment is exempt from income tax. Household expenses are expenses connected with the day-to-day running of the employee's home. Homeworking arrangements are arrangements between the employee and the employer under which the employee regularly performs some or all of the duties of the employment at home. [*ITEPA 2003, s 316A*]. It should be noted that it is only the additional expenses (eg light, heat, telephone) caused by the homeworking that qualifies for relief, not a proportion of any expenses that would have been incurred in any event. HMRC have said that they will accept an amount of up to £4 a week or £208 a year £3 a week (between 6 April 2008 and 5 April 2012) as reasonable without supporting evidence. If the employer pays more than this amount they will expect to see evidence to demonstrate that the payment is wholly in respect of additional expenses (Press Release, 9 April 2003).

(*u*) The Treasury have power by Regulation to exempt from *s 154* such minor benefit as they may specify. They cannot exempt a benefit under this power unless it is made available to an employer's employees generally on the same terms. [*ITEPA 2003, s 210*]. They have exempted welfare counselling (counselling of any kind, other than medical treatment of any kind or advice on finance (other than debt problems), on tax, on leisure or recreation, or legal advice) provided that it is made available to an employer's employees generally on similar terms (*Income Tax (Benefits in Kind) (Exemption for Welfare Counselling) Regulations 2000 (SI 2000 No 2080)*). HMRC have issued guidance (HMRC Guidance Note 3.12.2008) on the scope of this exemption. They say that where an Employee Assistance Programme includes a range of facilities and treatments, some of which fall outside the scope of the exemption, strictly the exemption does not apply to any of the services, as it does not provide any basis for apportionment. However common sense should be applied 'where the welfare counselling provided by the employer consists substantially of facilities that satisfy the terms of the exemption but also to a not significant proportion of the services provided which do not satisfy the exemption'. HMRC are particularly concerned about legal and financial advice. Incidental legal advice given by a non-lawyer where the employee's legal problem arises from his welfare problem is acceptable. However it is not acceptable for the initial call to be taken by a lawyer or for a lawyer to give legal advice subsequent to the initial call. The Guidance note sets out detailed rules and needs to be read if counselling is likely to include such advice. They have also exempted cyclist's breakfasts ('qualifying meals') provided for an employee in a tax year. This is food or drink provided by an employer in recognition of the employee having used a cycle to make a journey between their home and their workplace, and which is provided for consumption by the employee on their arrival at the workplace on that day. They have also exempted the benefit from the provision of a bus or minibus for conveying employees on a relevant journey, ie one which is a single journey of a distance of up to 10 miles made between the workplace and shops or other amenities and made on a working day. *(Income Tax (Exemption of Minor Benefits) Regulations 2002) (SI 2002 No 205)*. They also exempted one health screening (ie an assessment to identify employees who might be at a particular risk of ill health) and one medical check-up (ie a physical examination of an employee by a health professional which is limited to determine that employee's state of health) per employee each tax year, but only if health screenings were available to all employees and medical check-ups were available either to all employees or to all who health screening has identified as requiring a medical check-up. [*Income Tax (Exemption of Minor Benefits) (Amendment) Regulations 2007 (SI 2007 No 2090)*]. This exemption was repealed from 5 April 2009 by the *Income Tax (Exemption of Minor Benefits) (Revocation) Order 2009 (SI 2009 No 695)* and replaced by a new *ITEPA 2003, s 320B* (see **9.114**).

(v)   The provision of a benefit to a disabled employee if the main purpose of providing the benefit is to enable the employee to perform the duties of the employment, it consists in the provision of a hearing aid or other equipment, services or facilities (other than a benefit already excluded from tax under some other provision), it is provided under (or within the terms of) the *Disability Discrimination Act 1995 (DDA 1995)*, the Access to Work programme (under the *Employment and Training Act 1973, s 2* or its Scottish or Northern Irish equivalent) or some other statutory provisions (whether or not the employer has a legal duty to provide the benefit) and the benefit is made available to the employer's employees generally on similar terms. [*Income Tax (Benefits in Kind) (Exemption for Employment Costs resulting from Disability) Regulations 2002 (SI 2002 No 1596)*].

Payments to the employee's family

6.45   For the purpose of the benefit in kind provisions, all sums paid to an employee by his employer himself, and all benefits provided for an employee (or for members of his family or household) by his employer, must be treated as paid or provided by reason of the employment – even if it can be demonstrated that they are made for entirely unconnected reasons. There is an exception where the employer is an individual (but not if it is a partnership) and it can be shown that the payment or provision was made in the normal course of that individual's domestic, family or personal relationships. [*ITEPA 2003, s 201(3)*].

6.46   The people regarded as members of a person's family or household are his spouse, his sons and daughters, spouses of his sons and daughters, his parents, and his dependants, domestic staff and guests. [*ITEPA 2003, s 721(4)*].

6.47   As indicated at **6.42** above, the assessable amount is the cash equivalent of the benefit. This is the 'cost of the benefit' less any part of that cost which is made good by the employee to the person providing the benefit. [*ITEPA 2003, s 203*]. If the benefit is provided to a member of the employee's family there does not appear to be a right to reduce the cost by any payment made by the family member, but HMRC will undoubtedly allow this by concession.

The cost of the benefit

6.48   The 'cost of a benefit' is normally the amount of any expense incurred in (or in connection with) its provision. A proper proportion of any expense relating partly to the benefit and partly to other matters must be included. [*ITEPA 2003, s 204*]. Where an employee sells or transfers an asset to his employer or to a person nominated by the employer and the right or opportunity to make the transfer arose by reason of the employment, the employee is not taxable on the payment or reimbursement of expenses which are incidental to, and incurred wholly and exclusively as a result of, the transfer and which are of a kind not normally met by the transferor. [*ITEPA 2003, s 326*]. This excludes from the cost of the benefit the employer's legal and other costs of acquisition. It would not exclude any expense paid by the employer which would normally be borne by the vendor (*Press Release 27 April 1994*). There is no corresponding concession where the employer transfers an asset to the employee.

6.49   Where the benefit consists in the provision to the employee of a service provided by the employer in the normal course of its business, or the transfer to him of goods produced by the company, commonly called 'in-house' benefits, the cost of providing the benefit is the marginal cost. This was settled by the House of Lords in *Pepper v Hart [1992] STC 898*. That case was concerned with the provision by a private school of education for children of its teachers – a standard perk in the education field. The school argued that the cost to it of providing the education was the marginal cost and it cost virtually nothing to add another child to an existing class of children where there were vacancies in the class. HMRC contended that the total cost of running the school had to be apportioned amongst all the pupils, including the children of teachers, to arrive at the cost of the benefit. This would give a figure roughly equal to the standard fees charged by the school less the profit element included in such fees.

6.50   HMRC's contention was upheld in both the High Court and the Court of Appeal. In an exceptional seven-man hearing before the House of Lords, five of their Lordships supported HMRC's interpretation and two, including the Lord Chancellor, the taxpayer's, on a simple consideration of the statutory language. However, the House, in a landmark decision, opted to set aside the tradition that the courts could not consult Hansard to assist in determining what Parliament has intended in enacting the legislation. It felt that this should be permissible where:

(*a*)   legislation is ambiguous or obscure, or leads to an absurdity;

(*b*)   the materials relied on are statements by a Minister or other promoter of the *Bill*; and

(*c*)   the statements relied on are clear.

6.51   When what is now *s 204* was introduced in 1976 the original Bill contained a clause which sought to tax in-house benefits by reference to the price which the public would pay for the item. However, the Government withdrew that provision, the Minister stating, 'I will give some reasons which weigh heavily in favour of the withdrawal of this provision. The first is the large difference between the cost of providing some services and the amount of benefit which under the *Bill* would be held to be received ... I would point out that air and rail journeys are only two of a number of service benefits which have a number of problems attached to them. But there is a large difference between the cost of the benefit to the employer and the value of that benefit as assessed. It could lead to unjustifiable situations resulting in a great number of injustices and I do not think we should continue with it ... The second reason for withdrawing Clause 54(4) is that these services would tend to be much less used ... The third reason is the difficulty of enforcement and administration which both give rise to certain problems. Finally it was possible to withdraw this part of the legislation as the services cover not only a more difficult area, but a quite distinct area of these provisions, without having repercussions on some of the other areas ... .' (*Hansard Standing Committee E 17 June 1976, cols 893–895*).

6.52   He was then asked, 'Is he saying that these benefits will remain taxable but that the equivalent cost of the benefit will be calculated on some different basis? Or is he saying that these benefits will not be taxable at all?' The Minister responded, 'The existing law which applies to the taxation of some of these benefits will be retained. The position will subsequently be unchanged from what it is now before the introduction of the legislation'. He later said, 'The employee earning more than £5,000 or the director will be assessed on the benefit received by him on the basis of the cost to the employer ... If a company provides a service to the kind of employee which we have been talking about, and the company subsidises that service, the benefit assessable on the employee is the cost to the employer of providing that service ... Some companies provide services of a kind where the cost to them is very little. For example, an airline ticket, allowing occupation of an empty seat, costs an airline nothing – in fact, in such a case there could be a negative cost, as it might be an advantage to the airline to have an experienced crew member on the flight. The cost to the company, then, would be nothing ... sub-section (2) only re-states the existing position. It does not produce anything new.' (*Cols 930–932*).

6.53   On 22 June 1976 the Minister told the standing committee in response to a question on travel concessions for merchant seamen, 'This proposal concerns the employee of a company and his wife ... and the concession of a free passage or voyage in a company ship ... I think that I can satisfy the hon Gentlemen that these voyages will not now be subject to tax as a result of the withdrawal of sub-clause (4) apart from the nominal charge for food which is normally made and which would be assessable ... the only basis for charge would be on the cost to the employer, and in the example that we are considering that would be very small.' He was then specifically asked about concessionary fees for children of teachers at fee paying schools and replied, 'now the benefit will be assessed on the cost to the employer, which would be very small indeed in this case'. As indicated earlier, in *Pepper v Hart* itself HMRC were seeking to value the benefit to a teacher at a private school of cheap education of his child at the school, the very situation that had been envisaged in that question.

6.54   The previous rules had been explained to the Finance Bill standing committee by the Minister in 1975 in response to a question on the imposition of tax on certain vouchers. The railwayman travelling on his normal voucher will not be taxable either '... because the provision of the service that he provides falls upon the employer. Clearly, the railways will run in precisely the same way whether the railwaymen use this facility or not, so there is no extra charge to the Railways Board itself, therefore there would be no taxable benefits'.

6.55   Faced with these repeated assurances the House of Lords had no trouble in finding that, with the benefit of being able to consult *Hansard*, the reference to cost must be to marginal cost.

6.56   Following the decision in *Pepper v Hart* HMRC announced that its effect 'was that in the case of all in-house benefits the cost of the benefit to the employer is the additional or marginal cost only' (*Press Release 21 January 1993*). This Press Release made clear that in-house benefits include goods as well as services and facilities. It went on to state that the marginal cost depends on each employer's particular circumstances but that as a general guide HMRC accept that:

(*a*)   rail or bus travel on terms which do not displace fare-paying passengers involves no or negligible additional costs;

(*b*)   goods sold at a discount which leave employees paying at least the wholesale price involve no or negligible net benefit;

(*c*)   where teachers pay 15 per cent or more of a school's normal fees there is no net benefit; and

(*d*)   professional services which do not require additional employees or partners (eg legal and financial services) have no or negligible cost to the employer provided the employee reimburses any disbursements.

Transfer of assets

6.57   If the benefit consists of the transfer of an asset to the employee (or a member of his family or household) and the asset has been used or has otherwise depreciated since it was acquired by the employer (or other person who provides the benefit) the cost of the benefit is not the cost of the asset to the employer but its market value at the time of transfer, ie the price which it might reasonably have been expected to fetch on a sale in the open market at that time [*ITEPA 2003, s 206*], subject to **6.58** below. This works both ways. It would be unreasonable to tax an employee on the amount he paid for, say, a computer which has been used by the company for five years and is now obsolete and of very little value. It is only fair that if the employee buys the computer from the company at its current value no benefit should arise, and that if he does not pay for it the benefit should be limited to its current value, as the real benefit is what the employee has saved by not having to buy a machine in the same state from a second-hand shop. On the other hand some assets increase in value. If the employee takes home the painting that cost £500 and has been on his office wall for five years he may well find that he has a benefit charge on £1,200 or some similar figure because the painting has increased in value.

6.58   If the second-hand asset has previously been used by the company to provide a benefit to the employee, or to another higher-paid employee, by allowing him the use of it, the cost of the benefit is the higher of:

(*a*)   its market value at the time of transfer; or

(*b*)   the original cost of the asset (its market value at the time when it was first used by the employer (or other provider of the benefit) to provide benefits) less the aggregate of the amounts previously assessed on higher-paid employees in relation to the use of the asset. [*ITEPA 2003, s 206(5)*].

Example

On 5 July 2010, M Ployer Ltd purchased a video recorder for £800 which it installed at the house of Arthur, a higher-paid employee. On 5 December 2013 it sold the recorder to Ben, another higher-paid employee, at its then market value of £60.

Benefit charge on Arthur

	£
2010/11 20% of £800 × 9 months	120
2011/12 20% of £800	160
2012/13 20% of £800	160
2013/14 20% of £800 × 8 months	107
	£547

Benefit charge on Ben

	£	£	£
2013/14			
Higher of: Market value:		60	
Higher of: Cost	800		
Higher of: *Less*: Assessed on Arthur	(547)		
		253	253
Higher of: *Less*: Payment by Ben			
			60
Higher of: Benefit charge			£193

In this example Ben suffers a very heavy benefit charge even though he buys the asset at full market value. He would have been wiser to have let the employer sell the asset and bought a second-hand machine from a shop. Although the benefit has been pro-rated for parts of a year – which happens in practice – the *Act* appears to impose a full 20 per cent of cost charge even though the asset is not made available to the employee throughout the year. If Arthur had continued to have use of the asset for over five years the benefit would continue at 20 per cent of cost, so overall he would have been assessed on a figure greater than cost. An employee should be wary of his employer making very expensive assets with a long life, such as antiques or works of art, available for his use.

6.59   This charge does not apply to cars, or to a cycle or cyclists' safety equipment previously provided in circumstances where *ITEPA 2003, s 244* (see **9.93**) were met [*ITEPA 2003, s 206(3)(a)* as amended by *Finance Act 2005 (FA 2005), s 17*]. [Nor does it apply to an asset first used to provide benefits to higher-paid employees before 6 April 1980. [*ITEPA 2003, s 206(3) (c)*]. If such an asset, or a second-hand car, is transferred to an employee after having been used by the company, the cost of the benefit will be its market value at the time of the transfer, even if that use was by the employee himself.

6.60   It should not be overlooked that if the asset transferred is within the scope of capital gains tax the transfer will give rise to a capital gains tax charge on the employer. Where an asset is acquired in consideration for or in recognition of a person's (or another's) services or past services in any office or employment *TCGA 1992, s 17(1)(b)* requires the capital gain on the disposal to be calculated by reference to the market value at the time of the transfer.

Assets placed at the employee's disposal

6.61   If an asset is placed at the disposal of the employee (or of other members of his family or household) for his use without any transfer of the ownership of the asset, the cost of the benefit is the aggregate of:

(*a*)   the annual value of the use of the asset, namely (in most cases) 20 per cent of its market value at the time when it was first applied by the employer (or other provider of the benefit) in the provision of any benefit for any person; and

(*b*)   any expense incurred in (or in connection with) the provision of the benefit other than the cost of acquiring or producing it incurred by the owner, and any rent or hire charge payable for it by the person providing the benefit.

[*ITEPA 2003, s 205*].

6.62   In most cases the figure at (*a*) will be 20 per cent of the cost of the asset. If the asset is land the annual rental value of the use of the asset is its annual value under *ITEPA 2003, s 110* (see **8.4** below). If the asset was first used to provide benefits for higher-paid employees before 6 April 1980 only 10 per cent of the cost of the asset is charged instead of 20 per cent. [*ITEPA 2003, s 205(3)*]. If the asset is leased or rented and the rent exceeds the 20 per cent of cost figure (or in the case of land the annual value) the figure to be used at (*a*) will instead be the rent or leasing charges paid. [*ITEPA 2003, s 205(2)*].

6.63   If the service or asset is used in whole or part for business purposes the taxpayer can make an expenses claim under *ITEPA 2003, s 336* (and *s 343* if he is a clergyman), *section 346* if it is an employee liability payment (see **5.100**), or *section 343* if the benefit is the payment of a qualifying subscription, as if he had incurred expenditure out of his emoluments equal to the cost of the benefit from the asset. [*ITEPA 2003, s 365*].

6.64   Where an asset is used both in the business and for an employee's private purposes some fixed costs, such as road tax for a van, do not need to be taken into account where the private use of the asset is incidental to business use as it is only any additional expense incurred in connection with the provision of the asset that gives rise to a benefit (*Press Release 21 January 1993*).

Former employees

6.65   The main benefit in kind rules apply where the person is an employee at some point in the tax year in which the benefit is provided [*ITEPA 2003, s 201(4)*]. They accordingly cannot apply to benefits payable to a former employee after the end of the year of assessment in which the employment ceases. Indeed, HMRC used to take the view that they cannot apply to a benefit provided after the employment has ended but later in the same year of assessment. This does not mean such benefits escape tax. The benefit is part of the termination package and assessable as such (see **11.37**). A charge can also arise under other provisions. *ITEPA 2003, s 394* imposes tax on employment income (for the year the benefit is received) on a benefit in kind which is provided under a retirement benefits scheme. HMRC interpret 'retirement benefits scheme' very widely (see **11.34**). Any payment made as a result of a person's retirement – which could be deemed to occur if he leaves his job within a few years prior to retirement age – is likely to be within *s 394*. Benefits payable as part of a redundancy package would not normally be within *s 394*. The amount of such a benefit is calculated in the same way as for benefits in kind. [*ITEPA 2003, s 398*].

6.66   If the recipient of the benefit is a shareholder or an associate of a shareholder the benefit can also be a distribution, calculated on the same basis as for tax on employment income. [*ICTA 1988, s 418(1), (4)*]. Although the same benefit cannot be taxed under both *ITEPA 2003, s 203* and *ICTA 1988, s 418* [*ICTA1988, s 418(3)*] there is no such limitation where the benefit is taxable under *ITEPA 2003, s 394* (see **10.77**) or *s 402* (see **11.27**).

Time when benefit is provided

6.67   An interesting question arose in *Templeton v Jacobs [1996] STC 991*. The taxpayer, who lived in London, was offered employment from 1 May 1991 by a company in Kenilworth. He was not prepared to move and it was agreed that the taxpayer would, at the company's expense, convert his loft to an office. The builder sent his invoices to the company. These were all paid in full before 1 April 1991. HMRC sought to tax the whole cost of the loft conversion as a benefit in kind. The taxpayer contended that the benefit had been provided on 1 April 1991 and as the employment did not exist in 1990/91 could not be taxed under *s 203*. The High Court, reversing the decision of the Special Commissioners, held that no benefit is provided until it becomes available to be enjoyed by the taxpayer. In this case the work was not completed until after the employment had started so was not available until then. The judge also rejected an alternate claim that as the loft was rented to the company it was occupied by it and thus exempt under *s 316(1)* (see **6.44**(*o*)), holding that the benefit was the carrying out of the work, not the occupation of the office.

Lower-paid employees

6.68   The benefit in kind provisions (other than those described at **6.14–6.35** above, and **8.1–8.29** below do not apply to those in lower paid employment, ie where the earnings for the years are at a rate of less than £8,500. [*ITEPA 2003, s 217*]. In practice, with the average wage now £25,006 per annum, the number of lower-paid employees is diminishing and there are very few for whom employers might wish to provide benefits.

6.69   Furthermore, except for major companies that can provide in-house facilities for staff, a certain amount of ingenuity is needed, or a significant degree of inconvenience must be tolerated, to provide benefits for lower-paid employees without generating a tax charge on the cost of providing the benefit. This is because it is essential to avoid bringing into existence anything that might constitute a non-cash voucher (see **6.20** above) or a credit token (see **6.29** above). For example, suppose an employer enters into an arrangement with a local tailor to supply suits to his staff. How is the tailor to know who is entitled to a suit? If the employer gives the employee a letter addressed to the tailor saying that if he supplies a suit to the employee the employer will pay for it, the letter will be a non-cash voucher. If the employer says to the tailor that all his staff have official identification cards and he should supply a suit to whoever shows one, and send the employer a bill stating the name on the identity card, the card is probably a credit token. If the employee simply orders the suit himself and takes a cheque from the employer with him when he collects it, the cheque is a non-cash voucher – and in any event the cost of the suit is an emolument of the employee as he will have incurred the liability to pay for the suit. The employer could personally accompany the employee to the tailor and order the suit himself, but this does involve a certain amount of inconvenience.

6.70   If an employer does contrive to provide benefits to lower-paid employees without triggering a charge under the benefit rules the benefit does not, in theory at least, escape tax. The employee is taxable under general principles (see **3.2** above) on the money's worth into which the benefit can be converted. The leading case is *Wilkins v Rogerson 39 TC 344* where the employer arranged for an employee to collect a new suit from a tailor. It was held that he was taxable on the second-hand value of the suit, which was £5, and not its cost of £14.75. Whilst goods can normally be converted into cash – albeit at a figure significantly below cost – the same is not always true of services. For example, if an employer says to an employee, 'Come to the hairdressers with me and I will arrange for you to have your hair cut and styled', it is impossible for the employee to convert that benefit into cash because, by seeking to assign it, the employer would be aware that the person claiming the benefit was not the employee and would refuse to provide the benefit. Accordingly, the money's worth of the benefit would be nil.

Remuneration packages

6.71 Apart from company cars, where the quantum of the benefit has in the past been significantly below the cost of providing it and in some, but by no means all, cases still is, most benefits provided to higher-paid employees attract a tax charge equal to the cost of providing the benefit. In these circumstances the provision of benefits might be thought somewhat pointless. Admittedly, there is a National Insurance saving but in most cases this is only 10 per cent of the employee's salary (12.8 per cent less 28 per cent tax relief) or 11.4 per cent with a 21 per cent corporation tax rate, and it is questionable whether this is a sufficient benefit to justify the administrative costs. Probably the most common reason for providing benefits is that such provision is widespread in the UK and if other employers provide benefits it may be necessary to follow suit to attract the right calibre of staff. An employee may perceive the benefit to be worth more than an equivalent sum in cash even though he will suffer tax on it. He may also perceive an employer who provides benefits as having a more caring attitude towards staff than one who does not, although often such a perception is far from the case.

6.72 If an employer does decide that he wants to provide benefits it is obviously important to give staff the right benefits; those that will attract them to the employer or will motivate them in their work. Unfortunately, it is often difficult to determine what benefit to provide. It is also difficult to know whether the cost of the benefit is justifiable in terms of the incentive effect on staff. For example, an employee who does not drive, or one whose spouse already has a company car, would probably appreciate a rise far more than a company car. Many employees may be happier with a cash increase than a benefit. Other things being equal, it is better to have 60p in one's pocket to spend as one may wish than £1 spent on a benefit which generates a 40p tax charge that has to be met out of one's own pocket, and which may not be a benefit that one might have chosen for oneself. Even where an employee may appreciate a benefit, such as family medical insurance, if the expenditure on such an item is low on his list of priorities it is unlikely to motivate him significantly. These problems can be minimised by the use of remuneration packages.

6.73 The basic concept of a remuneration package is that the employer is prepared to pay a certain sum to obtain the services of the employee. This could be paid wholly in cash or it could be spent partly in cash and partly in the provision of benefits. In theory, provided that the total cost is the same, it should make no difference to the employer how the money is laid out but the provision of benefits could be advantageous to the employee.

Fixed packages

6.74   A remuneration package can be fixed or flexible. A fixed remuneration package generally comprises a standard package, the components of which the employer is normally prepared to convert into cash if the employee wishes. For example, he may say to the prospective employee, 'We will offer you £20,000 a year, plus a Ford Escort car, plus a non-contributory pension scheme; we think the car is worth £2,000 a year and we will put £1,000 a year into the pension scheme so we are really offering you £23,000'. If the employee were to say he would prefer to be paid £23,000 with no benefits, the employer ought to be prepared to accede to this. With a fixed remuneration package, therefore, the employer has to try to assess what benefits he thinks might be attractive to the employee and consequently takes a gamble on whether the employee might be indifferent to them. For example, whilst an employee is unlikely to actually refuse a company car unless he is positively offered extra salary in lieu, if the employee values the use of the car at £800 whereas the employer values it at £2,000, the cost of providing the car will have been largely wasted. The employee would find the job more attractive if he were given a £1,000 rise instead of the car.

Flexible packages

6.75   With a flexible remuneration package the employer fixes the amount he is prepared to spend to obtain or keep the employee and leaves the employee to decide how much of that he would like as salary and how much as benefits and what benefits he would like provided. This has a number of obvious advantages. It ensures that the employee realises what it costs to provide the benefit. It may also give the employer a competitive advantage, as some of the benefit he may be prepared to provide, if he is willing to respond positively to the employee's wishes, may not be available to the employee from other prospective employers.

6.76   There are dangers. If a large number of staff are involved, the administration costs of providing a range of benefits can be enormous. The provision of benefits could also give rise to staff jealousies. If one employee chooses an expensive car and a colleague a cheaper car and a larger salary, there is a risk that after a time the second employee may forget that his contemporary has a bigger car because he chose to forgo part of his salary and may come to see the difference in cars as reflecting a difference in status and thus become dissatisfied. What if an employee changes his mind? Should he be able to change the make up of his remuneration package and, if so, how frequently? There may be practical problems in ceasing to provide a benefit if the employer has had to enter into a long term contractual relationship with someone else to provide it. Consideration also needs to be given to the VAT position. Customs and Excise have been known to contend that there is a VATable supply to an employee if he has an entitlement to exchange his use of an asset for a cash sum. Although they have retreated from this in relation to cars (see **7.44**) they did so by changing the law so their argument could still run for other assets.

6.77 For these reasons fully flexible remuneration packages are rare. An employer would normally be wise to set some parameters on the employee's choice. He could have a limited list of benefits that he is prepared to provide, any or all of which the employee can opt to take as part of his remuneration package. Such schemes are often called 'cafeteria schemes' to reflect the fact that the employee chooses what he wants from the menu. If an employer opts for such a scheme, he should probably be prepared to consider the provision of benefits that are not on his list where these could be provided without undue trouble. He probably ought to provide a minimum amount that must be taken as salary, eg if the remuneration package is a total of £30,000 perhaps at least £20,000 must be salary. He also ought to set limits to avoid an undue risk of jealousy between employees, eg an employee with a £30,000 remuneration package might not be permitted to choose a company car costing more than say £20,000. He also ought to set limits to ease administration. For example, an employee could be allowed to choose what car he wants, provided that it is one that can be provided and serviced by one of the motor suppliers with which the employer already has an account.

6.78 Provided that these factors are borne in mind and both employer and employee are prepared to approach the provision of benefits with a degree of commonsense, the remuneration package can become an important tool in motivating employees. The choice of benefits that might be considered for inclusion in a remuneration package is very wide. The obvious ones are company cars, employee shareholdings and similar incentives, pensions and medical insurance. Some less obvious ones are considered at **9.115** below.

Form P11D, dispensations and PSAs

6.79 Where an employer provides benefits for, or reimburses expenses of a higher-paid employee, he must complete an annual return of expenses paid to each such employee by 7 July following the year of assessment concerned. [*TMA 1970, s 15(6)–(8)* and *Reg 85* of the *PAYE Regulations*]. This return is provided on a form P11D. The detailed requirements are considered at **17.80** onwards. If it is clear that a particular type of expense will not give rise to a benefit in kind charge on the employee, the employer can ask HMRC for a 'dispensation' from including the item on the forms P11D. The dispensation procedure is considered at **17.84**. For some types of small expenses the employer can volunteer to pay his employees' tax rather than incur the expense and trouble of allocating the expense between his employees. He does this by entering into a PAYE Settlement Agreement (PSA) with HMRC. The PSA rules are dealt with at **17.90** onwards. The circumstances in which a PSA can be used are fairly restricted.

Chapter 7

Benefits in Relation to Cars and Vans

Introduction

7.1   Probably the most popular benefit in kind in the UK is the company car. The tax treatment of cars provided to employees may conveniently be approached in five parts:

(*a*)   company cars for the exclusive use of a single higher-paid employee;

(*b*)   car fuel for company cars;

(*c*)   pool cars for higher-paid employees;

(*d*)   contributions to the running costs of an employee's own car; and

(*e*)   cars provided for lower-paid employees.

Company cars for exclusive use

7.2   The vast majority of company cars are provided for the exclusive or primary use of a single executive director or employee. Such cars attract a scale charge if they are available for private use and the employee is higher-paid (see **6.4** above), as most are. The scale charge figure is treated as earnings from the employment. [*Income Tax (Earnings and Pensions) Act 2003 (ITEPA 2003), s 120*]. The scale charge applies to a car made available (without any transfer of ownership) for the use of the employee (or of members of his family or household); if the car is made available by reason of the employment and it is available for private use. [*ITEPA 2003, s 114(1)*, Prior to 2014/15 there was also no charge if an amount constituted earnings from the employment in respect of the car or van by virtue of some other provision. This provision was originally intended to avoid double taxation. It was repealed by *Finance Act 2014 (FA 2014), s 23* following the FTT decision in *Apollo Fuels Ltd (TC 2753)*. The company hired its cars to its employees on arm's length terms. As the cars were second-hand, the hire charge was considerably less than the car benefit. The FTT held that the car lease was a transfer of ownership in the car, so the conditions for a benefit charge did not apply. The company had claimed that there could be no car benefit charge because the benefit of the leasing payments (if any) was taxable as earnings under general principles. Although the case was not decided on that point, the case highlighted a possible means of avoiding the car benefit charge, so this was blocked before it could be exploited. As with other benefits for higher-paid employees, if the car is provided by the employer himself it is automatically deemed to have been made available by reason of the employment unless the employer is an individual and it can be shown that it was made available to the employee or other person in the normal course of the employer's domestic, family or personal relationships. [*ITEPA 2003, s 117*].

7.3   Mr Vasilis sought to take himself out of the scope of these special rules by arranging for his company to sell him a 5 per cent interest in the car. He contended that the car had not been 'made available (without any transfer of ownership)' as there had been a transfer of ownership of the 5 per cent. Accordingly *section 114* could not apply and the benefit fell to be calculated under *section 205* (see **6.61**) (which in the case of an expensive car gave a more favourable result). This argument found favour with the Commissioners but Pumfrey J reversed their decision, holding that the words in parenthesis were not to be construed as taking the car outside the special regime for cars (*Christensen v Vasilis [2004] STC 935*). The taxpayer in *CPR Solutions Ltd v HMRC ([2013] UKUT 278)* sought to distinguish its position from *Vasilis*. The director bought the car personally and sold a 90 per cent interest to the company. The Upper Tribunal said that whether a car is made available to an employee does not depend on the existence of any agreement for the use of the car. Physical use is different from the co-extensive right to possession. Although a co-owner may enjoy a right of possession, he cannot exercise it while the car is being used by another co-owner. Availability for use must be considered in the light of the circumstances that exist in practice. A mere omission by the company as co-owner to assert its own rights of possession is sufficient to constitute an understanding amounting to the making available of the car to the employee.

Private use

7.4   'What is meant by a car being available for private use?' If a car is made available to an employee or members of his family or household by reason of his employment it is deemed to be available for private use as well as business use unless both:

(*a*)   the terms on which it is made available prohibit any private use; and

(*b*)   there was in fact no private use in the year of assessment.

[*ITEPA 2003, s 118*].

7.5   'Private use' means any use other than for the employer's business travel. [*ITEPA 2003, s 118(2)*]. The meaning of business travel is considered at **5.9** above. In *Gurney v Richards [1989] STC 682* a fire officer was required by his employment contract to be on call at all times and to drive his official car – equipped with a fixed flashing blue light – whenever he was on duty. He was forbidden from using the car for private use. The employer accepted that he had to use the car to drive to work (so as to be in it if he was called), but this did not prevent the High Court ruling that, as such travel was not in the course of his duties, it constituted private use so that car benefit was assessable on the employee. However, the case was remitted to the Commissioners to determine whether the existence of the flashing light might prevent the vehicle being a car at all, ie was it unsuitable to be used as a private vehicle? It is not known what the Commissioners decided. It is to be hoped that they held that it was a car, as the scale benefit is likely to be far less than 20 per cent of the cost of the car. The unfairness has to a huge extent subsequently been remedied by the introduction of a special relief for emergency vehicles where the only private use is while the employee is on call (see **7.71**).

Business travel

7.6   Business travel is travel for which the expense if incurred by an employee would be deductible under *ITEPA 2003, ss 337–342* (see **5.3**). [*ITEPA 2003, s 117(1)*]. Travel from a person's home to his place of employment is not normally travel in the performance of the duties. It is undertaken to put a person in a position to perform such duties, and as such is private mileage.

7.7   Where a chauffeur driven car is provided to take an employee to and from work so that he can work on confidential papers in the car HMRC do not accept that such work can of itself change the essentially private nature of the travel. They consider that the work being done is only one of the factors to be considered when deciding whether the journey is either a business one or is merely incidental to business use (*SP 2/96*). The Statement of Practice hints that it could well be business use if papers are needed for a meeting at the employee's home or have to be delivered to a client. This seems an odd test. It seems to be saying that if there is a business need to transport the papers then the fact that the employee goes with them does not prevent the transport having a business purpose. On the other hand, if there is a business need for the employee to work on the papers the fact that he chooses (or is obliged) to do this in his own time when he is travelling to work does not necessarily mean that this is a business need.

The car use benefit

7.8   The current system is based on the car's carbon dioxide emission level [*ITEPA 2003, s 59*]. The cash equivalent of the benefit is a percentage of the original list price of the car. [*ITEPA 2003, s 121*]. Up to 2010/11 where the original list price exceeded £80,000 the benefit was based on £80,000 only. [*ITEPA 2003, s 121(4)* repealed by *Finance Act 2009 (FA 2009), Sch 28, para 2*]. For most new cars this percentage is based on the carbon dioxide emission rating for the car. All cars sold in the EC that were first registered after 30 September 1999 have had to be sold with an EC or UK certificate that specifies a carbon dioxide emissions figure in terms of grams per kilometre driven. From November 2000 this figure has had to be shown on the car's log book (Vehicle Registration Document). Some cars registered between 1 January 1998 and 1 October 1999 also had to carry an emissions certificate. The car use charge for such cars is based on the emissions figure shown on the certificate. [*ITEPA 2003, ss 135, 136*].

Cars with a UK or EC emissions certificate

7.9   The legislation was substantially recast for 2012/13 onwards. If the car's carbon dioxide emission figure is less than the relevant threshold

(100g/km for 2012/13 and 95g/km thereafter) and the car's carbon dioxide emissions figure does not exceed 75g/km driven, the appropriate percentage for 2012/13 to 2014/15 is 5 per cent. For 2015/16 the 5 per cent rate applies only up to 50g/km with a higher 9 per cent rate applying thereafter and for 2016/17, these rates will increase by two percentage points. For 2010/11 to 2014/15, no benefit arises if the car does not have an internal combustion engine with reciprocating pistons and cannot in any circumstances emit carbon dioxide when driven, such as electric cars (see **7.14**). Where the emissions figure reaches the relevant threshold, the percentage is 11 per cent for 2012/13 and 2013/14, 12 per cent for 2014/15 and thereafter increases by 2 percentage points per annum. Where the emissions figure exceeds the threshold, the percentage is increased by one percentage point for each 5g/km of the excess up to a maximum of 37 per cent (35 per cent up to 2014/15) [*ITEPA 2003, s 139(1)-(4)* as substituted by *Finance Act 2010 (FA 2010, s 59* and as subsequently amended]. If the car's emissions figure is not a multiple of 5, it is rounded down [*ITEPA 2003, s 139(6)* as amended by *Finance Act 2011 (FA 2011), s 51*].

7.10 This gives the following percentages at the bottom and top ends of the scale:

Emissions	**2012/13**	**2013/14**	**2014/15**	**2015/16**	**2016/17**
Zero	0%	0%	0%	5%	7%
1–50g/km	5%	5%	5%	5%	7%
51–75g/km	5%	5%	5%	9%	11%
76–94g/km	10%	10%	11%	13%	15%
95–99g/km	10%	11%	12%	14%	16%
100–104g/km	11%	12%	13%	15%	17%
190–194g/km	29%	30%	31%	33%	35%
195–199g/km	30%	31%	32%	34%	36%
200–204g/km	31%	32%	33%	35%	37%
205–209g/km	32%	33%	34%	36%	37%
210–214g/km	33%	34%	35%	37%	37%
215–219g/km	34%	35%	35%	37%	37%
220–224g/km	35%	35%	35%	37%	37%

7.11 Prior to 2012/13, the percentage was based on the engine capacity of the car but using a lower percentage for older cars, for smaller cars first registered after 1 January 1998 and for imported cars without an official EC or UK emissions certificate (even if the figure was known) [*ITEPA 2003, s 140*]. The percentages for 2011/12 were as follows:

Emissions up to	125g/km	15%
	130 g/km	16%
	135 g/km	17%

and so on rising by 1% point per 5 additional g/km
(rounded down to the nearest multiple of 5) to

Emissions up to	220g/km	34%
	225 g/km	35%

If the car's emissions figure was not a multiple of five it was rounded down (other than for the purpose of determining whether the car was a qualifying low emissions car). [*ITEPA 2003, s 139(4), (5), (5A)*]. For 2005/06 to 2007/08 the 15 per cent rate applied where the emission level was below 140g/km, for 2008/09 and 2009/10 where it was below 135 and for 2010/11 where it was below 130. The maximum 35 per cent rate applied at correspondingly 5g/km higher levels.

7.12   Under the pre 2012/13 system, a number of concessionary rates applied from time to time. There was a discount of 6 per cent up to 2010/11 for electrically propelled vehicles, which was replaced by a 3 per cent discount for hybrid electric vehicles for 2011/12. There was also a 2 per cent discount (1 per cent before 2006/07) for gas or bi-fuel cars. The percentage was reduced to 10 per cent where the car was a 'qualifying low emissions car'. This is a car which has a low carbon dioxide emiussions figure for the year. Prior to 2010/11 it was one with a carbon dioxide emissions figure of 120g/km or less and which is not an electrically propelled vehicle (as defined in **7.13**). [*ITEPA 2003, s 139(3) (1A), (1B), (3A)*]. Cars propelled by alternative fuels such as hybrid and bi-fuel cars were capable of qualifying. For 2010/11 onwards it was reduced to 5 per cent if the emission level did not exceed 75g/km driven [*ITEPA 2003, s 139(3) (1B) as amended by FA 2010, s 58(4)*].

7.13   HMRC have power by statutory instrument to reduce the level at which the 15 per cent figure applies. [*ITEPA 2003, s 170(3)*].

Cars with no UK or EC emissions certificate

7.14

	First registered Before 1.1.1998	First registered After 31.12.1997
Up to 1400 cc	15%	15%
1401–2000 cc	22%	25%
over 2000 cc	32%	35%

If the car does not have an internal combustion engine with one or more reciprocating pistons there is no tax charge for 2010/11 to 2014/15 if the car cannot in any circumstances emit carbon dioxide by being driven and the charge is 35% in any other case. For 2015/16 onwards the percentage will be 9% if the car cannot emit carbon dioxide and 35% if it can. [*ITEPA 2003, s 140(3), (3A)* as amended by *FA 2010, s 58(8), (9)*]. Up to 2009/10 the percentage was 9 per cent for an electrically propelled car (15 per cent for one registered before 1 January 1998) and 32 per cent or 35 per cent (as applicable) in any other case ie the reduced percentages for cars under 2000cc does not apply. [*ITEPA 2003, ss 140, 142*]. A car was an electronically propelled vehicle for this purpose only if it was propelled solely by electrical power and that power was either derived from a source external to the vehicle or from an electrical storage battery which was not connected to any source of power when the vehicle is in motion. [*ITEPA 2003, s 140(4)* repealed by *FA 2010, s 58(10)*].

Diesel cars

7.15 A supplement of three percentage points is added to the scale figures up to 2015/16 subject to the normal 37 per cent (formerly 35 per cent) [*ITEPA 2003, s 141*]. This applies irrespective of whether or not the car has an emissions certificate but does not apply to cars first registered before 1 January 1998. Thus, for example, a diesel car with 168g/km emissions attracts a scale charge for 2014/15 of 28 per cent of original cost (25 + 3); one with 208 g/km would attract a scale charge of 36 per cent (33 + 3) but this is limited to 35 per cent); a post-1 January 1998 imported 2000cc car attracts a scale charge of 28 per cent (25 + 3) but a slightly larger car attracts the basic charge of 35 per cent (as the surcharge cannot increase the scale figure above 35 per cent, it will be ineffective). The supplement does not apply to a car propelled solely by diesel and which has been type-approved to the emission limit values set out in row B of the table in section 5.3.1.4 of Annex 1 to EC Directive 70/220/EEC [*Reg 3*]. From 2006/07 this exclusion does not apply if the car was first registered after 31 December 2005. From September 2015 a new European standard comes into force which will require diesel cars to have the same air quality emissions as petrol cars. Accordingly this supplement will be removed for 2016/17 onwards.

Bi-fuel cars

7.16 Where a car is registered on the basis of an EC or UK emissions certificate that specifies different emissions figures for different fuel the scale charge is based on the lowest figure (if there is more than one figure specified in relation to each fuel it is the lowest 'emissions (combined)' figure specified. [*ITEPA 2003, 137(2)*]. If a car meets the above test, or is first registered after 31 December 1997 and is propelled solely by road fuel gas, the scale figure is reduced by the aggregate of 1 per cent plus an extra 1 per cent for each 20gm/k by which the emissions figure is less than the lower threshold in the taxable (currently 145gm/k) [*Reg 6*]. In the case of a car first registered after 31 December 1997 which is capable of being propelled by electricity and petrol the scale charge is reduced by the sum of 2 per cent plus an extra 1 per cent for each 200gm/k [*Reg 5*]. The scale charge for other bi-fuel cars first registered after 31 December 1997 is reduced by 1 per cent [*Reg 7*]. From 2006/07 the reduction under *Reg* 5 is 3 per cent, that under *Reg* 6 is 2 per cent, and that under *Reg* 7 ceased to apply. From 2008/09 the reduction for a car which is constructed so as to be capable of being propelled by bioethanol (as defined in *Hydrocarbon Oil Duties Act 1979, s 2AB*) or a mixture of at least 85 per cent bioethanol and 15 per cent (or less) unleaded petrol (bioethanol E 85) is 2 per cent.

Automatic cars for disabled drivers

7.17   If:

(*a*)   the car has an official emissions figure;

(*b*)   the car has automatic transmission;

(*c*)   at any time in the tax year concerned the employee has a disabled person's badge;

(*d*)   by reason of his disability the employee can only drive a car with automatic transmission; and

(*e*)   the emissions figure for the car is greater than it would have been if the car had been an equivalent manual car,

the emissions figure applicable to the equivalent manual car can be used instead. [*ITEPA 2003, s 138*].

7.18   An equivalent manual car is one that is first registered on or about the same time as the employee's car and which is the closest variant available of the make and model of the employee's car (but does not have automatic transmission). [*ITEPA 2003, s 138(3)*]. A car has automatic transmission for the purpose of this provision only if the driver is not provided with any means whereby he can vary the gear ratio between the engine and road whether independently of the accelerator and brakes or, if he is provided with such means, these do not include a clutch pedal or lever that he can operate manually. [*ITEPA 2003, s 138(4)*].

7.19   From 2009/10 onwards if the price of an automatic car is more than an equivalent manual one, the disabled person has a disabled person's badge at any time during the tax year and his disability prevents him driving a manual car, the price of the automatic car is deemed to be that of the equivalent manual car [*ITEPA 2003, s 124A(1), (2)* inserted by *FA 2009, s 54*]. An equivalent manual car is one that is first registered at around the same time as the automatic, does not have automatic transmission and is otherwise the closest variant available of the make and model of the automatic car [*ITEPA 2003, s 124A(3)*]. A car is an automatic one if either the driver is not provided with any means to vary the gear ratio between the engine and the road wheels independently of the accelerator and brakes or, if it has such a means, these do not include a clutch pedal or a lever which the driver can operate manually [*ITEPA 2003, s 124A(4)*].

Discounts

7.20   The Treasury can by regulation reduce all or any of the above percentage figures other than those for cars first registered before 1 January 1998. [*ITEPA 2003, s 170(4)*]. They have done so by the *Income Tax (Car Benefits) (Reduction of Appropriate Percentage) Regulations 2001 (SI 2001 No 1123)* as amended by the *Income Tax (Car Benefits) (Reduction of Value of Appropriate Percentage) (Amendment) Regulations 2005 (SI 2005 No 2209)* and the *Income Tax (Car Benefits) (Reduction of Value of Appropriate Percentage) (Amendment) Regulations 2007 (SI 2007 No 3068)*. The provisions of these regulations are incorporated in the text above. Reductions made by Regulations prior to 22 March 2006 for cars capable of being propelled by petrol and road fuel gases, or by electricity and petrol, or solely by road fuel gas do not apply to qualifying low emissions cars, *FA 2006, s 59(9)*]. This is presumably intended to prevent the reductions made by the 2001 regulations applying to such cars.

For those for whom these calculations seem like a nightmare, HMRC have produced a ready reckoner which can be accessed on their website at www. hmrc.gov.uk/manuals/eimanuals/eim23410.htm. They have also produced two tables for supplements and reductions, the website address for which is the same but with the substitution of /eim23490.htm for the final part (Press Release 20.1.2006).

Original list price

7.21   It is important to note that the benefit is based on the original list price of the car, not its cost, even if it was bought new. In the past it has often been relatively easy to obtain discounts from list price so the benefit figure will often be based on a significantly greater figure than the cost of the car. The list price is the price published by the car's manufacturer, importer or distributor, as the case may be, as the inclusive price appropriate for a car of that kind if sold in the UK singly in a retail sale in the open market on the day immediately before the date of its first registration, ie the date on which it was first registered under the *Vehicle Excise and Registration Act 1994 (VERA 1994)* or under corresponding legislation of any country or territory. [*ITEPA 2003, ss 123(1), 171(2)*]. The inclusive price is the price including delivery to the showroom (or other place of business of the seller), tax and fitting standard accessories. [*ITEPA 2003, s 123(2)*]. Special rules apply where a car has no list price, eg it was not offered for sale in the UK at the time of first registration. A notional list price has to be used instead (see **7.27**).

7.22   The original list price has to include qualifying accessories. These are accessories which are made available for use with the car and by reason of the employee's employment, and are attached to the car but not necessarily provided for use in the performance of the employee's duties. [*ITEPA 2003, s 125*]. A mobile phone is not an accessory, but any other kind of equipment can be. [*ITEPA 2003, s 125(2)(d)*]. Accessories for the disabled are also excluded. This covers equipment designed solely for use by a chronically sick or disabled person, and also any other equipment which was made available for use with the car because it enabled the employee to use the car in spite of a disability which entitled him to hold a disabled person's badge, ie one issued to him under the *Chronically Sick and Disabled Persons Act 1970 (CSDPA 1970)* (or its Northern Ireland equivalent) and which is not required to be returned to the issuing authority under that provision (the familiar orange disabled sticker). The employee must actually hold a disabled person's badge, not merely be entitled to it, at the time the car is first made available to him. This exclusion does not extend to a car made available for a disabled member of the employee's family. [*ITEPA 2003, ss 125(2)(c), 171(4), 172*]. If at the time the car was first made available to the employee the only qualifying accessories available with the car were standard accessories, the list price of the car covers such accessories even if they were fitted after first registration, but to be a standard accessory it must have been available as such at the time of first registration. [*ITEPA 2003, ss 125(4), 126*]. If any qualifying accessory was available with the car as an optional extra (even if factually the accessory was not supplied with the car) then the list price to be used is that for a car which includes the accessory in question. [*ITEPA 2003, s 126(2)*]. If the accessory in question was available with the car when it was originally registered but there was no list price for such an accessory when supplied with the car, the list price is in the sum of that of the car without the accessory plus the list price of the accessory at that time (including fitting, delivery charges, customs duty, car tax and VAT). [*ITEPA 2003, ss 127(1)(a), 129*]. For 2011/12 onwards, where a car has a relevant security feature which is provided in order to meet a threat to the employee's personal physical security which arises wholly or mainly because of the nature of his employment, that security feature is treated as not being an accessory [*ITEPA 2003, s 135A* inserted by *Finance Act 2012 (FA 2012), s 14*]. The relevant security features are armour designed to protect the occupants from explosions or gunfire; bullet resistant glass; any modification to the fuel tank designed to protect its contents from explosions or gunfire (including making the tank self-sealing); and any modification to the car in consequence of any of the above [*ITEPA 2003, s 125A(3)*]. The Treasury have power by regulation to amend this list [*ITEPA 2003, s 125A(4)*].

7.23 If there was no list price including such charges a notional list price for the accessory has to be adopted instead. This is the price (inclusive of fitting, delivery and taxes) which the accessory might reasonably have been expected to fetch if sold in the UK singly in a retail sale in the open market immediately before it was first made available for use with the car – which will be either the time of its first sale or, if it was fitted between then and its first becoming available to the employee in question, the date it was fitted. [*ITEPA 2003, s 130*]. Where an accessory is fitted after the car was first made available to the employee, the list price (or notional list price) of that accessory, presumably at the time the accessory was fitted, must be added to the list price of the car. If the price of any such accessory was less than £100 it can be ignored. [*ITEPA 2003, s 126(3)*].

7.24 The HMRC view on 'cherished' number plates is that although the cost of the plate itself is a qualifying accessory, to be included in the value of the car, most of the value of a cherished number plate lies in the intangible right to use a particular registration mark, ie the cost of the number plate must be apportioned, the part attributable to the plate being part of the value of the car and the balance (the bulk) being the cost of a separate intangible right. Where the car is a company car *ITEPA 2003, s 239* it will prevent the value of that right being taxable as it is provided in connection with the provision of the car (*Tax Bulletin, Issue 14, December 1994*).

7.25   Equipment by means of which the car is capable of running on road fuel gas is not regarded as an accessory. [*ITEPA 2003, s 125(2)(b)*]. This removes a disincentive from converting cars to run on road fuel gases (ie compressed natural gas or liquid petroleum gas). If a car is manufactured so as to be capable of running on road fuel gases, the benefit is not calculated on the full list price of the car. It is on that figure less so much of that price as it is reasonable to attribute to the car being manufactured in that way rather than in such a way as to be capable of running only on petrol. [*ITEPA 2003, s 146*]. In most cases this is likely to give a figure equal to the list price of the equivalent petrol model. Road fuel gas is defined as any substance which is gaseous at a temperature of 15°C under a pressure of 1013.25 millibars and which is for use as fuel in road vehicles. [*ITEPA2003, s 171(1)*]. Any new types of gases which do not meet this tight test will therefore not qualify for this relaxation. From 2002/03 this does not apply to bi-fuel cars taxed by reference to carbon dioxide emissions (see **7.16**). [*ITEPA 2003, s 146(1)(b)*].

7.26   If an accessory replaces a previous one of the same kind and it is not superior to the old one the change is ignored in calculating the benefit. If the new accessory is superior to the old the value of the old accessory is excluded and the price of the new substituted. A new accessory is superior to the old if its price exceeds the price of the old (or if greater, the price of an equivalent accessory to the old. [*ITEPA 2003, s 131*].

Cars with no original list price

7.27   Where a car does not have an original list price a notional price must be adopted instead. [*ITEPA 2003, s 122(b)*]. This is the price which might reasonably have been expected to be its list price if the manufacturer, importer or distributor (as the case may be) had published an inclusive price appropriate for a car of the same kind (and with the same qualifying accessories as were fitted when the car was first made available to the employee in question, even if such accessories did not exist when the car was originally sold) if sold in the UK singly in a retail sale in the open market on the day immediately before the date of the car's first registration. [*ITEPA 2003, s 124*].

Practical solutions

7.28   Many employers do not have readily available the original list price of employees' cars or of any accessories bought before 5 April 1994. HMRC have said they will accept prices for such cars taken from published guides of actual list prices where the manufacturer's price is not available. They have also said that for such cars only major optional extras such as automatic gearboxes, air conditioning, etc. need be priced. Minor accessories can be treated as *de minimis* (*Press Release 27 September 1993*). Nevertheless, there is of course a legal obligation on the employer to provide the correct list price and a potential liability for penalties if he does not. Where a car does not have a list price – or despite all efforts the employer cannot discover it – it is apparently up to the employer to make his own estimate – and to be able to defend it if it is challenged by HMRC.

Classic cars

7.29   Special rules apply for classic cars. If the market value of the car and any qualifying accessories on the last day of the tax year (or if earlier the last day it is made available to the employee) exceeds the original list price the scale benefit must be based on that market value. [*ITEPA 2003, s 147(2)*]. A classic car for this purpose is one that has a market value of £15,000 or more and is 15 years old or more at the end of the fiscal year. [*ITEPA 2003, s 147(1)*]. It should particularly be noted that the value has to be recalculated – and if necessary agreed with HMRC – every year.

Capital contributions

7.30   If the employee contributes a capital sum towards the cost of the car or towards the cost of accessories whose value is added to the list price of the car, such contribution (or the aggregate of all such contributions) can be deducted from the list price but subject to a maximum deduction of £5,000. [*ITEPA 2003, s 132*]. The limitation is to prevent a full reimbursement eliminating any benefit in relation to the running costs of the car. In the case of a classic car the £5,000 is deducted from the market value calculated each year. [*ITEPA 2003, s 147(5)–(7)*]. If the employee is entitled to a repayment of part of the capital contribution on the sale of the car by reference to the disposal value in the same proportion as the original contribution bore to the cost of the car, this does not require a recalculation of the *section 168D* contribution figure, and does not give rise to a charge to tax as employment income on the amount repaid. If the agreement provides for the contribution to be repaid in full on the disposal of the car, however, HMRC do not regard it as a capital contribution at all (*Tax Bulletin, Issue 14, December 1994*).

Shared cars

7.31   If two employees have shared use of a car, one scale benefit is apportioned between them [*ITEPA 2003, s 148*]. The apportionment must be done on a just and reasonable basis. The car must be made available to all sharers by the same employer and it must be concurrently available to them.

What is a car?

7.32   A car is defined as any mechanically propelled road vehicle except:

(*a*)   a vehicle of a construction primarily suited for the conveyance of goods or burden of any description;

(*b*)   a vehicle of a type not commonly used as a private vehicle and unsuitable to be so used;

(*c*)   a motor cycle as defined in *s 190(4)* of the *Road Traffic Act 1972 (RTA 1972)*; and

(*d*)   an invalid carriage as defined in *s190(5)* of that *Act*.

[*ITEPA 2003, s 115*].

7.33   This definition was in issue in *County Pharmacy Ltd v HMRC [2005] STC (SCD) 729*. County purchased an Elddis Autostratus (a motorhome) for the use of its managing director, Mr Morris. He used it principally as a mobile office. The company had a shop in Wordsley Green Shopping Parade. Mr Morris was unable to access the office at the shop because of difficulties with climbing stairs. He would work from the motorhome in the mornings when it was parked outside his home. He would then drive to the shop at around 1.30, park the motorhome at the rear of the shop and continue working. He also used the motorhome to drive to the cash and carry to obtain stock for the business. The motorhome was registered with the DVLA as a 'Private Light Goods' vehicle. Mr Morris had been told by a VAT Inspector that the motorhome was not a car but a van. It accordingly did not attract the VAT scale fuel charge. The Special Commissioner held that the vehicle was a car. The construction of the vehicle was primarily for leisure purposes. It was irrelevant that it was fitted out as an office. The exceptions had to be interpreted subjectively. Doing so, the vehicle did not fall within any of the exceptions.

7.34   It should be noted that a slightly different definition – which does not contain the exclusion for invalid carriages – applies in relation mileage allowances and passenger payments (see **7.49**).

Income tax liability

7.35   If the scale benefit charge applies to a car, the tax on the charge satisfies the employee's income tax liability in respect of the use of the car (other than for car fuel or in connection with the provision of a chauffeur). He cannot be taxed in relation to the discharge of any liability of his in connection with the car (where, for example, the employee personally incurs a liability for repairs, insurance or road-fund licence and the employer reimburses it to him or pays the cost direct); nor under the provisions relating to non-cash vouchers and credit tokens in respect of items or services acquired in relation to the car; nor under *s 203* (see **6.46** above) in respect of expenses incurred by him in connection with the car. [*ITEPA 2003, s 239*].

7.36   Where two members of a family or household, eg father and son, are both employees of a family company, HMRC in the past took the view that they could assess either of them on a car made available by reason of either employment, ie they can assess the father both on his car and the son's although the son's car is clearly provided by reason of the son's employment (indeed strictly they can assess both on both cars but in practice do not do so) (see also **6.45** above). In such circumstances the car is regarded as provided by reason of the son's employment if it can be shown that the car is actually provided by reason of the son's employment and that either equivalent cars are made available to other employees holding similar posts with the employer or the provision of an equivalent car is in accordance with normal commercial practice for a job of that kind. [*ITEPA 2003, s 169*, enacting *ESC A71*]. It is not clear if the concession continues to apply after 2002/03. The car appears to fall within *s 148* (see **7.30**) ie it is available to father and son concurrently. It is available to the father because it is available to a member of his family, ie the son, and is available to the son by reason of his own employment. To continue with the concession it would need to be just and reasonable to apportion the entire benefit to the son and nothing to the father.

7.37   Some people felt that the decision in *Heaton v Bell* (see **7.77**) could be used in reverse to avoid the car benefit charge. The theory was that if a car is made available on terms that it could be surrendered at any time in exchange for a £1 a week salary increase, a charge would arise under *ITEPA 2003, s 62* based on the money's worth of the use of the car being £1 a week. Such a device will not now work as *ITEPA 2003, s 119* provides that the mere fact that an alternative to the benefit of the car is offered does not make the benefit taxable under *s 62*. There is a similar anti-avoidance rule for living accommodation (see **8.2**).

7.37A   In *HMRC v Apollo Fuels Ltd ([2014] UKUT 95)* the company leased cars which it owned to its employees. The lease rentals were agreed to be an arm's length price. The employees were entitled to mileage allowance payments for business mileage. The company offset such payments against the rental the employee owed under the car lease. The lease provided that the employee could cancel the agreement at any time subject to 7 days' notice. The company took the view that there was no taxable benefit as the employee paid for the use of the car and mileage allowance payments are not taxable. HMRC disagreed. They contended firstly that the company owned the car (as a car lease gave merely a contractual, not a proprietary interest in it) and had made it available for private use, so a car use benefit arose even though the employee had paid a full price for such use. Secondly that as the lease could be terminated, the amount of the lease payments by the employee constituted emoluments in accordance with *Heaton v Bell* (see **7.77**). Thirdly, that, as the company owned the car, the mileage payments were taxable, as freedom from tax depended on the employee owning the car. The Upper Tribunal thought that the car lease did not constitute a proprietary interest, but commented that if it did, there was no benefit because the right entitled the employee to 100 per cent use of the car so it could not then be 'made available' (see **7.3**) by the company. It went on to hold that *ITEPA 2003, s 114(3)* (see **7.2**) prevented the benefit provisions applying if 'an amount constituting earnings' in respect of the benefit is already taxable. It held that nil is an amount. The use of the car is earnings, but the lease payment reduces the earnings to nil. In any event it felt that it is implicit in the benefits code that there has to be a benefit so would hold that, if it were wrong, *ITEPA 2003, s114* could not apply. It went on to hold that the vehicle is not a company car for the purpose of mileage allowance payments as it does not meet the definition in *ITEPA 2003, s 236(2)* (see **7.53**). This case is a warning that just because something looks straightforward and commercial does not mean that HMRC will not seek to attack it if they think they can collect tax, however unmeritorious it may be to do so.

Car unavailable for part of the year

7.38   No benefit arises for any part of the year of assessment in which the car was unavailable for use. The scale figure is multiplied by the fraction that the number of days in the tax year on which the car is available bears to the number of days in that year (which will be 365 or 366 in a leap year). However, a car can only be regarded as unavailable on a particular day in three circumstances:

(*a*)   if it was not made available until after that date, eg a car provided to an employee on 1 October 2014 is unavailable to him from 6 April 2014 to 30 September 2014;

(*b*)   if it ceased before that date to be available, eg if a car is sold on 4 August 2014 it is unavailable to the employee from 5 August 2014 to 5 April 2015; or

(*c*)   the day falls within a period of 30 days or more throughout which it is not available to the employee.

[*ITEPA 2003, s 143*].

It appears that a car remains available to the employee even if it is incapable of being used throughout a period of more than 365 days. The test is if it has been made available to the employee or to members of his family or household, not whether it is capable of use. [*ITEPA 2003, s 116*]. It may well be unavailable if the employer specifically forbids the employee to use the car during a specified period though.

Replacement cars

7.39   If a car normally available to the employee is not available to him for a period of under 30 days and a second car is made available to replace the normal car during that period, the replacement car is treated as unavailable on the days on which it replaces the normal car, ie it is ignored. The replacement car must not be materially better than the normal car and must not be made available to the employee under an arrangement one of the main purposes of which is to provide the employee with the benefit of a car which is materially better than the normal car. A car is materially better for this purpose if it is materially better in quality or its cost (original list price plus accessories) is materially higher than that of the normal car. [*ITEPA 2003, 145*].

Payments for private use

7.40   If as a condition of the car being available for the employee's private use he is required to pay an amount of money for such use (whether by deduction from earnings or otherwise) the payment by the employee is deducted from what would otherwise have been the cash equivalent of the car. *[ITEPA 2003, s 144]*. For 2014/15 onwards this deduction applies only to the extent that the payment by the employee is made before the end of the tax year concerned *[ITEPA 2003, s 144(1)(b)* as substituted by *FA 2014, s 25]*.

Business use

7.41   The scale figures are based solely on the costs and emissions level of the car; the amount of the benefit does not vary according to the level of business mileage. The previous rules sometimes created an incentive to use the car for business purposes even if public transport would have been more sensible as the benefit reduced if business mileage exceeded 2,500 miles in a year, and reduced further if it exceeded 18,000 miles. The above scale figures also apply unaltered to second cars. Previously such cars attracted a higher benefit.

7.42   This does not mean that an expense claim cannot be made in respect of business use of the car although it seems probable that it will only be in rare circumstances that such a claim will be competent as the scale figure is a rough and ready way of arriving at a benefit where there is mixed use of the car. A reduction for business use was allowed in *Kerr v Brown and Boyd v Brown [2002] STC (SCD) 434, 2003 STC (SCD) 266*. Mr Kerr and Mr Boyd were senior officers in the fire brigade. They were each provided with a car which he was required to use in the performance of his duties. They worked in 24-hour shifts consisting of eight or 12 hours of managerial duties and 16 or 12 hours of standby duties (during which they had to be in their local area and available immediately in the case of fire). The cars were used to store and convey firefighting equipment. They were fitted with flashing blue lights and a sign reading 'Fire'. They were not used for personal use other than home to work travel when on duty. They were used for other brigade purposes when the officers were on leave. The taxpayers contended that the need to have their equipment at all times meant that the cars were not available for private use in the ordinary sense of that expression. Alternatively, their homes were their base as when they were on duty they undertook responsibility immediately they were called. The Special Commissioners considered the case with respect to *Gurney v Richards* (see **7.5**). They accordingly held that there was private use. However, they also accepted that on rest days and leave the cars were unavailable for private use. They accordingly held that the benefit should be reduced in the proportion that the days the cars were not available for private use bore to the total number of days in the year. At a later hearing they amplified this. An unbroken period of 24 hours should be treated as a day. A day should be regarded as a rest day even if part of it was spent in the car commuting. If a person does not work a full 24-hour shift (Mr Boyd did not always have to do stand by duty) the shift actually worked should be regarded as a day. It was not realistic to take the total hours worked and divide by 24.

Relaxations for the motor industry

7.43   Problems can arise in applying the rules to employees in the motor industry in relation to test and experimental cars, demonstrator and courtesy cars and employees who frequently change cars. For 2009/10 onwards HMRC have given guidance on the circumstances in which a benefit can arise in relation to test cars and demonstrator and courtesy cars and have devised a method of averaging to calculate the benefit where cars are changed frequently. As this is of limited interest, the rules are not considered here but can be found at *paras EIM 23650* to *EIM 23667* of HMRC's *Employment Income Manual*. Prior to 2009/10 there were a number of different local arrangements for averaging the benefit. These all ceased to have effect from 6 April 2009.

Salary sacrifice arrangements

7.44 A salary sacrifice arrangement under which an employee agrees to reduce his salary if his employer will provide him with a company car, or with a car of a better standard than it would otherwise have provided has no particular implications provided that there is no arrangement under which the car can be surrendered and the salary restored. A mere understanding that the salary will be restored if employer and employee were to agree at some future date that the company will no longer provide a car should not fall foul of *Heaton v Bell 46 TC 211* (see **7.77**). The salary surrendered will not constitute either a contribution towards the cost of the car or a payment for its use. All that has happened is that the employee's remuneration package has been varied. As with salary waivers, once an entitlement to income has arisen, ie the work has been done to earn the salary, it is probably not possible to sacrifice part of the salary. Only future salary can be sacrificed.

7.45 At one stage Customs and Excise contended that where a salary sacrifice was made VAT was chargeable by reference to the salary given up as this constituted consideration for the right to use the car. No such charge arises now, however. [*VAT (Treatment of Transactions) Order 1992 (SI 1992 No 630)*]. This applies irrespective of whether what is sacrificed is cash or other benefits provided that no specific charge is made for the use of the car. (*Business Brief 9/92*). Salary sacrifice is considered in more detail at **19.40**.

The car fuel benefit

7.46 If a higher-paid employee is provided with a car to which the scale benefit rules described above apply and he is also provided with fuel for that car by reason of his employment, he is also assessable on a fuel benefit. The cash equivalent of the benefit is the 'appropriate percentage' of £21,700, £16,900 for 2008/9 and 2009/10, £18,000 for 2010/11, £18,800 for 2011/12, £20,200 for 2012/13 and £21,100 for 2013/14). [*ITEPA 2003, s 150(1)*]. This is the percentage used to calculate the benefit in relation to the use of the car (see **7.8–7.19**). [*ITEPA 2003, s 150(2)*]. Fuel does not include any facility or means for supplying electrical energy or any energy for a car which cannot in any circumstances emit CO2 by being driven.[*ITEPA 2003, s 149(4)* as amended by *FA 2010, s 58(11)*]. Accordingly no fuel benefit arises in respect of such a car.

7.47   No fuel benefit arises if either the employee is required to make good to the employer the whole of the expenses incurred in connection with the provision of the fuel for private use or fuel is made available only for business travel. [*ITEPA 2003, s 151*]. In practice, many Inspectors of Taxes contend that it is impossible to meet the first of these conditions as the employee cannot demonstrate that he has not used any of his employer's petrol at any time during the year of assessment to drive home from work or for some similar private purpose. The benefit is not reduced at all if the employee reimburses some, but not the whole, of the cost of petrol for private use. Accordingly, if an employee is required to reimburse the cost of fuel for private motoring, detailed mileage records may need to be kept so as to be able to demonstrate that the full cost has in fact been reimbursed. It may be better to require the employee to pay for the fuel as a condition of the car being made available for his private use so that the payments can reduce the car use benefit (see **7.40** above). It appears that if the employee is required to reimburse the cost of all private petrol as a condition of the car being made available for private use and can show that he has reimbursed the full cost of such petrol the same payments will both eliminate the car fuel benefit and reduce the car use benefits. However, HMRC can be expected to resist such a contention.

7.48   The benefit is proportionately reduced if the car is unavailable for part of the tax year. [*ITEPA 2003, s 152(1)*]. It is also proportionately reduced if for part of the tax year either the facility for the provision of fuel for private use is not available, fuel is made available only for business travel or the employee is required to reimburse the cost of providing the fuel for private use. [*ITEPA 2003, s 152(2)*]. This latter reduction applies only if there is no time later in the year when one of these conditions is not met, ie it applies only where the employer stops providing fuel for private use in the tax year and does not recommence doing so in the same tax year. [*ITEPA 2003, s 152(3)*]. Where the cash equivalent is proportionately reduced it is reduced in the proportion that the days in the year for which fuel is made available bears to the number of days in the tax year. [*ITEPA 2003, s 152(4)*]. Where the use benefit in relation to a shared car is apportioned between two or more employees a corresponding reduction is also made in relation to the fuel benefit. [*ITEPA 2003, s 153*].

Employee-owned cars

Mileage allowance payments

7.49   There is an exemption from income tax for approved mileage allowance payments. [*ITEPA 2003, s 229(1)*]. These are amounts paid to an employee in respect of expenses in connection with the use for business travel (see **7.6**) of a privately owned car. [*ITEPA 2003, s 229(2)*]. The employee must obviously be the driver of the vehicle and it must not be a company vehicle. [*ITEPA 2003, s 229(4)*].

7.50   Mileage allowances are approved to the extent that they do not exceed in total specified limits. [*ITEPA 2003, s 229(3),*]. These are as follows:

Cars and Vans

On the first 10,000 miles, 45p per mile (40p up to 2010/11)

On the excess over 10,000 miles, 25p per mile

Motorcycles

24p per mile

Cycles

20p per mile

[*ITEPA 2003, s 230(2)*]

The Treasury have power by statutory instrument to amend these figures. [*ITEPA 2003, s 230(6)*].

7.51   If an employee uses his own vehicle for business travel and either is not paid mileage allowance payments (eg because his employer does not make such payments or the employee does not claim them) or the mileage allowance payments that he receives are less than the statutory limits he can claim a deduction (mileage allowance relief) for the shortfall against the emoluments from the employment. [*ITEPA 2003, ss 231, 232*]. If the emoluments are taxable (ie on a remittance basis) mileage allowances for an earlier year in which the employee was UK resident can also be deducted. [*ITEPA 2003, s 232(3)*]. This ensures that the relief is given when the remuneration is remitted if remittances during the year to which the allowances relate were insufficient. It should be noted that the relief can only be given against earning from the relevant employment; it is not given against employment income generally.

7.52   Business travel is of course travel for which expenses incurred by the employee would be deductible under *ss 337* to *342* (see **5.2**). [*ITEPA 2003, s 236(1)*]. A qualifying vehicle is a car, van, motorcycle or cycle. [*ITEPA 2003, s 235(1)*]. A car for this purpose is defined as a mechanically propelled road vehicle which is not a goods vehicle, a motor vehicle or a vehicle not commonly used as a private vehicle and unsuitable to be so used. [*ITEPA 2003, s 235(2)*]. It could, for example, therefore include a mobile home. It should be noted that this is not the normal definition of a car (see **7.32**). A van is a mechanically propelled goods vehicle with a design weight not exceeding 3,500 kilograms and which is not a motorcycle. [*ITEPA 2003, s 235(3)*]. Again this is not identical to the normal definition. The *Road Traffic Act 1988* definitions of a motorcycle (a mechanically propelled vehicle, not being an invalid carriage, with less than four wheels and the weight of which unladen does not exceed 410 kilograms) and a cycle – see **9.92** – are adopted. [*ITEPA 2003, s 235(4)*]. The allowance is not tied to an individual vehicle. What is looked at is the use of any vehicle of the particular kind during the year. [*ITEPA 2003, s 230(3)*]. For example, if an employee sometimes uses a van, sometimes uses his own car and sometimes uses his wife's car it is the combined business mileage for all three that needs to be looked at to determine whether the 10,000 mile limit is exceeded.

7.53   Furthermore, the 10,000-mile figure applies to the total number of business miles in relation to the employment or any associated employment (ie where the employer is the same, is an associated company (within *Income and Corporation Taxes Act 1988 (ICTA 1988), s 416*) or if the employers are partnerships or companies and controlled (within *ICTA 1988, s 840*) by the same person (or partnership)). [*ITEPA 2003, s 230(4), (5)*]. There are a couple of oddities in this definition. If a company controls two other companies the mileage in all three employments are aggregated. However, if an individual controls two companies, whilst mileage in the employments by the two companies is aggregated, mileage in an employment with the individual as a sole trader does not appear to be from an associated employment and is therefore not aggregated. Similarly, an employment with a partnership and one with a company owned by that partnership appear to have to be aggregated if a single individual (or another partnership) controls the partnership, but not otherwise. The legislation gives no guidance as to how the limit is to be applied where there are associated employments. This could be important in a dual contract arrangement for a non-UK domiciled taxpayer (see **13.13**) where remuneration from the overseas employment is not remitted to the UK. The normal rule is that where the legislation is silent the taxpayer is entitled to adopt whatever treatment is most favourable to him. This would enable him to treat mileage by his UK car attributable to his UK employment as being the first 10,000 miles of business travel and mileage by his overseas car attributable to his overseas employment as being the top slice of the total mileage. It also appears that business travel includes travel in a company car. As the benefit in respect of a company car is not affected by the proportion of business mileage, it appears that where a person owns a second car personally he could claim the 40p a mile for use of his own vehicle even where his business mileage in the company car exceeds 10,000 miles. A vehicle is a company vehicle (so no mileage allowance can be claimed for travel in it) even if it is a pool car or van, so that no taxable benefit arises on it. A cycle is a company vehicle if it is provided by the employer and the employee would have been taxable on its provision but for *s 244* (see **9.96**) [*ITEPA 2003, s 236(2)*]. Accordingly, an employee ought not to pay any of the maintenance costs of his company bicycle but these should be incurred direct by the company as only the company can obtain any tax relief (the employee would not be able to satisfy the wholly and exclusively test for, say, new tyres).

7.54   The statutory rates are maxima. Even if the employee can show that the actual costs applicable to business mileage exceed these mileage rates he/she cannot claim a deduction for the excess.

Mileage allowances for carrying passengers

7.55   There is an additional relief for an employee who carries a fellow employee with him or her in a car or van (but not on a motorcycle or cycle). No income tax charge will arise on a 'passenger payment' made to him by his employer. [*ITEPA 2003, ss 233, 234*]. A passenger payment is an amount paid to an employee because, while using a car or van (other than a company vehicle) for business travel, he carries one or more qualifying passengers in it. [*ITEPA 2003, s 233(3)*].

7.56   The passenger payment is 5p per mile. [*ITEPA 2003, s 234(1)*]. If the employee carries more than one qualifying passenger the allowance is 5p per passenger. The Treasury have power by regulation to alter the rate. [*ITEPA 2003, s 234(3)*]. It should be particularly noted that, unlike with the mileage allowance for the driver, the relief is dependent on the employer making a payment to the driver; it is not possible to claim a deduction against earnings where no payment is made. As the relief is intended to encourage car-sharing it is unclear why a passenger payment cannot be made if an employee carries a colleague in a company car.

7.57   A qualifying passenger is a passenger who is also an employee for whom the travel is business travel. [*ITEPA 2003, s 233(3)*]. It does not appear that the passenger has to be an employee of the driver's employer. The requirements that the travel must be business travel for the passenger probably means that in practice there will be few cases where it will apply in other circumstances, although it is possible to imagine some. For example, an employee who uses his own car to go to a business conference in another town might take with him friends who are going to the same conference. It is improbable that the employer would make him a passenger payment in such circumstances but the employers of the friends might do so. The definitions in **7.49** to **7.54** above also apply to passenger payments. So does *ITEPA 2003, s 117* (see **7.2**).

Discharge of employee's liability

7.58   If a liability in respect of fuel for a car is discharged (eg by the employer paying the garage bills), or a non-cash voucher or a credit token (such as a company credit card) is used to obtain fuel for the car or to obtain money which is spent on such fuel, or any sum is paid in respect of expenses incurred in providing fuel for the car, this must be regarded as constituting the provision of fuel for the car. [*ITEPA 2003, s 149(3)*].

7.59   Curiously, although *ITEPA 2003, s 239* prevents an employee being assessed both to the car use benefit and on the cost of repairs, etc. to the car, this is specifically expressed not to apply to a liability arising by virtue of *s 149*. In *Richardson v Worrall 58 TC 642* it was held that at the moment an employee filled his car with petrol he had incurred a liability to pay for that petrol and a subsequent payment for it by use of a company credit card amounted to the employer discharging that liability of the employee, so that the amount paid constituted emoluments. In practice HMRC are unlikely to seek to tax the employee on the cost of providing the fuel where the scale fuel benefit applies.

Advisory fuel rates for company cars

7.60   In January 2002 for the first time HMRC published guidelines on fuel only mileage rates for company cars. These can be used for 2001/02 onwards both where employers reimbursed employees for business travel in their company cars, and where they required employees to repay the cost of fuel used for private travel so as to avoid the fuel scale charge. It was open to an employer to seek to justify a higher figure in any particular case. The rates per mile from 1 June 2014 are:

Engine size	Petrol cars	Diesel cars	LPG cars
up to 1400 cc	14p	12p*	9p
1401–2000 cc	16p	14p	11p
over 2000 cc	24p	17p	16p

* The cut off point for diesel cars is 1600 cc not 1400 cc.

The rates alter frequently (normally four times a year) and at irregular intervals. The rates for earlier periods can be found on the HMRC website.

7.61   It should be stressed that these rates apply only to fuel for company cars. If an employee uses his own car for business travel the higher mileage allowance payments considered at **7.49** apply. The rates cannot be used for any other purpose. If an employer pays a higher rate for fuel used for business travel in a company car and can show that the cost of business travel is higher, eg where employees need to use particular types of car to cover rough terrain, there will be no benefit. If he cannot show this the excess will not trigger a need to pay the fuel scale charge provided that reimbursement is solely for miles of business travel but the excess will be taxed and charged to NIC as employment income. Similarly, HMRC will accept that no benefit arises where the employee reimburses the above rates (or higher) for private travel. HMRC do, however, reserve the right to contend that 'in exceptional cases', such as where a very large-engined company car achieves fewer than 16 miles to the gallon, a higher repayment rate should apply.

Pool cars

Meaning of 'pool car'

7.62   Neither the car use nor the car fuel benefit apply where an employee has the use of a pool car, ie one which has been included in a car pool for the use of the employees of one or more employers. [*ITEPA 2003, s 167(2)*]. A car can, however, only be treated as a pool car for a year of assessment if:

(*a*)   in that year it was made available to (and actually used by) more than one employee;

(*b*)   it was made available to each of those employees by reason of his employment (see **6.45** above);

(*c*)   it was not in that year ordinarily used by one of the employees to the exclusion of the others;

(*d*)   any private use of the car made by any of the employees entitled to use the car in that year was merely incidental to his business use of it; and (*e*) during that year the car was not normally kept overnight in (or in the vicinity of) any residential premises where any of the employees was residing (unless the place where it was kept was occupied by the employer or other person making the car available to the employees). [*ITEPA 2003, s 167(3)*].

7.63 If a car qualifies as a pool car it is treated as not being available for the private use of any of the employees entitled to use it, so that neither the car use nor the car fuel benefit will apply to any of the employees in relation to the car. [*ITEPA 2003, s 167(2)*]. Nor will there be any charge for the provision of a chauffeur (*Hansard 14 May 1993, col 585*).

7.64 When the provisions were introduced, the Minister gave as an example of head (*d*) above that if an employee takes a pool car home so that he can make an early start for a business meeting the next morning the private use, driving from the office to his home, would be merely incidental to the following day's business use. Whether such a journey is 'purely incidental' as interpreted in a different context in *Robson v Dixon 48 TC 527* seems questionable. Whether or not a car is a pool car. is a question of fact. There used to be a procedure under which this could be established in advance but this was abolished in the *Finance Act 1996 (FA 1996)*.

7.65 Some years later HMRC set out in *SP 2/96* what they believe parliament meant by 'merely incidental to', namely that it is necessary to consider whether:

(*a*) the private use of the car is independent of the employee's business use of the car; or

(*b*) the private use follows from the business use.

They regard this as 'a qualitative test which means that it is necessary to look at the nature of private use, over the year, by each employee who uses the car'. It is not clear what this means; logically such a test ought to be applied on a journey-by-journey basis so that only if every single journey falls within (*b*) could the car constitute a pool car. Applying their test, HMRC say that where an employee takes a car home in order to make an early start on a business journey the following morning, where that journey could not reasonably be undertaken the next day starting from the normal place of work, the journey home in the evening is purely incidental to the business travel next morning. Where an employee staying overnight on a business trip drives to a nearby restaurant such use is also merely incidental to the business use even though it is not necessary to use the car for the trip to the restaurant. They consider the incidental use of the car for an annual holiday as something falling within (*a*) and thus not incidental. This suggests that, once a business need to use a car is established, any private use while that business need subsists is likely to be incidental but any journey where there is no business need cannot be incidental. Where a chauffeur driven car is provided so that the employee can work in the car HMRC do not accept that travel between work and home is necessarily incidental to business use (see **7.6**).

7.66   Head *(c)* in **7.62** above seeks to ensure that, say, the managing director's Rolls Royce is not included in a car pool when, in reality, anyone other than the managing director using it does so at his peril.

7.67   It is not clear what happens if there is occasional use of a car for private purposes of an employee (not falling within **7.62**(d) above) but the employee is required to pay for such use. It is arguable whether such use can be 'private use' at all as the company is exploiting the car for payment in the course of its business. Furthermore, a charge in respect of a car can only arise if a benefit is provided to the employee; *s 157* (car available for private use) merely sets out a formula for calculating any benefit that arises under *ICTA 1988, s 154(2)*. It would be odd if use which does not in any event give rise to a benefit could prevent a car from being a pool car. It is also worth noting that *paragraph 10* of *SP 5/96* envisages a taxable benefit being provided from the use of a pool car, which is impossible if **7.62**(d) above is read literally.

Home to office travel

7.68   It should particularly be noted that a car cannot qualify as a pool car if it is used by any of the employees for home to office travel or for other private use except where such use is purely incidental to business use. There is accordingly no scope for avoiding the scale benefit charges by having a pool of similar cars none of which is allocated specifically to an individual but any of which can be used by the employees concerned as they wish. The pool car rules apply only where use of the cars is restricted to business use. There is an exception to this rule for government Ministers (see **5.82**). HMRC also accepts that if a chauffeur is required to take a pool car home for retention overnight that will not disqualify the car from being a pool car (*Employment Income Manual EIM 23480*).

Emergency vehicles

7.69   There is an exemption from the benefit rules for emergency vehicles. An emergency vehicle is defined as a vehicle which is used to respond to emergencies and which has fixed to it a lamp designed to emit a flashing light for use in emergencies (or which would have such a lamp but for the fact that if it did that would give rise to a special threat to the personal physical security of those using it by making it apparent that they were employed in an emergency service). [*ITEPA 2003, s 248A(3)*].

7.70   The exemption applies only where:

(a)   an emergency vehicle is made available to a person employed in an emergency service for the person's private use,

(b)   the terms on which it is made available prohibit its private use otherwise than when the person is on call or engaged in on-call commuting; and

(c)   the person does not make private use of it otherwise than in such circumstances [*ITEPA 2003, s 248A(1), (2)* inserted by *Finance Act 2004 (FA 2004) s 81*].

7.71 For this purpose private use means use other than for the person's business travel (ie travel the expenses of which, if incurred and paid by the employee would (if the rules on mileage allowances (see **7.49**) did not apply) be deductible in an expenses claim in relation to the employment. [*ITEPA 2003, s 171(1)*]. A person is employed in an emergency service if he is a constable or other person employed for police purposes, employed for the purposes of a fire or a fire and rescue service, or employed in the provision of ambulance or paramedic services. A person is on call when he is liable, as part of normal duties, to be called on to use the emergency vehicle to respond to emergencies. He is engaged in on-call commuting when he is using the vehicle for ordinary commuting (see **5.17**), or for travel between two places that is for practical purposes substantially ordinary commuting, and is required to do so in order that the vehicle is available for his use, as part of his normal duties, for responding to emergencies [*ITEPA 2003, s 248A(3)–(8)* inserted by *FA 2004, s 81*].

7.72 Mileage allowance payments (see **7.49**) cannot be claimed in relation to such a vehicle. [*ITEPA 2003, s 236(2)(c)* as amended by *FA 2004, s 81(2)*].

Volunteer drivers

7.73 Prior to 6 October 1991 HMRC generally turned a blind eye to any profit element in the motor mileage allowance paid to people who drive for the hospital car service and other volunteer organisations. Treasury Ministers decided to tax such profits from that date. 'To ensure that, so far as possible, neither people running volunteer car services nor drivers themselves are troubled at all when the tax liability, if any, is likely to be trivial' they have given such volunteers a choice between:

(*a*)   paying tax on the difference between the mileage allowance they receive and the fixed profit car scheme rates; or

(*b*)   paying tax on the difference between the mileage allowance they receive and their actual running costs.

'To ensure that ... voluntary work done by drivers ... should [not] be put at risk by sudden changes in tax liabilities or misunderstandings about them,' ie because no one dreamt that the Government would be so petty as to tax such amounts, the introduction of the new arrangements was phased in.

Is it better to have a company car?

7.74 The decision as to whether a person should be provided with a company car or whether he should provide his own car and claim a mileage allowance is not wholly tax driven. Even where the decision will be dependent on which alternative is more beneficial from a tax point of view, it is not always an easy one to make. The answer depends on many factors such as the cost of the car, the likely running costs, the total mileage, the proportion represented by private mileage, and the records that the employee is prepared to maintain.

Furthermore, the decision needs to be made at the start of the year: it cannot be made retrospectively. Accordingly, it will need to be made on the basis of estimates. There are a number of computer programmes available which will point to the correct decision for a particular car but, even so, the need to use estimates is likely to prevent the answer being wholly reliable. There are some simple rules that are likely to produce the right answer in many cases.

(*a*)   Is the employee prepared to keep detailed mileage records?

(*b*)   If he is not prepared to keep such records the car should probably be owned by the company. It is improbable that HMRC will accept a claim for a deduction for a privately owned car based on estimates.

(*c*)   Whilst mileage allowance payments can sometimes be realistic for the first 4,000 miles they are poor where business mileage exceeds that level. Accordingly, this method of recharging will not normally be attractive unless business mileage is low. It is in any event always necessary to know the actual business mileage in order to claim the mileage allowance from the company.

(*d*)   As mileage allowance payments are a fixed figure they are more attractive for small cars than for large, expensives ones.

(*e*)   If the employee is prepared to keep detailed records, whether or not it is better for the car to be owned by him or the company depends on:

  (i)   the proportion of business to private mileage;

  (ii)   the running costs; and

  (iii)   the emissions level of the car, or its original list price if it does not have an emission certificate.

  Unfortunately, as the decision has to be made before the start of the tax year and at that stage the first two of these factors are unknown they must be guessed. Whilst an estimate, or informed guess, can normally be made of (i) it is not normally possible to guess the size of repair bills with any degree of accuracy, particularly if insurance cover against accidents is limited. Nevertheless the estimate will give a ball park figure for the total cost of running the car. From this can be deducted the estimated mileage allowance payments for the estimated business mileage to produce the likely cost of private motoring if the car is owned personally. One thing that can be calculated in advance is the benefit figure. This is a known percentage of the emissions figure plus the same percentage of £16,900 (or a known percentage of the original list price plus £16,900) to cover both the use and car fuel. The resultant figure can be divided by the estimated private mileage to produce a benefit figure per mile of private motoring. It will normally be sensible to pay for private fuel on a company car unless business mileage is very high and private mileage (including home to work) exceptionally low.

Lower-paid employees

7.75   The car use and car fuel scale benefits apply only to higher-paid employees (and company directors). If a car is provided for a lower-paid employee no tax charge will arise except to the extent that the right to use the car represents 'money's worth'. Although in theory an employee could hire out his company car to a neighbour, even if expressly forbidden to do so by his employer, in practice he could not normally do so as the need to have the car available for business travel would prevent any meaningful bargain being struck. It might therefore be difficult for HMRC to show that there is any monetary value into which the right to use the car can be converted. If petrol is provided for the car, that will have a money's worth equivalent although it is likely to be below the retail price.

7.76   There are three problems in providing cars for lower-paid employees. The first is that the scale benefit must be assumed to apply for the purpose of determining whether or not the employee is lower-paid. There are likely to be very few employees earning under £8,500 less the benefit figure for whom employers might wish to provide cars.

7.77   Secondly, there must be no arrangements in existence under which the employee would be entitled to a salary increase if he were to give up the right to use the car. In *Heaton v Bell 46 TC 211* lower paid employees were able to borrow a car from their employer in return for agreeing to a reduction of £2 a week in their salary. It was held that an employee was assessable on a benefit of £2 per week as even if the deduction reduced the salary (rather than being an agreed deduction paid out of it) the employee could convert the right to use the car into a £2 a week salary increase at any time and this constituted money's worth.

7.78   Finally, the expenditure needs to be incurred by the employer. If it is incurred by the employee and merely paid by the employer the payments will themselves constitute emoluments. Care accordingly needs to be taken to ensure that repairs, etc. are clearly contracted for by the employer and that the garage is aware that it is carrying out the work for the employer not the employee.

Car parking

7.79   Expenditure incurred in paying (or reimbursing) expenses in connection with the provision of a car parking space at or near the employee's place of work is not regarded as an emolument of his employment. [*ITEPA 2003, s 237*]. This applies to the use of a company's own car park, a season ticket at a public car park, garage space rented for a specific executive and, it appears, even the reimbursement of one-off car park charges and parking meter charges including the excess charge but not a penalty charge. It applies irrespective of whether the employer or the employee provides the car. It also extends to parking for cycles (see **9.70**) and motorcycles. For 2005/06 onwards this exemption also applies to parking for a van. [*ITEPA 2003, s 237* as amended by *FA 2004, Sch 14, para 7*].

Car telephones

7.80   HMRC consider that the car scale charge covers the provision of a car telephone in the company car provided that the telephone cannot be used separately from the car (*SP 5/88* now obsolete). This view does not apply to a car telephone installed by the employer in a car owned by the employee. In such a case a benefit will arise unless either the employee is prohibited from using the telephone for private calls or he reimburses to the employer the full cost of private calls. The full cost for this purpose is not simply the call charges. An appropriate part of the rental charges, or the cash equivalent of the benefit in relation to the telephone (20 per cent of the cost), and of any administrative costs connected with the telephone, must also be included.

Vans and lorries

7.81   A new system of benefits in respect of vans applies for 2005/06 onwards. A van is defined as a mechanically propelled road vehicle of a construction primarily suited for the conveyance of goods or burden, of a design weight of up to 3,500 kilograms, and which is not a motorbike [*ITEPA 2003, s 115(1)*]. There is no benefit charge at all if the private use of a van during the tax year is 'insignificant'. Insignificant is not defined [*ITEPA 2003, s 114(3A)*, inserted by *FA 2004, Sch 14, para 2*]. HMRC's view is that private use is insignificant if it is 'very much the exception to the normal use, it is intermittent and irregular and it lasts only for short periods of time on odd occasions during the year'. They give as examples an employee who takes an old mattress or other rubbish to the tip once or twice a year, who regularly makes a slight detour to drop off a child at school or stop at a newsagent on the way to work or who calls at the dentist on the way home from work (HMRC factsheet: Tax on company vans). In addition, the cash equivalent of the benefit is nil if throughout the tax year (or the part of it for which the van is made available to the employee):

(*a*)   the terms on which the van is available to the employee prohibit its private use otherwise than for ordinary commuting (as defined in *ITEPA 2003, s 338(3)* – see **5.17**) or travel between two places that is for practical purposes substantially ordinary commuting;

(*b*)   neither the employee nor a member of the employee's family or household makes private use of the van otherwise than for such purposes; and

(*c*)   the van is available to the employee mainly for use for the purposes of the employee's business travel (as defined in *ITEPA 2003, s 171(1)* namely the travel costs of which would be deductible for tax purposes if the mileage allowance rules (see **7.55**) did not apply)

[*ITEPA 2003, s 155(1)–(7)* as amended by *FA 2010, s 58(12)*]. For 2010/11 to 2014/15 the benefit is also nil if the van cannot in any circumstances emit carbon dioxide by being driven [*ITEPA 2003, s 155(2)(b)* inserted by *FA 2010, s 58(12)*].

7.82   In all other cases the benefit is £3,000 pa from 2007/08 onwards.

7.83   The benefit is reduced for periods where the van is unavailable for private use, it is shared, or the employee makes a payment in relation to private use.

7.84   The calculation of the reduction where the van is unavailable for private use follows the rules on car benefits (see **7.38**), including the requirement that a car is treated as unavailable only if it is unavailable throughout a continuous period of 30 days (or during a period before or after which it was supplied to the employee). [*ITEPA 2003, s 156*]. If a van is available to the employee for a period of less than 30 days and during the period of unavailability a replacement van is provided, in order to avoid double taxation the replacement van is deemed not to have been made available on those days for which a benefit continues to accrue in relation to the original van. [*ITEPA 2003, s 159*].

7.85   For shared vans the benefit for each employee to whom the van is available for private use is calculated in the normal way and then reduced on a just and reasonable basis. However, if one of the employees who shares the van is a lower paid employee (ie outside the scope of the benefit code) and another who is within the benefit code is higher paid and is a member of the same family or household as the lower paid employee the availability to the lower paid employee is ignored in making this reduction. For example, suppose Jack who is a higher paid employee and his son Joe who is a lower paid employee have shared use of the van. Its availability to Joe must be ignored in arriving at Jack's benefit, so Jack will be regarded as having the entire private use of the van [*ITEPA 2003, s 157*]. It remains to be seen what will happen in circumstances in which Jack and Joe share the van with another employee, Fred. It is probably just and reasonable for Fred's benefit to be reduced by two-thirds. But is it then just and reasonable for Jack's benefit to be reduced by 50 per cent (on the basis that the van is deemed to be available only to him and Fred) or by a third (on the basis that if the availability to Joe is disregarded the use by Joe becomes use by virtue of the van being made available to Joe as a member of Jack's family)? The latter is more logical but it is difficult to fit into the clear wording that the availability of the van to Joe (not its availability to Joe by virtue of Joe's own employment) is to be disregarded.

7.86   If the employee is required to pay an amount of money as a condition of the van being available for his private use (or that of a member of his family or household) the payment can be deducted from the cash equivalent under *section 155* (after any reduction under *ss 156* and 157) but cannot reduce the benefit below nil [*ITEPA 2003, s 158*]. For 2014/15 onwards this deduction applies only to the extent that the payment by the employee is made before the end of the tax year concerned [*ITEPA 2003, s 144(1)(b)* as substituted by *FA 2014, s 25*].

7.87   For 2007/08 onwards a van fuel benefit charge also arises if fuel is provided for the van by reason of an employment and the £3,000 cash equivalent benefit applies in respect of the van. Fuel is treated as provided for a van if (in addition to any other way it may be provided) a liability in respect of the provision of fuel is discharged, a non-cash voucher or credit token is used to obtain fuel (or to obtain money which is spent on fuel), or a sum is paid in respect of expenses incurred in providing fuel. However, no van fuel benefit will arise in relation to any facility or means for supplying electricity for an electrically propelled van. [*ITEPA 2003, s 160*].

7.88   The fuel benefit is normally £550 (£500 up to 2009/10) but this is proportionately reduced if the van use benefit is reduced under *s 156* (van unavailable) or *s 157* (shared vans). Where a replacement van is supplied during a period of unavailability fuel supplied for the replacement van is obviously treated as relating to the normal van. The benefit is also proportionately reduced if for any part of the tax year the facility for the provision of fuel is not available, fuel is made available only for business travel (see **7.90**) or the employee is required to (and does) make good the whole of the expense incurred in connection with the provision of fuel for his private use, but only if there is no later time in the tax year in which that situation applies, ie a reduction can be made only if one of these three circumstances either applies for the entire tax year or starts to apply during the year and continues for the rest of the year. Where the benefit is proportionately reduced this is done on a daily basis, ie in the proportion in which the number of days for which the car is unavailable (or one of the other three circumstances applies) bears to the number of days in the tax year [*ITEPA 2003, s 163*].

7.89   In the case of a shared van the reduction in the fuel benefit follows that which applies to the use benefit. [*ITEPA 2003, s 164*].

7.90   No fuel benefit of course arises if the employee is required to make good the whole of the expense of providing the fuel for private use throughout the tax year or if fuel is made available only for business travel. [*ITEPA 2003, s 162*].

7.91   If a van or vans are made available to two persons who are both employees of the same employer and are members of the same family or household there is a potential for double taxation, ie A is taxable by reference to both his own and B's use and B is taxable by reference to both his and A's use. To avoid this A is not chargeable to either a van use or van fuel benefit by reference to B's use of the van if either B is chargeable in relation to the van or B:

(*a*)   is a lower paid employee;

(*b*)   has the use of the van in his own right as an employee (not by virtue of A's employment); and

(*c*)   either:

   (i)   equivalent vans are made available to employees who are in similar employment to B with the same employer and who are not members of the family or household of higher paid employees of the employer; or

   (ii)   the making available of an equivalent van is in accordance with the normal commercial practice for an employment of the kind held by B.

[*ITEPA 2003, s 169A*].

7.92   If an employee uses his own van for business journeys the authorised mileage rates that apply to cars (40p for the first 10,000 miles and 22.5p thereafter) (see **7.49**) also apply to vans.

Heavy goods vehicles

7.93   There is an exemption for lorries and other heavy goods vehicles, ie a mechanically propelled road vehicle which is primarily suited for the conveyance of goods and which has a design weight exceeding 3,500 kilograms when in normal use and travelling on a road laden [*ITEPA 2003, s 238*]. The exemption extends to the discharge of a liability of the employee in connection with the vehicle, to credit tokens used to obtain goods or services in connection with it, and to benefits and expenses incurred in connection with it. [*ITEPA 2003, s 239*]. The exemption does not, however, apply if the employee's use of the lorry is wholly or mainly for private use, eg he is a steam enthusiast and uses it to transport a steam engine to fairs. [*ITEPA 2003, s 238(3)*]. Nor does it apply to the provision of a chauffeur for the lorry! [*ITEPA 2003, s 239(5)*].

Motor cycles

7.94   There are few special rules for motor cycles. HMRC say that a motor cycle is a car for capital allowance purposes so that if it costs more than £12,000 the capital allowances may be restricted (Capital Allowance Manual, para 2398). On the other hand, they say that the CGT exemption for cars does not apply to motor cycles even with a sidecar (Capital Gains Manual, para 76907). It is unclear why, as that exemption applies to a mechanically propelled road vehicle constructed or adapted for the carriage of passengers and most motor cycles are designed to carry a passenger.

7.95   HMRC state that for industrial life agents the cost of protective clothing for business travel by motor cycle qualifies as a business expense (Schedule E Manual, para 7544, but now deleted). There is no logical reason why this should not equally apply to other employees who use a motor cycle for business travel.

7.96   The system of mileage allowances introduced for cars (see **7.49**) also applies to motorcycles, although the mileage rate remains 24p per mile.

Chapter 8

Benefits in Relation to Accommodation

Occasions of charge

8.1   Where living accommodation is provided for an employee, a charge to tax can arise under three headings.

(*a*)   There is a basic charge in relation to the accommodation that applies, irrespective of whether the employee is higher- or lower-paid, unless it can be shown that he is in 'representative occupation' of the property (ie he is occupying it on behalf of his employer, generally as an integral part of his duties).

(*b*)   There is an additional charge if the cost of the accommodation exceeds £75,000.

(*c*)   If the employee is in higher-paid employment the payment by the employer of the running costs of the property, such as rates, light and heat will give rise to a benefit in kind.

8.2   In certain circumstances a charge might arise under the basic rules for taxing employment income applying the *Heaton v Bell 46 TC 211* principle (see **7.77**). The charges described below under *Income Tax (Earnings and Pensions) Act 2003 (ITEPA 2003), ss 105, 106* applies in priority to any charge under other provisions and tax under the basic charging provision for employment income (*section 62*) is chargeable only to the extent, if any, that it would produce a greater taxable amount than *sections 105* and *106*. [*ITEPA 2003, s 109*]. This is an anti-avoidance provision. The effect of this provision is that these benefit-in-kind rules are disapplied if the rent paid by the employer is greater than the benefit figure.

8.3   This provision caused concern in *Toronto Dominion Bank v Oberoi [2004] STC 1197*. This was not a tax case although HMRC were joined to the proceedings. It was an application for rectification of a lease. The bank rented a property from Mr Oberoi for occupation by Mr Uggla, an employee of the bank. To avoid a benefit charge on Mr Uggla on the rent, the bank asked Mr Oberoi to agree to terminate the existing lease and grant a new one for a two-year period in consideration of the payment of a premium. Mr Oberoi agreed. Unfortunately, the new lease was based on the old and seems to have been carelessly drawn up as it described the premium as rent and contained a number of provisions that made sense only in the context of rent being payable. The bank sought rectification of the lease to substitute the word 'premium' for rent wherever it occurred or to delete the inappropriate provisions. HMRC argued that the label did not matter and the provisions of the lease were inconsistent with the payment being a premium – but did accept that it is possible to grant a lease for a period as short as two years for a premium and without rent. The judge both granted rectification and held that if rectified the payment would not be rent for the purpose of *s 109*.

The basic charge

8.4   If a person is provided with living accommodation by reason of his employment he is taxable on an amount equal to the 'rental value of the accommodation' less, if he pays rent or makes any other payment, so much as is made good to the employer (or other person who provides the accommodation) and less such amount as could have been deducted in an expenses claim under *s 336* (or *s 351* in the case of a clergyman) if the employer had paid for the accommodation himself. [*ITEPA 2003, ss 105, 327*].

Rental value

8.5   The rental value of the accommodation is the higher of:

(*a*)   any rent paid by the employer (or other person who provides the benefit) for the premises for the period they are provided to the employee; and

(*b*)   the rent that the employee would have paid for the period of occupation if the premises had been let to him at an annual rent equal to their annual value.

[*ITEPA 2003, s 105(3), (4), (4A)*].

8.6   Where the employer entered into a lease of the premises after 21 April 2009, and paid a lease premium (*a*) above applies as if the rent paid were the aggregate of the actual rent plus any amount attributed to the period in respect of the lease premium [*ITEPA 2003, s 105(4B)* inserted by *Finance Act 2009 (FA 2009), s 71(2)*]. An amount of premium is attributed to the period only if the term of the lease is 10 years or less and the premises are not normally used by the employer (or other person who provides the accommodation) for a purpose other than the provision of living accommodation to persons by reason of their employment [*ITEPA 2003, s 105A(1)*]. The amount to be attributed to a tax year is the proportion of the net premium that the number of days in the tax year for which the accommodation was provided to the employee bears to the term of the lease (in days) [*ITEPA 2003, s 105A(2)*]. A premium for this purpose is any premium payable under the lease (or otherwise under the terms on which the lease was granted). The net premium is the total amount (if any) that has been paid by the person as premium (or that is, or will become, payable) less any part of it, which has been repaid (or is, or will become, repayable) [*ITEPA 2003, s 105A(4), (5)*].

8.7   If a lease (including one exceeding 10 years) contains a break clause that is capable of being exercised so that the term of the lease becomes 10 years or less, it must be assumed that such break clause will be exercised [*ITEPA 2003, s 105B(1)–(3)*]. If it is not in fact exercised in such a way that the term of the original lease is as short as possible, the parties are treated as entering into a second notional lease the term of which begins immediately after the original lease would have ended had the break clause been exercised and ending at the tenth anniversary of the original lease or (if the break clause in the original lease can be further exercised) if earlier, at the earliest time the break clause can be exercised [*ITEPA 2003, s 105B(4), (5)*]. The premium for the notional lease is that for the original lease less any part that has already been attributed to a period under *ITEPA 2003, s 105B(4B)* [*ITEPA 2003, s 105B(6)*]. Where the notional lease is deemed to end on the tenth anniversary of the actual lease the notional premium is the proportion of the actual net premium that the term of the notional lease bears to the remainder of the length of the actual lease on the assumption that no further break clause is exercised [*ITEPA 2003, s 105B(7), (8)*].

Annual value

8.8   The annual value for this purpose is the rent which might reasonably be expected to be obtained on a letting from year to year if the tenant undertook to pay all usual tenant's rates and taxes and the landlord undertook to bear the cost of repairs, insurance and any other expenses necessary for maintaining the property in a state to command that rent. [*ITEPA 2003, s 110(1)*]. For this purpose the assumed rent is to be calculated on the basis that the only amounts that may be deducted in respect of services provided by the landlord are the costs to him of providing any relevant service, namely any service other than the repair, insurance or maintenance of the accommodation or of any other premises. [*ITEPA 2003, s 110(2)*]. If the accommodation is of a kind that might reasonably be expected to be let on terms that the landlord is to provide services which are either relevant services or the repairs, insurance or maintenance of any premises which do not form part of the accommodation but are occupied by the landlord, the notional rent is to be increased by the excess of the charge that could have been made for the relevant services over the cost of providing them plus the amount that could have been charged in respect of the repair etc of the other premises (with no deduction for any costs of such work). [*ITEPA 2003, s 110(3)–(5)*]. In practice, HMRC used to adopt the rateable value where the property was in the UK, as the definition of annual value for rating purposes was the same. Domestic rates were abolished from 1 April 1990 (1989 in Scotland). Despite this HMRC continue to base the benefit of living accommodation on the gross annual value for rating purposes – which actually represents 1973 values. For new, or materially altered buildings, employers are asked to supply an estimate of what the gross annual value would have been had domestic rates continued. HMRC will liaise as necessary with the District Valuer's office to confirm the employer's estimate. Unfortunately, *ITEPA 2003, s 110*, unlike the *ICTA 1988* provision which it replaced, makes no mention of the *Rating Act* so it is hard to see how *section 110* can legitimately be interpreted as requiring one to arrive at a notional rental value over 30 years ago! Nevertheless HMRC have said that they will continue with this practice. The charge under *s 106* (see **8.40**) was originally introduced as a rough and ready method of approximating the benefit to the market rent. Accordingly if HMRC were to seek to apply *section 110* to the charge under *s 105* it would create a double tax charge.

Accommodation costing over £75,000

8.9   The last domestic rating revaluation in England and Wales was in 1973 and the previous one was in 1963. Accordingly, while it was convenient for HMRC to adopt rateable values as the rental value for the purpose of what is now *s 105*, that figure long ago ceased to reflect the market rent that was envisaged by the legislature when the provision was first introduced. Therefore, in 1977 it was decided to supplement the basic charge with a further charge based on the cost of the property. If HMRC were to change their (non-statutory) practice and base the *s 105* or *106* (Step 1) charge on the actual market rental value of the property as the statute requires, the additional charge will become a penal impost if it is not repealed. However, HMRC have indicated that they will continue to use rateable values. In November 1995 HMRC recognised the inequity that arises where the charge under what is now *s 105* is based on the open market value of the property, for example because it is situated overseas so does not have a rateable value or an equivalent value. In such circumstances they will not seek to collect tax under *s 106* (*ESC A91*). If the *s 105* charge is greater than would apply with a UK property, but nevertheless below a market rent, it does not appear that the concession will allow a reduction in the *s 106* charge.

Occasions of additional charge

8.10   The additional charge arises where:

(*a*)   living accommodation is provided for a person in any period by reason of his employment (which has the same meaning as in **6.42** above); and

(*b*)   the cost of the accommodation exceeds £75,000.

[*ITEPA 2003, s 106*].

Amount of charge

8.11   The amount of the additional charge is the rent that would have been payable (for the period that the accommodation is made available to the employee) if the property had been let at an annual rent equal to the appropriate percentage of the excess of the cost of providing the accommodation over £75,000. [*ITEPA 2003, s 106*]. If the employee pays rent, etc. to the employer (or other provider of the accommodation) this is deducted first from the charge calculated under *s 105* but, to the extent that it exceeds the annual value, the balance is deducted from the amount that would otherwise have been chargeable under *s 106*. [*ITEPA 2003, s 106(3)*].

8.12   *Benefits in Relation to Accommodation*

The appropriate percentage

8.12   The appropriate percentage of the cost of providing the accommodation is the rate prescribed by the Treasury under *s 181* (beneficial loans – see **9.4** below) at the *beginning* of the year of assessment. This is 3.25% for 2014/15. It was 4.00 per cent for 2010/11 to 2013/14 and 4.75 per cent for 2009/10.

Cost of the accommodation

8.13   The 'cost of providing the accommodation' means the aggregate of:

(*a*)   the expenditure (including legal and other acquisition costs) incurred in acquiring the interest in the property held by a 'person involved in providing the accommodation'; and

(*b*)   any expenditure on improvements incurred by such a person before the year of assessment in relation to which the benefit arises.

[*ITEPA 2003, s 104*].

In other words, it is the cost of the property plus the cost of improvements up to the end of the previous year of assessment. A small benefit can be obtained by deferring until after 5 April improvements that are planned in February or March so that the cost does not increase the benefit for the next year of assessment.

Person involved in providing the accommodation

8.14   The following can be the 'person involved in providing the accommodation':

(*a*)   the person providing the accommodation;

(*b*)   the employer (if he is not the provider of the accommodation); and

(*c*)   any person who is connected (within the meaning of *s 839*) with a person falling within (*a*) or (*b*) above.

[*ITEPA 2003, s 112*].

Where more than one such person has an interest in the property, eg one holds a lease and another the freehold reversion, the expenditure incurred by each of them will need to be aggregated to arrive at the cost of providing the accommodation.

Property already owned by the employer

8.15   If an estate or interest in the property was held by a relevant person throughout the six years up to the date when the accommodation is first occupied by the employee, the cost of providing the accommodation is calculated differently. In these circumstances it is the aggregate of the market value of the property at the date when the employee first occupied the property plus expenditure on improvements by relevant persons between that date and the end of the year of assessment before that for which the benefit arises. This applies irrespective of whether during the six-year period the property was owned by the person who makes it available to the employee or by a different relevant person, or even by a succession of relevant persons. [*ITEPA 2003, s 107*]. The original cost of the accommodation in such circumstances was felt to be a historical figure unrelated to the need to acquire the property for occupation by the employee, and it would be unfair for the employee to be put in a substantially better position, by having his benefit calculated by reference to an out-of-date figure, than he would have been in had the house had to be bought specifically for his occupation. The market value of the property at the time it is first made available to the employee is the price which it might reasonably be expected to fetch on a sale in the open market with vacant possession. In arriving at this value any option in respect of the property held by the employee, or a connected person of his, or by a relevant person (as defined at **8.46** above) which would depress the value must be ignored. [*ITEPA 2003, s 107(3), (4)*]. Curiously this applies only for the purpose of calculating the amount of the benefit. The original cost continues to be used to determine whether or not the charge applies at all. For example, suppose that an employer bought a house in 1950 for £20,000 and a second identical one in 1980 for £200,000. In 2014/15, when both houses are worth £350,000, he allows employee A to occupy the first house and employee B to occupy the second. Employee A will not be liable to tax under *s 106* on his occupation but employee B will be taxed on 3.25% of £275,000 (£350,000 minus £75,000).

8.16   If the employee reimburses any part of the cost of acquisition of, or improvements to, the premises to the employer (or another relevant person), or pays a premium for the grant of a lease or sub-lease of the premises, that payment is deducted from the aggregate amount referred to at **8.42** above (or at **8.48** above, where the market value figure is adopted). [*ITEPA 2003, s 104*].

More than one property provided

8.17   If an employee is provided with more than one property, HMRC initially considered that the *s 106* charge was on the excess of the aggregate cost of both properties over £75,000. But they now accept that the two properties can be looked at separately so that a charge will only arise on the excess of the cost of an individual property over £75,000.

Property provided to more than one employee

8.18   Where a property is provided as living accommodation to more then one employee in the same period, the total charge under *s 106* on all of the employees concerned is limited to the amount that would have been taxable if it had been provided to a single employee during that period. The apportionment of the reduction between the employees must be done on a just and reasonable basis. [*ITEPA 2003, s 108*].

Exceptions

8.19   Neither the basic nor additional charge applies if the employee is covered by one of the following exemptions. These used to be known as representative occupation.

(*a*)   Where it is necessary for the proper performance of the employee's duties that he should reside in the accommodation, eg the caretaker of a block of flats will need to live in one of the flats to do his job properly so that he is on hand when the occupiers of other flats need him. [*ITEPA 2003, s 99(1)*].

(*b*)   Where the accommodation is provided for the better performance of the duties of his employment, and it is one of the kinds of employment in which it is customary to provide living accommodation for employees, eg a school caretaker does not need to live on or near the premises but because of the need to inspect the premises at intervals to ensure that they are secure, it makes sense for him to do so, and he will normally be provided with a house in the vicinity of the school. [*ITEPA 2003, s 99(2)*].

(*c*)   Where there is a special threat to the employee's security, and security arrangements are in force, and he resides in the accommodation as part of those arrangements, eg the Prime Minister does not have to live at 10 or 11 Downing Street to carry out his job (Harold Wilson did not) but because of the risk of terrorism the present Prime Minister needs to live there as special security arrangements have been made to protect the property. [*ITEPA 2003, s 100*].

8.20   Where one of these exemptions applies not only is there no charge in relation to the provision of the accommodation but no assessment can be made on the employee in respect of council tax or rates, water or sewerage charges paid by the employer (or any other person other than the employee), irrespective of whether these were paid by the employer or they were paid by the employee and reimbursed to him. [*ITEPA 2003, s 314*].

8.21   HMRC draw a distinction between board and lodging and living accommodation. They say that the exemption does not apply where the employee is provided with board and lodging. They interpret living accommodation as where 'the employee is provided with a self-contained living space with most of the facilities necessary for independent habitation' (Employment Income Manual para 1020). They say that living accommodation implies something which gives the occupant the necessary facilities to live domestic life independently without reliance on others to supply basic needs and that at a minimum they would expect an individual to have the use of a refrigerator and full cooking facilities, even if such facilities are shared (Employment Income Manual *para 11321*). It seems questionable whether the term 'living accommodation' would be given such a narrow meaning by the courts rather than the broader interpretation of a place where someone lives.

8.22   HMRC gives as examples of employees (who live on the premises concerned) who might be exempted under *para 8.6*:

(*a*)   (*para 11342*)

    agricultural workers who live on farms or agricultural estates;

    lock-gate and level crossing gate keepers;

    caretakers (with a genuine full-time caretaking job);

    stewards and green keepers;

    managers of pubs;

    wardens of sheltered housing schemes.

(*b*)   (*paras 11351* and *11352*)

    police officers;

    Ministry of Defence police;

    prison governors, officers and chaplains;

    clergymen and ministers of religion;

    members of HM Forces;

    members of the Diplomatic Service;

    managers of newsagents shops that have paper rounds;

    managers of traditional off-licence shops (ie which keep pub hours);

    head teacher, bursar, matron, nurse and doctor of boarding schools and other teachers at such schools with pastoral or other irregular contractual responsibilities outside normal school hours;

    stable staff of racehorse trainers;

    vets assisting in veterinary practices (but only if the better performance test can be individually justified);

    managers of camping and caravan sites (but only if the better performance test can be individually justified).

(*c*)   (*para 11362*)

    an employee under a genuine terrorist threat to his life – although they warn that the conditions are 'very difficult' to meet.

This is not of course an exhaustive list. Anyone in different circumstances who believes that they fall within one of the three circumstances is entitled to claim relief.

Council housing

8.23   No benefit arises to an employee of a local authority if accommodation is provided to him by that authority and the terms on which it is provided are no more favourable than those on which similar accommodation is provided by the authority for persons who are not their employees but whose circumstances are otherwise similar to those of the employee. [*ITEPA 2003, s 98*]. This ensures that a person who lives in a council house or flat and happens to be a council employee will not be charged to a benefit if the rent he pays is less than a market rent, provided that he pays the same rent as he would have done had he not been a council employee.

Directors

8.24 The exemption conferred by heads (*a*) and (*b*) in **8.8** above does not apply if the accommodation is provided by a company and the employee is a director of that company (or of an associated company) unless:

(*a*)   he does not have a material interest in the company; and

(*b*)   either:

    (i)   he is a full-time working director;

    (ii)   the company neither carries on a trade nor does its business consist wholly or mainly in the holding of investments or other property; or

    (iii)   the company is established for charitable purposes only.

[*ITEPA 2003, s 99(3)–(5)*].

8.25 The definition of director considered at **6.9** above applies. A person has a material interest in a company if he or associates of his (or he and his associates) is the beneficial owner of, or able to control, more than 5 per cent of the ordinary share capital or, if the company is a close company, possesses (or is entitled to acquire) such rights as would entitle him to more than 5 per cent of the assets on a winding-up. [*ITEPA 2003, s 68*]. A full-time working director is a director who is required to devote substantially the whole of his time to the service of the company in a managerial or technical capacity. [*ITEPA 2003, s 66(3)*]. HMRC interpret 'substantially the whole of his time' as meaning a normal working day (see **6.11**).

8.26 The restriction in **8.24** above also applies if the employee is a director of an associated company (ie one company controls the other or the two are under common control). [*ITEPA 2003, s 99(3), (5)*]. If he is a director of a number of associated companies the above tests must be met in relation to all such directorships. [*ITEPA 2003, s 99(3)*]. It is likely that in practice HMRC will look at all associated employments together in deciding whether or not the employee is a full-time working director, but there is no requirement for them to do so.

Running costs

8.27 If the employee is covered by one of the exemptions (see **8.19** above) there is a limit on the amount on which he can be assessed in respect of running costs. This applies to expenditure on:

(*a*)   heating, lighting or cleaning the premises;

(*b*)   repairs, maintenance and decoration; and

(*c*)   the provision of furniture and other appurtenances or effects which are normal for domestic occupation.

[*ITEPA 2003, s 315*].

Amount of charge

8.28   The total benefit in relation to all of the above items is limited to 10 per cent of the net amount of the emoluments of the employment for the year of assessment. If the property is not available for the employee for the entire year the figure is reduced proportionately. [*ITEPA 2003, s 315(4)*].

8.29   Expenditure incurred by the employee and reimbursed to him is treated as if it were expenditure by the employer for applying this limitation. On the other hand, if the employee reimburses expenditure by the employer (or anyone else other than the employee himself), the amount reimbursed is deductible from the 10 per cent of the emoluments figure. [*ITEPA 2003, s 315(4)*].

Net emoluments

8.30   The net amount of the employee's emoluments is the amount of those emoluments (excluding the expenditure at heads (*a*) to (*c*) in **8.27** above) less:

(*a*)   any capital allowances deductible from the emoluments;

(*b*)   any deduction for expenses under *ss 198, 199* and *332(3)*;

(*c*)   any deduction for fees and subscriptions under *s 201*;

(*d*)   contributions by the employee to a company pension scheme deductible under *ss 592(7)* and *594*; and

(*e*)   contributions to retirement annuities deductible under *s 619(1)(a)*.

(*f*)   mileage allowance relief (see **7.51**).

[*ITEPA 2003, s 315(5)*].

8.31   When personal pensions were introduced the need to amend this list to include payment to a personal pension scheme allowable under *section 639* seems to have been overlooked.

Associated companies

8.32   If the employer is a company, emoluments of any employment by an associated company (ie one which controls, or is controlled by, the employer company or is under common control with it) must be brought into account in calculating the 10 per cent limit as if they were emoluments of the employment in relation to which the accommodation is provided. [*ITEPA 2003, s 315(5)*].

8.33 This limitation of the benefit figure in respect of running costs applies only where a charge would arise under *s 105* or *106* (see **8.4** above) but for being excluded under the representative occupation rules (see **8.9** above). [*ITEPA 2003, s 315(2)*]. It will not apply if the employer pays the heating, lighting, etc. of a property owned by the employee himself.

Exceptions

8.34 It should be noted that telephone expenses are not included in the list of items to which the 10 per cent limit applies. Furthermore, only a proportion of gas and electricity bills are covered by this limitation, ie the part which relates to lighting, heating, and powering cleaning equipment. The part relating to cooking, heating hot water, powering TV, hi-fi equipment, power tools, etc. should be excluded from the calculation and assessed on the employee in full in addition to the 10 per cent figure.

8.35 It must also be remembered that expenditure on structural alterations and certain repairs does not give rise to a benefit at all (see head (*f*) at **6.44** above) and is therefore excluded from the expenditure under head (*b*) at **8.52** above.

8.36 Where the employee is in a representative occupation, no charge arises in respect of rates or, by concession, council tax (see **8.20** above). A charge will arise in relation to the community charge, however, if this was paid by the employer (and the 10 per cent limitation will presumably not apply to it).

Council tax

8.37 If the employer pays an employee's council tax the payment will be taxable on him as a benefit in kind unless he is in a representative occupation (see **8.19**). The payment will also attract both employer's and employee's National Insurance. If the employee's duties require him to work at home and he is entitled to deduct a proportion of his domestic expenses under *section 336* he may be able to deduct an appropriate proportion of his council tax if he has a room or rooms set aside exclusively for work (*IR Press Release 16 March 1993* and *DSS Press Release 9 November 1993*).

Ministers of religion

8.38 Where a clergyman or minister of religion is provided with a residence in premises owned or leased by a charity or ecclesiastical corporation from which to perform his duties and he is not a higherpaid employee, he is not taxed in respect of expenditure on heating, lighting, cleaning and gardening even though these are his contractual liability. This applies whether the church pays the sums on his behalf, reimburses them to him, or pays him an allowance towards such costs [*ITEPA 2003, ss 290A, 290B enacting ESC A61*].

Chevening House

8.39   The charges under *ss 105* and *106* do not apply in relation to the occupation of Chevening House which was put into trust for occupation by members of the Royal Family, or any other premises held on the trusts set out in the *Chevening Estate Act 1959*. [*ITEPA 2003, s 101*].

The employee's family

8.40   If living accommodation is provided for members of an employee's family or household, ie his spouse, his children and their spouses, his parents and his domestic staff (servants up to 2002/03), dependants or guests [*ITEPA 2003, s 721(5)*] by reason of the employee's job it must be treated as having been provided to him, so as to bring these provisions into operation. [*ITEPA 2003, s 97(1)*]. Living accommodation provided by the employer is automatically deemed to have been provided by reason of the employment unless either:

(*a*)   the employer is an individual and it can be shown that he has provided the accommodation in the normal course of his domestic, family or personal relationships; or

(*b*)   the employer is a local authority and the terms on which the accommodation is provided are no more favourable than those which apply to council tenants for similar accommodation in similar personal circumstances to the employee.

[*ITEPA 2003, s 97(2)*].

It should be noted that (*a*) will not include a partnership, even a husband and wife partnership, so other members of the family who live at the family home and work in the partnership business would be taxable if the home is a partnership asset – which could well be the case with a flat above the business premises.

Homes outside the UK

8.41   There is a limited exclusion from these provisions for overseas properties such as holiday homes owned through a company. This applies only where:

(*a*)   the company is wholly owned by a director or other officer of the company or by a member of his family or household (or by such a person and other individuals); and

(*b*)   the company has been 'the holding company of the property' at all times since the company first owned a relevant interest in it, namely an interest that confers (or would but for any inferior interest confer) a right to exclusive possession of the property at all times or at certain times.

[*ITEPA 2003, s 100A(1), (4), (5)* inserted by *Finance Act 2008 (FA 2008), s 45*].

8.42   A company is the holding company of the property for this purpose if:

(*a*)   it owns a relevant interest (as defined above) in the property;

(*b*)   its main or only asset is that interest;

(*c*)   the only activities undertaken by the company are ones which are incidental to its ownership of that interest (which will include the generation of rental income from the property).

[*ITEPA 2003, s 100A(2)*].

A holding company can also qualify as the holding company of the property if the property is owned by a wholly owned subsidiary, the subsidiary meets the above conditions, the subsidiary is the parent company's only or main asset and the only activities undertaken by the parent company are ones that are incidental to its ownership of the interest in the subsidiary. [*ITEPA 2003, s 100A(3)*].

8.43   If the shareholder acquired his interest in the company subsequent to the company acquiring the property, the conditions at **8.41**(b) have to be met only from the time that he first acquired any part of that interest, provided that he did not acquire any part of his interest directly or indirectly from a person connected with the director or other officer [*ITEPA 2003, s 100A(6)*]. This is an odd provision. It is not clear how it is intended to operate in practice. For example, suppose that the company acquired the property in 1980 and that in January 2004 the director and his brother purchased the company in equal shares. In January 2008 the director bought his brother's interest so he now owns 100 per cent. Between January 2004 and January 2008 *section 100A(6)* applies so the tests at **8.42** have to be met only from January 2004. The section ceases to apply from January 2008 as part of the director's interest has now been acquired from a connected person. Accordingly the tests at **8.42** have to be met from 1980 in looking at periods after January 2008. The question then arises as to whether HMRC can re-open earlier years on the basis that *s 100A(6)* does not specify the date at which the test is applied. As income tax is, in theory at least, an annual tax the answer is probably 'No' as regards years prior to 2007/08. But what about 2007/08 itself where the test was met for nine months but not the other three?

8.44   The above exclusion does not apply at all if either:

(*a*)   the company's interest in the property was acquired (or granted to it) directly or indirectly from a 'connected company' at an undervalue (or the company's interest in the property derives from an interest that was so acquired from a connected company);

(*b*)   expenditure in respect of the property has been incurred directly or indirectly by a connected company;

(*c*)   any borrowing of the company (other than a borrowing at a commercial rate or on which the director concerned has been taxed under the beneficial loan rules – see **9.1**) directly or indirectly from a connected company has been outstanding; or (*d*)   the living accommodation is provided in pursuance of an arrangement the main purpose, or one of the main purposes, of which is the avoidance of tax or NIC.

[*ITEPA 2003, s 100B(1)–(5), (7)*].

8.45   An interest is acquired at an undervalue within (*a*) above if the total consideration for it is less than that which might reasonably be expected to be obtained on a disposal of the interest on the open market. For this purpose consideration means consideration provided at any time and includes, for example, payments of rent. [*ITEPA 2003, s 100B(6)*]. For the purpose of (*d*) an arrangement includes any scheme agreement or understanding, whether or not enforceable. [*ITEPA 2003, s 100B(8)*]. A connected company means a company connected with the director or officer concerned or a member of his family or an employee of his, or a company connected with such a company. [*ITEPA 2003, s 100B(9)*]. A director of course includes a shadow director – see **6.10**.

8.46   This provision is deemed always to have had effect, and *Income and Corporation Taxes Act 1988 (ICTA 1988), s 145* (the predecessor provision) is treated as never having applied to such accommodation. [*FA 2008, s 42(2), (3)*]. This probably does not enable those who paid tax to now put in an error or mistake claim. Their tax would have been determined in accordance with the practice generally prevailing at the time. They could, however, put in such a claim on the basis that they were mistaken in believing that they were a shadow director. Nevertheless HMRC have said that any individual who can show that he has paid income tax for a year before 2008/09 (ie. has retained evidence of his tax payment) should write to them to claim a refund. HMRC Notice 28 8 2008). The notice does not indicate any limit on how far back a person can go.

8.47   The main limitations on the relief are:

(*a*)   any shareholding by a trust or company forfeits the relief for other shareholders;

(*b*)   in some cases it is necessary to deposit funds with a bank to raise a mortgage; such a deposit could well prevent the property being the only or main asset of the company;

(*c*)   as indicated at **8.43** the rules on acquisitions from other family members can operate erratically;

(*d*)   the rules prohibit joint ownership of the property by two companies, each of which is owned by individuals (or by the company and an individual) as neither company would have a right to exclusive possession.

8.48   It should particularly be noted that the exclusion does not apply to UK holiday homes. It should also be borne in mind that if the individual is not a director of the company (and the use of the property does not arise from a directorship or employment of another company) no benefit will arise even if the above conditions are not met unless the individual can be regarded as a shadow director, ie a person in accordance with whose instructions the directors are accustomed to act. Although in *R v Allen [2001] STC 1537* (see **6.10**) Mr Allen was held to be taxable as a shadow director, he accepted that he was such a person. Provided the issue is recognised initially, it is normally not too difficult to ensure that the shareholder/occupier of the property is not a shadow director.

Chapter 9

Other Benefits

Beneficial loan arrangements

Notional interest

9.1   If a higher-paid employee is granted an interest-free loan by reason of his employment, he is treated as receiving earnings from the employment of an amount equal to interest on the loan at 'the official rate' for the period that the loan is outstanding during each year of assessment. [*Income Tax (Earnings and Pensions) Act 2003, s 175*]. Similarly, if a loan carries interest at a rate below the official rate, a tax as employment income charge arises on the difference between interest at the official rate and that actually paid. [*ITEPA 2003, s 175*]. There is an option to aggregate all loans by the same lender and borrower where the lender is a close company, the borrower is a director of that company, the benefit of each loan is obtained by reason of his employment, the rate of interest on none of the loans exceeds the official rate at any time in the tax year, the loans are in the same currency, and none of them are qualifying loans. An election to aggregate must be made by 7 July after the end of the tax year. If there are several loans either all must be aggregated or none. [*ITEPA 2003, s 187*]. The notional interest is treated as paid by the employee at the end of the tax year or the earlier date on which the loan is repaid [*ITEPA 2003, s 184(4)*].

9.2   A replacement loan is treated as remaining the same loan as the original one if it is replaced, directly or indirectly by either a further employment-related loan from the same employer or a person connected with him, or by a third party loan which is itself replaced by such a further employment-related loan within the next 40 days. [*ITEPA 2003, s 186*].

9.3   An interesting issue arose in *Harvey v Williams [1998] STC (SCD) 215*. Mr Harvey was employed by Supergas Ltd. The company asked him to move from Newark to their Sittingbourne branch. He could not find a suitable house in Kent within his price range. Supergas agreed to 'lend' Mr Harvey £10,000 interest-free to buy a £70,000 house on the basis that when the house was sold they would receive 10/70ths of the sale proceeds. Mr Harvey contended that the £10,000 was not a loan, it was an investment by Supergas. The Special Commissioner held that as Supergas had agreed to make a loan, he had to hold it was a loan. Accordingly, *s 175* applied. This is a harsh decision. There seems no doubt that Supergas Ltd was obtaining a full commercial consideration for the outlay of its money. In no sense was it providing any benefit to Mr Harvey. It emphasises that great care needs to be taken if slightly unusual answers are found to commercial problems, as HMRC will not be slow to enforce a tax charge even in circumstances where there is little doubt that, had parliament foreseen them it would not have imposed a charge. It also emphasises the importance of getting the documents right.

The official rate

9.4   The official rate is fixed from time to time by the Treasury by statutory instrument. [*ITEPA 2003, s 181*]. It is arrived at by taking the average base rates of the main High Street banks, rounding this to the nearest whole number and adding 1.5 per cent. The rates are changed infrequently. The rate is currently 3.25 per cent. It was 4 per cent from 6 April 2010 to 5 April 2014, 4.75 per cent from 1 March 2009 to 5 April 2010 and 6.25 per cent from 6 April 2005 to 28 February 2009.

9.5   HMRC announced in January 2000 that in order to simplify record-keeping, valuation and reporting requirements in future, the official rate will be set in advance for the whole of the following tax year and will not be increased during that year even if typical mortgage rates (on which they say it is based) are increased. They recognise that 'this policy would need to be reviewed if typical mortgage rates were to fall sharply during a future tax year' (*Press Release 25 January 2000*). The rate was in fact varied during the course of 2002/03 and again during 2008/09, giving an average rate for those years of 5.94 per cent and 6.1 per cent respectively.

9.6   The Treasury are empowered to prescribe a different 'official rate' or rates for foreign currency loans. Such special rates can apply only where both the employee normally lives in the foreign country concerned and he has actually lived there at some time in the six years prior to the year of assessment concerned. [*ITEPA 2003, s 181(2)*]. HMRC consider that a holiday in the home country would not of itself be sufficient to show that the employee has actually 'lived' there; they consider that living connotes a degree of continuance (*Tax Bulletin, Issue 13*, October 1994). To date they have prescribed rates only for loans in Japanese Yen (3.9 per cent) and Swiss Francs (5.5 per cent). These rates have remained unchanged since 6 July 1994.

The employee's family

9.7   These provisions (and those in relation to waivers – see **9.25** below) apply not only to a loan to the employee himself but also to a loan to any relative of his. For this purpose a relative means the employee's spouse, his or his spouse's parents or remoter forebears, his or his spouse's children or remoter issue, his brothers and sisters, brothers or sisters of the employee's spouse, and a spouse of any of the above. [*ITEPA 2003, s 174(6)*]. This definition of relative is far wider than that which applies generally to the benefit in kind provisions.

Meaning of loan

9.8   The legislation defines 'loan' very widely. It includes 'any form of credit'. [*ITEPA 2003, s 173(2)(a)*]. However, advances against expenses need not be treated as a loan provided that the maximum amount outstanding does not exceed £1,000, the advances are spent within six months, and the employee accounts to his employer regularly for his expenditure. If any of these conditions are not met it must be treated as a loan. [*ITEPA 2003, s 179(1), (2)*]. HMRC have power to increase the £1,000 and six month limit in relation to an individual loan on the application of the employer. [*ITEPA 2003, s 179(3), (4)*]. The advance must be for the purpose of paying either necessary expenses (those which the employee is obliged to incur and pay as holder of the employment and are necessarily incurred in the performance of its duties) or incidental overnight expenses (expenses that are incidental to the employee's absence from the place where he normally lives, relate to a continuous period of absence within *s 240* (see **5.42**) and would not be deductible as an expense if the employee incurred and paid them [*ITEPA 2003, s 179(1), (5), (6)*]. The inclusion of the word 'not' in *section 179(6) (c)* looks odd. It may be because if the expenses were deductible they would constitute necessary expenses. Mention should also be made of *Aspect Capital Ltd v HMRC (2014 UKUT 81)*, which concerned the tax charge on a loan under *Income and Corporation Taxes Act 1988 (ICTA 1988), s 419* (now *Corporation Tax Act 2010 (CTA 2010, s 455)*. The company entered into a tripartite arrangement with the employee and an EBT. This required the employee to make a payment to the company only on the occurrence of a contingent event. It also provided that the company would provide a facility to the employee or on his behalf to enable the employee to acquire shares. This facility payment was made to the EBT, which sold the shares to the employer, not to the employee. Both the FTT and the UT held that the arrangement constituted a loan by the company to the employee and that although the facility payment was not an advance of money, under it the employee incurred a debt to the company equal to the facility payment.

9.9   Particular care needs to be taken with partnership service companies, as the case of *Andrew Grant Services Ltd v Walton [1999] STC 330* demonstrates. Mr Grant and his brother were in partnership as estate agents. Andrew Grant Services Ltd provided services to the partnership in return for a management charge. This was calculated annually by the company's accountants based on the expenses of the service company. The annual fee was the expenses of the company plus a mark-up. Sound familiar? That is how most such service companies operate. HMRC successfully contended that this was a form of credit. When the partnership consumed services it incurred a liability to pay for them. Such credit was extended from day to day (ie even before the service company paid its supplier!) Accordingly, there was a 'loan' from the time the services were consumed until the time the services were paid for. It appears from this that the only way to avoid a *section 175* liability in respect of a partnership service company is to pay for the services in advance! It may be relevant that in this case there was no agreement as to payment. The position may be different if there is an agreement between the partnership and the service company that the company will bill on a specific date.

Exceptions to the charge

9.10   There are a number of exceptions to this tax charge on notional interest.

(*a*)   There is no charge if the amount outstanding on the loan (or the aggregate of all the loans within *section 175*) does not exceed £10,000 at any time in the tax year (£5,000 up to 2013/14).

(*b*)   There is also no charge in respect of non-qualifying loans if the £10,000 limit is breached only because of the existence of qualifying loans (all or part of the interest on which is eligible for tax relief either under *section 393* (relief for interest paid – see **19.18**), or as a trading expense) and the £10,000 figure would not be exceeded if such loans are ignored. [*ITEPA 2003, s 180 as amended by Finance Act 2014 (FA 2014, s 22*]

Example

John has the following loans outstanding from his employer in 2013/14:

(i)   A second mortgage of £20,000 towards the purchase of shares in his family company. (John also has a building society mortgage of £25,000.)

(ii)   A season ticket loan which has averaged £2,300 during the year. The maximum amount was £4,800 in October 2011 and John is repaying it at the rate of £400 a month.

(iii)   A temporary loan of £1,000 made in February 2014 to clear credit card balances.

As loan (i) is a qualifying loan it does not need to be aggregated with loans (ii) and (iii). The highest amount of loan (ii), £4,800, was in October when loan (iii) did not exist. In February 2014 the amount of loan (ii) was £3,600 (£4,800 less three monthly repayments) and loan (iii) was £1,000, a total of £4,600. Accordingly, the *de minimis* exemption applies to loans (ii) and (iii) (but not loan (i)) because there was no point in the year at which the aggregate amount outstanding on the non-qualifying loans exceeded £5,000.

(*c*)   If a loan is made for a fixed and unvariable period and at a fixed and unvariable rate of interest, and 'the amount of interest paid on' the loan for the tax year in which it was made 'was equal to or greater than the interest that would have been payable at the official rate for that year', no charge arises merely because the official rate of interest in a subsequent year is higher than the fixed rate (although a charge could arise if, for example, the employee defaults in payment of the interest). [*ITEPA 2003, s 177*]. The words in inverted commas are taken from the legislation, as it appears to be defective. The concept of the relief was to confer exemption where the interest payable is at least equal to interest at the official rate at the time the loan was made. However, the wording seems to assume that the same official rate will apply throughout a year of assessment, which, of course, is not necessarily the case. Furthermore, the relief does not appear to apply at all if no interest was actually paid on the loan in the year it was taken out, eg if the interest is payable quarterly and the loan was made on 1 February, no interest would have been payable until 1 May in the following tax year. It may be that the courts would interpret 'paid ... for the year' as allowing one to accrue the interest on a day-to-day basis provided that it is actually paid at some time. If a loan is made at the official rate of interest and that rate increases before the end of the tax year, it will be apparent that the conditions for the relief cannot be met as interest calculated on a day-to-day basis at the official rate must exceed interest at the fixed rate actually applying to the loan.

(*d*)   Where a loan was made before 6 April 1978 (when there was no official rate) but is for a fixed and unvariable period and at a fixed and unvariable rate of interest, no charge will arise if it can be shown that the rate of interest payable is such as could have been expected to apply to a loan on the same terms (other than the rate of interest) made at that time between persons not connected with one another (within *s 839*) dealing at arm's length. [*ICTA 1988, s 161(3)*]. Unlike the exception in head (*c*) above, this rule seems to apply even if no interest is actually paid on the loan, eg because the employer opts not to pursue collection.

(*e*)   Where the loan is made not to the employee but to a relative, no tax charge will arise if the employee can show that he personally derived no benefit from it. [*ITEPA 2003, s 174(5), (b)*].

(*f*)   If the employee dies, the charge on notional interest ceases at the date of his death (ie the loan is deemed to have been repaid at that date). [*ITEPA 2003, s 190*].

(*g*)   There is no charge if the loan is made on ordinary commercial terms [*ITEPA 2003, s 176*]. For this purpose a loan is made on ordinary commercial terms if it is made by the lender in the ordinary course of a business carried on by him which includes the lending of money or the supplying of goods or services on credit provided that either:

(i)   at the time it was made comparable loans were available to all those who might be expected to avail themselves of the services provided by the lender, a substantial proportion of comparable loans made by the lender at or about the time the loan was made were made to members of the public at large with whom the lender dealt at arm's length, comparable loans generally made to the public at that time are (ie at the current time, not when the loan was made) still held on the same terms, and if those terms differ from those applicable immediately after the loan was made the changes were imposed in the ordinary course of the lender's business [*ITEPA 2003, s 176(3)*];

(ii)   if the loan has been varied since it was made but before 6 April 2000, at the time of that variation a substantial proportion of the aggregate of any existing loans were varied around the same time so as to be held on the same terms as the employee's loan after it was varied and any new loans by the lender around that time on the same terms were made to members of the public, a significant number of those loans and the employee's loan are now held on the same terms, and if those terms differ from those applicable immediately after the time of the variation the changes were imposed in the ordinary course of the lender's business [*ITEPA 2003, s 176(5)*]; or

(iii)   if the loan has been varied after 5 April 2000, at the time of that variation members of the public that had loans from the lender for similar purposes had a right to vary their loans on the same terms and conditions as the employee, any existing loans so varied are now held on the same terms, if those terms differ from those that applied immediately after the variation the changes were imposed in the ordinary course of the lender's business, and a substantial proportion of the aggregate of the loans varied at around the same time so as to be held on the same terms as the employee's loan after it was varied (and any new loans made by the lender at around that time which are held on those terms) were made to members of the public [*ITEPA 2003, s 176(6)*].

For the purpose of (i) above a loan is comparable to another if it is made for the same or similar purposes and on the same terms and conditions as the loan in question. [*ITEPA 2003, s 176(4)*] In determining whether loans made before 1 June 1994 were made (or are held) on the same terms and conditions, any fees, commission or other incidental expenses incurred by the borrower are ignored [*ITEPA 2003, s 176(8)*]. Similarly, in making the comparison for the purposes of (ii) and (iii) above, payments by a borrower or penalties, interest or similar amounts incurred as a result of varying the loan or on fees, commissions, or other incidental expenses incurred for the purpose of obtaining the loan are ignored to determine whether rights to vary loans are exercisable on the same terms or conditions or loans are held on the same terms. [*ITEPA 2003, s 176(9)*]. This is intended to exempt mortgages and loans by banks, building societies and other financial institutions where the loan to the employee is made on the same terms as loans to members of the public generally. Whether it achieved this is questionable. Banks do not have a single basis for lending money to all customers as is envisaged in (i). Their terms and the availability of some types of loan, will depend on their assessment of the risk involved so the 'same terms' will not be available to all their customers. It can be inferred from the wording of *ITEPA 2003, s 176(9)* that loans are made on the same terms only if the same fees, commissions and other incidental expenses are charged to staff. This was previously stated explicitly in *FA 1994, s 88(5)*. HMRC stress, 'The words "on the same terms" mean just what they say. If two loans are: made, or varied, on the basis of different lending criteria, or carry interest at different rates, or have different terms as to repayment or security, they are not held on the same terms' (Employment Income Manual para 26176). HMRC have also said that a loan does not qualify if the loan-to-income or loan-to-value ratio is relaxed for employees. However, they consider head (ii) above will be satisfied if over 50 per cent of the comparable loans are to the public at large and could be met at a lower figure. They say the public at large means the public in general as opposed to a specific section of the public, but does not require the loans to be available 'to everyone on the Clapham omnibus' (*Tax Bulletin, Issue 12*, August 1994). The question in *West v Crossland [1999] STC 147* was when is a loan not making a loan. Mr Crossland was an employee of Nationwide Building Society. He took a variable rate mortgage on preferential terms. He accepted that *section 160* applied. In early 1994 he asked the Nationwide to switch his mortgage into a fixed rate loan on the same terms as were available to the general public and claimed that henceforth the above exemption applied. 'No', said HMRC, 'at the time it was made the loan was on preferential terms. Those terms have changed; it is still the same loan and the test has to be applied at the time the loan was made'. 'I agree' said Lindsay J. 'Mr Crossland could have avoided the tax charge by repaying the loan and reborrowing on the new terms. The fact that Mr Crossland could so easily have satisfied the provisions ... does not point to any manifest injustice in [HMRC's] requirements that those demarcations apparently required by Parliament, have, indeed to be satisfied.' In *Amri v HMRC (TC 3451)* Ms Amri, an employee of HBOS plc, sought a £140,000 mortgage from Halifax, a subsidiary of HBOS. She was told that she could have a £35,000 staff loan. HMRC contended that although the remaining £105,000 was borrowed on normal commercial terms, it was tainted by the £35,000, and as the commercial rate of interest was at the time below the official rate, she was taxable to a benefit on the £140,000 borrowing. Fortunately the FTT took the common-sense approach and held that in reality there were two separate loans; a beneficial loan of £35,000 and a commercial loan of £105,000 and only the first had tax consequences.

(*h*) There is no charge on notional interest if, had interest been paid, the whole amount would have been either eligible for tax relief under *ICTA 1988, s 353* (relief for interest paid under MIRAS) or deductible in computing the profits of a trade, profession or vocation or of a Schedule A business. [*ITEPA 2003, s 178*].

Calculation of charge

The 'normal' method

9.11 There are two alternate methods of calculating the taxable amount. The first, the 'normal method', is to multiply the average amount outstanding in the year of assessment by the number of whole months during which the loan was outstanding, divide by 12, and multiply the result by the official rate of interest in force during the period the loan was outstanding. [*ITEPA 2003, s 182*].

9.12 Where a loan was outstanding for the entire year the average rate is:

2008/09	6.1%
2009/10	4.75%
2010/11–2013/14	4.0%

9.13 *Other Benefits*

The average rate for all of the years from 1999/00 to date for Sw Fr loans is 5.5 per cent and for Yen loans 3.9 per cent.

9.13   The average amount outstanding is arrived at by adding the amount of the loan outstanding on 5 April preceding the year of assessment and the amount outstanding on 5 April in the year of assessment and dividing by two, ie in most cases, by adding the loan at the beginning of the year and that at the end of the year, and dividing by two. If the loan commenced during the year the balance at the date the loan was made is used in place of that at the preceding 5 April, and if it is fully repaid in the year the balance at the date of such repayment is adopted in place of the balance at the following 5 April. If the amount of the loan varied on one of the two days used, ie because the loan was either increased or partly repaid on that day, the highest amount outstanding at any time on the relevant day must be used.

9.14   The number of whole months for which a loan is outstanding means tax months, ie months ending on the fifth day of a calendar month, not calendar months or 31-day periods. The average official rate is determined on a day-to-day basis.

Example

Joe is a higher-paid employee, and on 18 July 2008 his employer lent him £15,000. Joe repaid £5,000 on 5 April 2009, £4,000 on 16 June 2009 and the balance on 20 October 2009.

2008/09

		£
Loan at 18.07.2008		15,000
Loan at 05.04.2009	the highest balance on that day	15,000
		30,000
	half thereof	15,000
Complete tax months outstanding (from 6 August 2008)		8
Official rate in force for period loan outstanding (262 days)		
18.07.08–05.11.08 111/262 × 6.25%		2.648
06.11.08–28. 02. 09 115/262 × 6.25%		2,743
01.03.09–05.04.09 36/262 × 4.75		655
		6,046
Taxable amount £15,000 × 8/12 × 6.046% =		£604.60

2009/10

		£
Loan at 05.04.2009	the highest balance on that day (even though the loan was not that high at any time in 2008/09)	15,000
Loan at 20.10.2009	the highest balance on that day	5,000
		20,000
	half thereof	10,000
Complete tax months outstanding (to 5 September 2009)		5
Official rate in force for period loan outstanding (198 days)		
06.04.09–05.08.09 122/198 × 4.75%		2,927
06.08.09–20.10.09 76/198 × 4.75%		1,823
		4.75%
Taxable amount £10,000 × 5/12 × 4.75% =		£197.92

9.15   It will be seen that this is a somewhat rough and ready calculation. Either the taxpayer or the Inspector of Taxes can elect to use 'the alternative method' which is more accurate – but more time-consuming to compute. The election must be made by 31 January following the end of the tax year – so that the employee can use the correct calculation in his tax return.

The 'alternative' method

9.16   The alternative method involves taking each period for which the official rate remains fixed, taking the maximum amount of the loan outstanding on each day in that period, aggregating those figures, dividing by 365, multiplying by the official rate for the period, and adding together the results for each such period in the tax year. [*ITEPA 2003, s 183*].

Example

Using the same facts as the previous example, the calculation under the alternative method is as follows:

2008/09: there are two periods for which the official rate remains fixed and the loan is outstanding. The maximum amount outstanding remained at £15,000 on each day in both periods.

These are

18.07.08–28.02.09	226 days	6.25%
01.03.09–05.04.09	36 days	4.75%
		£
£15,000 × (226/365) days at 4.75%		441.16
£15,000 × (36/365) days at 4.75%		70.27
		511.43

2009/10: there are two periods for which the official rate is fixed and the loan is outstanding. The loan was £10,000 from 06.04.09 to 16.06.09 (the highest figure on that day) and £6,000 from 17.06.09 to 20.10.09. The calculation is accordingly:

06.04.09–16.06.09	73 days	4.75%
17.06.09–20.10.09	125 days	4.75%
		£
£10,000 × (73/365) days at 4.75%		95.00
£6,000 × (125/365) days at 4.75%		97.60
		192.60

9.17   It will be seen that in this example it is in the taxpayer's interest to opt to adopt the alternative method in both 2008/09 and 2009/10.

9.18   If two or more employees are chargeable to tax in respect of the same loan the cash equivalent must be apportioned between them in a fair and reasonable manner and the part apportioned to each is treated as the cash equivalent of the loan so far as he is concerned [*ITEPA 2003, s 185*].

Payment of interest

9.19   Where interest is actually paid on a loan for a year of assessment it can be deducted from the figure calculated above to determine the taxable amount. [*ITEPA 2003, s 175(3)*]. This is so even if the interest is paid in a subsequent year of assessment. HMRC take the view that a payment after the end of the tax year can be an amount 'paid on the loan for that year' only if the loan agreement specifically allows the employer to charge interest. It is difficult to see how they can read this requirement into the statutory wording though.

Loan made by reason of employment

9.20   Both for the purpose of the charge on notional interest and the charge on loan waivers, etc. described below, a loan must be regarded as made by reason of a person's employment if either:

(*a*)   it is made by his employer – unless the employer is an individual and the loan can be shown to have been made in the normal course of his domestic, family or personal relationships;

(*b*)   it is made by a company or partnership:

    (i)   over which his employer has control; or

    (ii)   by which his employer (if it is a company) is controlled; or

    (iii)   is controlled by the same person that controls his employer (if it is a company); or

(*c*)   if the employer is (or controls, or is controlled by) a close company, it is made by a person who has a material interest in that company (or the company which controls it) – unless that person is an individual and it can be shown that the loan was made in the normal course of his domestic, family or personal relationships.

[*ITEPA 2003, s 174(2), (5)*]. This is so even if it is clear that the loan was in fact made for some other reason, for example if (*a*) would have applied had the employer been the company's director/shareholder rather than the company.

9.21   For the purpose of determining whether a loan was made by reason of a person's employment a company includes a partnership (but the expression 'close company' does not) and references to the employer include a prospective employer. [*ITEPA 2003, s 174(2)*]. Furthermore, an employer or other person is deemed to have made a loan if either money was lent by someone else and the rights assigned to the employer etc., or the employer etc. arranges, guarantees or in any way facilitates the continuation of a loan already in existence. [*ITEPA 2003, s 174(4), Sch 7, para 2*].

9.22   HMRC regard a loan by an overseas employer to a foreign employee who comes to work in the UK as within the scope of this provision if it was made at a time when the employee's emoluments were taxable in the UK as employment income, it was made in contemplation of the employee working or living in the UK, or the loan was already in existence before the employee had UK taxable emoluments and the employer facilitated its continuation. They do not regard the employer as facilitating the loan merely because it is conditional on the employment continuing or the employer deducts the interest and repayments from the employee's salary and pays it over to the lender (*Tax Bulletin, Issue 13*, October 1994).

9.23   In applying the provisions on notional interest and on loan waivers, etc. references to a loan must be taken to include any form of credit, and a loan obtained by reason of a person's employment must be taken to include a fresh loan applied directly or indirectly in repaying an earlier loan obtained by reason of the employment. References to making a loan include arranging, guaranteeing or in any way facilitating a loan. [*ITEPA 2003, s 173(2)*].

9.24   In *Grant v Watton [1999] STC 330* it was held that a loan by the employer company to a partnership of which the employee is a member gives rise to a benefit charge on the employee. Furthermore if the arrangement between the company and the partnership provides for services to be provided by the company on the basis of its costs plus a percentage mark-up and those arrangements contain no provisions regarding the date of payments for such services, the company gives credit to the partnership each time it makes a payment to its suppliers, as that payment triggers the right to recover the sum plus the mark-up from the partnership.

Waivers, etc of the loan

9.25   If a loan to (or to a relative of) a higher-paid employee which was obtained by reason of the employment is released or written off (in whole or in part) the amount written off is taxable as income from the employment in the year it is written off. [*ITEPA 2003, s 188(1)*]. This charge applies not only to a loan within the charge to notional interest but also to one where interest was paid at or above the official rate, or which fell into one of the exceptions given at **9.10** above.

9.26   If the loan is written off after the employment has ceased, the employment is deemed to have continued in existence so as to trigger the tax charge at the time it is written off. [*ITEPA 2003, s 188(2)*]. This charge cannot be avoided by arranging for a replacement loan to the ex-employee to repay the employment-related one, with the replacement loan being waived or written off. [*ITEPA 2003, s 188(3)*]. As the deemed remuneration from such deemed employment is taxable as earnings it might perhaps be possible to pay real personal pension or retirement annuity payments against it.

Exceptions to the charge

9.27   There are some exceptions to this charge:

(*a*)   It does not apply if the loan was made to a relative of the employee and the employee can show that he derived no benefit from it (as such a loan is not an employment-related loan). [*ITEPA 2003, 174(5)(b)*]. HMRC say that this exemption 'will only rarely apply in a case where a company controlled by its directors lends money cheaply to a relative of a director. This is because the making of a loan by the company on uncommercial terms will reduce the value of the company's shares and the directors will only do this if there is a countervailing benefit to themselves'. [*Employment Income Manual para 26150*]. That is not necessarily correct. If a relative asks a director for a loan he may well decide that the company should make the loan so that the relative feels a greater obligation to repay it than if the director had made it personally; he is unlikely to even consider the effect on the value of his shares. Furthermore a small loan repayable on demand is in any event unlikely to have any effect on the value of the shares. HMRC also consider that 'the benefit referred to is not confined to monetary advantage. Anything that is beneficial to the employee concerned, such as a feeling of well being because (or the fulfilment of a wish that) a relative is assisted with a cheap loan, is a benefit.'. That is of equally questionable validity.

(*b*) It does not normally apply if the amount written off is already deemed to be income and chargeable to income tax under some other provision. However, if that other provision is *ITEPA 2003, s 403* (payment of compensation, etc. on termination of employment) so that there is a risk that no tax might actually be paid because of the exemption for the first £30,000 of compensation (see **11.19** below) then the charge under *section 403* will apply. [*ITEPA 2003, s 189(2)(b)*]. The exemption from the charge under *section 188* also does not apply where the other provision is *Income Tax (Trading and Other Income) Act 2005 (ITTOIA 2005), s 633* (sums paid to a settlor otherwise than as income) and the tax charge under that section is a future charge – which may never crystallise. In certain circumstances, *section 633* (as extended by *section 634*) treats a loan to a settlor by a company connected with the settlement (one in which the settlement holds shares) as income of the settlor up to the amount of the accumulated income of the settlement. If the loan exceeds such income the excess will cause undistributed income of future years to be regarded as income of the settlor until he has been taxed on the full amount of the loan. If a settlement has no income or no prospect of any (or all its income is distributed as it arises) no charge on the settlor can arise, which is why HMRC needs to be able to extract tax on a waiver of the loan. If tax is paid under *s 188* there is no exemption from tax under *s 633* in future years so double taxation can result.

(*c*) No charge will be made if the loan is written off or released on or after the death of the taxpayer. [*ITEPA 2003, s 190(2)*].

(*d*) If the loan is released in pursuance of arrangements made with a view to protecting the holder of shares acquired before 6 April 1976 from a fall in their market value no charge will arise. Before the law was altered on that date a popular form of employee incentives was the issue to executives of shares in the company in which they worked, the cost being financed by way of an interest-free loan repayable only when the executive wished to dispose of the shares. Such schemes often contained a provision that if the price of the shares fell, the difference between the amount of the loan and the market value of the shares would be waived so that the executive would not suffer a loss. [*ITEPA 2003, Sch 7, para 25(2)*].

Director's tax paid by employer

9.28 If a payment which attracts tax under PAYE is made to a person employed as a director of a company (but not otherwise), and the employer does not deduct the tax but it is paid to HMRC by some person other than the director, the amount so paid must be treated as emoluments of the director unless it is made good by him to that other person. [*ITEPA 2003, s 223*].

9.29 This is aimed at the situation where HMRC collect the tax by assessing the company under *Regulation 80* of the *PAYE Regulations*. As this is an assessment on the company the payment of the tax is not settling an obligation of the director – as a *Regulation 80* assessment is a liability of the company – and would not therefore be emoluments of his under general principles. It is also probably not a payment for the director's benefit as it is paid to settle an obligation of the company itself.

9.30   Accordingly, without this special provision the payment could escape tax (and was apparently held by the Commissioners to do so prior to the introduction of this provision) thus enabling the director to extract from the company his gross salary free of tax. By treating the payment as additional remuneration – the tax on which will be collected by HMRC from the director – the *section* restores the position.

9.31   If the company debits the payment to a director's current account, rather than treating it as a tax liability of the company, HMRC will normally regard the amount as having been made good by the director so no charge will arise. Strictly speaking, it has probably not been made good until the current account balance has been cleared.

9.32   The *section* does not apply at all to higher-paid employees who are not directors (within the meaning given at **6.9** above) or to a director who does not have a material interest in the company, and is not automatically brought into the higher-paid net simply by virtue of holding the directorship (see **6.7** above). [*ITEPA 2003, s 223(7)*]. It also does not apply to a director if he has died before the tax is paid over to HMRC. [*ITEPA 2003, s 223(6)*]. If he has ceased to be a director before the tax is paid over the payment must be treated as having been made in the year the employment ceased and will thus form part of the director's income for that year. [*ITEPA 2003, s 223(5)*]. However, in some circumstances a payment has to be grossed up and tax accounted for.

Mobile telephones

9.33   There is no benefit charge in relation to a mobile telephone being made available (without any transfer of the property in it) to the employee. [*ITEPA 2003, s 319 FA 2006, s 60(3)*]. A mobile telephone for this purpose is 'wireless telegraphy apparatus designed or adapted for the purpose of transmitting and receiving spoken messages so as to provide a telephone which is connected to a public telecommunication system (within the meaning of the *Telecommunications Act 1984*) and is not physically connected to a land-line'. It does not include a cordless telephone (ie one designed or adapted so as to provide a wireless extension to a telephone and which is used only as such an extension to a telephone that is physically connected to a land-line). The Minister confirmed 'the functions of the new generation of PDAs and Blackberrys made it more appropriate to include them in the exemption under computer equipment' (see **9.88**). They are accordingly not covered by this exemption.

9.34   Prior to 2006/07 the exemption also covered the provision of any number of mobile phones and also phones provided for the use of a member of the employee's family or household. This exemption continues to apply after 5 April 2006 to any such phone that was first provided to the person concerned before 6 April 2006 [*Finance Act 2006 (FA 2006), s 60(5)*].

9.35   The exemption extends to a telephone provided in connection with a car, van or other heavier commercial vehicle.

9.36   The exemption applies not only to the provision of the phone but also to the cost of calls (*Hansard, Standing Committee B, col 369*). However the exemption applies only where the mobile telephone is owned or rented by the employer. If the employee buys his own telephone and charges the cost of calls to the employer a benefit will arise. Care accordingly needs to be taken. If the phone account is in the name of the employee he will be taxable on the full cost of non-business calls.

9.37   Where an employee needs a telephone for business use it is now more attractive to provide him with a mobile phone (completely tax free) than with a fixed one on which he will be taxed on the full rental charge plus the cost of private calls. It should however be stressed that the exemption under *s 319* does not require any business use; it applies even if the phone is used wholly for non-business. Where a second mobile phone is provided primarily for business purposes private use of that phone would be ignored if it is not significant (*Hansard SCA 23.5.2006, Col 301*) so an employee can still be provided with several mobile phones without any benefit charge arising on any of them.

Scholarships

9.38   A scholarship provided for a child of an employee (or any other member of his family or household) must be treated as provided by reason of the employee's employment if it is provided under arrangements entered into by his employer or by any person connected with the employer. [*ITEPA 2003, s 212*]. This applies irrespective of whether or not the employer or a connected person contributes directly or indirectly to the cost of providing the scholarship. [*ITEPA 2003, s 212(2)*]. The *s 839* definition of connected persons applies. [*ITEPA 2003, s 718*].

9.39   No benefit will, however, arise in relation to a payment in respect of a scholarship which:

(*a*)   is provided from a trust fund or under a scheme;

(*b*)   is held by a person receiving full-time instruction at a university, college, school or other educational establishment; and

(*c*)   would not be regarded as provided by reason of the employment if *s 201(3)* and *s 212* (which deem any payment, etc. by the employer to have been made by reason of the employment – see **6.44** above) had not been enacted, provided that in the year it is paid, no more than 25 per cent of the total payments from the fund (or under the scheme) in respect of scholarships held by persons within (*b*) above is attributable to scholarships provided by reason of a person's employment. [*ITEPA 2003, s 213*].

9.40   A scholarship includes an exhibition, bursary or similar educational endowment. An employment includes one where the employee is lower-paid and also an employment not assessable to UK tax which would be so assessable had the employee been resident and ordinarily resident in the UK and all of the duties performed in the UK. [*ITEPA 2003, ss 211(3), 213(7)*]. This definition of employment does not enable HMRC to assess lower-paid employees or non-residents working overseas; it is needed to ensure that children of such employees are taken into account in determining whether the 25 per cent limit for relevant scholarships is breached. The exemption is intended primarily to cover scholarships provided by a company for children of the general public, or the public in a specified area, where the fact that one of the scholarships is won by a child of an employee is fortuitous.

9.41   *ITTOIA 2005, s 776I* (which exempts from income tax income arising from a scholarship held by a person receiving full-time instruction at a university, college, school or other educational establishment) must not be construed so as to confer an exemption from tax under the benefit in kind rules on anyone other than the scholar himself. [*ITEPA 2003, s 215*].

Removal expenses

9.42   A special relief applies to removal expenses, under which up to £8,000 can be paid tax-free to assist an employee with a move. The payment must be paid to the employee or to a third party on his behalf and be in respect of qualifying removal expenses, or must be incurred in the provision of a qualifying removal benefit for the employee or for members of his family or household. [*ITEPA 2003, s 271*]. The expense is ignored for employment income purposes, ie it does not create income and an offsetting deduction. [*ITEPA 2003, s 271(1)*]. Where the reimbursed expenses exceed the £8,000 limit, tax on the excess is collectible by direct assessment not under PAYE provided the reimbursement relates to qualifying removal expenses. [*Regulation 4* of the *PAYE Regulations*]. See HMRC leaflet *IR134* (*Income Tax and Relocation Packages*). The relief does not apply where *ITEPA 2003, section 22* (remittance basis where employee is UK ordinarily resident – see **12.39**) or *26* (foreign earnings where remittance basis applies and employee not UK ordinarily resident – see **2.47**) applies. [*ITEPA 2003, s 271(2)* as amended by *Finance Act 2008 (FA 2008), Sch 7, para 25*].

9.43   Qualifying removal expenses are 'those' reasonably incurred by the employee in connection with a change of residence and incurred on or before the end of the year of assessment following that in which the trigger event takes place. [*ITEPA 2003, ss 272(3), 274(1)*]. Qualifying removal benefits are benefits meeting the same conditions. HMRC have power in relation to individual cases to extend the period by another (or more) year of assessment. [*ITEPA 2003, s 274(2)*].

9.44   The change of residence must result from one of the following trigger events:

(*a*)   taking up employment with a new employer;

(*b*)   an alteration of the duties of an existing employment (which probably includes entering into a new employment with the same employer); or

(*c*)   an alteration of the place where the employee normally performs the duties of his employment.

In each case the time of the trigger event is when the employee begins to perform the new duties at the new place, not when he enters into the contract of employment. [*ITEPA 2003, s 273(2)*].

9.45   The change of residence must be made wholly or mainly to allow the employee to have his residence within a reasonable daily travelling distance of the place where he will normally perform his new duties (or the new place where he will perform his existing duties). [*ITEPA 2003, s 273(3)*]. The employee also needs to show that his previous residence was not already within a reasonable daily travelling distance of that place. [*ITEPA 2003, s 273(4)*].

9.46   To qualify as an eligible removal expense, expenditure must fall within one of the heads set out in **9.55** to **9.66** below. [*ITEPA 2003, s 272(1)*]. The Treasury have power by *regulations* to add items to these categories (but not to delete items). [*ITEPA 2003, s 286*].

Expenses of disposal

9.47   Where the employee (and/or a member of his family or household) has an interest in his current home and that interest is disposed of (or intended to be disposed of) in consequence of the move.

(*a*)   Legal expenses connected with the disposal of the employee's interest (including in relation to the redemption of a mortgage relating to the residence, ie either one for money borrowed to acquire it or one secured on it).

(*b*)   Any early redemption penalty on such a mortgage.

(*c*)   Fees of an estate agent or auctioneer.

(*d*)   Expenses of advertising the intended disposal.

(*e*)   Charges for disconnecting gas, electricity, telephone and other public utilities serving the residence.

(*f*)   Expenses of maintaining, insuring or preserving the security of the residence whilst it is unoccupied pending disposal.

(*g*)   Rent paid in respect of the residence whilst it is unoccupied pending disposal.

[*ITEPA 2003, s 279*].

Expenses of acquisition

9.48   Provided that the employee (and/or members of his family or household) acquires an interest in the new residence.

(*a*)   Legal expenses in connection with the acquisition (including in connection with a loan raised to acquire it).

(*b*)   Procurement fees in relation to a loan to acquire the interest in the new residence.

(*c*)   Mortgage indemnity insurance to protect a lender who lends the whole or a substantial part of the value of the employee's interest in the residence.

(*d*)   Survey or inspection fees in connection with the acquisition.

(*e*)   Land Registry fees (or the Northern Ireland equivalent).

(*f*)   Stamp duty.

(*g*)   Connection fees for gas, electricity, telephone and other public utilities.

[*ITEPA 2003, s 277*].

Expenses of abortive acquisition

9.49   Where expenses are incurred with a view to the acquisition of an interest in a residence which would have been the employee's new residence but where the employee (or other potential acquirer) reasonably declined to proceed with the acquisition or was prevented from doing so through circumstances beyond his control. The expense must have fallen within (*a*)–(*g*) in **9.51** had the acquisition proceeded. [*ITEPA 2003, s 278*].

Expenses of transporting belongings

9.50   Provided they are connected with transporting domestic belongings (of the employee and members of his family or household) from the employee's existing residence to the new one, or are insurance covering such transport. It is not clear whether assets of a hobby or other interest of the taxpayer qualify as domestic, ie whether belongings of the employee are automatically 'domestic', or if the test is first, are the items of a domestic nature and, if so, do they belong to the employee or his family or household.

(*a*)   Packing and unpacking.

(*b*)   Temporary storage if a direct move from the old to a new residence is not made (it is not clear what is temporary, it probably does not cover continuing storage where the new residence is too small to take all of the furniture and this is put in storage because a further transfer is envisaged at a future date).

(c)   Detaching fittings from the old residence – but only if they are to be taken to the new, not if they will be sold or otherwise disposed of.

(d)   Attaching fittings at the new residence, and also adapting them if they are brought from the old residence – but not if they are brought from elsewhere such as a second home.

[*ITEPA 2003, s 280*].

Travelling and subsistence

9.51

(a)   Travelling and subsistence of the employee and members of his family or household while making temporary visits to the new area (ie the area around or near the place where the employee's future duties will normally be performed) for purposes connected with the change of residence.

(b)   The employee's costs of travelling between his former residence and the place where he will normally perform his future duties.

(c)   Except where he is taking up employment with a new employer, the employee's costs of travelling between his new residence and his original place of work – if he will be employed in the new location by a different group company, consideration ought to be given to his being seconded by the original employer for an initial period.

(d)   Costs of the employee's subsistence (ie food, drink and temporary living accommodation).

(e)   The employee's costs of travelling between his former residence and any temporary living accommodation.

(f)   Except where he is taking up employment with a new employer, the employee's costs of travelling, prior to his change of residence, between his new residence and any temporary living accommodation.

(g)   Costs of travel of the employee and members of his family or household from his former residence to the new one provided that they are made in connection with the change.

(h)   The cost of subsistence of a child under 19 who is a member of the employee's family or household while staying in living accommodation around or near the former residence for the purpose of securing continuity of his education.

(i)   Such a child's cost of travelling between that accommodation and the employee's new residence.

(j)   The costs of subsistence for such a child while staying in living accommodation around or near the employee's new place of work before the change of residence in order to secure continuity of education. (Subsistence means food, drink and temporary living accommodation; boarding school fees at a school near the new residence for one or two terms may well be 'temporary' if the child will thereafter become a day pupil, but is probably not if the child will continue to board there.)

(*k*) The costs of travel by such a child between such temporary accommodation in the new locality and the employee's former residence.

[*ITEPA 2003, s 281*].

9.52 **Bridging loan expenses** ie interest payable by the employee (and/or members of his family or household) in respect of a loan raised by him wholly or partly because there was a gap between the time of acquisition of the new residence and the disposal of the old. The employee (and/or members of his family or household) must have had an interest in the old residence, dispose of it in consequence of the change of residence, and acquire an interest in the new one. If the new loan exceeds the market value of the interest in the old residence, interest on the excess does not qualify. Nor does interest on any part of the loan used for some purpose other than redeeming a loan on the old residence (ie one used to acquire it or for which the residence formed security) or acquiring the new one. [*ITEPA 2003, s 284*].

9.53 **Replacement of domestic goods** ie expenditure on the purchase of domestic goods intended to replace items used at the former residence but which are not suitable for use in the new. The employee (and/or members of his family or household) must have had an interest in the old residence, dispose of it in consequence of the move, acquire an interest in the new residence, and incur the expense as a result of the move. Any sale proceeds of the replaced goods must be deducted from the expenditure – although there is no requirement to deduct their market value if they are disposed of otherwise than by sale. [*ITEPA 2003, s 285*].

Benefits and expenses do not however fall into this head if they are deductible under *ss 341* (travel at start or finish of overseas employment), *342* (travel between employments), *370–372* (travel costs where duties performed abroad), or *373–375* (travel costs of non-domiciled employees). In other words if an expense can qualify as a deduction under some other provision it does not need to be included in the £8,000 limit. [*ITEPA 2003, s 282*]. Making a car or van available to the employee or members of his family or household for private use by reason of his employment is also excluded from this head (as it attracts a tax charge under other provisions). [*ITEPA 2003, s 283*].

9.54 Broadly speaking, the items that can constitute eligible removal benefits are the same as those in paragraphs **9.55** (disposal costs), **9.57** (acquisition costs), **9.58** (abortive acquisition costs), **9.58** (transport of belongings), **9.59** (travelling and subsistence) and **9.61** (duplicate expenses). However, if a car or van would otherwise constitute an eligible facility for travel it cannot do so if it is also available for other private use, ie it attracts the normal scale car and van use benefits. Also, if travel expenses already qualify for the special reliefs for overseas travel (see **13.23** and **13.32**) those reliefs take precedence and the expense is not to be treated as a removal expense.

9.55 Bridging loan expenses do not have an exact parallel in eligible removal benefits. However, there is a separate relief where a loan is raised by the employee (and/or members of his family or household) in connection with a move that satisfies the conditions in paragraph **9.60** above and *s 175* (beneficial loans, see **9.1**) would otherwise apply to the loan. [*ITEPA 2003, s 288*]. For this purpose a loan qualifies if the employee (and/or members of his family or household) had an interest in a former residence, disposed of it in consequence of the move, acquired an interest in the new residence, and raised the loan wholly or partly because of a gap between the acquisition of the new residence and the disposal of the old. [*ITEPA 2003, s 288(2)*]. Relief under *s 288* can be given only to the extent that qualifying removal expenses and qualifying removal benefits together fall short of the £8,000 maximum. [*ITEPA 2003, s 288(1), (3)*]. Where *s 288* applies the beneficial loan rules of *s 175* do not apply to that unrelieved amount for the 'exempted loan discharge period'. The number of days in this period is that produced by the formula:

where:

the unrelieved amount is the unrelieved balance of the £8,000;

the maximum amount of the loan is the maximum in the period from making the loan to, normally, the end of the year of assessment following that in which the change of employment occurs; and

the official rate is that in force at the time the loan is actually made.

If the formula produces a fraction it is rounded up. [*ITEPA 2003, ss 288(1), (4), 289*].

Overall limit

9.56 There is an overriding limit of relief on £8,000 for any change of residence. If husband and wife are both employees they can each attract £8,000 of relief on the same move. The Treasury have power to vary this figure but have never done so since it was introduced in April 1993. The benefit in kind rules apply for calculating the value of a qualifying removal benefit. [*ITEPA 2003, ss 287, 716(2)(d)*].

Interpretation

9.57 References in **9.50** to **9.64** above to a person's residence means his sole or main residence. [*ITEPA 2003, s 276*]. A member of a person's family or household means that person's spouse; son and his spouse; daughter and her spouse; parent; domestic staff; dependant or guest. [*ITEPA 2003, s 721(5)*]. It should be particularly noted that this does not include a 'common law wife' or other 'partner' who is not a spouse, unless such a person can qualify as a dependant or guest – which would probably not be the case if he contributes his share of the running costs of the residence. Nor does it appear to include a mother-in-law or father-in-law unless that person qualifies as a dependant or guest. Subsistence means food, drink and temporary living accommodation. [*ITEPA 2003, s 281(6)*].

Arrangements with relocation companies

9.58   If an employer operates an arrangement under which employees are able to sell their homes to either their employer or a relocation company for its current market value plus a share in any profit made by the relocation company when it resells the house, the profit share is, by concession, treated as covered by the capital gains tax private residence exemption even though it is a separate asset from the house. The house must be sold by the relocation company within three years of the employee's sale to that company. If the employee owns the property jointly with someone else, eg his spouse, the concession also applies to the profit share received by that other person (*ESC D37*). The sale to the relocation company must be made under arm's-length arrangements set up by the employer and the employee must have to sell his house because he has to move home, for example, on a transfer within the employer's organisation. Where the employee owns the home jointly with others, eg with his spouse, the concession also applies to the other joint holders. In addition, the costs borne by the employer or the relocation company will not be assessed as a benefit on the employee [*ITEPA 2003, s 326*]. This does not apply to any costs of the employee's transfer which would normally be borne by the vendor though.

Provision of meals

9.59   The provision by the employer (but not in theory at least, by a third party such as the employer's holding company) of free or subsidised meals (or light refreshments) in a canteen or on the employer's business premises does not attract a tax charge on the employee provided that:

(*a*)   they are provided on a reasonable scale;

(*b*)   all employees, or all of them at a particular location, can obtain either (or both) a free or subsidised meal or an equivalent meal voucher or token; and

(*c*)   if the meals are provided in the restaurant or dining room of a hotel, catering or similar business at a time when meals are being served to the public, the meals are taken in a part of the restaurant which is designated for the use of employees only.

[*ITEPA 2003, s 317* as amended by *FA 2004, Sch 17, para 1*].

9.60   A canteen does not have to be on the employer's premises. HMRC are sometimes prepared to treat the provision by the employer of meals at a local restaurant as within this exemption if the employer does not have his own canteen and has entered into an arrangement with the restaurateur to provide meals for his staff. They are unlikely to allow directors – and possibly higher-paid employees – to benefit from this concession, however. HMRC say that the word 'canteen' has its ordinary meaning.

9.61   Where a company has both a staff canteen and a directors' or executive dining room HMRC will normally regard the dining room as part of the canteen provided that the lunches are on a reasonable scale. If the two do not share the same kitchen they might resist this treatment.

Luncheon vouchers

9.62   HMRC do not tax luncheon vouchers if their value does not exceed 15p per working day. When the concession was introduced an employee could buy a reasonable meal for 15p. Today he would be lucky to get a cup of tea! The vouchers must be non-transferable, used only for meals, and available to lower-paid staff if they are not given to all staff. [*ITEPA 2003, s 89*]. This exemption will not apply after 5 April 2013 [*Finance Act 2012 (FA 2012), Sch 38, para 50*].

Training

Work-related training

9.63   No tax liability arises by virtue of the provision for an employee of work-related training or any benefit incidental thereto. [*ITEPA 2003, s 250(1)(a)*]. The exemption applies both where the cost is paid direct by the employer and where it is reimbursed by the employer to the employee. [*ITEPA 2003, s 250(1)*]. Work-related training is any training course or other activity designed to impart, instil, improve or reinforce any knowledge, skills or personal qualities which:

(*a*)   are likely to prove useful to the employee when performing the duties of the employment (or a related employment); or

(*b*)   will qualify, or better qualify, the employee to perform those duties (or to participate in any charitable or voluntary activities that are available to be performed in association with the employment).

[*ITEPA 2003, s 251(1)*].

9.64   A related employment for this purpose is another employment with either the same employer or with a person connected with the employer and which the employee is to hold, has a serious opportunity of holding or can reasonably expect to have such an opportunity to hold so in due course. [*ITEPA 2003, s 251(2)*].

9.65   The exemption also covers the payment of costs which are incidental to the employee undertaking the training, expenses incurred in connection with examinations (or other assessment of what the employee has gained from the training), and the cost of obtaining any qualification, registration or award to which the employee becomes (or may become) entitled as a result of the training or examination. [*ITEPA 2003, s 250(2)*]. It covers travelling and subsistence (which includes food, drink and temporary living accommodation) only to the extent that such expenses would either have qualified for relief under *ss 336* or *337* (see **5.2**) or attracted mileage allowance relief (see **7.51**) if the employee had undertaken the training as one of the duties of his employment and the employee had incurred and paid the expense. [*ITEPA 2003, s 253*].

9.66   It does not however extend to facilities or other benefits that are provided to the employee:

(*a*)   to enable him to enjoy the facilities or benefits for entertainment or recreational purposes which are unconnected with imparting skills or personal qualities within *s 251*;

(*b*)   to provide him with an inducement to remain in his employment (or to accept a new employment with the same or a related employer) where that inducement is unconnected with imparting such skills or personal qualities; or

(*c*)   to reward the employee for performing duties of his employment or performing them in a particular way.

[*ITEPA 2003, s 253*].

9.67   Nor does it extend to the cost of providing an employee with an asset (or the use of an asset) unless:

(*a*)   it is provided or made available for use only in the course of the training;

(*b*)   it is provided or made available both for such use and for use in the performance of the employee's duties but not for any other use;

(*c*)   it consists of training materials provided in the course of the training; or

(*d*)   it consists of, or is incorporated into, something made by the employee in the course of the training.

[*ITEPA 2003, s 254*].

This is very restrictive. If there is any possibility of the asset being used by the employee for leisure or at home, heads (*a*) and (*b*) cannot apply so a benefit will arise. Training materials means stationery, books or other written material, audio or video tapes, compact discs or floppy disks. [*ICTA 1988, s 200C(7)*]. It will not include, say, a bricklayer's trowel or similar small items. Nor would it include a personal stereo on which to play the training tapes.

9.68   In practice HMRC also do not normally assess the employee on the cost of courses or examinations which are directly related to his work provided that the cost is borne by the employer and he requires the employee to attend the course. In *Clayton v Gothorp 47 TC 168*, where an employer made a loan to an employee to enable her to take a nine-month training course (to enable her to gain promotion in her job) on terms that it would be waived if the employee served the employer for at least 18 months after the course, the amount waived was held to be taxable as remuneration.

Retraining courses

9.69   If an employer incurs expenditure in paying for (or reimbursing) expenses incurred in connection with a qualifying training course undertaken by an employee or ex-employee with a view to retraining the employee, the cost is not assessable on that employee. To qualify, a course must:

(*a*)   be designed to impart or improve skills or knowledge relevant to (and intended to be used in the course of) gainful employment or self-employment of any description;

(*b*)   be entirely devoted to the teaching or practical application of these skills and knowledge;

(*c*)   not exceed two years' duration (one year prior to 2005/06); and

(*d*)   take place wholly within the UK.

[*ITEPA 2003, s 311(1), (3)*].

9.70   The employee must have been employed by the employer for at least two years prior to starting the course (or prior to his ceasing the employment if earlier); the opportunity to take the course must have been available on similar terms to all employees or ex-employees (or all in the same category as the employee concerned); when the employee starts the course his employment must not have ceased more than 12 months earlier, and his employment must cease not later than two years after completing the course (and he must not be re-employed by the same employer within two years). [*ITEPA 2003, s 311(4)*].

Sporting and recreational facilities

9.71   There is an exemption from income tax in respect of any benefit consisting of a right or opportunity to make use of sporting or other recreational facilities provided by the employer for the use of employees generally. [*ITEPA 2003, s 261(1)–(3)*]. The exemption extends to vouchers which are exchangeable for such a benefit, and covers the provision of the benefit not only to employees but also to other members of their family or household, ie their spouse; children and their spouses; parents; servants; dependants and guests. [*ITEPA 2003, s 261(1)*].

9.72   A benefit will still arise to the employee if such benefits are provided to his grandchildren, or to his common law spouse or 'partner' unless that person qualifies as a dependant. In practice such benefits were frequently not assessed in earlier years either.

9.73   The relief does not cover:

(*a*)   A benefit consisting of the provision of, or of the use of, any mechanically propelled vehicle. As vehicle includes a ship, boat, aircraft or hovercraft this would normally include a yacht – even a sailing yacht normally uses its engine to get in and out of harbour. It would also seem to cover the use of a golf buggy at the company golf course.

(b) The provision of, or use of, holiday or overnight accommodation, or of accommodation provided in association with a right to make use of such accommodation. This would not impose a benefit in relation to the use of the hotel pool table when attending a training course as HMRC would regard the use as incidental to the course, not the course as incidental to the pool table, and would not seek to impose a benefit charge under normal rules provided, of course, that they accept that the course is wholly, exclusively and necessarily for the purpose of the employment.

(c) A facility provided on domestic premises – which includes land belonging to, or enjoyed with, a private dwelling. This seems to discriminate against small companies. If a major company can provide a company billiard room and company swimming pool on its premises without giving rise to a benefit on its employees, it is not clear why a benefit should arise if the managing director of a small firm allows his employees to use his personal swimming pool, tennis court or billiard room at his home.

(d) A facility provided so as to be available to, or for use by, members of the public generally. This will prevent the exemption applying to subscriptions to commercial sports or health clubs. However, it seems to go much further than that. If a company erects a sports complex which it makes available without charge to the local community it is unclear why there should be a benefit on its own employees who use it, whereas if it is not public spirited and limits use to its employees they will cease to be taxable. In practice, it may be that the marginal cost of the employees' usage is nil as the cost is incurred in providing the facility to the public – although the company would argue otherwise, as to obtain tax relief for the cost it may well need to show that use by the public is incidental to the provision for employees.

(e) A facility which is not used, either wholly or mainly, by people whose right or opportunity to use it derives from employment (whether with the same or with different employers). It derives from employment only if the facility is provided so as to be available generally to employees of a specific employer and the person using it is an employee or ex-employee of his or a member of the employee's family or household. The distinction between (d) and (e) seems to be that (d) excludes facilities provided for the benefit of the general public whereas (e) looks at facilities provided for employees but which in practice are also used by other people. It is not clear how the employer is supposed to monitor the facility's usage; how much public use is necessary to prevent the facility being mainly used by employees, although mainly is normally interpreted as meaning over 50 per cent; or whether mainly refers to the number of people who use the facility or the amount of time it is in use by employees and others respectively. A local amateur Olympic swimming hopeful who is allowed to use the company swimming pool for training is likely to use it far more intensively than any of the employees. Allowing the company sports ground to be used for the local village fête could well bring in a far greater number of non-employees than the company's total workforce.

[*ITEPA 2003, ss 261(4)–(6), 262*].

9.74 The Treasury have power both to limit these exclusions and further to restrict the scope of the exemption. [*ITEPA 2003, s 263*]. Sports facilities probably include sports kit and equipment, eg where the firm's football team plays on public pitches, as well as the provision of the pitch itself.

Redundancy, etc counselling

9.75 Expenditure on the provision of qualifying counselling services to an employee is exempt from tax. [*ITEPA 2003, s 310*]. To qualify:

(*a*) the main purpose of the counselling must be to enable the employee to adjust to the termination of his office or employment, or to help him to find other gainful employment or self-employment, or both;

(*b*) the counselling services must be either:

(i) giving advice or guidance;

(ii) imparting or improving skills; or

(iii) making available the use of office equipment or similar facilities;

(*c*) the employee must have been employed by the employer for at least two years (ending with the earlier of the termination of the employment or the commencement of the counselling);

(*d*) the opportunity to receive counselling on similar terms must be available generally either to all employees or to a particular class of employee – although HMRC accept that one person can form a class if his job is unique within the company.

[*ITEPA 2003, s 310(2)–(5)*].

9.76 The exemption extends not only to expenditure on the counselling services themselves (including the reimbursement of counselling fees incurred direct by the employee) but also to the payment or reimbursement of travelling expenses incurred in connection with the services – although only if such travel costs would have been deductible under *ss 336* or *337* (see **5.2**) if the receipt of the counselling services had formed part of the duties of the employment and the employment had continued (or from 2002/03 mileage allowance relief (see **7.51**) would have been available). [*ITEPA 2003, s 310(6)–(8)*]. The exemption covers counselling provided by a third party, eg the employer's holding company, as well as that provided by the employer itself. [*ITEPA 2003, s 310(1)*].

9.76A From 1 September 2013, when the employee shareholder scheme (see **14.201** onwards) came into effect, there is an exemption for the provision of advice which is provided for the purpose of advising the employee on the terms and effects of a proposed employee shareholder agreement. The exemption applies to tax advice only to the extent that it consists of an explanation of the tax effect of employee shareholder agreements generally [*ITEPA 2003, s 326B* inserted by *Finance Act 2013 (FA 2013, Sch 23, para 37*]. The advice must be provided by a relevant independent adviser (see **14.206**).

Computer equipment

9.77   Up to 2006/07 there was a limited exemption where the benefit consisted of the provision of computer equipment which was made available (without any transfer of the property in it) to a higher paid employee or a member of his family or household. [*ITEPA 2003, s 320*]. The exemption continues to apply to any computer equipment provided before that date. Computer equipment for this purpose included printers, scanners, modems, discs, and other peripheral devices designed to be used by being connected to or inserted in a computer. [*ITEPA 2003, s 320(7)*]. The exemption did not extend to the cost of access to, or the use of, public telecommunications systems. [*ITEPA 2003, s 320(7)(c)(ii)*]. Accordingly if the computer was used for Iinternet access the charges of the Internet Service Provider (ISP) were covered but the cost of the telephone company which links the computer to the ISP were not. The logic of this distinction is not readily apparent.

9.78   The computer equipment had to be made available under arrangements that did not favour directors of the company. [*ITEPA 2003, s 320(3)*]. If directors were included in the arrangements the computer equipment could not be made available to directors (or their families or household) on terms which favoured directors. Arrangements were taken to favour directors if, and only if, either under the arrangements the employee was required to be a director or, taking all such arrangements together, the terms on which the equipment was made available were more favourable in some cases where the employee was a director than in one or more cases where he was not. [*ITEPA 2003, s 320(6)*]. Under the original wording the effect seemed to be that the exemption could never apply if the only employees were directors or if, although there were other employees, only directors were provided with computer equipment. The *ITEPA 2003* wording seems to permit relief when the only employees are directors as the person is not 'required' to be a director. Curiously, if both employees and directors were provided with such equipment and a director was offered better terms (such as more expensive equipment) than any one of the other employees covered by the arrangements, it was not only the director who lost the exemption but all of the employees as well.

9.79   The exemption applied only to the first £500 of cash equivalent of the benefit made available in aggregate to an employee and members of his family or household. [*ITEPA 2003, s 320(5)*]. There was no requirement that the computer had to be used even partly for business. The idea was to encourage computer literacy generally. Where computer equipment or software was used solely for business it could be excluded in calculating the £500 figure.

9.80   The exemption also applied where the use of a computer would be taxed under the general employment income charging provision rather than as a benefit, such as where the employee has the choice of the use of a computer or extra salary. [*ITEPA 2003, s 320(1)*]. Curiously it appears that in such a case the £500 limit did not apply, although this appears to be unintentional.

9.81   This exemption was repealed by *FA 2006, s 61* except in relation to equipment first made available to the person concerned before 6 April 2006

[*FA 2006, s 62(3)*]. The Minister has given an assurance that the repeal 'does not change the position where an employer provides the use of computer equipment solely for work purposes and private use by the employee is not significant' (Hansard 2.5.2006 Col 876). This is presumably because of the exemption in *ITEPA 2003, s 316(2), (3)* (see **6.44(t)**).

Works transport services

9.82 No benefit charge arises in relation to an employee's use of a works transport service. [*ITEPA 2003, s 242*]. This is a service for conveying employees of one or more employers on qualifying journeys which is provided by means of a bus (a road passenger vehicle with a seating capacity of twelve or more) or a minibus (a vehicle constructed or adapted for the carriage of passengers which has a seating capacity of nine, ten or eleven – but ignoring any seats which do not meet the construction and use requirement of the *Road Traffic Act 1988*). [*ITEPA 2003, s 242*]. A qualifying journey is one between the employee's home and workplace, or between one workplace (any place at which the employee's presence is necessary in the performance of the duties of the employment) and another, which is made in connection with the performance of the employment. [*ITEPA 2003, s 249*]. The idea is to encourage employers to provide works buses for commuting to dissuade employees from driving. The government envisage that small employers could club together to hire a bus but this seems unlikely in practice. The government have said that a qualifying journey will include one that covers only part of the distance between the employee's home and his workplace (*Hansard, Standing Committee B, col 411*).

9.83 The transport service must be available generally to employees of the employer (or employers) concerned and the main use of the service must be for qualifying journeys by those employees. [*ITEPA 2003, s 242(1)(b), (c)*]. The exemption is subject to compliance with the conditions that the service must be used only by the employees for whom it is provided or their infant children (including step-children and illegitimate children but only those aged under 18). [*ITEPA 2003, s 242(1)(c)*].

Support for public bus services

9.84 If an employer gives financial or other support to a public transport road service (a public passenger transport service provided by means of a road vehicle) no benefit in kind charge arises for 1999/00 onwards on employees of that employer who happen to use the transport service. [*ITEPA 2003, s 243*]. Most people outside HMRC would be surprised at the suggestion that a benefit might arise on an employee simply because his employer chooses to subsidise or otherwise support a public bus service. A road vehicle is not defined. It could include a rural post office bus or even, presumably, a cycle rickshaw!

9.85 With the exception of local bus services, the transport service must not be available on favourable terms to employees of the employer concerned, ie they must pay the same fares as members of the general public, and the service must be available generally to employees of the employer concerned (it is hard to see how this condition could not be met if it is a public bus service). [*ITEPA 2003, s 243(4)*]. If the transport service is a local bus service as defined in *s 2* of the *Transport Act 1985 (TA 1985)*, ie a local stopping bus service, employees of the employer can receive free or reduced price travel provided of course that the service is available to employees generally.

Cycles

9.86   There are some specific exemptions to encourage cycling to work. No benefit arises in relation to facilities for parking a cycle provided that the parking space is at or near the employee's place of work. [*ITEPA 2003, s 237*]. In addition, no benefit charge arises in respect of the provision of:

(*a*)   a cycle (within *s 192(1), Road Traffic Act 1988 (RTA 1988)*, ie a bicycle, a tricycle or a cycle having four or more wheels, not being in any case a motor vehicle); or

(*b*)   cyclists' safety equipment,

provided that there is no transfer of the property in the cycle or equipment, ie provided that ownership remains with the employer (or the employer has contracted to hire the bicycle). [*ITEPA 2003, s 244*].

9.87   From 2005/06 this exemption also precludes any charge under the general employment income charging rules [*ITEPA 2003, 244(1)* inserted by *Finance Act 2005 (FA 2005), s 16(3)*]. The benefit or facility in question must be available generally to all employees of the employer concerned and the employee must use the bike mainly for qualifying journeys (ie from home to work and between one workplace and another). [*ITEPA 2003, ss 244(4), 249*]. It is not clear how the employer is to check that the bike is used mainly for business as he is obliged to do when he completes the employee's P11D. The answer apparently is that the government expects him to ignore the responsibility that it has placed on him to do so. As the Minister put it 'there is no intention to withdraw the relief if the employee also uses the bike for private or leisure use. Provided that the bike is mainly used for the commuting journey, the tax exemption will remain. By concession, employers will not be expected to check up on their employees' other cycling journeys (*Hansard 6 July 1999, Col 873*).

9.88   An employee is entitled to a tax-free mileage allowance payment of 20p a mile for business cycling. [*ITEPA 2003, s 230*].

9.89   There is also an exemption from the benefit in kind charge for cyclists' breakfasts. This is dealt with at **6.44**(v).

Childcare

9.90   There is an exemption from tax under the benefit in kind rules where childcare is provided by an employer. [*ITEPA 2003, s 318*]. There is a further exemption for up to £55 a week in respect of payments by the employer in respect of childcare provided by others or of childcare vouchers. [*ICTA 1988, s 318A*]. Both of these exemptions also preclude any charge under the general employment income charging rules [*ITEPA 2003, ss 270A(1), 318A(1)*].

9.91   Where the individual joins a childcare scheme after 5 April 2011 and is a higher rate taxpayer, the £55 maximum is reduced to £28 per week for higher rate taxpayers and £22 for additional rate payers so that the effective amount of the relief is the same as for basic rate taxpayers (20% of £55 = £11 as does 40% of £28 and 50% of £22 – the figure has not been amended to reflect the reduced 45% rate) [*ITEPA 2003, s 318A(6A)*]. The employer is required to make an estimate of the employee's tax liability when he joins the scheme and base the maximum on the estimate [*ITEPA 2003, s 318A(5C)* and *318AA*]. He must then make a new estimate at the beginning of each tax year [*ITEPA 2003, s 318AA(5)*]. If the estimate proves wrong, no adjustment needs to be made though.

9.92   In both cases the child must be a child or stepchild of the employee. In the case of childcare provision the child must be either resident with the employee or a person in respect of which the employee has parental responsibility. In the case of vouchers and payments the child must both be resident with the employee and the employee must have parental responsibility. [*ITEPA 2003, s 318(3), 318A(3)*].

9.93   A person remains a child for the purpose of these provisions until the last day of the week which contains 1 September following the child's 15th birthday – or 16th if the child is disabled. A child is regarded as disabled if either:

(*a*)   a disability living allowance or, for 2013/14 onwards, a personal independence payment, is payable in respect of him (or has ceased to be payable solely because he is receiving free in-patient treatment within the meaning of the *Social Security (Hospital In-Patients) Regulations 1975* and is not serving a sentence imposed by a court in a prison or youth custody institution);

(*b*)   he is registered as blind by a local authority under *National Assistance Act 1948* (welfare services) *s 29* or the corresponding Scottish or Northern Irish provisions;

(*c*)   he was formerly registered blind but has ceased to be so registered within the previous 26 weeks.

[*ITEPA 2003, s 318B(2)–(4) as amended by FA 2013, s 12*].

9.94   Parental responsibility means all of the rights duties, powers, responsibilities and authority which by law a parent of a child has in relation to the child and the child's property. [*ITEPA 2003, s 318(5)*]. It is clear from the context however that 'all' is not to be read literally, ie that relief will be due even if the parental authority is shared with the other parent [*ITEPA 2003, s 318B(5)*]. In both cases childcare means any form of care or supervised activity that is not provided in the course of the child's compulsory education [*ITEPA 2003, s 318B(1)*].

9.95   The relief for employer provided childcare is unlimited. However, it applies only if:

(*a*)   the premises on which the care is provided are not used wholly or mainly as a private dwelling;

(*b*)   any applicable registration requirement under *Part 3* of the *Childcare Act 2006* or in Wales (and previously in England also) the *Children Act 1989, Part 10A* (or the Scottish or Northern Irish equivalents) is met;

(*c*)   the premises on which the care is provided is either made available by the scheme employee or in the case of 'partnership arrangements' by one or more of the partners;

(*d*)   the childcare scheme is open to the scheme employer's employees generally (or generally to those of its employees at a particular location); and

(*e*)   the employee to whom the childcare is provided is either an employee of the scheme employer or is an employee working at the same location as those employees of the scheme employer to whom the scheme is open.

[*ITEPA 2003, s 318(3)–(8)*].

9.96   If the qualifying conditions are met in relation to part only of the costs the exemption applies to that part. [*ITEPA 2003, s 318(2)*]. Partnership arrangements exist where childcare is provided under arrangements made by two or more persons (including the scheme employer), the premises on which the care is provided are made available by one or more of those persons, and under the arrangements the scheme employer is wholly or partly responsible for financing and managing the provision of the care. [*ITEPA 2003, s 318(7)*].

9.97   The exemption is aimed at crèches and workplace nurseries – although the nursery does not have to be on the employer's premises. Partnership arrangements allow a group of neighbouring employees either to jointly set up a creche or for other employers to contribute to the cost of one employer's crèche in return for it looking after children of the contributors' employees. However, as all of the users of the crèche must be employees of someone, it probably does not permit an employer to enter into an arrangement with a nearby commercial crèche. Head **9.101(e)** will cover not only partnership arrangements but also cases where an employer allows his crèche to be used by neighbouring employers without requiring a contribution from them. The requirement that all the employees must work at the same location is an odd one. It seems to severely limit the scope for partnership arrangements. For example, two businesses adjacent to one another are clearly in the same location but it seems doubtful if two businesses half a mile from each other can meet this test.

9.98   One snag with a workplace crèche is that parents who commute do not necessarily wish to subject their young children to the delights of rush hour travel. They would prefer to use a childcare facility near where they live. The £55 a week relief helps in such cases – although £55 will not purchase much care

9.99   The conditions that must be met (in addition to that at **9.99**) are:

(*a*)   that the care is qualifying childcare; and

(*b*)   that it is provided under a scheme that is open either to the employer's employees generally or generally to those at a particular location.

[*ITEPA 2003, s 318A(4), (5)*]. It should also be noted that the childcare must be 'provided' by the employer [*ITEPA 2003, s 318A(1)*]. In other words, the contract with the nursery must be entered into by the employer. The relief does not apply if the employer merely reimburses the employee for payments by the employee or even makes a direct payment to the nursery if the contract is between the nursery and the employee. An employer contemplating using this relief ought to take legal advice on his liability, if any, if an employee's child is injured at the nursery. An employer who does not wish to undertake such a responsibility should use childcare vouchers (see **9.111**) as these can be used to settle a liability entered into by the employee.

9.100   Where the childcare (or vouchers where *ITEPA 2003, s 270A* applies) is provided in connection with relevant salary sacrifice arrangements (arrangements under which the employee gives up the right to an amount of employment income in return for the provision of the care or vouchers) or relevant flexible remuneration arrangements (arrangements under which the employee agrees with the employer to receive the care or vouchers rather than some other description of employment income) condition (*b*) is not prevented from being met merely because the scheme is not open to lower paid employees who are prevented from participation because such participation would be likely to reduce their earnings below the national minimum wages [*ITEPA 2003, ss 318A(5A), (5B), 270A(5A), (5B)* inserted by *Finance Act 2011 (FA 2011, s 36)*]. It will be seen that this provision was introduced with retroactive effect.

9.101   Qualifying childcare means registered or approved care, ie it must be provided either by:

(*a*)   a person registered under *Part 3* of the *Childcare Act 2006 or* the *Children Act 1989, Part 10A* (in England up to 18 July 2009 only but still applicable in Wales) *or*;

(*b*)   by or under the direction of the proprietor of a school on the school premises ;

(*c*)   prior to 18 July 2009 only, a childcare provider approved in accordance with the *Tax Credits (Approval of Child Care Providers) Scheme 2005* (prior to 5 April 2005, the 2003 Scheme);

(*d*)   a domiciliary care worker under the *Domiciliary Care Agencies (Workers) Regulations 2004*; or

[*ITEPA 2003, s 318C(1), (2), (3)* as amended by the a succession of regulations, the last being the *Income Tax (Qualifying Child Care) Regulations 2009 (SI 2009 No 1544)*]. For the purpose of head (*c*) the proprietor of a school is the Board of Governors or if there is no such body the person or persons responsible for the management of the school. A school qualifies only if it is one that HM Chief Inspector of Education, Children's Services and Skills is responsible for inspecting, and school premises means any premises that can be covered by such an inspection [*ITEPA 2003, s 318C(2A)* inserted by the *Income Tax (Qualifying Child Care) Regulations 2008 (SI 2008 No 2170)*]. In England care is not registered or approved care under head (*c*) if it is provided during school hours for a child who has reached compulsory school age or if it is provided in breach of a requirement to register under *Part 3* of the *Childcare Act 2006* [*ITEPA 2003, s 318C(2B)*]. Heads (*e*) and (*g*) continue to apply in Wales after 18 July 2009 (*The Income Tax (Qualifying Child Care) Regulations 2009 (SI 2009 No 1544)*). In Wales the equivalent approvals for heads (*e*) and (*f*) are under the *Domiciliary Care Agencies (Wales) Regulations 2004* and the *Tax Credits (Approval of Child Care Providers) (Wales) Scheme 2007*. The definition is different in Scotland and Northern Ireland, which have different child care-laws. The rules there can be found in *ITEPA 2003, s 318C(4), (5)*. Care provided for a child outside the UK qualifies only if it is provided by a childcare provider approved by an organisation accredited under the *Tax Credit (New Category of Child Care Provider) Regulations 2002* [*ITEPA 2003, s 318C(6)*].

9.102   However, the exemption does not apply to child care which is either:

(*a*)   provided by the partner (ie one of a married or unmarried couple) of the employee; or

(*b*)   provided by a relative of the child (parent, grandparent, aunt, uncle, brother or sister, whether by blood, half blood or marriage) if the care is provided wholly or mainly in the child's home or the home of the person having parental responsibility for the child;

(*c*)   although provided by a childcare provider within (*e*) above, is provided in the home of a relative of the child (parent, grandparent, aunt, uncle, brother or sister, whether by blood, half blood or marriage or a foster parent or step-parent) and the provider usually provides care there solely in respect of one or more children of which she is a relative even if that person is a registered or approved carer. [*ITEPA 2003, s 318C(7), (8)* as amended by the *Section 318C Regulations*].

9.103   The exempt amount was £55 for each qualifying week up to 5 April 2011. After that date the amximum exemption is limited to £38 a week for higher rate taxpayers and £22 a week for additional rate taxpayers The detailed rules are set out at **9.97**. A qualifying week is a tax week in which qualifying care is provided for a child. An employee is only entitled to one exempt payment, ie £55 per week, even if care is provided for more than one child. However, if both husband and wife is employed each can receive £55 even if there is only one child. [*ITEPA 2003, s 318C(6)–(8)* as amended by the *Income Tax (Exempt Amounts for Childcare Vouchers and for Employer Contracted Childcare)*

Order 2006 (SI 2006 No 882)]. If the payment in a week exceeds £55, the first £55 is exempt and the balance is taxable as a benefit. *[ITEPA 2003, s 318A(1)]*. If there are several payments some of which meet the qualifying conditions and some of which do not the exemption will be given for the qualifying payments (up to the £55 limit). *[ITEPA 2003, s 318A(2)]*.

9.104   The Treasury have power to vary the £55 figure by statutory instrument. They can similarly amend the qualifying conditions under both *sections 318* and *318A* as appears to them to be appropriate having regard to the corresponding regulations relating to the child care element of working tax credit.

9.105   As mentioned earlier there is also an exemption of up to £55 a week for childcare vouchers. *[ITEPA 2003, s 270A* as amended by the *Income Tax (Exempt Amount for Childcare and for Employer Contracted Childcare) Order 2006 (SI 2006 No 882)]*. So is the limitation on the relief described at **9.97A** where the employee is taxable at the higher or additional rate. *[ITEPA 2003, s 270A, 270B* inserted by *FA 2011, Sch 8, paras 2, 3]*. The qualifying conditions are identical to those under *section 318A*. A childcare voucher is a non-cash voucher, stamp or similar document or token intended to enable a person to obtain the provision of care for a child (whether or not in exchange for it). *[ITEPA 2003, s 84(2A)]*. The exemption also extends to the voucher administration cost, namely the difference between the cost of the voucher and its face value (the value of the childcare that can be obtained with it) *[ITEPA 2003, s 270A]*. This exemption also precludes any charge under the general employment income charging rules *[ITEPA 2003, s 270A(1)]*.

9.106   An employee is obviously not entitled both to exempt child care provision under *section 318A* and exempt vouchers under *section 270A* in the same week.

Eye tests and glasses, etc

9.107   There is an exemption (both from the benefit charge and from tax under the basic employment income charging rules) for the provision by an employee of an eye or eyesight test and for glasses, contact lenses or other corrective appliances that such a test shows are necessary *[ITEPA 2003, s 320A(1),]*. The provision of the test or appliance must be required by regulations made under the *Health and Safety at Work, etc Act 1974*. For example, *Reg 5* of the *Health and Safety (Display Screen Equipment) Regulations 1992 (SI 1992 No 2792)* enables an employee who habitually uses display screen equipment to request his employee to provide him with an eyesight test and any corrective equipment required as a result of that test. The employer must comply with such a request and must also make available further tests to such an employee at regular intervals. The relief applies only if tests and appliances are made available generally to those employees for whom they are required to be provided by the regulations. That is a somewhat odd provision as it is a statutory requirement to do so.

9.108   The Explanatory Notes to the Finance Bill 2006 said that HMRC would not normally have expected a tax charge on the benefit in kind unless the eye test or glasses were provided by means of a voucher. It is unclear why not as the test or appliances clearly gives a personal benefit where glasses or contact lenses are required as a result of the test. Nevertheless this means that in practice the exemption probably applies for earlier years also where no voucher was used.

Health-screening and medical check-ups

9.109   From 2009/10 onwards there is an exemption for the provision for an employee, on behalf of the employer (ie the employer must pay for it), of a health-screening assessment or a medical check-up [*ITEPA 2003, s 320B(1)*]. For this purpose a health-screening assessment is an assessment provided by an employee (or by any of a number of joint employers of the employee) to identify employees who might be at particular risk of ill-health. A medical check-up is a physical examination of the employee by a health professional solely for the purpose of determining the employee's state of health [*ITEPA 2003, s 320B(3)*]. The exemption applies only to one health-screening assessment or one medical check-up in a tax year as the case may be (ie it appears that it will enable an employee to have both a single screening and a single assessment) [*ITEPA 2003, s 320B(2)*].

Recommended medical treatment

9.109A   From a date to be fixed by the Treasury, there will be an exemption for the provision to an employee of recommended medical treatment (or the payment or reimbursement of the costs of such treatment up to £500 pa) [*ITEPA 2003, s 320C(1)(2)* inserted by *FA 2014, s 12*]. The exemption does not apply if the provision is pursuant to salary sacrifice or flexible remuneration arrangements though [*ITEPA 2003, s 320C(1)*]. Medical treatment is recommended for this purpose only if it is provided to the employee in accordance with a recommendation which is made for the purpose of assisting the employee to return to work after a period of absence due to injury or ill health, and is made to the employee as part of occupational health services provided to the employee by a service provided under the *Employment and Training Act 2003, s 2* (arrangements for the purpose of assisting persons to retain employment etc), or is made by such a service by (or in accordance with) arrangements made by the employer [*ITEPA 2003, s 320C(3)*]. The Treasury have power by regulation to add further requirement, such as that the employee must have been unfit for work for at least a specified number of consecutive days or in a specified manner [*ITEPA 2003, s 320C(3)(4)*].

9.109B   The £500 figure of course applies to the aggregate of actual earnings and benefits-in-kind [*ITEPA 2003, s 320C(6)*]. Medical treatment means all procedures for diagnosing or treating any physical or mental illness, infirmity or defect [*ITEPA 2003, s 320C(7)*]. The treatment has to be recommended by either the new Health and Work Service or by an occupational health service arranged or provided by the employee. The provision will come into force when the Health and Work Service is launched which is expected to be late 2014. It is probable that the Treasury will impose a requirement that the employee must be off work sick for a minimum period of four weeks (see Hansard, Public Bill Committee, 1.5.2014, Col 102). The DWP has estimated that the average cost of the treatment that is likely to be recommended will be £150-250, so the cap will allow the employer to fund two courses of such treatment for the employee per year. The government expect most recommended treatment to be physiotherapy for muscular conditions, or counselling for common mental health conditions (Public Bill Committee, Col 103).

Miscellaneous

9.110   Other benefits that an employer might consider are as follows.

(a)   *Health insurance*: The cost of BUPA, PPP, etc. premiums paid by the employer is taxable on the employee (unless he is lower-paid). The employer can normally obtain the cover cheaper than the employee himself through group scheme discounts, so this is a popular benefit. There is also an incidental benefit to the employer that an employee who is taken ill may be able to obtain the treatment quicker at a time convenient to him and the employer, and in a private room where he can be available for consultation by other staff.

(b)   *Death in service life assurance*: This will not give rise to a benefit in kind charge even if the policy is written in favour of the employee's spouse or dependants. The nominated beneficiary must be a member of the employee's family or household but need not be dependent on the employee. [*ITEPA 2003, s 307*].

(c)   *Permanent health insurance or serious illness insurance*: Whilst the premium is taxable on the employee, the employer can often buy the cover more cheaply, as a group scheme can benefit from the spread of risk that it provides.

(d)   *Professional subscriptions*: No benefit in kind charge arises if the employee pays on the employer's behalf a subscription that would qualify for tax relief under *ITEPA 2003, s 343* (see 5.84 above) if it were paid by the employee.

(e)   *Private minibus or coach*: Unless the works transport exemption (see 9.88) applies, a benefit in kind will arise on higher-paid employees if the employer provides a bus or coach to collect staff near their houses and bring them to and from work. However, the cost is likely to be well below the cost of equivalent public transport and the non-monetary benefit of avoiding changes of trains, etc. and avoiding the rush hour crush can be significant.

(f)   *Foreign travel*: If there is a business need for someone to take a trip abroad it may not always matter who goes. Accordingly, there might be scope for spreading this perk around the staff or for awarding the assignment to a specific employee who could derive an incidental benefit from it, eg if someone has to visit Australia to pay a goodwill visit to the company's agents there the employee with relatives there could be chosen, or the one who has long expressed a desire to visit Australia, so he can take a few days holiday (at his own expense) while he is in Australia.

(g) *Secondment to overseas branches*: Many staff like the concept of spending some months working overseas. If there is a need to second someone to an overseas office should it be such a person? There is no cost of providing such benefits, as the fare and accommodation has to be incurred for the business need that gives rise to the secondment. The incidental benefit can be very valuable to the employee but, because it has no cost and no money's worth, will not give rise to a tax charge on him.

(h) *Flexible hours*: Many people value being able to choose – within limits, of course – the hours they work. If the business is such that they can be given this choice without disrupting the business, this can provide a significant benefit, but again with no cost or money's worth. A problem is that in most organisations it is difficult to allow senior staff this flexibility.

(i) *Longer holidays*: Extra holidays are very important to some people and can accordingly be used to motivate them – particularly if the extra time has to be earned by meeting specific targets. It needs to be borne in mind that giving time off has a cost in lost productivity, unless, of course, it is given in recognition of increased productivity or the employee is not working at full capacity throughout the year, eg in a seasonal business extra time off in the off-season may have little or no real cost.

(j) *'No questions asked expense allowance'*: Although such an allowance is taxable on the employee as emoluments it can have a morale-boosting effect as it can be seen as a recognition that an employee is thought responsible enough to be expected to incur some business expenditure on his own initiative, and can make it easier for the employee to claim tax relief for business-related expenditure that he chooses to incur but does not feel able to ask his employer to reimburse.

(k) *Staff discounts on the employer's own goods, etc*: The tax charge on higher-paid employees is the marginal cost, which will often be very low (*Pepper v Hart [1992] STC 898*). HMRC accept that there is no benefit if the price paid is at least wholesale price. However, in most cases there should be no benefit (or a fairly nominal one) even if the price paid is significantly below that figure. Customs and Excise used to contend that VAT was due on the retail price of the goods where an employee had a contractual entitlement to the discount under his employment contract but now accept that it is only the price actually paid that attracts VAT (*Business Brief 8/92*).

(l) *Other staff discounts*: The employer may be in a position to negotiate significant discounts for his staff with suppliers and others – particularly if he is willing to give their staff discounts in return. There is little or no cost to the employer in providing such benefits.

(*m*) *Directors' indemnity insurance*: This does not normally give rise to a tax charge. The detailed rules are considered at **5.103–5.107**.

(*n*) *Free legal, financial or tax advice*: Although the employee will be taxable on the cost of such advice the employer will normally be able to negotiate special terms from his own accountant or solicitor to provide advice to his staff – particularly if this is provided on the employer's premises and there is a reasonable number of people involved so the professional adviser can obtain the benefit of economies of scale.

(*o*) *Use of office facilities*: If an employee is involved in outside interests, such as charities or community organisations, he may value being allowed to handle correspondence for such private activities from his office using the firm's photocopier, telephone, typing facilities, etc. Although in theory he is taxable on the cost this is likely to be negligible. The real benefit lies in the ability to handle such correspondence, etc. during working hours when it can often be done more effectively.

(*p*) *Use of other facilities*: In some types of business employees may be able to benefit from using the business facilities in 'down' time, eg a recording engineer may welcome the chance to use his employer's recording studio for personal projects when it is not booked by customers.

(*q*) *Christmas parties*: No tax is payable by an employee in relation to expenditure by his employer on a Christmas party or other annual function which is available to employees generally or available generally to those at a particular location provided that the cost per head of the party or function does not exceed £150. This is arrived at by dividing the total cost of providing the function (including VAT and transport or accommodation incidentally provided for persons attending it) by the total number of attendees. [*ITEPA 2003, s 264(2), (4)*]. If two or more functions are provided in a tax year and the total exceeds £150 but the aggregate of two or more does not, the cost of those functions is not taxed but that of other functions is. The cost per head includes VAT and transport or accommodation incidentally provided for persons attending the party (whether or not they are employees). [*ITEPA 2003, s 264(3)*]. It should be noted that the £150 is a *de minimis* figure, ie if the cost is £151 a head the entire £151 will be taxable. If expenditure is near the limit it should be carefully monitored to ensure that the £150 figure is not accidentally breached because of 'no shows' at a function for one reason or another.

(*r*) No income tax liability arises on:

  (i) the provision for the employee of overnight accommodation at or near the employee's permanent workplace (or a payment to the employee to reimburse such an expense); or

  (ii) the provision for the employee of transport for the purpose of ordinary commuting (or travel between two places that is for practical purposes substantially ordinary commuting) (or the reimbursement of such an expense);

where a strike or other industrial action disrupts a public transport service normally used by the employee. [*ITEPA 2003, s 345*]. This replaces a concession (ESC A58) under which HMRC did not tax the provision of travel or accommodation and subsistence during a period when public transport was disrupted due to industrial action.

There is also an exemption from 2003/04 for the provision or transport (or the payment or reimbursement of the expense) where the journey is from the employee's workplace to his home and either:

(i) the journey is made when the employee is required to work later than usual and until at least 9pm, such occasions occur irregularly, by the time the employee ceases work either public transport home is no longer available or it would not be reasonable to expect the employee to use it, and the transport is by taxi or similar private road transport; or

(ii) the employee regularly travels to work in a car with one or more other employees of the same employer under arrangements for the sharing of the car with them and the journey is made on an occasion when the employee is unable to use the car because of unforeseen and exceptional circumstances.

This exemption applies only to the first 60 journeys in the tax year. [*ITEPA 2003, s 248*]. Apparently, HMRC consider that where a supermarket manager is called out in the middle of the night because of the burglar alarm being triggered the taxi fare to the supermarket is taxable but the return fare is exempt under (i) above (*Taxline*, September 1994, item 108). For the purpose of (ii) unforeseen circumstances include where the employee travels home at the same time but cannot travel in the shared car, eg he has to use a taxi as he needs to take home with him files or computer equipment and there is insufficient room in the car for that equipment. It will not cover a case where inability to travel home in the shared car could reasonably have been anticipated. Nor curiously will it cover a journey from home to office, such as where the car breaks down and the employee needs to be in the office for an important meeting.

(s) *Disabled employees*: There is also an exemption for the provision of transport for a disabled employee (or the payment or reimbursement of expenses incurred on such transport) where that transport is for the purpose of ordinary commuting (or travel between two places that is for practical purposes substantially ordinary commuting). A disabled employee for this purpose is one who has a physical or mental impairment with a substantial and long-term adverse effect on the employee's ability to carry out normal day to day activities. [*ITEPA 2003, s 246*]. *Section 246* does not apply to the provision of the use of a car. Instead no car use or petrol benefit will apply (and there will be no benefit in respect of the payment or reimbursement of expenses incurred in connection with the car) provided that:

(i) the car has been adapted for the employee's special needs (or it has automatic transmission if the disability means that the employee can only drive such a car);

(ii)   the car is made available on terms prohibiting its use otherwise than for business travel, ordinary commuting (or substantially ordinary commuting) or travel to a place that would be covered by one of the training exemptions (see **9.63**); and

(iii)   in the tax year concerned the car is only used in accordance with those terms.

[*ITEPA 2003, s 247*]. These provisions replace a prior concession, *ESC A59*, which exempted home to work transport for disabled employees.

(*t*)   *Suggestion scheme award*: No tax charge arises in relation to certain awards under suggestion schemes. The scheme must be open on the same terms to employees of the employer generally (or to a particular description of them), the suggestion must relate to the activities carried on by the employer, the employee must not have been reasonably expected to have made the suggestion in the course of his duties (having regard to his experience) and the suggestion must not be made at a meeting held for the purpose of proposing suggestions. [*ITEPA 2003, s 321*]. In the case of an encouragement award (ie one made for a suggestion with intrinsic merit or showing special effort) any excess over £25 is taxable. In relation to a financial benefit award (ie one for a suggestion relating to an improvement in efficiency or effectiveness which the employer has decided to adopt and reasonably expects will result in a financial benefit) the reward is exempt, subject to a cap of £5,000, if it does not exceed the greater of:

(i)   50 per cent of the financial benefit reasonably expected to result from the adoption of the suggestion for the first year after its adoption; or

(ii)   10 per cent of the financial benefit reasonably expected to result for the first five years after its adoption.

If two or more awards are made on the same occasion for the same suggestion the maximum exempt amount is apportioned between them in proportion to their awards. If two or more awards for the suggestion are made to the same person on different occasions the limit is applied on a cumulative basis. [*ITEPA 2003, s 322*]. This replaces an earlier concession (*ESC A57*).

(*u*)   *Long service awards*: No tax liability arises in respect of a long service award (ie one to mark at least 20 years' service with the same employer) provided that:

(i)   it takes the form of either tangible moveable property, shares in the employer company (or another company in the same 51 per cent group) or the provision of a benefit other than cash, a cash voucher, a credit token, securities, shares other than in the employer company, or an interest in or rights over securities or shares (including in the employer company); and

(ii)   the chargeable amount does not exceed £50 for each year of service in respect of which the award is made.

[*ITEPA 2003, s 323(1)–(3)*]. If the amount exceeds the limit at (ii) only the excess is taxable. The exemption does not apply if a prior award was made to the same employee within the previous ten years. Service with two or more employers can be aggregated if one is a successor to the other or both are or have been in the same group or in the same group as a predecessor or successor of the other. [*ITEPA 2003, s 323(2), (4), (5)*]. This replaces a previous concession (*ESC A22*). The taxability of award is, in any event, questionable. It was held in *Ball v Johnson 47 TC 155* that a cash award made by a bank to employees who passed their banking examination did not constitute emoluments of the employment. However, HMRC consider that *Wicks v Firth 56 TC 318* has overruled this case as far as higher-paid employees are concerned. It is not clear how they have reached this conclusion!

This is arrived at by dividing the total cost of providing the function (including VAT and transport or accommodation incidentally provided for persons attending it) by the total number of attendees. [*ITEPA 2003, s 264(2), (4)*].

9.111   HMRC consider that if an employee receives commission (from his employment) in respect of his or her own insurance policy such commission is taxable remuneration, not a reduction in the cost of the policy. If he does not take the commission but requests, or allows, it to be invested for his or her benefit (eg to augment the policy) the commission that could have been taken is an emolument. If the employee is never entitled to commission but the employer forgoes commission due to him and it is used to augment the employee's policy, the value of such augmentation may not be an emolument. If the employee pays a net discounted insurance premium to his employer the amount of the discount is a benefit. If the benefit obtained by the employee is available to members of the general public on the same basis HMRC accept that no benefit arises (*SP 5/95*).

9.112   Although not a benefit that most employers are in a position to provide it should be mentioned for completeness that there is an exemption from income tax for 2003/04 onwards for the provision of coal or smokeless fuel or an allowance paid in lieu of such provision if the employee is a colliery worker and the amount of coal or fuel provided (or in respect of which the allowance is paid) does not substantially exceed the amount reasonably required for personal use. Curiously, it is for HMRC to prove that it exceeds such an amount, not for the taxpayer to show that it does not. A colliery worker for this purpose is a coal miner or any other person employed at or about a colliery otherwise than in clerical, administrative or technical work. [*ITEPA 2003, s 306*]. This replaced an earlier concession (*ESC A6*).

Chapter 10

Pension Provision

Introduction

10.1   To encourage saving towards one's retirement, tax relief is given for payments by both an employer and his employees to provide for pensions and other retirement benefits for employees. This pension provision obviously has to be in accordance with a scheme that satisfies statutory rules, and there are limits on the contributions that can qualify for tax relief. The current system of taxing pension funds and giving tax relief for pension contributions was introduced from 6 April 2006. The primary legislation was contained in the *Finance Act 2004 (FA 2004)* but much of the detail was fleshed out by regulations. Subsequent *Finance Acts* and regulations have made significant changes to these provisions, In particular, there have been cuts in the levels of contributions and pension funds on which relief is are granted. The pensions tax system does not seek to control how much can be contributed to a pension scheme or what the pension scheme does with the money, as the pre- 6 April 2006 system did. Instead it puts a limit on how much of the contributions to a scheme qualifies for tax relief and imposes a tax charge on money that comes out of the scheme other than in an approved form and on non-pension benefits provided by the scheme. There are two exceptions. Small pension schemes are prohibited from investing in residential property (other than through certain collective vehicles) and in tangible moveable property [*Finance Act 2006 (FA 2006), Sch 21*]. The rules on residential property in particular are very complex and are not considered here. The reader can find a detailed consideration of these rules in *Property Taxes 2014* (Bloomsbury Professional).

10.2   Currently pension provision is purely voluntary. However the *Pensions Act 2008* requires an employer to make arrangements to auto-enrol employees aged between 22 and state pensionable age (SPA) into membership of a workplace scheme or to join a Government Personal Account scheme. The SPA is currently 65 for men and 60 for women, although this is increasing gradually for women by three-monthly increments to reach 65 by November 2018 and will rise to 66 for both men and women by April 2020.

The Government scheme is NEST (National Employment Savings Trust). It is for individuals who earn more than £10,014 a year and work in the UK. Employers and employees must pay minimum contribution rates, as a percentage of a worker's pensionable earnings. The rates are:

Date	Minimum contributions
October 2012–September 2017	2% – the employer must pay at least 1% of this.
October 2017–September 2018	5% – the employer must pay at least 2% of this.
October 2018 onwards	8% – the employer must pay at least 3% of this.

Contributions are payable only to the extent that these fall into the earnings band from £5,772 pa to £41,865 pa. The employee can opt out of the pension scheme if he wishes. NEST has a contribution limit of £3,600 pa, so is not attractive to high earners. The obligation has been brought into effect gradually, starting from 1 November 2012 for large employers and gradually extending to smaller ones over the period to 1 April 2015. The staging dates exclude employers with fewer than 50 employees from legislation until next parliament. New employers setting up business from 1 April 2012–30 September 2017 have later dates ranging from 1 May 2017 to 1 February 2018. NEST is treated as an occupational pension scheme for the purpose of these provisions [*Finance (No 3) Act 2010 (F(No 3)A 2010), s 30*]. A maximum annual management charge is intended to be set at 0.3%, but for the first two years (under present intentions) it is set at 2% in order to meet the costs of establishing the scheme.

The basic rules

10.3   There are three limits on tax deductible contributions to a registered pension scheme, ie one in an approved form:

(*a*)   A lifetime allowance of the amount of pension savings that can benefit from tax relief. If the value of an individual's total pension funds (or of the parts of larger funds attributable to the individual) at the time benefits start to be paid out of the fund a tax charge will be imposed on the excess (see **10.25**). Accordingly this is not strictly a limit on contributions; it is a limit on the aggregate of contributions and growth within the fund up to that time. The lifetime allowance was initially £1,500.000. It rose annually, until 2011/12, but was cut back twice in later years, as follows:

2007/08	£1,600,000
2008/09	£1,650,000
2009/10	£1,750,000
2010/11	£1,800,000
2011/12	£1,800,000
2012/13	£1,500,000
2013/14	£1,500,000
2014/15	£1,250,000

[*FA 2004,s 218, FA 2011, Sch 17, FA 2013, s 48*].

An individual who was a member of the pension scheme during a period of non-residence has an enhanced lifetime allowance to reflect the fact the contributions during the period of non-residence will not attract tax relief (see **10.50**). [*FA 2004, ss 217–222*]. The £1,800,000 figure could be used up to 5 April 2012 to calculate the enhancement factor where the individual was relying on protection under *FA 2004, ss 220, 222, 223 or 224* (pension credits, relevant overseas individuals and transfers from recognised overseas pension schemes) or where he is relying on primary protection under *FA 2004, Sch 36, para 7* for pre-5 April 2006 rights (see **10.64**) [*FA 2004, s 218(5A), (5B) inserted by Finance Act 2011 (FA 2011), Sch 18, para 2*]. The £1,800,000 figure could also be used where a benefit crystallisation event (see **10.40**) arises because of the payment of a lump sum benefit after 6 April 2012 in respect of a death before that date [*FA 2004, s 218(5C)*].

(*b*) An annual allowance on the increase in value each year of an individual's pension fund. Under a money purchase scheme this will normally be the scheme contributions during the year. The amount was initially £215.000 and rose annually until 2011/12, but was cut back twice in later years as follows:

2007/08	£225,000
2008/09	£235,000
2009/10	£245,000
2010/11	£255,000
2011/12	£50,000
2012/13	£50,000
2013/14	£50,000
2014/15	£40,000

[*FA 2004, s 228 as amended by FA 2013 s 49, FA 2011, Sch 17, FA 2013, s 49*]

(*c*) An annual contribution limit of the greater of:

(i)   100% of a person's earnings; or

(ii)   £3,600.

[*FA 2004, s 190*]. Any excess over the annual allowance attracts a tax charge as an unauthorised payment though (see **10.20**).

If the individual has unused annual allowance available from any of the three previous years, the amount can be added to that of the current year, ie any shortfall between the annual allowance for a year and the pension contributions made in that year can be carried forward for up to three years [*FA 2004, s 228A(2), (3) inserted by FA 2011, Sch 17, para 5*]. The taxpayer must of course have been a member of a registered pension scheme (not necessarily the same one) in that earlier year though [*FA 2004, s 228A(4)*]. Where there are carried forward amounts from more than one year, that of the earliest year is treated as utilised first [*FA 2004, s 228A(7)*].

The special annual allowance charge (for 2009/10 and 2010/11 only)

10.4   In 2009 the Government announced an intention to limit tax relief on pension contributions from 2011/12. The value of the tax relief for contributions by employees (and the self-employed) was to be tapered down where the employee's income was £150,000 or more until it reached 20 per cent for those on incomes over £180,000. To prevent forestalling the special annual allowance charge was introduced for 2009/10 and 2010/11. This was payable by an individual whose 'relevant income' for the tax year was £130,000 or more if his 'total adjusted pension input amount' for that year exceeded the 'special annual allowance'. The charge was 20 per cent of the excess [*Finance Act 2009 (FA 2009), Sch 35, para 1* as amended by *Finance Act 2010 (FA 2010), s 48(2)*]. It was proposed to replace this charge with a new High Income Excess Relief Charge for 2011/12 onwards. The necessary legislation was contained in *FA 2010, s 23 and Sch 2*. However a change of government intervened and that charge was repealed by the *FA 2010, Section 23 and Schedule 2 (High Income Excess Relief Charge) (Repeal) Order 2010 (SI 2010 No 2938)* before it came into force. Accordingly as the legislation never took effect, it is not considered further. The charge was repealed because the incoming government instead decided to reduce the annual allowance (see **10.3**).

10.5   A person's relevant income for the purpose of the special annual allowance charge was his total income adding back any amount deducted in respect of pensions under a net pay arrangement and any deduction by virtue of *FA 2004, Sch 36, para 51* (individuals with a pre 6 April 2006 entitlement to corresponding relief) and adding in any amount that would have been income but for a post 22 April 2009 salary sacrifice in return for employer pension contributions and deducting:

(*a*)   any loss relief under *Income Tax Act 2007 (ITA 2007), s 24* other than in respect of pension payments;

(*b*)   the aggregate amount of any relevant contributions (subject to a maximum of £20,000);and

(*c*)   the grossed up amount of any gifts and payments,

[*FA 2009, Sch 35, para 2(1), (5)*]. If the result of this calculation was less than £150,000, the calculation had to be performed for each of the two previous tax years. If it was £130,000 or more in either of those years, then the relevant income for the current year had to be assumed to be £130,000 [*FA 2009, Sch 35, para 2(2)* as amended by *FA 2010, s 48(3)*]. If a scheme was entered into, one of the main purposes of which was to secure that the individual's income for the current year was less than £130,000, it again was deemed to be £130,000 [*FA 2009, Sch 35, para 2(3)*]. For the purpose of the calculation, relevant contributions were relievable pension contributions paid in the tax year, contributions in respect of which the individual was entitled to a tax reduction under *Income and Corporation Taxes Act 1988 (ICTA 1988), s 788* (double tax relief) which were paid in the year, and contributions paid in the year for which a deduction was given in accordance with *FA 2004, Sch 36, para 51* (individuals with a pre-6 April entitlement to corresponding relief) [*FA 2009, Sch 35, para 2(4)*].

10.6   The total adjusted pension input amount was the individual's pension input amount under *FA 2004, s 229* (see **10.29**) ie, broadly speaking, the total increase during the year of the individual's rights under all pension schemes (his contributions if there were no employer contributions) subject to a number of adjustments as follows:

(*a*)   *FA 2009, s 229(3)* (which provides that there is no pension input amount in the year in which a person dies or retires) (ie becomes entitled to all of the benefits that can be provided under the pension scheme) applied only if either:

  (i)   in the case of a deferred benefit arrangement, at that time there was at least 20 members of the scheme and the individual did not become entitled to the benefit as part of a scheme one of the main purposes of which was to reduce any of the special annual allowance charge, the annual allowance charge (see **10.29**) or the lifetime allowance charge (see **10.26**); or

  (ii)   the arrangement was an occupational pension scheme, public service pension scheme or a group personal pension scheme and the individual's entitlement to benefit arose only because of ill health (and one of the main purposes of the individual becoming entitled to the benefit was not to avoid liability to the special annual allowance charge, the annual allowance charge or the lifetime allowance charge),

[*FA 2009, Sch 35, para 4*].

(*b*)   The calculation had to be done by reference to the tax year, not the pension input period [*FA 2009, Sch 35, para 5*].

(*c*)   If there was a scheme one of the main purposes of which was to avoid or reduce liability to the special annual allowance charge, the annual allowance charge or the lifetime allowance charge, a further calculation had to be made of the increase during the tax year on the value of the consideration that might be expected to be received in respect of an assignment of the benefits to which the individual (or any dependent) had a prospective entitlement, on the assumptions that the benefits were capable of assignment, that the assignment was by a transaction between parties at arm's length and that any power to reduce entitlement to the benefits did not exist. If that amount exceeded what would otherwise have been the total pension input amount it had to be substituted for that amount [*FA 2009, Sch 35, para 6*].

This adjusted amount was then reduced by the aggregate of any protected pension input amounts (see **10.8**), any relevant refunded amounts (see **10.9**) and for 2009/10 only any pre 22 April 2009 pension input amounts (see **10.38**).

10.7   The special annual allowance was £20,000 [*FA 2009, Sch 35, para 1(4)*]. However if in calculating the total adjusted pension input amount an adjustment was made in respect of protected pension input amounts or a pre-22 April 2009 pension input amount under *FA 2009, Sch 35, para 16(3)* (or both), the £20,000 figure was reduced by that amount – or reduced to nil if such deductions exceeded £20,000 [*FA 2009, Sch 35, para 1(5)*].

10.8   The following were protected pension input amounts:

(*a*)   In the case of a defined benefit arrangement which was an occupational pension scheme or a public service pension scheme, any part of the total adjusted pension input amount that was attributable to contributions by the individual that were paid in pursuance of an agreement made before noon on 22 April 2009, had been paid on a quarterly or more frequent basis since before 22 April 2009 and were at the rate which had not increased with a view to securing that the calculation of the benefits was by reference to a period of service in excess of pensionable service by the individual (added year's contributions) (referred to below as the three conditions). If there was a material change in the rules of the pension scheme which affected at least 50 active members of the scheme, any additional amount as a result of that change was also protected [*FA 2009, Sch 35, para 8*].

(*b*)   In the case of a cash balance arrangement under an occupational pension scheme or a public service pension scheme, any part of the total adjusted pension input amount that was attributable to additional voluntary contributions by the individual that met the three conditions in (*a*) above [*FA 2009, Sch 35, para 9*]. The protection at (*a*) for a rule change again applied.

(*c*)   In the case of any other money purchase arrangement under an occupational pension scheme or public service pension scheme or a group personal pension scheme, any part of the total adjusted pension input amount that was attributable to additional voluntary contributions paid by the individual that met the three conditions in (*a*) above, or, if the individual has been a member of the scheme since before 22 April 2009, any other contributions by the individual that met those conditions [*FA 2009, Sch 35, para 10*].

(*d*)   In the case of other money purchase arrangements where the individual has been an active member of the pension scheme since before 22 April 2009 (or made a written application to join before that date), any part of the total adjusted input amount that met the three conditions in (*a*) above [*FA 2009, Sch 35, para 11*].

(*e*)   In the case of a hybrid arrangement, any part of the total adjusted input amount that would be applicable under *paras 8–11* in respect of the relevant benefits [*FA 2009, Sch 35, para 12*].

(*f*)   If the pension arrangement was made or reactivated after 22 April 2009 and it was under an occupational pension scheme or a public service pension scheme or a group personal pension scheme that related to an employment, there had been no rule change (other than one that affected at least 50 active members) and at least 20 members accrued benefits on the same basis as the individual, and any part of the total adjusted pension input amount that was attributable to the normal pattern of pension provision made by the employer in relation to his employees, ie a new joiner could obtain the same protection as applied to other members of the schemes. There was however no protection for added years' contributions or additional voluntary contributions [*FA 2009, Sch 35, para 13*].

(*g*)   None of the above protections applied if the individual was a party to a scheme one of the main purposes of which was to avoid or reduce liability to the special annual allowance charge, the annual allowance charge or the lifetime allowance charge [*FA 2009, Sch 35, para 14*].

10.9   The total adjusted pension input amount was a relevant refunded amount to the extent that it did not exceed the amount of a contribution refund lump sum paid to the individual (or to his personal representatives). This was any amount paid to the individual by the pension scheme (other than one within *FA 2004, s 66*) within 12 months after the end of the tax year. It was limited to the adjusted contributions amount for the tax year. This was the relevant relievable pension contributions less any relevant deductions. Relevant relievable pension contributions were the contribution by the individual for the year, but, in the case of an occupational scheme, public service scheme or group personal pension scheme, only if they were additional voluntary contributions (and did not fall within *para 9(3)* or *10(3)*) and, in any other case, only if they did not fall within *para 11(2)* (ie they were not protected pension input amounts). For 2009/10 contributions paid before 22 April 2009 were not relevant relievable pension contributions if they were paid pursuant to the payment of contributions on a quarterly or more frequent basis. Relevant deductions consisted of any previous contribution refund lump sum paid by the pension scheme since the end of the tax year, any pension debit to which the rights of the individual were subject in the tax year, any transfer of accrued rights from another registered pension scheme and the amounts crystallised by any benefit crystallisation event in the tax year [*FA 2009, Sch 35, para 15*].

10.10   A pre 22 April 2009 pension input amount in relation to a defined benefit arrangement was such part of the total adjusted pension input amount as on a just and reasonable basis related to the period 6–21 April 2009. In relation to a money purchase arrangement it was so much of the contributions as were paid in that period other than any paid pursuant to an agreement for the payment of contributions on a quarterly or more frequent basis [*FA 2009, Sch 35, para 16*]. A contributions refund lump sum was treated for the purposes of the pension scheme provisions of *FA 2004* as if it were a short service refund lump sum in excess of the limit in *FA 2004, s 205* (see **10.35**) [*FA 2009, Sch 35, para 18*].

10.11   Where money purchase contributions were paid less frequently than on a quarterly basis and the average of such contributions in 2006/07, 2007/08, and 2008/09 exceeded £20,000, the special annual allowance was increased to such average, subject to a maximum of £30,000 [*FA 2009, Sch 35, para 16*].

10.12   In most cases the effect of these rules was that where regular pension contributions were paid quarterly or more frequently under arrangements made before 22 April 2009 and continued to be paid at the same level, the special annual allowance was increased to the amount of such contributions so no special annual allowance charge applied. Where irregular contributions (or regular contributions at annual or half-yearly intervals) had been paid in the past, the special annual allowance was increased to a maximum of £30,000 and no special annual allowance charge arose if the payments during 2009/10 and 2010/11 were kept within that average. If they wee not the excess was taxable. If both regular and irregular (including annual or half-yearly) contributions were made and the regular contributions utilised the whole of the £20,000 normal special annual allowance, or reduced it, no increase was given for irregular contributions [*FA 2009, Sch 35, para 17(5)*].

10.13   The special annual allowance charge was payable by the employee [*FA 2009, Sch 35, para 1(6)*]. It was payable irrespective of where the employee and the pension schemewere resident, ordinarily resident or domiciled [*FA 2009, Sch 35, para 1(7)*]. The Treasury had power by statutory instrument to vary the rate of the charge. This required a positive resolution of the House of Commons [*FA 2009, Sch 35, para 19*]. The Treasury also had power by statutory instrument to apply *Schedule 35* to non-UK pension schemes subject to such modifications as they might specify [*FA 2009, Sch 35, para 20*]. *FA 2004, Sch 31, para 49* (annual allowance charge enhanced protection) (see **10.63**) did not apply to the special annual allowance charge [*FA 2004, Sch 36, para 49(3)* inserted by *FA 2009, Sch 35, para 22*].

10.14   The income cap was initially intended to be £150,000 but this was reduced by *FA 2010*. If the individual's relevant income for 2009/10 or 2010/11 would be less than £130,000 if the reference in *para 2(5)* (see **10.5**) to a scheme made after 22 April 2009 were to one made after 8 December 2009, and the individual's relevant income for 2009/10 was less than £150,000, it was treated as being less than £130,000 [*FA 2009, Sch 35, para 2(5A)* inserted by *FA 2010, s 48(4)*]. This avoided a retrospective charge on contributions made before 8 December 2009 that would have escaped the charge had the cap remained at £150,000. In applying the rules in such a case if an individual's relevant income for 2009/10 was less than £150,000, 9 December 2009 was substituted for the references above to 22 April 2009. Furthermore if a person's 2009/10 income was less than £150,000, but it exceeded £150,000 in either of the two previous years, (or there was a scheme to secure that it was less than £150,000) it was treated as £150,000 for 2009/10 [*FA 2009, Sch 35, para 16A* inserted by *FA 2010, s 48(6)*].

Pension scheme providers

10.15   A registered pension scheme can be established by employers and by financial institutions subject to regulation by the FSA (now the Financial

Conduct Authority (FCA) – which, with the Prudential Regulation Authority (PRA), replaced the FSA in 2013).

The Treasury has power by regulation to extend the class of providers [*FA 2004, s 154*]. From 6 April 2007 the person must have FCA permission to establish a personal pension scheme or stakeholder pension scheme. [*Financial Services and Markets Act 2000 (Regulated Activities) (Amendment) Order 2006 (SI 2006 No 1969)*]. However, an employer can establish an occupational pension scheme without such permission. The approval of HMRC is not needed to set up a pension scheme but the scheme has to register with HMRC to attract tax relief. HMRC must register it unless either

(*a*)   any information contained in the scheme or otherwise provided by the scheme administrator in connection with the application is inaccurate in a material respect;

(*b*)   any document produced to HMRC by the scheme administrator in connection with the application contains a material inaccuracy;

(*c*)   any declaration accompanying the application is false;

(*d*)   the scheme administrator has failed to comply with an information notice under *Finance Act 2014 (FA 2014), s 153A* given in connection with the application (including where he has concealed, destroyed or otherwise disposed of a document in breach of *Finance Act 2008 (FA 2008), Sch 36, paras 42* or *43* as applied by *s 153A(3)* and later changes to the rules (or arranged for such actions);

(*e*)   the scheme administrator has deliberately obstructed an HMRC officer in the course of an inspection under *s 153B* carried out in connection with the application where the inspection has been approved by the Tribunal;

(*f*)   the pension scheme has not been established (or is not being maintained) wholly or mainly for the purpose of making authorised payments within *FA 2004, s 164(1)(a)* or *(b)* (see **10.19**); or

(*g*)   any of the persons who is or are the scheme administrator is not a fit and proper person to be such an administrator

[*FA 2004, s 153* as amended by *FA 2014, Sch 5, para 3*]. Prior to 17 July 2014, they could refuse registration only if any information contained in the application was incorrect or any declaration accompanying it was false. Where an application for registration is made after 20 March 2014, HMRC can issue an information notice requiring the scheme administrator or any other person to provide them with such information or to produce such documents as they reasonably require in connection with the application. If the notice is given to someone other than the scheme administrator, HMRC must give a copy of it to the administrator. The provisions of *FA 2008, Sch 36*, in relation to information notices and appeals against such notices apply for this purpose. If the notice is given to someone other than the scheme administrator, he too has a right of appeal against the notice [*FA 2004, s 153A* inserted by *FA 2014, Sch 5, para 3*]. Where such an application is made, HMRC also have power from 20 March 2014 to enter any business premises and inspect documents that are on the premises if they reasonably require to inspect them in connection with the application. The *FA 2008, Sch 36*, inspection powers again apply. HMRC can get advance approval from the FTT for an inspection under this provision [*FA 2004, s 153B*].

10.15A If an application for registration contains information which is inaccurate, the inaccuracy is material, and it is careless or deliberate (or the scheme administrator knew of the inaccuracy at the time of the application or he later discovers it and fails to take reasonable steps to inform HMRC) the scheme administrator is liable to a penalty of up to £3,000 for each inaccuracy [*FA 2004, s 153D*]. The *FA 2008* penalties (again up to £3,000) apply if a reply to an information notice is inaccurate [*FA 2004, s 153E*]. There is also a penalty of up to £3,000 for a false declaration accompanying an application if it is careless or deliberate (or the scheme administrator knows or comes to know of it and does not tell HMRC). If there is more than one falsehood, a separate penalty applies for each falsehood [*FA 2004, s 153F*]. If a person other than the scheme administrator fails to comply with an information notice under *s 153A* or deliberately obstructs an HMRC officer in the course of an inspection which has been approved by the FTT, he is liable to the same penalties as apply under *FA 2008, Sch 36* [*FA 2004, s 153C*]. The *FA 2008, Sch 36* procedural rules on penalties, including the right of appeal, apply to all of these penalties [*FA 2004, ss 153C(3), 153D(8), 153E(2), 153F(4)*].

10.15B HMRC can withdraw the registration in the event of serious non-compliance with the tax rules [*FA 2004, s 157*]. Section 158 sets out the circumstances in which non-compliance is regarded as serious. From 20 March 2014, if HMRC do not make a decision on an application within six months, the scheme administrator has a right of appeal to the FTT as if the application had been refused. There is a right of appeal against both a refusal of registration and a decision to deregister [*FA 2004, ss 156, 159*].

10.15C From 1 September 2014, HMRC can by notice require the scheme administrator of a registered pension scheme or any other person to provide them with any information (or produce any document) that HMRC reasonably require for the purpose of considering whether any of the scheme administrators is a fit and proper person. They must give the administrator a copy of any notice given to a third party. There is a right of appeal against the notice or any requirement of the notice. The *FA 2008, Sch 36* rules in relation to appeals against information notices apply [*FA 2004, s 159A* inserted by *FA 2014, Sch 5, para 7*]. They can also enter business premises and inspect documents found therein if they reasonably require to inspect them for the purpose of considering whether a scheme administrator is a fit and proper person to be an administrator [*FA 2004, s 159B*]. The penalty provisions for failure to comply with an information notice or deliberately obstructing an HMRC officer in the course of an inspection that has been approved by the FTT are the same as those at **10.15A** [*FA 2004, ss 159C, 159D*].

10.15D Approved pension arrangements in existence at 5 April 2006 (A Day) automatically became registered pension schemes. If such a scheme did not wish to become a registered scheme it could opt out, but if it did so would suffer a tax charge of 40 per cent on the value of the assets held on A day. [*FA 2004, Sch 36, para 12*].

Payments by a registered pension scheme

10.16   Payments out of a pension scheme can fall into any of four categories, authorised member payments, unauthorised member payments, authorised employer payments and unauthorised employer payments. Unauthorised payments attract a tax charge (see **10.20**, **10.22** and **10.33**). HMRC can withdraw a scheme's registration if the unauthorised payments in any 12-month period exceed 25 per cent of the market value of the scheme's assets (although benefits-in-kind, compensation payments and payments made to comply with a court order are ignored in looking at the 25 per cent figure) [*FA 2004, ss 16, 164*].

10.17   A pension scheme is defined for the purpose of the legislation as a scheme or other arrangements comprised in one or more instruments or agreements having, or capable of having, effect so as to provide benefits to, or in respect of, persons on retirement, on death, on reaching a particular age, on the onset of serious ill-health or incapacity or in similar circumstances [*FA 2004, s 150(1)*]. An occupational pension scheme is one established by an employer or employers and which has (or is capable of having) effect so as to provide benefits to, or in respect of, all or any of the employees of that employer (or those employers) or any other employer (whether or not it also has effect of providing benefits to other persons, or is capable of doing so). [*FA 2004, s 150(5)*].

10.18   The legislation contains definitions of a member of a scheme (who can be an active member, pensioner, deferred member or pension credit member) [*FA 2004, s 151*]. It also contains definitions of an arrangement (the part of a scheme relating to an individual member) and of money purchase (where the provision is based on the contributions paid by or for the member) and defined benefit (where the benefits are fixed in advance and are unrelated to the amount of the contributions) arrangements [*FA 2004, s 152*]. These are largely self-explanatory.

Authorised member payments

10.19   The authorised (tax-free) member payments are:

(*a*)   Payments of pension. The minimum age at which pensions can start is 60 (50 up to 6 April 2010 and 55 up to 6 April 2013) (or earlier in the event of ill-health). There is no longer a requirement in all cases to buy an annuity by the age of 75. Instead the individual can draw income directly from the pension fund (a drawdown pension) as and when they wish subject to an annual cap. This is 150% of the amount of the equivalent annuity that could have been brought with the fund value (100% prior to 26 March 2013 and 120% prior to 27 March 2014). Between the ages of 60 and state pension age, this amount has to be re-determined at least every three years. After reaching state pension age it has to be re-determined annually by reference to the fund at the start of the year. The cap does not apply if the individual can show that he has secure pension income for life of at least £12,000 (£20,000 up to 27 March 2014). The amount drawn in a year is of course fully taxable as income. To prevent avoidance the amount drawn down in a year in which the individual is a temporary non-resident (ie he has become non-resident for a period of less than five years) is taxed as income of the year that he resumes UK residence [*Income Tax (Earnings and Pensions) Act 2003 (ITEPA 2003), ss 576A, 579CA inserted by FA 2011, Sch 16, para 21 as amended by FA 2013, ss 50, 51 and FA 2014, s 39*]. If the remittance basis applies, the remittance is also deemed to take place in that year [*ITEPA 2003, ss 576A(4), 579CA(2)*]. *Section 576A* overrides double tax agreements [*ITEPA 2003, ss 576A(7), 579CA(4)*]. Prior to 6 April 2011, pension benefit had to commence at age 75 at the latest (age 77 if the individual reached 75 after 21 June 2010). There is no limit on the size of the pension that can be paid. Control over this is in effect exercised by the tax charge where the employee's pension fund exceeds the lifetime allowance (see **10.39**). The scheme rules can of course also provide for payment of a pension to a pensioner's widow or dependant. Pension payments (other than for a widow or dependants) cannot normally continue beyond the date of the member's death with the exception that the scheme can provide for pension payments to continue for at least ten years (to cover a ten-year guaranteed annuity). If a scheme has fewer than 50 members the pension must normally be payable by an insurance company (ie by purchasing an annuity). The pensioner must be given an opportunity to select the insurance company. A short-term annuity or income withdrawals from the scheme itself can be used up to age 75 (or 77 as appropriate), when the final decision needs to be made. There is an alternative to buying an annuity at age 75 (or 77), namely to continue with income withdrawals, (an alternatively secured pension) but the maximum pension is then limited to 150 per cent of what would have been paid via an assurance company (70 per cent before 6 April 2007, 90% before 6 April 2011, 100% before 26 March 2013 and 120% before 27 March 2014). The Government Actuary's Department publish tables to allow schemes to calculate the allowable amount. These can be found at www.hmrc.gov.uk/pensionscharges/gad-tables.htm. Some commentators recommend this where the pensioner does not need his full pension to live on as after the pensioner's death the balance remaining in the fund can be used to fund a pension for someone else who is also a member of the scheme (but see **10.52**). [*FA 2004, ss 164, 165, 167* and *Sch 28* as amended by *FA 2013, s 50*]. From 6 April 2007 it ceased to be possible for an alternatively secured pension to continue to be paid as the facility to guarantee the pension for a period of up to ten years was withdrawn (although it is still possible for a guaranteed annuity to continue for the balance of that ten-year period). *Schedule 28* gives HMRC powers to make regulations to flesh out some of the rules. They have done so by the *Registered Pension Schemes (Relevant Annuities) Regulations 2006 (SI 2006 No 129)*, the *Pension Schemes (Reduction in Pension Rates) Regulations 2006 (SI 2006 No 138)* (as amended by the *Pension Schemes (Reduction in Pension Rates) (Amendment) Regulations 2009 (SI 2009 No 1311)*) and the *Registered Pension Schemes (Prescribed Manner of Determining Amount of Annuities) Regulations 2006 (SI 2006 No 568)*. A payment that would otherwise qualify as an authorised member payment is treated as a pension for the tax year in which it is paid if either –

(i)   it was paid by mistake, the member is still alive and the scheme administrator believed that the member was entitled to the payment;

(ii)   such a payment was made after the error was discovered and either the scheme administrator had taken reasonable steps to stop it being paid or it was paid during a time when the administrator was in the process of amending the rules to stop such payments (and had not taken an unreasonable time to do so);

(iii)   it was paid by mistake after, and within six months of, the member's death because the administrator was unaware of the death or had become aware of it too late to prevent the payment being made; or

(iv)   the payment is in respect of a defined benefit arrangement, the member had died, the member had not reached 75 and was not a controlling director (or connected person) and the payment represented arrears of scheme pension to which the administrator had not established the member's entitlement at the date of his death,

[*Registered Pension Schemes (Authorised Payments) Regulations 2009 (SI 2009 No 1171), Regs 4, 13–16*]. The government has announced a major reform of drawdown pensions from 6 April 2015. From that date a person will be able to take as much or as little pension from his fund as he wishes. He will be able to withdraw the whole amount as a lump sum if he wishes. However the amount drawn will be treated as taxable income to the extent that total withdrawals exceed the 25% tax-free limit (see **10.19**(*c*)(i)). The necessary legislation is likely to be in the 2015 Finance Bill.

Finance Act 2014, Sch 5, makes provision for a temporary relaxation to allow a transfer of pension rights after a lump sum is paid and a temporary relaxation to allow lump sum to be repaid to pension scheme that paid it. The provisions widen the six month lump sum window to 18 months in order to give defined contribution members who have already taken their pension commencement lump sum flexibility to delay drawing their pension until after April 2015. From that date, such members will have the option of taking their benefits in cash rather than by means of annuity purchase. However, HM Treasury announced on 21 July 2014 that the annual allowance will be cut from £40,000 pa to £10,000 pa for future pension contributions if individuals who have drawn cash under the new flexibilities subsequently reinvest the cash taken into a new pension and receive tax relief again. To deter this from happening, the £10,000 annual cap will apply to those who access their pensions from April 2015. The restriction will not apply to individuals who are already in capped drawdown – they will retain the £40,000 annual limit. However, HMRC's guide 'Pension flexibility 2015' provides that individuals who access their pension savings flexibly from a flexi-access drawdown fund will retain an annual allowance for defined benefit pension savings of up to £40,000, depending on the value of new DC pension savings.

(*b*)   A death benefit. This can be paid only to a dependant of the member. If a scheme is a defined benefit scheme (or prior to 2011/12 the dependant was over 75) it must take the form of a dependant's pension. Subject to this, a lump sum death benefit can be paid within two years of death. [*FA 2004, Sch 29, para 13* as amended by *FA 2011, Sch 16, para 33*]. The only permitted lump sums under a defined benefit arrangement are a pension protection lump sum which falls within the pension protection limit (which is defined in *Sch 29, para 14*) and a trivial commutation lump sum to extinguish the dependant's entitlement under the scheme (the 1 per cent limit at (*c*)(v) below applies). For a money purchase arrangement the lump sum can be an uncrystallised fund lump sum (which is defined in *FA 2004, Sch 29,para 15*), an annuity protection lump sum (which is defined in *FA 2004, Sch 29, para 16*), an unsecured pension lump sum (see *FA 2004, Sch 29, para 17*), a charity lump sum, which is paid to a charity nominated by the member and can only be paid if the member was over 75 when he died and there are no dependants (but can also be paid on the death of a dependant over 75), a trivial commutation lump sum, or, up to 5 April 2007 only, a transfer lump sum which is paid on the death of a member (or a dependant) where the member (or dependant) has no dependants and the funds become held for the benefit of another scheme member or members nominated by the deceased, and a trivial commutation lump sum [*FA 2004, ss 164, 167, 168* and *Sch 29, paras 13–20* as amended by *FA 2007, Sch 19, para 6*].

(*c*)   Certain lump sums paid to members. [*FA 2004, ss 164, 166* and *Sch 29*]. The only types of lump sum payment are:

(i)   A pension commencement lump sum. This can be paid when a member becomes entitled to a pension (but only if all or part of the member's lifetime allowance is available at that time (or, from 6 April 2011, the time the member becomes entitled to it if it is not paid to him until after he reached 75), the lump sum is paid within the period beginning six months before and ending one year after the member becomes entitled to it, the pension is not temporarily payable (or increased) only until the member becomes entitled to state retirement pension, and the sale or main purpose of providing for the pension was not to increase the member's entitlement to the lump sum [*FA 2004, Sch 29, para 1,* as amended by *Finance (No 2) Act 2010 (F(No 2)A 2010), Sch 3, para 7 and FA 2011, Sch 16 para 24*]. Prior to 6 April 2011, the member also had to be under 75 at the time of payment (77 if he reached 75 after 21 June 2010) but this requirement was repealed by *FA 2011, Sch16, para 24* The tax-free amount cannot exceed 25 per cent of the member's lifetime allowance. Any excess will be an unauthorised payment. The lump sum can be taken in instalments. Prior to 2011/12, the instalments had to cease by age 75. No lump sum can be taken under pension sharing arrangements on a divorce etc if the person giving up rights was already drawing the pension [*FA 2004, Sch 29, para 2* as amended by *FA 2011, Sch 16, para 25*]. Special rules apply where the member becomes entitled to income withdrawal or, from 6 April 2011, if the lump sum becomes payable after age 75 [*FA 2004, Sch 29, para 3* as amended by *FA 2011, Sch 16, para 26*]. If there are any remaining uncrystallised funds at the end of the six-month period or on the earlier death of the individual, they must be treated as having been designated under the arrangement as available for the payment of unsecured pension at that time. Remaining uncrystallised funds means such of the sums and assets held for the purposes of the arrangement which are not member-designated funds and have not been applied towards the provision of a scheme pension or dependants' scheme pension [*F(No 2)A 2010, Sch 3, para 8*]. If the scheme administrator has made an overpayment by way of a lifetime allowance charge, that overpayment is refunded to him by HMRC, and he pays all or part of that amount to the member, that payment is treated as a pension commencement lump sum provided that the member has part of his lifetime allowance available and the payment to the member is made within 12 months of the administrator receiving it (three months prior to 7 January 2008). [*FA 2004, Sch 29, para 1(6)* and *Registered Pension Schemes (Meaning of Pension Commencement Lump Sum) Regulations 2006 (SI 2006 No 135)* as amended by the *Registered Pension Schemes (Meaning of Pension Commencement Lump Sum) (Amendment) Regulations 2007 (SI 2007 No 3533)*]. A payment that would otherwise qualify as an authorised payment is treated as a pension commencement lump sum if either –

–   it was intended to represent such a lump sum but exceeded the permitted maximum because of an error in the calculation, the pension is reduced to reflect the error (so far as it had not already been paid) and the error arose because the administrator incorrectly thought that the member was entitled to a larger pension than was actually due;

–   it was intended to represent a lump sum but exceeded the permitted maximum because it was calculated by reference to an annuity or scheme pension purchase price, an error in the calculation meant that it was higher than it should have been and the overpayment was (as far as possible) used to reduce the purchase price of the annuity; or

–   the payment is made after the member's death, is in respect of a deferred benefit arrangement, the administrator had not established the member's entitlement at the date of death, it would have been a pension commencement lump sum if it had been paid before the date of death and the member had been entitled to it and the member was not a controlling director (or a connected person).

The member (or his estate) becoming entitled to such a lump sum must be treated as a benefit crystallisation event for the purpose of the lifetime allowance charge.

[*Registered Pension Schemes (Authorised Payments) Regulations 2009 (SI 2009 No 1171), Regs 5, 17, 18*].

(ii)   A serious ill-health lump sum,. This can be paid only where the scheme administrator has seen medical evidence that the member is expected to live for less than a year (the conditions in (i) above other than age also have to be met) [*FA 2004, Sch 29, para 4*]. Although such a payment can be made to a person over 75 it is unwise to do so as such a payment triggers a 55% tax charge (see **10.36**).

(iii) A short service refund lump sum. This is a payment by an occupational pension scheme where the member's service was terminated before normal pension age, the member is not entitled to short service benefit under *Pension Schemes Act 1993, s 71*, the payment extinguishes the member's entitlement under the scheme and the member under 75. The tax-free amount is limited to a refund of the member's contributions. Any excess is taxable (see **10.23**). [*FA 2004, Sch 29, para 5*].

(iv) A refund of excess contributions lump sum, where a repayment of some of a member's contributions for a tax year is refunded because it exceeds the contribution limit for that year. [*FA 2004,Sch 29, para 6*].

(v) A trivial commutation lump sum, which can be paid where the value of the member's pension rights does not exceed £30,000 (£18,000 up to 27 March 2014 and 1 per cent of the standard lifetime allowance up to 5 April 2012), the member is aged over 60 (and up to 2010/11 under 75), the member's lifetime allowance is available and the payment extinguishes the member's rights under the scheme. [*FA 2004, Sch 29, para 7* as amended by *FA 2011, Sch 18, para 4 and FA 2014, s 40*]. From 1 December 2009 a payment that would otherwise qualify as an authorised member payment is treated as a trivial commutation lump sum if either –

– a transfer has been made to the scheme in respect of the member and the payment to the member is made within six months of the transfer, does not exceed £10,000 (£2,000 up to 27 March 2014), (or the amount of the transfer if less) and exhausts the member's entitlement to benefit under the scheme;

– the payment does not exceed £10,000 (£2,000 up to 27 March 2014), it is made as compensation under the Financial Services Compensation Scheme and it exhausts the member's entitlement under the scheme;

– the payment is made to or in respect of a member who has reached 75, at that time the scheme administrator has not heard from the member for at least five years, the payment does not exceed £2,000, it extinguishes the member's entitlement to benefit under the scheme, and is paid within 12 months of the administrator discovering the member's whereabouts or learning of his death;

– although the member will continue to receive an annuity, the payment is made before the end of the commutation period under *FA 2004, Sch 29, para 7(2)*; or

–   the pension scheme is a public service scheme or an occupational pension scheme, the member is aged between 60 and 75, he is not a controlling director or a connected person, the payment does not exceed £2,000 and exhausts the member's entitlement under the scheme, no recognised transfer was made into the scheme during the previous three years, and the commutation value of the benefit to which the member is entitled does not exceed £2,000 (or in the case of a large scheme (at least 50 members) no excluded transfer, other than one within *FA 2004, Sch 36, para 12(8)(b)–(d)* (enhanced protection-permitted transfers), was made into the scheme in respect of the member during the previous five years)

[*Registered Pension Schemes (Authorised Payments) Regulations 2009 (SI 2009 No 1171), Regs 3–12 as amended by FA 2014, s 40(6)*].

(vi)   A winding up lump sum, which can be paid where an occupational pension scheme is wound up, the employer has made contributions under the scheme (and is not contributing to another scheme for the member), the member's lifetime allowance is available and the member is under 75. Such a lump sum is taxable to the extent that it exceeds £18,000 (1 per cent of the standard lifetime allowance up to 5 April 2012) [*FA 2004, Sch 29, para 10* as amended by *FA 2011, Sch 18, para 5*].

(vii)   A lifetime allowance excess lump sum, which is a payment to a member who has used up all his lifetime allowance, has reached normal minimum pension age and is under 75. Such a payment is taxable under the lifetime allowance charge (see **10.39**. [*Sch 29, para 11*].

(*d*)   A recognised transfer payment, ie a transfer of the funds to another registered pension scheme or to a recognised overseas pension scheme (see **10.55**) or to the Pension Protection Fund [*FA 2004, ss 164, 169* and *Registered Pension Schemes (Authorised Payments) (Transfers to the Pension Protection Fund) Regulations 2006 (SI 2006 No 134)*]. HMRC have power by regulation to make further rules in relation to recognised transfers. They have provided that those assets transferred which represent rights in respect of a pension in payment must be applied after the transfer towards the provision of a scheme pension (which is then treated as if it were the original scheme pension). This also applies if the original pension was being paid by an insurance company and the new pension is paid by a different insurance company. A reduction of the original scheme pension is a prescribed circumstance for the purpose of *FA 2004, Sch 28, para 2(4)* (pension payments) so as not to trigger a tax charge if the reduction in the rate of the initial pension payable under the new scheme reflects the reasonable administrative costs of the transfer and, if the original pension was payable until the end of a term certain, the term certain under the new scheme ends no later than the original date. If the transfer was the replacement of a lifetime annuity by a new one it is treated as a continuation of the old to the extent that the cost of the new annuity equals the assets transferred, but any excess annuity payment is treated as an unauthorised member payment. [*Registered Pension Schemes (Transfer of Sums and Assets) Regulations 2006 (SI 2006 No 499)*]. The regulations also contain special rules relating to transfers relating to short-term annuities, dependants' scheme pensions, dependants' annuities and alternatively secured pensions. Some of these can trigger unauthorised member payments.

(e)   A scheme administration member payments. This will be rare. It applies where a member is also involved in the administration of the scheme and is the arm's length salary for such work. [*FA 2004, ss 164, 171*].

(f)   A payment pursuant to a pension sharing order or provision, eg where there is an agreement or order to pass over pension rights to a spouse on a divorce. [*FA 2004, s 164*].

(g)   Such other payments as may be prescribed by regulation by HMRC. [*FA 2004, s 161*]. They have prescribed a payment in connection with the demutualisation of an insurance company in compensation for the loss of rights as a member of the scheme provided that it does not reduce the amount of the assets held for the purposes of the pension scheme [*Registered Pension Schemes (Authorised Member Payments) Regulations 2006 (SI 2006 No 137)*]. They have also prescribed lump sum payments arising from the commutation of equivalent pension benefits pursuant to the *Occupational Pension Schemes (Assignment, Forfeiture, Bankruptcy etc) Regulations 1997* (or its Northern Ireland equivalent), payment of state scheme premiums pursuant to *Pension Schemes Act 1993, s 55*, payments of contributions equivalent premiums pursuant to *Pension Schemes Act 1993, s 55(2)* and payments for restoring members' State Scheme rights pursuant to *Pension Schemes Act 1993, 2 Sch 5 (3B) (b)* (or their Northern Ireland equivalents) [*Registered Pension Schemes (Authorised Payments) Regulations 2006 (SI 2006 No 209)*]. They have also added a payment that satisfies *articles 39(1), 41(1) or 42(1)* of the *Taxation of Pension Schemes (Transitional Provisions) Order 2006 (SI 2006, No 572)* (see **10.70**) [*Registered Pension Schemes (Authorised Member Payments) (No 2) Regulations 2006 (SI 2006 No 571)*]. An amount paid to a member representing accrued arrears of pensions and which constitutes taxable income under *ITEPA 2003, s 579B* is an authorised payment except to the extent, if any, that it exceeds the amount accrued during the period from the earliest date that the member could have required the scheme administrator to make a payment of arrears of pensions under the scheme to the date on which he became entitled to the pension [*Registered Pension Schemes (Authorised Payments – Arrears of Pension) Regulations 2006 (SI 2006 No 614)*]. From 7 January 2008 a payment made as part of a scheme which makes a reattribution of the inherited estate of a person who carries on with-profits insurance business and which is made or sanctioned by the court, which is made to or in respect of the scheme's with-profits policy-holders in exchange for giving up rights over the inherited estate and which does not reduce the total value of the pension scheme's asset is an authorised member payment. [*Registered Pension Schemes (Authorised Member Payments) Regulations 2007 (SI 2007 No 3532)*].

(*h*) The transitional rules (see **10.62**) modify some of the above to authorise some extra payments under pre 6 April 2006 schemes.

Unauthorised member payments

10.20 An unauthorised member payment is any other payment by the scheme to a member. In addition the following transactions are deemed to give rise to an unauthorised member payment.

(*a*) If the member assigns or agrees to assign any of his pension benefits to a third party. The amount of the deemed payment is the consideration for the assignment (or the arm's length consideration if the assignment is not at arm's length). Where a charge is triggered under this section the subsequent actual pension payments are not themselves unauthorised payments. Where an annuity is payable for the balance of a ten-year period after the pensioner's death the continuing pension payments are not caught by this rule. [*FA 2004, s 172*]. If a person surrenders any such rights the pension scheme is treated as making an unauthorised payment to him equal to the consideration that he might be expected to receive if the rights surrendered has been assigned between parties acting at arm's length [*FA 2004, s 172A* inserted by *Finance Act 2005 (FA 2005), s 101*]. Similarly the pension scheme is treated as making an unauthorised payment if after the death of a member there is an increase in the rights of another member of the scheme which is attributable to the death, and the two are connected [*FA 2004, s 172B* inserted by *FA 2005, s 101*]. This is designed to thwart schemes under which a member does not draw a pension but attempts to use the pension scheme to pass the value of his contributions tax free to his children. A similar rule applies if a member surrenders or agrees to surrender any benefit or right under the scheme [*FA 2004, s 172A* inserted by *FA 2005, Sch 10, para 38*]. The detailed rules are supplemented by the *Registered Pension Schemes (Surrender of Relevant Excess) Regulations 2006 (SI 2006 No 211)*.

(*b*) A benefit-in-kind provided out of the assets of the scheme (unless it is already taxable as employment income or would have been but for the employee earning less than £8,500 pa). The amount of the unauthorised payment is normally the benefit that would arise under the employment income benefit code rules. However, HMRC have power by regulation to specify a different amount. [*FA 2004, s 173*]. They have done so in respect of co-ownership of residential property. The benefit to the employee is calculated in the same way as an employment benefit (see **8.1**). The benefit must be calculated on the property as a whole and apportioned amongst the co-owners. The pension scheme's share is taxed on the member as an unauthorised payment. If the accommodation is used by more than one member the pension scheme's share is apportioned amongst them [*Registered Pension Schemes (Co-Ownership of Living Accommodation) Regulations 2006 (SI 2006 No 133)*]. Because a benefit will give rise to an unauthorised payment the previous rules which limited the assets in which a scheme can invest to prevent a risk of a benefit arising are longer needed although there are anti-avoidance rules to prohibit some types of investment).

(*c*)   An event that creates a shift in value from an asset owned by the pension scheme to one owned by the member. The amount of the deemed payment is the amount by which the value of the pension scheme asset is reduced (or is reduced by more than would have occurred had the transaction been an arm's length one). [*FA 2004, s 174*].

(*d*)   An increase in the pension rights of a member (the transferee member) which is attributable to the death of another member where the two were connected persons immediately before the death; the rights of the deceased member included rights to benefits to which he (or a dependant) had a prospective entitlement or rights representing his unsecured pension fund, alternatively secured pension fund, dependant's unsecured pension fund or dependant's alternatively secured pension fund; and the consideration which might be expected to be received in respect of an assignment of his benefits by the transferee member immediately after the increase in the value of the pension rights exceeds the sum that might be expected to be received in respect of an assignment immediately before that time in consequence of the death. The scheme is treated as making an unauthorised payment to the transferee member equal to the increase in such consideration (but excluding any part of the excess that arises from the payment of a transfer lump sum death benefit (within *FA 2004, Sch 29, para 19*)) in respect of the deceased member from the transferee member becoming entitled to pension death benefit or lump sum death benefit in respect of the deceased member, or from something arising in a way prescribed by regulation by HMRC [*FA 2004, s 172B* inserted by *FA 2005, Sch 10, 38*]. *Section 172B* does not apply if at the time of the increase there are at least 20 members of the scheme and their benefits are all increased rateably or if the increase in pension rights of the transferee member is brought about by an assignment or agreement to assign within *s 172* [*FA 2004, s 172B (7), (8)*].

(*e*)   The allocation to a member of unallocated contributions in excess of the 'permitted maximum'. This occurs where contributions are paid to a scheme by an employer otherwise than in respect of an individual, at a later date any of these contributions come to be held for the benefit of an individual under a money purchase or hybrid arrangement, and the member and the employer (or the member and a connected person of the employer) are connected persons at any time during the tax year in which the allocation is made. The permitted maximum is the maximum amount of relief to which the member is entitled for contributions during the tax year (less contributions paid by the employer in that year). Where the individual is a member of more than one scheme this figure is divided by the number of such schemes. The unauthorised payment is of course the amount of the excess [*FA 2004, s 172C* inserted by *FA 2005, Sch 10, para 38*].

(*f*)   If the pension input amount for the pension input period in respect of a defined benefit, cash balance or hybrid arrangement relating to a member of an occupational pension scheme exceeds the notional unconnected pension input amount for that period, and at some time during that period the member and a sponsoring employer (or person connected with a sponsoring employer) are connected persons. The amount of the unauthorised payment to the member is the amount of the excess. The notional unconnected pension input amount is what the input amount under *ss 230–237* would have been if the member had not been connected with the employer (or connected person) at any time during the input period. [*FA 2004, s 172D* inserted by *FA 2005, Sch 10, para 38*].

(*g*)   Payments that would have been authorised payments but for a breach of the relevant qualifying conditions. [*FA 2004, s 164*].

(*h*)   From 1 November 2008 where one annuity is replaced by another because the funds are transferred to a different insurance company, the two are treated as being the same annuity for the purpose of *FA 2004, Sch 28, para 17(3)* (see **10.52**). However if the rights are simply surrendered, the pension scheme is treated as making an unauthorised payment in respect of the member [*Registered Pension Schemes (Regulation 10* of the *Transfer of Sums and Asset) Regulations 2006 (SI 2006 No 499)* as amended by the *Registered Pension Schemes (Transfer of Sums and Assets) (Amendment) Regulations 2008 (SI 2008 No 1946)*].

Authorised employer payments

10.21   The authorised employer payments are:

(*a*)   Public service scheme payments (which can only apply to a public service pension scheme). [*FA 2004, ss 175, 176*].

(*b*)   Authorised surplus payments. HMRC have power by regulation to permit (or presumably compel) a surplus to be repaid to the company – such a payment will however attract tax at 35 per cent payable by the scheme administrator (see **10.38**). [*FA 2004, ss 175, 177*]. They have so designated a payment made in compliance with *Pensions Act 1995 ss 37* (payment of surplus to employer) or *76* (excess assets on winding up); a payment to a sponsoring employer solely in respect of the death of a member where the member was not connected with the sponsoring employer at the date of his death and, in the case of an alternatively secured pension, the scheme administrator has been unable to identify any dependants of the deceased member; and any other payment to a sponsoring employer where the rules of the scheme permit the payment to be made, they contain a limit on the maximum benefits which can be paid to (or in respect of) a member (other than by reference to the size of the member's fund), if the scheme is being wound up the scheme liabilities have been fully discharged (and if it is not the requirement of *s 37* would have been satisfied had it applied), and, if the payment is solely in respect of the death of a member, the member was not connected to the sponsoring employer at the date of his death (and in the case of an alternatively secured pension the administrator has not been able to identify any dependants) [*Registered Pension Schemes (Authorised Surplus Payments) Regulations 2006 (SI 2006 No 574)*].

(c)   Compensation payments, ie a payment by the pension scheme to the employer to compensate the employer in respect of the member's liability for a criminal, fraudulent or negligent act or omission against the employer. [*FA 2004, ss 173, 178*]. Such a payment gives rise to a benefit to the employee of relieving him of the liability, so is of course taxable on the employee as an unauthorised member's payment.

(d)   Authorised employer loans. The pension fund will be able to lend up to 50 per cent of the value of its assets to the employer. Such a loan must be secured by a first charge on assets of adequate value (ie to cover the loan plus interest), the loan must carry interest at least equal to a rate to be prescribed by regulation, the loan must be repayable within five years and must be repayable by equal annual instalments over its term. The prescribed rate is one percentage point over the average of the base lending rates of the major clearing banks [*Registered Pension Schemes (Prescribed Interest Rates for Authorised Employer Loans) Regulations 2005 (SI 2005 No 3449)*]. If any of these conditions are breached the breach will give rise to an unauthorised employer payment equal to the amount or value of the breach. If the company is unable to make loan repayments the repayments can be deferred for up to a further five years from the 5th anniversary of the loan. If the amount is still not repaid after ten years the outstanding amount becomes taxable as an unauthorised employer payment. [*FA 2004, ss 175, 179* and *Sch 30*]. A borrowing in excess of the authorised limit creates a deemed scheme chargeable payment (see **10.44**).

(e)   Scheme administration employer payments, ie a payment to the employer to cover the arm's length cost of administering the scheme. [*FA 2004, ss 175, 180*].

(f)   HMRC have power by regulation to prescribe other types of payment. [*FA 2004, s 175*].

Unauthorised employer payments

10.22   Any other payment to the employer is an unauthorised payment. Value shifting transactions (ie which move value from an asset held by the scheme to one held by the employer) are also deemed to give rise to unauthorised employer payments. [*FA 2004, s 181*].

Interpretation

10.23   For the purpose of *ss 160–185* a payment includes any transfer of assets or of money's worth. [*FA 2004, s 161(2)*]. A payment or benefit provided out of assets acquired for the purpose of a registered pension scheme is deemed to be provided from funds held for such a purpose even after the scheme has been wound up. [*FA 2004, s 161(3), (4)*]. A payment to (or in respect of) a person connected (within *ICTA 1988, s 839*) with a member or sponsoring employer (or who was connected with the member at the date of the member's death), and who is not himself a member or sponsoring employer, must be treated as made in respect of the member or sponsoring employer. [*FA 2004, s 161(8)*]. An asset held by a person connected with a member or sponsoring employer (or the increase in value of such an asset or the reduction in a liability of such a person) is treated as held for the benefit of the member or sponsoring employer. [*FA 2004, s 161(6), (7)*].

10.24   The purchase of (or subscription for) debentures, debenture stock, loan stock, bonds, certificates of deposit or other instruments creating or acknowledging indebtedness which are listed or dealt in on a recognised stock exchange or are offered to the public does not constitute a loan for the purpose of those sections. [*FA 2004, s 162(2)*]. A guarantee of a loan made to (or in respect of) a member or sponsoring employer (or a person connected with such a person) is treated as a loan to (or in respect of) the member or sponsoring employer of an amount equal to the sum guaranteed. [*FA 2004, s 162(3)*]. If a member or sponsoring employer (or connected person) is liable to pay a debt to the pension scheme but is not required to pay it by the date on which a person at arm's length from the pension scheme might be expected to be required to pay it, the debt must be treated as a loan by the pension scheme to the member or sponsoring employer. [*FA 2004, s 162(4), (5)*]. A registered pension scheme is treated as borrowing money if the amount borrowed is repayable out of pension scheme assets. A liability that is to be met out of such assets is regarded as a liability of the pension scheme. [*FA 2004, s 163(2), (3)*]. Borrowing by a pension scheme is in respect of a particular arrangement under the scheme if it is properly attributable to that arrangement in accordance with the provisions of the pension scheme and any just and reasonable apportionment. [*FA 2004, s 163(4)*].

The tax position of the pension scheme

10.25   As under the previous regime, a registered pension scheme is exempt from tax on its investment income and underwriting income (but not on investment income held as a member of a property investment LLP). It is similarly exempt from capital gains tax on assets generating such income. [*FA 2004, ss 186, 187*].

10.26   A registered pension scheme cannot borrow more than 50 per cent of the value of the fund at the time of the borrowing in relation to a money purchase arrangement [*FA 2004, s 182*]. *Section 182* contains detailed rules for arriving at the value of the fund. If it exceeds this limit the scheme is treated as making a scheme chargeable payment equal to the excess [*FA 2004, s 183*]. The 50 per cent limit also applies to non-money purchase arrangements but the rules for calculating the value of the fund and the chargeable payment are obviously different. [*FA 2004, ss 184, 185*].

Contributions

10.27   Contributions by a member, or by a third party on behalf of the member, to the pension scheme attract tax relief in the year of payment to the extent that they do not exceed the limits at **10.3**(*c*). [*FA 2004, s 188*]. The individual must have UK earnings chargeable to income tax, be UK resident, have been UK resident (and a member of the pension scheme) at some time during the previous five tax years, or have general earnings from overseas Crown employment subject to UK tax [*FA 2004, s 189*]. No relief is given to the individual for contributions after age 75, for contributions by his employer or by HMRC under the *Pension Schemes Act 1993* (which cease at 5 April 2015) or from 6 April 2007 for life assurance premium contributions (see **10.28**). A pension credit (ie a transfer on divorce, etc) attracts relief only if it derives from a scheme that is not a registered pension scheme [*FA 2004, s 188* as amended by *Finance Act 2007 (FA 2007), Sch 18, para 2*]. From 1 September 2014, no relief is given if the contribution results from the transfer of property or money towards the pension scheme pursuant to an order under the *Pensions Act 2004, ss 16(1), 19(4)* or *21(2)(a)* (orders for money etc to be restored to pension schemes) or their Northern Irish equivalent (except to the extent that the contribution is greater than the amount of the unauthorised member payment) [*FA 2004, s 188(3A)-(3C)* inserted by *FA 2014, Sch 5, para 13*]. The Pensions Act 2004 gives the Pensions Regulator power to ask the court to make an order for restitution to the member. It was not felt appropriate to also give the member the relief for such a payment. Relief at the basic rate is given by deduction at source (except for a net scheme where it is given in full at source and a former retirement annuity scheme where payments can continue to be made gross). [*FA 2004, ss 192, 193*]. HMRC have power by regulation to attach conditions to the deduction and to regulate it [*FA 2004, s 192(7), (8)*]. They have done so by the *Registered Pension Schemes (Relief at Source) Regulations 2005 (SI 2005 No 3448)*. These require the individual (or the scheme employer if the pension scheme is connected with a specific employer) to provide specified information (name, address, date of birth, NI number and status (employed, pensioner, self-employed, child or other) to the scheme administrator before payment of the first net contribution. The scheme administrator can of course recover the tax deducted from HMRC [*FA 2004, s 192(3)(a)*]. The regulations provide for an annual repayment claim but also allow monthly interim claims.

10.28   Contributions are life assurance premium contributions (not eligible for tax relief) if rights under a non-group life policy (one under which the only benefits are payable in consequence, or in anticipation, of the death of the individual, or of a group of individuals which includes the individual, or of the deaths of more than one of a group of individuals which comprises the individual and persons connected with the individual) are (or later become) held for the purposes of the pension scheme and the contributions are treated as paid in respect of premiums under that policy. [*FA 2004, s 195A(1), (2)* inserted by *FA 2007, Sch18, para 3*]. The section contains detailed rules to determine what contributions are treated as paid in respect of such premiums. [*FA 2004, s 195A(3)–(5)*]. This removes relief for contributions paid by an individual for personal term assurance policies, ie policies that pay out only on the death or mortal illness of the insured person over a specified term, such as the term of a mortgage. [Finance Bill 2007 Explanatory Notes]. However, the wording also seems to exclude relief for premiums for whole of life assurance. HMRC have confirmed that relief is still given to the employer for contributions by the employer to such a policy. [*Budget Note BN18*]. The restriction applies to an occupational registered pension scheme only from 1 August 2007. [*FA 2007, Sch 18, para 6*]. It also does not apply to contributions to policies taken out before 1 August 2007 provided that the application for the policy was made before 14 December 2006, but contributions to such a policy will cease to be deductible if the policy is varied after 5 April 2007 to increase the sum assured or lengthen the term (other than by the exercise of an option in the policy). [*FA 2007, Sch 18, paras 5, 7*].

10.29   An employee can transfer shares acquired under an SAYE scheme or a SIP to the pension fund as contributions to the scheme (ie attracting tax relief) within 90 days of becoming entitled to the shares. [*FA 2004, s 195*].

10.30   Contributions to the scheme by an employer are deductible in calculating its profits. A contribution must be spread forward if it both exceeds 210 per cent of the contributions for the previous year and the excess is itself £500,000 or more. Relief is given only when the contributions are paid; they cannot be deducted on an accruals basis. [*FA 2004, ss 196, 197*]. Where contributions are being spread and the trade ceases the company can elect to spread them on a daily basis over open years up to the date of cessation [*FA 2004, s 198*]. HMRC can by regulation restrict the deduction in certain circumstances [*FA 2004, s 196A* inserted by *FA 2005, Sch 10, para 39*]. Statutory payments to make good a deficit in the scheme assets are also deductible. If the trade has ceased at the time of the payment they are deductible in the last period of trading. [*FA 2004, s 199*].

10.31   No deduction can be claimed for certain asset-backed pension contributions made after 29 November 2011 and a limited deduction only is allowed for others. Asset-backed arrangements are mainly used in defined benefit pension schemes where the cost to the employer of meeting a deficit in the pension scheme cannot be met within a reasonable period out of profits. Typically the employer will contribute to the pension scheme either properties which it leases back or dividend bearing shares in itself. The value of the asset contributed remains fully deductible in most cases, ie where the pension scheme obtains complete ownership of the asset on an irrevocable basis (Finance Bill 2012, Explanatory Notes). The disallowances is targeted at arrangements where the contribution effectively is returned in some way to the employer under the arrangements and the employee makes a series of payments over a period to clear the loan back or for use of the asset sold to the pension scheme. In such circumstances relief will be given when the periodic payments to the pension scheme are made instead of at the time of the initial asset-backed contribution. The legislation is complex and as it is of very limited application, is not considered here. It can be found in *FA 2004, ss 196B–196L* inserted by *FA 2012, Sch 13.*

10.32   Where under *Pension Schemes Act 1993, s 43* HMRC pays minimum contributions for the purpose of a registered pension scheme they must pay that amount grossed up at the basic rate. HMRC can by regulation specify circumstances in which this does not apply or make provisions supplementing the section [*FA 2004, s 202*]. *The Registered Pension Schemes (Minimum Contributions) Regulations 2005 (SI 2005 No 3450)* contain rules for the recovery of amounts that they pay in error. This provision will cease to apply from 6 April 2016 [*FA 2013, s 52(6)(12)*]

Charges to tax

10.33   An unauthorised member payment attracts an unauthorised payment tax charge of 40 per cent. The Treasury have power by regulation to vary this amount. The person liable for the tax is the member or, if the payment is made after his death, the recipient of the payment. If the total value of unauthorised payments in any 12-month period exceeds 25 per cent of the value of the fund there is in addition an unauthorised payment surcharge of 15 per cent. If payments are made to more than one member they are jointly and severally liable for this surcharge. [*FA 2004, ss 204–208*]. The surcharge applies to every payment in the 12-month period. The first 12-month period starts from the making of the first unauthorised member payment. Successive periods start from the first unauthorised member payment outside a 12-month period. If the 25 per cent threshold is reached earlier than 12 months the surcharge period ceases when it is reached. The legislation contains rules for valuing the fund [*FA 2004, ss 209–212*]. Payments in excess of the 25 per cent limit also trigger HMRC's right to de-register the fund. [*FA 2004, s 158(1)(a), (2)*].

10.34   An unauthorised employer payment gives rise to a 40 per cent tax charge on the employer. It also gives rise to the additional 15 per cent surcharge if total unauthorised employer payments in a 12-month period exceed 25 per cent of the fund value. [*FA 2004 s 209*]. The rules are the same as for member payments but member and employer payments are looked at separately to determine whether and when the 25 per cent threshold is reached [*FA 2004, s 213*].

10.35   The payment of a short-service refund lump sum ie a refund of contributions to a member who is not entitled to short service benefit and which extinguishes the member's entitlement to benefit under the scheme (see **10.19**(*c*)(iii)), attracts a tax liability of 20 per cent on the first £10,800 and 40 per cent of any excess. The Treasury have power by statutory instrument to amend these limits. The taxable amount is not treated as income for any tax purposes. The person liable to the charge is the scheme administrator. The charge arises irrespective of the residence and domicile of the recipient. [*FA 2004, s 205* and *Sch 29, para 5*].

10.36   For 2011/12 onwards, a 55% tax charge (the serious ill-health lump sum charge) arises if a serious ill-health lump sum (see **10.19**(*c*)(ii)) is paid to a person over 65. The person liable for the tax is the scheme administrator [*FA 2004, s 205A* inserted by *FA 2011, Sch 16, para 40*].

10.37   A special lump sum death benefit charge of 55 per cent (30 per cent prior to 6 April 2011) is imposed on the scheme administrator if the scheme pays a pension protection lump sum death benefit (a benefit payable on death before 75 which the member has specified is to be treated as such a benefit – which he is allowed to do up to a specified limit), an annuity protection lump sum death benefit (a capital refund under an annuity where the member dies under 75), an unsecured pension fund lump sum death benefit (a capital sum paid on death under 75 in respect of income withdrawal to which the member was entitled under an arrangement at the date of death),or, from 6 April 2011, a defined benefits lump sum death benefit or uncrystallised funds lump sum death benefit where the member was 75 or over at the time of his death [*FA 2004, s 202* and *Sch 29, paras 14, 16, 17* as amended by *FA 2011, Sch 16, para 41*]. The Treasury have power to amend the rate by statutory instrument. The taxable amount is not treated as income for any tax purpose. It is irrelevant where the recipient of the benefit is resident or domiciled [*FA 2004, s 206*]. It is proposed that from 2015/16, the 55% charge will be abolished. Instead where the deceased is over 75, any tax charge will be at the beneficiaries' top rate of income tax. Currently where a person dies under age 75 and has not yet started to draw (or has not otherwise crystallised) his pension, tax is paid at the beneficiaries' marginal rate on a pension for a dependant but there is no tax on the receipt of a lump sum by the dependent. The 55% tax charge applies on the receipt of a lump sum by a beneficiary after the pension has been crystallised or where the person has reached 75 by the time he dies and a lump sum is paid to his dependants. The proposal appears to be that where a person dies under 75, his whole fund can pass to his beneficiaries, either by way of lump sum or pension tax-free. However if he dies after reaching 75, the beneficiaries will be taxed at their marginal income tax rate on both a lump sum and a pension. For 2015/16, only a lump sum will be taxed at a flat rate of 45%.

10.38   An authorised surplus payment charge of 35 per cent arises where an authorised surplus payment (see **10.21**(*b*)) is made to a sponsoring employer (unless the sponsoring employer is a charity or outside the scope of UK tax). The scheme administrator is liable for the charge. The taxable amount is not treated as income for any tax purpose. It is irrelevant where the sponsoring employer is resident or domiciled. The Treasury have power by statutory instrument to amend the rate [*FA 2004, s 207*]. From 20 March 2014, the 35% charge does not apply to the extent that the payment is funded (directly or indirectly) by a surrender of benefits or rights which result in the pension scheme being treated as making an unauthorised payment under *FA 2004, s 172A* (see **10.20**) [*FA 2004, s 207(6A)* inserted by *FA 2014, Sch 5, para 11*].

10.39   If when benefit starts to be paid, or on any other 'benefit crystalisation event', the value of the fund attributable to a member exceeds his lifetime allowance (see **10.3**(*a*)) a lifetime allowance charge arises on the excess. The charge is 55 per cent if the excess is paid to the employee as a lump sum or 25 per cent if it will be paid in the form of pension. A lump sum is defined as so much of the basic amount (ie the excess over the available lifetime allowance) as is paid as a lump sum to the individual (or a lump sum death benefit in respect of the individual) plus any tax paid by the scheme administrator in respect of the payment. If the benefit is paid as a pension the tax charge is on 'the retained amount' ie any part of the basic amount not paid as a lump sum plus any tax paid in respect of it by the scheme administrator. The tax is payable by the member if the excess is paid to him as a lump sum. If it is not the liability is a joint and several liability of the member and the scheme administrator. A benefit crystallisation event may not trigger a charge on the entire surplus (eg where a person is a member of a number of pension schemes and starts to draw from one only). In such a case the charge is of course calculated on a cumulative basis. [*FA 2004, ss 210–216*]. If the scheme administrator is liable to the lifetime allowance charge he can apply to HMRC to be excused from it if he reasonably believed that there was no liability and in all the circumstances of the case it would be just and reasonable to excuse him. [*FA 2004, s 267*]. A similar relief applies to any person liable to the unauthorised payment surcharge or to the scheme administrator in relation to a scheme sanction charge [*FA 2004, s 268*]. *The Registered Pension Scheme (Discharge of Liabilities under Sections 267 and 268 of the Finance Act 2004) Regulations 2005 (SI 2005 No 3452)* sets out the rules for such application. The amount taxed is not treated as income for any tax purpose. It is irrelevant where the recipient of the payment or the member is resident or domiciled [*FA 2004, ss 215, 217*].

10.40 The benefit crystallisation events are:

(*a*) the designation of sums or assets held by a money purchase scheme as available for the payment of unsecured pension to the member,

(*b*) the individual becoming entitled to a scheme pension,

(*c*) an individual who is already in receipt of a scheme pension becoming entitled to an increase of more than the permitted margin,

(*d*) the individual becoming entitled to a lifetime annuity purchased under a money purchase arrangement,

(*e*) the individual reaching the age of 75 (77 if he did so after 21 June 2010) without having started to draw his pension or a lump sum, or, from 6 April 2011, where there is a money purchase arrangements and funds remain in the scheme

(*f*) the individual becoming entitled to a relevant lump sum,

(*g*) a person being paid a relevant lump sum death benefit in respect of the individual,

(*h*) the transfer of sums or assets by the scheme to a qualifying overseas pension scheme in connection with the individual's membership of the transferor scheme

[*FA 2004, s 216* as amended by *F(No 2)A 2010, Sch 3, para 6)* and *FA 2011, Sch 16, para 43*].

10.41 Each time a benefit crystallisation event occurs the assets in the scheme that are attributable to the member have to be compared to the member's lifetime allowance or the unutilised part of it. Where there have been previous benefit crystallisation events the amount utilised on a previous event is enhanced by multiplying it by the current standard lifetime allowance over the standard lifetime allowance at the time of the previous event, so the amount available in effect becomes the proportion of the allowance that was not utilised in earlier events. The payment of a death benefit is treated as occurring immediately before the death. The Treasury have power to fix the standard lifetime allowance. For 2012/13, it is £1,500,000. [*FA 2004, ss 218, 219*]. Where a person has become entitled to a pension credit (ie a transfer on divorce, etc) the pension credit is also enhanced for the purpose of the calculation [*FA 2004, s 220*]. Special rules apply where the individual was not UK resident and employed by a non-resident employer at some time during the period when the pension accrued, or where funds were transferred to the pension scheme from a recognised overseas pension scheme [*FA 2004, ss 221–226*].

10.42   An annual allowance charge arises if the total pension input amount for a tax year for an individual (his total contributions in relation to a money purchase scheme) exceeds the annual allowance for the year. The charge is at the rate found by aggregating the charge with the member's 'reduced net income' (ie taxable income less deductions and personal allowances) and applying the normal income tax rates treating the charge as the highest part of such income. Prior to 6 April 2011, it was 40 per cent of that excess. The funds can remain in the pension scheme though. The total pension input amount is the total increase during the year of the individual's rights under all registered pension schemes. The legislation provides how this is to be arrived at. Broadly speaking, it is the increase in the value of the funds during the year. This is not only the amount of contributions made during the year (except in the case of a money purchase arrangement). It will also include the fund income for the year and the increase in the value of the fund assets for the year whether realised or unrealised. There is no pension input amount if the individual dies or, from 6 April 2011, satisfies the severe ill-health conditions before the end of the tax year [*FA 2004, s 229(3)*]. He satisfies those conditions if either he becomes entitled to all of the benefits to which he is entitled under the scheme in consequence of a certificate from a doctor that he is unlikely to be able to work again, he becomes entitled to a serious ill-health lump sum or he is a member of the armed forces and becomes entitled to a tax-free benefit under *ITEPA 2003, s 641(1)* (see **2.27**) [*FA 2004, s 229(4)*]. The annual allowances are set out at **10.3**(*b*). The amount was reduced substantially from 2011/12 onwards. Contributions that do not qualify for tax relief are ignored in calculating the increase in value [*FA 2004, ss 227–238* as amended by *FA 2011, Sch 17, para 3*]. From 6 April 2011 where a member enters into flexible drawdown arrangements any subsequent pension input amount is subject to the annual allowance charge in full without the benefit of the annual allowance [*FA 2004, s 227A* inserted by *FA 2011, Sch 16, para 45*].

Special rules apply to determine the value of the opening and closing rights in a cash balance arrangement [*FA 2004, ss 230–233* as amended by *FA 2011, Sch 17, paras 7, 8*]. There are also detailed rules to determine such amounts for a deferred benefit arrangement and other types of arrangement [*FA 2004, ss 234–237* as amended by *FA 2011, Sch 17, paras 9–14*].

10.43   From 2011/12 onwards, the annual allowance charge is a liability of the individual, not the scheme administrator, even if the individual is non-UK resident or non-UK domiciled [*FA 2004, s 237A* inserted by *FA 2011, Sch 17, para 15*]. If an individual's liability for a year exceeds £2,000 and his pension scheme input amounts (his aggregate contributions to all schemes, plus the value of employer contributions) exceeds his annual allowance, he can serve a notice on the scheme administrator specifying that both he and the administrator are jointly liable to the charge (or to so much of it as is specified in the notice) [*FA 2004, s 237B(1)–(4)*]. Such a notice must be given by 31 July following the end of the tax year and must be in such form as may be specified by HMRC [*FA 2004, s 237B(5)*]. Although at first sight this might look odd, the purpose is to enable the scheme administrator to pay the charge out of the scheme assets without that payment being an unauthorised distribution. Such an election cannot be made if the scheme has entered the assessment period for the Pension Protection Fund [*FA 2004, s 237C*]. If the scheme administrator considers that paying the charge would be to the substantial detriment of scheme members and that in all the circumstances of the case it would not be just and reasonable for the scheme to pay the tax, he can apply to HMRC to exclude him from liability – so that the sole liability falls back onto the member [*FA 2004, s 237D*]. HMRC have power to modify the rules of a pension scheme to enable it to make such payments [*FA 2004, s 237F*]. They also have power to amend the annual allowances charge [*FA 2004, s 238A* inserted by *FA 2011, Sch 17, para 17*].

10.44 A scheme sanction charge of 40 per cent applies where the scheme makes a scheme chargeable payment. This is an unauthorised payment other than the exceptions set out below or an unauthorised borrowing (see **10.26**). If the payment has already attracted an unauthorised payment charge on either the member or the employer (see **10.33** and **10.34**) the charge is reduced by the lower of the tax paid or 25 per cent of the scheme chargeable payment. The charge does not arise on an unauthorised payment that is a benefit in kind (provided that the asset used to provide it is not a wasting asset), a compensation payment within *FA 2004, s 178* (see **10.21**(*c*)), a payment by or in anticipation of a court order on a divorce, or a payment of a type prescribed by HMRC by regulation [*FA 2004, s 241(2)*]. The charge is a liability of the scheme administrator. [*FA 2004, ss 239–241*]. HMRC have prescribed an unauthorised member payment made in exercise of the discretion conferred by *Reg 3(1)* of the *Registered Pension Schemes (Modification of the Rules of Existing Schemes) Regulation 2006 (SI 2006 No 364)* or which would be so made if those regulations applied to the scheme, if it is a payment of a type prescribed under *section 241(2)* and is referable to subsisting rights which accrued under defined benefit arrangements before 1 April 2006 [*Registered Pension Schemes (Unauthorised Payments by Existing Schemes) Regulations 2006 (SI 2006 No 365)*].

10.45 It should be noted that, apart from benefits, etc, the effective tax on unauthorised payments is 55 per cent (ie a 40 per cent unauthorised payment charge plus 15 per cent (after deduction for the unauthorised payment charge) – scheme sanction charge) plus a further 15 per cent unauthorised payment surcharge if the payment is over 25 per cent of the scheme assets.

10.46 Where, as will normally be the case, the scheme chargeable payment is or includes an unauthorised payment that has attracted un unauthorised payment charge under *FA 2004, s 208* and that tax has been paid, a credit can be claimed against the scheme sanction charge of the lower of 25 per cent of the scheme chargeable payment or the tax paid under *s 208* [*FA 2004, s 240(2)–(4)*]. The person liable for the tax is the scheme administrator. It is irrelevant whether the scheme administrator is UK resident or domiciled [*FA 2004, s 239(2)–(4)*].

10.47 A deregistration charge of 40 per cent of the assets of the scheme arises where the registration of a pension scheme is withdrawn. The person liable for the charge is the scheme administrator. It is irrelevant whether the administrator is UK resident or domiciled [*FA 2004, s 242*].

10.48 *FA 2010, Sch 2*, introduced a new 'high income' excess relief charge which was designed to claw back relief where the employee's income exceeded £150,000. This was intended to apply from 2011/12 onwards. However the incoming government repealed the charge by *F(No 2)A 2010, s 5* and the *High Income Excess Relief Charge (Repeal) Order 2010 (SI 2010 No 2938)* before it took effect.

Inheritance tax

10.49 A contribution under a registered pension scheme in respect of the member making the contribution is not a transfer of value for inheritance tax purposes [*Inheritance Tax Act 1984 (IHTA 1984), s 12* as amended by *FA 2004, s 203(1)*]. From 6 April 2011 if a member of a registered pension scheme, a qualifying non-UK pension scheme or an *ITEPA 2003, s 615(3)* scheme (certain overseas government pensions) omits to exercise pension rights under the scheme, the omission to exercise the right is not a transfer of value [*IHTA 1984, s 12(2ZA)* inserted by *FA 2011, Sch 16, para 47*]. An interest in a registered pension scheme and in certain pension schemes for non-residents which comes to an end on the death of the person entitled to it is not part of the deceased's estate (unless the right results from the application of a benefit provided under the scheme which is not a pension or annuity). [*IHTA 1984, s 151* as amended by *FA 2004, s 203(4)*]. Pension funds are excluded from the IHT rules on trusts [*IHTA 1984, s 58* as amended by *FA 2004, s 203(3)*].

10.50 Up to 5 April 2011 if a person under 75 omitted to exercise rights under the pension scheme (including an omission to do so before 6 April 2006) and he would have made a disposition under *IHTA 1984, s 3* but for *IHTA 1984, s 10* preventing it being a transfer of value, that omission was not a transfer of value (unless that person made an actual disposition of pension rights under the pension scheme (which was not exempted by *s 10*) within the two years prior to his death and it could not be shown that when he made that actual disposition he had no reason to believe that he would die within the following two years) [*IHTA 1984, s 12(2A)–(2C)* inserted by *FA 2006, Sch 22, paras 3, 12*]. For example, if a person under 75 deferred his pension at a time when he was in good health and subsequently (after two years) his health deteriorated but he continued to defer his pension, there was no disposition. In contrast, if when he deferred it he expected to die within the next two years the omission to take the pension was a taxable disposition. Even then there was an exemption to the extent that the disposition resulted in the provision of a lump sum death benefit (see **10.19**(*b*)), a pension death benefit (see **10.19**(*a*)) or both, to his spouse, civil partner or someone who was financially dependent on him at the time of his death, or in the making of a payment to charity [*IHTA 1984, s 12(2D)*]. The person liable to the tax was the scheme administrator of the pension scheme [*IHTA 1984, 200(1A)* inserted by *FA 2006, Sch 22, para 5*].

10.51   A disposition by a member of a pension scheme aged 75 or over was not a transfer of value if it consisted in his making an actual pension disposition under the scheme (ie he positively did something in relation to rights under the scheme which reduced the value of his estate) or in omitting to exercise pension rights under the scheme (ie he did not become entitled to the whole or part of a pension or lump sum or both under the scheme at a time when he was eligible to become entitled to the whole or part of a pension or lump sum or both under the scheme) [*IHTA 1984, s 12(2E)–(2G)*]. It is not wholly clear what this was trying to do. The intention was to impose an IHT charge on death where a person forbore from taking his pension. It may be based on the assumption that a person over 75 would be in receipt of an annuity, so omitting to exercise rights or passing part of his pension to his spouse would not normally result in a benefit to anyone other than the member or his spouse. These provisions were repealed by *FA 2011, Sch 16, para 47(3)*.

10.52   Up to 5 April 2011, where immediately before his death a member of a registered pension scheme had an alternatively secured pension (see **10.19**(*a*)) in respect of an arrangement under the scheme, he was treated for IHT purposes as being beneficially entitled to the assets forming part of his alternatively secured pension fund immediately before his death less the value of those assets which were expended on dependant's benefits within six months of the end of the month in which he died. Assets were so expended at any time if at that time they (or sums or assets directly or indirectly deriving from them) were applied either towards the provision of a dependant's scheme pension (see *FA 2004, Sch 28, para 16*) for the person's spouse, civil partner or a person who was financially dependent on that person; applied towards the provision of a dependant's annuity (see *FA 2004, Sch 28, para 17*) for such a person; designated as available for the payment of a dependant's unsecured pension (see *FA 2004, Sch 28, para 18*) for such a person; designated as available for the payment of a dependant's alternatively secured pension (see *FA 2004, Sch 28, para 19*) for such a person; or paid as a lump sum death benefit to a charity [*IHTA 1984, s 151A* inserted by *FA 2006, Sch 22, para 4*].

10.53   Where following the death of a member over 75 pension scheme assets were used to provide dependant's benefits within the six-month period and the dependant either died or ceased to be a dependant, a tax charge arose at that time on the value of the assets in the fund at the time of the dependant's death or ceasing to be a member (unless, in the case of death, the assets were paid to a charity within six months of the death). The rate of tax was determined by adding the taxable amount to the estate of the deceased member and treating it as the top slice of that estate (but using the rate tables at the time of the dependant's death) [*IHTA 1984, s 151B* and *Sch 2, para 6A* inserted by *FA 2006, Sch 22, para 11*]. The person liable for the tax was the scheme administrator of the pension scheme [*IHTA 1984, s 200(1A)*].

10.54 If *IHTA 1984, s 151B* did not apply on the death of a dependant of a deceased member of a registered pension scheme who was in receipt of a dependant's alternatively secured pension (such as where the scheme member died before age 75 and the dependant took an unsecured pension, which would have become an alternatively secured pension when the dependant reached 75 – see **10.19**(*a*)) the dependant's estate at the date of death was treated as including the assets in the pension fund (less any part paid to charity within six months of the death) [*IHTA 1984, s 151C*]. *IHTA 1984, ss 151A–151E* were repealed by *FA 2011, Sch 16, para 48* following the abolition of the rules as alternatively secured pensions from 6 April 2011.

Non-UK schemes

10.55 The unauthorised payments charge, unauthorised payments surcharge, short service refund lump sum charge, the special lump sum death benefit charge and the trivial commutation and winding-up lump sums and lump sum death benefit charges under *ITEPA 2003, s 636B* and *636C* apply to payments by a relevant non-UK scheme to (or in respect of) a relieved member of a relevant UK scheme (ie one who has obtained UK tax relief for any contributions to the scheme) or a transfer member of such a scheme (ie where funds in relation to the member were transferred to the scheme from either a registered pension scheme or another relevant non-UK scheme). A relevant non-UK scheme is one where relief from tax on contributions has been given under *FA 2004, Sch 33*, or relief has been given after 5 April 2006 under a double taxation agreement, a member has been relieved from tax on a benefit in kind under *ITEPA 2003, s 307* in respect of contributions to the scheme, or if there has been a transfer to the scheme from a registered pension scheme or another relevant non-UK scheme after 5 April 2006 [*FA 2004, Sch 34, para 1*]. The annual allowance charge and lifetime allowance charge also apply to a relevant non-UK scheme. The detailed provisions are set out in *Sch 34*. The amendments to the rules to adapt them to non-UK schemes are contained in the *Pension Schemes (Application of UK Provisions to Relevant Non-UK Schemes) Regulations 2006 (SI 2006 No 207)* as amended by the *Pension Schemes (Application of UK Provisions to Relevant Non-UK Schemes) (Amendment) Regulations 2009 (SI 2009 No 2047)*.

10.56 An individual who is a 'relevant migrant member' of a qualifying overseas pension scheme is entitled to relief under *section 188* (see **10.27**) in respect of contributions to the scheme if he has UK taxable earnings for that year, is UK resident when the contribution is paid and has notified the scheme manager that he intends to claim the relief. The contributions are of course paid gross [*FA 2004, Sch 33, para 1*]. The employer can obtain relief for contributions it makes too [*FA 2004, 33 Sch 2*]. Such contributions are not taxed as a benefit in kind [*ITEPA 2003, s 308A* inserted by *FA 2004, Sch 33, para 3*]. A relevant migrant member is an individual who is a member of an overseas pension scheme in relation to contributions and who was not UK resident when he first joined the scheme, was a member of the scheme when he became UK resident, immediately before becoming UK resident was entitled to tax relief for his contributions under the law of the place he was resident (or meets such alternative test as HMRC may prescribe) and has been notified by the scheme manager that information concerning benefit crystallisation events in relation to the individual and the pension scheme will be given to HMRC [*FA 2004, Sch 33, para 4*]. HMRC have prescribed an alternative test that the individual was entitled to tax relief for contributions to the pension scheme under the law of the place where he was then resident at some time in the ten years before he became UK resident [*Pension Scheme (Relevant Migrant Members) Regulations 2006 (SI 2006 No 212)*]. They have specified the required information by the *Pension Schemes (Information Requirements – Qualifying Overseas Pension Schemes, Qualifying Recognised Overseas Pension Schemes and Corresponding Relief) Regulations 2006 (SI 2006 No 208)*.

10.57   An overseas pension scheme is a pension scheme (other than a registered pension scheme) which is established in a country or territory outside the UK and satisfies any requirements prescribed by regulation by HMRC [*FA 2004, s 150(7)*]. They have prescribed that it must either:

(*a*)   be an occupational pension scheme which is regulated by a regulator of occupational pension schemes in its own country and be recognised for tax purposes under the tax legislation of the country in which it is established;

(*b*)   be a regulated pension scheme other than an occupational pension scheme in its own country and be recognised for tax purposes under the tax legislation of the country in which it is established;

(*c*)   be established in another EU country or in Norway, Iceland or Liechtenstein and the scheme rules provide that at least 70 per cent of a member's UK tax-relieved scheme funds will be designated for the purpose of providing the individual with a pension for life and the pension benefits payable to the member under that scheme (and any lump sum associated with those benefits) are not payable before the member reaches normal minimum retirement age (see **10.19**(*a*) or becomes entitled to a pension earlier because of ill health (within *FA 2004, Sch 28, para 1*) and be recognised for tax purposes under the tax legislation of the country in which it is established; or

(*d*)   be established by an international organisation for the purpose of providing benefit for its employees and the benefits from which meet the conditions in (*c*).

For this purpose a scheme is recognised for tax purposes under the legislation of the country in which it is established only if it is open to persons resident in the country or territory in which it is established; in that country there is a system of personal income taxation under which either tax relief is available in respect of pensions and that system does not allow relief for contributions made by the individual in question or his employer or all or most of the benefits paid by the scheme to members who are not in serious ill-health are taxable or, from 1 July 2007, the scheme is liable to taxation on its income and gains and is an Australian complying superannuation plan; and the scheme is approved or recognised by (or registered with) the tax authorities in its home country as a pension scheme (or if there is no system of such approval, recognition or registration it is resident in its home country and the benefits meet the conditions in (*c*) above. [*Pension Schemes (Categories of Country and Requirements for Overseas Pension Schemes and Recognised Overseas Pension Schemes) Regulations 2006 (SI 2006 No 206), Reg 2* and the *Pension Schemes (Categories of Country and Requirement for Overseas Pension Schemes and Recognised Overseas Pension Schemes) (Amendment) Regulations 2007 (SI 2007 No 1600)*]. The ECJ in *EC Commission v Kingdom of Denmark [2007] STC 38)* held that Denmark was in breach of EC law in limiting tax relief to pension schemes established in Denmark. Accordingly the UK might also be in breach of EC law to the extent that the above conditions may prove more onerous than those applicable to UK schemes.

10.58   An overseas pension scheme is also a recognised scheme if it meets the above conditions; is established in another EU country, Iceland, Liechtenstein or Norway or a country with which the UK has a double tax treaty containing an exchange of information and a non-discrimination provision; at the time of any transfer of sums which would constitute a recognised transfer (see **10.19**(*d*)), the rules of the scheme provide that at least 70 per cent of the sums transferred will be designated by the scheme manager for the purpose of providing the member with an income for life; the pension benefits (and any associated lump sum) payable to the member (to the extent that they relate to the transfer) are not payable before the member reaches normal minimum retirement age (or retires because of ill-health within *FA 2004, Sch 28, para 1*); the scheme is open to persons resident in the country or territory in which it is established and the scheme rules met the enhanced information requirements imposed by *FA 2013, s 53(1)* [*FA 2004, s 150(8)* as amended by *FA 2013, s 53* and the above *Regulations, Reg 3*].

Qualified Overseas Pensions Schemes (QROPS)

10.59   A scheme is a qualifying overseas pension scheme for the purpose of **10.40** above if:

(*a*)   the scheme manager has notified HMRC that it is an overseas pension scheme and has provided to HMRC such information as they may require;

(*b*)   the scheme manager has undertaken to HMRC to inform them if it ceases to be an overseas pension scheme;

(*c*)   the scheme manager has undertaken to HMRC to comply with any prescribed benefit crystallisation information requirements imposed on the scheme manager – these are prescribed by the *Pension Schemes (Information Requirements – Qualifying Overseas Pension Scheme, Qualifying Recognised Overseas Pensions Schemes and Corresponding Relief) Regulations 2006 (SI 2006 No 208)*; and

(*d*)   the overseas pension scheme is not excluded from being a qualifying overseas scheme because HMRC has decided that there has been a failure to comply with information requirements and because of this it is not appropriate to grant tax relief (there is a right of appeal against such a decision, and HMRC have power themselves to decide that the pension scheme should cease to be excluded).

[*FA 2004, Sch 33, para 5*]. HMRC also have power to exclude a recognised overseas pension scheme from being a qualifying scheme if they decide that there has been a failure to comply with any information requirement imposed on the scheme manager and they notify the person who they believe to be the scheme manager of that decision [*FA 2004, s 169(5), (7)*]. There is a right of appeal against such a decision [*FA 2004, s 170*].

10.60   HMRC publish a list of recognised QROPS on their website. In January 2008, HMRC removed a number of Singapore QROPS from that list with retrospective effect to 6 April 2006 on the basis that the schemes did not satisfy the requirement of the Regulations (see **10.57**) and were thus not eligible to be an 'overseas pension scheme'. This created consternation amongst taxpayers who had transferred funds in UK registered schemes to a Singapore QROPS in reliance on the HMRC website, and as a result of the retrospective withdrawal, were facing heavy tax charges as the transfer of the funds was therefore an unauthorised member payment, not the authorised one that everyone had believed at the time of the transfer. One of the Singapore trustees, Equity Trust (Singapore) Ltd, challenged HMRC's view that one of its pension schemes (ROSIIP) was not eligible for registration either because it was not open to residents of Singapore or because Singapore did not have a system that granted tax relief on contributions to ROSIIP, both of which are fundamental requirements (see **10.57**). The case, *TMF Trustees Singapore Ltd (formerly Equity Trust (Singapore) Ltd) v HMRC*, has reached the Court of Appeal (*[2012] EWCA Civ 192*). HMRC have won at all stages. It is understood that TMF Trustees (Singapore) Ltd sought judicial review of HMRC's conduct of the case and the court indicated that it would severely criticise HMRC's conduct unless HMRC conceded that taxpayers who had relied on the HMRC website listing had been entitled to do so.

10.61   HMRC has also warned the Guernsey government that Guernsey QROPS – a new innovation – cannot accept pension transfers from the UK unless they are for residents of the Channel Islands.

10.61A   *FA 2013, ss 53, 54* significantly increased HMRC's information and inspection powers in relation to QROPs.

Transitional

10.62   An approved pension scheme, statutory pension scheme, retirement annuity or personal pension scheme set up before 6 April 2006 automatically became a registered pension scheme from that date unless it notified HMRC before that date that it wished to opt out. As opting out triggered a 40 per cent tax charge on the scheme assets at 6 April 2006 it is unlikely that many schemes opted out. [*FA 2004, Sch 36, para 1*]. HMRC had power by regulation to modify the rules of such pension schemes from 6 April 2006 to fit them into the new regime. [*FA 2004, Sch 36, para 3*]. They did so by the *Registered Pension Schemes (Modification of the Rules of Existing Schemes) Regulations 2006 (SI 2006 No 364)* and *Reg 6* of the *Registered Pension Schemes (Surrender of Relevant Excess) Regulations 2006 (SI 2006 No 211)*. These changes did not however prevent HMRC from withdrawing approval of the scheme under *ICTA 1988, ss 591C, 591D, 650A* or *651* from a date prior to 6 April 2006. [*FA 2004, Sch 36, para 5*]. The timescale for the application of the modification regulations has now expired.

10.63   If the value of a scheme member's pension rights at 6 April 2006 exceeded £1,500,000 he could claim an enhanced lifetime allowance. [*FA 2004, Sch 36, para 7*]. The claim had to be made in the prescribed form by 5 April 2009 [*Reg 3, Registered Pension Schemes (Enhanced Lifetime Allowance) Regulations 2006 (SI 2006 No 131)*]. The individual's lifetime allowance then became the value of his rights at 6 April 2006 or, from 6 April 2012, if greater, £1,800,000. The detailed rules are contained in *FA 2004, Sch 36, paras 7–20* as amended by *FA 2011, Sch 18, para 10*, the above Regulations, the *Registered Pension Schemes (Uprating Percentage for Defined Benefits Arrangements and Enhanced Protection Limits) Regulations 2006 (SI 2006 No 130)*, the *Registered Pension Schemes (Surrender of Relevant Excess) Regulations 2006 (SI 2006 No 211)*, the *Registered Pension Schemes (Provision of Information) Regulations 2006 (SI 2006 No 567* and the *Registered Pension Schemes (Provision of Information) (Amendment) Regulations 2008 (SI 2008 No 720)*. Where such a claim has been made the annual allowance charge also does not apply to the member. [*FA 2004, Sch 36, para 49*]. This allows the member to retain his then existing pension rights (including rights to a lump sum) but he and his employer cannot be able to make further contributions to the scheme. HMRC are empowered to make regulations regarding the enhanced lifetime allowance. [*FA 2004, s 256*]. Similar rules apply to the reduction in the lifetime allowance from 2012/13 and 2014/15 [*FA 2013, s 47* and *FA 2014, Sch 4*].

10.64   HMRC did so by the *Registered Pension Schemes (Enhanced Lifetime Allowance) Regulations 2006 (SI 2006 No 131)* and the *Registered Pension Schemes (Enhanced Lifetime Allowance) (Amendment) Regulations 2006 (SI 2006 No 3261)*. They provide that if an individual's pension rights at 5 April 2006 exceed £1,500,000 and he wished to rely on *para 7*, or to claim enhanced protection under *para 12*, or to use pre-commencement credit under *para 18* to enhance his lifetime allowance, he had to give a notification to HMRC by 5 April 2009. They issued a certificate in response to such notification. A person who wishes to claim pension credits under *FA 2004, s 220* (pension sharing – see **10.41**), *s 221* (non-residence – see **10.3**(*a*)), or *s 224* (transfer from a recognised overseas scheme) must notify HMRC within five years after 31 January following the end of the tax year in which the profit sharing order or provision takes effect or the accrual period ends or the transfer takes place. The notification must be in the form prescribed by HMRC. A similar time limit applies where an enhanced allowance is claimed under *FA 2004, Sch 36, paras 7,11A* (where the individual has died) or *15A* (lump sum death benefit). HMRC can accept a late notification if the individual has a reasonable excuse. There is a right of appeal against their refusal to do so [*Registered Pension Schemes (Enhanced Lifetime Allowance) Regulations 2006 (SI 2006 No 131)* and the *Registered Pension Schemes (Block Transfers) (Permitted Membership Period) (Amendment) Regulations 2007 (SI 2007 No 838)*]. Similarly a person who does not have a primary protection enhancement factor under *para 7* or enhanced protection under *para 12*, could give notice to HMRC to treat his standard lifetime allowance as the greater of that allowance and £1,500,000 [*FA 2013, s 48 and Sch 22*]. There was a similar transitional rule on the 2014 changes, where an election needed to be made before 5 April 2014.

10.64A There is a personalised protection from the lifetime allowance known as IP 2014. HMRC and the Treasury have set out how IP 2014 will interact with the ever-growing protections which are already in place. *Finance Act 2014, Sch 6* contains the relevant provisions. *Paragraph 1(3)* of *Pt 1* provides that where an individual who has notified HMRC that they intend to rely on IP 2014 has one of three specified existing lifetime allowance protections, then as long as one of those more beneficial protections is valid, IP 2014 does not apply. Individuals with IP 2014 may also retain any FP 2014 or FP 2012. If they do, IP 2014 will apply if they subsequently lose their fixed protection. The deadline for applying for IP 2014 is 5 April 2017. The application form can be found online. Further information on IP 2014 is provided in HMRC's 'Pensions Individual Protection 2014: guidance note'.

Individuals who have pension savings above £1.25 million as at 5 April 2014, who do not already have primary protection, can apply for IP 2014. It is also available to individuals with enhanced protection – to protect them should such protection be lost. The lifetime allowance is the value of an individual's pension savings at 5 April 2014, up to £1,500,000. If the standard lifetime allowance should be increased in the future, the higher figure will apply. Individuals with pension savings above £1,500,0000 on 5 April 2014 will be able to apply for IP 2014, and they will have a protected LTA of £1,500,000. Under IP 2014, it is permitted to continue pension saving after 5 April 2014. Any pension commencement lump sum shall be limited to 25% of the individual's pension rights, subject to an overall cap of 25% of the personalised allowance.

In the event that the monetary value of savings falls below £1,250,000 following a pension sharing order on divorce, IP 2014 will cease. However, if the pension debit reduces the value to a figure above £1,250,000, IP 2014 will remain and the reduced level will apply from the date of the pension debit. The pension debit will be treated as reduced by 5% for each full tax year between 5 April 2014 and the date of the pension debit.

The valuation methods described in the consultation take into consideration different types of pension savings. For example, uncrystallised rights will adopt a method similar to that currently used for unauthorised payments. HMRC's guidance provides several examples of appropriate methods of calculation. IP 2014 will not be reduced in cases where any annual allowance charge is met by the scheme on the member's behalf (ie a 'scheme pays' arrangement).

10.65 If the pension scheme gave the member a right to retire before age 55 that right is also preserved, so is any right to take a lump sum on retirement in excess of £375,000 (25 per cent of the standard lifetime allowance).

The detailed rules are contained in *FA 2004, Sch 36, paras 21–36* and the *Registered Pension Schemes (Block Transfers) (Permitted Membership Period) Regulations 2006 (SI 2006 No 498).*

10.66   Those who had a retirement age under 50 at 6 April 2006 and were in a prescribed scheme or a prescribed occupation can continue with that early retirement date but have to take a reduced pension entitlement. [*FA 2004, Sch 36, para 19*]. The prescribed schemes are the Armed Forces Pension Scheme, The British Transport Police Superannuation Fund, the Firefighters' Pension Scheme (and its Northern Ireland equivalent), the Gurkha Pension Scheme and the Police Pension Scheme (and its Northern Ireland equivalent). The prescribed occupations are athletes, badminton player, boxers, cricketers, cyclists, dancers, divers (saturation, deep sea and free swimming), footballers, golfers, hockey players, jockeys (flat and National Hunt), members of the Reserve Forces, models, motor cycle riders (motocross or road racing) motor racing drivers, rugby players (League and Union), skiers (downhill), snooker or billiards players, speedway riders, squash players, table tennis players, tennis players (including real tennis), trapeze artistes and wrestlers [*Registered Pension Schemes (Prescribed Schemes and Occupations) Regulations 2005 (SI 2005 No 3451)*].

10.67   Payments under personal pension and retirement annuity contracts by a pre 6 April 2006 scheme in relation to ill-health contracts do not constitute unauthorised member payments [*FA 2004, Sch 36, para 27*]. Contributions under retirement annuity contracts are not required (but are permitted) to be made under deduction of tax after 6 April 2006 [*FA 2006, Sch 36, para 40*]. Annuities paid under such contracts can also continue to be paid gross until such time as the Treasury may by order appoint [*FA 2004, Sch 36, para 43*].

10.68   Where contributions to a 'corresponding' overseas pension scheme qualified for tax relief prior to 6 April 2006 they will continue to be deductible provided that HMRC are satisfied that the conditions of *ICTA 1988, s 355* continue to be met and that the scheme manager will provide them with the prescribed benefit crystallisation event information contained in the *Pension Schemes (Information Requirements – Qualifying overseas Pension Schemes, Qualifying Recognised Overseas Pensions Schemes and Corresponding Relief) Regulations 2006 (SI 2006 No 208).* The charges imposed by *Sch 34* (see **10.55**) apply to such a scheme.

10.69   Loans made before 6 April 2006 by an occupational pension scheme to a sponsoring employee qualify as authorised employer loans even if they exceed the normal 50 per cent limit provided that there is no alteration to the repayment terms. Where there is an alteration the pension scheme is treated as making a fresh loan at the date of the alteration equal to the existing loan. An extension of the repayment period for up to five years is not regarded as an alteration for this purpose provided that there has not been an earlier extension since 6 April 2006 [*FA 2004, Sch 36, para 38*].

10.70   The Treasury have power by statutory instrument to introduce such other transitional provisions as they think appropriate [*FA 2004, s 283(2)*].

They have done so by the *Taxation of Pension Schemes (Transitional Provisions) Order 2006 (SI 2006 No 572)* as amended by the *Taxation of Pension Schemes Transitional Provisions (Amendment)* and *(Amendment No 2) Orders (SI 2006 No 1962, SI 2009 No 1989)*, and the *Pension Schemes (Transfers, Reorganisations and Winding Up) (Transitional Provisions) Order 2006 (SI 2006 No 573)*. The first of these modifies a number of provisions, the second dealt primarily with transfers and reorganisations during the period 10 December 2003 to 5 April 2006 from pre 10 December 2003 schemes. The *Taxation of Pension Schemes (Transitional Provisions) (Amendment) Order 2008 (SI 2008 No 2990)* modified these regulations to prevent a reduction in pensions in payment triggering a tax charge where there are insufficient funds in the scheme to pay the pensions in full, the pension came into payment before 3 July 2007 and the reduction would not have prejudiced approval of the pension scheme under the pre *FA 2004* rules.

Information

10.71   HMRC can require a registered pension scheme to make a tax return [*FA 2004, s 250*]. They also have power to prescribe a requirement to provide other information or documents [*FA 2004, ss 251, 252*]. *The Employer-Financed Retirement Benefits Scheme (Provision of Information) Regulations 2005 (SI 2005 No 3453)* require the 'responsible person' (defined in *ITEPA 2003, s 399A*) to provide to HMRC the name of the scheme, the address of the responsible person and the date of the first contribution (or provision of the first benefit) by 31 January following the tax year in which that event took place. He is also required to provide details of relevant benefits (other than taxable pension payments) by 7 July following the end of the tax year in which it is provided.

10.72   *The Registered Pension Schemes and Employer-Financed Retirement Benefit Schemes (Information) (Prescribed Descriptions of Persons) Regulations 2005 (SI 2005 No 3455)* allow HMRC to obtain information from any person who is, or has been, the scheme administrator, a trustee, a sponsoring employer or a member of the scheme. *The Registered Pension Schemes (Audited Accounts) (Specified Persons) Regulations 2005 (SI 2005 No 3456)* specifies who is eligible to audit pension scheme accounts. There is a right of appeal against an information notice, but only as to whether the information is reasonably required by HMRC [*FA 2004, s 253*]. HMRC are also given power to prescribe the information that the scheme administrator is required to provide when he becomes liable for a tax payment, and rules concerning accounting for such payment and interest thereon [*FA 2004, ss 254, 255*]. They have done so in *The Registered Pension Schemes (Accounting and Assessment) Regulations 2005 (SI 2005 No 3454)*.

Administration

10.73   The detailed rules in relation to the administration of registered pension schemes are outside the scope of this book. They are contained in *FA 2004, ss 250–274* and a number of regulations made thereunder, namely the

Registered Pension Scheme (Accounting and Assessment) Regulations 2005 (SI 2005 No 3454), the *Pension Benefits (Insurance Company Liable as Scheme Administrator) Regulations 2006 (SI 2006 No 136)*, the *Registered Pension Schemes (Provision of Information) Regulations 2006 (SI 2006 No 567)* and the *Registered Pension Schemes (Splitting of Schemes) Regulations 2006 (SI 2006 No 569)*.

10.74 HMRC have power by regulations to require payments to be made electronically [*FA 2004, s 255* inserted by *FA 2005, s 101*]. A payment to HMRC is treated as made at the earliest time that everything that needs to be done before HMRC can receive the payment is capable of being completed [*FA 2004, s 255B*].

10.75 In recent years many employers have closed their final salary pension schemes either completely or to new entrants. Such schemes provide a pension equal to a proportion of the employee's final salary (usually two thirds after 40 years' service with the employer). They were popular in the 1960s. However they relied on a mixture of inflation and stock exchange growth in excess of salary growth, conditions which many consider to be no longer applicable. Some employers have offered employees an inducement to move from a final salary scheme to a money purchase scheme, ie one in which the pension will be whatever annuity an employee's earmarked fund can purchase at the date of his retirement. HMRC's view is that if such a cash inducement is paid to an employee (as opposed to an enhanced transfer value being paid to the new pension fund) the payment is employment income under *ITEPA 2003, s 394* (see **10.83**) and earnings for NIC purposes within *Social Security Contributions and Benefits Act 1992 (SSCBA 1992), s 3(1)(a)*. [*HMRC Press Release 24.1.2007*].

10.76 This view may well be open to challenge. *ITEPA 2003, s 394* applies to relevant benefits provided under an employer-financed retirement benefits scheme. [*ITEPA 2003, s 393*]. An employer-financed retirement benefits scheme is a scheme for the provision of benefits consisting of or including relevant benefits to, or in respect of, employees or former employees of the employer (but excluding a registered pension scheme). [*ITEPA 2003, s 393A*]. A relevant benefit is any lump sum, gratuity or other benefit (including a non-cash benefit) provided (or to be provided):

(*a*)   on or in anticipation of the retirement of an employee or former employee,

(*b*)   on the death of an employee or former employee,

(*c*)   after the retirement or death of an employee or former employee in connection with past service,

(*d*)   on, or in anticipation of, or in connection with, any change in the nature of service of an employee, or

(*e*)   to any person by virtue of a pension sharing order or provision relating to an employee or former employee.

[*ITEPA 2003, s 393B*]

10.77   HMRC consider the payment by the employer to be 'under' an employer-financed retirement benefit scheme. [*Technical Note* 9.2.2007]. They believe that this is wide enough to cover any payment of a relevant benefit. However, it is difficult to see how the payment is made under such a scheme. Indeed, it is the antithesis of such a payment. It is made to compensate a person for the reduction in his pension that will occur as a result of his agreeing to move to a less generous pension scheme. Furthermore it is not being paid 'in anticipation of the employee's retirement' (which is what HMRC claim where the employee is still working). It is being paid, if anything, in anticipation of his demurring from giving up existing pension rights. It is possible that the payment is taxable as employment income under general principles by virtue of the decisions in *Mairs v Haughey 66 TC 273* (see **11.59**) or *Hamblett v Godfrey 59 TC 694* (see **3.15**) but it does not fall readily into either of these principles. It does not replace the pension; the new scheme could produce a pension equal to or in excess of that which would have arisen under the old. It is not to give up employment rights. It is more akin to the payment in *Hochstrasser v Mayes 38 TC 673* (see **3.14**) where although the employment was held to be the factor that gave rise to the right to a payment, it was not the cause of the payment, but that was something outside the employment. Mention should also be made of the Court of Appeal decision in *Barclays Bank plc v HMRC [2008] STC 476* where the court felt it hard to conceive of a case where a payment to a pensioner was not in connection with the past employment. However, that case interpreted the phrase 'in connection with' whereas *section 393A* refers to 'a scheme for the provision of benefits ... in respect of ... former employees', which is a far tighter wording.

10.77A   This legislation was in issue in *Ballard v HMRC (TC 2503)*. Mr Ballard was made redundant and received a payment from a FURBS established by his former employer. He claimed that the payment was a relevant benefit within either (*c*) or (*d*) above. If it was, it would be taxable under *ITEPA 2003, s 394* (see **10.83**) but Mr Ballard was entitled to transitional relief under *FA 2004, Sch 36, para 22* (see **10.65**). The Tribunal held that it was a relevant benefit within (*c*) as it was a payment made after Mr Ballard's retirement in connection with past services. It thought that the word 'retirement' has no special meaning; it was not tied to pension age. It held that on the evidence, Mr Ballard had firmly decided to retire during the redundancy process. Although he was forced to accept redundancy, he was also entitled to retire from employment. That was a unilateral decision for him to make. The fact that the payment was also made as a result of his redundancy did not take it out of *s 393B*. In *Thomas v HMRC (TC 2463)* following a change of management, Mr Thomas, then 66 was made to feel unwelcome by his employer. The CEO sent him a letter saying, "it is our intention to retire you from the business on 1 February 2009 ... However you have a legal right to apply to work beyond that time". Mr Thomas decided to go quietly and "retired" on 1 February receiving a payment of 6 months' salary. The question was whether this was compensation for breach of Mr Thomas' employment rights taxable under *s 401* or a sum provided on or in anticipation of his retirement within *s 393*. It was held to be the latter as he had no contractual right to continue his employment, albeit that he may previously have been given an expectation of continued employment until 2010.

10.78   If the employee has already retired, HMRC consider that (*c*) in **10.69** applies, but it is stretching the words considerably to contend that a payment to move from one pension scheme to another is made 'in connection with past service'. It is nothing to do with the past service; it is a payment to agree to the alteration of existing contractual rights.

10.78A   The additional information powers at 15A onwards were introduced because a number of pension scheme promoters had set up schemes intended to enable people to 'liberate' their pension pots before the minimum pension age. Such withdrawals can attract very high tax charges. HMRC are anxious both to detect such schemes and to suggest to the Pensions Regulator that he might wish to appoint an independent trustee to the scheme. However because of the potential personal liabilities imposed on trustees, it might be difficult to find a person willing to act as such. Accordingly from 1 September 2014, if a person who is appointed as an 'independent trustee' is the scheme administrator or one of the scheme administrators, he does not assume any responsibility for tax charges on payments made prior to his appointment [*FA 2004, s 272A(3)–(11)* inserted by *FA 2014, Sch 5, para 19*]. An independent trustee for this purpose is a trustee of a pension scheme who is appointed by (or pursuant to) an order made by the Pensions Regulator under the *Pensions Act 1995, s 7* or by a court on an application made by the Pensions Regulator, and who was not at any previous time a trustee [*FA 2004, s 272A(2)*]. Furthermore any person who is appointed scheme administrator (or one of the administrators) at a time when the pension scheme has one or more independent trustees, is also exempted from such liabilities arising prior to the appointment of the independent trustee [*FA 2004, s 272B*]. This will enable the independent trustee to recruit new scheme administrators. The person or persons who were the scheme administrators immediately before the appointment of the independent trustee remain responsible for such past liabilities (but such liability ceases when the person dies or ceases to exist) [*FA 2004, s 272C(1)–(5)*]. If such persons cease to exist, the liability passes to the person or persons identified under *FA 2014, s 272(4)*, who are –

(*a*)   the trustees of the scheme who are UK resident, or if there are none,

(*b*)   the person or persons who control the management of the scheme or, if none,

(*c*)   the person or persons who established the scheme (normally the employer company) and any person by whom that person has been directly or indirectly succeeded in relation to the provision of benefits under the scheme or, if none,

(*d*)   any sponsoring employer of the scheme, or finally

(*e*)   any non-UK resident trustees.

HMRC can also impose the liability on members of the scheme under *FA 2004, s 273*, in certain circumstances [*FA 2004, ss 272C(6)–(9), 273(1A)*].

The Financial Assistance Scheme and the Financial Services Compensation Scheme

10.79   Where a final salary pension scheme was wound up between 1 January 1997 and 5 April 2005 because it was no longer able to meet all of its pension obligations, it may have qualified for assistance from the Financial Assistance Scheme (FAS) set up under *Pensions Act 2004, s 286*. The FAS is not a pension scheme. It makes top-up payments to members of other schemes. The Treasury are given power by regulation to introduce provisions in relation to the FAS [*FA 2009, s 73*]. This is because the government intend to amend the scheme so that in future it will make all of the payments that are currently made by the relevant pension scheme. When it does so, the Treasury will need to introduce provisions to ensure that payments to pensioners are taxed in the same way as those from a registered pension scheme. The Financial Services Compensation Scheme (FSCS) was established under the *Financial Services and Markets Act 2000 (FSMA 2000)*. As the FSCS is not a registered pension scheme provisions are similarly needed to cover payments to pensioners by the FSCS. The Treasury have accordingly also been given power by regulation to do this [*FA 2009, s 74*].

Unregisterable pension schemes

10.80   Schemes which do not qualify fro registration can either be funded or unfunded, ie the employer does not make contributions to a pension provider but simply enters into a commitment with the employee to provide him with specific pension benefits on retirement. When the pension is paid it will of course attract tax – but so will pension payments under a registered scheme. The major disadvantage is that an unfunded scheme provides little protection to the employee. His pension depends on the employer still being in existence at the time he retires, and on it then having the necessary financial resources to actually meet its commitments to ex-employees Contributions to a funded scheme (commonly called a FURBS (Funded Unapproved Retirement Benefit Scheme)) are not tax deductible to either the employer or the employee when paid but are not taxable on the employer either. [*FA 2004, ss 245, 247*]. The employer becomes entitled to a deduction up to the amount he has contributed when benefits are paid to, and taxed on, the member. [*Finance Act 2003 (FA 2003), Sch 24, para 1*]. However he never becomes entitled to tax relief on non-taxable payments to the member. The employee can never obtain tax relief for contributions that he makes, so it is rare for employees to contribute to a FURBS.

10.81   *FA 2003, Sch 24, para 1(2)* applies where the employer 'pays money or transfers an asset'. The predecessor provision, *ICTA 1988, s 595(1)*, applied where the employer 'pays a sum'. It was held by that Court of Appeal in *Irving v HMRC [2008] STC 597* that although a 'sum' normally implies a payment of money the context of the legislation is probably sufficient to require a broader interpretation and that it accordingly applied to a transfer of shares to the FURBS. The *FA 2003* wording of course reflects this wider meaning.

10.82   If an employer uses an unfunded registered scheme the benefit payments are deductible when paid, even though at that stage the member may no longer be an employee. If the benefits are taxable on the employee (but not otherwise) any expenses of providing them (other than contributions) are also deductible. [*FA 2004, ss 239, 240*]. If the employer under such a scheme insures against the risk that he may not be able to pay the pension because of his insolvency the cost of such insurance will be taxable on the employee as a benefit-in-kind. [*FA 2004, s 242*]. Pension payments from such a scheme remain taxable on the employee though (except where the scheme is an armed and reserve forces compensation scheme under *Armed Forces (Pensions and Compensation) Act 2004, s 1(2)*).

10.83   Any benefit received under an unapproved pension scheme is chargeable to income tax if it is not already taxable as a pension. [*ITEPA 2003, ss 393, 394*]. In the case of a benefit-in-kind the taxable amount is normally the cash equivalent of the benefit. [*ITEPA 2003, s 398*]. This is calculated in the same way as under the benefit in kind rules (see **Chapters 6–19**). [*ITEPA 2003, s 398(2)(b)*].

10.84   No tax charge however arises on:

(*a*)   benefits in respect of ill-health or disablement of an employee during service;

(*b*)   benefits in respect of the death by accident of an employee during service;

(*c*)   benefits under an excepted group life policy within *Income Tax (Trading and Other Income) Act 2005 (ITTOIA 2005), s 480*, or a life policy which provides for payment on the death of a single individual and, broadly speaking, satisfies *ITTOIA 2005, ss 480* and *481*; and

(*d*)   benefits of any description prescribed by regulations made by HMRC.

[*ITEPA 2003, s 393B(3)* inserted by *FA 2004, s 249*].

HMRC have prescribed under (*d*) the following benefits:

(i)   living accommodation provided by a local authority that is exempt if provided to an employee (see **8.23**);

(ii)   living accommodation that the employee occupied continuously during the five years prior to retirement, which was not taxed as being provided for the performance of the duties and which continues to be occupied after retirement (and which has not been materially improved);

(iii)   living accommodation provided to a member of the employee's family after the employee's death if it fell within *ITEPA 2003, s 99* (see **8.19**) or (ii) above at the time of the employee's death;

(iv)   living accommodation provided for a minister of religion or his family if it would have been exempt during his ministry (see **8.22**(*b*));

(v)   living accommodation provided within *ITEPA 2003, s 100* (see **8.19**);

(vi)   removal expenses that would have been exempt (see **9.42**) had the removal occurred during the employment;

(vii)   repairs and alterations within *ITEPA 2003, s 313* (see **6.44**(*f*));

(viii)   council tax within *ITEPA 2003, s 314(2)* (see **8.20**);

(ix)   welfare counselling within **6.44**(*v*);

(x)   recreational benefits within *ITEPA 2003, s 261* (see **9.32**);

(xi)   annual functions within *ITEPA 2003, s 264* (see **9.116**);

(xii)   will writing where the cash equivalent of the benefit does not exceed £150;

(xiii) equipment for disabled employees (see **6.44**(*w*));

[*Employer-Financed Retirement Benefits (Excluded Benefits for Tax Purposes) Regulations 2007 (SI 2007 No 3537)*].

HMRC issued a detailed guidance note on 14 January 2008 which gives greater detail.

10.85   From 6 April 2009 no tax charge arises on benefits provided by an employer-financed retirement benefit scheme if:

(*a*)   it was an approved pension scheme at 5 April 1980 under *ICTA 1970, s 222* but did not obtain continuing approval under FA 1970;

(*b*)   no material changes have been made to the terms on which benefits are provided under the scheme after 5 April 1980; and

(*c*)   no contributions have been made to the scheme after that date,

[*ITEPA 2003, s 395A* inserted by *Article 2, Enactment of Extra-Statutory Concessions Order 2009 (SI 2009 No 730)*]. This also applied by concession up to 2008/09.

10.86   An interesting point on *ICTA 1988, s 590A* (the predecessor to *s 394*) arose in *Trustees of Barclays Bank plc and Another v HMRC [2008] STC 476*. The pension fund was an approved scheme. Barclays has since 1955 provided widows of its pensioners on a concessionary basis with free tax-related services such as preparation of their tax returns by a group company. In 1977 it extended this concession to all its pensioners. It told its staff that this facility was a privilege, not part of the terms and conditions of service. In 1988 it decided to withdraw the concession but backed away from doing so in the face of threatened legal action by pensioners and trade unions. In 1997 it wished to sell Barclays Personal Taxation Services Ltd, the company that provided the services, and decided to pay compensation to pensioners to head off the problems it had experienced in 1988. It paid such compensation through the Pension Fund Trustees because they had the details of the pensioners. HMRC sought tax on the grounds that the payment to pensioners constituted benefits under an unapproved retirement scheme. The provision of the tax services had not themselves been taxed in the past as it was accepted by HMRC as an ex gratia service. The Special Commissioners held that for *s 394* to apply there has to be a 'scheme' for the provision of relevant benefits and the payments must have been received under that scheme. They held that the payments were not relevant benefits as they were not given in connection with past service by the pensioners. They were made to assuage the perceived hostility of pensioners and trade unions. They were motivated solely by the desire to avoid the consequences of such hostility. The Court of Appeal disagreed. If focussed on the phrase 'in connection with past service'. If felt that this could describe a range of links and felt that Parliament was unlikely to have intended to limit connection to a direct connection and that once a connection with the pension scheme could be shown, it would be rare for a connection with something else to displace it. It did however think that the definition is not unlimited; there has to be link with service. Arden LJ thought that 'It is difficult to think of a case where a benefit made available to persons chosen for their connection with an occupational pension scheme is not given in connection with their service.' She instanced 'a pensioner winning a quiz prize at the employer's annual party as one where the link with past service may be found to have been displaced ... The free tax service had clearly been provided because the pensioners were former employees. That link continued through the paying of compensation'. It is difficult to reconcile this decision with that of the House of Lords in *Hochstrasser v Mayes 38 TC 673* (see **3.14**) which distinguished between the employment being the nexus that gave rise to the opportunity to benefit and it being the thing which gave rise to the benefit. In any event the phrase 'in connection with', which was at issue in that case is not used in *s 394* so it is unclear to what extent, if any, this decision will apply after 5 April 2006.

10.87 In effect, with a FURBS the employer is simply making non-tax deductible contributions to a trust for the benefit of the employees, the only benefits of which is that income is taxed at the basic rate instead of the 40 per cent rate applicable to trusts and a tax deduction could become due at a future date..

10.88 A FURBS created before 6 April 2006 has inheritance tax benefits as *IHTA 1984, s 151* (which grants an IHT exemption for pension rights) applies not only to approved pension schemes but also to any other sponsored superannuation scheme set up by an employer for his employees. This latter exemption was withdrawn by *FA 2004, s 203(4)* which restricts the application of *s 151* to registered pension schemes and *ICTA 1988, s 615(3)* schemes (schemes for employees working wholly outside the UK so a FURBS set up after 6 April 2006 will not benefit from IHT relief. The IHT exemption for assets in a pre 6 April 2006 FURBS is preserved provided that no contributions are made to the scheme after that date. Where such contributions are made the exemption is preserved only for the proportion of the fund assets that the value of the assets at 6 April 2006 (increased in line with the RPI and reduced by payments of costs and expenses and payments taxed on the employee) bears to the total value of the fund at the time of the member's death [*FA 2004, Sch 36, paras 56–58*].

10.89 Other points to note are as follows:

(*a*) A FURBS can be run in conjunction with a registered scheme. Indeed it is normally sensible to make the maximum approvable provision first.

(*b*)   There is no point in funding for a pension which will be taxable. A FURBS should only pay out a lump sum – which is normally tax-free. If a pension is required the lump sum can be used to purchase an annuity, which being a purchased annuity will have a substantial tax-free element.

(*c*)   If the FURBS is self-administered the costs of setting up and running the scheme do not give rise to benefits in kind provided that they are funded by the company as separately identifiable contributions (*IR Booklet, The Tax Treatment of Top-up Pension Schemes, paragraph 2.2.4*).

(*d*)   The death benefit will attract inheritance tax if it is paid to the deceased's estate and may well do so if it is paid at the trustees discretion amongst a class that includes the estate (*IR Booklet, paragraph 2.5.5*).

(*e*)   The settlement anti-avoidance provisions can apply to a FURBS, thus negating the income tax and capital gains tax benefit, but this is 'not likely to be the case where the structure and operation of a scheme are broadly similar to an approved pension scheme' (*IR Booklet, paragraph 2.7.5*).

(*f*)   There is an obligation to report to HMRC the payment of a contribution to a FURBS within three months of its being paid. [*ICTA 1988, s 605(3)*]. The payment also needs to be shown on the employee's P11D.

10.90   *ICTA 1988, s 596A* makes offshore FURBS unattractive – although they still permit deferral of the tax – as it can increase the overall tax as compared with the UK-based FURBS as the calculation makes no allowance for the fact that some types of income and gains, eg capital gains on government securities, attract exemption from tax.

Individual savings accounts – old and new

10.91   An alternative form of top-up pension provision is to contribute regularly into an Individual Savings Account (ISA). For 1999/00 to 2009/10, an individual could put £7,000 per annum into an ISA. From 6 April 2010 (6 October 2009 for those aged over 50), the maximum annual contribution became £10,200. This again increased to £10,680 for 2011/12, £11,280 for 2012/13, £11,520 for 2013/14 and £15,000 for 2014/15. Like FURBS, there is no tax relief on contributions to an ISA. Unlike FURBS the growth within an ISA is tax-free as both its income and capital gains are exempt from tax. With a regulated pension scheme tax relief is given for the contributions, growth within the fund is tax-free, but the funds ultimately come out in a taxable form apart from the tax-free lump sum. With an ISA no tax relief is given for the contributions, growth within the fund is tax-free, and all withdrawals from the fund are tax-free also.

From 1 January 2011, a new form of Junior ISA was introduced under which a parent could contribute up to £3,840 for a child but only if the child was not eligible for a child trust fund. From 2014/15, the limit has increased to £4,000 and child trust funds have been converted to Junior ISAs.

Chapter 11

Termination Payments and Signing-on Fees

Introduction

11.1   Particular difficulties arise with lump sum payments either at the commencement or termination of an employment. A payment made before the employment commences to induce a person to take up an employment is part of the emoluments from that employment. However, if it is made for some other reason, such as to induce the person to give up something else – a profitable professional position in *Pritchard v Arundale* (see **11.68** below), amateur status in *Jarrold v Boustead* (see **11.69** below), or something similar – then it is not remuneration of the prospective employment.

11.2   A payment on the termination of an employment, either as compensation for breach of the employment contract or ex gratia, is not normally emoluments unless there is a contractual entitlement to it. Such payments are nonetheless generally taxable as employment income by virtue of *Income Tax (Earnings and Pensions) Act 2003, s 401*, but the tax treatment is more favourable than if the compensation itself constituted emoluments of the employment.

Compensation constituting emoluments

11.3   Compensation constitutes emoluments, and is thus taxable apart from the special provisions described below, if the employee is contractually entitled to it under the terms of his employment agreement. Where an employee is put on 'garden leave' that is not compensation. The employment continues until the expiration of the garden leave and the payments made to the employee are remuneration under the employment contract. All that happens is that the employer does not require the employee to carry out any duties of the employment during that period. The taxability of such a payment was challenged, unsuccessfully, in *Ibe v McNally [2005] STC 1426* which was a taxpayer in person fighting a hopeless case – albeit that she was told that she was being made redundant with immediate effect, so contended that the continuing salary payments during her notice period were a redundancy payment (see **11.58**).

Case law

Henry v Foster

11.4   Thus, in *Henry v Foster 16 TC 605*, the articles of association of the employer company provided that 'In the event of any director dying or resigning his office or in the event of any director ceasing to hold office for any cause ... the company shall pay to him or his representatives ... by way of compensation for the loss of office a sum equal to the total amount of the remuneration' for the previous five years. It was held that the substance of the matter was that in addition to his salary payments he became entitled to a further amount under the articles by way of deferred remuneration. Accordingly, the 'compensation' was taxable as employment income.

Hunter v Dewhurst

11.5   Another director of the same company, Mr Dewhurst, wished to retire in 1923 but the other directors wished him to remain. He offered to stay on the board (but not as an executive) on the basis that he would be paid £10,000, would waive his right to future compensation under the articles, and would take a reduced salary. It was held, albeit on a three-to-two majority, that the £10,000 was not satisfying the payment due under the articles at a later date. Nor was it in respect of past services. Mr Dewhurst was not required to remain a director for any specific period, so it could not relate to future services. It was a payment to induce him not to retire. As such it was not part of his remuneration (*Hunter v Dewhurst 16 TC 605*).

Prendergast v Cameron

11.6   By contrast, in *Prendergast v Cameron 23 TC 122*, a payment to induce a director not to resign was held to be taxable as remuneration as there is no difference between a promise not to resign and a promise to continue to serve as a director. Although Mr Cameron, like Mr Dewhurst, did not agree to continue as a director for any specific period, Viscount Caldecote thought it fair to assume that his fellow directors 'knew the man with whom they had to deal, and were confident that if he received the money they were prepared to pay him they would get good value for it'. He accordingly felt able to hold that the payment was remuneration for future services.

Hofman v Wadman

11.7   The importance of the documentation entered into is emphasised in *Hofman v Wadman 27 TC 192*. Mr Hofman had a five-year service agreement. The company wished to terminate his employment in order to facilitate a reorganisation but could not do so without breaching the contract. They entered into an agreement with him that the service agreement 'shall be cancelled forthwith, subject to the con-tinuance of the fixed remuneration provided for in Clause 4 ... it is understood [Mr Hofman] agrees to render such assistance to our staff ... as may be requested'. It was held that this did not cancel the service agreement, it cancelled some elements but preserved the salary. 'Although Mr Hofman ceased to hold the office of works manager ... the continuation in the office ... does not affect the question of his liability to income tax under Schedule E (which used to be the Schedule under which employment income was taxed).' Indeed McNaghten J indicated that even if the terms had been such that he was no longer under any obligation to render any services, he would still be liable to assessment in respect of all the payments made to him under the terms of the original service agreement.

Carter v Wadman

11.8   In *Carter v Wadman 28 TC 41* the taxpayer's employment agreement provided that, in the event of the agreement being terminated, he would be paid as compensation for loss of office £5 a week until the agreement would have expired. He was also entitled to a bonus of 25 per cent of the profits of the business. He could also prevent a sale of the business. On a disposal of the business he was paid £2,000 'in full settlement of all past, present and future claims under his service agreement'. It was held that this sum fell to be apportioned. To the extent that it related to giving up the claim to the £5 a week and the profit share, it was taxable; to the extent it related to giving up the ability to thwart a sale, it was not.

Dale v de Soissons

11.9   In *Dale v de Soissons 32 TC 118* the taxpayer's service agreement contained a provision that 'in the event of Mr de Soissons' appointment hereunder being so terminated there shall be paid to Mr de Soissons by way of compensation for loss of office the amounts following'. The compensation was held to be taxable. 'It seems to me the remuneration for the services took the form in part of a remuneration ... for the period he in fact served plus a further sum which he was contractually entitled to get under the terms of his agreement and as part of the bargain which he made ... The Colonel surrendered no rights. He got exactly what he was entitled to get under his contract of employment' (Sir Raymond Evershed, MR).

IR v Knight, Williams v Simmonds

11.10   In a Privy Council case, *Controller General of Inland Revenue v Knight [1973] AC 428*, Lord Wilberforce made the distinction 'Where a sum of money is paid under a contract of employment, it is taxable, even though it is received at or after the termination of the employment ... Where a sum of money is paid as consideration for the abrogation of a contract of employment, or as damages for the breach of it, that sum is not taxable'. The agreement in *Williams v Simmonds 55 TC 17* provided that, in the event of the company disposing of a substantial asset Mr Simmonds would be deemed to have lost his office as managing director and would be entitled to compensation calculated under a formula. It went on to say that Mr Simmonds could elect not to treat his office as terminated. He did not make such an election and was paid the compensation. It was held to be taxable. The judge described this result as 'unfortunate', as he pointed out that had Mr Simmons elected to treat his office as continuing and had then succumbed to pressure to resign, and had agreed to accept the same sum as compensation for the abrogation of his rights under the service agreement, it would probably not have been taxable.

Duff v Barlow

11.11   In *Duff v Barlow 23 TC 633* a payment to a director on the termination of his contract of employment was held not to be assessable as it was not for services rendered or to be rendered, the director having already received his agreed remuneration for such services. A similar decision was reached in *Hose v Warwick 27 TC 459* where a director of a company who was entitled to commission was paid to give up his rights to future commissions on being promoted to managing director of the company. The taxpayer in *Manduca v HMRC (TC 2648)* sought to rely on *Hose*. Mr Manduca and a colleague decided to set up a new hedge fund. They needed a sponsor and took the fund to Tilney Investment Management. Tilney later decided to withdraw from the hedge fund market. It gave Mr Manduca a time limit in which to find a new sponsor. Mr Manduca took the fund to Dexia who employed Mr Manduca (as Tilney had done previously). It also agreed to make a payment to him 'to recognise your role in transferring to Dexia the business' of the fund. Mr Manduca said that the payment was capital subject to CGT. HMRC said that it could not be capital as he had nothing to sell and that it was a payment for services. The FTT agreed. The essence of the decision in *Hose* was that Mr Hose had given up something valuable to the company (namely his business connections) but Mr Manduca had given up nothing.

Wales v Tilley

11.12   Great care needs to be taken with lump sum payments where the employment continues on amended terms. In *Wales v Tilley 25 TC 136* the taxpayer was entitled to a salary of £6,000 per annum and, when his service ceased, to a pension of £4,000 per annum for a period of ten years. He was paid £40,000 to release the company from the prospective obligation to pay the pension and to agree to serve the company in future at a salary of £2,000 per annum. It was held that in so far as the payment related to giving up the right to the pension it was not taxable. A pension is a separate head of charge under Schedule E and accordingly neither the pension nor the sum paid to commute it constituted profit from the office. To the extent that it related to the reduction in salary it was taxable. 'The ordinary way of remunerating the ... person employed is to make payments to him periodically, but I cannot think that such payments can escape the quality of income . . . because an arrangement is made to reduce for the future the annual payments while paying a lump sum down to represent the difference' (Viscount Simon). *Johnson v HMRC (TC 2656)* is an interesting case. In 2003 Mr Johnson and Mr Reid were invited to join RR Richardson Group Ltd. They were offered EMI options for which they each paid £30,000. In 2007, the company engaged a new managing director and it was agreed that both Mr Johnson and Mr Reid should leave the company. Mr Johnson received a compensation payment of £75,700. The termination agreement did not give a breakdown of how this figure was arrived at. Mr Johnson said that it included repayment of his £30,000 and the balance was six months salary in lieu of notice. HMRC asked the company how it had been arrived at and was not given a breakdown but was told that the payment was definitely not a refund of his investment. The FTT thought it inconceivable that Mr Johnson would have agreed a settlement without getting his £30,000 back, so held that it must be included in the £75,700. It also pointed out that the employment agreement did not entitle the company to make a payment in lieu of notice, so the balance was not employment income but an amount falling within *s 401*. The interesting side note is that in *Reid v HMRC (TC 1877)* an earlier Tribunal had held that Mr Reid's £30,000 had not been included in his compensation on the basis of HMRC's interpretation of Lord Hoffmann's comment in *Investors Compensation Scheme v West Bromwich Building Society [1998] WLR 894* that in construing an agreement one must only have regard to the terms of the agreement and not to any prior negotiations between the parties. The Johnson Tribunal said that HMRC had misconstrued Lord Hoffmann's comments (which were, in any event, obiter). He was referring to a court construing documents in the context of a contract where the parties were at odds as to the proper meaning to be attached to that contract. Here the Tribunal is concerned with HMRC's interpretation of a contract to which it was not a party. In circumstances where the party which had drawn up the agreement would not divulge its composition, it was not only open to HMRC to look outside the terms of the contract but they were obliged to do so. Sadly this decision was too late for Mr Reid to be able to appeal his own case.

Other cases

11.13   There is probably an inference that such a payment constitutes emoluments. Thus, in *Hamblett v Godfrey 59 TC 694* it was held that a payment to give up a right to be a member of a trade union was remuneration of the employment, as such rights were inseparable from the employment. In *Holland v Geoghegan 48 TC 482* payments to council dustmen to forego a right to sell materials salvaged from their collections were held to be emoluments. A payment to a director to relinquish a right under his employment agreement that the agreement could not be terminated without his consent was also held to be income under general principles (*Leeland v Boarland 27 TC 71*). So was a payment to a director to surrender his right to commissions due to him (*Bolam v Muller 28 TC 471*). In *McGregor v Randall 58 TC 110* a payment as compensation for the loss of future commission was held to be taxable. Redundancy payments were held to be taxable as earnings under general principles in *SCA Packaging Ltd v HMRC [2007] STC 1640* to the extent that they related to payments in lieu of notice. However, the facts were unusual. When the relevant trade unions were notified of proposed redundancies they negotiated with the company a number of memoranda of understanding covering the timing of redundancies and the compensation to be paid. These memoranda were held as a question of construction to have been incorporated into the employees' contracts of employment.

11.14 When compensation covers more than one thing, it is important to be able to split it. *Oti-Obihara v HMRC [2011] SFTD 202* provides an example of the problem. Mr Oti-Obihara claimed that he was subject to racial discrimination and harassment at work. He negotiated a settlement with his employer under which his employment was terminated and he was paid a sum of £500,000 in satisfaction of all claims against the employer. Mr Oti-Obihara reasoned that as he was entitled to three months' notice, he was taxable on three months' salary, £18,206, with the balance relating to the discrimination and harassment claim, which was outside the scope of income tax. The Tribunal held that on the facts the termination of the employment was related to the discrimination and to the extent that there was a nexus between the two, the compensation was taxable. It then assumed that in any negotiation for a settlement the employer would recognise that an employee of Mr Oti-Obihara's standing might take 18 months to find a comparable job, so allocated £165,000 to financial loss resulting from the termination of the employment while accepting that the balance of £335,000 was settlement for non-pecuniary loss. As neither party had contended for this figure of £165,000, the lesson seems to be that if the split is not agreed when the compensation is agreed, the taxpayer becomes dependent on the subjective opinion of the Tribunal as to what the split should be.

Compensation not constituting emoluments

11.15 Where the compensation does not otherwise constitute emoluments it will not escape tax. *ITEPA 2003, s 401* imposes an income tax charge on any payment (not otherwise chargeable to tax) made in consideration of (or in consequence of, or otherwise in connection with) the termination of an office or employment or any change in its functions (whether or not under any legal obligation and either directly or indirectly). [*ITEPA 2003, s 401(1)*]. It applies to all payments received, directly or indirectly, in consideration or in consequence of (or otherwise in connection with) the termination or change in the employment by either:

(*a*) the employee (or office-holder) or former employee;

(*b*) the spouse or any blood relative or dependant of the former employee; or

(*c*) the personal representatives of the former employee.

Any payment or other benefit provided on behalf of (or to the order of) the employee or former employee is also treated as received by him. [*ITEPA 2003, s 401(4)(a)*]. The tax is chargeable on the employee, not the recipient, where (*b*) above applies. [*ITEPA 2003, s 403(1)*]. There are, however, a number of exemptions, including one for the first £30,000. These are considered at **11.25**. Compensation taxable under *section 401* is taxed in the year of assessment in which it is received. [*ITEPA 2003, s 403(2)*].

11.16 The charge is specifically expressed to apply to benefit as well as payments. For this purpose a benefit includes anything which, if received for the performance of the duties of the employment, would be taxable as an emolument of the employment apart from any exemption. [*ITEPA 2003, s 402(1)*]. The right to receive the payment of compensation or benefit is obviously not itself regarded as a benefit for this purpose. [*ITEPA 2003, s 402(4)*]. A cash benefit is treated as received when it is paid (or a payment on account if it is made) or when the recipient becomes entitled to require payment of (or on account of) the benefit. A non-cash benefit is treated as received when it is used or enjoyed. [*ITEPA 2003, s 403(3)*].

Where compensation paid in connection with a change in the function of an employment includes benefits in kind, such benefits could be taxable under both *ITEPA 2003, s 201* (charge on benefits) and *ITEPA 2003, s 401*. In such circumstances HMRC consider that the charge under *section 201* takes precedence (*Tax Bulletin 65*, June 2003).

11.17   There are specific exemptions for:

(*a*)   a payment or benefit received in connection with a change in the duties of (or emoluments from) a person's employment which would have been exempt as qualifying removal expenses under *ITEPA 2003, s 271(1)* (see **9.48**) if it had been paid for the performance of the duties of the employment [*ITEPA 2003, s 402(3)*]; and

(*b*)   a payment or benefit received in connection with the termination of a person's employment, which, if it had been received in connection with the performance of the duties of the employment, would have been exempt under *ITEPA 2003*:

(i)   *section 269* expenses in relation to a car (see **6.44**(d));

(ii)   *section 319* mobile telephones (see **9.33**);

(iii)   *section 320* computer equipment (see **9.84**);

(iv)   *section 239(4)* expenses in relation to a car (see **7.31**), van (see **7.77**), or lorry (see **7.82**);

[*ITEPA 2003, s 402(2)*]

The specific exemptions under the following provisions of course also apply:

(v)   *section 317* meals in a canteen (see **6.44**(h));

(vi)   *section 250* work related training (see **9.63**);

(vii)   *section 255* individual learning accounts (see **9.68**);

(viii) *section 311* retraining courses (see **9.75**);

(ix)   *section 310* redundancy counselling (see **9.81**);

(x)   *section 308* employer's contributions under personal pension arrangements.

Income and Corporation Taxes Act 1988, s 148(5) provided that *section 148* applied irrespective of whether the payment or other benefit was provided by the employer (or former employer) or by some other person and irrespective of whether or not the payment or benefit was provided in pursuance of a legal obligation. [*Section 148(5)*]. The wording of *ITEPA 2003, s 401* was felt to be so widely drawn that there was no need to specifically repeat this wording.

11.18 In *Walker v Adams [2003] STC 269* Mr Walker, a Northern Irish Protestant, was constructively dismissed based on religious discrimination. A severance agreement was negotiated. It was not disputed that this attracted a charge under what is now *ITEPA 2003, s 403*. However, Mr Walker subsequently made an application to the Fair Employment Tribunal under the *Fair Employment (Northern Ireland) Act 1989*. He was awarded £77,446, £12,500 for injury to feelings and £63,946 in respect of net income loss both to the date of the decision and in the future and in respect of the loss of pension rights. HMRC accepted that the £12,500 was not a payment made 'in connection with' the termination of Mr Walker's employment but contended that the £63,946 was taxable. The Special Commissioner agreed. He accepted that the 1989 Act did not operate so as to import statutory terms into the contract of employment but created 'a free-standing right of action, basically tortious in nature, aimed against certain forms of discrimination'. Nevertheless, he felt that while the unlawful discrimination founded the tribunal's jurisdiction the chain of causation led back to the employment. 'The discrimination caused the termination of Mr Walker's employment; the termination caused the financial losses; and those losses gave rise to the £64,946 award'. He also felt that the words 'or otherwise' in what is now *ITEPA 2003, s 401* show that the relevant connection or link may be looser than would be required for a strict causation test.

11.19 The decision may well be wrong in the light of the later High Court decision in *Wilson v Clayton [2005] STC 157*. Mr Clayton was employed by a local authority. His employment was terminated and he was offered a new contract on different terms. Mr Clayton claimed unfair dismissal. The Employment Tribunal upheld his claim and ordered the local authority to reinstate Mr Clayton and pay him the amount of lost remuneration (under his old terms) between the date of termination of his employment and the date of reinstatement, which came to £5,060. It was held that the £5,060 fell within *s 401*. It was received 'in connection with' the termination of the employment. The effect of the reinstatement order was not that the termination never took place.

11.20 In *Porter v HMRC SpC 501; [2005] STC (SCD) 803* Mr Porter was made redundant in October 1988 and received an ex gratia payment from his employer. In addition in January 2001 the trustees of the employer's stock bonus plan made a payment to him of £64,726 being the amount that would have been due to him under the plan had his employment continued until that time. The issue was whether this payment was taxable under the basic employment income rules or as part of his compensation taxable under *section 401*. The Commissioner held that the payment was not from the employment. It was from the ending of the employment, from the settlement of claims relating to benefits that he might reasonably be expected to receive had the employment continued. Clearly it was 'in connection with the termination of' his employment. *Panesar v HMRC (TC 2359)* involved the compensation payment on the closure of a sub-post office. HMRC pointed the Tribunal to the breadth of the wording of *s 401*. They also said that the fact that they had treated the earnings as trading income was concessionary as Mrs Panesar ran a shop from the premises. They had made clear in EM68205 that this treatment does not extend to termination payments. The FTT held that *s 401* applied even though the official documents concerning the compensation scheme consistently described it as 'for loss of assets and investments'. The FTT thought that *s 401* will apply unless it can be shown that there is some independent reason for the payment apart from the office, which they described as a difficult hurdle to leap. The description in the documentation was a relevant factor but could not defeat *s 401*. In *Harrison v HMRC (TC 2397)* Mr Harrison was employed by the Financial Ombudsman Service as an adjudicator. He was dismissed and received a payment in lieu of notice. The Employment Tribunal held that he had been dismissed in breach of contract. Mr Harrison promptly contended that the payment from FOS could not have been made under his contract and was therefore taxable under *s 401*, so the first £30,000 was exempt. The Tribunal disagreed.

11.21   *Resolute Management Services Ltd v HMRC and Haderlein v HMRC [2008] STC (SCD) 1202* is interesting. Mrs Haderlein was employed by Resolute in 1996. She was a senior executive of the company. Resolute was formed at part of the Lloyds Insurance Market Reconstruction Plan and it was always envisaged that it would wind down and cease. Mrs Haderlein resigned from Resolute in July 2004 as she felt that in reality her job no longer existed. In November 2004 Resolute decided to make her an ex-gratia payment of £150,000. Even though by resigning Mrs Haderlein had forfeited a potential redundancy payment of £122,500, the Commissioner accepted that 'there are other things in life than money' and that Mrs Haderlein had accepted that she would lose her redundancy entitlement but was not looking for anything in return. The decision to make the ex-gratia payment was made subsequent to her resignation and was made because the company felt that she had 'done the right thing' in recognising that Resolute no longer needed her expertise or the cost of employing her. The Commissioner held that the payment was not earnings although the excess over £30,000 was taxable under *ITEPA 2003, s 401*. However Mrs Haderlein was a US citizen and she had returned home to the USA. She accordingly claimed that the UK was barred from taxing any part of the payment by virtue of the US/UK double tax agreement. If the payment was 'salaries, wages and similar remuneration' the UK had primary taxing rights; if it was not the USA had sole taxing rights. The Commissioner held that the payment lacked the necessary nexus with services rendered that characterises that phrase. Accordingly the USA had sole taxing rights.

11.22   In *A v HMRC [2009] STC (SCD) 269* the taxpayer resigned and filed a complaint alleging constructive unfair dismissal. He claimed compensation for loss of earnings and for damage to his reputation. He received £250,000. HMRC were prepared to accept that £10,000 of this related to damages but claimed that the remaining £240,000 was taxable subject to the exemption for the first £30,000. A claimed that £175,000 related to loss of reputation and £50,000 to injury to feeling, leaving only £50,000 relating to the termination of his employment. The Special Commissioners agreed with HMRC. They thought A's split 'conjecture' and seem to have been swayed by the facts that the claim for loss of earnings had been for £1.4million and that the settlement agreement was specified to be in consideration of A withdrawing his claims before the employment tribunal.

11.23   *HMRC v Colquhoun [2011] STC 394* was a case on payment to vary the terms of the employment. It is an interesting case. Mr Colquhoun was employed by Rosyth Royal Dockyard plc. In January 1997, he received an amount of £33,148 to change the terms of his contractual redundancy entitlement. £3,148 of this was taxed and the other £30,000 excluded under what is now *ITEPA 2003, s 403(1)* (see **11.25(a)**). In August 2005, Mr Colquhoun was made redundant and received a redundancy payment of £61,930 plus a payment in lieu of notice of £29,664. He claimed another £30,000 exemption. The FTT held that he was entitled to this. It had been untaxed in error in 1997, as there had been no change in the function or emoluments and no commutation of annual or periodic payments at the time. *Section 401* did not apply to a change in a contractual entitlement which was wholly contingent upon a future redundancy. Sadly the Upper Tribunal disagreed. *Section 401* is widely drawn; a payment 'received directly or indirectly … in connection with … the termination of a person's employment' is apt to include a payment to vary the right to a future redundancy payment. It also felt that the FTT had misinterpreted the reasoning in *Mairs v Haughey* (see **11.59**). It is unfortunate that Mr Colquhoun was a taxpayer in person. It would have been helpful to have seen his case fleshed out from a technical point of view.

11.24   An interesting issue arose in *Rubio v HMRC [2012] UKFTT 361(TC)*. In 1991, Mr Rubio was employed in Spain by a Spanish company, Symbol Technologies SL. In June 2000, he was asked to move to the UK and work for Symbol Technologies Ltd. It was anticipated that the UK job would last for approximately two years after which Mr Rubio would return to Spain. In June 2013, Symbol told Rubio that his employment with Symbol Technologies Ltd would be terminated and that there was no position available for him in the Spanish company. A termination payment of around £695,000 was agreed. HMRC accepted that Mr Rubio was not ordinarily resident in the UK and it was agreed that only 39.5% of his income was liable to UK tax. Symbol UK deducted £72,477 PAYE from the corporation. In 2005, HMRC opened an enquiry into the company and calculated that Symbol should have deducted an extra £17,165. In 2006, Symbol paid to HMRC £24,012 being that extra tax plus interest. The Tribunal held that no part of the termination payment constituted emoluments so that the whole amount fell within *ITEPA 2003, s 401* but that the foreign service exception under *ITEPA 2003, s 413* (see **11.28**) applied so no amounts were chargeable to tax. Mr Rubio was accordingly entitled to a refund of the PAYE that had been deducted. However, he was not entitled to a refund of the amount paid to HMRC in 2006 as that was not PAYE; it was a compromise payment, and, in any event, it had not been deducted from any amount due from him so he could not be entitled to it.

11.25   There are a number of exemptions from the tax charge under *ITEPA 2003, s 401*:

(*a*)   It applies only to the extent that the total payments and benefits in respect of an employment exceed £30,000. [*ITEPA 2003, s 403(1)*].

If an employee has different employments with the same employer or associated employers, a single £30,000 exemption applies in aggregate. [*ITEPA 2003, s 404*].

(*b*) It does not apply to a payment or benefit provided in connection with the termination of the employment by the death of the employee or on account of injury or disability of the employee. [*ITEPA 2003, s 406*].

(*c*) It does not apply to a payment or benefit under an approved retirement benefit scheme provided that either:

   (i) the payment or other benefit is by way of compensation for loss of employment, or for loss or diminution of emoluments, due to ill health; or

   (ii) the payment or other benefit is properly regarded as earned by past service. [*ITEPA 2003, s 407*].

(*d*) It does not apply to a payment or other benefit provided under a Royal Warrant, Queen's Order or Order in Council relating to members of Her Majesty's forces or by way of payment in commutation of annual or other periodical payments authorised by such a Warrant or Order, or, for 2006/07 onwards, to a payment or other benefit provided under a scheme established by an order under the *Armed Forces (Pensions and Compensation) Act 2004, s 1(1)*. [*ITEPA 2003, s 411* as amended by *FA 2007, s 63*].

(*e*) It does not apply to:

   (i) any benefit provided under a superannuation scheme administered by the government of another Commonwealth territory (as defined in the *Overseas Development and Co-operation Act 1980*); or

   (ii) any payment of compensation for loss of career, interruption of service or disturbance made in connection with any change in the constitution of any such territory to a person who before that change was employed in the public service of that territory. [*ITEPA 2003, s 412*].

(*f*) There is an exemption for foreign service (see **11.28**).

(*g*) It does not apply to a contribution to an unapproved pension scheme that is taxed on the employee under *ITEPA 2003, s 386*.

(*h*) It does not apply to a contribution to a personal pension which would have been exempt from tax under *ITEPA 2003, s 308* had it been paid for the performance of duties of the employment. [*ITEPA 2003, ss 405(1), 408*].

(*i*) Similarly it does not apply to a contribution to an approved pension scheme to provide benefits for the employee in accordance with the terms of the scheme. [*ITEPA 2003, s 408*].

11.26   The legislation contains detailed rules to identify the taxable payments where there are several payments and the aggregate exceeds £30,000. The £30,000 exemption must be set against receipts in earlier years before those of later years. If there is more than one payment or benefit in a single tax year, it is set first against cash payments in the order that they are received. If these do not exhaust the exemption, the balance is set against the aggregate of non-cash benefits received in the year. [*ITEPA 2003, s 404(4), (5)*].

11.27 Employers are associated for the purpose of aggregating payments if on the date of the termination or change in question in relation to any of the payments one of them is under the control of the other or one of them is under the control of a third person which either controls or is under the control of the other on that or any other date. The definition of control in *ICTA 1998, s 840* applies. References to any person include the successor of that person. [*ITEPA 2003, ss 404(2), 719*].

11.28 The exemption for foreign service applies:

(*a*)   if such service comprises either 75 per cent or more of the whole period of service down to the date of the termination of the employment or change in its duties; or

(*b*)   where the total period of service exceeds ten years, if the whole of the last ten are foreign service; or

(*c*)   where the total period of service exceeds 20 years, if 50 per cent or more of the total period is foreign service and that period includes any ten of the last 20 years. [*ITEPA 2003, s 413(1)*].

Foreign service for this purpose is:

(i)   employments for 2008/09 onwards for a tax year in which the employee is not ordinarily resident in the UK and for which the earnings are not general earnings within *ITEPA 2003, s 15* (see **2.47**) and would not be so even if the employee were to claim the remittance basis. [*ITEPA 2003, s 413(3A) inserted by Finance Act 2008 (FA 2008), Sch 7, para 30*].

(ii)   employments from 2003/04 onwards for which the earnings are not general earnings (ie earnings for a year when the employee was resident or ordinarily resident in the UK) or, if they were, the individual is a seafarer and the whole of the earnings attracts the 100 per cent deduction under *ITEPA 2003, s 378* (see **13.12**).

(iii) employment from 1974/75 to 2002/03, the emoluments for which were not chargeable under Case I of Schedule E;

(iv)   employment from 1974/75 to 1997/98 to which the 100 per cent foreign earnings deduction applied (this ceased from 16 March 1998);

(v)   employment before 1974/75 where the emoluments were not chargeable under Case I of Schedule E (or before 1956/57 were not chargeable under Schedule E). [*ITEPA 2003, s 413(2)–(6)*].

11.29 If an employment includes a period of foreign service but the above tests are not satisfied, a measure of relief is still due. The £30,000 standard exemption is first deducted from the compensation, etc. The balance is then reduced in the proportion that the length of foreign service bears to the whole period of service (up to the date of the termination or change). However, if the employee is entitled to deduct tax on making a payment to some other person (eg under a charitable covenant) the reduction is, if necessary, restricted to leave in charge to tax sufficient income to cover that deduction. [*ITEPA 2003, s 414*].

11.30   The value of a non-cash benefit is its cash equivalent. This is the greater of:

(*a*)   the amount of earnings that the benefit would have given rise to if it were received by an employee for the performance of the duties of his employment; or

(*b*)   the cash equivalent determined in accordance with *s 596B*, namely:

  (i)   in the case of a benefit other than living accommodation, the cash equivalent calculated under the benefit in kind rules for higher paid employees (see **Chapters 6, 7** and **9**);

  (ii)   in the case of living accommodation, the benefit calculated under the appropriate benefit rules (see **Chapter 8**).

[*ITEPA 2003, s 415*].

11.31   If a benefit consists of a cheap or interest-free loan the employee is treated as having paid interest on the loan – but only to the extent that the benefit is charged to tax (ie not if it is covered by the £30,000 exemption). This will enable him to claim a deduction against tax for that notional interest to the extent that the loan was one qualifying for tax relief on interest paid. [*ITEPA 2003, s 416*].

11.32   It is of course important to be able to evidence what a payment is for. HMRC will normally look at the contract of employment. They will also look for minutes of the employer, correspondence between the parties and the wording of any termination agreement. The importance of ensuring that the termination agreement supports what the taxpayer intends to argue is emphasised by *Appellant v Inspector of Taxes [2001] STC (SCD), 21*. The appellant had a number of disputes with his employer about alleged racial discrimination and took these to an industrial tribunal. He won two of his appeals. He agreed to settle the third on the basis that his employer would pay him £20,000 and that the taxpayer would then take voluntary redundancy – for which he would be paid an additional lump sum of £65,684. The taxpayer claimed that this additional sum was for loss of his human and civil rights and was not taxable. Unfortunately, the termination agreement described it as consideration for the Appellant's voluntary termination of his employment. The taxpayer's fall-back was that at least part of it related to a confidentiality clause and an agreement not to institute further industrial tribunal claims that were included in the agreement. The Commissioner held that the substance and reality of the termination agreement was that it was paid for the voluntary termination. The parties had not attributed any part of it to the other obligations under the agreement. He also agreed with HMRC that a payment that related to the confidentiality clause and the agreement not to institute proceedings would be taxable under *ITEPA 2003, s 225* (see **11.75**) as those obligations constituted restrictive covenants.

Other matters

11.33   As indicated in **11.14** above, *ITEPA 2003, s 401* applies to any payment in connection with the termination of an employment which is not otherwise chargeable as employment income whether or not it is made in pursuance of a legal obligation. It will apply to an ex gratia payment even where the employee has foregone his proper notice period or if he resigns. It will also apply to a payment made to compromise a legal action by the employee against his employer or to head off the threat of such an action. A payment in lieu of notice where someone is dismissed also falls within *ITEPA 2003, s 401*. Indeed it appears it can apply even if something is sold by the ex-employee to the employer at the time of the termination of the employment. Suppose for example an employee adapts his own car to make it especially suitable for use in his employment and when the employment terminates, he sells the car to the employer for £30,000. It appears that the £30,000 is taxable under *s 401*. It is well known that tax is not always logical, but that probably sounds incredible. Nevertheless that appears to be the result of the decision of the FTT in *Essack v HMRC (TC 3297)*. Mr Essack believed that he had an agreement that the company would grant him share options. When he was dismissed, he was paid £200,000 as 'compensation for loss of employment and any entitlement to shares in the company'. Both Mr Essack and his employer knew that the maximum he would get from an employment Tribunal as compensation for loss of his employment was £57,000. Clearly the remaining £143,000 related to the share rights. So what, said HMRC, *s 401* taxes any payment 'in connection with' the termination of the employment and income tax takes precedence over CGT. The FTT decided that Mr Essack did not have a right to shares; all that he had was 'an oral promise that an asset might be created in the future, which creates at best a contingent obligation on the promisor. However it then went on to say, 'Even if we are wrong in our CGT analysis and Mr Essack can be viewed as having a legally recognisable right over shares, we still do not consider that this is enough to take any of this sum outside the very wide ambit of s 401'.

11.34   Tax cannot be avoided by the employee ceasing to be UK resident prior to the determination of his employment. In *Nichols v Gibson [1996] STC 1008* the taxpayer's employment was terminated on 6 April 1994 after 31 years' service. He had been given prior warning of the termination and obtained employment in Jamaica. With the leave of his existing employer he started this on 1 April 1984. He contended that the compensation he received was not taxable as he was not UK resident in 1984/85 when the employment terminated, and none of the cases of Schedule E applied to him that year. It was held that *ITEPA 2003, s 401* imposes a charge independently of the basic employment income charging rules so it is irrelevant whether the ex-employee is UK resident or working in the UK in the tax year that the employment ceases.

11.35   *ITEPA 2003, ss 409, 410* exclude from *ITEPA 2003, s 401* for 1995/96 onwards any reimbursement by the former employer of a payment in respect of an employee liability or indemnity insurance premium which would have been deductible by the employee under *ITEPA 2003, s 555* (see **5.100**) had it not been reimbursed. If the employee has died a payment to his executors or administrators is similarly excluded. If the employer does not actually reimburse the expense but provides some other valuable consideration, the amount of such consideration is deemed to be a payment to the extent of the costs of the liability so as to preserve the exemption.

11.35A Mention ought also to be made of *HMRC v Knowledgepoint 360 Group Ltd ([2013] UKUT 7)*. This was a National Insurance case; the company applied PAYE but claimed no NIC was due. As the two generally run hand in hand, it is not surprising that HMRC challenged this. Knowledgepoint had set up an EBT some years previous. The shareholders sold the shares in Knowledgepoint, resulting in a separation of the EBT from the company. Following the sale, the EBT was left with a large sum of money. The trustees decided to distribute this to employees of Knowledgepoint who had contributed to the success of the Group prior to its sale. It is not clear why they believed that the payments were earnings for PAYE. The NIC rules say that the payment of a gratuity is not liable to NIC. The trustees contended that the payments to employees were gratuities. The FTT agreed but the UT disagreed. It held that the essential feature of a tip or gratuity is that it represents services rendered by the recipient personally to the taxpayer. This was established in *Calvert v Wainwright* (see **3.12**). As that is not the position here, the payments were not gratuities.

Information

11.36   The *PAYE Regulations* can require an employer or former employer to provide information in relation to these provisions. [*ITEPA 2003, s 684(4)*]. The *PAYE Regulations* impose an obligation to deduct tax on the excess of the payment over £30,000.

11.37   The reporting obligation was reintroduced in an extended form from 6 April 1999 by what is now *Reg 91* of the *PAYE Regulations*. This requires the employer (or former employer) to give details to HMRC of any award of payments combined with other benefits or consisting solely of such benefits where the total amount of the payments and other benefits exceed £30,000 and to give the same details to the employee. There is no obligation to remind either HMRC or the employee of benefits that are received by the employee in later years.

Ex gratia payments

11.38   Care needs to be taken with ex gratia payments to be able to demonstrate that the payment is not an emolument of the employee. HMRC will expect to see a minute authorising the payment and showing the reason for it. Many people recommend that the payment is made after the employment is terminated, to separate it from the employment. While it is doubtful if this is necessary, it is worth considering if it can be done without undue trouble.

It remains a question of fact whether or not a payment is emoluments of an employment; the timing of the payment cannot change its nature.

11.39 HMRC do however accept that it is unlikely that an implied contractual term to make a payment in lieu of notice can exist. This is because a contractual right to receive notice of termination of employment (whether specific or as a result of the *Employment Rights Act 1996 (ERA 1996)*) would conflict with an implied right to receive a payment in lieu of notice. They do however say that in certain circumstances an ex gratia payment can fall within the definition of earnings in *ITEPA 2003, s 7* because something can be an emolument even though it is non-contractual. If a payment in lieu of notice is paid as an automatic response to a termination, eg if every time there is a redundancy all employees receive a payment in lieu of any period of unworked notice, they consider that 'the payment is an integral part of the employer-employee relationship for the workplace, albeit non-contractual, and has its source in that relationship and nowhere else' (*Tax Bulletin 63*, Feb 2003).

11.40 In March 1991 the Pension Schemes Office (formerly the Superannuation Funds Office) stated (in *SFO/OPB Memorandum 104*) that HMRC have been advised that an arrangement by an employer to pay ex gratia 'relevant benefits' to an employee constitutes a retirement benefit scheme. Such a scheme will not be an approved scheme, so the contribution to it, ie the ex gratia payment, will constitute emoluments taxable as employment income. Accordingly, *s 401* and, more importantly, the £30,000 exemption (see **11.19(a)** above), will not apply to such a payment. 'Relevant benefits' are defined as 'any pension, lump sum, gratuity or other like benefit given or to be given on retirement or on death, or in anticipation of retirement, or in connection with past service, after retirement or death' or in connection with any change in the nature of the employee's service. [*ICTA 1988, s 612(1)*].

11.41 HMRC have said that 'self-evidently' there will be an 'arrangement' if the payment flows from any prior formal or informal arrangement with the employee. They also think that it includes any system, plan, pattern or policy for making such payments, such as a decision taken at a meeting to make an ex gratia payment, or where a personnel manager makes an ex gratia payment under a delegated authority or on the basis of some outline structure or policy, or where it is common practice for the employer to make ex gratia payments to a particular class of employee (*SP 13/91* – since withdrawn).

11.42 The payment must be made in respect of death or retirement to be caught. HMRC have said that an ex gratia payment on severance of the employment due to redundancy or loss of office (or because of death or disability due to an accident) is not affected 'where the arrangements for making the payment are designed solely to meet such a situation'. In particular, 'genuine redundancy payments' are not affected (*SP 13/91*). *SP 13/91* was withdrawn from 6 April 2006 but it seems likely that this exclusion still applies.

11.43 They have also confirmed to the ICAEW (*Tax 15/92*) that:

(*a*)   a senior executive who changes jobs at age 45, obviously as part of his normal working career, is not retiring so any ex gratia payment is not affected by the approach;

(*b*)   if, however, at the time he changes jobs he is aged 60 'this might well be regarded as retirement', but would depend on the precise circumstances;

(*c*)   if a division of a company is sold and the 55-year-old manager responsible for running it leaves to take a job with the purchaser, this 'does not look to be consistent with retirement but with maximising his opportunities to continue working until normal retirement age' so it would probably not be caught;

(*d*)   if a person in his 50s has a heart attack and is advised by his doctor to leave work and seek a less stressful position that 'may well be viewed as retirement' – although if the ex gratia payment is made purely as compensation for the loss of health it would not be regarded as made in connection with the retirement; and

(*e*)   if an employee aged 50 leaves to take a job nearer home to be able to nurse her aged parents it would probably not be viewed as retirement bearing in mind the age of the employee and the fact that she obtains further work – but may well be regarded as retirement if she does not seek a further job.

11.44   They have told the Law Society (*Law Society Press Release 7 October 1992*) that whether an individual continues to work, or make him or herself available for work after employment is terminated is not conclusive. It is simply a factor to take into account. So is the age of the individual. 'An ex gratia payment made to a man moving on to a further full-time employment in his middle years will obviously not be made "on or in anticipation of retirement". However, an ex gratia payment to a man of older years who has no other full-time employment in prospect could fall on the other side of the line'. They also say that 'provided the situation has not been contrived for the purpose of obtaining favourable tax treatment, then termination of employment in circumstances which amount to unfair dismissal, whether that comes about because the employee is sacked or is forced to resign, will not constitute "retirement"'.

11.45   Pension Schemes Services (the new name for the Pension Schemes Office) say the only benefits affected are lump sums, gratuities and similar benefits given:

(*a*)   where a person retires or dies;

(*b*)   in anticipation of retirement;

(*c*)   after a person has retired or died (if the payment is in recognition of past services); or

(*d*)   as compensation for any change in the conditions of a continuing employment.

11.46   Pension Schemes Services were willing to grant approval (so that the lump sum would become a non-taxable capital payment under an approved pension scheme) for an ex gratia lump sum payment if:

(*a*)   it was the only lump sum relevant benefit potentially payable in respect of the employment (ie the employee was not a member of an approved pension scheme unless the payment was on retirement and the other scheme provided benefits only on death-in-service); and

(*b*)   it satisfied the normal requirements for approval of a retirement benefit scheme; in particular the lump sum on retirement did not exceed 1½ times salary – or the appropriate lower figure where the employee had less than 40 years' service.

Payments in lieu of notice

11.47   Care also needs to be taken with payments in lieu of notice (PILONs). If the payment is compensation for a breach of the employment agreement or, probably, even agreed liquidated damages it will not be emoluments. However, if there is a contractual entitlement it will be general earnings within *ITEPA 2003, ss 7* and *62* to which the £30,000 exemption will not apply. The trap is well illustrated by the case of *EMI Electronics Ltd v Coldicott (1999) STC 803*, a Court of Appeal decision. The employment agreement provided for six months' written notice but went on to say 'The company reserves the right to make payment of the equivalent of salary in lieu of notice'. It was held that this was sufficient to make the PILON a contractual payment assessable under *s 62*.

11.48   This principle was carried a step further in *Richardson v Delaney (2001 STC 1328)*. The employment agreement provided for an 18-month notice period but entitled the company to terminate the employment 'with immediate effect' by paying salary in lieu of notice. On 1 December 1995 it gave the 18-months' notice and put the employee on garden leave. At the same time it suggested an alternative, namely that the employment should terminate by mutual agreement on 28 December 1995, and the company would make a payment to the employee of £68,001 in compensation for the premature termination of the employment. After negotiation the compensation payment was agreed at £75,000 plus the taxpayer would keep his company car worth £10,000. Lloyd J could see no breach of contract. The company was entitled to give notice to terminate the contract. It was entitled to make a payment in lieu of notice. That payment could not become compensation simply because the employment had continued for a month, and the payment in lieu covered only 17 months. Whilst that is logical, it is hard to reconcile with the terms of the employment agreement. The employment was not terminated by the company with immediate effect. It was terminated by notice and, as a separate agreement, it was subsequently mutually agreed that the notice period would not be worked and that a payment would be made. It may well be that this agreement varied the employment contract and would be taxable as such, but that was not the basis of the decision.

11.49   Lloyd J was strongly influenced by dicta of Lord Browne-Wilkinson in *Delaney v Staples [1992] 1 AC 687*, an unfair dismissal case. Lord Browne-Wilkinson had there identified four principle categories of case in which a payment is made that could be described as in lieu of notice:

(*a*)   where proper notice is given, the employee is put on garden leave, and he is paid the whole of his wages up-front instead of month by month;

(*b*)   where the contract of employment provides expressly that the employment may be terminated either by notice or on payment of a sum in lieu;

(*c*)   where at the end of the employment the employer and employee agree that the employment is to terminate forthwith on payment of a sum in lieu of notice; and

(*d*)   where without the agreement of the employee the employer summarily dismisses the employee and tenders a payment in lieu of proper notice.

Lord Browne-Wilkinson was concerned to determine whether or not a payment was wages, not if it was compensation. Lloyd J could not fit the payment to Mr Delaney into any of the four categories. He thought it was 'to some extent ... closer to Lord Browne-Wilkinson's third category although not entirely foreign to his second category'.

11.50   This is a somewhat worrying decision. Many terminations fall between categories (*c*) and (*d*). The employee agrees to prematurely terminate his employment by resigning and the employer agrees to make a payment. This is generally a cosmetic procedure as the employee is anxious to avert falling within category (*d*). If category (*d*) is the only true case of a breach of contract, as Lloyd J clearly implies, can the employee resign and yet still be within (*d*)? He probably could do if the employer summarily dismisses him and the payment (and the resignation) is made in settlement of a challenge by the employee against the validity of the purported dismissal and in settlement of his claim against that challenge.

11.51   In *Brander and others v HMRC [2007] STC (SCD) 582* clause 18.5 of the employment agreement allowed the company to terminate the employment forthwith by paying salary and the value of all other contractual benefits in lieu of the required period of notice. Three directors of the company, Mr Bocker, Mr McGrotty and Mr Brander, were asked to resign as it needed new institutional investment and a condition of such investment was that a new management team should be brought in. Mr Bocker and Mr McGrotty each received as part of their settlement package a payment of £9,273 for 'loss of share option rights'. The Special Commissioner decided that the company did not in fact terminate the employment by operating clause 18.5. It invited the directors to resign. He also held that there was in fact no loss of share option rights and that aside from the compensation agreement there was no contractual entitlement to the £9,273. The compensation packages also contained a payment described as 'pension contributions' for which there was no contractual entitlement. It was held that both the £9,273 and the pension contribution were 'not otherwise chargeable to tax' so were taxable under *ITEPA 2003, s 401* (see **11.15**) but subject to the £30,000 exemption (see **11.25**(a)).

In *Cornell v HMRC [2009] STI 2199, FTT(Tax)* Mrs Cornell had to serve a three-month probationary period during which she was entitled to a week's notice. The contract provided that at the end of this period her performance would be assessed and if satisfactory she would be confirmed in the post. Thereafter she would be entitled to three months' notice. The company was entitled to pay in lieu of notice. Mrs Cornell was made redundant about 4½ years after starting the job. She was paid three months' salary on termination of her employment. She contended that her performance had never been assessed, so her probationary period had not ceased and thus only one week's salary could be in lieu of notice; the rest must be redundancy pay. The Tribunal disagreed. It held that once the probationary period had come to an end the probationary provision ceased to have effect irrespective of whether or not it had been properly performed.

11.52   HMRC issued further guidance in *Tax Bulletin 63, February 2003* in the light of a January 2001 employment case, *Cerberus Software Ltd v Rowley [2001] IRLR 160*. In that case the Court of Appeal held that a provision in the contract that an employer 'may' make a PILON meant that the employer was free to give neither notice nor a PILON but instead to breach the contract and pay damages for the breach. HMRC do not consider that this conflicts with the *EMI* decision, as in *EMI* 'the employer had exercised his discretion and so ensured that the source of the payment was the employer-employee relationship' whereas in *Cerberus* it had suited the employer to breach the contract as the ex-employee had found alternative employment during the notice period.

11.53   HMRC say that it is crucial to establish and examine the facts to decide whether the discretion has been exercised. Factors that may be relevant include:

(*a*)   A settlement that is substantially the same in value as an exercise of the discretion would have produced is likely to be viewed as made by exercise of the discretion, as happened in *Richardson v Delaney* (although each case will depend on its own facts).

(*b*)   A payment resulting from a decision not to exercise discretion could be expected to have characteristics normally associated with compensation or damages for breach of contract (such as the employee by securing alternative employment had reduced the loss or damage caused by the employer's breach).

(*c*)   Other adjustments are common when calculating payments for a breach (such as the application of the decision in *British Transport Commission v Gourley [1955] 3 All ER 796* that the real loss is the after-tax income that the employee would have received), and

(*d*)   A decision by an employer not to exercise its discretion might be evidenced in writing.

Legal expenses

11.54   Legal expenses incurred in connection with a claim for compensation for loss of office are not deductible from the compensation. The charge under *s 401* is on the actual amount of the payment (*Warnett v Jones 53 TC 283*). It will not help if the settlement requires the employer to pay the legal costs. As this relieves the employee of an obligation to settle an expense that he has incurred, the payment of such fees is itself a benefit within *s 401*. However, by concession HMRC will not seek tax on the receipt of legal costs recovered by a successful ex-employee under a court order (including one following a compromise of action), or where a dispute is settled without court action on terms that include a specific undertaking to pay the ex-employee's costs. In the latter case the payment must be made direct to the ex-employee's solicitor and the costs to which it relates must be exclusively in connection with the termination of the employment (*ESC A81* and *Law Society Press Release 3 November 1993*). The concession does not apply to other professional fees – in particular, accountancy fees – but if the accountant, valuer or other professional is engaged by the solicitor and his fees are shown as disbursements on the solicitor's bill (or absorbed by the solicitor in his own costs) HMRC accept that they form part of the legal costs (*Tax Bulletin, Issue 13, October 1994*).

Lump sums under registered pension schemes

11.55   Lump sums paid (whether on retirement or otherwise) either:

(*a*)   in pursuance of an approved pension scheme (except where it is compensation paid for loss of office or for loss or diminution of emoluments where such loss is not due to ill health);

(*b*)   in pursuance of a retirement benefits scheme within *ICTA 1988, s 611*; or

(*c*)   under approved personal pension arrangements within *ICTA 1988, ss 630–655* (**10.80–10.86**),

are specifically exempted from income tax. [*ITEPA 2003, s 637*]. This will exempt such payments not only from the general charging provisions but also from *s 401*. However, in the case of a personal pension scheme if the member's death occurred after his normal pension date, ie if he was taking income withdrawals from the fund, the lump sum is taxable. The tax is at a flat rate of 35 per cent, payable by the pension scheme administrator and is not income for any other tax purposes. [*ICTA 1988, s 648B*]. The reason for the charge is that the lump sum (which will be a return of contributions with interest) is in lieu of future annuity payments, which would themselves have been taxable.

Members of Parliament and of the Greater London Authority

11.56   Grants and payments made by the House of Commons to a person who ceases to be an MP on dissolution of Parliament, under *s 5(1)* of the *Parliamentary Standards Act 2009* (formerly under *s 131* of the *Parliamentary*

Pensions Act 1984) to persons ceasing to hold certain ministerial and other offices, or under *s 3* of the *European Parliament (Pay and Pensions) Act 1979* which provides for resettlement grants to persons ceasing to be Euro MPs, or from 2009/10 under *Article 13* of the *Statute of the European Parliament* which provides for payment of transitional allowances, are similarly exempted from tax. Curiously, such grants remain taxable under *s 401* to the extent they exceed £30,000. The first £30,000 of payments made to a person after 5 April 2008 under the *Greater London Authority Act 1999 (GLAA 1999)* on ceasing to be the Mayor of London or a member of the Greater London Assembly are similarly exempt [*ITEPA 2003, s 291* as amended by *Finance Act 2012 (FA 2012), s 15*].

Redundancy payments

11.57   Statutory redundancy payments are specifically exempted from tax as earnings, except under *s 401*. [*ITEPA 2003, s 309*]. So is any additional voluntary payment by the employer, but only up to a figure equal to the statutory payment, ie twice the statutory payment can be paid tax-free. [*ITEPA 2003, s 309(2)*]. See **11.13** for a case where redundancy payments were held to be taxable to the extent that they related to payments in lieu of notice.

11.58   On the privatisation of Harland & Wolff employees were offered new employment by a proposed buy-out company, Harland & Wolff 1989 Ltd. To induce him to accept, an employee was given an ex gratia payment consisting of two elements, 30 per cent of the sum to which he would have been entitled under Harland & Wolff's non-statutory redundancy scheme, and £100 per complete year of service with Harland & Wolff. HMRC contended that the entire payment was an inducement to accept the new employment and as such was an emolument of it. The House of Lords unanimously held that the sum was severable; the 30 per cent element being a payment in reality to give up the employee's rights under the Harland & Wolff redundancy scheme and as such 'derives its character from the nature of the payment which it replaces', and the £100 per annum payment being taxable as employment income (*Mairs v Haughey [1993] STC 569*).

11.59   Their Lordships criticised HMRC for not applying *SP 1/81* (which said that HMRC would not assess the first £30,000 of non-statutory redundancy pay, even if it was part of the conditions under which the employees agreed to give their services or they had an expectation of it). They also held that in any event in law a redundancy payment is not an emolument. It has 'a real element of compensating or relieving an employee for the consequences of his not being able to earn a living in his former employment. The redundancy legislation reflects an appreciation that an employee who has remained in employment ... has a stake in his employment which justifies his receiving compensation if he loses that stake. It is distinct from the damages to which he would be entitled if his employment were terminated lawfully. It is also unlike a deferred payment of wages in that the entitlement to a redundancy payment is never more than a contingent entitlement, which no doubt both the employer and employee normally hope will never accrue'. A redundancy payment is not a payment from being or becoming an employee (per *Shilton v Wilmshurst* – see **11.72**); it is to compensate or relieve an employee for what can be the unfortunate consequences of becoming unemployed. It is also paid after the employment has come to an end, a *prima facie* indication that it is not an emolument from that employment.

11.60   Following that decision HMRC withdrew *SP 1/81* and replaced it by *SP 1/94*. This accepts that non-statutory redundancy is taxable only under *ITEPA 2003, s 401* (ie only on the excess over £30,000) whether the scheme is a standing one which forms part of the terms on which the employees give their services or is an *ad hoc* scheme devised to meet a specific situation. It goes on to warn that payments 'which are not genuinely made to compensate for loss of employment through redundancy … In particular payments which are in reality a form of terminal bonus' are taxable in full. It instances as terminal bonuses payments for meeting production targets or doing extra work in the period leading up to a redundancy, and payments conditional on continual service in the employment for a time after the issue of the redundancy notice. It concludes by suggesting that employers might wish to submit redundancy schemes to their local Inspector (enclosing the scheme document plus the text of any intended letter to employees) for advance clearance as to whether the payments are taxable.

11.61   It is important that the employee actually becomes redundant as is shown by *Allan v IRC [1994] STC 943*. An old established company operating two stores decided to close down its business and sell its assets. It resolved to make redundancy payments to a number of employees. After closing the first store it received an offer for the company which was accepted. The shareholders felt that the redundancy payments should still be made irrespective of whether an employee was kept on by the purchaser. The company was sold in March 1982 and in May 1982 it paid a redundancy payment to Mr Allen. Mr Allen continued to be employed by the company. It was held that, although originally intended as a redundancy payment, the payment had changed its character by the time it was made. At that stage it was a payment by an employer to its employee. The payment arose from the employment and from nothing else as Mr Allen had never, in fact, been made redundant.

11.62   In *Antelope v Ellis [1995] STC (SCD) 297* the taxpayer was employed as managing director of a subsidiary company within a group from around 1986. In 1991 the group wished him to relinquish that post and become managing director of a second group company. He did not want the new job but eventually agreed to the transfer on condition that if he were to leave the group before March 1993 he would receive a substantial redundancy payment. He ceased the employment within that period and received the payment. The Special Commissioner held that it was not a termination payment (to which the £30,000 exemption would apply) but an inducement to take the employment with the second company. It is hard to reconcile this decision with *Mairs v Haughey*. It does not appear that the case was cited to the Commissioner, who accepted the Crown's submission based on *Prendergast v Cameron 23 TC 122* – see **11.6**.

11.63   Where an employment terminated between 6 April 1996 and 6 April 1998, the employee could, by concession, show on his tax return for the year of termination any cash sum received plus the amount of the benefit enjoyed for that year only, calculated by reference to *ITEPA 2003, s 398* (see **10.87**). In most cases these follow the benefit in kind rules for employees. No benefits then needed t be shown on the return in later years. Instead, HMRC will raise an assessment on the taxpayer each year for the benefit enjoyed in that year. If the taxpayer can show that the aggregate amount assessed exceeds the amount that would have been taxable on the statutory basis the assessments will be limited to that amount. As this cut off depends on the valuation exercise which the concession is designed to circumvent it is unlikely that many people claimed it. If the taxpayer opted to adopt the statutory basis of valuing the right to the future benefit at the date of termination, HMRC said that the amount adopted could not subsequently be re-opened if it proves excessive, eg because the benefit ceases earlier than was anticipated. It is not wholly clear that such an incorrect assumption cannot trigger an entitlement to the taxpayer to re-open the return under *Taxes Management Act 1970, s 33*. This concession is no longer needed following the changes introduced in the *FA 1998* (see **11.15**) which have broadly the same effect as the concession.

11.64   Where, as part of the arrangements for the termination of a person's employment, the employer agrees to make a special payment into an occupational pension scheme for the employee (or purchases an annuity from a life office, which is approved as a pension scheme) HMRC cannot charge tax under *ITEPA 2003, s 401* in relation to the payment as *ITEPA 2003, s 308* specifically exempts from income tax a payment by an employer to a registered pension scheme. For 2013/14 onwards, this applies only to a contribution in respect of the employee himself. It will not extend to a contribution in respect of a family member (*ITEPA 2003, s 308* as amended by *Finance Act 2013 (FA 2013, s 11*).

Golden handcuffs

11.65   Particular problems arise where the employment is not the only reason for a payment. Thus, on the sale of a business the price to be paid for the goodwill or for shares could be tied to the length of the vendor's service with the purchasing company. This was a popular ploy when firms of stockbrokers were sold in the mid-1980s. The partners would be issued with loan stock or a similar security of the purchaser which would be redeemable at the time he ceased to work for the purchaser. The redemption terms would vary according to the length of service, eg the loan stock could be redeemable at par within the first year, at £1.20 if redeemed in the second, £1.40 if redeemed in the third, and so on. It was usually a term of the agreement that the company would be entitled to redeem the loan stock if the partner ceased to work for it.

11.66   This sort of arrangement has the same effect as paying the employee a loyalty bonus if he remains with the company for more than a year. Nevertheless, it is likely that, in normal circumstances, the full redemption price of the loan stock would be a capital gain, not income. Such arrangements are probably only viable in certain types of business. It would need to be established that the ultimate redemption price reflects the real value of the business at the time of acquisition and that the requirement for the vendor to remain with the company was felt necessary to enable that value to be fully realised. If this cannot be shown, HMRC might well be able to show that the increase in the price to be paid for the loan stock arose from the employment.

Signing-on fees

Case law

Riley v Coglan

11.67 If a payment is made to a person on, or prior to, taking up an employment it is necessary to analyse the real reason for the payment. If it is to induce him to take up the job, the payment will be regarded as an emolument of that employment. This is particularly likely to be the case if the payment is tied to the employee remaining in the employment for a specified period. In *Riley v Coglan 44 TC 481* an amateur rugby player received a signing-on fee on joining a rugby league club as a professional. The agreement provided that part of the fee was to be returnable if he did not remain with the club for a specified period. It was held that the payment was remuneration, being a reward for remaining in the club's employment for the period.

Jarrold v Boustead

11.68 In contrast, if the payment is to induce the person to give up some existing benefit that is incompatible with the employment, that payment may not constitute emoluments. The leading case is *Jarrold v Boustead 41 TC 701*, another case where an amateur rugby player received a signing-on fee for joining a rugby league club. It was held that the payment was not a reward for his future services to the club; it was to compensate him for having to give up his amateur status. He attached value to this as, once lost, it could not be regained.

Pritchard v Arundale, Vaughan-Neil v CIR

11.69 In *Pritchard v Arundale 47 TC 680* a senior partner in a successful firm of accountants was approached to become managing director of a company. He was not prepared to give up his professional practice without the company showing sufficient commitment to him to give him the confidence to leave his partnership. The major shareholder of the company accordingly transferred to him a substantial block of shares in the company. HMRC claimed that those shares were a reward for the future services he was to perform for the company. It was held that it was to induce him to give up professional practice and did not constitute emoluments. Similarly, in *Vaughan-Neil v IRC 54 TC 223* a payment to a practising barrister who gave up the bar and took employment with a company was held to be an inducement to accept the professional and social consequences flowing from taking up an employment. Interestingly, in that case HMRC conceded that the payment was not remuneration of the employment but contended that it was assessable as a restrictive covenant as he agreed to cease his practice at the bar. The court did not feel this was tenable as the bar's rules of conduct prevent an employed barrister from continuing in practice, and the payment could not, in reality, be to prohibit him from doing something that he was powerless to do.

11.70   Unfortunately, this does not always hold good. Each case needs to be looked at on its own merits. In *Glantre Engineering Ltd v Goodhand 56 TC 165*, a payment of £10,000 made to Mr Wells, an employee of a leading firm of accountants, to induce him to take up employment with an engineering company was held to be taxable. Warner J distinguished the case from that of *Pritchard v Arundale* on three grounds. The payment to Mr Wells was made by the prospective employer; that to Mr Arundale was made by a third party. Mr Arundale was not merely changing from one employment to another; he was exchanging the status of senior partner in a firm of chartered accountants for that of joint managing director of, and shareholder in, a company. Mr Arundale was entitled to his shares on signing the agreement but was not to start work until some time later and if he had died in the interim his estate would have been entitled to retain the shares; Mr Well's payment was one of the specific terms of his new employment. As Warner J reversed the decision of the Commissioners this suggests that the circumstances in which an inducement payment is not taxable are likely to be fairly limited. Mr Wells did give up the security of working for a major firm of accountants and the likelihood of a future partnership with it and the payment was specifically stated to compensate for the losses.

Shilton v Wilmshurst

11.71   In *Shilton v Wilmshurst [1990] STC 55* Nottingham Forest FC agreed with Southampton FC to transfer to Southampton the contract of the footballer, Peter Shilton, in return for a substantial transfer fee. This transfer would only go through if Shilton himself agreed satisfactory terms of employment with Southampton. Nottingham Forest made a payment to Shilton to induce him to agree to join Southampton. HMRC contended that their payment was remuneration for his future services with Southampton, whereas Shilton claimed that it was taxable under *s 148* (subject to the first £30,000 being exempt) as a payment on the termination of his employment with Nottingham Forest. The Court of Appeal observed that Nottingham Forest would obtain no benefit from Shilton's services to Southampton so it was hard to see why they should remunerate him for such services. Their only interest was in obtaining the transfer fee from Southampton, and the payment was to induce Shilton to undertake the necessary steps to enable this to be paid to them. However, the House of Lords dismissed this distinction. The question to be asked was whether the payment was an emolument 'from employment', ie from being or becoming an employee. The fact that Nottingham Forest had a different motive for making the payment did not stop it being a payment in return for the taxpayer agreeing to become an employee of Southampton. It was made available to Shilton in return for his agreeing to render services to Southampton. It was putting a gloss on the legislation to suggest that payment by a third party could only be an emolument if that party has an interest in the performance of the duties.

Teward v CIR

11.72   In *Teward v IRC [2001] STC (SCD) 36* Mr Teward was employed by Glaxochem Ltd. That company sold one of its plants to Synpac Chemicals Ltd. The taxpayer agreed to join Synpac. A stumbling block was Mr Teward's share options in Glaxo Holdings plc, the parent company of Glaxochem. Synpac agreed to pay Mr Teward £24,103, the amount of the loss Mr Teward would suffer on being forced to abandon his share options, in consideration of his entering into a service agreement with Synpac. Mr Teward argued that the payment was compensation for giving up his advantages under the Glaxo share option schemes and was unconnected with his employment with Synpac. The Commissioners thought it clear from the evidence that the payment formed part of the package of arrangements whereby Mr Teward became an employee of Synpac. Accordingly the new employment was the source of the payment.

11.72A   The issue in *Martin v HMRC (TC 2460)* was what happens if part of the signing-on fee has to be repaid. Mr Martin received a signing-on fee of £250,000 for committing to work for a company for at least five years. If he left during that period, part of the fee would become repayable. He received the fee in 2005/06 and had to repay £162,500 when he left in 2006/07. HMRC taxed the £250,000, but said that no relief could be given when the bulk of it had to be repaid. The FTT agreed that the £250,000 was assessable in full. At 5 April 2006, the money belonged to Mr Martin. He had no expectation of having to repay it. However it decided that the £162,500 was negative earnings. *Income Tax Act 2007, s 128* (see **2.55A**) allows relief against general income for a loss in an employment or office. *ITEPA 2003, s 11* (see **2.5**) taxes earnings less any deduction allowed under specified provisions (which include *s 128*) and *s 11(3)* specifically recognises that taxable earnings can be a negative figure. Accordingly although Mr Martin could not alter the 2005/06 assessment, he could set the £162,500 against his 2006/07 earnings from the employment in arriving at taxable income from the employment for that year. That would leave £22,500 unrelieved, which he could set against general income of that year under *s 128*.

11.73   In spite of the above cases, it is unsafe to assume that a signing-on fee can be paid tax-free. HMRC are likely to take the stance that any such payment relates to future services and the taxpayer may well have to pursue his case before the courts if he is to show otherwise.

Payments for a restrictive covenant

11.74   If an employee, ex-employee or potential employee (or director) gives, in connection with holding that employment or office, an undertaking the tenor or effect of which is to restrict him as to his conduct or activities, any sum that is paid to him in respect of giving the undertaking (or of its total or partial fulfilment) must be treated as an emolument of the employment if it would not otherwise be so. [*ITEPA 2003, s 225(3)*]. This applies whether or not the undertaking is legally valid. It applies not only to a payment to the employee himself but also to a payment to any other person. If the employee dies before receiving the payment it must be treated as having been paid immediately before his death. [*ITEPA2003, s 225(5)*]. This provision applies only where general earnings are taxed under the normal rule of *ITEPA 2003, s 15* (see **2.48**) in the tax year in which the payment is received (and would still be such if the individual were to claim the remittance basis) or if the employee is non-UK resident and his general earnings are taxed under *ICTA 1988, s 27* (see **2.8**). It does not apply where the earnings are eligible to be taxed on the remittance basis. [*ITEPA 2003, s 225(6) inserted by Finance Act 2005 (FA 2005), Sch 7, para 24*]. For this purpose, the mere assumption of an obligation to make over or provide valuable property, rights or advantages does not constitute valuable consideration – but anything done in the discharge of such an obligation does. [*ITEPA 2003, s 226(2)*].

11.75 It is, therefore, not possible to avoid income tax on a signing-on fee or termination payment by paying it for a restrictive covenant. In *RCI (Europe) Ltd v Woods (2004 STC 315)*, Mr Haylock agreed to be bound by a restrictive covenant up to December 1995. The agreement provided that he could elect for the restrictive covenant to continue to apply to December 1996 and December 1997, in which case he would be entitled to further payments. His contention that such further payments did not fall within *ITEPA 2003, s 226* as they were derived from the elections, not from the employment, was dismissed by Lightman J. The elections were a continuation of covenants given in relation to the termination of the office. The reason the continued undertakings were given was that Mr Haylock had held the office of director. Mr Haylock also contended that even if the payments arose from his employment he was not gainfully employed by RCI Europe at the time they were received so the payment could not be taxed. Lightman J held that the payment did not fall within what is now *Reg 8(5)* of the *Social Security (Contributions) Regulations 2001 (SI 2001 No 1004)* (earnings period for payments made after a person ceased to be a director in relation to periods in which he was a director to be the year in which they are paid) as the payment did not relate to any particular period. Accordingly the normal rules, which gave a one-week earnings period, applied. In *Kent Foods Ltd v HMRC [2008] STC (SCD) 307* the non-compete undertaking was set out in a separate document. The taxpayer contended that as that document made no mention of the employment and his employer was not a party to it, it could only be tied to the sale of his shares, not to either past or prospective employment. The Special Commissioner felt that there was plainly a connection between the employment and the giving of the undertakings, so *section 225* applied and the payment was also earnings for NIC. This looks like a case of the taxpayer trying to be too clever; the deal was originally structured such that the £500,000 allocated to the non-compete agreement was part of the sale price of the shares, so the taxpayer managed to convert capital into income!

11.76 At one stage there was evidence that some Inspectors were seeking to tax payments as termination of employment as consideration for a restrictive covenant on the basis that as part of the arrangements for the termination of the employment it is common for an employee to agree not to take any further action for damages against the employer – and fairly common for him to sign an acknowledgement that the compensation is in full and final settlement of all claims against the employer. HMRC argue that this restricts the employee's future conduct and thus the payment is within *s 226 (Taxline, November 1994, Item 149)*. In most cases such an argument does not accord with the facts. The compensation is not paid 'in respect of the giving of the undertaking', it is paid in respect of the premature cessation of the employment. HMRC now accept that no chargeable value should be attributed to such undertakings. This applies not only where the employee accepts the termination settlement in full and final settlement of his claims but also where the agreement expressly provides that the employee should not commence, or should discontinue, legal action in respect of his claims, and where it re-affirms undertakings about the individual's conduct or activity after termination which formed part of the terms on which the employment was taken up (*SP 3/96*).

11.77   HMRC still consider that a charge would arise if an employer were to make a payment specifically for an undertaking not to litigate. What if there is no such provision but the compromise agreement contains a 'repayment clause', ie a requirement for the employee to repay some or all of the compensation if he subsequently initiates litigation in respect of the employment or its termination? HMRC say this should not trigger a tax charge. If the settlement sum is paid in consideration of settling the employee's genuine claim 'the settlement sum is exhausted by reference to those claims and no sum remains to be attributable to the undertaking not to litigate … whether or not a repayment clause exists'. They will however challenge the entire arrangement if the employee's claims appear spurious. HMRC also point out that if a repayment clause is activated that has no affect on the taxation of the original compromise payment; there is no provision to allow relief for the repayment (*Tax Bulletin 67*, Oct 2003).

Transfer of assets

11.78   If an asset is transferred to the employee as part of his termination arrangements the market value of the asset will be taxed in accordance with the above rules. In addition there may be capital gains tax or capital allowance consequences. *Taxation of Chargeable Gains Act 1992 (TCGA 1992), s 17(1) (b)* requires the capital gain to be calculated by reference to market value where an asset is disposed of in connection with a person's (not necessarily the transferee's) loss of office or employment or diminution of emoluments or otherwise in consideration for, or in recognition of, past services in an office or employment. If the asset has qualified for capital allowances as plant and machinery, eg it is a company car, and it is sold below market value the actual sale price is used as the disposal value for capital allowance purposes where there is a charge to tax as employment income on the disposal. [*Capital Allowances Act 2001 (CAA 2001), s 61(2)*]. This does not appear to envisage a charge on the full amount of the undervalue, but if the whole amount is excepted from tax by *ITEPA 2003, 403(1)* (see **11.20(a)**), the disposal value appears to be the market value, not the price paid if less.

Chapter 12

Foreign Nationals Working in the UK

Reliefs available

12.1   There are a number of special reliefs for foreign nationals working in the UK. Some of these can also apply to a UK national who is not domiciled in the UK or returns to the UK after having been resident and ordinarily resident overseas for a period of years.

Employment in the UK for short periods

12.2   If a person is neither resident nor ordinarily resident in the UK he will be taxable only on earnings for duties performed in the UK. Accordingly, if any duties of the employment are performed outside the UK the salary has to be apportioned between UK and non-UK work, with only the part attributable to the former being chargeable to UK tax.

12.3   The meaning of residence is considered in **2.12** above. It must also be borne in mind that the 'tie-breaker' clause of a double taxation agreement may prevent a person from being regarded as UK resident even though he would be resident in the UK under the normal rules (see **13.4** below).

12.4   Where a person came to the UK to take up employment prior to 6 April 2013 he is treated as resident from the date of his arrival if he comes to work for at least two years and ordinarily resident from the same date if it is clear that he intends to stay for at least three (*Booklet HMRC6 paras 7.7.1, 7.2*). If these tests are not met at the time of his arrival the normal residence rules apply, ie he will normally be UK resident in the tax year of arrival only if he is physically present in the UK for over 183 days. He will be regarded as ordinarily resident from the start of the tax year following the third anniversary of his arrival, unless prior to then he makes a decision to remain in the UK for at least three years (from the date of his arrival) or buys accommodation or acquires it on a lease of three years or more – in which case he will normally be regarded as UK ordinarily resident from the start of the tax year in which the event occurs (or from the date of arrival in the UK if it occurs in the tax year in which he comes to the UK) (*Booklet HMRC6 paras 7.7.3, 7.7.4*).

Double taxation agreements

12.5   If a resident of a country with which the UK has entered into a double taxation agreement works in the UK the double tax agreement will usually exempt him from UK tax on his salary provided that:

(*a*)   he is not present in the UK for more than 183 days during the year of assessment (or a 12-month period commencing or ending in that year);

(*b*)   the remuneration is paid by, or on behalf of, an employer who is not a resident of the UK; and

(*c*)   the remuneration is not borne as such by a permanent establishment or a fixed base of the employer in the UK.

12.6   See, for example, *Article 15* of the *UK/USA Double Taxation Convention* (*SI 2002 No 2648*). As the wording of double taxation agreements differs, the applicable agreement needs to be referred to in each case to ascertain the exact scope of the exemption. In particular, it will often not apply to artists, athletes and entertainers, or to merchant seamen crewing a UK registered ship or aircraft engaged in international trade.

12.7   In the past HMRC accepted that head (*b*) was satisfied if the non-resident remained an employee of an overseas employer where he was seconded by that employer to a UK associated company. They now consider this wrong and interpret the reference to the employer as meaning the 'economic employer' rather than the legal one. Accordingly, they do not consider that the exemption applies when the cost of the employee's salary has been borne by a UK company that uses his services. (*Tax Bulletin, Issue 17, June 1995*). In applying the 183-day test in head (*a*) HMRC say that a day must be counted if the employee is in the UK for any part of it. Previously they took the number of working hours and divided by 24 (*HMRC Brief 9.4.2009*).

12.8   Double taxation agreements can also exempt certain other types of earnings. For example, several of the UK's double tax agreements exempt earnings of professors or teachers who visit the UK for a period of up to two years for the purpose of teaching or research, although it was suggested in the case of *IRC v Vas [1990] STC 137* that this relief can apply only to earnings in the 24 months from the time of the person's first such visit to the UK even if that was of very short duration. In any event, if a visit exceeds two years the exemption does not apply at all; the earnings for the whole period, not merely the excess over two years, will be taxable. Payments to students who are in the UK for the purpose of full-time education or training are also generally exempted. So, normally, is remuneration of employees of the foreign government (or a political subdivision thereof) unless they are UK nationals.

Overseas earnings

12.9   Overseas earnings (formerly called 'foreign emoluments') are earnings of a person not domiciled in the UK from an office or employment with an employer resident outside the UK and the Republic of Ireland (provided he is not also UK resident – ie is not dual resident). [*Income Tax (Earnings and Pensions) Act 2003 (ITEPA 2003), s 22*].

12.10   If the duties of an office or employment are performed wholly outside the UK and the emoluments therefrom constitute overseas earnings, the income is excepted from the basic rules on taxing earnings under *ITEPA 2003, s 9* (see **2.5**), but it will then be assessable under *s 23* (see **2.6**) on a remittance basis. From 5 April 2008 this applies only where the relevant conditions are met. These are considered at **12.17** onwards.

12.11   Where an employee is resident and ordinarily resident in the UK but not UK domiciled he is taxable on a remittance basis in relation to 'chargeable overseas earnings'. [*ITEPA 2003, s 22(2)*]. 'Overseas earnings' for this purpose are earnings from an employment with a foreign employer the duties of which are performed wholly outside the UK. A foreign employer for this purpose is an individual, partnership or body of persons resident outside the UK and not resident in the UK (ie not dual resident). Up to 2007/08 a person resident in the Republic of Ireland could not be a foreign employer if the employee was UK resident. [*ITEPA 2003, ss 23(2), 721(1)* as amended by *Finance Act 2008 (FA 2008), 7 Sch 39*]. If the duties are not performed wholly outside the UK, or if the employer is a UK company, partnership or individual, the whole of the earnings from the employment are taxable in the UK whether or not they are remitted to the UK.

12.12   If an employee is resident but not ordinarily resident in the UK (irrespective of where he is domiciled) he is also taxable on a remittance basis but only in respect of earnings for duties performed outside the UK (other than an overseas Crown employment subject to UK tax). [*ITEPA 2003, s 26(2)*]. Such a person is taxable on his earnings for work performed in the UK irrespective of whether or not he is paid in the UK or remits the earnings to the UK.

12.13   It should be stressed that in such a case the earnings – or at least the part attributable to non-UK work – need to be paid outside the UK. If the salary is paid in the UK this will have the effect of remitting the part attributable to non-UK work and thus bringing it within the charge to UK tax.

12.14   As indicated at **12.2**, if the employee is neither resident nor ordinarily resident in the UK he is taxable in the UK only on earnings from work done in the UK.

Associated employments

12.15   If during a tax year an employee holds an associated employment as well as the employment with a foreign employer which gives rise to overseas earnings, and the duties of the associated employment (or employments) are performed wholly or partly in the UK, the earnings from the two employments need to be aggregated and re-apportioned on a reasonable basis if that would result in a lower amount being regarded as overseas earnings within **12.9** above. [*ITEPA 2003, s 24*]. The detailed rules are considered at **13.24** below.

Payments out of overseas earnings

12.16   If an employee makes payments out of his overseas earnings or foreign emoluments in circumstances corresponding to those in which the payments would have reduced his liability to income tax, the Board of HMRC can allow those payments as a deduction in calculating the amount of the emoluments. [*ITEPA 2003, s 355*]. In the past they exercised this discretion to allow a deduction for foreign alimony or maintenance payments, mortgage interest relief and pension contributions, to the extent that such payments would have been deducted if they had been made in the UK under a UK source agreement. A deduction for an annuity or other annual payment cannot be allowed unless it would have been within the charge to income tax as an annual payment had it arisen in the UK. [*Finance (No 2) Act 1992 (F(No 2)A 1992), s 60*]. This prevents a deduction being given for, in particular, foreign maintenance where a deduction would not be allowed for UK maintenance. The main item to which this relief now applies is foreign pension contributions to a scheme whose terms correspond to a UK approved pension scheme. Where such deductions, or a deduction for foreign travel expenses, other expenses incurred in relation to the employment, or for pension payments under a UK pension scheme, are allowed the emoluments are treated as reduced by those deductions (so only the net amount is capable of being remitted).

The remittance basis

12.17   As indicated at **12.10** above, some earnings are taxable only to the extent, and at the time, that they are remitted to the UK. From 2008/09 onwards the remittance basis applies to general earnings for the tax year to the extent that:

(*a*)   they are 'chargeable overseas earnings' for that year; and

(*b*)   the employee is ordinarily resident in that year and *Income Tax Act 2007 (ITA 2007), ss 809B, 809D* or *809E* apply to the employee for that year.

[*ITEPA 2003, s 22(1)* as amended by *FA 2008, Sch 7, para 14*].

12.18   *ITA 2007, ss 809B, 809D* and *809E* set out who is entitled to use the remittance basis. This is an individual who is UK resident and either not UK domiciled or not ordinarily resident in that year and who either:

(*a*)   makes a claim for the remittance basis to apply for that year. (If the individual is 18 or over during that year and has been UK resident in seven out of the nine tax years immediately preceding that year in order to make a claim, the individual has to pay a charge of £50,000 (£30,000 if he has been UK resident for between seven and 12 years) in relation to his unremitted income for that year and must nominate unremitted income or gains to which that charge is to apply. He does not have to nominate sufficient income or gains as to give rise to £50,000 of tax, but if he does not do so the charge is still 50,000. [*ITA 2007, ss 809B, 809H*];

(*b*) whose unremitted foreign income and gains for the year is less than £2,000. [*ITA 2007, s 809D*];

(*c*) has no UK income or gains in the tax year and has remitted no overseas income or gains and who either has been UK resident in not more than six of the nine tax years immediately preceding that year, or is under 18 throughout the year. [*ITA 2007, s 809E*].

12.19 Where the remittance basis applies the full amount of such earnings which are remitted to the UK in a tax year is the taxable earnings from the employment in that year, irrespective of whether or not the employment is held when the earnings are remitted. [*ITEPA 2003, s 22(2), (3)* as amended by *FA 2008, Sch 7, para 14*].

12.20 General earnings for a tax year are overseas earnings for that year if:

(*a*) one of *ITA 2007, ss 809B, 809D or 809E* applies to the employee for that year;

(*b*) the employee is ordinarily resident in the UK in that year, and

(*c*) the duties of the employment are performed wholly outside the UK.

[*ITEPA 2003, s 23(2)* as amended by *FA 2008, Sch 7, para 15*].

12.21 The 'chargeable earnings' for the year are the overseas earnings for that year less any amounts that would be deductible under *ITEPA 2003, ss 232* (mileage allowance relief – see **7.51**) or *327–385* (deductions from employment income), *Finance Act 2004 (FA 2004), ss 188–194* (contributions to registered pension schemes) and *Capital Allowances Act 2001, s 262* (capital allowances deductible from earnings). [*ITEPA 2003, s 23(3)*]. The balance, if any, of the general earnings is of course taxable under *ITEPA 2003, s 15(1)* (see **2.47**). [*ITEPA 2003, s 22(7)* inserted by *FA 2008, Sch 7, para 14(6)*].

12.22 For this purpose no account is to be taken of the effect of *ITEPA 2003, s 41D* (limit on foreign securities income where duties of associated employment performed in the UK (see **12.39**)). [*ITEPA 2003, s 24(8)* inserted by *FA 2008, Sch 7, para 16*].

Overseas Workday Relief

12.23 Where a person comes to the UK and works both in the UK and overseas, a special relief applies for the first three tax years of UK residence (provided that he has not been UK resident for any of the three tax years prior to coming here). Provided that such a person is non-UK domiciled (as will normally be the case), he can use the remittance basis for those three years in respect of overseas earnings from an employment with a non-UK resident employer even if that employment is not carried on wholly outside the UK. The earnings are apportioned between UK and overseas work on a just and reasonable basis

(ITEPA 2003, ss 15, 23, 26A, 41ZA as amended or inserted by Finance Act 2013 (FA 2013), Schs 6 and 44). In practice HMRC are likely to contend that this requires the apportionment to be made on a time basis. The proportion attributed to UK work is taxed irrespective of whether or not it is remitted but the part attributed to overseas work is taxed here only if and when it is brought into the UK. The operation of this rule creates an identification problem with remittances to ensure that the part attributable to UK work is not taxed twice. Accordingly a taxpayer who wants to use this relief can nominate a separate overseas bank account into which his earnings will be paid and to which simplified identification rules can apply. Such a nomination must be made by 31 January following the end of the first tax year to which it applies. The account must be an ordinary bank account. It cannot be the nominated account of more than one person (so spouses cannot use a joint account). Nothing must be paid into the nominated account other than earnings from the employment, disposal proceeds of employment-related securities and interest on the account. If something else is accidentally paid into the account it must be transferred out within 30 days of its being discovered (together with any later prohibited receipts). However this applies only to the first two mistakes. A third mistake cannot be remedied; the account will cease to be a nominated account. Where an individual has such a nominated account special identification rules apply. The total amount remitted to the UK in the year is first identified and treated as a single transfer made at the end of the tax year. All other transfers out of the account are treated as a second single transfer made immediately after the first. The normal mixed account rules are then applied to those two deemed single transfers. These treat employment income (ie UK earnings) for a tax year as being remitted in priority to foreign employment income for that year. Having determined the deemed make up of the two deemed single payments, each individual transfer is treated as containing the same proportions of the different types of income *(ITA 2007, ss 809RA–809RD inserted by FA 2013, Sch 6, para 6)*.

12.23A Overseas workday relief is intended to largely preserve the position that previously applied where a person was resident but not ordinarily resident in the UK. Up to 2012/13 where the employee was not ordinarily resident in a tax year but the remittance basis applied by virtue of any of *ITA 2007, ss 809B–809D* the taxable earnings from the employment for that year was the amount of general earnings which were remitted in that year which were neither general earnings in respect of duties performed in the UK, nor general earnings from overseas Crown employment subject to UK tax (see **2.24**). *[ITEPA 2003, s 26(1), (2)]*. This applied whether or not the employment was held when the earnings were remitted. *[ITEPA 2007, s 26(3)]*. To the extent that the general earnings were in respect of UK duties or Crown employment they were of course taxable under *ITEPA 2003, s 15(1)* in the normal way. *[ITEPA 2003, s 26(6)]*.

Remittances

12.24 Earnings are remitted to the UK if either:

(a) Money or other property is brought to (or received or used in) the UK by, or for the benefit of, a 'relevant person' (or a service is provided in the UK to or for the benefit of a relevant person), if either:

  (i)   the property or consideration for the service (or the service itself if it is the income) is (wholly or partly) the earnings;

  (ii) the property or consideration is property of a relevant person (or consideration given by a relevant person) that derives (wholly or partly and directly or indirectly) from the earnings; or

  (iii) the earnings (or anything deriving (wholly or partly and directly or indirectly) from the earnings are used outside the UK (directly or indirectly) in respect of a 'relevant debt'.

(*b*)   Qualifying property of a 'gift recipient' either is brought to (or received or used in) the UK and enjoyed by a relevant person, is consideration for a service that is enjoyed in the UK by a relevant person, or is used outside the UK (directly or indirectly) in respect of a relevant debt.

(*c*)   Property of a third party (other than a relevant person) is either brought into the UK and enjoyed by a relevant person, is consideration for a service enjoyed in the UK by a relevant person or is used outside the UK (directly or indirectly) in respect of a relevant debt in circumstances where there is a connected operation.

[*ITEPA 2003, s 22(5); ITA 2007, s 809L(1)–(5), (9)*].

12.25   For this purpose a relevant person is any of:

(*a*)   the employee;

(*b*)   the employee's spouse or civil partner (and for this purpose a man and woman living together as husband and wife are treated as if they were married and a same sex couple living together as civil partners as if they were civil partners);

(*c*)   an infant child or grandchild of the employee or a person within (*b*);

(*d*)   a close company (or one which would be close if it were UK resident) in which a person falling within any of (*a*)–(*c*) or (*e*) is a participator;

(*e*)   the trustees of a settlement in which a person falling within any of (*a*)–(*d*) is a settlor or beneficiary, or a body connected with such a settlement (within *ITA 2007, s 993(3), (c), (d), (e)* or (*f*)).

[*ITA 2007, s 809M*].

12.26   For the purpose of **12.24(b)** a gift recipient is someone (other than a relevant person) to whom the employee makes a gift of money or other property that is earnings of the individual or derives (in whole or part and directly or indirectly) from such earnings. [*ITA 2007, s 809N(2)*]. The question of whether someone is a relevant person is determined at the time of the gift but if the donee subsequently becomes a relevant person he ceases to be a gift recipient. [*ITA 2007, s 809N(3), (4)*]. An individual is regarded as making a gift of property if he disposes of it either for no consideration or at below market value (in which case the gift is of course of the undervalue). [*ITA 2007, s 809N(5)*]. There is a gift even if the individual retains an interest in the property or an interest, right or arrangement enables or entitles him to benefit from it. [*ITA 2007, s 809N(6)*].

12.27 Qualifying property in relation to a gift recipient is:

(*a*)   the property gifted;

(*b*)   anything that derives (wholly or partly and directly or indirectly) from that property (including any asset that does not belong to the individual but from which he can benefit by virtue of any interest, right or arrangement);

(*c*)   any other property (including any asset that does not belong to the individual but from which he can benefit by virtue of any interest, right or arrangement) which either is brought to (or received or used in) the UK and enjoyed by a relevant person, is consideration for a service enjoyed in the UK by a relevant person, or is used outside the UK (directly or indirectly) either in respect of a relevant debt, by virtue of an operation which is effected with reference to the gift to the gift recipient or with a view to enabling or facilitating the gift to be made to the gift recipient.

[*ITA 2007, s 809N(7), (8)*].

12.28 Enjoyment of property or service by a relevant person is ignored if either:

(*a*)   the property or service is enjoyed by someone else virtually to the entire exclusion of all relevant persons;

(*b*)   full consideration in money or money's worth is given by a relevant person for the enjoyment; or

(*c*)   the property or service is enjoyed by relevant persons in the same way, and on the same terms, as it can be enjoyed by the general public or a section of the general public.

[*ITA 2007, s 809N(9)*].

12.29 A relevant debt is one that relates (wholly or partly and directly or indirectly) to:

(*a*)   money or other property brought to (or received or used in) the UK by, or for the benefit of, a relevant person (or which is enjoyed by a relevant person); or

(*b*)   a service provided in the UK by, or for the benefit of, a relevant person (or which is enjoyed in the UK by a relevant person)

if the property or service would have constituted a remittance under **12.24**. [*ITA 2007, s 809L(7)*]. A relevant debt includes a debt for interest on a borrowing. [*ITA 2007, s 809L(8)*]. The remittance is deemed to take place at the time that the property or service is first enjoyed by a relevant person by virtue of its importation or use. [*ITA 2007, s 809L(6)*]. Accordingly if it is subsequently re-exported and remitted for a second time the second remittance does not trigger a further tax charge.

12.30   For the purpose of **12.24(c)** the question of whether or not the owner of the property is a relevant person must be determined at the time the property or service is imported or used. [*ITA 2007, s 809O(2)*]. A connected operation is one which is effected with reference to a qualifying disposition or with a view to enabling or facilitating a qualifying disposition. [*ITA 2007, s 809O(3)*]. A qualifying disposition is one that is made by a relevant person to or for the benefit of the owner of the property, and is a disposition of money or other property that is, or derives (wholly or partly and directly or indirectly) from the earnings of the employee (unless the disposition is itself (or is part of) the giving of full consideration in money or money's worth for the event that triggers the remittance). [*ITA 2007, s 809O(4), (5)*]. The exception at **12.28** above also applies for the purpose of **12.24(c)**. [*ITA 2007, s 809O(6)*].

12.31   The amount of earnings remitted is determined as follows:

(*a*)   If the property or consideration is the earnings, that is the amount remitted. [*ITA 2007, s 809O(2)*].

(*b*)   If the property or consideration derives from the earnings, the amount remitted is the amount of the earnings from which it derives. [*ITA 2007, s 809O(3)*].

(*c*)   If the earnings are used outside the UK to pay a relevant debt the amount remitted is the earnings so used (but if the debt is only partly in respect of the property or service used in the UK the remittance is of course limited to the part of the debt that relates to that property or service). [*ITA 2007, s 809P(4), (10)*].

(*d*)   If something deriving from the earnings is used outside the UK to pay a relevant debt the amount remitted is the earnings from which it was derived. [*ITA 2007, s 809P(5), (10)*].

(*e*)   If the remittance is triggered by enjoyment by a gift recipient the amount remitted is the earnings of which the qualifying property consists, or from which it is derived, or from which the property given to the gift recipient consists or was derived. [*ITA 2007, s 809O(6), (7), (10), (11)*].

(*f*)   If the remittance is triggered by a connected operation within 12.24(*c*), the amount remitted is the earnings from which the disposition of money or other property derives (wholly or partly or directly or indirectly). [*ITA 2007, s 809P(8), (9), (10)*].

(*g*)   If the amount remitted (together with any previous remittances) would otherwise exceed the earnings, the total remittances is limited to the earnings. [*ITA 2007, s 809P(12)*].

(*h*)   The payment to HMRC of the £30,000 or £50,000 annual charge for the privilege of using the remittance basis is not itself a remittance if the payment is made direct to HMRC from an overseas bank account either by bank transfer or cheque. (*ITA 2007, s 809V*). Nor is there a remittance if works of art, collectors' items or antiuqes are brought inot the UK solely for public display in a museum, gallery or other establishment approved by HMRC. [*ITA 2007, ss 809X(3), 809Z.*].

12.32   Special rules apply to determine the amount remitted if money or other property is brought to, or received or used in, the UK by, or for the benefit of, a relevant person (or a service is provided in the UK to or for the benefit of such a person), and the property (or consideration for the service) is derived (wholly or partly and directly or indirectly) from a transfer from a mixed fund (or a transfer from a mixed fund or something deriving from it is used outside the UK in respect of a relevant debt). [*ITA 2007, s 809Q(1), (2)*]. The remittance is first identified in the order set out below against the following type of income or gains to the extent that such items have been paid into the fund in the tax year concerned and prior to the time of the remittance.

(*a*)   employment income (ie earnings chargeable to UK tax on an arising basis) not chargeable to foreign tax;

(*b*)   relevant foreign earnings not subject to foreign tax;

(*c*)   foreign specific employment income (ie deemed income under the share scheme rules – see **12.35**) not subject to foreign tax;

(*d*)   foreign investment income not subject to foreign tax;

(*e*)   foreign chargeable gains not subject to foreign tax;

(*f*)   employment income subject to foreign tax;

(*g*)   foreign investment income subject to foreign tax;

(*h*)   foreign chargeable gains subject to foreign tax;

(*i*)   income or capital not within any of the above heads.

If the remittance is not fully identified against income from the year under this procedure the balance has to be identified against income for the previous year in the same order and so on. [*ITA 2007, s 809Q(3), (4)*].

12.33   However, this is subject to a proviso that if by reason of an arrangement the main purpose (or one of the main purposes) of which is to secure an income tax advantage or capital gains tax advantage, a mixed fund would otherwise be regarded as containing income or capital within any of paragraphs (*f*) to (*i*) above it must be identified with a particular category only to the extent that it is just and reasonable to do so. [*ITA 2007, s 809S(2)*]. If a debt in respect of a mixed fund has been satisfied (wholly or partly and directly or indirectly) from income or capital within one of the heads (or from something deriving directly or indirectly from it) the fund must be treated as containing that income or capital to the extent that it is just and reasonable to do so. [*ITA 2007, s 809R(3)*]. It is not wholly clear what is meant by 'a debt in respect of a mixed fund'. It probably means money borrowed that has been paid into the fund. If so, it appears that what the provision seeks to achieve is to ensure that once the debt has been repaid the income or capital that is used to repay it should be treated as the item that was paid into the mixed fund instead of the borrowed money.

12.34   Where an offshore account holds only the income or gains relating to a single employment, a simplified method can be used. HMRC will accept that employees who are resident but not ordinarily resident in the UK and who perform duties of an office or employment both in the UK and overseas do not have to apply the statutory mixed fund rule to that account provided that:

(*a*)   the account is held solely by the employee; and

(*b*)   the only things that the account contains are employment income from a single employment, interest arising only on that account, gains from foreign exchange transactions in respect of the funds in that account, any gains arising on employee share scheme related transactions and any proceeds from employee share scheme related transactions in respect of amounts paid by the employee in acquiring the shares.

Where the account contains such eligible items covering more than one year, they are identified with remittances on a last in first out basis. Subject to this, amounts remitted from the account are treated as comprising the kinds of income or gains in the order set out at **12.32** for the tax year as a whole, instead of the identification having to be made each time funds are withdrawn from the account (*SP 1/09* (replacing *SP 5/84*)).

Employment related securities

12.35   If an amount constitutes employment income of an individual under the employment related security rules in relation to restricted securities (see **14.26**), convertible securities (see **14.59**), securities acquired for less than their market value (see **14.88**), securities disposed of for more than their market value (see **14.96**), shares in research institution spin off companies (see **14.120**) or securities options (see **14.102**) and the remittance basis applies to the individual for any part of 'the relevant period' special rules apply to determine the taxable amount (*ITEPA 2003, s 41A(1), (2)* inserted by *FA 2008, Sch 7, para 22*), the taxable specific income for the tax year in which the amount constitutes employment income (ie the amount chargeable to tax – see **2.5**) is the aggregate of the UK of the UK securities income plus any amount of 'foreign securities income' (see **12.38**) remitted in the year (irrespective of whether or not the employment is still held when the earnings are remitted). [*ITEPA 2003, s 41A(4)–(7)*].

12.36   For remittance purposes, if the event that gives rise to the remittance is the disposal of foreign securities or of a foreign option, the consideration for the disposal (or the then market value of the securities or option if there is no consideration) is treated as arising from the foreign securities income. If some other event generates the remittance (for example the securities are sold and the proceeds remitted) the securities or option is treated as deriving from the foreign securities income. HMRC say that where the employee acquires shares in a UK company, the shares are UK assets and therefore they are 'used in the UK by and for the benefit of the employee' (*HMRC Technical Note 1.8.2008*). This appears to mean that if shares are acquired in an overseas company, which is subsequently taken over by a UK one on a share exchange, the share exchange will trigger a remittance of any foreign securities income relating to those shares.

12.37   The relevant period in relation to restricted or convertible securities is the period from the date of acquisition to the events that generate the deemed employment income (under the employment-related securities rules). [*ITEPA 2003, s 41B(1), (2)*]. If the deemed employment income arises under *ITEPA 2003, s 446* (discharge of notional loan where securities acquired at an undervalue – see **14.93**) the relevant period is the year from the date that the notional loan was deemed to be made, ie from the time the securities were acquired (unless the securities were acquired on the exercise of an option and at that time the employee was not resident in the UK, in which case it is the period from the acquisition of the option to the day of the event that gives rise to the deemed income - which is normally when the option is exercised or sold – or, if earlier, the day the option vests, ie the time when it is first capable of being exercised. [*ITEPA 2003, s 41B(1), (3), (7)*]. If the deemed employment income arises from the disposal of securities at an overvalue or from a post-acquisition benefit it is such period as is just and reasonable. [*ITEPA 2003, s 41B(1), (4)*]. Where the securities derive from the exercise of an option the relevant period begins when the option was acquired and ends with the event that gives rise to the deemed employment income, which is normally when the option is exercised or sold (or, if earlier, the day the securities option vests). [*ITEPA 2003, s 41B(1), (5)*].

12.38   For the purpose of determining the extent to which the deemed employment income is foreign securities income, the income is deemed to accrue evenly over the relevant period (see **12.38**). [*ITEPA 2003, s 41C(1), (2)*]. The part attributed to a tax year in which the individual is ordinarily resident in the UK and is taxed on a remittance basis and in which the employment is with a foreign employer and the duties of the employment are performed wholly outside the UK is foreign securities income. [*ITEPA 2003, s 41C(3), (4)*]. So is any part attributed to services performed outside the UK in a tax year in which the individual is not ordinarily resident in the UK and is on a remittance basis (or is non-UK resident) and some or all of the duties are performed outside the UK (any necessary apportionment between UK and non-UK duties being made on a just and reasonable basis). [*ITEPA 2003, s 41C(5)–(7)*]. The legislation does not specify how the apportionment is to be done. HMRC say that they would expect that a split based on overseas and UK workdays will be the most commonly used method of arriving at a just and reasonable apportionment but that they will accept any method that achieves a just and reasonable result. This applies also to the apportionment under *ITEPA 2003, ss 41D* (see **12.39**) and *41E* (see **12.40**) (*HMRC Technical Note 1.8.2008*). Where *ITEPA 2003, s 24A* (see **13.14A**) applies (the income is treated as not being foreign securities income) it must be assumed for the purpose of *s 41C* that it is just and reasonable for none of the securities income accruing in the tax year to be treated as foreign [*ITEPA 2003, s 41C(4A)(9)* inserted by *Finance Act 2014 (FA 2014), Sch 3, para 4*].

12.39   Where *s 41C(3)* applies and at the same time the employee holds associated employments the duties of which are not performed wholly outside the UK the foreign securities income is limited to such amount as is just and reasonable, having regard to:

(*a*)   the earnings for the period from all of the associated employments;

(*b*)   the proportion of those earnings that are chargeable overseas earnings (within *ITEPA 2003, s 22* – see **12.9**);

(*c*)   the nature of, and time devoted to, the duties performed outside the UK and in the UK respectively; and

(*d*)   all other relevant circumstances.

For this purpose associated employments are employments with the same employer or with associated employers (as defined in *ITEPA 2003, s 24(5), (6)* – see **12.15**). [*ITEPA 2003, s 41D*].

12.40   If having regard to all the circumstances, the proportion of the securities income that would otherwise be regarded as foreign is not one that is just and reasonable, a just and reasonable apportionment must be adopted instead [*ITEPA 2003, s 41E*]. HMRC say that the reason for this override is that there may be circumstances where the relevant period in *ITEPA 2003, s 41B* does not match the reality of the period over which the gain can fairly be said to have been earned. There may also be circumstances where the gain could not fairly be said to have been earned in equal amounts over each day of the relevant period (*HMRC Technical Note 1.8.2008*). HMRC say that these new rules do not apply to securities acquired after 5 April 2008 in pursuance of an option granted before that date. Furthermore where an option granted after that date replaces a prior option in accordance with *ITEPA 2003, s 483* (see **14.119**) the new option continues in the old regime (*HMRC Technical Note 1.8.2008*).

Overseas savings, etc

12.41   Where an employee has overseas earnings or foreign emoluments outside the UK and also has other funds, such as savings from a period before he came to the UK, it should be noted that the onus is on the taxpayer to disprove an assessment. Once the funds become mixed, for example, by putting the savings and the earnings, or amounts derived from the sale of investments made out of the earnings, into the same bank account, it becomes impossible to show that remittances out of that account are not remittances of the earnings. Accordingly, the foreign emoluments should be paid into a separate overseas bank account from other funds. It would be sensible to use the earnings account to meet non-UK expenditure, so maximising the amount of savings that are available to be remitted to the UK.

Relief for delayed remittances

12.42   Where a person who is taxable on the remittance basis and brings earnings into the UK in a particular year and could not have remitted them earlier because of either:

(*a*)   the laws of the country or territory where the earnings were received;

(*b*)   executive action of its government; or

(*c*)   the impossibility of obtaining in that country currency (other than the currency of that country or territory) that could be transferred to the UK;

he can claim to treat the earnings as having been remitted to the UK in the year in which they were received in the overseas country. [*ITEPA 2003, s 35*]. Such an election would avoid a bunching of taxable income.

12.43   If the taxpayer already has unremittable earnings for an earlier year or years he can choose which year's earnings his deemed remittance represents (up to the amount of the previously unremitted earnings for each particular year). Such an election must be included in the *ITEPA 2003, s 35* claim and is irrevocable. If the person has died before the earnings become remittable the election can be made by personal representatives. [*ITEPA 2003, s 36*].

12.44   A claim under *ITEPA 2003, s 35* must be made by the fifth anniversary of 31 January following the tax year in which the funds are remitted to the UK. The resultant adjustments to the earlier year's tax can be made even though the normal time limit for doing so has expired. If the taxpayer has died before the funds become remittable the claim can be made by his personal representatives and the personal representatives are liable for the tax as a debt due from and payable out of the estate. [*ITEPA 2003, s 36*]. It should be noted that the relief applies only to the extent that the funds are actually remitted to the UK in the tax year in which the restrictions on remitting them cease to apply. There is no relief if the remittance is delayed to a later year.

Travelling expenses

Special relief

12.45   There is a special relief for travelling expenses of an employee who is not domiciled in the UK and is in receipt of emoluments for duties performed in the UK. [*ITEPA 2003, s 337(1)*]. It applies if one of the following conditions is satisfied on the date on which the employee arrives in the UK to perform duties of the office or employment, (the qualifying arrival date), namely:

(*a*)   the employee was not resident in the UK in either of the two years of assessment immediately prior to that in which the qualifying arrival date (or the first such date in the year of assessment if there is more than one) falls; or

(*b*)   he was not in the UK for any purpose at any time during the period of two years ending immediately prior to that arrival in the UK.

[*ITEPA 2003, s 375*].

12.46   Once one of these conditions is met, the reliefs set out below apply for a period of five years beginning with that date. [*ITEPA 2003, s 373(3)*].

12.47   It is difficult to envisage when head (*b*) might apply. It seems to assume that the person was resident in the UK in the two preceding years of assessment but nonetheless did not visit the UK at all for a period of two years. It is unlikely that he would be held to be UK resident in the year immediately prior to the start of the employment in such circumstances.

Amounts exempted

12.48   During the five-year period for which *s 373* applies, the employee is not taxed on travelling expenses for any journey made either:

(*a*)   from the country (outside the UK) in which he normally lives to any place in the UK in order to perform any duties of the office or employment there; or

(*b*)   to the country in which he normally lives from any place in the UK after performing duties there,

provided that the cost of the travel facilities is borne by his employer or is paid by the employee and reimbursed by his employer (and that the expenses form part of the earnings from the employment). [*ITEPA 2003, s 373(4)*].

Meaning of 'usual place of abode'

12.49   It should be noted that if the employee comes from Paris but takes his summer holiday in Nice, the travel to and from Nice would qualify for relief. If he takes his holiday in Barcelona, travel to and from Barcelona would not qualify as Spain is a different country. If he flies to and from Nice and motors to Barcelona the cost of the travel to and from Nice will qualify but the expenses from Nice to Barcelona will not. It appears that if the employee flies to Paris to catch another plane to Nice, only the expenses of the flight to Paris will qualify as it is the cost of returning to the country where the employee normally lives, not to any particular place in that country, that are relieved.

12.50   The purpose of these reliefs is to allow a non-UK national to visit his family and friends during his early years of residence in the UK without having to do so out of taxed income. Once the employee has been working in the UK for five years he ought to have adjusted his life sufficiently so that this special relief is no longer needed. The requirement for the expense to be borne, or reimbursed, by the employer arose because the government in 1986, when the relief was introduced, felt that the employer would not be prepared to meet the cost unless in all the circumstances it were reasonable. Accordingly, this would reduce the risk of abuse.

The employee's family

12.51   The relief that is given for visits by an employee's spouse and infant children when he is working abroad for a continuous period of at least 60 days (see **13.32–13.36** below) also applies where a non-UK domiciled employee is working in the UK and is himself entitled to relief under *section 373*, ie during the five years from the time he first meets the qualifying conditions. This relief for journeys by the spouse and children is given for journeys:

(*a*)   made to accompany the employee at the beginning of the continuous 60-day period, or to visit him during it; or

(*b*)   to return to the home country following a journey within (*a*).

[*ITEPA 2003, s 374*].

12.52   The rules set out in **13.32–13.36** below, apply to this relief. As with the employee's own travel expenses, the cost must be borne by the employer or incurred by the employee and reimbursed to him by his employer. [*ITEPA 2003, s 374(1)*].

12.53   If a journey within either **12.51** above, or **13.32** below, is made partly for the purpose specified therein and partly for some other purpose, only so much of the expenses as is attributable to the specified purpose can be deducted from the emoluments (so the balance will give rise to a benefit in kind). [*ITEPA 2003, ss 373(6), 374(7)*].

12.54   If an expense qualifies as a deduction under both *s 373* and some other provision it obviously cannot be deducted twice. [*ITEPA 2003, s 330*].

Administrative procedure

12.55   In the past there were practical problems in handling the affairs of people coming to work temporarily in the UK as many Inspectors of Taxes insisted on obtaining formal domicile rulings even though it was clear that the person was in the UK for a temporary purpose only. The residence form, P86, now includes a section on domicile so that 'in straightforward cases' an individual's residence and domicile status will be dealt with together. HMRC have indicated that this will apply where a person who has never been UK domiciled has come here only to work and intends to leave the UK once the employment ceases. (*IR Press Release, 8 September 1994*). Following the introduction of self-assessment it is less important to know one's residence and domicile position in advance of completing a tax return – although it is of course desirable in order to plan one's finances effectively. Pre-self-assessment there was a special return, form 11K, for non-UK domiciled taxpayers. This is no longer the case. Now a non-UK domiciled or non-UK resident taxpayer completes the normal tax return form (if asked to complete a return) and attaches to it a 'Residence' page on which the taxpayer claims his non-UK domiciled or non-UK resident status.

Tax equalisation payments

12.56   It is common for multi-national employers to operate tax equalisation schemes where a foreign national is sent to work in the UK. Under such a scheme the employer pays the employee, in addition to his salary, the difference, if any, between the tax that he would have paid on his salary in his home country and the tax that he pays in the UK. In effect it indemnifies him again, his UK tax burden exceeding that in his home country. It is well-established that such payments are taxable as additional salary. Where the employee has both emoluments for work performed in the UK and earnings taxable on a remittance basis for overseas work HMRC have always considered that to the extent that a tax equalisation payment is to meet a tax liability in respect of earnings for UK work it is itself taxable as UK earnings. The alternative view is that as it relates to the employee's overall income it should be apportioned between UK and overseas income in proportion to such income. HMRC said that anyone who wished to dispute their approach for 1997/98 onwards would need to litigate the position (*Tax Bulletin 27, Feb 1997*). Miss Perro duly did so *(Perro v Mansworth [2001] STC (SCD) 179, SpC 2865)*. The Special Commissioner upheld the HMRC view, holding that the payment was in respect of the UK duties.

12.57   HMRC are prepared to operate modified PAYE and NIC procedures where tax equalisation is used. The employer must obtain the permission of HMRC to use this procedure. Details of the procedure and the undertaking that needs to be given by the employer to HMRC are set out in Appendices 6 and 7 of HMRC's Employment Procedures Manual, which can be found on their internet site.

Champions League Final

12.58   If an employee of an overseas team which competed in the 2011 UEFA Champions League final was neither UK resident or ordinarily resident at the time of the final, he was exempted from income tax in respect of income which related to duties performed in the UK in connection with the final [*Finance Act 2010 (FA 2010), Sch 20, para 1*]. For this purpose an overseas team was a football club which is not a member of the Football Association, the Scottish Football Association, the Football Association of Wales or the Irish Football Association [*FA 2010, Sch 20, para 6*]. The exemption extended to employment with a company which was a member of the same group of companies as the team [*FA 2010, Sch 20, para 6*].

12.59   The exemption did not apply to income which arises as a result of a contract entered into after the final, or to income arising as a result of any amendment after the final of a prior contract [*FA 2010, Sch 20, para 2*]. Nor did it apply if arrangements had been made which would have resulted in a person being entitled to the exemptions if those arrangements had as one of their main purposes the obtaining of the exemption [*FA 2010, Sch 20, para 3*]. An identical exemption applies to overseas teams that compete in the 2013 UEFA Champions League Final [*Finance Act 2012 (FA 2012), s 13*]. These exemptions are of course granted as a condition of the final being held in the UK.

Chapter 13

Working Overseas

Introduction

13.1 Special reliefs apply to UK residents working overseas. It should be borne in mind that these only apply if the employee remains resident or ordinarily resident in the UK. If he is working overseas for several years he is likely to have become non-UK resident in which case his salary will be outside the scope of UK tax.

13.2 It should also be noted that earnings from a Crown employment for duties performed outside the UK are normally subject to UK tax as if the duties were performed in the UK. [*Income Tax (Earnings and Pensions) Act 2003 (ITEPA 2003), ss 25(1)(b), 26(1)(b), 27(1)(b), 28*]. A Crown employment is employment under the Crown which is of a public nature and the earnings from which are payable out of the public revenues of the UK or of Northern Ireland. [*ITEPA 2003, s 28(2)*]. HMRC have power to make an order excepting from the operation of *ITEPA 2003, ss 25(2)* and *27(2)* general earnings of any description of employee (or any description of employment) specified in the order. This can be done if they consider that such earnings should not be subject to UK tax having regard to the international obligations of the government and such other matters as appear to HMRC to be relevant. [*ITEPA 2003, s 28(5), (6)*]. They have done so by an Order of 6 April 2003 which excludes earnings of employees engaged locally (ie not based in the UK) if they are not UK resident and the maximum pay for their grade is less than that of an executive officer employed in the same department of the UK Civil Service working in Inner London.

Year of departure

13.3 Where a person goes overseas to take up full-time employment under a contract of employment for a period that includes a complete tax year, HMRC's practice is to regard him as ceasing to be both resident and ordinarily resident in the UK from the time of his departure (*Booklet IR20, paragraph 2.2*). Obviously, if his employment terminates prematurely and he comes back within that tax year this concession will not be applied. The same applies to his spouse if she goes with him, or if she joins him later (in which case her non-residence will date from the time of her departure (*paragraph 2.4*)). HMRC say 'full-time' for this purpose must be interpreted in accordance with its ordinary non-technical meaning, ie putting in what a layman would clearly recognise as a full working week. They also consider that where someone has several part-time jobs overseas concurrently, or an employment and self-employment concurrently, it might be reasonable to aggregate the total working time (*Tax Bulletin, Issue 6, page 57*).

Advantages of non-residence

13.4   When a person works overseas but continues to spend a significant time in the UK he may be resident in both countries. In such a case thought may need to be given to whether it is sensible to seek to give up his UK residence and, if so, how this might be done. If he is working in a country with which the UK has a double taxation agreement that agreement probably prevents him being resident in both of the contracting countries at the same time for the purpose of that treaty.

13.5   For example, if a person would be regarded as US resident under US law and as UK resident under UK law the UK/US double taxation agreement contains the following rules to determine which country is entitled to treat him as a resident – with the other country agreeing to treat him as non-resident in relation to income covered by the double taxation agreement.

(*a*)   If he has a permanent home available to him in only one of the countries he is treated as a resident of that country.

(*b*)   If he has a permanent home in neither or both countries he is treated as resident in the country with which his personal and economic relations are closest (his centre of vital interests).

(*c*)   If his centre of vital interests cannot be determined he is treated as a resident of the country in which he has a habitual abode.

(*d*)   If he has a habitual abode in both countries, or neither of them, he is treated as being a resident of the country of which he is a national.

(*e*)   If he is a national of both countries, HMRC and Internal Revenue Service must agree between themselves which country is to treat him as a resident.

(*Article 4(4), UK/USA Double Taxation Convention (SI 2002 No 2648)*).

13.6   This 'tie-breaker' clause is not the same in all of the UK's double taxation agreements although they broadly follow this pattern.

13.7   If a UK resident intends to work in the USA for two years and will also have significant earnings in another country it may sometimes be sensible to try to arrange his affairs so that the above tests will result in his remaining UK resident. This is not difficult to achieve provided that he meets the UK tests of residence, as such a person's centre of vital interests is likely to remain in the UK. It used to be easy to ensure that a person met the UK residence requirement by ensuring that he retained a UK house and a UK directorship and visited the UK every year for a board meeting. Now that the retention of available accommodation is no longer a test of UK residence, this has become far more difficult to achieve.

13.8   Establishing UK residence will not take the US earnings out of charge to US tax as the US is entitled under the agreement to tax US earnings if a UK resident is present in the US for more than 183 days in a calendar year (or he is present for a shorter period but the salary is claimed as a deduction in calculating US taxable profits of his employer). It will, however, take non-US income, such as the third-country salary, out of US tax.

Relief for seafarers for long absences abroad

13.9   Prior to 17 March 1998 the earnings of a UK resident from work performed overseas effectively escaped UK tax if that person was working overseas for a period of 365 days or more (with fairly generous visits back to the UK being permitted during the period). This special relief was abolished by *s 63(1)* of the *Finance Act 1998 (FA 1988)* except for seafarers (see below). There was no transitional relief. If an employee was working overseas at 17 March 1998 he retained the right to his relief in respect of earnings paid before that date in respect of work done before that date, provided that he remained overseas for as long as was necessary to complete the requisite 365-day period. However, earnings for work done after 16 March 1998 and for work done before that date but paid after 16 March became taxable in full.

13.10   The relief (with some modifications) continues to apply to employment as a seafarer. This is defined as an employment (other than Crown employment) consisting of the performance of duties on a ship (or of such duties and others incidental to them). [*ITEPA 2003, s 384(1)*]. A ship for this purpose is not defined, but is expressed not to include any offshore installation. Prior to 2004/05 an offshore installation was defined as one within the meaning of the *Mineral Workings (Offshore Installations) Act 1971* or what would be such an installation if the reference in that *Act* to controlled waters was to any waters. It is now defined in *Income Tax Act 2007 (ITA 2007), ss 1001* and *1002*. This excludes those employed on oil rigs and gas installations – or at least on some of them! In *Clark v Perks [2001] STC 1254* the Court of Appeal had to consider the meaning of a ship. It was held that this is an ordinary English word and its application to the facts of a particular case is a question of fact for the Commissioners to decide. In that case the General Commissioners had held that a moveable 'jack-up' oil rig which had no motive power of its own and had to be towed by tugs was a ship. It was held that this was a decision that they were entitled to come to. In *Lavery v Macleod [2000] STC (SCD) 118* the Special Commissioners held that a different jack-up rig had sufficient characteristics to be a ship. They noted that HMRC accept that two other types of moveable drilling rigs, a drillship and a semi-submersible unit are ships. They were also clearly impressed that the jack-up rig has been moved several times including one journey of 2,500 miles which took 27 days. They emphasised that their decision depended on the individual facts of that case. In *Palmer v HMRC 77 TC 738* the Court of Session held, on *Edwards v Bairstow* principles, that the General Commissioners had been entitled to hold that the ship in that case was an offshore installation. In *Langley v CIR [2008] STC (SCD) 298* the Special Commissioners decided that a self-propelled drilling rig was not a ship until the 'thrusters' had been attached so that it could move under its own power; it then became both a ship and an offshore installation, but once it had been used as a drilling rig (but not before) it would cease to be an offshore installation (while remaining a ship) if it was being renovated, 'mothballed' or awaiting charter. In *Torr v HMRC [2009] STC (SCD) 772* the Special Commissioners held that a self-propelled, dynamically positioned, semi-submersible vessel which operated as a workover/support vessel was not a ship. The ship moved between wells in an oilfield to carry out repairs to other rigs. In *Spowage v HMRC [2009] SFTD 393* the First-tier Tribunal similarly held that a vessel that had functioned as an offshore installation was a ship during periods in which it was used as a multi-purpose maintenance and construction support vessel. In *Gouldson v HMRC [2011] STC 1902* the UT held that a vessel used principally as a 'flotel', housing workers engaged in the construction of oil storage tankers was not a ship while doing so. Although the tankers were not at the time engaging in mineral exploitation, the legislation did not contain a temporal limitation so it was permissible to look at the future intended use.

13.11   If in any year of assessment the duties of an employment as a seafarer are performed wholly or partly outside the UK and any of those duties are performed in the course of a qualifying period which falls wholly or partly in that year and consists of at least 365 days, a deduction of 100 per cent of the emoluments attributable to the chargeable period, or to so much of it as falls within the year of assessment, is allowed from those emoluments. [*ITEPA 2003, ss 378, 379*]. The earnings must be taxable as general earnings under *ITEPA 2003, s 15* (see **2.48**) or, in relation to a qualifying period beginning after 5 April 2011, EEA-resident earnings even if the employee were to claim the remittance basis. [*ITEPA 2003, s 378(5)* as amended by *Finance (No 3) Act 2011 (F(No 3)A 2011), s 4*]. EEA-earnings are general earnings within *ITEPA 2003, ss 15* or *27* from a period in which the employee is tax resident in another EEA State and which falls within a tax year in which the employee is not ordinarily resident in the- UK [*ITEPA 2003, s 378(6)*].

Apportionment of UK and non-UK duties

13.12   In practice, if a person had a single employment embracing both UK and overseas duties HMRC rarely accept that any method other than a straight time apportionment is appropriate to ascertain the earnings qualifying for the deduction. If there are separate employments for UK and non-UK duties it is more difficult for HMRC to mount a challenge under this provision, particularly if the earnings from the non-UK employment can be shown to be directly related to the profits of the overseas employer, such as where, for example, the employee is paid on a commission basis.

13.13   It has been held that the attribution of the emoluments of a single employment between UK and overseas duties must be made by reference to the employee's contractual rights (subject to the ceiling in *Sch 12, para 2*). When the contract does not specifically allocate part of the remuneration to the overseas duties, the remuneration contractually accrues on a day-to-day basis under the *Apportionment Act 1870*. (*Varnam v Deeble 58 TC 501*). For this purpose the daily salary is 1⁄365 of the annual salary, irrespective of the number of days in the year that an employee is contractually required to work (*Platten v Brown 59 TC 408; Leonard v Blanchard [1993] STC 259*).

13.13A For 2014/15 onwards, none of an employee's general earnings from an employment for a tax year can be treated as overseas earnings if:

(*a*) one or more of the following applies:

    (i) general earnings from the employment would otherwise be chargeable overseas earnings,

    (ii) employment income in respect of the employment arises under *ITEPA 2003, s 41C* (employment-related securities – see **12.38**) and would otherwise be foreign earnings to which the remittance basis applies, or

    (iii) employment income in respect of the employment arises under *ITEPA 2003, s 41H* and would otherwise be chargeable foreign securities income,

    (iv) *ITEPA 2003, s 554Z9* (disguised remuneration) applies to employment income in respect of the employment which corresponds to the value of a relevant step

(*b*) the employee holds a UK employment at some time in the tax year (or if it is a split year, in the UK portion) when he also owns the overseas employment,

(*c*) the UK employer is the same as, or is associated with, the overseas employer,

(*d*) the UK employment and the overseas employment are related to each other,

(*e*) X% is less than Y% (see **13.14C**)

[*ITEPA 2003, ss 23(1A), 24A(1)(5)-(8)(13)* inserted by *Finance Act 2014 (FA 2014), Sch 3, para 3*]. For this purpose a UK employment is any employment the duties of which are not performed wholly outside the UK [*ITEPA 2003, s 24A(4)*].

13.13B The UK and overseas employments must, in particular, be assumed to be related to each other for the purpose of (*d*) if either:

(*a*) it is reasonable to suppose that the relevant employee would not hold one employment without holding the other (or that the employment will cease at the same time or one employment will cease in consequence of the other ceasing),

(*b*) the terms of one employment operate to any extent by reference to the other employment,

(*c*) the performance of duties of one employment is (wholly or partly) dependent upon, or otherwise linked (directly or indirectly) to the performance of duties of the other, (*d*)   the duties of the employments are wholly or mainly of the same type (ignoring the fact that they may be performed (wholly or partly) in different locations),

(*e*)   the duties of the employments involve (wholly or partly) the provision of goods or services to the same customers or clients,

(*f*)   the employee is either:

   (i)   a director of the UK employer or the overseas employer and has a material interest (over 5%) in either employer company,

   (ii)   a senior employee of either company (senior employee is not defined), or

   (iii)   one of the employees of either company who receives the higher or highest levels of remuneration.

[*ITEPA 2003, s 24A(9)*]. The reference in (*f*) to the UK employer or the overseas employer includes references to any person with which that employer is associated and, if either employer is a company, that company and all of the companies with which it is associated taken together as if they were one company [*ITEPA 2003, s 24A(10)*]. The Treasury have power by statutory instrument to amend these relationship tests [*ITEPA 2003, s 24A(11)(12)*].

13.13C   For the purpose of **13.14A** X% is the amount given by the formula

$$\frac{C}{1} \times 100\% \text{ where}$$

C = the total amount of double tax relief credit that would be allowed under *Taxation (International and Other Provisions) Act 2010 (TIOPA 2010), s 18(2)* against income tax in respect of all the employment income falling within **13.14A(*a*)** if none of that income was chargeable overseas earnings (or fell within the other heads of that paragraph); and

Y is the total employment income falling within **13.14)(a)**.

[*ITEPA 2003, s 24A(14), 24B(1)(2)(4)*]. For this purpose it must be assumed that all DTR is claimed within the applicable time limit and that all reasonable steps are taken to minimise any amounts of tax payable as required by *TIOPA 2010, s 33* [*ITEPA 2003, s 24B(3)*]. Y is 65% of the additional rate (the 45% top rate of income), ie currently Y% is 29.25% [*ITEPA 2003, s 24A(15)*]. The Treasury have power by statutory instrument to amend the definition of Y [*ITEPA 2003, s 24A(16)*].

Example

John has an employment in the UK in which he earns £60,000. He has a related employment in Utopia of £40,000. He paid income tax in Utopia for the year of £17,000.

$$\text{X is } \frac{17,000\%}{40,000} = 42.5\%$$

As this is not less than 29.25%, *ITEPA 2003, s 24A* does not apply and the overseas employment can be dealt with on a remittance basis. It will be apparent that *s 24A* will always apply if the overseas employment is not chargeable to tax in the country where the employment takes place as X will then be nil.

13.13D *Section 24A* does not apply if:

(a)   were the duties of the overseas employment instead duties of the UK employment, all or substantially all of them could not lawfully be performed in the overseas country (whether on the meeting of any condition or otherwise) by virtue of a regulatory requirement imposed under the laws of that country, and

(b)   were the UK duties of the UK employment to instead be duties of the overseas employment, all or substantially all of them could not lawfully be performed in the part of the UK in which they are in fact performed (whether in the meeting of any condition or otherwise) by virtue of any UK regulatory requirements.

[*ITEPA 2003, s 24A(17)*].

Emoluments qualifying for deduction

13.14   If there is a single employment with both UK and non-UK duties, what qualifies for the deduction is the amount of the emoluments attributable to the qualifying period, not the emoluments attributable to the duties performed abroad. [*ITEPA 2003, s 379(1)*]. In other words, the earnings for intervening days spent in the UK qualify for the 100 per cent deduction even if the employee worked in the UK on those days. For this reason it may well be better for a seafarer to have a single employment for both UK and overseas work if the job involves UK duties and there are no special circumstances which could justify a far higher proportion of the emoluments as attributable to overseas work than would apply on a strict time basis.

13.15   It should be noted that the deduction applies to emoluments attributable to (ie earned in) the qualifying period. The relief will, of course, be given in the year that those earnings are assessed where they are received in a later year than that in which they were earned.

13.16   The emoluments qualifying for relief are the net amount after deduction of capital allowances; overseas travel expenses within *ITEPA 2003, ss 341, 342, 370* or *371*; allowable expenses under *s 336*; professional subscriptions under *s 343*; the special relief for expenditure by ministers of religion under *s 351*; contributions to a registered pension scheme under *s Finance Act 2004 (FA 2004), ss 188–194*; the special reliefs for corresponding payments out of foreign emoluments under *s 355*, travel expenses for non-UK domiciled individuals under *s 373* or *374* and mileage allowance relief under *s 232*. [*ITEPA 2003, s 381*]. It is not clear in what circumstances *s 355* can apply as foreign emoluments do not attract the relief.

13.17   Earnings for a period of leave immediately after the qualifying (or eligible) period are treated as attributable to the eligible period if (or to the extent that) they are earnings for the tax year in which that qualifying period ends. [*ITEPA 2003, s 379(2)*].

Incidental duties

13.18   Duties which a seafarer performs on a ship engaged on a voyage beginning or ending outside the UK (or on part of a journey beginning or ending outside the UK) are to be treated as performed abroad notwithstanding that they may be performed on a UK registered ship (or aircraft). However, where the journey, or any part of it, both begins and ends in the UK (including the Continental shelf), those duties will not be covered by *s 193(1)* to the extent that they are actually performed in the UK. [*ITEPA 2003, s 382*].

13.19   Duties of a seafarer performed outside the UK must be treated as performed in the UK if in the tax year in which they are performed the employment is in substance one whose duties fall to be performed in the UK and the work outside the UK is merely incidental to the performance of UK duties. [*ITEPA 2003, s 383*].

Share options

13.20   HMRC take the view that a gain on a share option is not an 'emolument' and therefore cannot attract the deduction (*IR Press Release 7 March 1994*). This is unlikely to be a problem except where the individual normally works in the UK for the same employer and is temporarily sent overseas. This is because the tax charge on the exercise of an option (see **14.13**) applies only where at the time the option is granted the employee is taxable under as a person who is resident and ordinarily resident in the UK. Accordingly the only income tax charge will be on the value of the option at the time of its grant in accordance with *Abbott v Philbin* (see **3.19**). This is usually a very low figure.

Returning expatriates

13.21   HMRC interpret the legislation as requiring the employee to be UK resident and ordinarily resident throughout the qualifying period. HMRC's view was challenged, unsuccessfully, in *Carstairs v Sykes [2000] STC 1103*. It was held there that the statutory context was that *Income and Corporation Taxes Act 1988 (ICTA 2008), s 193* was an exception to *ICTA 1988, s 19*, which provided that tax is chargeable under Case I of Schedule E where an individual is resident and ordinarily resident in the UK. Accordingly the most natural construction of 'absent' from the UK is 'not physically present in the UK as the country of residence and ordinary residence'.

Deduction for travelling expenses

Expenditure qualifying for deduction

13.22   If a person who is resident and ordinarily resident in the UK holds an employment the duties of which are performed *wholly* outside the UK (and the emoluments are not overseas earnings or foreign emoluments, see **12.9** above) expenses of the employee:

(*a*)   in travelling from any place in the UK to take up the employment; or

(*b*)   in travelling to any place in the UK on its termination,

are deductible from the earnings.

[*ITEPA 2003, s 341(1)–(4)*].

13.23   Accordingly, travel from the UK to take up the overseas employment and travel back to the UK following its termination will not give rise to a benefit in kind if paid by the employer (and will qualify for a deduction if paid by the employee). At least, that is the intention and what happens in practice. If travel is partly for one of the above purposes and partly for another purpose the deduction obviously applies only to the part that is properly attributable to the employment. [*ITEPA 2003, s 341(5)*].

Board and lodging expenses

13.24   If, for the purpose of enabling an employee within **13.23** above, to perform the duties of the overseas employment:

(*a*)   board and lodging outside the UK is provided for him and the cost is borne by or on behalf of his employer; or

(*b*)   he incurs expenses out of his emoluments on such board and lodging and those expenses are reimbursed by or on behalf of his employer,

the amount of such expenditure can be deducted from the emoluments (provided, of course, that such expenses are taxed as part of the emoluments). [*ITEPA 2003, s 376*]. If board and lodging is partly to enable the employee to perform the duties of the overseas employment and partly for some other purpose, only the part attributable to the former qualifies for a deduction. [*ITEPA 2003, s 376(3)*].

Multiple employments

13.25   If a person who is resident and ordinarily resident in the UK holds two or more employments, the duties of at least one of which are performed *wholly or partly* outside the UK, and travels from one place (having performed there duties of one office or employment) to another place for the purpose of performing duties of another office or employment (the emoluments from which are not overseas earnings or foreign emoluments), and either or both of those places are outside the UK, a deduction from the earnings of the employment to which he is travelling so as to trigger the right to claim the travel as deductible expenses is given for the travel expenses. [*ITEPA 2003, s 342(1)–(7)*]. If travel is partly for the purpose of performing the duties and partly for some other purpose, only the part of the expense attributable to the employment is allowable. [*ITEPA 2003, s 342(8)*]. The intention of this deeming is to ensure that the travel expenses do not give rise to a benefit in kind if paid by the employer and that they qualify for a deduction if paid by the employee.

Duties performed partly outside UK

13.26 Where a person holds an employment the duties of which are performed partly outside the UK travel expenses borne by his employer (or incurred by him and reimbursed by his employer) on any journey by him:

(*a*) from any place in the UK to the place of performance of any of the duties outside the UK; or

(*b*) from the overseas place of performance of any of the duties to any place in the UK,

he can deduct the expenses from the earnings (or up to 2002/03 was not taxable on the travel expenses) provided that the duties concerned can only be performed outside the UK and the expense was incurred wholly and exclusively for the purpose of performing the duties (for expenditure within (*a*)) or of returning after performing the duties (for expenditure within (*b*)). [*ITEPA 2003, s 370(1), (2), (4)*]. The employee must be ordinarily resident in the UK and the earnings must be taxable as general earnings under *ITEPA 2003, s 15* (see **2.48**) even if the employee were to claim the remittance basis [*ITEPA 2003, s 370(6)* inserted by *FA 2008, Sch 7, para 27*].

13.27 The requirement that the duties can only be performed outside the UK is obviously to prevent the controlling director of a family company opening an office overlooking the beach in the south of France and choosing to work from that office in the summer. The requirement that the expenditure must be borne or reimbursed by the employer is because the Chancellor of the Exchequer at that time believed that if the employer pays for the expenditure he will ensure that it is a reasonable amount. This assumption is of dubious validity in many cases, particularly where the employer is a company controlled by the employee.

13.28 If a person is absent from the UK for the purpose of performing the duties of one or more offices or employments (whether or not performed wholly overseas) he is similarly not assessable on travel expenses borne by his employer (or incurred by him and reimbursed by his employer) in respect of:

(*a*) any journey by him from the place of performance of the overseas duties to any place in the UK; or

(*b*) any return journey following a journey within (*a*),

provided that the duties concerned can only be performed outside the UK and the absence from the UK was occasioned wholly and exclusively for the purpose of performing the overseas duties. [*ITEPA 2003, s 370(1)–(3)*].

Duties performed on a vessel

13.29   For the purpose of *s 370* (and *371* below), duties which are performed on a vessel cannot be treated as performed outside the UK if the voyage is simply from one UK port to another [*ITEPA 2003, ss 40(1), 372*] but the relief under *s 370* (see **13.27** above) applies if the reason for the travel was not merely to perform the duties concerned (ie the overseas duties) but also if it was to perform those duties and other duties of the employment, eg it was to join the vessel overseas for a voyage to a UK port. [*ITEPA 2003, s 370(5)(e)*].

13.30   If an expense qualifies for relief under both *s 342* and *s 370* it obviously cannot be deducted twice. However, the taxpayer can choose under which *section* he wants the relief to be given. [*ITEPA 2003, s 330(1)*].

Family travel

13.31   A special relief is given for expenses of an employee's family in visiting him, where the employee is working overseas for 60 days or more. The employee must be absent from the UK for a continuous period of 60 days or more for the purpose of performing the duties of one or more offices or employments. [*ITEPA 2003, s 371(1)–(4)*]. 'Continuous' means that even a single day back in the UK, for whatever reason, will debar the relief (or start a fresh 60-day period after the employee returns overseas). From 6 April 2008 the employee must be ordinarily resident in the UK and the earnings must be taxable as general earnings under *ITEPA 2003, s 15* (see **2.48**) even if the employee were to claim the remittance basis. [*ITEPA 2003, ss 371(6), 370(6)* inserted by *FA 2008, Sch 7, para 28*].

13.32   If travel facilities are provided for travel for the employee's spouse or infant children and the cost is borne by or on behalf of the employer (or the expense is incurred by the employee and reimbursed to him by the employer) the expenditure is allowed as a deduction in calculating the earnings from the employment (provided it constitutes part of such earnings). [*ITEPA 2003, s 371(1)*]. The effect is that the employee will not be assessed on a benefit in kind in relation to the expenditure.

Travel eligible for relief

13.33   This relief applies only to travel between a place in the UK and the place of performance of the duties (or any of them) outside the UK, being either:

(*a*)   a journey by the employee's spouse or any infant child of his accompanying him at the beginning of the 60-day period or to visit him during that period; or (*b*)   a return journey following a journey falling within (*a*).

[*ITEPA 2003, s 371(5)*].

13.34   It applies to not more than two outward and two return journeys by the same person in the same year of assessment. A child includes a stepchild and an illegitimate child, but the child must be under 18 at the beginning of the outward journey. [*ITEPA 2003, s 371(6), (7)*].

Example

On 1 January 2014, Keith is sent by his employer to work on a contract in Indonesia. The contract lasts until 31 October 2014. Keith's employer pays for the following trips for Keith's wife, Katie, and his children Ken and Kelly. Ken is 16 and Kelly's 18th birthday is on 12 September 2014.

1 January 2014 – initial visit by Katie and Ken

15 January 2014– return trip by Katie and Ken

10 February 2014 – visit by Ken and Kelly

21 February 2014 – return trip by Ken and Kelly

31 March 2014– visit by Ken and Kelly

14 April 2014 – return trip by Ken and Kelly

9 September 2014 – visit by Katie and Kelly

18 September 2014 – return trip by Katie and Kelly

(1)   Travel for both Katie and Ken on 1 January 2014 and 15 January 2014 qualifies for relief.

(2)   Travel for both Ken and Kelly on 10 February 2014 and 21 February 2014 qualifies for relief.

(3)   Travel by Kelly on 31 March 2014 qualifies for relief. That by Ken does not as Ken has already made two return journeys in 2013/14. It is assumed that there was no previous overseas tour (in the same or a different country) by Keith in 2013/14. If Keith had been on an earlier tour, any trips by Katie, Ken or Kelly during that previous tour would have to be taken into account to determine which visits breached the two-trip limit.

(4)   Travel by Kelly on 14 April 2014 qualifies for relief. It is not clear whether Ken's travel does. Although it is his first trip in 2014/15 the expression 'two outward and two return journeys' could be interpreted as requiring both the outward and return journey to qualify to obtain relief for either.

(5)   Travel by both Katie and Kelly on 9 September 2014 and 18 September 2014 qualifies for relief. It does not matter that Kelly is over 18 on 18 September 2014 as she was under that age on 9 September.

13.35   It should be noted that the visit must be to the place of performance of the duties. Thus, if Keith had been worried about Ken and Kelly coming to Indonesia and had suggested that instead they all fly to Singapore to see one another, the relief would not apply and Keith would be assessed on the cost of Ken and Kelly's fares. Indeed, if he had suggested they visit him in Djakarta, the capital of Indonesia, rather than going to the remote jungle site where Keith was actually working it again appears that the relief would not apply as Djakarta would not be 'the place of performance' of the duties. *Section 371* does not give relief for the employee's own travel expenses if he comes back to the UK to visit his family. However, in most cases such expenses will fall within *ITEPA 2003, s 370* (see **13.27**). *Section 370* does not contain any limit to the number of journeys. It does however carry an additional requirement that the duties performed outside the UK can only be performed there.

13.36   Where the duties to be performed by an individual can readily be segregated it can sometimes be attractive to create two employments, one for UK work and the other for non-UK work, with the non-UK employer being an overseas company and all or part of the earnings from such an employment being kept outside the UK. However anti-avoidance legislation has been introduced from 2014/15 which will prevent such an arrangement in most cases (see **13.14A** onwards). HMRC accept that such 'dual contract' arrangements can work but have warned that they believe that 'the commercial reality may in some cases be that the employee has just one employment' (*Tax Bulletin* 76, April 2005). It is questionable whether a person can be taxed by reference to 'reality' unless HMRC show that the agreements are a sham. They may be able to show this where the nature of the work is such that part of the duties of the overseas employment must inevitably be done from the UK. Accordingly when entering into such arrangements it is important to consider the duties in detail and satisfy oneself that the duties can properly be split. Where a person for example makes telephone appointments in the UK to visit customers outside the UK that is not necessarily fatal to a dual contract arrangement if the appointments could have been made by someone else. Dual contracts would not normally be viable if a person is required to give continuing advice and some is given in the UK and some elsewhere. If a person will do some free-standing work overseas and other work will be done largely overseas but partly in the UK it may be sensible to limit the duties of the overseas employment to the free-standing work and put the remaining overseas work into the UK contract. There is no reason why the UK contract (the earnings from which are fully taxable) should not include overseas work; the key thing is that the work under the overseas contract must be performed wholly outside the UK. Even where the duties can be split HMRC is likely to challenge the split of the earnings using *s 24*.

Pensions

13.37   Normally, where a person receives a relevant benefit from an unapproved retirement benefit scheme it is chargeable to tax unless the contributions to the scheme were themselves taxed as a benefit in kind. [*ITEPA 2003, ss 394, 396*]. Obviously, this provision was not intended to apply to pension provision for overseas work where the pension scheme was established abroad. Accordingly, by concession HMRC do not seek tax on a lump sum benefit receivable by an employee (or his personal representative or a dependant) from an overseas pension scheme if his foreign service (see **11.28**) comprises either:

(*a*)   at least 75 per cent of his total service in the employment;

(*b*)   the whole of the last ten years' service in the employment (where it exceeds ten); or

(*c*)   at least 50 per cent of his total service where that exceeds 20 years and the foreign service includes at least ten of the last 20 years.

Where these conditions are not met only the proportion of the lump sum that the period of UK service in the employment bears to the total period of the employment will be taxed (*ESC A10*).

Chapter 14

Employee Shareholdings

Introduction

14.1   There is a great deal of legislation in relation to employee shareholdings. This can be split into two broad categories: approved share schemes, and other transactions.

14.2   Approved share schemes are considered in Chapters 15 and 16. These enable limited benefits to be provided to employees without attracting a tax charge provided that a large number of fairly stringent conditions are complied with. There are five types of approved share scheme. Approved profit sharing schemes and savings-related share option schemes cannot be used to provide benefits to selected employees, they must be directed at virtually the entire workforce. Accordingly, whilst they encourage wide share ownership they are not generally suitable as employee incentives. They cannot be targeted to specific employees and cannot be tied to the performance of the employee. CSOP schemes (often called executive share option schemes) can often provide an attractive benefit to selected employees but other than for start-ups this is fairly modest, is limited to future growth in the value of the shares, and will not enable the employee to actually obtain a shareholding in the company for at least three years. Enterprise Management Incentives, whilst selective, are limited to a small number of employees and are aimed primarily at unquoted companies, where there is normally a share valuation problem and the tax incentive could turn out to be an incentive to leave the company rather than to tie the employee to it. Share Incentive Plans are attractive and flexible. However they are all-employee schemes and most growing companies are not attracted to such schemes. Furthermore it is questionable whether there is a real incentive in giving financially unsophisticated employees unmarketable shares whose value is not readily apparent.

14.3   Because of the severe limitations on the use of approved schemes, many employers and their employees who wish to use share ownership as a means of providing incentives for senior executives, opt to accept the tax charges that arise where benefits from shares in the employer company are provided without resort to an approved scheme. Unapproved share schemes can be particularly attractive in a start-up situation where the shares have little value. If any tax charge can be triggered immediately, such as by giving the employee shares immediately – or preferably by selling them to him at a very low market value – with an obligation to resell them at a low price should the employee leave the company within a specified period, it is attractive to accept that tax charge and avoid any inhibitions on the development of the business that the need to comply with conditions for approval would otherwise generate.

14.4   A then Treasury Minister, Dawn Primarolo, has stated that the government intend 'to deal with any arrangements that emerge in future designed to frustrate our intention that employers and employees should pay the proper amount of tax and NICs on the rewards of employment. Where we become aware of arrangements which attempt to frustrate this intention we will introduce legislation to close them down, where necessary from today' (2 December 2004). Accordingly schemes designed to frustrate this legislation are likely to be countered by retrospective legislation back to 2 December 2004. It should also be borne in mind that since 1 August 2004 there has been an obligation to disclose to HMRC details of tax or NIC avoidance schemes which involve securities, payments to trustees and intermediaries or loans. Such notification has to be given when the scheme is first marketed or used. [*Finance Act 2004 (FA 2004), ss 306–318*].

Occasions of charge on unapproved schemes

14.5   There are a number of potential occasions of charge to income tax in relation to unapproved employee share schemes:

(*a*)   If the shares are restricted securities (see **14.23**) an income tax charge arises:

    (i)   if they cease to be restricted securities (other than on a transfer to an associated person;

    (ii)   the restrictions are varied; or

    (iii)   the shares or securities are sold (see **14.23**).

(*b*)   If the shares are convertible securities (see **14.51**) an income tax charge arises on:

    (i)   their conversion;

    (ii)   their disposal (other than to an associated person);

    (iii)   a sale of the right to convert; or

    (iv)   the receipt of any other benefit in respect of the entitlement to convert (see **14.53**).

(*c*)   If the initial market value of the shares is artificially depressed (see **14.62**) an income tax charge arises at the time of acquisition of the securities (see **14.63**).

(*d*)   If such shares are restricted securities an income tax charge arises at the end of the first tax year in which they are held as if the restrictions had been lifted at that time (see **14.65**).

(*e*)   If the value of the shares is artificially enhanced an income tax charge arises at the end of the tax year in which such enhancement takes place (see **14.74**).

(*f*)   If the shares are acquired at an undervalue a tax charge will either arise:

    (i)   at the time of acquisition under the basic employment income charging provision (*ITEPA 2003, s 62*) on the amount of the undervalue; or

    (ii)   if the payment due at that time is less than the market value of the securities, as if a notional interest free loan equal to the amount of the undervalue had been made to the employee by the employer at that time (see **14.81**).

(*g*)   Where (*f*)(ii) applies there is an annual income tax charge on notional interest on the notional loan (unless had interest been paid it would have qualified as a charge on income) (see **14.79** and **9.1**).

(*h*)   In such a case if the shares are sold or no further payment becomes due in respect of them and at that time all or part of the notional loan is still outstanding an income tax charge arises at that time on the outstanding amount (see 14.87).

(*i*)   If the shares are sold for a consideration greater than their market value an income tax charge arises on the excess (see **14.89**).

(*j*)   If the employee receives any benefit by virtue of holding the shares that benefit is taxed as income (see **14.91**).

(*k*)   If the shares are acquired under an option no tax charge arises on the grant of the option but an income tax charge can arise on:

    (i)   the exercise of the option;

    (ii)   an assignment or release of the option;

    (iii) receipt of a benefit in connection with the option (see **14.93**).

Effect of the provisions

14.6   Accordingly, the effect of most of these provisions is to subject to income tax gains that would otherwise have been liable to capital gains tax. Where the rate of tax is the same for both taxes, treating the amount as income usually merely results in a loss of the ability to utilise the employee's £10,100 annual capital gains tax exemption against the gain (if he has not already utilised it on other transactions). A more serious problem is that share options (other than under the EMI scheme – see **16.67**) defer the start of taper relief on the shares themselves until the option is exercised. With a two-year indexation period for business assets, which includes all unquoted shares and virtually all quoted shares held by employees, the sooner the taper period starts the better from the employee's point of view, although it may not be a great hardship for an employee to have to hold the shares for two years after exercising their option – unless they do not have the necessary outside finance to acquire the shares in the first place. From the company's perspective a three-year option period ties the employee to the company for five years if he wants the full 90 per cent taper relief, but the loss of the employee's goodwill by extending the period in this way needs to be weighed against this benefit. In most cases the tax is collected from the employee. There is in general no obligation on the employer to apply PAYE, although the decision of the Special Commissioners in *Paul Dunstall Organisation Ltd v Hedges [1999] STC SCD 26, Sp C 179* has cast doubt on this. PAYE does need to be applied where the shares are readily convertible assets. Normally this will only apply on an acquisition of shares, not on one of the other transactions described below which trigger a tax charge. However, it is specifically provided that PAYE must be applied on the trigger events under the employee share scheme rules.

Share acquisitions included

14.7　Many people expect tax charges to arise where an employee subscribes for shares at an undervalue. It should not be overlooked, however, that the various provisions outlined below apply not only where an employee subscribes for new shares or is granted an option to do so. They equally apply if he acquires existing shares from one of the shareholders or is granted an option by a shareholder to acquire shares from him.

Phantom shares

14.8　Before considering the legislative provisions in detail, mention should be made of phantom shares (sometimes called shadow shares), which are becoming increasingly popular. As the name suggests these are notional shares. The employee is allotted an agreed number of phantom shares. When the company declares a dividend he is paid a bonus equal to the dividend he would have received had he held that number of shares. When he wants to 'dispose' of his shares the company will pay him a bonus equal to the gain he would have made had that number of actual shares been sold on the open market. If the company makes a scrip issue the employee will be 'issued' with further phantom shares. In the event of a rights issue, as he is not expected to make a cash payment, he will either receive the cash sum for which he could have sold his rights, or such additional shares as could have been acquired with the proceeds of the sale of the rights attaching to the remainder. If desired the company's articles of association can give the holder of phantom shares the right to vote at general meetings.

14.9　The concept is, of course, that if the employee is going to pay income tax on all the benefits he would obtain from ownership of the shares he might as well simply be paid income. This is convenient for the employee as the 'gain' can be taxed under the PAYE system at the time he receives the income rather than face a large tax bill at a later date when he may well have already spent the funds. It is convenient to the employer because it simplifies administration and does not affect the size of holdings of other shareholders. As share incentives generally aim to give the employee a stake in the growth of the company, phantom shares meet this objective as well as actual shares. The main difference is that the cost of the incentive is met by the company (but as such triggers a corporation tax deduction for the company) whereas with real shares the cost is effectively met by the shareholders (as they are giving the employee part of the growth that would otherwise have accrued to their own shares). With an unquoted company the interests of the shareholders and the company are usually identical and the shareholders will usually realise that they are providing the value of share options, whereas with a listed company many shareholders probably do not realise this.

Shares in private companies

14.10   Employee shareholdings are not generally of great incentive value in private companies except in two circumstances. The first is where there is a strong likelihood that the company will be sold or a public quotation obtained for its shares in the reasonably near future. In such circumstances very substantial benefits can be obtained by the employee as the sale or flotation will itself result in a significant increase in the value of the shares. The second is that the ownership of shares in the employer company can have a strong psychological effect on some employees, even though the shares have little real value.

14.11   The reason that such shares are not generally of value to employees in other circumstances is, of course, that, as there is no market for the shares, the employee cannot realise their value. If he wishes to dispose of them, the only potential purchasers are likely to be the other shareholders, and the size of the employee's holding is likely to be such that those other shareholders will be indifferent as to whether or not they acquire those shares. Furthermore, many private companies do not pay dividends so the employee is unlikely to receive any other benefit from his ownership of the shares.

14.12   Although the value of the employee's shares – both on acquisition and disposal – is likely to be small, that value has to be agreed with the Shares Valuation Division of HMRC, which can be both time-consuming and costly, and if HMRC's figure differs significantly from the company's, a tax charge under one of the provisions outlined below will arise in relation to that difference in value.

Simple share acquisitions

14.13   It also needs to be borne in mind that in most cases the special rules considered below do not displace the charge under the basic charging provision, *Income Tax (Earnings and Pensions) Act 2003 (ITEPA 2003), s 62*. This states that earnings includes 'any ... other profit or incidental benefit of any kind obtained by the employee if it is money or money's worth'. [*ITEPA 2003, s 62(2)(b)*]. Money's worth is the monetary value at the time of receipt of something that is capable of being converted into money. For example, if a person is given ordinary shares in the company for which he works at a time when they have a value of £1,000 he will in most cases be taxable under *s 62* on that £1,000. The special rules described below are intended to impose an additional tax charge in circumstances where the value of the shares, or in the case of shares acquired under an option the value of the option, at the time of acquisition does not properly represent the benefit obtained by the employee.

14.14   In many cases the charge under *s 62* will be the only charge. This is likely to be the case where the shares are ordinary shares not subject to any restrictions and not attracting any rights other than those attaching to all of the shares. It is only if there is something unusual about the shares as a result of which they are likely to increase in value disproportionately to those shares held by other shareholders that the special rules considered below are likely to bite.

14.15   Before looking at the specific rules on employee share schemes it should be stressed that these extend the general rules on taxation of earnings and those rules can themselves impose a charge on earnings paid in the form of share incentives without a need fro recourse to the special provisions. A case in point is *PA Holdings Ltd v HMRC* [2012] STC 582. PA created a Jersey-based employee benefit trust (EBT). The trustees set up a Jersey company, Ellastone Ltd. They subscribed for redeemable preference shares which carried a right to dividends but thereafter to nothing other than repayment at par. The EBT distributed these shares to employees. PA Holdings made a contribution to the EBT and the EBT used the money to make a capital contribution to Ellastone. Ellastone paid a large dividend on the special shares. The First-tier Tribunal made finding of fact that the payment received by employees were both earnings and distributions. The First-tier and Upper Tribunals both said that dividends could not be taxed as earnings for income tax purposes as there is a separate tax code for taxing dividends, and that must take priority over any earnings charge. They relied on *Income and Corporation Taxes Act 1988 (ICTA 1988), s 20(2)*: 'no distribution which is chargeable under Schedule F shall be chargeable under any other provisions of the Income Tax Acts'. However, the Court of Appeal held that the tribunals had been in error in thinking that both Schedules E and F could be relevant. They sought to rely on the case *Fry v Salisbury House Estate 15 TC 266* to say that 'They cannot both be relevant, income falls either into the one or the other. The factual conclusion that the income falls within Schedule E precludes any finding that the income also falls within Schedule F' (Moses LJ). Moses went on to say that *ICTA 1988, s 20(2)* – 'no distribution which is chargeable under Schedule F shall be chargeable under any other provisions of the Income Tax Acts' – merely 'resolves the conflict where income from one and the same source is charged under different schedules', and that 'Schedule F does not take priority over Schedule E. It does not charge emoluments at all'. That begs a very big question. It surely could equally be said that Schedule E does not take priority over Schedule F where dividends are received by virtue of an employment; it does not charge dividends at all. Furthermore the decision seems to undermine the integrity of the tax credit system. When Schedule F was originally introduced tax at the basic rate had to be deducted at source from dividend payments and handed over to HMRC. This was changed by *Finance Act 1972 (FA 1972)*, which introduced tax credits. *ICTA 1988, s 20(2)* started life as *FA 1972, s 87(3)*. From the context of that section it seems clear that it was intended as an essential part of the tax credit system. It would be unreasonable to force a company to pay ACT equivalent to basic rate tax and then deny the recipient of the dividend credit for that tax. *Section 87(1)* gave the shareholder the right to a tax credit to reflect the collection of the ACT from the company under *section 84*. In that context a dividend had to be taxable under Schedule F. If it were not there was no machinery to allow the tax credit so the payment of the dividend would effectively have resulted in double taxation. Although the tax credit is nowadays less significant this principle still ought to apply. The Court of Appeal decision undermines it. If a dividend can be taxed under the rules relating to earnings the tax credit is lost. Although Moses LJ suggested a possible need for *section 20(2)*, he did not address how it fits in with tax credits or that the effect of taxing a dividend as earnings is to deny the tax credit. A similar dividend scheme was used in *Sloan Roninson Investment Services Ltd v HMRC (TC 2132)*. It failed because the tribunal held that the employees had already become entitled to the money prior to the issue of the shares. However the FTT said that if that were wrong it felt the case indistinguishable from *PA*, and felt that the companies were just money box companies.

Unapproved employee share schemes: the current rules

14.16   The special rules that apply to unapproved employee share schemes were substantially recast by *s 139* and *Sch 22* to *Finance Act 2000 (FA 2000)*. These are now contained in *ITEPA 2003*, new *ss 417–484*.

14.17   They impose an income tax charge where:

(*a*)   securities or an interest in securities is acquired by a person;

(*b*)   the right or opportunity to acquire the securities (or interest) is available by reason of an employment of either the acquirer or of any other person; and

(*c*)   that person does not pay the full, unrestricted market value for the security (*Hansard*, SCB, 22.5 2003, col 256).

[*ITEPA 2003, s 421B(1)*]

14.18   For this purpose:

(*a*)   securities (or an interest) are acquired at the time when the person becomes beneficially entitled to the securities or interest in them (if that is different from the time when the securities are conveyed or transferred). [*ITEPA 2003, s 421B(2)(a)*];

(*b*)   references to an employment include a former employment and a prospective employment. [*ITEPA 2003, s 421B(2)(b)*];

(*c*)   a right or opportunity to acquire securities (or an interest in securities) which is made available by a person's employer (or a person connected with his employer) is deemed to have made available by reason of his employment (unless the person who makes the opportunity available is an individual and that opportunity is made available in the normal course of his domestic, family or personal relationships) [*ITEPA 2003, s 421B(3)*]; and

(*d*)   an interest in shares or securities means an interest which is less than full beneficial ownership (including an interest in the proceeds of sale) but excluding a right to acquire the shares or securities. [*ITEPA 2003, s 420(8)*].

14.19   There is a potential problem in relation to earn-outs where a company is sold to another with the price payable dependent on profit targets over the next few years being met. It is usual for at least some of the existing management to remain with the company or become employees of the new company. Despite the wording of (*c*) above HMRC have said that where it can be shown that the earn-out is further consideration for the disposal of the target company rather than value obtained by reason of employment the value of the shares of the new company received under the earn-out will be taken to be equal to the value of the shares sold so that no liability to income tax will arise (*Press Release 22.7.2003*). The press release sets out the sort of factors that HMRC will take into consideration.

Tyrer v Smart

14.20   In *Tyrer v Smart 52 TC 533* the courts had to consider whether shares were obtained 'as a director or employee'. In 1969 a company made a public offer of shares by tender. Employees were given a preferential right to acquire shares at the minimum tender price of £1. Mr Tyrer applied for and was allotted 5,000 such shares. The striking price was £1.25 and dealing commenced at £1.30. The High Court and the Court of Appeal held that Mr Tyrer had obtained his shares not as an employee but as the result of his willingness to take a commercial risk in investing. This was reversed by the House of Lords who held that the Special Commissioners were entitled to find that he had acquired the shares as an employee.

14.21   The question in *Smith v HMRC [2009] UKFTT 210 (TC)* was whether Mr Smith had acquired his shares in pursuance of a right or opportunity obtained by reason of his employment. Mr Smith was initially employed by Sensormatic Electronics and was awarded share options in that company. If there was a change of control of Sensormatic he had a right to require Sensormatic to buy back his shares. He exercised the option. Sensormatic was subsequently taken over by Tyco and Mr Smith received Tyco shares in return for his shares in Sensormatic. He then required Tyco/Sensormatic to buy back his Tyco shares. The price was roughly £1.5million more than their then market value. By that time Mr Smith had become an employee of Tyco. He contended that he did not acquire his shares as an employee of Tyco; he acquired them as a shareholder of Sensormatic. The Tribunal held that the £1.5million was income. Mr Smith was an employee of Tyco, he had received a benefit and that benefit was provided at the cost of Tyco. 'By reason of' is a very wide expression (*Wicks v Firth* – see **6.39**). Accordingly the benefit was taxable under the benefit-in-kind rules (see **6.39**). It indicated that, but for this, Mr Smith would have won. His employment with Sensormatic furnished him with the opportunity to acquire his Sensormatic shares but by the time he acquired his Tyco shares he was no longer an employee of Sensormatic – although he was an employee of Tyco – and he did not acquire his Tyco shares by reason of his employment with Tyco.

14.22 *Chapters 2 to 4 (ss 422–450)* (see **14.23–14.92**) cease to apply to securities or an interest in securities:

(*a*) immediately after the securities are disposed of (other than to an associated person) (see **14.31**). [*ITEPA 2003, s 421B(5)*];

(*b*) immediately before the death of the employee [*ITEPA 2003, s 421B(6)*]; or

(*c*) seven years after the first date following the acquisition of the securities on which the employee is no longer an employee of either the employer, if the securities are issued by a company that company, or a person connected with the employer or such a company. [*ITEPA 2003, s 421B(7)*].

'Securities' for the purpose of these provisions includes:

(*a*) shares (or stock) in a body corporate, wherever incorporated, or in an unincorporated body constituted under the laws of a foreign country or territory;

(*b*) debentures, debenture stock, loan stock, bonds, certificates of deposit and other instruments creating or acknowledging indebtedness (other than contracts of insurance);

(i) HMRC say that this includes gifts (Press Release 2.7.2003).

(*c*) warrants and other instruments entitling their holder to subscribe for securities (whether or not in existence or identifiable);

(ii) HMRC say that where a warrant simply gives a right to acquire shares it will be excluded under **14.20**(*e*) but if a warrant gives other rights, such as a current right to receive dividends in respect of the shares to which it relates, it will be a security (Press Release 2.7.2003).

(*d*) certificates or other instruments conferring rights in respect of securities held by third parties and the transfer of which may be effected without the consent of such third parties;

(*e*) units in collective investment scheme (ie arrangements which are made with effect to property of any description (including money) the purpose of which is to enable people taking part in the arrangements to participate in any way from (or receive profits or income arising from) the acquisition, holding, management or disposal of the property or sums paid out of such profits or income);

(*f*) options and futures (ie rights under a contract for the sale of a commodity, or other property, under which delivery is to be made at a future date at a price agreed when the contract is made – which includes where the contract is expressed to be by reference to a standard lot or quality with the price being variable to take account of such variations and also where the price is not specified in the contract but is left to be determined by reference to the price at which a contract is to be entered into on a market or exchange (or could be entered into at a time and place specified in the contract));

(*g*)   rights under a contract for differences (or similar contract the purpose or pretended purpose of which is to secure a profit or avoid a loss by reference to fluctuations in the value or price of property or of an index or some other factors designated in the contract) (other than contracts of insurance);

(*h*)   arrangements falling within *Finance Act 2005 (FA 2005), s 48A* (alternative finance arrangements - alternative finance investment bond); and

(*i*)   rights under contracts of insurance (other than excluded contracts, namely an annuity contract which will be pension income; a contract of long-term insurance (within the meaning of the *Financial Services and Markets Act 2000 (FSMA 2000) (Regulated Activities) Order 2001*) (other than an annuity contract) which does not have a surrender value and is not capable of acquiring one (whether a conversion or otherwise); and a contract of general insurance (other than one which falls under generally accepted accounting practice (GAAP) to be accounted for as a financial asset or liability).

[*ITEPA 2003, (s 420(1)–(4), (8)* as amended by *Finance (No 2) Act 2005 (F(No 2)A 2005), Sch 2, para 2, Finance Act 2006 (FA 2006), s 92(2)* and the *Employment Income (Meaning of Securities) Order 2007 (SI 2007 No 2130)*].

14.23   However, the following are not securities:

(*a*)   cheques (and bills of exchange other than bills accepted by a banker), banker's drafts and letters of credit;

(*b*)   money and statements showing balances on a current, deposit or savings account;

(*c*)   leases and other dispositions of property and saleable securities;

(*d*)   securities options (ie a right to acquire securities – but from 2 December 2004 such a right which is made available under arrangements the main purpose or one of the main purposes of which is the avoidance of tax or NIC is not a securities option and will therefore constitute a security by virtue of **14.19**(*f*)); and

(*e*)   prior to 2 December 2004 other options were also not securities.

[*ITEPA 2003, s 420(5), (8)* as amended by *FA 2006, s 92(3)*]. Rights under contracts of insurance were also excluded from the scope of these provisions up to 2 December 2004 but were brought within the definition of securities from that date. The charge applies to insurance policies taken out both before and after that date but where a charge arises under *ITEPA 2003, s 446K* (securities with artificially enhanced market value) the first relevant period (see **14.73**) starts on 2 December, and for the purpose of *ITEPA 2003, s 420(1A)(c)* (**14.18**(*h*) above) the *FA 2004, s 50* meaning of GAAP applies even for times before 1 January 2005 (when it came into effect). [*F(No 2)A 2005, Sch 2, para 2(8)*]. The change was to counter schemes under which the market value of an insurance policy was artificially enhanced subsequent to its acquisition by an employee.

14.24   The Treasury have power to amend by statutory instrument the definition of what is and is not a security for the purpose of the unapproved share schemes legislation. [*ITEPA 2003, s 420(6), (7)*].

14.25   The amount of the tax charge depends on the trigger. Different rules apply to:

(*a*)   restricted securities (*Chapter 2* of *Part 7* of *ITEPA 2003* – see **14.26**)

(*b*)   convertible securities (*Chapter 3* – see **14.59**)

(*c*)   securities with artificially depressed market value (*Chapter 3A* – see **14.68**)

(*d*)   securities with artificially enhanced market value (*Chapter 3B* – see **14.80**)

(*e*)   securities acquired for less than market value (*Chapter 3C* – see **14.88**)

(*f*)   securities disposed of for more than market value (*Chapter 3D* – see **14.98**)

(*g*)   post acquisition benefit from securities (*Chapter 4* – see **14.98**)

(*h*)   shares acquired under securities options (*Chapter 5* – see **14.102**).

Some of these new provisions apply only to securities acquired on or after 16 April 2003 whereas others affect shares acquired before that date also.

Chapter 2:   Does not apply to securities or interests in securities acquired before 16 April 2003. It applies to securities acquired after that date from a date to be appointed by the Treasury by statutory instrument. [*Finance Act 2003 (FA 2003), Sch 22, para 3(2)*]. This was fixed as 1 September 2003 (*Finance Act 2003, Schedule 22, para 3(1) (Appointed Day) Order 2003 (SI 2003 No 1997*).

Chapter 3:   Applies irrespective of the date of acquisition of the securities but only applies from 1 September 2003. [*FA 2003, Sch 22, para 4(2)*].

Chapter 3A: Generally applies irrespective of the date of acquisition of the securities but *sections 446E* (see **14.71**) and *446I(1)(a)* (see **14.78**) do not apply to securities or interests in securities acquired before 16 April 2003 and for securities acquired from that date apply only from 1 September 2003. [*FA 2003, Sch 22, para 5(2), (3)*].

Chapter 3B: Generally applies irrespective of the date of acquisition of the securities but *ss 446M* (see **14.84**) and *446N* (see **14.85**) do not affect securities or interests in securities acquired before 16 April 2003 and for securities acquired from that date apply only from 1 September 2003. [*FA 2003, Sch 22, para 6(2), (3)*].

Chapter 3C: Does not apply to securities acquired before 16 April 2003. [*FA 2003, Sch 22, para 7(2)*].

Chapter 3D: Applies to securities and interests in securities disposed of after 15 April 2003 irrespective of when they were acquired. [*FA 2003, Sch 22, para 8(2)*].

Chapter 4:   Applies from 16 April 2003 irrespective of when the securities were acquired, but for shares acquired before 16 April 2003 the following provisions of *ITEPA 2003* as originally enacted continue to apply: *s 450* (other than *subs 3(b)–(e)* and *6(b)*) (see **14.142**), and as far as is relevant for the purposes of *s 450*, *ss 447–449, 451, 452* (other than *subs (4)* and *(5)*) *461* (other than *subs (3)*), *464–466* and *468–470*. [*FA 2003, Sch 22, para 9(3)(a),(4)*]. These provisions also apply up to 1 September 2003 for shares acquired after 15 April 2003. [*FA 2003, Sch 22, para 9(3)(b), (4)*].

Chapter 5:   Applies to share options as originally defined under *ICTA 1988, s 254(1)* from 1 September 2003 and to other options from 16 April 2003. [*FA 2003, Sch 22, para 10(2)*].

Restricted securities (Chapter 2)

14.26   If the securities concerned are restricted securities at the time of their acquisition a tax charge arises when a chargeable event occurs in relation to the securities (see **14.33**). [*ITEPA 2003, s 422*]. The chargeable amount is of course income for the year in which the chargeable event occurs. [*ITEPA 2003, s 426*]. The issue of the securities is not a chargeable event. However, an election can be made to treat the securities as unrestricted on issue (see **14.31**). With an unquoted company this can be attractive as there is often little difference in value between a tiny holding of restricted and unrestricted shares. Paying tax on the full initial value takes the future growth in value wholly out of the charge to income tax and into capital gains tax, which is normally at a lower rate. HMRC have said that as no consideration was received when either Northern Rock plc or Bradford and Bingley plc was taken into public ownership, there was no chargeable event at that time (22.2.2008 and 29.9.2008 respectively) and that the disposal will give rise to a capital loss to employees who purchased shares. No loss arises in relation to the free shares issued on conversion from a building society (*HMRC Briefs 32/2008, 4/2009*).

14.27   'Employment-related' shares or securities are restricted securities if there is any contract, agreement, arrangement or condition which reduces the market value of the securities and which either:

(1)   provides for:

    (*a*)   transfer, reversion, or forfeiture of the employment-related securities (or the interest in them) if certain circumstances arise (or do not arise);

    (*b*)   as a result of that transfer, reversion or forfeiture the person by whom the employment-related securities are held will cease to be beneficially entitled to them; and (*c*)   that person will not be entitled to receive an amount which would have been at least equal to that market value at the time of the transfer, reversion or forfeiture if there had been no such provision for transfer, reversion or forfeiture [*s 423(2)*]; or

(2)   restricts:

    (*a*)   the freedom of the holder of the securities to dispose of them or of their sale proceeds;

    (*b*)   the right of the holder to retain the securities or their sale proceeds; or

    (*c*)   any other right conferred by the securities [*s 423(3)*], or

(3)   creates a disadvantage (or possible disadvantage) to the holder, the employee (if different) or any person connected with either as a result of either retaining or disposing of the shares [*s 423(4)*].

[*ITEPA 2003, s 423*].

This definition potentially creates a problem with 'ratchet' shares. These normally provide for the shares to increase in value if performance targets are met. Such shares are commonly used in management buy-outs. Such shares were not within the scope of *Finance Act 1988 (FA 1988), s 78* (see **14.142**) as the right giving rise to the increase is not created or varied after issue; it is inherent in the shares from the outset. They do however seem to fall within *s 423(3)*. HMRC have entered into a Memorandum of Understanding with the British Venture Capital Association (dated 25 July 2003) covering various aspects of *s 423*. In it they accept that where the management of an investee company hold ratchet shares the ratchet arrangement should be taken into account in arriving at the unrestricted market value of the shares (see **14.37**) provided that:

(*a*)   the ratchet rights of the managers depend on the overall performance of the company not on the individual performance of any particular shareholder;

(*b*)   the ratchet arrangements of the managers are in place when the Venture Capitalists acquire their shares;

(*c*)   the price the managers pay for their shares reflects, at the time of acquisition, their maximum economic entitlement (which HMRC accept is met if the managers pay the same price as the venture capitalists); and

(*d*)   the managers' shares are ordinary shares.

Although the Memorandum does not deal with other ratchet shares the principle seems to be that if the price paid for ratchet shares is at least the full market value of ordinary shares having the same rights apart from the ratchet no tax will arise. Further guidance is given in the HMRC Press Release of 22.7.2003. References to a restriction mean provisions relating to the securities and interest which is made by any contract, agreement, arrangement or condition to which any of the heads in (2) above applies [*ITEPA 2003, s 432(5)*].

14.28 However employment-related securities are not restricted securities by reason only that:

(*a*) they are unpaid or partly paid and as such are liable to forfeiture for non-payment of calls (and there is no restriction on the holder's right to meet such calls); or

(*b*) the holder can be required to sell the securities (or offer them for sale) if he ceases to be employed by the employer (or a person connected with the employer) as a result of misconduct.

[*ITEPA 2003, s 424(1)* as amended by *F(No 2)A 2005, Sch 2, para 4(2)*]. From 2 December 2004 neither of these exemptions applies if the main purpose (or one of the main purposes) of the arrangement under which the right or opportunity to acquire the securities arises is the avoidance of tax or NIC. [*ITEPA 2003, s 424(2)* inserted by *F(No 2)A 2005, Sch 2, para 4(3)*]. Prior to 2 December 2004 there was an exclusion where the securities were restricted securities solely because they were redeemable. The change is to counter schemes by which additional value was transferred to the employee at the time of redemption. Where such securities were acquired prior to 2 December 2004 *ITEPA 2003, s 422* (see **14.26**) applies even though the securities were not restricted securities at the time of their acquisition. [*F(No 2)A 2005, Sch 2, para 4(4)*].

14.29 It will be apparent that the market value of a restricted security is usually very low as the restrictions artificially depress that value. The legislation accordingly aims to impose a tax charge when the restriction is lifted.

14.30 There can still be a tax charge on acquisition if the securities fall within heads 2 or 3 of para **14.27**. However, the restrictions within head 1 are likely to render the shares completely valueless (or almost so). Accordingly, no charge arises on the issue of such shares. There is no initial charge even if the shares would still be restricted under heads 2 or 3 following the lifting of the head 1 restrictions (as the lifting of those restrictions will trigger a tax charge by reference to the value at that time of the shares subject to the head 2 or 3 restrictions). [*ITEPA 2003, s 425(1)*].

Election to pay tax on acquisition

14.31 This is subject to two caveats. Any charge imposed under *Chapter 3*, (see **14.59**) *3C* (see **14.88**) or *5* (see **14.102**) of *Part 7* to the *Act* will still arise. [*ITEPA 2003, s 425(2)*]. Secondly the employer and employee can jointly elect for the normal charge to arise on acquisition. [*ITEPA 2003, s 425(3)*]. Such an election is irrevocable, must be made within 14 days of the acquisition of the shares and must be in a form approved by HMRC. [*ITEPA 2003, s 425(4), (5)*]. HMRC have said that there is no scope for accepting an election made outside the 14-day period. They have published the form of election on their website. They have not given it a number. The easiest way to find it is to search under '*s 425*'. The election does not need to be sent to HMRC. They only want to see it in the context of an enquiry. If an employer wishes to make any amendments to this form they need to be approved in advance by HMRC (Press Release 2.7.2003). For 2015/16 onwards, the election cannot be made unless, at the time of the acquisition, the earnings from the employment are (or would be if there were any) general earnings to which any of the charging provisions of *ITEPA 2003, ss 14-41* applies [*ITEPA 2003, ss 425(6), 428(7)(bb), 430(4)* inserted by *Finance Act 2014 (FA 2014), Sch 9, para 9/para 10/para 11*].

14.32   At first sight it is hard to imagine why anyone should want to avail themselves of this election, but it can give a saving overall. The government say that an employee may prefer to pay some tax on acquisition to reduce the charge on a future chargeable event. The reason is that the rules seek to tax as income the part of the growth in value after the time of acquisition of the shares that is attributable to the restrictions. If there is no initial tax charge the growth in value up to the time of the removal of the restrictions (or the first occasion on which any of them is removed) is split between the part attributable to the actual cost of the shares and the part attributable to the restrictions. Any amount taxed on acquisition is added to the actual cost and this increases the proportion of the growth that is attributable to such cost. In the vast majority of cases falling within head 1 in para **14.26** the initial value of the restricted shares is likely to be very low, with the result that any initial undervalue by reference to the value of the shares in the light of the restrictions is also likely to be very low. Accordingly, although electing to trigger a tax charge on that undervalue is likely to create a small benefit when the restrictions are removed, the tax saving will normally be so small that it is unlikely to justify the administrative costs of triggering the charge on acquisition of the shares.

The chargeable events

14.33   There are three chargeable events that can trigger an income tax charge subsequent to the acquisition of the securities. These are:

(*a*)   the securities (or interest) ceasing to be restricted securities in circumstances in which an associated person is beneficially entitled to them (or to the interest) after the event;

(*b*)   the variation (or removal) of any restriction relating to the securities in such circumstances; and

(*c*)   the disposal for consideration of the securities (or any interest in them) by an associated person (otherwise than to another associated person) at a time when they are still restricted securities.

[*ITEPA 2003, s 427(3)*]. There are, however, a number of exceptions to the basic rule. These are considered at **14.54**.

14.34   The reference to an associated person is confusing as most people would assume this to mean someone who is not the employee but has some connection with him. That is not however the case. Associated persons are defined as:

(*a*)   the person who acquired the securities on the acquisition;

(*b*)   the employee (if different); and

(*c*)   any relevant linked person (a person who either is (or has been) connected with or is (or has been) a member of the same household as, either the employee or the person who initially acquired the shares – but a company is not a relevant linked person if it is the employer, the issuer (or original vendor) of the shares, or the person by whom the opportunity to acquire them was made available).

[*ITEPA 2003, s 421C* as amended by *FA 2004, s 90(2)*]. A former connected person or member of the employee's household was not a linked person prior to 18 June 2004 but is from that date even if the shares were acquired earlier.

14.35   Accordingly the tax charge will in most cases be triggered by:

(*a*)   the shares ceasing to be restricted securities at a time when they are still held by the employee (or a connected person);

(*b*)   some or all of the restrictions being varied or removed at a time when the shares are still held by the employee (or a connected person); or

(*c*)   the shares being sold by the employee to an unconnected person at a time when they are still restricted shares.

14.36   The definition of a connected person in *ICTA 1988, s 839* applies. [*ITEPA 2003, s 718*]. The extension to members of the same household as the employee or as the person who holds the shares should be noted. It might well make a common-law spouse a relevant linked person so that a disposal to such a person will not trigger the charge but the later removal of the restrictions will do so.

The taxable amount

14.37   The taxable amount is:

$$\text{UMV} \times (\text{IUP} - \text{PCP} - \text{OP}) - \text{CE}$$

Where:

UMV = Unrestricted Market Value = the market value of the securities immediately after the chargeable event but for any restrictions.

IUP = Initial Uncharged Portion = the proportion of what would have been the market value at the time of the acquisition but for any restrictions that were either not initially paid for or not previously charged to tax.

PCP = Previously Charged Proportion = the amount charged to tax on a previous chargeable event.

OP = Outstanding Proportion = the proportion of the share value that is still reduced by restrictions.

CE = Consideration and expenses = any amount paid (or expenses incurred) in connection with the lifting or variation of the restrictions. [*ITEPA 2003, s 428(1), (2)* new].

14.38 The *Act* requires the calculation of the IUP, PCP, and OP by reference to further formulae and further terms IUMV (Initial Unrestricted Market Value), DA (Deductible Amounts) and AMV (Actual Market Value). IUMV is what the market value of the securities would have been at the time of acquisition had they not been subject to restrictions [*ITEPA 2003, s 428(3)*]. AMV is their actual market value immediately after the chargeable event [*ITEPA 2003, s 428(5)*]. The CGT definition of market value applies. [*ITEPA 2003, s 421(1)*].

The following are Deductible Amounts:

(*a*)   any consideration given for the acquisition of the shares (which presumably includes any amounts given for the acquisition of any shares from which they derived including any payments pursuant to an option in respect of such shares);

(*b*)   any amount that constituted earnings from the employment in respect of the acquisition of the shares (see **14.13**);

(*c*)   any amount that constituted earnings from the employment under *Chapter 2* (conditional interest in shares) or *Chapter 4* (post-acquisition benefits from shares) as originally enacted (or their predecessors, *ICTA 1988, ss 140A–140C*, and *FA 1988, ss 78–87*);

(*d*)   if the shares were acquired on a conversion of other employment-related securities, any amount taxed on the employee as employment income on the conversion; and

(*e*)   if the acquisition of the shares was pursuant to an option, any amount taxed on the employee as income of the employment on the exercise of the option (but, for chargeable events after 12 March 2008, not any amount exempted from tax). [*ITEPA 2003, s 428(7)* as amended by *FA 2008, s 46(4)*].

It should be noted that the amount taxed on a previous application of the current rules where the restrictions are withdrawn in stages is not deducted. This is because the formula effectively allows for this. The exclusion of exempt income by FA 2008 is to put the position beyond doubt from 12 March 2008. HMRC believe that it has always been necessary to exclude such income.

14.39 The formula to arrive at IUP is:

$$\frac{\text{IUMV} - \text{DA}}{\text{IUMV}}$$

That to arrive at PCP is the aggregate of the results of the application of the formula IUP – PCP – OP on each previous chargeable events (or nil if there were no previous chargeable events).

That to arrive at OP is:

$$\frac{\text{UMV} - \text{AMV}}{\text{UMV}}$$

14.40

Example

Fred Bloggs is issued with A shares in Wonder Consultants Ltd on 10 August 2006. The A shares rank pari passu with the ordinary shares with the exception that they are subject to the following restrictions.

(*a*)   Wonder Consultants Ltd. is entitled to forfeit the shares without compensation at any time within the first three years; and

(*b*)   If the holder wishes to dispose of the shares at any time within the first five years he must first offer them for sale to employees of Wonder Consultants Ltd at par.

Fred acquired 5,000 shares at 10p a share. The value of the ordinary shares on 10 August 2006 was £5 a share. The value subject to the restrictions was 15p a share. The value of ordinary shares at 9 August 2009 is £8 per share and that at 9 August 2011 £10 per share. The value of the A shares immediately after the removal of restriction (a) was £3 a share.

There is no charge on Fred on the acquisition of the A shares (see **14.26**) but there are two chargeable events, on the cessation of the (*a*) restriction on 9 August 2009 and on the cessation of the (*b*) restriction on 9 August 2011.

Taxable on 9 August 2009:

UMV $= 5{,}000 \times £8 = £40{,}000$

IUP $= \dfrac{\text{UMV } (5{,}000 \times £5 = £25{,}000) - \text{DA } (5{,}000 \times 10p = £500)}{\text{IUMV } (£25{,}000)}$

$= 0.98$

PCP $=$ nil (as there were no previous chargeable events)

OP $= \dfrac{\text{UMV } (£40{,}000) - \text{AMV } (5{,}000 \times £3 = £15{,}000)}{\text{UMV } (£40{,}000)}$

$= 0.625$

CE $=$ nil (as no payment is required to remove the restriction).

The taxable amount is therefore

£40,000 × (0.98 – nil – 0.625) – nil

£40,000 × 0.355 = £14,200

Taxable on 9 August 2011:

UMV $= 5,000 \times £10 = £50,000$

$$\text{IUP} = \frac{\text{IUMV (£25,000 as before)} - \text{DA (£500} + £14,200 = £14,700)}{\text{IUMV (£25,000)}}$$

$= 0.412$

PCP $= 0.355$ (as above)

$$\text{OP} = \frac{\text{UMV £50,000} - \text{AMV (5,000} \times £10,000 = £50,000)}{\text{UMV (£50,000)}}$$

$= 0.625$

CE $=$ nil (as no payment is required to remove the restrictions).

The taxable amount is therefore

$£50,000 \times (0.98 - 0.355 - \text{nil})$ $= \text{nil}$

$£50,000 \times 0.625$ $= £31,250$

14.41 The calculation effectively splits the increase in value of the shares as follows:

part of value initially paid for	2.0%
part taxed in 2009/10	62.5%
part taxed in 2011/12	35.5%
	100%

2% of growth in value is accordingly subject only to capital gains tax.

The growth of the remaining 98% up to 2009/10 is subject to income tax, part in 2009/10 and the rest in 2011/12. The growth between August 2009 and 2011 in value of the 62.5% charged to income tax in 2009/10 attracts only capital gains tax because once it attracts the income tax charge on removal of the relevant restrictions that part of the value ceases to be regarded as employment related.

14.42 If Fred and Wonder Consultants had elected under *s 425(3)* (see **14.31**) to trigger the charge on the real undervalue in August 2003 when the shares were issued to Fred the charge would have been on £250 (5,000 × 15p value less 10p cost). However, that £250 would then have been become part of DA making DA £750 and IUMV 0.97%. This would have reduced the tax charge in 2009/10 to £40,000 × 0.345% or £13,800 but left that in 2011/12 unchanged. In effect the formula apportions the part of the initial value attributable to the restrictions not 'paid for' between the events that trigger a cessation of those restrictions. Nevertheless it will be seen that by paying tax on £250 upfront Fred would have reduced the taxable amount on the removal of the first restrictions by £400. Whether a £150 overall saving would have justified the extra work is another question.

14.43   The employer and employee can jointly elect to calculate the gain on a chargeable event by ignoring the reference to OP (which effectively means ignoring the existence of any restrictions that continue to attach to the shares after that chargeable event). *[ITEPA 2003, s 430(1)(a)]*. This triggers the entire charge as if all of the restrictions on the shares had been removed at the time of the chargeable event. In return it treats the shares as ceasing to be restricted securities for the future. For 2015/16 onwards, the election cannot be made unless, at the time of the acquisition, the earnings from the employment are (or would be if there were any) general earnings to which any of the charging provisions of *ITEPA 2003, ss 14-41* applies *[ITEPA 2003, ss 425(6), 428(7) (bb), 430(4) inserted by FA 2014, Sch 9, para 9/para 10/para 11]*.

14.44   It might be sensible to make such an election if the remaining restrictions are unlikely to have much effect on the value of the shares. A good example is a provision that in the event of the person ceasing to be an employee the shares must be offered for sale to other employees or the company before they are offered to other people. In reality it is unlikely that anyone who is not an employee would be in the market for the shares in such circumstances so the restriction is unlikely to significantly affect the value of the shares. It would probably be worthwhile in such circumstances to trigger the tax charge and save the administrative costs of having to do a second calculation when the shares are eventually sold.

14.44A From 17 July 2014, if an associated person disposes of the employment-related securities (the old securities) for consideration (otherwise than to another associated person), and

(*a*)   the whole or part of the consideration consists of (or includes) restricted securities (the new securities) being acquired by an associated person,

(*b*)   the 'value of the consideration' is no more than what would have been the market value of the old securities immediately before the disposal but for any restrictions,

(*c*)   the avoidance of tax or NI is not the main purpose (or one of the main purposes) of the disposal, and

(*d*)   the consideration consists partly of the new securities and partly of other consideration,

the disposal must be treated as being two separate disposals, namely a disposal of the appropriate amount of the old securities for such part of the consideration as does not consist of the new securities (which is a chargeable event within *s 427(3)(c)*) and a disposal of the remaining old securities for consideration consisting wholly of the new securities (to which **14.44A** applies)

[ITEPA 2003, s 430A(1)(3) inserted by FA 2014, Sch 9, para 36]. For this purpose the value of the consideration is the sum of what would have been the market value of the new securities immediately before the disposal but for

any restrictions, plus the value of the rest of the consideration (if any) [*ITEPA 2003, s 430A(2)*]. The appropriate amount of the old securities is of course the proportion that the value of the part of the consideration that does not consist of the new securities bears to the value of the consideration.

14.44B If the consideration consists wholly of the new securities, neither the disposal of the old securities nor the acquisition of the new securities gives rise to any liability to income tax, the disposal is not a chargeable event within *s 427(3)(c)*, and the employment-related securities rules apply to the new securities as they apply to the old (with the exception that *ITEPA 2003, ss 425* (see **14.31**) and *431* (see **14.45**) do not apply to the new securities) [*ITEPA 2003, s 430A(5)(6)*]. If at the time of the disposal *ITEPA 2003, ss 426-429* do not apply to the old securities by virtue of an election under *ITEPA 2003, s 430* or *431* (or by virtue of a previous application of *s 430A*) *ss 426-430* do not apply to the new securities [*ITEPA 2003, s 430A(7)*].

14.44C If there is a chargeable event for the purposes of *ITEPA 2003, s 426* (see **14.26**) in relation to any of the new securities, for the purpose of the calculation under *s 428* (amount of charge – see **14.37**):

(*a*)   the initial uncharged portion (IUP) is equal to what IUP was for the purpose of determining the taxable amount for the purpose of *s 426* in relation to chargeable events relating to the old securities that occurred before the disposal (or what it would have been had there been any such chargeable events), and

(*b*)   the previously charged proportion (PCP) is the aggregate of PCP determined in accordance with *s 428(4)*, and what PCP would have been (for the purposes of determining the taxable amount for the purposes of *s 426*) if a chargeable event relating to the old securities had occurred immediately before the disposal but after any chargeable events relating to the old securities that actually did occur before the disposal

[*ITEPA 2003, s 430A(8)–(10)*].

14.44D If *ITEPA 2003, s 423(2)* (no liability to income tax on acquisition of certain securities subject to forfeiture) applied in relation to the old securities and at the time of the disposal, there is still a restriction relating to those securities (so that they are still restricted securities by virtue of *s 423(2)*:

(*a*)   these provisions apply to any of the new securities that are not restricted securities as if there were a restriction relating to them corresponding to the restriction relating to the old securities (the deemed restriction) and that deemed restriction were removed immediately after their acquisition [*ITEPA 2003, s 430A(11), (12)*], and

(*b*)   if there is a restriction by virtue of which some or all of the new securities are (at the time of the disposal) restricted securities by virtue of *s 423(2)* and within five years after the acquisition of the old securities the restriction is not removed or varied so that the new securities cease to be restricted securities, that restriction must be treated as being removed five years after the acquisition of the old securities [*ITEPA 2003, s 430A(13), (14)*].

14.44E If at the time of the disposal there is a restriction relating to the old securities such that they are restricted securities and *s 430A(13), (14)* apply in relation to the old securities:

(*a*) *s 430A(12)–(14)* apply in relation to the new securities as if the reference in *s 430A(11)* to the deemed restriction were a reference to the actual restriction relating to the old securities, and

(*b*) the references in *s 430A(13), (14) to* the acquisition of the old securities must be read as if it were to the acquisition of the original forfeitable securities, ie the restricted securities to which *s 430A(13), (14)* apply by virtue of the application of *ITEPA 2003, s 423(2)* to the old securities [*ITEPA 2003, s 430A(15)–(17)*].

14.45 The employer and employee can also jointly elect either:

(*a*) to calculate the tax charge under *ITEPA 2003, s 62*, on the issue of the employment-related securities by ignoring the restrictions in valuing these securities. [*ITEPA 2003, s 431(1)*]; or

(*b*) to calculate the tax charge under *section 62* by ignoring some but not all of the restrictions, specifying in the election which are to be ignored. [*ITEPA 2003, s 431(2)*].

14.46 Such an election results in tax being paid at the time of issue of the shares on the amount by which the restrictions (or the specified restrictions) reduce the market value of the shares. It might be sensible to make the election if the shares are expected to grow rapidly in value. If the company is newly formed the shares may well have little or no value at the time the shares are issued irrespective of whether they are restricted or not. In such circumstances it would clearly be worth triggering the charge at a time when it will result in little or no tax becoming due, so as to be able to treat the shares as unrestricted shares for the future for tax purposes. If the restrictions were not included in an attempt to avoid tax, but were attached to the shares for good commercial reasons, the restricted value is unlikely in most cases to be much different to the unrestricted value so again it might make sense to trigger any tax charge at the time of issue of the shares to avoid having to cope with the legislation for the future. For 2015/16 onwards, the election cannot be made unless, at the time of the acquisition, the earnings from the employment are (or would be if there were any) general earnings to which any of the charging provisions of *ITEPA 2003, ss 14–41* applies [*ITEPA 2003, s 425(6)* inserted by *FA 2014, Sch 9, paras 9–11*].

14.47 HMRC have said that where shares are issued under an EMI option an election under *s 431* to ignore any restrictions on the shares acquired will increase the acquisition cost of the shares but will not normally result in a tax charge because of the exemption in *s 530* (see **16.105**). As the election will prevent any future charge to income tax if the restrictions are lifted or varied, it will normally be in the employee's interest to make the election. They warn, however, that while they are happy with normal commercially driven restrictions on such shares, such as employee pre-emption rights, 'one would not expect to see an EMI option linked to other restrictions that materially depress the market value of the shares under option ... the purpose of the option would need to be considered and the option would not be a qualifying EMI option if it was issued as part of a scheme or arrangement one of the main purposes of which was the avoidance of tax through the use of restrictions' (Press Release 5.9.2003). If the market price on exercise is lower than the market value at the time the option was granted a *s 431* election will increase the tax payable on exercise as the limit on the charge under *s 531* (see **16.106**) will then operate by reference to the unrestricted market value, not the actual value (Press Release 10.9.2003).

14.48   If the shares are in a research institution spin-out company to which the special rules at **14.121** onwards apply, a *s 431* election is deemed to have been made. [*ITEPA 2003, s 454(1)* inserted by *FA 2005, s 20*]. The intention of those rules is that no income tax charge should arise on the initial value of the intellectual property. The shares in such a company are in many cases restricted securities, so that intention would be frustrated if a charge on such a value arose on the removal of restrictions. Deeming the election to have been made means that the only occasion of charge becomes the time of issue of the securities, at which time the special rules take the value of the intellectual property out of the charge to tax.

14.49   It is possible that the deemed election could be disadvantageous. For example the value of the intellectual property might be low in relation to the overall value of the spin-out company or the value of the intellectual property may have increased substantially between its transfer to the company and the date the employee acquires the shares, which may make it attractive to the employee to defer the tax charge until the restrictions are removed. Accordingly a joint agreement can be made by the employer and employee to disapply *s 451(1)*. Such an agreement must be in a form approved by HMRC, must be made within 14 days of the acquisition of the shares (or by 15 October 2005 for shares acquired before 1 October 2005) and is irrevocable. [*ITEPA 2003, s 454(2), (3), FA 2005, s 20(7)*]. It does not need to be sent to HMRC. Where such an agreement is entered into the initial unrestricted market value of the shares (IUMV in **14.38** above) is calculated disregarding the effect on that value of the intellectual property agreement or any transfer under it. [*ITEPA 2003, s 454(4), (5)*].

14.50   An election under both *ss 430* and *431* is irrevocable, must be made within 14 days of the acquisition of the shares (or of the chargeable event if it is under *s 460*), and must be in a form approved by the Board of HMRC. [*ITEPA 2003, ss 430(2), (3), 431(4), (5)*]. There is a form of election on HMRC's website. The comments at **14.31** apply equally to this form. The Explanatory Notes to the *Finance Bill 2003* state that the election does not need to be notified to HMRC at the time. Presumably it merely needs to be reflected in the employee's tax return and in the return that needs to be made to HMRC by the company under *s 421K* (see **14.137**). For shares or securities issued between 16 April 2003 and 1 September 2003 (the appointed day) the election needed to be made within 14 days after 1 September 2003. [*ITEPA 2003, s 432(3)*].

14.51   Where employment-related securities are restricted securities (or a restricted interest in securities) the employer and employee are deemed to have made an election under *s 431* if the acquisition occurs after 17 June 2004, and the securities are shares (or an interest in shares) which are either:

(*a*)   awarded or acquired under an approved SIP (see **15.1**) in circumstances in which no liability to tax arises because of s *490* (see **15.43**);

(*b*)   acquired by the exercise of an option under an approved SAYE option scheme (see **16.5**) in circumstances in which no liability to income tax arises because of *s 519* (see **16.11**(*b*));

(*c*)   acquired by the exercise of an option under an approved CSOP scheme (see **16.8**) in circumstances in which no liability to income tax arises because of *s 524* (see **16.11**); or

(*d*)   acquired by the exercise of an EMI option (see **16.67**) in circumstances in which no liability to income tax arises because of *s 530* (see **16.106**).

[*ITEPA 2003, s 431A* inserted by *FA 2004, s 88(3)*]. Where the shares were acquired before 18 June 2004 the deemed election is treated as made on that date and where applicable *s 446O* (see **14.83**) has effect as if the shares were acquired on that date. [*FA 2004, s 88(12), (13)*].

14.52   They are also deemed to have made the election under *section 431* if the main purpose or one of the main purposes of the arrangement under which the right or opportunity to acquire the securities is made available is the avoidance of tax or NIC and the securities are acquired after 1 December 2004. [*ITEPA 2003, s 431B* inserted by *F(No 2)A 2005, Sch 2, para 7*].

14.53   If the shares are convertible securities (see **14.59**) or an interest in convertible securities the market value for the purpose of the above calculation is to be determined as if they were not. [*ITEPA 2003, s 428(8)*] It is not wholly clear what this means. The explanatory notes to the 2003 Finance Bill stated that it is 'the value ignoring those conversion rights' which suggests that the conversion rights are to be ignored completely although the wording appears equally apposite to require an assumption to be made that the conversion had already taken place. The former interpretation is undoubtedly the intention as the conversion will trigger a charge under *Chapter 3* (see **14.56**). If the chargeable event occurs on a disposal within *s 427(3)(c)* (see **14.33**) and the consideration for the securities is less than their actual market value only an appropriate proportion of the taxable amount calculated at **14.37** is taxable (ie that amount multiplied by the consideration over the actual market value). [*ITEPA 2003, s 428(9)*]. This does not apply if something which affects the securities has been done (at or before the time of the chargeable event and after 1 December 2004) as part of a scheme or arrangement the main purpose (or one of the main purposes) of which is the avoidance of tax or NIC [*ITEPA 2003, s 428(10)* inserted by *F(No 2)A 2005, Sch 2, para 5*].

14.54   The occurrence of a chargeable event does not trigger a tax charge if:

(*a*)   the employment-related securities are shares (or an interest in shares) [*s 429(1)(a)*];

(*b*)   the restrictions attaching to the employment-related securities attach to all of the company's shares of the same class [*s 429(1)(b)*];

(*c*)   all of the shares of that class (other than the employment-related securities in question) are affected by an event similar to the event that is the chargeable event in relation to the employment-related securities (ie the restrictions are removed, or varied, or the shares are disposed of (depending on which type of chargeable event triggers the occasion of charge to tax) [*s 429(1)(c),(2)*];

(*d*)   immediately before the trigger event either:

   (i)   the company is 'employee-controlled by virtue of holdings of shares of that class' [*s 429(3)*]; or

   (ii)   the majority of the shares of that class are not employment-related securities (for events prior to 7 May 2004 the test was that the majority was not held by (or for the benefit of) employees of the company, persons who are related to employees of the company, associated companies of the company, employees of any 'associated company' of the company or persons who are related to an employee of any such associated company). [*s 429(4)* as amended by *FA 2004, s 86(5)*]; and

(*e*)   for chargeable events after 1 December 2004 nothing which affects the securities has been done (at or before the time of the chargeable event) as part of a scheme or arrangement the main purpose or one of the main purposes of which was the avoidance of tax or NIC. [*ITEPA 2003, s 429(1)(ba), (1A)* as amended by *F(No 2)A 2005, Sch 2, para 6*].

[*ITEPA 2003, s 429*]. Head (*e*) did not apply prior to 7 May 2004 and between that date and 1 December 2004 it only needed to be shown that the avoidance of tax or NIC was not the main purpose or one of the main purposes of the arrangement under which the opportunity to acquire the securities was made available. This exemption is disapplied in certain cases – see **14.79**.

14.55   For the above purpose a company is employee-controlled by virtue of shares of a class if:

(*a*)   the majority of the shares of that class (other than any held by, or for the benefit of, any associated company) are held by, or for the benefit of, employees of the company or of a company controlled by the company (or ex-employees or prospective employees of such companies); and

(*b*)   those employees are together able as holders of the shares to control the company.

[*ITEPA 2003, s 421H(1)*].

The definition of associated company contained in *ICTA 1988, s 416* applies. [*ITEPA 2003, s 421H(2)*]. For events prior to 7 May 2004 a person was related to an employee if either he acquired the shares pursuant to a right or opportunity available by reason of the employee's employment or he was connected with a person who so acquired the shares (or with the employee) and acquired the shares from the employee or from another person who was related to the employee other than under a disposal made by way of a bargain at arm's length. [*ITEPA 2003, s 429(5)*].

14.56   The *National Insurance Contributions and Statutory Payments Act 2004, s 3* amends *SSCBA 1992, Sch 1, para 3B* to permit an employer to recover employers NIC from an employee if the employer and employee agree and the NIC relates to deemed income under *ITEPA 2003, s 426* or s *438* (see **14.59**) or an election to transfer the liability to the employee is made. This election mirrors that for share options (see **14.116**). It needs HMRC approval. Such an election cannot be made where the NIC liability arises under *ITEPA 2003, s 446A* (see **14.67**) or, from 30 March 2006, under retrospective anti-avoidance provisions. [*SSCBA 1992, Sch 1, para 3B(7B)*]. From 1 September 2004, where such an agreement is entered into the amount taxable under *s 426* is reduced by any amount recovered from the employee before 5 June following the end of the tax year (and any amount that has become the employee's liability as a result of the election). The deduction is obviously not to be taken into account in determining the NIC itself. If HMRC withdraw approval of the election the liability transferred to the employee is limited to any amount actually paid before 5 June following the end of the tax year. [*ITEPA 2003, s 428A*]. *The Social Security (Contributions) Regulations 2001, Sch 4, paras 7(9), (11)–(12A)* enable the employer to retain and sell sufficient of the securities to meet the employee's obligation under an agreement provided that he accounts to the employee for any excess. HMRC have issued model forms of election (www.hmrc.gov.uk/manuals/ersmmanual/ERSM170750.htm). These do not have to be used but HMRC say that if one is not they need to approve the form of election. They have given guidance on what the election needs to contain and also some things which, if included, will prevent their approving the election (Press Release 10.11.2008).

14.57   The application of these rules was in issue in *UBS AG v HMRC [2010] SFTD 1257*. UBS wished to pay various bonuses to its employees. A third party set up a Jersey company. This created a class of restricted shares which were issued to UBS and distributed by UBS to employees. The restrictions lasted for only three weeks. During this period the shares could not be sold but were liable for forfeiture on payment of 90% of their market value if the FTSE 100 index exceeded a specified figure. However, the Jersey company also took an option to hedge the index so that in the event of it exceeding the specified level, the company would receive a sum of money. The effect was that in that event, the 90% figure would be 99.2% of what the employee would receive on redemption of the shares if there were no forfeiture. The Tribunal held that the effect of this arrangement was that the securities were not restricted securities within the meaning of *ITEPA 2003, s 423* (see **14.27**) as the restrictions did not reduce the market value of the shares. It also held that where an employee was entitled contractually to a guaranteed bonus, a tax liability arose at the time the bonus was awarded, not at the later time of the transfer of the shares in satisfaction of that bonus.

14.58 A similar arrangement was used in *Deutsche Bank Group Services (UK) Ltd v HMRC 2011 SFTD 406*. The idea was that no tax charge would arise on the grant of the beneficial interest as *ITEPA 2003, s 425(1)* would apply (see **14.30**). No charge would arise on the removal of the restrictions because the restrictions attached to all of the Z shares, so *ITEPA 2003, s 429* would apply (see **14.52**). The charge on redemption would be to CGT, not income tax. The Deutsche Bank restrictions were different to the UBS restrictions and the Tribunal accepted that they reduced the value of the shares. However it also decided that the scheme as a whole and each aspect of it was created and co-ordinated purely for tax avoidance purposes. While that of itself does not prevent the scheme from having effect, it calls into question whether it falls within the intention of parliament so the Tribunal held that the scheme was not entitled to the tax exemption on the issue of restricted securities.

14.58A The two cases were heard together by the Upper Tribunal [2012] UKUT 320 (TCC). That Tribunal disagreed with the FTT in UBS. It felt that the securities were restricted securities because the hedging was not a condition of the securities. However the restriction ceased on 19 February 2004, when the securities ceased to be subject to the forced sale provision, so a tax charge would arise at that time unless the exemption in *ITEPA 2003, s 429* applied (see **14.54**). It was common ground that the first three conditions were satisfied. The fourth required UBS not to be an associated company of the Jersey company. The FTT had held that it was not and that was a decision that it was entitled to reach. Accordingly the scheme worked. However with Deutsche Bank (by then renamed DB Group Services (UK) Ltd) the Tribunal felt that the Jersey company was under the control of DB, so the exemption did not apply. The Court of Appeal [2014] EWCA Civ 452, dismissed HMRC's appeal against the Upper Tribunal's decision and allowed DB's appeal on the basis that the question of control was a question of fact and that the Upper Tribunal had no power to interfere with the FTT's finding that there was no control. Both the UT and Court of Appeal held that the transaction was not a sham and that the scheme worked technically so that *s 425* applied. In the case of UBS, both also found that the exemption in *s 429* applied but in the case of DB Deutsche Bank, DB was held by the UT to have control of the offshore company so its scheme failed technically. The Court of Appeal reversed the UT decision in DB and held that both schemes succeeded. Both the UT and Court of Appeal held that neither scheme was caught by the *Ramsay* principle.

14.58B There have since been a spate of tax avoidance cases before the FTT focused on restricted shares. *Tower Radio Ltd v HMRC (TC 2784)* was a scheme under which employees were issued shares in an SPV (not controlled by the employer). The Articles of Association of the SPV required the employee to sell the shares to his employer (at 95% of their market value) if he were to leave within a specified period. Following the lapse of that period, the company was liquidated and the cash passed to the employee. The Tribunal held that, applying that *Ramsay* approach, 'the only coherent analysis of the transaction is that the surplus cash of the employer was paid to the relevant employees'. t felt that virtually all of the steps in the scheme were carried out for tax avoidance purposes and should be regarded as irrelevant in interpreting the legislation. In *L M Ferro Ltd v HMRC (TC 2853)* the company subscribed for B shares in an SPV at a substantial premium and transferred the shares to Mr. Ferro. The shares were subject to forfeiture (at 95% of their value) if Mr. Ferro were to cease to be an employee within the following 12 months. The FTT held that 'the transactions which took place, when realistically appraised, amounts to an artificial contrived scheme, whose essence was to pay money'. Accordingly the share scheme rules were not engaged as 'money' is not included in the definition of employment-related securities. 'The scheme amounts to a bonus of money rather than shares'.

Convertible securities (Chapter 3)

14.59   If the employment-related securities are convertible securities:

(*a*)   the conversion rights are ignored in ascertaining the market value of the shares for income tax purposes at the time of their acquisition – and thus in ascertaining any tax payable under *ITEPA 2003, s 62*; but

(*b*)   a tax charge arises if a chargeable event occurs in relation to the securities.

[*ITEPA 2003, ss 437(1), 438*]. Head (*a*) does not apply on an acquisition after 1 December 2004 if the main purpose (or one of the main purposes) of the arrangement under which the right or opportunity to acquire the securities is made available is the avoidance of tax or NIC and it produces a lower market value figure than the amount determined as follows. In such a case the market value of the securities has to be determined as if the securities were immediately and fully convertible and the entitlement to convert were both immediate and unconditional (if the securities fall within **14.60**(*a*) and that entitlement is not both immediate and conditional) or the circumstances are such that an entitlement to convert arises immediately (if the securities fall within **14.60**(*b*) and the entitlement is not immediate) or provision were made for their immediate conversion (if the securities fall within **14.60**(*c*)). [*ITEPA 2003, s 437(2), (3)*]. For this purpose immediately and fully convertible means convertible immediately after the acquisition of the securities so as to obtain the maximum gain that would be possible on a conversion at that time without giving any consideration for the conversion or incurring any expenses in connection with it and assuming that the securities into which they are convertible existed at that time if that is not the case and it is appropriate to do so. [*ITEPA 2003, s 437(4)*].

14.60   Securities are convertible for this purpose if:

(*a*)   they confer on the holder an entitlement (whether immediate or deferred and whether conditional or unconditional) to convert them into securities of a different description (for acquisitions prior to 2 December 2004 securities were not within this head if the entitlement was unconditional or was a deferred, immediate or conditional entitlement) to convert them into securities of a different description;

(*b*)   a contract, agreement, arrangement or condition authorises or requires the grant of such an entitlement to the holder if certain circumstances arise (or do not arise); or (*c*)   a contract, agreement, arrangement or condition makes provision for the conversion of the securities (otherwise than by the holder) (eg automatically on the happening of a specified event) into securities of a different description.

[*ITEPA 2003, s 436*].

14.61   There are four possible chargeable events:

(*a*)   the conversion of the employment-related securities into securities of a different description in circumstances in which the employee (or an associated person) is beneficially entitled to the new securities [*s 439(3) (a)*];

(*b*)   the disposal for consideration of the employment-related securities (or any interest in them) by the employee (or an associated person) otherwise than to another associated person at a time when they are still convertible securities [*s 439(3)(b)*];

(*c*)   the release for consideration of the entitlement to convert [*s 493(3)(c)*]; and

(*d*)   the receipt by the employee (or an associated person) of a benefit in money or money's worth in connection with the entitlement to convert (but ignoring the benefit of a conversion within (*a*) to (*c*) and a benefit received on account of any disability of the employee within the meaning of the *Disability Discrimination Act 1995*). [*s 493(3)(d), (4)*].

[*ITEPA 2003, s 439*].

Associated person has the meaning considered at **14.34** above.

14.62   The taxable amount on the occurrence of a chargeable event is the difference between the gain realised on that event and the aggregate of any consideration given for the entitlement to convert and any expenses incurred by the holder of the securities in connection with the conversion, disposal or receipt. However both of these items have special meanings (see **14.63** and **14.64**) [*ITEPA 2003, s 440(1)–(3)*]. If *s 437(1)* (see **14.59**(*a*)) was displaced by the alternative method of calculating the market value at the time of acquisition the taxable amount is reduced by the excess of the market value calculated under *s 437(2), (3)* over that which would have been produced under *section 437(1)* (less the aggregate of any amount by which the taxable amount on any previous chargeable event has been reduced under this provision). [*ITEPA 2003, s 440(3A)* inserted by *F(No 2)A 2005, Sch 2, para 10*]. This avoids that difference being doubly taxed as the charge on the acquisition will already have reflected the value of the conversion rights.

14.63   The amount of gain realised on the occurrence of a chargeable event within *s 439(3)(a)* (an actual conversion) is calculated using the formula:

$$CMVCS - (CMVERS + CC)$$

where:

CMVCS	=	Current Market Value of the Converted Securities = the market value at the time of the chargeable event of the securities into which they are converted (ignoring any conversion rights that those new securities may themselves have).
		In the case of an interest in securities it is the proportion of the market value of the securities which the value of the interest bears to the value of the securities.
CMVERS	=	Current Market Value of the Employment-related Securities = what would have been the market value of the securities at the time of the chargeable event if they were not convertible securities.
CC	=	Consideration for Conversion = the amount of any consideration given for the conversion.
		The amount of gain realised on an event within *s 439(3)(b)* (disposal prior to conversion) is calculated using the formula:
DC	=	CMVERS

where:

DC	=	Disposal Consideration

The amount of gain realised on an event within *s 439(3)(c)* (sale of the right) or (*d*) (receipt of a benefit) is the consideration received or the market value of the benefit as the case may be. [*ITEPA 2003, s 441*].

14.64 The consideration given for the entitlement to convert is the excess, if any, of the consideration given to acquire the securities (AES) over what the market value of the securities would have been at the time of the acquisition if the conversion rights had not existed (NCMV). [*ITEPA 2003, s 442*]. In other words the employee is treated as having bought the conversion rights only if and to the extent that his actual acquisition price exceeded the then value of the shares ignoring the right to convert. If the shares were restricted shares and an election was made under *s 431* (see **14.45**) to ignore the restrictions in valuing the shares it is that uplifted value that has to be compared with the subscription price. In effect, there will be no consideration within *s 442* if any income tax charge arose on the issue of the shares. If the shares are in a research institution spin-out company the special rules at **14.121** apply to determine the market value at the time of acquisition, ie CMVCS. [*ITEPA 2003, s 452(2)(b)* inserted by *FA 2005, s 20*].

Example

14.65 Peter Pan acquired 1,000 A shares in Wendy Enterprises Ltd on 5 October 2009 for £2,000. The shares were subject to restrictions and convertible to ordinary shares on 5 October 2008. The value of the A shares on 5 October 2009 was £1,800. The value ignoring the conversion rights was £300 and that ignoring both the conversion rights and the restrictions was £1,400. The value on 5 October 2011 of the ordinary shares into which Peter's A shares were converted was £10,000. The value of the A shares immediately prior to conversion was £7,000. The restrictions were removed in June 2012 at which time the unrestricted value ignoring the conversion rights was £6,000.

Peter paid £2,000 for shares that, ignoring the conversion rights, were worth £300. Accordingly he has given consideration of £2,000 − £300 = £1,700.

The gain realised on conversion is:

CMVCS − CMVERS + CC

£10,000 − £7,000 + nil (as no consideration was given for the conversion)

= £3,000

The taxable amount on conversion is:

Gain realised − consideration given

£3,000 − £1,700 = £1,300

Peter will have also suffered a charge on the removal of the restrictions of:

UMV × (IUP − PCP − OP)

$$£6,000 \times \frac{(1,400 - 300 - \text{nil} - \text{nil})}{1,400}$$

= £6,000 × 78.57% = £4,714

If Peter had elected under *s 431* to ignore all of the restrictions the position would have been:

taxable on acquisition = value of unrestricted shares − consideration paid
ignoring conversion rights
£1,400 − £2,000
= nil

taxable on removal of restrictions = nil

taxable on conversion = gain realised − consideration given
£3,000 − (£2,000 − £1,400 = £600)
£2,400

14.66   No charge arises on the happening of a chargeable event if:

(*a*)   the employment-related securities are shares in a company;

(*b*)   all the company's shares of the same class are convertible;

(*c*)   all of the company's remaining shares of that class are affected by an event similar to that which is the chargeable event in relation to the employment-related securities (ie converted, disposed of, the conversion right is released or a benefit is received as the case may be); and

(*d*)   immediately before the trigger event either:

    (i)   the company was employee-controlled by virtue of holdings of shares of that class; or

    (ii)   the majority of the company's shares of that class were not employment-related securities (for events prior to 7 May 2004 the test was that the majority was not held by (or for the benefit of), employees of the company, persons who are related to such employees, associated companies of the company, employees of any associated company of the company and persons who are related to such employees.

    and

(*e*)   where the chargeable event occurs after 1 December 2004, nothing which affects the securities has been done (at or before the time of that event) as part of a scheme or arrangement the main purpose or one of the main purposes of which is the avoidance of tax or NIC. [*s 443(1)(ba), (1A)* as amended by *F(No 2)A 2005, Sch 2, para 11*].

[*ITEPA 2003, s 443*].

The definitions of employee-controlled, associated company and related person considered at **14.55** above again apply. [*ITEPA 2003, ss 443(5), 444(6)*]. Head (*e*) did not apply prior to 6 May 2004. For chargeable events between that date and 1 December 2004 it applied only if the avoidance of tax or NIC was not the main purpose or one of the main purposes of the arrangement under which the opportunity to acquire the securities was made available.

14.67   If an election under *SSCBA 1992 Sch 3A* is made for the employee to bear the employer's NIC liability in relation to the deemed income under *s 438* the taxable amount can be reduced by that NIC. The detailed rules are the same as apply to *s 426*. These are considered at **14.56**. [*ITEPA 2003, s 442A* inserted by *FA 2004, Sch 16, para 2*].

Securities with artificially depressed market value (Chapter 3A)

14.68   Further charges can arise where the market value of employment-related securities (or other relevant securities) is reduced by things done other than for genuine commercial reasons. [*ITEPA 2003, s 446A(1)*]. This applies in particular to:

(*a*)   anything done as part of a scheme or arrangement the main purpose, or one of the main purposes, of which is the avoidance of tax or NIC; and (*b*)   any transaction between companies which are members of the same group (51 per cent subsidiaries) on terms which are not such as might have been expected to be agreed between persons acting at arm's length (other than a payment for group relief).

[*ITEPA 2003, s 446A(2), (3)*].

14.69   A charge to income tax arises on the acquisition of such an artificially depreciated security if at the time of acquisition the market value has been reduced by at least 10 per cent as a result of things done other than for genuine commercial purposes within seven years prior to the time of the acquisition. [*ITEPA 2003, s 446B(1), (2)*]. The charge is additional to that arising under any other provision. [*ITEPA 2003, s 446B(4)*]. The amount is calculated by the formula FMV – MV, where FMV is what the market value at the time of acquisition would have been if those things had not been done and MV is the actual market value of the securities at that time (or, if greater, the amount of the consideration given for the acquisition of the securities). [*ITEPA 2003, s 446C*].

14.70   If the artificially depreciated securities are restricted securities (see **14.26**) (or an interest in such securities) the full market value (but not the market value) must be determined as if the employment-related securities were not restricted securities. [*ITEPA 2003, s 446D(1)*]. This effectively taxes the full value of the restriction. Accordingly the charge on the removal of the restrictions (or other chargeable event) will not apply in such a case. [*ITEPA 2003, s 446D(1)*]. If the artificially depreciated securities are convertible securities (or an interest in convertible securities) both the full market value and market value are determined as if they were not (so the charge on conversion will also apply in such a case). [*ITEPA 2003, s 446D(2)*].

14.71   If the market value of employment-related securities which are restricted securities (or an interest in such securities) is artificially low immediately after an event which is a chargeable event for the purpose of *s 426* (charge on restricted securities – see **14.26**) the UMV (market value of the securities) for the purpose of *s 428(2)* (see **14.37**) is calculated as if the depreciating events had not taken place (as well as ignoring the restrictions) and on, events after 6 May 2004, also ignoring the event that gave rise to the reduction and the fact that the employment-related securities are about to be disposed of or cancelled. [*ITEPA 2003, s 446E(1)(a),(6)–(8)* as amended by *FA 2004, s 87*]. The market value is artificially low for this purpose if it has been reduced by at least 10 per cent as a result of anything done otherwise than for genuine commercial reasons within seven years prior to the occurrence of the chargeable event (and if *s 425(2)* (see **14.31**) precludes a tax charge arising on acquisition, the seven-year period instead runs to the date of acquisition of the shares). [*ITEPA 2003, s 446E(2)–(5)* as amended by *FA 2004, s 87*].

14.72   If the market value is artificially low on 5 April in any year a chargeable event is deemed to occur on that 5 April under *s 427(3)(a)* (lifting of restrictions) (see **14.33**) in respect of the securities. The seven-year period to determine whether the value is artificially low in such a case is the seven years to the 5 April concerned (or to the date of acquisition where *s 425(2)* applies). [*ITEPA 2003, s 446E(1)(b), (2)–(6)* as amended by *FA 2004 s 87*]. This does not mean that there is an annual charge. Once the charge under *s 427(3)(a)* has been triggered the shares are no longer regarded as restricted shares (see **14.33**) so no further charges can arise under that provision. This provision applies only to shares acquired after 15 April 2003 and applies to such shares only from 1 September 2003 [*ITEPA 2003, s 446J(3)*]. *Section 446J(3)* does not apply to securities acquired before 16 April 2003. [*FA 2003, Sch 22, para 5(3)*].

14.73   From 7 May 2004 if immediately before the employment-related securities are disposed of (other than by a chargeable event), or are cancelled without being disposed of, the market value of the securities is artificially low, a chargeable event under *s 427(3)(a)* (see **14.33**) is treated as occurring on the date on which the disposal or cancellation occurs. In such a case no deduction for OP can be made in the calculation under *s 428* (see **14.39**).

14.74   If the securities were acquired before 7 May 2004 a charge under *section 446E(1)(aa)* is triggered only if their market value would be artificially low immediately before the disposal or cancellation if the seven-year relevant period began on 7 May 2004 (if that is later than its normal starting date). [*FA 2004, s 87(5)*].

14.75   If the market value of an employee's interest in shares which is only conditional (see **14.163**) is artificially low immediately after a chargeable event under *ITEPA 2003, s 427*, as originally enacted (see **14.166**) the reference to market value in *s 428(1)* as originally enacted must be taken as referring to what that value would have been but for the action giving rise to the depreciation in value. The market value of shares is artificially low for this purpose if it has been reduced by at least 10 per cent as a result of things done otherwise than for genuine commercial purposes within the seven years before the chargeable event or, if later, within the period beginning with 16 April 2003. [*ITEPA 2003, s 446F*].

14.76   If the market value of employment-related shares which are convertible securities (see **14.59**) (or an interest in such securities) has been reduced by at least 10 per cent as a result of things done otherwise than for genuine commercial purposes in the seven years preceding the acquisition, the market value of the securities in the definition of NCMV in *s 442(5)* (value of convertible securities at time of acquisition) (see **14.64**) is what the value would have been but for those depreciatory events (as well as ignoring the conversion rights). [*ITEPA 2003, s 446G*].

14.77   If the market value of securities into which employment-related securities are converted is artificially low at the time of a chargeable event under *s 439(3)(a)* (conversion) (see **14.61**) the references to market value in the definition of CMVCS in *s 441(6)* (amount of gain realised by conversion) (see **14.63**) must be taken to refer to what that market value would have been had the depreciatory events not taken place. The market value of such securities is artificially low for this purpose if it has been reduced by at least 10 per cent as a result of things done other than for genuine commercial reasons in the seven years prior to the occurrence of the chargeable event. [*ITEPA 2003, s 446H*].

14.78   If any consideration or benefit mentioned in:

(*a*)   *s 428(9)* (consideration on disposal of restricted securities) (see **14.53**);

(*b*)   *s 441(4),(5)* or *(9)* (consideration for disposal of convertible securities, release of entitlement to convert, or benefit received in respect of entitlement to convert) (see **14.63**);

(*c*)   *s 446C(4)* (securities with artificially depressed market value) (see **14.69**);

(*d*)   *ss 446X* and *446Y(3)* (consideration for disposal of securities exceeding market value) (see **14.98**); or

(*e*)   *s 448* (securities benefit not otherwise subject to tax) (see **14.99**)

consists in whole or part in the provisions of securities or an interest in securities the market value of which is artificially low, the market value of the consideration or benefit must be taken to be what it would have been if the depreciatory event had not taken place. The seven-year period in this case ends with the receipt of the consideration or benefit. [*ITEPA 2003, s 446I(1)*]. Head (*a*) does not apply if the securities were acquired before 16 April 2003. [*FA 2003, Sch 22, para 5(3)*].

Disapplication of exceptions

14.79   In some circumstances the occurrence of a chargeable event does not trigger a tax charge. However such exceptions do not apply in some circumstances where the value is artificially manipulated, namely:

(*a*)   *section 429* (see **14.54**) does not apply where *ss 446E* (see **14.69**) or *446I(1)(a)* apply;

(*b*)   *section 443* (see **14.66**) does not apply where *ss 446G* (see **14.76**), *446H* (see **14.77**) or *446I(1)(b)* apply;

(*c*)   *section 446R* (see **14.96**) does not apply where *s 446B* (see **14.69**) applies; and

(*d*)   *section 449* (see **14.100**) does not apply if *s 446I(1)(c)* applies.

[*ITEPA 2003, s 446IA inserted by FA 2004, s 86(6)*].

Securities with artificially enhanced market value (Chapter 3B)

14.80   Adjustments may also be required to be made where the market value of an employment-related security is increased by things done otherwise than for genuine commercial purposes (a non-commercial increase), including in particular:

(*a*)   something done as part of a scheme or arrangement the main purpose, or one of the main purposes, of which is the avoidance of tax or NIC; and (*b*)   a transaction between companies in a group (51 per cent subsidiaries) on terms which are not such as might be expected to be agreed between persons acting at arm's length (other than a payment for group relief).

[*ITEPA 2003, s 446K*].

14.81   If the shares are in a research institution spin-out company to which the special rules at **14.121** onwards apply, neither the entering into of the intellectual property agreement, nor the transfer of rights pursuant to it are things done otherwise than for genuine commercial purposes. [*ITEPA 2003, s 455* inserted by *FA 2005, s 20*].

14.82   If the market value of the securities (IMV = Increased Market Value) is at least 10 per cent more than what that value would have been if the non-commercial increase had been disregarded (the MV) on a 'valuation date' in relation to a 'relevant period' (normally 5 April), the employee is taxable on employment income of the difference between the two amounts (IMV – MV) for the tax year in which the valuation date falls. [*ITEPA 2003, s 446L (1)–(6)*]. In arriving at both the IMV and MV of the securities any restrictions having effect in relation to the employment-related securities and any non-commercial reductions (ie reduction in the market value as a result of something done otherwise than for genuine commercial purposes) must both be ignored. [*ITEPA 2003, ss 446L(6), (7), 446K(4)*].

14.83   A relevant period is a tax year. In the first year it is the period from the acquisition of the securities (or from 16 April 2003 if they were acquired before that date) to the following 5 April. In the year in which the securities cease to be within the charge to income tax (eg because they are sold or all restrictions are removed, etc.) it is the period from 6 April to the date that the securities cease to be taxable. A valuation date is the last day of a relevant period. [*ITEPA 2003, s 446O; FA 2003, Sch 22, para 6(4)*].

14.84   If on the valuation date the securities are relevant restricted securities (ie restricted securities in respect of which no election has been made under *s 430* or *431(1)* to crystallise the tax charge up-front – see **14.43–14.45**) the above amount determined under *s 446L* (see **14.82**) must be multiplied by CP(Chargeable Proportion) where CP = I – OP.

OP (Outstanding Proportion) is the amount that would be determined under *s 428(5)* on the valuation date if there had been a chargeable event on that date (see **14.37**). If an election has been made under *s 431(2)* (to crystallise up front part of the tax charge in relation to the restriction) the reference above to the amount under *s 428(6)* is of course what that amount would be applying *s 431(2)*. [*ITEPA 2003, s 446M*]. *Section 446M* does not apply to securities acquired before 16 April 2003. [*FA 2003, Sch 22, para 6(3)*].

14.85   If the employment-related securities have been restricted securities (or an interest in such securities) at any time during the relevant period a deduction needs to be made from the amount determined under *s 446L* (where applicable applying *s 446M*). This Deductible Amount (DA) is TA – ARTA, where

TA   = Taxable Amount = the amount determined under *s 428* in relation to the chargeable event (see **14.37**).

ARTA = Artificially Reduced Taxable Amount = the figure that would have been the taxable amount under *s 428* in relation to the chargeable event if any non-commercial increases during the period beginning at the same time as the relevant period and ending immediately before the chargeable event had been disregarded.

[*ITEPA 2003, s 446N*]. *Section 446N* does not apply to securities acquired before 16 April 2003. [*FA 2003, Sch 22, para 6(3)*].

14.86   From 7 May 2004 none of the exemptions in *s 429* (see **14.54**), *s 443* (see **14.66**), *s 446R* (see **14.96**) or *s 449* (see **14.97**) apply if the market value of the employment-related securities at the time of the acquisition has been increased by 10 per cent or more by non-commercial increases within the seven years prior to the acquisition of the securities. If a charge arises under *s 446L* (see **14.82**) *s 429* cannot subsequently apply in relation to those securities. [*ITEPA 2003, s 446NA* inserted by *FA 2004, s 86(7)*].

14.87   It will be seen that *s 446L* imposes an annual charge. However, this is not cumulative as the MV disregards only those non-commercial increases that take place during the tax year itself. The 10 per cent *de minimis* limit is applied on a cumulative basis though. The adjustment under *s 446N* is designed to eliminate amounts already taxed under *s 446L* from the taxable increase in value on the removal of the restrictions (or other trigger event).

Securities acquired for less than market value (Chapter 3C)

14.88   Where no payment is made for employment-related securities at or before the time of the acquisition, or the payment made is less than the market value of the securities, a notional interest-free loan is treated as having been made to the employee by the employer at the time of the acquisition (unless **14.96** below applies). [*ITEPA 2003, ss 446Q(1), 446S(1)*]. This is based on *ITEPA 2003, s 175* (see **9.1**) but goes wider as it is not restricted to higher paid employees. At first sight it would appear to apply to a situation where an employee is gifted unrestricted ordinary shares. However that is not the case because 'employment-related securities' is defined to mean securities or an interest in securities to which *Chapters 2–4* of *Part 7, ITEPA 2003, (ss 442– 470)* apply (*ITEPA 2003, s 421B(8)*). Accordingly it applies only where the securities already fall within the rules described at **14.15** onwards. If the shares are in a research institution spin-out company the special rules at **14.121** apply to determine the market value at the time of acquisition. [*ITEPA 2003, s 452(2) (c)* inserted by *FA 2005, s 20*].

14.89   HMRC say that where shares or other securities are acquired by reason of employment for less than market value there will normally be a general earnings charge on the undervalue. This charge takes priority over the *s446Q* charge. So do the charges under *ITEPA 2003 ss 201–210* (benefits in kind: residual liability to charge), *s 437* (convertible securities - see **14.59**), *s 446A* (securities with artificially depressed market value – see **14.68**) and *s 471* (securities options – see **14.102**). [*Employment Related Securities Manual 70030*]. Accordingly this provision is a sweep-up charge. It could apply where securities are acquired on the exercise of an option where the grantee is resident but not ordinarily resident in the UK. [*Employment Related Securities Manual 70010*]. It was introduced to deal with the issue of partly paid shares.

14.90 The notional loan is treated as an employment-related one, which brings into play the rules on such loans set out in *ITEPA 2003, ss 175–187* (see **9.1**). [*ITEPA 2003, s 446S(2), (3)*].

14.91 The amount of the notional loan is of course the difference between the market value of the securities at the time of the acquisition and the total of any 'deductible amounts'. [*ITEPA 2003, s 446T(1)*]. If the securities are not fully paid the market value is what the value would have been if they were fully paid. [*ITEPA 2003, s 446T(2)*].

14.92 The deductible amounts are:

(*a*) any payment made by the employee (and or if different by the person who acquired the securities) at or before the time of the acquisition;

(*b*) any amount taxed as earnings on the employee under *ITEPA 2003, s 62* (the basic charging provision on earnings) in respect of the acquisition of the securities (but, for acquisitions after 12 March 2008, not any amount exempted from tax);

(*c*) where *ITEPA 2003 s 425(2)* (see **14.31**) applies, any amount taxed as employment income under *s 426* on the first chargeable event in relation to the securities (*s 425(2)* defers the tax charge on the issue of restricted securities until the happening of a chargeable event);

(*d*) if the securities were acquired on a conversion of other employment on related securities any amount taxed as employment income under *ITEPA 2003, s 438* (see **14.59**) on the conversion; and

(*e*) if the securities were acquired under an option any amount taxed as employment income under *ITEPA 2003, s 476* (see **14.107**).

[*ITEPA 2003, s 446T(3)* as amended by *Finance Act 2008 (FA 2008), s 46(5)*].

The amount of the notional loan outstanding at any later time is obviously the difference between the amount initially outstanding and the amount of any further payments made for the securities up to that time. [*ITEPA 2003, s 446T(4)*].

14.93 The notional loan is treated as discharged when either:

(*a*) the securities are disposed of (other than to an associated person within the meaning given in *ITEPA 2003, s 421C* (see **14.34**); or (*b*) if there is an outstanding contingent liability to pay for the employment-related securities, that liability is released, extinguished, transferred or adjusted so as no longer to bind any associated person (except where (*e*) applies (prior to 17 July 2014, it read if the securities were not fully paid up at the time of acquisition, the outstanding or contingent liability to pay for them is released, transferred, or adjusted so as to no longer to bind the holder or any associated person);

(*c*) something which affects the securities is done after 1 December 2004 as part of a scheme or arrangement the main purpose (or one of the main purposes) of which is the avoidance of tax or NICs;

(*d*) the total payments for the securities come to equal the amount initially outstanding, ie the notional loan is 'repaid' by an associated person;

(*e*) the employment-related securities, together with the liability to make such further payment or payments, are disposed of otherwise than to an associated person and for consideration of an amount that reflects the transfer of the liability; or

(*f*) the employee dies.

[*ITEPA 2003, s 446U(1), (4)* as amended by *F(No 2)A 2005, Sch 2, para 14*].

Where the loan is treated as discharged under (*a*), (*b*), or (c) above (but not (*d*)) the balance of the notional loan outstanding at the time of the trigger event is treated as employment income of the employee for the tax year in which that event occurs. [*ITEPA 2003, s 446U(2), (3)*]. This applies even if the employment has terminated by that time. Head (*a*) does not apply after 17 July 2014 if, at the time of the acquisition, there was an actual or contingent liability to make one or more further payments equal to the amount initially outstanding for the employment-related securities [*ITEPA 2003, s 446U(1A)* inserted by *FA 2014, Sch 9, para 37*].

14.94 No charge in relation to such a notional loan arises if the securities are shares, all of the shares of the same class are acquired for a payment below their market value (or for no payment) and at the time of their acquisition either the company is employee-controlled (within *ITEPA 2003, s 421H* – see **14.55**) by virtue of holdings of shares of that class or the majority of the company's shares of the same class are not employment-related securities (for events prior to 7 May 2004 the test was that the majority was not held by, or for the benefit of, employees, related persons of employees, associated companies of the company, employees of such associated companies and related persons of such employees). [*ITEPA 2003, s 446R* as amended by *FA 2004, s 86*]. A person was related to an employee for this purpose if either that person acquired his shares pursuant to a right or opportunity available by reason of the employee's employment or he was connected (within *ICTA 1988, s 839*) with such a person or with the employee and acquired his shares from the employee or another person who was related to the employee other than by way of a bargain at arm's length. [*ITEPA 2003, s 446R(5)*]. For chargeable events after 1 December 2004 the exemption applies only if nothing has been done (at or before the time of the acquisition) as part of a scheme or arrangement the main purpose, or one of the main purposes, of which was the avoidance of tax or NICs. [*s 446R(1) (ba), (1A)* as amended by *F(No 2)A 2005, Sch 2, para 13*]. This restriction did not apply prior to 6 May 2004. On chargeable events between that date on 1 December 2004 the exemption was lost only if the avoidance of tax or NICs was not the main purpose or one of the main purposes of the arrangements under which the opportunity to acquire the securities was made available.

14.95   If the main purpose or one of the main purposes of the arrangement under which the right or opportunity to acquire the securities is made available is the avoidance of tax or NICs and the acquisition takes place after 1 December 2004 the whole amount of the notional loan by virtue of *ss 444S* and *446T* is instead treated as income of the tax year in which the acquisition takes place (in place of the above tax charges). [*ITEPA 2003, s 446UA* inserted by *F(No 2) A 2005, Sch 2, para 15*].

Securities disposed of for more than market value (Chapter 3D)

14.96   If employment-related securities are disposed of by the employee (or an associated person within *s 421C* – see **14.34**), other than to another associated person, for a consideration which exceeds the market value at the time of the disposal the excess gain is taxed as income for the tax year in which the disposal takes place. [*ITEPA 2003, ss 446X, 446Y(1), (2)*]. The amount of the excess gain is the difference between the consideration received on the disposal and the aggregate of the market value of the securities at the time of the disposal plus any expenses incurred in connection with the disposal. [*s 446Y(3)*]. Up to 5 April 2008 HMRC took the view that where an employee was resident but not ordinarily resident in the UK the exercise of a securities option could be charged to tax by virtue of this provision on a notional loan based on the value of the securities at the time the option was exercised and on the 'discharge' of that loan at the time the securities were sold, even though the option provision specifically excluded employees who are not ordinarily resident in the UK. However their practice was not to pursue the liability where at the time of the grant of the option the employee was resident 'wholly overseas' and the grant was not in prospect of taking up the UK employment or otherwise in respect of duties performed in the UK. For example if a US resident was granted options in the US and his employer subsequently transferred him to the UK to work in its UK subsidiary, HMRC accepted that the right or opportunity arose in respect of an employment outside the scope of UK tax, and such an employment is outside the intention behind the provision (*Employment Related Securities Manual, para 70410*).

14.97   *Gray's Timber Products Ltd v HMRC [2010] STC 782* provides a salutary lesson. On 9 December 1999, a Mr G was allotted 14,465 shares in the company, a 5 per cent holding, for £50,000 having become an employee on the previous day. He entered into a shareholders' agreement with the major shareholders. This provided that in the event of a sale of the company they would accept a lower price per share than other shareholders and the amount foregone would enhance the price payable for Mr G's holding. The company was duly sold. Mr G received from the purchaser £1.451million. If the purchase price had been divided pro rata amongst the whole share capital he would have received £1.027million. HMRC contended that the £424,000 difference fell within *ITEPA 2003, s 446Y*. Both the Inner House of the Court of Sessions and the Supreme Court agreed, in spite of the fact that as between Mr G and the purchaser the disposal was an arm's-length transaction. They felt that the purchaser would have been indifferent as to how the price for the company was split. More importantly, they felt that the market value of the shares depended on the rights given by the Company's Memorandum of Association. A shareholders agreement (particularly one not entered into by the 14 per cent minority shareholders) could not change the market value of the shares. The lesson here is obviously to amend the Memorandum of Association if it is wished to vary share rights, not do so by an outside document.

Unquoted companies

14.98 Where an employee has a small minority interest in an unquoted company the market value of his holding is likely to be very low. Most private companies contain a formula in their Articles of Association to fix the value at which shares are to be sold in certain specified circumstances. The formula under many, if not most, such pre-emption rights will ignore the fact that the shares constitute a minority interest. Accordingly, a disposal under the pre-emption rights is invariably at an overvalue.

Post-acquisition benefits from securities (Chapter 4)

14.99 If the employee or an associated person (within *ITEPA 2003, s 421C* – see **14.34**) receives a benefit in connection with the employment-related securities the amount or market value of that benefit is taxed as employment income of the tax year in which it is received. [*ITEPA 2003, ss 447, 448*]. If the benefit is otherwise chargeable to income tax this provision does not apply unless something which affects the securities has been done as part of a scheme or arrangement the main purpose (or one of the main purposes) of which was the avoidance of tax or NIC [*ITEPA 2003, s 447(4)* as substituted by *F(No 2)A 2005, Sch 2, para 18*].

14.100 The charge on benefits does not apply if the securities are shares, a similar benefit is received by the owners of all of the shares of the same class and, immediately before the receipt of the benefit, either the company is employee-controlled by virtue of holdings of shares of that class or the majority of the company's shares of that class are not employment-related securities (see **14.96** above). [*ITEPA 2003, s 449*]. If the chargeable event occurs after 1 December 2004 this exemption does not apply if something which affects the securities has been done as part of a scheme or arrangement the main purpose (or one of the main purposes) of which is the avoidance of tax or NIC. [*ITEPA 2003, s 449(1)(ba), (1A)* as amended by *F(No 2)A 2005, Sch 2, para 19*]. This restriction did not apply prior to 6 May 2004 and between that date and 1 December 2004 it applied only if the avoidance of tax or NIC was the main purpose or one of the main purposes of the arrangement under which the opportunity to acquire the securities was made available. It appears from the wording that the new *subsection (4)* enables HMRC to charge PAYE and NICs on a dividend paid by a family business in circumstances where the directors/shareholders have opted to take little or no remuneration so as to boost the profits available out of which dividends can be paid to them on their shares. The receipt of the dividend is a benefit received in connection with the employment-related securities and the arrangement under which dividends are taken instead of remuneration has as one of its main purposes the avoidance of NIC. However whether declaring a dividend is 'doing something' in relation to the shares seems questionable. It is equally questionable whether not paying NIC on a dividend, because Parliament chose not to impose it on a dividend, can constitute avoidance. Certainly HMRC have not indicated that the provision can apply in such circumstances. To do so would attract double income tax which is undoubtedly not the intention of Parliament. Furthermore the Explanatory Notes to the 2005 Finance Bill indicated that the changes had been introduced to stop schemes of which HMRC had become aware under the disclosure rules which used shares in order to pass remuneration value to employees in a way that attempts to avoid income tax and NIC. It seems doubtful whether paying dividends rather than remuneration is either something that would have been disclosed as an avoidance scheme or something of which HMRC were unaware prior to such a disclosure.

14.101   If the shares are in a research institution spin-out company (see **14.123**) to which the special rules at **14.121** onward apply, the shares (or interest) are acquired before the intellectual property agreement is made (or before any transfer of intellectual property pursuant to it) and a benefit deriving from the intellectual property agreement is received by the employee in connection with the shares, the taxable amount under *s 448* (see **14.99**) is nil. [*ITEPA 2003, s 453(1)* inserted by *FA 2005, s 20*]. This does not apply if something which affects the shares or interest has been done as part of a scheme or arrangement the main purpose (or one of the main purposes) of which is the avoidance of tax or NIC. [*ITEPA 2003, s 453(2)*].

Share options (officially called securities options) (Chapter 5)

14.102   The next set of rules applies where a securities option is acquired by a person and the right or opportunity to acquire the option is available by reason of an employment (or former or prospective employment) of that or any other person. [*ITEPA 2003, s 471(1), (2)*]. A securities option is any right to acquire securities. [*ITEPA 2003, s 420(8)*]. A right or opportunity to acquire a securities option which is made available by a person's employer (or a connected employer within *ICTA 1988, s 839*) must be regarded as being made available by reason of that person's employment unless it is provided by an individual in the normal course of his domestic, family or personal relationships. [*ITEPA 2003, s 471(3)*]. A right or opportunity to acquire a securities option which is available by reason of holding employment-related securities must be regarded as being available by reason of the same employment as gave rise to the opportunity to acquire the employment-related securities. [*ITEPA 2003, s 471(4)*].

14.103 The basic rule is that no income tax charge arises in respect of the acquisition of the option (other than the charge under *ITEPA 2003, s 526*, on an option under an approved CSOP scheme which was granted at a discount). [*ITEPA 2003, s 475*].

14.104 An income tax charge can however arise:

(*a*)   on the acquisition of the securities pursuant to the option, under any of *ITEPA 2003*:

    (i)   *s 446B* (see **14.69**)

    (ii)   *s 446S* (see **14.90**)

    (iii)   *s 476* (see **14.107**)

(*b*)   under *ITEPA 2003, s 476* on an assignment or release of the option;

(*c*)   under *ITEPA 2003, s 476* on the receipt of a benefit in connection with the option.

[*ITEPA 2003, s 473(2), (3)*].

14.105 Special rules relate to options acquired under:

(*a*)   an approved SAYE option scheme (see **16.11**);

(*b*)   an approved CSOP scheme (see **16.11**);

(*c*)   an enterprise management incentive scheme (see **16.72**).

[*ITEPA 2003, s 473(4)*].

14.106 No income tax charge (other than any charge under *ITEPA 2003, s 66*) arises in relation to the acquisition or exercise of an employment-related securities option if either:

(*a*)   at the time of the acquisition the earnings (if any) from the employment were not general earnings taxable under *ITEPA 2003, ss 15* (see **2.48**), 22 (see **12.9**) or 26 (see **2.48**) (ie the employee is non-UK resident). [*ITEPA 2003, s 474(1)* as amended by *FA 2008, Sch 7, para 31*] (or prior to 2008/09 the employee was not both resident and ordinarily resident in the UK);

(*b*)   the option is employment-related by reason of a former employment and no charge would have arisen if the acquisition of the option had taken place in the last tax year in which the employment was held;

(*c*)   the option is employment-related by reason of a prospective employment and no charge would arise if the acquisition of the option had taken place in the first tax year in which the employment is held; or

(*d*)   the option is a new option (within *ITEPA 2003, s 483* – see **14.119**) and one of the above exceptions applies in relation to the old option.

[*ITEPA 2003, s 474*].

14.107 Subject to these exceptions an income tax charge arises on the acquisition of securities under the option (or the happening of some other chargeable event). [*ITEPA 2003, s 476(1), (2)*]. The following are chargeable events:

(*a*) the acquisition of securities pursuant to the option by either the employee or some other associated person (see **14.34**);

(*b*) the assignment or release of the option for consideration by the employee or another associated person (other than to another associated person or for payment by an associated person);

(*c*) the receipt by the employee (or an associated person) of any other benefit in money or money's worth in connection with the option.

[*ITEPA 2003, s 477 (3)* as amended by *FA 2004, s 90(4)*].

However, such an event is not a chargeable event if it occurs after the death of the employee. [*ITEPA 2003, s 477(2)*]. If the employee was resident and ordinarily resident at the time the option was granted a tax charge will arise on its exercise even if at that stage the employee has ceased to be resident and ordinarily resident in the UK.

14.108 For the purpose of (*a*) above securities are acquired at the time when a beneficial interest in them is acquired. [*ITEPA 2003, s 477(4)*]. For the purpose of (*c*) above:

(i) a benefit received on account of any disability (within the *Disability Discrimination Act 1995 (DDA 1995)*) is ignored; and

(ii) a benefit in money or money's worth received as consideration for (or in connection with) either failing to exercise the option (or undertaking not to do so) or granting to another person a right to acquire the securities which are the subject of the option, must be regarded as having been received in connection with the option.

[*ITEPA 2003, s 477(5), (6)*].

14.109 For the purpose of the share option rules the person who initially acquired the option, the employee (if different) and any relevant linked person are associated persons. [*ITEPA 2003, s 472(1)*]. A person is a relevant linked person if he either is (or has been) connected with or is (or has been) a member of the same household as the employee (or if different the person who initially acquired the option). However, a company is not a relevant linked person if it is the employer (or, if different, the person who granted the option or the person by whom the right or opportunity to acquire it was made available). [*ITEPA 2003, s 472(2), (3)* as amended by *FA 2004, s 90(3)*]. A former connected person or member of the employee's household was not a linked person prior to 18 June 2004 but is from that date even if the options were acquired earlier. The *ICTA 1988, s 839* definition of connected persons applies. [*ITEPA 2003, s 718*].

14.110 If the employee has been divested of the option by operation of law, eg he has become bankrupt, the person who exercises the option or receives the consideration is the taxable person rather than the employee. In such a case the tax charge is under Case VI of Schedule D. [*ITEPA 2003, ss 476(5), 477(7)*].

14.111 The taxable amount is:

AG – DA

Where   AG = the gain realised on the occurrence of the chargeable event (see **14.107**); and

DA = the total of any deductible amounts (see **14.113**).

[*ITEPA 2003, s 478*].

14.112 The amount of gain realised on the exercise of the option is the market value of the shares at the date of such exercise less the price payable for the shares under the option. [*ITEPA 2003, s 479(2), (3)*]. This does not of course apply if the option is an enterprise management incentive option as *ITEPA 2003, ss 531* and *532* contains different rules in relation to such options (see **16.105**). [*ITEPA 2003, s 479(4)*]. The amount of gain realised on an assignment or release of the option is the consideration received for the assignment or release. The amount of gain realised on the receipt of any other benefit is the amount received or the market value of the benefit. [*ITEPA 2003, s 479(5), (6)*]. This is subject to the proviso that if a benefit, or the consideration for releasing or assigning an option, consists in whole or part in the receipt of securities (or an interest in securities) the market value of which has been reduced by at least 10 per cent as a result of something done otherwise than for genuine commercial purposes within the prior seven years, the market value of such securities must be taken as what it would have been but for the reduction. In particular anything done as part of a scheme or arrangement, one of the main purpose of which is the avoidance of tax or NIC, must be treated as not having been done for genuine commercial purposes. So must any transaction (other than a payment for group relief) between companies which are members of the same group (51 per cent subsidiaries) on terms which are not such as might be expected to be agreed between persons acting at arm's length. [*ITEPA 2003, s 479(7)–(9)*]. If the shares are in a research institution spin-out company the special rules at **14.121** apply to determine the market value at the time of acquisition. [*ITEPA 2003, s 452(2)(c)* inserted by *FA 2005, s 20*].

14.113 The deductible amounts are:

(*a*)   any consideration given for the acquisition of the option itself [*s 480(2) (a)*];

(*b*)   any expenses incurred in connection with the acquisition of the securities or the assignment, release or receipt which gives rise to the chargeable event [*s 480(2)(b)*];

(*c*)   any amount taxed as employment income under *ITEPA 2003, s 526* (option under approved CSOP scheme granted at a discount – see **16.11**) to the extent that it is attributable to the shares in question [*s 480(4)*];

(*d*)   any amount taxed as earnings under *ITEPA 2003, s 66* (the basic charging provision on employment income) in respect of the acquisition of the option [*s 480(5)(a)*];

(*e*)   any amount charged to income tax as a benefit in kind in respect of the option (but, for chargeable events after 12 March 2008, not any amount exempted from tax). [*s 480(5)(b)*];

(*f*)   the amount of any gain by a previous holder on an assignment of the option which would have been a deductible cost under *s 479(2)(c)* as originally enacted on an exercise of the option at a time when that section was in force [*s 480(5)(c)*]; and

(*g*)   any amount deductible under *sections 481 or 482* (see **14.116**) in relation to employer's National Insurance contributions borne by the employee. [*s 480(7)*].

[*ITEPA 2003, s 480(2), (4), (5), (7)* as amended by *FA 2008, s 46(6)*].

Curiously there seems to be no relief for any expenses in connection with the grant of the option. The exclusion of exempt income by *FA 2008* is to put the position beyond doubt from 12 March 2008. HMRC believe that it has always been necessary to exclude such income.

14.114   If there is more than one chargeable event in relation to an option (including if *ss 476* or *477* as originally enacted applied to that earlier event) amounts deducted in calculating the gain realised on an earlier event obviously cannot be deducted again. [*ITEPA 2003, s 480(6)*].

14.115   It should be noted that a charge under *ITEPA 2003, s 478* will arise even if the employee pays a market price for the option and the exercise price is the market value of the securities at the time the option is granted. In contrast if the employee were granted partly paid shares, so that *ITEPA 2003, s 446Q* applied (see **14.88**), the only charge would have been to notional interest or if the shares were restricted shares an election could have been made under *ITEPA 2003, s 431* (see **14.45**) to ignore the restrictions so that no income tax charge would have arisen. Unfortunately the option rules take priority as a right to acquire shares is excluded from being an interest in shares – see **14.18**(*d*).

14.116   If the employer and employee have entered into an agreement under *Social Security Contributions and Benefits Act 1992 (SSCBA 1992), Sch 1, para 3A*, for the employee to reimburse the employer's NIC on the exercise of the option, or made an election under *Sch 1, para 3B* to that Act to transfer responsibility for payment of such NIC to the employee, any amount reimbursed to the employer under that agreement before 5 June following the tax year in which the gain is realised, and the amount of any liability transferred to the employee, are deductible under **14.113**(*g*) above). [*ITEPA 2003, s 481(1), (2)*]. If HMRC withdraw their approval to an election under *Sch 1, para 3B* the amount deductible is limited to any NIC liability actually met by the employee before 5 June in the tax year following that in which the gain is realised. [*ITEPA 2003, s 481(3)*]. The deduction obviously cannot be made to arrive at the amount chargeable to the NIC. [*ITEPA 2003, s 481(4B)* inserted by *FA 2004, Sch 16, para 3*].

14.117 HMRC say that the distinction between an agreement and an election is that under an agreement the employer remains the person liable for the NIC but he has a contractual right to recover the amount from the employee, whereas with an election the NIC liability is transferred from employer to employee. HMRC approval is not needed for an agreement because it is a private arrangement between employer and employee (Press Release 23.8.2004). *The Social Security (Contributions) Regulations 2001, Sch 4, paras 7(9),(11)– (12A)* authorise the employer to retain and sell sufficient of the securities to meet the employee's obligation under an agreement provided that he accounts to the employee for any excess.

14.118 If the employee becomes liable to pay a special contribution under *Social Security Contributions (Share Options) Act 2001, s 2* in respect of the option that contribution is deductible under **14.113**(*g*) above. Such a contribution can be payable only where the option was granted between 6 April 1999 and 19 May 2000. The special contribution was an amount equal to employer's NIC on the gain that would have been made had the option been exercised on 7 November 2000. In return for that payment no NIC is payable on exercise of the option. The appropriate notice of the election must have been given to HMRC by 11 August 2001, the person (or one of the persons) who gave the notice must have been liable for the employer's NIC (either as the employer or by virtue of an election under *Contributions and Benefits Act 1992, Sch 1, para 3B*), and the special contribution must actually have been paid by 11 August 2001 (or such later date as HMRC may have agreed). [*ITEPA 2003, s 482*].

14.119 If an employment-related securities option (the old option) is assigned or released and all or part of the consideration for that assignment or release consists of another securities option (the new option), the value of the new option is not treated as consideration for the assignment or release of the old. Instead the above rules apply to the new option as they applied to the old. [*ITEPA 2003, s 483(1)–(3)*]. In such a case the amount of the consideration given for the acquisition of the new option is the sum of:

(*a*)   the consideration given for the old option (or if any amount (other than the new option) was received for its assignment or release, the amount if any by which the cost of the old option exceeded such receipt); and

(*b*)   any valuable consideration (other than the old option) given for the acquisition of the new option.

[*ITEPA 2003, s 483(4)*].

14.120 Two or more transactions must be treated as being a single transaction by which one option is assigned for a consideration which consists of or includes another option if they result in a person ceasing to hold an option and either that person or a connected person (within *ICTA 1988, s 839*) coming to hold another option, and one or more of those transactions is effected under arrangements to which two or more persons holding employment-related securities options which would attract income tax under the above rules are parties. [*ITEPA 2003, s 483(5)*].

Shares in research institution spin-out companies

14.121 Special rules apply to determine the market value of shares (or an interest in shares) in a research institution spin-out company. The market value at the time of acquisition of the shares or right is calculated disregarding the effect on value of the intellectual property agreement and any transfer of intellectual property pursuant to it. [*ITEPA 2003, s 452* inserted by *FA 2005, s 20*].

14.122 These apply where:

(*a*) an agreement is made for one or more transfers of 'intellectual property' (called an intellectual property agreement) from one or more 'research institutions' to a company (a spin-out company);

(*b*) a person acquires shares (or an interest in shares) in the spin-out company either before the intellectual property agreement is entered into or within 183 days after it;

(*c*) the right or opportunity to acquire the shares or interest was available by reason of employment by the research institution or the spin-out company;

(*d*) the person is 'involved in research' in relation to any of the intellectual property that is the subject of the intellectual property agreement; and

(*e*) the avoidance of tax or NICs is not the main purpose (or one of the main purposes) of the arrangements under which the right or opportunity to acquire the shares or interest is made available.

[*ITEPA 2003, s 451* inserted by *FA 2005, s 20*].

14.123 For this purpose a research institution is a university (or other publicly-funded institute within *s 41(2), Higher Education Act 2004 (HEA 2004)*) or any institution that carries out research activities otherwise than for profit and is not controlled (or wholly or mainly funded) by a person who carries on activities for profit. [*ITEPA 2003, s 457(1)*]. The Treasury have power by statutory instrument to amend this definition. [*ITEPA 2003, s 457(2)*]. A person is involved in research in relation to any intellectual property transferred (or to be transferred) from a research institution if he has been actively engaged for the research institution in connection with research which is relevant to something to which the intellectual property relates. The person does not have to have been an employee of the institution; he could be a sub-contractor. The sole test is whether he has been actively involved in the research. [*ITEPA 2003, s 458*]. If a research institution (or two or more research institutions) controls a company (within *ICTA 1988, s 416*) a transfer of intellectual property by that company to a spin-out company is treated as a transfer by the institution (or institutions). [*ITEPA 2003, s 459*]. It will be seen from **14.122**(*a*) that the research institution does not need to control the spin-out company. It is accordingly possible for intellectual property to be transferred by two or more institutions (or companies controlled by them) to the same spin-out company. Where this occurs the individual obviously only needs to have been engaged in the research by one of them. [*ITEPA 2003, s 458(a)*]. A transfer of intellectual property includes a sale, the grant of a licence or other right, and the assignment of a licence or other right in relation to that property. [*ITEPA 2003, s 456(3)*].

14.124 Intellectual property covers all or any of:

(*a*) any patent, trade mark, registered design, copyright, design right or plant breeders right (including rights under *s 7, Plant Varieties Act 1997*) (those are statutory rights governed by the *Copyright Designs and Patents Act 1988 (CDPA 1988)*);

(*b*) any right under the law of an overseas country or territory corresponding to (or similar to) one of the above rights;

(*c*) know-how (ie information or techniques not protected by a right within (*a*) or (*b*) but having industrial, commercial or other economic value;

(*d*) any licence or other right in respect of anything within (*a*) to (*c*); and

(*e*) goodwill (which has the meaning it has for accounting purposes) associated with something within (*a*)–(*d*)

[*ITEPA 2003, s 456(1)*]. The Treasury have power by statutory instrument to amend the definition. [*ITEPA 2003, s 456(2)*].

14.125 These special rules apply only if either the date of acquisition of the shares or the date of the intellectual property agreement is after 1 December 2004. [*FA 2005, s 20(5)*]. If the shares were acquired before 1 December 2004 (but the intellectual property agreement was entered into after that date) the deemed election under *ITEPA 2003, s 431(1)* (see **14.45**) is treated as made on 2 December 2004. [*FA 2005, s 20(6)*]. It is not clear what the effect of this deeming is. The election must be made within 14 days of the acquisition of the shares. [*ITEPA 2003, s 431(5)(b)*] so it appears to have no effect if the shares were acquired before 18 November 2004. It seems unlikely that is the intention. However it seems equally unlikely that the intention is to reduce the initial value of the shares by the value of the intellectual property at 2 December 2004 rather than that at the time of acquisition, but it may have that very limited intention.

14.126 Where shares in a spin-out company were acquired before 2 December 2004 and the above rules would have applied had they been acquired after that date a joint election could be made by the employer and employee to treat the above rules as applying for the purpose of the basic charging provisions (see **2.5**), *ITEPA 2003, ss 446Q, 446S* (see **14.89**) and *ITEPA 2003, s 471* (see **14.102**) (but not for the purpose of a conversion charge under *ITEPA 2003, s 439(3)(a)* (see **14.61**). [*FA 2005, s 21(2)*]. Such an election had to be made by 15 October 2005, had to be in a form specified by HMRC (but did not have to be sent to HMRC) and is irrevocable. [*FA 2005, s 21(1), (7)*].

14.127 Where such an election was made, the above rules apply on the acquisition but a chargeable event in relation to the shares is deemed to occur at the time of disposal of the shares (or interest in them) for consideration to someone other than an associated person (see **14.34**) (or on such earlier date as may have been specified in the election). [*FA 2005, s 21(3), (4)*]. The taxable amount at that time is the market value of the shares or interest immediately before the actual chargeable event less the total of any deductible amounts. These are the deductible amounts set out at **14.38** plus the disposal costs of the shares if the chargeable event is deemed to occur on the date of the disposal. [*FA 2005, s 21(5), (6)*]. The chargeable event under the three provisions is always the acquisition of the shares but it appears that the legislation is seeking to draw a distinction between market value at acquisition and market value at the time of the deemed chargeable event, so that the deemed chargeable event will trigger a tax charge on the value of the intellectual property. The effect accordingly seems to be simply to defer the tax charge until the shares are disposed of. The intention is that no tax charge should arise unless the spin-out company is successful so the employee realises an actual gain. Even then the taxable amount will be limited to that gain.

The rules prior to 2003/04 that can still apply

14.128 The changes made by the *FA 2003* had a twofold aim, to block some avoidance opportunities in the existing legislation and to simplify the rules so that they would operate more fairly. As indicated at **14.25** some of these provisions are still relevant as they continue to apply to trigger a tax charge in relation to securities issued before 16 April 2003 and in some cases to securities issued between that date and the appointed day under *FA 2003, Sch 22, para 3(2)*. These are:

Acquisitions at an undervalue: paragraphs **14.140–14.151** continue to apply to securities acquired before 16 April 2003. They have been replaced by the provisions considered at **14.88–14.97** above for acquisitions after that date.

Unapproved share schemes: paragraphs **14.152–14.161** ceased to apply from 16 April 2003 with the exception that the charge on the removal or variation of a restriction applying to the shares under *ITEPA 2003, s 450(3)(a)* (as originally enacted) (see **14.155**(*a*)) and *s 450(1), (3), (4)* and *(5)* which relate to it, continue to apply in relation to shares and interests in shares acquired before 16 April 2003 (and to other shares until 1 September 2003). To the extent that they relate to *s 450, ss 447–449, 451(1)* to *(3), 461(1)(e), 464–466* and *468–470* also continue to apply so far as relevant. They have been replaced by the provisions considered at **14.68–14.79** above.

Ancillary provisions: paragraphs **14.163–14.171** ceased to apply from 16 April 2003 except to the extent that they relate to the provisions listed above under unapproved share schemes.

The provisions that can still apply are considered at **14.140** onwards.

Additional matters

14.129 For the purpose of *Chapters 2–4* (**14.26–14.101**) but not *5* (options), 'associated persons' in relation to employment-related securities means the person who acquired the securities on the acquisition, or if different, the employee and any relevant linked person. A person is a linked person if he and either the person who acquired the securities on the acquisition or, if different, the employee are connected (within *ICTA 1988, s 839*) or are members of the same household (the person's domestic staff and guests – *ITEPA 2003, s 721(5)*). A company is not however a relevant linked person if it is the employee, the person from whom the employment-related securities were acquired), the person by whom the right or opportunity to acquire the employment-related securities was made available, or the person by whom the securities were issued. [*ITEPA 2003, s 421C* inserted by *FA 2003, Sch 22, para 2*].

14.130 If an associated person is entitled to employment-related securities and either:

(*a*) as a result of the conversion of those securities (or of any other transaction or series of transactions) he ceases to be entitled to the original securities but he or another person acquires replacement securities; or

(*b*) by virtue of his being entitled to the original securities he or an associated person acquire other securities (the additional securities);

the replacement securities or the additional securities must be treated as acquired pursuant to the same right or opportunity as the original securities. [*ITEPA 2003, s 421D(1), (2)* inserted by *FA 2003, Sch 22, para 2*]. If the market value of the original securities is reduced by reason of the issue of the replacement securities or additional securities (or the securities in which they are an interest) that reduction is treated for the purposes of *Chapters 2* (restricted securities) (see **14.26**) and *3* (convertible securities) (see **14.59**) as consideration or additional consideration given for the acquisition of the additional securities or the replacement securities. [*ITEPA 2003, s 421D(3)*]. *Subsections (2)* and *(3)* apply irrespective of whether or not any actual consideration was given for the additional or replacement securities. [*ITEPA 2003, s 421D(4)*]. Where *Chapters 2* to *4* (**14.26–14.101**) apply to an interest in securities an increase of that interest is treated as a separate interest acquired pursuant to the same right or opportunity as the original interest and a reduction of that interest (other than by a disposal to an associated person) is treated as a disposal otherwise than to an associated person of a separate interest proportionate to the reduction. [*ITEPA 2003, s 421D(5), (6)*]. Such a disposal is a chargeable event which potentially triggers a tax charge.

14.131 *Chapters 2, 3* and *4* of *Part 7* of *ITEPA 2003* do not apply in relation to employment-related securities if, at the time of acquisition, the earnings (if any) from the employment are not general earnings taxable under *ITEPA 2003, ss 15* (see **2.48**), *22* (see **12.9**) or *26* (see **2.48**) (ie the employee is non-UK resident. [*ITEPA 2003, s 421E(1)* substituted by *FA 2008, Sch 7, para 31*]. Where the split year concession (ESC A11) applies to a person, HMRC used to take the view that these provisions applied to shares or rights obtained at any time in the year of arrival in the UK. However they now accept that the concession applies in that year. It also applies in the year of departure other than to securities acquired for less than market value. However they reserve the right to depart from this position in cases of avoidance. They also say that where a right to acquire securities was obtained prior to 6 April 2008 in the non-resident part of the year of arrival, and that right is not 'money's worth' (ie it is not a legal option), there will however be a charge to tax under basic principles [*ITEPA 2003, s 62*] on acquisition of the shares. If there is a legal option a tax charge can arise on exercise if the value of the shares at that time is less than the option price and the option was granted in respect of UK duties (HMRC Concession 4.7.2008). Up to 2007/08 they did not apply if the employee was not both resident and ordinarily resident in the UK and *Chapters 3A* to *3D* did not apply if at that time the earnings from the employment were not taxable in the UK (or would not have been taxable if there had been any earnings). [*ITEPA 2003, s 421E(1), (2)*]. None of *Chapters 2* to *4* apply to a former employment if they would not have applied if the acquisition of the securities had taken place in the tax year in which the employment was held, or to a prospective employment if they would not have applied to an acquisition in the first year in which the employment was held. [*ITEPA 2003, s 421E(3), (4)*]. In the case of additional and replacement securities this residence test applies to the acquisition of the original securities. [*ITEPA 2003, s 421E(5)*]. The special rules that apply where the recipient of employment related securities is non-UK domiciled are dealt with at **12.35** onwards.

14.132 There is an exemption from *Chapter 2* (restricted securities – see **14.26**), *3* (convertible securities – see **14.59**) and *3C* (securities acquired at an undervalue – see **14.88**). For employment-related securities that are shares acquired under the terms of an offer to the public (or an interest in shares so acquired), but only if the avoidance of tax or NICs was not the main purpose (or one of the main purposes) of the arrangements under which the right or opportunity under which the shares were acquired or for which they are held arose. Up to 18 June 2004 the exemption also extended to *Chapters 3A, 3B, 3D* and *4* and the main purpose test did not apply. Where shares within *Chapter 3B* (securities with artificially enhanced value – see **14.80**) were acquired before 18 June 2004 they are treated for the purpose of *s 446L* (see **14.82**) as if they had been acquired on that date. [*ITEPA 2003, s 421F(1)* as amended by *FA 2004, s 89*]. The rules on priority share allocations set out at **14.150** continue to apply to shares issued under the new rules. In a case within *ITEPA 2003, s 544(1)* (exemption for priority share allocations where different offers are made to public and employees) (see **14.150**) the exemption covers an acquisition made under the terms of either the public or the employee offer, irrespective of whether or not there is any benefit within *s 544(2)*. [*ITEPA 2003, s 421F(2), (3)*].

14.133 Prior to 18 June 2004 none of *Chapters 2* to *4* of *Part 7* of *ITEPA 2003* applied to:

(*a*)   shares awarded or acquired under an approved Share Incentive Plan (see **Chapter 16**);

(*b*)   shares acquired by the exercise of a share option granted under an approved SAYE option scheme; or

(*c*)   shares acquired by the exercise of a share option granted under an approved CSOP scheme.

[*ITEPA 2003, s 421G* inserted by *FA 2003, Sch 22, para 2* and repealed by *FA 2004, s 88(2)*].

14.134   For the purposes of *Chapters 2* to *4* a company is employee-controlled by virtue of shares of a class if the majority of the company's shares of that class (other than any held by or for the benefit of any associated company – within *ICTA 1988, s 416*) are held for the benefit of employees (or ex-employees or prospective employees) of the company or of a company controlled by that company, and those employees are together able as holders of the shares to control the company. [*ITEPA 2003, s 421H*].

14.135   For the purposes of *Chapters 2*, (see **14.26**) *3*, (see **14.59**) and *3A* (see **14.68**) references to consideration given for the acquisition of the employment-related securities cover consideration given both by the employee and, if different, the person by whom the securities were acquired. [*ITEPA 2003, s 421I(1), (2)*]. Consideration given for a right to acquire the securities is regarded as part of the consideration for their acquisition. [*ITEPA 2003, s 421I(2)*]. If the right to acquire the securities (the new option) is the whole or part of the consideration for the assignment or release (or for agreeing to a restriction of the exercise of the right) of another right to acquire them (the old option), the consideration given for the new option is the sum of the amount by which the consideration for the old option exceeds any consideration received for the assignment or release of the old option (apart from the new option) and any valuable consideration given for the new option (apart from the old one). [*ITEPA 2003, s 421I(4), (7)*]. For this purpose two or more transactions are treated as a single transaction by which a right to acquire the securities is assigned for a consideration which consists of or includes another right to acquire the securities if:

(*a*)   the transactions result in a person ceasing to hold a right to acquire the securities and that person or a connected person coming to hold another right to acquire them; and

(*b*)   one or more of the transactions is effected under arrangements to which two or more persons who hold rights to acquire the securities in respect of which a tax liability could arise under *Chapter 5* (options) (see **14.102**) are parties.

[*ITEPA 2003, s 421I(5)*].

Information

14.136   A person who is (or has been) a responsible person in relation to reportable events (see **14.137**) must make to HMRC a return falling wholly or partly within that person's reportable event period, ie the period from the occurrence of the first reportable event for which he is a responsible person to the time when that person will no longer be a responsible person in relation to reportable events [*ITEPA 2003, s 421JA(1)-(3)* inserted by *FA 2014, Sch 8, para 228*]. The return must be made by 6 July following the end of the tax year and must contain (or be accompanied by) such information as HMRC may require. The information that they can require includes in particular information to enable them to determine the liability to tax (including CGT) of any employee [*ITEPA 2003, s 421JA(4)(5)*]. The return need not contain (or be accompanied by) duplicate information, and no return is required if it would only contain such information [*ITEPA 2003, s 421JA(7)*]. This is information which is contained in (or accompanies)

(*a*)   an annual return which another person gives for the tax year under *s 421JA*,

(*b*)   an annual return which any person gives for a tax year under the provisions relating to SIPs, Schedule 3 SAYE option schemes, Schedule 4 CSOP schemes, or EMI options

[*ITEPA 2003, s 421JA(8)*]. If after submitting an annual return, a person becomes aware that something which should have been included was omitted (or something was included which should not have been included), or becomes aware of any other error or inaccuracy in relation to the return, he must submit an amended return correcting the position without delay [*ITEPA 2003, s 421J(6)*]. The return must be submitted electronically (but HMRC have power to permit some other method where they consider it appropriate) [*ITEPA 2003, s 421JB(1)(2)*]. HMRC must prescribe how returns and accompanying information are to be given electronically [*ITEPA 2003, s 421JB(3)*].

14.136A   The responsible persons are:

(*a*)   the employer;

(*b*)   any 'host employer' of the employee;

(*c*)   the person from whom the securities (or interest or option) was acquired; and

(*d*)   if the securities are not 'excluded securities' the person by whom the securities were issued.

[*ITEPA 2003, s 421L(2), (3)*]. A host employer is a person for whom the employee works at the time of the reportable event and who would be treated for PAYE purposes under *ITEPA 2003, s 689(2)* (see **2.63**) as making a payment of PAYE income of the employee in question if a payment were made by the employer in respect of the period in which the employee works for the employer and the conditions of *s 689(1)(c), (d)* were satisfied in relation to the payment. [*ITEPA 2003, s 421L(4), (5)*]. Excluded securities are:

(i)   loan stock, bonds or other instruments creating or acknowledging indebtedness issued by (or on behalf of) a national or regional government or local authority (of the UK or elsewhere) or any body whose members consist of states, national or regional governments or local authorities, or

(ii)   securities which are listed or dealt in on a recognised stock exchange and were issued by a person who (at the time of the reportable event) is not connected with the employer in question.

[*ITEPA 2003, s 421L(6)*].

14.137 The reportable events are:

(*a*)   an acquisition of securities, an interest in securities or a securities option pursuant to a right or opportunity available by reason of the employment of the person who acquires the securities, interest or option or of any other person (or an event which is treated as such an acquisition);

(*b*)   an event which is a chargeable event within *ITEPA 2003, s 426* (restricted securities) (see **14.26**);

(*c*)   an event which is a chargeable event for the purposes of *ITEPA 2003, s 438* (convertible securities) (see **14.59**);

(*d*)   the doing of something which gives rise to a taxable amount under *ITEPA 2003, s 446L* (artificial enhancement of value) (see **14.82**);

(*e*)   an event which discharges a notional loan under *ITEPA 2003, s 446U* (securities acquired at an undervalue) (see **14.94**) or would have done so but for the exemption for research institution spin-out companies (see **14.101**);

(*f*)   a disposal of securities or an interest in securities within *ITEPA 2003, s 446X* (disposal at an overvalue) (see **14.98**);

(*g*)   the receipt of a benefit which gives rise to a taxable amount under *ITEPA 2003, s 447* (benefits from securities) (see **14.99**);

(*h*)   the assignment or release of a securities option acquired pursuant to a right or opportunity available by reason of the employment of the person who acquires the option or of any other person (see **14.107**); and

(*i*)   the receipt of a benefit in money or money's worth which is received in connection with such a securities option (or treated as being so received under *ITEPA 2003, s 477(6)*) (see **14.111**).

[*ITEPA 2003, s 421K* inserted by *FA 2003, Sch 22, para 2*].

14.138 In addition, HMRC can by notice require a responsible person to provide them with such particulars of any reportable event which takes place in a period specified in the notice as are required by the notice, or if no reportable events in relation to which person served with the notice is a responsible person have taken place in that period, to state that fact. [*ITEPA 2003, s 421J(4)*]. Any such notice must specify a date within which it must be complied with. This must not be less than 30 days after the date when the notice is given. [*ITEPA 2003, s 421J(5), (6)*]. Once a person has complied with such a notice this absolves any other responsible person from the obligation to notify the chargeable event. [*ITEPA 2003, s 421J(8)*].

14.139 HMRC have power to prescribe the form of a notice under both *subsections (3)* and *(4)*. The prescribed form is Form 42. It is important to realise the very wide scope of the wording of **14.137**(*a*). HMRC say that this is not intended merely to require a report of share etc issues within the rules outlined above. It requires details of all share issues where the right or opportunity to acquire the shares arose or was deemed to arise, 'by reason of the individual's employment (or prospective employment). A right or opportunity made available by a person's employer, or a connected person of the employer, is automatically deemed to be by reason of the employment (subject to an exception where the employer is an individual) (see **14.18**(*c*)). Accordingly, in HMRC's view the paragraph requires details of all issues of shares in family companies where the recipient is or will become a director of the company. It probably also requires details of transfers of shares by an existing controlling shareholder, eg to his children, if the recipient is, or will become, a director. Whether HMRC's view is right seems questionable. The structure of the rewrite legislation is that the opening section of a Chapter, in this case *s 417*, sets out the scope of the Chapter and the later provisions define that scope. Accordingly, there is a strong argument that *s 421K* can only require details of transactions within the scope of *ss 417–548*. Unfortunately, the penalty for not completing the return is up to £300 (plus daily penalties of up to £60 a day) and that for completing it negligently (which the Commissioners might well hold includes omitting something which HMRC had publicly said needs to be included) is up to £3,000, so it is probably wisest to comply with the HMRC view.

14.139A If a person fails to make the annual return by 5 July (containing or accompanied by all of the required information) he is liable to a penalty of £100. There is then a further penalty of £300 if it is more than three months late with a further £300 if it is over 6 months late, ie a total penalty of £700 [*ITEPA 2003, s 421JC(1)-(4)*]. If the return is not filed within 9 months of the due date, HMRC have power to impose a daily penalty of £10 a day for each day the failure continues. They must give a notice to the person specifying the penalty period. This can begin earlier than the day on which the notice is given but not before the end of the nine-month period. Where a previous such penalty notice was given, the next one cannot begin before the expiry of the earlier one [*ITEPA 2003, s 421JC(5)-(7)*]. A penalty cannot be imposed if the person satisfies HMRC (or on appeal, the Tribunal) that there is a reasonable excuse for the failure. An insufficiency of funds is not a reasonable excuse unless attributable to events outside the person's control. Reliance on another person to do anything is not a reasonable excuse unless the delegator took reasonable care to avoid the failure. Where a person had a reasonable excuse for the failure but the excuse ceased, it is treated as continuing if the failure is remedied without unreasonable delay after it ceased.

14.139B If the annual return (or information accompanying the return) is not given electronically (and HMRC have not agreed some other method), or it contains a material inaccuracy which is careless or deliberate and which is not corrected without delay once it is discovered, the person in question is liable for a penalty of up to £5,000. A penalty is careless if it is due to a failure by the person in question to take reasonable care [*ITEPA 2003, s 421JD*].

14.139C HMRC must assess a penalty and notify the person of the assessment. The assessment must be made within 12 months after the date on which the person becomes liable for the penalty or, in the case of a penalty for a material inaccuracy, within 12 months after HMRC become aware of the inaccuracy and within 6 years from the date on which the person becomes liable for the penalty [*ITEPA 2003, s 421JE(1)-(4)*]. The penalty must be paid within 30 days of the penalty notice or, if it is appealed, within 30 days from the date the appeal is determined or withdrawn [*ITEPA 2003, s 421JE(5)*]. The penalty can be enforced as if it were income tax or corporation tax [*ITEPA 2003, s 421JE(6)*].

14.139D There is a right of appeal both against the decision to impose a penalty and the amount of the penalty. Notice of appeal must be given to HMRC within 30 days of the notice of the assessment. On appeal, the Tribunal can affirm or cancel the HMRC decision and can substitute a different penalty amount. The provisions of *Taxes Management Act 1970 (TMA 1970)*, relating to appeals apply to appeal under this provision [*ITEPA 2003, s 421JF*].

Internationally Mobile Employees

14.139E For 2015/16 onwards, if an amount is treated as employment income under *ITEPA 2003, Part 7, Chapters 2-5* (employment-related securities – see **14.16–14.120**) and one or more of the mobility conditions is met, an amount equal to $S1 - FS1$ (where $S1$ is the amount of the securities income and $FS1$ is the part of it which is 'foreign') is treated as taxable specific income from the employment for the year [*ITEPA 2003, s 41F(1)(3)* inserted by *FA 2014, Sch 9, para 5*]. So is the full amount of any chargeable foreign securities income which is remitted to the UK in the tax year (irrespective of whether or not the relevant employment income is still held at the time of the remittance) [*ITEPA 2003, s 41F(6)(7)*]. The international mobility conditions are

(*a*)   that any part of the 'relevant period' (see **14.139C**) is within a tax year for which the remittance basis applies to the individual,

(*b*)   a part of the relevant period is within a tax year for which the individual is not UK resident, or

(*c*)   a part of the relevant period is within the overseas part of a split tax year

[*ITEPA 2003, s 41F(2)*]. The amount of the securities income that is foreign is the sum of any chargeable foreign securities income and any unchargeable foreign securities income (see **14.139D**) [*ITEPA 2003, s 41F(5)*].

14.139F In applying the remittance basis, the relevant securities or relevant securities option (the one by virtue of which the amount is treated as employment income) is treated as deriving from the chargeable foreign securities income [*ITEPA 2003, s 41F(8)(11)*]. If the chargeable event is the disposal of the relevant securities, or assignment or release of the option, and the individual receives consideration for the disposal, assignment or release which is equal to or exceeds its market value, the consideration is instead treated as so deriving [*ITEPA 2003, s 41F(9)*].

14.139G   The relevant period depends on the event which gives rise to the income. In the case of restricted or convertible securities, it is the period from the date of acquisition to the date of the chargeable event (unless *s 41G(4)* applies) [*ITEPA 2003, s 41G(2)*]. If the amount is treated as employment income by virtue of *ITEPA 2003, s 446B* (securities with artificially depressed market value – see **14.69**) the relevant period is the tax year in which the securities are acquired. If *ITEPA 2003, s 446C(1)(aa)* or *(b)* applies (see **14.69**) it is the period from the start of the tax year in which the chargeable event is treated as occurring to the day on which it is so treated [*ITEPA 2003, s 41G(4)*]. If the amount is treated as employment income under *ITEPA 2003, s 446L* (securities with artificially enhanced market value – see **14.82**) the relevant period is that from the start of the tax year in which the valuation date falls to the valuation date [*ITEPA 2003, s 41G(5)*]. If the amount is treated as income under *ITEPA 2003, s 446U* (discharge of notional loan – see **14.93**) or *446UA* (avoidance cases – see **14.93**) and the relevant securities were acquired on the exercise of a securities option, the relevant period is that from the date the option was acquired to the day on which it vests. In any other case, it is the tax year in which the notional loan is treated as made (or the part of the tax year up to the date of the chargeable event if that occurs in the same year) [*ITEPA 2003, s 41G(6)*]. If the deemed income arises under *ITEPA 2003, chapter 3D* (securities disposed of for more than market value – see **14.96**) or *chapter 4* (post-acquisition benefits), it is the tax year in which the chargeable event occurs [*ITEPA 2003, s 41G(7)*]. If the deemed income arises under *ITEPA 2003, chapter 5* (employment-related securities option – see 14.102), it is the periods from the date of the acquisition of the option to the earlier of the date of the chargeable event that triggers the income or the day the option vests, ie either becomes exercisable or becomes exercisable subject only to a period of time expiring [*ITEPA 2003, s 41G(8), (11)*]. If the relevant period under the above rules would not, in all the circumstances, be just and reasonable, the relevant period is instead such period as is just and reasonable [*ITEPA 2003, s 41G(9)*].

14.139H   The extent to which the securities income (ie the chargeable amount) is chargeable foreign securities income or unchargeable foreign securities income is determined arithmetically. The income is first treated as accruing evenly over the relevant period [*ITEPA 2003, s 41H(2)*]. If any part of the relevant period is within a tax year for which:

(*a*)   the remittance basis applies to the individual,

(*b*)   the individual does not meet the requirements of *ITEPA 2003, s 26A* for the year (requirement for three-year period of non-residence – see **12.23**),

(*c*)   the relevant employment is with a foreign employer, and

(*d*)   the duties of the employment are performed wholly outside the UK in the year

and *ITEPA 2003, s 24A* (see **13.14A**) does not apply in relation to the employment in that year, the securities income is chargeable foreign securities income [*ITEPA 2003, s 41H(3)–(5)*]. If this provision does not apply to a tax year because *ITEPA 2003, s 24A* applies to the year, it must be assumed for the purpose of *s 41L* (see **14.139J**) that it is just and reasonable for none of the securities income treated as accruing in that tax year to be chargeable foreign securities income [*ITEPA 2003, s 41H(10)*].

14.139I   If any part of the relevant period is in a tax year where:

(*a*)   the remittance basis applies to the individual for that year, and

(*b*)   he meets the requirements of *ITEPA 2003, s 26A* for the year,

the securities income accruing in that part of the period is chargeable foreign securities income if the duties of the employment are performed wholly outside the UK, and if only part of the duties are performed outside the UK the securities income must be apportioned between UK and non-UK duties on a just and reasonable basis with the part apportioned to non-UK duties being chargeable foreign securities income [*ITEPA 2003, s 41H(6), (7)*].

14.139J   If any part of the relevant period is in a tax year for which the individual is non-UK resident (or is the overseas part of a split tax year) and the duties of the employment are performed wholly outside the UK, the securities income treated as accruing in that period is uncharged foreign securities income. If some of the duties are performed in the UK, the securities income is apportioned on a just and reasonable basis and the part attributable to non-UK duties is unchargeable foreign securities income [*ITEPA 2003, s 41H(8), (9)*]. If the proportion of the securities income that would otherwise be regarded as chargeable foreign securities income or unchargeable foreign securities income under the above calculation is not, having regard to all the circumstances, just and reasonable it must be replaced by such amounts as is just and reasonable [*ITEPA 2003, s 41L*].

14.139K   If the individual holds associated employments as well as the relevant employment (ie another employment with the same or an associated employer (within *ITEPA 2003, s 24(5), (6)* – see **12.39**) and the duties of the associated employments are not performed wholly outside the UK, the amount of the securities income that can be regarded as chargeable foreign securities income is limited to such amount as is just and reasonable having regard to:

(*a*)   the employment income from all of the employments,

(*b*)   the proportion of that income which is chargeable overseas earnings (see **12.21**),

(*c*)   the nature of, and time devoted to, the duties performed outside the UK and those performed in the UK, and

(*d*)   all other relevant circumstances

[*ITEPA 2003, s 41I*].

14.139L   *ITEPA 2003, ss 39(2)* (incidental duties – see **2.21**) and *40* (Crown duties deemed performed in the UK – see **13.2**) apply for the purpose of these provisions [*ITEPA 2003, s 41J(1)*]. Duties of an employment performed in the

UK sector of the continental shelf in connection with exploration or exploitation activities(see **17.98**) must be treated for the purpose of these provisions as being performed in the UK [*ITEPA 2003, s 41J(2)(3)*]. If securities income is from overseas Crown employment subject to UK tax (see **2.23A**), it is not foreign. Such securities income is to be regarded as subject to UK tax rules unless it falls within an exception contained in a Treasury Order under *ITEPA 2003, s 28(5)*. Such an order excepting general earnings from UK tax also has effect for excepting securities income from *s 41K* [*ITEPA 2003, s 41K*].

The rules up to 2002/03 that can still apply

Shares acquired at an undervalue (continues to apply to shares acquired before 16 April 2003)

14.140   If a person who was employed (or about to be employed) in director's or higher-paid employment (as defined at **6.4–6.6** above), or a person connected with him, acquired shares 'at an undervalue' before 16 April 2003 (whether in his employer or some other company) in pursuance of a right or opportunity available by reason of his employment, and the undervalue was not otherwise taxable as employment income, he was treated as having received a notional loan equal to the amount of the undervalue by reason of the employment. [*ITEPA 2003, s 194, s 193*]. The effect is to bring the beneficial loan provisions into play (see **9.1** above). These impose a tax charge on employment income on the notional interest that would have had to be paid if the notional loan had carried real interest at a market rate (fixed by the Treasury). In practice, the charge on notional interest would not normally arise if the company is a close company. This is because there is an exemption if the loan was used for a qualifying purpose (see **9.10** above) and, in most cases, the purchase of shares in a close company by an employee of the company will come within this exemption.

14.141   However, the beneficial loan provisions also impose an income tax charge on the waiver of a loan obtained by reason of a person's employment (whether or not it was on beneficial terms) (see **9.32** above). This is far more significant in relation to employee shareholdings because the notional loan under *ITEPA 2003, s 193* is treated as remaining outstanding until one of a number of specified events occurs, with any outstanding balance at that time regarded as then being written off or waived. [*ITEPA 2003, s 195*]. In other words, an income tax charge will arise at that stage on the amount of the undervalue. The chargeable amount is then treated as part of the cost of the shares in such circumstances. [*Taxation of Chargeable Gains Act 1992 (TCGA 1992), s 120(3)*].

14.142   When were shares acquired at an undervalue? This expression was far wider than the day-to-day meaning of the words might imply. Shares could be acquired at an undervalue for the purpose of *ITEPA 2003, s 193* even though a liability to pay the full market price arose – or indeed even if the price was greater than the market value of the shares, perhaps to reflect the fact that payment would not be made immediately. Shares were acquired at an undervalue for the purpose of the section if they were acquired either:

(*a*)   without payment for them at the time of acquisition; or

(*b*)   for an amount paid at the time of acquisition which was less than the market value of fully paid up shares of the same class.

[*ITEPA 2003, s 193(1)*].

14.143   In considering whether an acquisition fell into one of the above heads, the value of any obligation to make further payments for the shares at a later date had to be ignored. The amount of the undervalue on acquisition was the market value of fully paid up shares of the same class, less any payment made for the shares at the time of acquisition. [*ITEPA 2003, ss 193(2), 194*].

14.144   *ITEPA 2003, s 193* did not apply to a straightforward acquisition of shares with the price being immediately payable, or to a gift of shares as, in such circumstances, the difference between the market value of the shares and the price paid for them, if any, is taxable under general principles. It will represent money's worth in accordance with *Weight v Salmon 19 TC 174* (see **3.6** above).

Occasions of charge

14.145   It will be apparent that many common transactions under which employees or potential employees frequently acquire shares will be within *ITEPA 2003, s 193*. For example:

(*a*)   the acquisition of partly paid shares; and

(*b*)   the purchase of shares from an existing shareholder with the price being payable at a future date or by instalments.

14.146   If payments in respect of the shares, such as calls or payments of instalments on the purchase price, are made subsequent to the acquisition of the shares (and before the notional loan is deemed to terminate) such payments are regarded as repayment of part of the notional loan and deducted from it. [*ITEPA 2003, s 194(3)*]. *ITEPA 2003, s 193* will not apply where shares are given to an employee or are sold to him at an undervalue with the price being immediately payable, as the benefit obtained by the employee in such circumstances will already be taxable under the basic income tax rules on earnings.

Deemed waiver of the loan

14.147   The events that bring about the termination (and deemed waiver) of the notional loan are as follows:

(*a*)   The whole of the outstanding amount being made good by means of payment for the shares. If the price for the shares is at least equal to their market value at the time of their acquisition by the employee, payment for the shares will wholly extinguish the notional loan. Accordingly, the only effect of *ITEPA 2003, s 193*, will be the charge to notional interest which, as indicated above, will normally only create a tax liability if either the company is a non-close company or the employee does not work full-time for it and does not, (with his associates) own at least 5 per cent of the ordinary shares. [*ITEPA 2003, s 195(1)(a)*].

(*b*) If the shares were initially partly paid, an occasion on which any outstanding obligation to pay for them is released (or is transferred or adjusted so as to no longer bind the employee or a connected person of his). For example, suppose an employee is issued with shares at a price of £2 per share of which 10p is payable initially and that the market price of ordinary shares at the time was £2 per share. The market price of the shares subsequently falls to 50p and the company agrees to reduce the price of the employee's shares to £1 per share, in other words, it waives the premium. A tax charge will arise at the time that the company agrees to reduce the price. It appears that the charge will be on £1.90 per share (as that will be the notional loan still outstanding at the time) even though the employee has a continuing obligation to pay a further 90p per share when the company makes a further call on them. [*ITEPA 2003, s 195(1)(b)*].

(*c*) The disposal of the shares (including a surrender of the right to them) so that neither the employee nor a connected person of his has a beneficial interest in the shares. A disposal to a connected person, even by way of an arm's length sale, will not bring about a deemed waiver of the notional loan (see **9.25** above). A sale of partly paid shares (at arm's length to a non-connected person) will trigger a tax charge on the full amount of the undervalue even though the price received for the shares will reflect the fact that the purchaser is assuming the obligation to meet future calls. [*ITEPA 2003, s 195(1)(c)*].

(*d*) The death of the employee – but no income tax charge in relation to the deemed waiver is imposed in this instance. [*ITEPA 2003, s 195(1), (2)*]. If the shares are acquired (or held) not by the employee but by a connected person of his the death of that connected person will not give rise to a deemed waiver of the loan.

Cessation of employment

14.148 If the employment has ceased at the time the notional loan is deemed to terminate, it is treated as continuing so that the tax charge can be made. [*ITEPA 2003, s 195(3)*]. *ITEPA 2003, s 192* applies to the acquisition and disposal of an interest in shares, such as an interest in the proceeds of sale of part of the shares, in the same way as to shares. Obviously, in such a case, the market value to be used is not the value of fully paid shares, but the proportion of such value attributable to the interest that the employee holds in the shares. [*ITEPA 2003, s 194*]. The *section* did not apply to share options – which were dealt with by *ICTA 1988, s 135*. [*ITEPA 2003, s 197(1)*].

14.149 References to shares includes stock and also securities (as defined in *ICTA 1988, s 254(1)*). An acquisition of shares includes their receipt by way of allotment or assignment. Reference to payment for shares includes giving any consideration in money or money's worth or making any subscription, whether in pursuance of a legal liability or not. The capital gains tax definition of market value [*CGTA 1979, s 150*] applies, as does the *section 839* definition of connected person. [*ITEPA 2003, s 197(1)*]. The *section* does not apply to any amount which is already liable to tax under some other provision. [*ITEPA 2003, ss 64(1), (2), 196*].

Priority allocation of shares

14.150 It is specifically provided that where there was an offer to the public of shares in a company at a fixed price or by tender and a director or employee (of that or any other company) was entitled to an allocation of shares in priority to members of the public, the benefit of that priority was not to be treated as an emolument (either under general principles or the benefit in kind rules). [*ITEPA 2003, s 542*]. This did not apply to the extent that the price payable by the employee was below the fixed offer price or the lowest successful tender price (or, in a case falling within **14.151** below, the appropriate notional price). [*ITEPA 2003, s 543*]. The total number of shares allocated as priority shares to employees could not exceed 10 per cent of the shares on offer, all the persons entitled to priority allocations had to be entitled on similar terms, and the priority applicants could not be restricted to directors or those whose remuneration exceeded a particular level. [*ITEPA 2003, s 542(3), (5)*]. If the offer was one of a series of offers to the public of shares of the same class the 10 per cent limit applied to the aggregate of all the offers, and the priority shares in an individual offer could not exceed 40 per cent of the shares in that offer. [*ITEPA 2003, s 544(3)*]. From August 1990 the fact that directors or employees of the company were entitled to a larger allocation per person than others (eg employees of a related company) was not to be taken to mean that they were not entitled on similar terms, provided that those other persons were similarly entitled to a larger allocation of shares in a different company which was offered to the public at the same time and the aggregate value of the package offered to both sets of people was comparable. [*ITEPA 2003, s 546(3)–(6)*]. This extension was to cover employee shares issued on the electricity privatisation.

14.151 Offers made after 15 January 1991 had to be genuine. [*ITEPA 2003, s 542(1)(a), FA 1988, s 68(1)(a); Finance Act 1991 (FA 1991), s 44(2)*]. It is not clear what this means; it is hard to envisage an offer to the public not being genuine. From the same date, in determining whether the price payable by the employee is less than the offer price to the public, any 'registrant discount' made to the employee is ignored, provided that at least 40 per cent of the shares issued to the public attract a discount or other benefit of a similar value. A 'registrant discount' is a discount (or other benefit) given to employees who comply with the same conditions as members of the public who are entitled to a discount, and is given in the same circumstances as to members of the public. [*ITEPA 2003, ss 543(1)(b), 545(1)(b), 547*]. If the public are offered a combination of shares in two or more companies (as happened with Powergen and National Power) and a separate offer is made to employees which does not extend to shares in both (or all) companies, the public offer and the offer to employees are regarded as together constituting a single offer of shares to the public. [*ITEPA 2003, ss 544, 545(2)*]. In such a case the exemption has to be calculated by reference to 'the appropriate notional price'. This is the price at which the shares might reasonably have been offered to the public if they had been offered individually instead of as a package. [*ITEPA 2003, s 545(3), (5)*]. If such prices for all of the shares do not come to the aggregate price for the combined offer (as will almost always be the case as the shares would probably not have been offered as a package unless one component of it was unattractive on its own), the notional price of each is to be reduced or increased in proportion to the difference. [*ITEPA 2003, s 545(4)*].

Unapproved employee share schemes

14.152 A further tax charge could arise where, on or after 26 October 1987, a person acquired shares (or an interest in shares) in a company in pursuance of a right conferred on him, or an opportunity offered to him, by reason of a directorship or an employment. [*ITEPA 2003, ss 447, 449* (old)]. These provisions applied to lower-paid as well as higher-paid employees. They did not, however, apply if the employment was not within Case I of Schedule E. [*ITEPA 2003, s 447(4)* (old)]. Nor did they apply to an acquisition which was made in pursuance of an offer to the public or, after 16 January 1991, was treated as an offer to the public under *ITEPA 2003, s 544* (see **14.150** above) or which would have been so treated if no benefit had been given to the employee. [*ITEPA 2003, s 448(2)* (old)]. Where a tax charge arose under *ITEPA 2003, s 422* (see **14.26**), this obviously displaced the *s 449* charge.

Occasions of charge

14.153 There were three occasions of potential tax charges:

(*a*)   where restrictions were removed;

(*b*)   where the shares were in a dependent subsidiary; and

(*c*)   where a special benefit was received.

14.154 Only the first of these is still relevant. A charge to tax is triggered under this head if a 'chargeable event' occurred in relation to the shares at a time when the employee still had a beneficial interest in them. [*ITEPA 2003, s 449* (old)]. If the company was a dependent subsidiary at the time of the chargeable event (or was one at the time the shares were acquired), *s 449* (old) did not apply, but a charge under *s 453* (old) arose instead. [*ITEPA 2003, s 445(4)* (old)].

Meaning of 'chargeable event'

14.155 A 'chargeable event' was the occurrence of any of the following, but only if it increased the value of the shares (or would have done so but for something else happening at the same time):

(*a*)   the removal or variation of a restriction to which the shares were subject;

(*b*)   the creation or variation of rights relating to the shares;

(*c*)   the imposition of a restriction on other shares in the company (which could increase the value of the employee's shares);

(*d*)   the variation of a restriction to which such other shares were subject; and

(*e*)   the removal or variation of a right relating to other shares in the company.

[*ITEPA 2003, s 450(1), (3)* (old)].

Exceptions

14.156   There were a number of exceptions. The above events were chargeable events only if the shareholder has been a director or employee of the company (or, if different, of the company which gave rise to the acquisition of the shares, or of an associated company) at some time during the seven years ending with the occurrence of the event. In other words, a removal of restrictions, etc. did not trigger a tax charge if the shareholder ceased to be a director or employee more than seven years earlier. [*ITEPA 2003, s 452(3)* (old)]. It is difficult to envisage a company that wants to provide a benefit to an ex-employee by varying rights attaching to his shares waiting to do so until three or four years after he has left, let alone seven!

14.157   A removal of restrictions or variation of rights was not a chargeable event if it affects all of the shares of the same class (and falls into one of the following categories) and at the time of the variation, etc., either:

(*a*)   the majority of the shares of the same class as were held by the employee were not held by (or for the benefit of):

   (i)   directors or employees of the company,

   (ii)   an associated company of the company (such as its parent company), or

   (iii)   directors or employees of any such associated company;

(*b*)   the company was employee-controlled by virtue of holdings of shares of the same class as were held by the employee; or

(*c*)   the company was a subsidiary which was not a dependent subsidiary and its shares were of a single class.

[*ITEPA 2003, s 450(4)* (old)].

Associated companies

14.158   For the purpose of head (*a*) in **14.157** above a company was an associated company of another at a given time if at that time (or at any other time in the previous year) one had control of the other or both were under the control of the same person or persons. [*ITEPA 2003, s 470(1)* (old)]. Head (*a*) was aimed at the situation where a variation affected a class of shares mainly held by non-employees and the increase in value accrued to all, so that it could not have been designed as a benefit for employees as such. If the company was a subsidiary it was not normally possible to meet head (*a*) as the majority of the shares of the class held by employees would have been held by the parent company within (*a*)(ii).

Employee-controlled companies

14.159 A company was employee-controlled by virtue of holdings of shares of the same class (and thus within head (*b*) of **14.157**) if the majority of the shares of that class (excluding any held by or for the benefit of an associated company, such as the parent company) were held by (or for the benefit of) employees or directors of the company or of another company under its control (ie shares held by employees of a subsidiary of the company could be included), and those people were together able as holders of the shares to control the company. [*ITEPA 2003, s 468* (old)]. Shares in a subsidiary could not normally satisfy this test as the shares held by the parent did not count towards the shares which controlled the company. It is possible to envisage a single class of shares in a subsidiary which have, say, double the voting rights attaching to them when they are held by employees than when they are held by other people, so that employees could control the company even though it is a subsidiary of another company, although this would be somewhat unusual.

14.160 Where a chargeable event took place, an income tax charge arose on the amount by which the value of the shares was increased by that event (or would have increased but for the occurrence of some other event such as a coincidental fall in the Stock Exchange value of the shares (*ICAEW Memorandum 739 13 December 1989*)). [*ITEPA 2003, ss 449(2), 451* (old)]. If the employee's interest in the shares was less than their full beneficial ownership, the charge was on an appropriate part of such amount only. [*ITEPA 2003, ss 451(2), 455(4)* (old)].

Restrictions on shares

14.161 References above to restrictions to which shares were subject, or to rights relating to shares, included restrictions imposed (or rights inferred) by any contract or arrangement or in any other way. [*ITEPA 2003, s 450(6)* (old)]. They did not have to be restrictions inherent in the shares themselves. Thus, if the shares were pledged as security for a loan, restrictions in the loan agreement needed to be considered. Restrictions in dealing with the shares might be imposed by an employee's service agreement or by a shareholders' agreement.

Shares subject to forfeiture, etc (continues to apply to shares acquired before 16 April 2003)

14.162 *ITEPA 2003, s 422* as originally drafted, formerly *ICTA 1988, s 140A* applied where after 16 March 1998 a person acquired a beneficial interest in shares or securities in a company as a director or employee of that or any other company (called the 'employee's interest') on terms that his interest in the shares was 'only conditional'. [*ITEPA 2003, ss 422(1), 423(2), 428(3)* (old)].

14.163 A beneficial interest in shares was only conditional for this purpose so long as the terms on which the holder was entitled to the interest (whether imposed by contract or by any arrangement or in any other way):

(*a*)   provided that if certain circumstances arose (or did not arise) that person would cease to be entitled to any beneficial interest in the shares – either by way of transfer, reversion or forfeiture; and

(*b*)   on that event he would not be entitled to receive by virtue of his interest an amount equal to (or exceeding) the then open market value of the shares (or, to be precise, the amount that might reasonably be expected to be obtained from a sale of his interest in the shares in the open market if there were no provision for transfer, reversion or forfeiture of his beneficial interest in the shares).

[*ITEPA 2003, s 424(1)* (old)].

14.164 A person's interest was not to be treated as only conditional merely because:

(*a*)   the shares were unpaid or partly paid and as such liable to forfeiture for non-payment of calls (provided, of course, that there was no restriction on the holder's meeting such calls) [*ITEPA 2003, s 424(2)(a)* (old)]; or

(*b*)   the company's Articles of Association required a shareholder to offer his shares for sale or, if the shares were issued after 26 July 1999 transfer them, if he ceased to be an officer or employee of the company or of one or more companies which were members of the same 51 per cent group [*ITEPA 2003, s 424(2)(b)* (old)]; or

(*c*)   in the case of a security, the security could be redeemed on payment of any amount [*ITEPA 2003, s 424(2)(d)* (old)]; or

(*d*)   the employee could be required to offer the shares for sale, or transfer them, if he ceased to be an officer or employee of the company or of one or more companies in the same 51 per cent group (ie over 50 per cent common control) as a result of misconduct. [*ITEPA 2003, s 424(2)(c)* (old), formerly *ICTA 1988, s 140C (3A)* inserted by *FA 1999, s 43* with retroactive effect]. In most cases it would have benefitted the employee for this change to have always had effect. However, if the value of the shares had fallen since issue, the employee was adversely affected as excluding the shares left the value at issue taxable at that time under normal Schedule E rules (*Hansard, 6 July 1999, col 867*).

14.165 The reference in **14.163** to 'circumstances arising' included the expiration of a period specified in (or determined under) the terms by which the holder was entitled to his interest, the death of the holder, the death of any other person and the exercise by any person of any power conferred on him by (or under) the terms on which the interest in the shares was held. [*ITEPA 2003,* *s 424(3)* (old)]. If the shares or security were issued between 17 March 1998 and 26 July 1999 and could remain only conditional for more than five years, the section also imposed an income tax charge on the value of the interest at the time of its acquisition. *[ICTA 1988, s 140A(2)]*. If the terms on which the employee acquired his interest were such that the interest had to either cease or cease to be only conditional within that five-year period, there was no charge under *ITEPA 2003, s 423* (old) on the acquisition of the employee's interest but there could, of course, still be a tax charge under *ITEPA 2003, s 479* (old) if the shares were acquired pursuant to an option or *ITEPA 2003, s 193* if the shares were acquired at an undervalue.

14.166   *ITEPA 2003, s 427* (old) imposed an income tax charge for the year in which the shares ceased to be only conditional if at that time either the employee's beneficial interest in the shares continued (ie his interest was expanded to an unconditional one) or the employee sold or otherwise disposed of the interest that was granted to him (ie the 'employee's interest') or any other beneficial interest in the shares. *[ITEPA 2003, s 427(1), (3)* (old)]. The charge was, of course, on the difference between the open market value of the 'employee's interest' immediately after it ceased to be only conditional (or at the time of the sale or other disposal) over the aggregate of:

(*a*)   the consideration given for the acquisition of the employee's interest (see **14.162**);

(*b*)   any amount taxed as employment income in respect of that acquisition; and

(*c*)   any amount taxed as employment income under *ITEPA 2003, ss 449, 453* (old) (see **14.152**) (by reference to an event occurring before the shares ceased to be only conditional). *[ITEPA 2003, s 428* (old)].

FA 2008, s 46(3) amended the wording of this provision to ensure that no amount of tax-exempt income can be included in (*a*)–(*c*). The Act does not give an effective date so it is probably 21 July 2008, the date of Royal Assent to that Act. The exclusion of exempt income by *FA 2008* is to put the position beyond doubt from 12 March 2008. HMRC believe that it has always been necessary to exclude such income.

14.167   If the employee died while his interest in the shares or securities was still only conditional, the tax charge was triggered at that time as if he had disposed of his interest immediately before his death, and the market value was calculated on the assumption that it was known that the employee would die immediately afterwards and disregarding any restriction that terminated on the death. *[ITEPA 2003, s 431* (old)].

14.168   For the purpose of this charge a person acquired shares or securities as a director or employee of a company both if he acquired them in pursuance of a right conferred on him (or an opportunity offered to him) by reason of his employment and if he acquired them (or acquired a right to acquire them) from some other person and that person himself acquired them by reason of his (ie the assignee's) office or employment. *[ITEPA 2003, s 423* (old)].

14.169 A right acquired after a person ceased to be a director or employee was nevertheless regarded as conferred by reference to his employment unless, had that right been offered or conferred in the last tax year in which the employment was held, it would not have fallen to be treated as received by reason of the employment. [*ITEPA 2003, s 423(2)* (old)]. For a right to be acquired or conferred by reason of an office or employment, the remuneration from that employment had to be taxable on a worldwide basis, ie under Case I of Schedule E. [*ITEPA 2003, s 425(1)* (old)].

14.170 If a person acquired shares or securities (or an interest in them) as a director or employee and as a result of any two or more transactions he ceased to be entitled to his interest and either he or a connected person (within *ICTA 1988, s 839*) became entitled to an interest in any shares or securities which was only conditional (or he or a connected person became entitled to any convertible shares), the interest in those new shares or securities was treated as having been acquired by reason of the office or employment. [*ITEPA 2003, s 423(3)–(5)* (old)]. The consideration given for the employee's interest obviously included any consideration given by the connected person in such a case. [*ITEPA 2003, s 429(2)(b)* (old)].

14.171 In calculating the tax charge on the interest ceasing to be only conditional, the consideration given for the acquisition of the interest included any value or consideration given for a right to acquire the shares or for anything by virtue of which the employee's interest in the shares ceased to be wholly conditional (eg if he made a payment to have the condition removed). [*ITEPA 2003, s 429(3)* (old)]. Consideration given partly for one thing and partly for another had to be apportioned on a just and reasonable basis. [*ITEPA 2003, s 429(4)* (old)]. The performance of any duties of or in connection with the employment in question was not consideration for this purpose. [*ITEPA 2003, s 429(5)* (old)]. Obviously, no amount could be counted as consideration more than once. [*ITEPA 2003, s 429(6)* (old)]. *ITEPA 2003, s 485*, which dealt with consideration on assignments, etc, and on share exchanges, also applied for this purpose. [*ITEPA 2003, s 430* (old)]. So did *ITEPA 2003, s 487(1)*, which defines director and employee, with the modifications that references to a body corporate were limited to a company. References to the release of a right included agreeing to the restriction of its exercise and 'shares' included stock and any other interest of a member of a company. [*ITEPA 2003, s 430(6)* (old)].

Capital gains tax

14.172 The effect of many of the above provisions is to treat as income part of the proceeds or value of shares, which is capital under general principles. Accordingly, relief against capital gains tax is needed to avoid double taxation. Where the income tax charge arises on an actual disposal, of either shares or rights, relief is given by *TCGA 1992, s 37(1)*, which excludes from the consideration for capital gains tax purposes the amount taxed as income.

14.173 Where the income tax charge arises on a notional disposal, relief is given by *TCGA 1992, ss 119A, 120*. *Section 120* allows a capital gains tax deduction either on the disposal or on the first disposal of the shares or interest in shares after the trigger event for the amount on which tax was charged under:

(*a*)   *ITEPA 2003, ss 447, 555* (old) (see **14.152** onwards) (including where the disposal is made by someone other than the employee) [*TCGA 1992, s 120(1)–(2)*];

(*b*)   *ITEPA 2003, s 195(2)* (share options) [*TCGA 1992, s 120(3)*];

(*c*)   *ITEPA 2003, ss 476, 477* (old) (see **14.107**) [*TCGA 1992, s 120(4)*];

(*d*)   *ICTA 1988, s 138* (which applied between 6 April 1972 and 25 October 1997 and was replaced by the *Finance Act 1998* provisions) [*TCGA 1992, s 120(5)*];

(*e*)   *ITEPA 2003, s 423* (old) [*TCGA 1992, s 120(5A)*];

(*f*)   *ITEPA 2003, s 439* (old) (convertible shares) [*TCGA 1992, s 120(5B)*];

(*g*)   *ITEPA 2003, s 526* (see **16.12**) [*TCGA 1992, s 120(6)*].

14.174   *Section 119A* (inserted by *FA 2003, Sch 22, para 50*) similarly treats 'the relevant amount' as part of the consideration for the acquisition of the securities on a disposal if it is the event giving rise to a relevant income tax charge or the first disposal after such an event. [*TCGA 1992, s 119A(1), (2)*]. The relevant amount for this purpose is of course the amount, or the aggregate of the amounts, treated as employment income by reason of events occurring no later than the disposal (and where there has been an earlier disposal of the employment-related securities, after that disposal – or the last such disposal. [*TCGA 1992, s 119A(4)*]. A relevant income tax charge is one resulting in an amount being treated as employment income under *FA 2005, s 21(3)* or one of the following provisions of *ITEPA 2003*.

(*a*)   *Section 426* (restricted securities) (see **14.26**)

(*b*)   *Section 438* (convertible securities) (see **14.59**)

(*c*)   *Section 446U* (discharge of notional loan) (see **14.94**)

(*d*)   *Section 447* (receipt of benefit) (see **14.99**) where the benefit is an increase in the market value of the securities (unless they were disposed of before 6 April 2005).

(*e*)   *Section 476* by virtue of *s 477(3)(a)* (acquisition pursuant to an option) (see **14.107**)

[*TCGA 1992, s 119A(3)* as amended by *FA 2005, s 22*].

Where the relevant amount arises under *s 476* it is increased by the aggregate of any amounts deducted under *ITEPA 2003, s 480(5)(a)* or (*b*) (see **14.113**(*d*) and (*e*)), and any relief under *ITEPA 2003, ss 428A* (see **14.55**), *442A* (see **14.67**), *481* (see **14.116**) or *82* (see **14.118**) (relief for NIC met by employee) is ignored. [*TCGA 1992, s 119A(5)* as amended by *FA 2004, 16 Sch 6* and *FA 2005, s 22(2)*]. The adjustment for NIC effectively prevents an employer's liability met by the employee from reducing the capital gains tax charge. For disposals prior to 1 September 2004 such NIC paid under *ss 481 or 482* could be deducted. [*TCGA 1992, s 119A(5)*]. If securities cease to be employment-related securities by reason of *ITEPA 2003, s 421B(6)* (see **14.21**(*b*) or *(7)* (see **14.21**(*c*)) they are treated for the purpose of *s 119A* as continuing to be employment-related (so as to not trigger the section) until the next occasion on which they are disposed of. [*TCGA 1992, s 119A(6)*].

14.175 Where after 31 August 2003 an individual acquires employment-related securities which are (or are an interest in) restricted securities (see **14.26**) or convertible securities (see **14.59**), the consideration for the acquisition is the aggregate of the price actually paid plus any amount taxed as earnings under the unapproved share scheme rules in *ITEPA 2003* (see **14.33** and **14.61**). Prior to 12 March 2008 the Act referred to any amount that 'constituted' earnings but the wording was amended by *FA 2008, s 46(1)* to make clear that it does not include exempt earnings within *ITEPA 2003, s 8*, ie amounts statutorily exempted from tax. No corresponding adjustment is made to the vendor's disposal price if the securities were not acquired by issue. [*TCGA 1992, s 149AA inserted by FA 2004, Sch 16, para 52*]. This provision is subject to *s 119A* (see **14.174**), ie *s 119A* applies where the disposal is the event giving rise to the tax charge and *s 149AA* applies to other disposals.

14.176 Where an individual has acquired shares or an interest in shares to which the special rules applying to research institution spin-out companies apply (see **14.121**) which are disposed of after 6 April 2005, if *s 149AA* does not apply in relation to the shares the consideration for the acquisition is the aggregate of the actual cost of the shares plus any amount taxed as earnings under the share scheme rules. This is subject to *s 119A* and does not affect the vendor's disposal proceeds if the shares were acquired other than by subscription. [*TCGA 1992, s 149AB inserted by FA 2005, s 22*]. This gives relief for income tax paid under the transitional rules for such shares acquired before 2 December 2004.

14.177 The capital gains tax legislation contains a general rule that where an asset is acquired or disposed of in consideration for, or in recognition of, the services or past services of the taxpayer or any other person in any office or employment, the transaction is deemed to be for a consideration equal to the market value of the asset. [*TCGA 1992, s 17*]. This is not appropriate where some of the special provisions outlined above apply. Accordingly, *TCGA 1992, s 149A* displaces this rule (for both parties) where the shares are acquired under a share option scheme. The effect is to calculate the tax by reference to the actual consideration. The section also makes clear that the value of the services themselves does not form part of the consideration. [*TCGA 1992, s 149A(3)*]. Similarly *TCGA 1992, s 149B* displaces the general rule where an individual acquires an interest in shares which are restricted securities within *ITEPA 2003, s 423*. Instead the acquisition cost is the consideration given for the interest as calculated under *ITEPA 2003, s 429* (old) (see **14.194**). [*TCGA 1992, s 149B(2)*]. The general rule is also displaced by *ITEPA 2003, s 520*, formerly *ICTA 1988, s 185(3)* (see **16.11**(*d*)) where shares are acquired under an approved share option scheme, and by *TCGA 1992, s 149C* inserted by *ITEPA 2003, Sch 6, para 212* (formerly *FA 1988, s 68(4)*) where shares are acquired under an employee priority share application within *ITEPA 2003, s 542*.

14.178 For capital gains tax purposes an option is a separate asset to the shares. [*TCGA 1992, s 144(1)*]. However, its exercise does not give rise to a disposal. Instead the acquisition of the option merges into that of the shares to become a single transaction taking place at the time of the acquisition of the shares, the option money (and any other allowable costs of acquiring the option) becoming part of the cost of the shares [*TCGA 1992, s 144(2)*]. Any amount taxed as employment income at the time of disposal is excluded from the disposal proceeds of the shares. If an option is not exercised it is a wasting asset, wasting over the period during which it is capable of being exercised. This does not apply if the option is a quoted one, but that is rare in the context of employee incentives. [*TCGA 1992, s 146*]. Where an option is granted in consideration of services in an employment or office *TCGA 1992, s 17* would normally treat it as acquired at market value. However, unless the option was granted before 15 March 1993 this section is disapplied and only the actual price paid for the option is deductible. [*TCGA 1992, s 149A*]. It is not permissible to attribute a value to the services in calculating the actual consideration. [*TCGA 1992, s 149A(3)*].

14.179 The effect of *TCGA 1992, s 17* in relation to share options was considered by the Court of Appeal in *Mansworth v Jelley [2003] STC 53* where it was held that if the grant of an option fell within *s 17*, the acquisition of the shares in pursuance of the option also does so. This is because *TCGA 1992, s 144*, the special rules on options, provides that where an option is exercised the grant of the option and its exercise are to be treated as a single transaction. [*TCGA 1992, s 144(2)*]. Accordingly if one of those transactions falls within *s 17* both must do so. Chadwick LJ thought that the particular issue raised by the appeal was unlikely to be of widespread concern and said that the effect of *TCGA 1992, s 149A* may have the effect that *s 17(1)* can have no application on the grant of an option to an employee.

14.180 HMRC thought otherwise. In a press release of 8 January 2003 they stated that the decision will generally increase the capital gains acquisition cost of the asset for people exercising options granted otherwise than by way of bargain at arm's length or by reason of employment. Most of the people affected would be employees who had sold shares that they acquired by exercising unapproved share options or Enterprise Management Incentive options. The base cost for such people would be the market value of the shares at the time the option was exercised plus the amount charged to income tax on the exercise (by virtue of *TCGA 1992, s 120*). Accordingly where an option was exercised and the shares immediately sold the overall result would be that the taxpayer would realise a CGT loss equal to the amount on which he was assessed to income tax. The other side of the coin however is that people who disposed of the shares on exercise of the option would have an unexpected CGT liability based not on the option price but on the value of the shares at the date the option was exercised. However HMRC subsequently changed their mind and now say that the CGT base cost is not augmented by any amount chargeable to income tax on the exercise of the option (HMRC Brief 30/2009). HMRC have pointed out that where a loss calculated in accordance with their 8 January 2003 press release arose on a disposal before 1996/97 (when self-assessment started) there was no mechanism for the loss to become final; it is only when the loss is utilised that it can be formally quantified. Accordingly such 'losses' cease to be available for use if they have not already been utilised. Where the loss arose after 5 April 1996 (and before 9 April 2003 – see **14.182**) but in a year for which the enquiry window is closed, that loss is still available to be utilised against future gains. HMRC consider that where a pre 5 April 1996 loss has been set against gains for which the enquiry window is still open, a taxpayer should amend his return to disallow the loss relief (Business Brief 60/2009).

14.181 HMRC amplified their view in two further press releases of 17 March 2003 and 8 August 2003. The decision does not affect people who acquired shares through approved option schemes as they are exempt from tax on exercise of the option, except on the comparatively rare occasions where there was an income tax charge under *ITEPA 2003, s 526* (see **16.12**). They consider that:

(*a*)   losses resulting from the *Mansworth v Jelley* decision for years up to 1995/96 can be brought forward and set against capital gains in the earliest 'open' year;

(*b*)   losses arising in 1996/97 cannot be utilised unless a claim to do so was made before 31 January 2003;

(*c*)   losses arising in 1997/98 could only be utilised if a claim was made before 31 January 2004; and

(*d*)   it is too late to amend a return for 1996/97 to 2000/01 and an error or mistake claim is not competent as the assessment was made in accordance with the practice generally prevailing at the time; in effect this means that if the application of *Mansworth v Jelley* would have resulted in a smaller capital gain or results in a larger loss the excess cannot be reclaimed but if it turns a gain into a loss that loss (or increased loss) can be claimed (presumably under *TMA 1970, Sch 1A*) within the normal time limits.

Under self-assessment a loss must be quantified and, if necessary, established in the year in which it arises not that in which it is sought to utilise it, so it is now too late to establish a loss in relation to any relevant year.

14.182 The law was changed in relation to the exercise of an option after 9 April 2003 by *FA 2003, s 157* to restore the position to what most people had thought it to be before the decision in *Mansworth v Jelley*. This introduced a new *TCGA 1992, s 144ZA*. This provides that where the grant of an option and its exercise are treated as a single transaction under *TCGA 1992, s 144(2)* or *(3)* *TCGA 1992, s 17* does not apply for determining the consideration for the sale, or the cost to the person exercising the option, but does apply in accordance with *s 144(3)(a)* to determine the consideration for the option. Similarly, in the less common case of a put option it does not affect the consideration received on the sale but does apply to the grant of the option itself. Where *s 17* is disapplied the value of the consideration is of course the actual price paid for the shares. [*TCGA 1992, s 144ZA(4)*]. This is a logical approach. The market value of an option reflects the consideration that would be paid on its exercise, eg if the market value of an option to acquire shares for £5 in three years time is £1 that is the price that someone would be prepared to pay for the right to buy the shares at £5. If the actual cost of the option is 10p and at the time the option is exercised the shares are worth £8 it is logical to charge income tax on 90p and capital gains tax on £2 (£8 less 10p + 90p + £5). It is not logical to charge income tax on 90p, and allow the taxpayer a 90p loss!

14.183 Where a charge to tax on employment income arises on the grant or exercise of an option, special rules are needed to treat the taxed amount as a deduction in calculating the chargeable gain. *TCGA 1992, s 120* grants such relief. If an option obtained by virtue of an individual's employment is released in consideration of the grant of a fresh option after 28 November 1995 a form of roll-over relief applies, the new option merging in with the old and any expenditure on the acquisition of the new option becoming part of the cost of the old. [*TCGA 1992, s 237A*]. Prior to 28 November 1994 this only applied where the option was granted under an approved scheme and the reason for the exchange was a company takeover. [*TCGA 1992, s 238(4)* repealed by *FA 1996, s 112(2)*].

14.184 If the company obtains consideration for the grant of the option this is taxable as a capital gain (subject to the possibility of merging into a single transaction when the option is exercised). [*TCGA 1992, s 144*]. The grant of the option may well constitute a bargain made otherwise than at arm's length – and is in any event a disposal made partly in consideration of services in the employment – with the result that the market value of the option falls to be substituted as the consideration in calculating that gain. [*TCGA 1992, s 17(1)*]. In practice, HMRC have not taken this point. However, *Finance Act 1993 (FA 1993), s 104* introduced a specific exemption from such a charge but in relation to approved schemes only. Accordingly, there seems a risk that HMRC might as a result change their practice in respect of unapproved schemes.

Corporation tax

14.185 There was generally no statutory right to a corporation tax deduction for payments to the trustees of employee share schemes prior to 1 January 2003. It had to be shown that the payment satisfied the normal wholly and exclusively test that applies to business expenses. In practice such payments were normally deductible following the decision of the Court of Appeal in *Heather v P & E Consulting Group Ltd 48 TC 293* which held that annual contributions to a trust set up by the company to give its staff the opportunity to acquire shares in the company and to remove the possibility of the company coming under the control of outside shareholders was deductible. Later cases which mainly concern trusts where the intention was that the trustees should hold the shares, not necessarily transfer them to individual employees are reviewed at **19.43**. However no deduction could be claimed where no expense is actually incurred. In *Lowry v Consolidated African Selection Trust Ltd 23 TC 259* certain employees of the company were entitled to be issued with ordinary shares in the company at par in consideration of their services. The House of Lords refused a deduction for the difference between the market value of the shares and their cost on the basis that no expense had been incurred by the company.

14.186   A deduction can no longer be claimed under general principles for the cost of providing the shares if the following rules apply (or would have done so but for *Corporation Tax Act 2009 (CTA 2009), s 1009*) (see **14.187**(4)). [*CTA 2009, s 1038(1)*]. Instead there is a statutory relief. This is in most cases far more generous than the old position as it allows a deduction for the market value of the shares at the time they are issued or otherwise acquired by the employee less the payments actually made by the employee to acquire the shares (or an option pursuant to which the shares were acquired). The government say that the new relief has been widely welcomed as a set of clear, well-written rules that work effectively to deliver what companies want; they give companies certainty against a background of uncertain accounting treatment (*Hansard Standing Committee B, 12 June 2003, col 494*). The new rules enable companies to dispense with the complex and costly trust structures that used to be needed to generate a tax deduction (*Hansard SCB, 12 June 2003, col. 495*).

14.187   The new rules give a corporation tax deduction where by reason of his (or someone else's) employment with the company a person acquires shares or obtains an option and acquires shares in exercise of that option. [*CTA 2009, s 1007(1)*]. Four conditions need to be met:

(1)   The business for the purpose of which the award of shares or grant of the option is made must be carried on by the employing company and must be within the charge to corporation tax. [*CTA 2009, s 1007(2)*].

(2)   The shares must be fully paid, irredeemable ordinary shares and must be either of a class listed on a recognised stock exchange, shares in a company that is not under the control of another company or shares in a company that is under the control of a listed company which is not a close company (and would not be one if it were resident in the UK). [*CTA 2009, s 1008(1)*].

(3)   The shares must be shares in the employing company, or in a company which at the time of the award (or of the grant of the option) is either its parent company, a company that is a member of a consortium that owns the employing company or its parent company or, if the employing company or its parent is a member of a consortium that owns another company (C), a company that is a member of the consortium (or the parent of a member) and is a member of the same commercial association of companies as C or from 17 July 2014, shares within *s 1016(1A)*. In the case of an option the shares can also be shares in a qualifying successor company (see **14.188**). [*CTA 2009, ss 1008(2), 1016*].

(4)   The employee must:

(*a*)   in the case of an award of shares be subject to income tax in respect of the award under *ITEPA 2003* (or would be subject to such tax if at all material times he were resident and ordinarily resident in the UK and the duties of the employment were performed in the UK) and *ITEPA 2003, s 446(UA)* (tax avoidance – see **14.92**) must not apply to the shares;

(*b*)   in the case of the grant of an option, be subject to income tax under *ITEPA 2003*, either in respect of the grant of the option or by virtue of *ITEPA 2003, ss 476* (or would be subject to an income tax charge on the exercise of the option if at all material times he were resident and ordinarily resident in the UK and the duties of the employment by virtue of which the option was granted were performed in the UK); or

(*c*) if the recipient acquires shares which are subject to forfeiture, is subject to income tax under *ITEPA 2003, s 427* (see **14.33**) on the shares ceasing to be subject to forfeiture or on the recipient disposing of the shares or dying without the shares having ceased to be subject to forfeiture (or would be subject to such a charge if at all material times he were resident and ordinarily resident in the UK and the duties of the employment by reason of which the award was made or the option was granted were performed in the UK).

[*CTA 2009, ss 1009, 1017*].

14.188 For the purpose of (3) above a qualifying successor company is one that acquires control of the company in which the option was granted and agrees with the option holder that he will release his right in consideration of the grant to him of a new option over shares in a qualifying company, ie one that would fall within (3) above if the acquiring company were the employing company. [*CTA 2009, ss 1022(1)–(3), 1025*]. Where there is such a takeover shares acquired in exercise of the new option are treated as having been acquired in exercise of the old one and any consideration given in respect of the grant or exercise of the new option is treated as if it had been given in respect of the old. [*CTA 2009, s 1022(4)*]. Shares are within *s 1016(1A)* if after the option is obtained the company in which the shares are to be acquired (the relevant company) ceases to be controlled by another company (the takeover), immediately before the takeover the shares met one of the other qualifying conditions but ceased to do so as a result of the takeover, the shares are acquired pursuant to the option within 90 days of the takeover, and the avoidance of tax is not one of the main purposes of the takeover [*CTA 2009, s 1016(1A)* inserted by *FA 2014, Sch 9, para 44*].

14.188A   For 2015/16 onwards if –

(*a*) a person has an employment (the actual employment) with a non-UK resident company not within the charge to corporation tax (the overseas employer),

(*b*) in performing any of the duties of the actual employment the person works in the UK for (but is not employed by) another company (the host employer), and

(*c*) the host employer is a UK resident company (or a non-resident company within the charge to corporation tax

the person is treated as having an employment with the host employer (the deemed employment), the duties of which consist of the work that the person does for the host employer [*CTA 2009, s 1007A(1)(2)* inserted by *FA 2014, Sch 9, para 42*]. A person works for another person for this purpose if he provides, and is obliged to provide, personal service to the other person [*CTA 2009, s 1007A(8)*].

14.188B   If shares (the relevant shares) are acquired because of the actual employment and, because of the work the person does for the host employer an amount of employment income is charged to tax under *ITEPA 2003* in relation to the acquisition of the shares, the shares are treated for the purpose of *s 1007* (so far as would not otherwise be the case) as if they are acquired because of the deemed employment (regardless of when the acquisition takes place) [*CTA 2009, s 1007A(3)(4)*]. References to the employing company in *s 1008* include references to the overseas employer [*CTA 2009, s 1007A(5)*]. If in relation to an acquisition of shares the amount of relief would otherwise be greater than the total amount of employment income of the employee in relation to the acquisition, the relief is limited to that amount [*CTA 2009, s 1007A(6)*]. If relief is available to more than one company in respect of the same acquisition of shares, relief can be given to only one of them [*CTA 2009, s 1007A(7)*].

14.188C   Similarly if –

(*a*)   a person has (or had) an employment with a non-UK resident company (the overseas employment),

(*b*)   he or another person obtains an option to acquire shares because of the overseas employment,

(*c*)   he has an employment (the UK employment) with a UK resident company (or an overseas company within the charge to corporation tax),

(*d*)   the person who obtained the option acquires shares pursuant to it, and

(*e*)   the employee is charged to tax under *ITEPA 2003* on an amount of employment income in relation to the acquisition because of the UK employment (or it is because of the UK employment that the employee or another person is able to acquire the shares pursuant to the option)

the option is treated for the purpose of *s 1015(1)* as if it is obtained because of the UK employment (regardless of when it is obtained) [*CTA 2009, s 1015A(1)-(3)*]. In *s 1016* references to the employing company include the company referred to in (*a*) above [*CTA 2009, s 1015A(4)*]. As with *s 1007A*, the relief is limited to the total amount of employment income taxed on the employee in relation to the acquisition, and if relief is available to more than one company it can be given to only one of them [*CTA 2009, s 1015A(5)(6)*].

14.188D   If the conditions of *CTA 2009, s 1007A(1)(2)* (see **14.188A**) are met in relation to an employment, an option to acquire shares (the relevant option) is obtained because of the actual employment, shares are acquired pursuant to that option, and because of the work the person does for the host employer an amount of employment income is chargeable to tax in relation to the acquisition of the shares, the relevant option (regardless of when it is obtained) is treated as obtained because of the deemed employment (so far as would not otherwise be the case) [*CTA 2009, s 1015B(1)-(4)*]. References to the employing company in *s 1016* include the overseas employer [*CTA*

2009, s 1015B(5)]. As with *s 1007A*, the relief is limited to the total amount of employment income taxed on the employee in relation to the acquisition, and if relief is available to more than one company it can be given to only one of them [*CTA 2009, s 1015B(6)(7)*].

14.189 Except in the case of restricted or convertible shares for which special rules apply (see **14.191** and **14.194** respectively), the amount of the corporation tax relief is the difference between:

(*a*)   the market value of the shares at the time of the award (or the exercise of the option) or the time of the disposal or death where the shares are sold or the recipient dies without the shares having ceased to be subject to forfeiture; and

(*b*)   the total amount or value of any consideration given by the recipient or any other person in respect of the shares (or in respect of the grant or exercise of the option or, in the case of shares subject to forfeiture in respect of the shares, the grant or exercise of the option (if applicable) or the shares ceasing to be subject to forfeiture).

[*CTA 2009, ss 1010, 1018*]. The consideration cannot include the performance of any duties of, or in connection with, the employee's employment with the employing company. In the case of an option (including in respect of shares subject to forfeiture) it also does not include employer's National Insurance paid by the employee by virtue of an agreement or election under *paras 3A(2)* or *3B* of *Sch 1* to the *Social Security Contributions and Benefits Act 1992* (or its Northern Irish equivalent). [*CTA 2009, ss 1010, 1018*].

Restricted shares

14.190 The rules in **14.190** are modified in the case of restricted shares (and options over such shares). The employee must either be subject to income tax in respect of the award of the shares or option or be subject to it under *ITEPA 2003, s 426* (see **14.26**) on the occurrence of a chargeable event (or he would have been so subject if at all material times he were UK resident and ordinarily resident and all of the duties of the employment were performed in the UK). [*CTA 2009, s 1009*]. In the case of an EMI option (see **16.65**) the relief is increased by the difference between the amount on which the employee would have been taxable had the option not been an EMI option and any amount taxed on the employee under the EMI code (see **16.105** and **16.106**). [*CTA 2009, s 1019(2)–(4)*].

14.191 The relief is given on the award of the shares or the occurrence of the chargeable event and the amount is the amount that is taxable on the employee on that occasion (ignoring NIC that the employee has elected to pay and excluding in relation to awards after 12 March 2008 any amount that is exempt from tax). On the death of the employee the relief is that amount that would have been taxed on him as employment income had a chargeable event occurred immediately before his death. [*CTA 2009, ss 1011, 1025, 1026*]. In determining the relief due *ITEPA 2003, ss 428(9)* (see **14.53**) and *446E(6)* (see **14.71**) must be disregarded – so must the amount of any non-commercial increase (an increase in the market value as a result of anything done otherwise than for genuine commercial purposes – see **14.80**) in the market value of the shares since their acquisition [*CTA 2009, s 1027(4)*]. The exclusion of exempt income by *FA 2008* is to put the position beyond doubt from 12 March 2008. HMRC believe that it has always been necessary to exclude such income.

14.192 If the award or grant was made partly for the purpose of the business and partly for the purpose of a business not within the charge to corporation tax the relief is reduced to such extent as is just and reasonable. [*CTA 2009, s 1012*].

14.192A This additional relief for restricted shares was extended by *FA 2014* to the situation where the shares were acquired because of an overseas employment with a non-UK company and the employee also has an employment with a UK company and tax is charged in relation to a chargeable event in relation to the shares because of the UK employment [*CTA 2009, ss 1025A, 1025B* inserted by *FA 2014, Sch 9, para 445*].

Convertible shares

14.193 If the shares are convertible shares the rules in **14.190** are again modified. Relief is given on the award of the shares (or their acquisition if they are acquired under an option), on any chargeable event in relation to the shares or at the time of the employee's death. The amount of the relief is the amount on which the employee was taxed (or would have been taxed had he been UK resident and ordinarily resident and worked wholly in the UK). [*CTA 2009, s 1031*]. In the case of an EMI option (see **16.65**) the relief is increased by the difference between the amount on which the employee would have been taxable had the option not been an EMI option and any amount taxed on the employee under the EMI code (see **16.105** and **16.106**). [*CTA 2009, s 1019(3)*]. No account is to be taken of any relief under *ITEPA 2003, ss 481* or *482* for employer's National Insurance which the employee elected to pay. [*CTA 2009, s 1019(4)*]. If the shares are also restricted shares the total relief in respect of the acquisition is limited to the greater of that due under each head. [*CTA 2009, s 1011(5)*]. On death the relief is on the amount that would have been taxed on the employee on the first chargeable event after his death had he survived. [CTA 2009, s 1019(6)]. *Sections 446G* and *446H* –securities with artificially depressed market value (see **14.65–14.76**) – must be disregarded in determining the relief due. [*CTA 2009, s 1034*]. If the award or grant is made partly for the purpose of a business that is outside the scope of corporation tax the relief is reduced to such amount as is just and reasonable. [*CTA 2009, s 1020*]. The normal meaning of chargeable event (see **14.61**) applies with the modification that a conversion of the shares into something not satisfying *CTA 2009, s 1008* (see **14.190**(2), (3)) is not a chargeable event for the purpose of this relief. [*CTA 2012, s 1032*].

Other matters

14.194 A just and reasonable apportionment must be made of any consideration given partly in respect of the shares (or grant and exercise of the option or, in the case of shares subject to forfeiture, the shares, the grant and exercise of the option or the shares ceasing to be subject to forfeiture) and partly in respect of other matters. [*CTA 2009, ss 1010(3), 1018(3)*]. If the award was made partly for the purpose of a business within **14.187**(1) above and partly for the purpose of a business in relation to which those requirements are not met the amount of the relief must be reduced to such extent as is just and reasonable. [*CTA 2009, ss 1012, 1020*].

14.195 The corporation tax deduction is given by treating the amount as an allowable business expense of the business for the purpose of which the award was made or option granted (or as a management expense in the case of an investment company or life insurance company). If the award was made (or option granted) for the purposes of more than one business within the charge to corporation tax the deduction is apportioned between them on a just and reasonable basis. [*CTA 2009, s 1013*]. Except in the case of convertible shares for which special rules apply (see **14.194**), the deduction is made in the accounting period in which the recipient acquires the shares (ie when he acquires a beneficial interest in the shares, not, if different, the time they are transferred or conveyed to him). [*CTA 2009, s3 1013(1), 1021(1)*].

14.196 In the case of convertible shares or securities the relief is the amount that constitutes earnings of the employment in respect of an award of the shares (or their acquisition pursuant to an option) but disregarding *s 437(2), (3)* (see **14.59**), any relief for employer's NIC met by the employee and in relation to awards after 12 March 2008 excluding any amount that is exempt from tax. [*CTA 2009, ss 1011(4), 1018(2), 1019(4)*]. Where the convertible shares are also restricted shares the total relief in respect of the acquisition is limited to the greater of the relief under each head. [*CTA 2009, s 1019(5)*]. The relief on a chargeable event (within *s 439(3)(a)* (see **14.61**) is the amount taxed on the employee, ignoring any relief for employer's NIC met by the employee. However a conversion into anything other than shares which meet the requirement of *CTA 2009, s 1008* (see **14.187**). [*CTA 2009, s 1032(2)*]. The relief on the death of an employee is the amount that would have counted as employment income in relation to the first event following his death had he still been alive. [*CTA 2009, s 1034*]. *Sections 446G* (see **14.76**) and *446H* (see **14.77**) must be disregarded for the purpose of both *paras 22C(6)* and *(7)*. [*CTA 2009, s 1033(4)*]. If the award or grant is made partly for the purposes of a business within the charge to corporation tax and partly for a different business the relief is reduced to such extent as is just and reasonable. [*CTA 2009, s 1035*]. Where the employee is not resident and ordinarily resident in the UK the relief is the amount on which he would have been taxable if he were. [*CTA 2009, s 1009(3), (4)*]. The relief for convertible shares is given in the accounting period in which the recipient acquires a beneficial interest in the shares under the award (or in pursuance of the option), or in which the chargeable event or the event following the employee's death takes place, as the case may be. [*CTA 2009, s 1031*]. The exclusion of exempt income by *FA 2008* is to put the position beyond doubt from 12 March 2008. HMRC believe that it has always been necessary to exclude such income. This additional relief for convertible shares was extended by *FA 2014* to the situation where the shares were acquired by virtue of an employment with an overseas company, and the employee subsequently takes up employment with (or works for) a UK company and tax is charged on a chargeable event in relation to the shares by virtue of the UK employment [*CTA 2009, s 1030A, 1030B* inserted by *FA 2014, Sch 9, para 46*].

14.197 If between the award of the shares (or the grant of the option) and the relief-triggering event (ie that mentioned in paragraph **14.187**) there is a 'qualifying transfer' (or transfers) of the whole or substantially the whole of the business for the purposes of which the award or grant was made and, as a result of that transfer or transfers, the whole or substantially the whole of that business is carried on by a successor company at the time of the relief-triggering event the deduction is obviously given to the successor company. If there is more than one successor company the relief is not apportioned. The companies must jointly nominate one of their members to receive the entire relief. A transfer is a qualifying transfer only if the transferor and transferee companies are members of the same group (51 per cent subsidiaries). [*CTA 2009, s 1036*].

14.198 If a deduction for a payment can be given under *ICTA 1988, Sch 4AA, para 2* (see **15.60**), *3* (see **15.62**), *9* or *10* (see **15.68**) in relation to a SIP such relief is given instead. [*CTA 2009, s 1037*].

14.199 Where a deduction is available under these rules for any accounting period that is the only way of giving relief for the 'cost of providing the shares'. This is the case even if a deduction could otherwise have been claimed in a different accounting period or could have been claimed by some other company. The cost of providing the shares means expenses directly related to the provision of the shares including any amount paid or payable by the employing company in respect of the participation of the employee in an employee share scheme (ie any scheme or arrangement for enabling shares to be acquired by reason of employees' employment where the shares are acquired under such a scheme). It does not however include the expenses of setting up an employee share scheme, the costs of borrowing for the purposes of the scheme, or fees, commission, stamp duty and similar incidental expenses of acquiring the shares. [*CTA 2009, s 1038*].

14.200 For the purposes of these provisions

(*a*)   An employment includes an office and members of a company whose affairs are managed by the members themselves are treated as office-holders. [*CTA 2009, s 1002*].

(*b*)   If an option to acquire shares obtained by reason of an employee's employment is exercised by the recipient after the employee's death the condition in para 14 (income tax position of the employee see **14.187**(4)) is treated as met if it would be met were the employee still alive. If an option is exercised after the death of the recipient the Schedule applies as if the recipient were still alive and the acquisition of the shares were made by him. [*CTA 2009, ss 1015(3), 1030(5)*].

(c)   Companies are members of the same group only if one is a 51 per cent subsidiary of the other or both are 51 per cent subsidiaries of a third company. A company is a parent company of another if that other is its 51 per cent subsidiary. [*CTA 2009, s 1004(1)–(4)*].

(d)   A company is a member of a consortium owning another company if it is one of five or fewer companies that between them beneficially own at least 75 per cent of the other company's ordinary share capital and each of which owns at least 10 per cent of that capital. [*CTA 2009, s 1004(5)–(8)*].

(e)   A commercial association of companies mean a company together with such of its associated companies (within *CTA 2010, s 449*) as carry on businesses that are of such a nature that the businesses of the company and the associated companies, taken together, may be reasonably considered to make up a single composite undertaking. [*CTA 2009, s 1004(9)*].

(f)   The *CTA 2010, s 1124* definition of control applies.

(g)   Market value has the same meaning as in *TCGA 1992, ss 272* and *273*. [*CTA 2009, s 1005*].

(h)   An option includes any right to acquire shares and shares includes an interest in shares and stock or an interest in stock. [*CTA 2009, s 1003(1)*].

Chapter 15

Share Incentive Plans

Introduction

15.1   Share Incentive Plans, or SIPs (formerly called All Employee Share Ownership Plans (AESOPs)) are a form of all-employee share incentive. They can be very attractive, not only because the benefits that can be obtained by employees are very generous but also because they are very flexible. Most companies will find that a SIP enables them to devise a form of incentive that is particularly suitable for their employees. However, like any all-employee share scheme, a SIP cannot be used to benefit selected employees only. For unlisted companies it also suffers from the usual problem that to obtain the full benefits of the scheme it needs to be shown that the issue price is not less than the market value of the shares at the date they are issued. This involves having to agree a value with HMRC. Not only does this incur professional fees but in practice the company is generally anxious to get the scheme off the ground and is reluctant to enter into prolonged negotiations over the valuation. This creates pressure to accept the HMRC figure, or more likely to compromise at somewhere near the HMRC figure, even though the company believes this to be excessive. Such a forced compromise could adversely affect the agreement of what the company believes to be more realistic valuations on subsequent transactions.

15.2   For this and other reasons most private companies are reluctant to introduce all-employee share schemes. However, a SIP is so attractive in other ways that it may be worthwhile to seek to overcome the problems in order to introduce such a scheme.

15.3   A SIP can provide the following:

(*a*)   free shares of up to £3,600 (£3,000 prior to 2014/15) in value each tax year for each employee;

(*b*)   'partnership shares', which are paid for by the employee out of pre-tax income, at their current value, of up to £1,800 (£1,500 prior to 2014/15) in each year;

(*c*)   'matching shares' of up to £3,600 (£3,000 prior to 2014/15) in each year (these are free shares awarded to purchasers of partnership shares; an employee can give up to two matching shares for every partnership share); and

(*d*)   for dividends per employee to be invested in purchasing (at market value) dividend shares with no higher rate tax then being payable on the dividend. Up to 2013/2014 the maximum dividend shares that could be acquired was £1,500 in each year but the maximum is now at the company's discretion,(see **15.38**).

[*Income Tax (Earnings and Pensions) Act 2003 (ITEPA 2003), Sch 2, paras 35(1), 46(1), 60* as amended by *Finance Act 2014 (FA 2014), s 49*]. The Treasury have power by Statutory Instrument to amend these figures [*ITEPA 2003, ss 35(2A), 46(6), 60(4)* inserted by *FA 2014, s 50*].

15.4   Subject to a minimum holding period, the growth in value of all of the above types of shares is completely tax-free whilst the shares remain within the SIP. When they are taken out the employee starts with a capital gains tax base cost equal to the value of the shares at the time they leave the SIP. The issue of shares can if desired be tied to performance targets although the legislation is fairly prescriptive as to how this is done.

Conditions of establishment

15.5   An SIP must meet the following conditions:

(*a*)   It must be established by a company and must provide either:

    (i)   for shares (free shares) to be appropriated to employees without payment; or

    (ii)   for shares ('partnership shares') to be acquired on behalf of employees out of sums deducted from their salaries. [*ITEPA 2003, Sch 2, para 2*].

(*b*)   It can also provide for shares ('matching shares') to be appropriated without payment in proportion to partnership shares. [*ITEPA 2003, Sch 2, para 3*].

(*c*)   The plan must be notified to HMRC. The notification must be given by 6 July in the tax year following that in which the first award date falls. If it is notified late, the scheme is a SIP only from the beginning of the tax year in which the notice is given (or the previous year if it is given before 6 July in a tax year) [*ITEPA 2003, Sch 2, para 81A(5)(6)* inserted by *FA 2014, Sch 8, para 28*]. For example if a SIP is created in 2014/15 and notification is given in August 2015, shares issued in 2014/15 will not attract tax benefits; the SIP benefits will apply only to shares issued from 6 April 2015. The notice must be accompanied by such information as HMRC may require and must contain a declaration that the requirements of *Sch 2* are met in relation to the SIP and, if shares have been awarded prior to the notification, that those requirements were met in relation to the award of the shares and have continued to be met [*ITEPA 2003, Sch 2, para 81A(2)–(4)* inserted by *FA 2014, Sch 8, para 28*]. Prior to 5 April 2014 the application had to be approved after the scheme had been established and before shares were issued [*ITEPA 2003, Sch 2, para 81*]. If HMRC refused to approve a plan there is a right of appeal to the Special Commissioners, who can backdate the approval (but not before the application for approval. [*ITEPA 2003, Sch 2, para 82*]. HMRC have published model plan rules, a model trust deed, specimen free share agreement and specimen partnership share agreement. These can be found on their website.

(*d*)   The purpose of the plan must be to provide benefits to employees in the form of shares in a company which give them a continuing stake in that company. [*ITEPA 2003, Sch 2, para 7(1)*]. It must not provide benefits to employees otherwise than in accordance with *Sch 2*. In particular it must not provide cash to the employees as an alternative to shares. It can however permit an employee to receive a benefit from a company as a result of any shares in that company being held on the employees' behalf under the SIP where the employee would have obtained the same benefit had the shares been acquired by the employee otherwise than by virtue of the plan [*ITEPA 2003, Sch 2, para 7(1A)-(1C) inserted by FA 2014, Sch 8, para 19*]. Up to 2013/14 it could not contain features which were not essential (or reasonably incidental) to the purpose of the plan [*Sch 2, para 7(2) repealed by FA 2014, Sch 8, para 19*].

(*e*)   The plan must provide that every employee who is eligible to be awarded shares under the plan and is a UK resident taxpayer (ie an employee for whom the earnings from the employment are general earnings taxable under *ITEPA 2003, s 15* (see **2.48**)) and who is resident and ordinarily resident in the UK) must be invited to participate in the plan. [*ITEPA 2003, Sch 2, para 8(1) (2)*]. It can, if so desired, allow eligible employees who are not UK-resident taxpayers to join also. [*ITEPA 2003, Sch 2, para 8(5)*]. This requires that each time shares are issued under the scheme every eligible employee must be entitled to participate. [*ITEPA 2003, Sch 2, para 5*]. The meaning of eligible employees is considered at **15.6** below.

(*f*)   The plan must not contain any features which discourage any description of eligible employees from participating in it. [*ITEPA 2003, Sch 2, para 8(3)*].

(*g*)   Every employee entitled to participate in an award of shares must do so on the same terms. [*ITEPA 2003, Sch 2, para 9(1)*]. This requirement is not infringed by the awarding of free shares by reference to an employee's remuneration, length of service or hours worked. [*ITEPA 2003, Sch 2, para 9(3)*]. However, if more than one of these criteria is used each factor must give rise to a separate entitlement and the total entitlement must be the sum of the separate entitlements. [*ITEPA 2003, Sch 2, para 9(4)*].

Example

X Ltd wishes to allocate 1,000 shares. It has eligible employees as follows:

Name	Salary	Weekly hours	Years of Service
Arthur	40,000	40	4
Barry	35,000	35	8
Charles	15,000	35	6
Doreen	45,000	40	10
Evelyn	20,000	35	10
Fanny	8,000	15	15
	163,000	200	53

It decides to issue 500 by reference to remuneration, 250 by reference to hours worked and 250 by reference to length of service. It must therefore offer Arthur 40/163 × 500 (123), 40/200 × 250 (50) and 4/53 × 250 (19) a total of 192 shares. It must offer Fanny 8/163 × 500 (24), 15/200 × 250 (19) and 15/53 × 250 (71) a total of 114 shares. It could not, for example, allocate 500 by reference to salary and 500 by reference to weekly hours multiplied by the years worked.

The company cannot award free shares by reference to any other factor. [*Sch 2, para 9(2)*]. It can, however, make the number of shares awarded to an individual subject to performance targets (called 'performance allowances'). [*Sch 2, para 9(5)*]. Such allowances are explained at **15.23**.

(*h*) No feature of the plan must have the effect of conferring benefits wholly or mainly on directors or employees receiving higher levels of remuneration (except of course to the extent that they do so because the shares are awarded by reference to salary). [*ITEPA 2003, Sch 2, para 10*]. If the company is a member of a group the plan must not confer benefits wholly or mainly on such directors or employees of the group as a whole either. [*Sch 2, para 10(2), (3)*].

(*i*) The shares must form part of the ordinary share capital of the scheme company, a company that controls it or a company which is (or controls) a member of a consortium which owns the company (or its parent company). [*ITEPA 2003, Sch 2, para 26*].

(*j*) The shares must either be of a class listed on a recognised stock exchange, shares in a company which is controlled by a listed company which is not a close company (and if it is non-UK resident would not be close were it UK resident) or shares in a company which is not under the control of another company. [*ITEPA 2003, Sch 2, para 27*]. In other words, shares in a subsidiary company can be used only if the parent company is listed and non-close or the subsidiary is itself a listed company.

(*k*) The shares must be fully paid up and (unless they are shares in a works co-operative, ie a registered industrial and provident society which meets specified conditions set out in *para 128*) not redeemable and not subject to terms which could make them redeemable at a future date. [*ITEPA 2003, Sch 2, para 28*].

(*l*) Up to 16 July 2013 the shares could not be subject to any restrictions other than that:

(i) they could be subject to a minimum holding period – it appears that this permitted only a holding period under *para 36* (see **15.21**), *61* (see **15.37**) or *67* (see **15.41**) and that there was no minimum holding period for partnership shares (see **15.35**);

(ii) they could carry restrictions which affect all ordinary shares in the company;

(iii) they could have no, or limited, voting rights;

(iv) free or matching shares could be subject to forfeiture during a period of up to three years from the date of issue of the shares on the participant ceasing to be in relevant employment or the participant withdrawing the shares from the plan (or in the case of matching shares, on the participant withdrawing the matching partnership shares from the plan); but the shares could not be subject to forfeiture by reason of an event within *ITEPA 2003, Sch 2, para 32(2)* (the terms of which were identical to *s 498*) (see **15.50**(*b*)), forfeiture must not be linked to the performance of any person or persons, and the same provision for forfeiture had to apply in relation to all free or matching shares included in the same award under the plan;

(v)   they could be subject to pre-emption rights requiring shares awarded to an employee under the plan (and which were held by the employee or a person to whom he was permitted to transfer the shares under the company's Articles of Association) to be offered for sale on the employee ceasing to be employed by his employer company or an associated company, provided that the pre-emption required was contained in the Articles of Association and applied to all employees of the company (or of the company and any company that it controlled), required the shares to be offered for sale at a specified consideration and also required non-employee holders of the same class of shares who dispose of shares to do so on the same (or not better terms).

[*ITEPA 2003, Sch 2, paras 30–33* repealed by *Finance Act 2013 (FA 2013), Sch 2, para 48*].

(*m*)   The shares must not be shares in a 'service company' (originally called an 'employer company') or in a company that controls such a company and is itself under the control of the people who make the subsidiary a service company. A 'service company' for this purpose means one whose business consists substantially in the provision of services of persons employed by it where the majority of such services are provided either to persons who control the company (including a partnership) or to an associated company. For this purpose a company is associated if both are under the control of the same person or persons (determined in accordance with *ICTA 1988, s 416 (2)–(6)*). If a partner (either alone or together with others) controls a company the partnership must also be treated as controlling it. [*ITEPA 2003, Sch 2, para 29*].

(*n*)   No conditions can be imposed on the employee's participation in an award of shares under the plan other than those specifically permitted by *Sch 2*. [*ITEPA 2003, Sch 2, para 11*].

(*o*)   The arrangement for the plan must not make any provision for loans to be made to some or all of the employees of the company (or in the case of a group plan – see **15.9** below) of any participating company. Nor can those arrangements (which includes any scheme, agreement undertaking or understanding) or the operation of the plan be associated with any such provision. [*ITEPA 2003, Sch 2, para 12*].

Eligible employee

15.6   The plan must provide that an individual can participate in an award of shares only if:

(*a*)   in the case of free shares he is eligible to participate in it at the time the award is made; and

(*b*)   in the case of partnership or matching shares he is eligible to participate in the award at the time the partnership share money relating to it (or to the matched partnership shares) is deducted from his salary (or if there is an accumulation period (see **15.31**)) at the time of the first deduction of partnership share money relating to it [*ITEPA 2003, Sch 2, para 14*].

15.7   The individual must be an employee of the company (or in the case of a group plan (see **15.9**) of a participating company). [*Sch 2, para 15*]. If the plan provides for a qualifying period he must at all times during that period have been an employee of a qualifying company, namely of the company itself or of some other company that at the time the individual was employed by it was an associated company of either the company or another company qualifying under *para 15*. [*Sch 2, para 17(2)*]. In the case of a group plan a qualifying company is:

(*a*)   a company that is a participating company at the end of the qualifying period; or

(*b*)   a company that when the individual was employed by it was a participating company; or

(*c*)   a company that when the individual was employed by it was an associated company of one within (*a*) or (*b*) or of another company qualifying under *para 15*.

[*ITEPA 2003, Sch 2, para 17(3)*].

Heads (*b*) and (*c*) were introduced to ensure that a person who moves around within a group of companies is not thereby disqualified from participating. Where a reservist is called up for service under the *Reserve Forces Act 1996* HMRC will by concession treat the employment with the Ministry of Defence as fulfilling these employment conditions. [*ESC A103*].

15.8   Such a qualifying period cannot be longer than 18 months before the date on which the award is made. In the case of partnership or matching shares it cannot be longer than 18 months before the deduction of the partnership share money or, if there is an accumulation period, longer than six months before the start of that period. [*ITEPA 2003, Sch 2, paras 16(2)–(6)*]. As an accumulation period cannot be longer than 12 months before the issue of the shares this means that in no case can the qualifying period exceed 18 months before entitlement to the shares arise. The plan can authorise the company to specify different qualifying periods in respect of different awards of shares, but for each award the same qualifying period must apply to all employees. [*ITEPA 2003, Sch 2, para 16(7), (8)*].

15.9   An employee share ownership plan established by a company that controls other companies can extend to the employees of those other companies. [*ITEPA 2003, Sch 2, para 4*]. Such a plan is called a group plan and the companies to which it extends are known as participating companies. Where a group plan is used, the identity of the participating companies must not be such that the plan is likely to confer benefits wholly or mainly on directors of group companies or on employees of group companies who receive higher levels of remuneration. [*ITEPA 2003, Sch 2, para 10*].

15.10   A group plan can also extend to employees of a jointly owned company (and of a company controlled by such a company) if one of the 50 per cent shareholders is a member of the group. A jointly owned company for this purpose is one 50 per cent of the issued share capital of which is owned by one person and 50 per cent by another and which is not controlled by any one person. A jointly owned company cannot participate in more than one plan. Nor can a company controlled by a jointly owned company (unless it was a member of the second plan prior to 24 July 2002). [*ITEPA 2003, Sch 2, para 91*].

15.11   Up to 17 July 2013, the plan had to exclude from participation any individual who had a material interest in the company. From that date such an individual is eligible to participate, and an existing SIP has effect with the omission of those exclusions [*FA 2013, Sch 2, paras 33-38*]. The rules prior to 17 July 2013 were that the plan had to exclude an individual from participation in an award of shares under the scheme if at the time (or at any time within the previous 12 months) he had a material interest in:

(*a*)   a close company whose shares can be awarded under the plan; or

(*b*)   a company which controlled such a company or was a member of a consortium which owned such a company. [*ITEPA 2003, Sch 2, para 19 repealed by FA 2013, Sch 2, para 36*].

For this purpose a material interest was beneficial ownership of over 25 per cent of the ordinary share capital of the company. [*ITEPA 2003, Sch 2, para 20 repealed by FA 2013, Sch 2, para 36*]. The ability to control directly or through the medium of other companies or by any other indirect means, more than 25 per cent of the ordinary share capital was also treated as a material interest. [*ITEPA 2003, Sch 2, para 20*]. If the company was a close company (or would have been one if the exclusions in *Income and Corporation Taxes Act 1988 (ICTA 1988), s 414(1)(a)* (non-resident companies) or *s 415* (certain quoted companies) did not apply) a person also had a material interest in the company if he possessed or was entitled to acquire such rights as would in the event of a winding up or in any other circumstances give an entitlement to receive over 25 per cent of the assets then available for distribution among the participators. [*ITEPA 2003, Sch 2, para 20(1), (3), (4)*].

15.12   An individual was also treated as having a material interest if he and associates of his had such an interest or if an associate or associates of his had a material interest in the company. [*ITEPA 2003, Sch 2, para 19(2)*]. An associate for this purpose was:

(*a*)   any relative (spouse, parent or remoter ancestor, child or remoter issue, brother or sister) or partner of the individual;

(*b*)   the trustees of a settlement (within *ICTA 1988, s 660G(2)*) in relation to which the individual or any relative of his, living or dead, was the settlor; or

(*c*)   where the individual was interested in any shares or obligations of the company which are subject to any trust (or are held in the estate of a deceased person), the trustees (or personal representatives). [*ITEPA 2003, Sch 2, para 22* repealed by *FA 2013, Sch 2, para 36*].

15.13   If the individual was previously a discretionary object of a trust, the trust owned (or had at any time in the past owned) shares or obligations of the company, and the individual ceased to be a beneficiary as the result of an irrevocable disclaimer or release, or of an irrevocable exercise by the trustees of a power to exclude him as a beneficiary, the individual was not regarded as having been interested in the shares or obligations during the 12 months prior to the award of shares, provided that both immediately after he ceased to be a beneficiary no associate of his was interested in the trust's shares or obligations and neither the individual nor any associate of his received any benefit from the trust within the 12 months prior to the individual ceasing to be a beneficiary. [*ITEPA 2003, Sch 2, para 24* repealed by *FA 2013, Sch 2, para 36*].

15.14   If the individual had an interest in shares or obligations of a company as a beneficiary of an employee benefit trust (*ITEPA 2003, ss 550, 551* – see **15.15**), the trustees were not regarded as associates of his for the purpose of **15.13**(*b*) if neither the individual nor he and associates of his (or any associate or associates of his) had at any time after 13 March 1989 been the beneficial owner of (or able to control) more than 25 per cent of the ordinary share capital of the company (either directly or through the medium of other companies or by any other indirect means). In certain circumstances a beneficiary could however be treated as owning some of the shares held by the EBT (see **15.16**).

[*ITEPA 2003, Sch 2, para 23* repealed by *FA 2013, Sch 2, para 36*].

15.15   A trust was an employee benefit trust (EBT) in relation to a company for this purpose if:

(*a*)   all or most of the employees of the company were eligible to benefit under it ; and

(*b*)   since 13 March 1989 either there had been no disposals (by way of sale, loan or otherwise) of any property subject to the trust, or all such disposals had been disposals in the ordinary management of the trust or disposals of ordinary shares in the company or of money paid outright, and such shares or money had been either:

(i)   applied for the benefit of specified individuals;

(ii)   applied for charitable purposes; or

(iii)   transferred to another EBT, a qualifying ESOT within *Finance Act 1989 (FA 1989), Sch 5*, the trustees of an approved savings related share option scheme (within *ITEPA 2003, Sch 3*) or the trustees of a CSOP Scheme (within *ITEPA 2003, Sch 4*) (see **16.13**)

[*ITEPA 2003, ss 550, 551*]

The specified individuals were:

(*a*)   employees or former employees of the company (or of another company controlled by the company);

(*b*)   spouses, former spouses, widows or widowers of such individuals; or

(*c*)   relatives (parent or remoter forebears, child or remoter issue, brother, sister, nephew or niece) of any of the individuals within (*a*) or (*b*)

[*ITEPA 2003, s 551(2), (6)*]. A SIP approved before 17 July 2013 (and any provision for forfeiture in an award made before that date) has effect with any modifications needed to reflect the amendments made by *FA 2013, Sch 2, paras 2–6* [*FA 2013, Sch 2, para 17*].

15.16   The following tests applied to determine whether the trustees of the EBT were to be regarded as associates of an individual who was a beneficiary of the trust. [*ITEPA 2003, s 549(1)*]. In applying these tests the *ICTA 1988, s 417(3), (4)* definition of associate applied, not the definition in **15.12** above, except that it did not include the trustees of an EBT as a result of the beneficiary having an interest in shares or obligations of the company which are held by the trust. [*ITEPA 2003, s 549(4)*]:

(*a*)   If the beneficiary (or an associate of his) had received a payment from the EBT and, at any time in the three years prior to making the payment, the property in the trust included any part of the ordinary share capital of the company, the beneficiary (or associate) was treated as the beneficial owner of the appropriate percentage of the ordinary share capital held by the EBT at that date (in addition to any shares held by him personally). [*ITEPA 2003, s 552*]. The appropriate percentage was:

$$\frac{P \times 100}{D}$$

Where P = the aggregate of the relevant payment and any other payments received from the EBT by that beneficiary or any associate of his during the previous 12 months (or, if greater, the aggregate of any distributions by the company to the EBT in respect of its ordinary share capital during the three years ending with the date of the payment to the beneficairy); and

D = the aggregate of any distributions made to the EBT by the company in respect of its ordinary share capital during the 12 months ending with the date of the payment to the beneficiary, and any such distributions made in the previous 12 months or the 12 months preceding that, divided by the number of such 12-month periods in which distributions were made, ie it is a third if distributions were made in each of the three years, a half if they were made in only two and the entire distributions if they were all made in a single year. If there were no distributions in the three-year period, $D = 1$.

[*ITEPA 2003, s 553*]

(*b*)   If the beneficial ownership of shares held by an EBT was attributed to a beneficiary under (*a*), and during the 12 months prior to the receipt of the payment the benficiary (or an associate of his) has received a payment from any other EBT which owned ordinary share capital in the company, the payments (or if more than one the last of them) from each of the EBTs had to be aggregated in arriving at the appropriate percentage of the shares held by each of the EBTs concerned. [*ITEPA 2003, s 554*].

(*c*)   Although not specifically stated, it is clear that if the beneficiary or any associate of his has received no payments from an EBT in the three-year period he was not regarded as associated with the trustees of the EBT.

15.17   *ITEPA 2003, ss 549–554* applied in relation to the individual for this purpose. [*ITEPA 2003, Sch 2, para 21(4)*]. In testing whether an employee benefit trust could be ignored as an associate, another employee benefit trust which also held shares in the company was treated as not being an associate of the first trust. [*ITEPA 2003, Sch 2, para 21(5)*]. In determining whether an individual had a material interest in a company he was treated as having a right to control shares if he had a right to acquire them (such as an option). [*ITEPA 2003, Sch 2, para 21(2)*]. This required option shares to be brought into account even if the option was not immediately exercisable. If the option was over unissued shares which the company was contractually bound to issue on the exercise of the option the ordinary share capital of the company had to be increased by the number of such shares in applying the 25 per cent test. [*ITEPA 2003, Sch 2, para 21(4)*]. Although irrational, it appears that only options held by the individual or by an associate were reflected in this adjustment. For example, suppose an individual owned 240 out of 1,000 issued shares. Twenty employees, including that individual had an option to acquire 15 new shares each. If all the options were exercised the individual would hold 255 out of 1,300 shares which is under 25 per cent. However, it appears that only his option can be taken into account. He was therefore deemed to hold 255 out of 1,015 shares which is over 25 per cent, so he had to be excluded from participation in the employee share ownership plan.

In considering whether an individual has a material interest in a company, shares held by the trustees of either a qualifying profit sharing scheme (see **16.4**) or another SIP which had not been appropriated to or acquired on behalf of an individual could also be ignored [*ITEPA 2003, Sch 2, para 21(6)*], ie a person was not interested in shares held generally by such a scheme merely because at a future date the trustees could decide to allocate some of them to him.

15.18   An employee cannot participate at the same time in two or more qualifying share schemes established by the same company. The plan must therefore provide that an individual is not to be awarded free shares under the plan in a tax year if in that year either:

(*a*)   shares have been (or are being) appropriated to him in accordance with a qualifying profit sharing scheme established by the company or a connected company (ie one which controls, or is controlled by, the company, one which is controlled by a third company which also controls the scheme company, or one which is a member of a consortium which owns the company or which is owned in part by the scheme company as a member of a consortium); or

(*b*)   he has (or is about to) participate in another *Sch 2* SIP established by the company or a connected company – or would have done so but for his failure to meet a performance target. [*ITEPA 2003, Sch 2, para 18*].

(*c*)   if the employer participates in an award of shares in a tax year and he has already participated in an award under another SIP established by the same or a connected company *ITEPA 2003, Sch 2, paras 35* (maximum award), *46* (maximum partnership share money deductions) and *64* (limit on amount reinvested) apply as if both (or all) of the plans were a single plan. [*ITEPA 2003, Sch 2, para 18A*].

The shares

15.19   Different rules apply to free shares, partnership shares and matching shares.

Free shares

15.20   If the plan provides for free shares it must provide that the initial market value of free shares awarded to a participant (the market value on the date of the award, but up to 16 July 2013 ignoring the existence of any restrictions or any risk of forfeiture if the shares are restricted shares) cannot exceed £3,600 £3,000 up to 5 April 2014). Shares are restricted for this purpose if there is any contract, agreement, arrangement or condition that would bring them within *ITEPA 2003, s 423* (see **14.27**) if they were employment-related securities. [*ITEPA 2003, Sch 2, para 35* as amended by *FA 2013, Sch 2, para 49* and *FA 2014, s 49*]. The Treasury have power by statutory instrument to amend the £3,600 figure [*ITEPA 2003, Sch 2, para 35(2A)* inserted by *FA 2014, s 50*]. It is not clear whether or not a risk of forfeiture under *ITEPA 2003, Sch 2, para 32(1)(b)* or (*c*) (which permits a provision for forfeiture in certain circumstances in the event of the participant withdrawing free or matching shares from the plan or withdrawing the partnership shares that triggered the right to matching shares) needs to be ignored; that risk would probably not make the acquisition 'only conditional'. *Section 424* itself provides that a risk of forfeiture in the event of the employee ceasing to be an employee does not make the shares 'only conditional'. It is not clear if that risk can be ignored or must be taken into account in valuing the shares. It appears from the wording that it is the latter, but as it would substantially devalue the shares the intention is probably that that risk should be ignored.

15.21 The plan must require the company in respect of each award of free shares to specify a holding period during which a participant is contractually bound to permit his free shares to remain in the hands of the trustees and not to assign, charge or otherwise dispose of his beneficial interest in the shares. [*ITEPA 2003, Sch 2, para 36(1)*]. The holding period must be between three and five years, must begin on the date of the award and must be the same in respect of all shares in the same award (although different periods can apply to different awards). [*ITEPA 2003, Sch 2, para 36(2), (3)*]. The participant's obligation in relation to the holding period ceases if during that period he ceases to be an employee and they are subject to the provisions of *para 37* (see **15.22**) *79* (see **15.77**) and *90(5)* (see **15.86**). [*ITEPA 2003, Sch 2, para 36(4)*].

15.22 During the holding period a participant can direct the trustees:

(*a*)   to accept a takeover bid that will result in the new holding being treated as the same as the old (ie as not giving rise to a CGT disposal by virtue of *Taxation of Chargeable Gains Act 1992 (TCGA 1992), ss 135* and *136*);

(*b*)   to accept an offer of a qualifying corporate bond for his free shares under a general offer which is made to holders of shares of the same class in the company and which is made in the first instance on a condition which if satisfied would give the offeror control of the company (within *Corporation Tax Act 2010 (CTA 2010), s 450*);

(*c*)   to accept an offer of cash (with or without other assets) for the shares which is made under such a general offer;

(*d*)   to agree to a transaction affecting the shares pursuant to a compromise, arrangement or scheme affecting all of the ordinary shares of the company (or all of those of the same class as the free shares or all of the shares which are held by a class of shareholders identified otherwise than by reference to their employment or to their participation in a SIP).

[*ITEPA 2003, Sch 2, para 37*]. From 17 July 2013, it does not matter if the general offer is made to different shareholders by different means. If in the course of a take-over offer (as defined in *Companies Act 2006 (CA 2006), s 974*) there arises a right to require the offeror to acquire the participant's free shares (or such of them as are of a particular class) the participant can direct the trustees to exercise that right. A SIP approved before 17 July 2013, has affect with any modifications needed to give effect to these changes [*ITEPA 2003, Sch 2, para 37(7), (8)* inserted by *FA 2013, Sch 2, para 20*].

15.23 If the plan provides for the issue of free shares (or the number to be awarded) being conditional on performance targets being met, the following conditions must apply:

(*a*)   the performance measure used must be based on business results or other objective criteria and must be fair and objective measures of the performance of the units to which they are to be applied [*ITEPA 2003, Sch 2, para 39(3)*];

(*b*)   the performance targets must be set for performance units comprising one or more individuals and an individual must not be a member of more than one performance unit in relation to a particular award [*ITEPA 2003, Sch 2, para 39(2), (4)*];

(*c*)   the performance allowance must be calculated by one of the two methods described below [*ITEPA 2003, Sch 2, para 34(1)*]; and

(*d*)   the plan must require the company (as soon as reasonably practicable):

     (i)   to notify each employee participating in the award of the performance targets and measures which will be used to determine the number of free shares awarded to him, and

     (ii)   to notify all qualifying employees (ie those eligible to participate in an award) in general terms of the performance measures to be used to determine the number or value of the free shares to be awarded to each employee participating in the award – but there is no need to tell employees in general any information which the company reasonably considers would prejudice commercial confidentiality. [*ITEPA 2003, Sch 2, para 40*].

Performance allowance – method 1

15.24

(*a*)   At least 20 per cent of the shares in the award must be awarded without reference to performance (and as if they were the only shares included in the award);

(*b*)   the remaining shares must be awarded by reference to performance (participation in these shares needs to be on the same terms under *ITEPA 2003, Sch 2, para 9*) (see **15.5**(*g*)); and

(*c*)   the highest number of shares within (*b*) awarded to an individual must not be more than four times the highest number of shares within (*a*) awarded to an individual. [*ITEPA 2003, Sch 2, para 41*].

Presumably head (*c*) requires an individual award to be capped at the four times figure. As the performance targets have to be set in advance it would not be possible to adopt criteria which ensures that the four times figure will not be exceeded.

If free shares of more than one class are awarded the shares of each class must separately meet these rules.

Performance allowance – method 2

15.25

(*a*)   Some or all of the shares must be awarded by reference to performance; and

(*b*)   The awarding of the shares to qualifying employees who are members of a performance unit must be on the same terms within *ITEPA 2003, Sch 2, para 9* (see **15.5**(*g*)), but the same terms need not apply to different performance units.

[*ITEPA 2003, Sch 2, para 42*].

15.26   *Paragraph 42* is a peculiar provision. As a performance unit can be a single person it appears to permit different targets being set for each individual and for the bulk of the shares to go to senior executives, ie it could be used as a highly attractive executive share scheme by giving the executives fairly easy targets and attracting 95 per cent of the available shares to executives and giving the rest of the staff tougher targets to meet to get the remaining 5 per cent. Presumably it is hoped that the need to tell all employees what is going on under *para 40* would prevent this as it would result in a lot of very disgruntled employees.

Partnership shares

15.27   If the plan provides for partnership shares it must require each qualifying employee to enter into a partnership share agreement with the company under which the employee authorises the company to deduct money from his salary (called partnership share money) for the purchase of partnership shares, and the company undertakes to arrange for partnership shares to be awarded to the employee in accordance with the plan. [*ITEPA 2003, Sch 2, para 44*]. The agreement must specify what amounts (or what percentage of salary) are to be deducted and at what intervals – although the employee and the company can subsequently agree to vary both the amounts and the intervals. [*ITEPA 2003, Sch 2, para 45(3)*]. The deduction must not exceed either £1,800 in any tax year (£1,500 up to 5 April 2014) or ten per cent of the salary payment from which it is being deducted (or if the plan provides for an accumulation period – see **15.32** – ten per cent of the aggregate of the salary payments over that period). [*ITEPA 2003, Sch 2, para 46* as amended by *FA 2014, s 49*]. Salary for this purpose is the amount subject to PAYE but excluding expenses and benefits in kind. [*Sch 2, para 43(4)*]. This appears to be the amount net of pension contributions where these are deducted from salary. If these limits are exceeded the excess must be repaid to the employee as soon as practicable. [*ITEPA 2003, Sch 2, para 46(5)*]. 'Salary' also includes any amount that would have been subject to tax as employment income (and less any expenses that would have been deductible) if the individual were within the scope of such tax. [*ITEPA 2003, Sch 2, para 43(4)(b)*]. Different limits can be set for each award of shares. [*Sch 2, para 46(4)*]. The plan can provide that the deduction must not be less than £10 on any occasion (or such lower figure as the company may decide). [*Sch 2, para 47*]. The Treasury have power by statutory instrument to amend the £1,800 figure [*ITEPA 2003, Sch 2, para 46(6)* inserted by *FA 2014, s 50*]. From 17 July 2013, the plan must provide that partnership shares are not to be subject to any provision for forfeiture [*ITEPA 2003, Sch 2, para 43(2A)* inserted by *FA 2013, Sch 2, para 50*]. From 6 April 2014, partnership shares can however be subject to provisions requiring them to be offered for sale provided that the consideration on such a sale is at least equal to the lower of the amount of partnership share money applied in acquiring the shares on behalf of the employee and the market value of the shares at the time they are offered for sale [*ITEPA 2003, Sch 2, para 43(2B) (2C)* inserted by *FA 2014, Sch 8, para 23*].

15.28   A partnership share agreement must include a notice in a prescribed form containing prescribed information as to the possible effect of deductions on an employee's entitlement to social security benefits, statutory sick pay and statutory maternity pay. [*ITEPA 2003, Sch 2, para 48*]. The prescribed information is set out in the *Employee Share Ownership Plans (Partnership Shares – Notice of Effects on Benefits, Statutory Sick Pay and Statutory Maternity Pay) Regulations 2000 (SI 2000 No 2090)*.

15.29   The plan must provide that partnership share money deducted by the employer must be paid to the trustees as soon as practicable and held by them on the employee's behalf pending investment. It must require the trustees to keep such money in a bank (authorised under the *Banking Act 1987*) building society or relevant European institution (within *ICTA 1988, s 840A(2)*). If interest is earned on the monies the trustees must be required to account for it to the employee. [*ITEPA 2003, Sch 2, para 49*].

15.30   If the plan does not provide for an accumulation period the partnership share money must be applied by the trustees in acquiring shares on behalf of the employee on 'the acquisition date'. This is set by the trustees. It must be within 30 days of the last date on which the partnership share money was deducted. The number of shares to be awarded to each employee must be determined by reference to the market value of the shares on the acquisition date. If there is a surplus (eg because the money will not buy an exact number of shares) this must be repaid to the employee unless he agrees to it being carried forward and added to the amount of the next deduction. [*ITEPA 2003, Sch 2, para 50*].

15.31   Most companies will not want to issue new shares every month. Even if the trustees can buy shares in the market they may feel that the costs of doing this on a monthly basis are prohibitive. Accordingly, the plan can provide for accumulation periods. An accumulation period cannot exceed 12 months. [*ITEPA 2003, Sch 2, para 51(1)*]. If the plan provides for accumulation periods the partnership share agreement must specify when each such period begins and ends (the first obviously beginning not later than the date of the first deduction. [*ITEPA 2003, Sch 2, para 51(3)*]. The accumulation period in respect of each award must be the same for all participants. [*ITEPA 2003, Sch 2, para 51(4)*]. The plan can also provide that in the event of a share for share exchange in relation to the company during an accumulation period the employee can agree that the money accumulated can be used to buy shares in the acquiring company. [*ITEPA 2003, Sch 2, para 51(5)*].

15.32   Where the plan provides for an accumulation period it must provide for the partnership share money to be used by the trustees in acquiring shares on 'the acquisition date', which in this instance is 30 days after the end of the accumulation period. [*ITEPA 2003, Sch 2, para 52(2), (5)*]. From 17 July 2013, the number of shares awarded to the employee must be determined in one of three ways and the partnership share agreement must specify which is to apply

[*ITEPA 2003, Sch 2, para 52(2A)* inserted by *FA 2013, Sch 2, para 79*]. The options are –

(a)   The number of shares awarded to each employee can be based on the lower of the market value of the shares at the start of the accumulation period and that on the acquisition date. [*Sch 2, para 52(3)*].

(b)   the number of shares awarded can be determined in accordance with the market value of the shares at the start of the accumulation period [*ITEPA 2003, Sch 2, para 52(3A)* inserted by *FA 2013, Sch 2, para 79*], or

(c)   the number of shares awarded can be determined in accordance with the market value of the shares on the acquisition date [*ITEPA 2003, Sch 2, para 52(3B)* inserted by *FA 2013, Sch 2, para 79*].

Any surplus must be repaid to the employee as soon as practicable after the acquisition or, if the employee agrees, carried forward to the next accumulation period. [*ITEPA 2003, Sch 2, para 52(6)*]. If the employee leaves before the end of the accumulation period the full amount deducted must be repaid to him. [*ITEPA 2003, Sch 2, para 52(7)*]. If an accumulation period comes to an end on the occurrence of a specified event the plan can provide that the partnership share money can be returned to the employee rather than used to purchase shares. [*ITEPA 2003, Sch 2, para 52(8)*]. It is not readily apparent what this is intended to cover.

15.33   The plan can, and usually will, allow the company to place a ceiling on the shares to be included in an award of partnership shares. [*ITEPA 2003, Sch 2, para 53(1)*]. For example, it could provide that no more shares are to be issued in a particular award than amounts to two per cent of the company. Without such a provision if the performance targets are significantly exceeded the company could find itself having to dilute existing shareholdings by a greater amount than was authorised by the shareholders. The partnership share agreement not surprisingly needs to contain an undertaking to notify the employees of any such restriction. [*ITEPA 2003, Sch 2, para 53(3)*]. Again, not surprisingly, the employees must be notified of the limit before any money is deducted from their salaries. [*ITEPA 2003, Sch 2, para 53(4)*]. If the ceiling is reached the entitlement of each individual included in the particular award of shares must be reduced proportionately. [*ITEPA 2003, Sch 2, para 53(5)*].

15.34   The employee must be entitled to tell the company to stop making deductions in pursuance of his partnership share agreement. He can also subsequently tell it to resume deductions – but may not make up the amounts that would have been deducted whilst the agreement was suspended. Where the plan provides for accumulation periods, it can if desired prevent the employee restarting deductions more than once in any such period. If an employee asks for deductions to stop or to restart, the request must be actioned within 30 days (a restart requiring a deduction on the first pay day after the expiry of the 30 days). [*ITEPA 2003, Sch 2, para 54*].

15.35   The employee must have an entitlement to withdraw at any time from the partnership share agreement on giving 30 days' notice in writing. In such an event any deductions held on his behalf must be repaid to him. [*Sch 2, para 55*]. Any deductions held on behalf of an employee must also be repaid to the employee if the plan ceases to qualify because of *ITEPA 2003, Sch 2, para 81H* (see 15.100) or *81I* (see **15.101**) or up to 2013/14 approval of the plan was withdrawn or a plan termination notice (see **15.83**) was received in respect of the plan). [*ITEPA 2003, Sch 2, para 56* as amended by *FA 2014, Sch 8, para 25*]. In all cases the repayment must be made as soon as practicable after the trigger event. The employee must also be entitled to withdraw all or any of his partnership shares from the plan at any time. [*ITEPA 2003, Sch 2, para 57*]. If he does so within five years of acquiring the shares a tax charge will arise (see **15.47**). From 17 July 2013, the plan must provide that partnership shares are not to be subject to any provision for forfeiture [*ITEPA 2003, Sch 2, para 43(2A)* inserted by *FA 2013, Sch 2, para 50*].

Matching shares

15.36   If the plan provides for matching shares it must provide for them:

(*a*)   to be of the same class and carry the same rights as the partnership shares to which they relate;

(*b*)   to be awarded on the same day as the partnership shares; and

(*c*)   to be awarded to all employees who participate in the award on exactly the same basis. [*ITEPA 2003, Sch 2, para 59*].

The partnership share agreements need to specify the ratio of matching shares to partnership shares for the time being offered by the company (which must not exceed two matching shares for each partnership share and must be applied by reference to the number of shares not the percentage holdings); the circumstances and manner in which the company can change the ratio; and that the company will inform the employee of any change in the ratio before partnership shares are awarded to him under the agreement. [*ITEPA 2003, Sch 2, para 60*]. The Treasury have power by statutory instrument to amend the prescribed ratio [*ITEPA 2003, Sch 2, para 60(4)* inserted by *FA 2014, s 50*].

15.37   The holding period that relates to free shares (see **15.21**) must also apply to matching shares. [*ITEPA 2003, Sch 2, para 61*].

Reinvestment of dividends

15.38   The plan can either require or permit (at the company's option) any cash dividends in respect of plan shares held by the trustees on behalf of participants to be applied in acquiring further shares ('dividend shares'). [*ITEPA 2003, Sch 2, para 62*]. However, the total dividend reinvestment per employee prior to 2013/14 was limited to £1,500 in any tax year. [*ITEPA 2003, Sch 2, para 64*]. If the employee is a participant in more than one SIP established by the company or an associated company, the £1,500 applied to the aggregate dividends from all of those SIPs. [*ITEPA 2003, Sch 2, para 64(2), (6)*]. *Para 64* was repealed by *FA 2013, Sch 2, para 88*. From 17 July 2013 if the company opts to issue further shares it must tell the trustees the amount of the cash dividends to be applied in buying further shares and how that amount is to be determined [*ITEPA 2003, Sch 2, para 62(1A)* inserted by *FA 2003, Sch 2, para 83*].The company can revoke or modify its decision to require or permit the acquisition of dividend shares. [*ITEPA 2003, Sch 2, para 62(4)*]. Any dividends in excess of the investment limit or which the company opts not to re-invest must be paid to the participant as soon as practicable. [*ITEPA 2003, Sch 2, paras 64(3),69*].

15.39   Dividend shares must be of the same class and carry the same rights as the shares on which the dividend is paid and must not be subject to any provision for forfeiture – even apparently in the event of the employee leaving the employment in circumstances that his main shares become subject to forfeiture. [*ITEPA 2003, Sch 2, para 65(1)*]. For 2014/15 onwards, dividend shares can however be subject to provisions requiring them to be offered for sale provided that the sale consideration is at least equal to the lower of the amount of the cash dividends applied in acquiring the shares on behalf of the employee and the market value of the shares at the time they are offered for sale [*ITEPA 2003, Sch 2, para 65(2)* inserted by *FA 2014, Sch 8, para 26*].

15.40   In exercising their power in relation to the acquisition of dividend shares the trustees must treat participants fairly and equally. [*ITEPA 2003, Sch 2, para 66(1)*]. They must acquire the dividend shares on 'the acquisition date', which for this purpose is a date fixed by the trustees which must be within 30 days of the receipt of the dividend by the trustees. [*ITEPA 2003, Sch 2, para 66(2), (4)*]. The number of dividend shares must be determined by the market value of the shares on the acquisition date. [*ITEPA 2003, Sch 2, para 66(3)*]. If the dividend is insufficient to allow the acquisition of any shares (or there is a surplus after the acquisition of such shares) the excess dividend can be retained by the trustees (whether the participant likes it or not!) and carried forward to add to the next cash dividend. They must identify such cash separately to ensure that it is only used for this purpose. [*ITEPA 2003, Sch 2, para 68(1)–(3)*]. Any carried forward amount that is not invested in dividend shares within three years from the date the dividend was paid must be paid over to the recipient. If the employee leaves the employment before the amount is invested or a plan termination notice (see **15.83**) is received the cash in hand must similarly be paid to the participant. [*ITEPA 2003, Sch 2, para 68(4)*]. Up to 5 April 2013 where cash was held from more than one dividend the cash from the earliest dividend was deemed to be invested first. [*ITEPA 2003, Sch 2, para 68(6)* repealed by *FA 2013, Sch 2, para 90*].

15.41   The minimum holding period requirement that applies to free shares (see **15.21**) also applies to dividend shares with the proviso that the holding period for dividend shares must be three years. [*ITEPA 2003, Sch 2, para 67*].

The tax position

15.42   In general no tax is payable in relation to free shares, partnership shares, matching shares, dividend shares or cash awaiting investment while the shares or cash remain in the hands of the trustees. If shares are taken out of the plan during the holding period their removal will trigger a tax charge though. The detailed rules are considered below. From 18 June 2004 these tax exemptions do not apply if the main purpose (or one of the main purposes) of the arrangements under which the shares are awarded or acquired is the avoidance of tax or NIC. [*ITEPA 2003, s 489(4)*].

Income tax

15.43

(*a*) The value of the shares at the time of an award or acquisition of shares under the plan is not treated as taxable income. [*ITEPA 2003, s 490*].

(*b*) An income tax charge will arise on any capital sum received by a participant if it relates to dividend shares that were acquired within three years prior to the receipt of the capital sum, or if it relates to other plan shares that were acquired within the prior five years. [*ITEPA 2003, s 501*]. A 'capital receipt' for this purpose includes any amount of money's worth other than proceeds of disposal of the shares, new shares received on a take-over or an amount which constitutes income of the recipient (or would do but for *Schedule 2*). [*ITEPA 2003, s 502*]. If the participant asks the trustees to sell some of his shares in order to take up the rights on the remainder under a rights issue (to acquire shares in the same company only) those sale proceeds are not a capital receipt. [*ITEPA 2003, s 502(5)*].

(*c*) Partnership share money deducted from an employee's salary is not taxable as employment income [*ITEPA 2003, s 492*], ie partnership shares are brought out of pre-tax income.

(*d*) Nevertheless, up to 5 April 2006 the deduction of partnership money did not reduce the salary for the purpose of determining the amount of the employee's pensionable earnings under either a retirement benefit scheme (ie a company pension scheme) a retirement annuity or a personal pension. [*ITEPA 2003, s 492(2)*].

(*e*) An income tax charge will arise on any amount paid over to the employee under *ITEPA 2003, Sch 2, para 46(5)* (see **15.27**), *50(5)(b)* (see **15.30**), *52(6)(b)* (see **15.32**), *52(7)* (see **15.32**), *52(8)* (see **15.32**), *55(3)* (see **15.35**) or *56(1)* (see **15.35**). The amount is taxable as income of the year in which the amount is paid over to the employee. [*ITEPA 2003, s 503*].

(*f*) An income tax charge arises on the amount or value of any money or money's worth received by the participant in respect of the cancellation of his partnership share agreement. [*ITEPA 2003, s 504*].

(*g*) The amount applied by the trustees in acquiring dividend shares is not treated as income of the participant for any tax purpose and the recipient has no entitlement to tax credit in respect of any such amount. [*Income Tax (Trading and Other Income) Act 2005 (ITTOIA 2005), s 770* formerly *ITEPA 2003, s 493*].

(*h*)   Similarly, no income tax charge (and no tax credit) arises on the amount of a dividend that is retained by the trustees under *Sch 2, para 68(2)* (see **15.40**) pending investment. [*ITTOIA 2005, s 770(2)*]. However, if any such amount is subsequently paid over to the participant under *Sch 2, para 68(4)* (see **15.40**) the participant is taxable on that amount for the tax year in which it is paid over to him and the tax credit is at the rate in force in that year not the year in which the dividend was received by the trustees. [*ITTOIA 2005, ss 392, 393*]. A tax charge similarly arises on the participant if the shares cease to be subject to the SIP within the three-year minimum holding period (see **15.21**). The dividends are deemed to have been distributed to the participant in the tax year in which that condition is breached. [*ITTOIA 2005, s 394*]. If the shares cease to be subject to the plan by virtue of *para 65(2)* (provision requiring dividend shares to be offered for sale) the amount of the distribution treated as made is the proportion of the market value of the shares at the time they are offered for sale that so much of the amount of cash dividends applied to acquire the shares as represents a cash dividend paid in respect of plan shares in a UK resident company, bears to the amount of the cash dividend, if that is less than the above amount [*ITTOIA 2005, s 394(3A) (3B)* inserted by *FA 2014, Sch 8, para 57*].

(*i*)   Dividends or other distributions received by the trustees are not liable to tax in their hands under *ITA 2007, s 479* (tax at the rate applicable to trusts) except to the extent that:

    (i)   the shares to which they relate are not awarded to participants (treating earlier acquisitions as awarded first) within two years of their acquisition (five years if at the time of their acquisition none of the shares in the company in question are readily convertible assets but if they subsequently become so the two-year period again applies from the date of the change) and ten years if a deduction is allowed under *Corporation Tax Act 2009 (CTA 2009), s 989* (formerly *ICTA 1988, Sch 4AA, para 9*) *(see **15.68**)* or

    (ii)   if earlier, the shares are disposed of by the trustees (other than by being awarded to a participant).

[*ITA 2007, ss 488–490*].

Where the trustees acquire shares because they are forfeited by the participant the date of acquisition by the trustees is the date of forfeiture. [*ITA 2007, s 490(3)*].

(*j*)   *ICTA 1988, s 234A(4)* (information relating to distributions to be provided by nominee) does not apply in relation to any amount applied by the trustees in acquiring dividend shares on behalf of a participant. [*ITEPA 2003, s 493*]. However, it (and *s 234A(5)–(11)*) does apply to an amount chargeable to tax under *ITEPA 2003, Sch 2, para 68*, (see **15.40**), or *s 502* (see **15.43**(*b*)). [*ITEPA 2003, s 493, Sch 2, para 80(4)*]. *ICTA 1988, s 234A(4)–(11)* also applies in relation to the balance of any cash dividend paid over to the participant under *ITEPA 2003, Sch 2, para 64*, (see **15.38**). [*ITEPA 2003, Sch 2, para 80(4)*].

(*k*)   Incidental expenditure of the trustees or the employer in operating the plan (ie the running costs) does not give rise to any charge to income tax on employees. [*ITEPA 2003, s 499*].

Charge on shares ceasing to be subject to plan

Free or matching shares

15.44   If free or matching shares cease to be subject to the plan (eg because they are removed by the participant, sold by the trustees at his direction, or the plan ceases to be a qualifying one) less than three years after the date they were awarded to the participant an income tax charge arises on the market value of the shares when they cease to be subject to the plan. [*ITEPA 2003, s 505(1), (2)*]. The market value of shares for SIP purposes is determined in the same way as for capital gains tax under *TCGA 1992, ss 272–274*. [*ITEPA 2003, Sch 2, para 92(1)*]. This is subject to *para 35(3)* (see **15.20**) which requires any risk of forfeiture (and up to 16 July 2013 any restriction) to be ignored [*ITEPA 2003, Sch 2, para 92(2)*]. HMRC and the trustees can agree a valuation date [*ITEPA 2003, Sch 2, para 92(3)* as amended by *FA 2013, Sch 2, para 55*].

15.45   If they have been in the plan for at least three years but less than five, an income tax charge still arises but in this case it is on the lower of the market value at the date the shares were awarded to the participant or at the date when they ceased to be subject to the plan. [*ITEPA 2003, s 505(3)*]. If the shares cease to be subject to the plan by virtue of *ITEPA 2003, Sch 2, para 43(2B)*, the reference to market value of the shares must be read as the market value of the shares at the time they are offered for sale [*ITEPA 2003, s 506(3A)* inserted by *FA 2014, Sch 8, para 8*]. If the charge is on the market value on the date of the award and a charge has previously arisen under *ITEPA 2003, s 501* (see **15.43**(*c*)) in relation to a capital receipt from the shares, the tax due under *section 505(3)* is reduced by that already paid under *section 501*. [*ITEPA 2003, s 505(4)*]. It should be noted that this relief is given by reducing the tax not the income. The tax due is reduced by any tax paid under *section 446L* (see **14.75**) where the shares have an artificially enhanced market value. [*ITEPA 2003, s 505(4A)*].

15.46   If the shares cease to be subject to the plan by virtue of the participant assigning, charging or otherwise disposing of his beneficial interest in the shares in breach of *ITEPA 2003, Sch 2, para 36(1)(b)* (see **15.21**) the full market value of the shares at the date they cease to be subject to the plan is taxed irrespective of how long they have been held in the plan [*ITEPA 2003, s 507*]. As the tax charge is calculated on the value of the shares when they leave the plan no relief needs to be given for tax previously paid on capital receipts under *section 501*.

Partnership shares

15.47   If partnership shares cease to be subject to the plan less than three years from their acquisition date (see **15.30** and **15.32**) the employee is again taxable as income on the relevant amount (the market value of the shares when they cease to be subject to the plan up to 2013/14). [*ITEPA 2003, s 506(1), (2)*]. The relevant amount is the market value of the shares when they cease to be subject to the plan, except that if they cease to be subject to the plan by virtue of *ITEPA 2003, Sch 2, para 43(2B)* (provision requiring partnership shares to be offered for sale – see **15.27**) then it is the lower of the amount of partnership share money used to acquire the shares and the market value of the shares at the time they are offered for sale [*ITEPA 2003, s 506(2B)*] inserted by *FA 2014, Sch 8, para 8*]. *ITEPA 2003, Sch 2, para 92(2)*, which requires any restriction to be ignored in valuing the shares, (see **15.44**) also applies for this purpose [*ITEPA 2003, s 506(2C)*]. If the shares have been held for at least three years but less than five the income tax charge is on the lower of the amount of partnership share money used to acquire the shares or the market value of the shares when they cease to be subject to the plan. [*ITEPA 2003, s 506(3)*]. If the tax charge is on the partnership share money and there has been a previous charge under *s 501* on a capital receipt the tax payable under *s 506(3)* is reduced by that previously paid under *s 501*. [*ITEPA 2003, s 506(4)*]. The tax due is reduced by any tax paid under *s 446L* (see **14.85**) where the shares have an artificially enhanced market value. [*ITEPA 2003, s 506(4A)*].

15.48   As the partnership share money should be equal to the value of the shares at the time of acquisition it will be seen that for all practical purposes the charge on partnership shares is the same as that on free or matching shares. It is reasonable that no deduction should be allowed for the cost of the shares as the shares were purchased out of pre-tax income so by taxing the entire value the legislation both claws back the initial tax exemption and if the shares were in the plan for less than three years taxes the growth in value.

Dividend shares

15.49   If dividend shares cease to be subject to the plan within three years from the date they were acquired, the participant is taxable on the amount of the dividend used to acquire the shares, but in the tax year in which they cease to be subject to the plan. [*ITTOIA 2005, s 394*]. The charge is not as employment income. It imposes tax on the dividend used to acquire the shares. Any tax credit to which the participant is entitled is calculated by reference to the tax credit fraction in force when the shares leave the plan, not when the initial dividend was paid. [*ITTOIA 2005, s 394(5)*]. At least that seems to be the intention. Any tax due under *ITTOIA 2005, s 394* (after deduction of any related tax credit) can be reduced by the tax previously paid under *ITEPA 2003, s 501* (see **15.43**(*b*)) on a prior capital distributions. [*ITTOIA 2005, s 395*].

Exceptions

15.50   No income tax charge arises on shares ceasing to be subject to the plan:

(*a*)   if the shares have been held in the plan for at least five years – three in the case of dividend shares. [*ITEPA 2003, ss 497, 505, 507*]; or (*b*) if the shares cease to be subject to the plan on the participant ceasing to be in relevant employment if this is:

    (i) because of injury or disability,

    (ii) on dismissal by reason of redundancy,

    (iii) by reason of a transfer to which the *Transfer of Undertakings (Protection of Employment) Regulations 1981* apply,

    (iv) by reason by a change of control or other circumstance which ends the associated company status of his employer company,

    (v) by reason of his retirement (before 17 July 2013) only if this was on or after reaching the retirement age specified in the plan (which had to be the same for men and women and could not be less than 50), or

    (vi) on his death

    [*ITEPA 2003, s 498* as amended by *FA 2013, Sch 2, para 2*]; or

(*c*) if the participant is not chargeable to tax as employment income in respect of the employment at the time of the award giving rise to the shares. [*ITEPA 2003, s 500*].

15.50A From 17 July 2013, a participant is not liable to income tax on shares (the relevant shares) in a company being withdrawn from the plan if the withdrawal of the shares from the plan relates to:

(*a*) a transaction resulting from a compromise, arrangement or scheme which is applicable to (or affects) all the ordinary share capital of the company (or all of the shares of the same class as the relevant shares), or all the shares (or shares of the same class) which are held by a class of shareholders identified otherwise than by reference to their employment or their participation in a SIP [*ITEPA 2003, s 498(3), (9)* inserted by *FA 2013, Sch 2, para 19*];

(*b*) an offer (which can be made to different shareholders by different means) forming part of a general offer which is made to holders of shares of the same class as the relevant shares (or to holders of shares in the company) and which is made in the first instance on a condition such that, if it is satisfied, the person making the offer will have control of the company (within the meaning of *CTA 2010, s 450*) [*ITEPA 2003, s 498(3)(10)(11)(12)*];

(*c*) the application of *Companies Act 2006, ss 979 – 982* or *983 – 995* in the case of a take-over offer which relates to the company and, if it has more than one class of shares, the class or classes to which it relates includes the relevant shares [*ITEPA 2003, s 498(3)(13)*];

and as a result of which the participant receives cash (and no other assets) in exchange for the relevant shares [*ITEPA 2003, s 498(3)*]. It does not matter if the participant receives other assets in exchange for other shares [*ITEPA 2003, s 498(4)*].

15.50B This exception does not apply to the relevant shares if in connection with the offer etc, a course of action was open to the participant which, had it been followed, would have resulted in other assets being received for the relevant shares (eg the participant has the option of taking either cash or shares in the offer and chose to take cash) [*ITEPA 2003, s 498(5)*]. Nor does it apply to the relevant shares if it is reasonable to suppose that the relevant shares would not have been awarded to the participant if the offer etc had not been made (or if any arrangements for the making of the offer etc which were in place or under consideration at any time not been in place or under consideration) [*ITEPA 2003, s 498(6)*]. Arrangements for this purpose includes any plan, scheme, agreement or understanding, whether or not legally enforceable [*ITEPA 2003, s 498(8)*]. In the case of dividend shares, the references to shares being awarded to participants includes their being acquired by the trustees on the participant's behalf [*ITEPA 2003, s 498(7)*].

PAYE

15.51 Where a participant becomes chargeable to income tax as a result of shares ceasing to be subject to the plan, *ITEPA 2003, s 696* (readily convertible assets) applies as if he were being provided with assessable income in the form of those shares at the time the shares cease to be subject to the plan and in respect of the relevant employment and *s 696* applies as if the taxable amount were the amount referred to in that provision. [*ITEPA 2003, s 509*].

15.52 Where an obligation to make a PAYE deduction arises on the shares ceasing to be subject to the plan (which will be the case if they are readily convertible assets) the trustee must pay over the necessary sum to the company unless the plan requires the employee to make such a payment to the company. [*ITEPA 2003, s 510*]. If the amount so paid to the employer exceeds the PAYE due, the excess is repayable to the employee. [*ITEPA 2003, s 511*]. *Section 710* applies to the PAYE. Accordingly, if the amount of the PAYE is not paid by the employee to the employer within 90 days the taxable amount must be grossed up. If the trustees transfer the shares to the employee they clearly ought to insist on his paying over the money to them before transferring the shares to him. They also have power to sell some of the shares, or other shares they hold for the employee, to raise the funds to pay the PAYE (see **15.77**).

15.53 If at the time the shares cease to be subject to the trust there is no employer company to which the PAYE Regulations apply, or HMRC consider that it is impracticable for any such company to account for the PAYE and direct that the trustees should do so, the trustees must themselves deduct PAYE and account for it as if the participant were a former employee of the trustees. This will require them to deduct tax at the basic rate. [*ITEPA 2003, s 511*]. If a participant disposes of his beneficial interest in any of his plan shares to the trustees (and they are deemed by *TCGA 1992, Sch 7D, para 6* (see **15.80**) to have disposed of the shares) PAYE must be applied as if the consideration paid by the trustees to the participant had been an amount received by them as the proceeds of disposal of plan shares [*ITEPA 2003, s 512*]. The same provisions apply to the receipt by the trustee of money which constitutes (or forms part of) a capital receipt on which a participant is chargeable to income tax (see **15.43**(*b*)). [*ITEPA 2003, s 514*].

Capital gains tax

15.54   The increase in value of the shares is not chargeable to capital gains tax on either the beneficiary or the trustees while the shares remain 'subject to the plan', ie until the earliest of the times at which either the shares are withdrawn from the plan, the employee ceases to be employed by the company without remaining or immediately becoming employed by an associated company, or the trustees dispose of the shares under *ITEPA 2003, Sch 2, para 79* (see **15.79**) to meet a PAYE obligation. [*TCGA 1992, Sch 7D*]. Shares are withdrawn from the plan for this purpose if they are transferred to the employee (or another person) on the direction of the employee, the employee assigns, changes or otherwise disposes of his beneficial interest in the shares, or the shares are disposed of by the trustees on the direction of the participant with the trustees having an obligation to account for those proceeds to the participant or some other person.

15.55   It accordingly appears that if the employee wishes (and the trustees agree) he can leave the shares in the plan indefinitely and thus prolong the period of this capital gains tax exemption.

15.56   When the shares cease to be subject to the plan there is a deemed (tax-free) disposal and reacquisition at the market value at that time. [*TCGA 1992, Sch 7D, para 2(1)* inserted by *ITEPA 2003, Sch 6, para 221*]. Notwithstanding, this, the beneficiary is (and must be) treated as becoming absolutely entitled to the shares as against the trustees at the initial date that the shares are awarded to him under the plan. [*TCGA 1992, Sch 7D, para 3*]. This relieves the trustees of any risk of CGT from that date. So that plan shares do not distort the CGT identification rules, whilst they remain subject to the plan they are treated as being of a different class to other shares in the company held by the employee. [*TCGA 1992, Sch 7D, para 4*]. If the trustees acquire shares from an *Finance Act 1989 (FA 1989)* ESOT such shares are also treated as a separate class from other unallocated shares held by the trustees while they have not been appointed to an employee. [*TCGA 1992, Sch 7D, para 4*]. Shares acquired by virtue of a payment for which a deduction was allowed under *CTA 2009, s 989* (see **15.68**) which have not yet been awarded under the plan must be treated as of a different class from other shares held by the trustees which were not acquired out of that payment [*TCGA 1992, Sch 7D, para 4(6)*].

15.57   The exemption of the trustees on gains accruing prior to the shares being awarded to employees is dependent on the shares having been awarded to employees (or acquired on their behalf as dividend shares) under the plan within a specified period. If none of the shares in the company are readily convertible assets this is five years from the date of their acquisition. If they are, it is two years (and if they become readily convertible during the trustees' period of ownership they must be awarded within two years of that time if that is earlier than the expiry of the five-year period). [*TCGA 1992, Sch 7D, para*

2(2), (3)]. In applying this test, shares acquired by the trustees are deemed to be awarded to employees on a first in/first out basis. [*TCGA 1992, Sch 7D, para 2(5)*].

15.58   If shares allocated to an employee are subsequently forfeited they are treated as having been disposed of by the employee to the trustees (as a tax-free disposal) and reacquired by the trustees at their then market value. [*TCGA 1992, Sch 7D, para 7*]. If the trustees acquire shares from an existing qualifying profit sharing scheme the disposal and acquisition is deemed to be at a no gain/no loss price and, for the purpose of determining whether they are taxable when they dispose of the shares, the plan trustees are treated as acquiring the shares when the profit sharing scheme trustees did so (ie to avoid tax they need to allocate the shares to employees within five or two years as appropriate of the profit sharing trustees having acquired them). [*ITEPA 2003, Sch 7, para 86*]. If a CGT charge does arise on the SIP trustees the date of the transfer from the profit sharing scheme must be used as the acquisition date for taper relief purposes though. [*ITEPA 2003, Sch 7, para 86*].

15.59   If on a rights issue the SIP trustees sell some of the rights in order to take up the others (see **15.70**) the gain on that disposal is not taxable provided that the rights issue extends to all ordinary shares in the company. [*TCGA 1992, Sch 7D, para 8*]. This is an odd provision. It is clearly intended to stop rights being offered to the trustees only, but where a company has more than one class of ordinary shares a rights issue will often be confined only to the class which comprises the rights shares. The meaning of 'ordinary shares' is unclear. Although 'ordinary share capital' is defined 'ordinary shares' is not and there is no logical reason to assume that the two expressions have the same meaning.

Corporation tax

15.60   The employer company (eg the subsidiary company that employs a participant not the parent company whose shares he is awarded) is allowed a deduction in calculating its trading profits for the market value of free or matching shares awarded to its employees. The amount deductible is the value at the time the shares are acquired by the trustees (not when they are awarded to the employee if that is a later date) but is allowed only in the accounting period in which they are awarded to employees. [*CTA 2009, s 994*]. That is the only way in which relief can be given in respect of the provision of the shares, eg if a deduction falls to be made under generally accepted accounting principles as the cost of providing an employee benefit, that deduction is specifically disallowed for tax purposes. In determining what shares are awarded to employees the shares held by the trustees are deemed to be awarded on a first in/first out basis. [*CTA 2009, s 994(6)*].

15.61   If the shares are awarded under a group plan the market value is the relevant proportion (that which the number of shares awarded to employees of the company concerned bears to the total number of shares in the award) of the total market value of all of the shares included in the award. [*CTA 2009,* *s 994(4)*]. In theory this is helpful in the case of unquoted shares, as the total award is likely to have a greater value per share than if the shares awarded to employees of a single company had to be looked at separately. In practice it may be unworkable. It appears to assume that all of the shares included in an award will have been acquired by the trustees on the same date, which need not necessarily be the case.

15.62 A corporation tax deduction is also allowed to the employer company in relation to partnership shares to the extent, if any, that the market value of those shares at the time that they were acquired by the trustees exceeds the partnership share monies (see **15.27**) paid by the employees. Again, the deduction is given only in the accounting period in which the award is made. [*CTA 2009, s 995*].

15.63 Clearly, a corporation tax deduction cannot be given (unless it appears that it would have been due apart from these SIP rules) if at the time the shares are awarded to an employee he is not taxable on them as employment income (or would not be so taxable if his earnings were remitted), ie if the shares are awarded in breach of the SIP rules. [*CTA 2009, s 996*]. No deduction can be allowed if either the company or an associated company has already had a deduction for the same shares on providing them to the same or any other trust (even apparently to one which is not for the benefit of qualifying employees). A first in/first out basis applies to determine which shares are caught by this provision. [*CTA 2009, s 996(5)*].

15.64 No deduction is allowed for shares that are acquired on behalf of employees as dividend shares. [*CTA 2009, s 997*]. No deduction is allowed either for 'funny' shares that are liable to depreciate substantially in value for reasons that do not apply generally to shares in the company. [*CTA 2009, s 996(4)*]. This is obviously an anti-avoidance provision to prevent the rights of shares being rigged so that the company would obtain a far greater deduction than the benefit accruing to the employee. If plan shares are forfeited they are treated for corporation tax purposes as having been acquired by the trustees at that time for no consideration and no deduction is given to the company in respect of any subsequent award of those shares under the plan (as relief will already have been given when they were previously awarded). [*CTA 2009, s 984(4)*].

15.65 A corporation tax deduction is allowed to the company which establishes the SIP for expenses incurred in doing so. [*CTA 2009, s 987*]. This deduction is lost (and no deduction can be claimed even if one would otherwise have been due under general tax law) if any shares are acquired by the trustees or rights are granted to employees before HMRC approve the plan. [*CTA 2009, s 987(3)* formerly *ICTA 1988, Sch 4AA, para 7(2)*]. If HMRC approve the SIP more than nine months after the end of the period of account in which an expense is incurred, relief is given at the time of approval not when the expense is incurred. [*CTA 2009, s 987(4)*]. It is unclear why a taxpayer should be penalised for HMRC delays.

15.66 It should particularly be noted that if in the case of a group plan the parent company recharges a proportion of the costs to the subsidiaries (as it would naturally do if it wants each subsidiary to have budgetary responsibility for its own employee costs) the subsidiary cannot obtain a deduction for the amount borne by it. It may well be that the parent cannot do so either as it is questionable whether it has incurred an expense which it has entered into on behalf of the subsidiary and which is not borne by the parent.

15.67 No specific right of deduction is given for any contribution by a company towards the expenses of the trustees in respect of operating the SIP (including interest on sums borrowed to acquire shares and any fees, commission, stamp duty and similar incidental costs attributable to the acquisition of shares, but excluding the purchase price of the shares themselves). However, it is specifically provided that such a deduction is not disallowed. [*CTA 2009, s 988*]. Accordingly, a deduction can be claimed for such a contribution if it satisfies the normal trading income wholly and exclusively test.

15.68 For contributions to a SIP after 6 April 2003 a deduction is specifically allowed where:

(*a*) the payment is to enable the SIP to acquire shares in the paying company or a company which controls it;

(*b*) the payment is applied by the trustees to acquire such shares;

(*c*) the shares are not acquired from the company;

(*d*) at the end of the period of 12 months following the acquisition the trustees hold shares that constitute at least 10 per cent of the ordinary share capital of the company and carry rights to not less than ten per cent of any profits available for distribution to shareholders and of any assets of the company available for distribution to shareholders in the event of a winding-up; and

(*e*) the payment is not made pursuant to tax avoidance arrangements.

[*CTA 2009, s 989(1)* as amended by *Finance Act 2010 (FA 2010, s 42(5)*]. For the purpose of (*d*) above, shares that have been appropriated to and acquired on behalf of an individual under the plan are treated as held by the trustees while they remain subject to the plan [*CTA 2009, s 989(3)* formerly *ICTA 1988, Sch 4AA, para 9(3)*]. The deduction is claimable at the time that condition (*d*) is met, not at the time of the payment if earlier [*CTA 2009, s 989(4)* formerly *ICTA 1988, Sch 4AA, para 9(1)*]. For the purpose of (*e*) a payment is made pursuant to tax avoidance arrangements if it is made pursuant to arrangements entered into by the paying company one of the main purposes of which is to onbtain a tax deduction or an increased deduction. [*CTA 2009, s 989(6A)* inserted by *FA 2010, s 42(6)*]. This change was aimed at schemes where as a result of a change in share capital the employees received very little real value byt the company obtained a high tax deduction.

15.69 HMRC can by notice direct that the benefit of a deduction under *s 989* should be withdrawn if either:

(*a*) 30 per cent of the shares acquired by virtue of the payment in respect of which the deduction was made have not been awarded under the plan within five years of their acquisition; or (*b*)   all of the shares acquired by virtue of that payment have not been awarded within ten years of their acquisition.

[*CTA 2009, s 990(2)–(3)*]. Where such a direction is made the withdrawal of the relief is made by treating the amount as a trading receipt for the period of account in which the direction is given [*CTA 2009, s 986(2)* formerly *ICTA 1988, Sch 4AA, para 10(2)*]. If the requisite shares are subsequently awarded under the plan the sum again becomes deductible, in this case in the period of account in which the requisite condition is met [*CTA 2009, s 991*]. If any of the qualifying shares are awarded to a person who is not taxable on them as employment income, part of the deduction is withdrawn by treating as a trading receipt for the period of account in which that award was made the proportion of the payment that the shares awarded to that taxpayer bears to the total number of shares acquired out of the payment [*CTA 2009, s 992*]. Where shares are acquired on different days they are treated as awarded to employees on a first in, first out basis [*CTA 2009, s 990(6)*].

15.70   If the employer company is an investment company relief is again given both for the value of free shares (and the excess value of partnership shares) and for expenses, but as a management expense. *CTA 2009, s 985(3)*].

15.71   If a SIP is terminated under *ITEPA 2003, Sch 2, Para 81H* (see **15.100**) or *81I* (see **15.101**) (or prior to 2014/15 the approval of a SIP was withdrawn) HMRC can direct that the cost of the shares (but not the expenses of setting up the scheme) should be disallowed. If they do so the company is treated as receiving a trading receipt (or miscellaneous income in the case of an investment company), at the time that HMRC give notice of withdrawal of approval, equal to the deductions previously allowed to the company. [*CTA 2009, s 998* as amended by *FA 2014, Sch 8, para 83*]. There is a right of appeal against such a direction. [*ITEPA 2003, Sch 2, para 85(1)(c)* – see **15.103**].

Stamp duty

15.72   There is no stamp duty or stamp duty reserve tax on a transfer after 11 May 2001 (ie where the relevant instrument is executed or the agreement to transfer the shares is made after that date) of partnership shares or dividend shares by the trustees of a SIP to an employee. [*Finance Act 2001 (FA 2001), s 95*]. The transfer of free shares and matching shares being for no consideration is exempt under general principles as a transfer from trustees to a beneficiary.

The trustees

15.73   The plan must provide for the establishment of a body of trustees resident in the UK to operate it. [*ITEPA 2003, Sch 2, para 71*]. Their functions must be regulated by a trust deed constituted under the law of some part of the UK and complying with the requirements of *Schedule 2*. [*ITEPA 2003, Sch 2, para 71(3)*]. The trust deed must not contain any terms that are neither essential nor reasonably incidental to complying with the requirements of

Schedule 2. [ITEPA 2003, Sch 2, para 71(4)]. It can contain terms that define who is a professional trustee and who a non-professional one, can provide that the trustees include at least one person who is a professional trustee and at least two non-professional ones, can provide that at least half of the non-professional trustees are to be selected in accordance with a specified process of selection and can provide that trustees so selected are to be employees of the company (or of a participating company in the case of a group plan. *[ITEPA 2003, Sch 2, para 71(5)].* The trust deed must also require the trustees to maintain records of participants who have participated in one or more SIPs established by the company or a connected company. *[ITEPA 2003, Sch 2, para 71A].*

15.74   The deed has to require the trustees to give notice to the employee of any award of shares to him as soon as practicable after that award. In the case of free or matching shares the notice must specify the number and description of the shares, their market value in accordance with which the number of shares awarded was determined (before 17 July 2013 the market value on the date they were awarded), the holding period applicable to them (which must be between three and five years – see **15.21** and **15.37**) and (from 17 July 2013) details of any restrictions to which they are subject. *[ITEPA 2003, Sch 2, para 75* as amended by *FA 2013, Sch 2, para 52].* It is unclear how the trustees are expected to know the market value of unquoted shares. In the case of partnership shares it needs to state the number and description of the shares, the amount of partnership share money applied in acquiring the shares, and their market value on the date of acquisition. *[ITEPA 2003, Sch 2, para 75(3)* as amended by *FA 2013, Sch 2, para 80].* For the purpose of the SIP code shares are subject to a restriction if there is any contract, agreement, arrangement or condition which makes provision to which any of *ITEPA 2003, s 423(2)-(4)* (restricted securities – see **14.27**) would apply *[ITEPA 2003, Sch 2, para 99(4)* inserted by *FA 2013, Sch 2, para 56].*

15.75   The trustees must similarly give the employee notice of the acquisition of dividend shares on his behalf. This must specify the number and description of the shares, their market value on the date of acquisition, their holding period (which must be three years – see **15.41**) and any uninvested amount of the dividend carried forward. If the shares are in a non-UK company the notice must also show the amount of any foreign tax deducted. *[ITEPA 2003, Sch 2, para 75(4)].*

15.76   The trust deed must also require the trustees to dispose of a participant's plan shares and to deal with any right conferred in respect of them as directed by or on behalf of the participant. *[ITEPA 2003, Sch 2, para 72(1)].* The plan can authorise employees to give general directions to the trustees. *[ITEPA 2003, Sch 2, para 72(3)].* Subject of course to the rights of the trustees to dispose of the shares to subscribe for a rights issue or pay PAYE, the deed must prohibit the trustees from disposing of free, matching or dividend shares – even to the employee – at any time during the holding period (other than where the employment terminates during that period. *[ITEPA 2003, Sch 2, para 73].* It must also require the trustees to pay over to the participant any money or money's worth received in respect of the shares. *[ITEPA 2003, Sch 2, para 74].*

15.77   The trustees can be given power to borrow to acquire shares for the purpose of the plan and for such other purposes as may be specified in the trust deed. [*ITEPA 2003, Sch 2, para 76*]. They are entitled to dispose of some of the rights arising under a rights issue in order to take up the remainder, but only if the employee directs them to do so. [*ITEPA 2003, Sch 2, para 77*].

15.78   Up to17 July 2013 the trust deed had to provide that if there was a transfer of shares to the plan from an *FA 1989* ESOT which was a qualifying transfer under *FA 1989, s 69(3AA)* those shares could not be awarded to anyone as partnership shares but had to be awarded as free or matching shares at the next award in priority to any other shares. [*ITEPA 2003, Sch 2, para 78* repealed by *FA 2013, Sch 2, para 92*].

Tax obligations

15.79   The deed must ensure that where a PAYE obligation is imposed on the trustees as a result of any of an employee's plan shares ceasing to be subject to the plan the trustees can raise the cash either by selling some of those shares (including to themselves), by selling other plan shares held on behalf of the employee, or by receiving an appropriate sum from the employee. [*ITEPA 2003, Sch 2, para 79*].

15.80   If at any time an employee disposes of a beneficial interest in plan shares, those shares are deemed to have been disposed of at that time by the trustees for an amount equal to the consideration for the disposal of the beneficial interest. If that disposal is not at arm's length the market value of the shares is adopted instead. If the employee becomes insolvent the operation of the insolvency rules is deemed to give rise to a disposal of his beneficial interest in the shares. [*TCGA 1992, Sch 7D, para 6*].

15.81   The trust deed must require the trustees to maintain such records as are needed for both themselves and the company to meet their PAYE obligations in relation to the plan and to be able to notify the employee of any amounts on which he becomes liable to tax by reason of the occurrence of any event (it presumably means only in relation to the plan) such as on a failure to acquire dividend shares within the relevant period. [*ITEPA 2003, Sch 2, para 80*].

Withdrawal of approval

15.82   Up to 2013/14 HMRC had power to withdraw approval of a SIP on the occurrence of any disqualifying event. Such withdrawal could be from the time of that event or such later time as they specified. [*ITEPA 2003, Sch 2, para 83*]. There was a right of appeal by the company to the Special Commissioners. [*ITEPA 2003, Sch 2, para 85*]. Notice of appeal had to be given within 30 days after notice of the decision to withdraw approval was given to the company. [*ITEPA 2003, Sch 2, para 85(3)*]. There was a similar right of appeal against a refusal by HMRC to approve an alteration to the plan. [*ITEPA 2003, Sch 2, para 85(1)(b)*].

15.83   The disqualifying events were:

(*a*)   Any contravention of *Schedule 2*, the plan rules or the trust deed.

(*b*)   Any alteration in a key feature of the plan or in the trust deed without HMRC approval. A key feature for this purpose was something relating to a provision that was necessary to meet the requirement of *Schedule 2*. HMRC could not withhold approval to a change unless it appeared to them that if approval were then sought for the amended plan it would not qualify.

(*c*)   If the plan provided for performance allowances under method two (see **15.25**), performance targets being set in respect of an award of shares that could not reasonably be regarded as comparable (such targets were comparable only if they were comparable in terms of the likelihood of their being met by the performance units to which they applied).

(*d*)   Any alteration being made in the share capital of a company (or the rights attaching to any of its shares) any of whose shares were subject to the plan trust that materially affected the value of shares that were subject to the plan trust.

(*e*)   Shares subject to the plan trust receiving different treatment to the other shares of the same class. This applied in particular to differences in dividends, repayment, up to 16 July 2013 the restrictions attaching to the shares, or any offer of substituted or additional shares, securities or rights of any description in respect of the shares. It did not apply where the difference in treatment was a key feature of the plan or resulted from an employee's plan shares being subject to restriction (forfeiture prior to 17 July 2013). Nor did it apply if the only difference was that newly issued shares received less favourable treatment to existing shares in relation to dividends payable for a period beginning before the date of their issue.

(*f*)   The trustees, the scheme company or any participating company (in the case of a group scheme) failing to furnish information in accordance with *para 93* (which enabled HMRC to seek such information as they reasonably required for the purpose of their functions under *Schedule 2*).

[*ITEPA 2003, Sch 2, para 84* as amended by *FA 2013, Sch 2, para 53* repealed by *FA 2014, Sch 8, para 28*]. Prior to 24 March 2010, the references in (*d*) and (*e*) to shares subject to the plan trust were to shares held by participants. The change was to make it clear that approval can be withdrawn even if no shares have been issued under the plan.

15.84   The withdrawal of approval did not affect the operation of the plan in relation to shares that were awarded to participants in the plan before the time of such withdrawal (and at a time when the plan was approved. [*ITEPA 2003, Sch 2, para 83(3)*].

Termination of plan

15.85   The SIP can provide for the company to issue a plan termination notice. If it does it must also provide that where such a notice is issued a copy must be sent without delay to HMRC, the trustees and each individual who either owns plan shares or has entered into a partnership share agreement. [*ITEPA 2003, Sch 2, para 89*].

15.86 If a company issues a plan termination notice no further shares can then be awarded under the plan and the trustees must remove all of the plan shares from the plan as soon as practicable at the end of the notice period (three months after the date on which the copy notices under *para 89* are issued – if these are sent on different dates it is probably three months after the last) or, if later, the first date on which they can be removed from the plan without triggering an income tax charge on the participant, ie three years after they were acquired in the case of dividend shares and five years after they were awarded in relation to other shares. [*ITEPA 2003, Sch 2, para 90*].

15.87 The trustees can remove the shares from the plan earlier if the participant consents, ie if he agrees to accept a tax charge, but only if that consent is given after he receives a copy of the plan termination notice. [*ITEPA 2003, Sch 2, para 90(5), (6)*]. They remove the shares from the plan either by transferring them to the employee (or to whoever else he may direct) or by selling them and accounting to the employee for the proceeds. [*ITEPA 2003, Sch 2, para 90(8)*]. If the employee has died the transfer or payment of the funds is obviously to be made to his personal representatives. [*ITEPA 2003, Sch 2, para 90(9)*]. The trustees must also of course pay the employee any uninvested partnership share money or dividends in accordance with *para 56* (see **15.35**) and *68(2)* (see **15.40**) and any other money held on the employee's behalf. [*ITEPA 2003, Sch 2, para 90(7)*]. Such money must be paid over on receipt of the plan termination notice, not at the end of the three-month notice period. For 2002/03 onwards if a deduction has been allowed under *CTA 2009, s 989* (see **15.68**) and not withdrawn under *CTA 2009, s 990* and not all of the shares acquired by virtue of the payment have been awarded before the issue of the plan termination notice there must be treated as a trading receipt for the period of account in which the termination notice is given the proportion of the payment that the awarded shares bears to the total shares purchased from the payment. [*CTA 2009, s 993*].

15.88 It is unclear why a company should want to issue a plan termination notice. If it simply decides not to make any further awards under the plan it will die a natural death and the same results will accrue but without the statutory time pressure on the trustees. The termination notice procedure might be desirable if the company is sold or ceases trading and it is wished to stop ongoing duties for the trustees where, for example, a few employees have left the shares with the trustees for more than five years to obtain the capital gains tax benefits.

Company reconstructions

15.89 A company reconstruction is treated as not involving a disposal of shares comprised in the original holding but the new shares are treated as having been awarded or acquired to the employee when the original ones were awarded. [*ITEPA 2003, Sch 2, para 86*]. The new shares do not have to meet the tests in *paras 25–33* (see **15.5**(*i*)–(*m*)) provided that the original ones did. [*ITEPA 2003, Sch 2, para 87(2)(c)*]. The income tax and capital gains tax rules apply in relation to the new shares as they would have applied to the old. [*ITEPA 2003, Sch 2, para 87(2)(d)*]. Any reference in the rules to an employee's plan shares become of course a reference to his new shares that replace or supplement the old. [*ITEPA 2003, Sch 2, para 87(6)*].

15.90 A company reconstruction for this purpose means a transaction which results in a new holding being equated with the original holding for CGT purposes (ie one within *TCGA 1992 ss 132–137*) or which would have done so but for the fact that the new holding consists of or includes a qualifying corporate bond. [*ITEPA 2003, Sch 2, para 86*]. Such a transaction is excluded from being a company reconstruction if the new holding includes shares which are taxable as income on the recipient under *ICTA 1988, s 209(2) (c)* (redeemable shares issued otherwise than wholly for new consideration), *s 210(1)* (bonus issue following repayment of share capital) or *s 249* (stock dividends). [*ITEPA 2003, Sch 2, para 86(4)*]. It is not clear what happens where a transaction includes both such shares and other shares. *Para 86(2)* suggests that the transaction is not a company reconstruction at all but *para 86(3)* suggests that it is not one only in relation to those shares which attract the income tax charge. If, as part of a reconstruction the trustees receive cash, that cash is deemed to arise before the new holding comes into being. [*ITEPA 2003, Sch 2, para 87(5)*]. It is not immediately apparent what this deeming is intended to achieve.

Rights issues

15.91 Where the trustees acquire shares under a rights issue in respect of an employee's plan shares the rights shares are treated as identical to the original shares and as having been appropriated to (or acquired on behalf of) the employee in the same way and at the same time as the original shares. [*ITEPA 2003, Sch 2, para 88*].

15.92 This rule does not apply where either:

(*a*) the funds used to acquire the rights shares were not raised by the trustees selling the rights in some of the shares in order to take up the remainder (eg where the employee put the trustees in funds to take up the rights issue); or

(*b*) similar rights are not conferred in respect of all ordinary shares in the company (as indicated earlier it is not at all clear that 'ordinary shares' – which is not defined – is the same as 'ordinary share capital', which is). [*ITEPA 2003, Sch 2, para 88(4), (5)*]. In both of these cases the new shares will not be plan shares and they are excluded from *TCGA 1992, s 127–130*, ie they are not treated as forming a single asset with the original shares.

Administration

15.93   Once notice of the establishment of the SIP has been given to HMRC (see **15.5**(*c*)) the company must make an annual return to HMRC for the tax year in which the scheme takes effect and subsequent years [*ITEPA 2003, Sch 2, para 81B(1)-(3)*]. The return must be made by 6 July in the following tax year and must contain such information as HMRC may require [*ITEPA 2003, Sch 2, para 81B(4), (5)*].

15.94   If during a tax year an alteration is made in a key feature of the SIP or of the plan trust, the annual return for that year must contain a declaration that the alteration has not caused the SIP rules to cease to be met. A key feature is any provision which is necessary in order for the requirements of *Sch 2* to be met [*ITEPA 2003, Sch 2, para 81B(6)–(8)*].

15.95   A return is not required for any year after the termination condition has been met, ie a plan termination notice has been issued under *para 89* (see **15.85**) and all of the requirements of *paras 56(3), 68(4)* and *90* have been met by the trustees [*Finance Act 2003 (FA 2003), Sch 2, para 81B(9), (10)*].

15.96   If the company becomes aware that something which should have been included in any annual return was not included (or something that should not have been included was included) or that any error or inaccuracy has occurred in relation to a return for a tax year, it must make an amended return correcting the position without delay [*ITEPA 2003, Sch 2, para 81B(11)*].

15.97   If a company fails to make its annual return by the due date, it is liable to a penalty of £100 and a further penalty of £300 if the return is over three months late, with a further £300 if it is more than six months late. If the return is not submitted within nine months of the due date, HMRC can, by notice to the company, impose a penalty of £10 a day for such period as they may specify starting not earlier than the date of the notice. They can issue as many such notices as are needed to induce the company to deliver the return [*ITEPA 2003, Sch 2, para 81C(1)–(7)*]. No penalty can be charged if the company has a reasonable excuse for the failure. An insufficiency of funds is not a reasonable excuse unless attributable to events outside the company's control. Nor is reliance on another person unless the company took reasonable care to avoid the failure. Where the company had a reasonable excuse which ceases, it is treated as continuing if the failure is then remedied with unreasonable delay [*ITEPA 2003, Sch 2, para 81C(8), (9)*].

15.98   Both notification of the SIP under *para 81A* (see **15.5**(*c*)) and the annual return and any accompanying information must be given electronically (although HMRC have power to enable it to be given in a particular case in some other way if they consider it appropriate to do so) [*ITEPA 2003, Sch 2, para 81D*]. If the return is not made electronically (without HMRC consent to another method) or it contains a material inaccuracy which is careless or deliberate and is not corrected as required by *para 81B(11)* (see **15.96**) the company is liable to a penalty of up to £5,000 [*ITEPA 2003, Sch 2, para 81E*].

15.99 HMRC have power to enquire into a *para 81A* notice or an alteration under *para 81B(7)*. They must give notice of their intention to do so by 6 July following the tax year in which the notice was given (or by 6 July in the next tax year if it was given late). They can of course open an enquiry even after they have terminated the SIP [*ITEPA 2003, Sch 2, para 81F*]. They close an enquiry by giving a closure notice. The SIP can ask the Tribunal to require the issue of a closure notice within a specified time [*ITEPA 2003, Sch 2, para 81F*].

15.100 If HMRC thinks that the SIP requirements are not (or have not been) met and that the situation is (or was) so serious that this provision should apply, the closure notice can withdraw the SIP status from such time as is specified in the closure notice (or from the date of the closure notice) [*ITEPA 2003, Sch 2, para 81H(1), (2)*]. Such a withdrawal does not affect the operation of the SIP code in relation to shares appropriated to an individual (or acquired on his behalf) before the date of the withdrawal; the SIP continues in force in relation to such shares [*ITEPA 2003, s 81H(3)(4)*]. In addition the company is liable for a penalty of such amount as HMRC may decide, but not exceeding twice HMRC's reasonable estimate of the total income tax and NIC saved in consequence of the SIP during the period (up to the date of giving the closure notice) for which the conditions were not met (including the future tax and NIC benefits that will apply to shares for which the SIP code remains in force under *para 81H(3)(4)*) [*ITEPA 2003, Sch 2, para 81H(2), (5)–(7)*].

15.101 If HMRC consider that the SIP rules have not been complied with but the breach is not serious enough to warrant withdrawal of SIP status, the company is liable to a penalty of up to £5,000 and must secure that the SIP rules are met in relation to the SIP within 90 days of the end of the period during which notice of appeal against the enquiry notice can be given or, if later, within 90 days of the date on which any appeal is determined or withdrawn (unless the breaches have already been met before the expiration of the 90-days period) [*ITEPA 2003, Sch 2, para 81I(1)–(5)*]. If the company fails to comply with this requirement, HMRC can give it a notice (a default notice) stating that it has not complied. The SIP status will then be withdrawn from such time as is specified in the notice (or the date of the notice) and the company becomes liable to an additional penalty of the amount at **15.100** above [*ITEPA 2003, Sch 2, para 81I(6)–(12)*].

15.102 If a company is liable for a penalty under these provisions, HMRC must assess the penalty and notify the company of the assessment [*ITEPA 2003, Sch 2, para 81J(1), (2)*]. Such an assessment must be made within 12 months of the date on which the company became liable for the penalty. In the case of a penalty under *para 81E(1)(b)* (inaccuracy in a return – see **15.98**) the time-limit is 12 months from the date on which HMRC became aware of the inaccuracy, but not later than six years after the date on which the company became liable for the penalty (ie when it submitted the return) [*ITEPA 2003, Sch 2, para 81J(4)*]. If the penalty is under *para 81H(2)* (see **15.100**) or *81I(2)* or *(7)* (see **15.101**) the assessment must be made within 12 months of the date on which the appeal is determined or withdrawn [*ITEPA 2003, Sch 2, para 81J(5)*]. The penalty is payable 30 days from the date on which the company is notified of the penalty or, if it is appealed against, within 30 days of the appeal being determined or withdrawn [*ITEPA 2003, Sch 2, para 81J(6)*]. The penalty can be enforced as if it were corporation tax (or income tax, as the case may be) charged in an assessment. *Taxes Management Act 1970 (TMA 1970), ss 100-103* do not apply to a penalty under these provisions [*ITEPA 2003, Sch 2, para 81J(7)(8)*].

15.103 The company has a right of appeal against a penalty under *para 81C* (see **15.97**) or *81E* (see **15.98**), a decision under *81H* (see **15.100**) or *81I* (see **15.101**) (including a decision not to specify a date in the closure notice), a decision by HMRC under *para 81I* to give the company a default notice (including a decision not to specify a date in the closure notice), and against the amount of any such penalty [*ITEPA 2003, Sch 2, para 81K(1)–(4)*]. It can also appeal against a decision of HMRC to give a direction under *CTA 2009, s 998* (withdrawal of corporation tax deductions in relation to a *Schedule 2* SIP) [*ITEPA 2003, Sch 2, para 81K(5)*]. Notice of appeal must be given to HMRC within 30 days of the notice of assessment, closure notice, default notice or notice of the Officer's decision, as the case may be [*ITEPA 2003, Sch 2, para 81K(6)*]. On appeal, the Tribunal can affirm or cancel the HMRC decision and can vary the amount of the penalty (but in the case of one within *paras 81H* or *81I(1)*, only to the extent to which HMRC has power to do so) [*ITEPA 2003, Sch 2, para 81K(7)-(9)*]. The provisions of *TMA 1970*, relating to appeals apply to appeals under these provisions [*ITEPA 2003, Sch 2, para 81K(10)*].

15.104 An HMRC Officer can by notice require a person to provide him with any information which he reasonably requires for the performance of any functions of HMRC under the SIP code, and which the person to whom the notice is addressed has, or can reasonably obtain [*ITEPA 2003, Sch 2, para 93(1)* as substituted by *FA 2014, Sch 8, para 31*]. This extends in particular to information to enable a HMRC Officer to check anything contained in a notice under *para 81A* (see **15.5**(*c*)) or a return under *para 81B* (see **15.93**) or to check any information accompanying such a notice or return; or to determine the liability to tax (including CGT) of any person who has participated in a SIP, or any other person for whom the operation of a SIP is relevant to his liability to tax; and to information about the administration of a SIP or any proposed alteration to the terms of a SIP. The notice must specify the period within which the information is to be supplied, which must not be less than three months after the date the notice is given [*ITEPA 2003, Sch 2, para 93* as amended by *FA 2014, Sch 8, para 31*].

Chapter 16

Tax-Advantaged Share Option and EMI Schemes

Introduction

16.1   Although Chancellors of the Exchequer have often been suspicious of employee share incentives, seeing them as little more than a device to enable an employee to receive part of his remuneration in a capital form, attempts have been made in recent years to encourage employee share ownership provided that this is done in a politically acceptable way. There are currently five approved ways to enable employees to take shareholdings in the company for which they work:

(*a*)   Share Incentive Plans (SIP) (formerly called All Employee Share Option Plans (AESOP)). These are the most attractive ways to provide a tax incentive but can be used only where it is proposed that all of the employees of an enterprise should have the opportunity to acquire shares. SIPs are dealt with in **Chapter 15** and are not considered further here.

(*b*)   Approved SAYE option schemes (formerly called savings-related share option schemes). Again such a scheme can be used only where it is proposed to include in the scheme all of the employees of an enterprise.

(*c*)   Approved CSOP (company share option plan) Schemes (formerly called executive share option schemes, or sometimes *Finance Act 1984 (FA 1984)* share option schemes or discretionary share option schemes). Selected employees only can participate in a CSOP scheme.

(*d*)   Enterprise Management Incentives (EMI schemes). These are aimed at selected, generally senior, employees.

(*e*)   Employee Shareholder Shares. These can be used for selected employees.

16.2   Under all such schemes, in return for accepting restrictions on the benefits that can be provided, the tax charges that would otherwise arise under the various provisions considered in **Chapter 14** are disapplied.

16.3   Many of the conditions that must be met by the two types of approved share option schemes are identical, or virtually so. On consolidation of the income tax legislation in 1988 the draftsman collected these together in *Schedule 9* to the *Act*. This treatment seems sensible and is followed below, albeit that it was abandoned by the tax law rewrite team, the basic principles of the two types of scheme being considered before the qualifying conditions for both are examined.

16.4   There used to be a further type of plan, approved profit sharing schemes, but the use of such schemes was discouraged following the introduction of SIPs in April 2001 and such schemes no longer confer tax benefits except to the extent that shares were appropriated to employees before 1 January 2003.

Share option schemes

16.5   There are two types of approved share option schemes: SAYE option schemes and CSOP schemes. There are also Enterprise Management Incentive options which are considered at **16.67**. Under a SAYE option scheme the employee enters into a Save As You Earn contract with a bank, building society or other approved financial institution. This commits him to save a regular monthly amount for at least three years. The maximum permissible monthly figure is £250. At the end of the contract (which can be for three or five years) he is credited with a tax-free bonus. If he leaves the funds to accumulate for a further two years he will be entitled to a second bonus. At the same time as he starts his SAYE scheme the employee is granted an option to subscribe for (or acquire) shares in the employer company. The option price must be satisfied out of the proceeds of the SAYE scheme. Accordingly, the amount he can acquire must be based on the estimated value of the scheme in five years' time (or seven years if he opts to tie up his savings for that longer period). Three-year savings schemes can also be used but the £250 per month limit still applies. From 29 May 2009 the tax-free bonus is 0.3 times the monthly contribution for three-year contracts, 2.2 times for five-year ones and 5.2 times for seven-year contracts. With monthly payments of £250 this will produce £9,075 at the end of three years, £15,550 after five years or £22,300 after seven years. As the shares can be issued at 80 per cent of their market value at the time the option is granted (see **16.15**(*j*)), this will allow an employee to acquire options over £27,875 worth of shares. As interest rates have fallen, so has the bonus rate. Accordingly now may not be the best time to start a SAYE option scheme. At one time during 2008 the bonus on a seven-year contract was 12.7 times giving a total fund of £24,175, £1,875 more than would be produced under a current contract.

Employees eligible to join scheme

16.6   All full-time employees with at least five years' service must have a right to participate in the scheme. Accordingly, a SAYE option scheme cannot be targeted at specific employees.

16.7   Furthermore, the employee cannot normally exercise his option for at least three years. SAYE option schemes are aimed at enabling a broad spread of employees to acquire a share stake in their employer company. They are generally used by major listed companies who feel that providing an employee with a share stake will enable him to identify more closely with the company.

They are not really suitable for unquoted companies where an employee will acquire a tiny, unmarketable holding which is unlikely to have any value. As a profit sharing scheme does not require the employee to do anything other than to continue in his employment, such a scheme is likely to be more acceptable to employees than a SAYE option scheme under which the employee has to save money out of his post-tax income, which in most cases he will 'repay' to the employer company to acquire the shares.

Executive share option schemes

16.8   A CSOP scheme is very different. The scheme can be targeted at executives only; indeed, it is possible to grant options to a single person.

16.9   Such schemes are no longer attractive in many cases as the limit on the benefit that can be provided is comparatively small. Such schemes might still be attractive for junior and middle range executives and in other circumstances where it is not wished to motivate the entire workforce by the grant of share option. Most of the tax benefits are common to both types of schemes.

Tax benefits of approved schemes

16.10   If, in accordance with the provisions of an approved share option scheme, an individual obtains an option (or other right) to acquire shares in a company by reason of his employment as a director or employee (of that or any other company) tax is not to be charged, under any provision of the *Tax Acts*, in respect of the receipt of the option (subject to a minor exception considered at **16.12** below).

16.11   The tax position under the tax-advantaged option schemes is as follows:

Schedule 3 SAYE option scheme:

(*a*)   No income tax liability arises on the grant of an option. This is now the normal rule in relation to options under *Income Tax (Earnings and Pensions) Act 2003 (ITEPA 2003), s 475* (see **14.103**).

(*b*)   No income tax liability arises on the exercise of the option provided that it is exercised in accordance with the terms of the scheme and, unless the option was exercised before 18 June 2004, the avoidance of tax or NIC is not the main purpose (or one of the main purposes) of any arrangements under which the option was granted or is exercised: and either:

   (i)   it is not exercised within three years of being granted; or

   (ii)   although it is exercised in the first three years this is by virtue of *ITEPA 2003, Sch 3, para 34(5)* (which allows options to be exercised within six months after the termination of the employment where the ownership of a company or business is transferred) (see **16.16**(*d*)) or *37* (which allows options to be exercised within six months of a takeover of the company) (see **16.20**) [*ITEPA 2003, s 519*].

(*c*)   The general exemption from tax on the exercise of an option by personal representatives under *ITEPA 2003, s 477(2)* (see **14.107**) applies to an SAYE option in the same way as any other option.

From 17 July 2013 in relation to any shares acquired by the exercise of the share option, no liability to income tax arises in respect of its exercise if-

(*a*)   the individual exercises the option before the third anniversary of the date on which it was granted (and at a time when the SAYE option scheme is approved),

(*b*)   the option is exercised by virtue of a provision included in the scheme under *ITEPA 2003, Sch 3, para 37(1)* or *(6)* (general offer, arrangements, etc – see **16**.

(*c*)   as a result of the offer, etc the individual receives cash (and no other assets) in exchange for the shares,

(*d*)   when the decision to grant the option was taken, the offer, etc had not been made,

(*e*)   when that decision was taken, no arrangements were in place or under consideration for the making of the offer, etc,

(*f*)   if the scheme includes a provision under *ITEPA 2003, Sch 3, para 38* (takeovers etc – see **16.19**) no course of action was open to the individual which, had it been followed, would have resulted in the individual making an agreement under that provision which would have prevented him from acquiring the shares by the exercise of the option, and

(*g*)   the avoidance of tax or NIC is not the main purpose (or one of the main purposes) of any arrangements (including any plan, scheme, agreement or understanding, whether or not legally enforceable) under which the option was granted or exercised

[*ITEPA 2003, s 519(3A)(3C)* inserted by *Finance Act 2013 (FA 2013), Sch 2, para 21*]. A general offer falls within this provision if it is a general offer to acquire the whole of the issued ordinary share capital of the company (other than capital already held by the offeror or a connected person of his) which is made on a condition such that (if it is met) the person making the offer will have control of the company. It does not matter if the offer is made to different shareholders by different means. A person is to be treated as having control of a company if he and others acting in concert together gain control of it [*ITEPA 2003, s 519(3D)–(3G)*]. A compromise or arrangement, or, from 6 April 2014, a non-UK company reorganisation arrangement, falls within the provision if it is applicable to or affects all the ordinary share capital of the relevant company or all of the shares of the same class as those acquired by the exercise of the option (or all of the shares or shares of the same class which are held by a class of shareholders identified otherwise than by reference to their employment, directorships or participation in a *Schedule 3 SAYE option scheme*) [*ITEPA 2003, s 519(3H)* as amended by *Finance Act 2014 (FA 2014), Sch 8, para 101*]. A takeover falls within the provision if it relates to the relevant company (and if it has more than one class of shares, the class or classes to which it relates includes the class acquired under the option) [*ITEPA 2003, s 519(3I)*]. The relevant company is that whose shares are acquired under the option [*ITEPA 2003, s 519(3J)*]. A non-UK company re-organisation arrangement is an arrangement made in relation to a company under the law of a territory outside the UK which gives effect to a reorganisation of the company's share capital by the consolidation of shares of different classes or the division of shares into different classes (or both) and which is approved by a resolution of members of the company [*ITEPA 2003, ss 47A, 35ZA inserted by FA 2014, Sch 8, paras 119, 181*]. The members who vote in favour of the arrangement must however represent over 50% of the total voting rights of all the members having the right to vote on the issue [*ITEPA 2003, ss 47A(2), 35ZA(2)*].

Schedule 4 CSOP schemes:

(*a*)   No liability to income tax arises on the grant of the option except where it was granted at a discount (see below). [*ITEPA 2003, s 475*].

(*b*)   No liability to income tax arises on the exercise of the option in accordance with the provisions of the scheme provided that the avoidance of tax or NIC is not the main purpose (or one of the main purposes) of any arrangements under which the option was granted or is exercised, and either:

  (i)   it is not exercised within the first three years or more than ten years after it was granted; or

  (ii)   If the option is exercised within the first three years, this is in accordance with *ITEPA 2003, Sch 4, para 24* (see **16.18**) and the individual exercising the option does so within six months of ceasing to be in qualifying employment because of redundancy or retirement, a relevant transfer under the *Transfer of Undertakings (Protection of Employment) Regulations 2006*, or the company ceasing to be controlled by the scheme organiser (prior to 17 July 2013 ceasing to be a full-time director or employee because of injury, liability, redundancy (within the *Employment Rights Act 1976 (ERA 1976)*)) or retirement (up to 17 July 2013 retirement after reaching a retirement age specified in the scheme);

[*ITEPA 2003, s 524 as amended by FA 2013, Sch 2, paras 14, 26*]. An individual is in qualifying employment if he is a full-time director or qualifying employee (as defined in **16.15**(*h*)) of the scheme organiser or (in the case of a group scheme) a constituent company [*ITEPA 2003, s 524(2BA) inserted by FA 2013, Sch 2, para 26*]. The reference to the company being controlled by the scheme organiser does not cover a case where such control was by virtue of *ITEPA 2003, Sch 4, para 34* (jointly owned companies – see **16.22**) [*ITEPA 2003, s 524(2D) inserted by FA 2013, Sch 2, para 26*].

(*c*)   The general exemption from tax on the exercise of an option by personal representatives under *ITEPA 2003, s 477(2)* (see **14.107**) applies to a CSOP option scheme in the same way as any other option.

16.11A In the case of a CSOP scheme, in relation to any shares acquired by the exercise of the share option, no liability to income tax arises in respect of its exercise if –

(a) the individual exercises the option before the third anniversary of the date on which the option was granted (at a time when the CSOP scheme was approved),

(b) the option is exercised by virtue of a provision included in the scheme under *ITEPA 2003, Sch 4, para 25A* – see **16.18A**),

(c) the individual receives cash (and no other assets) in exchange for the shares as a result of a general offer, compromise or arrangement or takeover offer (as defined in *Companies Act 2006 (CA 2006), s 94*) giving rise to the application of *CA 2006, ss 979 – 982 or 983 – 985*,

(d) the decision to grant the option was taken at a time when that offer, etc had not been made,

(e) when that decision was taken, no arrangements (including any plan, scheme agreement or understanding, whether or not legally enforceable) were in place for (or under consideration for) the making of a general offer, compromise or arrangement, or takeover offer which would fall within *ITEPA 2003, s 524(2H)–( )–(2N)* (see below),

(f) the scheme includes a provision under *ITEPA 2003, Sch 4, para 26 (see 16.19)* in connection with the general offer etc, no course of action was open to the individual which (had it been followed) would have resulted in the individual making an agreement under the *para 26* provision which would have prevented him from acquiring the shares by the exercise of the option, and

(g) the avoidance of tax or National Insurance contributions is not the main purpose (or one of the main purposes) of any arrangements under which the option was granted or exercised

[*ITEPA 2003, s 524(2E)–(2G)* inserted by *FA 2013, Sch 2, para 26*].

16.11B A general offer falls within (e) above if it is a general offer to acquire the whole of the issued share capital of the relevant company (other than any already held by the offeror or a connected person) which is made on a condition that (if met) the person making the offer will have control of the company; or it is a general offer to acquire all the shares in the company (other than any already held by the offeror or a connected person) which are of the same class as those acquired by the exercise of the option. It does not matter if the general offer is made to different shareholders by different means. A person is to be treated as obtaining control of a company if he and others acting in concert together obtain control of it [*ITEPA 2003, s 524(2H)–(2K)*]. A compromise or arrangement falls within (e) if it is applicable to (or affects) all of the ordinary share capital of the relevant company (or all the shares of the same class as those acquired by the exercise of the option, or all the shares (or all those of the same class) which are held by a class of shareholders identified other than by reference to their employment or directorships or their participation in an approved CSOP scheme) [*ITEPA 2003, s 524(2L)*]. A takeover offer falls within (*e*) if it relates to the relevant company and, if there is more than one class of share, the class or classes to which it relates is (or includes) the class acquired by the exercise of the option [*ITEPA 2003, s 524(2M)*]. The relevant company is of course the one whose shares are being acquired by the exercise of the option [*ITEPA 2003, s 524(2N)*].

16.12   For the purpose of (*a*) above an option is granted at a discount if at the time when it was granted the aggregate of any consideration given for the option under a CSOP scheme, plus the option price, is less than the market value of the same quantity of issued shares of the same class at the time the option is granted. This taxable amount is treated as employment income if it would not otherwise have been so – it is difficult to envisage circumstances in which it would not. [*ITEPA 2003, s 526*]. This is intended to cover small accidental undervalues. One of the conditions for approval of a CSOP scheme is that the option price must not be manifestly less than the value of the shares at the time the option is granted. Accordingly, if the difference is significant this would probably lead to the complete withdrawal of approval of the scheme.

Circumstances in which the tax charge is reduced

16.13   If a charge to tax arises under *s 526* on the grant of the option (see **16.12**) and because, for example, one of the conditions in *ITEPA 2003, Sch 4* is breached, the tax exemptions for approved option schemes do not apply, the amount on which the participant is taxable under *s 526* can be deducted in calculating the gain on a later chargeable event, such as on the exercise of the option (see **14.107**). [*ITEPA 2003, ss 480(4), 526(4)*].

16.14   To qualify for approval both types of option scheme must satisfy the conditions at **16.15** below. A savings-related option scheme must also satisfy the further conditions set out at **16.16** below, and an executive share option scheme those at **16.17** below.

Conditions to be met

16.15   This paragraph describes the conditions common to both types of scheme. *ITEPA 2003, Sch 3* deals with SAYE option schemes and *Sch 4* deals with CSOP schemes.

(*a*)   Scheme shares must form part of the ordinary share capital of either:

   (i)   the scheme organiser (formerly called the grantor) (ie the company that set up the scheme);

   (ii)   a company which controls the scheme organiser; or

   (iii) a company which is (or controls a company that is) a member of a consortium that owns the scheme organiser or a company that controls it (prior to 27 July 1989, the consortium member also had to own at least 15 per cent of the share capital of the grantor company).

[*ITEPA 2003, Sch 3, para 18, Sch 4, para 16*].

'Ordinary share capital' means all the issued shares other than those entitled to a dividend at a fixed rate with no further right to share in the profits of the company. [*ITEPA 2003, Sch 3, para 49, ITA 2007, s 989* formerly *Income and Corporation Taxes Act 1988 (ICTA 1988), s 832(1)*].

(*b*)   The shares must be either:

(i)   of a class quoted on a recognised stock exchange, or

(ii)   shares in a company which is not controlled by another company.

[*ITEPA 2003, Sch 3, para 19, Sch 4, para 17*].

In relation to options granted before 23 September 2010, there was a third alternative, namely shares which, although unquoted, were in a company which was under the control of one whose shares were quoted and which was not a close company (and if it was an overseas company would not be close if it were UK resident). This test was abolished by *Finance Act 2010 (FA 2010), s 39.* The change effectively applied also to share options granted between 24 March 2010 and 23 September 2010 over shares in a company which was under the control of a listed company (and not quoted on a recognised stock exchange) as such option were treated as not being CSOP options [*FA 2010, s 39(4)*]. A company which permitted such options had until 23 September to obtain HMRC approval to a change of the scheme rules, but only in respect of option granted after that date. [*FA 2010, s 39(6)–(8)*].

This prevents shares in a subsidiary company being scheme shares unless they are quoted shares

(*c*)   The shares must be fully paid. [*ITEPA 2003, Sch 3, para 20(a), Sch 4, para 18(a)*].

(*d*)   The shares must not be redeemable. [*ITEPA 2003, Sch 3, para 20(b), Sch 4, para 18(b)*].

(*e*)   Up to 17 July 2013 the shares could not be subject to any restrictions, other than:

(i)   restrictions attaching to all the shares of the same class; or

(ii)   a restriction imposed by the Articles of Association (or equivalent document in the case of an overseas company) requiring:

(A)   all shares held by directors or employees of the company or of any other company of which it has control to be disposed of (or offered for sale) immediately the holder ceases to be a director or employee; and

(B)   all shares acquired by non-directors or employees (or ex-directors or employees) in pursuance of rights or interests obtained by directors or employees to be disposed of (or offered for sale) on acquisition;

and providing that any such disposal must be by way of sale for a consideration in money on terms specified in the Articles, and that the Articles also require any other person who disposes of shares of the same class to sell their shares on those same terms. [*ITEPA 2003, Sch 3, para 21(1)–(3), (7), Sch 4, para 19(1)–(3), (8)* both repealed by *FA 2013, Sch 2, paras 61, 71*].

Points to note are that it appears that the Articles needed to contain both provisions (A) and (B) in (ii) above even if the scheme did not permit options to be exercised after a person ceased to be an employee; and that all holders of shares of the same class had to be obliged to sell the shares under the formula (or at the price) fixed in the Articles if they sold under the pre-emption clause in the Articles. The intention was to ensure that an employee was not deprived of the value of his shares when he ceased his employment. It was felt that if other non-employee shareholders (including the major shareholders) are prepared to accept the same terms, such terms are likely to be fair. This is not necessarily the case as the formula in the Articles can be such as to produce a different value per share depending on the size of the holding. It should be stressed that the restrictions under head (ii) had to be contained in the Articles. It was not sufficient to impose them under a shareholders' agreement. Restrictions under head (i) did not need to be contained in the Articles but could be imposed by some outside document.

Any contract, agreement, arrangement or condition by which the employee's freedom to dispose of his shares (or an interest in them, or of the sale proceeds) or to exercise any right conferred by them, or under which a disposal or exercise of rights could result in a disadvantage to the employee (or a connected person of his), had to be regarded as a restriction attaching to the shares. [*ITEPA 2003, Sch 3, para 21(4), Sch 4, para 19(4)*]. This did not apply:

(I)   in relation to any terms of a loan covering how the loan was to be repaid or the security to be given for it if the scheme was a CSOP scheme; or

(II) to a restriction on disposal imposed by the Financial Services Authority's Model Code for Securities Transactions by Directors of Listed Companies (the 'yellow book') or by any agreement having the same purpose or effect;

(III) to a discretion of the directors under the Articles of Association of the company to refuse to accept a transfer of shares if the directors had undertaken to HMRC not to exercise it in such a way as to discriminate against persons participating in the scheme and had notified all those who were eligible to participate in the scheme of the existence of the undertaking.

[*ITEPA 2003, Sch 3, para 21(5)–(6), Sch 4, para 19(5)–(7)*].

(f) Unless the grantor company has only one class of shares (or only one class of ordinary shares plus fixed rate preference shares) the majority of the issued shares of the same class as the scheme shares must either be:

(i)   employee-controlled shares, ie held by employees or directors (or ex-employees or directors) of the company (or of a company controlled by it) and who (by virtue of their holdings of such shares) are together able to control the company; or

(ii) open market shares, ie held by persons other than:

(A) directors or employees (or rather, persons who acquired their shares in pursuance of a right conferred on them or an opportunity afforded to them as a director or employee of the grantor or some other company and not in pursuance of an offer to the public);

(B) trustees of people who acquired their beneficial interest in the shares as directors or employees (within (A) above); and

(C) in the case of shares which are not of a class listed on a recognised stock exchange but which are in a company which is under the control of a listed company (as defined in (*b*)(iii) above), companies which control the grantor company or with which the grantor is associated.

[*ITEPA 2003, Sch 3, para 22, Sch 4, para 20*].

In other words, the company must either be under the control of directors and employees (including former directors and employees) and the scheme shares must be part of the class that gives control, or the class of shares used for the scheme (which does not need to control the company) must be held by a spread of shareholders the majority by value of whom are not, and have not at any time been, directors or employees (with the exception that an employee's shares can be regarded as held by non-employees if he acquired them in pursuance of an offer to the public). Some people contend that the people who set up a company acquire their initial shares not as persons who are to become directors or employees but rather as entrepreneurs. However, HMRC do not subscribe to this view (*Press Release 26 October 1987*). Accordingly, it would be rare for a company to meet the test in head (ii) unless it is a listed company. Unquoted companies will normally need to satisfy head (i). In approaching this test care needs to be taken. Where a company is formed by two 'partners' it is not uncommon to have two classes of shares, A shares and B shares, with separate but identical rights. It appears that such a structure will result in no class of shares controlling the company so that the test in head (i) could not be met.

(*g*) Up to 17 July 2013 in the case of a SAYE option scheme it had to specify what age was to be the specified age, ie the retirement age. This had to be between 60 and 75 and had to be the same for men and women. [*ITEPA 2003, Sch 3, para 31* repealed by *FA 2013, Sch 2, para 10*]. There was no requirement for a CSOP scheme to specify a retirement age but from 10 July 2003 if it did so it had to be the same for men and women and not be less than 35. [*ITEPA 2003, Sch 4, para 35A* repealed by *FA 2013, Sch 2, para 15*].

(*h*) The only people eligible to participate in the scheme at a particular time must be employees or directors of the scheme organiser (or in the case of a group scheme a constituent company) – which can include part-time employees and can also include part-time directors in a SAYE option scheme but not in a CSOP scheme. [*ITEPA 2003, Sch 3, para 10, Sch 4, para 8*]. A CSOP scheme approved before 1 May 1995 had to exclude an employee who was not required under the terms of his employment to work for the company for at least 20 hours a week but this restriction was removed by *Finance Act 1995 (FA 1995), s 137(3)*. If such a scheme is altered to extend it to part-time employees that alteration will have effect from the date of that change. [*FA 1995, s 137(7), (8)*]. A full-time director is not defined. HMRC have indicated that they consider it to mean a director who works for at least 25 hours a week on average. The meaning of 'full-time' is considered in more detail at **6.11**. Although an ex-director or ex-employee cannot be granted options under the scheme this does not prevent such a person from exercising an option acquired whilst he was a director or employee. [*ITEPA 2003, Sch 4, para 24*]. Where a reservist is called up for service under the *Reserve Forces Act 1996* HMRC will by concession treat the employment with the Ministry of Defence as fulfilling these employment conditions. [*ESC A103*]. They have asked to be informed (Sahd.Ullah@ir.gsi.gov.uk) when this concession is used.

(*i*)   Up to 17 July 3013 no person with a material interest in a close company which was either the company whose shares could be acquired under the option, a company which had control of such a company or a company which was a member of a consortium which owned a company which in turn has control over such a company (or who had such an interest within the previous 12 months) could be eligible to participate in the scheme. [*ITEPA 2003, Sch 3, para 11(1), Sch 4, para 9(1)*]. This provision was repealed by *FA 2013, Sch 2, para 41*, in relation to SAYE option schemes. It still applies in relation to CSOP schemes. The rules are accordingly considered at **16.18B** onwards. The same rules applied to SAYE option schemes up to 16 July 2013. The relevant legislation was in *ITEPA 2003, Sch 3, paras 11 to 16*. From 17 July 2013, an existing SAYE option scheme has effect with the omission of this restriction.

(*j*)   The price at which shares may be acquired on exercise of the option:

(i)   must be stated at the time when the option is granted; and

(ii)   must not be manifestly less than 80 per cent of the market value of shares of the same class at that time in the case of a SAYE option scheme or less than 100 per cent of the value in the case of a CSOP scheme.

HMRC and the scheme organiser can agree in writing that the not manifestly less test is to be applied by reference to an earlier time or times stated in the agreement. This will enable a value to be agreed with HMRC in advance of issuing the option. The scheme can (but need not) provide for the option price, the number of shares covered by the option or the description of shares covered by the option to be varied so far as necessary to take account of a variation in the company's share capital. [*ITEPA 2003, Sch 3, para 28, Sch 4, para 22*]. From 17 July 2013, The market value of shares subject to a restriction must be determined as if they were not so subject [*ITEPA 2003, Sch 3, para 28(6); Sch 4, para 22(6)* both inserted by *FA 2013, Sch 2, paras 62, 72*].

(*k*) Share options granted to a participant must not be assignable. [*ITEPA 2003, Sch 3, para 29, Sch 4, para 23*].

(*l*) A SAYE option scheme must provide that if a participant dies before exercising his option, it can be exercised within 12 months after the date of death if he dies before the bonus date or within 12 months after the bonus date if he dies on or within 12 months after that date. A CSOP scheme does not have to allow an option to be exercised after the individual's death but if it chooses to do so must provide that it must be exercised at any time within the 12 months after the death. [*ITEPA 2003, Sch 3, para 32, Sch 4, para 25* as amended by *FA 2014, Sch 8, para 175*].

Further conditions to be met by SAYE option schemes

16.16 This paragraph describes further conditions to be met by SAYE option schemes.

(*a*) The scheme must provide for the scheme shares to be paid for out of the proceeds (including interest and either including or excluding as the participant chooses any bonus, such choice to be made at the time that rights under the option scheme are obtained) of a certified contractual savings scheme which has been approved by HMRC. [*ITEPA 2003, Sch 3, paras 24, 26*].

(*b*) The rights obtained under the scheme must not be capable of being exercised before the bonus date or more than six months after that date, ie the date on which repayments under the certified contractual savings scheme are due. [*ITEPA 2003, Sch 3, para 30*]. Where the proceeds of the scheme are regarded as including the maximum bonus (ie where the scheme will continue for at least seven years), the bonus date is the end of seven years. If they are not, it is the earliest date on which any bonus is payable under the scheme (which is the fifth anniversary of the scheme). For 2014/15 onwards, the scheme can provide that if on the occurrence of such an event the shares cease to be qualifying shares, the option can be exercised within 20 days after that event occurs, even though the shares no longer meet the relevant conditions [*ITEPA 2013, Sch 3, paras 17(1A), 37(6B); Sch 4, paras 15(1A), 25A(7B)* inserted by *FA 2014, Sch 8, paras 109, 114, 171, 176*].

(*c*) The scheme must provide that if an option holder ceases to hold his office or employment (namely, the one under which he is eligible to participate in the scheme, together with any other office or employment in the grantor company or in any associated company over which the grantor has control [*ITEPA 2003, Sch 3, para 35*]) by reason of either:

(i) injury, disability, or redundancy within the meaning of the *Employment Rights Act 1996*; or

(ii) retirement (up to 17 July 2013 on reaching the age specified in (*f*) below or, for schemes approved before 26 July 1991, pensionable age (or any other age at which he was bound to retire under the terms of his contract of employment));

(iii) from 17 July 2013, a relevant transfer (under *Transfer of Undertakings (Protection of Employment) Regulations 2006*, or

(iv) from 17 July 2013, by reason of the employer company ceasing to be an associated company of the scheme organiser by reason of a change of control (as defined in *Corporation Tax Act 2010 (CTA 2010), ss 450, 451)*

the option must be exercised within six months of the employment ceasing (or it must then lapse). [*ITEPA 2003, Sch 3, para 34(2* as amended by *FA 2013, Sch 2, paras 12, 23)*].

(*d*) The scheme must provide that if an option holder ceases to hold his office or employment for any other reason within three years of having been granted the option, it must lapse. [*ITEPA 2003, Sch 3, para 34(4)*].

If the cessation is solely because the business or part of a business is transferred to a person which is not an associated company of the scheme organiser where the transfer is not a relevant transfer within the *Transfer of Undertakings (Protection of Employment) Regulations 2006* (up to 2014/15 if it was solely because the scheme organiser ceased to have control of the employer company, so that the employment ceased to be an eligible employment (eg it is with a subsidiary of the grantor which is sold), or it was with a division of a company which was transferred to a person who was not an associated company of (or under the control of) the grantor,) the scheme can allow the option to be exercised within six months of the participant ceasing to be an eligible employee. [*ITEPA 2003, Sch 3, para 34(5)* as amended by *FA 2014, Sch 8, para 113*].

The scheme can also permit an option holder to exercise his option within six months of the bonus date (see (*b*) above) if at that time he is a director or employee of a company which, although not a participating company, is an associated company of the scheme organiser or a company over which the scheme organiser has control. [*ITEPA 2003, Sch 3, para 36*].

(*e*) The scheme must provide that if an option holder ceases to hold his office or employment for any reason (other than those in (*d*) above) more than three years after being granted the option it must either immediately lapse or the option holder must exercise it, if at all, within six months of the employment ceasing. [*ITEPA 2003, Sch 3, para 34(3)*].

(*f*) Up to 17 July 2013 the scheme had to provide that if the option holder's employment continued after he reaches a specified age between 60 and 75 which is selected by the employer but which had to be the same for men and women or, for schemes approved before 25 July 1991, after he reaches pensionable age, he could nevertheless exercise the option within six months of reaching that age. [*ITEPA 2003, Sch 3, paras 31, 33*]. These provisions were both repealed by *FA 2013, Sch 2, paras 10, 11* although *para 33* continues to apply to options granted before that date [*FA 2013, Sch 2, para 16*].

(*g*) The scheme must provide for a person's contributions under the certified contractual savings scheme to be of such amount as to produce (as near as may be) the purchase money for the shares under the option scheme. [*ITEPA 2003, Sch 3, para 25(1), (2)*].

(*h*) The scheme must not permit the aggregate amount of a person's contributions under all contractual savings schemes linked to approved savings-related share option schemes (with the same or other employees) to exceed £250 per month and if it imposes a minimum on the amount of a person's contributions this must not exceed £10 per month. The Treasury have power to amend these figures. [*ITEPA 2003, Sch 3, para 25(3), (4)*].

(*i*) Every person who has been an employee (whether full or part-time) or full-time director of the grantor or other participating companies (other than one having a material interest in the company if it is close) for a qualifying period (which can be determined by the grantor but must not exceed five years) and who is taxable on his remuneration under *ITEPA 2003, s 15* as general earnings of a person who is resident and, from 5 April 2008, ordinarily resident in the UK, must be eligible to be granted options (and to exercise them) on similar terms [*ITEPA 2003, Sch 3, para 6(2)*] . There is nothing to prevent options being granted to a person who is resident and not ordinarily resident provided the scheme rules contain a power to do so (HMRC Notice 25.7.2008). Part-time employees could be excluded from participating in schemes which were approved before 1 May 1995 but this was prohibited by *FA 1995, s 137(2), (7)*. All those who actually participate in the scheme must in fact do so on similar terms. [*ITEPA 2003, Sch 3, para 7(1)* as amended by *Finance Act 2008 (FA 2008), Sch 7, para 38*]. It is permissible to determine the number of shares over which a person is to be granted options by reference to levels of remuneration, length of service or similar factors. [*ITEPA 2003, Sch 3, para 7(2)*].

(*j*) A person must not be eligible to participate in the scheme at any time (except as permitted by (*d*)–(*f*) above) unless at that time he is a director or employee of the grantor or another participating company. [*ITEPA 2003, Sch 3, para 10(1)*]. For 2014/15 onwards, if the scheme includes such a provision, the variation or variations made must in particular secure that the total market value of the shares which can be acquired by the exercise of the option is (immediately after the variation) substantially the same as what it was immediately before the variation and that the total option price is substantially the same as it was immediately before the variation [*ITEPA 2003, Sch 3, para 28(3A), Sch 4, para 22(3A)* inserted by *FA 2014, Sch 8, paras 111, 4*. Such a variation of course must not result in any of the eligibility conditions ceasing to be met in relation to the option [*ITEPA 2003, Sch 3, para 28(3B); Sch 4, para 22(3B)*].

(*k*) There must be no features of the scheme (other than those required by any of the above conditions) which have the effect of discouraging any description of employees or former employees who fulfil the conditions in (*m*) above from actually participating in the scheme. [*ITEPA 2003, Sch 3, para 6(3)*].

(*l*)   If the grantor is a member of a group of companies, the scheme must not have the effect of conferring benefits wholly or mainly on directors of companies in the group or on those employees of companies in the group who are in receipt of the higher or highest levels of remuneration. [*ITEPA 2003, Sch 3, para 8*]. This would prevent, for example, the inclusion in the scheme only of companies with higher-paid employees or the exclusion as a participating company of a subsidiary with a large number of lower-paid employees. There is no definition of higher or highest levels of remuneration. This is presumably a question of fact to be determined by reference to each individual group of companies.

A SAYE option scheme or CSOP scheme approved before 17 July 2013 has affect with any modifications needed to give effect to the above changes made by *FA 2013, Sch 2, paras 7-15, 23, 24, 25* [*FA 2013, Sch 2, para 17(1)*].

Further conditions to be met by CSOP schemes

16.17   The scheme must provide that the aggregate market value of the shares over which a participant has options under the scheme (and any other executive share option scheme established by the grantor or by any associated company of the grantor) at the time the option is granted must not exceed £30,000. From 17 July 2013, the market value of shares subject to a restriction must be determined as if they were not subject to that restriction [*ITEPA 2003, Sch 4, para 6(4)* inserted by *FA 2013, Sch 2, para 68*].

16.17A   The terms of a *Schedule 4* CSOP option granted after 5 April 2014 must state, at the time the option is granted:

(*a*)   the price at which shares can be acquired under the option,

(*b*)   the number and description of the shares which can be acquired by the exercise of the option,

(*c*)   the restrictions (if any) to which these shares may be subject,

(*d*)   the times at which the option can be exercised (in whole or part), and

(*e*)   the circumstances under which the option will lapse or be cancelled (in whole or part), including any conditions to which the exercise of the option is subject

[*ITEPA 2003, Sch 4, para 21A(1)* inserted by *FA 2014, Sch 8, para 173*]. These terms can be varied after the option is granted but in the case of the price only as provided for in *para 22* (see **16.15**(*j*)); in the case of the number or description of shares only as provided for in *para 22* or by way of a mechanism which is stated at the time the option is granted; and in any other case only by way of such a mechanism [*ITEPA 2003, Sch 4, para 21A(2)*]. Any such mechanism must be applied in a way that is fair and reasonable [*ITEPA 2003, Sch 4, para 21A(3)*]. The terms and any such mechanism must be notified to the participant as soon as practicable after the grant of the option [*ITEPA 2003, Sch 4, para 21A(4)*].

16.18   If desired a CSOP scheme can allow an individual to exercise his share options after ceasing to be a full-time director or employee. [*ITEPA 2003, Sch 4, para 24*]. There is no time limit for doing so but the exercise will not attract tax benefits unless it falls within **16.11**(*b*)(iii). It can also provide that if a participant dies before exercising the options, they can be exercised within 12 months of the date of the death [*ITEPA 2003, Sch 4, para 25*].

16.18A   From 16 July 2013, the scheme can provide that the share options can be exercised within six months after the date when a person has obtained control of the company as a result of a general offer that meets the conditions in *ITEPA 2003, s 524(2H)–(2J)* (see **16.11A**) and any condition subject to which the offer is made has been satisfied [*ITEPA 2003, Sch 4, para 25A(1)–(5)* inserted by *FA 2013, Sch 2, para 29*]. It can similarly provide that the options can be exercised within six months after the court sanctions a compromise or arrangement under *CA 2006, s 899*, which is applicable to (or affects) all the ordinary share capital of the company (or all the shares of the same class as the option shares or all (or all of the same class) which are held by a class of shareholders identified other than by reference to their employment or directorships or their participation in an approved CSOP scheme) [*ITEPA 2003, Sch 4, para 25A(1)(6)*]. A person is to be treated as obtaining control of a company if he and others acting in concert together obtain control of it [*ITEPA 2003, Sch 4, para 25A(8)*]. The scheme can also provide that options can be exercised at any time when any person is bound or entitled to acquire shares in the company under *CA 2006, ss 979-982* or *983-985* (takeover offers: right of buyer to buy-out minority shareholders [*ITEPA 2003, Sch 4, para 25A(7)*].

16.18B   No person with a material interest in a close company which is either the company whose shares can be acquired under the option, a company which has control of such a company or a company which is a member of a consortium which owns a company which in turn has control over such a company (or who has such an interest within the previous 12 months) can be eligible to participate in the scheme. [*ITEPA 2003, Sch 4, para 9(1)*].

A individual has a material interest in a close company for this purpose if he beneficially owns or has the ability to control more than 30 per cent (25 per cent up to 16 July 2013) of the ordinary share capital of the company (either directly or through the medium of other companies or by any other indirect means) in the case of a SAYE option scheme or a CSOP scheme. He also has a material interest if he owns or is entitled to acquire such rights as would in the event of a winding up of the company or in any other circumstances give an entitlement to receive more than 25 per cent or 10 per cent of the assets as the case may be that would then be available for distribution among the participators (as defined in *ICTA 1988, s 417(1)*). [*ITEPA 2003, Sch 4, para 10* as amended by *FA 2013, Sch2, para 44*].

An individual is treated as having a material interest if either he, he together with one or more of his associates (see below) or any such associates (with or without any other associates) does so. A non-UK company which would be close if it were resident in the UK and a quoted company which is not close only because at least 35 per cent of the voting power is held by the public under *ICTA 1988, s 415* must be treated as close companies for this purpose. [*ITEPA 2003, (4), Sch 4, para 9(2), (4)*].

For the purpose of deciding whether a person has a material interest a right to acquires shares, however arising, is regarded as a right to control them. If a person would be entitled to subscribe for new shares in the event of his exercise of a right, the issued share capital must be treated as increased by that number of shares in applying the 25 per cent of ordinary share capital test at a time prior to their issue. However the interests of the trustees of an approved SIP in any shares held by them in accordance with the plan but which have not been appropriated to, or acquired on behalf of, an individual, and any rights exercisable by the trustees as a result of that interest are ignored. [*ITEPA 2003, Sch 4, para 11*].

An associate of an individual for the purpose of the material interest test means:

(i)   any relative (spouse, parent, child or remoter relation in the direct line, brother or sister) or partner of that individual;

(ii)   the trustee or trustees of any settlement in relation to which that individual (or any relative of that individual, living or dead), is or was a settlor; and

(iii)   where that individual is interested in any shares or obligations of the company concerned which are subject to any trust, or are part of the estate of a deceased person, the trustees or personal representatives.

[*ITEPA 2003, Sch 4, para 12*].

For this purpose the trustees of an employee benefit trust are not to be regarded as associates of the individual merely because of the individual being so interested if neither the individual, he and one or more associates (as defined above but excluding an employee benefit trust within this exception) or any associate or associates has at any time after 13 March 1989 been the beneficial owner of (or able, directly or through the medium of other companies or by any other indirect means, to control) more than 25 per cent of the ordinary share capital of the company. Chapter 11 of Part 7 of *ITEPA 2003* which contains further rules about employee benefit trusts applies for this purpose. [*ITEPA 2003, Sch 4, para 13*]. These are dealt with at **15.15–15.16**. Also for the purpose of (iii) if the individual was formerly a beneficiary of a discretionary trust which at any time held shares or obligations of the company concerned but ceased to be a beneficiary, either as a result of an irrevocable disclaimer or release executed by the beneficiary or the irrevocable exercise by the trustees of a power to exclude the beneficiary from the object of the trust, the individual is not regarded as having an interest in shares or obligations of the company held by the trust at any time during the previous 12 months, provided that immediately after he ceased to be a beneficiary no associate of his (as defined above) was interested in those shares or obligations and neither the beneficiary or any associate received any benefit under the trust in the 12 month period. [*ITEPA 2003, Sch 4, para 14*].

Exchange of options

16.19   Both a SAYE option scheme and a CSOP scheme can provide that if a company either:

(i)   obtains control of the grantor company as a result of making a general offer:

    (A)   to acquire the whole of the issued ordinary share capital of the company (and the offer is made on a condition that if satisfied would give the offeror control of the company); or

    (B)   to acquire all of the shares of the same class as the scheme shares; or

(ii)   obtains control of the grantor company in pursuance of a compromise or arrangement sanctioned by the courts under *CA 2006, s 899* or for 2014/15 onwards of a non-UK company re-organisation arrangement which has become binding on the shareholders governed by it; or

(iii)   becomes bound or entitled to acquire shares in the grantor company under *CA 2006, ss 979–982*;

    a participant may release his option under the scheme ('the old rights') in consideration of the grant to him of an option relating to shares in a different company (which can either be the acquiring company or a company which controls it or a consortium company within head *(a)*(iii) of **16.15** above) ('the new rights'). [*ITEPA 2003, Sch 3, paras 38(1), (2), 39(2), Sch 4, para 26(1), (2), 27(2)* as amended by *FA 2013, Sch 2, para 25*]. From 17 July 2013, the references to the issued ordinary share capital and to shares in the company do not include any shares already held by the offeror or a connected person, and it does not matter if the general offer is made to different shareholders by different means [*ITEPA 2003, Sch 4, para 26(2A)(2B)* inserted by *FA 2013, Sch 2, para 30*]. From 17 July 2013, the market value of shares subject to a restriction must be determined as if they were not subject to the restriction [*ITEPA 2003, Sch 3, para 39(7); Sch 4, para 27(7)* both inserted by *FA 2013, Sch 2, paras 63, 73*]. Shares are subject to a restriction for SIP purposes if there is any contract, agreement, arrangement or condition which makes provision to which any of *ITEPA 2003, s 423(2)–(4)* (restricted securities – see **14.27**) would apply [*ITEPA 2003, Sch 3, para 48(3); Sch 4, para 36(3)* both inserted by *FA 2013, Sch 2, paras 65, 75*].

The new option must be equivalent to the old; in particular:

(i)   the new option shares must satisfy the conditions in heads *(c)–(f)* in **16.15** above;

(ii)   the new rights must be exercisable in the same manner as the old rights, and subject to the provisions of the scheme as it had effect immediately before the release of the old;

(iii)   the total market value immediately before the release of the old rights of the option shares must be substantially the same (equal to up to 2013/14) as the total market value immediately after the grant of the new rights of the new option shares; and

(iv)   the total amount payable to acquire the shares under the new option must be substantially the same (equal to up to 2013/14) as was payable to acquire shares under the old.

[*ITEPA 2003, Sch 3, para 39(4), Sch 4, para 27(4)* as amended by *FA 2014, Sch 8, paras 116, 178*].

The exchange of options must take place within six months from the time that the person making the offer obtains control of the company (and any condition subject to which the offer was made is satisfied) or within six months of the non-UK reorganisation becoming binding. In the case of an arrangement under *CA 2006, s 899* it must take place within six months of the court approving the compromise or arrangement; and in the case of an acquisition under *CA 2006, ss 979–982* (formerly *Companies Act 1985 (CA 1985), ss 428–430*) within the period during which the company is bound or entitled to acquire the shares. [*ITEPA 2003, Sch 3, para 38(3), Sch 4, para 26(3)* as amended by *FA 2014, Sch 8, paras 115, 177*].

The new option is regarded as having been granted at the time the corresponding old option was granted. [*ITEPA 2003, Sch 3, para 39(5), (6), Sch 4, para 27(5), (6)*]. From 2014/15 the market value of shares for this purpose has to be determined using a methodology agreed by HMRC [*ITEPA 2003, Sch 3, para 39(8); Sch 4 para 27(8)* inserted by *FA 2014, Sch 8, paras 116, 178*].

16.20   In the case of an SAYE option scheme (but not a CSOP scheme), if it is wished, the scheme can provide that:

(i)   if any person obtains control of the grantor company as a result of a general offer falling within **16.19**(*i*) above, the options can be exercised within six months of the time that he does so (and any condition subject to which the offer was made is satisfied);

(ii)   if the court sanctions an arrangement under the *CA 2006, s 899* applicable to or affecting all the ordinary share capital of the company (or all of the shares of the same class as those to which the option relates or all of the shares (or of the class) which are held by a class of shareholders identified other than by reference to their employment or directorships or their participation in an approved SAYE option scheme), the options can be exercised within six months of the court sanctioning the compromise (prior to 17 July 2013 the scheme had to be for the reconstruction of the grantor company or its amalgamation with another company);

(iii)   if any person becomes bound or entitled under *CA 2006, ss 979–982* the options can be exercised at any time during the period that person remains bound or entitled to acquire shares; and

(iv)   if the grantor company passes a resolution for voluntary winding up, the options can be exercised at any time within six months of the passing of the resolution.

(v)   from 2014/15 onwards, if a non-UK company re-organisation arrangement applies to or affects all of the ordinary share capital of the company or all of the shares of the class to which the option relates (or all of such shares which are held by a class of shareholder identified otherwise than by reference to their employments or directorships or their participation in a *Sch 3 SAYE scheme*), the option can be exercised within six months of the scheme becoming binding on the shareholders covered by it.

[*ITEPA 2003, Sch 3, para 37* as amended by *FA 2013, Sch 2, para 24 and FA 2014, Sch 8, para 114*]. The application of (i)) above was in issue in *Tailor v HMRC (TC 2614)*. The company was acquired by a Newco in an MBO. The Newco made an offer to acquire the shares held by the non-management shareholders as required by the Takeover Code. This was held to be a general offer. However it was not an offer to acquire the whole of the issued ordinary share capital as it did not include the shares already held by the management. Accordingly Mrs Tailor's shares were not acquired 'under' the SAYE scheme. As she had held her options for less than three years (see **16.11**) an income tax charge arose on the exercise of the options. As the options were employment-related securities options (see **14.102**) the acquisition of the shares was a chargeable event (see **14.107**) giving rise to employment income. As quoted shares are readily convertible assets, the company was under an obligation to apply PAYE. Accordingly HMRC could not assess Mrs Tailor as Reg 185(6) of the PAYE Regulations gives her a credit for the PAYE that should have been deducted.

In the event of a takeover, the option holder can be given a choice to exchange his option for a new option in the acquiring company (under the above provision), to exercise his option prematurely to enable him to accept the offer in relation to the shares, (see **16.16**(*d*) above) or to do nothing and exercise the option when it would otherwise be exercisable (although in practice the terms of the takeover are likely to require the options to be cancelled if they are not immediately either exercised or exchanged). Although the exercise of the option, either in due course or prematurely, can be permitted by the scheme such an exercise will not normally attract the tax benefits expected from the use of an approved scheme as the shares will not usually qualify as eligible shares. An exchange of options will preserve the tax benefits. The scheme can also provide that if in consequence of one of the above events, shares in the company to which the option relates cease to qualify as *Schedule 3* SAYE shares, the option can be exercised within 20 days of the event (ie the beginning of the six-month period) notwithstanding that the shares are no longer qualifying shares [*ITEPA 2003, Sch 3, para 37(6A)–(6D)* inserted by *FA 2014, Sch 8, para 114*]. It can also provide that an option exercised in that 20-day period can be treated as exercised under *para 37(1)* or *(6)*, provided that it also provides that if the option is exercised in anticipation of the relevant event (or of a person becoming bound or entitled to acquire shares within *para 37(6)*) the exercise is to be treated as having had no effect unless that event occurs within the following 20 days [*ITEPA 2003, Sch 3, para 37(6E)(6F)*].

16.21   The provisions for notification of an option scheme, annual returns, enquiries, penalties and appeals considered at **15.93–15.103** apply also (with any necessary modifications) to *Schedule 3 SAYE option schemes* and *Schedule 4 CSOP option schemes* [*ITEPA 2003, Sch 3, paras 40A-40K; Sch 4, paras 28A–28K*, inserted by *FA 2014, Sch 8, paras 117, 178*].

Administration

16.21A   Prior to 2014/15 HMRC had to approve a SAYE option scheme or a CSOP scheme if the scheme organiser applied for approval and the scheme fulfilled the necessary requirements. [*ITEPA 2003, Sch 3, para 40(1), Sch 4, para 28(1)*]. An application for approval had to be made in writing and contain such particulars and be supported by such evidence as HMRC required. [*ITEPA 2003, Sch 3, para 40(2), Sch 4, para 28(2)* repealed by *FA 2014, Sch 8, paras 117, 178*]. The requirement for prior approval was abolished as a simplification measure. However it has a very large downside. HMRC used to scrutinise schemes vigorously and even tried to insert amendments to suit their own internal requirements even where a scheme met the statutory requirements. Now if a scheme fails to meet the HMRC requirements, that fact will not be known until after the scheme has been notified to HMRC and possibly until after HMRC have enquired into an annual return. The company is now at risk that options issued prior to HMRC discovering defects in the scheme will turn out to be unapproved share options with no tax advantages. This is likely to result in very unhappy option-holders! Of course unexercised options can be surrendered and new ones granted, but in many cases the value of the shares will have increased in the interim, so that will still disadvantage the employee.

Groups of companies

16.21B   A scheme can be expressed to extend to all or any subsidiaries of the company setting up the scheme (or other companies of which it has control). [*ITEPA 2003, Sch 3, para 3, Sch 4, para 3*].

16.22   Each joint owner of a jointly owned company can include that company (and any company controlled by it) in its own group scheme. A jointly owned company for this purpose is one of which 50 per cent of the issued share capital is owned by one person and 50 per cent by another, or which is otherwise controlled by two persons taken together. Each joint owner is treated as controlling the jointly owned company (and any company controlled by it). A company cannot however be a constituent company in more than one group scheme. Nor can it be a constituent company in a particular group scheme if another company in the jointly owned group is a constituent company of another scheme. Accordingly once one of the companies in the jointly owned group becomes a member of the group scheme of one of the joint owners, no other company in that group can join the group scheme of the other joint owner. [*ITEPA 2003, Sch 3, para 46, Sch 4, para 34*].

16.23   All the companies covered by a scheme are referred to as constituent (formerly participating) companies and such a scheme is called a group scheme.

Prohibited features

16.24   The purpose of the scheme must be to provide, in accordance with *Schedule 3*, benefits for employees or directors in the form of share options. It must not provide benefits to employees or directors otherwise than in accordance with that Schedule. In particular, it must not provide cash as an alternative to share options or to shares which might otherwise be acquired by the exercise of share options [*ITEPA 2003, Sch 3, para 5, Sch 4, para 5* as substituted by *FA 2014, Sch 8, paras 108, 169*]. Up to 5 April 2014, HMRC were prohibited from approving a scheme if in their view it contained any features which were not essential to the purpose of providing for directors' and employees' rights to acquire shares, or which were not reasonably incidental to that purpose. [*ITEPA 2003, Sch 3, para 5, Sch 4, para 5* as originally enacted].

16.25   In *IRC v Burton Group plc [1990] STC 242* an option scheme incorporated tasks which the employee had to meet before he became entitled to acquire shares. The company wished to amend the scheme to ensure that it operated effectively as an incentive scheme by enabling it to vary such tasks after an option had been granted. HMRC refused to approve the change. They contended that for an employee to 'have obtained a right to acquire shares' the machinery by which his entitlement to them could be identified must be known at the time the option is granted. They also claimed that the amendment was neither essential nor reasonably incidental to the purpose of providing share benefits. Both these claims were dismissed in the High Court. The new conditions did not affect the number of shares the employee could acquire and there was no objection to the requirement that he should meet subsequently imposed conditions. On the second point, the scheme has to be looked at as a whole. The changes were designed to ensure that the scheme worked more effectively. Accordingly, HMRC could not refuse approval for the amendments.

Withdrawal of approval

16.26   HMRC had power to withdraw approval if an alteration was made in a key feature of the scheme (one necessary to meet the requirements of this *Act*) without their approval and they would not have approved the change if it were a new scheme, or the company refused to provide information requested by HMRC under *ITEPA 2003, Sch 3, para 45* or *Sch 4, para 33* (see **16.34** below). Such withdrawal could be retrospective to the date that the conditions ceased to be met or from any later date that HMRC chose. [*ITEPA 2003, Sch 3, para 42(1), (2), Sch 4, para 30* repealed by *FA 2014, Sch 8, paras 117*].

16.27   If approval of a SAYE option scheme (but not a CSOP scheme) is withdrawn, the tax benefits are preserved in relation to options granted before the withdrawal. [*ITEPA 2003, Sch 3, para 42(3)*].

Alterations to scheme

16.28   If the scheme is altered in any way after approval, the approval lapses from the date of the change unless the alteration is approved by HMRC. [*ITEPA*

2003, Sch 3, para 43, Sch 4, para 31]. It is not clear if HMRC have power to approve an alteration retrospectively. In any event, it is obviously wise to seek approval for an alteration before putting it into effect.

Right of appeal

16.29   The company has a right of appeal if HMRC do not approve a scheme or an alteration to a scheme or withdraw approval (or in the case of a savings-related share option scheme, decide that a condition subject to which approval was given is satisfied). This appeal is to the Special Commissioners and must be made within 30 days of the company being informed of the HMRC decision. [*ITEPA 2003, Sch 3, paras 41, 44, Sch 4, paras 29, 32*].

In *IRC v Eurocopy plc [1991] STC 707*, the court upheld HMRC's refusal to allow the application to existing options of an alteration that reduced the period before which options could be exercised from nine to six years. HMRC's stance was based on the fact that the rights attaching to the options prior to the alteration were not the same as the rights attaching to them after it. The Eurocopy decision was distinguished in *IRC v Reed International plc 67 TC 552*. Before the alteration an option holder would have had to exercise his option within six months of the merger of Reed and Elsevier NV, albeit that such a merger had not been in contemplation when the option was granted. The alteration removed that as a trigger. The Court of Appeal felt that the removal of one out of ten or 11 events on the earliest of which an existing right would be exercisable could not realistically be described as the obtaining of a new and different right to acquire shares (as could the bringing forward of the exercise date in *Eurocopy*); it was simply a variation of an existing right.

Information

16.30   HMRC can by notice require any person to supply such information as they reasonably require for the performance of any functions under the SAYE or CSOP code and which the person to whom the notice is addressed has or can reasonably obtain. They must allow him at least three months to provide the information. The information they can request includes that necessary to check whether anything contained in a notice under *Sch 3, para 40A* (or *Sch 4, para 28A*) or a return under *Sch 3, para 40B* (or *Sch 4, para 28B*) or any information accompanying it to determine the liability to tax of any participant in the scheme or any other person whose liability to tax the operation of the scheme is relevant to, and to monitor the administration of the scheme and any alteration to it. [*ITEPA 2003, Sch 3, para 45, Sch 4, para 33* as amended by *FA 2014, Sch 8, paras 118, 180*].

Approved profit-sharing scheme (up to 1 January 2003)

16.31   It was possible to set up approved profit sharing schemes between 5 April 1999 and 31 December 2002. The legislation is still on the statute book, presumably to ensure that any clawback of relief arising from later actions can still be taxed. However new schemes can no longer be set up. An approved profit sharing scheme was actually something of a misnomer as there was no requirement that the benefits should be related to profits. The company set up a trust to which it allocated money which the trustees used to subscribe for shares in the company (or to buy such shares on the open market). Immediately on acquisition of the shares, the trustees had to allocate them among participating employees, whilst retaining ownership of the shares.

16.32 HMRC can withdraw approval of a profit sharing scheme if at any time:

(*a*)   any participant was in breach of his obligations under *ICTA 1988, Sch 9, para 2(2)(a), (c), (d))*;

(*b*)   any contravention of any of the relevant requirements in *ICTA 1988, Sch 10*, the scheme itself, or the terms of the trust, took place;

(*c*)   any shares of a class of which shares had been appropriated to participants received different treatment in any respect from any other shares of that class, particularly in relation to:

    (i)   the dividend payable (which would seem to include one holder waiving his dividend);

    (ii)   repayments (as the shares cannot be redeemable shares this presumably meant repayment on a winding up);

    (iii) the restrictions attaching to the shares; or

    (iv)   any offer of substituted or additional shares (or securities or rights of any description) in respect of the shares;

(*d*)   HMRC ceasing to be satisfied that the scheme complied with *ICTA 1988, Sch 9, para 2(3)* (see heads (*l*) and (*m*) at **16.63** below) or *Sch 9, para 36*; or

(*e*)   the trustees or the grantor (or another participating company) failing to furnish any information which they were required to furnish under *Sch 9, para 6* (see **16.34**) [*Sch 9, para 3(2)*];

(*f*)   the trustees appropriating shares to a participant who has had free shares awarded to him at an earlier time in the same year of assessment under a SIP (see **Chapter 15**) established by the grantor company or a connected company (or would have done so but for his failure to meet a performance target (see **15.23**);

(*g*)   HMRC ceasing to be satisfied that the arrangements for the scheme prohibited loans to employees within *ICTA 1988, Sch 9, para 2(2A))*. [*ICTA 1988, Sch 9, para 3(2)*].

For the purpose of (*f*) above a connected company was one which controlled the grantor company; one which was controlled by the grantor company or by a company which also controlled the grantor company; or one which was a member of a consortium which either owned the grantor or of which the grantor was one of its part owners. [*ICTA 1988, Sch 9, para 3(6)*].

16.33   HMRC have discretion as to whether to withdraw approval with effect from the time of the trigger event or from a later date. They could not, however, withdraw approval merely because shares which have been newly issued receive a lesser dividend than shares issued earlier in respect of a period beginning before the date of their issue. [*ICTA 1988, Sch 9, para 3(3)*].

Tax benefits of the schemes

16.34   The tax benefits of such schemes derived from the fact that when the trustees of an approved profit sharing scheme appropriated to a participant in the scheme shares which had previously been acquired by the trustees (and as to which the qualifying conditions of *ICTA 1988, Sch 9* were met):

(*a*)   the value of the shares at the time of appropriation was not treated as employment income of the individual (even though the beneficial interest in the shares passed to him) provided that such appropriation was made before 6 April 2002; and

(*b*)   the individual was not taxed under *ITEPA 2003, ss 449, 455* (see **14.149** and **14.159** above) or by virtue of *ITEPA 2003, ss 193, 194* (see **14.141** above) in respect of the shares.

[*ICTA 1988, s 186(1), (2)*].

Capital receipt before release date

16.35   If either the trustees or the participant (ie the individual to whom shares were appropriated) became entitled before the release date (see **16.61** below) to receive any money or money's worth ('a capital receipt') in respect of any of a participant's shares, the participant was taxable on employment income for the year of assessment in which such entitlement arose on the 'appropriate percentage' of so much of the receipt as exceeded the 'appropriate allowance' for that year. [*ICTA 1988, s 186(3)*].

Meaning of 'appropriate allowance'

16.36   The appropriate allowance was £20 multiplied by one plus the number of years of assessment between the time of the appropriation of the shares and the start of the year of assessment in which the capital receipt arises. [*ICTA 1988, s 186(12)*]. It could not, however, exceed £60. If the trustees or the participant became entitled to more than one capital receipt in any year of assessment (and before the release date) the appropriate allowance was set against them in the order in which they were received. [*ICTA 1988, s 186(12)*].

Items not regarded as capital receipts

16.37   Money or money's worth was not to be regarded as a capital receipt for this purpose to the extent that either:

(*a*)   it constituted income of the recipient for income tax purposes;

(*b*)   it consisted of the proceeds of a disposal falling within *ICTA 1988, s 186(4)* (see **16.41** below);

(*c*)   it consisted of new shares within *ICTA 1988, Sch 10, para 5* (see **16.49** below) [*ICTA 1988, Sch 10, para 4(1)(a)–(c)*];

(*d*)   it was the proceeds of disposal of some of the rights arising under a rights issue (provided that the disposal was pursuant to a direction given to the trustees by the participant or any other person in whom the participant's beneficial interest in the shares vested) [*ICTA 1988, Sch 10, para 4(2)*]; or

(*e*)   the entitlement to the receipt arose after the death of the participant. [*ICTA 1988, Sch 10, para 4(4)*].

16.38   If the amount of a capital receipt exceeded the locked-in value of the shares (see **16.41** below) immediately before the entitlement to the receipt arose, the charge under *s186(3)* was limited to tax on the locked-in value. [*ICTA 1988, Sch 10, para 4(3)*].

Disposal before release date

16.39   If the trustees disposed of any of a participant's shares at any time before the release date (or, if earlier, the date of the participant's death) the participant was taxable on employment income, for the year of assessment in which the disposal occurred, on the appropriate percentage of the locked-in value of the shares at the time of disposal. [*ICTA 1988, s 186(4)*]. The locked-in value was normally the initial market value of the shares. If the participant had previously been taxed under *s 186(3)* in relation to a capital receipt from the shares, it was the initial market value less the amount of that receipt (or aggregate receipts). [*ICTA 1988, s 186(5)*]. If the locked-in value exceeded the disposal proceeds of the shares the locked-in value had to be treated as being equal to the proceeds. [*ICTA 1988, s 186(6)*]. The release date was the third anniversary of the date on which the shares were appropriated to the employee. [*ICTA 1988, s 187(2)*]. The appropriate percentage was 100 per cent except where the employee has reached retirement age, been made redundant or left because of injury or disability, when it was 50 per cent. [*ICTA 1988, Sch 10, para 3*].

16.40   If the disposal was made out of a holding of shares which were appropriated to the participant at different times, the shares were deemed to be disposed of in the order of acquisition (ie on a first in, first out basis) for the purpose of determining the initial market value, the locked-in value, and the appropriate percentage in relation to the shares. [*ICTA 1988, s 186(8)*].

16.41   This assumption applied even if the different acquisitions and disposals were identifiable (by reference to numbered share certificates, for example) or the participant specified to the trustees that they were to dispose of shares appropriated to him at a particular time. [*ICTA 1988, s 186(9)*].

Payment for rights

16.42   If at any time prior to the disposal a payment was made to the trustees to enable them to take up rights on a rights issue, the proceeds of disposal first had to be reduced by an amount equal to the proportion of that rights payment (or of the aggregate of all such payments if more than one) which the market value of the shares immediately before the disposal bore to the market value of all the participant's shares held by the trustees at that time. [*ICTA 1988, s 186(7)*]. In other words, if the participant (or, indeed, anyone else) had previously made a payment to the trustees to enable them to take up a rights issue, that payment was, not unnaturally, deducted in arriving at the taxable amount.

16.43   However, a payment that was previously made to the trustees from, say, stockbrokers arising from a sale of rights, for example, where some of the rights were sold to provide funds to take up the rest, obviously could not be deducted from the disposal proceeds of the shares as it was not an extraneous sum but derived from those shares. [*ICTA 1988, s 186(8)(a)*]. If there have been earlier share disposals any amount deducted from those proceeds clearly could not be deducted again. [*ICTA 1988, s 186(8)(b)*].

Disposal of beneficial interest

16.44   If the participant's beneficial interest in any of his shares was disposed of, *s 186(4)* (see **16.41** above) applied as if the shares themselves had been disposed of by the trustees for the consideration that was received on the disposal of the beneficial interest. The vesting of the beneficial interest on the insolvency of the participant or by operation of law did not trigger this tax charge, however. [*ICTA 1988, s 186(9)*].

16.45   If the disposal by the trustees was a transfer of shares (before the release date) to the participant himself, or the Board of HMRC considered that the disposal was not at arm's length, or the disposal was a disposal of the beneficial interest only and took place within the period of retention, the income tax charge had to be calculated by reference to the market value of the shares at the time of the disposal, not the disposal proceeds. [*ICTA 1988, s 186(10)*].

Additional rate tax

16.46   Provided that the trustees of an approved scheme appropriated qualifying shares in accordance with the scheme within 18 months from the date of their acquisition, the 40 per cent tax rate applicable to trusts that applies to discretionary and accumulation trusts was not payable on dividends from the shares. Shares were deemed to be appropriated to participants on a first in, first out basis. [*ICTA 1988, s 186(11)*].

Company reconstructions

16.47   If the participant's shares were disposed of on a reconstruction or amalgamation that qualified as a company reconstruction for capital gains tax purposes, any part of the new holding (ie the new shares received in exchange for (or in addition to) the old) which consisted of:

(*a*) redeemable shares or securities issued otherwise than wholly for new consideration (eg as a scrip issue);

(*b*) a scrip issue of shares where the company previously repaid any share capital since 6 April 1965; or

(*c*) share capital which was taxed as a stock dividend,

were not to be treated as forming part of the new holding. [*ICTA 1988, Sch 10, para 5(1), (2)*]. In each of the above circumstances the value of the shares was already taxed as income under other provisions (under (*a*) or (*b*) it was a distribution and under (*c*) taxable under *section 249*). This provision accordingly prevented double taxation. By taking the shares out of the new holding their value became a capital receipt – but one that was excluded from tax under *ICTA 1988, Sch 10, para 4* (see **16.39** above).

16.48   A company reconstruction was not treated as involving a disposal of the original holding, but the new shares received on the reconstruction had to be treated as having been appropriated to the participant at the time the old shares were appropriated. Provided that the conditions in *ICTA 1988, Sch 9, paras 10–12, 14* were fulfilled with respect to the old shares, they were treated as also being fulfilled with respect to the new. [*ICTA 1988, Sch 10, para 5(4)*].

Market value of shares after reconstruction

16.49   *Section 186(5)* (see **16.41** above) applied to the new holding as if the initial market value of the shares were equal to their locked-in value immediately after the reconstruction. This was arrived at as follows:

(*a*) Ascertain the aggregate amount of locked-in value (immediately before the reconstruction) of those shares comprised in the original holding which at the time had the same locked-in value.

(*b*) Distribute that amount among:

(i) such of the original shares as are retained as part of the new holding; and

(ii) the new shares received on the reconstruction;

in proportion to their market values immediately after the date of the reconstruction. [*ICTA 1988, Sch 10, para 5(5)*]. *Section 186(5)(a)* then applied only to capital receipts after the date of the reconstruction.

Capital receipt on reconstruction

16.50   If, as part of the reconstruction, the trustees became entitled to a capital receipt (eg there was a cash payment to shareholders), that receipt was treated as having arisen before the new holding came into being and before the date on which the locked-in value of shares comprised in the original holding fell to be ascertained. [*ICTA 1988, Sch 10, para 5(6)*]. In the context of a new holding, references in *Sch 10, para 5* to shares included securities and rights of any description (eg warrants) which formed part of the new holding. [*ICTA 1988, Sch 10, para 5(7)*].

16.51   The rules in **16.49–16.52** also applied where qualifying corporate bonds were received on a reconstruction, provided that the trust deed had been altered to prohibit the trustees from disposing of the bonds in such circumstances in accordance with *Sch 9, para 33(a)*). [*ICTA 1988, Sch 10, para 5A* and *FA 1994, s 101(4)–(13)*].

Value of shares exceeding relevant amount

16.52   If the total amount of the initial market value of all the shares appropriated to an individual in a year of assessment (whether under one or more approved schemes) exceeded the relevant amount:

(*a*)   the appropriate percentage in relation to the excess shares (see **16.55** below) for the purpose of any charge to income tax by reason of the occurrence of an event relating to the shares was 100 per cent (and the event had to be treated as relating to shares which were not excess shares in priority to those that were) [*ICTA 1988, Sch 10, para 6(4)*];

(*b*)   excess shares that had not been disposed of before the release date (or, if earlier, the death of the participant) had to be treated as disposed of by the trustees immediately before that date at their market value – so as to trigger an income tax charge on 100 per cent of that value [*ICTA 1988, Sch 10, para 6(5)*]; and

(*c*)   the locked-in value of the excess shares at any time was their market value at that time. [*ICTA 1988, Sch 10, para 6(6)*].

Meaning of 'excess shares'

16.53   For this purpose the 'excess shares' were the shares which caused the relevant amount to be exceeded and any further shares appropriated subsequently. [*ICTA 1988, Sch 10, para 6(2)*]. If shares were appropriated to an individual at the same time under two or more schemes the excess shares were treated as coming rateably from both schemes. [*ICTA 1988, Sch 10, para 6(3)*]. Where there had been a company reconstruction a new share received on the reconstruction had to be treated as an excess share if the original share from which it derived was an excess share. [*ICTA 1988, Sch 10, para 6(7)*].

16.54   If the trustees appropriated shares to an individual at a time when he was ineligible to participate in the scheme those 'unauthorised shares' were taxed in the same way as described above in relation to excess shares. [*ICTA 1988, Sch 10, para 6(1)(b)*].

PAYE deductions

16.55   If the trustees received a sum of money which constituted (or formed part of) either:

(*a*)   the proceeds of a disposal of shares falling within *section 186(4)* (see **16.41** above); or

(*b*)   a capital receipt (see **16.37** above),

in respect of which a participant was taxable on employment income by virtue of *s 186*, they had to pay that money not to the participant but to the employer company. If he was employed by more than one company, both of which were participants in the scheme, they had to pay it to such of the companies as HMRC directed. The company had to deduct tax under PAYE and pay the balance to the participant. [*ICTA 1988, Sch 10, para 7(1), (3)*]. If at the time the trustees received the money there was no company which both employed the individual and was a participant in the scheme, or if HMRC considered it impractical to require the employer company to make a PAYE deduction and directed the trustees to do so, the trustees themselves had to deduct tax under PAYE when paying the money to the participant. For this purpose the participant was treated as if he were a former employee of the trustees, so the PAYE deduction was made at the basic rate. [*ICTA 1988, Sch 10, para 7(4)*]. HMRC were empowered to direct the trustees to pay the capital sum to any company that they specified (eg the participant's current employer) even though that company may have had nothing to do with the scheme, in which case that company had to apply PAYE when paying the amount over to the employee. However, such a direction required the consent of the trustees, all the employer company or companies that were participants in the scheme (if any), and the company on which HMRC wished to impose the obligation to deduct PAYE. [*ICTA 1988, Sch 10, para 7(5)*]. The *PAYE Regulations* obviously applied to the payment as if it were remuneration. [*ICTA 1988, Sch 10, para 7(6)*].

16.56   If a participant disposed of his beneficial interest in his shares to the trustees, so that there was a deemed disposal by the trustees under *s 186(9)* (see **16.43** above) the amount had to be subjected to PAYE in the same way as on an actual disposal by the trustees. [*ICTA 1988, Sch 10, para 7(2)*]. If the participant directed the trustees to transfer the shares to himself before the release date, and therefore had to make a payment to them of tax at the basic rate on the appropriate percentage of the locked-in value (see **16.41** above), that amount had to be accounted for by the trustee as if it were an amount deducted under PAYE in respect of the disposal proceeds of the shares. [*ICTA 1988, Sch 10, para 7(7)*].

16.57   In determining the amount on which PAYE was payable the trustees could ignore the fact that some of the shares might be excess shares unless HMRC otherwise directed. [*ICTA 1988, Sch 10, para 7(8)*]. The trustees would not necessarily know that they were excess shares. This accordingly relieved them of the obligation to account for tax on a higher amount than, on the face of things, appeared due.

16.58   For capital gains tax purposes the employee was treated as owning the shares while they were held by the trustees. [*Taxation of Chargeable Gains Act 1992 (TCGA 1992), s 238(1)*].

Definitions

16.59   There are a number of special definitions for the purpose of those provisions. Where the meanings are not obvious, these have generally been inserted in the text above where appropriate. It may be helpful to list the main expressions for which specific definitions are included together with the paragraphs above where the definition can be found:

appropriate percentage

associated company: two companies are associated companies at a given time if at that time or at any time within the previous year one has control of the other or both are under the control of the same person or persons [*ITEPA 2003, Sch 3, para 47(1), Sch 4, para 35(1)*]

bonus date: (**16.16**(*b*))

capital receipt: (**16.37**)

certified contractual savings scheme: an approved SAYE scheme

connected person: the *s 839* definition applies [*ITEPA 2003, s 718*]

consortium: a company is a member of a consortium owning another company if it is one of a number of companies which between them beneficially own at least 75 per cent of the other company's ordinary share capital and each of which beneficially owns at least 5 per cent of that capital [*ITEPA 2003, Sch 3, para 48(2), Sch 4, para 36(2)*]

control: the *ICTA 1988, s 416* definition of control applies from 6 April 2003. The *section 840* definition applied previously. [*ITEPA 2003, Sch 3, para 47(2), Sch 4, para 35(2)*].

grantor: the company that established the scheme

initial market value

locked-in value: (**16.41**)

market value: as defined in *TCGA 1992, s 272* [*ITEPA 2003, Sch 3, para 48(1), Sch 4, para 36(1)*]

material interest: (**16.15**(*i*))

participant: an employee who participates in the scheme

pensionable age: as defined in *Social Security Contributions and Benefits Act 1992 (SSCBA 1992), s 122(1)* as amended by *Pensions Act 1995 (PA 1995), Sch 4*

period of retention

release date: the third anniversary of the date on which shares are apportioned under a profit sharing scheme. [*FA 1996, s 116*)]

relevant amount

shares: includes stock.

Capital gains tax

16.60   If a tax charge arises under *ITEPA 2003, s 526* (see **16.12**) the taxable amount is treated as part of the cost of the shares for capital gains tax purposes. [*TCGA 1992, s 120(2), (6) Sch 7D, para 12*]. This applies whether or not the option is exercised in accordance with the terms of the scheme and irrespective of whether or not the scheme is still a tax advantaged scheme at the time the option is exercised. The charge under *s 526* is, of course, one that would not have arisen but for the scheme being a tax advantaged scheme, so it is reasonable to expect relief to be given in such circumstances. Where *TCGA 1992, s 17(1)* would apply to require the company to calculate its capital gain on the grant of the option by reference to its market value, that provision is not to apply but the company is treated as granting the option only for the actual consideration received (if any). Furthermore, the value of the employee's services to the company is not to be treated as consideration for either a SAYE or CSOP option. The scheme must be treated as still being a tax advantaged scheme when the option is exercised if that is not the case. [*TCGA 1992, s 149A, Sch 7D, paras 10, 13* as amended by *FA 2014, Sch 8, paras 128, 189*]. This ensures that the company is not taxed on a notional capital gain if it grants the option at an undervalue – as would frequently be the case.

Corporation tax relief

16.61   A company is entitled to corporation tax relief for expenditure that it incurs on establishing a share option scheme within *ITEPA 2003, Sch 3* (SAYE option scheme) or *Sch 4* (CSOP option scheme) (but only if no employee or director obtains rights under the scheme prior to such approval).

[*Income Tax (Trading and Other Income) Act 2005 (ITTOIA 2005), s 94A* as amended by *FA 2014, Sch 8, para 140*]. Prior to 6 April 2014 relief was given only if the scheme had been approved by HMRC.

16.62   The deduction is given as a trading expense (or management expense if the company is an investment company). Relief is normally given in the period of account in which the expenditure is incurred but if the scheme is not approved within nine months after the end of that period it is instead given in the period in which the approval is given. [*ITTOIA 2005, s 94A(3), CTA 2009, s 1221(1)(c)* formerly *ICTA 1988, s 84A(2), (3)*].

Enterprise Management Incentives

16.63   Enterprise Management Incentives (EMIs) aim to help 'young, growing businesses which often have insufficient cashflow to reward their employees, recruit and retain the people they need' (*IR Press Release 21*

March 2000). They are share options granted after 27 July 2000 'to reward key people who are prepared to take a risk and use their skills and talents in helping those companies achieve their potential'. EMIs allow a small unquoted trading company to issue employees with options up to £100,000 of shares each. The scheme is fairly complex.

16.64   Actually it seems doubtful whether they will often be attractive in that context. An employee of a young and growing company would often be better off to acquire his shares immediately on joining the company unless it has by then already become very valuable. Whilst companies are often reluctant to allow executives to acquire shares before they have proved their worth, it is normally not that difficult to issue the shares with an obligation to sell them back for a nominal figure if the executive leaves the company within a specified period, and companies are increasingly willing to do this. EMI options can be useful within an established valuable company where a new executive does not have the funds to acquire shares but wants to participate in the growth in value, or where the shareholding is small and the shares will qualify for entrepreneurs' relief only if they are issued on exercise of an EMI option.

Purpose of granting the option

16.65   An EMI option is a qualifying option only if:

(*a*)   it is granted for commercial reasons in order to recruit or retain an employee of the company; and

(*b*)   it is not granted as part of a scheme or arrangement one of the main purposes of which is the avoidance of tax.

[*ITEPA 2003, Sch 5, para 4*].

16.66   There is no guidance as to when an option is granted in order to recruit or retain a person rather than, for example, simply to incentivise him, and no indication as to whether there are circumstances in which an option might be regarded as having a purpose of avoiding tax by virtue of the knowledge that the gain will be taxed less heavily than salary.

16.67   One of the problems of the absence of an advance clearance procedure, namely the question of whether a company is carrying on a qualifying business, has been alleviated informally. The company can submit written details of the company to the Small Company Enterprise Centre (HM Revenue and Customs, 1st Floor, Ferrers House, Castle Meadow Road, Nottingham NG2 1BB, tel: 0115 974 1250) before the EMI options are granted and HMRC will give written confirmation if they believe, on the basis of the information provided to them, that the company qualifies.

Maximum entitlement

16.68   An employee must not hold unexercised qualifying options which were granted by reason of his employment with a single company (or group of companies) in respect of shares with a total value (at the date of the grant of the option) of more than £120,000 (£100,000 up to 5 April 2008). [*ITEPA 2003, Sch 5, para 5(1)*].

16.69   If the grant of an option causes that limit to be exceeded the excess is not a qualifying option. [*ITEPA 2003, Sch 5, para 5(3)*]. If an employee has been granted options up to the £120,000 limit and, for example, exercises or releases some he cannot be granted further qualifying options (by either the company or another member of the same group) within three years of the date of the last qualifying option, ie the one that brought the total up to £120,000. [*ITEPA 2003, Sch 5, para 6*].

16.70   If at the time an option is granted to an employee he holds unexercised options under an approved CSOP scheme (see **16.11** granted by reason of employment with the same company (or another member of its group) those executive share options must be brought into account in testing the £120,000 limit. [*ITEPA 2003, Sch 5, para 5(4), (5)*].

16.71   The value of shares under option is the market value at the time the option is granted of the maximum number of shares of the same class as those which may be acquired on its exercise. If the shares are restricted shares the restrictions or risk must be ignored in valuing the shares. Shares are restricted shares if there is any contract, arrangement or condition that would bring them within *ITEPA 2003, s 423* (see **14.24**). [*ITEPA 2003, Sch 5, para 5(8)*].

Maximum value of options

16.72   The total 'value' of shares in the company in respect of which qualifying options exist must not exceed £3 million. [*ITEPA 2003, Sch 5, para 7(1)*]. This test is applied at the time each option is granted. [*ITEPA 2003, Sch 5, para 7(2)*]. The value of shares for this purpose is the sum of the market values of shares of the same class as the option shares at the time each option was granted. Para **16.79** applies in ascertaining such values. [*ITEPA 2003, Sch 5, para 7(6)*].

16.73   If the grant of an option causes the limit to be exceeded it is only the excess that is non-qualifying. If two or more options are granted at the same time such an excess is divided amongst them in proportion to the value of the shares over which each option is granted. [*ITEPA 2003, Sch 5, para 7(3)–(5)*].

Qualifying company

16.74   The company must satisfy the following conditions at the time the options are granted:

(*a*)   It must not be a 51 per cent subsidiary of another company (or otherwise under the control (within *ICTA 1988, s 840*) of another company, or of another company together with any other person connected with that company). Also no arrangements must exist (other than arrangements within para 40 – see **16.116**) by virtue of which the company could become a 51 per cent subsidiary or fall under such control. [*ITEPA 2003, Sch 5, para 9*].

(*b*) If the company has subsidiaries they must all be qualifying subsidiaries, i.e:

   (i) the company must possess at least 75 per cent of the issued share capital and 75 per cent of the voting power in the subsidiary;

   (ii) in the event of a winding up of the subsidiary (or in any other circumstances) the company (or another of its subsidiaries) must be beneficially entitled to at least 75 per cent of the assets which would then be available for distribution to the shareholders of the subsidiaries;

   (iii) the company (or another of its subsidiaries) must be beneficially entitled to at least 75 per cent of any profits of the subsidiary which are available for distribution to its shareholders;

   (iv) no other person (other than another subsidiary of the company) must have control (within *ICTA 1988, s 460 (s 840* prior to 5 April 2003)) of the subsidiary; and

   (v) there must be no arrangements in existence by virtue of which any of the above conditions could cease to be met.

   [*ITEPA 2003, Sch 5, paras 10, 11*].

(*c*) The value of the company's gross assets must not exceed £30 million If the company has subsidiaries the consolidated value of the group assets (the aggregate value of the gross assets of the group disregarding any that consist in rights against, shares in or securities of another group company) must not exceed £15 million. [*ITEPA 2003, Sch 5, para 12*].

(*d*) The company must exist wholly for the purpose of carrying on one or more qualifying trades, disregarding any incidental purposes (see below), or of preparing to do so. The meaning of a qualifying trade is considered at **16.81** below. In the case of a parent company the business activities of the group as a whole must not consist wholly or to a substantial extent in the carrying on of non-qualifying activities (see below) and at least one group company must satisfy the above qualifying purpose and qualifying trade test. [*ITEPA 2003, Sch 5, paras 13, 14*].

(*e*) In relation to options granted after 15 December 2010, the company must either have a permanent establishment in the UK or it must be a parent company and some other member of the group must meet the trading activities test in (*d*) above and have a permanent establishment in the UK [*ITEPA 2003, Sch 5, para 14A* inserted by *Finance (No 3) Act 2010 (F(No 3)A 2010), s 6*].

16.75 For the purpose of (*b*) above a subsidiary will not be treated as ceasing to be a qualifying one at a time when it (or another company) is being wound up if the subsidiary would have qualified but for the winding up and the winding up is for commercial purposes and not part of a scheme or arrangement one of the main purposes of which is the avoidance of tax. [*ITEPA 2003, Sch 5, para 11(5), (7)*, formerly *FA 2000, Sch 14, para 15(3)*]. Similarly it will not cease to be a qualifying subsidiary if arrangements are in existence for the disposal of the group's entire interest in the subsidiary provided that the disposal will be for commercial purposes and not part of a tax avoidance scheme. [*ITEPA 2003, Sch 5, para 11(6), (7)*].

16.76   For the purpose of determining under head (*d*) whether a company exists wholly for the purpose of carrying on one or more qualifying trades the holding or management of property used in its trade can be ignored. In the case of a group so can the holding of shares in (or lending money to) other group companies, holding or managing property used for the purposes of a qualifying trade by a group company, and incidental activities of a company that meets the trading requirements applicable to a single company. [*ITEPA 2003, Sch 5, para 13(2), 14(3)*]. The reference in head (*d*) to non-qualifying activities means excluded activities (see **16.89**) other than the letting of ships or the receiving of royalties or licence fees and any activities carried on otherwise than in the course of a trade. [*ITEPA 2003, Sch 5, para 14*]. Incidental activities means activities carried on in pursuance of incidental purposes, and incidental purposes means purposes having no significant effect (other than in relation to incidental matters) on the extent of the company's activities. [*ITEPA 2003, Sch 5, paras 13, 14*].

Meaning of qualifying trade

16.77   To be a qualifying trade it must:

(*a*)   be conducted on a commercial basis and with a view to the realisation of profits; and

(*b*)   not consist wholly or to a substantial part in the carrying on of excluded activities.

[*ITEPA 2003, Sch 5, para 15(1)*]. Prior to 16 December 2010 the trade also had to be carried on wholly or mainly in the UK but this has been replaced by the permanent establishment test at **16.78**(*d*).

HMRC say that whether a trade is carried on wholly or mainly in the UK will depend on the relevant facts and circumstances. A company will satisfy the test if over half of the trading activities taken as a whole is carried on in the UK (*SP3/00*).

16.78   Research and development from which it is intended that a qualifying trade will be derived (or will benefit) is treated as carrying on a qualifying trade provided that the intended trade will be carried on by the company carrying out the research and development or by another group company. [*ITEPA 2003, Sch 5, para 15(2), (4)*]. Curiously if A Ltd is carrying out research and development with the intention that a new subsidiary, B Ltd will carry on the trade, that research and development will not qualify unless A Ltd is already a member of a group. Preparing to carry out research and development cannot however be regarded as the carrying on of a qualifying trade. [*ITEPA 2003, Sch 5, para 15(3)*].

Excluded activities

16.79 The activities which are prohibited (unless they are insubstantial) are:

(*a*) dealing in land, commodities or futures or in shares, securities or other financial instruments;

(*b*) dealing in goods otherwise than in the course of an ordinary trade of wholesale or retail distribution (see **16.84**);

(*c*) banking, insurance, moneylending, debt factoring, HP financing or other financial activities;

(*d*) leasing (including letting ships on charter or other assets on hire (see **16.85**);

(*e*) receiving royalties or licence fees (see **16.87**);

(*f*) providing legal or accountancy services;

(*g*) property development (see **16.88**);

(*h*) farming or market gardening;

(*i*) holding, managing or occupying woodlands, any other forestry activity or timber production;

(*j*) operating or managing hotels or comparable establishments (ie a guest house, hostel or other establishment the main purpose of maintaining which is the provision of facilities for overnight accommodation (with or without catering) or managing property used as a hotel or comparable establishment, where the company has an estate or interest in (or is in occupation of) the hotel, etc in question [*ITEPA 2003, Sch 5, para 21*];

(*k*) operating or managing nursing homes (ie establishments that exist wholly or mainly to provide nursing care for persons suffering from sickness, injury or infirmity or for women who are pregnant or have given birth to children) or residential care homes (ie establishments that exist for the provision of residential accommodation, together with board and personal care, for persons in need of such care by reason of old age, mental or physical disability, past or present dependence on drugs or alcohol, any past illness or past or present mental disorder), or managing property used as a nursing home or residential care home, where the company has an estate or interest in (or is in occupation of) the home in question [*ITEPA 2003, Sch 5, para 22*];

(*l*) providing services or facilities by a business carried on by another person if that business consists to a significant extent of excluded activities (within (*a*) to (*k*)) and the same person has a controlling interest in both the company and that other business [*ITEPA 2003, Sch 5, para 23*].

[*ITEPA 2003, Sch 5, para 16*].

16.80   A trade of retail distribution is one in which the goods are offered for sale and sold to members of the general public for their use or consumption. A trade of wholesale distribution is one where the goods are sold to an intermediary for resale (including after processing) to members of the general public. [*ITEPA 2003, Sch 5, para 17(2), (3)*, formerly *Finance Act 2000 (FA 2000), Sch 14, para 20(1), (2)*]. A trade is likely to be an ordinary trade if the goods are bought by the trader in quantities larger than those in which he sells them, the goods are bought and sold in different markets and the trader employs staff and incurs expenses in the trade in addition to the costs of the goods and any remuneration paid to a person connected with the trader (if it is a company). [*ITEPA 2003, Sch 5, para 17(5), (6)*]. Factors that suggest that a trade is not an ordinary one are if there are purchases or sales from or to connected persons, purchases are matched with onward sales, the goods are held for longer than is normal for goods of that kind, the trade is carried on somewhere not commonly used for wholesale or retail trade, and the trader does not take physical possession of the goods. [*ITEPA 2003, Sch 5, para 17(5), (7)*]. A trade cannot be an ordinary trade if it consists to a substantial extent in dealing in goods of a kind which are collected or held as an investment if a substantial proportion of those goods are held for a longer period than a vendor seeking to dispose of them at their market value would keep them. [*ITEPA 2003, Sch 5, para 17(4)*].

16.81   A trade of leasing ships (but not oil rigs or pleasure craft) can be a qualifying one if:

(*a*)   every ship it lets on charter is beneficially owned by the company;

(*b*)   every ship beneficially owned by the company (including any not let on charter) is registered in the UK;

(*c*)   the company is solely responsible for arranging the marketing of the services of its ships (this probably prevents it using an agent);

(*d*)   in relation to every letting of a ship on charter by the company:

  (i)   the letting is for 12 months or less (and no provision is made for extending it beyond 12 months other than at the option of the charterer);

  (ii)   during the period of the letting there is no provision in force for the grant of a new letting which would extend beyond that 12-month period (other than at the option of the charterer);

  (iii)   the letting is to an unconnected person and under a bargain made at arm's length (unless the letting is between a company and its qualifying subsidiary or between two qualifying subsidiaries of the trader); and

  (iv)   under the terms of the charter the company is responsible for taking the management decisions in relation to the ship (other than those generally regarded in the trade as matters of husbandry) and for defraying substantially all expenses in connection with the ship throughout the charter period other than those directly attributable to particular voyages (and no arrangements exist by virtue of which someone other than the company could be appointed to be responsible for such matters).

[*ITEPA 2003, Sch 5, para 18*].

16.82   If any of these requirements are not met but non-qualifying lettings (together with any other excluded activities carried on by the company) do not amount to a substantial part of the trade it can be treated as a qualifying trade. [*ITEPA 2003, Sch 5, para 24*].

16.83   A company that receives royalties or licence fees can nevertheless be treated as carrying on a qualifying trade if the royalties and licence fees (or all except a part that is not substantial in terms of value) are attributable to the exploitation of relevant intangible assets. [*ITEPA 2003, Sch 5, para 19*]. A relevant intangible asset is one the whole or greater part (in terms of value) of which has been created by either the company carrying on the trade ('the relevant company') or a company which was a qualifying subsidiary of the relevant company throughout a period during which it created the whole or greater part (in terms of value) of the intangible asset. For this purpose, if the relevant company acquired all of the shares in another company on a share exchange at a time when the only issued shares in that company were subscriber shares, the reference to the relevant company includes that other company. [*ITEPA 2003, Sch 5, para 19*]. Prior to 6 April 2007 the value had to be created by the relevant company or by a company which at all times during which it created the asset was the parent or a fellow qualifying subsidiary of the relevant company. The change applies to options granted after 5 April 2007 and to earlier unexercised options from 6 April 2007 for the purpose only of determining whether an activity is an excluded activity. [*Finance Act 2007 (FA 2007), s 61(2)–(4)*]. However, if immediately before 6 April 2007 the right to exploit the assets was vested in the relevant company or a subsidiary of it (either alone or jointly with others) and the asset was a relevant tangible asset, but ceases to be so as a result of the *FA 2007* changes, the activity will not become an excluded activity in relation to that option. [*FA 2007, s 61(5), (6)*]. If the asset is intellectual property (which is defined, restrictively, as any patent, trademark, registered design, copyright, design right, performer's right, plant breeder's right or any corresponding or similar right under the laws of another country) the creation of the asset means its creation in circumstances in which the right to exploit it vests in the company (whether alone or jointly with others). Thus, for example, if A is commissioned by B to write a book in return for a royalty so that the entire copyright vests in B the royalty does not derive from a relevant intangible asset of A.

16.84   Property development means the development of land by a company which has an interest in the land (or did so at any time) with the sole or main object of realising a gain from the disposal of an interest in the land when it is developed. [*ITEPA 2003, Sch 5, para 20(2)*]. For this purpose an interest in land is any estate, interest or right in or over land (including any right affecting the use or disposition of land), and any right to obtain such an estate, interest or right from another which is conditional on the other's ability to grant it. [*ITEPA 2003, Sch 5, para 20(3)*]. An option to acquire land does not appear to fall within this definition but probably would do so on exercise. The interest of a creditor (other than for a rentcharge) whose debt is secured on land is not an interest in land. [*ITEPA 2003, Sch 5, para 20(4)*].

16.85   For the purpose of **16.83**(*l*) a person has a controlling interest in a business carried on by a company if either:

(*a*)   he controls the company (applying *CTA 2010, ss 450, 451*),

(*b*)   the company is a close company and he (or an associate of his) is a director and beneficially owns over 30 per cent of the ordinary share capital of the company (or is able directly or indirectly to control over 30 per cent), or

(*c*)   not less than half of the business could (in accordance *with CTA 2010, s 942*) be regarded as belonging to him for the purpose of *CTA 23010, s 941* (disallowance of losses following a change in ownership of a company). [*ITEPA 2003, Sch 5, para 23(4)*].

A person has a controlling interest in an unincorporated business if he is entitled to at least half of the assets used for the business or half of the income arising from the business. [*ITEPA 2003, Sch 5, para 23(5)*]. In applying these tests there must be attributed to a person any rights or powers of any associate of his (within *ICTA 1988, s 417(3), (4)*) but excluding a brother or sister. [*ITEPA 2003, Sch 5, para 23*].

Eligible employees

16.86   An employee is eligible to participate in EMIs only if:

(*a*)   he is an employee of the relevant company (the one over which he will be granted the option) or a qualifying subsidiary (see **16.78**(*b*)) of it [*ITEPA 2003, Sch 5, para 25*];

(*b*)   the time that he is required to spend on the business of the relevant company (or of its group if it is a parent company) is either:

(i)   at least 25 hours a week, or

(ii)   if less, 75 per cent of his working time,

(including any time that he would have been required to spend but for injury, ill health or disability, pregnancy, childbirth, maternity or paternity leave or parental leave, reasonable holiday entitlement, and garden leave). Interestingly time counts towards this test both if the income from it is taxed as general earnings of a UK resident under *ITEPA 2003, s 15* (see **2.48**) and if it is taxed as self-employment income under Case I or II of Schedule D. For 2008/09 onwards the employee must also not be taxable on a remittance basis. [*ITEPA 2003, Sch 5, paras 26, 27* as amended by *Finance Act 2008 (FA 2008), Sch 17, para 39*]. This is called the 'commitment of working time';

(*c*)   he does not have a material interest – broadly over 30 per cent – in the company (or if it is a parent company in any group company. [*ITEPA 2003, Sch 5, paras 26–28*].

Where a reservist is called up for service under the *Reserve Forces Act 1996* HMRC will by concession treat the employment with the Ministry of Defence as fulfilling these employment conditions. [*ESC A103*]. They have asked to be informed (Sahd.Ullah@ir.gsi.gov.uk) when this concession is used.

16.87   For the purpose of (*c*) above an individual has a material interest in a company if he (or he together with one or more associates, or one or more associates alone) is either:

(*a*)   the beneficial owner of more than 30 per cent of the ordinary share capital of the company (or able to control, directly or indirectly more than 30 per cent), or

(*b*)   if the company is a close company, he possesses (or is entitled to acquire) such rights as would in the event of a winding up of the company or in any other circumstances give an entitlement to receive more than 30 per cent of the assets that would then be available for distribution among the participators (as defined in *ICTA 1988, s 417(1)*). [*ITEPA 2003, Sch 5, para 29*].

16.88   In applying these tests the option shares themselves are ignored until the option is exercised. [*ITEPA 2003, Sch 5, para 30(3)*]. A person with 29 per cent of the shares could therefore be granted an option that would bring him well above 30 per cent but once he exercises it could not be granted a new qualifying option. A company is treated as a close company if it would be close but for being non-UK resident or because it is a listed company and 35 per cent of the shares are held by members of the public. [*ITEPA 2003, Sch 5, para 29(4)*]. A right to acquire shares (other than under the EMI or other approved schemes) must be treated as a right to control them. [*ITEPA 2003, Sch 5, para 30(2)*]. If the right is to acquire unissued shares, the issued share capital must be increased by the option shares (but not it appears by option shares held by other people) in applying the 30 per cent test. [*ITEPA 2003, Sch 5, para 30(4), (5)*]. The interest of the trustees under a SIP (see **Chapter 15**), and any rights exercisable by those trustees by virtue of any such interest, are ignored to the extent that the shares have not been appropriated to, or acquired on behalf of, the individual concerned. [*ITEPA 2003, Sch 5, para 30(7)*].

16.89   In applying *paras 26–28* (see **16.90**) 'associate' in relation to an individual means:

(*a*)   any relative (spouse, parent or remoter forebear and child or remoter issue, but not a brother or sister) or partner of that individual;

(*b*)   the trustees or trustees of any settlement in relation to which that individual or any of the above relatives of his (living or dead) was a settlor;

(*c*)   if the individual is interested in any shares or obligations of the company which are subject to a trust (or are part of a deceased estate) the trustees or personal representatives.

[*ITEPA 2003, Sch 5, para 31*].

16.90 However, the trustees of an employee benefit trust (are not regarded as associates by reason only of the individual being interested as a beneficiary of that trust if the individual (or the individual together with associates of his – other than the trustees of another employee benefit trust – or associates of his on their own) has at any time since 13 March 1989 been the beneficial owner (or able to control directly or indirectly) over 30 per cent of the ordinary share capital of the company. [*ITEPA 2003, Sch 5, para 32*]. However in certain circumstances the beneficiary can be deemd to own some of the shares held by the EBT. These rules are considered at **15.15–15.16**.

16.91 In applying *para 31* (see **16.94**) the trustees of a discretionary settlement of which the individual was formerly a beneficiary are not treated as his associates if at some time within the following 12 months he ceases to be a beneficiary by an irrevocable release or disclaimer of his interest or by the irrevocable exercise by the trustees of a power to exclude him, and:

(*a*) immediately after he ceased to be a beneficiary no associate of his was interested in the shares held by the trust; and

(*b*) neither the individual nor any associate of his received any benefit from the trust in the 12 months ending with his ceasing to be a beneficiary. [*ITEPA 2003, Sch 5, para 33*].

Terms of options, etc

16.92 The option itself has to satisfy the following conditions:

(*a*) it must be over shares that are fully paid up, irredeemable (and not becoming redeemable at a future date) and forming part of the ordinary share capital of the relevant company [*ITEPA 2003, Sch 5, para 35*];

(*b*) the option must be capable of being exercised within ten years from the date of its grant – or if its exercise is subject to conditions they must be capable of being fulfilled within that ten-year period [*ITEPA 2003, Sch 5, para 36*];

(*c*) the option must take the form of a written agreement and this must state:

   (i) the date on which the option is granted;

   (ii) that it is granted under the provisions of *Sch 5*,

   (iii) the number (or maximum number) of shares that may be acquired;

   (iv) the price payable by the employee to acquire them (or the method by which that price is to be determined);

   (v) when and how the option may be granted;

   (vi) details of any conditions, such as performance conditions, affecting the terms or extent of the employee's entitlement;

   (vii) details of any restrictions attaching to the shares;

(viii) whether the shares are subject to risk of forfeiture (ie if the interest that may be acquired is restricted within *ITEPA 2003, s 426* – see **14.26**).

[*ITEPA 2003, Sch 5, para 37*].

(*d*) the terms on which the option is granted must prohibit the employee from transferring any of his rights under it [*ITEPA 2003, Sch 5, para 38(a)*]; and

(*e*) if the terms permit the option to be exercised after the employee's death they must require this to be done within 12 months after the death. [*ITEPA 2003, Sch 5, para 38(b)*].

Notification to HMRC

16.93 EMI options do not have to be approved in advance by HMRC. Indeed there is no procedure for them to do so. However for the option to be a qualifying option it must be notified to HMRC within 92 days of the grant of the option days. [*ITEPA 2003, Sch 5, para 44*]. HMRC do not have power to extend this 92-day period. Failure to notify timeously will negate the EMI tax benefits. Notification is given by completing a Form EMI 1 (which can be either completed online or downloaded from the HMRC website and sent to: Small Company Enterprise Centre, HM Revenue and Customs, 1st Floor, Ferrers House, Castle Meadow Road, Nottingham NG2 1BB.

16.94 The notice must:

(*a*) be given by the employer (not the relevant company if different);

(*b*) contain (or be accompanied by) such information as HMRC may require for the purpose of checking that the conditions of *ITEPA 2003, Schedule 5* are met;

(*c*) contain a declaration by a director or the secretary of the employer company that in his opinion the requirements of *ITEPA 2003, Schedule 5* are met and that the information provided is, to the best of his knowledge and belief, correct and complete and that the employee has made and signed a written declaration that he meets the commitment of working time (see **16.96**).

[*ITEPA 2003, Sch 5, para 44* as amended by *FA 2014, Sch 8, para 217*]. The employing company must retain the declaration by the employee and if requested to do so by HMRC, must produce it to HMRC within seven days of the request, and it must also give a copy of the declaration to the employee within seven days of its being signed [*ITEPA 2003, Sch 5, para 44(5A)* inserted by *FA 2014, Sch 8, para 218*]. The notice and any information supporting it must be given electronically (although HMRC have power if they consider it appropriate to allow the notice and any supporting information to be given in some other way). HMRC must prescribe how notices and supporting information are to be given electronically [*ITEPA 2003, Sch 5, para 44(8)–(10)* inserted by *FA 2014, Sch 8, para 217*].

16.95   HMRC can amend the notice (by notice to the employer) within nine months of receiving it to correct obvious errors or omissions. The employer can override that correction by giving notice to HMRC rejecting it within three months from the date it is issued. [*ITEPA 2003, Sch 5, para 45*].

16.96   HMRC are entitled to enquire into the notice at any time within 12 months after the end of the 92 day notification period (30 days for options granted before 12 May 2001). They do so by giving notice to the employer company. If they intend to enquire into the employee's commitment of working time they must instead give the notice to the employee. The 12-month limit does not apply if HMRC discover that any of the information provided in, or in connection with, the notice was false or misleading in a material particular. In the absence of such a discovery they cannot enquire more than once into the same notice. [*ITEPA 2003, Sch 5, para 46*].

16.97   When HMRC complete their enquiry they must inform the employer company and tell it whether or not in their opinion the conditions for the option to qualify as an EMI option are met. If they agree that they are they must also notify the employee of that fact. On completion of an enquiry into the commitment of working time they must notify both employer and employee. At any time after an enquiry has been opened the employer (or if it related to the commitment to working time the employee) can apply to the First-tier Tribunal for a direction that HMRC should give a closure notice within a specified period. [*ITEPA 2003, Sch 5, para 47, 48*].

16.98   If HMRC do not give an enquiry notice the EMI conditions are taken to be met. If they do, their decision following their enquiry is conclusive as to whether or not they are met – subject, if they decide that they are, to any later discovery. [*ITEPA 2003, Sch 5, para 49*].

16.99   If HMRC decide that the EMI conditions are not met, or that the notice under *para 2* was not properly given, the employer company can appeal against that decision within 30 days of the issue of the closure notice under *para 5*. If the decision is that the commitment of working time is not met the employee can similarly appeal. The appeal goes to the First-tier Tribunal. [*ITEPA 2003, Sch 5, para 50*].

16.100   Those familiar with self-assessment will recognise this procedure. There is however one notable difference. There is no protection against discovery for documents sent with the notice. This is an odd procedure for an 'incentive'. It leaves the employee in a state of uncertainty as to whether HMRC may at a later date make a discovery and deny him the tax benefits that he anticipated from his EMI option.

Income tax position

16.101   Income tax is not charged on the grant of an EMI option, provided that it is exercised within ten years of the grant (or of the grant of the original option if it is a replacement option. This is not giving much away as that is the normal rule that applies to any option (see **14.96**).

16.102 Income tax is not charged on the exercise of the option either provided that the option price is not less than the market value of the shares at the time the option was granted (or if it is a replacement option, the time the original one was granted). [*ITEPA 2003, s 530*]. If the option price is less than the original market value of the shares an income tax charge arises at the time the option is exercised but this is limited to the excess of the 'chargeable market value' over the aggregate of the consideration for the grant of the option and the option price paid for the shares. The chargeable market value for this purpose is the lower of the market value of the shares at the time the option was granted (or if it is a replacement option – see **16.112** – at the time the original option was granted) and their market value at the time the option is exercised. [*ITEPA 2003, s 531*]. In other words the employee is taxed on the lower of the discount or the profit he can realise by immediately selling the shares. If the price paid exceeds the then value of the shares there is obviously no tax charge. [*ITEPA 2003, s 530*, formerly *FA 2000, 14*]. If the shares are subject to restrictions, such as a requirement to sell them if the employee leaves the employment, it will normally be sensible to make an election under *ITEPA 2003, s 431* (see **14.45**). If the option price is nil the tax charge is on the difference between the chargeable market value and any consideration given for the grant of the option (and no charge arises if that consideration exceeds the value of the shares). [*ITEPA 2003, s 531*].

Disqualifying events

16.103 If a disqualifying event occurs before the option is exercised and it is not then exercised within 90 days of that event (40 days for events occurring before17 July 2013) the amount which is taxable on exercise of the option is increased by the amount, if any, by which the market value of the shares when the option is exercised exceeds their market value immediately before the disqualifying event (called 'the post-event gain') less the amount of any consideration given for the grant of the option. [*ITEPA 2003, s 532* as amended by *FA 2013, Sch 2, para 94*]. If the option was granted at below the then market value of the shares the taxable amount is the difference between the chargeable market value under *s 531* (see **16.106**) (broadly, the market value of comparable shares at the time the option was granted) plus the post-event gain and the aggregate of the option price (if any) plus any consideration given for the grant of the option. [*ITEPA 2003, s 532*]. This is of course the aggregate of the undervalue on the grant of the option and the growth in the value of the shares subsequent to the disqualifying event.

Example

Joan was granted an EMI option on 12 December 2008 to acquire £50,000 worth of shares for £50,000 at any time within the next ten years. She exercised the option on 10 April 2014 when the shares were worth £600,000. A disqualifying event occurred in June 2012 when the shares were worth £400,000.

Joan is taxable on the exercise of the option on:

(*a*) the lower of:

(i) the option price £50,000 less the 2008 value of the shares

$$£50,000 \quad = \quad \text{NIL}$$

(ii) the option price £50,000 less the 2014 value of the shares

$$£600,000 = £550,000$$

the lower is   NIL

plus

(*b*) the excess of the 2014 value £600,000 over the 2012 value £400,000

$$\underline{£200,000}$$
$$\overline{£200,000}$$

In other words the increase in value since the disqualifying event is taxed as employment income in addition to any tax charge arising by reference to the grant of the option at an undervalue.

16.104 The following are disqualifying events.

(*a*) The relevant company becoming a 51 per cent subsidiary of another company (or coming under the control of another company, or of another company and any person connected with it, without becoming a subsidiary). If a replacement option is granted (see **16.112**) and at some time during the six-month period referred to in **16.112**(*b*) (and before the surrender of the old option) such a loss of independence occurs in relation to the old option that will not be a disqualifying event. That is commonsense. A loss of independence is bound to occur as a result of the takeover and the qualifying conditions for the replacement option to be treated as such are as stringent as those that apply on the grant of the original option.

(*b*) The relevant company ceasing to meet the trading activities requirement (see **16.81**).

(*c*) The employee ceasing to be eligible either by ceasing his employment with the company (or group) or by failing to meet the commitment of working time (see **16.90**). A disqualifying event also occurs if that commitment is not satisfied in any tax year. [*ITEPA 2003, s 535(2), (4)*]. This must be tested on a monthly basis, ie at the end of each calendar month the 25 hours per week and 75 per cent of time tests are applied on a cumulative basis from the beginning of the tax year. If these tests are not met in any month the disqualifying event is deemed to have incurred at the end of the previous month (and if they are not met in April it is deemed to have occurred at the end of the previous tax year). The tests are applied from the beginning of the tax year in which the option is granted. If they are not met at a month end prior to the grant the option is disqualified *ab initio*. If the employment begins during the year (or ceases during a month) the test period obviously starts when the employment starts (or ends when it ceases) [*ITEPA 2003, s 535(2), (6)*].

(*d*)   The terms of the option being varied if the effect of the variation is either to increase the market value of the shares that are subject to the option or to prevent the option satisfying the requirement *of ITEPA 2003, Sch 5*.

(*e*)   An alteration to the share capital of the relevant company if it:

    (i)   affects the value of the shares subject to the option (or but for the occurrence of some other event would do so);

    (ii)   consists of (or includes) the creation, variation or removal of a right relating to any shares in the company (including rights conferred by any contract or arrangement or in any other way), the imposition of a restriction relating to any shares (or which is imposed by any contract, etc.) or the variation or removal of a restriction to which any shares are subject; and

has the effect either:

(1)   that the requirements of *ITEPA 2003, Sch 5* would no longer be met in relation to the option; or

(2)   unless the alteration is made for commercial reasons or its main purpose (or one of its main purposes) was not to increase the market value of option shares, of increasing the value of the shares that are subject to the option.

[*ITEPA 2003, s 537*].

(*f*)   A conversion of any of the shares to which the option relates into shares of a different class, unless:

    (i)   the conversion is a conversion of one class only ('the original class') into shares of one other class only ('the new class');

    (ii)   all of the shares of the original class are converted into shares of the new class; and

    (iii)   immediately before the conversion either:

        (A)   the majority of the shares of the original class were not held by (or for the benefit of) an associated company or directors or employees of the company or of an associated company; or

        (B)   the company was employee-controlled (within *ITEPA 2003, s 421H* – see **14.55**) by virtue of holdings of shares of the original class.

[*ITEPA 2003, s 538*].

(*g*)   The grant to the employee of an option under a CSOP scheme (see **16.11**) in relation to the same company or any other company in the same group if immediately after it is granted the employee holds unexercised employee options (ie under the EMI scheme, a different EMI scheme relating to employment with the same group, or under the CSOP scheme) in respect of shares with a total initial value of over £100,000. [*ITEPA 2003, s 539*].

(*h*)   If when the option was granted the relevant company was a qualifying company by reason only of preparing to carry on a qualifying trade, its ceasing such preparations or it (or if it is a parent company it or another group company) not commencing that trade within two years of the grant of the option. [*ITEPA 2003, s 534(3)–(5)*].

[*ITEPA 2003, ss 533–537*].

16.105   No tax charge arises on the grant of a qualifying EMI option or on the exercise of the option by a UK resident employee provided that the earnings from the employment are taxable as general earnings under *ITEPA 2003, s 15* (see **2.48**) [*ITEPA 2003, s 540*]. However any other income tax charges under *ITEPA 2003, ss 422–470* (see **14.26** onwards) in relation to the shares apply in the normal way. [*ITEPA 2003, s 541*.

Capital gains tax relief

16.106   On a disposal of shares acquired under an EMI option taper relief is calculated as if the shares had been acquired when the original option was granted. [*TCGA 1992, Sch 7D, para 15*]. This also of course applies to replacement shares on a company reorganisation within *TCGA 1992, s 127* provided that they meet the conditions of *Sch 5, para 35* (see **16.96**(*a*)). [*TCGA 1992, Sch 7D, para 14(3)*]. HMRC take the view that if under a reorganisation the EMI shares are replaced by loan notes (that constitute non-qualifying corporate bonds) the EMI continuity provisions do not apply as the term 'replacement shares' is not apt to cover securities.

If a disqualifying event (see **16.107**) occurs in relation to a qualifying option this treatment applies only if the option is exercised within 40 days of that event. If it is not, taper relief runs only from the time the shares are actually acquired. [*TCGA 1992, Sch 7D, para 14(4)*].

16.107   If there is a rights issue in respect of shares acquired under an EMI option the rights shares are not treated as a single holding with the option shares. [*TCGA 1992, Sch 7D, para 16*]. Accordingly the date of acquisition for taper relief purposes of the rights shares is the date of the rights issue; it does not relate back to the grant of the option.

Company reorganisations

16.108   If there is a takeover of the relevant company and:

(*a*)   the holder of a qualifying option by agreement with the acquiring company releases his rights under that option ('the old option') in consideration of the grant to him of equivalent rights ('the new option') over shares in the acquiring company; and (*b*)   the new option is granted within six months of the takeover (or if the acquirer becomes bound or entitled to acquire the shares under a court order within the time specified in that order); and

(*c*)   the new option meets the specified conditions (see **16.96**);

the new option is treated as a 'replacement option' and is treated as if it had been granted on the date the old option was granted (and references in *Sch 5* to a qualifying option include a replacement option). [*ITEPA 2003, Sch 5, paras 39, 40, 42*].

16.109   The conditions that the new option must meet to qualify as a replacement option are:

(*a*)   it must be granted to the holder of the old option by reason of his employment with the acquiring company, or if that company is a parent company another group company – so a replacement option cannot be granted to a person who leaves his employment as a result of the takeover;

(*b*)   at the time of the release of the old option the requirements of *paragraph 4* (purpose of granting the option) (see **16.74**) and *paragraph 7* (£3 million overall limit) (see **16.76**) are met in relation to the new option;

(*c*)   at that time, the independence requirement (see **16.78**(*a*)) and the trading activities requirement (see **16.84**(*d*)) are met in relation to the acquiring company;

(*d*)   at that time the individual to whom the new option is granted is an eligible employee (see **16.90**) in relation to the acquiring company;

(*e*)   at that time the requirements as to the terms of the option, etc. (see **16.96**) are met in relation to the new option;

(*f*)   immediately before the release of the old option the total market value of the shares subject to that option is equal to the total market value, immediately after the grant, of the shares to which the new option relates; and

(*g*)   the total amount payable by the employee to acquire the shares in pursuance of the new option is the same as that payable under the old.

[*ITEPA 2003, Sch 5, para 43*].

16.110   In effect the old option can be replaced by the new with effect from the initial date only if the employee would have been able to acquire an EMI option over shares in the acquiring company had the old option not been granted.

16.111   A takeover (or 'company reorganisation' as the legislation terms it) will trigger these replacement option rules only where a company ('the acquiring company') either:

(*a*)   obtains control of the relevant company (ie the one to which the option relates) either as a result of making a general offer to acquire all of the issued ordinary share capital and which is made on a condition which, if satisfied, will give the acquiring company control of the relevant company, or as a result of making a general offer to acquire all of the shares of the same class as those to which the option relates; or

(*b*)   obtains control of the relevant company in pursuance of a compromise or arrangement sanctioned by the court under *CA 2006, s 899* (formerly *CA 1985, s 425*); or

(*c*)   becomes bound or entitled under *CA 2006, ss 979–982* (formerly *CA 1985, ss 428–430*) to acquire shares of the same class as those subject to the option; or

(*d*)   obtains all the shares of a company whose shares are subject to an EMI option as a result of a qualifying exchange of shares (which is where a new holding company with virtually identical shareholdings is put over the top of the existing company by means of a share exchange).

[*ITEPA 2003, Sch 5, para 39*]. From such date as the Treasury may appoint, the references to the issued ordinary share capital and to shares in the company in (*a*) do not include any shares already held by the offeror or a connected person, and it does not matter if the general offer is made to different shareholders by different means [*ITEPA 2003, Sch 5, para 39(4)(5)* inserted by *FA 2013, Sch 2, para 31*].

16.112   For the purpose of (*d*) above a qualifying exchange of shares is where a company acquires all of the shares in another ('the old company'), and:

(*a*)   the consideration for the old shares consists wholly of the issue of shares in the acquiring company;

(*b*)   the new shares are issued in consideration of old shares only, at a time when there are no issued shares in the acquiring company other than subscriber shares and new shares previously issued in consideration of old shares;

(*c*)   the consideration for new shares of each description consists wholly of old shares of the corresponding description (ie on the assumption that they were shares in the same company they would be of the same class and carry the same rights);

(*d*)   the new shares of each description are issued to the holders of old shares of the corresponding description in proportion to their holdings; and

(*e*)   the exchange of shares does not constitute a disposal by virtue of *TCGA 1992, s 127*.

[*ITEPA 2003, Sch 5, para 40*].

Information powers

16.113   HMRC have power by notice to require any person to provide them within such time as they may direct (which must not be less than three months) with such information as they think necessary for the performance of their functions under *Schedule 15* that the person has or can reasonably obtain. [*ITEPA 2003, Sch 5, para 51*].

16.114 The company whose shares are subject to EMI options must make a return to HMRC for each tax year falling (wholly or partly) in the company's qualifying option period (the period starting when the first qualifying option is granted and ending when the company's shares are no longer subject to qualifying options (and will no longer become subject to them) ie until the scheme is closed) [*ITEPA 2003, Sch 5, para 52(1)–(4)* as substituted by *FA 2014, Sch 8, para 218*]. The return must be made by 6 July in the following tax year and contain (or be accompanied by) such information as HMRC may require. The information they can require includes in particular information to enable them to determine the liability to tax (including CGT) of any person who has been granted a qualifying option to which the company's shares are subject [*ITEPA 2003, Sch 5, para 52(5)(6)*]. The return and any information accompanying it must be made electronically (although if they consider it appropriate to do so, HMRC have power to allow some other method). HMRC must prescribe how returns and accompanying information is to be given electronically [*ITEPA 2003, Sch 5, para 52A*]. If after a return has been made, the company becomes aware that something which should have been included was omitted (or something which should not have been included was included) or discovers any other error or inaccuracy, it must make an amended return correcting the position without delay [*ITEPA 2003, Sch 5, para 52(7)*]. Up to 2013/14, the requirement was to make an annual return for each tax year in which such options are unexercised containing such information as HMRC may require. This must be submitted within 92 days after the end of the year. [*ITEPA 2003, Sch 5, para 52*].

Market value of shares

16.115 Subject to *Sch 5, para 5(7)* (see **16.75**) the market value of shares has the same meaning as for capital gains tax purposes under *TCGA 1992, ss 272* and *273*. [*ITEPA 2003, Sch 5, para 55*]. Where the market value on any date falls to be determined HMRC and the employer company can agree that it should be determined by reference to a different date or dates, or to an average of the value on a number of dates. [*ITEPA 2003, Sch 5, para 56*]. This will enable a value to be agreed in advance of the grant of the option subject to the option being granted within an agreed time of the date of the agreement.

16.116 If HMRC and the employer company cannot agree on the value of shares the employer company can require the valuation to be referred to the General Commissioners (or if it so elects the Special Commissioners). If it does not do so HMRC can determine the value. The employer company then has a right of appeal to the Commissioners against that determination. [*ITEPA 2003, Sch 5, para 57*].

Penalties

16.116A A company is liable for a penalty of £500 if it fails to produce a declaration to HMRC as required by *para 44(5A)* (see **16.98**), or to give a copy of the declaration to the employee within the prescribed period and HMRC decide that such a penalty should be payable [*ITEPA 2003, Sch 5, para 57A* inserted by FA *2014, Sch 8, para 220*].

16.116B   If a company fails to submit its annual return for a tax year (containing or accompanied by all required information) by 6 July following the end of the tax year, it is liable for a penalty of £100. If the failure continues for three months, it becomes liable to a further penalty of £300, and another £300 if it is more than six months late (ie the penalties will total £700) [*ITEPA 2003, Sch 5, para 57B(1)–(4)*]. If the return is more than nine months late, the company becomes liable to further penalties of £10 a day for each day the failure continues. The notice must specify the period for which the penalty is to run. It can apply retrospectively from the end of the nine-month period. If HMRC impose a further penalty under this provision, it cannot start before the expiry of the previous penalty period [*ITEPA 2003, Sch 5, para 57B(5)–(7)*].

16.116C   If the annual return and all accompanying information is not filed electronically (other than if HMRC have consented to a different method) or the return contains a material inaccuracy which is careless (ie which is due to a failure by the company to take reasonable care), or deliberate, or which is not corrected promptly as required by *para 52(7)* (see **16.118**), the company is liable to a penalty of up to £5,000 [*ITEPA 2003, Sch 5, para 57C*].

16.116D   Where a company is liable for a penalty, HMRC must assess it and notify the company of the assessment. Such an assessment must be raised within 12 months of the date the company becomes liable for the penalty or, in the case of one for a material inaccuracy, within 12 months of HMRC becoming aware of the inaccuracy and within six years from the date on which the company becomes liable for the penalty (it is not clear if this is the due date of the return or the date the return was submitted) [*ITEPA 2003, Sch 5, para 57D(1)–(4)*]. A penalty is payable within 30 days after the day on which the assessment was notified to the company or, if notice of appeal is given against it, within 30 days of the date on which the appeal is determined or withdrawn [*ITEPA 2003, Sch 5, para 57D(5)*]. The penalty can be enforced as if it were income tax or corporation tax as the case may be [*ITEPA 2003, Sch 5, para 57D(6)*].

16.116E   The company can appeal against both an HMRC decision that it is liable for a penalty and the amount of the penalty. Notice of appeal must be given to HMRC within 30 days of the penalty notice. On appeal the Tribunal can affirm or cancel the HMRC decision and can substitute a different amount of penalty [*ITEPA 2003, Sch 5, para 57E(1)–(5)*]. The TMA provisions relating to appeals apply for this purpose too [*ITEPA 2003, Sch 5, para 57E(6)*].

Other matters

16.117   The Treasury have power to amend *paras 17–26* (the trading activities requirement) (see **16.78**(*d*)) and to substitute different sums for the £100,000 limit in *para 5* (see **16.72**) or the £15m gross asset figure in *paragraph 16* (see **16.78**(*c*)). [*ITEPA 2003, Sch 5, para 54*].

For the purpose of *ITEPA 2003, Sch 5, paras 44–59* (but not for the rest of the *Schedule*) a person is not taken to have failed to do something required to be done within a limited time if:

(*a*)   he had a reasonable excuse for not doing it within that time; and

(*b*)   if the excuse ceased, he did without unreasonable delay after it did so.

[*ITEPA 2003, Sch 5, para 53*]. An insufficiency of funds cannot be a reasonable excuse unless it is attributable to events outside the person's control. Reliance on another person to do anything is not a reasonable excuse unless the person (ie the delegator) took reasonable care to avoid the failure [*ITEPA 2003, Sch 5, para 53(3)* inserted by *FA 2014, Sch 8, para 219*].

Entrepreneurs' relief

16.118   Entrepreneurs' relief can be claimed on a disposal after 6 April 2013 of 'relevant EMI shares' (even where the employee holds less than five per cent of the company) if either –

(*a*)   the option grant date was at least a year prior to the time of the disposal and throughout the year prior to the disposal,

    (i)   the company is a trading company of the holding company of a trading group, and

    (ii)   the individual is an officer or employee of the company (or if it is a member of a trading group of one or more group of companies); or

(*b*)   the relevant EMI shares were acquired by the individual before the cessation date, the option grant date was at least 12 months before the cessation date, conditions (i) and (ii) in (*a*) above are met during the 12 months prior to the date of disposal and the cessation date is within the three years ending with the date of the disposal

[*TCGA 1992, s 169I(7A)(7B)* inserted by *FA 2013, Sch 24, para 3*]. The cessation date is the date on which the company ceases to be a trading company without continuing to be (or becoming) a member of a trading group, or ceases to be a member of a trading group without continuing to be or becoming a trading company [*TCGA 1992, s 169I(70)*]. Head (*b*) mirrors that in *TCGA 1992, s 169I(7)*, which is designed to preserve the relief for a company that ceases its trade, provided that it is wound up within three years of the cessation.

16.119   Relevant EMI shares are –

(*a*)   shares of a company acquired by an individual on or after 6 April 2013, as a result of exercising a qualifying EMI option where the option is exercised on or before the tenth anniversary of the date of grant, or

(*b*)   shares of a company which are a new holding received on a company reconstruction (ie acquired after 5 April 2013) to which *TCGA 1992, s 127* applies to only by virtue of *TCGA 1992, ss 126* (reorganisation of a company's share capital) or *135(3)* (acquisition of over 25 per cent of the ordinary shares in a company in consideration of the issue of shares or debentures of the acquirer).

[*TCGA 1992, s 169I(7E),(7A),(7F)*]. Head (*a*) does not apply to shares acquired as a result of the exercise of a qualifying option if a disqualifying event (see **16.107**) occurs before its exercise and it is exercised more than 90 days after the day on which the event occurred [*TCGA 1992, s 169I(7E)*]. In the case of a *TCGA 1992, s 135(3)* acquisition, the shares are relevant EMI shares only if the exchange of shares in question is a qualifying exchange of shares (see **16.116**) and when it occurs the independence requirements (see **16.78**(*a*)) and the trading activities requirement (see **16.79**(*d*)) are met in relation to the new company [*TCGA 1992, s 169I(7G)*]. If the shares disposed of are relevant EMI shares by virtue of *TCGA 1992, s 189I(7F)* (**16.122**(*b*) above) references to the company in relation to times before the reorganisation mean (if different) the company whose shares are the original relevant EMI shares or, if there has been more than one reorganisation since the original relevant EMI shares were acquired, the company whose shares are the original relevant EMI shares (or, if at the time in question the individual is holding relevant EMI shares which are shares of another company, that other company) [*TCGA 1992, s 169I(7I)*].

16.120   If the shares disposed of are relevant EMI shares by reference to *TCGA 1992, s 169I(7F)* the question whether the requirement of *TCGA 1992, s 169I(7B)(a)* is met (that the assets disposed of are relevant EMI shares acquired by the individual before the cessation date) must be determined by reference to the date of acquisition of the original relevant EMI shares [*TCGA 1992, s 169I(7J)*].

16.121   In *TCGA 1992, s 169I(7A)(b)* and *7B(b)*, the option grant date is normally the day on which the qualifying options in question were granted. However if the qualifying option is a replacement option (see **16.112**) the option grant date instead means the date on which the old option was granted (or if that was also a replacement option, the date of the earlier old option and so on) [*TCGA 1992, s 169I(7M)*]. In relation to any time during the currency of an old option so taken into account reference to the company in *TCGA 1992, s 169I(7A)(c)* must be read as references to the company whose shares were the subject of the old option.

16.122   If the relevant EMI shares were acquired as a result of the exercise of a qualifying option where a disqualifying event (see **16.107**) occurred in relation to the option before it is exercised but it is exercised within the permitted 90-day period (or if the shares are relevant EMI shares by virtue of *TCGA 1992, s 169I(7F)* (reorganisations) the original EMI shares were so acquired), *TCGA 1992, s 169I(7A)(b)*, it has effect as if the reference to the date of disposal were a reference to the date of the disqualifying event, and if the disqualifying event is within *ITEPA 2003, s 534(1)(c)* (see **16.108**(*b*)) has effect as if the reference to the cessation date were to the first day after the end of the 90 days' exercise period if that is later than the cessation date [*TCGA 1992, s 169I(7P)–(7R)*].

16.123 For the purpose of the CGT identification rules, in *TCGA 1992, s 105*, if an individual acquires shares of the same class on the same day and in the same capacity and some of those shares are relevant EMI shares, the EMI shares must be treated as acquired by a single transaction separate from the remainder of the shares, and the remainder shares must be treated as disposed of before the EMI shares [*TCGA 1992, s 105(5)(5)* inserted by *FA 2013, Sch 24, para 3*]. Similarly in applying *TCGA 1992, s 106A* (identification of securities for CGT purposes) where securities of the same class are reacquired within 30 days of the disposal, shares acquired which are not relevant EMI shares must be identified with the disposal before those which are such EMI shares [*TCGA 1992, s 106A(5)(aa)* inserted by *FA 2013, Sch 24, para 4*]. Subject to *TCGA 1992, s 106A(4)* (securities to be identified on a first in, first out basis) and *106A(5)* (securities reacquired within 30 days of a disposal) shares disposed of must be identified with relevant EMI shares (rather than with other shares) and with relevant EMI shares on a first in, first out basis [*TCGA 1992, s 106A(6A)*]. No shares identified with relevant EMI shares by virtue of *TCGA 1992, s 106A(6A)* are to be regarded as forming part of an existing *TCGA 1992, s 104* holding or as constituting such a holding [*TCGA 1992, s 106A(6B)*].

16.124 If an individual acquires shares in a company which would be relevant EMI shares if the reference in **16.122**(*a*) to 6 April 2013, had referred to 6 April 2012 and the individual makes no disposal of shares of the same class in the company (whether or not EMI shares) during 2012/13, the shares are treated as if they were relevant EMI shares. If the individual disposes of some shares of that class in 2012/13, he can elect for the shares acquired to be treated as if they were relevant EMI shares [*FA 2013, Sch 24, para 6(1)–()–(3)*]. The election had to be made by 31 January 2014 [*FA 2013, Sch 24, para 6(6)*].

Employee Shareholder Shares

16.125 *FA 2013, s 55* and the *Finance Act 2013, Schedule 23 (Employee Shareholder Shares) (Appointed Day) Order 2013 (SI 2013/1755)* introduced a new type of tax advantaged employee share scheme; employee shareholder shares. From 1 September 2013, such shares must be acquired under an employee shareholder agreement. This is an agreement between the employee and the company in return for which the employee agrees to forgo some of his employment rights in return for the issue of the shares at no cost to the employee.

16.126 An Employee Shareholder is defined in *Employment Rights Act 1996 (ERA 1996), s 205A*, which was inserted into that Act by the *Growth and Infrastructure Act 2013, s 31*. This provides that an individual becomes an employee shareholder if –

(*a*)   the company and the individual agree that he is to be an employee shareholder,

(*b*)   in consideration of that agreement the company issues or allots to the individual fully paid ordinary shares in the company which have a value (see **16.135**) on the day of issue or allotment of at least £2,000 (or it procures that its parent undertaking issues or allots such shares), (*c*)   the company gives the individual a written statement of the particulars of the status of employee shareholder and of the rights attached to the shares being issued to him, and

(*d*)   the individual gives no consideration (other than by entering into the agreement)

[*ERA 1996, s 205A(1)*].

16.127   The rights that an employee shareholder forgoes are:

(*a*)   the right under *ERA 1996, s 63D* to undertake study or training,

(*b*)   the right under *ERA 1996, s80F* to request flexible working (but not the right to make an application within 14 days from which the employee returns to work from a period of parental leave) [*ERA 1996, s 205A(8)*],

(*c*)   the right under *ERA 1996, s 94* not to be unfairly dismissed, and

(*d*)   the right to a redundancy payment under *ERA 1996, s 135* (other than where the employee is dismissed while he is suspended on full pay on medical grounds in consequence of a requirement or recommendation under *ERA 1996, s 64(2)* [*ERA 1996, s 205A(10)*].

[*ERA 1996, s 205A(2)*]. In addition some other rights are modified, namely

(*e*)   if an employee shareholder wishes to return to work during maternity leave (or during adoption leave) she (or he) must give her employer 16 weeks advance notice instead of the normal eight weeks [*ERA 1996, s 205A(3)*].

(*f*)   Similarly if an employee shareholder wishes to return to work during a period of additional paternity leave, he must give 16 weeks' notice instead of the normal six [*ERA 1996, s 205A(4)*].

16.128   The statement at **16.130(c)** must:

(*a*)   state that, as an employee shareholder, the individual will not have the above rights,

(*b*)   specify the extended notice period that will apply to maternity leave, adoption leave and additional paternity leave,

(*c*)   state whether any voting rights attach to the employee shares,

(*d*)   state whether the employee shares carry any right to dividends,

(*e*)   state whether the employee shares would confer any right to participate in the distribution of any surplus of assets on a winding up,

(*f*)   if the company has more than one class of shares and the employee shares carry a right to vote, to dividends or to participation in a surplus on a winding up, explain how those rights differ from the equivalent rights that attach to the shares in the largest class (or the next largest if the employee shares are included in the largest class),

(*g*)   state whether the employee shares are redeemable and, if so, at whose option, (*h*)   state whether there are any restrictions on the transferability of the employee shares and, if there are, what those restrictions are,

(*i*)   state whether any of the requirements of *CA 2006, ss 561 and 562* (pre-emption rights) are excluded in the case of the employee shares,

(*j*)   that whether the employee shares are subject to drag-along (the right of the main shareholders on a sale of the company to require other shareholders to sell too) or tag-along rights (the right on a sale of the company to require the main shareholders to also procure an offer for the employee shares) and, if so, to explain the effect of the shares being so subject

[*ERA 1996, s 205A(5)*].

16.129   It should particularly be noted that the only right that the employee shares need have is a right to payment at (or possibly below) par on redemption or on a winding up. They do not need to be ordinary share capital. Nor do they have to have any other rights provided that the agreement spells out that they have no rights. It should also be noted that it is compulsory to give up all of the rights specified at **14.203**. The employer and employee cannot agree that only some of them should be given up. However they can agree to reinstate some of them contractually (although that might give rise to a different tax treatment).

16.130   Before an employee shareholder agreement is entered into, the employee must be given the statement at **14.202(c)** and must receive advice from a 'relevant independent advisor' as to the terms and effects of the proposed agreement [*ERA 1996, s 205A(6)*]. There is then a mandatory seven-day cooling-off period after the employee has received the advice before he can sign the agreement. Failure to comply with these two requirements renders the agreement of no effect [*ERA 1996, s 205A(6)*]. The company must pay the reasonable costs incurred by the individual in obtaining such advice – even if as a result the employee decides not to become an employee shareholder [*ERA 1996, s 205A(7)*]. A relevant independent advisor means a qualified lawyer; or an officer, official, employee or member of an independent trade union who has been certified in writing by the union as competent to give advice and is authorised to do so by or on behalf of the union; or a person who works at an advice centre (whether as an employee or volunteer) who has been certified by that centre as competent to give advice and is authorised to do so by the centre; or a person of a description specified by the Secretary of State by statutory instrument under *ERA 1996, s 203* [*ERA 1996, ss 203(3A), 205(13)*]. Such a person must not however be an employee of the employer or an associated employer and be acting for the employer or an associated employer [*ERA 1996, s 203(3B)*]. The benefit of the advice is of course not itself taxable on the employee (see **9.82A**).

16.131   The Secretary of State for Employment can increase the £2,000 minimum figure and can require that a buy-back of employee shares by the company in the event that the employee ceases to be an employee or ceases to be an employee-shareholder must be on terms which meet specified conditions, in each case by statutory instrument [*ERA 1996, s 205A(11)(12)*].

An overseas company which has a share capital and a Societe European can enter into an employee-shareholder agreement in the same way as a UK one [*ERA 1996, s 205A(13)*]. The value of shares must be determined in the same way as market value under *TCGA 1992, ss 272 and 273* [*ERA 1996, s 205A(14)*].

16.132 An employee has a right not to be subjected to a detriment by an act (or deliberate failure to act) of the employer done on the grounds that the employee refused to accept an offer by the employer for the employee to become an employee-shareholder [*ERA 1996, s 47G* inserted by *Growth and Infrastructure Act 2013, s 31(2)*]. The dismissal of an employee must be regarded as unfair if that is the reason (or principal reason) for the dismissal [*ERA 1996, s 104G* inserted by *Growth and Infrastructure Act 2013, s 31(4)*].

16.133 For the purpose of the income tax charge on employment income (but not for any other income tax purpose) the employee is treated as having paid £2,000 for the shares [*ITEPA 2003, s 226B(1)(7)* inserted by *FA 2013, Sch 23, para 3*]. However the excess (if any) of the market value of the shares over £2,000 is taxable as earnings of the employment [*ITEPA 2003, s 226A(1)–(3)*]. This tax charge does not apply if the shares are acquired pursuant to an employment-related securities option – presumably because in such a case the employee share option rules take precedence [*ITEPA 2003, s 226A(4)*].

16.134 If all of the shares acquired in consideration of the agreement are acquired on the same day, the employee is treated as having made the £2,000 payment on that day [*ITEPA 2003, s 226B(2)*]. If they are acquired on different days but at least £2,000 worth is acquired on the first such day, the £2,000 is again deemed to have been paid on that day. If the market value of the shares initially acquired exceeds £2,000, the £2,000 figure is apportioned to the shares by reference to their market value, eg if the employee is issued with 1,000 shares worth £3,000, each is treated as having a deemed cost of £2 and each attracts a tax charge on the remaining £1 of value [*ITEPA 2003, s 226B(4)(5)*].

16.135 An employee can get the benefit of only one deemed £2,000 payment if he acquires shares under a number of employee-shareholder agreements either with the same employer or with an associated company of the employer [*ITEPA 2003, s 226C(1)–(3)*]. For this purpose companies are associated if one has control of the other (applying *CTA 2010, ss 450 and 451*) or both are under the control of the same person or persons [*ITEPA 2003, s 226C(4)(a),(6)*]. If a company controls another at the time the employee shareholder agreement is entered into, this limitation continues to apply by reference to that company even if that control ceases [*ITEPA 2003, s 226C(4)*]. There is an exception where control ceases because one of the companies has been dissolved, the dissolution was at least two years earlier and at no time during that two-year period has the employee been engaged (either as an employee, an officer, or a self-employed person) by any company which is an associated company of the dissolved company [*ITEPA 2003, s 226C(5)*].

16.136 The £2,000 deemed payment does not apply if either:

(*a*)   on the date the shares are acquired (or at any time within the previous 12 months) the employee had a material interest in the employer company or its parent undertaking (as defined in *CTA 2006, s 1162*), or

(*b*)   on the date the shares are acquired, the employee is connected with an individual who has (or had at any time within the previous 12 months) a material interest in the employer-company (or its parent undertaking)

[*ITEPA 2003, s 226D(1)(2)*]. An individual has a material interest in a company for this purpose if at least 25 per cent of the voting rights is controlled by him and persons connected with him [*ITEPA 2003, s 233D(4)*]. In the case of a close company (or one which would be close but for being resident overseas or excluded by *CTA 2006, ss 446, 447* (quoted companies)) an individual also has a material interest in it if he and persons connected with him possess such rights as would, in the event of a winding up or in any other circumstances, give an entitlement to receive at least 25 per cent of the assets that would then be available for distribution among the participants [*ITEPA 2003, s 226D(5)*].

16.137 A person also has a material interest in a company (whether or not it is a close company) if either –

(*a*)   the employee and/or an individual connected with him have an entitlement to acquire such rights as would (together with any existing rights held) give the employee a material interest in the company, or

(*b*)   there are arrangements in place between the employer company (or, a parent undertaking) and the employee (and/or individual connected with the employee) which enable the employee or the connected person to acquire such rights as would (together with any existing rights held) give the employee a material interest in the company

[*ITEPA 2003, s 226D(6)–(8)*]. For this purpose arrangement includes any agreement, understanding, scheme, transaction or series of transactions (whether or not legally enforceable) [*ITEPA 2003, s 226D(9)*]. It should be noted that in looking at whether the relief applies at all, the test is whether an individual (whether the employee or a connected person) has a material interest, but in looking at what is a material interest account has to be taken of votes exercisable by all connected persons, including companies and trusts. However this may be a distinction without a difference. If A is a connected individual of B and A has a material interest in the company, B does not get the deemed £2,000 payment because A controls 25 per cent of the company even though B may have no other interest in it.

16.138 The charge to tax under *ITTOIA 2005, s 383* on dividends and other distributions of UK companies does not apply to the amount or value of a payment by a company on the purchase of its own shares from an individual if the payment is made in respect of shares in the company (see *CTA 2010, s 213*), the shares are exempt employee shareholder shares (ie exempt from CGT – see **14.215**) and at the time of the disposal, the individual is not an employee or office holder of the company or an associated company (see **14.211**) [*ITTOIA 2005, s 385A* inserted by *FA 2013, Sch 23, para 16*].

16.139 A capital gain which accrues on the first disposal of an exempt employee-shareholder share is exempt from CGT [*TCGA 1992, s 236B(1)* inserted by *FA 2013, Sch 23, para 20*]. Where shares are acquired under a number of different agreements, this exemption applies only if, immediately after its acquisition, the total value of qualifying shares (ie employee-shareholder shares in the employer company which entered into the agreement or an associated company) acquired by the employee does not exceed £50,000, and if they were acquired in stages so there is a time when the total is less than £50,000 and a later acquisition brings the total over £50,000, that later acquisition is split into two, the proportion of the new acquisition which brings the total to £50,000 being exempt (and treated as acquired before the remaining shares) and the balance being taxable [*TCGA 1992, s 236C(6), (7)*]. The meaning of associated company at **16.139** applies for this purpose [*TCGA 1992, s 236C(4), (5)*].

16.140 Curiously if the first of the related acquisitions of employee shareholder shares exceeds £50,000, it does not appear that any part is exempt. Equally odd it appears that if a person is entitled to shares under only a single agreement there is also no exemption if the £50,000 limit is breached. It is not clear why. The value of a share for this purpose (at any time) is its unrestricted market value at the time when it was acquired by the employee, ie what that value would be immediately after the acquisition but for any restriction (within *ITEPA 2003, s 432(8)* – see **14.27**) [*TCGA 1992, s 236C(8)(9)*].

16.141 The exemption does not apply if on the date on which the share is acquired or at any time within the previous 12 months, the employee (or a connected individual) has a material interest in the employer company or its parent undertaking [*TCGA 1992, s 236D(1)(2)*]. The definition of a material interest is the same as that under *ITEPA 2003, s 226D(4)–(8)* (see **14.212W**).

16.142 *TCGA 1992, ss 104* (share pooling), *105* (disposal on or before acquisition) and *106A* (identification of securities) do not apply to exempt employee-shareholder shares [*TCGA 1992, s 236E(1)*]. Instead of an employee holding shares of the same class in a company, some (but not all) of which are exempt employee shareholder shares and the employee disposes of part of the holding, the employee can determine which of the shares disposed of are exempt employee-shareholder shares [*TCGA 1992, s 236E(2)(3)*].

16.143 The CGT roll-over rules in relation to mergers and re-organisation of share capital (*TCGA 1992, ss 127, 135* and *136*) do not apply to exempt employee shareholder shares. As the reorganisation triggers a disposal but no chargeable gains in relation to such shares, there is no need for a tax deferral. However it needs to be realised that the reorganisation creates a disposal, so the new shares obtained will not themselves be employee-shareholder shares, and the future gain on such shares will be taxable. This means that on a merger, care needs to be taken. It may be that the exempt employee shareholder shares will have to be retained intact to avoid disadvantaging employees.

16.144   The relinquishment of employment rights as consideration for the employee shareholder agreement is not itself to be regarded as a disposal of an asset for CGT purposes [*TCGA 1992, s 236G*].

Chapter 17

Pay As You Earn (PAYE)

Requirements for employers

17.1   The legislation requires an employer to deduct income tax (in accordance with *regulations*) on the making of any payment of, or on account of, any income assessable to tax as earnings. [*Income Tax (Earnings and Pensions) Act 2003 (ITEPA 2003), s 684*]. The meaning of payment for this purpose was in issue in *Aberdeen Asset Management plc v HMRC [2012] UKUT 43 (TCC)*. Aberdeen entered into a tax avoidance scheme designed to provide benefits to senior employees without triggering tax or National Insurance. It was ultimately accepted that the scheme was flawed and that the benefit obtained by the employees was liable to tax and NIC (National Insurance Contributions). The issue before the Upper Tribunal was whose liability the tax was, the employer's or the employees'. The scheme involved a payment by Aberdeen to an employee benefit trust (EBT), the formation of a company for each employee into which the EBT injected value, the transfer of the shares in that company from the EBT to the employee, and the company either lending its funds to the employee or, if the employee preferred, buying assets at the behest of the employee and allowing the employee or his family use of such assets. The First-tier Tribunal held that 'there was a composite transaction consisting of a series of steps which began with the establishment of, and transfer of money into, the EBT and ended with the transfer of the shares to the employee'. The question was whether that transfer was a 'payment' within the meaning of what is now *ITEPA 2003, s 684*. The judge, Warren J, noted that the fact that the overall purpose of the employment income legislation is to tax the material rewards of the employment is not a pointer, one way or the other, to whether a money emolument can be a 'payment' within *section 684*. 'Payment' is one of those words that take its meaning from its context. The judge did 'not consider that the provision of an emolument can be the subject of an obligation to deduct income tax unless, at the least, there is a mechanism by which the required deduction can be made from the emoluments'. With a cheque or a credit to a bank account or a director's loan account, a deduction can be made. He rejected an HMRC suggestion that the EBT could have caused the company to pay a dividend to meet the tax immediately before the transfer of the shares to the employee. He held that *section 684* cannot apply at all to a non-money emolument. In the context of the tax scheme, the transfer of shares in a 'money-box company' was not a 'payment' for the purpose of *section 684* because it did not create an immediate right to obtain money; the money needs to be at the unconditional disposal of the employee for there to be a payment within *section 684*.

17.2   The judge then went on to consider what is now *ITEPA 2003, s 696* (see **17.42**). This depended on whether trading arrangements were in existence (see **17.43**(*f*)). Warren J held that there were. When the employee received the shares, the company held its assets in cash which the employee could have obtained by declaring a dividend or winding up the company. Apart from a small amount of costs, the money he would have received would be similar to the original payment by Aberdeen (see **17.44**). Accordingly Aberdeen should have applied PAYE and accounted for NIC.

17.3   In addition payment for this purpose (and for the purpose of the *PAYE Regulations*) is specifically stated to have the same meaning as under the taxation of employment income rules, ie the five rules set out in **2.50** above apply (with the substitution of 'paid' for 'received') to determine the date on which PAYE needs to be deducted, or in the case of a 'net payment', accounted for. [*ITEPA 2003, s 686*]. It does not matter if the income is assessable in the year of receipt or some other year (eg because *ITEPA 2003, ss 17* or *30* applies, see **2.18** above). Nor does it matter that no assessment may have been made in respect of the tax. Obviously, in most cases no assessment will have been made as the information needed to raise an assessment will not become available until after the end of the tax year. It was held in *R (on the application of Oriel Support Ltd) v HMRC [2009] STC 1397* that HMRC can require an employer to account for PAYE under its own PAYE reference. Oriel managed a large number of companies and for convenience wanted to put the PAYE for all of their employees through its own PAYE scheme. It was held that it was not entitled to do this. It paid such employees as agent of each individual's employer's company and as such had to account for PAYE as agent of that company. That meant that it had to comply with the employer's tax obligations.

17.4   Before looking at some specific areas of the PAYE rules, it is worth mentioning a number of general points of interest which arose in *Buller v Hemmer Investments Ltd [2010] STC 1779*. Hemmer provided scaffolders during the refit of an offshore oil-drilling platform. The rig was moved to Nigeria and Hemmer was contracted to continue to work on it. It sent workers from the UK on terms that Hemmer would continue to pay them their standard net UK salary and that the employee would work for four weeks at a time followed by four weeks' unpaid leave. This pattern of employment created a problem as the PAYE tables spread the personal allowance evenly throughout the year. Accordingly missing out the non-working weeks would only give half the personal allowance due. The company accordingly treated the non-working weeks as work weeks in which there were no earnings, thus calculating a tax refund due to the employee. It did not pay this 'refund' to the employee, but sought to deduct it from the PAYE due to HMRC. HMRC challenged this. They would be happy if the rebate were paid to the employee, but Hemmer believed that the 'net pay arrangement' entitled it to retain the benefit of the rebate. The High Court confirmed that 'it is permissible as a matter of both employment and tax law for the employment to be on net pay terms'. It pointed out that HMRC's own guidance stated, 'free of tax arrangements are agreed between the employer and the employee. The Inland Revenue office takes no part in these arrangements and will not discuss them'. Unfortunately many of the employees to whom HMRC spoke were unclear whether or not they had been told of the net pay arrangement. In these circumstances the court held that Hemmer could not make out its case that net pay or free of tax terms, were 'agreed' with employees. It accordingly upheld HMRC's claim. The effect is that HMRC collected the tax 'rebate' twice; it would not allow Hemmer to reclaim it and said that it need pay it to employees only if they chose to make a claim – and if they were not aware that they were entitled to a rebate, they obviously would not make such a claim. This can be contrasted with HMRC's approach to missed P11D items where they invite the employer to pay the tax due by all of the affected employees to save work. The words, sauce, goose and gander spring readily to mind. Another big lesson from this case is that it is unwise to allow staff to talk to HMRC unless the employer is confident that the person concerned has the knowledge and capacity to do so and to resist HMRC putting words into his mouth. If the employer offers the employees free professional representation, the avoidance of confusion may justify the cost!

17.5   From 6 April 2013 all employers (other than those employing only nannies or other household staff) have had to deal with PAYE electronically under RTI (Real Time Information). This effectively means that they must either use payroll software or will need to transfer the information regularly into such software. HMRC provide free software for very small employers (those with nine or fewer employees) but most are expected to use a payroll bureau or purchase the necessary software. In theory a return needs to be made to HMRC every time that a payment of, or an account of, remuneration is paid, as the obligation is to report the amount on or before the date of payment. However for some employees this will require 365 returns as casual staff can be engaged and paid for a single day. Accordingly HMRC have temporarily relaxed this requirement. They will accept monthly returns from employers with less than 50 employees. In order to report under RTI, an employee needs to know (before he pays the employee) the employee's full and official name, date of birth, National Insurance Number, current gender, address, and date employment started. Without this information, the HMRC computer may not accept a submission.

17.6   Penalties for late filing of RTI returns apply from 6 November 2014 (except for small employers to whom they will apply from 6 April 2015). They are monthly penalties. The rate depends on the number of employees, namely:

1–9	£100
10–49	£200
50–249	£300
250 or more	£400.

Penalty notices will only be issued quarterly. An employer will be allowed one late submission per tax year before penalties are imposed. No penalty is chargeable if the employer has a reasonable excuse for the late submission. Where an employee has to submit more than one return for a month, only one monthly penalty is chargeable, however many of them are late.

Payments by intermediaries

17.7   Where a payment of assessable income is made by an intermediary, the employer (not the intermediary) is treated as making the payment, and thus becomes liable to deduct PAYE from it, unless the intermediary has himself applied PAYE. [*ITEPA 2003, s 687*]. An intermediary for this purpose is a person acting on the employer's behalf and at his expense (or at the expense of a person connected with him) or a trustee holding property for persons (or a class of persons) including the employer.

17.8   *Section 687* was considered by the High Court in *DTE Financial Services Ltd v Wilson [1999] STC 1061*. The decision in favour of HMRC in that case was upheld by the Court of Appeal (*[2001] ECWA Civ 455, [2001] STC 777*) on the basis of the *Ramsay* principle (see below). It accordingly held that the analysis involving *section 687* did not arise. As the Court of Appeal did not consider the correctness or otherwise of Hart J's analysis, it is still good law. In that case the company entered into a marketed National Insurance avoidance scheme which involved the following steps:

(*a*)   the company decided that a director, Mr McDonald, should be paid a £40,000 bonus;

(*b*)   an unconnected Manx company, GV, set up a discretionary trust with £40,300;

(*c*)   three days later the trustees appointed the whole capital of the trust to GV contingent on its remaining in existence for a further four days;

(*d*)   the next day DTE Financial paid GV £40,600 in consideration of its assigning to Mr McDonald its interest in the settlement; and finally

(*e*)   the interest in the settlement duly fell in and the £40,000 trust capital was paid to Mr McDonald.

HMRC contended that the trustees had made a payment of assessable income to Mr McDonald within *section 687*. Hart J quickly dismissed this claim. The emolument received by Mr McDonald was the contingent interest; the £40,000 was not the emolument, it was a fruit of that emolument. However it was also held that if the principles enunciated by the House of Lords in *W T Ramsay Ltd v IRC [1981] STC 174* and subsequent cases applied (which enables steps inserted into a composite transaction solely for tax avoidance purposes to be excised to identify the real transaction) the payment of £40,000 made by the trustees would clearly have fallen within *section 687* (as the real transaction would have been a decision by the company to pay a bonus of £40,000 to Mr McDonald combined with the payment to him of £40,000 by the trustees). The *Ramsay* principle was held to apply so PAYE should have been accounted for under *section 687*.

17.9   If an employee works for someone other than his employer and the *PAYE Regulations* do not apply to the employer (or other person who pays his salary), for example, because he is a non-UK resident, the person for whom the employee works is deemed to have paid the salary for PAYE purposes. [*ITEPA*

2003, s 689]. Accordingly a business that uses workers engaged through a non-UK agency needs to take care to ensure that the agency applies PAYE. This provision even appears to bring within the scope of PAYE employees of overseas companies who are seconded to their UK subsidiaries, although when it was introduced the Minister assured Parliament that it 'creates no new liabilities to tax' but merely 'will remove doubt' about the validity of the *PAYE Regulations* (*Hansard 19 April 1994, cols 748* and *749*). Where the provision applies and the person who paid the worker deducted PAYE but did not account for it to HMRC, the engager is liable for tax on the grossed up amount of the payment actually made to the worker. If the worker was paid gross, PAYE is due on that gross amount [*ITEPA 2003, s 689(3)*]. The charge applies if the payment to the employee is made by the employer or by a person acting on behalf of either the employer or the UK engager (and at the expense of the employer or the UK engager or a person connected with either) or by trustees holding property for persons who include the employee (or for a class of persons which includes the employee) [*ITEPA 2003, s 689(5)*].

17.9A If by virtue of *ITEPA 2003, ss 687A* (payment of disguised remuneration – see **3.28**) or 693–700 (special types of income) the overseas employer would be treated under the PAYE regulations (had they applied to him) as making a payment to the employee, he must also be treated as having actually made such a payment so as to trigger the application of this provision (but PAYE is due only on that actual payment with no grossing up) [*ITEPA 2003, s 689(1A), (4)*]. For 2014/15 onwards, where PAYE is due on the earnings of a non-employee under the agency rules (see **19.1**) and the agency (or other third party liable to account for PAYE) did not make the payment of PAYE income of the worker but the PAYE regulation would apply to the agency if it had made the payment, the agency is treated as having made a payment of PAYE income of the worker equal to the amount given by *s 689(3)* [*ITEPA 2003, s 689(1B), (1C)* inserted by *Finance Act 2014 (FA 2014), s 20*]. In such a case, the engager is relieved of liability [*ITEPA 2003, s 689(2)* as amended by *FA 2014, s 20*].

17.10 If the employer is treated as making a payment of any amount to the employee under any of *ITEPA 2003, ss 696–702* (see **17.42–17.58**) he is also deemed to have made an actual payment of that amount so as to trigger an obligation on the person for whom the employee works to account for PAYE. [*ICTA 1988, s 203C(3A)*]. An interesting issue arose in *Demon Internet Ltd v Young [2005] STC (SCD) 233, SpC 449*. Demon was acquired by Scottish Power on 30 April 1998. As part of the process Scottish Power agreed to make payments to employees of Demon to cancel share options held by them in that company. On 30 April 1998, Scottish Power wrote to the then Finance Director of Demon instructing him personally to make payments to the employees out of money provided by Scottish Power. No tax was deducted from the payment but the employees were told that it was taxable as employment income. HMRC demanded PAYE from Demon. Demon contended that it could have no obligation to deduct PAYE until the *Finance Act 1998* became law. Accordingly at 30 April 1998, there was no power – and no lawful authority – for it to deduct tax. The Special Commissioners held that the duty implied by *FA 1998* was to comply with the *PAYE Regulations* that were extant at any time. The relevant PAYE regulation was not introduced until 4 August 1998. The budget resolutions similarly only gave power to amend the *PAYE Regulations*, it was not until the regulation was amended that there was an obligation to deduct tax.

17.11   Where an employee who is not both resident and ordinarily resident in the UK works partly in the UK and partly overseas he is taxable only on the proportion of his salary that relates to UK duties (see **2.7**). The whole of the salary payable to such a person is within the scope of PAYE – with the employee having a right to reclaim the tax overdeducted. However, the employer (or a person designated by him for the purpose of the section) can apply to HMRC for authority to deduct tax on only a proportion of the salary, ie the proportion that is estimated to be applicable to UK duties. The application must obviously give all available information relevant to the calculation of the relevant proportion. [*ITEPA 2003, s 690*]. HMRC can calculate the deduction on the assumption that the remittance basis applies, even though the taxpayer will not yet have claimed it [*ITEPA 2003, s 690(2A)*]. Curiously, prior to 2003/04 it appeared that HMRC could not grant such a request unless the proportion of the salary applicable to UK duties was not ascertainable at the time the application was made. If it could be ascertained PAYE had to be applied to the entire payment, including the part applicable to non-UK duties! [*Income and Corporation Taxes Act 1988 (ICTA 1988), s 203D(2)(b), (8)*]. It is difficult to believe that this was intended. The rewrite Act has corrected this anomaly. Following the *Demon* decision HMRC assessed the employees, who promptly appealed, contending that the tax was Demon's liability. The case *Clifton & others v HMRC [2007] STC (SCD) 386* was heard by a different Commissioner. He agreed that Demon had no obligation, or indeed power, to deduct tax, but nevertheless held that *Finance Act 2006, s 67(3)* imposed on Demon an obligation to account for the PAYE that would have been deductible if they had the power to deduct. Sadly he went on to hold that in his self-assessment the employee can claim credit only for tax which the employer has deducted or should have deducted. Accordingly, irrespective of whether the employer had accounted for the PAYE, as it had no obligation to deduct, the tax was properly assessable on the employees.

17.12   If a person ('the relevant person') enters into an agreement that employees of another person ('the contractor') shall work for the relevant person and 'it is likely that' the contractor will not apply PAYE, HMRC can direct the relevant person to apply PAYE to payments that he makes to the contractor in respect of work done by the employees. The direction must specify the name of the relevant person and the contractor, must be given by notice (which means that it must be in writing – see *Hansard 19 April 1994, col 754*) and a copy must be given to the relevant person (unless HMRC cannot find him). The relevant person must apply PAYE to the entire payment, ie including the contractor's profit loading, as if it were remuneration of the employee. [*ITEPA 2003, s 691*]. It is not clear how he is to apportion the payment if it is in respect of work done by more than one employee. The Minister said that 'it is not part of our purpose to provide as a normal state of affairs that a farmer should be required to provide for PAYE for labour employed by a gang master' (*Hansard 19 April 1994, col 753*). The purpose is obviously to ensure that HMRC can collect the tax where they believe that the contractor will disappear before they can collect the PAYE from him. It is not clear that either the relevant person or the contractor can challenge HMRC's belief that it is likely that the contractor will not account for PAYE. Although the side-heading to the section is 'mobile UK workforce' there is nothing in the section itself to so limit its application. There seems no reason why HMRC should not give a direction under it simply because the contractor is tardy with accounting for PAYE or HMRC fear that he could become insolvent. There are two slight protections against this. First, it is the belief of the Board, not an officer of the Board, that is required before a notice can be given. Secondly, an assurance was given by the then Minister that 'it is not our intention to create in the new clause an obligation which does not already exist within the piece of secondary legislation to which I referred in my opening remarks' (*Hansard 19 April 1994, col 753*). He did not specify what that piece of legislation is. It was probably *regulation 4* of the *PAYE Regulations* which was revoked by *FA 1994, s 133* so that is not much comfort.

17.13 Prior to the enactment of the above rules where a person worked under the general control and management of a person who was not his immediate employer, that person ('the principal employer') was deemed by *regulation 4* of the *PAYE Regulations 1993* (which was repealed by *section 133* of the *Finance Act 1994* as it is replaced by the above provisions) to be the employer for PAYE purposes. *Regulation 4* provided that if the emoluments were actually paid by the immediate employer, the principal employer had to notify him of the tax to be deducted and to himself deduct the tax out of the payment that he made to the immediate employer. This effectively treated the immediate employer as a mere agent of the principal employer. It was accepted in *Andrews v King [1991] STC 481* (see **17.22** and **4.55** above) that *regulation 4* overrode *regulation 2* so that the immediate employer ceased to be an employer altogether for the purpose of the *PAYE Regulations. Regulation 4* seemed apt to cover, for example, a site foreman who was given the aggregate net wages of each of the employees at that site and paid the money over to the individual employees. As none of the above provisions seem to cover such a case it is not readily apparent why the *regulation* has been repealed or if this is still good law.

17.13A If the remuneration receivable by an individual in consequence of providing services falls to be treated under *ITEPA 2003, s 44* (agency workers) as earnings from an employment (see **19.1**) the PAYE rules (except *ITEPA 2003, ss 691, 693–702*) (special types of income) and *710*) apply as if the individual held the employment with or under the deemed employer [*ITEPA 2003, s 688(1), (1A)* as substituted by *FA 2014, s 16*]. This provision also applied before 2014/15 but was limited to deeming the employment to be held with or under the agency because *s 44* was so limited.

17.13B If the remuneration receivable by an individual under (or in consequence of) a contract falls to be treated as employment income under *s 44* and a payment of (or of an amount of) PAYE income of the individual is made by a person acting on behalf of the client and at the expense of the client (or a person connected with the client), *ITEPA 2003, ss 687* and *710* (in relation to a payment treated as made by the client under *s 687*) have effect in relation to the payment as if the client and not the agency were the deemed employer [*ITEPA 2003, s 688(2)*].

The PAYE Regulations

17.14   The Board of HMRC have power to make regulations with respect to the assessment, charge, collection and recovery of income tax. Such regulations can include provisions:

(*a*)   requiring any person who makes a payment of (or on account of) remuneration to deduct tax (either at the basic rate or other rates in such cases or classes as the regulation may provide) by reference to tax tables prepared by the Board, and making such persons liable to account for such tax to HMRC;

(*b*)   for the production to persons authorised by the Board of wages sheets and other documents and records for their inspection to satisfy themselves that income tax is being deducted in accordance with the regulations;

(*c*)   for the collection and recovery of income tax in respect of remuneration which has not been deducted during the year;

(*d*)   requiring the payment of interest on tax due to the Board which is not paid by the due date, for determining the date from which interest is to be calculated (provided that it is not earlier than 14 days after the end of the year of assessment) and for enabling the repayment or remission of such interest;

(*e*)   requiring the payment of interest on repayments due from the Board and for determining the date from which such interest is to be calculated (which cannot be earlier than one year after the end of the year of assessment);

(*f*)   for the assessment and charge of income tax by the Inspector in relation to income subject to PAYE; and

(*g*)   for appeals in relation to matters arising under the *regulations* where there would not otherwise be a right of appeal.

[*ITEPA 2003, s 684*]. HMRC say that a person who is registered for PAYE but is not due to make a payment for a month must tell them that nothing is due (HMRC Notice 5.8.2008). This does not appear to be a statutory requirement but if it is not followed HMRC's computer will issue a demand for payment, which will create problems for the business.

17.15   Interest under head (*d*) of **17.14** above, must be paid without deduction of income tax and is not to be taken into account in computing income, profits or losses for any tax purpose. [*ITEPA 2003, s 684(6)*].

17.16   The Board must construct the tax tables with a view to securing that, as far as possible:

(*a*)   the total income tax payable in respect of any income taxable as employment income for any year of assessment is deducted from such income payable during the year – it can be assumed for the purpose of estimating the total income tax payable that the income will continue to accrue for the rest of the year at the same rate as has been earned from 6 April to the date of making the payment from which the deduction falls to be made; and

(*b*) the income tax deductible (or repayable) on the occasion of any payment of income is such that the total net income tax deducted from the beginning of the year of assessment bears the same proportion to the total income tax payable for the year that the part of the year which ends with the date of the payment bears to the whole year. [*ITEPA 2003, s 685*].

17.17 The total income tax payable for the year means, for the purpose of heads (*a*) and (*b*) of **17.14** above, the total income tax estimated to be payable in respect of the income from the employment subject to a provisional deduction for allowances and reliefs, and subject also (if necessary) to an adjustment for amounts overpaid or underpaid in respect of previous years. [*ITEPA 2003, s 685(2)*].

17.18 An interesting point arose in *Blackburn v Keeling [2003] EWHC 754 (Ch), [2003] STC 1162*. Mr Keeling incurred a loss as a Lloyd's underwriter. Under special rules that apply to underwriters this was a 2003/04 loss but the figure was provisional and would not be finalised until May 2003. In February 2002 Mr Keeling elected to carry back the loss to 2002/03 under *ICTA 1988, s 380* and asked HMRC to amend his 2003/03 PAYE coding to reflect the loss. HMRC refused on the grounds that the loss had not by then been 'established' and would not be established until after the end of 2002/03. The Commissioners and the judge both disagreed. Peter Smith J thought that the Inspector, (and, on appeal, the Commissioners), was entitled to 'take into account all matters known to him at the time he prepares the code to arrive at the fairest and most realistic code that is likely to be the nearest to the true position of the taxpayer when the taxpayer's affairs for that tax year are finally worked out'. Unfortunately, the Court of Appeal disagreed. Although, it felt it arguably contrary to the spirit of the PAYE system that tax should be deducted in 2002/3 when everyone knew that Mr Keeling would in due course be entitled to claim loss relief for that year, it felt the wording of *Regulation 7(2)(a)* ('the release from income tax to which the employee is entitled for the year ... so far as his title to those reliefs has been established at the time of the determination') meant that the appeal had to be rejected.

17.19 The regulations may provide that no repayment of tax is to be made to any person if at the time:

(*a*) he has claimed jobseeker's allowance in respect of a period including that time;

(*b*) he is disqualified from receiving jobseeker's allowance because he is on strike (or would be so disqualified if he satisfied the other qualifying conditions); or

[ITEPA 2003, s 708].

17.20   The Board have made regulations covering all of these matters. They are now the *Income Tax (Pay As You Earn) Regulations 2003 (SI 2003 No 2682)*. It is not proposed to consider all of these regulations in detail but there are a number of them that are of particular importance.

17.21   *Regulation 2*, 'Interpretation' adopts the definition of employment in *ITEPA 2003, ss 4* and *5* (see **4.1** and **4.12**) and specifies that employer has a corresponding meaning. However this is subject to *Regulations 10* to *12* which provide respectively that agencies, pension payers and 'other payers' are to be treated as employers (except for specified purposes). An agency is deemed to cease to employ the worker (so must issue form P45) if it makes no relevant payments to the worker for a period of three months [*Reg 10(2)*]. *Prima facie Regulation 12* seems to impose the responsibility of applying the *PAYE Regulations* on many people who are not employers in the normal sense of the word at all. For example, if A collects B's wage packet for him because B is sick on payday, A may become B's employer because he is paying the emoluments to B. The wages clerk of a company may become an employer if wages are paid in cash as he is the person making the payment. Fortunately, in *Andrews v King [1991] STC 481*, where HMRC put forward a similar claim, it was held that *Regulation 4* (see **17.13** above) overrides the definition of employer in *Regulation 2*. It was held in *R v Walton General Commrs, ex p Wilson [1983] STC 464* that the reference in the *PAYE Regulations 1993* to emoluments was wide enough to cover benefits in kind. The *2003 Regulations* no longer refer to emoluments but to PAYE income [*Reg 2*]. This is defined in *ITEPA 2003, s 683* as any PAYE employment income for the year, any PAYE pension income for the year and any PAYE social security income for the year. PAYE employment income is in turn defined as income which consists of any taxable earnings from an employment in the year and any taxable specific income from an employment for the year (ie the full amount of any specific income which by virtue of any enactment counts as employment income for that year in respect of the employment), which is probably as broad as the previous concept of emoluments [*ITEPA 2003, ss 10(3), 683(2)*]. PAYE does not in general apply to benefits as there is an obligation to deduct tax only 'on making a relevant payment' [*Reg 21(1)*] and a relevant payment is a payment 'of, or on account of PAYE income' [*Reg 4(1)*]. The provision of a benefit is not the making of a payment. The December 1998 Special Commissioners' decision in *Paul Dunstall Organisation Ltd v Hedges [1999] STC SCD 26* casts some doubt on the position in relation to benefits. The company negotiated a sale of a piece of land for £1.5m. It was advised that if it transferred the land to its director prior to exchange of contract it would avoid National Insurance. It did not wish to give the whole value to the director. It accordingly voted him a bonus of £800,000 to be paid in the form of a proportion of the land. It contracted to sell the remainder of the land to the director for £680,000. The director then entered into the sale contract and sold the site for £1.5m, making a £20,000 property dealing profit (a capital gain in the eyes of the Commissioners). HMRC contended that PAYE should have been applied to the payment of emoluments of £800,000 and the Special Commissioners upheld this.

17.22   The basis of their decision was that 'payment' is a word that takes its meaning from its context. As the PAYE Regulations 1993 referred to 'any payment of emoluments', and it is well established that emoluments can take the form of perquisites, they inferred that payment did not mean 'payment in money'. The director received a perquisite that could be turned into money. They accepted that if a deduction was to be made from perquisites there had to be machinery enabling this to be done. They also accepted that there could be difficulties in valuing benefits in kind that could not be turned into money. They concluded that where something was capable of valuation PAYE fell to be deducted from the amount for which the perquisite could be sold when received and that the machinery for deduction was through the coding notice. The transactions took place in 1998.

17.23 In some ways this is an understandable decision. The accepted wisdom now has long been that if a person is voted a bonus of a specified amount to be satisfied by the transfer of an asset to him there is a risk that the amount is pay for PAYE purposes. Nowadays most 'advisers' would have suggested a bonus of the piece of land without placing a figure on it. It is unclear whether the Special Commissioners would have arrived at the same conclusion if that had been done. Worryingly, their reasoning suggests that they would have. This is somewhat frightening. In most cases HMRC have been content to assess the director. It appears that they could now go back and raise a *Regulation 72* assessment on the company – and collect from it interest on overdue tax – and repay the tax assessed on the director. They are not constrained by the 'general view of the law' principle, as they have always contended that there was a liability on the employee even though they have generally not enforced it. Some companies have voluntarily paid the tax 'on behalf of' the employees on the PAYE due date. Even such companies may not be safe.

17.24 In other ways the decision is extraordinary. The concept that the coding notice provides a machinery for deduction is far fetched. In most cases the bonus would exceed a year's basic salary, so the deduction is impracticable. It would almost certainly be *ultra vires* for the *PAYE Regulations* to require an employer to account to HMRC for an amount that it is in practice impossible for him to deduct. Parliament provided in 1994 a procedure for applying PAYE to tradeable assets. In 1998 it extended this to readily convertible assets (see **17.48**). It would hardly have done so if it had all along 'intended' that the PAYE system should apply to such assets. Yet in applying the law the courts seek to reflect the intention of Parliament. In *Aberdeen Asset Management plc v HMRC [2012] UKUT 43(TCC)*, Warren J expressed strong reservations on the reasoning of the Special Commissioners in this case, so it is questionable whether the decision is correct.

17.25 The Special Commissioners relied heavily on *Garforth v Newsmith Stainless Ltd [1979] STC 129*, where an amount credited to a director's current account was held to have been paid 'when money is placed unreservedly at the disposal of directors'. Although Walton J there referred to 'money', the Special Commissioners took his wording as authority for the view that 'payment' has no settled meaning, which somewhat stretches what was actually said. There was a problem with *IRC v Herd* (see **17.29**), where the court held that PAYE could not be applied where only part of a payment was assessable, but the Commissioners resolved that by holding that that was a narrow point which did not greatly assist them! They also got round the small problem that the £800,000 bonus voted at 11.00am on 22 June 1998 differed from the £820,000 sale price achieved at 12.50pm on the next day by ascribing this to 'the volatility of the market', even though the value of the balance of the land did not apparently move during that 26-hour period.

17.26   Subject to the above case and to the statutory exceptions described below, the provision of a benefit will not make the provider an employer under the *regulations* and he will not be a person 'paying' emoluments. On the other hand, in *Booth v Mirror Group Newspapers plc [1992] STC 615* where Mirror Group Newspapers made a payment to an employee of a subsidiary, Pergamon Media Trust plc, to induce him to enter into employment with Pergamon it was held that Mirror Group Newspapers was liable to deduct tax (by reference to an emergency coding) because by making the payment it was itself deemed to be an employer of Mr Booth by virtue of *Regulation 2*. As a result, everyone who tips a waiter or an employed taxi driver without deducting PAYE should be aware that he is committing an offence under the *PAYE Regulations*!

17.27   *Regulation 49* deals with new employees (other than those producing a form P45 (which will show the employee's code number) or who are former full-time students). It imposes an obligation on the employer to complete a form P46 and send it to HMRC when he makes the first relevant payment. The *1993 Regulations* only required this to be done where the person was being paid at an annual rate which exceeded the personal allowance (or at a rate of more than £1 a week or £4 a month if the employee had other employment). The employer must also of course deduct tax on the cumulative basis using the emergency code (which grants the personal allowance) if the employee was formerly a full-time student or using the basic rate code if he was not. This is another change. Under the *1993 Regulations* the basic rate code was used only if the employee had other employment.

17.28   In *Burton v HMRC* [2010] STC 2410 Mr Burton, a higher rate taxpayer was taxed at the basic rate under the *PAYE Regulations* for many months. He contended that HMRC had to show compliance with the Regulations by both his employer and HMRC itself before they could seek to collect from him the tax underdeducted. The Tribunal said that there was no such test. In any event the tax that had been deducted was precisely that required by the regulations.

17.29   If the employer fails to deduct tax from a payment of emoluments, *Regulation 72(1), (3)* empowers HMRC to recover the tax that should have been deducted under PAYE from the employee concerned, if they are satisfied that the employer took reasonable care to comply with the *PAYE Regulations* and the under-deduction was due to an error made in good faith. They have a similar power to require the employee to pay the tax if they believe that he knew that the employer 'has wilfully failed to deduct' PAYE. [*Reg 72(1), (4)*]. If they direct that the employee should pay the tax under either provision the employer ceases to have any liability to pay it. Notice of a direction under *Regulation 72* must be given both to the employer and the employee (unless HMRC are not aware of the employee's address). The employer is entitled to request a direction under *Regulation 72(3)*. The employer has a right of appeal against the refusal of such a request and the employee has a right of appeal against the direction. The employee also has a right of appeal against a direction under *Regulation 72(4)*. *[Regs 72A–72D]* In *IRC v Herd [1993] STC 436* it was held that unless a direction has been made under *Regulation 42* HMRC have no power to recover the tax from the employee, ie they cannot assess him direct under the employment income rules for tax which ought to have been deducted under PAYE. However, Lord Mackay felt that neither *ITEPA 2003, s 684* nor the regulations were wide enough to impose an obligation to apply PAYE to a payment only part of which was assessable under PAYE. In that case the payment was the purchase price of shares, the gain on which was assessable as employment income but the element of the price that reflected their original cost was not. Accordingly, PAYE could not apply. Logically, the same principle should apply to other mixed payments, such as compensation for loss of office where the first £30,000 is exempt from tax, if anyone is brave enough to take the point. A problem can arise in a family business where directors' drawings are voted as net salary at the end of the year. This appears to have been what happened in *R v IRC ex p McVeigh [1996] STC 91*. May J held that including the tax liability in creditors in the accounts and the amount net of deductions in the loan account would no doubt constitute a deduction of tax if the tax were paid over to HMRC. However, he felt it would 'be a misuse of language to say that the bookkeeping and accounting alone, without actual payment and without any of the procedures which the Regulations require, constituted a deduction of tax from the gross payment'. Accordingly, HMRC were entitled to assess Mr McVeigh as he knew that the company had failed to 'deduct' PAYE.

17.30 The harshness of the principle is well illustrated by the Special Commissioners decision in *Black v Inspector of Taxes [2000] STC (SCD) 540*. Black, Brown, Green and White were directors of a subsidiary company. Jones, the chairman and chief executive, promised them each bonuses of a specified sum. At a board meeting of the parent company it was resolved to pay these bonuses by way of transfer of units in a unit trust HMRC assessed Black and his colleagues on the value of the units as benefits in kind. Black and his colleagues appealed, contending that the company ought to have deducted tax under PAYE before providing the units to them. It was agreed that for PAYE purposes 'payment' was the transfer of money or money's worth where quantified in money (eg cheque or credit card). Accordingly, if there was a legal entitlement to payment of money prior to the transfer of the units the satisfaction of that entitlement constituted payment; if there was no legal entitlement the transfer could not amount to payment but would be a benefit in kind (it would now of course be subject to PAYE under the readily convertible asset rules – see **17.42** – but these did not exist at the time). If there is such a general principle it is curious that it was not annunciated in the *Paul Dunstall* case (see **17.21**). Nevertheless, the parties were content to adopt it. It was held that Mr Jones had power to bind the company and his agreement to pay the bonuses created a legal entitlement to the appropriate sum of money. Accordingly, PAYE should have been deducted. The Commissioner considered that the agreement was not to pay a net amount; the directors were entitled to bonuses of £250,000 and if the company had deducted tax when paying the bonus they would have no complaint. Nevertheless she held that PAYE should have been deducted from the whole sum. It is not wholly clear why. If the legal entitlement was to receive £250,000 less tax – say £150,000 – and the taxpayer received value of £250,000 it is hard to see how the additional £100,000 can be in satisfaction of the legal entitlement. On the face of it that £100,000 ought to be a benefit in kind.

17.31 *Regulation 73* deals with the submission of the end of year return, form P35. *Regulation 73* requires the return to be rendered within 44 days after the end of the tax year, ie by 19 May. The form P35 is no longer required under RTI. The last return in the tax year provides HMRC with all of the information that was previously required by the form. Prior to the introduction of RTI, failure to file the P35 so rendered the employer liable to a heavy penalty, namely £1,200 for each 50 employees plus a further penalty of £100 a month per 50 employees for each month the failure continued after a penalty had been imposed (up to the end of the year after that to which the P35 relates only), plus, if the failure continued for more than a year, 100 per cent of the PAYE for the year. If the number of employees was not a multiple of 50 the £100 figure applied to the excess number (or the lesser number if the total was under 50). If a return was made, but it was incorrect because it was made fraudulently or negligently, the penalty was an amount equal to the tax omitted from the return. These penalties were maxima; they were fully mitigable. The penalty for the first 12 months in business was a fixed non-mitigable amount of £100 a month per 50 employees for each month the failure continued. Such penalties have been imposed virtually automatically by HMRC. [*TMA 1970, s 98A*].

17.32 *Regulation 90* requires an employer to make a quarterly return of cars provided to employees and available for their private use. This must be done within 28 days of the end of each income tax quarter (ie 5 April, 5 July, 5 October, 5 January). The return must show for each car that becomes available to an employee (or ceases to be available to him) in that quarter the employee's name and National Insurance number, the car and its original list price, any capital contribution by the employee, any amount the employee is required to pay during the tax year as a condition of the car being available for his private use, and whether fuel is provided for private use.

17.33 The tax is normally payable to HMRC 14 days after the end of each income tax month. [*Reg 69*]. If no payment is made within that period, *Regulation 77* gives the Collector of Taxes power to require the company to make a return of emoluments paid in that month and of the tax payable thereon. Alternatively, *Regulation 78* gives the Collector power to estimate the tax that he thinks is likely to be due, demand it from the employer and, unless the employer pays the tax actually due within seven days or convinces the Collector that nothing is due, enforce payment of that estimated sum. If the total of PAYE, National Insurance and construction industry subcontractors' deductions is likely to be below £1,500 per month on average for a tax year, *Regulation 70* allows the employer to account quarterly (the first payment falling due on 5 July) instead of monthly. The £1,500 figure relates to the aggregate of PAYE, National Insurance, student loan deductions and building industry sub-contractors' deductions less tax credits payable (Working Families Tax Credit (WFTC) or Disabled Persons Tax Credit (DPTC)) – see **Chapter 20**.

17.34 *Regulation 80*, 'Determination of unpaid tax', is increasingly being used by HMRC. Where it appears to HMRC that there may be tax due under PAYE that has not been paid to the Collector, they can 'determine the amount of that to the best of judgement' and serve notice of that determination on the employer. Subject to the normal right of appeal, the amount of the determination is recoverable as if the determination were an assessment and the amount of tax determined were tax payable by the company. An Inspector will frequently make a *Regulation 80* determination on the directors' remuneration shown in accounts submitted to him or on amounts of untaxed emoluments found as a result of a PAYE inspection. There are a number of points to note.

(*a*)   HMRC consider that it is not open to the employer to appeal against a determination on the grounds that the code number used by the Inspector does not fully reflect the allowances due to the employee, as the obligation on the employer under the regulations is to deduct tax in accordance with the code number that has been issued to him. As no time limit within which an appeal against a coding notice must be made is specified this is of dubious validity.

(*b*)   As the tax payable on a *Regulation 80* determination is a liability of the employer, he has no right to recover it from the employee and the employee is not entitled to any credit for it in his income tax self-assessment. In practice the employee is normally given credit for it, but is not allowed a repayment of any excess unless he can show that he has reimbursed the tax to the employer.

17.35   A more serious consequence of a *Regulation 80* determination is that it carries interest. This interest runs not from the date of the determination but from 19 April following the year of assessment to which it relates. [*Reg 82*].

17.36   If a *Regulation 80* assessment is not paid within 30 days from the date on which the determination becomes final HMRC can recover the tax from the employee if either they consider that the employee received the income knowing that the employer had wilfully failed to deduct the tax or the tax is tax on a notional payment [*Reg 81*]. For 2004/05 onwards (but not for earlier years) the employee has a right of appeal against such a direction [*Reg 81A* inserted by the *Income Tax (PAYE) (Amendment) Regulations 2004 (SI 2004 No 851)*].

17.37   In the past where a person was treated as self-employed and was ultimately agreed (or held) to be an employee HMRC allowed the tax paid by the employee as a self-employed person to be set against the tax due under the *Regulation 80* determination. For a period they stopped doing so on the basis of the Special Commissioner, Mr Clark's, decision in *Demibourne Ltd v CIR [2005] STC (SCD) 687, SpC 486*. In that case HMRC itself argued that Demibourne Ltd did not have a legitimate expectation that the *Regulation 81* determination, if upheld, should be reduced by the tax that Mr Bone (the worker) had paid on the disputed income, and in any event the Special Commissioners had no jurisdiction to decide this. The taxpayer had claimed such legitimate expectation because when HMRC initially challenged Mr Bone's status HMRC had told the company, 'Please note that it is not HMRC practice to charge tax twice and any tax already paid on Mr Bone's earnings will be taken into consideration'. HMRC explained that away to the Commissioners on the ground that the statement had been made at a time when the Officer thought that the case would be settled by agreement. The Commissioner agreed that he had no jurisdiction but commented, 'It would be preferable for the determinations confirmed by this decision to be adjusted by negotiation between the parties and Mr Bone so as to allow for the tax already paid by him to the extent that it is incapable of adjustment. Ideally agreement should also be reached as a basis for dealing with the tax in subsequent years'.

17.38   It hardly seems reasonable for HMRC to change their practice on the basis that in Demibourne they refused to apply that practice, apparently to punish Demibourne for having exercised its right of appeal to the Commissioners. In that case Mr Bone had apparently indicated that he was not prepared voluntarily to disclose his income to Demibourne. HMRC's concern was that if they allow an offset to Demibourne (or another employer) Mr Bone (or the worker) might reclaim the tax he had paid on the basis that it was repaid in error, so leaving HMRC out of pocket. HMRC produced no evidence to demonstrate that this had happened in past cases. In his decision in *Parade Park Hotel* (see **4.44**), Mr Clark stated, 'In the light of comments made following my decision in *Demibourne Ltd v HMRC* I would like to emphasise that in my view there is nothing to prevent HMRC from entering into such arrangements [ie that if the employment position were to be conceded they would enter into a negotiated settlement which would take into account the fact that the worker declared the income for self-assessment], using their 'collection and management' powers under the Commissioners for Revenue and Customs Act 2005.'

17.39   As a result of an outcry over the practical problems caused by this approach, new *Regulations 72E* to *72G* were added to the *PAYE Regulations* by the *Income Tax (PAYE) (Amendment) Regulations 2008 (SI 2008 No 782)* with effect from 6 April 2008. These enable HMRC to direct that part of the PAYE liability should be transferred from the employer to the employee. The part that can be transferred is the amount on which tax was paid by the employee on the income that he treated as self-employment income. The employee has a limited right of appeal on the grounds only that he did not receive the amount of income determined by HMRC, the amount specified is incorrect because all or part does not fall within *Regulation 72E*, or no trigger event has occurred (or if it has it occurred before 6 April 2008). This removes the right of the employee to make an error or mistake claim on the basis that the employer ought to have deducted tax under PAYE and recover the tax paid by the employee, no matter how negligent the employer might have been.

17.40   It has been held that an employer is liable to operate PAYE even if non-UK resident provided that it has 'a trading presence in the UK' (*Clark v Oceanic Contractors 56 TC 183*). In that case an overseas company was engaged, through a Belgian branch, in installing pipelines in the UK sector of the North Sea. It had a permanent establishment in the UK but paid the employees direct from Belgium in US dollars. The House of Lords held that the critical factor in implying a territorial limitation into a section establishing a method of tax collection is whether, in the circumstances, it could be made effective. As Oceanic had a permanent establishment in the UK to which a *Regulation 80* determination could be issued, this was a sufficient tax presence to bring it within the scope of PAYE.

Organised arrangements for sharing tips (Troncs)

17.41   In some industries, such as hotels and catering, tips and gratuities are shared out not by the employer but by a third party, such as the head waiter. In such circumstances the employer cannot apply PAYE to the tips as he does not know what has been paid to each employee. Instead the person responsible for sharing out the money (called the troncmaster) is required to apply PAYE when making payments to individual employees. There must be 'an organised arrangement' for gratuities or service charges' to be shared [*Reg 100*]. There is no corresponding provision for National Insurance. Accordingly tips, gratuities and service charges paid to employees via a tronc escape both employer's and employees' NIC. Although it is the responsibility of the troncmaster to account for PAYE the employer must notify HMRC of the existence of the tronc, and, if he knows it, the name of the troncmaster immediately he becomes aware that a tronc is being operated [*Reg 100(2)*]. HMRC have power to require the employer to operate PAYE if they believe that the troncmaster has failed to carry out his obligations [*Reg 100(5)*]. They cannot make such a direction retrospectively though. If a director of an employer company acts as troncmaster it is important to document that he does so personally, not on behalf of the employer (as if the company is troncmaster the normal PAYE rules apply). That is what happened in *Figael v Fox 64 TC 441*. The Court of Appeal said that the General Commissioners were entitled to infer that the director was acting in his capacity as director so that the company was liable for the PAYE. For NIC purposes. the National Insurance Contributions Office (NICO) differentiate between a voluntary service charge and a mandatory one. Their view is that if the service charge is mandatory and is paid to the employer NICs are due even if the money is passed to the troncmaster for division between the staff. They also take the view that if the employer influences how the money is shared out, including if he guarantees a minimum level of tips, NIC is payable. Both of these views are questionable. It was held in *Annabels's (Berkeley Square) Ltd v HMRC [2009] STC 1551* that where an employer hands over payments to the tronc master for distribution as the tronc master may decide, the amount allocated to an employee is not earnings for the purpose of the employer's obligation to pay the national minimum wage.

Readily convertible assets

17.42   If assessable income of an employee is paid in the form of a readily convertible asset, the employer is treated as making a payment to which he must apply PAYE of the amount which, on the best estimate that can reasonably be made, is the amount of income likely to be taxable as employment income in respect of the provision of the asset. [*ITEPA 2003, s 696*]. This appears to apply irrespective of whether the asset is provided by the employer, an intermediary, or a third party.

17.43   A readily convertible asset is:

(*a*)   any asset capable of being sold or realised on a recognised investment exchange (within the meaning of the *Financial Services Act 1986 (FSA 1986)*) or the London Bullion Market;

(*b*)   any asset capable of being sold or otherwise realised on the New York Stock Exchange or on a market for the time being specified in *PAYE Regulations*;

(*c*)   the rights of an assignee (or any other rights) in respect of a money debt that is or may become due to the employer or any other person (eg a trade debt which is assigned to the employee);

(*d*)   any property (or right in such property) that is subject to a 'warehousing regime';

(*e*)   an asset consisting of anything that is likely (without anything being done by the employee) to give rise to (or to become) a right enabling a person to obtain an amount of money which is likely to be similar to the expense of providing the asset;

(*f*)   an asset for which 'trading arrangements' are in existence; or

(*g*)   an asset for which trading arrangements are likely to come into existence in accordance with any arrangements of another description existing when the asset is provided (or in accordance with any understanding existing at the time).

(*h*)   shares or securities which do not fall within the above heads must be treated as readily convertible assets unless they are shares which are corporation tax deductible (see **2.106**).

[*ITEPA 2003, s 702(1), (5A), (5B)*].

17.44   A warehousing regime for this purpose means that the item is held within a Customs warehouse within *Value Added Tax Act 1994 (VATA 1994), s 18*, a fiscal warehouse within *VATA 1994, s 18A* or any corresponding regime in another EEA (European Economic Area) State. [*ITEPA 2003, s 702(6)*]. There are trading arrangements for an asset if any arrangement exists, the effect of which is to enable the employee, or a member of his family or household (as defined in *ITEPA 2003, s 721(4)* – see **6.46**), to obtain an amount of money that is (or is likely to be) similar to the expense incurred in the provision of the asset. [*ITEPA 2003, s 702(2)*].

17.45   The reference in **17.43**(*e*) and **17.44** to obtaining an amount of money means enabling an amount to be obtained by any means at all, including in particular:

(*a*)   by using the asset or other property as security for a loan or advance; or

(*b*)   by using any rights comprised in or attached to the asset or other property to obtain any asset for which trading arrangements exist.

The term includes references to cases where the employee (or some other person) is enabled to obtain an amount as a member of a class or description of persons as well as where he is enabled to obtain it in his own right. [*ITEPA 2003, s 702(4)*].

17.46   An amount is similar to the expense incurred in the provision of an asset if it is equal to or exceeds such expense or is not substantially less than it. [*ITEPA 2003, s 702(5)*].

17.47   An asset for this purpose includes any property (particularly any right or interest falling within *Part 3* of the *Financial Services and Markets Act 2000 (FSMA 2000) (Regulated Activities) Order 2001 (SI 2001 No 544)*, other than a non-cash voucher, credit token or cash voucher (see **6.20**, **6.30** and **17.59** respectively), a payment subject to PAYE, or certain shares issued under approved share schemes. There is also power for the PAYE Regulations to lay down further exclusions. [*ITEPA 2003, s 701*]. The excluded shares are shares acquired by the employee under an approved SAYE scheme (see **16.5**), an approved profit sharing scheme (see **16.35**), an approved CSOP scheme (see **16.8**) (provided that the option was exercised between three and ten years of its grant or was exercised in accordance with the relevant rules – see **16.11**(*b*)(ii)) or on the exercise of a pre-27 November 1996 option. The shares must be ordinary share capital of a company which is the employer company, one which controls that company, or a company which is a member of a consortium which owns the employer company or a company which controls it (or which controls a member of such a consortium). The exclusion for pre-27 November 1996 options applies only where the avoidance of tax or NIC is not the main purpose (or one of the main purposes) of any arrangements under which the option was obtained or exercised. The exclusion of such shares applies only to their acquisition. It does not apply to anything that changes their value subsequent to the acquisition. [*ITEPA 2003, s 701(2) (c),(3)–(5)*].

17.48   Shares will of course normally be readily convertible assets only if they are quoted or trading arrangements are in place in respect of them at the time they are transferred to the employee. The exemption includes shares whose value has been enhanced as mentioned in *ITEPA 2003, s 696*, (see **17.54**) and it also applies to *ITEPA 2003, ss 696–700*.

17.49   This provision was considered in *DTE Financial Services Ltd v Wilson [2001] STC 777, [2001] EWCA Civ 455*. The scheme adopted there is set out at **17.8**. HMRC contended that the appointment of the contingent interest to Mr McDonald constituted an arrangement, the purpose of which was to enable him to obtain an amount similar to the expense incurred in the provision of the asset (see **17.46**). Whilst Hart J thought this a possible interpretation the Court of Appeal disagreed. It felt that the legislation contemplates trading arrangements which are extraneous to the asset itself. It is not possible to find trading arrangements relating to an asset by analysing the incidents of the asset itself. Trading arrangements were held to exist in *Aberdeen Asset Management plc v HMRC [2012] UKUT 43(TCC)*.

17.50 In *Spectrum Computer Supplies Ltd v HMRC; Kirkstall Timber Ltd v HMRC [2006] STC (SCD) 668* the Special Commissioners held that the collection by the company of book debts that had been assigned to employees did not give rise to trading arrangements. This was a pyrrhic victory though, as they found that the transfer of the debt was a 'mechanism to deliver cash' and as such was a 'payment' for PAYE purposes, not a benefit in kind.

17.51 An asset consisting of shares or securities which is not a readily convertible asset must be treated as one unless it is shares that are corporation tax deductible, ie for which the company is entitled to relief under *Finance Act 2003 (FA 2003), Sch 23* (see **14.186**). A scrip or rights issue on such shares (or any other shares acquired by virtue of holding such shares) is treated as corporation tax deductible. So are shares received on a share exchange for such shares provided that it constitutes a new holding for capital gains tax purposes. [*ITEPA 2003, s 702(5A)–(5D)*].

17.52 This provision is designed to prevent the avoidance of PAYE – and thus the deferral of payment of the tax until it can be collected by assessment – by the payment of bonuses in gold bars and similar assets. Such payments became popular in the late 1980s primarily to avoid National Insurance but the PAYE benefit was a useful bonus. Curiously, such devices seem to have attracted the ire of HMRC more than that of the Contributions Agency (the predecessor of HMRC's NICO). The former regularly attacked such schemes whereas the Contributions Agency tolerated them until the loss of revenue became sufficiently serious to seek a change in the law.

17.53 Shares or securities which do not fall within **17.43**(*a*)–(*g*) must nevertheless be treated as readily convertible assets unless they are shares which are corporation tax deductible. Shares are corporation tax deductible for this purpose if they are acquired by a person by reason of his (or another person's) employment with a company (or pursuant to an option so acquired) and the company is entitled to corporation tax relief in respect of the shares under *FA 2003, Sch 23* [*ITEPA 2003, s 702(5A), (5B)*]. If a person acquires additional shares by virtue of holding shares that are corporation tax deductible they are also treated as corporation tax deductible. [*ITEPA 2003, s 702(5C)*]. If a person ceases to be beneficially entitled to shares that are corporation tax deductible and acquires other shares that constitute a new holding within *Taxation of Chargeable Gains Act 1992, ss 127–130* (company reorganisations and share exchanges) the new holding is treated as if it were corporation tax deductible. [*ITEPA 2003, s 702(5D)*].

17.54 If assessable income is provided by enhancing the value of an asset in which the employee or a member of his family or household already has an interest and the asset as enhanced is a readily convertible asset, *section 696* is to apply as if the employee had been provided with the enhanced asset. [*ITEPA 2003, s 697(1)*]. Such deeming merely triggers the operation of the section. The amount on which PAYE is payable is the best estimate that can reasonably be made of the amount assessable in respect of the enhancement – which will, of course, normally be the cost of making the enhancement. [*ITEPA 2003, ss 696, 697(2)*].

17.55 An asset is enhanced for this purpose if either:

(*a*) the asset, or any right or interest in it, is improved or otherwise made more valuable by the provision of any service (eg improvements are made to the employee's house); or

(*b*) property is added to the asset which improves it or otherwise increases its value (eg an additional premium is paid to an existing insurance policy); or

(*c*) money or other property is applied to the improvement of the asset in question, or to securing an increase in its value or in the value of any right or interest in it.

The exclusions set out at **17.44** also apply for this purpose, the exclusion, of course, being of the improved shares. [*ITEPA 2003, ss 697(3)* and *710(2) (a)*, and *Reg 3* and *3B* of the *Income Tax (Employments) (Notional Payments) Regulations 1994 (SI 1994 No 1212)*]. So does the transitional relief where the enhancement took place between 6 April and 31 July 1998. [*FA 1998, s 64(6)*].

17.56 The obligation to deduct PAYE under *section 696* applies also to transactions which give rise to income tax charges in relation to employment-related securities (see **Chapter 14**) as if the employee were provided with PAYE income [*ITEPA 2003, s 698*]. It also applies to gains from share options assessable on an employee under *ITEPA 2003, ss 473* (see **14.104**), *476* (see **14.107**) and *477* (see **14.107**). In both cases the employee is treated as if he were provided at the relevant time by the employer with assessable income in the form of such shares and as if that income were being provided in respect of the employment by reason of which he was granted the benefit or option. The amount to which PAYE has to be applied is the amount on which tax is likely to be chargeable under the relevant provision. [*ITEPA 2003, ss 698(2), 700(4)*]. The amount likely to be chargeable under *s 426* (see **14.26**), *428* (see **14.37**) or *476* (see **14.107**) is the amount after deducting any relief for secondary Class 1 contributions met by the employee [*ITEPA 2003, s 698 (2A); 700(4A)*]. If the employment related securities are not readily convertible assets and the consideration or benefit does not take the form of a payment, *ITEPA 2003, s 696* (readily convertible assets) applies as if the provision of the asset (ie the consideration) were the provision of PAYE income in the form of the shares (so that PAYE has to be applied even though the shares are not a readily convertible asset) [*ITEPA 2003, s 698(4)*].

17.57 If the trigger event is the assignment or release of an option (or of any other right to acquire shares), PAYE must be applied on the amount of any payment for the assignment or release, or, if less, the amount assessable under *section 476*. If the consideration consists not of cash but of the provision of an asset which is either a readily convertible asset under *section 702* or a non-cash voucher, credit token or cash voucher, the employee is treated as receiving assessable income from the employment in respect of which the right was granted in the form of that asset and PAYE must be applied to the amount on which tax is likely to be chargeable under the trigger provisions

The employee shareholding rules were substantially recast from 1 September 2003. Under the prior legislation if the trigger event was the shares ceasing to be wholly conditional under *section 422* (old), PAYE was applied as if the employee had been provided at that time with a further interest in the shares which was not wholly conditional. [*ITEPA 2000, s 698* (old)]. If the trigger was the conversion of shares PAYE was applied as if the original provision of the convertible shares included the ones into which they are converted (ie as if the converted shares were received by reason of the employment for which the employee was granted the convertible shares). The exclusions for shares received under an approved share scheme described at **17.47** also applied to amounts within *section 700*.

17.58 The amount on which PAYE is applied is the amount likely to be chargeable by virtue of the relevant provision. If there are a series of conversions, the amount is, of course, related back to the issue of the initial holding of convertible shares. [*ITEPA 2003, s 700(4)*]. Where the employee agrees to pay the employer's NIC (see **14.56**, **14.67** and **14.116**) the amount on which PAYE is due is the amount after deducting that NIC. [*ITEPA 2003, s 698(2A), 700(4A)* inserted by *FA 1994, Sch 16, para 4*].

17.58A If *ITEPA 2003, ss 698* or *700* applies and all or part of the amount treated as employment income is (or is likely to be) foreign securities income (see **12.38** up to 2014/15 and **14.139A** thereafter) the amount of the payment treated under *s 696* (see **17.54**) as made is limited to the amount that (on the basis of the best estimate that can reasonably be made) is likely to count as employment income, minus the amount that (on the same basis) is likely to be foreign securities income.

Vouchers and credit tokens

17.59 PAYE must also be applied by the employer where a 'cash voucher' is received by an employee. [*ITEPA 2003, s 693(1)*]. Again it appears irrelevant whether the voucher is provided by the employer, an intermediary or a third party. PAYE does not apply to either the provision of the voucher or its use if it is used to meet expenses and the expenses would not have been taxable as earnings had they been paid direct by the employee. The *PAYE Regulations* can provide for further exclusions [*ITEPA 2003, s 693(2)–(4)*]. A cash voucher is deemed to be provided to an employee for this purpose when it is appropriated to him (whether by attaching it to a card held for him or in any other way). [*ITEPA 2003, s 693(5)*].

17.60 A cash voucher is any voucher, stamp or similar document capable of being exchanged (either on its own or together with other vouchers, stamps or documents) for a sum of money equal to (or greater than, or not substantially less than) the expense incurred in providing it. It includes a voucher exchangeable only after a time and also a voucher that is capable of being exchanged either for cash or for goods or services. [*ITEPA 2003, s 75*]. The taxable amount is of course the amount for which the voucher can be exchanged. [*ITEPA 2003, s 81*]. As tax cannot physically be deducted from a voucher it must of course be deducted from the cash element of the employee's salary. [*ITEPA 2003, s 710(1)*]. Any money, goods or services obtained in exchange for the voucher is obviously not also taxable as a benefit under the basic definition of emoluments. [*ITEPA 2003, s 95*].

17.61 PAYE must also be applied by the employer when an employee receives a non-cash voucher – again, apparently, irrespective of whom he receives it from – if at the time the voucher is provided either:

(*a*)   it is capable of being exchanged for anything which, if it had been provided to the employee at the time the voucher was received, would have been a readily convertible asset for the purpose of *ITEPA 2003, s 696* (see **17.42**); or

(*b*)   but for *ITEPA 2003, s 701(2)* (which excludes non-cash vouchers from being readily convertible assets), the voucher would itself have fallen to be regarded as a readily convertible asset.

There is power for vouchers to be excluded from these provisions under the *PAYE Regulations* but no such exclusions have so far been made. The voucher is deemed to have been provided to the employee at the time that it is appropriated to him (whether by attaching it to a card held by him or in some other way). [*ITEPA 2003, s 694(7)*].

17.62   The employer must also be treated as making a payment subject to PAYE on each occasion on which an employee uses a credit token provided to him (by anyone) by reason of his employment. [*ITEPA 2003, s 695*]. This is something which would fall to be regarded as a readily convertible asset within *section 702*. Prior to 6 April 1998, PAYE fell to be applied only if the credit token was used to obtain money or goods which were capable of being sold or otherwise realised on an exchange or market falling within *s 203F(2)(a)* or (*b*), or goods for which trading arrangements existed. [*ICTA 1988, s 203H*]. The meaning of a credit token and the ascertainment of the assessable amount are considered at **6.29–6.34**. It is not clear how an employer is expected to know that the credit token has been exchanged, particularly where it is provided by a third party. PAYE need not be deducted from a credit token which is used to obtain money to defray expenses and would not have been taxable as earnings if the money had been paid direct to the employee and he had incurred the expense. The *PAYE Regulations* can provide for further exclusions [*ITEPA 2003, s 695(2), (3)*].

The mechanics of the deduction

17.63   Where PAYE is payable by virtue of any of paragraphs **17.7–17.13** or **17.42–17.58** above, the obligation to deduct PAYE arises at such time as may be prescribed by the *PAYE Regulations* and is an obligation to deduct it from any payment or payments that the employer actually makes of 'PAYE income' of that employee. [*ITEPA 2003, s 710(1), (2)*]. It is not possible to make a real deduction from notional income. It is obviously intended to mean other income assessable under the employment income rules which is paid in cash. HMRC are empowered to prescribe the time at which this deduction is to be made. [*ITEPA 2003, s 710(5)*]. They have prescribed the occasion of any salary payment made in the same income tax month as the notional payment and falling on or after the time of that payment. If the employer accounts quarterly for PAYE it is any salary payment in the same quarters. [*Reg 62*]. Where the liability arises under retrospective legislation the deduction is against salary payments in the tax year in which Royal Assent of the legislation creating the charge is given and which fall on or after the date of Royal Assent [*ITEPA 2003, ss 684(2), 710 (7A) inserted by FA 2006, s 94(3), (4)*]. It will be apparent that in many, if not most, cases, salary payments in that period will be insufficient to enable the deduction to be made. Accordingly, HMRC have turned these rules into an '*in terrorem*' provision, ie they are not to collect tax but to dissuade employers from making such payments. However, HMRC do have power to substitute an alternative date. The *National Insurance Contributions Act 2006* empowers the Treasury by regulation to apply the PAYE rules on retrospective payments to NIC. They did so by the *Social Security (Contributions) (Amendment No 2) Regulations 2007 (SI 2007 No 1057)* but only in relation to the changes to the employee share rules made by *Finance (No 2) Act 2005 (F(No 2)A 2005)* and *FA 2006*.

17.64   If because of an insufficiency of salary payments in the same tax month the employer is unable to deduct the full amount of tax on the notional payment, he must nevertheless account to HMRC for the PAYE on it 14 days after the end of the month in the normal way. [*ITEPA 2003, s 710(3), (4)*].

17.65   If the employee does not reimburse such tax within 90 days of the end of the tax year in which the relevant date falls the tax is itself deemed to be emoluments of the employment (which arise on the date of the notional payment) and is assessable on him as employment income. [*ITEPA 2003, s 222 as amended by FA 2014, s 19*]. Where the employer was treated as making the notional payment before 6 April 2014, the money had to be reimbursed within 90 days the date on which the notional payment was deemed to be made (30 days for payments made before 9 April 2003) Where a tax charge is applied retrospectively in accordance with the previous government's threat to backdate anti-avoidance legislation to 2 December 2004, the 90 days run from the end of the tax year in which Royal Assent is given to the Act that introduces the provision.. The amount was originally deemed to be income of the employee. The change to deem it emoluments is apparently to ensure that the amount is brought into account to determine whether the employee is in higher paid employment (see **6.4**). It also appears to subject the amount to National Insurance. It is not clear what can amount to reimbursement – 'make good' is actually the statutory wording. An agreement by the employee that the tax should be debited to an account of his with the employer on which there is a credit balance is almost certainly making good; but debiting to an already overdrawn account, or the employer making a loan to the employee to satisfy the obligation, may well not be. The provision applies only where the employer is treated as having made a payment of employment income under *ITEPA 2003, ss 687* (see **17.7**), *687A* (disguised remuneration – see **3.28**) or *693–700* (see **17.59**) or from 2014/15, *689A* (workers on the continental shelf – see **17.98**).

17.66   This question was in issue before the Special Commissioners in *Ferguson v IRC [2001] STC (SCD) 1*. The taxpayers were awarded a bonus in the form of rhodium metal. This was sold on 26 September 1995 and the proceeds credited to the company's bank account and posted to the directors' current accounts. Mr Ferguson had been erroneously advised that the tax was payable on 16 April 1996 (instead of 19 October 1995). HMRC contended that Mr Ferguson had not made the requisite payment to the company that he was required to make before 25 October 1995. The Special Commissioner had no hesitation in finding that he had done so. While, in theory, he could have withdrawn the tax money erroneously credited to the current account it was clear from the evidence that this would and could not have happened.

17.67   Prior to 2014/15 this legislation was very harsh. In *Chilcott v HMRC [2010] EWCA Civ 1538* is correct. Mr Chilcott, a director of Evolution Capital Ltd, exercised various share options in the company in June 2001. The company did not apply PAYE as it did not believe that Mr Chilcott had acquired the options by reason of his employment (it took the view that they were obtained by reason of his being a founder shareholder). After prolonged arguments, in August 2006 HMRC made a *Regulation 80* determination that PAYE was due. Meanwhile in October 2003, Mr Chilcott had paid the tax on the option by declaring it as income on his self-assessment tax return. So why the case? Because, said HMRC, it was a company liability so a payment by Mr Chilcott was irrelevant (although if he was agreeable HMRC would give the company credit for the tax paid by Mr Chilcott). More importantly, the law requires Mr Chilcott to have refunded the tax to the company within 90 days of June 2001. He had not done so (obviously, because at that time he was disputing that any tax was due). Accordingly HMRC said the law entitles them to tax on a grossed-up basis if it is not refunded to the company within the 90 days; they demanded their pound of flesh. Unfortunately John Clark is not a latter day Portia and could find no way to frustrate such an unreasonable demand, nor could the High court or the Court of Appeal. Indeed Lord Nueberger retorted, 'Section 144A of the Taxes Act is, as Mr Yerbury accepts, clear in its terms and has the meaning for which the Revenue contends, as the Special Commissioner and Proudman J held. It is time that its meaning could at least in some circumstances be regarded as penal, as it applies even if "the due amount" is "made good" on the 31st day, but that does enable this court to rewrite such a clear statutory provision. The fact that some might regard the operation of s 144A, according to its terms, as penal merely emphasises that the court should construe it with care and if there is a narrower construction less beneficial to the Revenue, more beneficial to the taxpayer, available then the court should at least seriously consider it and, if appropriate, adopt it. The fact that there is a time limit, as there is in sections of many Acts, merely carries with it the inevitable consequence that if an event occurs just before the time limit expires, it will produce a different result (sometimes a radically different result) from that which applies if the event happens just after the time it expired. Neither of these two points, taken on their own or together, entitle this court to rewrite what is, and as is accepted by the Appellant, to be a clearly drafted section.' Sedley LJ added that the fact that parliament chose not to debate the provision at all does not mean that it has to be taken as not having approved it. Sadly, therefore this is a penal provision arising as a result of the

Gordon Brown/Dawn Primarolo habit of bulldozing badly drafted legislation through parliament in such volumes as to leave little opportunity for debate. In *Manning v HMRC (TC 2666)* the company neatly circumvented this trap by providing in the scheme rules that 'it is a condition of the exercise of the ... Warrant that Participant ... will ... deliver cash or a cheque to the Employer sufficient to pay the PAYE by the due date'. The FTT held that the effect of this was that the beneficial ownership of the shares was held in suspense until that condition was satisfied.

17.68 Where a notional payment takes the form of a non-cash voucher which is a cheque voucher the payment is treated as made when the cheque is handed over in exchange for money, goods or services – or the time it is posted if sent by post. In the case of any other non-cash voucher, it is the later of the time when the chargeable expense is incurred or the voucher is received by the employee. [*ITEPA 2003, s 694(5), (6)*].

Definitions

17.69 An 'employee' means a person who holds or has held an office or employment under or with another person and 'employer' means a person under or with whom that employee holds or has held the office or employment. In relation to any assessable income of an employee, his employer means the person who is the employer in relation to the office or employment in respect of which that income is provided or by reference to which it falls to be regarded as assessable. [*ITEPA 2003, s 712(1)*].

17.70 If the remuneration receivable by an individual is treated as emoluments under the agency rules in *section 44* (see **19.1**), *ITEPA 2003, ss 687–692* (but not *691*), *ss 693–702* and *s 710* apply as if that individual held an employment with the agency. However, if in such a case a payment of (or on account of) assessable income of that individual is made by a person acting on behalf of the client (and at the expense of the client or a person connected with him), *ITEPA 2003, ss 687* and *710* apply in relation to that payment as if the client, not the agency, were the employer for the purposes of those provisions. [*ITEPA 2003, s 688(1), (2)*].

Pensions

17.71 PAYE is also applicable to certain pensions. It has always applied to pensions paid direct by the employer. Where, however, the pension was paid by an insurance company or other pension provider it was previously generally treated as an annuity and tax deducted at the basic rate only. The insurance company must apply PAYE to such pensions paid under a company pension scheme. [*ITEPA 2003, s 683(3)*]. [*ITEPA 2003, s 683(3)*].

Collection from the employee

17.72 As indicated in **17.29** above it was held in *IRC v Herd [1993] STC 436* that where an item is within the scope of PAYE HMRC's recourse is normally only against the employer. There is no right of recovery from the employee unless either he was aware that tax had not been deducted or the Collector absolves the employer from liability.

17.73   Tax on items such as benefits in kind, any taxable element of expenses that are outside the PAYE scheme, and deemed employment income under the share incentive rules, etc. is collectable from the employee either under the self-assessment procedure or by direct collection.

17.74   The due date of payment for tax on directly collected earnings is 14 days after the date on which the Collector first makes an application for payment of the tax. [*Reg 147*]. Interest on overdue tax runs from that date irrespective of whether an appeal is made. [*TMA 1970, s 86(1), (3)*].

17.75   Where an assessment relates to income which has been taken into account for PAYE and was received at least 12 months before the start of the year of assessment in which it was made, it must be made in accordance with the practice generally prevailing at the end of the year following the year of assessment to which it relates if it is raised after that time. [*ITEPA 2003, s 709*]. The meaning of this provision was considered by the Court of Appeal in *Walters v Tickner [1993] STC 624*. In that case an assessment for 1983/84 was made on 22 August 1988, more than 12 months after 1983/84. The taxpayer contended that *section 206* merely required HMRC to raise the assessment in accordance with the generally prevailing practice and did not affect the taxpayer's right of appeal.

17.76   Nolan LJ was reluctant to hold that the taxpayer's right to challenge a generally prevailing practice should depend on whether or not HMRC chose to make the assessment within 12 months rather than whether the taxpayer asked them to do so. Finding the wording to be 'ambiguous and obscure' he resorted to the *Pepper v Hart [1992] STC 898* principle (namely that a court can look at Hansard to assist in the interpretation of legislation which is ambiguous or obscure or the literal meaning of which leads to an absurdity) and referred to the *1991 Hansard* where he found 'If a taxpayer has been formally assessed and the assessment is regarded as settled, he cannot reopen the assessment. If however he has not been assessed, he can, at any time within five years, demand an assessment. Therefore, there is liable to be the anomalous position … in which there is a change in practice which follows from a decision of one of the superior courts. The taxpayer who has not been formally assessed can then demand an assessment … while somebody else in an exactly comparable position will be precluded if he has been formally assessed to tax. *Subsection (1)* removes that anomaly and ensures that the rule of practice shall be that which obtained at the expiration of the period of twelve months immediately following the year of assessment.'

17.77   This inclined him towards HMRC's interpretation but as the case dealt with scholarship income he was able to hold that the specific exemption for such income overrode what is now *section 709* so he did not have to decide what that *section* means. He added a plea to Parliament to amend the wording. Unfortunately the rewrite did not take the opportunity to do so.

17.78 HMRC do not need to issue assessment for a tax year if the tax deducted in accordance with the PAYE tables is the same as it would have been if all the relevant circumstances had been known to all parties throughout the year, ie a formal assessment is not necessary if the correct amount of tax has been deducted under PAYE. In practice they do not normally issue an assessment if the tax deducted is correct to within about £30. The taxpayer can, however, ask to be issued with a tax return – which will trigger the normal self-assessment procedures. The time limit for such a request is five years after 31 October following the year of assessment. [*ITEPA 2003, s 711*].

Security for PAYE

17.79 From 19 July 2011, HMRC have been given power by statutory instrument to require security (or further security) to be given for PAYE and NIC. It is a criminal offence attracting a fine of up to £5,000 to fail to provide such security [*ITEPA 2003, s 684(2), (4B), (4), (4A) inserted by Finance Act 2011 (FA 2011), s 85*].

Form P11D, dispensations and PSAs

17.80 Where an employer provides benefits for, or reimburses expenses of a higher-paid employee, he must complete an annual return of expenses paid to each such employee by 7 July following the year of assessment concerned. [*Taxes Management Act 1970 (TMA 1970), s 15(6)–(8)* and *Reg 85* of the *PAYE Regulations*]. This return is provided on a form P11D. A separate form strictly needs to be completed for each employee, but if there is a dispensation for travelling and subsistence payments, then P11D lists of, typically, cars, car fuel and medical insurance are perfectly acceptable to HMRC, and indeed may be preferred for large employers.

17.81 *TMA 1970, s 15(5), (9)* and *(11)* impose additional obligations. *Subsections (5)* and *(9)* allow the P11D to require details of payments by third parties. If the provision of the benefit or payment has been arranged or guaranteed or in any way facilitated by the employer he must provide particulars of the payment or benefit and the name and address of the third party. If they were not arranged by him but he is aware of their existence he must provide the name and address of the third party. *Subsections (9)* and *(11)* require the employer to calculate the amount of any benefit and to determine the amount of any expenses, etc. that are chargeable to tax. In doing so, he cannot make any deductions, eg for allowable expenses under *ITEPA 2003, s 336*, which he is unable to substantiate by reference to information in his possession and – even if he can do this he must not make any deductions due under *ITEPA 2003, ss 328(1), 362, 363, 364* or *365*. [*TMA 1970, s 15(11)(a)*].

17.82 Prior to 1990/91 HMRC were content for forms P11D to be completed on the basis of the expenses in a company's accounting year ending in the fiscal year. However, they now refuse to accept this practice, insisting that forms P11D must reflect the expenses paid in the fiscal year.

Purpose of the form

17.83   Initially the form P11D was solely an information return. The inclusion of an item on it was not an indication that it was taxable. All expenses reimbursed to the employee or incurred on his behalf had to be included on the return even if the expenditure was clearly for *bona fide* business reasons. It now tries to combine several things. It is a report of taxable benefits – or at least the employer's perception of the nature and amounts of taxable benefits. In addition, it is a report of expenses made to and on behalf of the employee. This is a report of total expenses, not merely of taxable expenses. It is for the employee to submit a *section 198* claim to establish the amount that is taxable in relation to expenses.

Dispensations

17.84   HMRC have power to grant a dispensation from including expenses on a form P11D if the Inspector of Taxes is satisfied that they will not give rise to a tax charge on the employee. [*ITEPA 2003, s 65*]. The procedure is that the employer (or other person who incurs the expenditure) applies to the Inspector for a dispensation. The application, which can be done by way of letter, must list the employees, or categories of employee in respect of whom the dispensation is sought, the type of expenses concerned and the circumstances in which the expenditure is incurred. If the dispensation is granted, expenses of the agreed type paid to the person or class of person concerned do not have to be included on the form P11D in future years. A form P11D obviously still has to be completed if any expenditure is incurred in relation to the employee of a type not covered by the dispensation. However, only such expenditure need then be shown on the form. HMRC must grant the dispensation if they are satisfied that no tax is payable under the relevant parts of the benefit code. [*ITEPA 2003, s 65(2)*]. Where a dispensation is given nothing in that provision is to apply to the payments or benefits covered by it. [*ITEPA 2003, s 65(5)*].

17.85   HMRC will not normally grant a dispensation for round sum allowances. They are granted for such things as travelling and subsistence, home telephones where the employer reimburses business calls only, and similar items where no personal benefit is likely to arise. HMRC will need to be satisfied that the employer has a satisfactory system for authorising expenses and controlling reimbursements to employees. The Inspector is obviously unlikely to entertain any consideration of a dispensation if there are outstanding P11Ds for earlier years. There is a separate dispensation for non-cash vouchers and credit tokens. This is dealt with at **6.35**. Where a dispensation granted before 6 April 2002 covered car mileage allowance that part of it ceases to have effect from that date if mileage allowance payments (see **7.49**) are made to the employee. [*Finance Act 2001 (FA 2001), s 58*]. The dispensation is unnecessary as the mileage allowance payments are not taxable up to a statutory limit and the intention is to tax any payments in excess of that limit. There is an interesting discussion in *Reed Employment plc v HMRC [2014] UKUT 160 (TCC)* (see **5.38A**) in relation to the validity of dispensations where HMRC are mistaken as to the nature of the expenditure when they grant the dispensation.

Director's expenses

17.86   There is no reason why dispensations should not be claimed by small private companies for director's expenses, but HMRC are likely to be reluctant to grant a dispensation in such cases unless similar types of expense are also paid to employees and the system used for controlling reimbursements to employees is also applied to the directors. As the concept of a dispensation is to cover recurrent expenses that are clearly of a business nature and which are properly authorised this is not unduly surprising. The expenses of a director tend to be more variable and, in most cases, there is no independent scrutiny of the validity and reasonableness of such expenses. The HMRC guidance on dispensations states: 'You must have an independent system in place for checking and authorising expenses claims. At a minimum, this means having someone other than the employee claiming the expenses check that the amount claimed isn't excessive [and] the claim doesn't include disallowable items. If it is not possible for you to operate an independent system for checking and authorising expenses claims – for example, because you are the sole director of your company and you have no other employees – you will only be able to obtain a dispensation if you ensure all expenses claims are supported by receipts for the expenditure [and] demonstrate that the claim relates to expenditure that can be covered by a dispensation – your receipts may be sufficient for this purpose, but if not you must retain additional information'.

17.87   HMRC have power to revoke a dispensation either retrospectively to the time it was granted or from such later date as he may specify. [*ITEPA 2003, s 65(6)–(9)*].

Form P11D(a)

17.88   Where all the expenses paid to higher-paid employees are covered by a dispensation – or none are paid in relation to particular employees – the employer does not need to complete a form P11D showing nil expenses. He can instead complete a form P11D(a) which is a list of employees with a certificate appended stating that no forms P11D are due in respect of such people.

Form P9D

17.89   If benefits or round sum expenses are provided to lower-paid employees or payments in kind are made to such people, the employer has to complete another form, P9D, in relation to each such employee. This is an information return. It gives details of the items concerned so that HMRC are aware of them and can determine what sum, if any, is assessable on the employee in relation to such expenditure.

PAYE Settlement Agreements (PSAs)

17.90   There is a procedure under which an employee can settle in a single payment the income tax liabilities of his employees on minor or non-recurrent benefits in kind and expenses payments. The employer agrees to accept responsibility for the tax, and the amounts covered by the PSA then cease to be income of the employees concerned. The legislation is contained in *Regulations 105–117* of the *PAYE Regulations* on the authority of *ITEPA 2003, ss 703–707*.

17.91   The items that can be covered by a PSA are expenses and benefits that are agreed by HMRC to be either:

(*a*)   minor as regards the amounts of the sums paid or the type of benefit provided;

(*b*)   irregular as regards the frequency in which (or the times at which) the sums are paid or the benefit is provided; or

(*c*)   paid provided or made available where:

    (i)   in the case of a payment it is impracticable to apply PAYE; and

    (ii)   in the case of a benefit it is shared by more than one employee and apportionment between them is impracticable.

[*Reg 106*].

The Regulations are deliberately vague to allow HMRC and employers scope to be reasonable in agreeing what should be included in a PSA [*SP 5/96, para 6*]. HMRC do not wish to dictate to Inspectors what can and cannot be included in a PSA and say that even the items shown as eligible in *SP 5/96* will not always be appropriate for inclusion [*para 7*].

17.92   HMRC say that an objective judgement must be made in applying head (*a*); they interpret minor as meaning minor in value, not a small part of the individual's earnings. Items that could fall into this category might include:

long service awards outside *ITEPA 2003, s 323* (see **9.116**(*v*))

incentive awards

reimbursement of late night taxis home outside *ITEPA 2003, s 248* (see **9.116**(*s*))

personal incidental overnight hotel expenses in excess of the statutory daily limit

a present for an employee in hospital

staff entertaining, such as a ticket to Wimbledon

use of a company van

use of a pool car where the conditions for exemption are not met

subscription to gyms, sports clubs, etc.

telephone bills

gift vouchers and small gifts.

[*SP 5/96, para 10*].

17.93 If an item is not minor it could still be irregular. In deciding whether something is irregular HMRC will take account of the nature of the item, the normal frequency of its payment and how often it was given to the employee in question. A payment could be irregular in relation to employee B even if it is regular in relation to employee A. Normally, HMRC will look only at the year, but something provided to an employee once a year every year would probably be regarded as regular. The sort of thing HMRC believe this head might cover is:

> occasional attendance at an overseas conference where the whole expense does not satisfy the test under *ITEPA 2003, ss 336–338* (see **5.2**)

> expenses of a spouse occasionally accompanying an employee abroad

> occasional use of a company holiday flat

> one-off gifts which are not minor

[*SP 5/96, para 13*].

Another obvious example is removal expenses in excess of the statutory limit.

17.94 To come within head (*c*) the employer will need to show that it is not possible to apply PAYE or enter the item on form P11D without a disproportionate amount of effort or record-keeping taking account of the value of the item concerned, the number of employees involved and the nature of the item. HMRC give as examples:

> free chiropody care

> hairdressing services

> shared use of the firm's bus to work

> Christmas parties and similar entertainment outside *ITEPA 2003, s 264* (see **9.116**(*r*))

> the cost of shared taxi fares home outside *ITEPA 2003, s 248* (see **9.115**(*s*))

> shared cars

[*SP 5/96, para 15*].

17.95 A PSA is incorporated in a formal written agreement between the employer and HMRC. [*Reg 111*]. It can be entered into before the start of a tax year, during the year or between 6 April and 5 July following the end of the tax year. [*Reg 112*]. However, it cannot cover emoluments paid before the agreement is made or benefits already reflected in the PAYE coding for the year. [*Reg 112(2)*]. An agreement can be varied within the same time limits. [*Reg 113*]. *Regulation 108* lays down rules for the calculation of the tax. This must be paid by 19 October following the end of the tax year. [*Reg 109*]. Interest runs on tax paid late [*Reg 115*] and interest is payable from the 19 October date on any overpayment. [*Reg 116*]. The employer must keep specified records and make them available for inspection by HMRC. [*Reg 117*]. Any serious breach of this requirement, or a serious failure to pay the tax on the PSA or pay over PAYE regularly, will entitle HMRC to cancel the PSA. [*Reg 114*].

17.96 It should be stressed that once an item is included in a PSA it ceases to be income of the employee for all tax purposes – and the employee is not entitled to credit for any of the tax or repayment of it [*Reg 107*]. Unfortunately, there is no obligation to tell employees what is covered by a PSA or even that one has been entered into. If the employee incorrectly puts the amount on his return as income HMRC will collect tax on it; they cannot tell him that the employer has already paid tax on the item under a PSA.

17.97 *Section 53* of the *Social Security Act 1998 (SSA 1998)* introduced a new Class 1B National Insurance payable by employers in respect of a PSA. This NIC charge makes a PSA unattractive as the employer still needs to do much of the administrative work that the PSA is designed to avoid.

Oil and Gas Workers on the Continental Shelf

17.98 For 2014/15 onwards, if

(*a*)   a payment of (or an account of) PAYE income of a continental shelf worker in respect of a period is made by a person who is the employer or an intermediary of either the employer or of the 'relevant person',

(*b*)   the PAYE regulations do not apply to the person making the payment (or if that person is an intermediary, to the employer, and

(*c*)   income tax and any 'relevant debts' are not deducted (or not accounted for) in accordance with the PAYE regulations

the relevant person is treated for the purpose of the PAYE regulations as making a payment of PAYE income of the continental shelf worker of the amount of the payment (or if tax was deducted or the employee is entitled to a net payment, the grossed up amount).

[*ITEPA 2003, s 689A(1), (3), (4)* inserted by *FA 2014, s 21(5)*]. For this purpose a continental shelf worker is a person in an employment some or all of the duties of which are performed in the UK sector of the continental shelf (as defined in *ITEPA 2003, s 41* – see **3.48**) and in connection with exploration or exploitation activities (as so defined) [*ITEPA 2003, s 689A(W)*]. If the employer has an associated company (as defined in *Corporation Tax Act 2010 (CTA 2010), s 449*) with a place of business or registered office in the UK, that associated company is the relevant person. If it does not, the relevant person in relation to a continental shelf worker is the person who holds the licence under *Part 1* of the *Petroleum Act 1998* in respect of the area of the UK sector of the continental shelf where some or all of the duties of the continental shelf worker's employment are performed [*ITEPA 2003, s 689A(11)*]. A relevant debt is a sum payable by the payee to HMRC under or by virtue of any enactment (other than an excluded debt) or such a sum payable under a contract settlement [*ITEPA 2003, s 684(7AA)*]. The excluded debts are child tax credit or working tax credit overpayments and, if the payee is an employer, any amount that the payee is required to deduct from the PAYE income of employees for a tax year [*ITEPA 2003, s 684(7AB)*].

17.99 If by virtue of *ITEPA 2003, ss 687A* (disguised remuneration – see **3.28**) or *693–700* (vouchers – see **17.59**), an employer would be treated for the purposes of the PAYE regulations (if they applied to it) as making a payment of any amount to a continental shelf worker, *s 689A* has effect as if the employer had also made an actual payment of that amount [*ITEPA 2003, s 689A(5)*].

17.100 For the purpose of *s 689A*, a payment of (or on account of) PAYE income is made by an intermediary of the employer or of the relevant person if it is made by a person acting on behalf of the employer or of the relevant person and at the expense of the employer or the relevant person or of a person connected with either, or if it is made by trustees holding property for any persons who include the continental shelf worker (or for a class of persons which includes him) [*ITEPA 2003, s 689A(6)*]. If there is more than one relevant person in relation to a continental shelf worker and in consequence of the same payment each of them is treated as making a payment of PAYE income of the worker, and one of them complies with *ITEPA 2003, s 710* (notional payments: accounting for tax – see **17.60**), that payment clears the liability of all of them [*ITEPA 2003, s 689A(9), (10)*].

Chapter 18

Provision of Services through an Intermediary or Managed Service Company

18.1   A taxpayer who operates through a personal services company (or other intermediary) and would have been an employee of the intermediary's client had he worked direct for it is taxed on employment income of a notional amount to the extent that such notional amount falls short of his deemed earnings. This was described by the government as an anti-avoidance provision in its well-known *IR 35 1999 Budget Day Press Release*, although many people would question whether choosing a particular method of structuring a transaction over a different method and accepting the normal tax consequences of that structure can properly be described as avoidance. The real reason for the provision appears to be that the government, having introduced legislation to make it more attractive to receive dividends than remuneration, became concerned that people were 'avoiding' National Insurance by opting to pay those lower tax rates on dividends.

18.2   The tax charge arises where:

(*a*)   an individual ('the worker') personally performs services for another person ('the client') (or is under an obligation personally to perform such services);

(*b*)   the services are provided under a contract directly between the client and the worker but under arrangements involving a third party ('the intermediary'); and

(*c*)   the circumstances (including the terms on which the services are provided, having regard to the terms of the contracts under the arrangements) are such that if the services were provided under a contract directly between the client and the worker, the worker would be regarded for income tax purposes as an employee of the client.

[*Income Tax (Earnings and Pensions) Act 2003, s 49(1)*].

18.3   A typical example is the one-man company which loans out its sole employee. The company contracts with a client to provide services which are then personally performed by its sole employee. The provision applies if that employee would have been an employee of the client had the company not existed. The normal tests of employment set out at **4.12** onwards apply.

Accordingly, if the individual is providing a service rather than his labour the provision will not apply. HMRC have said that where a contract requires workers to work where the client requests, for an agreed number of hours per week, at an agreed rate of pay and to keep a timesheet checked by the client, be subject to the directives of the client and not subcontract the work to any one else, and the engagement is for a month or more, they consider that the legislation will apply unless the worker can demonstrate a recent history of work including engagements which have the characteristics of self-employment (*IR Press Release 7 February 2000*).

18.4   Some people feel that following the Court of Appeal decision in *Brook Street Bureau (UK) Ltd v Dacas [2004] EWCA Civ 217* and *Cable and Wireless plc v Muscat [2006] EWCA Civ 220* this legislation, which imposes a PAYE obligation on the service company, may be ineffective as in law the true employer, with the obligation to account for PAYE and NIC may be the end user. These two cases are considered at **4.74–4.82**. As discussed there, it is not clear to what extent, if any, they are applicable to tax law. Even if they are, it is doubtful if the effect is to shift the liability to deduct PAYE from service company to end-user. It is more likely that both would have the obligation to apply PAYE and NIC as one would have entered into an actual contract of employment and the other into a deemed contract, so both would meet the test of being an employer under *ITEPA 2003*. Indeed even if it is permissible to look for the existence of an implied contract, *ss 49(1) and 50(1)* (see **18.12**) seem to require that contract to be ignored and for PAYE to be applied by reference to a deemed contract between the worker and his service company (ie the intermediary).

18.5   In *R (on the application of Professional Contractors Group Ltd) v IRC [2001] EWHC Admin 236, [2001] STC 629* the judge emphasised that it is not correct to look simply at the contract between the client and the intermediary because what has to be ascertained is what the contractual relationship between the client and the worker would have been if they had contracted direct. 'It appears to me clear that [HMRC] must bear in mind that under IR 35 they are not considering an actual contract between the service company and the client, but imagining or constructing a notional contract which does not in fact exist. In those circumstances, of course the terms of the contract between the agency and the client as a result of which the service contractor will be present at the site are important, as would be the terms of any contract between the service contractor and the agency. But, particularly given the fact that, at any rate at present, a contract on standard terms may or may not be imposed by an agency, or may be applicable not by reference to a particular assignment, but on an ongoing basis and may actually bear no relationship to the (non-contractual) interface between the client and the service contractor, such document can only form a part, albeit obviously an important part, of the picture'. The Professional Contractors Group decision was appealed to the Court of Appeal (*[2001] EWCA Civ 1945*) (*[2002] STC 165*) but the issues under appeal were not Schedule E ones.

18.6   The first case to be litigated under these provisions, or rather their National Insurance equivalent, was *Battersby v Campbell [2001] STC (SCD)*

189), SpC 287. This was an appeal by a taxpayer in person who seems to have mainly argued that he took the risks of self-employment and had not sought to avoid tax. It is unsurprising in those circumstances that the Commissioner accepted HMRC's view that had the taxpayer been employed under a contract with the client it would have been a contract of service. The second was *F S Consulting Ltd v McCaul [2002] STC (SCD) 138, SpC 305.* This was another National Insurance case. The taxpayer challenged the interpretation of the regulation rather than addressing the deemed relationship between the worker and the client, so again the Commissioner considered that relationship based only on the HMRC arguments. In *Synaptic v Young [2003] STC 543* the case was fully argued before the General Commissioners, who held that, on balance, if there had been a contract it would have been a contract of employment. On appeal Hart J felt that the identification and characterisation of the arrangements is a matter of fact for the fact-finding tribunal. The fact that the tribunal is then asked to hypothesise a contract comprising those arrangements directly between the worker and the client does not by itself convert the question from being a question of mixed fact and law into a pure question of law. Accordingly the court can interfere only if it concludes that the decision reached by the Commissioners is an impossible one on the facts found by them, or that they have misdirected themselves. He felt there was evidence on which they had been entitled to conclude that the notional contract was a contract of employment.

18.7   The taxpayer also won in *Lime-IT Ltd v Justin [2003] STC (SCD) 15, SpC 542* but in that case the Commissioners pointed out that no evidence had been called from the client and warned that 'In future cases on this legislation (and its income tax equivalent) the Special Commissioners will wish to explore at a preliminary hearing whether it is possible to obtain evidence from the client'. In *Tilbury Consulting Ltd v Gittins [2004] STC (SCD) 1, SpC 379.* HMRC duly sought, and were given, a witness summons for someone from the client to attend the hearing of the appeal to give oral evidence, albeit that he had already written twice to HMRC in response to letters they had sent to the client. The taxpayers won despite such evidence, although the facts were a little unusual. Ford Motor Co had contracted with a company called Compuware Ltd to set up, service and staff a particular IT contract. Tilbury Consulting Ltd was engaged by Compuware to provide services to it by making available Mr Tilbury's services. Accordingly, Mr Tilbury was not answerable to Ford; he was answerable to Compuware. Similarly, Ford dealt with Compuware. It was of no concern of Ford what particular individuals Compuware used in the contract. In these circumstances a notional contract between Ford and Mr Tilbury would not have been a contract of employment. Ford did not exercise control over the performance of Mr Tilbury's services and was happy to accept a substitute if Compuware wanted to send along someone else. This may point to a lacuna in the legislation or, more likely, an error of judgement by HMRC. Mr Tilbury might well have been an employee under a notional contract between himself and Compuware but HMRC did not seek to apply the provisions by reference to such a contract. A case won by the taxpayer in spite of the evidence of the end user is *Ansell Computer Services Ltd v Richardson [2004] STC (SCD) 472, SpC 425.* In that case the Special Commissioner placed most significance on the fact that the end user, Marconi, was not obliged to keep Mr Ansell in work throughout the period of the engagement; Mr Ansell was not obliged to put in a particular amount of work; he did not need the permission of Marconi to take time off; both Mr Ansell and Marconi gave evidence that they regarded a substitution right as genuine (albeit unlikely that the situation would ever arise); and Mr Ansell did not obtain normal Marconi staff benefits such as a company car, sick pay or membership of the social club. He accepted that although the work had to be carried out at Marconi's premises this was for security reasons. The taxpayer also won in *First Word Software Ltd v HMRC [2008] STC (SCD) 389*. Again the facts were unusual. Mr Atkins, the worker, heard that Reuters were looking for a specialist skill which he possessed and First Word approached Reuters, sending them Mr Atkins' CV. Reuters had given an overall software consultancy to Plexus, and Reuters, having interviewed Mr Atkins, put him into contact with Plexus. First Word contracted with Plexus 'for the design, development and migration of Reuters subsidiary human resource and payroll computer systems onto a single global instance of Oracle Applications III'. Accordingly the agreement was to provide a computer package, not the services of Mr Atkins. The taxpayer again won in *Datagate Services Ltd v HMRC [2008] STC (SCD) 453*. The contract there was for consultancy services; there was a right of substitution; the worker had to work on the end user's premises for security reasons; the end user did not integrate the consultants into his business but gave him specified, mainly self contained projects; and it 'wished to learn from him'.

18.8   The taxpayer was less successful in *Usetech Ltd v Young [2004] STC 1671*, another National Insurance case. In that case two employees of the client gave evidence that whilst Mr Hood (the worker) had some flexibility over the hours he worked he was expected to agree them with the client. Mr Hood worked as a member of a team and was expected to accept the work allocated to him at weekly meetings. They also made clear that although the contract allowed for substitution they would not have accepted a substitute without interview and would not have done so at all if Mr Hood was available. The Commissioners stressed in particular that 'there must be mutuality of obligations, but that does not imply that the "employer" is required to provide work ... the requirement of mutuality may be satisfied by the obligation, on the one hand to work and, on the other, to remunerate'. The taxpayer also lost in *Netherlane Ltd v York [2005] STC (SCD) 305, SpC 457*, a case in which the Commissioner was scathing about the paucity of evidence put forward by the taxpayer. On appeal the judge said that whether a relationship is an employment requires an evaluation of all of the circumstances. The presence of a substitution clause is an indicium that points towards self-employment but is not necessarily determinative of the issue (although he in fact agreed with the Commissioners that Mr Hood's hypothetical contract would not have contained a substitution clause). He also said that the case indicates that 'the mutuality requirement for a contract of employment to exist would be satisfied by a contract which provided for payment (in the nature of a retainer) for hours actually worked. It is only where there is both no obligation to provide work and no obligation to pay the worker for time in which work is not provided that the want of mutuality precludes the existence of a continuing contract of employment'. The client also gave evidence in *Future Online Ltd v Faulds [2005] STC 198* where HMRC again won. The Special Commissioner commenting 'it seems to me ... that the mutual obligations that actually existed between Mr Roberts and E D S were above the irreducible minimum'. HMRC also won in *Island Consultants Ltd v HMRC [2007] STC (SCD) 700* where the Commissioner felt that 'the factors predominately point to an employment, although a somewhat unusual one'. He also commented that although not much control is expected for an expert there must still be some control and it was sufficient that there was some control over where he worked. The taxpayer again lost in *MKM Computing Ltd v HMRC [2008] STC (SCD) 403*, where the contract was held not to be for the delivery of the project but for expert time to be spent in the development and delivery of a project; in *Dragonfly Consultancy Ltd v HMRC [2008] STC 3030*, where it was held that the worker 'worked on parts of a project which were allocated to him as part of the AA's teams, who was integrated into the AA's business and who had a role similar to that of a professional employee' and in *Alternative Book Co Ltd v HMRC [2008] STC (SCD) 830* which involved an IT contractor working under a succession of short-term contracts. In *HMRC v Larkspur Data Ltd [2009] STC 1161* the judge felt that the General Commissioners had misdirected themselves on the principles relating to control and remitted the case to the Commissioners for a rehearing.

18.9   However although HMRC seems to be on a winning streak at the Tribunal, the taxpayer can still win occasionally. *MBF Design Services Ltd v HMRC [2011] SFTD 383* provided (through an agency) the design services of Mr Fitzpatrick to Airbus UK Ltd under a series of contracts. The Tribunal felt that the overall impression was of a series of relationships typical of that in a contract for services. It then looked at the 'practical reality of working' and concluded that Mr Fitzpatrick was not 'part and parcel' of Airbus' organisation in any but the most temporary and limited sense.

18.10   HMRC have said that if, as part of an employer compliance review, they feel they need to check information about working practices with the client to check that the service company has reached a correct view on the application of IR 35 they will ask the worker's permission. If the worker is unhappy for HMRC to speak to the client HMRC are willing 'to explore a mutually acceptable other way for the contact to be made'. But, if a mutually acceptable way cannot be agreed HMRC will approach the client direct 'for information on the details of the day-to-day working arrangements' where they think this necessary (Press Release 7.1.2004). It is of course up to the client what information he is willing to volunteer to HMRC, although at the end of the day *Taxes Management Act 1970 (TMA 1970), s 20(3)* enables them to require the client to provide information.

18.11   The charge initially applied only to supplies to a business but that limitation (and *s 49(2)*) was removed by *Finance Act 2003 (FA 2003), s 136(2)*. The government apparently envisaged hordes of nannies and other domestic staff forming companies to seek to avoid tax, albeit that the level of earnings of such people is generally such that the cost of operating the company would be likely to cancel out any tax saving. The change is not limited to domestic staff. It could potentially apply to anyone who provides services to private householders, such as builders, gardeners, personal secretaries and even financial managers, although it is unlikely to do so in most cases as such people are usually genuinely self-employed.

18.12   The intermediary is treated as making a deemed salary payment to the worker if in any tax year the worker (or an associate of the worker) either:

(*a*)   receives from the intermediary (directly or indirectly) a payment or other benefit that is not taxable as employment income, or

(*b*)   has rights which in any circumstances would entitle him to receive from the intermediary (directly or indirectly) any such payment or other benefit.

[*ITEPA 2003, s 50(1)*].

18.13   The deemed salary is not related to the payment or benefit received; it is 95 per cent of the income from relevant engagements after deducting expenses and capital allowances that would be allowable under the rules relating to employment income, pension contributions, salary and benefits already paid to the worker and the related employer's NI and the NI generated by the notional salary itself. It is calculated as follows:

(*a*)   ascertain the total of all payments and benefits received by the intermediary in the tax year in respect of relevant engagements (ie engagements within **18.2** above which do not fall within any of the exceptions set out in **18.21** below);

(*b*)   reduce that figure by 5 per cent;

(*c*)   add any payments or other benefits (calculated as for employment income purposes, ie under Chapters 6–9) received direct by the worker in respect of relevant engagements;

(*d*)   deduct expenses met in that year by the intermediary that would have been deductible from the emoluments of the employment if the worker had been employed by the client (see **Chapter 5**) – for 2002/03 onwards also include expenses met by the worker and reimbursed by the intermediary and, where the intermediary is a partnership of which the worker is a partner, expenses met by the worker on behalf of the partnership;

(*e*)   deduct any capital allowances on expenditure incurred by the intermediary that could have been deducted by the worker if he had been employed by the client and had incurred the expenditure;

(*f*)   deduct any pension contributions made by the intermediary to an approved pension scheme, either a company pension scheme or personal pension in respect of the worker (but excluding of course any excess contributions later repaid);

(*g*)   deduct any employee's National Insurance paid by the intermediary for the tax year in respect of the worker;

(*h*)   deduct the amount of any payments or other benefits received in the tax year by the worker from the intermediary which are taxable as earnings from employment;

(*i*)   the resultant figure is the notional salary plus related employer's National Insurance, so the notional salary is the figure remaining after deducting the employer's National Insurance element.

[*ITEPA 2003, s 54*].

18.14   If the intermediary provides a car or other vehicle for the worker and he would have been entitled to mileage allowance relief (see **7.52**) in respect of the use of the vehicle had he been an employee of the client, and the vehicle had not been a company vehicle (see **7.54**), the amount of such mileage allowance relief is treated as an expense deductible at (*d*) above [*ITEPA 2003, s 54(4)*]. If the intermediary is a partnership of which the worker is a partner and he provides a vehicle for the purpose of the partnership business it is treated as provided by the intermediary to the worker so as to trigger the right to this relief [*ITEPA 2003, s 54(5)(b)*]. If the worker receives exempt mileage allowance payments or passenger payments (see **7.50** and **7.56**) from the intermediary those are treated as taxable (and thus as deductible at (*h*) above) for the purpose of calculating the deemed salary payment [*ITEPA 2003, s 54(7)*]. As the payments will have been treated as income at step (*a*) this adjustment effectively excludes them from the calculation.

18.15   The government have confirmed that 'a worker who is continuously employed by his service company, and undertakes contracts for clients of the service company in different places, can claim the costs of travelling to and from those clients' premises. That is because a client's premises can be treated as a temporary place of work, provided that the worker does not expect to work there for more than 40 per cent of the time in a period exceeding 24 months. The legislation will allow this more generous treatment to continue, even where there is the same employee relationship'. The minister pointed out that this is a more generous treatment than if a person had a series of short employments with different clients in different parts of the country. *Hansard SCH 6 July 2000 Column 465.*

18.16

Example

Jim is a computer programmer. He is a single parent with two children and cannot do a full-time job as he needs to collect his children from school. He has a concept for a new internet product. Jim is trying to devote as much time as he can to the product which is being developed by his company, Internet Wizard Ltd. In order to support his family Jim advertises his services as a computer consultant. Jim has also registered with an agency. During 2013/14 the agency found him a three-month contract servicing the computers of Alpha Ltd, a two-month contract as a member of a development team for Beta plc and a contract to develop a stock control system for Gamma plc which took Jim three months. All these contracts were entered into by Internet Wizard Ltd. The accounts of Internet Wizard Ltd for the year to 5 April 2014 contains the information set out below.

18.16 *Provision of Services through an Intermediary*

At the end of the assignment Alpha Ltd gave Jim a laptop which had cost them £3,000 and had a then value of £1,800.

		£
Income:	computer consultant – home computer	9,000
	business computer	11,000
	Alpha Ltd	12,000
	Beta plc	9,000
	Gamma plc	10,000
		51,000
Expenses:	Salary for Jim	5,000
	NI on salary	1,600
	Pension contribution	1,000
	Agency commission – 15%	3,600
	Motor expenses	12,000
	Computer disks etc	3,000
	Stationery	1,000
	Training courses to keep up to date	2,500
	Administrative costs of company	3,000
		32,700

	£
Net profit before depreciation (which Internet Wizard Ltd needs to buy more equipment)	18,300

The capital allowances on Jim's company car (which was first registered before 1.1.1998) for the year to 5 April 2014 amount to £2,000. The car was used 10 per cent of the time on travelling in the course of the Alpha Ltd contract, 8 per cent for the Beta contract, and 12 per cent for the Gamma contract, and 40 per cent on consultancy work. The other 30 per cent was private use. The capital allowances on the company's computer equipment were £6,000. Jim did not use the computers on the Alpha and Beta contracts as those companies will not permit outside disks to be input into their systems. 40 per cent of the computer usage was private. The cost to the company of the computers was £40,000 and the cost of the car was £26,000.

It seems likely that the work done for Alpha Ltd and Beta plc are relevant engagements. The consultancy work on business computers and the work done for Gamma plc are unlikely to be relevant engagements as in those cases Internet Wizard Ltd is selling services of troubleshooting and system creation respectively, not Jim's labour. On this basis the notional salary is as follows:

			Alpha Ltd	Beta Ltd	Total
Income from relevant engagements			12,000	9,000	21,000
Less 5%			(600)	(450)	(1,050)
			11,400	8,550	19,950
Value of gift from Alpha Ltd.			1,800	–	1,800
			13,200	8,550	21,750
Less	Jim's salary	5,000			
	Benefits:				
	Use of computers	2,400			
	Use of car				
	22% of 26,000	5,720			
	Petrol	2,850			
		15,970	(9,692)	(6,278)	(15,970)
National Insurance			(996)	(604)	(1,600)
Pension Contributions			(622)	(378)	(1,000)
Motor Expenses			(1,200)	(960)	(2,160)
Capital Allowances on car			(200)	(160)	(360)
Taxable amount			490	170	660
Of which NI					
$\frac{13.8}{113.8} \times 660$			59	21	80
Notional Salary			438	152	590

Notes

1   It appears that the whole of Jim's earnings from Internet Wizard Ltd and the related National Insurance can be deducted even though only 41 per cent of the company's income is from relevant engagements

2   The engagements have been considered separately above for clarity. However, the notional salary from all relevant engagements is calculated globally. Accordingly a loss in one will reduce the notional salary payment in relation to the others.

3   The Class 1A NIC-free band has been ignored for simplicity.

18.17   Where tax is deducted under the building industry sub-contractors scheme the income from the relevant engagements is of course the gross receipt before such deductions. [*ITEPA 2003, s 54(2)*]. Many people would see this as double taxation. HMRC do not. They say that the sub-contractors' deductions is a payment on account of the company's corporation tax liability and the PAYE and NI on the notional salary relates to the worker's tax liability. Whilst in theory that is right, in most cases the notional salary will eliminate the corporation tax liability so the single amount of income has to bear two tax deductions albeit that the sub-contractor's deductions will fall to be repaid in due course. To avoid this, sub-contractor deductions suffered by a company can be set against its PAYE liabilities [*Finance Act 2004 (FA 2004), s 62(3), (4)*].

18.18   Where an amount received by the intermediary either relates to the services of more than one worker or relates partly to the services of the worker and partly to other matters any necessary apportionment is to be made on a just and reasonable basis. [*ITEPA 2003, s 54(8)*]. This should enable VAT to be excluded from the calculation. It is not clear whether it will allow materials to be excluded where a single price is charged to cover both labour and materials.

18.19   In calculating the notional payment a 'payment or other benefit' includes anything that if received by an employee for performing the duties of his employment would be taxed as an emolument of that employment. [*ITEPA 2003, s 55(2)*]. The amount of a non-cash benefit is the greater of the amount that would be taxable under *ITEPA 2003, ss 6, 62* (the charging provision on earnings) if the benefit were an emolument (normally the resale value of the benefit) or the cash equivalent of the benefit under *ITEPA 2003, ss 19* or *398*. [*ITEPA 2003, s 55(3), (4)*]. A payment or cash benefit is treated as received when a payment is made of or on account of it. (Where a payment on account is received it is probably only that receipt, not the full 'payment', that is deemed to be received at that time). A non-cash benefit is deemed to be received when it is used or enjoyed. [*ITEPA 2003, s 55(5)*]. Where a benefit is enjoyed over a period it is presumably deemed to be received on a day-by-day basis.

18.20   The calculations are all on a cash basis, ie the notional income is based on the cash received during a tax year, not fees earned in relation to services performed during that year. Similarly, only salary actually paid during a tax year can be deducted in arriving at the notional salary payment.

Exceptions

18.21   There are a number of exceptions to the personal service company rules.

(*a*)   As indicated at **18.2** the provision does not apply to the extent that the income of the company does not derive from relevant engagements.

(*b*)   If the intermediary is a company, the provision applies only if *both*:

    (i)   the intermediary is not an associated company of the client by reason of both of them being under the control of the worker (or of the worker and another person); and

    (ii)   either:

        (A)   the worker has a material interest in the intermediary (see below); or

    (B)   all payments or benefits received or receivable by the worker come directly from the intermediary and can reasonably be taken to represent remuneration for services provided by the worker to the client.

[*ITEPA 2003, s 51*].

(*c*)   If the intermediary is a partnership, the provisions apply only if either:

    (i)   the worker, alone or with one or more relatives (spouse, parent or remoter forebear, child or remoter issue or brother or sister) is entitled to 60 per cent or more of the profits of the partnership; or

    (ii)   most of the profits of the partnership derive from the provisions of services under relevant engagements to a single client or to a single client together with associates (see **18.24**) of that client; or

    (iii)   under the profit-sharing arrangements the income of any of the partners is based on the amount of income generated by that partner by the provision of services under relevant engagements.

[*ITEPA 2003, s 52(2)*].

(*d*)   If the intermediary is a partnership and the worker is not a partner, or it is an individual, the provisions apply only if the payment or benefit is received or receivable by the worker directly from the intermediary and can reasonably be taken to represent remuneration for services provided by the worker to the client. [*ITEPA 2003, s 52(3)*].

(*e*)   The provision does not apply to payments subject to deduction of tax under *Income Tax Act 2007 (ITA 2007), s 966* (payments to non-resident entertainers or sportsmen). [*ITEPA 2003, s 48(2)(b)*]. Nor does it apply to services provided by managed service companies, which have their own tax deduction scheme (see **18.57**) [*ITEPA 2003, s 48(2)(aa)*]. It does apply to payments subject to deduction of tax under *ITEPA 2003, s 44* (workers supplied by agencies – see **19.1**) [*ITEPA 2003, s 48(2)(a)*] or under *FA 2004, ss 57–77* (subcontractors in the construction industry), although it does not affect the operation of those provisions.

18.22   For the purpose of **18.21(*b*)** a worker has a material interest in a company if either:

(*a*)   he himself has a material interest in the company (either alone or with one or more associates); or

(*b*)   an associate (see **18.24**) (or associates) of his has a material interest in the company (even though the worker himself has no interest in it).

[*ITEPA 2003, s 51(3)*].

18.23   A material interest for this purpose means either:

(*a*)   beneficial ownership of more than 5 per cent of the ordinary share capital of the company (or the ability to control, directly or indirectly – such as through the medium of other companies – more than 5 per cent); or (*b*)   possession of (or entitlement to acquire) rights entitling the holder to receive more than 5 per cent of any distributions that may be made by the company; or

(*c*)   if the company is a close company, possession of (or entitlement to acquire) rights that in the event of a winding up or in any other circumstances would entitle the holder to receive more than 5 per cent of the assets that would then be available for distribution among the participators (as defined in *Income and Corporation Taxes Act 1988 (ICTA 1988), s 417(1)*).

[*ITEPA 2003, s 51(4)*].

18.24   For the purpose of *ITEPA 2003, ss 48–61*, the *Corporation Tax Act 2010 (CTA 2010), s 448* definition of an associate applies in relation to an individual. [*ITEPA 2003, s 60(1)*]. However, where the individual has an interest in shares or obligations of the company as a member of an employee benefit trust within *ITEPA 2003, ss 550, 551* the trustees are not regarded as associates of his by reason only of that interest unless the individual (either on his own or within one or more associates – excluding the trustees of an employee benefit trust merely because the individual has an interest in the trust) or associates of the individual have at any time since 13 March 1989 been the beneficial owner of or able to control (directly, through the medium of other companies or by any other indirect means) more than 5 per cent of the ordinary share capital of the company. [*ITEPA 2003, s 60(2)–(6)*]. However in certain circumstances the beneficary can be treated as owning some of the shares held by the EBT. The relevant rules are considered at **15.15–15.16**.

18.25   It is doubtful if this exception includes shares allocated to the employee under a SIP (see **Chapter 15**) as the participant appears to be the beneficial owner of (or at least has the ability to control) such shares.

18.26   In the case of a company an associate means a person connected with the company within *ICTA 1988, s 839* [*ITEPA 2003, ss 60(1)(b), 718*]. In the case of a partnership associate means an associate of any member of the partnership. [*ITEPA 2003, s 60(1)(c)*].

18.27   It should be noted that **18.21(*b*)** excludes from the IR 35 rules a loan-out where the intermediary is an associated company of the client. This will ensure that intra-group charges in respect of staff, particularly where there is a central payroll function, are not accidentally caught. It might logically also let out the situation where the intermediary is the service company of a partnership. Unfortunately it does not appear to do so. The use of the expression 'associated company' rather than associate and the definition in *ICTA 1988, s 416* imply that both intermediary and client must be companies. Of course in most cases it will not matter as an employee of a partnership service company is unlikely to have a shareholding in it, let alone own over 5 per cent. Care may, however, be needed where the spouse of a partner is an employee of the service company.

18.28   The let out for partnerships in **18.21(*c*)** appears to leave significant scope for avoidance. Whether this will occur probably depends on clients.

Currently, most clients seem reluctant to engage a partnership, preferring to engage someone via a company, but the possibility of behavioural changes should not be ruled out.

18.29   The obvious situation is if two friends enter into partnership sharing profits equally and each works for one customer. This will be exempt as it satisfies all three sub-heads of **18.21(c)**. Some people think this an unlikely scenario. Will someone willingly take on the risks of joint and several liability inherent in a partnership and are they prepared to share profits equally? In practice, the answer to both questions is likely to be 'Yes'. Most people do not realise the risks of entering into a partnership and the variation between earnings of two friends in the same line of business will not generally be significant. There is nothing to stop the profit-sharing ratio being changed in subsequent years if incomes diverge significantly, provided that the entitlement of any one individual never reaches 60 per cent and no attempt is made to tie the profit-sharing to the income generated by each partner.

18.30   The restrictions relate to the profit-sharing arrangements. There is nothing to prevent drawings being tied to the income generated by each partner if profits are shared equally. There is probably also nothing to stop this being supplemented with an agreement that the tax of both partners will be paid by the partnership and in the event of a dissolution of the partnership, the assets at the time of the dissolution will be shared equally irrespective of the balances on partners' capital accounts.

18.31   There also seems nothing to prevent a partnership between two friends and their respective spouses with profits being shared equally up to twice the amount of income generated by the lowest earning of the two workers and the spouse of the other being entitled to the balance of the profits (which will be the excess income generated by the higher earning worker). The 60 per cent figure will not be breached; there will be at least two clients of the partnership, and the income of no partner is based on the profits generated by that partner. Although head (*a*) looks at the worker and his relatives, head (*c*) does not do so. Nor does *ITEPA 2003, s 61(3)(b)* seem to apply, which provides that a payment provided to a member of an individual's family is treated as provided to the worker, as this is looking at payments whereas head (*c*) is looking at profit-sharing arrangements.

Timing of notional payments

18.32   The notional payment is normally deemed to be made at the end of the tax year concerned (ie on 5 April). [*ITEPA 2003, s 50(3)*]. However, if one of the following events occurs during the tax year that will trigger a notional payment at the time of that event:

(*a*)   If the worker is employed by the intermediary, his ceasing to be so employed.

(*b*)   If the worker is a member of the intermediary company, his ceasing to be a member, egeg by disposing of all of his shares, even if the disposal is to a trust of which he is the principal beneficiary. A disposal of shares will often not signify a cessation of the worker's association with the company, so the logic of its triggering an interim notional payment is not readily apparent.

(c)   If the worker holds an office with the intermediary company, his ceasing to hold that office. Take care if the worker agrees to be company secretary temporarily to fill a casual vacancy, perhaps for a few days only, as when he hands over the reins to a permanent incumbent this will trigger a tax charge.

(d)   If the intermediary is a partnership, its dissolution.

(e)   If the intermediary is a partnership its ceasing to trade. (Curiously, if the intermediary is a company a cessation of the trade will not trigger the notional payment.)

(f)   If the intermediary is a partnership, a partner ceasing to act as such – apparently even if the worker is not a partner or, if he is, is not the partner ceasing to act. It is not clear what is meant by ceasing to act as a partner. For example, if a general partner becomes a limited partner does he cease to act as a partner as he becomes prohibited from taking part in the management of the partnership business?

(g)   The company ceasing to trade.

[*ITEPA 2003, s 57*].

18.33   It is not clear how the notional salary payment is calculated on the occurrence of one of the above events. Logically it ought to be based on the income from relevant engagements from the previous 6 April up to the date of the trigger event, with a further notional salary payment being calculated (where relevant) from that time up to the following 5 April. However, *ITEPA 2003, s 57(5)* states, 'The fact that the deemed payment of earnings is treated as made before the end of the tax year does not affect what receipts and other matters are taken into account in calculating its amount'. This seems to imply that only a single notional payment is calculated at the end of the year and that the entire payment is deemed to be made at the time of the trigger event. As interest on PAYE runs only from 5 April after the end of the tax year it may not matter unduly for income tax purposes but would have an affect on employees' National Insurance as the 'pay period' would appear to end at the date of the trigger event.

Relief for distributions

18.34   If the intermediary is a company and it makes a distribution either during the same tax year or in a year subsequent to that in which a notional payment is deemed to be made the intermediary (not the worker) can make a claim for relief. It is an odd claim. It is the worker that is doubly taxed not the intermediary. It is not for any particular relief. It is for such relief as appears to HMRC to be appropriate in order to avoid a double charge to tax. [*ITEPA 2003, s 58(5)*]. The claim must be made within five years after the 31 January following the tax year in which the distribution is made. [*ITEPA 2003, s 58(2)(b)*].

18.35 If HMRC are satisfied that some sort of relief is appropriate (ie it is for the company to convince them that some relief should be given) they must give this by treating the amount of the distribution as reduced, not the amount of the deemed employment income payment. [*ITEPA 2003, s 58(3), (4)*]. They must exercise the power so as to secure that, as far as practicable, relief is given against relevant distributions of the same tax year before those of other years, against relevant distributions received by the worker before those received by another person, and against relevant distributions of earlier years before those of later years. [*ITEPA 2003, s 58(5)*]. Where a distribution is reduced the related tax credit is obviously correspondingly reduced. [*ITEPA 2003, s 58(6)*].

18.36 Where Parliament gives a wide discretion to HMRC such as here there is no effective right of appeal against their decision. The taxpayer can apply for judicial review but not only is this costly but he has to show (probably without HMRC having to explain the reason for their decision) that the decision was unreasonable in the sense that nobody acting judicially could have arrived at it on the facts or that it was made maliciously. It is accordingly likely to be virtually impossible to challenge a refusal to give relief.

18.37 Although at one stage there was doubt whether HMRC would grant relief where the dividend is received by a third party they have confirmed that relief can be given against any distributions.

18.38 A distribution is a dividend or certain other payments to shareholders or, in the case of a close company, expenses incurred in providing benefits to shareholders [*ICTA 1988, ss 209–211, 418, 832; ITEPA 2003, Sch 1*]. A loan is not a distribution so relief could not be given against tax due under *ICTA 1988, s 419* (loans to participators).

18.39 Worse, a payment of salary is not a distribution. This creates a major problem where the profits of the intermediary are distributed as bonuses subsequent to 5 April – perhaps at or shortly after the end of the intermediary's accounting period, which is what very often happens with personal service companies. The bonus cannot be deducted in calculating the notional payment as it is not a payment received by the worker in the relevant year (which is all that *step 7* of *para 7* will allow to be deducted). It can be deducted in calculating the notional salary payment for the following year, but apart from the fact that there will be double taxation in the year of payment this is likely to lead to anomalies as if in a particular year no notional payment arises excess actual salary payments cannot be taken into account in calculating the notional payment of a different year. Accordingly, once a notional payment has arisen it may be that the only safe way to avoid double taxation is to stop paying remuneration and pay only dividends to the worker in future years!

Corporation tax or income tax deduction

18.40 Corporation tax or income tax relief is given for the amount of the notional payment and related employer's National Insurance by allowing it as a deduction in calculating the profits of the intermediary's business. [*Corporation Tax Act 2009, s 139(2); Income Tax (Trading and Other Income) Act 2005 (ITTOIA 2005), s 163(2)*]. The deduction must be taken into account for the period of account in which the notional salary payment is made. [*CTA 2009, s 139(3); ITTOIA 2005, s 163(3)*]. No deduction can be claimed under any other provision in respect of the notional payment. [*CTA 2009, s 139(4); ITTOIA 2005, s 163(4)*]. It should be noted that the notional salary payment does not have to satisfy the normal 'wholly and exclusively' test.

18.41   This provision creates a mismatch.

Example

Personal Services Ltd prepares its accounts to 31 March. These show the following profits.

Year to 31.3.2012	£50,000
Year to 31.3.2013	£70,000
Year to 31.3.2014	£80,000

It is deemed to make the following notional salary payments:

5.4.2012	£40,000
5.4.2013	£60,000
5.4.2014	£70,000

The corporation tax position (ignoring National Insurance) will be as follows:

Year to 31 March	*2012*	*2013*	*2014*
Profits	£50,000	£70,000	£80,000
Less notional salary paid			
In the accounting period	nil	£40,000	£60,000
Chargeable to corporation tax	£50,000	£30,000	£20,000

Over the three years the company has received £200,000, of which the employee has been taxed on £170,000. One would therefore expect the company to have a corporation tax liability on £30,000 not on the £100,000 that in fact applies.

18.42   HMRC appear unsympathetic to this problem. They point out that if the company calculates the notional salary every month (before the end of the month of course) and actually pays it as real salary the notional salary calculation at the end of the year will produce a nil figure. Most people will not find the suggestion of having to do monthly calculations particularly helpful. If the company has a 31 March year end consideration might be given to calculating the notional salary immediately before the year end and making an actual salary payment of an equivalent amount. A more practical solution might be to change the company's accounting date to 5 April so that the notional payment date falls in the accounting period.

18.43   The notional payment can create a trading loss for a company, which can of course be dealt with like any other trading loss.

Example

Suppose that in the Example in **18.41** the profit for the year to 31 March 2015 is £30,000. The corporation tax position for that year (ignoring National Insurance) will be:

	£
Profit	30,000
Notional salary payment 5.4.2014	(70,000)
Loss	(40,000)

£20,000 of this loss can be carried back and set against the £20,000 profits for the year to 31 March 2014 and the balance can be carried forward. It might be worth considering a cessation so that the full £40,000 can be carried back under a terminal loss relief claim.

18.44   In contrast, if the intermediary is a partnership the notional salary payment cannot create a loss. The deduction is limited to the amount that reduces the profits of the partnership for the tax year to nil. Worse, if the expenses of the partnership in connection with the relevant engagement exceed the sum of:

(*a*)   the amount deductible at **18.13**(*d*) above in calculating the notional salary; and

(*b*)   '5 per cent of the amount taken into account in Step One of the calculation in paragraph 7' (this is probably intended to be 5 per cent of the gross income not 5 per cent of the 95 per cent of the gross income which is the figure at Step One);

the excess expenses must be left out of account in calculating the profits of the business. [*CTA 2009, s 140; ITTOIA 2005, s 164*].

18.45   The reason for this is probably that if a loss could be created by deducting the notional payment a partner who was deemed to receive that notional payment would claim to set the loss against the notional payments. It operates very unfairly if there is a mismatch between profit share and notional payment, or if the worker to whom the notional payment relates is not a partner at all. This can be illustrated by comparing the position between a corporate and partnership intermediary.

18.46   *Provision of Services through an Intermediary*

Example

An intermediary has the following profile for the year to 5 April 2014.

	£	£
Income (wholly from relevant engagements)		100,000
Business expenses relating to relevant engagements		
Within employment income rules	8,000	
Not within employment income rules	20,000	
Other business expenses	10,000	38,000
		62,000
The notional salary payment is:		
95% of income	95,000	
Less employment income expenses	8,000	
	87,000	
Less employer's National Insurance on		
notional salary payment at 13.8%	10,550	
Notional salary payment	76,450	
If the intermediary is a company its corporation tax position will be:		
Profit as adjusted for tax purposes		62,000
Less notional salary and NI		87,000
Adjusted loss available for carry back or forward		(25,000)

If the intermediary is a partnership of which the worker is not a partner the position will be:

	£	£
Profit as adjusted for tax purposes		62,000
Add back expenses	38,000	
Less allowable under employment income	(8,000)	
5% of 100,000	(5,000)	25,000
		37,000
Less notional payment (restricted)		37,000
		NIL

Application of employment income rules

18.46   The government of course want to collect real tax and real National Insurance in respect of the notional payment. To achieve this rules in relation to the taxation of employment income, and in particular the PAYE provisions, apply as if the worker were employed by the intermediary and the relevant engagements were undertaken by the worker in the course of that employment. [*ITEPA 2003, s 56(2)*]. The notional payment is also treated as an emolument of the employment to determine whether the worker is higher paid for benefit-in-kind purposes (see **6.4**) and for the purpose of *ITEPA 2003, ss 336* and *337* (see **5.2**) (and from 2002/03 mileage allowance relief (see **7.52**)). [*ITEPA 2003, s 56(3)*]. Where the intermediary is a partnership or unincorporated association the deemed salary payment is of course treated as received by the worker in his personal capacity and not as income of the partnership or association. [*ITEPA 2003, s 56(6)*].

18.47   The notional salary payment is treated as relevant UK earnings of the worker for pension purposes [*FA 2004, s 189(2)(a)* applying *ITEPA 2003, s 7(5)*. It was also treated as relevant earnings for the purpose of *ICTA 1988, s 644* (relevant earnings for personal pension purposes). [*ITEPA 2003, s 56(8)*]. It is unclear why it was not also statutorily treated as relevant earnings for the purposes of *section 623* (retirement annuities) or indeed for the purposes of *ss 592* and *593* (occupational pension schemes). HMRC have always indicated that it would do so. On the face of it the deeming requirement under *ITEPA 2003, s 56(1)* would automatically make it earnings for those purposes, but it should have automatically made it earnings under *s 644* as well.

18.48   The worker is not chargeable to tax in respect of a notional salary payment if (or to the extent that) the payment would not be taxable as employment income on an actual payment by the client of emolument from an actual employment with him by reason of any combination of:

(*a*)   the worker being resident, ordinarily resident, or domiciled outside the UK;

(*b*)   the client being resident or ordinarily resident outside the UK; or

(*c*)   the services in question being provided outside the UK. [*ITEPA 2003, s 56(5)*].

18.49   This is an interesting provision. It is not possible to remit a notional amount to the UK. Accordingly, if the worker is non-UK domiciled, the client is non-UK resident and the services are performed outside the UK no tax charge will arise in respect of that relevant engagement even if the duties of the worker's real employment with the intermediary are partly carried on in the UK (egeg for other clients). Furthermore, the subsection does not prevent the notional salary payment arising; it merely excludes it from tax. Accordingly, the intermediary will still be entitled to claim a deduction for the payment.

18.50   If the worker is resident in the UK, and the services in question are provided in the UK the intermediary is treated as having a place of business in the UK, whether or not it in fact does so. [*ITEPA 2003, s 56(7)*]. This will allow HMRC to require the intermediary to apply PAYE, although how they will enforce this obligation is another matter if the intermediary is non-UK resident and does not in fact have a place of business in the UK. HMRC consider that this provision supplements rather than replaces their power to require the client to apply PAYE under *ITEPA 2003, s 689*.

Other matters

18.51   If the arrangement for an engagement involves more than one relevant intermediary, ie one which is within the scope of the personal service provisions, *ss 48–61* must be applied separately to each of them. [*ITEPA 2003, s 59(6)*]. However, where a payment or other benefit passes from one of those intermediaries to the other (or another) in relation to the same engagement the amount of income brought into the calculation must be reduced to such extent as is necessary to avoid double-counting. [*ITEPA 2003, s 59(4), (5)*]. The legislation does not indicate which intermediary is to make the adjustment. Nor does it require either to notify the other of any adjustment to ensure that both do not claim the relief. It probably does not matter unduly as all of the relevant intermediaries in relation to an engagement are made jointly and severally liable for the tax attributable to it (other than one which receives no payment or benefit in relation to that or any other relevant engagement). [*ITEPA 2003, s 59(2), (3)*].

18.52   For the purpose of the IR 35 provisions a man and a woman living together as husband and wife are treated as if they were married to each other. [*ITEPA 2003, s 61(4)*].

18.53   Anything done by (or in relation to) an associate of an intermediary is treated as done by the intermediary. [*ITEPA 2003, s 61(3)(a)*].

18.54   A payment or other benefit provided to a member of an individual's family or household is treated as provided to that individual. [*ITEPA 2003, s 61(3)(b)*].

18.55   References to payments or benefits received or receivable from a partnership obviously include those to which a person is or may be entitled in his capacity as a partner. [*ITEPA 2003, s 61(2)*].

The HMRC Guidance

18.56   In May 2012, HMRC published a guidance booklet, 'Intermediaries Legislation (IR35)'. This is in two parts. Part 1 lays down a number of tests to determine whether a person is employed or not and allocates points to signify how important HMRC regards each. The tests and the HMRC points are set out below. I have also added my own points based on case law.

	HMRC View	My View
Do you have business premises separate From your home?	10	1
Do you need Professional Indemnity Insurance?	2	negligible

	HMRC View	My View
Has your business had an opportunity in the last 2 years to increase your income by working more efficiently (tip: if you agree a target delivery time and deliver earlier you can answer 'Yes'?	10	negligible
Do you engage any workers who bring in at least 25% of your yearly turnover (tip: if you agree to produce a report and your wife will type it, answer 'Yes' as you will not generate any income without her labour)?	2	10
Has the current client engaged you as an employee within the last 12 months with no major changes to your working arrangements (tip: choosing where and when to perform the work is probably a major change)?	(15)	negligible
Does your business both:		
(a) Have a regularly updated business plan		
(yes, that is really the test even though very few businesses have one), and		
(b) Does your business have a business bank account identified as such by the bank (tip: don't let them label it 'No 2 account')?	1	negligible
Do you have to bear the cost of having to put right any mistakes (tip: put it in the contract as HMRC does not understand that in practice virtually everyone – obviously, outside HMRC – including employees, is expected to do this)?	4	negligible
Have you had any bad debts exceeding 10% of your turnover in the last 2 years (I don't understand the relevance of that either)?	10	negligible
Do you render an invoice before being paid and negotiate payment?	2	negligible
Do you have the right to send a substitute?	2	negligible
Have you ever done so within the last 2 years?	20	37
	48	48

Note: The tips in brackets are not part of the HMRC questions.

It is hard to see any legal basis for HMRC's points allocation.

The law on employment status is very clear, albeit that its application is often far from easy. There cannot be a contract of employment unless:

(*a*)   the contract imposes an obligation on a person to provide work personally;

(*b*)   there is mutuality of obligation between the purported employer and employee; and

(c) there is some element of control, ie the ultimate authority over the purported employee in the performance of their work resides in the employer.

The first and third of these derive from the case of *Ready Mixed Concrete (South East) Ltd v Minister of Pensions and National Insurance [1968] 1 All ER 433* (see **4.17**) and the second from that of *Nethermere (St Neots) Ltd v Gardner [1984] 1 CR 612* (see **4.40**) as an explanation of the Ready Mixed Concrete test. It is only if all three of these elements are present that one moves to the next stage and stands back and asks if the facts point most closely to the employment. This legal basis was reaffirmed most recently in the Employment Appeal Tribunal in *Quashie v Stringfellows Restaurants Ltd* (UK EAT/0289/11/RN) (see **4.47**).

Having a real right to send a substitute (and proving that it is a real right by having done so) accordingly means that there is not an employment as head (a) above is not met. A test that allocates a mere 22 out of 48 points to the lack of an obligation to perform personal services accordingly does not conform with the law. Similarly, using someone else to do part of the work is indicative that one is not required to do the work personally. However, if HMRC wish to lay down a non-statutory 'safe harbour' test of employment, it is sensible to seek to come within it even though that safe harbour test is simply a concession and not an interpretation of the law.

HMRC say that if a client scores more than 20 points on their scale, he is regarded as low risk. If when they open an IR35 review if the worker has kept a copy of his scorecard and evidence to support the answers, they will close the review and go away unless the information given was inaccurate.

Part 2 of the booklet gives some examples. These are well worth a study. For example, take Emma. Emma works for X Ltd for 18 months on three successive six-month contracts. She works for nobody else during that period. They are fixed price contracts. If Emma works overtime (which obviously implies fixed hours) she is paid extra but has to negotiate the extra payment. She is highly skilled and has no right to send a substitute. Before engaging Emma, X Ltd has checked her background and interviewed her. Emma is highly skilled and X Ltd gives her a completely free hand over how and where she works. In practice X Ltd provide all of the equipment Emma needs. Emma reports to a manager of X Ltd every Friday afternoon. She tells X Ltd 'out of courtesy' if she cannot attend for any reason.

On the basis of past Tribunal decisions, Emma looks very much like an employee, yet HMRC say that she is self-employed.

Similarly with Juanita. Juanita has worked for a single client for eight years. She is paid by the hour and the client would not accept a substitute as her services are so highly specialised. The client directs the scope of the project which Juanita has to deliver and by when. The end client provides all of the equipment. Juanita works as part of a team. The client has to give her notice if it wants to terminate the agreement.

Juanita is the sort of lady that HMRC would normally say is an employee, but in this case they say that her circumstances are borderline.

Managed service companies

18.57   In 2006 the Government became concerned about the use of managed service companies (MSCs) to avoid, or rather, (in HMRC's view at least) evade the IR 35 legislation. Although in the view of HMRC the engagement of workers through a MSC attracted the IR 35 legislation, such companies were not applying the rules. HMRC found that enforcing those rules with MSCs 'was difficult because of the large number of workers involved and the resource-intensive nature of the legislative test. Furthermore even when a debt had been established as the result of an investigation by HMRC, MSCs can escape payment because they have no assets and can generally be wound up or simply cease to trade'. [*Tackling Managed Service Companies, December 2006*]. Whether that justified legislative action is questionable. HMRC could have almost always taken action under insolvency law had they chosen to do so, both to seek to recover the tax from the directors of the MSC for trading while insolvent and to ask the court to ban those directors from involvement in new MSCs. Instead *Finance Act 2007 (FA 2007), s 25* and *Sch 3* introduced a new Chapter dealing with MSCs into *ITEPA 2003*.

The charge to PAYE and NIC

18.58   This provides that if:

(a)   the services of an individual ('the worker') are provided, directly or indirectly, by an MSC;

(b)   the worker (or an associate of the worker) receives from any person a payment or benefit (see **18.60**) which can reasonably be taken to be in respect of the services; and

(c)   the payment of the benefit is not earnings received by the worker directly from the MSC (at the time that the payment or benefit at (b) is received);

the MSC is treated as making a payment to the worker which must be treated as being earnings from an employment. [*ITEPA 2003, s 61D*].

18.59   The amount of the deemed payment plus the employer's NIC thereon is the amount of the payment or benefit at (b) above less any expenses met by the worker that would have been deductible from the deemed earnings had the worker been employed by the client to provide the relevant services. [*ITEPA 2003, s 61E(1)*]. The deemed employment payment is of course that amount less the employer's National Insurance element. The client for this purpose is the person to whom the relevant services are supplied. The relevant services are the services referred to at **18.56(a)**. [*ITEPA 2003, s 61D(4)*]. If the MSC is a partnership of which the worker is a partner, the deduction is of expenses met by the worker for and on behalf of the partnership, but only if such expenses would have been deductible had the worker been employed by the client. [*ITEPA 2003, s 61E(2)*]. If the MSC supplies the worker with a car or other vehicle the expenses deductible include any mileage allowance relief (see **7.50**) to which the worker would have been entitled had the vehicle been a company vehicle. [*ITEPA 2003, s 61E(3)*].

18.60   For the purpose of these provisions a payment or benefit is anything that, if received by an employee for performing the duties of an employment, would be general earnings from the employment. [*ITEPA 2003, s 61F(1)*]. In the case of a non-cash benefit the amount of the benefit is the cash equivalent of the benefit. This is the amount that would be treated as earnings if the benefit derived from an employment (see **Chapters 6–9**) except in the case of the provision of living accommodation, when it is the higher of that amount or the cash equivalent under *ITEPA 2003, s 398(2)* (which is the higher of the cash equivalent under the benefits code and the amount of earnings that the benefit would give rise to if it were received for performance of the duties of the employment). [*ITEPA 2003, s 61F(3), (4)*]. A non-cash benefit is treated as received at the time that it would have been so treated under the benefit code. [*ITEPA 2003, s 61F(5)*].

18.61   The *Income Tax Acts*, particularly the PAYE provisions, applies in relation to the deemed employment payments as if the worker were employed by the MSC to provide the services and the deemed employment payment were a payment by the MSC of earnings from that employment. [*ITEPA 2003, s 61G(1), (2)*]. However, no deduction for expenses or mileage allowance relief can be made from the deemed employment payment because, of course, these have already been deducted in arriving at the amount of that deemed payment. [*ITEPA 2003, s 61G(3)*]. Where the MSC is a partnership of which the worker is a member, the deemed employment payment is of course treated as received by the worker in a personal capacity, not as income of the partnership. [*ITEPA 2003, s 61G(6)*].

18.62   The worker is not chargeable to tax in respect of the deemed employment payment if, or to the extent that, he would not be taxable if he were employed by the client because either:

(*a*)   the worker is resident, ordinarily resident or domiciled outside the UK;

(*b*)   the client is resident or ordinary resident outside the UK; or

(*c*)   the relevant services are performed outside the UK; or

(*d*)   there is a combination of two or more of these factors.

[*ITEPA 2003, s 61G(4), (5)*].

18.63   Where the worker is resident in the UK and the relevant services are provided in the UK, the MSC is treated as having a place of business in the UK, whether or not it in fact does so. [*ITEPA 2003, s 61G(7)*]. This imposes on it an obligation to deduct PAYE and NIC. Of course in many cases HMRC have no ability to enforce payment of a debt due from a non-UK resident person (although the UK is increasingly entering into mutual assistance agreements with other countries that give it the ability to do so). The real impact of such deeming is to enable HMRC to recover the tax due from UK residents involved with the MSC under the transfer of debt provisions (see **18.73**).

What is an MSC?

18.64   A company (as defined at **18.66**) is an MSC if:

(*a*)   its business consists wholly or mainly of providing (directly or indirectly) the services of an individual (or individuals) to other persons;

(*b*)   payments are made (directly or indirectly) to the individual, or associates (see **18.67**) of the individual, of an amount equal to the greater part (or all) of the consideration for the provision of the services;

(*c*)   the way in which those payments are made result in the individual (or associate) receiving a greater net sum (ie net of tax and National Insurance) than he would have received had all of the payments constituted employment income; and

(*d*)   a person who carries on a business of promoting or facilitating the use of companies to provide the services of individuals ('an MSC provider') is involved with the company.

[*ITEPA 2003, s 61B(1)*].

18.65   For the purpose of (*d*) above an MSC provider is involved with the company if he (or an associate of his) either:

(*a*)   benefits financially on an ongoing basis from the provision of the services of the individual;

(*b*)   influences or controls the provision of those services;

(*c*)   influences or controls the way in which payments to the individual (or associates of the individual) are made;

(*d*)   influences or controls the company's finances or any of its activities; or

(*e*)   gives or promotes an undertaking to make good any tax loss (see **18.66**).

[*ITEPA 2003, s 61B(2)*]. However a person is not regarded as influencing or controlling the company's finances (see (*d*)) merely by virtue of providing legal or accountancy services in a professional capacity. [*ITEPA 2003, s 61B(3)*]. Nor is a person regarded as doing so merely by virtue of carrying on a business consisting only of placing individuals with persons who wish to obtain their services (including by contracting with companies which provide their services) unless that person (or an associate of his) also does something within (*c*) or (*e*) or something else within (*d*) by doing something within (*b*). [*ITEPA 2003, s 61B(4), (5)*]. The Treasury have power by statutory instrument to exclude other types of person from (*d*). [*ITEPA 2003, s 61C(1)*].

18.66   For the purpose of **18.64** a company includes a partnership as well as a body corporate. [*ITEPA 2003, s 61C(3)*]. For the purpose of **18.65**(*e*) an undertaking to make good any tax loss means an undertaking (in any terms) to make good in whole or in part (and by any means) any cost to the individual (or an associate of his) resulting from a provision of the Tax Acts (or an enactment relating to National Insurance or a provision of subordinate legislation in relation to either) applying in relation to payments made to the individual or associate. [*ITEPA 2003, s 61C(5), (6)*].

18.67   For the purpose of these provisions an associate in relation to an individual is any of:

(*a*)   a member of the individual's family or household;

(*b*)   a relative of the individual;

(*c*)   a partner of the individual; or

(*d*)   the trustee of any settlement in relation to which the individual, or a relative of the individual or member of the individual's family (living or dead) is or was the settlor. [*ITEPA 2003, s 61I(2)*].

A relative for this purpose is an ancestor, lineal descendant, brother or sister of the individual. [*ITEPA 2003, s 61I(6)*]. A man and woman living together as husband and wife are treated as if they were married to each other, and two persons of the same sex living together are treated as if they were civil partners of each other. [*ITEPA 2003, s 61I(7)*]. The reference to deemed civil partners, which applies only for the purpose of *section 61I(2)*, is a little odd as there is no reference to civil partnerships in *subsection (2)*. It is presumably intended to make clear that the two together constitute a 'family', although as a person living with another is almost certainly already a member of that other's 'household' this seems unnecessary. For the purpose of *section 61B* only (meaning of MSC), the reference to an associate of a person also includes a person who, for the purpose of securing that the individual's services are provided by a company, acts in concert with the person (or with that person and others). [*ITEPA 2003, s 61C(4)*].

18.68   In the course of the 2007 Finance Bill debates the Minister, John Healey, told Parliament in relation to the definition of an MSC: 'It is essential that this subsection is read carefully and in its entirety … The first element that must be satisfied is that a person is carrying on a business of promoting or facilitating companies to provide the services of individuals, not a business to promote or facilitate companies generally. For that reason, those promoting or facilitating companies generally – for example company formation agents – are not MSC providers. The same would be true of training providers and a number of companies that may provide advice. Some have asked whether a person who promotes their business and who provide services to those working through service companies is an MSC provider. The answer is no. There is a clear distinction between a person who promotes themselves or their business and someone who is, as a business, promoting the use of companies to provide the services of individuals. Even if a person fulfils the criteria of being an MSC provider, it does not automatically follow that their client companies are MSCs. That depends on the relationship with their client companies – namely whether they are involved with the client companies.' [*Hansard, Finance Bill Committee, 15.5.2007, col 172*]. Mr Healey later expanded on the meaning of being involved with the client company: 'We are aware that MSC providers seeking to circumvent the legislation will claim that each relationship with their thousands of client companies is unique and does not constitute being involved. Let me try and be clear about how HMRC will approach this. First and foremost it will look at the nature of the product provided by an MSC provider. Where it is clearly a standardised product constituting the MSC being involved with client companies, it will take the starting view that all client companies are MSCs. The onus will then be on the individual companies to demonstrate no involvement.' [*Hansard, Finance Bill Committee, 15.5.2007 cols 173/174*].

18.69   Mr Healey also said: 'Let me turn to new *s 61B(3)* (see **16.83**) and reinforce the fact that a person who merely provides legal or accountancy services in a professional capacity is not an MSC provider involved with their client. There is a specific exclusion ... Let me try to make this absolutely clear: even when the specific exclusion does not apply, the purpose of the legislation is not to include within the definition of MSC providers, accountants, tax advisors, lawyers and company secretaries who provide advice or other professional services to companies in general. Those persons are not in the business of promoting or facilitating the use of companies to provide the services of individuals, nor are they regarded as involved with the company in the way the legislation envisages ... When an individual asks a tax advisor for help or advice in setting up a business to provide that individual's services to end users, the tax advisor considers the individual's position and might recommend a corporate structure that includes the payment of dividends to the individual as a shareholder worker. The tax advisor is not acting as an MSC provider.' [*Hansard, Finance Bill Committee, 15.5.2007, cols 175/176*].

18.70   The Minister also confirmed that: 'Freelancers or agency workers who are engaged directly by an agency or who are in some way in business on their own account and run their own affairs either through a personal service company or some sort of umbrella company are simply not affected by the legislation.' [*Hansard, Finance Bill Committee, 15.5.2007, col 176*]. HMRC say: 'An MSC is a form of intermediary company through which workers provide their services to end clients. The definition of an MSC in the legislation encompasses both "composites" and "managed personal service companies". In essence a scheme provider promotes the use of these companies and provides the structure to workers. The worker (although a shareholder) does not exercise control over the company.' [*HMRC Guidance Note 5.6.2007*]. They later say in the same note: 'If you are in business on your own account and control your company's finances and how the company operates, your company is not an MSC.' This seems to be the main test of whether a company is an MSC, ie is it controlled by the worker or by an MSC provider?

18.71   HMRC have set out what they call indications of whether a service provider may be an MSC provider, namely:

(*a*)   Do all of the companies the service provider supports have a unique identifier (egeg John Smith (well-known provider) Ltd, Pete Brown (well-known provider) Ltd?

(b) Does the service provider determine, or seek to determine, terms and conditions relating to the client company, or individual? EgEg:

    (i)   format of contract;

    (ii)   payment arrangements;

    (iii) payment rates;

    (iv) invoicing arrangements;

    (v)   terms under which the individual will work.

(c) Is authority for any aspect of the company's trading/provision of the individual's services delegated to the service provider? EgEg:

    (i)   receipt, or payment, of company funds (particularly payment into a common bank account);

    (ii)   contractual arrangements.

(d) Does the service provider interpose themselves between the individual/company and the recruitment business in any other way whatsoever?

(e) Does the service provider interpose themselves between the individual/company and the client in any other way whatsoever?

(f) Does the service provider only support service company clients?

(g) Is the individual work seeker unable to change service provider and retain their company?

(h) If the answer to any of the above questions is 'yes', particularly questions (b), (c), (d) and (e), the service provider may be an MSC provider.

[*HMRC Technical Note, 29.5.2007*].

18.72 They have also said that they are actively considering the development of an Audit Standard which 'would enable a suitably qualified person, not associated with the Service Provider, to review a Service Provider's business model using the Audit Standard. This would determine whether the Service Provider's client companies were MSC or not.' However, this proposal is at an early stage and there are a number of issues to be resolved before a final decision as to whether to develop such a standard is made. [*HMRC Statement, 15.10.2007*].

18.73 HMRC have warned that their view is that a company or partnership that meets the necessary criteria but claims not to be an MSC because the provider of the services is an officer of or partner in the company/partnership is in fact an MSC. They are looking to litigate this issue (*HMRC Guidance Note 3 December 2008*).

The transfer of debt provisions

18.74 The reason why accountants, employment agencies and others are so concerned about whether or not they might be deemed to be MSC providers is that legislation provides that the *PAYE Regulations* can provide for the collection of the tax from certain third parties. [*ITEPA 2003, s 688A(1)*, inserted by *Finance Act 2007 (FA 2007), Sch 3, para 3, 6*]. The relevant Regulations (see **18.76**) came into force on 6 August 2007. The tax and NIC can be recovered from any of the following people:

(*a*)   a director (as defined in *ITEPA 2003, s 67* – see **6.9**) or other office holder, or an associate (as defined in *ITEPA 2003, s 611* – see **18.67**) of the MSC;

(*b*)   an MSC provider (who is involved with the MSC);

(*c*)   a person who (directly or indirectly) has encouraged or been actively involved in the provision by the MSC of the services of the individual; and

(*d*)   a director or other office holder, or an associate of, a person (other than an individual) within (*b*) or (*c*) above.

[*ITEPA 2003, s 688A(2)*].

18.75   It is specifically provided that a person does not fall within (*c*) above merely by virtue of:

(*a*)   providing legal or accountancy services in a professional capacity; or

(*b*)   placing the individual with persons who wish to obtain the services of the individual (including by contracting with the MSC for the provision of those services).

[*ITEPA 2003, s 688A(3)*].

18.76   The *PAYE Regulations* state that if an MSC has a 'relevant PAYE debt' and an Officer of HMRC is of the opinion that the relevant PAYE debt or part of the relevant PAYE debt is irrecoverable from the MSC within a reasonable period, HMRC can make a direction authorising the recovery of that amount from the persons specified in *ITEPA 2003, s 688A* and that upon making such a direction those persons become jointly and severally liable for the PAYE debt. However, HMRC cannot recover the amount from any person until they have served a transfer notice on that person. There is a right of appeal to the Special Commissioners against such a transfer notice, but only on one or more of ten grounds specified in the Regulations. [*Regs 97C–97G*]. A relevant PAYE debt is defined in *Reg 97B*. It is tax that has been determined under *Reg 80* or that has been determined or assessed by HMRC under *Regs 76, 77(6), 78(4)* or *79(2)*. Corresponding rules apply to NIC debts of the MSC. [*Social Security (Contributions) Regulations 2001 (SI 2001 No 1004), Sch 4, paras 29A–29L*].

18.77   The Minister told Parliament: 'Let me reassure the Committee on the transfer of debt. Given that the transfer notices are expected to be issued infrequently, HMRC intend to vest such work in a central, specialised team that undertakes work of a similar nature ... only those who have encouraged or been actively involved in the provision by the MSC of the services of the individual will fall within its scope. Both tests require the third party to have an active role, so those who simply use MSC workers will not be caught. If an end client did more than simply use MSC labour, for example by telling those who it employed that they must move to an MSC, it would fall within the scope of the measure as that would be regarded as encouragement - the Hon. Lady asked about that point. That was the reason why we included the word "actively", which I am glad she welcomed ... The Hon. Lady also voiced her concern about the notion of the power given to an officer who "considers" being rather broad. It is not as broad as it appears; it simply reflects that fact that under existing PAYE legislation, debts may arise both as a result of an employer failing to pay a sum declared as due, and on a sum estimated to be due by HMRC. Proposed new *section 688A* does not provide for HMRC to create a PAYE debt, but for regulations to enable the transfer of debts that have been created by virtue of existing legislation.

'Government amendments Nos. 99 and 100 reflect the consideration that we have given to concerns that employment businesses or agencies might be within the scope of the debt transfer provision, simply as a result of carrying on their normal business of placing individuals. We have ... decided to remove that risk by expanding the exclusion, as set out in proposed new *s 688A(3)*, so that the mere placing of individuals with clients is not within the scope of the provisions. An employment business will be within that scope where it is involved beyond such activity, perhaps by advising workers to use an MSC.

'**Mrs Villiers:** If a recruitment company holds a list of approved suppliers and advisers that it makes available to the contractors with which it works, such as a list of approved suppliers of corporate structures, would that bring it within the scope of the third-party debt rules?

'**John Healey:** I cannot be specific about the judgement to which an HMRC officer might come in those circumstances, but they would increase the potential for a company to fall within the scope of the rules ...

'The Hon. Lady was rightly concerned about the position of those she termed "ordinary employees" of MSCs. Let me make it clear that we do not intend ordinary employees of MSCs or third parties to be caught by the debt transfer provision. Defining an ordinary employee would be difficult, however, and her attempt to do so made that point for me. Except for MSC directors, providers and associates, the debt transfer provisions cover only those who have encouraged or been actively involved with the supply of labour services through MSCs. It is important to recognise that the transfer of debt regulations include a specific right of appeal on the grounds that "the amount specified in the transfer notice does not have regard to the degree and extent to which the transferee ... has encouraged ... or been involved." On those grounds, the Special Commissioners may reduce the amount specified in the transfer notice to a level that, in their opinion, is just and reasonable.' [*Hansard, Finance Bill Committee 15.5.2007 cols 190/191*].

Relief in case of distributions by MSC

18.78   If an MSC which is a body corporate is treated as making a deemed employment payment in any tax year and either in that year (either before or after the payment is deemed to have been made) or in a subsequent tax year it makes a distribution, it can claim to set the amount of the deemed employment payment against the distribution so as to reduce the amount of the distribution. [*ITEPA 2003, s 61H(1), (4)*]. The claim must be made within five years after 31 January following the tax year in which the distribution is made. [*ITEPA 2003, s 61H(2)*]. HMRC can give the relief only if they are satisfied that it should be given in order to avoid a double charge to tax. [*ITEPA 2003, s 61H(3)*]. If there is more than one distribution the relief is to be given as far as practicable:

(*a*)   against distributions in the same tax year before those of other years;

(*b*)   against distributions received by the worker before those received by another person; and

(*c*)   against distributions of earlier years before those of later years.

[*ITEPA 2003, s 61H(5)*]. Where a distribution is reduced the corresponding tax credit is obviously reduced too. [*ITEPA 2003, s 61H(6)*].

Other matters

18.79   The MSC provisions do not affect the operation of *ITEPA 2003, ss 44–47* (agency workers – see **19.1**). Nor do they apply to payments or transfers to which *ITA 2007, s 966* applies (deduction of tax from payments to non-resident entertainers and sportsmen). [*ITEPA 2003, s 61A(2)*].

18.80   Where a payment by an MSC is within the scope of the IR 35 rules it appears that tax must be accounted for in accordance with the MSC rules, not those under IR 35.

18.81   It should be noted that the MSC rules treat the whole of the payment to the worker as earnings plus employers NIC whereas IR 35 allows a 5 per cent reduction. However, the difference is probably not that significant. The IR 35 rules impose tax on the gross income generated by the worker (less allowable deductions) whereas the MSC provisions charge it only on the payments to the worker. Accordingly they effectively allow a deduction for the fees of the MSC provider for running the company. If those fees are 5 per cent of the income generated by the worker the PAYE and NIC due under the two provisions would be identical.

18.82   The MSC itself can of course deduct the deemed employment payment and the related employer's NIC in calculating its own taxable profits. The deduction is allowed for the period of account in which the deemed employment payment is made but cannot create a loss for income tax purposes. Curiously it does seem to create a loss for corporation tax except where the MSC is a partnership. [*ITTOIA 2005, s 164A* inserted by *FA 2007, Sch 3, para 9* for income tax and *FA 2007, Sch 3, para 10* for corporation tax].

Chapter 19

Miscellaneous

Workers supplied by agencies

19.1   If –

(*a*)   an individual (the worker) personally provides services (other than excluded services) to another person (the client),

(*b*)   there is a contract between the client (or a connected person of the client) and someone other than the worker, the client or a person connected with the client (the agency) and

(*c*)   the services are provided under or in consequence of that contract (or the client or a person connected with the client pays (or otherwise provides) consideration for the services) then, unless it is shown that the manner in which the worker provides the services is not subject to (or to the right of) supervision, direction or control by any person (or the remuneration for the services already constitutes employment income of the worker)

    (i)   the worker must be treated for income tax purposes as holding an employment with the agency (the duties of which consist of the services that the worker provides to the client) and

    (ii)   all remuneration receivable by the worker (from any person) in consequence of providing the services must be treated for income tax purposes as earnings from that employment.

[*Income Tax (Earnings and Pensions) Act 2003 (ITEPA 2003), s 44(1)–(3)* as substituted by *Finance Act 2014 (FA 2014), s 16*].

19.2   The excluded services are

(*a*)   Services as an actor, singer, musician or other entertainer or as a fashion, photographic or artist's model. Such people traditionally obtain work through agencies but such work is normally one-off assignments which are not analogous to a continuous employment.

(*b*)   Services rendered wholly in the individual's own home – or at other premises which are neither under the control or management of the client, nor premises at which the worker is required, by reason of the nature of the service, to render them. This is because where the work is not done on the client's premises the element of control that would be normal between employer and employee is generally lacking.

[*ITEPA 2003, s 47(2)*].

19.3   If the client provides the agency with a fraudulent document which is intended to constitute evidence that *section 44* does not apply because the manner in which the worker provides the services is not subject to (or to the right of) supervision, direction or control by any person, the worker must instead be treated for income tax purposes as holding the deemed employment with the client [*ITEPA 2003, s 44(4)(a),(5)*]. Similarly if a relevant person provides the agency with a fraudulent document which is intended to constitute such evidence, the worker is treated as holding the deemed employment with that relevant person in relation to services by the worker after the fraudulent document is provided [*ITEPA 2003, s 44(4)(b),(5)*]. A relevant person for this purpose is anyone (other than the worker, the client, or a person connected with the client or the agency) who is resident (or has a place of business) in the UK and is a party to a contract with the agency (or with a connected person of the agency) under (or in consequence of which) either the services are provided or the agency (or a connected person) makes payments in respect of the services [*ITEPA 2003, s 44(6)*]. In other words, the person responsible for applying PAYE is normally the agency or, if there is a chain of agencies, the one that contracts with the end client. However if someone such as the client or an agency earlier in the chain, has fraudulently misled that agency, the obligation to deduct PAYE shifts to the person who provided the fraudulent document to the agency (and if he himself was provided with a fraudulent document, to his provider, and so on until the obligation ultimately rests with the fraudster). However in the case of agencies, this applies only to the extent that the person who provided the false document is resident in the UK or carrying on a business here. If he is not, the obligation to apply PAYE will end up with the first UK agency that accepted the fraudulent document. Accordingly a UK agency that contracts with a non-UK one for the provision of the worker's services needs to take care to satisfy itself that there is no control.

19.4   It should be stressed that this provision can require PAYE to be deducted from the remuneration of someone who is self-employed, ie it converts his self-employment income into employment income. This is because the right of supervision, direction or control is not the test of whether an employment exists. Control is simply one of the tests to determine whether an employment exists – and even then such control must be of sufficient degree to make the controller the worker's master (see **4.17**). The concept of supervision, direction or control over the manner in which the worker provides his services, is a completely new concept. Accordingly there is no case law available to demonstrate what it means. There is some HMRC guidance. It would be a brave agency that does not rigidly follow that guidance, particularly where the agency is not the person paying the worker, as in such a case the potential PAYE and NI risk to the agency will far exceed the fee it obtains for placing the worker.

19.5   HMRC say that the legislation is 'looking at whether or not that person has the freedom to choose how they do their work, or instead, does someone have the power or authority over the worker to dictate how the work is done, by imposing controls over them, subjecting them to supervision or giving them directions'. They define supervision as 'someone overseeing a person doing their work, to ensure that person is doing the work they are required to do and it is being done correctly to the required standard. That sounds like what most of us do if we engage someone to paint our house! HMRC say that supervision can also involve helping the person where appropriate in order to develop their skills and knowledge. Most people would surely call that teaching or training rather than supervision. HMRC define direction as 'someone making a person do his/her work in a certain way by providing them with instructions, guidance or advice as to how the work must be done'. That sounds like what I tell my decorator too! They define control as 'someone dictating what work a person does and how they go about doing their work'. They go on to say that control includes someone having the power to move the person from one job to another.

19.6   HMRC quote the Court of Appeal decision in *Autoclenz Ltd v Belcher & others [2009] EWCA Civ 1046*, an employment Tribunal appeal, to support their case. But it must be borne in mind that the test there was whether the individual 'has entered into or works under … a contract of employment … or any other contract … whereby the individual undertakes to do or perform personally any work or services for another party to the contract [whose status is not that of a client or customer of any profession or business undertaking carried on by the individual]'. It is questionable to what extent, if any, tests applied to define that concept can be transposed to this legislation, even if, in an attempt to illustrate that concept, the judges referred to a right of supervision, direction or control, as that explanation must derive its meaning from the context in which it is given. HMRC similarly refer to *Talentcore* (see **19.7**) but again the context was that the Tribunal were seeking to establish whether an individual was an employee and the Tribunal held that they were not. Many people think that this legislation was introduced specifically to reverse the decision in *Talentcore* because HMRC tend to be bad losers. However that means that they would think that the legislation achieves that intention, wouldn't they! Whether it does, may well be for a later Tribunal to decide. HMRC also refer to *Serpol Ltd v HMRC (TC 1043)*. The question in *Serpol* was whether the company was acting as an agency. The agency rules before amendment by *FA 2014* referred to 'supervision, direction or control, as to the manner in which the services are provided'. That is far more limited than the *FA 2014* wording. The Tribunal in a very brief decision held there that even if in practice the individual is so experienced that there is no need for supervision, direction or control, a right of control nevertheless existed. In a very brief decision the Tribunal held that those individuals the nature of whose duties were 'prescribed by the nature of the services' which seems to mean had to be carried out at a particular place, were within the agency legislation whereas those who could work at home were not. The reasons for the distinction are unclear. FTT decisions of course have no precendential value.

19.7   HMRC give a number of examples: These are worth looking at, but some of them are a bit far-fetched. For example scenario one relates to Paul, a website designer, who is specifically told that 'he has a completely free role to design and build the website as he sees fit without anyone being able to intervene to instruct Paul what the website must look like … The only specific requirement … is that the new website is completed, placed on line and activated before his engagement ends'. That is so divorced from life as to be completely unhelpful. The second scenario is as impractical as the first.

19.8   The legislation contains its own anti-avoidance provision. If an individual (W) personally provides services (other than excluded services – see **19.2**) to another person (C); a third person (A) enters into arrangements one of the main purposes of which is to secure that the services are not treated for income tax purposes under *ITEPA 2003, s 44*, as duties of an employment held by W with A; and but for this anti-avoidance provision, *s 44* would not apply to the services, *s 44* applies in relation to the services (with W being treated as the worker, C as the client and A as the agency) [*ITEPA 2003, s 46A(1)(3)(4)* inserted by *FA 2014, s 16*]. The rules at **19.3** where an agency is provided with a fraudulent document are specifically disapplied in such a situation [*ITEPA 2003, s 46A(4)(d)*]. The government presumably feel that when faced with both a fraudster and a tax avoider, the latter is the more heinous so should be responsible for the tax. Arrangements include any scheme, transaction or series of transactions, agreement or understanding, whether or not legally enforceable, and any associated operations [*ITEPA 2003, s 46A(2)*].

19.9   Where tax is recoverable under *s 44(4)* to *(6)* (see **19.3**) from the person who provided a fraudulent document or under *s 46A* (the anti-avoidance rule – see **19.6**) the tax can be collected from any director of the company (as defined in *ITEPA 2003, s 67* – see **6.9**) or member of the LLP if the agency does not account for the PAYE and it is a company or an LLP [*ITEPA 2003, s 688(2A)* inserted by *FA 2014, s 17*]. The procedure is that HMRC can serve a personal liability notice on any person who was a director (the definition includes the members of an LLP) of the company or LLP at the time at which the fraudulent document was provided to an agency (or the time when the *s 46A* arrangements were entered into) specifying the amount of PAYE that should have been accounted for and requiring the director to pay to HMRC that specified amount plus specified interest on it [*PAYE Regulations 2003, Regs 97ZA, 97ZB(1)(2)* inserted by *FA 2014, s 17*]. The interest is at the normal rate for interest on overdue tax and runs from the date the notice is served on the director [*Reg 97ZA(3)*]. A director who is served with a personal liability notice is liable to pay the tax and interest within 30 days of the service of the notice [*Reg 97ZA(4)*]. If HMRC serve personal liability notices on more than one director in respect of the same debt, they are jointly and severally liable [*Reg 97ZA(5)*].

19.10   There is a limited right of appeal against a personal liability notice. The only permitted grounds of appeal are that all or part of the specified amount does not represent an amount of relevant PAYE debt of the company or LLP (ie an amount within *ss 44(4)-(6)* or *46A*), or that the person was not a director of the company on the relevant date. An appeal on the grounds that it is not a relevant PAYE debt cannot be made if it has already been determined on an appeal by the company that the specified amount is a relevant PAYE debt of the company and the company did not deduct, account for, or (as the case may be) pay the debt by the time by which it was required to do so [*Reg 97ZC(1)(3)(4)*]. Notice of appeal must be given within 30 days of the date on which the notice is served on the director and must specify the grounds of appeal [*Reg 97ZC(2)*]. On an appeal the Tribunal can either uphold or quash the personal liability notice. It can also vary the specified amount so that it properly represents the relevant PAYE debt if the appeal raises the ground that the specified amount does not represent that debt [*Reg 97ZC(5)(6)*]. HMRC have power to withdraw a personal liability notice if they consider it appropriate to do so. If a notice is withdrawn or quashed by the Tribunal, HMRC must give notice of that fact to the director [*Reg 97ZD*].

19.11 The *Taxes Management Act 1970 (TMA 1970)*, rules on collection and recovery apply as if the personal liability notice were an assessment and the specified amount and interest on it were income tax charged on the director [*Reg 97ZE(1)*]. Summary proceedings for the recovery of the specified amount and interest thereon can only be brought within 12 months of the date on which the personal liability notice is served on the director [*Reg 97ZE(2)*]. Curiously, the period is not extended where an appeal is brought. If one or more personal liability notice are served in relation to a debt and the amounts paid to HMRC (whether under such notices or by the company) exceed the amount of the debt, HMRC must repay the excess on a just and equitable basis and without unreasonable delay, ie it is for HMRC to decide who to repay provided that decision is made fairly [Reg 97ZF(1)(2)]. They must also pay interest (at the repayment interest rate) on the amount repaid from the date that the excess occurred [*Reg 97ZF(3)(4)*].

19.12 HMRC can by regulations make provisions to require a specific employment intermediary to keep and preserve specified information, records or documents for a specified period and to provide specified information, records or documents to HMRC within a specified period or at specified times [*ITEPA 2003, s 716B(1)* inserted by *FA 2014, s 18*]. For this purpose an employment intermediary is any person who makes arrangements under (or in consequence of) which an individual either works (or is to work) for a third person, or an individual is (or is to be) remunerated for work done for a third person [*ITEPA 2003, s 716B(2)*]. An individual works for a person if either he performs any duties of an employment for that person (whether or not that person employs the individual), or he provides (or is involved in the provision of) a service to that person [*ITEPA 2003, s 716B(3)*]. There will be an initial penalty for failure to provide information, documents or records in accordance with the regulations of up to £3,000 and further penalties of up to £600 a day after the initial penalty has been imposed [*TMA 1970, s 98(4F)* inserted by *FA 2014, s 18*].

19.12A The legislation was more narrowly drawn prior to 2013/14. It provided that if an individual

(*a*) personally provided (or was under an obligation personally to provide) services to another person ('the client');

(*b*) was supplied to the client by or through a third party ('the agency');

(*c*) provided (or was under an obligation to provide) his services under the terms of a contract between the individual and the agency; and

(*d*) was subject to (or to the right of) supervision, direction or control as to the manner in which he rendered such services;

those services had to be treated as if they were the duties of an employment held by the individual. Accordingly, the remuneration arising under (or in consequence of) the contract was emoluments of that deemed employment and was taxable as employment income. [*ITEPA 2003, s 44*].

19.12B The agency legislation does not apply if the remuneration is already taxable as employment income under some other provision. [*ITEPA 2003, s 44(1)(d)*]. Accordingly, it would not apply where the individual is an employee of the intermediary. However other anti-avoidance rules (see **19.35**) have been introduced to deal with that situation. An agency includes an unincorporated body, such as a trade union, of which the individual is a member. [*ITEPA 2003, s 46(1)(b)*]. All remuneration which the client pays or provides by reason of the individual supplying the services has to be treated as receivable in consequence of the contract between the individual and the agency. [*ITEPA 2003, s 44(2)(b)*]. For the purpose of the section remuneration includes every form of payment and all perquisites, benefits and profits whatsoever, other than anything that would not have been taxable under Schedule E, if the individual had held a real employment. [*ITEPA 2003, s 47(3)*].

19.12C *ITEPA 2003, s 44* applies even if the individual performs the services in question as a partner in a firm or a member of an unincorporated body. In such circumstances, as the income is treated as earnings of the individual from his deemed employment, it ceases to be taxable income of the partnership or body. [*ITEPA 2003, s 46(1)(a), (2)*].

19.12D If an individual enters into arrangements with another person with a view to the rendering of personal services by that individual, and the effect of such an arrangement is that remuneration for those services is taxable on that other person under *ITEPA 2003, s 44*, all remuneration receivable under (or in consequence of) the arrangement must be treated as emoluments of a deemed employment held by the individual. [*ITEPA 2003, s 45*]. This prevents the interposition of someone else with a lower tax rate. It is not clear if this provision can apply if the other person is a limited company or, indeed, if by interposing a limited company the services can be taken out of *ITEPA 2003, s 44* entirely. The probability is that they can although that is unlikely to help unduly as the IR 35 legislation (see **19.35**) will then apply to the company.

19.12E *ITEPA 2003, s 44* is, of course, an anti-avoidance provision aimed at thwarting the non-operation of PAYE where the employer/employee relationship is broken by interposing the agency. Many workers, having been paid fees by the client, omitted to declare such fees to HMRC with a substantial resultant loss in tax. However, it does not merely impose a PAYE liability. It changes the assessable nature of the income for all tax purposes.

19.12F The provision fell to be considered by the First-tier Tribunal in *Talentcore Ltd (t/a Team Spirits) v HMRC [2010] SFTD 744*. Talentcore provided individuals for counter and promotional work to major cosmetic companies at duty-free shops at airports. The individual would be subject to control by the cosmetic company. Once the individual accepted an assignment, she was expected to carry it out or to find a replacement out of the pool of people approved by Talentcore. The Tribunal held that there was an unfettered right of substitution. As long as someone was there and capable of doing the work, the cosmetic company was indifferent as to the identity of that person. Accordingly the individual was not obliged to personally provide the services so head (*a*) above was not satisfied. On head (*d*), the Tribunal thought that it did not matter whether Talentcore or the cosmetic company had the right of supervision, as long as someone did.

19.12G The FTT also considered this legislation in *Oziegbe v HMRC (TC 3733)*. Mr Oziegbe provided security services, generally on construction sites. He would obtain a contract to provide X people on a site and would then find the necessary number of workers. HMRC first sought to contend that the guards were employees of Mr Oziegbe. When they accepted that they were not, they assessed him under the agency legislation instead. The FTT commented, 'This section is designed essentially to deal with the position of agency workers who are neither employed by the agency, nor by the client to which they are provided (in the latter case largely because there will probably be no contractual relationship at all between the worker and the client), but nevertheless the workers fit into the infrastructure of the client, albeit possibly only on a temporary basis, and work under the control of the client as if they were employees. It thought that the provision is most likely to be engaged when the agency worker fulfils a role in which it is natural and obvious that the client will exercise control over how the worker performs his or her services', eg secretaries provided by an agency who perform an identical function to the secretaries that the client might directly employ, and who will be expected to fit in with all the work practices of the particular client. It went on to say, 'The most obvious situation in which the "control" requirement will not be satisfied is where the particular service being rendered is one that is extraneous to the basic activity of the client, such that it is entirely natural that the client will have no control or right of control over the way in which the services are provided', eg if a construction company has various items of equipment on site and contracts an independent entity to service it, a sub-contractor of the maintenance firm would not generally be working under the control of the construction company, albeit that 'the construction company would obviously indicate that it was time to service some particular vehicle, or that one vehicle had suffered some defect, but the worker would then do the required maintenance work on his own account, and not remotely in accordance with the direction or control of the client'. In the case of security, the construction company would point out to the guards the relevant access point to the site, any particular danger and the type of security provision that it was contracting to receive but would thereafter have no involvement with how the licenced and specialist security guards performed their function.

19.12H A particular problem arises with travelling expenses. Although the Act does not provide that the deemed employment is with either the agency or the client, there is an inference that it is with whoever pays the individual, which will normally be the agency. Unfortunately, HMRC consider that the place where this deemed employment is carried on is not the office of the agency; it is the premises of whichever client the individual may from time to time be working for, the cost of travel from the individual's home (or the agency's office) to the client's premises is not travel in the course of the duties of the deemed employment. It is an expense incurred to put the individual into a position to carry out the duties. It is accordingly not an expense wholly, exclusively and necessarily incurred in the course of the employment. Many types of activity where workers are supplied through an agency require skills that are in short supply, so the clients serviced by an individual frequently cover a wide geographical area and extensive travel can be required. The cost of such travel is generally reimbursed to the individual in addition to his fee. An unwelcome side-effect of deeming the engagements to be in the course of an employment is to tax the employee on such reimbursed travel costs. These would normally have constituted business expenses had the individual actually been an employee of the agency. Furthermore, they consider that the premises of the client will normally be the place at which the duties are performed and say that this will typically be a permanent workplace (Employment Status Manual (ESM), para 2016) (see **5.18**). This is questionable. It is clearly based on the premise that each assignment is a separate employment. It is arguable that if there is a deemed employment with the agency the workplace for that deemed employment is wherever the agency sends the worker from time to time. A client's premises seem to fit more comfortably within the definition of a temporary workplace (see **5.18**) than a permanent one. HMRC do accept that if the worker is 'genuinely required to work temporarily away from the normal base at the client's premises' travel to and from that second place of work will be allowable, but they warn their staff that that would be exceptional. They also accept (albeit pragmatically) that if an agency sends a worker to two or more clients in the course of a single day travel between the two is allowable provided that the clients were all obtained through the same agency and the worker starts and finishes the day at his or her own home (ESM, para 2017).

Salaried members of LLPs

19.13   The government also became concerned that LLPs were disguising remuneration by making the employee a member of the LLP. Accordingly *FA 2014, s 74* and *Sch 17, Part 1* introduced a deeming provision to treat the member as an employee in certain circumstances. From 6 April 2014, a member of an LLP is treated as employed by the LLP under a contract of service (instead of being a member of the partnership), and his rights and duties as a member must be treated as rights and duties under the contract of service if –

(*a*)   it is reasonable to expect that at least 80% of the total amount payable by the LLP in respect of the individual's performance of services for the partnership will be 'disguised salary',

(*b*)   the mutual rights and duties of the members of the LLP (and of the partnership and its members) do not give the individual significant influence over the affairs of the partnership, and

(*c*)   the individual's contribution to the LLP is less than 25 per cent of the disguised salary.

19.13A *Miscellaneous*

[*Income Tax (Trading and Other Income) Act 2005 (ITTOIA 2005), ss 863A, 863B inserted by FA 2014, Sch 17, para 1*].

19.13A The question as to whether condition (*a*) is met must be determined at the following times –

(*a*)   if 'relevant arrangements' are then in place, at 6 April 2014 or, if later, when the individual becomes a member of the LLP,

(*b*)   at any subsequent time when relevant arrangements are put in place, and

(*c*)   if the question of whether the condition is met has previously been determined and the relevant arrangements were expected to come to an end or be modified at a particular time, immediately after that time.

[*ITTOIA 2005, s 863B(1)*]. Relevant arrangements are arrangements (including any agreement, understanding, scheme, transaction or series of transactions, whether or not legally enforceable) under which amounts are payable (or may be paid) by the LLP in respect of the individual's performance of services for the partnership in his capacity as a member of the partnership [*ITTOIA 2005, s 833B(2)(5)*]. This effectively means that relevant arrangements are in place at any time at which the individual is entitled to participate as a member in the LLP's profits.

19.13B A payment is disguised salary if either –

(*a*)   it is fixed,

(*b*)   it is variable but is varied without reference to the overall amount of the profits or losses of the LLP, or

(*c*)   it is not, in practice, affected by the overall amount of the LLP's profits or losses

[*ITTOIA 2005, s 863B(3)*]. It should in particular be noted that the individual must have a share of the profits of the LLP. For example if a tax partner of a firm of accountants is entitled to 70 per cent of the profits of the tax department, that amount will be disguised salary even though it is wholly dependent on the performance of the tax department. Once condition (*a*) has been found to apply, it is treated as continuing to apply until such time as one of the situations in **19.12** comes about [*ITTOIA 2005, s 863B(4)*].

19.13C The question of whether condition (*c*) in **19.11** is met must be determined on 5 April 2014 (or, if later, the date the individual became a member of the LLP) and then at the beginning of each subsequent tax year [*ITTOIA 2005, s 863D(3)*]. For the purpose of condition (*c*), the individual's contribution to the LLP is the total amount which he has contributed to the LLP as capital (less so much of that amount, if any, which (directly or indirectly) he has previously withdrawn or received back, he is (or may be) entitled to draw out or receive back at any time when he is a member of the LLP, or to which he is (or may become) entitled to require someone else to reimburse to him [*ITTOIA 2005, s 863E(1)(2)(6)(7)*]. For this purpose, the individual's share of any profits of the LLP (calculated in accordance with UK GAAP, not his share of taxable profits) is regarded as capital to the extent that it has been added to the partnership capital [*ITTOIA 2005, s 863E(3)(4)*].

19.13D If at the time that the test is applied, the individual has given an undertaking (whether or not legally enforceable) to make a contribution to the capital of the LLP but he has not yet made the contribution, the undertaking requires him to make it within two months of becoming a member of the LLP (or by 5 July 2014, if later); and the contribution will be a capital contribution when it is made, the individual can be treated as having made the contribution at the time the test is applied [*ITTOIA 2005, s 863F(1)(2)*]. Obviously the test does not have to be reapplied when he actually makes the contribution (but if he does not make it within the two month period, the test has to be reapplied ab initio as if he had never given the undertaking) [*ITTOIA 2005, s 863F(3)(4)*]. If he makes a partial payment, that part can be taken into account as if the undertaking referred to that amount [*ITTOIA 2005, s 863F(5)*].

19.13E The comparison is not technically with the amount of the disguised salary as the test has to be applied at the beginning of the tax year, whereas the earnings will not be ascertainable until the end of that year. It is the amount of the disguised salary which it is reasonable to expect will be payable by the LLP in respect of the individual's performance of services for the partnership in his capacity as a member of the LLP during the relevant tax year [*ITTOIA 2005, s 863D(2)*].

19.13F In effect this test requires the individual to maintain a capital account in the LLP at least equal to 25 per cent of his annual earnings from the LLP. As there is nothing to stop him borrowing to make the contribution, it is the easiest of the conditions to ensure fails. Failure to meet any one of the three conditions will prevent the provision from applying.

19.13G If during the tax year there is a change in the member's contribution to the LLP or a change of circumstances which might affect the question of whether condition (*c*) is met, the question whether the condition is met has to be revisited at that time [*ITTOIA 2005, s 863D(4)*]. If a time at which the test falls to be applied coincides with an increase in the member's contribution to the LLP, and as a result of that contribution the condition ceases to be met, it must be treated as nevertheless being met unless it is reasonable to expect that it will fail to be met throughout the rest of the tax year [*ITTOIA 2005, s 863D(7)*]. In practice this probably means that an increase in the individual's capital contribution can be taken into account only if it is likely that he will not withdraw the money again before the end of the tax year.

19.13H If the individual becomes a member of the LLP during the tax year, the reference to his capital contribution is to that contribution multiplied by the number of days in the tax year for which the person is a member of the LLP over the number of days in the tax year.

19.13I *Miscellaneous*

Example

John became a member of an LLP on 18 June 2014, so he was a member for only 292 days in the tax year. He made a capital contribution to the LLP of £50,000.

John's contribution is treated as $\dfrac{£50,000 \times 292}{365} = £40,000$

The reason for this reduction is that John will only have earnings for 292 days in the tax year (80 per cent of the year) so will only receive 80 per cent of his annual earnings. The reduction compares 80 per cent of his contribution to that 80 per cent of annual earnings.

19.13I The same calculation has to be made if the individual ceases to be a member of the LLP during the year [*ITTOIA 2005, s 863D(10)(11)*].

19.13J In determining whether *ITTOIA 2005, s 863A* applies to an individual no regard is to be had to any arrangements the main purpose (or one of the main purposes of which is to secure that the section does not apply to either the individual or to the individual and one or more other individuals [*ITTOIA 2005, s 863G(1)*].

19.13K If:

(*a*) an individual personally performs services for an LLP at a time when he is not a member of the LLP,

(*b*) he performs the services under arrangements involving a member of the LLP who is not an individual,

(*c*) the main purpose (or one of the main purposes) of those arrangements is to secure that *ITTOIA 2005, s 863A* does not apply to the individual (or to the individual and one or more other individuals), and

(*d*) in relation to the individual's performance of the services, an amount arises to the member referred to at (*b*) in respect of his membership of the LLP, which would be employment income of the individual if he were performing the services under a contract of service by which he was employed by the LLP and the amount arose directly to the individual from the LLP,

then in relation to the individual's performance of the services, the individual must be treated as if he were a member of the LLP to whom *s 863A* applies, and as having directly received the amount arising to the member at (*b*) as employment income in respect of the deemed employment under *s 863A* [*ITTOIA 2005, s 863G(2)-(4)*]. Obviously neither that amount nor any amount representing it is income of the individual for income tax purposes on any other basis [*ITTOIA 2005, s 863G(4)(d)*].

Example

John works for an LLP. He is not a member of the LLP but John Enterprises Ltd is a member. John Enterprises Ltd is owned by John and his wife in equal shares. During 2014/15, John Enterprises received £80,000 in respect of John's services. It pays corporation tax of £16,000 and distributes the remaining £64,000 dividend.

John is treated as receiving the £80,000 as earnings of an employment with the LLP. However he is not then taxed on the £32,000 dividend he received. As this is an anti-avoidance provision, it should be noted that the corporation tax does not appear to be repayable and that Mrs John appears to remain taxable on her dividend even though the income that generated it has been taxed on John.

19.13L   Where *ITTOIA 2005, s 863A* applies, the amount of deemed employment income (and other allowable expense in relation to the employment such as employers' NIC) is allowed as a deduction in calculating the profits of the LLP [*ITTOIA 2005, s 94AA; CTA 2009, ss 92A, 1273A* inserted by *FA 2014, Sch 17, paras 2-4*].

The payroll deduction scheme

19.14   The payroll deduction scheme allows an employee tax relief at source for regular charitable payments that he requests his employer to deduct from his salary. The deductions must be made in accordance with an approved scheme. This involves the employer entering an arrangement with an 'agency charity'. The agency charity – which has to be approved by HMRC for the purpose – receives the weekly or monthly contributions from the employer, deducts a handling fee and pays the money over to the charity or charities that the employee has selected. [*ITEPA 2003, ss 713–715*].

19.14A The scheme is voluntary. Employees cannot force an employer to start up a scheme and if he opts not to do so they cannot obtain tax relief for direct charitable payments (other than under a charitable deed of covenant or the special rules for gift aid donations). If an employer sets up a scheme he cannot require employees to participate in it or require any particular level of contribution. The agency charity may impose a minimum contribution level, however. The employee must have complete freedom as to which charity or charities he wishes to assist (although the agency charity can set a minimum donation to any one charity). Accordingly, a scheme cannot be set up to benefit a particular charity only. Payroll giving donations can also be made to the national heritage bodies set out in *Corporation Tax Act 2010 (CTA 2010), s 468*. [*ITEPA 2003, s 714(2)*].

19.14B The deduction must be made from emoluments taxable under PAYE. Accordingly, anyone who is taxable under PAYE can participate even if he is not an employee, eg if he is a pensioner.

19.14C The regulations with which the employer must comply, and the obligations placed on him, are very onerous. They are not considered in detail here. Consequently, it is not surprising that, although the legislation has been in force since 1987/88, in the first ten years only around 9,000 such schemes had been introduced and HMRC had stopped publicising the number of schemes.

Ministers of religion

19.15   Special reliefs apply to clergymen and ministers of religion (of whatever religious denomination), holding a full-time office as a clergyman or minister. That described at **19.15** applies only where a charity or ecclesiastical corporation has an interest in the premises and (in right of the charity's interest) the clergyman has a residence in these premises from which to perform his duties. [*ITEPA 2003, s 290(4)*].

19.15A HMRC give as examples of cases where they consider that the relief will not apply, premises privately leased by the minister from a charity, premises in which the minister lives rent-free but which are not his or her official residence (for example, a country cottage provided by the congregation), and premises occupied by a minister holding an appointment that could be filled by a layman (for example a school teacher). (Employment Status Manual (ESM), para 60009). Some of these seem questionable. In the first the minister surely has a residence in the premises 'because of [the charity's interest and by reason of holding the employment'. The legislation does not say that his occupation has to be rent free. In the third test it is whether he is 'in full-time employment as a minister of a religious denomination', not whether his duties could have been carried out by someone other than a minister.

19.15B The following items in relation to the property do not constitute emoluments:

(*a*)   the making good to the clergyman of statutory amounts payable in connection with the premises or statutory deductions falling to be made in connection with them (except insofar as any such amount is referable to part of the premises which the clergyman lets out);

(*b*)   the payment on his behalf of any such statutory amount; and

(*c*)   unless he is in director's or higher-paid employment, any expenses incurred in connection with the provision in the premises of living accommodation for him including heating, lighting, cleaning and gardening expenses (*ESC A61*) (and which are incurred in consequence of his holding his office).

[*ITEPA 2003, s 290(1), (2)*].

19.16   The following deductions can be made from a clergyman's emoluments. This is a separate relief from the above and there is no requirement for the premises to be owned by a charity.

(*a*)   Any payment or expenses incurred by him wholly, exclusively and necessarily in the performance of his duties (this is a relaxation of the general expenses rule which also requires the taxpayer to be necessarily obliged to incur the expense);

(*b*)   if the minister pays rent in respect of a dwelling house any part cf which is used mainly and substantially for the purposes of his duties 25 per cent of that rent or, if less, the part that on a just and reasonable apportionment is attributable to that part of the house; and

(*c*)   if an interest in the premises belongs to a charity or ecclesiastical corporation, 25 per cent of the expenses borne by the minister on the maintenance, repair, insurance or management of premises in which he has a residence from which to perform his duties. (Any such expenses deductible under (*a*) must obviously be deducted first.)

[*ITEPA 2003, s 351*].

No deduction can be claimed in respect of qualifying travelling expenses in relation to a vehicle (other than a company vehicle) if mileage allowance payments (see **7.49**) are made or mileage allowance relief (see **7.51**) is available in respect of the clergyman's use of the vehicle.

[*ITEPA 2003, s 359*].

19.17   Where the clergyman is in beneficial occupation of his residence the 'business' element of the running costs is deducted from his salary before calculating the ten per cent limitation on the benefit on such expenses (see **8.53**). The relief under *ITEPA 2003, s 351(1)* (**19.16**(*a*) above) is, however, calculated on the full amount of the expenses ignoring such limitation. HMRC have said that they will not necessarily accept 25 per cent as the right figure but might adopt a different amount (*Taxation, 22 October 1992, page 95*). It is not clear on what basis, as the Act specifies 25 per cent, not up to 25 per cent, other than in relation to rent. Even in relation to rent it is difficult to envisage any figure other than 25 per cent being just and reasonable except where part of the premises is used for some purpose other than that of the ministry. HMRC say that the position on council tax needs to be looked at carefully. If the tax is imposed on the church as occupier of the premises it is a liability of the church and, as such, cannot be assessed on the minister if the property is used by the minister to perform his duties. [Employment Income Manual, para 60014].

19.17A   Where a clergyman or minister of religion is provided with a residence in premises owned or leased by a charity or ecclesiastical corporation from which to perform his duties and he is not a higher paid employee, he is not taxed in respect of expenditure on heating, lighting, cleaning and gardening even though these are his contractual liability. This applies whether the church pays the sums on his behalf, reimburses them to him, or pays him an allowance towards such costs [*ITEPA 2003, ss 290A, 290B* enacting *ESC A61*].

Relief for loan interest

19.18   In certain circumstances a director or employer (both higher and lower-paid) can obtain tax relief for interest paid on a loan to acquire shares in (or make a loan to) the company for which he works. This applies where the employer is either a close company (or, from 2014/15, a company that is resident in another EEA state which would have been a close company had it been UK resident) or a co-operative or employee-controlled company [*ITA 2007, s 392 as amended by FA 2014, s 13(2)*]. A number of conditions must be met both initially and throughout the period up to the time of each interest payment.

19.19   In the case of a close company these are that:

(*a*)   the company must be a trading company or if it is an investment company must not be a close investment-holding company;

(*b*)   the individual must own part of the ordinary share capital of the company;

(*c*)   he must either have worked for the greater part of his time in the actual management or conduct of the company or of an associated company or must have a material interest in the company (broadly, own over 5 per cent of the ordinary share capital);

(*d*)   he must not have recovered any capital from the company (other than capital which has already triggered a restriction of the relief); and

(*e*)   if the company is an investment company and the individual does not meet the first test in (*c*), ie he qualifies only under the material interest test, the company must not own a property that is occupied as a residence by the individual.

[*Income Tax Act 2007 (ITA 2007), ss 393*].

HMRC interpret actual management or conduct for the purpose of (*c*) above as requiring the individual to be involved in the overall running and policy-making of the company as a whole, not merely having responsibility for one particular area. They also consider that the individual must either be a director or have significant managerial or technical responsibilities (*Tax Bulletin, Issue 9*).

19.20   The loan must have been borrowed to defray the cost of acquiring part of the ordinary share capital of the company (broadly, any shares other than fixed rate preference shares), or lending money to the company which is used wholly and exclusively for its business (or that of an associated company) or replacing an earlier loan that satisfied one of these tests or replaced another that satisfied them. [*Income and Corporation Taxes Act 1988 (ICTA 1988), s 360(1)*]. Shares acquired after 13 March 1989 that attracted Business Expansion Scheme relief or Enterprise Investment Scheme relief cannot also attract loan interest relief. [*ICTA 1988, s 360(3A)*].

19.20A   The relief does not apply if the company is a close investment-holding company (or would have been if it were UK resident [*ITA 2007, s 392(2)(a), 393A(7)*]. A close company is a close investment-holding company in an accounting period if throughout that period it does not exist wholly or mainly for one or more of the following purposes.

(*a*)   carrying on a trade or trades on a commercial basis, (*b*) making investment in land or estates or interests in land, where the land is or is intended to be 'let commercially',

(*c*) holding shares in (and securities of), or making loans to, one or more companies which is a 'qualifying company' and is under the control of the close company (or of a company which controls the close company) and exists wholly or mainly for the purpose of holding shares in (or securities of), or making loans to, one or more qualifying companies,

(*d*) co-ordinating the administration of two or more qualifying companies,

(*e*) the making of investments within (*b*) by one or more qualifying companies or by a company which has control of the close company, or

(*f*) a trade or trades carried on, on a commercial basis by one or more qualifying companies or by a company which controls the close company.

[*ITA 2007, s 393A(3)* inserted by *FA 2014, s 13(3)*]. Prior to 2014/15, the similar definition in *Corporation Tax Act 2010 (CTA 2010), s 34* previously applied. For the purpose of (*b*) above, a letting of land is commercial unless it is let to a connected person of the close company, or to the spouse or civil partner, or a relative (or the spouse or civil partner of a relative) of a connected person, or a relative of the spouse or civil partner of a connected person (or the spouse or civil partner of such a person) [*ITA 2007, s 393A(3)*]. For the purpose of (*c*) to (*f*), a qualifying company is one which is under the control of the close company (or of a company that controls the close company) and exists wholly or mainly for the purpose of carrying on a trade or trades on a commercial basis or for the purpose of making investments in land (or estates or interests in land) where the land is to be let commercially [*ITA 2007, s 393A(6)*]. If a company is wound up and was not a close investment-holding company in the accounting period ending immediately before the winding-up starts, it cannot be a close-investment holding company in a later accounting period [*ITA 2007, s 393A(5)*].

19.21 For the purpose of (*c*) in paragraph **19.18** an individual has a material interest in a company if he is the beneficial owner of over five per cent of the ordinary share capital of the company; or is able to control, directly or through other companies, over five per cent or possesses or is entitled to acquire such rights as in the event of a winding up of the company or in any other circumstance would give him a right to over five per cent of the assets available for distribution to participators (broadly, shareholders). [*ITA 2007, s 394* formerly *ICTA 1988, s 360A(1)*]. For this purpose the individual is deemed to own shares held by any associate (or to be able to exercise rights of an associate). An associate means for this purpose:

(*a*) the individual's spouse; parent or remoter issue; child or remoter issue; brother or sister; or partner (in the commercial sense, not in the sense of a live-in companion);

(*b*) the trustees of a settlement of which the individual or any of his above relatives (or deceased relatives) is or was the settlor; and (*c*)   if the individual is interested in any shares or obligations of the company which are subject to a trust (other than an approved profit sharing scheme – within Chapter 16 – unless the loan was made before 6 April 1987 or an employee benefit trust – see **15.15** – unless the loan was made before 27 July 1989 or at some time after that date the 5 per cent test had been met), or are part of the estate of a deceased person, the trustees or personal representatives.

[*ITA 2007, s 395*].

19.22   In the case of a co-operative the loan must have been either to acquire a share or shares in the co-operative or to lend to it money which was used wholly and exclusively for the purpose of its business (or a subsidiary's business) or to replace a previous qualifying loan. The conditions that need to be met throughout the entire period up to each loan interest payment date are:

(*a*)   the body continues to be a co-operative;

(*b*)   the individual has worked for the greater part of his time as an employee of the co-operative (or of a subsidiary); and

(*c*)   he must not have recovered any capital from the company (other than capital which has already triggered a restriction).

[*ITA 2007, s 401*].

A co-operative for this purpose means a common ownership enterprise or a co-operative enterprise within the *Industrial Common Ownership Act 1976 (ICOA 1976), s 2*.

19.23   In the case of an employee-controlled company the loan must have been to acquire part of the ordinary share capital or to replace a previous loan. [*ITA 2007, s 396(2)*]. There is no relief for a borrowing to lend to such a company An employee-controlled company is one where over 50 per cent of both the issued ordinary share capital and the voting power is beneficially owned by full-time employees (including directors) – but for this purpose where an individual owns over ten per cent of the ordinary shares or voting power the excess over 10 per cent is deemed not to be held by employees. [*ITA 2007, s 396(3), (4)*]. A person works full-time if he works for the greater part of his time as an employee or director of the company or a 51 per cent subsidiary. [*ITA 2007, s 396(5)*]. This definition appears to include part-timers provided that working for the company is their only occupation. The shares must have been acquired either before the company became employee-controlled or within 12 months after that time, and the company must be employee-controlled for at least nine months of the tax year in which the interest payment is made (unless it first became employee-controlled during that year). [*ITA 2007, ss 396(2), 397(3)*]. In addition, and throughout the entire period up to each interest payment date:

(*a*)   the company must have been unquoted, resident in the UK or another EEA state and not also resident in a non EEA country (UK resident and not dual resident prior to 2014/15) and a trading company or the holding company of a trading group (a group, the business of whose members, taken together, consists wholly or mainly of carrying on one or more trades);

(*b*)   the individual must have been a full-time employee of the company – this condition is deemed to be met if he ceased to be such an employee within the previous 12 months and satisfied the condition up to the date of such cessation; and

(*c*)   the individual must not have recovered any capital from the company, other than capital that has already triggered a reduction in the relief.

[*ITA 2007, s 397* as amended by *FA 2014, s 14*, formerly *ICTA 1988, s 361(4) (a), (d), (e)*].

19.24   It should be noted that a full-time employee will not qualify under the close company test unless he is employed in a managerial or technical capacity, but all employees are eligible for the co-operative or employee-controlled company test.

19.25   For the purpose of all three tests an individual is regarded as recovering capital from the company if either:

(*a*)   he receives any consideration for the sale, exchange or assignment of any of his shares, or any of his shares are redeemed by the company;

(*b*)   the company repays a loan or advance from him; or

(*c*)   he receives consideration for assigning a debt to him by the company.

[*ITA 2007, s 407(1)*].

19.26   Where this happens if he does not use the amount so received to reduce the loan he is treated as if he had done so – so that thereafter the interest applicable to the amount deemed to have been repaid will not attract tax relief. If the transaction giving rise to the capital repayment was not a bargain at arm's length, the amount of capital deemed repaid is the market value of the consideration. [*ITA 2007, ss 406, 407(4)*]. Obviously, if there is a subsequent replacement loan the restriction carries through to the new loan. [*ITA 2007, s 408*].

19.27   It was held in *Lord v Tustain [1993] STC 755* that if a company is set up with the intention that it should acquire a trade but at the time of the subscription for the shares it had not yet done so, it is nevertheless a company which exists 'for the purpose of' carrying on a trade.

Diplomats, etc

19.28   Diplomatic Agents, ie heads of missions or members of diplomatic staff of foreign states, are exempt from UK tax on their UK earnings under the *Diplomatic Privileges Act 1964*. This exempts a diplomatic agent 'from all dues and taxes, personal or real, national, regional or municipal' (with some exceptions that do not affect earnings). [*Schedule 1, Article 34*]. Article 33 provides a similar exemption from National Insurance. *Article 37(2)* extends this exemption to members of the administrative and technical staff of the diplomatic mission and *Article 37(3), (4)* exempts from tax, and National Insurance earnings of members of the service staff of the mission and of private servants of members of the mission provided that they are neither UK nationals nor permanently resident in the UK. This exemption is extended by *ITA 2007, s 841* to an Agent General for any state or province of a country within *Schedule 3* to the *British Nationality Act 1981*, the Republic of Ireland, or any self-governing colony and to an employee who is either:

(*a*)   a member of the personal staff of an Agent-General;

(*b*)   an official agent for any of the countries mentioned in *Schedule 3* to the *British Nationality Act 1981* or the Republic of Ireland (of any state or province of such a country); or

(*c*)   an official agent for a self-governing colony.

The exemption for such staff applies only if the High Commissioner of the country, or Agent-General for the state, province or self-governing colony in question certifies that the employee is ordinarily resident outside the UK and is resident here solely for the purpose of the performance of his diplomatic duties. [*ICTA 1988, s 320*]. It will not therefore normally apply to staff recruited in the UK. In *Jiminez v CIR [2004] STC (SCD) 371* Mrs Jiminez, a cook at the Namibian High Commission in London, was held liable for UK tax. She was a Filipino national and claimed not to be permanently resident in the UK. The Special Commissioner thought that Mrs Jiminez was permanently resident in the UK but held that in any event her claim had to fail as the Namibian High Commission had not given the appropriate certificate to the Foreign and Commonwealth Office. It may seem unreasonable that Mrs Jiminez's tax position should depend on action by a third party. The logic is probably that the High Commission should be aware whether a person is a permanent resident of the UK for the purpose of the provision (the FCO guidance states that the test is whether the person would be in the UK but for the requirement of the sending State). In fact Mrs Jiminez was recruited in the UK and regarded by the High Commission as locally recruited staff and thus as being a permanent resident of the UK.

19.29   There is a similar exemption for foreign consuls. The income from a person's employment as a consul or an official agent in the UK for any foreign state is exempt from UK tax, and also ignored for the purpose of calculating UK tax on other income. A consul for this purpose is a person recognised by Her Majesty as being a consul-general, consul, vice-consul or consular agent. An official agent is a person who is not a consul, but is employed on the staff of any consulate, official department or agency of a foreign state – other than a department or agency that carries on a trade, business or undertaking carried on for the purposes of profit. [*ITEPA 2003, ss 300, 301*]. It has been held that for a country to be a foreign state for the purpose of *section 300* it does not have to be one recognised by the UK (*R v IRC ex parte Caglar [1995] STC 741*).

19.30   The income from a person's employment in the UK as a consular employee of a foreign state (to which the section applies) is similarly exempt from income tax (but not excluded to calculate the tax rate on other income) unless the employee is a British citizen, a British Dependent Territories citizen, a British national (overseas) or a British overseas citizen and is not a citizen of the foreign state concerned. [*ITEPA 2003, s 302*]. A consular employee includes any person employed for the purposes of the official business of a consular office at any consulate, consular establishment, or any other premises used for such purposes. [*ITEPA 2003, s 302(4)*]. Subsistence allowances paid by the European Commission to experts seconded to the Commission by their employers are also exempt from tax (see **5.84**).

19.31   There is also an exemption for the UK earnings of personnel of the armed forces of designated foreign countries, namely, Belgium, Canada, Denmark, Germany, France, Greece, Italy, Luxembourg, the Netherlands, Norway, Portugal, Turkey and the USA; and for persons attached to a designated NATO allied headquarters, namely, the Channel Committee, Channel Command, Eastern Atlantic Area Command, Supreme Headquarters Allied Powers and Allied Command Atlantic Headquarters. [*ITEPA 2003, s 303*, formerly *ICTA 1988, s 323* and *Visiting Forces and Allied Headquarters (Income Tax and Death Duties) (Designation) Order (SI 1961 No 580* and *SI 1964 No 924)*]. The salary must be paid by the foreign government and the employee must not be a British citizen, British Dependent Territories citizen or British National (Overseas) or British Overseas citizen (except to the extent that the NATO treaty requires the earnings of such people to be exempted). The exemption extends to civilian employees of a visiting force. A period while a person is a member of a visiting force or allied headquarters is ignored in considering his residence or domicile position (but not so as to deny him personal allowances).

19.32   Similarly the *International Organisations Act 1968, s 1(2)(b)* and *Sch 1* provides representatives, members of subordinate bodies, high officers, experts and persons on missions of designated International Bodies, the same exemption from income tax (and National Insurance) as applies to the head of a diplomatic mission [para 9]. It also exempts from income tax the emoluments received by any other officer or servant of the organisation [para 15]. The bodies concerned are those designated by Order in Council to be an organisation of which the UK is a member or of which any other sovereign power is a member. The *International Organisations Act 2005* ensures that the exemption also applies to staff of the Commonwealth Secretariat, the Organisation for Security and Co-operation in Europe, bodies established under the EU Treaty, the International Criminal Court, the European Court of Human Rights and the International Tribunal for the Law of the Sea. The appropriate Order in Council will need to be looked at to determine the exact scope of the exemption.

Capital gains tax

19.33   For capital gains tax purposes where a person acquires or disposes of an asset wholly or partly in connection with:

(*a*)   his or another's loss of office or employment or diminution of emoluments; or (*b*)   in consideration for (or recognition of) his or another's services (or past services) in any office or employment;

the asset is deemed to be acquired or disposed of for a consideration equal to its market value. [*Taxation of Chargeable Gains Act 1992 (TCGA 1992), s 17(1)(b)*]. This does not apply to the acquisition of an asset if there is no corresponding disposal of it and no consideration in money or money's worth is given. If there is such consideration the deemed cost cannot exceed that amount [*TCGA 1992, s 17(2)*]. Nor does it apply:

(i)   in respect of certain priority share allocations to employees [*TCGA 1992, s 149C* – see **14.177**];

(ii)   in relation to employee share options [*TCGA 1992, s 149A* – see **14.177**]; or

(iii) on a disposal by a close company or an individual to an employee trust [*TCGA 1992, s 239(2)* – see **19.112**].

Defalcations by close company directors

19.34   An interesting area is the tax effect of defalcations by a director of a company. What is the correct tax treatment of the funds in the hands of the director? HMRC tell their staff 'If the evasion has been extractive, decided tax cases support either settlement with the company, as omitted profits liable to Corporation Tax (and possible consequential *section 455, ITA 2007* liability), or with its directors as undisclosed employment income paid out of the evaded profits. The basis of settlement depends on the particular facts and circumstances of each case ... In the normal case there will be no evidence that an unexplained source of money or a capital reconciliation deficiency is anything other than a misappropriation of company funds by a director or participator. *Curtis v J & G Oldfield Ltd 9 TC 319* provides general authority for director misappropriations being taxed as company profits. The Tax Cases decided subsequently have been, in many cases, about the source of the money required to explain a capital reconciliation deficiency, rather than whether extractions should be assessable on the company (with *CTA 2010, s 455* (loans to participators) or on the individual directors personally as employment income. The fact that these cases have involved both approaches to settlement shows that either route is possible. The facts of a case are important in deciding the correct approach. As soon as extractions, either by diversion of company receipts or by false description or inflation of expenses in the company accounts, are established all the evidence should be considered to decide what those extractions represent. This will include whatever documentary evidence is available and the oral evidence of the director(s) who should be asked to explain how the extractions took place and what they and the company believe the extractions represent. If the extractions are recorded or passed through a loan account which has been disguised in the accounts or is outside the accounts, or there are references to loans, or there is some indication or expectation that the company would be reimbursed in certain circumstances, the extractions might be assumed to possess the characteristics of a loan rather than anything else ... amounts taken from the company on a regular basis, particularly weekly or monthly, with no reference to a loan, or irregular amounts but there is some reference to off-record remuneration being paid, might possess more of the characteristics of remuneration rather than anything else … Where, after enquiry, there is little evidence one way or another, the department's preferred line is to treat money extracted as additional company profits with the extractions treated as loans to the participators. The circumstances of the case may play a very important part in your decision. If the company is insolvent, and/or the directors seem prepared to let it go into liquidation or allow it to cease trading and become dormant, corporation tax, *section 455* liability remains the preferred settlement route. A 'joint and several' corporation tax/*section 455* offer may still be possible for a company in liquidation. The offer has to be made by the liquidator and the participators who extracted the money from the company'. [Enquiry Manual, paras 8601/8605].

19.35 They go on to instruct their staff that Head Office approval is required before the employment income route is chosen unless there is clear evidence that extractions were in the nature of remuneration. [Enquiry Manual, para 8701].

19.36 HMRC also say 'company funds misappropriated by a director are normally assessable upon the company. There is judicial support for this' [Enquiry Manual, para 8510]. The judicial support is probably not support for anything other perhaps than it is for the taxpayer to overturn the assessment. None of the cases seem to have questioned whether the approach HMRC took was the correct one. Indeed taxpayers seem, not unnaturally, to have concentrated on seeking to show that no defalcation took place and a contention that defalcations should be taxed in a particular way would somewhat undermine such a contention. For what it is worth HMRC ran the money belongs to the company argument in *Erddig Motors Ltd v McGregor 40 TC 95*, *Frederick Lack Ltd v Doggett 46 TC 524*, *Bamford VATA Advertising Ltd 48 TC 359* and *Fen Farming Co Ltd v Dunsford 49 TC 246*. They ran the remuneration argument in *Hudson v Humbles 42 TC 380*, *Frowd v Whalley 42 TC 599*, *James v Pope 48 TC 142*, *Murphy & Elders 49 TC 135* and *Bamford (Inspector of Taxes) v ATA Advertising Ltd 51 TC 1*. They took a third approach in *New Fashions (London) Ltd v CIR [2006] STC 175*, contending that it was remuneration but seeking to collect the tax not from the individual but rather from the company under the *PAYE Regulations*. The General Commissioners in that case do not seem to have addressed at all the question of whether the amount was remuneration. They expressed the question for determination as whether certain payments were in settlement of legitimate trading invoices and, having decided that they were not, merely determined that the determinations should stand good. The appeal was largely on procedural grounds and did not address whether the defalcations could on the evidence have been reasonably considered as remuneration. Most small companies adopt a variant of Table A in the *Companies (Tables A to F) Regulations 1985 (SI 1985 No 805)*. This states: 'The directors shall be entitled to such remuneration as the company may by ordinary resolution determine'. It is hard to see how funds withdrawn from the company can constitute remuneration in the absence of such a resolution. Under company law a director who disposes of the company's property in breach of his fiduciary duties towards the company is treated as having committed a breach of trust and if the director himself is a recipient of the property he will hold it on trust for the company (*J J Harrison (Properties) Ltd v Harrison [2002] 1 BCLC 162, CA*).

19.37   It is interesting to note that where HMRC take the view that the defalcations belong to the company and give rise to a 'loan' by the company to the director, they consider that this deemed loan does not come into being until it is accepted that liability arises on misappropriations and accordingly they cannot seek tax on a benefit in kind in relation to interest on the notional loan under *ITEPA 2003, s 175* (see **9.1**) for periods prior to that time [Enquiry Manual, para 8610].

Electronic communications

19.38   The Government wants to encourage the use of electronic communications, which they believe increase efficiency for business. They have adopted the slogan 'digital by default', but this does not appear to have its everyday meaning of ensuring that everyone is able to communicate with HMRC electronically when they wish to do so. It seems to mean that taxpayers should be compelled to communicate electronically with HMRC when that suits HMRC but are expected to use the postal system when HMRC consider it too expensive to produce the necessary software or prefer not to communicate electronically as has long been the case with e-mails. *Finance Act 2002 (FA 2002), s 136* gives HMRC power to require returns to be filed electronically and to make regulations regarding such returns. *FA 2003, s 204* similarly gives them power to require tax payments to be made electronically. They have required PAYE to be dealt with electronically. They have also required all pension scheme returns to be made electronically from 16 October 2007 by a direction made on 13 April 2007 under the *Registered Pension Schemes and Overseas Pension Schemes (Electronic Communication of Returns and Information) Regulations 2006 (SI 2006 No 570)*. The *FA 2014* has also required notices and returns in relation to employee share schemes to be made electronically.

Losses in an employment or office

19.39   An employee who makes a loss in his employment or office in a tax year can claim relief for that loss against his total income for that year, the previous year or both. If he claims for both he must specify which year's income is to be relieved first. The claim must be made within 12 months of the normal self-assessment filing date, ie by 31 January two years after the end of the tax year [*ITA 2007, s 128(1)–(5)*]. Employment losses are comparatively rare though as *ITEPA 2003, s 329* limits the amount of a deduction allowable under *ITEPA 2003, ss 327–385* (deductions allowed from earnings) to the amount of earnings from which it is deductible. There are however exceptions for ministers of religion, business travel, advances for necessary expenses, incidental overnight expenses, counselling, retraining courses and mainland transfers for oil and gas workers [*ITEPA 2003, ss 329(4), (5), 322*]. Apart possibly from the first of these, they are unlikely to create a loss though. Accordingly the relief must be aimed at specific provisions elsewhere in *ITEPA 2003*. Curiously *ITA 2007, s 128(5A)* (inserted by *FA 2009, s 68(1)*), which disallows a loss arising as a result of arrangements one of the main purposes of which is the disallowance of tax, was aimed against artificial transactions triggering a deduction under *ITEPA 2003, s 346*. The legislation contains no definition of a loss. It is presumably an excess of deductions over income from the employment. If the whole of a loss cannot be relieved against general income, an election can be made to treat the excess as a capital gains tax loss, but such a loss cannot be offset against capital gains of a later year [*ITA 2007, s 130; TCGA 1992, s 261B*]. This legislation was considered in *Martin v HMRC* (see **11.73A**).

Salary sacrifice

19.40   There has been a growth in salary sacrifice arrangements in recent years, as the government has introduced more and more tax-free benefits such as childcare vouchers. These are generally intended to encourage employers to provide what the government consider to be socially desirable objectives that the government does not itself have the funds to provide. Unfortunately these are rarely attractive to employers, not least because the government often insist on such benefits being available to all staff and employers do not wish to incur either the cost or the administrative burden that the provision of universal benefits often entails. Salary sacrifice arrangements move the cost of providing the benefit to the employee. It is attractive to an employee because he exchanges gross income for a benefit that he would otherwise have had to provide himself out of taxed income. For senior employees salary sacrifice arrangements can also provide a means to enhance the employee's pension by exchanging gross salary for an employer pension contribution that the employer would not otherwise have paid.

19.41   HMRC are concerned both about the growth of salary sacrifice arrangements and that employees may not fully appreciate what such an arrangement entails. They have issued a guidance note (11 August 2008) explaining salary sacrifice. This stresses that to be effective, a salary sacrifice entails a permanent alteration to the employee's terms of employment. He reduces the amount of his remuneration. That change is legally binding and could affect an employee's entitlement to other earnings related payments. In particular if the employee is in a final salary pension scheme, the scheme rules will often look only at salary, excluding benefits, so a salary sacrifice can reduce the employee's pension entitlement. If at a future date the employer ceases to provide the benefit, or it becomes taxable so that the employee no longer wants it, the employee must not be entitled to opt to take back his original salary. Such an option would create a tax liability on the benefit equal to the amount foregone (*Heaton v Bell 46 TC 211*, see **7.77**). This does not apply to employer provided childcare, workplace parking or employer provided cycles and cycle safety equipment as the legislation for such payments specifically excludes the application of the *Heaton v Bell* principle. HMRC consider that if a salary sacrifice arrangement is specified to last for a fixed period of time and it is ended prematurely, the *Heaton v Bell* principle might well apply. Accordingly great care may need to be taken. They also point out that benefits are not dealt with under PAYE so the employee's payslip needs to show only the reduced salary as pay (although there is of course nothing to stop the employer showing the benefit elsewhere on the payslip). They also stress that benefits are not taken into account in determining whether a person has been paid at least the national minimum wage. The case of *Reed Employment plc v HMRC [2014] UKUT 160(TCC)* which is considered at **5.38** dealt with a purported salary sacrifice that proved to be ineffective.

Employee benefit trusts

19.42   Employee benefit trusts (EBT) have been used from time to time to enable a company to set aside funds to incentivise employees. They became increasingly popular in the1980s as a means for a family company to set aside funds for its directors in a form that was tax deductible to the compay but did not attract a tax charge on the directors if the trust lent the money to the directors or used it to purchase assets that could be used by the directors or simply accumulated it. The government became concerned about the growth of such trusts. They successfully challenged the tax deduction in *Macdonald v Dextra Accessories Ltd [2004] STC 339* – see **19.46**) and in 2011 introduced the legislation on disguised remuneration considered at **3.26** onwards, which was primarily aimed at loans by EBTs.

19.43   EBTs rely for their tax efficiency on general law. A contribution by a company to a trust set up for the benefit of its employees is normally wholly and exclusively incurred for the benefit of the company's trade and thus an allowable corporation tax deduction. In *Heather v P-E Consulting Group Ltd 48 TC 293* the Court of Appeal held that annual contributions to such a trust were allowable. This was followed in *Jeffs v Ringtons Ltd 58 TC 680* and *E Bott Ltd v Price 59 TC 437*. In the latter case the payments were not a specific annual amount and lasted for only three years, so it is likely that regularity is unimportant and a single payment would be deductible. Although a deduction was denied in *Rutter v Charles Sharpe & Co Ltd 53 TC 163* the facts in that case were peculiar. Only the dividends were to be distributed to staff, with the capital being returnable to the company after 80 years. In these circumstances it is not surprising that the contributions were regarded as capital as they would ultimately result in an enduring asset for the company. It did not seem to do so.

19.44   The contributions will not normally have a revenue nature as far as the trustees are concerned provided that the arrangements do not create 'annual payments' in the tax sense. Assuming that the trust is a discretionary one, the income will be taxable on the trustees at the 45 per cent rate applicable to trusts in the normal way but is not assessable on the employees as no part belongs to any individual employee. A distribution from the trust to an employee is income at the time of the distribution – even if at that stage the employment has ceased. As this was a concession, no repayment supplement was given. The trustees must have completed tax returns each year and produce evidence of the tax that they have suffered if they want to claim the benefit of this concession. If the employee trust was non-UK resident *ESC A68* did not apply but *ESC B18* gave broadly the same effect. This taxed the employee on the grossed up amount of the distribution but gave him credit for the underlying tax (*Taxline, November 1994, Item 139*). This was given statutory effect from 6 April 2010 by *ITA 2007, ss 496A* and *496B*. These provide that if in a tax year the trustees of a UK resident settlement make a 'discretionary employment income payment', *ITA 2007, ss 496A* and *496B* allow the trustees to claim repayment from HMRC of the lower of amount A or B where

A = the trust rate of tax on the total of the amounts that are employment income of beneficiaries of the settlement because of the discretionary employment income payments made in the tax year by the trustee, and

B = the amount of the trustees' tax pool available for the year reduced by the total amount of income tax (if any) treated under *ITA 2007, s 494* (grossing up of discretionary payment) as having been paid as a result of payments made by the trustees in the tax year

[*ITA 2007, s 496B(1)-(3)*]. The claim cannot be made before the end of the tax year to which it relates [*ITA 2007, s 496B(4)*]. Prior to 2010, HMRC made a repayment to the trustees by concession (ESC A68). A discretionary employment income payment is a payment to a person (the beneficiary) that is made out of income in the exercise of a discretion (whether exercisable by the trustees or any other person if either

(a) what is paid to the beneficiary is employment income of the beneficiary only because of the payment and it is not exempt income (ie not exempted from income tax by any provision of ITEPA 2003), or

(b) the payment is made at a time when the settlement is an employee benefit settlement [*ITA 2007, s 496A(2)-(4)*]. A settlement is an employee benefit settlement for this purpose if the trusts on which the settled property is held do not permit funds to be applied otherwise than for the benefit of persons defined by reference to one or more of employment in a particular trade or profession; employment by (or holding office with) a body carrying on a trade, profession or undertaking; or marriage to (or civil partnership with), or relationship to (or dependence on) persons in such a class [*ITA 2007, s 496A(5)(6)*]. The trust can also include charitable purposes [*ITA 2007, s 496A(5) (6)*]. If the trusts are so limited only for a period, it is an EBT for that period only [*ITA 2007, s 496A(7)*].

19.45   An EBT does not have to include all employees – although if it only covers a few it may be difficult to show that the contributions are wholly for the purpose of the company's trade, particularly if those few are already shareholders. There is no difficulty in the directors being the trustees. The beneficiaries can include former employees. There is flexibility on when shares are acquired and an ability to invest other than shares in the employee company. The main disadvantage is that the capital gains tax roll-over relief considered at 19.96 onwards did not apply to the transfer of shares to an EBT.

19.45A The most recent case on EBTs is *HMRC v Murray Group Holdings Ltd and others (2014 UKUT 292)*. This relates to an EBT set up by Glasgow Rangers Football Club. The trust deed in that case gave the trustees power to create sub-trusts on the recommendation of the employer. A sub-trust would be for the benefit of the family of an individual employee, but the employee himself was not a beneficiary. The employer would advance money to the EBT which would in turn advance it to the sub-trust. The sub-trust would lend the money to the employee. The loan was normally for ten years. It was granted on a discounted basis reflecting LIBOR plus 1.5–2 per cent. At the end of the ten years, there was an expectation that the loan would be renewed. HMRC contended that the loan was a sham as in practice it would never have to be repaid and the payment was in reality emoluments. In a split decision, the FTT disagreed. It did not regard the liability to make repayment as a remote contingency which might in the context of a purposive construction fall to be disregarded. The Tribunal noted that it had asked HMRC's Counsel whether HMRC would regard the loans as debts on an employee's estate in the event of his death and that Counsel had responded two days later that 'HMRC preferred not to commit itself'! In a surprisingly brief decision, the UT held that the Tribunal had not misdirected itself and the decision was one they had been entitled to reach. This case is a set-back for HMRC who have been seeking to settle outstanding EBT loan cases on the basis that the company should account for tax and NIC (and interest) on the 'loan' and HMRC would allow the company a corporation tax deduction. *The Murray Holdings'* case does not necessarily mean that other EBT loan schemes will succeed. It is dependent on the facts. A scheme where the loan was interest-free and repayable only on death could well be in a different position.

Timing of the corporation tax deduction

19.46 A major problem with an EBT is the period in which contributions by the company attract a corporation tax deduction. Urgent Issues Task Forces abstract No 13 (UITF 13) states that for accounting purposes cash and shares held by the trustees should be treated as assets of the employer until the rights in the shares is transferred to employees. This means that contributions by the company to the EBT will not be recognised as an expense until the time of such transfer, which may be several years distant. The HMRC view is that UITF 13 needs to be followed in calculating profits for tax purposes. They do not consider that this principle of timing is affected by the fact that UITF 13 'strays' from the legal form of transactions, ie it ignores the fact that the ESOT is a legal entity distinct from the employer (*Tax Bulletin 27, Feb 1997*). Paragraph 8 of UITF13 states, 'The Task Force reached a consensus that the principles of FRS5 require the sponsoring company of an ESOP trust to recognise certain assets and liabilities of the trust as its own whenever it had de facto control of the shares held by the ESOP and bears their benefit or risks. This will generally be the case when the trust is established in order to hold shares for an employee remuneration scheme and may do so in other circumstances'. If the references to 'shares' is replaced by 'assets' the logic of this approach seems compelling. It is nevertheless likely that the HMRC approach will be challenged in the courts at some stage. Until that is done most employee trusts have little or no tax benefit. The main issue is whether accountants can alter the tax effect of a transaction by treating assets belonging to A as if they belonged to B. Tax law follows accountancy principles only to the extent that these are not over-ridden by law. It probably makes no difference if the trustees of the employee trust are all non-directors as paragraph 2(*d*) of UITF 13 points out that 'most ESOP trusts (particularly those established as a means of remunerating employees) are specifically designed so as to serve the purposes of the sponsoring company, and to ensure that there will be minimal risk of any conflict arising between the duties of the trustees and the interest of the company. Where this is so, the sponsoring company has de facto control'. It probably also does not matter that UITF 13 is expressed not to apply to small companies as the HMRC view (which is believed to reflect that of the Accounting Standards Board) is that where small companies are exempted from following the details of a standard they are still expected to comply with its spirit.

19.47 Particular care is needed where the trust will buy shares from a controlling shareholder. In *Mawsley Machinery Ltd v Robinson [1998] STC (SCD) 236* Mr Kimbell, the controlling shareholder, did not wish his employees and fellow directors, who could not afford to buy his shares, to lose control of the company on his death. The company accordingly set up a discretionary trust for the benefit of employees with the intention that it should buy Mr Kimbell's shares on his retirement. It was held that although the trust was for the benefit of employees it was also a convenience for Mr Kimbell so the company's contributions to it could not be said to have been incurred wholly and exclusively for the purposes of its trade. It is not clear to what extent UITF 13 applies where an employee trust is not set up to hold shares in the employer company but holds other assets. In principle this should make no difference.

19.48 HMRC took a different point in *Macdonald v Dextra Accessories Ltd and others [2004] STC 339*, namely the application of *Finance Act 1989 (FA 1989), s 43*. This prohibits a deduction in respect of emoluments or potential emoluments (amounts reserved in the accounts of an employer or held by an intermediary with a view to their becoming relevant emoluments) from an office or employment if the emoluments are not paid within nine months after the end of the accounting year. HMRC contended that payments into an employee benefit trust were potential emoluments and as such no deduction was due until the potential emoluments became actual emoluments and were paid. The company contended that, as the trustees of the employee benefit trust had powers entitling them to deal with the funds other than by making payments of emoluments to the beneficiaries, the contributions were not paid to the trustees 'with a view to their becoming potential emoluments'. In fact the trustees had allocated the funds to sub-trusts for each director and made loans from the sub-trust to the director. The Commissioners and Neuberger J agreed that the payments were not potential emoluments but the Court of Appeal disagreed. The words 'with a view to' coupled with 'potential' indicate a future event that may or may not occur. This test is to be applied not by reference to the intention of the trustees but by looking at the terms on which the funds are held by the trustees. The phrase is accordingly apt to embrace the whole range of possibilities open to the trustees under the trust deed, one of which was the payment of emoluments. The Court did, however, stress that 'it is not possible to lay down any hard and fast rule applicable to all cases, as to how the expression 'with a view to' is intended to apply to any given set of facts. Each case will turn on its own facts'. It is interesting to note that HMRC do not seem to have argued at any stage that the company's accounting treatment is not in accordance with UITF 13. It may be that they felt that they could not show that the company had de facto control over the trustees. If so that would seem to call into question much of what HMRC say in their *Tax Bulletin* article.

19.49   A similar issue arose in *JT Dove Ltd v HMRC [2011] SFTD 348*. The company was initially held by a pensions trust company for the enduring benefit of all of the employees of the company. Following a change in the pension rules, which prohibited self-investment by a pension scheme, it was decided to move the shares into an employee benefit trust (EBT). The machinery used was that the company contributed £3million to the EBT and the EBT used this to buy the shares from the pension scheme. There was no tax avoidance or even tax saving motive; the intention was simply to preserve the company in perpetuity for the benefit of its employees. Sadly the EBT trust deed gave the trustees a fall-back power to transfer shares to employees but only with the consent of all of the trustees, the directors of the company, and the employees. This reserve power was held to be enough to make the £3million 'potential emoluments' and deny the corporation tax deduction. In constructing the deed, the Tribunal held that all the background knowledge reasonably available to the parties at the time of the establishment of the EBT (other than the negotiations of the parties and their declarations of subjective intent) should be taken into account but that the views of the parties as to how the trustees' powers were likely to be exercised had to be ignored.

19.50   If a close company or an individual transfers assets to an employee trust and the exemption under *Inheritance Tax Act 1984 (IHTA 1984), s 13* or *s 28* applies, *TCGA 1992, s 17* (see **19.34**) does not apply. Instead, the actual consideration paid is adopted for capital gains tax purposes. If the disposal is by way of gift or sale at less than the transferor's CGT base cost it is treated as taking place at a no gain/no loss price and the trustees inherit the transferor's CGT history. [*TCGA 1992, s 239(1), (2)*]. Such a disposal by a close company will not trigger a charge on the shareholders under *TCGA 1992, s 125* if the actual disposal proceeds is at least equal to the company's base cost of the shares. [*TCGA 1992, s 239(3)*].

19.51   The above no gain/no loss rule applies to a disposal by a non-close company in certain circumstances. The disposal must not be an arm's-length sale to the trustees and the trusts must not only satisfy *IHTA 1984, s 86(1)* but the persons for whose benefit the trust permit the property to be applied must include all or most of the directors or employees of the company (or if preferred the company and its subsidiaries). This is subject to the proviso that it must not permit the trust property to be applied for a participator in the company (or in any other company that has transferred assets to the trust), a person who has been such a participator at any time in the previous ten years or a connected person of such a person. A participator owning less than five per cent of any class of share (or the issued share capital as a whole) and who would be entitled to less than five per cent of the assets on a winding up need not be excluded. The fact that income can be distributed to a participator is also ignored as is the possibility of the trustees appropriating shares to such a person under an approved profit sharing scheme (see **Chapter 16**). [*TCGA 1992, s 239(4)–(7)*].

19.52   There are also inheritance tax reliefs on the transfer of assets to an employee trust. The settled property must be held on trusts which, either indefinitely or until the end of a period (which can be defined by reference to a fixed date or in some other way), do not permit any of that property to be applied otherwise than for the benefit of:

(*a*)   persons of a class defined by reference to employment in a particular trade, or profession (or employment by, or office with, a body carrying on a trade profession or undertaking); or

(*b*)   persons of a class defined by reference to marriage or relationship to (or dependence on) persons of such a class.

[*IHTA 1984, s 86(1)*].

It is acceptable to also include a power to apply the property for charitable purposes. Where the class is defined by reference to employment with a particular body the class must either comprise all or most of the employees and directors of that body or the trust must hold its property for the purpose of an approved profit sharing scheme within **Chapter 16** above. [*IHTA 1984, s 86(2), (3)*].

19.53   A transfer of property by a close company to such an employee trust is not a transfer of value if the beneficiaries include all or most of the directors and employees of that company – or if preferred of the company and any one or more of its subsidiaries. [*IHTA 1984, s 13(1)*]. The exemption is lost if the trust permits any of the property to be applied at any time (including after the trust ceases to qualify as an employee trust) for the benefit of a participator in the company (other than one owning less than five per cent), a participator in another close company that made a transfer to the same trust which was exempt under *section 13*, a person who was a participator in the company or such company at any time within the previous ten years, or a connected person of one of the above. A power to pay income to a participator will not lose the relief though. Nor will the relief be lost if the trust is an approved profit sharing scheme within **Chapter 16**. [*IHTA 1984, s 13*].

19.54   A transfer of shares or securities by an individual to an employee trust (within *IHTA 1984, s 86(1)*) is also exempt provided that the potential beneficiaries include all or most of the directors and employees of the company (subject to the exclusion for participators described at **19.53**). At the date of the transfer (or at some time within the following 12 months) the trustees must hold over half of the ordinary shares in the company and have powers of voting on all questions affecting the company as a whole which, if exercised, would yield a majority of the votes capable of being exercised (and there must be no power under which these conditions could cease to be exercised without the consent of the trustees). If the company has shares or securities of a class which confers powers of voting only on the question of a winding up and/or questions primarily affecting shares or securities of that class those shares can be ignored in applying the control test. [*IHTA 1984, s 28*]. This relief is intended to allow a shareholder to transfer a controlling interest in the company to an employee trust. A similar exemption from the tax charge on property ceasing to be held on discretionary trust applies where a trust owning shares or securities of a company becomes an employee trust within *IHTA 1984, s 86(1)*. The above conditions again apply. [*IHTA 1984, s 75*].

19.55 Where property is held in an employee trust (within *IHTA 1984, s 86(1)*) all the property in treated as comprised in a single settlement (even if it was settled by different settlors at different times) and an interest in possession is less than five per cent of the assets will not trigger IHT charges. [*IHTA 1984, s 86(4)*]. If assets are transferred from one employee trust to another they are treated for IHT purposes as remaining in the first trust. This also applies to an indirect transfer provided the gap during which the assets are not comprised in an employee trust does not exceed one month. [*IHTA 1984, s 86(5)*]. If the trust ceases to qualify as an employee trust an IHT charge arises on the whole of the settled property at a special rate, dependent on how long the property has been in the trust. This reaches a maximum of 30 per cent where the property has been in the trust for 50 years or more. [*IHTA 1984, s 72(2)(a), (5)*]. This special charge also arises on a distribution by the trust to a person who has directly or indirectly provided property to it (unless it did not exceed £1,000 in any one year) or if the beneficiary is an employee of a close company to a participator owning five per cent or more of the company, or to a person who bought his interest in the settlement or to a connected person of such people. [*IHTA 1984, s 72(2)(b), (3)*]. It also applies if the trustees make any other disposition which reduces the value of the settled property. [*IHTA 1984, s 72(2)(c)*]. There is an exemption for the appropriation of shares under an approved profit sharing scheme. [*IHTA 1984, s 72(4)*].

19.56 Where a person (the employer) makes an 'employee benefit contribution' to an employee benefit trust and a deduction would otherwise be allowed for that contribution in computing his taxable profits the deduction is allowable only to the extent that:

(*a*)   during the accounting period in question, or within nine months after it, qualifying benefits are provided (or qualifying expenses paid) out of the contributions; or

(*b*)   where the making of the contributions is itself the provision of qualifying benefits, the contributions are made during the accounting period or within nine months thereafter.

[*CTA 2009, s 1290; Income Tax (Trading and Other Income) Act 2005 (ITTOIA 2005), s 38*].

19.57   For this purpose a person makes an employee benefit contribution if, as a result of any act or omission, property is held (or can be used) under an employee benefit scheme, or there is an increase in the total value of property that is so held or can be so used (or a reduction in any liabilities under an employee benefit scheme). [*CTA 2009, s 1291(1)*]. An employee benefit scheme (EBS) means 'a trust, scheme or other arrangement for the benefit of persons who are, or include, employees of the employer'. [*CTA 2009, s 1291(2)* formerly *Finance Act 2003 (FA 2003), Sch 24, para 9(1); ITTOIA 2005, s 39(2)*]. This makes clear that the restriction cannot be avoided by declaring a trust over assets which the company already controls, such as funds held in a bank account. It also makes clear that any other action which has the effect of creating or enhancing the value of employee benefit contributions are subject to these anti-avoidance rules (*Explanatory Notes to Finance Bill 2007*).

19.58   Qualifying benefits are provided where there is a payment of money or transfer of assets (other than by way of loan) that either:

(*a*)   gives rise to both an income tax charge (either on the recipient or someone else) under *ITEPA 2003*, and to an NIC charge;

(*b*)   would have given rise to such charges if the duties of the employment in respect of which the payment was made were performed in the UK and the person in respect of whose employment it was made fulfilled the conditions of residence to attract NIC (ie the only reason that an income tax and NIC charge do not arise is because the employee is resident or ordinarily resident outside the UK); or

(*c*)   is made in connection with the termination of the recipient's employment with the employer.

[*CTA 2009, s 1292*]. Where the qualifying benefit takes the form of the payment of money it is treated as provided at the time that the money is treated as received under *ITEPA 2003, s 18* (see **2.51**). [*CTA 2009, s 1293(1); ITTOIA 2005, s 41*].

19.59   Qualifying expenses include any expenses of a scheme manager (prior to 21 March 2007 of the third party) (other than the provision of benefits to employees of the employer) in operating the employee benefit scheme in question but cannot include expenses that, if they had been incurred by the employer, would not be deductible by the employer for tax purposes (in any accounting period). A scheme manager means a person who administers an employee benefit scheme (acting in that capacity). [*CTA 2009, s 1296(1); ITTOIA 2005, ss 41, 44(1)*].

19.60   If the provision of a qualifying benefit takes the form of a transfer of an asset to the employee the amount provided is the aggregate of the amount (if any) expended on the asset by the scheme manager (formerly the third party) and, if the asset was transferred to the scheme manager (prior to 21 March 2007, to the third party) by the employer, the amount that would have been deductible by the employer on making the transfer if *Schedule 24* had not been enacted. [*CTA 2009, s 1293(2); ITTOIA 2005, s 41*].

19.61   When the deduction is restricted the relief is not lost. The deduction can be claimed in a subsequent period (or periods) in which qualifying benefits (but curiously not qualifying expenses) are paid. [*CTA 2009, s 1294; ITTOIA*

2005, s 42]. Qualifying benefits provided (or qualifying expenses paid) by the scheme manager (formerly the third party) after the recipient of an employee benefit contribution are deemed to be provided or paid out of that contribution up to the amount of the contribution (as reduced by the amount of any benefits or expenses previously paid or provided in the accounting period or within nine months thereafter). [*CTA 2009, s 1294; ITTOIA 2005 s 42*]. This appears to deny relief completely to the extent that the scheme manager makes a payment in anticipation of receiving the employee benefit contribution before he receives it.

19.62 If the employer's tax computations are submitted before the end of the nine month period a deduction can be claimed only for qualifying benefits or expenses paid before the computations are submitted, and relief for later payments within the nine month period is claimed by amending the computations. [*CTA 2009, s 1295; ITTOIA 2005, s 43*]. Obviously if it is believed that subsequent payments will be made it is likely to make more sense in most cases to delay submitting the computations until the nine-month period has expired.

19.63 The restriction does not apply to a payment or transfer which constitutes:

(*a*) the consideration for goods or services provided in the course of a trade or profession;

(*b*) contributions under an approved retirement benefit scheme;

(*c*) contributions under an approved personal pension scheme;

(*d*) contributions under an accident benefit scheme (ie an employee benefit scheme under which benefits can be provided only by reason of a person's disablement or death caused by an event occurring during his services as an employee of the employer);

(*e*) contributions to a SIP;

(*f*) a payment which attracts corporation tax relief under *FA 2003,Sch 23*.

[*CTA 2009, s 1290(4); ITTOIA 2005, s 38(4)*].

19.64 These provisions effectively both nullify for the future the decision in *Dextra Accessories* (see **19.48**) and override the accounting treatment permitted by UK GAAP. It should particularly be noted that if the employee benefit scheme makes a payment that is neither a qualifying benefit nor a qualifying expense no deduction will ever be obtained by the employer for that part of the contributions even if the employer would have obtained a deduction had he made the payment direct. Accordingly such a scheme should not in future make charitable donations or payments that do not relate to an identifiable employee and so do not attract an income tax charge as earnings of anyone.

19.65 In recent years HMRC have actively sought to discourage the use of EBTs. They set out their interpretation of the inheritance tax consequences in Revenue & Customs Brief 18/11. This includes a warning that where a close company makes a payment to an EBT an inheritance tax charge arises under *IHTA 1994, s 94* unless it is excluded from being a transfer of value under *IHTA 1984, s 10* (transactions not intended ot transfer gratuitous value), *section 12* (dispositions qualifying for a tax deduction) or *section 13* (disposition by close company for the benefit of employees). They go on to say that in their view *section 10* is not met 'if there is the slightest possibility of gratuitous intent' at the date the contribution is made; that the relieving effect of *section 12* 'cannot be given provisionally while waiting to see whether the contribution will become allowable for corporation tax purposes'; and that *s 13* cannot apply unless the participators in the company and any person connected with them are excluded from benefit under the terms of the EBT. The HMRC interpretation is not generally accepted but the uncertainty it causes is sufficient to deter most people from setting up new EBTs.

19.66 In November 2009, HMRC said that in their view 'at the time the funds are allocated [by the EBT] to the employee or his/her beneficiaries, those funds become earnings on which PAYE and NICs are due and should be accounted for by the employer. In addition HMRC's view is that an Inheritance Tax charge may arise on the participators of a close company.' (Spotlight 5). They followed this up in 2011 by offering a 'settlement opportunity' to EBTs, pointing out that the proposed disguised remuneration legislation was being introduced to 'put beyond doubt that such arrangements or schemes [ie EBTs] do not work'. However the Upper Tribunal decision in the taxpayer's favour in *Murray Group Holdings* (see **19.45A**) suggests that at least in some cases HMRC's view may well be incorrect.

Employee share ownership trusts (obsolete)

19.67 Curiously at one stage the government sought to encourage the setting up of such vehicles, although only on an all-employee basis. The *FA 1989* introduced a new form of employee incentive; the employee share ownership trust or ESOT (renamed QUEST – qualifying share trusts – immediately prior to their abolition). The Chancellor of the day, however, felt that some employers were deterred from using EBTs because of uncertainties as to the tax treatment. Whether a complex statutory code was likely to encourage the use of such trusts is open to question. The 1989 legislation has not been included in *ITEPA 2003* but it has been retained on the statute book. However as tax relief for contributions ot a statutory ESOT was withdrawn in relation to contributions after 31 December 2002 there is no longer any point in using such a trust. [*FA 2003, s 142*].

19.68 The ESOT legislation granted a tax deduction for a contribution by a UK resident company to a qualifying ESOT at a time when the company (or a company under its control within *s 840*) had employees who were eligible to benefit under the ESOT – provided that before the end of the 'expenditure period' the contribution is expended by the trustee for a 'qualifying purpose' and a claim for relief was made before the end of the 'claim period'. [*FA 1989, s 67(1)–(3)*]. As indicated earlier this statutory tax relief ceased to apply from 31 December 2002 – or in some cases a little later, it is withdrawn for payments during accounting periods beginning after that date. [*FA 2003, s 142*]. That does not mean that contributions to an ESOT can no longer qualify for relief. It means that an employer needs to rely on general tax law to obtain a deduction. Because of the provisions outlined in paras **19.54** onwards, which delay relief for the employer until the benefits are actually paid, the effect of general tax law will in most cases be to defer the relief.

19.69   The contribution was treated as a deduction in computing the company's trading profit, or as management expenses if it was an investment company. [*FA 1989, s 67(2)*]. If it was neither, no tax relief was due. It appears that the contribution could not be in kind, but had to be in money, as it is stated in *FA 1989, s 67(1)(a)* that the *section* applies where the company 'expends a sum in making a payment by way of contribution'. The conditions that must be satisfied to constitute a qualifying ESOT are considered at **19.94** below.

19.70   An ESOT must be set up by a company (called the founding company) for the benefit of its employees and employees of members of its group. A non-UK resident company cannot set up a qualifying ESOT. Nor could it obtain a deduction for a payment to an ESOT under these special provisions even if it was liable to corporation tax because it was carrying on a trade in the UK. Most people consider that the 1989 legislation was unnecessary as payments to an employee share trust qualify for tax relief under general principles, as being wholly and exclusively for the purpose of the company's trade and not for a capital purpose. The legislation does not displace the pre-existing law so a non-UK company might well be able to obtain a deduction under general principles. A qualifying ESOT will not be able to rely on general principles where the legislation is unfavourable. It will obviously be bound by the specific legislative provisions. In practice few companies have used statutory ESOTs because these are very restrictive. Anyone considering using one ought first to consider whether its objective might be better met by a SIP (see **Chapter 15**).

19.71   A number of expressions used in **19.68** above call for explanation. The 'expenditure period' is the nine months following the end of the period of account in which the contribution was charged as an expense. [*FA 1989, s 67(5)*]. As the trustees had from the date they receive the contribution to the end of the expenditure period to expend the money this allowed them a period of between nine and 21 months (longer if the period of account exceeded a year) depending on when in the period of account the contribution was made. If the money was not spent in this period, or was spent other than for a qualifying purpose, the company could not deduct the contribution (or so much of it as had not been spent).

Qualifying purposes

19.72   There are five 'qualifying purposes' on which the ESOT can expend its funds:

(*a*)   the acquisition of shares in the founding company;

(*b*)   the repayment of sums borrowed;

(*c*)   the payment of interest on sums borrowed;

(*d*)   the payment of any sum to a beneficiary (ie a qualifying employee); and

(*e*)   the meeting of expenses.

[*FA 1989, s 67(4)*].

Deemed order in which receipts spent

19.73   If it is necessary to determine what funds are spent (eg because the ESOT receives contributions from more than one company and does not spend them all, or spends some for a non-qualifying purpose) contributions must be regarded as having been spent in the order in which they are received by the trustees. [*FA 1989, s 67(7)*]. *Section 67* does not say whether other income, such as bank deposit interest, for instance, is to be treated as spent in the same way in priority to contributions from participating employers or after them, but *FA 1989, Sch 5, para 6* requires the rules of the ESOT to provide that all receipts must be treated as spent in the order that they are received.

Time limit on claim

19.74   The relief had to be claimed within the 'claim period', ie within two years after the end of the period in which the contribution was charged as an expense by the company.

19.75   Although an ESOT can only purchase shares in the founding company, it is possible for it to hold debentures or similar securities of the company if it receives these on a share exchange or company reorganisation, or as a result of a scrip or rights issue. Accordingly, the Act uses the expression 'securities' rather than shares, and defines this as meaning shares and debentures. [*FA 1989, s 69(12)*]. References below to securities have the same meaning.

Charges to tax

19.76   Although the company obtained a deduction, a charge to tax can be made on the trustees in certain circumstances to withdraw this relief. This charge is intended to claw back the tax relief given to the company if the funds are used for a non-qualifying purpose. If the trustees do not pay it the tax can be collected from the company. The 'chargeable events' that trigger a tax charge are as follows:

(*a*)   A transfer of securities by the trustees, unless it is a qualifying transfer. [*FA 1989, s 69(1)(a)*]. Subject to (*b*) below, a transfer to a beneficiary of the ESOT is a qualifying transfer and does not attract tax. [*FA 1989, s 69(2)*]. So is a transfer to the trustees of an approved profit sharing scheme provided that it is made for a consideration which is not less than the price the shares might reasonably be expected to fetch on a sale in the open market. [*FA 1989, s 69(3)*]. It would probably be a breach of trust for the trustees of the profit sharing scheme to pay more than the market price, so in practice such a transfer would have to take place at market value. This will, for example, allow a listed company to fund an ESOT to buy in shares on the open market which can be passed on in due course to the company's profit sharing scheme, although if the profit sharing scheme has the necessary funds there is no reason why it should not itself buy shares in the open market. A disposal in exchange for shares is also a qualifying transfer provided that it qualifies for roll-over relief under *TCGA 1992, s 135*. [*Finance (No 2) Act 1992 (F(No 2)A 1992), s 36*]. A transfer is also a qualifying transfer if it is a transfer of relevant shares made to the trustees of a SIP (see **Chapter 15**) provided that any consideration received does not exceed the market value of the shares. [*FA 1989, s 69(3AA)*]. Where the trustees dispose of part of a holding of shares (whether or not by way of a qualifying transfer) the 'relevant shares' in the holding must be treated as disposed of before other shares. [*FA 1989, s 69(3AB)*]. Relevant shares for this purpose means shares held by the trustees at midnight on 26 November 2002 or shares purchased by them out of money held in a bank or building society account at that time (treating all payments (for anything) by the trustees after that time as coming first out of such money. [*FA 1989, s 69 (3AC), (3AD)*].

(*b*)   A transfer of shares (or debentures) by the trustees to a beneficiary of the ESOT if the transfer is not made on qualifying terms. [*FA 1989, s 69(1) (b)*]. A transfer is made on qualifying terms only if:

(i)   all the shares transferred at the same time are transferred on similar terms (except where they are transferred under an approved savings-related share option scheme);

(ii)   shares have been offered to everyone who is a beneficiary of the ESOT (other than those who are beneficiaries only by virtue of an approved savings-related share option scheme) at the time the transfer is made; and

(iii)   shares are transferred to all such beneficiaries who have accepted the offer.

[*FA 1989, s 69(4)*].

It will be seen that this prevents an ESOT transferring shares to selected employees only, without triggering a tax charge – or rather without triggering the charge to claw back the company's tax relief, as the trustees will have a capital gains tax charge even where the transfer to beneficiaries is on qualifying terms, except where the concession discussed at **19.88** below applies. For the purposes of condition (i) it is permissible to allocate shares according to levels of remuneration, length of service or similar factors. [*FA 1989, s 69(6)*]. In the case of a large company it will be very difficult to meet condition (ii) if it is interpreted literally, as it does not allow for the possibility of people becoming eligible beneficiaries between the date a decision to pass shares to beneficiaries is made and the date that the transfer actually takes place.

A transfer from an ESOT established after 28 April 1996 is also made on qualifying terms if it is made to a person exercising an option under an approved savings-related share option scheme established by the company which established the ESOT (or a company controlled by it), the option is exercised in accordance with that scheme, and the consideration for the transfer is payable to the trustees. [*FA 1989, s 69(4ZA)*]. This allows the trustees to grant options for an employee to buy his shares from the ESOT rather than the employing company, so giving greater flexibility. Such options will not be granted under the company's savings-related share option scheme itself. Membership of that scheme is merely a test of eligibility. However, the legislation requires the ESOT to grant options in accordance with the requirement of *ITEPA 2003, Sch 3*], ie to mirror what would be required under an approved scheme (see **19.94**(*h*)).

(*c*) The retention of shares or debentures by the trustees for more than 20 years (seven years where the trust was established before 3 May 1994). [*FA 1989, s 69(1)(c) and 4A*]. For this purpose shares or debentures are treated as disposed of by the trustees in the order that they acquire them. [*FA 1989, s 69(7)*]. The expiration of seven years from the time of acquisition of the shares will trigger the tax charge. The concept is to discourage the use of an ESOT to hold shares for long periods, perhaps so as to have a block of shares held in friendly hands.

(*d*) The expenditure of any sum by the trustees other than for a qualifying purpose. [*FA 1989, s 69(1)(d)*]. The qualifying purposes are the same as those specified in **19.72** above. [*FA 1989, ss 67(4), 69(5)*]. In applying the above rules the trustees of the ESOT acquire shares or debentures when they become entitled to them, with the exceptions that:

(i) if they are new shares or debentures obtained on a share exchange [*TCGA 1992, s 135(1)*] or a reorganisation [*TCGA 1992, s 126*] which constitutes a company reorganisation for capital gains tax purposes they are treated as having been acquired at the time the original securities were acquired [*FA 1989, s 69(9)*]; and

(ii) if the trustees agree to take a transfer of shares or debentures they are treated as having become entitled to them at the date of the agreement, not the later date of transfer. [*FA 1989, s 69(10)*].

Similarly they transfer shares to another person when that other person becomes entitled to them (or if earlier, when they agree to make the transfer), and retain shares if they remain entitled to them. [*FA 1989, s 69(8), (11)*].

(*e*) If after 27 July 2000 the trustees make a qualifying transfer within *s 69(3AA)* (see (*a*) above) for a consideration and they do not expend the entire consideration for one or more qualifying purposes within nine months after the end of the period of account (of the grantor company) in which the qualifying transfer took place. [*FA 1989, s 69(1)(e) and 69(5A)* inserted by *Finance Act 2000 (FA 2000), s 55*].

Meaning of chargeable amount

19.77 Where the chargeable event is one of those described in heads (*a*)–(*c*) at **19.76** above, and the transaction constitutes a disposal of the shares by the trustees for capital gains tax purposes, the amount on which this special tax charge is assessed, the 'chargeable amount', is the sums allowable under *TCGA 1992, s 38(1)(a), (b)*, ie the cost of the shares (including acquisition costs) plus any enhancement expenditure. If the chargeable event is not a disposal for capital gains tax purposes the chargeable amount is the sum that would have been allowable under *s 38(1)(a), (b)* had it constituted such a disposal. [*FA 1989, s 70(1), (2)*]. *FA 1989, s 72* (see **19.88** below) can impose an overriding limit on the chargeable amount. [*FA 1989, s 72(2)(c)*].

19.78   If the chargeable event is the expenditure of money for a non-qualifying purpose (ie within head (*d*) at **19.76** above) the chargeable amount is the sum so spent. [*FA 1989, s 70(3)*].

19.79   If the chargeable event is the failure to invest money received from a *FA 2000* qualifying ESOP (ie within head (*e*) at **19.76** above) the chargeable amount is the part of that consideration not used for a qualifying purpose within nine months after the end of the period of account. [*FA 1989, s 70(4)* inserted by *FA 2000, s 55(6)*].

19.80   The tax charge is imposed by treating the trustees as receiving on the occurrence of a chargeable event annual profits or gains taxable as miscellaneous income for the year of assessment in which the event occurs equal to the chargeable amount. [*FA 1989, s 68(1), (2)*]. Tax is chargeable at the rate applicable to trusts, thus giving, on current rates, a charge at 34 per cent. [*FA 1989, s 68(2)(c)*].

Late payment of tax

19.81   If any part of the tax is not paid by the trustees within six months from the date on which assessment becomes final and conclusive, a notice of liability to tax can be served on the founding company, or on any other company that has paid a sum to the trustees and obtained a tax deduction for it, and the unpaid tax (together with any accrued interest and interest accruing after the service of the notice of liability) then becomes payable by that company instead of by the trustees. [*FA 1989, s 68(3), (4), (6), (7)*]. If the company does not pay the full amount due within three months from the date of service of the notice of liability the amount outstanding again becomes recoverable from the trustees although HMRC still have a continuing right to recover it instead from the company. [*FA 1989, s 68(5)*].

Potential future liability to tax

19.82   It should be noted that once a company has obtained a deduction for a contribution to an ESOT, however small that contribution may be, it is thereafter potentially liable for all tax payable by the trustees at any time in the future even though that tax may arise in relation to funds deriving from some other company and may far exceed the contributions that the unfortunate company made to the ESOT. Anyone purchasing a company that has contributed to an ESOT needs to be aware of this risk. As it is an open-ended and unquantifiable commitment an indemnity from the vendor against such tax may not be a sufficient protection. It may be that the purchaser should consider requiring the ESOT trust to be wound up as that seems to be the only way to limit the risk.

Borrowing by the ESOT

19.83   If a chargeable event (within **19.76** above) (called 'the initial chargeable event') occurs in relation to an ESOT at a time when any amount borrowed by the trustees is outstanding, and it is one to which *FA 1989, s 72(2)(b)* (see **19.85** below) applies (ie the chargeable amount was restricted), a further chargeable event is deemed to occur at the end of the year of assessment in which any part of the borrowing is repaid. [*FA 1989, s 71(1)–(3)*]. The chargeable amount on that further chargeable event is the amount of the loan repayments in the year of assessment. [*FA 1989, s 71(5)*]. The tax consequences are the same as for an actual chargeable event, ie there is a charge under the miscellaneous income provisions at 45 per cent. [*FA 1989, s 71(4)*].

19.84   Although, on the face of it, this creates a double charge – once when the chargeable event occurs and again when the loan is repaid – this is not in fact the case as *FA 1989, s 72* (which is considered at **19.88** below) puts a limit on the total sums that can be treated as chargeable amounts. The intention of *FA 1989, s 71* is to ensure that a tax charge cannot be avoided by the ESOT borrowing funds, using them to make non-qualifying transfers, etc., and then receiving contributions from the employer company to repay the borrowing. It effectively treats the chargeable event as occurring when the borrowing is repaid only if a charge cannot be made when the actual non-qualifying transfer or payment takes place.

19.85   If *FA 1989, s 72(2)(b)* had effect at the time of the initial chargeable event the chargeable amount on the deemed further chargeable event is the smaller of:

(*a*)   the aggregate of the loan repayments made in the year of assessment; and

(*b*)   the result of the formula A minus B minus C, where:

A = the sum which would be the chargeable amount for the initial chargeable event apart from *s 72(2)*,

B = the chargeable amount for the initial chargeable event (ie applying *s 72(2)*), and

C = an amount equal to the aggregate of the chargeable amounts for any prior chargeable events, ie any loan repayments in earlier years of assessment but subsequent to the initial chargeable event.

[*FA 1989, s 71(6)–(8)*].

19.86   If, after the occurrence of a further chargeable event (within **19.85** above), a second chargeable event occurs in circumstances within *FA 1989, s 71(1)* (so that there is potentially a second 'further chargeable event') at a time when the borrowing at **19.83** above is still outstanding, that borrowing (ie that was outstanding at the time of the first event) is ignored to determine whether a deemed further chargeable event can arise in relation to that second event. In other words, only any additional borrowing since the time of the first chargeable event will generate a charge under *s 71*. [*FA 1989, s 71(9)*].

19.87 In ascertaining what borrowings are repaid, amounts borrowed earlier (even, apparently, if from a different lender) must be treated as repaid before later borrowings. [*FA 1989, s 71(10)*].

Limit on chargeable amounts

19.88 Where a chargeable event within *FA 1989, s 69* (see **19.76** above) or a deemed further chargeable event within *FA 1989, s 71* (see **19.83** above) occurs:

(*a*)   the amount which would otherwise be the chargeable amount must be aggregated with the chargeable amounts for all prior chargeable events; and

(*b*)   if such aggregate amount exceeds 'the deductible amount' the chargeable amount on that event must be reduced by that excess.

[*FA 1989, s 72(1), (2)*].

For the purpose of head (*b*) above, the deductible amount is the total of all sums received by the trustees before the occurrence of the event in question which either:

(i)   has qualified for a deduction under *FA 1989, s 67(2)* (see **17.24** above) by the company that paid it; or

(ii)   would qualify for a deduction if a claim for a relief were made immediately before the occurrence of that event.

[*FA 1989, s 72(3), (4)*].

19.89 The purpose of *FA 1989, s 72* is to limit the total amounts that can be taxable on the trustees to the sums which have qualified for a deduction by the company or companies that have made contributions to the ESOT. This test is looked at over the entire life of the ESOT.

Tax position of the ESOT

19.90 The legislation does not confer any tax exemption on the ESOT itself. The trustees will be liable to income tax on their investment income, such as dividends from the shares or bank deposit interest, in the normal way. The trustees will also be liable to capital gains tax when they transfer shares to beneficiaries, or if they make any non-qualifying transfers of shares. By concession HMRC do not charge the trustees to capital gains tax on a transfer of assets to a beneficiary for no consideration if the employee is liable to income tax on the full market value of the assets transferred (*IR Press Release*

5 December 1990). This concession applies even if the employee trust is not a qualifying ESOT, provided that it qualifies as a trust for the benefit of employees for inheritance tax purposes under *IHTA 1984, s 86* (see **19.54**) (or would do but for *section 86(3)*) and that the employee does not own more than five per cent of the company (within *IHTA 1984, s 28(4)–(6)*).

19.91   A company that contributes funds to the ESOT is not liable for the tax on such liabilities of the trustees. It can only be called upon to pay the tax arising in relation to chargeable events.

19.92   Curiously, the payment of tax does not seem to be a qualifying purpose. The reason is probably because there is no need to pay such tax out of funds provided by the company as the existence of the tax liability predicates the trustees themselves having generated either income or capital gains out of which the tax can be met. Unfortunately, *FA 1989, Sch 5, para 9* states that the trust deed must require all sums received by the trustees (not merely contributions from the company) to be expended only for qualifying purposes. It may be that the draftsman considered that tax can qualify as an expense of the trustees.

Tax position of the beneficiary

19.93   The legislation does not confer any tax exemption on the beneficiary. The value of shares he receives from the ESOT will constitute emoluments in the normal way. This is why the government envisages that an ESOT might be combined with an approved profit sharing scheme. If the beneficiary receives shares under the profit sharing scheme, the company should obtain a corporation tax deduction for such payments in any event, so, if a company has an approved profit sharing scheme, it is difficult to see why it should want an ESOT as well. If the company's profits fluctuate, a combination of the two types of scheme will enable funds to be set aside in good years in excess of the profit sharing scheme limits so that the ESOT can 'warehouse' shares which can be appropriated to beneficiaries of the profit sharing scheme in years when the company is less able to make payments to that scheme.

Qualifying conditions

19.94   A trust will be a qualifying ESOT at the time it is established if it satisfies the following conditions. [*FA 1989, Sch 5, para 1*]. If a trust established before 4 May 1994 is a qualifying ESOT at the time it is established it will continue to be an ESOT throughout its life, but will not be a qualifying ESOT during any period that condition (*d*) below is not met. [*FA 1989, Sch 5, para 12, 13*]. Similarly, one established after 3 May 1994 will continue to be an ESOT throughout its life other than for any period during which all of the conditions about trustees are not met. [*FA 1989, Sch 5, para 12A*]. The distinction seems to be that once a trust is an ESOT it must comply with all the regulations governing ESOTs, but a company can obtain a corporation tax deduction for a contribution to an ESOT only if it is a qualifying ESOT at the time the contribution is made.

19.94 *Miscellaneous*

(*a*)   It must be established under a trust deed. [*FA 1989, Sch 5, para 2(1)*]. It is not possible to have an oral ESOT even though under general law it is possible to have an oral trust.

(*b*)   It must be established by a company (the founding company) which at the time is resident in the UK and is not under the control of another company [*FA 1989, Sch 5, para 2(2)*], ie an ESOT cannot be set up by a subsidiary; it must be established by the holding company of a group. An ESOT cannot be established for the employees of a UK branch of an overseas company or even for those of a UK subsidiary of such a company. In the light of the substantial amount of investment by overseas companies in the UK in recent years this seems a somewhat strange restriction as it prevents large numbers of employees from being able to participate.

(*c*)   The trust deed must provide for the establishment of a body of trustees, must appoint the initial trustees, and must contain rules for the retirement and removal of trustees and the appointment or replacement of additional trustees. [*FA 1989, Sch 5, para 3(1), (2)*]. If the trustee is to be a trust company the deed must provide that only such a company can be the trustee. [*FA 1989, Sch 5, para 3C*].

(*d*)   The trust deed must provide either that:

   (i)   there must be at least three trustees all of whom must be UK residents; or

   (ii)   the trustee must be a company controlled by the founding company;

   and in the case of individual trustees that either (*e*) or (*f*) below must apply.

(*e*)   In the case of individual trustees either:

   (i)   the trustees must include one person who is a trust corporation, a solicitor, or a member of such other professional body as HMRC may allow (which is likely to include all the main UK accountancy bodies);

   (ii)   most of the trustees must be persons who are not, and never have been, directors of the founding company or any other UK resident company that at the time is controlled by the founding company;

   (iii)   most of the trustees must be employees of the founding company (or of another UK resident company controlled by the founding company) who do not have a material interest in any of such companies and have never had such an interest; and

   (iv)   the trustees within (iii) above must have been selected (before being appointed) by a majority of the employees falling within the founding company's group (ie that company and all UK resident companies controlled by it at that time) at the time of the selection, or by persons elected to represent those employees.

[*FA 1989, Sch 5, para 3(3), (4)*]; or

(*f*)   (i)   the trustees must include at least one professional trustee and two non-professional ones;

      (ii)   at least half of the non-professional trustees must have been selected (by a majority of votes, or by elected representatives of the employees) by all of the employees of the founding company's group other than any having a material interest in the company; and

      (iii)   such trustees must be employees of the founding company (or of another group member) who do not have a material interest in the company. [*FA 1989, Sch 5, para 3B(4), (7), (8)* inserted by *Finance Act 1994 (FA 1994), Sch 13, para 3*].

Trusts established before 3 May 1994 had to comply with head (*e*) (i). Even after that date a trust company can be used only if the board of directors satisfies the test at (*f*)(i) above with the substitution of a reference to the directors for the trustees. [*Sch 5, para 3C*].

For the purpose of (*f*)(i) a professional trustee means a trust corporation, a solicitor, or a member of any other professional body that HMRC may designate, who has been selected by (and only by) the non-professional trustees (trustees designate in the case of the initial appointment), and who is not a director or employee of the founding company. [*Sch 5, para 3B(5), (6)*].

For the purpose of (*e*)(iii) and (*f*)(iii) above, a person has a material interest in a company if he (with his associates), or any one or more associates of his:

(A)   is the beneficial owner of, or able to control (directly or indirectly) more than five per cent of the ordinary share capital of the company; or

(B)   possesses, or is entitled to acquire, such rights as would in the event of a winding up or in any other circumstances give an entitlement to receive more than five per cent of the assets which would then be available for distribution among the participators.

[*FA 1989, Sch 5, para 16(1)*].

The definition of control in *section 840* and that of participator in *section 417* apply. [*FA 1989, Sch 5, para 16(2)*]. An associate of a person means:

(i)   any relative (ie spouse, parent or remoter forebear, child or remoter issue, or brother or sister) of that person;

(ii)   a partner of that person;

(iii)   the trustees of any settlement in relation to which the person is a settlor (or any relative of his, living or dead, is or was a settlor);

(iv)   where the person is interested in any shares or obligations of the company which are subject to any trust (or are part of the estate of a deceased person):

      (1)   the trustees of the settlement (or the personal representatives of the deceased), and

    (2)   if that person is a company, any other company that is interested in those shares or obligations.

[ICTA 1988, s 417(3), (4), FA 1989, Sch 5, para 16(2)(a)].

It should be noted that the majority of the trustees must be elected by the employees or their representatives, eg their trade union. The idea is that the employees, not the directors or senior executives, should control the votes attaching to the shares from time to time held by the ESOT. One of the trustees must be a trust corporation or a professional person. HMRC will require him to ensure that the trust operates properly and any aggrieved employees will probably look to him for recompense as the employee trustees (the majority) might not be expected to have the necessary expertise. This does not appear to be an enviable role for a professional person to accept!

(*g*)   The trust deed must provide that a person is a beneficiary at a particular time (the relevant time) if:

    (i)   at that time he is an employee or director of a company which falls within the founding company's group;

    (ii)   at each given time in (ie throughout) a qualifying period he was an employee or director of a company falling within the founding company's group; and

    (iii)   in the case of a director at that given time he worked at the rate of at least 20 hours a week (ignoring holidays and sickness).

[FA 1989, Sch 5, para 4(2)].

A qualifying period for this purpose is a period of up to five years which is specified in the trust deed and which ends at the relevant time. *[FA 1989, Sch 5, para 4(5)].* In other words, the founding company can choose what qualifying period of service is needed before a person can be a beneficiary, but this cannot be more than five years. A company falls within the founding company's group at a particular time if it is UK resident at that time and either it is the founding company or it is controlled by the founding company (within *section 840*). *[FA 1989, Sch 5, para 4(9)].* It should be noted that for the purpose of (ii) the company needs to meet these tests throughout the qualifying period. For example, if the company selects a qualifying period of five years, an employee of a company purchased by the founding company within the five years prior to the relevant time cannot be a beneficiary at the relevant time – even though he may have worked for his employer company for over five years.

(*h*)   The deed can allow a person to be a beneficiary at a given time if at that time he is eligible to participate in an approved savings-related share option scheme established by a company within the founding company's group. The deed must provide that the trustees of the ESOT must conform with the *ICTA 1988, Sch 9* requirements in relation to such a beneficiary.

[FA 1989, Sch 5, para 4(2A), (2B)].

(i) The deed can allow a person to be a beneficiary at a particular time (the relevant time) if:

(1) he was an employee or director of a company in the founding company's group throughout a qualifying period, and

(2) he ceased to be such an employee or director, or the company left the group, less than 18 months before the relevant time.

[*FA 1989, Sch 5, para 4(3)*].

A qualifying period in this case means a period equal in length to that adopted under head (*g*), above, but which ends when the person ceased to be an employer or the company left the group. [*FA 1989, Sch 5, para 4(3)*].

In other words, it is permissible (but, unlike with existing employees, not mandatory) to include ex-employees who ceased to be employed by the group within the previous 18 months provided that they qualified as beneficiaries at the date the employment ceased or the employing company left the group. The deed can also allow a charity to be a beneficiary but only as a long-stop, ie if there are no qualifying employees or directors in existence and the ESOT is in consequence being wound up. [*FA 1989, Sch 5, para 4(4)*]. Subject to this the deed must not permit any person not falling within heads (*g*) or (*h*) to be a beneficiary. [*FA 1989, Sch 5, para 4(7)*]. It should be particularly noted that a statutory ESOT must include all employees as beneficiaries including part-time employees (but not part-time directors) with more than five years' service. It can if it wishes include those with shorter service, and can include pensioners and other ex-employees but only for the first 18 months after their employment ceases. A non-statutory employee trust can include all pensioners and can pick and choose which employees to include.

(*j*) The deed must provide (other than by virtue of an approved savings-related share option scheme) that a person cannot be a beneficiary at a particular time (the relevant time) if either at that time or at any time within the previous 12 months he had a material interest in the founding company. [*FA 1989, Sch 5, para 4(8)*]. The meaning of material interest is considered in head (*f*) above.

(*k*) The functions of the trustees must be so expressed in the trust deed that it is apparent that their general functions are:

(i) to receive sums from the founding company (and other sums – by way of loan or otherwise);

(ii) to acquire securities, ie shares and debentures;

(iii) to transfer securities or money (or both) to beneficiaries;

(iv) to grant rights to acquire shares to persons who are beneficiaries;

(v) to sell securities to the trustees of approved profit sharing schemes at open market value; and

    (vi)   pending transfer, to retain securities and to manage them (whether by exercising voting right or otherwise).

[*FA 1989, Sch 5, para 5*].

(*l*)   The deed must require all sums received by the trustees:

    (i)   to be expended within nine months from the day the sum is received (except where it is received from the founding company or a company under its control, when it must be expended within nine months from the end of the period of account in which the sum is charged as an expense);

    (ii)   to be expended only for qualifying purposes (as listed in **19.72** above);

    (iii) whilst retained by the trustees, to be kept as cash or kept in an account with a bank or building society.

[*FA 1989, Sch 5, para 6(1)–(3)*].

It must also provide that, in ascertaining whether a particular sum has been expended, sums received earlier by the trustees must be treated as expended before those received by them later. [*FA 1989, Sch 5, para 6(4)*].

(*m*) The deed must provide that where the trustees pay sums to different beneficiaries at the same time all the sums must be paid on similar terms (but the fact that terms vary according to levels of remuneration of beneficiaries, the length of their service, or similar factors does not mean that the terms are not similar). [*FA 1989, Sch 5, para 6(5), (6)*].

(*n*)   The trust deed must provide that the only securities that can be acquired by the trustees are shares in the founding company, which:

    (i)   form part of the ordinary share capital;

    (ii)   are fully paid up;

    (iii) are not redeemable; and

    (iv)   are not subject to restrictions – other than restrictions attaching to all shares of the same class or a restriction which:

        (A)   is imposed by the founding company's Articles of Association;

        (B)   requires all shares held by directors or employees of the founding company (or of any other company which it controls) to be disposed of on ceasing to be so held; and

        (C)   requires all shares acquired by other people in pursuance of rights or interests obtained by such directors or employees to be disposed of on acquisition.

[*FA 1989, Sch 5, para 7(1), (2)*].

A restriction within (iv) above must require that any disposal under it must be by way of sale for a consideration in money on terms specified in the Articles, and the Articles must provide that any person disposing of shares of the same class (whether or not a director or employee) must be required to sell them on the same terms. [*FA 1989, Sch 5, para 7(3)*].

The deed can, if desired, provide that the trustees can acquire other securities if they are issued to the trustees on a share exchange or company reorganisation which does not constitute a disposal for capital gains tax purposes. [*FA 1989, Sch 5, para 8*]. Clearly the deed ought to contain such a power.

(*o*) The deed must provide that shares in the founding company cannot be acquired by the trustees at a price in excess of their open market value. [*FA 1989, Sch 5, para 7(4)*].

(*p*) The deed must provide that shares in the founding company must not be acquired by the trustees at a time when that company is under the control (within *section 840*) [*FA 1989, Sch 5, para 15*] of another company. [*FA 1989, Sch 5, para 7(5)*].

(*q*) The trust must provide that:

(i) where the trustees transfer shares (or other securities) to a beneficiary they must do so on qualifying terms; and

(ii) the trustees must transfer all securities within 20 years from the date they acquire them (seven years if the trust was created before 3 May 1994). [*FA 1989, Sch 5, para 7(1)*].

For the purpose of (i), a transfer is made on qualifying terms only if:

(A) all the securities transferred at the same time (other than by virtue of an approved savings-related share option scheme) are transferred on similar terms (however, they may vary according to levels of remuneration, length of service or similar factors);

(B) securities have been offered to all persons who are beneficiaries (other than solely by virtue of an approved savings related share option scheme) when the transfer is made; and

(C) securities are transferred to all those beneficiaries who have accepted the offer.

[*FA 1989, Sch 5, para 9(1)–(3)*].

A transfer is also made on qualifying terms if it is made to a person exercising an option granted under an approved savings-related share option scheme established by the founding company (or a company controlled by it), the option is being exercised in accordance with the provisions of that scheme and the consideration for the transfer is payable to the trustees. [*ICTA 1988, Sch 5, para 9 (2ZA)*].

The deed must also specify that in determining whether particular securities have been transferred in accordance with the rules, securities must be treated as transferred in the order in which they were acquired. [*FA 1989, Sch 5, para 9(4)*].

(r)   The trust deed must not contain features which are not essential (or reasonably incidental) to the purpose of acquiring sums and securities, granting share options to persons who are eligible to participate in approved savings-related share option schemes, transferring shares to such persons, transferring sums and securities to employees and directors, and transferring securities to the trustees of approved profit sharing schemes. [*FA 1989, Sch 5, para 10*].

(s)   The deed must provide that the trustees acquire securities when they become entitled to them, transfer securities to another person when that person becomes entitled to them, and retain securities if they remain entitled to them. [*FA 1989, Sch 5, para 11(1)*]. If it permits trustees to acquire on a share exchange, etc., securities other than qualifying shares in the founding company (see head (*m*) above) the deed must provide that such securities must be treated as acquired when the trustees become entitled to the original shares for which they were exchanged or in respect of which they were issued. [*FA 1989, Sch 5, para 11(2)*]. The deed must also state that if the trustees agree to take (or to make) a transfer of securities, the acquisition (or disposal) takes place when the agreement is made, not when the transfer takes place. [*FA 1989, Sch 5, para 11(3)*].

Information

19.95   An Inspector of Taxes can require the trustees of an ESOT (whether a qualifying one or not) to make a return if they have at any time received (from anyone) a contribution that has qualified for a corporation tax deduction by the payer. [*FA 1989, s 73(1)*]. The request for a return must specify the information that it is to contain. This must only be information that the Inspector needs for the purposes of *FA 1989, ss 68–72* but may include information about:

(a)   sums received by the trustees, including borrowings (and the persons from whom the sums were received);

(b)   expenditure incurred by the trustees (including the purpose of the expenditure and the recipient);

(c)   assets acquired by the trustees (including the person from whom they were acquired and the consideration given by the trustees); and

(d)   transfers of assets made by the trustees (including to whom they were transferred and the consideration, if any, furnished by them).

[*FA 1989, s 73(2)–(7)*].

19.96   When a company is granted a corporation tax deduction for a contribution to an ESOT, the Inspector of Taxes must send the trustees a certificate stating:

(a)   that a deduction has been allowed; and

(b)   the amount of the deduction.

[*FA 1989, s 73(8)*].

19.97   It is somewhat unusual for HMRC to be required to provide information to taxpayers. However, the trustees need this information to determine whether the limit on the size of a chargeable amount applies (see **19.78** above).

19.98   Failure by the trustees to make a return when required to do so renders them liable to a penalty of up to £300, plus a further £60 a day after it has been declared by the court or Commissioners before whom proceedings for the penalty have commenced. [*TMA 1970, ss 73(9), 98*].

Transfers of Shares to Share Incentive Plans

19.99   *Schedule 7C* to the *TCGA 1992* grants a form of roll-over relief where shares are transferred to a SIP. SIPs are dealt with in **Chapter 15**.

19.100   It applies as where:

(*a*)   An individual or trust (ie a person other than a company, which will of course include an unapproved ESOT) (called 'the claimant') makes a disposal of shares to the SIP. [*TCGA 1992, Sch 7C, para 2(1)*].

(*b*)   Those shares can qualify as eligible shares under *ITEPA 2003, Sch 2, paras 25–33* (see **15.5**(*j*)) but as if the parts of *paragraph 27* which apply only to listed shares were omitted ie they can be awarded as plan shares to participants in the SIP. [*TCGA 1992, Sch 7C, para 2(2)*].

(*c*)   At any time in the 12 months following the date of that disposal the SIP holds for the benefit of plan beneficiaries shares in the company that constitute at least ten per cent of its ordinary share capital (within *ICTA 1988, s 832(1)*) and carry rights to at least ten per cent of any profits available for distribution to shareholders and of any assets available for distribution to shareholders in the event of a winding up. [*TCGA 1992, Sch 7C, paras 2(3), 4(2)*].

(*d*)   At all times in the period from the date of the disposal to the trustees to the date that the claimant acquires his new assets (or, if later, to the date that the ten per cent test in (*c*) above is fulfilled) there are no unauthorised arrangements under which the claimant (or a connected person) could be entitled to acquire (directly or indirectly) from the SIP trustees any shares or any interest or right deriving from shares. [*TCGA 1992, Sch 7C, paras 2(5), 4(A)*]. All arrangements are unauthorised for this purpose unless they only allow shares to be appropriated to or acquired on behalf of an individual under the plan. [*TCGA 1992, Sch 7C, para 4(5)*].

(*e*)   The claimant obtains consideration for the disposal, ie he sells the shares to the SIP rather than gifts them. [*TCGA 1992, Sch 7C, para 3(1)*].

(*f*)   At some time during the six months from the date of the disposal or, if later, the six months from the time that the SIP meets the ten per cent ownership test at (*c*) the entire consideration for the disposal is applied in acquiring assets, or an interest in assets, which:

(i)   are chargeable assets of the claimant; and

(ii)   are not shares in (or debentures of) the scheme company or another company in the same group as the scheme company.

[*TCGA 1992, Sch 7C, para 3(1), 4(3)*].

19.101   If all of the above conditions are met the claimant can claim (within two years from the date of acquisition of the replacement assets) to be treated as if he had sold the shares for a price that gives neither a gain nor a loss and as if the consideration for the replacement assets were reduced by the excess of the actual consideration over the no gain/no loss price. [*TCGA 1992, Sch 7C, para 5(1)*].

19.102   If conditions (*a*) to (*e*) above are met but the whole of the consideration is not reinvested in acquiring the replacement assets, partial relief is given if the amount not reinvested is less than the gain accruing on the disposal. [*Sch 7C, para 3(2)*]. In such a case the claim will be to reduce the gain accruing on the disposal to the amount not invested and to reduce the acquisition cost of the replacement assets by the same amount. [*TCGA 1992, Sch 7C, para 5(2)*].

19.103   The replacement assets are treated as meeting condition (*f*) if an unconditional contract for their acquisition is entered into during the six-month period. [*TCGA 1992, Sch 7C, para 3(1)*]. It should particularly be noted that, if the SIP does not satisfy the ten per cent test at the date of the disposal, an acquisition of replacement assets before it meets that test will not qualify for the roll-over relief. The acquisition must be delayed until after the ten per cent test is satisfied. The rollover relief of course only affects the claimant; the deeming does not flow through to the other party to the transaction. [*TCGA 1992, Sch 7C, para 5(3)*]. Any provision of the *TCGA 1992* which fixes the consideration deemed to be given on a disposal or acquisition is applied before the rollover relief. [*TCGA 1992, Sch 7C, para 5(4)*].

19.104   Roll-over relief cannot be claimed if the replacement asset is land or a dwelling house (or part of a dwelling house) and at any time in the period from its acquisition to the time that relief is given under *Sch 7C* the house qualifies for CGT exemption as being the principal private residence of the claimant or his spouse. [*TCGA 1992, Sch 7C, para 6(1), (2)*]. It is not clear if this limitation applies where the shares are disposed of by an employee trust. It probably does. The doubt is because the legislation refers to the new asset being within *TCGA 1992, s 222(1)*. A gain by a trust on a residence occupied by a beneficiary falls within *section 225*. However, as that applies *sections 222–224* the courts will probably hold that the restriction applies.

19.105   Where this exclusion does not apply on the acquisition of land or of a dwelling house (or interest in a dwelling house) but after the rollover relief claim has been allowed it becomes the principal private residence of the claimant or his spouse, it must be treated as never having been eligible for rollover relief but the resultant gain (or additional gains) in relation to the disposal to the SIP is deemed to arise at the time that the property first qualifies for the principal private residence exemption, not at the time of the sale to the SIP. [*TCGA 1992, Sch 7C, para 6(3), (4)*].

19.106 If the replacement asset was an option to acquire a dwelling house or land and after that option is exercised the dwelling house or land becomes the principal private residence of the claimant or his spouse the above restrictions again apply. [*TCGA 1992, Sch 7C, para 6(5)–(8)*]. The restrictions also apply if the dwelling house or land qualifies as the principal private residence of a person entitled to occupy it under the terms of a settlement. [*TCGA 1992, Sch 7C, para 6(9)*].

19.107 A similar restriction applies if the replacement asset is shares on which enterprise investment scheme (EIS) income tax relief is claimed (this carries with it exemption from capital gains tax on a disposal of the shares). [*TCGA 1992, Sch 7C, para 7*]. Again, rollover relief is not given at all if the EIS relief claim has been made before the roll-over relief claim. [*TCGA 1992, Sch 7C, para 7(2)*]. If the EIS relief claim is made subsequently the rollover relief claim must be adjusted, but in this case the capital gain is deemed to arise at the time of the actual disposal to the ESOP, not when the EIS claim is made. [*TCGA 1992, Sch 7C, para 7(4)*].

19.108 Rollover relief cannot be claimed if at the time of the acquisition of the replacement asset the taxpayer is neither resident nor ordinarily resident in the UK unless he would be chargeable to CGT on a gain on the replacement asset because it is used in connection with a trade carried on in the UK through a branch or agency. Nor can it be claimed if the claimant will not be liable to CGT in respect of the replacement asset under the terms of a double taxation agreement. [*TCGA 1992, Sch 7C, para 8*].

Exemption for fees relating to monitoring schemes

19.109 For 2010/11 onwards, no liability to income tax arises on the payment (or reimbursement) by an employer (or by a contractor for a sub-contractor) of a fee in respect of an application to join the scheme administered under the *Protection of Vulnerable Groups (Scotland) Act 2007* (scheme to collate and disclose information about individuals working with children or with vulnerable adults) [*ITEPA 2003, s 326A* inserted by *Finance Act 2011 (FA 2011), s 39*]. The Treasury have power by statutory instrument to extend the exemption to any future corresponding schemes for England and Wales or Northern Ireland [*ITEPA 2003, s 326A(2)*].

Chapter 20

National Insurance

20.1   Although not, in theory at least, a tax, the taxation of income from employment is incomplete without a brief consideration of National Insurance. Because it is nto a tax changes to it cannot be made through the Finance Bill but require separate legislation. In practice most changes are made by secondary legislation. Although this is a social security contribution, the rates can be high. Indeed, in many cases the National Insurance contributions generated by a person's earnings will exceed the income tax thereon. This might be an appropriate place to mention that the National Insurance legislation provides that where a company fails to account for National Insurance contributions (NIC) and that failure is attributable to fraud or neglect by an officer of the company (such as a director or the company secretary) that officer can be made personally liable for payments of the NIC plus interest [*Social Security Administration Act 1992 (SSAA 1992), s 121C*].

20.2   National Insurance is administered by HMRC's National Insurance Contributions Office (NICO). The main reason for giving responsibility to HMRC was to make it easier to align the rules for income tax and National Insurance. The1999 government formed the view that industry wanted such an alignment. Actually, what industry wanted was to be able to use the same base for payroll deductions, which requires an alignment of National Insurance with PAYE, not with income tax. While PAYE is dealt with on a cumulative basis and National Insurance on a non-cumulative one even alignment with PAYE would probably not achieve a great deal.

20.3   Fifteen years on the promised alignment seems a far off dream. NICO still seems to operate semi-autonomously within HMRC and although PAYE visiting staff also look for NIC errors the interpretation of similar legislation still seems to differ considerably between income tax and NIC. In these circumstances it has been assumed that practices of the former Contributions Agency (who were previously rsponsible for National Insurance) continue under NICO so they are referred to below as NICO practices.

Gross pay

20.4   National Insurance contributions are based on an employee's 'gross pay'. This is not necessarily the same thing as earnings for income tax purposes. In particular where an employer incurs an expense to provide a benefit for an employee, or relieves the employee of a pecuniary liability, such as where he settles the bill for an expense incurred by the employer, the cost is normally regarded as pay for National Insurance purposes, whereas for income tax it would normally give rise to a benefit in kind on the employer. *Section 4* of the *Social Security Contributions and Benefits Act 1992 (SSCBA 1992)* specifically treats as earnings for National Insurance purposes statutory sick pay, statutory maternity pay, sickness benefit, gains on the exercise of share options taxed under *ITEPA 2003, ss 479* (see **14.112**) and sums received for restrictive covenants, taxed under *Income Tax (Earnings and Pensions) Act 2003 (ITEPA 2003), ss 225* or *226* (see **11.75**). In *P A Holdings Ltd v HMRC 2011 EWCA Civ 1414* (see **3.27**) it was held that dividends on shares issued to employees were pay for both income tax and NIC purposes.

20.5   HMRC have attacked schemes designed to avoid NIC by paying bonuses by means of the transfer of some exotic commodity with arrangements in place to enable the commodity to be immediately sold by the employee. One such case is *EDI Servicess Ltd v HMRC [2006] STC (SCD) 392,* where the bonus was paid by the purchase and transfer of gold Napoleons. Adopting the purposive approach towards tax avoidance schemes of the House of Lords in *Barclays Mercantile Finance Ltd v Mawson [2005] STC 1* the Commissioners held that the overall scheme was a mechanism designed to deliver cash and as such was not what Parliament had in mind when exempting payments in kind from NIC. Accordingly NIC was payable.

20.6   The Contributions Agency took a far harder line than HMRC on business expenses incurred by employees although NICO seem to be mellowing a little. Recent editions of *CWG2 Employer's Further Guide to PAYE and NICs,* are far less prescriptive than in the past as to what evidence is acceptable to substantiate that an expense is a business expense. After listing the evidence it would ideally like for different types of expense it adds 'This is not a complete list and any evidence will be considered'. On the other hand there are some items, such as a payment to an employee on his birthday or marriage, and ex gratia payments, which NICO do not consider should be included in gross pay but which the rest of HMRC generally consider to be part of emoluments. Whilst NICO have accepted that payments made to cover business expenses incurred by an employee are not gross pay, they still insist that the employer must have evidence to identify the business expenses actually incurred and to demonstrate both the amount and that the expense was incurred as part of the employee's work, but accept that a log is not the only acceptable way to identify business telephone calls or business car mileage. They also accept that expenses covered by an HMRC dispensation do not attract an NIC liability. (*Taxline, January–April 1995*). Hopefully, a benefit of the Contributions Agency moving to HMRC will in time be a move towards the HMRC approach.

20.7   It is understood that NICO sometimes contend that where a termination agreement is signed in advance of cessation of the employment, that is a variation of the employment agreement so that the receipt of compensation attracts National Insurance (*Taxline, July 1998*). In most cases that is probably incorrect. Agreement of compensation for breach of contract is not a variation of the contract and the receipt of an ex gratia payment is often unconnected with the employment. It is of course generally convenient to everyone to seek compensation for breach of the employment agreement while the employee is still at work if at all possible and it would be unfortunate if the tax system discourages people from common-sense procedures. Most of the exclusions from earnings for tax purposes, such as payment of qualifying travelling expenses, mileage allowance payments and passenger payments, are also excluded from earnings for NIC purposes. In recent years exemptions from income tax have been mirrored by NIC exemptions, but some old exemptions may not have yet been brought into line. However, as discussed in **Chapter 11** this is a contentious area of law in general.

20.8   Where an employee is taxable under *ITEPA 2003, s 473* on a gain on the exercise of an unapproved share option (see **14.112**) the employee and employer can jointly elect that the employee should be liable for all or part of the employer's National Insurance on the share option (visit www.hmrc. gov.uk/nic/forms.htm). HMRC have to approve in advance both the form of the election and the arrangements made for ensuring that the employee will in fact pay the National Insurance (*SSCBA1992, s 38* inserted by *Child Support, Pensions and Social Security Act 2000 (CSPSSA 2000, s 78*). They have published a model form of election. It is obviously sensible, although not essential, to use this. The effect of the election is completely to relieve the employer of the liability. Where such an election is made the employer's National Insurance liability can be deducted from the gain taxable under *s 478* (but it does not reduce the employee's own National Insurance liability (if any) on the gain (*ITEPA 2003, s 481*).

20.9   This provision was introduced because many 'dot-com' companies were worried that the gain on exercise of share options is unquantifiable until the option is exercised and might be so large that it could force the employer into insolvency. Whether many employers will actually ask employees to take on part of their tax liability is questionable. However, there seems no reason why the employee should not be asked to enter into the election at the time the option is granted. If it is explained that it means that he has to pay the current value of the shares plus 8.68 per cent of the growth in value to acquire the shares (1 per cent additional primary percentage plus 12.8 per cent of 60 per cent after the tax relief (see **20.7**) of 40 per cent assuming the option is exercised after 2002/03) this is likely to still appear very attractive to the employee.

20.10   NICO consider that most payments into FURBS (see **10.80**) prior to 5 April 1999 and all contributions after that date are earnings for National Insurance purposes. As the Contributions Agency guideline did not initially make this clear where a FURBS takes the form of a discretionary trust they only sought to enforce this liability in such cases from 6 April 1998 (*Press Release 17 November 1997*). The basis for their view was that the contribution was 'remuneration or profit derived from an employment' within *SSCBA 1992, s 3*. They did accept that if the FURBS was a 'truly discretionary' trust *s 3* could not apply as no part of the payment could be attributed to any one individual. To solve this problem *s 3(2A)* of the *Social Security and Benefits Act 1992* inserted by *s 48* of the *Social Security Act 1998 (SSA 1998)* enables regulations to be made to apportion a payment for the benefit of two or more employees. The resultant regulation is now the *Social Security (Contributions) Regulations 2001, Sch 2, para 13*. It provides for the apportionment to be made on a factual basis where appropriate and, if that cannot be done, equally between all the employees who are members of the FURBS. In *Tullet & Tokyo Forex International Ltd and others v the Secretary of State for Social Security [2000] EWHC Admin 350* the High Court held that payments by the employer of short-dated gilts to a life assurance policy held by the employee were not earnings 'paid to or for the benefit of' the employee; what was paid for the benefit of the employee was what the employee received, namely the enhancement in the value of the life assurance policy which was a payment in kind that fell to be disregarded under the *Social Security (Contributions) Regulations 2001, Sch 3, para 2(1)*. HMRC do not accept that this reasoning applies to a payment into a FURBS and successfully established that before the Special Commissioners in *Telent plc v HMRC [2008] STC (SCD) 202*. The Commissioner thought it clear that what was being considered in *Tullet* was a payment in kind. He felt that a payment of pension contribution is fundamentally different and did not consider that a pension contribution could constitute a payment in kind. However he did consider it to be 'earnings' paid 'for the benefit of' the employee, which is the test as to whether something attracts NIC. The Court of Appeal in *Forde & McHugh Ltd v HMRC [2012] EWCA Civ 692* (a lead case for a number of other appeals) thought that *Tullett* had been wrongly decided. In that case the Upper Tribunal held that 'on general principles, there are no emoluments' for income tax purposes when the employer pays a sum into a conditional or contingent fund for the ultimate benefit of the employee, although in the case of income tax, but not NI, statute has intervened to treat contributions to the scheme as income of the employee. In that case the company's contribution was primarily satisfied by the transfer of a holding of gilts and relied also on the *Tullett & Tokyo Forex International Ltd* case. In the Supreme Court [2014] UKSC 14, the taxpayer accepted that earnings had a wider meaning than emoluments but contended that it did not extend to a transfer of assets to a fund in which at the time of the transfer the earner had only a contingent interest (as it would be defeated if he died before his retirement). The Court said that it was right to accept that as from the outset of NI in 1946, the word 'earnings' had included benefits in kind. However it decided (reversing the decision of the Court of Appeal) that the Upper Tribunal was correct that the transfer did not give rise to earnings. The payment of a pension is deferred earnings, so in the absence of clear wording to the contrary, it would be wrong to treat a payment into the fund as earnings too; 'earnings' looks at the receipt by the employee, not the payment by the employer and the earner received nothing other than the contingent right to future relevant benefits; and simply treating the payment into the trust as earnings ignores both the existence of the contingency and the trustees' future performance in valuing the fund. It was improbable that such a difficult calculation was intended by parliament.

Contributions to a FURBS after 6 April 2006 no longer attract an income tax charge. Curiously, the social security legislation does not appear to have been amended to eliminate the NIC charge as well.

20.11   Where a retrospective change is made to *ITEPA 2003* the Treasury have power by regulation also to amend the NIC legislation to impose a corresponding retrospective NIC charge provided that the charge is in an area that they already have power to make regulations under *SSCBA 1992, ss 3* (power to prescribe the manner and basis of the calculation or estimation of earnings), *4(6)* (power to treat amounts chargeable to income tax under *ITEPA 2003* as earnings for NIC purposes) or *4A* (power to treat payments or benefits to workers supplied by service companies etc as earnings) [*SSCBA 1992, s 4B* inserted by *National Insurance Contributions Act 2006*]. Parliament has in the past rarely changed tax law retrospectively. However the Minister in a Parliamentary Statement on 2 December 2004 said that she was 'giving notice of our intention to deal with any arrangements that emerge in future designed to frustrate our intention that employers and employees should pay the proper amount of tax and NICs on the rewards of employment. Where we become aware of arrangements which attempt to frustrate the intention we will introduce legislation to close them down where necessary from today'. Subsequent anti-avoidance changes to the share scheme rules in particular have generally been made with effect from 2 December 2004.

Benefits in kind

20.12   Prior to 6 April 2000, benefits in kind did not, in general, attract National Insurance. [*Social Security (Contributions) Regulations 1979, Regulation 19(1)(d) (SI 1979 No 591)*]. There were, however, a growing list of exceptions where the benefit was regarded as pay. All benefits in kind are liable to National Insurance from 6 April 2000, unfortunately in a somewhat odd manner. The items that were treated as pay prior to 6 April 2000 are still treated as pay. This means that they attract both employers' and employees' contributions by reference to the week (or month or other pay period) in which they are paid. Other benefits attract only employers' contributions and these are not collected weekly or monthly through the PAYE system. Instead, they are NICable under Class 1A (see **20.19**) which is collected in a single payment after the end of the tax year.

20.13   The benefits that are taxed as pay are:

(*a*)   The conferment of any interest in any of the following assets.

    (i)   Shares and stock of any company (including a non-UK one).

    (ii)   Debentures, bonds, certificates of deposit and other instruments creating or acknowledging indebtedness.

    (iii)   Loan stock, bonds and other instruments creating or acknowledging indebtedness issued by or on behalf of a government, local authority or public authority.

    (iv)   Warrants or other instruments entitling the holder to subscribe for assets within (*a*)(i)–(iii).

    (v)   Unit trusts and interests in other collective investment schemes including OEICs.

    (vi)   Options to acquire or dispose of:

       (A)   an asset within (*a*)(i);

       (B)   UK or foreign currency;

       (C)   gold, silver, palladium or platinum.

  (vii)   A contract for the sale of a commodity or any other property under which delivery is to be made at a future date at a fixed price.

 (viii)   Any contract whose purpose is to generate a profit or loss by reference to fluctuations in the price of any property or an index or similar factor.

  (ix)   Any alcoholic liquor in respect of which no duty has been paid under *Alcoholic Liquor Duties Act 1979 (ALDA 1979), s 1.*

   (x)   Any gemstone such as diamond, emerald, ruby, sapphire, amethyst, jade, opal or topaz and organic gemstones such as amber or pearl, whether cut or uncut and whether or not having an industrial use.

  (xi)   Certificates or other instruments which confer:

       (A)   property rights in respect of any asset within (*a*)(i)–(iv) above, and after 24 August 1994 (ix) and (x);

       (B)   a right to acquire, dispose, underwrite or convert an asset where such right would be exercisable by a person who owned the asset direct;

       (C)   a contractual right to acquire any such asset.

  (xii)   Any voucher capable of being exchanged for such an asset falling into one of the above paragraphs.

 (xiii)   Any voucher stamp or similar document which is capable of being exchanged (either singly or together with other vouchers or documents) for an asset falling within (i) to (ix) or (xi) above.

(*b*)   The conferment of an interest in any long-term (life insurance, etc.) insurance contract.

(*c*)   Company cars – see **20.22**.

(*d*)   Any amount on which an employed earner is taxable under *ITEPA 2003, ss 417–446* (see **Chapter 14**) in respect of the acquisition of shares or an interest in shares. The taxable amount is the same as for income tax purposes. Broadly speaking, the same exemptions apply.

(*e*)   A readily convertible asset (as defined from income tax) is one, readily convertible under *ITEPA 2003, s 701* or a voucher capable of being exchanged for such an asset. Prior to that date, only assets for which trading arrangements existed were subject to National Insurance. [*Sch 3, para 2* and *Parts III & IV Social Security (Contributions) Regulations 2001 (2001 No 1004)*].

Other payments in kind, or by way of the provision of services, board and lodgings or other facilities are exempt from NIC. It was held in *Tullet & Tokyo Forex International Ltd and others v the Secretary of State for Social Security*

[2000] EWHC Admin 350 (see **20.10**) that payments that enhanced the value of an insurance policy already held by an employee did not fall within (*b*) above.

20.14   There are a number of specific exemptions from National Insurance including the transfer to an employee of ordinary shares in the company for which he works (or its parent, etc.) and options over such shares provided that either the shares are issued under an approved scheme or they are non-tradeable shares; reimbursement of travel and lodging expenses incurred as the result of the disruption to public transport by industrial action; reimbursement of taxi or car hire costs where an employee works beyond 9pm at the request of his employer on exceptional occasions (not more than 60 times a year); reimbursement of overseas travel expenses where these are deductible for income tax under *ITEPA 2003, ss 341, 342, 370* and *371* (see **13.23–13.36**) and most benefits that are exempted from income tax. [*Sch 3, Parts I & II Social Security (Contributions) Regulations 2001 (SI 2001 No 1004)* and *Social Security (Contributions) (Amendment No 2) Regulations 2008 (SI 2008 No 607), para 4*]. There is also an exemption for holiday pay schemes by groups of employers. [*SSCR 2001, Sch 3, para 12, Part X*]. This was withdrawn for most employers from 30 October 2007 by the *Social Security (Contributions) (Amendment No 9) Regulations 2007 (SI 2007 No 2905)*. It still applies where the employer is a person carrying on a business which includes construction operations and the employee is personally engaged in such operations, but only for a transitional period to 30 October 2012.

20.15   There is also an exemption for 'gratuities and offerings' where either the payment is not made directly or indirectly by the employer (and does not represent sums previously paid to the employer) or the employer does not allocate the payment, directly or indirectly to the earner (*Social Security (Contributions) Regulations 2001, Sch 3, Part X (5)*). This was in issue in *Channel 5 TV Group Ltd v Morehead [2003] STC (SCD) 327, SpC 369*. One of the shareholders of Channel 5 sold its shares at a substantial profit. It decided to give some of its profits to the staff of Channel 5. It paid $4.9 million to a firm of solicitors who made out cheques to the individual staff members. The solicitors deducted tax but not National Insurance on the basis that the payments were gratuities not provided or allocated by Channel 5. HMRC contended that the word 'gratuity' meant 'tip'. The Special Commissioners held that it is not so limited. A gratuity is 'a voluntary payment given in return for services rendered where the amount of the payment depended on the donor and where there was no obligation on the part of the donor to make the payment'. Channel 5 did not make or allocate the payments. The US company allocated the payments, albeit on the recommendation of the chief executive of Channel 5 acting in a personal capacity after consulting his fellow executive directors. That did not mean that they have been acting for Channel 5 though. Nor did the assistance given to the solicitors by Channel 5's payroll department amount to allocating the payments. Accordingly no National Insurance was payable.

20.16   This provision was also in issue in *Knowledgepoint 360 Group v HMRC [2011] SFTD 977*. The company had established two discretionary employee benefit trusts, one in 1992 and the second in 1997. Both held shares in the company. The company was sold in December 2001. During 2002, 2003 and 2004, the trustees of the EBTs decided to make payments to former employees of the company. The company deducted PAYE but not NI, relying on the Channel 5 case. The Tribunal held that the payments were gratuities; there was no obligation on the trustees to make the payment and the decision was made by the trustees independently of the company. There was no 'allocation' by the company and the fact that the original funds had derived from the company was not sufficient to mean that the far larger sums paid to the employees were indirect payments by the company.

Earnings periods

20.17   Unlike PAYE, National Insurance is not calculated on a cumulative basis. It is based on the employee's pay in an earnings period. This is the period for which earnings are normally paid if they are paid on a regular basis. In other words, if a person is paid weekly, the earnings period is a week, if he is paid monthly it is a month. Company directors have a special earnings period, namely the fiscal year. Accordingly, their National Insurance is effectively calculated on a cumulative basis. From 6 April 1999 National Insurance can be applied to directors during the year as if this special rule did not apply, provided that any necessary adjustment is made at the end of the year. This will enable the National Insurance deductions to be spread, whereas the special rule bunches the entire deductions into the early part of the year. Once the earnings period has been identified National Insurance is calculated on the aggregate of all payments of gross pay made in the period.

Contributions

20.18   National insurance is payable by both the employer and the employee. The weekly employer's contribution for 2014/15 (called the secondary contribution) is as follows.

Gross pay
per week

first £153   nil

excess over £153   13.8% (of the excess only)

The employee's contribution for 2014/15 (called the primary contribution) is:

Gross pay
per week

First £153   nil

Next £153–£805   12%

excess over £805   2%

The limits (called respectively the secondary threshold and the upper earnings limit) for 2013/14 were £148 and £797 per week.

For 2009/10 onwards there are five separate National Insurance thresholds, the lower earnings limit (LEL), the primary threshold, the secondary threshold, the upper accrual point (which is fixed at £770 per week) and the upper earnings limit (UEL). The lower earnings limit is tied to the amount of the State pension. For 2014/15 it is £111 a week. Once that level is reached, the employee's earnings count towards his pension entitlement. However earnings between the LEL and the earnings threshold do not attract National Insurance. That is payable only on earnings in excess of the primary threshold (for employee contributions) or the secondary threshold (for employer contributions). The two thresholds are the same for 2014/15, but were slightly different in earlier years. The upper accrual limit is the point at which earnings cease to attract pension entitlement. Nevertheless full National Insurance contributions are still payable on the band of earnings between that limit and the UEL. The UEL is tied to the income tax system. It is the point at which higher-rate tax becomes payable after personal allowances have been taken into account, ie for 2014/15 it is £41,865 (£10,000 personal allowance and £31,865 basic rate threshold).

20.19   It used to be possible to contract out of the earnings related portion of the State pension scheme provided that there was a pension scheme in place that promised greater benefits than the State scheme and, from 2012/13 onwards, the pension was salary related. Where this was done, both employer and employee paid a reduced rate on up to £770 per week earnings. However this facility was abolished from 6 April 2012.

Maximum contributions

20.20   The maximum weekly contribution by an employee for 2014/15 is £78.24 plus two per cent of the excess earnings over £805. There is no limit on the employer's contribution. The contributions are collected by being deducted by the employer from the employee's pay. The contributions are collected by HMRC, the employer paying them over monthly along with his PAYE tax deductions.

Employees excluded

20.21   No National Insurance is payable (by either employer or employee) if the employee is under 16 at the time the earnings are paid to him. The employee's contributions are not payable where the employee is over the State retirement age (65 for men and between 60 and 65 for women depending on their date of birth) but the employer's contribution is still payable in respect of such people. Where a man underwent a sex change it was held that she remained a man until such tiem as a gender reconition certificate was issued under the Gender Recognition Act 2004 (*M v HMRC [2010] SFTD 1141*). A married woman who was married before 6 April 1977 and has remained in employment (not necessarily the same employment) since that date, may be entitled to pay contributions at a reduced rate. This does not affect the amount of the employer's contribution, however.

Class 1A contributions

20.22   The employer, but not the employee, also has to pay a Class 1A contribution in relation to:

(*a*)   employees to whom he provides company cars; and

(*b*)   those benefits in kind not treated as pay (see **20.10**) and not specifically excluded from National Insurance (see **20.20**).

[*SSCBA 1992, s 10*].

The Class 1A contribution is at the same rate as the employer's Class 1 contribution (12.8 per cent for 2003/04 to 2010/11 and 13.8 per cent for 2011/12 to 2014/15) but is payable annually in arrears. The Class 1A contribution in relation to cars is payable on the car use and car fuel benefits assessable for income tax purposes (see **7.8** and **7.46** above).

20.23   The Class 1A charge on benefits in kind does not apply to:

(*a*)   certain amounts which are excluded from earnings under the *Social Security (Contributions) Regulations 2001, (2001 No 1004)* as awarded, namely:

(i)   meal vouchers of 15p per working day [*Reg 40(2)* and *Sch 3, Pt V para 6A*];

(ii)   a gratuity from someone other than the employer (eg a tip by a passenger to an employed taxi driver) [*Reg 40(2)* and *Sch 3, Pt X para 5*];

(iii)   a payment to a minister of religion which does not form part of his stipend or salary (eg Christmas donations by parishioners [*Reg 40(2)* and *Sch 3, Pt X para 13*];

(iv)   (A)   a payment by way of a right to acquire securities [*Reg 40(2)* and *Sch 3, Pt IX para 3, 3A*];

(B)   a payment deducted from earnings under a partnership share agreement (see **15.27**) [*Reg 40(2)* and *Sch 3, Pt IX para 6*];

(C)   free shares awarded under a SIP (see **15.20**) [*Reg 40(2)* and *Sch 3, Pt IX para 7*];

(v)   the benefit of a priority application of shares which is not treated as an emolument by *ITEPA 2003, s 542* (see **14.150**) [*Reg 40(2)* and *Sch 3, Pt IX para 5*];

(vi)   a payment of travel expenses that is excluded from tax under *ITEPA 2003, ss 341, 342* and *370–375*) (see **13.15–13.25**) [*Reg 40(2)* and *Sch 3, Pt VIII para 4*];

(vii)   a cost of overseas living allowance paid to a member of the Commonwealth War Graves Commission or the British Council [*Reg 40(2)* and *Sch 3, Pt VIII para 13*];

(viii) travel expenses of a person not domiciled in the UK which are taxable under *ITEPA 2003, s 373* [*Reg 40(2)* and *Sch 3, Pt VIII para 5*];

(ix) a payment of a benefit under an unapproved pension scheme attributable to contributions before 6 April 1998 or which derives from contributions which were assessed on the employee [*Reg 40(2)* and *Sch 3, Pt VI paras 4, 5*];

(x) a contribution to a pension scheme which is awaiting HMRC approval [*Reg 40(2)* and *Sch 3, Pt VI para 6*];

(xi) a payment to a French, Irish or Danish or US pension scheme which is exempted from tax under the relevant double tax agreements [*Reg 40(2)* and *Sch 3, Pt VI para 7*];

(xii) a subscription etc exempt from tax under *ITEPA 2003, s 343* (see **5.87**) [*Reg 40(2)* and *Sch 3, Pt X para 11*];

(xiii) the VAT on any supply of goods or services by the employer to the employee where the remuneration includes a sum for that supply [*Reg 40(2)* and *Sch 3, Pt X para 9*];

(xiv) a payment made by an issuer of charge cards, cheque guarantee cards, credit cards or debit cards as a reward to an individual who assists in identifying or recovering lost or stolen cards in the course of his or her employment (other than employment by the issuer) [*Reg 40(2)* and *Sch 3, Pt X para 15*];

(xv) holiday pay paid (or reimbursed) from a fund to which more than one employer contributes and which is not under the control of the employer in question [*Reg 40(2)* and *Sch 3, Pt X para 12*];

(xvi) a payment to an employed earner receiving full-time instruction at a university, technical college or similar establishment provided specified conditions are met in relation to the course [*Reg 40(2) and Sch 3, Pt VII para 12*];

(*b*) payments of qualifying travelling expenses or other expenses incurred in carrying out the employment [*Reg 40(3)*];

(*c*) a payment in respect of removal expenses not within **9.57** [*Reg 40(4)*];

(*d*) benefits under some approved pension schemes [*Reg 40(6)*];

(*e*) an amount exempted from income tax under the following extra-statutory concessions [*Reg 40(7)*]:

A11 residence in the UK-year of commencement or cessation

A37 directors fees received by partnerships

A56 accommodation in Scotland

A91 living accommodation provided by reason of employment

[*Social Security (Contributions) Regulations 2001 (SI 2001 No 1004), Reg 40 and Sch 3*].

20.24   For the purpose of (*d*) above 'childcare' included:

(*a*)   care provided by a childminder or day carer under *Part X* and *Sch 9, Children's Act 1989 (CA 1989)* (child minding and day care for young children);

(*b*)   where the child is eight or over, care provided by a child minder;

(*c*)   where the child is under eight, care provided by a child minder but only if it does not exceed in total two hours in any day;

(*d*)   care provided by a relative (within *CA 1989, s 71(13)*) or a nanny (within *s 105(1)* of that *Act*);

(*e*)   care provided during out-of school hours and school holidays;

(*f*)   full-time and part-time care.

[*Social Security (Contributions) Regulations 2001 (SI 2001 No 1004), Regulation 40(8)*].

20.25   A third party who provides a benefit for the employee of someone else can agree with HMRC to account for Class 1A National Insurance on that benefit. [*Social Security Contributions and Benefits Act 1992, s 10ZA,*]. If the third party has entered into an arrangement with HMRC to pay the employee's tax liability, that tax payment does not itself attract Class 1A contributions (*s 10ZA(2)*).

20.26   It is accordingly still necessary to determine whether the provision of a benefit constitutes 'pay' or if it is a benefit within Class 1A. The normal HMRC test is whether the payment by the company satisfies a liability of the employee, in which case it is pay (see **20.4**) or whether it is a liability of the employer, in which case Class 1A applies. *Frost Skip Hire (Newcastle) Ltd v Woods [2004] STC (SCD) 387, SpC 420* concerned school fees. Mr Frost applied for his son to be admitted to a private school. He paid the school fees for the Summer term 1997. Thereafter he asked the school to address its invoices to the company and the company paid the fees. It was held that Mr Frost had undertaken to the school to pay the fees. The change to billing the company did not alter the parents' continuing contractual liability for the fees. Accordingly the payment of the school fees was NICable as pay of Mr Frost.

PAYE Settlement Agreements (Class 1B Contributions)

20.27   *Section 53* of the *SSA 1998* introduced a new Class 1B National Insurance contribution. This is payable by employers only. The rate is 13.8 per cent (12.8 per cent for 2003/04 to 2010/11) (the same as the employer's Class 1 contributions). It is payable on the aggregate of:

(*a*)   the amount of emoluments included in a PAYE Settlement Agreement which relates to items which would otherwise be subject to NIC if they had not been included in the PSA; and

(*b*)   the income tax due on the PSA.

Head (*a*) is obviously reasonable. Head (*b*) has given rise to a great deal of adverse comment. The tax on a PSA is a liability of the employer; it is not employees' liabilities which are being settled by the employer. Accordingly, this element is contrary to the basic principle that National Insurance is payable only on emoluments of employees.

Occupational pension schemes

20.28   If an employer has an occupational pension scheme that provides salary-related benefits above a defined level, he can contract his employees out of the earnings related element of the State pension scheme. The occupational pension scheme needs to provide benefits at least equivalent to those under the State scheme. In return the contributions of both employer and employee are reduced.

Multiple employments

20.29   Where a person has more than one job, National Insurance is calculated separately for each of them in most cases, even if they are with associated employers. If it is clear that the employee's earnings from one of the employments will exceed £805a week (or £41,865 per annum) NICO can authorise the other employer not to deduct the employee's contributions, (or only to deduct two per cent) although the employer's contribution will obviously still have to be paid. In other cases, if the total contributions by an employee exceed £4,146.72 (53 × £(805 − 153) × 12 per cent) plus two per cent of the excess over £805, the excess will be refunded direct to the employee by NICO after the end of the fiscal year. There is an exception where two or more employers are 'carrying on business in association'. In such a case the earnings are aggregated unless it is 'not reasonably practicable to do so'. Both of these expressions were considered by the Special Commissioners in *Samuels & Samuels Limited v Richardson [2005] STC (SCD) 1, SpC 431*. It was held that five companies (three wholly owned by a fourth, which also owned 40 per cent of the fifth) were carrying on business in association. The business of all five related directly or indirectly to insurance broking, they were all administered from Samuels & Samuels Ltd's (S & S) office, S & S employed all the staff of the group (as opposed to directors) and supplied administrative services to the other company. Mr Samuels was a director of all of the companies and the companies were under common ownership (including the fifth, which was ultimately controlled by Mr Samuels). It was also held that it was reasonably practicable to aggregate Mr Samuel's earnings from the five companies; all it required was a simple calculation.

Overseas employers

20.30   If an overseas employer does not have a place of business in the UK, the employer's contributions are not payable in respect of UK-based employees. A UK office is not necessarily a place of business for this purpose if management is not exercised from it. An employee who has come from the European Economic Area, or from Austria, Australia, Barbados, Bermuda, Canada, Cyprus, Finland, Guernsey, Iceland, Israel, Jamaica, Japan, Jersey, Korea, Malta, Mauritius, New Zealand, Norway, Philippines, Sweden, Switzerland, Turkey, the USA or Yugoslavia (including Bosnia, Croatia and Slovenia) and who continues to pay social security in his own country can claim exemption from National Insurance. Where a person who previously worked in another country is sent to the UK by his overseas employer (ie he is recruited overseas) National Insurance is not payable for the first 12 months that he is in the UK, provided that the overseas employer has a place of business outside the UK (whether or not he also has one in the UK).

20.31 If an employee who is ordinarily resident in the UK works overseas and his employer has a place of business in the UK, his overseas earnings remain within the scope of National Insurance. If he is working overseas for more than 12 months, liability for National Insurance ceases after 52 weeks.

20.32 In *Stevens and others v CIR [2004] STC (SCD) 310, SpC 411* individuals who were working for other employers in the UK agreed to work for Premmit Engineering Services Ltd, a UK company with a place of business in the UK. They were engaged by the company to work in Switzerland and were required to make their way to Switzerland at their own expense. They signed their employment contracts with Premmit in London but did no work for the company in the UK. Mr Stevens and his colleagues challenged a decision of HMRC that they were liable for NIC rather than Swiss social security contributions for the first two years. It was held that UK NIC was due. The employer had a place of business in the UK, Mr Stevens was 'sent' to Switzerland by Premmit, at the time he went to Switzerland he was in the service of Premmit and his employment was expected to last for less than two years.

20.33 In *Oleachem (Scotland) Ltd v HMRC [2009] STC (SCD) 205* the company set up a Jersey subsidiary (OISL) to engage chemists which OISL seconded to Oleachem to work for its clients, mainly in the UK Continental Shelf. There was no dispute that PAYE was due. However NIC could apply only if OISL was resident or present in the UK. HMRC sought to apply the Ramsay principle to look through OISL and treat Oleachem as the employer. The Special Commissioners held that the chemists were mariners and that as the PAYE Regulations contain specific rules for mariners, these override the general rules and the Ramsay principle cannot affect that conclusion.

Employee shareholdings

20.34 *Social Security Contributions and Benefits Act 1992, Sch 1, para 3B* enables employer and employee to make a joint election to enable the employer's NIC to be recovered from the employee in certain circumstances. This election is dealt with at **14.56**, **14.67** and **14.116**.

Meaning of 'employee'

20.35   The meaning of an employee for National Insurance purposes is the same as for income tax (see **Chapter 4**). If a person's status is established with HMRC this will be accepted by NICO (in theory at least) and vice versa. In practice NICO seem to refuse to accept that a person's status has been 'established' unless there had been a very thorough HMRC investigation. The *Social Security (Categorization of Earner) Regulations 1978 (SI 1978 No 1689)* deem certain categories of people to be employees for National Insurance purposes even if they can show that they are actually self-employed. The categories concerned are office cleaners, ministers of religion, lecturers and teachers and a husband or wife working for their spouse. In HMRC's view lecturers and teachers includes anyone who is giving instruction on courses which result in the attainment of a recognised qualification, licence or skill which provides access to a particular job or authority to conduct a particular activity in the workplace, even though the instruction does not take place in a school or similar establishment. (HMRC Brief 25/2009).

20.36   An anomaly existed for a long time in relation to actors and musicians, where NICO regarded all performers as employees and insisted on the theatre, promoter, TV company, etc. deducting National Insurance even though the rest of HMRC accepted that many such persons were self-employed. This caused a great deal of resentment, particularly as the logic for this approach was never clear. In a parliamentary reply the Minister answered that the Agency had taken legal advice to the effect that this approach was not sustainable and that under the existing law entertainers should generally be regarded as self-employed. The *Social Security (Categorisation of Earners) Regulations 1978 (SI 1978 No 1689)* were therefore amended to make entertainers employees for National Insurance purposes except where 'the remuneration does not include any payment by way of salary with 'salary' being defined as payments made for services rendered under a contract for services, computed by reference to the amount of time for which work has been performed and, where there is more than one payment, payable at a specific period or interval. [*Social Security (Categorisation of Earners) Amendment Regulations 2003 (SI 2003 No 736)*]. The Minister's intention was to 'require the majority of performers to be treated as employees for National Insurance purposes'. It is beneficial to many performers to be treated as employees so as to have a right to unemployment benefit when they are 'resting'. The reason for the 2003 amendment is that the original wording was largely ineffective. Many entertainers receive, as part of the remuneration package, pre-purchase payments as compensation for the loss of future repeat fees and rights or royalties which far exceed the salary element. Very few actors are therefore paid wholly or mainly by salary.

20.37   HMRC have revisited the position in the case of *ITV Services Ltd v HMRC [2013] EWCA Civ 867*. ITV had split its contracts with actors into six categories, bespoke agreements, the ITV/Equity contract, the PACT/Equity contract, All Rights agreements, memo fees and walk-ons. It contended that the actors' remuneration did not include any payment by way of salary (as defined in the regulations). The actors were paid for being available for work; the fee was calculated by reference to the time for which work was expected to be performed, not time for which work was actually performed. This was rejected by the Tribunal. It held that the test had to be applied when the contract was entered into, so the reference in the regulations to 'performed' has to be interpreted as 'to be performed' as it can only be looking at future work. Accordingly time expected to be worked was the real test. It then concluded that, other than the All Rights agreement (which provided for a single inclusive fee), all of the contractual arrangements, including even walk-ons, included a 'payment by way of salary', so ITV was liable for secondary National Insurance contributions on them. The Upper Tribunal agreed (*[2012] UKUT 47 (TCC)*). ITV changed tack in the Court of Appeal. They accepted that walk-ons paid at a daily rate attract NIC. Rimer L J thought the FTT and UT interpretation was incorrect and the legislation had in contemplation contracts which include provisions for either a daily, weekly or other periodical rate for work to be done on an identifiable day or days (although his fellow judges expressed reservations). Unfortunately all of the disputed contracts incorporated industry-wide collective agreements and those agreements provided, inter alia, 'production day payments' which met Rimer's definition of salary. Accordingly the contract included provision for payment of salary and NI was due.

IR 35

20.38 The IR 35 rules considered in **Chapter 18** apply also for NIC by virtue of the *Social Security Contributions (Intermediaries) Regulations 2000 (SI 2000 No 727)* as amended by the *Social Security Contributions (Intermediaries) (Amendment) Regulations 2003 (SI 2003 No 2079)*.

Drawings by directors

20.39 In many family companies, directors are not paid a regular salary but take money from the company during the year which is posted to a current account pending a decision when the accounts are prepared how much is to be voted as salary, or as dividend or whether the overdrawn balance on the current account is to be left outstanding as loan. NICO have in the past been known to claim that such drawings constituted 'earnings' at the time of each individual payment unless the current account is in credit at the time. Their view was based on *Reg 22(2)* of the *Social Security (Contributions) Regulations 2001 (SI 2001 No 1004)*. This provides that 'any payment made by a company to or for the benefit of any of its directors' is to constitute earnings if it would not otherwise do so and the payment is made on account of, or by way of an advance on, a sum which would be earnings.

20.40 This view seems of doubtful validity. When a drawing is made it is not drawn on account of remuneration. It is not normally drawn on account of anything! It is simply a payment which will fall to be reimbursed to the company if it is not at a later date offset by an entitlement coming into existence at a future time to a payment from the company. It is understood that this was confirmed by an unpublished appeal decision given by the Minister in 1990. They seem to have backed away from this position though. They now tell their staff 'You need to identify to what remuneration a director is entitled and when that entitlement arises. The entitlement could be under a service agreement or some other agreement. If there are no remuneration agreements between directors and the company, and the company has adopted Table A ..., remuneration is normally voted at the annual general meeting, ... Class 1 NICs are due at the time of payment of earnings so that, normally, the time of payment of remuneration is when it is voted ... Until the remuneration is voted, or otherwise authorised, there are no earnings within *sections 3* and 6 *SSCBA 1992*. If however payments are made on account of the expected remuneration, those payments are treated as earnings because of *regulation 22*. It is important to note that *regulation 22* cannot change a loan, or partial or full repayment by the company of a loan, into a payment of earnings. The payment has to be on account of earnings' (National Insurance Manual, para 12014).

Dividends

20.41   NICO have also been known to claim that where a company pays a dividend to a director or employee and the dividend turns out to be unlawful, eg because the company does not have sufficient distributable reserves or because it has not been properly declared, it constitutes earnings for NIC purposes (letter of 7 December 1993 reproduced in *ICAEW Tax 5/94*). This also seems of very doubtful validity. If a dividend is declared it cannot change its nature if it transpires that it should not have been paid. Nor is it clear how a payment in respect of shares can be earnings if the shareholder happens to be an employee but something different if it is not. Furthermore, company law enables the company to call for repayment, which is inconsistent with the amount being earnings – or indeed income at all. And in the same letter NICO indicate that a trust cannot exist without a document, which is clearly wrong, and that in the absence of a specific power in the trust deed trustees have no legal right to waive a dividend however much they believe this to be in the interests of the beneficiaries, which is almost certainly wrong, there must at least be a question mark over the quality of the legal input, if any, into the letter. Indeed their current position is that, 'Dividends are derived from a shareholding and not employment. They cannot therefore be classed as earnings and do not attract NICs' Even where a dividend is unlawful 'this is a matter which can only be taken up by the shareholders themselves under company law. There is no action open to [NICO] under social security legislation. The fact that a dividend has not met the requirements of company law does not make it earnings for NICs purposes'. They do however tell their staff that, 'To decide whether a dividend is genuine rather than a disguised payment of earnings you need to see: the Memorandum and Articles of Association, the minutes of the meeting at which the dividend declaration was made; and·the profit and loss account/balance sheet for the years in question' (National Insurance Manual, para 2115).

20.42   In *P A Holdings Ltd v HMRC 2011 EWCA Civ 1414* (see **3.27**) it was held that dividends on shares issued to employees were pay for both income tax and NIC purposes. The shares in that case carried very artificial dividend rights. The Court of Appeal said that whether dividends are remuneration is a question of fact. The mere fact that an employee acquires shares by reason of his employment will not make dividends on them earnings as he receives the dividend qua shareholder not qua employee. In the PA case the intention was to pay earnings in the guise of dividends.

Income from property

20.43   NICO have also been known to claim that where a property owner collects the rents, furnishes and maintains the property and carries out repairs, or contracts for them to be carried out, he is gainfully employed as a self-employed earner and therefore liable to Class 2 National Insurance contributions. This is presumably on the basis that his property investments constitute a business. NICO can draw a degree of support for this view from VAT Tribunal decisions. It is probably a question of fact and degree but in *American Leaf Binding Co Sdn Bhd v Director-General of Inland Revenue [1978] STC 561*, a Privy Council case, Lord Diplock said, albeit *obiter*, 'In the case of a private individual it may well be that the mere receipt of rents from property that he owns raises no presumption that he is carrying on a business'. This is worth quoting to NICO if they contend that National Insurance is due unless the provision of services is effectively a full-time job *(Taxline, April 1998)*. However this does not appear to be a general policy. In *Rashid v Garcia [2003] STC (SCD) 36* Mr Rashid who received income from letting properties sought to pay Class 2 contributions but HMRC decided that he was not entitled to do so. The Special Commissioners felt that whether property rental was a business in any particular case was a matter of degree. Whilst Mr Rashid clearly had responsibilities when things went wrong he did nothing more than what a landlord normally did. They were accordingly not satisfied that there was sufficient activity to constitute a business; it was an investment which by its nature required some activity to maintain it.

Statutory sick pay, maternity pay and paternity pay

20.44   One of the benefits provided under the National Insurance scheme is statutory sick pay (SSP). However, SSP is not payable in the first three qualifying days in such a period (called a PIW or period of incapacity for work). A qualifying day means a day on which the employee is required to be available for work, so weekends and public holidays will not be qualifying days for most employees. If there was a previous period of sickness within the previous 56 days (even if the employee was then working for a different employer) the two periods are linked together to form a single PIW, so that statutory sick pay will be payable for all of the qualifying days in the second period.

20.45   An employee is not entitled to SSP for more than 28 weeks in a tax year. SSP paid by a previous employer needs to be taken into account for this purpose.

20.46   The current weekly rates of SSP are £NIL if the employee's average earnings are below £111 per week and £87.55 if they are at least that amount.

The average earnings are calculated over a two-month period prior to the date the sickness starts. SSP is payable for each qualifying day (at one-seventh of the weekly rate).

20.47 For 2014/15 onwards no part of the SSP is recoverable from the government.

A pregnant employee is entitled to statutory maternity pay (SMP) for a period of up to 39 weeks off work, starting between the eleventh and sixth week before the expected confinement provided that she earns at least £111 per week on average during the eight weeks prior to commencing 2014/15 she is entitled to 90 per cent of her normal weekly pay for the first six weeks (provided she has worked for the same employer for at least six months) and to the lower of £138.18 or 90 per cent of normal weekly pay per week for the other 33. The SMP is paid by the employer who can recover 92 per cent of the SMP from the government. A small employer can recover 100 per cent of the SMP plus an additional 3 per cent of the gross SMP as compensation for the NIC paid on the SMP. A small employer is one whose NI contributions for the previous tax year (ie both employers and employees Class 1 contributions) did not exceed £45,000.

20.49 There is also a right to statutory adoption pay (SAP) and statutory paternity pay (SPP). Statutory adoption pay is payable for 39 weeks. Only one of an adopting couple is entitled to SAP but they can choose which is to claim it. The other is entitled to statutory paternity pay. The partner of a woman entitled to SMP (whether or not the biological father) is also entitled to SPP. SPP is payable only for two weeks. The employee can choose which two but they must be consecutive and must fall within eight weeks of the birth. The qualifying conditions for both SAP and SPP and the right of recovery of all or part of the payments are the same as for SMP. The weekly rate of both SAP and SPP for 2014/15 is the lower of £138.18 or 90 per cent of the employee's average weekly earnings. An employee can also claim Additional Statutory Paternity Pay of the same amount for the unused balance of his spouse's entitlement if she does not take her full entitlement.

Student loans

20.50 Employers are also required to deduct student loan repayments from salary payments. Such loans are made to university students towards the cost of their courses. This obligation is not a tax but needs to be borne in mind as it will involve administration responsibilities and penalties can be incurred if these are not carried out properly. Broadly speaking, for 2014/14 once the former student's earnings exceed £16,910 pa (£1,409.16 a month or £325.19 a week) the employer has to deduct 9% of the excess of his salary over that figure.

Personal Liability Notice

20.51 HMRC have power under the *SSAA 1992, s 121C* to recover contributions that a company has failed to pay from any culpable officer. A person is a culpable officer if it appears to HMRC that the failure to pay the contributions is attributable to fraud or neglect on the part of an individual who was at the time an officer of the company. In *Zubair v HMRC (TC 2324)* the FTT held Mr Zubair liable to pay £244,195 in his absence. Mr Zubair was the sole director of the company. The FTT said that he 'was bound to take that degree of care in and about the management of the company's affairs as would be taken by a reasonably prudent company director. Such a director would ensure that the proper tax payments were made timeously'. The fact that he did not do so is sufficient to constitute neglect (although it is clear that the FTT thought that his actions might well amount to fraud).

Chapter 21

VAT

Motor vehicles

21.1 There is a deemed supply on which VAT is accountable to HMRC where fuel that was supplied to a taxable person in the course of his business is provided to an individual by reason of his employment or office for use in his own vehicle or in a vehicle allocated to him (ie a company car which is not a pool car – the definition [*Value Added Tax Act 1994 (VATA 1994), s 56(9)*] is the same as the income tax one). [*VATA 1994, s 56(1)(a)*]. The VAT is calculated on a scale charge. [*VATA 1994, s 57*]. This is different from the income tax charge, which applies only to company cars whereas the VAT charge applies to all cars for which fuel supplied by the employer is used for private motoring.

21.2 The figures are also different. This is because the derogation that the UK has from the EC rules only permits it to increase the charge in line with inflation, whereas the income tax increases are now deliberately in excess of inflation. For an accounting period beginning after 30 April 2007 the scale figures are based on the carbon dioxide emissions for the car. From 1 May 2014 these are as follows (the rates are VAT inclusive figures):

Emissions figure g/km	*Quarterly rate £*	*VAT thereon £*	*Annual rate £*	*VAT thereon £*
120 or less	156	26.00	627	104.00
125	234	39.00	939	156.00
130	251	41.83	1,004	167.32
135	266	44.33	1,064	177.32
140	282	47.00	1,129	188.00
145	297	49.50	1,190	198.00
150	313	52.17	1,255	208.68
155	328	54.67	1,315	218.68
160	345	57.50	1,381	230.00
165	360	60.00	1,441	240.00
170	376	62.67	1,506	250.68
175	391	65.17	1,567	260.68

Emissions figure g/km	Quarterly rate £	VAT thereon £	Annual rate £	VAT thereon £
180	408	68.00	1,632	272.00
185	423	70.50	1,692	282.00
190	439	73.17	1,757	292.68
195	454	75.67	1,818	302.68
200	470	78.33	1,883	313.32
205	485	80.83	1,943	323.32
210	502	83.67	2,008	334.68
215	517	86.17	2,069	344.68
220	533	88.83	2,134	353.32
225 or more	548	91.33	2,194	365.32

21.3 If a vehicle's emission figure is not a multiple of five it is rounded down. If the car does not have an official emissions figure the emissions figure is treated as 140g/km or less if the vehicle is 1400cc or less, as 175g/km if it is between 1401cc and 2000cc and as 225g/km if it exceeds 2000cc. [*VATA 1994 s 51* as amended by the *VAT (Consideration for Fuel Provided for Private Use) Order 2009 (SI 2009 No 1030)*].

21.4 The charge does not apply if the employee pays an amount at least equal to the cost of the fuel to the employer. [*VATA 1994, s 56(2)*]. If fuel is provided for a car used by a third party by reason of the individual's employment, such as to a member of his family, the scale figure will apply to that car also. [*VATA 1994, s 56(3)(d)*]. Any fuel provided by an employer for private use in a company car is automatically deemed to be provided by reason of the individual's employment. [*VATA 1994, s 56(3)(e)*]. Where the scale charge applies, the whole of the input tax is of course treated as being for the purpose of the employer's business; it is not necessary to disallow the private element as being for non-business use. [*VATA 1994, s 56(5)*]. The fuel is treated as supplied to the employee at the time it is put into the car's fuel tank. [*VATA 1994, s 56(6)*]. If the employee changes his car during a VAT accounting period (normally a three-month period), only one scale charge applies for that accounting period. [*VATA 1994, s 56(8)*]. If the two cars fall into different bands, the appropriate figure for each is apportioned on a daily basis to arrive at a scale figure for that accounting period. [*VATA 1994, s 57(5), (6)*].

21.5 If an employer charges an employee for the use of a car, including under a salary sacrifice arrangement, the charge is treated as outside the scope of tax provided that the input VAT on the acquisition of the car was wholly or partly blocked. [*Business Brief 10/95*]. Salary sacrifice arrangements are, in any event, statutorily outside the scope of VAT where the right to private use of a car is given in lieu of the salary (except to the extent of any actual cash payment). [*VAT (Treatment of Transactions) Order 1992 (SI 1992 No 630)*]. Where an employee pays the employer an amount so that he can be provided with a more expensive car than would otherwise be the case, HMRC regard the payment as consideration for a supply. [*Business Brief 9/92*].

21.6 In *EC Commission v UK (Case C-33/03) [2005] STC 582* the ECJ held that by granting taxable persons the right to deduct VAT on certain supplies of fuel to non-taxable persons the UK had failed properly to implement the Sixth Directive. The UK contended that in carrying out their work employees generally act on behalf of their employer so there must exist a right for the employer to deduct VAT in respect of the fuel bought by the employee for the purpose of the employer's taxable transactions. Whilst accepting that as a truism, the ECJ held that the UK legislation did not make it a condition for eligibility for deduction of VAT that the fuel bought by the employee should be used for the purpose of the employer's business. On the contrary it specifically allowed a deduction whether or not the travel was business travel (because, of course, the scale charged effectively turns all travel into business travel because input tax in relation to private travel is used for a taxable purpose, namely to generate the scale charge).

21.7 In *Auto Lease Holland BV v Bundesamt fur Finanzen (Case C-185/01) [2005] STC 598* the ECJ held that there is no supply of fuel by the lessor of a vehicle to the lessee where the lessee fills up the leased vehicle at filling stations, even if the vehicle is filled up in the name and at the expense of the lessor. In that case the company as lessor entered into a 'fuel management agreement' with the lessee under which the lessee could pay for fuel using an Auto Lease credit card, Auto Lease would pay the garage and would charge the lessee a monthly amount (based on a twelfth of the estimated annual fuel cost) with an annual adjustment to the actual cost for the year. The ECJ held that the fuel could not be regarded as having been supplied to Auto Lease as the lessee had power to dispose of the fuel as if he owned it. Accordingly the fuel was supplied by the garage to the lessee not to Auto Lease.

21.8 Following these cases the UK revoked the 1991 Order and replaced it with the *VAT (Input Tax) (Reimbursement by Employers of Employees' Business Use of Road Fuel) Regulations 2005 (SI 2005 No 3290)*. This gives an employee the right to deduct input tax where 'road fuel is supplied to a taxable person (employer) in circumstances where it is delivered to and paid for by his employee acting in his name and on his behalf for use by him (employee) either in whole or in part for the purpose of the taxable person's business'. Where all the fuel is used for that purpose the whole amount is deductible. Where only part is so used the whole is deductible if the scale charge applies but only a part (determined by reference to the distance covered by the vehicle and the cylinder capacity of the vehicle) is deductible where it does not. In either case the taxable person must hold a VAT invoice which, where so required, must be made out to him as the recipient of the supply.

21.9 HMRC say that the effect of the new Regulation is that 'the current arrangements in practice for businesses to recover VAT on fuel purchased by employees are unchanged, except that businesses must now retain VAT invoices to support their claims' (*Business Brief 22/2005*). The new Regulation may well satisfy the ECJ. However, it is questionable whether in English law it is possible for the supply of petrol to be made to the employer and thus for a VAT invoice to be issued in the employer's name. This is because the High Court held in *Richardson v Worral 58 TC 6421* (see **3.4**) that the supply of fuel is made to the employee not the employer, even where it is paid for using a company credit card.

Demonstrator cars

21.10   HMRC have agreed with the Retail Motor Industry Federation a simplified method of calculating the VAT due on the private use of stock in trade cars (ie cars for which the deduction of input tax is not blocked) provided to directors and employees free of charge where the list price is under £80,000. Where the list price is over £80,000 the figure has to be agreed with HMRC based on VAT on 25% for the running costs including depreciation. The scale figures are as follows:

List price	Annual VAT	Quarterly VAT
£	£	£
0–9,000	63.09	15.77
9,000–12,000	82.99	20.75
12,000–17000	113.01	28.25
17,000–23,000	153.85	38.46
23,000–31,000	203.55	50.89
31,000–40,000	259.47	64.87
40,000–50,000	321.61	80.40
50,000–65,000	419.35	104.84
65,000–80,000	513.60	128.40

21.11   Some businesses abused this agreement by charging the director a nominal figure, such as 0.50p a year, for the use of the car. The effect was that as the car is supplied for a consideration VAT can be charged only on that consideration. HMRC have accordingly been given power in such a case to direct that the value of the supply must be taken to be its market value [*VATA 1994, Sch 6, para 1A*]. The market value could well be greater than the value agreed with the Retail Motor Industry Federation.

Blocking of input tax recovery

21.12   VAT incurred on the acquisition or importation of a motor car cannot be treated as input tax unless either:

(*a*)   the car is a qualifying car (ie one on which VAT recovery has not previously been blocked), acquired from a taxable person, and intended for use exclusively for business or as a hire car, (*b*)   the car is stock in trade of a car manufacturer or dealer,

(*c*)   the car is not a qualifying car but has been let on hire to the same person since before 1 August 1995, or

(*d*)   the car is unused and is supplied to a car hire business for leasing at a commercial rent

[*VAT (Input Tax) Order 1992 (SI 1992 No 3222), para 7*].

For the purpose of (a) a taxable person must be taken not to intend to use the car exclusively for business if he 'intends to make it available … to any person (including where the taxable person is an individual, himself, or where the taxable person is a partnership, a partner) for private use, whether or not for a consideration' [*para 7 (2G)*].

21.13   This proviso has spawned a great deal of litigation. This has almost wholly been resolved in HMRC's favour. There are two Court of Appeal decisions which set out the current state of the law, *C & E Commrs v Upton (t/a Fagomatic) [2002] STC 640* and *C & E Commrs v Elm Milk Ltd [2006] STC 792*. HMRC won in *Fagomatic*; the taxpayer won in *Elm Milk*.

21.14   Mr Upton was a sole trader. His business was as a cigarette vending machine operator. He had no visible private life worth mentioning. He worked seven days a week, 8am to midnight or later. He had not had a holiday for five years, was 61 and had no wife or family. On the occasions when he did find a little time for socialising he drank a lot and would not have dreamed of driving; he used taxis. He ran his business from home. The car was parked in a car park 300 yards away. It was insured for both business and private use, but only because his insurance agent had told him that it is not possible to obtain insurance for business use only. Peter Gibson LJ said that 'it is plain that the test for the disqualifying condition … is of intention at the time of acquisition. The fact that a car is available or is made available to a person for private use subsequent to the acquisition is not determinative. However, that fact may be highly relevant to an inference that the taxable person has the intention to make the car available to himself for private use'. In the High Court the judge had remarked that:

> 'there is a particular difficulty in the way of [a] person if he is to escape from the qualifying condition that "he intends to … make it available … to …himself … for private use". The very fact of his deliberate acquisition of the car whereby he makes himself the owner of the car and controller of it means that at least ordinarily he must intend to make it available to himself for private use, even if he never intends to use it personally'. Buxton LJ stressed this distinction between the car, as a question of fact, being 'available' for private use however little Mr Upton had any intention of so using it. 'Mr Upton did not restrict the general nature of that availability by deciding that he would only use the car for one of the two purposes for which at the time of purchase it became available'.

The court indicated that it might well be impossible for a sole trader to bring a car within the exception.

21.15   Mr Phillips was the sole director of Elm Milk, a company wholly owned by him and members of his family. He had no written contract of employment. He drove considerable distances in the course of the company's business. On 1 February 2003 the company (acting by Mr Phillips), passed a board resolution noting that it was about to purchase the car and stating that the car was to be bought with the intention that it should be used for business purposes only by Mr Phillips, that the company did not intend to make the car available for private use, and that any private use would be a breach of the employee's terms of employment. The VAT and Duties tribunal found that both the company and Mr Phillips intended to be bound by the board resolution. The board resolution also recited that the insurance policy for the car would not permit anyone other than the company to use it for social, domestic or pleasure purposes. The tribunal felt this evidenced the company's intention albeit that the actual insurance cover was not so limited. The car was kept locked in a car park near the company's office and within 50 yards of Mr Phillips' home. The keys to the car were kept in the company's office (but as sole director Mr Phillips clearly had access to them at all times). All private motoring by Mr Phillips was in fact done in a different car owned by Mrs Phillips. Arden LJ distinguished the case from Fagomatic. She felt that one needs to start from the overall scheme of the legislation. This is to disallow input tax relief. Accordingly:

> 'the taxpayer has a high threshold to cross if he wishes to bring himself first within the exception and then within the exception to the exception. For this purpose he must show that the intention is to use the car exclusively for business use. Then ... he has to show not that he does not intend to use the car for private use ... but it is not his intention even to make it available for private use'.

She also noted that Parliament had not said that an availability requires that the car is not physically available for private use. That is accordingly a question of fact. 'There is no reason why a car cannot be made unavailable for private use by suitable contractual restraints'. She later noted 'there is no doubt that a company can enter into a binding employment contract with its sole director, even where that director is also the controlling shareholder'. She rejected an HMRC contention that the restrictions were worthless as they could in practice be revoked by Mr Phillips at any time; 'It would not necessarily follow that the intention of the company would be to lift the restrictions rather than to enforce any remedy for breach'. She also felt that neither the terms of the insurance, nor the fact that the employer recognised that the car might be used for a non-business purpose in a genuine emergency situation in breach of the condition but that few reasonable employers would do anything about it, did not mean that an intention not to make the car available for private use could not be shown.

21.16   The current position accordingly seems to be that it is possible, but very difficult, for a family company to avoid the input tax block, but it is probably impossible for a sole trader to do so. Many of the earlier tribunal decisions have failed on the insurance point. They have also given weight to the location of the car keys as a test of availability. Elm Milk is not the only case where a company has succeeded in showing that a car made available to a director was contractually not available for private use. The taxpayer succeeded in *Squibb & Davies (Demolition) Ltd (VTD 17829), Masterguard Security Services Ltd (VTD 18631)* and *Peter Jackson (Jewellers) Ltd (VTD 19474)*. It also succeeded in *Neil Macleod (Prints & Enterprises) Ltd (VTD 17144)*, although in that case the car was made available not to a director but to a disabled employee and the employee confirmed to the tribunal that he had been told that he must only use the vehicle for business and not for personal use, and that a log book and petrol receipts should be kept.

Entertaining

21.17 An employer cannot deduct input tax on goods or services used for the purposes of business entertainment. [*VAT (Input Tax) Order 1992 (SI 1992 No 3222), Article 5(1)*]. If he makes an onward supply of such items he need charge VAT only on the excess of the consideration, if any, over his own cost. [*Article 5(2)*]. Business entertainment includes hospitality of any kind, but does not include the provision of entertainment for employees or directors (or other persons engaged in the management of the employer) unless that provision is incidental to its provision for others. [*Article 5(3)*]. HMRC interpret this restrictively. For example, if a company throws a party for staff at which the staff are entitled to bring a guest either free or at a small charge, HMRC accept that the cost of entertaining the employee is not business entertaining but contend that input tax attributable to the cost of entertaining his guest is disallowable as business entertaining.

21.18 Following the VAT Tribunal decision in *Ernst & Young v Customs and Excise Comrs [1997] V&DR 183 (VAT Decision 15/00)*, HMRC accept that where a business provides entertainment to its employees in order to maintain and improve staff relations, it does so wholly for business purposes. However, if the expenditure 'has no discernible business purpose and no connection with the business activity' they will seek to disallow the input tax.

21.19 Where a company arranged a lunch to mark the opening of new premises which was attended by 25 senior employees and 130 actual or potential customers, the staff entertaining was held to be incidental to the provision of entertaining for customers so that the input tax was not deductible (*Wilsons Transport Ltd 1983 (VAT Decision 1468)*). A similar decision was reached in *Elizabethan Banquets (1985) (VAT Decision 1795)*, where employees attended banquets to maintain the expected atmosphere for paying customers. In contrast, where a promoter of rock concerts provided free beer at the concerts for both customers and staff the whole of the input tax was allowed, that for customers because they had paid for the beer in the ticket price so that it was not business entertaining and that for staff as staff entertaining (*D Lumby (1995) VAT Decision 12972*).

21.20 In the case of *Julius Fillibeck Sohne GmbH & Co KG v Finanzamt Neustadt (Case C-258/95) [1998] STC 513*, the European Court of Justice held that free transport for employees from home to work is in principle a supply of services within *Article 6(2)* of the *Sixth Directive*, so that output tax falls to be accounted for on the value of that supply. The company was a building company which transported workers from their homes to building sites in company vehicles. The employees made no payment for the transport. The ECJ indicated that in certain circumstances the needs of the business might necessitate the provision of transport, eg if there was no alternative public transport, in which case the personal benefit accruing to the employees would be of secondary importance compared to the needs of the business. The fact that only the employer was able to provide suitable transport or that the workplace was liable to change could be indications of such circumstances. So could the fact that a building firm has special characteristics and that the transport was provided under a collective agreement. In practice, HMRC do not normally seek output tax in relation to transport in company vehicles, but are coming under some pressure from the European Commission to do so in the light of this case.

21.21 It should be noted that the exemption does not apply to volunteers or the self-employed. However, there is an Extra-Statutory Concession (*para 3.10* of *Notice 48*) in relation to sports clubs. HMRC allow the deduction of input tax necessarily incurred on the provision of meals and accommodation for team members selected to represent their country or county and to committee members of the club even though such persons are not employees. This concession does not extend to alcoholic drinks or tobacco.

Other benefits

21.22 If an employer provides, free of charge to his employees, food or beverages in the course of catering (eg in a staff canteen) or accommodation in a hotel, inn, boarding house or similar establishment, the consideration for that supply is deemed to be nil – but as it is a supply in the course of the employer's business this will entitle him to recover the related input tax. If the supply is for a consideration consisting wholly or partly of money, the supply is deemed to be for a consideration equal to that money (any other consideration being ignored). [*VATA 1994, Sch 6, para 10*]. This treatment conforms with the ECJ decision in *Hotel Scandic Gasaback AB v Riksskatteverket [2005] STC 1311 (Case C-412/03)* that the EC Sixth Directive precludes a notional rule that treats an application of goods or services as being for private use where actual consideration is paid even where that consideration is less than the cost price of the goods or services

21.23 HMRC accept that the provision of goods (such as overalls or tools) to employees for the purpose of their employment is not a supply if no charge is made. [*para 4.4* of *Notice 700*]. There is accordingly no input tax restriction and no requirement to account for any notional output tax. A gift of a free meal to an employee is similarly not a supply. [*para 8.9.3* of *Notice 700*].

21.24 In contrast, if an employee is allowed to use a business asset for his personal use, such as use at weekends or for holidays, that is a supply on which VAT needs to be accounted. If such use is permanent and there is no consideration, eg the employer gives the employee a redundant computer, the value of such supply is the amount that would have to be paid by the employer to purchase an identical item (including age and condition) at the time of the supply. If an identical item cannot be purchased, it is the cost of a similar item. If there is no similar item, it is the cost of making the item at the time of the supply. [*VATA 1994, Sch 4, para 5, Sch 6, para 6*].

21.25 If the private use is temporary, eg the provision of a computer for as long as the employee continues with the company, the supply is a supply of services. The consideration is the full cost to the employer of providing the service. [*VATA 1994, Sch 4, para 5, Sch 6, para 7*]. HMRC say that this is the amount of depreciation on the goods, plus any other standard-rated costs related to the goods, multiplied by the proportion that the private use bears to total use. [*para 9.3.1* of *Notice 700*]. However between January 2004 and 15 August 2007 HMRC took the view that there would be wider benefits to the business and so as long as there was some business use the VAT incurred could be deducted in full. When the Government's Home Computer Initiative was withdrawn in April 2006 HMRC 'reviewed the VAT position' and discovered that they had been wrong and announced that from 15 August 2007 VAT could be recovered in full only where the provision of the computer is necessary for the employee to carry out the duties of the employment - as in such circumstances it is likely that any private use will not be significant when compared with the business need for providing the company. By a happy coincidence this mirrors the direct tax position. In any other case the VAT needs to be apportioned. Where a computer was provided under the Home Computer Initiative full VAT recovery can continue until the agreement for its use expires. [*Business Brief 55/2007*].

21.26 If an employer provides domestic accommodation free of charge to an employee, any VAT incurred is deductible as input tax. [*para 12.2.1* of *Notice 700*]. However, input tax is not deductible on the provision of accommodation for a director, except to the extent that the accommodation is used for business purposes. There is neverthless a deemed taxable supply under *VATA 1994, Sch 4, para 5*.

21.27 If an employee receives a prize, eg for exceeding sales targets or selling more than anyone else in a month, HMRC accept that that is not a supply for a consideration so no notional output tax needs to be accounted for. If the reward extends to a non-employee, such as the employee's spouse, the input tax on the non-employee element is, however, blocked as business entertainment. [*para 3.3* of *Notice 700/7, Business Promotion Schemes*].

21.28 If a person gives goods to someone else's employees, eg free goods to a customer's staff for selling that person's goods, VAT is due on a deemed supply unless the value of the goods is less than £50 or they form part of a series of gifts to the same person. [*VATA 1994, Sch 4, para 5, SI 2001 No 735*].

21.29   For input tax to be deductible the supply of goods or services has to be to the person claiming the deduction and the goods or services must be used for the purpose of that person's business [*VATA 1994, s 24(1)*]. To what extent is the VAT deductible where the employer picks up a charge that relates to an employee? In *C & E Commrs v Redrow Group plc [1999] STC 161* where Redrow, a housebuilder, paid the selling costs of a purchaser who sold his existing house and replaced it with a Redrow House, the House of Lords accepted that a service could be supplied both to Redrow and to the prospective purchaser. However in that case Redrow instructed the estate agents and, so long as the prospective purchaser bought a Redrow house, they were paid by Redrow. They were doing what Redrow instructed them to do, for which they charged a fee which was paid by Redrow. In *HMRC v Jeancharm Ltd [2005] STC 918* a young employee of Jeancharm drove his company car in such a way as to kill two people. He pleaded guilty to a charge of causing death by dangerous driving. The company picked up the legal costs and related VAT to the extent that they were not paid by its insurers. Lindsay J held that there had been no supply to the company. 'It was not the company that was charged with causing death by dangerous driving but Damian and it was not the company but Damian that needed defending'. In this case it was the insurers who instructed the solicitors and the company had no right to influence their conduct in Damian's defence and had no means of doing so. Accordingly, there could be no supply to them. It was therefore irrelevant whether or not the supply was for the purpose of its business.

Index

[All references are to paragraph number]

A

Accommodation
  appropriate percentage, 8.12
  associated companies, 8.32–8.33
  basic charges
    annual values, 8.8
    rental value, 8.5–8.7
    statutory provisions, 8.4
  Chevening House, 8.39
  clergymen, 8.38
  council tax, 8.37
  definitions
    'cost of providing accommodation',
      8.13
    'persons involved in providing
      accommodation', 8.14
  directors, 8.24–8.26
  exceptions, 8.34–8.36
    council housing, 8.23
    general provisions, 8.19–8.22
  family benefits, 8.40
  net emoluments, 8.28–8.31
  occasions of charge, 8.1–8.3
  overseas holiday homes, 8.41–8.48
  property details
    more than one property provided,
      8.17
    property already owned by
      employer, 8.15–8.16
    property provided to more than one
      employee, 8.18
  running costs, 8.27
Accountants
  deductible subscriptions, 5.91
  employment status, 4.96
Agency workers
  anti-avoidance rules, 19.8–19.9,
    19.12E, 19.12F–19.12G
  appeals, 19.10
  collection and recovery rules, 19.11
  control test, 19.5–19.7
  excluded services, 19.2
  fraudulent documents, 19.3

Agency workers – *contd*
  information and reporting, 19.12
  managed service companies, 18.70
  PAYE deductions, 19.4
  statutory provisions, 19.1
  taxable remuneration, 19.12A–19.12D
  travelling expenses, 19.12H
**All Employee Share Option Plans
    (AESOPs)** *see* **Share incentive
    plans (SIPs)**
Anti-avoidance rules
  agency workers, 19.8–19.9,
    19.12F–19.12G
  defalcations by close company
    directors, 19.34–19.37
  'disguised remuneration'
    acquisitions out of sums or assets,
      3.89–3.90
    approved share schemes, 3.60–3.62
    benefit packages, 3.67–3.68
    car ownership schemes, 3.85–3.86
    commercial loans, 3.65–3.66
    death of employee, 3.55–3.56
    deferred remuneration, 3.69–3.72
    earmarked sums or assets, 3.88
    employee management incentive
      schemes (EMIs), 3.63
    employee share schemes, 3.73–3.80
    employment income exemptions,
      3.87
    employment-related securities,
      3.82–3.84
    Members of Parliament, 3.64
    pensions, 3.91–3.101
    relief where no further relevant step,
      3.58–3.59
    retrospectivity, 3.102
    statutory provisions, 3.28–3.47
    subsequent income tax liability, 3.57
  introduction of legislation, 1.9
  National Insurance (NI), 20.5–20.6
  provision of services through
    intermediaries, 18.1